INTERNATIONAL AWARD WINNING
HARRIS REFERENCE
CATALOG

POSTAGE STAMP PRICES

of the
UNITED STATES
UNITED NATIONS
CANADA & PROVINCES

Plus: Confederate States, U.S. Possessions,
U.S. Trust Territories,
Albums and Accessories,
Comprehensive U.S. Stamp Identifier

Serving the Collector Since 1916

H.E. Harris & Company was founded by Henry Ellis Harris. Harris began the business in 1916 at an early age of fourteen and took advantage of free advertising in the Washington Post to begin his mail-order business. He built an enormously successful stamp company and garnered the support and confidence of the philatelic community. This annual US/BNA Catalog began publication in 1935 and was 64 pages.

Stock No. 0794819060
ISBN: 0-7948-1906-0

Copyright © 2004 Whitman Publishing, LLC.
All Rights Reserved. Designed in U.S.A.

"The marks SCOTT and SCOTT'S are Registered in the U.S. Patent and Trademark Office, and are trademarks of Amos Press, Inc., dba Scott Publishing Co. No use may be made of these marks or of material in this publication which is preprinted from a copyrighted publication of Amos Press, Inc., without the express written permission of Amos Press, Inc., dba Scott Publishing Co., Sidney, Ohio 45365."

ABOUT OUR CATALOG PRICES

The prices quoted in this catalog are the prices for which H.E. Harris offers stamps for retail sale at the time of publication.

These prices are based on current market values as researched by our staff, but, more importantly, on our day-to-day buying and selling activities in the stamp market.

Although you may certainly use this catalog as a guide to current market prices, you must keep in mind the fact that prices can change in response to varying levels of collector demand, or dealer promotions, and/or special purchases. We are not responsible for typographical errors.

You should also remember that condition is always the key factor in determining the value and price of a given stamp or set of stamps. Unlike some other stamp catalogs, we price U.S. stamps issued up to 1935 in three different condition grades for unused and used examples. For these earlier issues, we have also shown the percentage premium that would apply to Never Hinged Mint examples.

Our illustrated definitions of condition grades are presented on pages X-XII.

We have not found it possible to keep every stamp in stock that is listed in this catalog, and we cannot guarantee that we can supply all of the stamps in all conditions that are listed.

However, we will search for any stamp in any condition that a customer may want if that stamp is not in our stock at the time the customer places an order for it.

Serving the Collector Since 1916

INDEX

UNITED STATES STAMPS

Air Mail	140-145
Air Mail Special Delivery	146
Certified Mail	146
Envelope Cut Squares & Entires	150-159
General Issues	1-138
Hunting Permit	181-184
Hunting Permit, State	185-190
Offices in China	147
Officials	148-149
Parcel Post	149
Parcel Post Due	149
Postage Due	147
Postal Cards	164-172
Postal Cards, Air Mail	173-174
Postal Cards, Official	175
Postal Cards, Reply	174-175
Postal Notes	149
Postal Stationery	150-159
Postal Stationery, Air Mail	160-162
Postal Stationery, Official	163
Registration	146
Revenues	176-180
Special Delivery	146
Special Handling	149

UNITED STATES RELATED AREAS

Canal Zone	191-195
Confederate States	195
Cuba	196
Guam	196
Hawaii	196-197
Marshall Islands	198-207
Micronesia	208-215
Palau	216-224
Philippines	225
Puerto Rico	225
Ryukyu Islands	226-231

UNITED NATIONS

Geneva Issues	244-247
Geneva Air Letter Sheets & Postal Cards	247
New York Air Post	241
New York Issues	232-240
New York Postal Stationery	242-243
Vienna Issues	248-250
Vienna Air Letter Sheets & Postal Cards	251

CANADA & PROVINCES

British Columbia & Vancouver Island	290
Canada Air Post	287
Canada Air Post Special Delivery	288
Canada General Issues	252-286
Canada Phosphor Tagged Issues	287
Canada Postage Due	289
Canada Registration	288
Canada Semi-Postal	287
Canada Special Delivery	288
Canada War Tax	288
New Brunswick	301
Newfoundland	291-299
Newfoundland Air Post	299-300
Newfoundland Postage Due	300
Nova Scotia	301
Prince Edward Island	302

OTHER FEATURES

Catalog Pricing Policy	I
Guide for Collectors	III-IX
Pictorial Guide to Centering	X
Quality and Condition Definitions	XI-XII
Stamp Identifier Section	XIII-XXXII
Discount Coupon	**305**

A GUIDE FOR COLLECTORS

In this section we will attempt to define and explain some of the terms commonly used by stamp collectors. Instead of listing the terms in an alphabetical dictionary or glossary format, we have integrated them. In this way, you can see how an individual term fits within the total picture.

PRODUCTION

The manufacture of stamps involves a number of procedures. We will discuss the major steps here, with emphasis on their implications for stamp collectors. Although we present them separately, modern printing presses may combine one or more operations so that the steps tend to blend together. There also are steps in the process that we do not cover here. While they may be important to the production process, their direct implications for most collectors are minimal.

PLATE MAKING

Before anything can be printed, a printing plate must be made. Using the intaglio printing process (which is explained under **printing**) as an example, the steps involved in plate production are as follows:

- A **master die** is made. The design is recess engraved in a reverse mirror-image. Most master dies consist of only one impression of the design.
- The next step is to prepare a **transfer roll**. The soft steel of the transfer roll is rocked back and forth under pressure against the hardened master die and a series of multiple impressions, called **reliefs**, are created in the transfer roll. Note that the impression on the transfer roll will be raised above the surface, since the roll was pressed into the recesses of the master die.
- Once the transfer roll has been made and hardened, it is used to impress designs in to the soft steel of a **printing plate** that can fit up to 400 impressions of small, definitive-sized stamps or 200 impressions of large, commemorative-sized stamps. This time, the raised design on the transfer roll impresses a recessed design into the plate.

The process is much more complex than this, but these are the basics. Once the printing plate is hardened, it is almost ready to be used to create printed sheets of stamps. Depending on the printing equipment to be used, the printing plate will be shaped to fit around a cylinder for rotary press printing or remain flat for flat-bed press printing. In either form, the plate is then hardened and is ready for use in printing.

DESIGN VARIETIES

The complexity of the platemaking process can result in major or minor flaws. The inspection process will catch most of these flaws, but those that escape detection will result in **plate varieties**.

The early United States Classic issues have been examined in minute detail over the decades. Through **plating** studies, minor differences in individual stamps have been used to identify the position on the printing plate of each design variety. Sometimes called **"flyspeck philately"** because it involves the detection of minute "flyspeck" differences, such plating work has resulted in the identification of some of our greatest rarities. Compare the prices for the one cent blue issues of 1851 and 1857 (#s 5-9 and 18-24) and you will see the tremendous dollar difference that can result from minute design variations. (The Harris Stamp Identifier in this catalog explains the design differences.)

During the plate making or subsequent printing process, plate flaws that are detected will be corrected, sometimes incompletely or incorrectly. Corrections or revisions in an individual die impression or in all plate impressions include the following:

- **Retouching**—minor corrections made in a plate to repair damage or wear.
- **Recutting** or **re-engraving**—similar to, but more extensive than, retouching. Recutting usually applies to changes made before a plate has been hardened, while re-engraving is performed on a plate that has had to be tempered (softened) after hardening.
- **Redrawing**—the intentional creation of a slightly different design. The insertion of secret marks on the National Bank Notes plates when they were turned over to the Continental Bank Note Company in 1873 can be considered redrawings.
- **Reentry**—the reapplication of a design from a transfer roll to the plate, usually to improve a worn plate. If the reentry is not done completely, or if it is not done precisely on top of the previous design, a double transfer will result. Such double transfers will show on the printed stamp as an extra line at one or more points on the stamp.

Other design varieties may result from undetected plate flaws. A **plate crack** (caused by the hardened plate cracking under wear or pressure) or a **plate scratch** (caused by an object cutting into the plate) will show as an ink line on the printed stamp.

One other group that can be covered here to avoid possible confusion includes **reissues, reprints, special printings** and **reproductions**. None of these are design varieties that result from plate flaws, corrections or revisions. In fact, reissues, reprints and special printings are made from the same, unchanged plates as the originals. They show no differences in design and usually can be identified only by variations in paper, color or gum.

Reproductions (such as U.S. #3 and #4), on the other hand, are made from entirely new plates and, therefore, can be expected to show some variation from the originals.

ERRORS, FREAKS, ODDITIES

"EFOs", as they are called, are printed varieties that result from abnormalities in the production process. They are design varieties, but of a special nature because the result looks different from the norm. When you see them, you know something went wrong.

Basically, freaks and oddities can be loosely defined as minor errors. They include the following:

- **Misperforations**, that is, the placement of the perforations within the design rather than at the margins.
- **Foldovers**, caused be a sheet being turned, usually at a corner, before printing and /or perforating. The result is part of a design printed on the reverse of the sheet or placement of perforations at odd angles. Such freaks and oddities may be of relatively minor value, but they do make attractive additions to a collection. Truly major errors, on the other hand, can be of tremendous value. It would not be overstating the case to argue that many collectors are initially drawn to the hobby by the publicity surrounding discoveries of valuable errors and the hope that they might someday do the same. Major errors include the following:
- **Inverts.** These are the most dramatic and most valuable of all major errors and almost always result from printing processes that require more than one pass of a sheet through the presses. If the sheet inadvertently gets "flipped" between passes, the portion printed on the second pass will emerge inverted.

Two definitions we should introduce here are **"frame"** and **"vignette"**. The vignette is the central design of the stamp; the frame encloses the vignette and, at its outer edges, marks the end of the printed stamp design. Oftentimes, stamps described as inverted centers (vignettes) actually are inverted frames. The center was properly printed in the first pass and the frame was inverted in the second pass.

- **Color errors.** The most noticeable color errors usually involve one or more omitted colors. The sheet may not have made it through the second pass in a two-step printing process. In the past such errors were extremely rare because they were obvious enough to be noticed by inspectors. In modern multi-color printings, the chances of such errors escaping detection have increased. Nonetheless, they still qualify as major errors and carry a significant premium.

*Other color errors involve the use of an incorrect color. They may not seem as dramatic as missing colors, but the early issues of many countries include some very rare and valuable examples of these color errors.

Although technically not a color error, we can include here one of the most unusual of all errors, the United States 1917 5-cent stamps that are supposed to be blue, but are found in the carmine or rose color of the 2-cent stamps. The error was not caused by a sheet of the 5-centers being printed in the wrong color, as you might expect. Rather, because a few impressions on a 2-cent plate needed reentry, they were removed. But an error was made and the 5-cent design was entered. Thus it is a reentry error, but is described in most catalogs as a color error because that is the apparent result. Whatever the description, the 5-cent denomination surrounded by 2-cent stamps is a real showpiece.

- **Imperfs.** A distinction should be drawn here between imperforate errors and intentionally imperforate stamps. When the latter carry a premium value over their perforated counterparts, it is because they were printed in smaller quantities for specialized usages. They might have been intended, for example, for sale to vending machine manufacturers who would privately perforate the imperforate sheets

On the other hand, errors in which there is absolutely no trace of a perforation between two stamps that were supposed to be perforated carry a premium based on the rarity of the error. Some modern United States coil imperforate errors have been found in such large quantities that they carry little premium value. But imperforate errors found in small quantities represent tremendous rarities.

Be they intentional or errors, imperforate stamps are commonly collected in pairs or larger multiples because it can be extremely difficult—often impossible, to distinguish them from stamps that have had their perforations trimmed away in an attempt to pass them off as more valuable imperfs. Margin singles that show the stamp and a wide, imperforate selvage at one of the edges of the sheet are another collecting option.

PRINTING

There are three basic printing methods:

1. **Intaglio,** also known as **recess** printing. Line engraved below the surface of the printing plate (that is, in recess) accept the ink and apply it to damp paper that is forced into the recesses of the plate. Intaglio methods include **engraved** and **photogravure** (or **rotogravure**). Photogravure is regarded by some as separate from intaglio because the engraving is done by chemical etching and the finished product can be distinguished from hand or machine engraving.
2. **Typography.** This is similar to intaglio, in that it involves engraving, but the action is in reverse, with the design left at the surface of the plate and the portions to be unprinted cut away. Ink is then applied to the surface design, which is imprinted onto paper. **Typeset** letterpress printing is the most common form of typography.
3. **Lithography.** This method differs from the previous two in that it involves **surface printing**, rather than engraving. Based on the principle that oil and water do not mix, the design to be printed is applied with a greasy ink onto a plate that is then wet with a watery fluid. Printing ink run across the plate is accepted only at the greased (oiled) points. The ink applies the design to paper that is brought in contact with the plate. **Offset** printing, a modern lithographic method, involves a similar approach, but uses a rubber blanket to transfer the inked design to paper.

The printing method that was used to produce a given stamp can be determined by close inspection of that stamp.
1. Because the paper is pressed into the grooves of an intaglio plate, when viewed from the surface the design appears to be slightly raised. Running a fingernail lightly across the surface also will reveal this raised effect. When viewed from the back, the design will appear to be recessed (or pressed out toward the surface). Photogravure stamps have a similar appearance and feel, but when viewed under a magnifier, they reveal a series of dots, rather than line engravings.
2. Because the raised design on a plate is pressed into the paper when the typograph process is used, when viewed from the surface, the printing on the stamp does not have the raised effect of an intaglio product. On the other hand, when viewed from the reverse, a raised impression will be evident where the design was imprinted. Overprints often are applied by typography and usually show the raised effect on the back of the stamp.
3. Unlike either of the previous two methods, lithographed stamps look and feel flat. This dull, flat effect can be noticed on any of the United States 1918-20 offset printings, #s 525-536.

Overprints and **surcharges** are inscriptions or other markings added to printed stamps to adapt them to other uses. A **surcharge** is an overprint that changes or restates the value of the stamp. The United States Offices in China (K1-18) issues carry surcharges.

Some foreign semi-postal issues are stamps with a printed denomination that is applied to the postage fee and an overprinted surcharge that is applied to a specified charity.

Overprints can be applied for reasons other than to change their value. Examples would be for commemorative purposes (#s 646-648), to hinder the use of stolen stamps (#s 658-679 the Kansas-Nebraska issues), to change or designate the usage of the stamp (modern precancels), or to indicate usage in a distinct political unit (Canal Zone, Guam and Philippines overprints on United States stamps used during the early period of U.S. administration until new stamps could be printed).

Overprints can be applied by handstamp or even typewriter, but the most efficient and commonly used technique seen on stamps is typeset press printing.

WATERMARKS

This actually is one of the first steps in the stamp production process because it is part of paper manufacturing. A **watermark** is a slight thinning of the paper pulp, usually in the form of a relevant design. It is applied by devices attached to the rolls on papermaking machines. Without getting involved in the technical aspects, the result in a watermark that can sometimes be seen when held to the light, but more often requires watermark detector fluid.

A word of caution here. Such detector fluids may contain substances that can be harmful when inhaled. This is particularly true of lighter fluids that often are used by collectors in lieu of specially made stamp watermark detector fluids.

Watermarks are used to help detect counterfeits. Although it is possible to reproduce the appearance of a watermark, it is extremely difficult. The authorities have at times been able to identify a counterfeit by the lack of a watermark that should be present or by the presence of an incorrect watermark.

On the other hand, there are occasions when the incorrect or absent watermark did not indicate a counterfeit, but a printing error. The wrong paper may have been used or the paper may have been inserted incorrectly (resulting in an inverted or sideways watermark). The United States 30 cent orange red that is listed among the 1914-17 issues on unwatermarked paper (#467A) is an example of a printing error. It was produced on watermarked paper as part of the 1914-15 series, but a few sheets were discovered without watermarks.

Unfortunately, the difficulty encountered in detecting watermarks on light shades, such as orange or yellow, makes experts very reluctant to identify single copies of #476A. Although not visible, the watermark just might be there.

Because an examination of a full sheet allows the expert to examine the unprinted selvage and all stamps on that sheet at one time, positive identification is possible and most of the stamps that come down to us today as #476A trace back to such full sheets.

GUMMING

Gumming once was almost always applied after printing and before perforating and cutting of sheets into panes. Today, pregummed paper may be used, so the placement of this step in the process cannot be assured—nor is it the sequence of much significance.

The subject of gum will be treated more fully in the **Condition** section of this catalog. At this point, we will only note that certain stamps can be identified by their gum characteristics. Examples include the identification of rotary press stamps by the presence of gum breaker ridges or lines and the detection of the presence of original gum on certain stamps that indicates they can not be a rarer issue that was issued without gum, such as #s 40-47. Others, such as #s 102-111 can be identified in part by their distinctive white, crackly original gum.

PERFORATING

We have already discussed the absence of perforations in the **Errors** section. Here we will concentrate on the perforating process itself.

All perforating machines use devices to punch holes into the printed stamp paper. The holes usually are round and are known as perforations. When two adjacent stamps are separated, the semicircular cutouts are the **perforations**; the remaining paper between the perforations forms **perf tips**, or "**teeth**".

Most perforations are applied by perforators that contain a full row of punches that are driven through the paper as it is fed through the perforating equipment. **Line Perforators** drive the punches up and down; **rotary perforators** are mounted on cylinders that revolve. There are other techniques, but these are the most common.

To clear up one point of confusion, the **perforation size** (for example, "perf 11") is not the size of the hole or the number of perforations on the side of a given stamp. Rather, it describes the number of perforations that could be fit within two centimeters.

A perf 8 stamp will have visibly fewer perforations than a perf 12 stamp, but it is much harder to distinguish between perf 11 and perf 10-1/2. **Perforation gauges** enable collectors to make these distinctions with relative ease.

TAGGING

Modern, high-speed, mechanical processing of mail has created the need for "tagging" stamps by coating them with a luminescent substance that could be detected under ultraviolet (U.V.) light or by printing them on paper that included such substances. When passed under a machine capable of detecting these substances, an envelope can be positioned and the stamp automatically cancelled, thereby eliminating time-consuming and tedious manual operations. The tagged varieties of certain predominantly untagged stamps, such as #s 1036 and C67, do carry modest premiums. There also are technical differences between phosphorescent and fluorescent types of luminescent substances. But these details are primarily of interest to specialists and will not be discussed in this general work.

PAPER

The fact that we have not devoted more attention to paper should not be an indication of any lack of interest or significance. Books have been written on this one subject alone, and a lack of at least a rudimentary knowledge of the subject can lead to mis-identification of important varieties and resultant financial loss.

The three most common categories of paper on which stamps are printed are **wove**, **laid**, and **India**. The most frequently used is machine-made **wove paper**, similar to that used for most books. The semiliquid pulp for wove paper is fed onto a fine wire screen and is processed much the same as cloth would be woven. Almost all United States postage stamps are printed on wove paper.

Laid paper is formed in a process that uses parallel wires rather than a uniform screen. As a result, the paper will be thinner where the pulp was in contact with the wires. When held to the light, alternating light and dark lines can be seen. Laid paper varieties have been found on some early United States stamps.

India paper is very thin and tough, without any visible texture. It is, therefore, more suited to obtaining the sharp impressions that are needed for printers' pre-production proofs, rather than to the high-volume printing of stamps.

Other varieties include **bluish** paper, so described because of the tone created by certain substances added to the paper, and silk paper, which contains threads or fibers of silk that usually can be seen on the back of the stamp. Many United States revenue stamps were printed on silk paper.

COLLECTING FORMATS

Whatever the production method, stamps reach the collector in a variety of forms. The most common is in sheet, or more correctly, pane form.

Sheets are the full, uncut units as they come from a press. Before distribution to post offices, these sheets are cut into **panes**. For United States stamps, most regular issues are printed in sheets of 400 and cut into panes of 100; most commemoratives are printed in sheets of 200 and cut into panes of 50. There are numerous exceptions to this general rule, and they are indicated in the mint sheet listings in this catalog.

Sheets also are cut in **booklet panes** for only a few stamps—usually four to ten stamps per pane. These panes are assembled in complete booklets that might contain one to five panes, usually stapled together between two covers. An intact booklet is described as **unexploded**; when broken apart it is described as exploded.

Coils are another basic form in which stamps reach post offices. Such stamps are wound into continuous coil rolls, usually containing from 100 to 5,000 stamps, the size depending on the volume needs of the expected customer. Almost all coils are produced with perforations on two opposite sides and straight edges on the remaining two sides.

Some serious collectors prefer collecting coils in pairs or strips—two or more adjacent stamps—as further assurance of genuineness. It is much easier to fake a coil single that shows only portions of each perforation hole than a larger unit that shows the complete perf hole.

A variation on this theme is the **coil line pair**—adjacent stamps that show a printed vertical line between. On rotary press stamps the line appears where the two ends of a printing plate meet on a rotary press cylinder. The joint is not complete, so ink falls between the plate ends and is transferred onto the printed coil. On flat plate stamps the guideline is the same as that created for sheet stamps, as described below.

Paste-up coil pairs are not as popular as line pairs. They were a necessary by-product of flat plate printings in which the coil strips cut from separate sheets had to be pasted together for continuous winding into roll form.

The modern collecting counterpart to coil line pairs is the plate **number strip**—three or five adjacent coil stamps with the plate number displayed on the middle stamp. Transportation coil plate strips have become particularly sought after. On most early coil rolls, the plate numbers were supposed to be trimmed off. Freaks in which the number remains are interesting, but do not carry large premiums since they are regarded as examples of miscut oddities rather than printing errors.

Miniature sheets and **souvenir sheets** are variations on one theme—small units that may contain only one or at most a much smaller quantity of stamps than would be found on the standard postal panes. Stamps may be issued in miniature sheet format for purposes of expedience, as for example the Bret Harte $5 issue (#2196), which was released in panes of 20 to accommodate the proportionately large demand by collectors for plate blocks rather than single stamps.

As the name implies, a souvenir sheet is a miniature sheet that was released as a souvenir to be saved, rather than postally used—although such sheets or the stamps cut out from them can be used as postage. Note: **souvenir cards** are created strictly for promotional and souvenir purposes. They contain stamp reproductions that may vary in size, color or design from the originals and are not valid for postal use.

Often, a common design may be produced in sheet, coil and booklet pane form. The common design is designated by collectors as one **type**, even though it may be assigned many different catalog numbers because of variations in color, size, perforations, printing method, denomination, etc. On the other hand, even minor changes in a basic design represent a new type.

Sheet stamps offer the greatest opportunity for format variation and collecting specialization. Using the following illustration for reference, the varieties that can be derived include the following:

Block (a)—this may be any unit of four stamps or more in at least 2 by 2 format. Unless designated as a different size, blocks are assumed to be blocks of four.

Specialized forms of blocks include:

Arrow block (b)—adjacent stamps at the margin of a sheet, showing the arrow printed in the margin for registration in the printing process, as, for example, in two-color printings. When the arrow designates the point at which a sheet is cut into panes, the result will appear as one leg of the arrow, or V, on each pane.

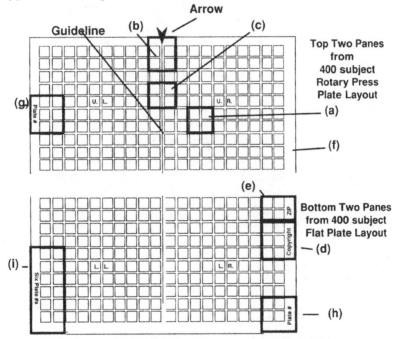

(This diagram is for placement purposes only, and is not an exact reproduction of margin markings)

Guideline block (c)—similar to arrow block, except that it can be any block that shows the registration line between two rows of two stamps each.

Gutter block—similar to guideline block, except that an uncolored gutter is used instead of a printed line. The best known United States gutter blocks are those cut from full-sheet "Farley printings". Pairs of stamps from adjacent panes on each side of the gutter form the gutter block.

Imprint, or **inscription blocks (d)** include **copyright, mail early** and **ZIP (e)** blocks. On most modern United States sheets, the **selvage**, that is, the margin that borders the outer rows of stamps **(f)**, includes one or more inscriptions in addition to the plate numbers. It may be a copyright protection notice or an inscription that encourages mail users to post their mail early or to use the ZIP code on their mail.

Because the inscription appears along the margin, rather than in one of the corners, it is customary to collect copyright blocks and mail early blocks in two rows of three stamps each, with the inscription centered in the margin. The ZIP inscription appears in one of the corners of each pane, so it is collected in corner margin blocks of four.

Plate number block—this is by far the most popular form of block collecting. On each sheet of stamps, a plate number (or numbers) is printed to identify the printing plate(s) used. Should a damage be discovered, the plate can easily be identified.

On flat plate sheets, where the plate number appeared along the margin, the format usually is plate blocks of six, with the plate number centered in the margin **(g)**.

On rotary press and other sheets where a single plate number appears in one of the four corners of the margin, the customary collecting format is a corner margin block of four **(h)**. This also is true for plate blocks with two plate numbers in two adjacent corner stamps and for modern plates where single digits are used to designate each plate number and the complete series (containing one digit for each printing color) appears in the corner.

Before single digits were adopted for modern multi-color printings, the five-digit numbers assigned to each plate might run down a substantial portion of the sheet margin. **Plate strips** are collected in such instances. Their size is two rows times as many stamps as are attached to the margin area that shows all plate numbers **(i)**.

Because a sheet of stamps is cut into separate panes, printing plates include plate numbers that can be seen on each of the cut panes. On modern sheets the plate numbers would be located in each of the four corners of the uncut sheet. Once cut, each of the four panes would show the same plate number in one of its corners. The position of the plate number, which matches the position of the pane on the uncut sheet, is designated as upper left or right and lower left or right. Some specialists seek matched sets. A **matched set** is one of each of the four positions for a given plate number. A **complete matched set** is all positions of all plate numbers for a given issue.

Other definitions that relate in one way or another to the format in which stamps are produced include:

Se-tenant—from the French, meaning joined together. A pair, block or larger multiple that contains different designs. The 1967 Space Twins issue is an example of a se-tenant pair in which the two different stamps are part of an integral design. The 1968 Historic Flags se-tenant strip contains ten separate designs, each of which can stand alone.

Tete-beche pair—from the French, meaning head-to-tail. Such pairs show adjacent stamps, one of which is upside down in relation to the other.

Proof—any trial impression used in the evaluation of prospective or final designs. **Final die proofs**—that is, those made from a completed die preparatory to its being used in the production of printing plates—are the standard proof collecting form.

Essay—a partial or complete illustration of a proposed design. In the strict philatelic sense, essays are printed in proof form.

Color trials—a preliminary proof of a stamp design in one or more colors. Trial color proofs are used to select the color in which the stamp will be printed.

Grill—a pattern of embossed cuts that break the stamp paper. See the information at the head of the 1861-67 Issue listings and the section of grills in the Harris Stamp Identifier.

POSTAL MARKINGS

The extensive subject of cancellations and postal markings on stamps and covers is too specialized to present in detail here. Volumes have been written on individual categories of markings—straight line markings, ship cancels, foreign mail cancels, flight covers, etc. In this section we will limit ourselves to the basic definitions related to the stamp and the manner in which it is cancelled, rather than the specialized usage of the envelope to which the stamp is affixed.

- **Manuscript**, or **pen cancels** were the earliest form of "killing" a stamp—that is, marking it to indicate it had been postally used.
- **Handstamps** were created shortly after the first stamps were issued. The early devices might only show a pattern such as a grid and often were carved from cork.
- **Fancy cancels** were an extension of the handstamp. Local postmasters carved cork cancelers that depicted bees, kicking mules, flowers and hundreds of other figures. Stamps with clear strikes of such fancy cancels usually carry hefty premiums over those with standard cancels.
- **Machine cancels** are applied by mechanical rather than manual means.
- A stamp is **tied** to a cover (or piece) when the cancellation, whatever its form, extends beyond the margins of the stamp onto the cover. Such a tie is one indication of the authenticity of the cover.

Specialized cancellations include the following:

- **Cut cancel**—as the name implies, a cancel that actually cuts the stamp, usually in the form of a thin, straight incision. The most common usage of cut cancels on United States stamps is on Revenue issues.
- **Perfin**, or perforated initial—usually not a cancellation as such, but rather a privately administered punching into the stamp of one or more initials. Most often, the initials were those of a large firm that wished to prevent personal use of their stamps by employees.
- **Precancel**—a cancellation printed on stamps in advance of their sale. The primary purpose of precancels is for sale to large volume mailers, whose mail is delivered to post offices and processed in bulk without necessarily receiving further cancellation.
- **Non-contemporary cancel**—a cancellation applied to a stamp long after the normal period of use for that stamp. A stamp that is worth more used than unused or a damaged unused stamp that would be worth more on cover are examples of candidates for non-contemporary markings.
- **Cancel-to-order**, or **C.T.O.**—a cancel that is printed on a stamp by an issuing country to give it the appearance of having been used, or to render it invalid for postage in that country. Special fancy cancels or "favor cancels" have been applied at various times in the countries for philatelic reasons.

CATEGORIES

The number of specialized categories into which stamps can be slotted is limited only by the imagination of the individual collector. Some collectors have attempted to collect one of each and every stamp ever issued by every nation that ever existed. Other collectors have concentrated on all the possible varieties and usages of only one stamp. Between these two extremes, stamps can be divided into certain generally accepted categories, whether or not they are used as boundaries for a collection. These categories are as follows:

- **Definitives**, or **regulars**—stamps that are issued for normal, everyday postage needs. In the United States, they are put on sale for a period limited only by changing rate needs or infrequent issuance of a new definitive series. Post offices can requisition additional stocks of definitives as needed.
- **Commemoratives**—stamps issued to honor a specific event, anniversary, individual or group. They are printed in a predetermined quantity and are intended for sale during a limited period. Although they can be used indefinitely, once stocks are sold out at a local post office, commemoratives usually are not replenished unless the issue has local significance.
- **Pictorials**—stamps that depict a design other than the portrait of an individual or a static design such as a coat of arms or a flag. While some collectors think of these strictly as commemoratives (because most commemoratives are pictorials), some definitives also can be pictorials. Any number of definitives that depict the White House are examples.
- **Airmails**, or **air posts**—stamps issued specifically for airmail use. Although they do not have to bear a legend, such as "airmail", they usually do. Airmail stamps usually can be used to pay other postage fees.

When air flights were a novelty, airmail stamp collecting was an extremely popular specialty. Part of this popularity also can be ascribed to the fact that the first airmail stamps usually were given special attention by issuing postal administrations. Produced using relatively modern technology, they often were among the most attractive of a nation's issues.

- **Zeppelin stamps**—although these do not rate as a major category, they deserve special mention. Zeppelin issues were primarily released for specific use on Zeppelin flights during the 1920s and 1930s. They carried high face values and were issued during the Great Depression period, when most collectors could not afford to purchase them. As a result, most Zeppelin issues are scarce and command substantial premiums. United States "Zepps" are the Graf Zeppelins (C13-C15) and the Century of Progress issue (C18).
- **Back-of-the-book**—specialized stamps that are identified as "back-of-the-book" because of their position in catalogs following the listings of regular and commemorative postal issues. Catalogs identified them with a prefix letter.

Some collectors include airmail stamps in this category, in part because they carry a prefix letter (C) and are listed separately. Most collectors treat the airmails as part of a standard collection and begin the back-of-the-book section with semi-postals (B) or, for the United States, special deliveries (E).

Other frequently used "b-o-b" categories include postage dues (J), offices in China, or Shanghais (K), officials (O), parcel posts (Q), newspapers (PR), and revenues (R), the latter including "Duck" hunting permit stamps (RW).

Postal stationery and postal cards are the major non-stamp back-of-the-book categories. A complete envelope or card is called an **entire**; the cutout corner from such a piece, showing the embossed or otherwise printed design, is described as a **cut square**.

Some collecting categories do not relate to the intended use of the stamps. Examples include **topicals** (stamps collected by the theme of the design, such as sports, dance, paintings, space, etc.) and **first day covers**. (Modern first day covers show a stamp or stamps postmarked in a designated first day city on the official first day of issue. The cancel design will relate to the issue and the cover may bear a privately-printed cachet that further describes and honors the subject of the stamp.

One of the oddities of the hobby is that **stampless covers** are an accepted form of "stamp" collecting. Such covers display a usage without a stamp, usually during the period before stamps were required for the payment of postage. They bear manuscript or handstamps markings such as "due 5," "PAID," etc. to indicate the manner in which postage was paid.

Although they do not constitute a postal marking, we can include **bisects** here for want of a better place. A bisect is a stamp cut in half and used to pay postage in the amount of one-half of the stamp's denomination. The 1847 ten cent stamp (#2) cut in half and used to pay the five cent rate is an example.

Bisects should be collected only on cover and properly tied. They also should reflect an authorized usage, for example, from a post office that was known to lack the proper denomiination, and sould pay an amount called for by the usuage shown on the cover.

Not discussed in detail here is the vast subject of **covers**, or postal history. Envelopes, usually but not necessarily showing a postal use, are described by collectors as covers. Early "covers" actually were single letter sheets with a message on one side and folded into the form of an enclosing wrapper when viewed from the outside. The modern aerogramme or air letter is similar in design to these early folded letters.

H.E. Harris Pictorial Guide to Centering

Cat #	Very Fine	Fine	Average
1 to 293 1847 to 1898	Perfs clear of design on all four sides. Margins may not be even.	Perfs well clear of design on at least three sides. But may almost touch design on one side.	Perfs cut into design on at least one side.
294 to 749 1901 to 1934	Perfs clear of design. Margins relatively even on all four sides.	Perfs clear of design. Margins not even on all four sides.	Perfs touch design on at least one side.
750 to Date 1935 to Present	Perfs clear of design. Centered with margins even on all four sides.	Perfs clear of design. Margins may be uneven.	Perfs may touch design on at least one side.

Note: Margins are area from edges of stamp to the design. Perfs are the serrations between stamps to aid in separating them.

CENTERING

One major factor in the determination of a stamp's fair value is its **centering**, the relative balance of the stamp design within its margins. Whether the stamp has perforations or is imperforate, its centering can be judged. Because the stamp trade does not have an established system for grading or measuring centering, "eyeballing" has become the standard practice. As a result, one collector's definition may vary from another's. This can create some confusion, but the system seems to work, so it has remained in force.

Centering can range from poor to superb, as follows:

- **Poor**—so far off center that a significant portion of the design is lost because of bad centering. On a poorly centered perforated stamp, the perforations cut in so badly that even the perf tips may penetrate the design.
- **Average**—a stamp whose frame or design is cut slightly by the lack of margins on one or two sides. On a perforated stamp, the perf holes might penetrate the stamp, but some margin white space will show on the teeth. Average stamps are accepted by the majority of collectors for 19th century stamps and early 20th century stamps, as well as for the more difficult later issues.
- **Fine**—the perforations are clear of the design, except for those issues that are known to be extremely poorly centered, but the margins on opposite sides will not be balanced, that is, equal to each other. (Note: a stamp whose top and bottom margins are perfectly balanced may still be called fine if the left and right margins differ substantially from each other.)
- **Very fine**—the opposite margins may still appear to differ somewhat, but the stamp is closer to being perfectly centered than it is to being fine centered. Very fine stamps are sought by collectors who are particularly interested in high quality and who are willing to pay the premiums such stamps command.
- **Superb**— perfect centering. They are so scarce that no comprehensive price list could attempt to include a superb category. Superb stamps, when they are available, command very high premiums.
- **"Jumbo"**—an abnormal condition, in which the stamp's margins are oversized compared to those of the average stamp in a given issue. Such jumbos can occur in the plate making process when a design is cut into the printing plate and excessive space is allowed between that design and the adjacent stamps.

Note: Some collectors also define a "fine to very fine" condition, in which the margin balance falls into a mid-range between fine and very fine. In theory it may be an attractive compromise, but in practice the range between fine and very fine is too narrow to warrant a separate intermediate category.

Quality and Condition Definitions

In determining the value of a given stamp, a number of factors have to be taken into consideration. For mint stamps, the condition of the gum, whether or not it has been hinged, and the centering are all major factors that determine value. For used stamps, the factors to consider are cancellation and centering. The following H.E. Harris guidelines will enable you to determine the quality standards you may choose from in acquiring stamps for your collection.

Mint Stamps Gum

Unused—A stamp that is not cancelled (used), yet has had all the original gum removed. On early U.S. issues this is the condition that the majority of mint stamps exist in, as early collectors often soaked the gum off their stamps to avoid the possibility of the gum drying and splitting.

Original Gum (OG)—A stamp that still retains the adhesive applied when the stamp was made, yet has been hinged or had some of the gum removed. Mint stamps from #215 to date can be supplied in this condition.

Never Hinged (NH)—A stamp that is in "post office" condition with full gum that has never been hinged. For U.S. #215 to #1241 (1963), separate pricing columns or percentages are provided for "Never Hinged" quality. From #1242 (1964) to date, all stamps are priced as Never Hinged. Hinged Stamps 1964 to date are available at 20% off the NH price.

Cancellations

The cancellations on Used stamps range from light to heavy. A lightly cancelled stamp has the main design of the stamp clearly showing through the cancel, while a heavy cancel usually substantially obliterates the design elements of the stamp. In general it should be assumed that Very fine quality stamps will have lighter cancels than average cancellation stamps.

Heavy Cancel

Light Cancel

GUM

The impact of the condition of the back of an unused stamp (i.e., the gum) upon that stamp's value in today's market needs careful consideration. The prices for 19th century stamps vary widely based on this element of condition.

Some traditional collectors feel that modern collectors pay too much attention to gum condition. Around the turn of the century, some collectors washed the gum off the stamps to prevent it from cracking and damaging the stamp themselves. But that generation is past and the practice not only is no longer popular, it is almost unheard of.

To some extent the washing of gum is no longer necessary, since modern gums are not as susceptible to cracking. A more important development, however, has been the advent of various mounts that allow the collector to place a stamp in an album without the use of a hinge. With that development, "never hinged" became a premium condition that could be obtained on stamps issued from the 1930s to date. As a result, gum took on added significance and its absence on 20th century stamps became unacceptable.

The standard definitions that pertain to gum condition are as follows:
- **Original gum**, or **o.g.**—the gum that was applied when the stamp was produced. There are gradations, from "full" original gum, through "partial" o.g. down to "traces". For all intents and purposes, however, a stamp must have most of its original gum to be described as "o.g."
- **Regummed**— the stamp has gum, but it is not that which would have been applied when the stamp was produced. Many collectors will avoid regummed stamps because the gum may hide some repair work. At best, regumming may give the stamp an appearance of completeness, but a premium should not be paid for a stamp that lacks its original gum.
- **Unused**—while many collectors think of this as any stamp that is not used, the narrow philatelic definition indicates a stamp that has no gum or is regummed.
- **Unhinged**—as with "unused", the term has a specific meaning to collectors: a regumming that shows no traces of a hinge mark. Unfortunately, in their confusion some collectors purchase stamps described as "unused" and "unhinged" as if they bore original gum.
- **No gum**—the stamp lacks its gum, either because it was intentionally produced without gum (also described as **ungummed**) or had the gum removed at a later date. It is customary to find 19th century stamps without gum, and the condition is acceptable to all but the most fastidious collectors. On 20th century stamps, original gum is to be expected.

- **Hinged**—the gum shows traces of having been mounted with a hinge. This can range from **lightly hinged** (the gum shows traces, but none of the hinge remains) to **heavily hinged** (a substantial portion of one or more hinge remnants is stuck to the stamp, or a significant portion of the gum has been lost in the removal of a hinge).
- **Thinned**—not only has the gum been removed, but a portion of the stamp paper has been pulled away. A thin usually will show when the stamp is held to a light. One of the faults that may be covered over on regummed stamps is a thin that has been filled in.
- **Never hinged**—as the name implies, the stamp has its original gum in post office condition and has never been hinged. Although some collectors think of **"mint"** stamps as any form of unused, o.g. stamps, the more accepted "mint" definition is never hinged.

USED STAMPS

For used stamps, the presence of gum would be the exception, since it would have been removed when the stamp was washed from the envelope, so gum is not a factor on used stamps.

The centering definitions, on the other hand, would be the same as for unused issues. In addition, the cancellation would be a factor.

We should point out here that we are not referring to the type of cancellation, such as a fancy cancel that might add considerably to the value of a stamp or a manuscript cancel that reduces its value. Rather, we are referring to the degree to which the cancellation covers the stamp.

A **lightly cancelled** used stamp, with all of the main design elements showing and the usage evidenced by an unobtrusive cancel, is the premier condition sought by collectors of used stamps. On the other hand, a stamp whose design has been substantially obliterated by a **heavy cancel** is at best a space filler that should be replaced by a moderate to lightly cancelled example.

PERFORATIONS

The condition of a stamp's perforations can be determined easily by visual examination. While not necessarily perfect, all perforations should have full teeth and clean perforation holes. A **blunt perf** is one that is shorter than it should be, while a **pulled perf** actually shows a portion of the margin or design having been pulled away. **Blind perfs** are the opposite: paper remains where the perforation hole should have been punched out.

One irony of the demand for perforation is that **straight edges**, that is, the normal sheet margin straight edge that was produced when flat-plate sheets were cut into panes, are not acceptable to many collectors. In fact, many collectors will prefer a reperforated stamp to a straight edge. (Technically, **"re"perforated** can only apply to a stamp that is being perforated again, as when a damaged or excessive margin has been cut away and new perforations are applied, but we will follow the common practice of including the perforation of normal straight edges in this category).

As a result of this preference, many straight edges no longer exist as such. When one considers that they were in the minority to start with (a pane of 100 flat plate stamps would include 19 straight edges) and that even fewer come down to us today, an argument could be made that they may someday be rarities...although it is hard to conceive of anyone paying a premium for straight edges.

FAKES, FAULTS, AND EXPERTIZING

Below the first quality level—stamps free of defects—a range of stamps can be found from attractive **"seconds"** that have barely noticeable flaws to **space fillers** that may have a piece missing and which ought to be replaced by a better copy—unless we are talking about great rarities which would otherwise be beyond the budget of most collectors.

The more common flaws include **thins, tears, creases, stains, pulled perfs, pinholes** (some dealers and collectors used to display their stamps pinned to boards), **face scuffs** or erasures, and **fading**.

Stamps with faults sometimes are **repaired**, either to protect them from further damage or to deceive collectors.

While the terms that are applied to stamps that are not genuine often are used interchangeably, they do have specific meaning, as follows.
- **fakes**–(in French, faux; in German, falsch)–stamps that appear to be valuable varieties, but which were made from cheaper genuine stamps. Trimming away the perforations to create an imperforate is a common example of a fake.
- **bogus** stamps, **phantoms, labels**–outright fantasies, usually the product of someone's imagination, produced for amusemenr rather than deception.

While most stamps are genuine, and the average collector need not be concerned about the possibility of repairs, **expertizing** services do exist for collectors who are willing to pay a fee to obtain an independent opinion on their more valuable stamps.

The UNITED STATES STAMP IDENTIFIER

Shows you how to distinguish between the rare and common U.S. stamps that look alike.

Types of 1¢ Franklin Design of 1851-60

TYPE I—has the most complete design of the various types of stamps. At top and bottom there is an unbroken curved line running outside the bands reading "U.S. POSTAGE" and "ONE CENT". The scrolls at bottom are turned under, forming curls. The scrolls and outer line at top are complete.

TYPE Ia—is like Type I at bottom but ornaments and curved line at top are partly cut away.

TYPE Ib—(not illustrated) is like Type I at top but little curls at bottom are not quite so complete nor clear and scroll work is partly cut away.

TYPE II—has the outside bottom line complete, but the little curls of the bottom scrolls and the lower part of the plume ornament are missing. Side ornaments are complete.

 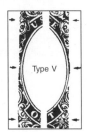

TYPE III—has the outside lines at both top and bottom partly cut away in the middle. The side ornaments are complete.

TYPE IIIa—(not illustrated) is similar to Type III with the outer line cut away at top or bottom, but not both.

TYPE IV—is similar to Type II but the curved lines at top or bottom (or both) have been recut in several different ways, and usually appear thicker than Type IIs.

TYPE V—is similar to Type III but has the side ornaments partly cut away. Type V occurs only on perforated stamps.

Types of 3¢ Washington & 5¢ Jefferson Designs of 1851-60

3¢ WASHINGTON
TYPE I—has a frame line around the top, bottom and sides.

TYPE II—has the frame line removed at top and bottom, while the side frame lines are continuous from the top to bottom of the plate.

TYPE IIa—is similar to Type II, but the side frame lines were recut individually, and therefore are broken between stamps.

5¢ JEFFERSON
TYPE I—is a complete design with projections (arrow) at the top and bottom as well as at the sides.

TYPE II—has the projections at the top or bottom partly or completely cut away.

Types of the 10¢ Washington Design of 1851-60

  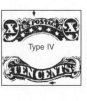 

TYPE I—has the "shells" at the lower corners practically complete, while the outer line below "TEN CENTS" is very nearly complete. At the top, the outer lines above "U.S. POSTAGE" above the "X" in each corner are broken.

TYPE II—has the design complete at the top, but the outer line at the bottom is broken in the middle and the "shells" are partially cut away.

TYPE III—has both top and bottom outer lines cut away; similar to Type I at the top and Type II at the bottom.

TYPE IV—has the outer lines at the top or bottom of the stamp, or at both place, recut to show more strongly and heavily.

Types I, II, III and IV have complete ornaments at the sides and three small circles or pearls (arrow) at the outer edges of the bottom panel.

TYPE V—has the side ornaments, including one or two of the small "pearls" partly cut away. Also, the outside line, over the "X" at the right top, has been partly cut away.

Types of the 12¢ Washington issues of 1851-60

PLATE 1 has stronger, more complete outer frame lines than does Plate 3. Comes imperforate (#17 or perf #36).

PLATE 3 has uneven or broken outer frame lines that are particularly noticeable in the corners. The stamps are perf 15. (#36b)

The REPRINT plate is similar to plate 1, but the Reprint stamps are greenish black and slightly taller than plate 1 stamps (25mm from top to bottom frame lines versus 24.5 mm) The paper is whiter and the perforations are 12 gauge.

The UNITED STATES STAMP IDENTIFIER

Shows you how to distinguish between the rare and common U.S. stamps that look alike.

Types of the 1861 Issue, Grills & Re-Issues

Shortly after the outbreak of the Civil War in 1861, the Post Office demonitized all stamps issued up to that time in order to prevent their use by the Confederacy. Two new sets of designs, consisting of six stamps shown below plus 24¢ and 30¢ demonitized, were prepared by the American Bank Note Company. The first designs, except for the 10¢ and 24¢ values, were not regularly issued and are extremely rare and valuable. The second designs became the regular issue of 1861. The illustrations in the left column show the first (or unissued) designs, which were all printed on thin, semi-transparent paper. The second (or regular) designs are shown at right.

Types of the 1861 Issues

1st

SECOND DESIGN shows a small dash (arrow) under the tip of the ornaments at the right of the figure "1" in the upper left-hand corner of the stamp.

2nd

1st

SECOND DESIGN, 3¢ value, shows a small ball (arrow) at each corner of the design. Also, the ornaments at the corners are larger than in the first design.

2nd

1st

SECOND DESIGN, 5¢ value has a leaflet (arrow) projecting from the scrolled ornaments at each corner of the stamp.

2nd

1st

FIRST DESIGN has no curved line below the row of stars and there is only one outer line of the ornaments above them.
SECOND DESIGN has a heavy curved line below the row of stars (arrow); ornaments above the stars have double outer line.

2nd

2nd

FIRST DESIGN has rounded corners.
SECOND DESIGN has a oval and a scroll (arrow) in each corner of the design

Types of the 15¢ "Landing of Columbus" Design of 1869

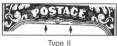
Type I   Type II

TYPE I has the central picture without the frame line shown in Type II.
TYPE II has a frame line (arrows) around the central picture; also a diamond shaped ornament appears below the "T" of "Postage".
TYPE III (not illustrated) is like Type I except that the fringe of brown shading lines which appears around the sides and bottom of the picture on Types I and II has been removed.

IDENTIFIER CHART
1861-1867 Bank Notes

Description and Identifying Features				1¢	2¢	3¢	5¢	10¢	12¢	15¢	24¢	30¢	90¢
1861. National. First designs. Thin, semi-transparent paper. No grill.				55		56	57	58[1], 62B	59		60	61	62
1861-62. National. Modified designs[3]. Thicker, opaque paper. No grill.				63		64[2], 65[2], 66[2]	67	68	69		70[2]	71	72
1861-66. National. Thicker, opaque paper. No grill. a. New designs.					73					77			
b. Same designs, new shades.						74[2]	75[2], 76[2]			78[2]			
1867. National. Grills. All on thick, opaque paper.													
Grills	Pts. as seen from stamp face	Area of covered Horiz. x Vert.	# of rows of Pts.										
A	Up	All over	—				79	80				81	
B	Up	18 x 15 mm	22 x 18				82						
C	Up	c. 13 x 16 mm	16-17 x 18-21				83						
D	Down	c. 12 x 14 mm	15 x 17-18		84		85						
Z	Down	c. 11 x 14 mm	13-14 x 17-18	85A	85B	85C		85D	85E	85F			
E	Down	c. 11 x 13 mm	14 x 15-17	86	87	88		89	90	91			
F	Down	c. 9 x 13 mm	11-12 x 15-17	92	93	94	95	96	97	98	99	100	101
1875. National. Re-issues. Hard, white paper. White crackly gum. No grill.				102	103	104	105	106	107	108	109	110	111

FOOTNOTES:
1. #58 does not exist used. Unused, it cannot be distinguished from #62B.
2. Different from corresponding 1861-66 issues only in color.
3. See diagrams for design modification.

The UNITED STATES STAMP IDENTIFIER

Shows you how to distinguish between the rare and common U.S. stamps that look alike.

Types of the 1870-71 Through 1887 Bank Notes

The stamps of the 1870-71 issue were printed by the National Bank Note Company. The similar issue of 1873 was printed by the Continental Bank Note Company. When Continental took over the plates previously used by National, they applied the so-called "secret marks" to the designs of the 1¢ through 15¢ denominations by which the two issues can be distinguished as shown below. The illustrations at the left show the original designs of 1870-71; those at the right show secret marks applied to the issue of 1873.

 1¢ Secret mark is a small curved mark in the pearl at the left of the figure "1".

 7¢ Secret mark is two tiny semicircles drawn around the end of the lines which outline the ball in the lower right-hand corner.

 2¢ 1870-71 are red brown. The 1873 issue is brown and in some copies has a small diagonal line under the scroll at the left of the "U.S." (arrow).

 10¢ Secret mark is a small semicircle in the scroll at the right-hand side of the central design.

 3¢ Secret mark is the heavily shaded ribbon under the letters "RE".

 12¢ Secret mark shows the "balls" at the top and bottom on the figure "2" crescent-shaped (right) instead of nearly round as at the left.

 6¢ Secret mark shows the first four vertical lines of shading in the lower part of the left ribbon greatly strengthened.

 15¢ Secret mark shows as strengthened lines (arrow) in the triangle in the upper left-hand corner, forming a "V".

IDENTIFIER CHART
1870-1887 Bank Notes

Description and Identifying Features	1¢	2¢	3¢	5¢	6¢	7¢	10¢	12¢	15¢	21¢	30¢	90¢
1870-71. National. No secret marks. White wove paper, thin to medium thick. With grills.	134	135	136		137	138	139	140	141	142	143	144
1870-71. National. As above, except without grills.	145	146	147		148	149	150	151	152	153	154[2]	155[2]
1873. Continental. White wove paper, thin to thick. No grills.												
a. With secret marks.	156	157	158		159	160	161	162	163			
b. No secret marks.											165[2]	166[2]
1875. Continental. Special Printing. Same designs as 1873 Continental. Hard, white wove paper. No gum.	167	168	169		170	171	172	173	174	175	176	177
1875. Continental. New color or denomination. Hard yellowish, wove paper.		178		179								
1875. Continental. Special printing. Same designs as 1875 Continental. Hard, white wove paper. No gum.		180		181								
1879. American. Same designs as 1873-75. Continental. Soft, porous paper.	182	183[3]	184[3]	185	186[3]		188		189[3]		190[3]	191[3]
a. Without secret mark.							187[3]					
1880. American. Special printing. Same as 1879 issue. Soft, porous paper. No gum.	192	193, 203[3]	194[3]	204	195[3]	196	197[3]	198	199[3]	200	201[3]	202[3]
1881-82. American. Designs of 1873. Re-engraved[4]. Soft, porous paper.	206		207[5]		208		209					
1887. American. Same designs as 1881-82. New colors.		214[5]									217	218

FOOTNOTES:
1. See diagrams for secret marks.
2. Corresponding denominations differ from each other only in color.
3. Corresponding denominations differ from each other only in color and gum. The special printings are slightly deeper and richer. The lack of gum is not positive identifier because it can be washed from the 1879 issues.
4. See diagrams for re-engravings.
5. Corresponding denominations differ from each other in color.

The UNITED STATES STAMP IDENTIFIER

Shows you how to distinguish between the rare and common U.S. stamps that look alike.

Re-Engraved Designs 1881-82

1¢ has strengthened vertical shading lines in the upper part of the stamp, making the background appear almost solid. Lines of shading have also been added to the curving ornaments in the upper corners.

3¢ has a solid shading line at the sides of the central oval (arrow) that is only about half the previous width. Also a short horizontal line has been cut below the "TS" of "CENTS".

6¢ has only three vertical lines between the edge of the panel and the outside left margin of the stamp. (In the preceding issues, there were four such lines.)

10¢ has only four vertical lines between the left side of the oval and the edge of the shield. (In the preceding issues there were five such lines.) Also, the lines in the background have been made much heavier so that these stamps appear more heavily linked than previous issues.

2¢ Washington Design of 1894-98

TYPE I has horizontal lines of the same thickness within and without the triangle.

TYPE II has horizontal lines which cross the triangle but are thinner within it than without.

TYPE III has thin lines inside the triangle and these do not cross the double frame line of the triangle.

2¢ Columbian "Broken Hat" Variety of 1893

231

As a result of a plate defect, some stamps of the 2¢ Columbian design show a noticeable white notch or gash in the hat worn by the third figure to the left of Columbus. This "broken hat" variety is somewhat less common than the regular 2¢ design.

Broken Hat variety, 231c

4¢ COLUMBIAN BLUE ERROR

Collectors often mistake the many shades of the normal 4¢ ultramarine for the rare and valuable blue error. Actually, the "error" is not ultramarine at all, but a deep blue, similar to the deeper blue shades of the 1¢ Columbian.

$1 Perry Design of 1894-95

TYPE I shows circles around the "$1" are broken at point where they meet the curved line below "ONE DOLLAR" (arrows).

TYPE II shows these circles complete.

10¢ Webster design of 1898

TYPE I has an unbroken white curved line below the words "TEN CENTS".

TYPE II shows white line is broken by ornaments at a point just below the "E" in "TEN" and the "T" in "CENTS" (arrows).

2¢ Washington Issue of 1903

Die I
319, 319g, 320

The rounded inner frame line below and to the left "T" in "TWO" has a dark patch of color that narrows, but remains strong across the bottom.

Die II
319f, 320a

2¢ "cap of 2" Variety of 1890

Cap on left "2"

Plate defects in the printing of the 2¢ "Washington" stamp of 1890 accounts for the "Cap of left 2" and "Cap on both 2s" varieties illustrated.

Cap on right "2"

XVI

The UNITED STATES STAMP IDENTIFIER

Shows you how to distinguish between the rare and common U.S. stamps that look alike.

FRANKLIN AND WASHINGTON ISSUES OF 1908-22

Perforation	Watermark	Other Identifying Features		1¢ Franklin	2¢ Washington	1¢ Washington	2¢ Washington	3¢ thru $1 denominations	8¢ thru $1 denominations
PERF. 12	USPS (double)	White paper		331	332			333-42	422-23
		Bluish gray paper		357	358			359-66	
	USPS (single)	White paper		374	375	405	406	376-82, 407	414-21
COIL 12	USPS (double)	Perf. Horizontal		348	349			350-51	
		Perf. Vertical		352	353			354-56	
	USPS (single)	Perf. Horizontal		385	386				
		Perf. Vertical		387	388			389	
IMPERF.	USPS (double)			343	344			345-47	
	USPS (single)	Flat Plate		383	384	408	409		
		Rotary Press					459		
	Unwmkd.	Flat Plate				481	482-82A	483-85	
		Offset				531	532-34B	535	
COIL 8-1/2	USPS (single)	Perf. Horizontal		390	391	410	411		
		Perf. Vertical		392	393	412	413	394-96	
PERF. 10	USPS (double)								460
	USPS (single)					424	425	426-30	431-40
	Unwmkd.	Flat Plate				462	463	464-69	470-78
		Rotary Press				543			
COIL 10	USPS (single)	Perf. Horizontal	Flat			441	442		
			Rotary			448	449-50		
		Perf. Vertical	Flat			443	444	445-47	
			Rotary			452	453-55	456-58	
	Unwmkd.	Perf. Horizontal				486	487-88	489	
		Perf. Vertical				490	491-92	493-96	497
PERF. 11	USPS (double)				519				
	USPS (single)						461		
	Unwmkd.	Flat Plate				498	499-500	501-07	508-18
		Rotary Press				*544-45	546		
		Offset				525	526-28B	529-30	
Perf. 12-1/2	Unwkmd.	Offset				536			
11 x 10	Unwmkd.	Rotary				538	539-40	541	
10 x 11	Unwmkd.	Rotary				542			

* Design of #544 is 19 mm wide x 22-1/2 mm high. #545 is 19-1/2 to 20 mm wide x 22 mm high.

Size of Flat Plate Design — 18-1/2 to 19mm, 22mm

Stamps printed by rotary press are always slightly wider or taller on issues prior to 1954. Measurements do not apply to booklet singles.

HOW TO USE THIS IDENTIFICATION CHART

Numbers referred to herein are from Scott's Standard Postage Stamp Catalog. To identify any stamp in this series, first check the type by comparing it with the illustrations at the top of the chart. Then check the perforations, and whether the stamp is single or double line watermarked or unwatermarked. With this information you can quickly find out the Standard Catalog number by checking down and across the chart. For example, a 1¢ Franklin, perf. 12, single line watermark, must be Scott's #374.

The UNITED STATES STAMP IDENTIFIER

Shows you how to distinguish between the rare and common U.S. stamps that look alike.

Types of The 2¢ Washington Design of 1912-20

Type I

Type I where the ribbon at left above the figure "2" has one shading line in the first curve, while the ribbon at the right has one shading line in the second curve. Bottom of toga has a faint outline. Top line of toga, from bottom to front of throat, is very faint. Shading lines of the face, terminating in front of the ear, are not joined. Type I occurs on both flat and rotary press printings.

Type Ia is similar to Type I except that all of the lines are stronger. Lines of the Toga button are heavy. Occurs only on flat press printings.

Type Ia

Type II

Type II has ribbons shaded as in Type I. Toga button and shading lines to left of it are heavy. Shading lines in front of ear are joined and end in a strong vertically curved line (arrow). Occurs only on rotary press printings.

Type III where ribbons are shaded with two lines instead of one; otherwise similar to Type II. Occurs on rotary press printings only.

Type III

Type IV

Type IV where top line of toga is broken. Shading lines inside the toga bottom read "Did". The Line of color in the left "2" is very thin and usually broken. Occurs on offset printings only.

Type V in which top line of toga is complete. Toga button has five vertical shaded lines. Line of color in the left "2" is very thin and usually broken. Nose shaded as shown in illustration. Occurs on offset printings only.

Type V

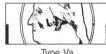
Type Va

Type Va is same as Type V except in shading dots of nose. Third row of dots from bottom has four dots instead of six. Also, the Overall height of Type Va is 1/3 millimeter less than Type V. Occurs on offset printings only.

Type VI is same as Type V except that the line of color in left "2" is very heavy (arrow). Occurs in offset printings only.

Type VI

Type VII

Type VII in which line of color in left "2" is clear and continuous and heavier than Types V or Va, but not as heavy as in Type VI. There are three rows of vertical dots (instead of two) in the shading of the upper lip, and additional dots have been added to hair at top of the head. Occurs on offset printings only.

Types of The 3¢ Washington Design of 1908-20

Type I

TYPE I in which the top line of the toga is weak, as are the top parts of the shading lines that join the toga line. The fifth shading line from the left (arrow) is partly cut away at the top. Also the line between the lips is thin. Occurs on flat and rotary press printings.

Type II

TYPE II where top line of toga is strong and the shading lines that join it are heavy and complete. The line between the lips is heavy. Occurs on flat and rotary press printings.

Type III

TYPE III in which top line of toga is strong, but the fifth shading line from the left (arrow) is missing. The center line of the toga button consists of two short vertical lines with a dot between them. The "P" and "O" of "POSTAGE" are separated by a small line of color. Occurs on offset printings only.

Type IV

TYPE IV in which the shading lines of the toga are complete. The center line of the toga button consists of a single unbroken vertical line running through the dot in the center. The "P" and the "O" of "POSTAGE" are joined. Type IV occurs only in offset printings.

COMMEMORATIVE IDENTIFIER

The following handy identifier is a list of commemoratives organized alphabetically by key words on the stamp which are the most prominent after "U.S. Postage" and matches the stamp with its corresponding Scott number.

Abbey, Edwin Austin ... 3502k
Abbott & Costello ... 2566
Abraham Lincoln ... 2975j
Abyssinian Cat ... 2373
Acadia National Park ... 746, 762
Acheson, Dean ... 2755
Acoma Pot ... 1709
Adams
    Abigail ... 2146
    John ... 806, 841, 850, 1687a, 2201, 2216b
    John Quincy ... 811, 846, 2201, 2216f
Addams, Jane ... 878
Admiralty Head Lighthouse (WA) ... 2470, 2474
Adopting a Child ... 3398
Adventures of Huckleberry Finn, The ... 2787
African
    Americans 873, 902, 953, 1085, 1233, 1290, 1361, 1372, 1486, 1490-1491, 1493, 1495, 1554, 1560, 1772, 1791, 1860, 1865, 2027, 2043, 2051, 2083, 2084, 2097, 2164, 2211, 2223, 2275, 2420, 2496, 2746, 2766, C97, C102, C103, C105
    Elephant Herd ... 1388
    Violet ... 2495
Agave Cactus ... 1943
Aging Together ... 2011
AIDS Awareness ... 2806
Air
    Air Service Emblem ... C5
    -Cushion Vehicle ... C123, C126
    Force ... 1013, C49
    Force, U.S. ... 3167
    Mail Service, US ... C74
    Save Our ... 1413
    Service Emblem ... C5
Airborne units spearhead attacks ... 2838d
Aircraft ... 3142
Aircraft Gun 90mm, Anti ... 900
Airlift ... 1341
Airliner, Hypersonic ... C122, C126
Alabama ... 1654, 1953
    Statehood ... 1375
Alamo, The ... 776, 778, 1043
Alaska ... 1681, 1954
    (Cook, Captain James) ... 1732, 1733
    Highway ... 2635
    Purchase ... C70
    Statehood ... 2066, C53
    Territory ... 800
    -Yukon Pacific Exposition ... 370-371
Alaskan
    Malamute ... 2100
    Brown Bear ... 2310
Albania ... 918
Alcoholism, You Can Beat It ... 1927
Alcott, Louisa May ... 862
Alexandria ... C40
Alger, Horatio ... 2010
All Aboard ... 3333-37
All in the Family, TV Series ... 3189b
Allegiance, Pledge of ... 2594
Allen, Ethan ... 1071
Alley Oop ... 3000n
Alliance for Progress ... 1234
Alliance, French ... 1753
Allied forces retake New Guinea ... 2838a
    Nations ... 537, 907
    Victory ... 537
Allies
    attack Sicily ... 2765c
    battle U-Boats ... 2765a
    Break Codes ... 2697f
    free Rome, June 4: Paris, August 25 ... 2838f
    in Normandy, D-Day ... 2838c
    Land in North Africa ... 2697j
    Liberate Holocaust survivors ... 2981e
Alligator ... 1428
Allosaurus ... 1390, 3136g
Alpha ... 3142e
Alpha Airplane ... 3142a
Alta, California, 1st Civil Settlement ... 1725
Amateur Radio ... 1260
Ambulance ... 2128, 2231
America
    Beautification of ... 1318, 1365, 1366
    Smiles ... 3189m
    Survives the Depression ... 3185k
America's Libraries ... 2015
America PUAS ... 2426, 2512, C121, C127
America/PUASP ... C131

American ... 1596, 1597, 1598, 1599, 1603-1606, 1608, 1610-1615
Architecture ... 1779-1782, 1838, 1839-1841, 1928-1931, 2019-2022
Art ... 3236
Arts ... 1484-1487, 1553-1555
Automobile Association ... 1007
Bald Eagle ... 1387
Bankers Association, Jan. 3 ... 987
Bar Association ... 1022
Bicentennial ... 1432, 1456-1459, 1476-1479, 1480-1483, 1543-1546, 1559-1568, 1629-1631, 1633-1647, 1648-1667, 1668-1674, 1676-1682, 1686-1694, 1704, 1716-1720, 1722, 1726, 1728, 1753, 1789, 1811, 1813, 1816, 1937-1938, 2052
Cats ... 2372-2373, 2374-2375
Chemical Society ... 1002
Child ... 3151e
Circus ... 1309
Credo ... 1139-1144
Crocodile ... 3105d
Dance ... 1749-1752
Dance, Ballet ... 1749
Dogs ... 2098-2101
Elk ... 2328
Flag ... 1623, 2116
Folklore ... 1317, 1330, 1357, 1370, 1470, 1548
Foxhound ... 2101
Gothic by Grant Wood ... 3236q
Horses ... 2155-2158
Illustrators ... 3502
Indian ... 565, 695, 1364
Indian Dances ... 3072-3076
Institute of Architects ... 1089
Kestrel ... 2476-2477, 3044
Legion ... 1369
Lobster ... 2304
Militia ... 1568
Music ... 1252, 2721-2737, 2767-2778, 2849-2861, 2982-2992, 3154-3165
Owls ... 1760-1763
Philatelic Society ... 730-731, 750, 766, 770
Realism ... 3184n
Red Cross ... 702, 967, 1910
Revolution ... 551, 645, 651, 653, 657, 689, 690, 727, 734, 752, 1010, 1729, 1851, 1937-1938
Revolution Battles ... 617-619, 629-630, 643-644, 646, 688, 1003, 1361, 1563-1564, 1686, 1722, 1728, 1826
Samoa ... 3389
Shoals Lighthouse (FL) ... 2473
Shorthair Cat ... 2375
Sign Language ... 2784
Society of Civil Engineers ... 1012
Sports ... 1932-1933, 2046, 2097, 2376-2377, 2417
Streetcar, First ... 2059
Trees ... 1764-1767
Turners Society ... 979
Washington ... 1675
Wildlife ... 2286-2287, 2288-2307, 2308-2316, 2322-2335
Woman ... 1152
Wool Industry ... 1423
Americana Issue ... 1581-1582, 1584-1585, 1590-1594, 1616-1619, 1622, 1623, 1625
Americans, African ... 873, 902, 953, 1085, 1233, 1290, 1361, 1372, 1486, 1490-1491, 1493, 1495, 1554, 1560, 1772, 1790, 1791, 1860, 1865, 2027, 2043, 2051, 2083-2084, 2097, 2164, 2211, 2223, 2275, 2420, 2496, 2746, 2766, C97, C102-C103, C105
AMERIPEX ... 2145
'86 ... 2198-2201, 2216-2219
Amethyst ... 1540
Amish Quilt ... 3524-27
Ammendment, 19th ... 3184e
Amphipod ... 3442
Anemone ... 3029
Angels ... 1268, 1276, 1363, 1471
Angus and Longhorn Cattle ... 1504
Animals,
    Humane, Treatment of ... 1307
Annapolis Tercentenary, May 23 ... 984
Antarctic Expedition, Byrd ... 733, 735, 753, 768
Antarctic Explorers ... 2386, 2387, 2388, 2389
Antarctic Treaty ... 1431, C130
Anthem, Flag and ... 1890, 1891, 1892, 1893
Anthony, Susan B. ... 784, 1051
Anti-Aircraft Gun, 90mm ... 900
Antibiotics saves lives ... 3186b
Antillean Euphonia ... 3222
Anti-Pollution ... 1410-1413

Antioch Dunes Evening Primrose ... 1786
Antique Automobiles ... 3019-3023a
Apgar, Virginia ... 2179
Apollo 8 ... 1371, 2633, 2634
Apollo, Soyuz ... 1569-1570
Appaloosa ... 2158
Appleseed, Johnny ... 1317
Appomattox, Civil War Centennial ... 1182
Apprenticeship ... 1201
Apte Tarpon Fly ... 2547
Arbor Day ... 717
Arc de Triompe ... 934
Architects, Institute of American ... 1089
Architecture, American ... 1779-1782, 1800-1802, 1838-1841, 1928-1931, 2019-2022
Archives, National ... 2081
Arctic
    Explorations ... 1128
    Fox ... 3289
    Hare ... 3288
Arizona ... 1680, 1955
    National Park (Grand Canyon) ... 741, 757, 2512
    Statehood ... 1192
Ark and The Dove, The ... 736
Arkansas ... 1657, 1956
    River Navigation ... 1358
    Statehood ... 782, 2167
Arlington Amphitheater ... 570, 701
Armadillo ... 2296
Armed
    Forces ... 926, 929, 934-936, 939, 1026, 1067
    Forces Reserve ... 1067
Armstrong,
    Edwin ... 2056
    Louis ... 2982, 2984
Army
    and Navy ... 900
    Issue ... 934, 985, 998, 1013, 1067
    Issue, Continental ... 1565
    Issue, Salvation ... 1267
Arnold, Gen. H.H. "Hap" ... 2191
Arrival of Lafayette ... 1010
Arrows ... E22-E23
Art
    Deco Style (Chrysler Building) ... 3184j
    Glass ... 3328
Arthur, Chester A. ... 826, 2218c
Articles of Confederation ... 1726
Artists ... 884-888, 1187, 1207, 1241, 1243, 1322, 1335, 1361, 1370, 1386, 1433, 1486, 1553, 1863, 1934, 2182, C71
Asia ... C131
Assassin bug ... 3351g
Assiniboine Headdress ... 2501
Aster ... 2993
Astronauts ... 1331, 1434-1435, 1912, 2419, 2632, C76
Atlantic
    Cable ... 1112
    Cod ... 2206
Atomic Energy Act ... 1200
Atoms For Peace ... 1070
Audubon, John James ... 874, 1241, 1863, C71
Austin, Stephen F. ... 776, 778
Australia Bicentennial ... 2370
Austria ... 919
Authors ... 859-863, 980, 1250, 1281, 1294, 1327, 1487, 1733, 1832, 1848, 1856-1857, 2010, 2047, 2073, 2094, 2168, 2196-2197, 2350, 2418, 2538
Auto Tail Fin ... 2908-2910
Automobile ... 296, 1162, 1286A, 1511, 1906, 2437, 2438d, 2905-2906
    Antique ... 3019-3023a
    Electric ... 1906
Avant-garde art, 1913 ... 3183d
Aviation
    Commercial ... 1684
    Naval ... 1185
    Pioneers of ... C91-C95, C99-C100, C113-C114, C118-C119, C128-C129
Aviator ... 2998
Azurite ... 2700
B-10 ... 3142f
B-24's hit Ploesti refineries ... 2765d
Baby Buggy ... 1902
Baby Coos ... 3151f
Babyland Rag ... 3151i
Badger ... 1922, 2312
Bailey, Mildred ... 2860
Balboa, Vasco Nunez de ... 397, 401
Bald Eagle ... 1909, 2309

Baldwin, Abraham	1850
Ball, Lucille	3523
Ballet	1749, 3237
Balloon Jupiter	C54
Ballooning	2530
Balloons, Hot Air	2032-2035
Ballot Box, Early	1584
Baltimore	
& Ohio Railroad	1006
Cathedral	1780
Bankers Association, American	987
Banking and Commerce	1577-1578
Banneker, Benjamin	1804
Bar Association, American	1022
Bara, Theda	2827
Barber, Samuel	3162
Barbie Doll	3188i
Barcelona	235
Barn Swallow	2286
Barney Google	3000i
Barred Owl	1762
Barrel Cactus	1942
Barry, John	790
Barrymores, The	2012
Bartholdi, Frederic Auguste	2147
Barton, Clara	967, 2975c
Bartram, John & William	3314
Baseball	855
Olympic	2619
Professional	1381, 2016, 2046, 2097, 2417
Basketball	
Centennial	2560
Naismith—	1189
Bass, Largemouth	2207
Bastogne and Battle of the Bulge	2838j
Battle for Leyte Gulf	2838i
Battle of	
Bennington	643, 644
Braddock's Field	688
Brooklyn	1003
Bunker Hill	1361, 1564
Chancellorsville	2975p
Coral Sea	2697c
Fallen Timbers	680
Fort Stanwix	644
Gettysburg	2975t
Lexington and Concord	1563
Mobile	1826
New Orleans	1261
Oriskany	644, 1722
Saratoga	644
Shiloh	2975e
White Plains	629, 630
Beach Clean-Up	2954
Beach Umbrella	2443
Beacon on Rocky Mountains	C11
Beagle	2098
Beale, Boggs, Lincoln and S. Douglas Debating	1115
Bearberry	2687
Bear	
Black	2299
Brown	1884
Polar	1429, 3291
Smokey, the	2096
Beatles, The "Yellow Submarine"	3188o
Beau Geste	2447
Beaugregory Fish	1827
Beautification of America	1318, 1365-1368
Beaver	2316
Beavertail Cactus	1944
Beckwourth, Jim	2869q
Belgium	914
Bell,	
Alexander Graham	893, 1683
Liberty	1518, C57, C62
Bella	
Bella Tribe, Heiltsuk	1834
Coola Tribe	1837
Benedict, Ruth	2938
Benet, Stephen Vincent	3221
Bengal Tiger, White	2709
Benny, Jack	2564
Bergen	
& McCarthy	2563
Edgar	2563
Bering Land Bridge	C131
Berlin Aircraft	3211
Berlin Wall, Fall of the	3190k
Bernstein, Leonard	3521
Bessie Coleman	2956
Best	
Friend of Charleston	2363
Wishes	2271, 2396
Bethune, Mary McLeod	2137
Betsy McCall	3151l
Bicycle	1460, 1901
Tandem	2266
Big Band	
Leaders	3096-99
Sounds	3186j
Big Brothers/Big Sisters	2162

Bighorn Sheep	1467, 1880, 1949, 2288
Bill of Rights	1312
Drafting of the	2421
Biltmore House	1929
Biplane	2436, 2438, 2438c, 2781
Bird of Paradise	3310
Bird Treaty, Migratory	1306
Birds	
& Flowers, State	1953-2002
Bison	1883, 2320
Bissell, Emily	1823
Black	
and Tan Coonhound	2101
Bear	2299
Heritage	1744, 1771, 1804, 1875, 2016, 2044, 2073, 2137, 2203, 2249, 2371, 2402, 2442, 2567, 2617, 2746, 2816, 2956, 3058, 3371
Hugo L.	2172
Widow	3351a
Black-footed Ferret	2333, 3105a
Black-tailed	
Jack Rabbit	2305
Prairie Dog	2325
Blacksmith	1718
Blackwell, Elizabeth	1399
Blair, Montgomery	C66
Blake, Eubie	2988
Bliss, Fort	976
Blondie	3000l
Blood Donor	1425
Blue Flag	2663
Blue Jay	1757, 1757d, 2318, 2483
Blue Paloverde	3194
Bluebird, Eastern	2478, 3033
Bluefin, Tuna	2208
Bluets	2656
BMX Biking	3322
Boatmen on the Missouri by George Caleb Bingham	3236f
Bobcat	2482, 2332
"Bobtail" Horsecar	2061
Bobwhite	2301
Bogart, Humphrey	3152
Bolivar, Simon	1110-1111
Bombardier beetle	3351m
Bon Homme Richard	983
Bonds and Stamps help	2765g
Books, Bookmark and Eyeglasses	1585
Boone, Daniel	1357
Borglum, Gutzon, Sculptured Head by	1114
Boston	
State House	1781
Tea Party	1480-1483
Terrier	2099
Botanical Congress	1376-1379
Boulder Dam	774
Bow, Clara	2820
Boxing	2766, 3182h
Box Turtle	2326
Bowling	2963
Boy Scouts	995, 1145, 2161, 3183j
Boys' Clubs of America	1163
Brachiosaurus	3136d
Bradley, Omar N.	3394
Brain Coral, Beaugregory Fish	1827
Bread Wagon	2136
Breakfast in Bed by Mary Cassatt	3236o
Breast Cancer Awareness	3081
Brice, Fanny	2565
Bridge	293, 961, 1012, 1109, 1258, 1721
at Niagara Falls	297
Brooklyn	1012, 2041
Bridger, Jim	2869c
Bright Eyes	3230-3234
Bringing Up Father	3000d
Broad-billed Hummingbird	2643, 2289
Broadbill Decoy	2138
Broadway Songwriters	3345-50
Brontosaurus	1390, 2425
Brooklyn Bridge	1012, 2041
Brooklyn, Battle of	1003
Brother Jonathan	2365
Brown	
Bear	1884
Horse with Green Bridle	2979
Pelican	1466, 3105h
Brussels Universal and International Exhibition	1104
Bryan, William Jennings	2195
Bryant, Bear	3143, 3148
Buchanan, James	820, 2217f
James (Wheatland)	1081
Buchanan's No. 999	2847
Buck, Pearl	1848
Buckboard	2124
Buffalo	287, 569, 700, 1392, 1883
Bill Cody	2178, 2869
Soldiers	2818
Buggy	1360, 1370, 1505, 1902
Baby	1418, 1902
Bullfinch, Charles	1781
Bull, John	2364

Bunchberry	2675
Bunche, Ralph	1860
Bunker Hill	1034, 1056
Flag	1351
Burbank, Luther	876
Bureau of Engraving and Printing	2875
Burgoyne Campaign	644, 1728
Burmese	2374
Butte	2902, 2902B
Butterflies	1712-1715
By 1945, World War II has uprooted millions	2981g
Byrd Antarctic Expedition II	733, 735, 753, 768
Richard E.	2388
Cab, Hansom	1904
Cabbage Patch Kids	3190i
Cable	
Car	1442
San Francisco	1442, 2263
TV	3190f
Caboose, RR	1905
Cabrillo, Juan Rodriguez	2704
Cadillac, Landing of	1000
Cagney, James	3329
Calder, Alexander	3198-3202
Calico Scallop	2120
California	1663, 1957, 3438
Condor	1430, 3105i
Gold	954
Gold Rush	3316
Pacific International Exposition	773, 778
Poppy	2651
Sea Lion	2329
Settlement	1373
Statehood	997
(Yosemite National Park)	740, 751, 756, 769
Calliope Hummingbird	2646
Camarasaurus	3136c
Camel	2392
Camellia	1877, 1935
Cameras, Motion Picture	1555
Camp Fire Girls	1167, 2163
Camptosaurus	3136b
Canada	1324
Goose	1757, 1757c, 2334
-US Friendship	961
Canal	298, 681, 856
Boat	2257
Erie	1325
Cancer	
Cancer, Crusade Against	1263
Detection, Early	1754
Candle	1205, 2395
Holder, Rush Lamp and	1610
Cannon	629-630, 1178, 1181
Canoe	1356, 2163, 2353A, 2453, 2454
Canvasback Decoy	2140
Cape Hatteras	1448-1451, 2471
CAPEX '78	1757-1757h
Capitol	572, 989, 992, 1202, 1365, 1503, 1590-1591, 1616, 1623, 2114, 2115, 2116, 2561, C64-C65
National Sesquicentennial	989-992
—Statue of Freedom on Dome	989
Cardinal	1465, 1757, 1757a, 1965-1966, 1969, 1985, 1987, 1998, 2000, 2480, 2489
in Snow	2874
Honeyeater	3225
CARE	1439
Carlson, Chester	2180
Carlyle House, John	C40
Carmel, Man and Children of	1485
Carnegie, Andrew	1171
Carolina Charter	1230
Carolina-Charleston	683
Carousel	
Animals	2390-2393
Horses	2976-2979a
Carpenters' Hall	1543
Carreta	2255
Carriage, Steam	2451
Carrier, Letter	1238, 1490, 1497, 2420
Cars, Classic	2381-2385
Carson	
Kit	2869n
Rachel	1857
Rachel Valley, NV	999
Carter Family, The	2773, 2776
Carteret, Philip, Landing of	1247
Caruso, Enrico	2250
Carver, George Washington	953, 3183c
Cashman, Nellie	2869k
Cassatt, Mary	1322, 2181
Catfish	2209
Cather, Willa	1487
Cats, American	2372-2375
Cats, Musical Smash	3190b
Catt, Carrie C.	959
Cattle	
Angus and Longhorn	1504
Western, in Storm	292
Celebrate the Century	

1900's	3182
1910's	3183
1920's	3184
1930's	3185
1940's	3186
1950's	3187
1960's	3188
1970's	3189
1980's	3190
1990's	3191
Cellular Phones	3191o
Centennial Olympic Games	3068, 3068a-68t
Century	
Of Progress Exposition	728-731
Flight	C18
20th, Limited	3335
Ceratosaurus	3136a
Certified Public Accountants	2361
Chalic Coral	1829
Challenger Space Shuttle	2544
Champions of Liberty	1096, 1110-1111, 1117-1118, 1136-1137
Guiseppe Garibaldi	1168-1169
Gustaf Mannerheim	1165-1166
Ignacy Jan Paderewski	1159-1160
Mahatma Gandhi	1174-1175
Masaryk	1147-1148
San Martin	1125-1126
Chancellorsville	2975p
Chaney, Lon	2822
Chaney, Lon, Jr.	3172
Chanute, Octave	C93-C94
Chaplin, Charlie	2821
Charles Mingus	2989
Charleston Carolina	683
Charleston, Best Friend of	2363
Charlie Parker	2987
Charlotte Amalie Harbor, St. Thomas, Virgin Islands	802
Charter	2559
Oak	772
Chaplin, Charlie as the Little Tramp	3183a
Chavez, Dennis	2186
Checkerspot	1713
Chemical Society, American	1002
Chemistry	1685
Chennault, Claire Lee	2187
Cherokee	
Seal	972
Strip	1360
Strip Land Run	2754
Cherub	2948
Chesapeake Bay Retriever	2099
Chestnut, Mary	2975o
Cheyenne Headdress	2502
Chicago, Century of Progress,	
Exposition	728-731, 766
Flight	C18
Chicksaw Seal	972
Children's Stamp	1085
Chief Joseph	1364, 2869f
Chief Shadoo	683
Child labor reform	3183o
Child on Hobby Horse	1769
Children	230, 235, 651, 717, 796, 855, 963, 995, 1005 1007, 1015, 1024, 1073, 1082, 1085, 1087, 1093, 1135, 1149, 1152, 1163, 1167, 1199, 1238, 1273, 1321-1322, 1336, 1342-1343, 1385, 1414, 1426, 1444, 1453, 1455, 1468, 1470, 1483, 1485, 1507, 1549, 1559, 1701, 1703, 1768-1769, 1772, 1788-1799, 1824, 1842, 1910, 1939, 2010-2011, 2026-2027, 2028-2029, 2030, 2063, 2104, 2106-2108, 2153, 2160-2165, 2199, 2244, 2251, 2275, 2367, 2399, 2427
Children's Friendship	1085
Chilkat Tlingit Tribe	1835
China Clipper	C115
Over the Pacific	C20-C22, C115
Republic of	1188
Chinese	
Hibiscus	3313
New Year	2876
Resistance	906
Chipmunk	1757f
Choctaw Seal	972
Christmas	3003-3018
4¢ '62	1205
5¢ '63	1240
5¢ '64	1254-1257
5¢ '65	1276
5¢ '66	1321
5¢ '67	1336
6¢ '68	1363
6¢ '69	1384
6¢ '70	1414-1418
8¢ '71	1444-1445
8¢ '72	1471-1472
8¢ '73	1507-1508
10¢ '74	1550-1552
10¢ '75	1579-1580
13¢ '76	1701-1703
13¢ '77	1729-1730
13¢ '82	2025
15¢ '78	1768-1769
15¢ '79	1799-1800
15¢ '80	1842-1843
20¢ '81	1939-1940
20¢ '82	2026-2030
20¢ '83	2063-2064
20¢ '84	2107-2108
22¢ '85	2165-2166
22¢ '86	2244-2245
22¢ '87	2367-2368
25¢ '88	2399-2400
25¢ '89	2427-2429
25¢ '90	2514-2516
29¢ '91	2578-2585
29¢ '92	2710-2719
29¢ '93	2789-2803
29¢ '94	2871-2874
32¢ '95	3003-3018
32¢ '96	3107-3117
32¢ '97	3176-3177
32¢ '98	3244
33¢ '99	3355-67
34¢ '01	3536
Churchill, Winston	1264, 2559, 2559d
Cigar-Store Figure	2243
Cinco de Mayo	3203, 3309
Circuit Board, Printed	1501
Circus	2750-2753
Circus	
American	1309
Wagon	2452-2452D
Cities, Save Our	1411
City	
Mail Delivery	1238
of Refuge National Park	C84
Civil	
Aeronautics Conference, International	649, 650
Service	2053
War	2975
War Centennial, Appomattox	1182
War Centennial, Fort Sumter	1178
War Centennial, Gettysburg	1180
War Centennial, Shiloh	1179
War Centennial, The Wilderness	1181
War, Grand Army of the Republic	985
War, United Confederate Veterans	998
Civilian Conservation Corps	2037
Clara Barton	2975c
Claret Cup Cactus	2660
Clark	
Expedition, Lewis and	1063
George Rogers	651
Grenville	1867
Classic	
American Aircraft	3142
American Dolls	3151
Books	2785-2786, 2788
Cars	2381-2385
Films	2445-2448, 2722
Mail Transportation	2434-2438
Clay, Henry	140, 151, 162, 173, 198, 227, 259, 274, 284, 309, 1846
Clemens,	
Samuel L.	863
Samuel L. (Mark Twain)	1470
Clemente, Roberto	2097, 3408j
Clermont	370-373, 1270
Cleveland, Grover	564, 693, 827, 2218d
Cliff Palace	743, 759
Cliffs of Green River by Thomas Moran	3236l
Cline, Patsy	2772, 2777
Clipper, 314	3142r
Clown	1390, 2750
Coal Car	2259
Coast and Geodetic Survey	1088
Coast Guard	936
Cobb, Ty	3408d
Cochrane, Mickey	3408g
Cobb, Col. David	1686, 1686d
Cochran, Jacqueline	3066
Cocker, Spaniel	2099
Cod, Atlantic	2206
Cody, Buffalo Bill	2177, 2869b
Coffeepot	
Curved Spout	1778
Straight-Spout	1775
Cog Railway Car	2463
Cohan, George M.	1756
Coil Stamps	2902, 2905, 2908, 2912, 2909
Cole, Nat "King"	2852
Coleman	
Bessie	2956
Hawkins	2983
Collective Bargaining	1558
College Football	1382, 2089
Collie	2100
Collins, Eddie	3408b
Colonial	
American Craftsmen	1456-1459
Post Rider	2779
Colorado	1670, 1958
(Mesa Verde National Park)	743, 759
Statehood	1001, 1711
Coltrane, John	2991
Columbia	
District of	2561
University	1029
Columbian	
Doll	3151b
Exposition	230-245, 2624-2629
Exposition, World Stamp Expo '92	2616
World Stamp Expo '92	2624, 2626-2629
Columbus	240, 2616, 2620-2623
Christopher	118-119, 230-245, 2616, 2620-2629, 2805
First Voyage of	2620-2623
Landing	118-119
Landing in Puerto Rico	2805
Monument	1076
Comanche Headdress	2503
Comedians	2562-2566
Comic Strip Classic	3000
Comiskey Park, Chicago	3517
Commerce, Banking and	1578
Commercial Aviation	1684
Commodity Rationing	2697b
Common	
Dolphin	2511
Sunflower	2666
Communications	
for Peace, Echo I—	1173
in Colonial Times	1476-1479
Compact Discs	3190h
Composers	879-883, 962, 1372, 1484, 1755-1756, 1845, 2044, 2110, 2177, 2211, 2371, 2550
Computer	
Technology	3106
Art and Graphics	3191f
Comstock, Henry	1130
Concord / German Immigration	2040
Concord, Lexington and	617-619, 1563
Condor, California	1430
Conestoga, Wagon	2252
Congratulations!	2267
Congress	
Liberty of	2004
Congressional	3334
Conifer, Sprig of	1257
Connecticut	1637, 1959
Settlement	772, 778
Statehood	2340
Conservation	
Corps, Civilian	2037
Energy	1547, 1723
Forest	1122
Range	1176
Soil	1133
Soil and Water	2074
Water	1150
Waterfowl	1362
Wildlife	1077-1079, 1098, 1392, 1427-1430, 1464-1467, 1760-1763
Constellation Airplane	3142m
Constitution	
Bicentennial	2336-2348, 2355-2360, 2412-2415, 2421
Drafting of the	2355-2359
Nineteenth Amendment	1051
Nineteenth Amendment (Suffrage)	784
Ratification	835, 2336-2348
Signing of the	798, 2360
Thirteenth Amendment	902
US Frigate	951
Construction toys	3183n
Consumer Education	2005
Contemplation of Justice	1592, 1617
Continental	
Army	1565
Colors, 1776	3403d
Congress, First	1543-1546
Marines	1567
Navy	1566
Contra Costa Wallflower	1785
Contributors to the Cause	1559-1562
Cook, Captain James	1732-1733
Coolidge, Calvin	834, 2219b
Coon Cat, Maine	2374
Coonhound, Black and Tan	2101
Cooper	
Gary	2447
James Fenimore	860
Cooperative for American Relief Everywhere (CARE)	1439
Copernicus, Nicolaus	1488
Copley	
Elizabeth	1273
John Singleton	1273
Copper	2701
Coral Reefs	1827-1830
Cord	2383
Cornwallis	
at Yorktown, Surrender of	703
Surrender of	1686

Cornwell, Dean	3502j
Coronado Expedition	898
Corregidor (Philippines)	925
Corsair Airplane	3142g
Corythosaurus	3136m
Cosby Show, The Hit Comedy	3190j
Costa's Hummingbird	2644
Cottontail	2290
Country & Western Music	2723, 2771-2778
Crane	
Black-Necked	2867
Ichabod	1548
Whooping	2868
Crater Lake National Park	745, 761
Crayola Crayons, introduced, 1903	3182d
Crazy Horse	1855
Creatures of the Sea	2508-2511
Credit Union Act	2075
Crested Honeycreeper	3224
Crime Prevention	2102
Crippled, Hope for the	1385
Crockett, Davy	1330
Crocus	3025
Crosby, Bing	2850
Crosley Field, Cincinnati	3512
Cross-Country Skiing	2810
Crusade Against Cancer	1263
Cub Airplane	3142c
Curtiss	
Glenn	C100
Jenny	C1-C3, C74, 3142s
Curved-Spout Coffeepot	1778
Cushing, Harvey, M.D.	2188
Cutler, Manasseh	795
Cycling	3119
Czechoslovakia	910
Daffodil	2761
Dahlia	1878, 2995
Dam	
Boulder	774
Grand Coulee	1009
Norris	1184
Dances, American Indian	3072-3076
Dante	1268
Dare, Virginia	796
Dartmouth College Case	1380
Daspletosaurus	3136k
David Farragut	2975g
Alexander J.	1841
Dr. Allison	2816
Jefferson	1408, 2975f
Davis	
Sr., Benjamin O.	3121
Jefferson	2975f
Daye Press, Stephen	857
Daylight	3333
DC-3 Airplane	3142q
DC-4 Skymaster	C32-C33, C37, C39, C41
de Grasse, Count	703
De Haviland Biplane	C6
Dean, James	3082
Decatur House	1440
Decatur, Stephen	791
Declaration of Independence	120, 1545, 1687
by John Trumbull	1691-1694
of War	2559j
Deer	2390
Mouse	2324
White-Tailed	1888
DeForest Audions	C86
Delaware	1633, 1960
Statehood	2336
Delivery of Letter	E20-E21
Delta Wing Plane Silhouette	C77
Dempsey, Jack wins title, 1919	3183m
Denmark	920
Dental Health	1135
Department	
of Agriculture	O1-O9, O94-O95
of Justice	O25-O34, O106-O107
of State	O57-O71
of the Air Force 1947-1997	3167
of the Interior	O15-O24, O96-O103
Desegregation public schools	3187f
Desert	
Five Spot	2690
Plants	1942-1945
Shield/Desert Storm	2551
Destroyer "Reuben James"	2559f
Detroit	1000
Development Energy	1724
Devils Tower National Monument	1084
Dewey	
George	793
John	1291
Diabetes	3503
Diamond Head, HI	C46
Dick Tracy	3000m
Dickinson	
Emily	1436
John	1687e, 1694
Dickson, William	3064
Dinosaurs (Prehistoric Animals)	2422-2425
Dirksen, Everett	1874
Disabled	
American Veterans and Servicemen	1421-1422
International Year of	1925
Disco Music	3189d
Discovery	1733
Disney, Walt	1355
District of Columbia	2561
Diver	
Coral	2866
Motorboat	2863
Ship	2864
Ship's Wheel	2865
Dix, Dorothea	1844
Dizzy Dean	3408s
Doctors	949, 1138, 1251, 1399, 1754, 1865, 2013, 2038, 2170, 2188
Dog Sled	1128, 2135
Dogbane beetle	3351e
Dogface	1714
Dogs	239, 619, 1128, 1307, 1468, 2202
American	2098-2101
Seeing Eye	1787
Dogwood	2347
Blossoms Lace Design	2354
Dolls	3151
Dolls by	
Martha Chase, "Alabama Baby"	3151a
Izannah Walker	3151h
Ludwig Greiner	3151k
Martha Chase	3151d
Albert Schoenhut	3151o
Dolphin, Common	2511
Dorchester, SS	956
Douglas Debates, Lincoln-	1115
Douglas Fir	1376
Douglass, Frederick	1290, 2975h
Dove	2877-2878
Dr. Seuss "The Cat in the Hat"	3187h
Dracula	3169
Drafting of the	
Bill of Rights	2421
Constitution	2355-2359
Drew M.D., Charles R.	1865
Drive-in movies	3187i
Drug Abuse, Prevent	1438
Drum	1615, 1629-1630
Dunn, Harvey	3502o
Drummer	1479, 1629, 1630
Du Sable, Jean Baptiste Pointe	2249
DuBois, W.E.B.	2617
Duck Decoys	2138-2141
Duck Stamps	
American Eider	RW24
American Merganser	RW23
Baldpates	RW9
Black Mallards	RW7
Black-Bellied Whistling Duck	RW57
Blue Geese	RW22
Blue-winged Teal	RW20
Buffleheads	RW15
Canada Geese	RW3, RW25, RW43
Canvasback Decoy	RW42
Canvasback Drake	RW32
Canvasbacks	RW2, RW42, RW49
Cinnamon Teal	RW38, RW52
Duckling	RW28
Emperor Geese	RW39
Fulvous Whistling Duck	RW18, RW53
Goldeneye Ducks	RW16
Green-winged Teal	RW6, RW46
Harlequin Ducks	RW19
Hawaiian Nene Geese	RW31
Hooded Merganser Drake	RW45
Hooded Mergansers	RW35
King Eider	RW58
Labrador Retriever	RW26
Lesser Scaup	RW56
Mallard Drake	RW26
Mallard Hen	RW28
Mallards	RW47
Mallards Alighting	RW1
Old Squaw Ducks	RW34
Pair of Brant	RW30
Pintail Drake and Hen Alighting	RW5
Pintail Drakes	RW29
Pintails	RW50
Redhead Ducks	RW13, RW27
Redheads	RW54
Ring-necked Ducks	RW27
Ross's Geese	RW37, RW44
Ruddy Ducks	RW8, RW48
Scaup Ducks	RW4
Shoveller	RW12
Snow Geese	RW14, RW55
Spectacled Eider	RW59
Steller's Eiders	RW40
Trumpeter Swans	RW17
Whistling Swans	RW33
White-fronted Geese	RW11
White-winged Scoters	RW36
Widgeons	RW51
Wood Ducks	RW10, RW41
Duck, Wood	2484-2485, 2493, 2494
Duesenberg	2385
Dulles	
Airport	2022
John Foster Memorial	1172
Dunbar, Paul Laurence	1554
Dung beetle	3351n
Dutchman's Breeches	2682
Eagan, Eddie	2499
Eagle	1743, 2598
and Shield	116, 1596, 2431, 2595-2597, 2602-2604, 2907, CE1-CE2
Bald	314A, 775, 909-921, 1090, 1131, 1140, 1313, 1344, 1387, 1424, 1831, 1909, 2111-2113, 2122, 2355, 2356-2359, 2394, 2431, 2534-2542, 2605-2606, C67
from Great Seal of the US	1369
in Flight	C48, C50
Nebula	3384
Weather Vane	1344
with Shield and Quill Pen	2421
with Shield, Olive Branch and Arrows	2413, C23
Eakins, Thomas	1335
Earhart, Amelia	C68
Early	
Ballot Box	1584
Cancer Detection	1754
Earp, Wyatt	2869j
Earth	1173, 1193, 1371, 1434, 1569-1570, 1913-1914, 1917, 1919, 2277, 2279, 2282, 2526, 2535, 2570, C122-C123, C125, C126
Clean-Up	2951
Day Issue	2951-2954, 3189a
Eastern	
Bluebird	2478, 3033
Chipmunk	2297
Hercules beetle	3351l
Eastman, George	1062
Ebbets Field, Brooklyn	3510
Ebony jewelwing	3351h
Echo I—Communications for Peace	1173
Eddie Rickerbacker	2998
Eddy's No. 242	2845
Edison	
Thomas (Electric Light's Golden Jubilee)	654-656
Thomas A.	945
Edmontonia	3136i
Education	
Consumer	2005
Higher	1206
Improving	3191e
(Land Grant Colleges)	1065
(Learning Never Ends)	1833
(Nation of Readers)	2106
(Parent-Teachers Association)	1463
Public	2159
Teachers of America	1093
Educators	869-873, 1093, 1291, 1824, 1850, 1852, 1854, 1861, 1920, 2137, 2169, 2171, 2194
Egalite	C120
Egg Nebula	3387
EID	3532
Einosaurus	3136j
Einstein, Albert	1285, 1774
Eisenhower, Dwight D.	1383, 1393-1395, 1401-1402, 2219g, 2513
El Capitan	740, 751, 756, 769
Elderberry longhorn	3351b
Electric	
Automobile	1906
Light's Golden Jubilee	654-656
Streetcar, Early	2060
Theories	2055
Toy Trains	
Electronics, Progress in	1500-1502, C86
Elephant	
Circus	2753
Herd, African	1388
Elevator	2254
Eliot	
Charles W.	871
T.S.	2239
Elk 1886	
Elkhorn Coral	1828
Elks, Support our Youth	1342
Ellington, Duke	2211
Ellsworth, Lincoln	2389
Ely's No. 10	2846
Emancipation Proclamation	1233
Emerson, Ralph Waldo	861
Emigration	290
Emily Post's Etiquette	3184f
Empire State Building	3185b
Empire State Express	296
Employ the Handicapped	1155
Endangered	
Flora	1783-1786
Species	3105

Energy	1723-1724
Conservation	1547, 1723
Development	1724
Engineering	1012
Engineers, American Society of	1012
English Sundew	3531
Envelopes, Sealed	2150
Environment, Preserve the	1527
Eohippus	3077
Ericsson Memorial, John	628
Erie Canal	1325
Erikson, Leif	1359
Erroll Garner	2992
E.T. the Extra-Terrestrial	3190m
Eubie Blake	2988
Everglades National Park	952
Ewry, Ray	2497
Executive	
Branch	2414
Department	O10-O14
Mansion	990
Exotic Shorthair Cat	2372
Experiment	2405
Explorer II	2035
Explorers	285, 288
Antarctic	2386-2389
Armstrong	C76
Balboa	397
Byrd	733, 735, 768, 2388
Cabrillo	2704
Cook	1732-1733
Coronado	898
de Leon	2024
Ellsworth	2389
Erikson	1359
Greely	2221
Henson	2223
Kane	2220
Lewis and Clark	1063
Marquette	1356
Nicolet	739, 755
Palmer	2386
Peary	1128, 2223
Polar	2220-2223
Powell	1374
Stefansson	2222
Verrazano	1258
Wilkes	2387
Expo '74	1527
Expositions	230-245, 285-293, 323-330, 370-371, 397-400, 401, 404, 630, 728-731, 735, 750-751, 766, 773, 778, 852-853, 948, 1075-1076, 1104, 1196, 1244, 1310-1311, 1340, 1342-1344, 1527, 1632, 1757, 2006-2009, 2086, 2410, 2616, 2624-2629
Express	
International	2542
Mail	1909, 2122, 2394, 2541
Extreme Sports	3191d
Eyeglasses, Books, Bookmark	1585
Fairbanks, Douglas	2088
Fall of Corregidor	2697d
Fallingwater	2019
Family	
Planning	1455
Unity	2104
Famous Americans	860-868, 870-893, 945, 953, 960, 965, 975, 980, 986, 988, 1062, 1072, 1121, 1138, 1170-1172, 1177
Fantasy, Space	2741-2745
Farley, Cal	2934
Farmers of America, Future	1024
Farming	286
Farnsworth, Philo T.	2058
Farragut, David G.	311, 792, 2975g
Fashion, 1970's	3189k
Faulkner, William	2350
Fawcett, Robert	3502d
Fawn	2479
FDR's New Deal	3185e
Federal	
Deposit Insurance Corporation	2071
Hall	1086
Reserve system created, 1913	3183b
Federated States of Micronesia	2506
Fenway Park, Boston	3516
Fermi, Enrico	3533
Ferryboat	2466
Fiedler, Arthur	3159
Fields, W.C.	1803
Fierce fighting frees Manila	2981b
Fife Player	1631
Fifth World Forestry Congress	1156
Fiftieth Anniversary of Statehood (Montana, North Dakota, South Dakota, Washington)	858
Fifty State Flags	1633-1647, 1648-1667, 1668-1682
Fifty-Star and 13-Star Flags	1509
Fifty-Star Runway	C72-C73
Figure Skating	3190e
Fillmore, Millard	818, 2217d
Films, Classic	2445-2448, 2722
Fine Arts	1259
Finger Coral	1830
Finland Independence	1334
Finnish Settlement, Swedish-	836
Finnish Settlement, Swedish (Stamp Collecting)	2200
Fir, Douglas	1376
Fire	
Engine Truck	971, 2264
Pumper	1908
Truck	971
Firemen, Volunteer	971
Fireweed	2679
Fireworks	2276
First	
Automated Post Office	1164
Baseball World Series, 1903	3182n
Civil Settlement—Alta, California	1725
Continental Congress	1543-1546
Crossword puzzle, pub., 1913	3183l
Kentucky Settlement	1542
Moon Landing	2841
Navy Jack	1354, 1566
Stars and Stripes	1350
Supersonic Flight 1947	3173
Television Camera	2058
Transcontinental telephone line, 1914	3183e
Voyage of Christopher Columbus	2620-2623
Fischer's Lovebirds	2537
Fish	2205-2209
(Anti-Pollution)	1412
Fanfin Anglerfish	3439
Fangtooth	3441
(Louisiana World Exposition)	2086
Medusa	3443
Pumpkinseed Sunfish	2491
Sea Cucumber	3440
(Wildlife Conservation)	1427
Fishing	
Boat	2529, 2529C
Flies	2545-2549
Fitzgerald, F. Scott	3104
Flag	2880, 2882-2892
and Anthem Issue	1890
29-Star, 1847	3403t
38-Star	3403q
49-Star, 1912	1132
50-Star	1153, 3403t
Bennington, c. 1820	3408h
Brandywine, 1777	3403f
Centennial, 1876	3403p
Easton, 1814	3403j
Forster, 1775	3403c
Fort Sumter, 1861	3403o
Francis Hopkins, 1777	3403e
Great Star, 1837	3403m
Indian Peace, 1803	3403i
John Paul Jones, 1779	3403g
New England, 1775	3403b
Over Capitol	2115, 2116
Over Field	2919
Over Porch	2897, 2913-2916, 2920-2921
Over Yosemite	2280
Peace, 1891	3403r
Pierre L'Enfant, 1783	3403h
Plane and Globes	C90
Sons of Liberty, 1775	3403a
With Clouds	2278, 2285A
With Fireworks	2276
Flagg, James Montgomery	3502a
Flags	231-233, 329, 372-373, 537, 614, 629-630, 690, 775, 778, 909-921, 923, 938, 942, 1000, 1010, 1034, 1069, 1088, 1123, 1239, 1271, 1275, 1407, 1625, 1645-1647, 1648-1667, 1668-1682, 2097, 2204, 2616
and Anthem	1892-1893
on Parade	2531
Over Capitol	1623, 2114
Over Mt. Rushmore	2523, 2523A
Over Supreme Court	1894-1895, 1896
Over White House	1208, 1338-1338G, 2609
US	288, 372-373, 537, 629, 630, 690, 727, 752, 775, 778, 929, 938, 944, 962, 990-991, 1004, 1010, 1094, 1115, 1132, 1153, 1208, 1249, 1261, 1320, 1338-1338G, 1345-1354, 1383, 1406, 1447, 1509, 1519, 1597-1598, 1618C, 1622, 1630, 1631, 1686, 1686d, 1688, 1890-1891, 1893-1896, 1952, 2103, 2114-2216, 2276, 2278, 2280, 2409, 2419, 2421, 2475, 2522, 2523, 2523A, 2528, 2531, 2605-2609, 2879-2893, C34, C54, C76, C115, C122-C125, C126
with Olympic Rings	2528
Flags, State	1633-1682
Alabama	1654
Alaska	1681
Arizona	1680
Arkansas	1657
California	1663
Colorado	1670
Florida	1659
Hawaii	1682
Idaho	1675
Illinois	1653
Indiana	1651
Iowa	1661
Kansas	1666
Kentucky	1647
Louisiana	1650
Maine	1655
Michigan	1658
Minnesota	1664
Mississippi	1652
Missouri	1656
Montana	1673
Nebraska	1669
Nevada	1668
New Mexico	1679
North Dakota	1671
Ohio	1649
Oklahoma	1678
Oregon	1665
Rhode Island	1645
South Dakota	1672
Tennessee	1648
Texas	1660
Utah	1677
Vermont	1646
Washington	1674
West Virginia	1667
Wisconsin	1662
Wyoming	1676
Flamingo	2707
Flanagan, Father	2171
Flappers do the Charleston	3184h
Flash Gordon	3000p
Flathead Headdress	2504
Flies, Fishing	2545-2549
Flight, Powered	C47
Flora and Fauna	2476-2483, 2486-2492
Flora, Endangered	1783-1786
Floral Piece, Lace	2352
Florida	1659, 1961
Settlement	1271
Huguenot-Walloon Monument	616
Statehood	927, 2950
manatee	3105o
panther	3105m
Flower fly	3351f
Flowers	1158, 1183, 1192, 1256, 1318, 1337, 1365, 1366, 1367, 1375, 1377-1379, 1711, 1737, 1783, 1784-1786, 1807, 1876-1879, 1942, 1944, 1951, 2014, 2074, 2076-2079, 2166, 2268, 2273, 2285, 2347, 2378-2379, 2395, 2416, 2517-2520, 2524-2527, 3025-3029
Fall Garden	2993-2997
Garden	2760-2764
State Birds and	1978-2002
Summer Garden	2829-2833
Winter Garden	3025-3029
Flushing Remonstrance, the	1099
Flying Fortress Airplane	3142k
Fog Warning, The by Winslow Homer	3236j
Folk	
Art, American	1706-1709, 1745-1748, 1775-1778, 1834-1837, 2138-2141, 2238, 2240-2243, 2351-2354, 2390-2393, 2501-2505
Dance	1751
Heroes	3083-3086
Folklore, American	1317, 1330, 1357, 1370, 1470, 1548, 1578
Food for Peace—Freedom from Hunger	1231
Football, College	1382, 2089, 2376
Forbes, Brig. Gen. John	1123
Forbes Field, Pittsburgh	3515
Ford, Henry	1286A
Ford Mustang	3188h
Foreign Countries	398, 856, 906, 909-921, 925, 961, 1021, 1104, 1131, 1157-1158, 1188, 1313, 1324, 1334, 1431, 1569, 1570, 1721, 1753, 1757, 2003, 2036, 2040, 2091, 2349, 2370, 2532, C120
Forest	
Congress, Fifth World	1156
Conservation	1122
Fire Prevention	2096
"...for purple mountain majesties"	1893
Fort	
Bliss	976
Dearborn (Chicago)	728, 730, 766
Duquesne (Pitt)	1123
Harrod	1542
Kearney	970
McHenry	962
McHenry, Flag	1346, 1597, 1598, 1618C
Moultrie Flag	962, 1345
Nisqually	1604
Orange, Landing at	615
Sackville, Surrender of	651
Snelling	1409
Stanwix	644
Sumter, Civil War Centennial	1178
Ticonderoga	1071
Fossil Fuels	2009
Foster, Stephen Collins	879
Four	
Chaplains	956
Freedoms	908, 2840
Horsemen of Notre Dame	3184l
4-H Club	1005

49-Star Flag	1132
Foxhound, American	2101
Foxx, Jimmie	3408n
Fragrant Water Lily	2648
France	915, 934
Francis of Assisi	2023
Francisco, Peter	1562
Frankenstein	3170
Franklin, Benjamin	1, 3, 5, 18-24, 38, 40, 46, 63, 71, 81, 85A, 86, 92, 100, 102, 110, 112, 134, 145, 156, 167, 182, 192, 206, 212, 219, 246-247, 264, 279, 300, 314, 316, 318, 331, 357, 374, 383, 385, 390, 392, 414-423, 431-440, 460, 470-479, 497, 508-518, 523-524, 547, 552, 575, 578, 594, 596-597, 604, 632, 658, 669, 803, 947-948, 1030, 1073, 1393D, 1474, 1687b, 1690, 1693, 1753, 2036, 2052, 2145, 2779
Franklinia	1379
Fraternity	C120
Frederick Douglass	2975h
Free-Blown Glass	3325
Freedom from Hunger, Food for Peace	1231
of the Press	1119, 1476-1477, 1593
Wheels of	1162
Freedoms, Four	908, 933
Frémont, John C.	288, 2869j
French Alliance	1753
Daniel Chester	887
Revolution	C120
Frequency Modulation	2056
Friendship Apollo 7	1193
with Morocco	2349
Frilled Dogwinkle	2117
Fringed Gentian	2672
Frost A.B.	3502g
Robert	1526
Fulbright Scholarships	3065
Fulton Celebration, Hudson-	372-373
Ferry House	1003
Robert	1270
Fur Seals	1464
Furness, Frank	1840
Future Farmers of America	1024
Mail Transportation	C122-C126
Spacecraft	2543
Gable, Clark	2446
Gadsby's Tavern	C40
Gadsden Purchase	1028
Galaxy NGC1316	3388
Galliard Cut	856
Gallatin, Albert	1279
Gallaudet, Thomas H.	1861
Galvez, Gerneral Bernardo de	1826
Games, World University	2748
Gandhi, Mahatma	1174-1175
Garden Flowers	2760-2764, 2829-2833
Aster	2993
Chrysanthemum	2994
Dahlia	2995
Hydrangea	2996
Rudbeckia	2997-2997a
Garden, International Peace	2014
Gardening—Horticulture	1100
Garfield, James A.	205, 205C, 216, 224, 256, 271, 282, 305, 558, 587, 638, 664, 675, 723, 825, 2218b
Garibaldi, Guiseppe	1168-1169
Garland, Judy	2445
Garner, Erroll	2992
Gasoline Alley	3000h
Gato Class	3377
Gatsby style, The	3184b
GeeBee Airplane	3142i
Gehrig, Lou	2417, 3408t
Gemini 4	1332, 2634
General Federation of Women's Clubs	1316
Geodetic, Coast and, Survey	1088
Geophysical Year, International	1107
George, Sen. Walter F., Memorial	1170
Georgia	726, 1636, 1962
Georgia Statehood	2339
German Immigration, Concord	2040
Germany surrenders at Reims	2981f
Geronimo	2869m
Gershwin George	1484
Ira & George	3345
Get Well!	2268
Gettysburg Address	978
Battle of	1180, 2975t
GI Bill, 1944	3186i
Giannini, Amadeo P.	1400
Giant Panda	2706
Giant Sequoia	1764
Gibson Girl	3182m
Josh	3408r
Gila trout	3105j
Gilbert, John	2823
Gilbreth, Lillian M.	1868
Giraffe	2705
Girl in Red Dress with Cat and Dog by Ammi Phillips	3236c
Girl Scouts	974, 1199, 2251
Giving and Sharing	3243
Glacier National Park	748, 764
Gladiola	2831
Glassblower	1456
Globes	650, 702, 1016, 1066, 1070, 1112, 1128-1129, 1151, 1156, 1162, 1410-1413, 1439, 1576, 2535-2536, C12, C16-C17, C19, C24, C42-C44, C89-C90
Gloriosa Lily	3312
Goddard, Robert H.	C69
Goethals, Gen. George W.	856
Gold Stars	2765i
Gold Star Mothers	969
Golden Gate	399, 567, 698
Bridge	3185i
International Exposition	852
Golf 1932-1933, 2377, 2965	
Gompers, Samuel	988
Gone with the Wind	2446, 3185i
Goniopholis	3136e
Goode, Alexander D.	956
Goodnight, Charles	2869l
Gottschalk, Louis Moreau	3165
Gowan & Marx	2366
Graces, The Three	895
Graf Zeppelin	C13-C15, C18
Grand Army of the Republic, Aug. 29	985
Canyon	741, 757, 2512, 3183h
Coulee Dam	1009
Union Flag	1352
Grange, National	1323
Grant, Ulysses S.	223, 255, 270, 281, 303, 314A, 560, 589, 640, 666, 677, 787, 823, 2217i, 2975d
Grassland Habitats	1922
Gray Birch	1767
Owl	1760
Squirrel	2295
Wolf	2322, 3292
Great Americans Issue	1844-1869, 2167-2173, 2176-2182, 2183-2184, 2184A, 2185-2186, 2188, 2190-2194, 2194A, 2195-2197, 2933, 2938, 2940, 2943
Smoky Mountains National Park	749, 765, 797
White Throne	747, 763
Blue Heron	1921
Head	746, 762
Horned Owl	1763
Lakes	1069
Lakes Lighthouses	2969-2973
Plains Prairie	3506
River Road	1319
Salt Lake, Valley of	950
Seal of the United States	1194
Train Robbery, The 1903	3182c
Greatest Show on Earth, Circus	2750-2753
Greece	916
Greeley Adolphus W.	2221
Horace	1177
Green Bay, (WI)	739, 755
Bay Packers	3188d
Mountain Boys	643
Nathanael	785
Throated Carib	3223
Greetings	3245-52
Griffith, D.W.	1555
Grizzly Bear	1923
Grofé, Ferde	3163
Gropius House	2021
Walter	2021
Grosbeak, Owl	2284
Grosvenor, Lt. Thomas	1361
Guggenheim Museum	1280
Guitar	1613
Gulf War	3191b
Gunston Hall (Home of George Mason)	1108
Gutenberg Bible	1014
Guthrie, Woody	3213
Haida Ceremonial Canoe, Tlingit, Chief in	1389
Halas, George	3146, 3150
Hale, Nathan	551, 653
Haley, Bill	2725, 2732
Half Moon	372-373
Hamilton Alexander	143, 154, 165, 176, 190, 201, 217, 1053, 1086, 1686e
Alice	2940
Hamilton's Battery, Alexander	629, 630
Hammarskjold, Dag	1203-1204
Hancock John	1687d, 1694
Winfield	2975n
Handcar 1880s	1898
Handicapped, Employ the	1155
Handy, W.C.	1372
Hansom Cab	1904
Hanson, John	1941
Hanukkah	3118, 3352, 3547
Happy Birthday	2272, 2395
New Year	2720, 2817, 2876, 3060, 3120, 3179, 3120, 3179, 3272
Harbor NY, New Amsterdam	1027
Seal	1882
Harding, Warren G.	553, 576, 582, 598, 605, 610-613, 631, 633, 659, 670, 684, 686, 833, 2219a
Hardy, Stan Laurel & Oliver	2562
Harebell	2689
Harlequin Lupine	2664
Harness Racing	2758
Harnett, William M.	1386
Harriet Tubman	2975k
Harris Joel Chandler	980
Patricia Roberts	3371
Harrison Benjamin	308, 622, 694, 828, 1045, 2218e
William Henry	814, 966, 2201, 2216i
Harrod, Fort	1542
Hart, Lorenz	3347
Harte, Bret	2196
Hartford, USS	792
Hartlley, David	2052
Harvard, John	2190
Hatter	1459
Hatteras, Cape	1448-1451, 2471
Hawaii	1682, 1963
City of Refuge National Park	C84
(Cook, Captain James)	1733
Diamond Head	C46
Discovery of	647
Statehood	2080, C55
Territory	799
Hawaiian Wild Broadbean	1784
Monk seal	3105c
Hawkins, Coleman	2983
Hawthorne, Nathaniel	2047
Hayes, Rutherford B.	563, 692, 824, 2218a
Head of Freedom, Capitol Dome	573
Headdresses	230, 237, 783, C117
Indian	2501-2505
Headless Horseman	1548
Health Research	2087
Healy, George, Portrait by	1113
Heitsuk, Bella Bella Tribe	1834
Held, John Jr.	3502t
Help End Hunger	2164
Helpping Children Learn	3125
Hemingway, Ernest	2418
HemisFair '68	1340
Henry, Patrick	1052, 1144
Henson, Matthew	2223
Herb Robert	2657
Herbert, Victor	881
Herkimer at Oriskany, by Frederick Yohn	1722
Brig. Gen. Nicholas	644, 1722
Hermitage, The	786, 1037, 1059
Herrmann, Bernard	3341
Hershey, Milton S.	2933
Hiawatha	3336
Hickok, Wild Bill	2869o
Higher Education	1206
Highlander Figure	2240
Himalayan Cat	2373
Hines, John L.	3393
Hip-hop Culture	3190o
Hispanic Americans	2103
Hispanics	801, 895, 898, 983, 1043, 1110-1111, 1125-1126, 1157, 1234, 1271, 1437, 1826, 2024, 2097, 2103, 2173, 2185, 2247, 2255, 2704, C56, C104, C116
Historic Flags	1345-1354
Preservation	1440-1443
Hitchcock, Alfred	3226
Hoban, James	1935-1936
Holiday, Billie	2856
Holly	1254
Buddy	2729, 2736
Hollywood Composers	3339-44
Holmes, Oliver Wendell	1288, 1288B, 1305E
Home on the Range	2869a
Homemakers	1253
Hometowns honor their returning veterans	2981j
Homer, Winslow	1207
Homestead Act	1198
Honeybee	2281
Honorable Discharge Emblem	940
Honoring Those Who Served	3331
Hoover, Herbert	1269, 2219c
Hope for the Crippled	1385

XXIV

Hopi Pot	1708
Hopkins	
Johns	2194
Mark	870
Hornsby, Rogers	3408f
Horse	
and Rider	2715
Racing	1528
Horses	
American	2155-2158
Carousel	2391
Racing	1528
Sports	2756-2759
Horticulture—Gardening	1100
Hospice Care	3276
Hospitals, Public	2210
Hostages Come Home	3190d
Hot Air Ballooning	2033, 2034
Household conveniences	3185g
House of Representatives, US	2412
Houston, Sam	776, 778, 1242
Howe	
Elias	892
Julia Ward	2176
Huckleberry Finn, the Adventures of	2787
Hudson	
-Fulton Celebration	372-373
General	2843
River	372-373, 752
Hughes, Charles Evans	1195
Huguenot-Walloon Tercentenary	614-616
Hull, Cordell	1235
Human Treatment of Animals	1307
Hummingbirds	2642-2646
Humphrey, Hubert H.	2189
Hunger	
Freedom From—Food for Peace	1231
Help End	2164
Hunt, Richard Morris	1929
Huntington, Samuel	1687
Hyacinth	2760
Hyde Park	930
Hypersonic Airliner	C122, C126
I Love Lucy	3187l
Ice	
Dancing	2809
Hockey	2811
Iceboat	2134
Idaho	1675, 1964
Statehood	896, 2439
Iiwi	2311
Illinois	1653, 1965
Institute of Technology	2020
Statehood	1339
(Windmill)	1741
Immigrants arrive	3182i
Independence	
Declaration of	1687
Finland	1334
Hall	1044, 1546, 1622, 1625, 2779
Mexican	1157
Sesquicentennial Exposition	627
Skilled Hands for	1717-1720
Indiana	1651, 1966
Statehood	1308
Territory	996
Indian	
Paintbrush	2647
Pond Lily	2680
Indians	230-231, 237-238, 240, 285, 287, 328, 565, 680, 682-683, 695, 739, 755, 783, 972, 1063, 1187, 1360, 1389, 1426, C117
American	1364
American Art, Navajo Blanket	2238
Centennial	972
Chief Joseph	1364
Crazy Horse	1855
Head Penny	1734
Headdresses	2501-2505
Masks, Pacific Northwest	1834-1837
Red Cloud	2176
Sequoyah	1859
Sitting Bull	2184
Thorpe, Jim	2089
Induction Motor	2057
Industry	
Agriculture for Defense	899
Petroleum	1134
Poultry	968
Science &	2031
Wool	1423
Inkwell and Quill	1535, 1581, 1811
Inline Skating	3324
Insects & Spiders	3351
Integrated Circuit, The	3188j
International	
Civil Aeronautics Conference	649-650
Cooperation Year	1266
Geophysical Year	1107
Naval Review—Jamestown Festival	1091
Philatelic Exhibition	630
Philatelic Exhibitions	778, 1075-1076, 1310-1311
Red Cross	1016, 1239
Style of Architecture	3186k
Telecommunication Union	1274
Women's Year	1571
Year of the Child	1772
Year of the Disabled	1925
Youth Year	2160-2163
Interphil 76	1632
Intrepid	2032
Inventors	889-893, 945, 1062, 1270, 1286A, 2055, 2567, C45, C69, C91-C94, C113-C114, C118-C119
Inventors, American	2056-2058
Iowa	1661, 1967
Statehood	942, 3088
Territory	838
Iris	2763
Irish Immigration	3286
Irving, Washington	859, 1548
Isabella, Queen	234, 236-238, 241-244, 2620
Islands, Northern Mariana	2804
Itlay invaded by Allies	2765f
Ives, Charles	3164
Ives, Frederic E.	3063
Iwo Jima (Marines)	929
Jack-in-the-Box	2791, 2798, 2801
Jack-in-the-Pulpit	2650
Jackson,	
Andrew	73, 85B, 87, 93, 103, 135, 146, 157, 168, 178, 180, 183, 193, 203, 211, 211D, 215, 221, 253, 302, 786, 812, 941, 1209, 1225, 1286, 2201, 2216g
(Battle of New Orleans)	1261
Gen. Stonewall	788, 1408, 2975s
(Hermitage)	1037, 1059
Mahalia	3216
Washington and	2592
Jackson Pollack, Abstract Expressionism	3186h
Jacob's Ladder	2684
Jamestown	
Exposition	328-330
Festival, International Naval Review	1091
Founding of	329
Japan	
Invades Aleutians	2697e
Opening of	1021
Treaty, US-	1158
US Declares War on	2559j
Japanese Bomb Pearl Harbor	2559i
Jay, John	1046, 2052
Jazz and Blues Singers	2854-2861
Jazz Flourishes	3184k
Jazz Musicians	2983-2992
Jeffers, Robinson	1485
Jefferson	
Memorial	1510, 1520
Thomas	12, 27-30A, 42, 67, 75-76, 80, 105, 139, 150, 161, 172, 187-188, 197, 209, 228, 260, 275, 310, 324, 561, 590, 641, 667, 678, 807, 842, 851, 1011, 1033, 1055, 1141, 1278, 1299, 1299b, 1687b, 1693, 1779, 2185, 2201, 2216c, 2523, C88
Thomas (Monticello)	1047
Jelly Roll Morton	2986
Jenny Airplane	3142s
Jet Liner	C51-C52, C60-C61, C78, C82
Over Capitol	C64-C65
Jitterbug sweeps nation	3186g
John Coltrane	2991
John Henry	3085
Johnson, Andrew	822, 2217
Johnson,	
James P.	2985
James Weldon	2371
Lyndon B.	1503, 2219i
Robert	2857
Johnston, Joseph E.	2975m
Joliet, Louis	1356
Jolson, Al	2849
Jones	
Bobby	1933, 3185n
Casey	993
John Paul	790, 1789
Joplin, Scott	2044
Joseph	
E. Johnston	2975m
Pulitzer	946
Journalism—Freedom of the Press	1119, 1476-1477, 1593
Juke Box	2911-2912A
Julian, Percy Lavon	2746
Jupiter	2573
Balloon	C54
Pioneer 10	1556
Just, Ernest E.	3058
Justice	313
Contemplation of	1592
(Scales of)	1139, 1186
Jumbo Jets	3189n
Jumping spider	3351t
Jurassic Park	3191k
Kahlo, Frida	3509
Kamehameha, King	799
Kane, Elisha Kent	2220
Kansas	1666, 1968
City, MO	994
Statehood	1183
Territory	1061
Karloff, Boris	3170, 3171
Katzenjammer Kids	3000b
Kearney	
Expedition, Gen. Stephen Watts, Oct. 16	944
Fort	970
Keaton, Buster	2828
Keep in Touch	2274
Keller, Helen/Anne Sullivan	1824
Kelly, Grace	2749
Kennedy	
John F.	1287, 2219h
Memorial	1246
Robert F.	1770
Kent, Rockwell	3502q
Kentucky	1647, 1969
Settlement, First	1542
Statehood	2636
Kern, Jerome	2110
Kerosene Table Lamp	1611
Kestrel, American	2476-2477, 3044
Key, Francis Scott	962
Keystone Cops	2826
Kids Care	2951-2954
Kii Statue	C84
Killer Whale	2508, 2511
Kindred Spirits by Asher B. Durand	3236g
King	
John's Crown	1265
Martin Luther, Jr.	1771, 3188a
Penguins	2708
Salmon	1079
Kitten and Puppy	2025
Klondike Gold Rush	3235
Knox, Henry	1851
Knoxville World's Fair	2006-2009
Koala	2370
Korea	921
Korean Veterans	2152
Korean War	3187e
Korngold, Enrich Wolfgang	3344
Kosciuszko, General Thaddeus	734
Kossuth, Lajos	1117-1118
Krazy Kat	3000e
Kwanzaa	3175, 3368, 3548
La Fortaleza, PR	801
Labor Day	1082
(A. Phllip Randolph)	2402
(Collective Bargaining)	1558
(Gompers, Samuel)	998
Organized	1831
(Perkins, Francis)	1821
Lacemaking	2351-2354
Lady beetle	3351c
Ladybug	2315
Lady's Slipper	1377, 2077
Lafayette	1010, 1097
Indiana	C54
Marquis de	1686d, 1716
Lagoon Nebula	3386
LaGuardia, Fiorello	1397
Lake	
Erie	1069
Huron	1069
Michigan	1069
Ontario	1069
Placid, NY, Olympic—Winter Games '32	716
Placid, NY, Olympic—Winter Games '80	1795-1798
Superior	1069
Lamps	1206, 1386
Kerosene Table	1611
Rush	1610
Whale Oil	1608
Land-Grant Colleges	1065
Landing	
Craft	1434
of Cadillac	1000
of Carteret	1247
of the Pilgrims	549, 1420
Landsat	2570
Langley, Samuel P.	C118
Lanier, Sidney	1446
Lantern, Railroad	1612
LaRabida	239
Lasers	3188k
Last of the Buffalo, The by Alfred Bierstadt	3236m
Large-Flowered Trillium	2652
Latrobe, Benjamin	1780
Laubach, Dr. Frank	1864
Laurel & Hardy	2562
Laurens, John	1686e
Law and Order	1343
Law, World Peace through	1576
Leadbelly	3212
Leatherworker	1720
Lee	
General Robert E.	788, 982, 1049, 1408
Jason	964

Entry	Number(s)
Robert E.	2975b
Lefty Grove	3408k
Lefty's Deceiver	2548
Legend of Sleepy Hollow, The	1548
Legends	
of Baseball	3408
of Hollywood	2967
of the West	2869, 2870
Leigh, Vivian	2446
Leon, Ponce de	2024
Lerner & Loewe	3346
Letter Writing Issue	1806-1810
Letter	1310, 1511, 1805, 2150, 2618
Carriers	1490, 1497, 2420
Lift Spirits	1807
Preserve Memories	1805
Shape Opinions	1809
Levendecker, J.C.	3502c
Lewis	
and Clark Expedition	1063
Francis	1687c
Meriwether	1063
Sinclair	1856
Lexington and Concord	617-619, 790, 1563
Liberte	C120
Liberty	1034-1042A, 1043-1044A, 1045-1054A, 1055-1059A, C120
Bell	627, 1518, 1595, 1618, C57, C62
Birth of	618
Head of	1599, 1619
Ship	2559h
Statue of	566, 696, 899, 908, 946, 995, 1035, 1041-1042, 1044-1044A, 1057, 1075, 1320, 1594, 1599, 1619, 1816, 2147, 2224, C35, C58, C63, C80, C87
Torch	1008, 1594, 1816, 2531A
Libraries, America's	2015
Library	
Low Memorial	1029
of Congress	2004, 3390
Life Magazine, 1st Issue of	3185c
Lighthouse, Sandy Hook	1605
Lighthouses	1391, 1449, 1605, 1891, 2470-2474
Lightning Airplane	3142n
Lightning Whelk	2121
Li'l Abner	3000q
Lilac	2764
Lily	1879, 2829, 3530
Lincoln	
Abraham	77, 85F, 91, 98, 108, 122, 137, 148, 159, 170, 186, 195, 208, 222, 254, 269, 280, 304, 315, 317, 367-369, 555, 584, 600, 635, 661, 672, 821, 902, 906, 978, 1036, 1058, 1113-1116, 1143, 1233, 1282, 1303, 2081, 2106, 2217g, 2410, 2433, 2523, 2523A, 2975j, C59, C88
-Douglas Debates	1115
Gen. Benjamin	1686b
Memorial	571
Tad	2106
Lindbergh, Charles	1710, 2781, C10
Lindbergh flies the Atlantic	3184m
Lions International (Search for Peace)	1326
Lippman, Walter	1849
Literary Arts	1773, 1832, 2047, 2094, 2239, 2350, 2418, 2449, 2538, 2698
Little	
American (Antarctic)	733, 735, 753, 768
House on the Prairie	2786
Nemo in Slumberland	3000c
Orphan Annie	3000j
Women	2788
Livingston, Robert R.	323, 1020, 1687a, 1693
Lloyd, Harold	2825
Lockheed Constellation	C35
Locks at Sault Ste. Marie	298
Lockwood, Belva Ann	2178
Locomobile	2381
Locomotives	114, 922, 947, 961, 993, 1006, 1415, 1506, 1511, 1573, 1755, 1897A, 2226, 2362-2366, 2402, 2843-2847
Loesser, Frank	3350
Lombardi, Vince	3145, 3147
London, Jack	2182, 2197
Long, Dr. Crawford W.	875
Long-billed Curlew, Numenius Longrostis by John James Audubon	3236e
Longfellow, Henry W.	864
Longhorn Cattle, King and	1504
Los Angeles, CA. Olympic Issue '32	718, 719
Los Angeles Class	3372, 3374
Louis	
Armstrong	2982, 2984
Joe	2766
XVI, King	1753
Louisiana	1650, 1970
Purchase Exposition	323-327, 1020
Statehood	1197
World Exposition	2086
Love	1475, 1951, 2072, 2143, 2202, 2248, 2378-2379, 2440-2441, 2535-2537, 2618, 2814, 2814C, 2948-2949, 3030, 3274-75
Birds	2813, 2815
(Cherubs)	2957-2960
Love You	2398

Entry	Number(s)
Dad!	2270
Mother!	2273
Lovebirds, Fischer's	2537
Low	
Juliette Gordon	974
Memorial Library	1029
Lowell, James Russell	866
Ludington, Sybil	1559
Luge	2808
Lugosi, Bela	3169
Luna Moth	2293
Lunar	
Orbiter	1435, 2571
Rover	1435
Lunch Wagon	2464
Lunt, Alfred & Lynn Fontaine	3287
Luther, Martin	2065
Luxembourg	912
Lyndhurst	1841
Lyon, Mary	2169
Maass, Clara	1699
MacArthur, Gen. Douglas	1424
Macdonough, Thomas	791
MacDowell, Edward A.	882
Mackinac Bridge	1109
Madison	
Dolley	1822
Helene	2500
James	262, 277, 312, 479, 808, 843, 2201, 2216d, 2875a, 3545
Madonna and Child	2789, 2790, 2871, 3003
Madonna and Child, della Robbia	1768
Maggie Mix-up	3151n
Magna Carta	1265
Magsaysay, Ramon	1096
Mahoning by Franz Kline	3236s
Mail	
Car	2265
Car (Postal People)	1489
Car (USPS)	1396
Delivery, City	1238
Express	1909, 2122, 2394, 2541
International Express	2542
Order Business	1468
Overland	1120
Planes and US Map, Two	C7, C8, C9
(Pony Express)	894, 1154
Priority	2419, 2540
Railroad	2265
Transportation, Future	C122-C123, C125, C126
Truck	2781
Wagon	1903
Mailbox, Rural	1703, 1730
Maine	1655, 1971
(Christmas)	1384
Coon Cat	2374
(Great Head National Park)	746, 762
Statehood	1391
Makeup Rate	2521
Malamute, Alaskan	2100
Malaria Eradication	1194
Malcolm X	3273
Mallard	1757b
Decoy	2139
Mammoth, Woolly	3078
Man Walks on the Moon	3188c
Mann, Horace	869
Mannerheim, Gustaf	1165-1166
Maps	327, 733, 735, 753, 768, 783, 795, 858, 906, 927, 933, 942, 952, 955, 957, 984, 1018, 1067, 1069, 1071, 1092, 1112, 1120, 1131, 1154, 1206, 1232, 1247-1248, 1258, 1274, 1306, 1308, 1319, 1340, 1431, 1690, 1937, 1938, 2220-2223, 2386-2389, 2620, C7-C9, C14, C53, C55, C116-C117
Marathon	3067
Marblehead (Lake Erie)	2972
Marbois, Marquis Francois de Barbe	1020
Marconi's Spark Coil and Spark Gap	1500
Marigold	2832
Marilyn Monroe	2967
Marin, Luis Munoz	2173
Marine	
Corps	1013
Corps Reserve	1315
Mariner	
2	2569
10	2568
10/Venus, Mercury	1557
Marines	929
assault Tarawa	2765j
Continental	1567
on Guadalcanal	2697i
raise flag on Iwo Jima	2981a
Maris, Roger, 61 in '61	3188n
Marquette, Jacques	285, 1356
Mars	2572, 2631-2632
Pathfinder and Sojourner	3178
Viking Missions to	1759
Marsh Marigold	2658
Marshall	
George C.	1289

Entry	Number(s)
Islands, Republic of the Federated States of Micronesia	2506-2507
James W.	954
John	263, 278, 313, 480, 1050, 2415
Plan	3141
Plan, Acheson, Dean	2755
Martin, Roberta	3217
Marx, Gowan &	2366
Mary Chestnut	2975o
Maryland	1639, 1972
Settlement	736
Statehood	2342
Masaryk, Thomas G.	1147, 1148
Masks, Pacific Northwest Indian	1834, 1835, 1836, 1837
Mason	
George	1858
George (Gunston Hall)	1108
Massachusetts	1638, 1973
Bay Colony	682
Flag	1034, 1056
Statehood	2341
Windmill	1740
Masters, Edgar Lee	1405
Masterson, Bat	2869h
Mastodon	3079
Mathewson, Christy	3408c
Matzeliger, Jan	2567
Maybeck, Bernard	1930
Mayflower	548
Compact, Signing of	550
(Landing of the Pilgrims)	549, 1420
Mayo, Doctors William J. and Charles H.	1251
Mazzei, Philip	C98
McCarthy	
& Bergen	2563
Charlie	2563
McCormack, John	2090
McCormick, Cyrus Hall	891
McDowell, Dr. Ephraim	1138
McGruff the Crime Dog	2102
McHenry Flag, Fort	1346
McKinley, William G.	326, 559, 588, 639, 665, 676, 829, 2218f
McLoughlin, John	964
McMahon, Sen. Brien	1200
McMein, Neysa	3502m
McPhatter, Clyde	2726, 2733
McQueen's Jupiter	2844
Mead, Margaret, anthropologist	3184g
Meadow Beauty	2649
Meany, George	2848
Medal of Honor	2013, 2045, 2103
Medical Imaging	3189o
Medics treat wounded	2765b
Mellon, Andrew W.	1072
Melville, Herman	2094
Memorial	1318
Poppy	977
Merchant Marine	939
Mercury	1557, 2568, 2634
Helmet and Olive Branch	E7
Project	1193
Mergenthaler, Ottmar	3062
Mermaid	1112
Merman, Ethel	2853
Mesa Verde National Park	743, 759
Messenger	
on Bicycle	E6, E8-E11
Running	E1-E4, E5
Metropolitan Opera	2054
Mexican	
Hat	2688
Independence	1157
Michael, Moina	977
Michigan	1658, 1974
Landing of Cadillac	1000
State College	1065
Statehood	775, 2246
Micronesia, Federated States of/ Republic of the Marshall Islands	2506-2507
Microphone	1502
Microscope	1080, 1263, 1754, 1925
Mighty Casey	3083
Migratory	
Bird Hunting & Conservation Stamp Act	2092
Bird Treaty	1306
Miquel Locks, Pedro	398
Military Uniforms	1565-1568
Militia, American	1568
Milk Wagon	2253
Millay, Edna St. Vincent	1926
Millikan, Robert	1866
Mineral Heritage	1538-1541
Minerals	2700-2703
Mingus, Charles	2989
Mining Prospector	291
Minnesota	1664, 1975
(Hubert Humphrey)	2190
Statehood	1106
Territory	981
Minute Man, The	619
Mirror Lake	742, 750, 758, 770

Entry	Number(s)
Missiing in Action	2966
Mission Belfry, CA	1373
Missions	1373, 1443, C116
Mississippi	1652, 1976
(Great River Road)	1319
River	285, 1356
River Bridge	293
Statehood	1337
Territory	955
Missouri	1656, 1977
Kansas City	994
River	1063
Statehood	1426
Mistletoe	1255
Mitchell	
Billy	3330
Margaret	2168
Pass, NE	1060
Mobile, Battle of	1826
Mockingbird	2330
Model B Airplane	3142b
Model T Ford	3182a
Modern Dance	1752
Mold-Blown Glass	3326
Monarch Butterfly	2287, 3351k
Monarch caterpillar	3351j
Monday Night Football	3189l
Monitor and Virginia	2975a
Monmouth, Battle of (Molly Pitcher)	646
Monongahela River	681
Monorail	1196
Monroe	
James	325, 562, 591, 603, 642, 668, 679, 810, 845, 1020, 1038, 1105, 2201, 2216e
Marilyn	2967
Monopoly Game, The	3185o
Montana	1673, 1978
(Glacier National Park)	748, 764
Statehood	858, 2401
Monticello	1047
Monument, George Washington	2149
Moon	126, 1021, 1192, 1345, 1371, 1434-1435, 1548, 1909, 2122, 2246, 2394, 2404, 2419, 2571, 2631, 2634, C124
First Landing	2841
Landing	2419, 2842, C76
Rover	1435
Moore	
John Bassett	1295
Marianne	2449
Moorish Idol	1829
Moose	1757e, 1887, 2298
Morgan	
Charles W.	1441, 2340
Horse	2156
Silver Dollar	1557
Morning Light, S.S.	1239
Morocco, Friendship with	2349
Morris, Robert	1004
Morro Castle, San Juan, Puerto Rico	1437
Morse, Samuel F.B.	890, 924
Morton	
Jelly Roll	2986
Julius Sterling, (Arbor Day)	717
Moses	
Grandma	1370
Horace A.	2095
Moss Campion	2686
Mothers	
Gold Star	969
of America	737-738, 754
Motion	
Pictures	926, 1555, 1727
-Picture Camera	1555
Motorcycle	1899
Mott, Lucretia	959
Moultrie Flag, Fort	1345
Mount	
Davidson	1130
Hood	1124
McKinley National Park	800, 1454
Ranier	2404
Ranier National Park	742, 750, 758, 770
Rockwell (Mt. Sinopah)	748, 764
Rushmore	2523-2523A, C88
Rushmore Memorial	1011
Surabachi	929
Vernon	785, 1032
Mountain	
Bluebird	2439
Goat	2323
Habitats	1923
Lion	2292
Nonprofit	2903-2904A
Movies go 3-D	3187o
Mrs Elizabeth Freake and Baby Mary by the Freake Limner	3236b
Muddler Minnow	2549
Muir, John	1245, 3182j
Mule Deer	2294
Mummy, The	3171
Murphy, Audie L.	3396
Murrow, Edward R.	2812
Muscogee Seal	972
Museum	
National Postal	2779
Smithsonian Institution	3059
Music	
American	1252
and Literature by William Harnett	3236i
Big Band	3096-3099
Musicals	2767-2770
Musicians Rock & Roll/Rhythm & Blues	2721, 2724-2737
Muskellunge	2205
Mustang Airplane	3142a
Muybridge, Eadweard	3061
My	
Fair Lady	2770
Old Kentucky Home State Park	2636
Myron's Discobolus	719
Naismith—Basketball	1189
Nancy	3000o
Narrows Bridge, Verrazano-	1258
Nassau Hall (Princeton University)	1083, 1704
Nation of Readers, A	2106
National	
Apprenticeship Program	1201
Archives	227, 2081
Capitol	990-992
Defense	899-901
Education Association	1093
Farmer's Bank	1931
Grange	1323
Guard	1017
Park Service	1314
Parks	740-751, 756-765, 769-770, 952, 1448-1454, 2018, C84
Postal Museum	2779-2782
Recovery Act	732
Stamp Exhibition	735, 768
Native American Culture	2869e
Nativity, by John Singleton Copley	1701
NATO	1008, 1127, 3354
Natural History	1387-1390
Nautical Figure	2242
Nautilus	1128
Navajo Blanket	2235-2238
Naval	
Academy, US	794
Aviation	1185
Review, International	1091
Navigation, Lake	294
Navigation, Ocean	299
Navy	790-794
Continental	1566
Department	O35-O45
US	935, 1013, 1067
Nebraska	1669, 1979
Statehood	1328
Territory	1060
Nelson, Thomas, Jr.	1686d, 1687c
Neptune	1112, 2576
New England	2119
Netherlands	913, 2003
Nevada	1668, 1980
Settlement	999
Statehood	1248
Nevelson, Louise	3379-83
Nevin, Ethelbert	883
New	
Amsterdam Harbor, NY	1027
Baseball Records	3191a
England Neptune	2119
Hampshire	1068, 1641, 1981
Hampshire Statehood	2344
Jersey	1635, 1982
Jersey, Settlement	1247
Jersey, Statehood	2338
Mexico	1679, 1983
Mexico (Chavez, Dennis)	2185
Mexico, Statehood	1191
Orleans	2407
Sweden	C117
Year, Chinese	2817
Year, Happy	2720, 3370, 3500
York	1643, 1984, C38
York City	1027
York City Coliseum	1076
York, Newburgh	727, 731, 767
York, Skyline	C35
York Statehood	2346
York Stock Exchange	2630
York World's Fair '39	853
York World's Fair '64	1244
Newburgh, New York	752
News of victory hits home	2981i
Newspaper Boys	1015
Newman, Alfred	3343
Niagara by Frederic Edwin Church	3236n
Niagara Falls	568, 699
Railway Suspension Bridge	961
Nicolet, Jean	739
Nieu Nederland	614
Nighthawks by Edward Hopper	3236p
Nimitz, Chester W.	1869
Nineteenth Amendment	1406, 2980
(Suffrage)	784, 1051, 1406
Nisqually, Fort	1604
Nixon, Richard	2955
No. 12 by Mark Rothko	3236t
Nobel Prize, The	3504
Nonprofit	2902
Norris	
Dam	1184
Sen. George W.	1184
Norse-American	620, 621
North	
Carolina	1644, 1985
Carolina (Great Smoky Mountains National Park)	749, 765
Carolina Statehood	2347
Dakota	1671, 1986
Dakota Statehood	858, 2403
Pole	1128
Northern	
Mariana Islands	2804
Sea Lion	2509
Northwest Territory	
Ordinance	795
Sesquicentennial	837
Norway	911
Numismatics	2558
Nurse	702, 1699, 1910
Nursing	1190
NYU Library	1928
Oakland Bay Bridge, Plane Over	C36
Oakley, Annie	2869d
Ocelot	3105e
Ochs, Adolph S.	1700
Ocotillo	1378
Official	
Postal Savings Mail	O121-O143
Stamps	O1-O56, O57-O120
Ohi'a Lehua	2669
Ohio	1649, 1987
Class	3375
River Canalization	681
Statehood	1018
Oil	
Derrick	1134
Wagon	2130
O'Keeffe, Georgia	3069
Okinawa, the last big battle	2981c
Oklahoma	1678, 1988
(Cherokee Strip)	1360
Statehood	1092
Oklahoma!	2722, 2769
Old	
Faithful	744, 760, 1453
Man of the Mountain	1068, 2344
North Church	1603
Oglethorpe, General	726
Olmstead, Fredrick Law, Landscape Artist	3338
Olympians	2496-2500
Olympic	3068, 3087
Games '32	716, 718-719
Games '60	1146
Games '72	1460-1462, C85
Games '76	1695-1698
Games '80	1790-1798, C97
Games '84	2048-2051, 2067, 2070, 2082-2085, C101-C112
Games '88	2369, 2380
Games '92	2553-2557, 2611-2615, 2637-2641
Games '96	3068
Games, Diver	1695
Games, Runner	1697
Games, Skater	1698
Rings	2539-2542
Rings and Snowflake	1146
Rings, Flag with	2528
Special	1788
Special, Winter	2142
Omithominus	3136n
Omnibus	1897, 2225
O'Neil, Capt. William O. "Bucky"	973
O'Neill, Eugene	1294, 1305C
O'Neill, Rose	3502i
One-Room Schoolhouse	1606
Opening of Japan	1021
Opera, Metropolitan	2054
Opisthias	3136h
Orange, Landing at Fort	615
Orange-Tip	1715
Orbiter	
Lunar	2571
Viking	2572
Orchids	2076-2079
Order, Law and	1343
Ordinance, Northwest Territory	795
Oregon	1665, 1989
(Crater Lake National Park)	745, 761
SS	997
Statehood	1124

Territory	783, 964
Trail	964, 2747
Organ & Tissue Donation	3227
Organized Labor	1831
Oriskany	644
Herkimer at	1722
Mail Transportation	C124
Ormandy, Eugene	3161
Orson Welles, "Citizen Kane"	3186o
Osprey	2291
Osteopathic Medicine	1469
Otter, Sea	2510
Ouimet, Francis	2377
Overland Mail	1120, 2869t
Overrun Countries	129, 909-921
Owens, Jesse	2496, 3185j
Owl/Grosbeak	2284-2285
Owls, American	1760-1763
Oxen	950, 958, 964, 970, 981, 997, 1019, 1061, 1426, 1487, 1542
P-51's escort B-17's on boming raids	2838b
P.S. Write Soon	1806, 1808, 1810
Pacific	
Calypso	2079
Coast Rain Forest	3378
Dogwood	3197
Exposition, Alaska-Yukon-	370-371
Exposition, California	773, 778
Northwest Indian Masks	1834-1837
Trust Territories, Northern Mariana Islands	2408
'97	3130-3131
Packard	2384
Paddlewheel Steamer	1187, 2435, 2438
Paderewski, Ignacy Jan	1159-1160
Paige, Satchel	3408p
Paine, Thomas	1292
Painting, American	1187, 1207, 1241, 1243, 1273, 1322, 1335, 1361, 1386, 1433, 1553 C71
Palace	
of the Arts	1930
of the Governors, Santa Fe, NM	1031A, 1054A
Palaeosaniwa	3136l
Palmer, Capt. Nathaniel B.	2386
Palomar Mountain Observatory	966
Pamphleteers	1476
Pan American	
Exposition	294-299
Games	2247, C56
Inverts, The	3505
Union	895
Union Building	C34
Panama	
Canal	398, 856, 3183f
Pacific Expedition	401
Pacific Exposition	397-400A
Panda, Giant	2706
Pansy	3027
Papanicolaou, Dr. George	1754
Parcel Post Postage Due Stamps	JQ1-JQ5
Parent Teacher Association	1463
Paris, Treaty of	2052
Parker	
Al	3502f
Charlie	2987
Dorothy	2698
Parkman, Francis	1281, 1297
Parrish, Maxfield	3502b
Partridge, Alden	1854
Pasqueflower	2676
Pass, NE, Mitchell	1060
Passionflower	2674
Patrol Wagon, Police	2258
Patton, Jr., General George S.	1026
Paul, Alice	2943
Paul Bunyan	3084
Peace	
Atoms for	1070
Bridge	1721
Corps	1447, 3188f
Garden, International	2014
of 1783	727, 731, 752, 767
Symbol	3188m
Through Law, World	1576
Through World Trade, World	1129
Peacetime Draft	2559b
Peach	2487, 2493, 2495
Peale, Charles Wilson	1789
Peanuts	3507
Pear	2488, 2494, 2495A
Peary, Admiral Robert	1128, 2223
Peashooter Airplane	3142o
Pecos Bill	3086
Pelican, Brown	1466
Pember, Phoebe	2975r
Penguins, King	2708
Penn	
Academy	1840
William	724
Pennsylvania	1634, 1990
Academy of Fine Arts	1064, 1840
Avenue	2561
State University	1065
Statehood	2337
Toleware	1775-1778
Perasaurolophus	3136o
Percy Crosby's "Skippy"	3151m
Performing Arts	1755-1756, 1801, 1803, 2012, 2088, 2090, 2110, 2211, 2250, 2411, 2550
Periodical cicada	3351r
Perisphere	853
Perkins, Frances	1821
Perry	
Commodore	144, 155, 166, 177, 191, 202, 218, 229, 261
Commodore Oliver Hazard	276-276A
Matthew C.	1021
Pershing, Gen. John J.	1042A
Persian Cat	2375
Persistent Trillium	1783
Personal Computers	3190n
Petrified Wood	1538
Petroleum Industry	1134
Phantom of the Opera, The	3168
Pharmacy	1473
Pheasant	2283
Philadelphia	
Exchange	1782
Light Horse Flag	1353
Philatelic	
Americans, Society of	797
Exhibition, International Centenary	948
Exhibition, Third International	778
Exhibitions	948, 1632, 1757, 2145, 2216-2217, 2218-2219
Exhibitions, Centenary International	948
Exhibitions, Fifth National	1075-1076
Exhibitions, Trans-Mississippi	751
Society, American	730-731, 750, 766, 770
Phillips, Coles	3502e
Philippines (Corregidor)	925
Phoebe Pember	2975r
Phoenix	2406
Photography	1758
George Eastman	1062
Physical Fitness	2043
—Sokols	1262
Piano	1615C
Pickett, Bill	2869g
Pierce	
-Arrow	2382
Franklin	819, 2217e
Pika	2319
Pilgrim Tercentenary	548-550
Pilgrims	548-550
Landing of the	1420
Pine Cone	2491
Pink Rose	2492
Pioneer	
10	3189i
10 Jupiter	1556
11	2573
Pioneers	
of Aviation	C91-C96, C99-C100, C113-C114, C118-C119, C128-C129
of Communication	
Piper	
Cub	C129
William T.	C129, C132
Piping plover	3105n
Pitcher, Molly (Battle of Monmouth)	646
Pitts, Zasu	2824
Plains	
Indian	3151g
Prickly Pear	2685
Plane	C77
and Globes	C89
Globes and Flag	C90
Pledge of Allegiance	2593-2594
Pluto	2577
Pocahontas	330
Poe, Edgar Allan	986
Poets	864-868, 986, 1405, 1436, 1446, 1485, 1526, 1554, 1926, 2239, 2449
Poinsettia	1256
Poland	909
(von Steuben, General)	689
Poland's Millennium	1313
Polar	
Bear	1429, 1885, 3291
Explorers	1128, 1431, 2220-2223
Police, Patrol Wagon	2258
Poling, Clark V.	956
Polio	1087, 3187a
Polk, James K.	816, 2217b, 2587
Polo	2759
Polo Grounds, New York City	3514
Pons, Lily	3154
Ponselle, Rosa	3157
Pony Express	894, 1154
Rider	2780
Poor, Salem	1560
Popcorn Wagon	2261
Popeye	3000k
Popular Singers	2849-2853
Porgy & Bess	1484, 2768
Porkfish	1828
Porter	
Cole	2550
David D.	792
Portrait of Richard Mather by John Foster	3236a
Post	
Office Department	O47-O56, O108
Office Department Building	C42
Office, First Automated	1164
Office, Truck	E14, E19
Rider	113, 1478
Wiley	C95-C96
Stamp Centenary	947, 948
Postwar Baby Boom	3186l
Postal	
Conference, International	C66
Service	1164, 1238, 1396, 1489-1498, 1572-1575, 2420, 2539
Posting a Broadside	1477
Postman and Motorcycle	E12-E13, E15-E18
Potomac River	1366
Poultry Industry	968
POWs-MIAs	1422, 2966
Powatan, USS	792
Powered Flight	C47
Prairie Crab Apple	3196
Preamble to the Constitution	2355-2359
Prehistoric Animals	2422-2425
Preservation of Wildlife Habitats	1921-1924
Preserve the Environment (Expo '74)	1527
Presidential Issue '38	803-804, 806-824, 826-831, 832-834, 839-851
Presidents Miniature Sheets '86	2216-2219
Presidents Miniature Sheets '86 (Stamp Collecting)	2201
Presley, Elvis	2721, 2724, 2731
Pressed Glass	3327
Prevent Drug Abuse	1438
Priestley, Joseph	2038
Prince Valiant	3000s
Princeton	
George Washington at	1704
University (Nassau Hall)	1083
Printed Circuit Board	1501
Printing	857
Press	857, 1014, 1119, 1476, 1593, 2779
Priority Mail	2419, 2540
Prisoners of War	2966
Proclamation	
Emancipation	1233
of Peace, American Revolution	727, 752
Professional	
Baseball	1381
Management	1920
Progress	
Alliance for	1232, 1234
in Electronics	1500-1502, C96
of Women	959
Prohibition enforced	3184c
Project Mercury	1193
Prominent Americans	1278-1283, 1283B, 1284-1286A, 1287-1288, 1288B, 1289-1294, 1299, 1303-1304, 1304C, 1305, 1305C, 1393-1395, 1397-1402
Pronghorn Antelope	1078, 1889, 2313
Propeller, Wooden, and Airplane Radiator	C4
Prostate Cancer Awareness	3315
Providence, RI	1164
Pteranadon	2423
PUAS, America	2426, 2512, C121, C127
PUASP, America/	C131
Public	
Education	2159
Hospitals	2210
Pueblo Pottery	1706-1709
Puerto Rico	
(Clemente, Roberto)	2097
Columbus Landing in	2805
(De Leon, Ponce)	2024
Election	983
(Marin, Luis Munoz)	2173
San Juan	1437
Territory	801
Pulaski, General	690
Pulitzer, Joseph	946
Puma	1881
Pumper, Fire	1908
Pumpkinseed Sunfish	2481
Puppy and Kitten	2025
Pure Food and Drug Act	1080, 3182f
Pushcart	2133
Putnam, Rufus	795
Pyle	
Ernie	1398
Howard	3502h
Quarter	
Horse	2155
Seated	1578
Quill	
Inkwell and	1535, 1581, 1811
Pen	1099, 1119, 1230, 1250, 2360, 2421

Quilts	
American	1745-1748
Basket Design	1745

Quimby, Harriet C128
Raccoon 1757h, 2331

Racing
- Car 2262
- Horse 1528

Radiator, Airplane, and Wooden Propeller C4

Radio
- Amateur 1260
- entertains America 3184i
- Waves 1260, 1274, 1329

Raggedy Ann, by Johnny Gruelle 3151c

Railroad
- Baltimore & Ohio 1006
- Engineers 993
- Lantern 1612
- Mail Car 2265
- Transcontinental 922

Railway
- Car, Cog 2463
- Mail Car 2781

Rainey, "Ma" 2859
Rand, Ayn 3308
Randolph, A. Philip 2402
Range Conservation 1176
Raphael Semmes 2975i
Ratification of the Constitution 835, 2336-2348
Rayburn, Sam 1202
Read, George 1687e, 1694
Readers, A Nation of 2106
Rebecca of Sunnybrook Farm 2785
Recognizing Deafness 2783
Recovering Species 3191g
Recreational Sports 2961-2965
Red Ball Express speeds vital supplies, 1944 .... 2828h
Redding, Otis 2728, 2735

Red
- Cloud 2175
- Cross, American 702, 967, 1910
- Cross, International 1016
- Fox 1757g, 2335
- Maids 2692
- -Nosed Reindeer 2792, 2797, 2802
- Squirrel 2489
- -winged Blackbird 2303

Redding, Otis 2728, 2735
Redhead Decoy 2141
Red-headed Woodpecker 3032
Reed, Dr. Walter 877
Refuge National Park, City of C84
Register and Vote 1249, 1344
Religious Freedom in America 1099
"Remember the Maine" 3192
Remington, Frederic 888, 1187, 1934, 3502p
Renwick, James 1838
Representatives, House of 2412

Republic of
- China 1188
- Palau 2999
- Texas 776, 778, 2204
- the Marshall Islands 2507

Research, Health 2087
Resolution 1733
Restaurantionen 620
Retarded Children 1549
Reticulated Helmet 2118
Retriever, Chesapeake Bay 2099
Return to Space 3191h
Reuter, Ernst 1136-1137
Revel, Bernard 2193
Revere, Paul 1048, 1059A
Rhode Island 1645, 1991
- Flag 1349
- Settlement 777
- Statehood 2348
- Windmill 1739

Rhodochrosite 1541
Rhythm & Blues/Rock & Roll 2724-2737
Ribault Monument, Jan 616
Richard Nixon 2955
Richardson, Henry Hobson 1839
Rickenbacker, Eddie 2998, 2998a
Riley, James Whitcomb 868
Ring Nebula 3385
Ringmaster 2751
Ringtail 2302
Rise of the Spirit of Independence 1476-1479
Riverboats 3091-3095
River Otter 2314
Roanoke Island Settlement, Virginia Dare 796
Roanoke Voyages 2093
Robert E. Lee 2975b
Robie House, Chicago 3182o

Robinson
- Edward G. 3446
- Jackie 2016, 3186c, 3408a

Rochambeau, Count de 703
Rock 'n Roll 3187m
Rock & Roll/Rhythm & Blues Musicians 2721-2737

Rockne, Knute 2376
Rockwell, Norman 2839, 3502s
Rocky Marciano, undefeated 3187k
Rocky Mountains 288
- Beacon on C11

Rodgers, Jimmie 1755
Rodgers & Hammerstein 3348
Rogers, Will 975, 1801

Roosevelt
- Eleanor 1236, 2105, 3185d
- Franklin D. 930-933, 1284, 1298, 1305, 1950, 2219d, 2559d, 3185a
- (Rough Riders) 973
- (Sagamore Hill) 1023
- Theodore .. 557, 586, 602, 637, 648, 663, 674, 830, 856, 1011, 1039, 2218g, 2523, 3182b, C88

Roses 1737, 1876, 2378-2379, 2490, 2492, 2833, 3049, 3054
Roseate Spoonbill 2308
Rosebud Orchid 2670
Rosetta, Sister 3219

Ross
- Betsy 1004
- George 1004

Rotary International 1066
Rough Riders 973
Round-lobed Hepatica 2677

Rover
- Lunar 1435
- Surface C124, C126C

Royal
- Poinciana 3311
- Wulff 2545

RR Caboose 1905
Rube Goldgerg's Inventions 3000f
Rubens Peale with Geranium by Rembrandt Peale 3236d
Ruby-throated Hummingbird 2642
Rue Anemone 2694
Ruffled Grouse 1924
Rufous Hummingbird 2645

Rural
- America 1504-1506
- Electrification Administration 2144
- Free Delivery 3090
- Mailbox 1730

Rush Lamp and Candle Holder 1610
Rushing, Jimmy 2858
Rushmore, Mount 1011, 2523-2523A, C88

Russell,
- Charles M. 1243
- Richard 1853

Ruth, Babe 2046, 3184a, 3408h
Rutledge, Edward 1687e, 1694
S Class 3373
S.S. Adriatic 117
Saarinen, Eeno 2022
Sabertooth Blenny 1830
Saber-tooth Cat 3080
Sacagawea 1063, 2869s
Sackville, Surrender of Fort 651
Saddlebred Horse 2157

Safety 1007
- Traffic 1272

Sagamore Hill (Home of Theodore Roosevelt) 1023
Saguaro Cactus 1192, 1945, 1955

Saint
- Augustine 927
- Charles Streetcar 2062
- Gaudens, Augustus 886
- Lawrence Seaway 1131, 2091

Salem, Peter 1361
Salomon, Haym 1561
Salute to Youth 963
Salvation Army 1267
Sampson, William T. 793
San Diego, CA 773, 778
San Francisco 567, 698
- 49ers 3190c
- Bay 400-400A
- Cable Car 1442, 2263
- Discovery of 400A, 404
- Garter snake 3105k
- (Golden Gate) 567, 698
- -Oakland Bay Bridge, Plane over C36

San
- Gabriel Mission, CA C116
- Idlefonso Pot 1707
- Juan, Puerto Rico 1437
- Martin, Jose de 1125-1126
- Xavier del Bac Mission 1443

Sandburg, Carl 1731
Sandy Hook Lighthouse 1605, 2474

Santa
- Claus .. 1472, 1508, 1800, 2064, 2108, 2579, 2580-2585, 2873, 3004
- Fe, NM 944, 1031A, 1054A
- Maria 232

Saratoga
- Battle of 1728
- US 791
- Victory at 2590

Sargent, Gov. Winthrop 955

Saroyan, William 2538
Satellite 1575
Saturn 2574
Sault Ste. Marie 1069
Savannah 923

Save Our
- Air 1413
- Cities 1411
- Soil 1410
- Water 1412

Savings
- and Loans 1911
- Bonds, US 2534
- Bonds—Servicemen 1320

Saw-Whet Owl 1761, 2284
Sawtooth Mountain, ID 2439
Sawyer, Tom 1470
Saxhorns 1614
Scarlet Tanager 2306
Schaus swallowtail butterfly 3105f
Schley, Winfield S. 793

School
- Bus 2123
- Teachers 1093

Schoolhouse, One-Room 1606
Schurz, Carl 1847
Science & Industry 2031
Sciences, The 1237
Scientists 874-878, 953, 1074, 1080, 1285, 1488, 1774, 2699, 2746

Scooties 3151j
Scorpionfly 3351s

Scott
- Blanche Stuart C99
- General Winfield 24, 142, 153, 164, 175, 200, 786
- Jock 2546

Scotts Bluff, NE 1060

Sea
- Creatures of the 2508-2511
- Lion, Northern 2509
- Otter 2510

Seal .. 683, 775, 778, 794, 897, 927, 940, 955, 972, 974, 979, 995, 1001-1002, 1005, 1015, 1018, 1066, 1091, 1095-1096, 1127, 1131, 1151, 1156, 1167, 1194, 1234, 1266, 1308, 1314, 1419, 1421, 1432, 1525, 1559, 1560, 1561, 1565-1570, 1825, 2142, 2336, C40
- Fur 1464
- Harbor 1882

Sealed Envelopes 2150
Seamstress 1717
Seaplane 2468
Search for Peace (Lions International) 1326
Seashells 2117-2121
Seated Liberty Quarter 1578
SEATO 1151
Seattle World's Fair 1196
Secretariat Wins Triple Crown 3189g
Seeing Eye Dogs 1787
Sego Lily 2667
Seinfeld Sitcom Sensation 3191c
Self-adhesive 2915, 2919-2920, 2957, 3008-3010, 3012, 3014-3017, 3019

Seminole Seal 972
Semmes, Raphael 2975i
Senate, US 2413
Sequoyah 1859
Serra, Father Junipero C116
Service Women 1013

Servicemen
- Disabled American Veterans and 1421-1422
- Savings Bonds 1320

Sesame Street 3189c
Sessile Belwort 2662
Sevier, Gov. John 941
Seward, William H. 370, 371
Shadoo, Chief 683
Shakespeare, Wiliam 1250
Sheridan, Gen. Philip 787

Sherman
- General William T. 225, 257, 272, 787, 2975q
- Roger 1687a, 1693

Shibe Park, Philadelphia 3518
Shield, Eagle and Flags 121
Shiloh, Civil War Centennial 1179, 2975e
Shot Heard Round the World, The 3187c
Shooting Star 2654

Ship
- Figurehead 2241
- Liberty 2559h

Shipbuilding 1095
Shiprock, NM 1191
Shorthair Cat
- American 2375
- Exotic 2372

Shoshone Headdress 2505
Show Boat 2767
Showy Evening Primrose 2671
Shuttle 1913-1914, 1917, 1919, C125, C126a, C126d
Siamese Cat 2372
Sign Language, American 2783-2784

Signing of the		
Constitution		798, 2360
Mayflower Compact		550
Sikorsky, Igor		C119
Silver Centennial		1130
Silversmith		1457
SIPEX		1310-1311
Sisler, George		3408e
Sitting Bull		2183
Skateboarding		3321
Skiing, Alpine		3180
Skilled Hands for Independence		1717-1720
Skylab		1915
Skylab I		1529
Sled, Dog		1128, 2135
Sleepy Hollow, Legend of		1548
Sleigh		1384, 1551, 1900, 2400, 2428
Slinky, 1945		3186m
Sloan, John		1433
Slolam		2807
Smith		
Alfred E.		937
Bessie		2854
Captain John		328
Jessie Willcox		3502l
Smithsonian Institution		943, 1838, 3059
Smokey the Bear		2096
Smooth Solomon's Seal		2691
Snelling, Fort		1409
Snowboarding		3323
Snowdrop		3028
Snowman		2793, 2796, 2799, 2803
Snow White and the Seven Dwarfs		3185h
Snowy		
Egret		2321
Owl		3290
Social Security Act		2153
Society of Philatelic Americans		797
Softball		2962
Soil		
Conservation		1133
Conservation, Water and		2074
Save our		1410
Sokols, Physical Fitness—		1262
Solar Energy		2006, 2952
Solo Transatlantic Flight, Lindbergh's		1710, C10
Songwriters		3100-3103
Sonoran Desert		3293
Soo Locks		1069
Sound Recording		1705
Sousa, John Philip		880
South Carolina		1640, 1992
Settlement		1407
Statehood		2343
South Dakota		1672, 1993
Statehood		858, 2416
South-East Asia Treaty Organization (SEATO)		1151
Southern Magnolia		3193
Southwest Carved Wood Figure		2426, C121
Soyuz, Apollo		1569-1570
Space		
Accomplishment in (Apollo 8)		1371
Accomplishments in		1331-1332
Achievement Decade		1434-1435
Achievements		1912-1919
Achievement and Exploration		3412
Adventure		2631-2634
(Apollo Soyuz)		1569-1570
Discovery		3238-42
(Echo I—Communications for Peace)		1173
Escaping the Gravity of Earth		3411
Exploration		2568-2577
Exploring the Solar System		3410
Fantasy		2741-2745
(Fort Bliss)		976
(Future Mail Transportation)		C122-C125, C126
(Goddard, Robert H.)		C69
(Mariner 10/Venus, Mercury)		1557
(Moon Landing)		2419, C76, 3413
Needle		1196
(Palomar Mountain Observatory)		966
(Pioneer 10/Jupiter)		1556
Probing the Vastness of Space		3409
(Project Mercury)		1193
Shuttle		2544-2544A, 2631, C125, C126a, C126d
Shuttle Program		3190a
(Skylab I)		1529
Vehicle		2543
(Viking Missions)		1759
(von Karman, Theodore)		2699
Spacecraft		C122, C125, C126
Spaniel, Cocker		2099
Spanish Settlement of the Southwest 1598		3220
Speaker		1502
Speaker, Tris		3408l
Speaker's Stand		1582
Special		
Occasions		2267-2274, 2395-2398
Olympics		1788, 3191i
Olympics, Winter		2142
Spectacle Reef (Lake Huron)		2971

Sperry, Lawrence and Elmer		C114
Spinybacked spider		3351q
Spirit of '76		1629-1631
"Spirit of St. Louis", Lindbergh's		1710, C10
Split Rock (Lake Superior)		2969
Sport Utility Vechicles		3191m
Sportin' Life		1484
Sports		
American		2376-2377
Recreational		716-719, 855, 1146, 1189, 1262, 1381-1382, 1460-1462, 1528, 1695-1698, 1702-1703, 1788, 1790-1798, 1932-1933, 2016, 2027, 2029, 2033-2034, 2043, 2046, 2048-2051, 2067-2070, 2082-2085, 2089, 2097, 2142, 2247, 2369, 2376-2377, 2380, 2417, 2496-2500, 2560, 2756-2759, 2766, 2807-2811, 2962, 2965, C56, C85, C97, C101-C112
Summer		3397
Spotted water beetle		3351o
Spreading Pogonia		2078
Squashblossoms Lace, Design		2351
St. John's College		
St. Joseph (Lake Michigan)		2970
St. Louis World's Fair, 1904		3182e
Stagecoach		1120, 1572, 1898A, 2228, 2434, 2438a, 2448
Staggerwing Airplane		3142j
Stamp		
Collecting		1474, 2198-2201, 2410, 2433
Expo '89		2410, 2433, 2433a-2433d
Expo '92, World Columbian		2616
Stand Watie		2975l
Standing Cypress		2695
Stanley Steamer		2132
Stanton		
Edwin M.		138, 149, 160, 171, 196
Elizabeth		959
Star-Spangled Banner, 1814		3403k
Star Route Truck		2125
Star Trek		3188e
Stars		
and Stripes		2531, 3403
of the Silent Screen		2819-2828
"Stars and Stripes Forever"		3153
Starr, Brenda		3000t
State		
Birds & Flowers		1953-2002
Capitols		782, 838, 896, 903-904, 927, 941, 957, 996, 1001, 1232, 1308, 1407, 2337, 2342
Statehood Anniversary		858
Statehood		
Alabama		1375
Alaska		2066, C53
Arkansas		2167
California		997
Colorado		1001, 1711
Connecticut		2340
Florida		927, 2950
Georgia		2339
Hawaii		2080, C55
Idaho		896, 2439
Illinois		1339
Indiana		1308
Iowa		942
Kansas		1183
Kentucky		2636
Louisiana		1197
Maine		1391
Maryland		2342
Massachusetts		2341
Michigan		775, 778, 2246
Minnesota		1106
Mississippi		1337
Missouri		1426
Montana		858, 2401
Nebraska		1328
Nevada		1248
New Hampshire		2344
New Jersey		2338
New Mexico		1191
New York		2346
North Carolina		2347
North Dakota		858, 2403
Ohio		1018
Oklahoma		1092
Oregon		1124
Rhode Island		2348
South Carolina		2343
South Dakota		858, 2416
Tennessee		941
Texas		938
Vermont		903, 2533
Virginia		2345
Washington		858, 2404
West Virginia		1232
Wisconsin		957
Wyoming		897, 2444
Statesman, Acheson, Dean		2755
Statue of Liberty		566, 696, 899, 908, 946, 995, 1035, 1041-1042, 1044, 1044A, 1057, 1075, 1320, 1594, 1599, 1619, 1816, 2147, 2224, 2599, C35, C58, C63, C80, C87
Steam Carriage		2451
Steamboats		2405-2409, 2435, 2438b

Steamship (Savannah)		923
Stearman Airplane		3142l
Steel Industry		1090
Steelers Win Four Super Bowls		3189e
Steeplechase		2756
Stefansson, Vihjalmur		2222
Stegosaurus		1390, 2424, 3136f
Steinbeck, John		1773
Steiner, Max		3339
Steinmetz, Charles		2055
Stevenson, Adlai E.		1275
Stewart, Walter		1686e
Stock car racing		3187n
Stock Exchange, New York		2630
Stock Market crash, 1929		3184o
Stocking		2872
Stone		
Harlan F.		965
Lucy		1293
Mountain Memorial		1408
Stonewall Jackson		2975s
Stourbridge Lion		2362
Stokowski, Leopold		3158
Straight-Spout Coffeepot		1775
Stratford Hall		788
Stratojet Airplane		3142h
Stravinsky, Igor		1845
Stream Violet		2655
Streamline design		3185k
Streetcars		2059-2062
Streetcar Named Desire, A 1947		3186n
Strickland, William		1782
Stuart, Gilbert Charles		884
Stutz Bearcat		2131
Stuyvesant, Peter		971
Submarines shorten war in Pacific		2838e
Suffrage, Woman		1406
(Belva Ann Lockwood)		2179
(Lucy Stone)		1293
(Susan B. Anthony)		784, 1051
Sugar Bowl		1777
Sullivan		
Anne & Helen Keller		1824
Expedition, Maj. Gen. John		657
Louis		1931
Sun		616, 906, 950, 968, 1016, 1188, 1434, 1710, 1723-1724, 1915, 2340
Tower of the		852
Yat-Sen		906, 1188
Super Bowl I		3188l
Super Chief		3337
Superman arrives		3185f
Supersonic Flight		3173
Support Our Youth—Elks		1342
Supreme Court		991, 1895, 1896, 2415
(Black, Hugo)		2172
Flag Over		1894
Frieze (American Bar Association)		1022
(Holmes, Oliver Wendell)		1288, 1288B, 1305E
(Jay, John)		1046
(Marshall, John)		312, 1050
(Moore, John Bassett)		1295
(Warren, Earl)		2184A
Surface Rover		C124, C126c
Surrender		
at Saratoga		644, 1728
of Cornwallis at Yorktown		703, 1686
Surrey		1907
Sutter's Mill		954
Swallowtail		1712
Swedish		
-Finnish Landing		836
Pioneer		958
(Stamp Collecting)		2200
Sweet White Violet		2659
Switzerland		2532
Synthetic Fuels		2007
Szell, George		3160
Taft		
Sen. Robert A. Memorial		1161
William H.		685, 687, 831, 2218h
Tail fins, chrome		3187g
Talking Pictures		1727
Tandem Bicycle		2266
Tanner, Henry O.		1486
Taylor, Zachary		179, 181, 185, 204, 817, 2217c
Tea Caddy		1776
Teachers of America		1093
Teddy bear created		3182k
Teen fashions		3187b
Telecommunication Union, International		1274
Telegraph		890, 924
Telephone		893, 1683
Telescope		1919
Television Camera, First		2058
Tennessee		1648, 1994
Statehood		941, 3070-3071
Valley Authority		2042
Williams		3002
Tennis		2964
Terrier, Boston		2098

Entry	Number(s)
Territorial Issues	799-802
Territories, Pacific Trust, Northern Mariana Islands	2408
Terry, Sonny	3214
Terry and the Pirates	3000r
Tesla, Nikola	2057
Texas	1660, 1995
(HemisFair '68)	1340
Republic of	776, 778, 2204
Statehood	938, 2968
Windmill	1742
Thank You!	2269
That's All Folks	3534a, 3535a
Thayer, Sylvanus	1852
Theater Dance	1750
Thelonious Monk	2990
Thick-billed parrot	3105b
Thinking of You	2397
Thirteenth Amendment	902
13-Star Flags, 50 Star and	2216, 2552, 2608
Thirty Mile Point (Lake Ontario)	2973
Thomas A. Edison	945
Thomson, Charles	1687, 1694
Thoreau, Henry David	1327
Thorpe, Jim	2089, 3183g
Three Graces	895
314 Clipper Airplane	3142r
Thurber, James	2862
Tibbett, Lawrence	3156
Tickseed	2653
Ticonderoga, Fort	1071
Tidal Basin	1318
Tiger Stadium, Detroit	3511
Tiger, White Bengal	2709
Tiger Swallowtail	2300
Tilghman, Bill	2869
Tiomkin, Dimitri	3340
Titanic Blockbuster Film	3191l
Tlingit	
Chief in Haida Ceremonial Canoe	1389
Tribe	1836
Tokyo Bay	1021
Tokyo Raid	2697a
Toleware, Pennsylvania	1775-1778
Toonerville Folks	3000g
Torch	978-979, 1015, 1066, 1096, 1110-1111, 1117-1118, 1125-1126, 1136-1137, 1144, 1147-1148, 1159-1160, 1165-1166, 1168-1169, 1174-1175, 1234, 1308, 2336
Liberty	1594, 1816, 2531A
of Enlightment	901
Toscanini, Arturo	2411
Tourmaline	1539
Touro Synagogue	2017
Tow Truck	2129
Tower of the Sun	852
Toy	
Ship	2714
Soldier	2794-2795, 2800
Steamer	2713, 2717
Train	2712, 2716, 2719
Track Racing	2757
Tractor	1162, 2127
Trailer	2547-2548
Traffic Safety	1272
Trail, Oregon	2747
Trans-Mississippi	
Exposition	285-293
Philatelic Exposition	751, 769
Reissue	3209-3210
Transatlantic	
Airmail	C24
Flight, Solo	1710, C10
Transcontinental Railroad	922
Transistors	1501
Transpacific Airmail	C20-C22, C115
Transport Plane, Twin-Motor	C25
Transportation	1897-1897A, 1898-1908, 2252-2256, 2258-2266, 2451, 2453, 2457, 2463-2464, 2466, 2468, 2905
Air-Cushion Vehicle	C123, C125, C126b
Airplane	649, 650, 934, 947, 1185, 1511, 1574, 1684, 1710, 2433, 2436, 2438c, 2468, C1, C2-C9, C10-C11, C20-C22, C25-C33, C35-C41, C44-C47, C68, C74, C91-C96, C99, C100, C113-C115, C118-C119, C128-C129
Ambulance	2128, 2231
Automobile	1162, 1286A, 1511, 1906, 2131-2132, 2262, 2381-2385, 2437, 2438d
Balloons	2032-2035, 2530, C54
Bicycle	1460, 1901, 2266, C110
Buggy	1360, 1370, 1505, 1902, 2124
Bus	1897, 2123, 2225
Cable Car	1442, 2263
Caboose, RR	1905
Canoe	2453
Carriage, Steam	2451
Cart	981, 2133
Classic (Mail)	2434-2438
Coal Car	2259
Cog Railway Car	2463
Elevator	2254
Ferryboat	2466
Fire Engine	971, 1908, 2264
Handcar	1898
Horses	235, 240, 287, 289, 400, 400A, 404, 618, 645, 783, 835, 894, 898, 944, 947, 950, 973, 1001, 1003, 1006, 1012, 1028, 1061, 1120, 1123, 1130, 1154, 1176, 1243, 1261, 1360, 1384, 1408, 1416, 1478-1479, 1505, 1528, 1548, 1551, 1559, 1686, 1689, 1794, 1934, 2059, 2341, 2345-2346, 2391, 2400, 2401, 2448
Jeep	2559c
Jet	1017, 1574, 2022, 2047, C49, C51-C52, C57-C65, C75, C77-C78, C81-C82, C87, C89-C90, C98, C122, C126a
Locomotive	922, 947, 961, 993, 1006, 1506, 1573, 1755, 1897A, 1905, 2226, 2362-2366, 2402
Lunar Rover	1435
Lunch Wagon	2464
Mail Car	2265
Monorail	1196
Motorcycle	1899
Railway Car, Cog	2463
Series	1898A, 2123-2132, 2134-2136
Ships and Boats	230-233, 235, 293, 329, 372-373, 398-399, 402-403, 548-549, 567, 614-615, 620-621, 683, 698, 736, 739, 746, 755, 762, 790, 792-793, 802, 836, 856, 923, 936, 939, 947, 951, 956, 984, 994, 997, 1000, 1003, 1010, 1017, 1021, 1027, 1063, 1069, 1088, 1091, 1095, 1109, 1128, 1197, 1207, 1239, 1258, 1270, 1271, 1322, 1325, 1335, 1356, 1358, 1374, 1389, 1409, 1420, 1433, 1441-1442, 1448, 1480-1483, 1567-1568, 1688, 1733, 1793, 1937, 1938, 2040, 2080, 2085, 2091, 2093, 2134, 2163, 2200, 2220, 2260, 2336, 2340, 2342, 2386-2387, 2404-2409, 2435, 2506-2507, 2529, 2529C, 2559, 2621, 2623, C130
Shuttle	C125, C126d
Sled	1128, 1461, 1702-1703, 2027, 2135
Sleigh	1384, 1551, 1900, 1940, 2400
Stagecoach	1120, 1572, 1898A, 2228, 2434, 2438, 2448
Steam Carriage	2451
Streetcar	2059-2062
Surface Rover	C124, C126
Tank	1026, 2559e
Tractor	1162, 2127
Tractor-Trailer	2457
Tricycle	2126
Truck	1025, 1162, 1572, 2125, 2129, 2457, 2559a, 2635
Wagon	240, 286, 289-290, 323, 783, 950, 958, 964, 970, 981, 997, 1018-1019, 1028, 1061, 1120, 1124, 1360, 1426, 1487, 1542, 1744, 1897, 1903, 1907, 2124, 2128, 2130, 2136, 2253, 2255, 2258, 2261, 2341, 2345-2346, 2403, 2448, 2452, 2452D, 2464
Wheelchair	1155, 1385, 2153, 2256
Zeppelin	C13-C15, C18
Trapeze, Circus	2752
Traynor, Pie	3408o
Treasury Department	O72-O82, O114-O120
Treaty	
Antarctic	1431, C130
of Paris	2052
US-Japan	1158
Tree Planting	2953
Trees	1240, 1245, 1376
American	1764-1767
Trego, William T.	1689
Tricycle	2126
Tri-Motor Airplane	3142p
Trinity Church	1839
Troops Guarding Train	289
Trout	1427
Truck	
Star Route	2125
Tow	2129
Trucking Industry	1025
True katydid	3351p
Truman, Harry S.	1499, 1862, 2219f, 2981h, 3186d
Trumball, John	1361, 1686, 1686d
Trumpet Honeysuckle	2683
Truth, Sojourner	2203
Trylon	853
Tube, TV	1502
Tuberculosis	1823
Tubman, Harriet	1744, 2975k
Tucker, Richard	3155
Tugboat	2260
Tulip	2425-2427, 2517-2520, 2524-2527, 2762
Tuna, Bluefin	2208
Turk's Cap Lily	2681
Turners Society, American	979
TV Camera, Tube	1502
TV entertains America	3186f
(Twain, Mark), Samuel L. Clemens	863, 1470
Twinflower	2665
Twin-Motored Transport Plane	C25-C31
Two Against the White by Charles Sheeler	3236r
Two Medicine Lake	748, 764
Tyler, John	815, 847, 2217a
Tyrannosaurus	2422
Ulysses S. Grant	2975d
Umbrella Beach	2443
Underground Railroad	2975k
United	
Confederate Veteran	998
(Dag Hammarskjold)	1203-1204
Headquarters	1203-1204
International Cooperation Year	1266
Nations	907, 1419, 2974
Nations Conference	928
Nations Memorial,	
States enters WWI	3183i
(Stevenson, Adlai E.)	1275
Way	2275
Universal	
(Classic Mail Transportation)	2434-2437
(Future Mail Transportation)	C126
Postal Union	1530-1537, 3332, C42-C44
Postal Union (Future Mail Transportation)	C122-C125
Uranus	2575
Urban Planning	1333
US	
Air Mail Service	C74
-Canada Friendship	961
Capitol	649-650, 989, 992, 1013, 1152, 1202, 1365, 1368, 1503, 2114-2116, 2532, 2561, C64
Celebrates 200th Birthday	3189f
Congress	2559j
Frigate Constitution, Oct. 21	951
House of Representatives	2412
-Japan Treaty	1158
Launches satellites	3187d
Map and Two Mail Planes	C7
Military Academy	789
(Morocco, Friendship With)	2349
Naval Academy	794, 3001
Postage Stamp Centenary	947
Savings Bonds	2534
Senate	2413
Servicemen	1421-1422
& Soviets link up at Elbe River	2981d
-Sweden Treaty	2036
Troops clear saipen bunkers	2838g
USA	2193, 2608A, 2608B
and Jet	C75, C81
Netherlands	2003
USS Holland	3376
USS Yorktown Lost	2697g
Utah	950, 1677, 1996
Settlement	950
Statehood	3024
(Zion National Park)	747, 763
Valens, Ritchie	2727, 2734
Valentino, Rudolph	2819
Valley	
Carson, NV	999
Forge	645, 1689, 1729
of the Great Salt Lake	950
Van	
Buren, Martin	813, 2201, 2216h
der Rohe, Mies	2020
Varela, Padre Felix	3166
Variscite	2702
VCR's Transform Entertainment	3189h
Vega Airplane	3142d
Vehicle, Space	2543
Velvet ant	3351i
Venus Flytrap	3528
Venus Mercury, Mariner 10/	1557
Vermont	1646, 1997
Battle of Bennington and Independence	643
Statehood	903, 2533
Verrazano-Narrows Bridge	1258
Verville, Alfred	C113
Veterans	
Administration	1825
Administration of Foreign Wars	1525
Civil War	985, 998
Disabled American	1421
Honoring	3508
Korean	2152
of Foreign Wars	1525
of World War II	940
Vietnam	1802, 2109
World War I	2154
Victory, Allied	537
Video Games	3190l
Vietnam	
Veterans	1802
Memorial	2109, 3190o
War	3188g
Viking	
Mission to Mars	1759
Orbiter	2572
Ship	621
Vincennes	651
Violet, African	2495
Violins, Weaver	1813
Virgin Island	802
Virginia	1642, 1998
Bluebells	2668
Capes, Battle of the	1938
of Sagadahock	1095
Rotunda	1779
Windmill	1738
Virtual Reality	3191i
Voice of America	1329
Volleyball	2961
Voluntarism	2039

Volunteer Firemen	971
von	
Karman, Dr. Theodore	2699
Steuben, Gen. Frederich	689, 1686, 1686d
Vote, Register and	1249
Voyager 2	2574-2576
V-mail	2765e
Wagner, Honus	3408q
Wagon	
Bread	2136
Circus	2452, 2452D
Lunch	2464
Mail	1903
Oil	2130
Walk in the Water	2409
Walker, Dr. Mary	2013
Walker, Madam C.J.	3181
Wallenberg, Raoul	3135
Walloon, Huguenot	614-616
Walter Johnson	3408i
Wapiti	1886
War	
Department	O83-O93, O114-O120
Win the	905
Ward, Clara	3218
Warner, Pop	3144, 3149
Warren, Earl	2184
Washington	
and Jackson	2592
and Lee University	982
at Cambridge	617
at Princeton	1704
at Valley Forge	645, 1729
Bicentennial Issue	704-715
Booker T.	873, 1074
Bridge	1012
Crossing the Delaware	1688
D.C.	943, 989-992
Dinah	2730, 2737
(Executive Branch)	2414
George	2, 4, 10-11, 13-17, 25-26, 31-37, 39, 41, 43-45, 47, 62B, 64-66, 68-70, 72, 74, 78-79, 82-83, 85, 85C-85E, 88-90, 94, 96-97, 99, 101, 104, 106-107, 109, 111, 115, 136, 147, 158, 169, 184, 194, 207, 210, 211B, 213-214, 219D, 220, 248-252, 279B, 301, 319-322, 332-342, 353-356, 358-366, 375-382, 384, 386, 388-389, 391, 393-396, 405-413, 424-430, 441-450, 451-459, 461-469, 481-496, 498-507, 519, 525-536, 538-546, 554, 577, 579, 583, 595, 599-599A, 606, 634-634A, 645-647, 660, 671, 688, 703-715, 720-722, 785, 804, 839, 848, 947-948, 982, 1003-1004, 1011, 1031, 1054, 1123, 1139, 1213, 1229, 1283, 1283B, 1304, 1304C, 1686, 1686c, 1688b, 1689, 1689b, 1729, 1952, 2081, 2201, 2216a, 2523, C88
Headquarters	727, 730, 752, 766
Inauguration	854, 2414
John P.	956
Martha	306, 556, 585, 601, 636, 662, 673, 805, 840, 849
Monument	649-650, 1158, 1366
(Mount Ranier National Park)	742, 750, 758, 770
State	1674, 1999
Statehood	858, 2404
(Steamboat)	2408
Territory	1019
(Touro Synagogue)	2017
Water	
Conservation	1150
Conservation, Soil and	2074
Save Our	1412
Waterfowl Conservation	1362
Waters	
Ethel	2851
Muddy	2855
Watie, Stand	2975l
Waxman, Franz	3342
Wayne	
Gen. Anthony	680
John	2448
We Give Thanks	3546
Weaver Violins	1813
W.E.B. DuBois, social activist	3182l
Webster, Daniel	141, 152, 163, 174, 189, 199, 226, 258, 273, 282C, 283, 307, 725, 1380
Webster, Noah	1121
Wells, Ida B.	2442
West	
Benjamin	1553
Gen. Joseph	683
Point, US Military Academy	789
Quoddy Head (ME)	2472
Virginia	1667, 2000
Virginia Statehood	1232
Western Wildlife	2869p
Westport Landing, MO	994
Westwood Children, The by Joshua Johnson	3236h
Wetland Habitats	1921
Whale	
Killer	2508
Oil Lamp	1608
Wharton	
Edith	1832
Joseph	1920

Wheat Fields	1506
Wheatland (Home of James Buchanan)	1081
Wheel Chair	1155, 1385, 2153, 2256
Wheels of Freedom	1162
Wheelwright	1719
Whistler, James A. McNeill	737-738, 754, 885
Whistler's Mother	737-738, 754
Whitcomb, Jon	3502n
White	
Bengal Tiger	2709
Cloud, Head Chief of the Iowas, The by George Catlin	3236k
House	809, 844, 932, 990, 1208, 1240, 1338, 1338A, 1338D, 1338F, 1338G, 1935-1936, 2219, 2219e, 2609, 3445
House, Little	931
Josh	3215
Mountain Avens	2661
Oak	1766
Paul Dudley, Dr.	2170
Pine	1765
Plains, Battle of	629-630
Sanford	1928
William Allen	960
White-Tailed Deer	1888, 2317
Whitman, Walt	867
Whitney, Eli	889
Whittier, John Greenleaf	865
Whooping Cranes	1098
Wightman, Hazel	2498
Wigmaker	1458
Wild	
Animals	2705-2709
Columbine	2678
Flax	2696
Pink	2076
Turkey	1077
Wildcat Airplane	3142t
Wilder, Thornton	3134
Wilderness, Civil War Centennial	1181
Wildflowers	2647-2696
Wildlife	1757, 1880-1889, 2478, 3033
American	2286-2335
Conservation	1077-1079, 1098, 1392, 1427-1430, 1464-1467, 1760-1763
Habitats, Preservation of	1921-1924a
Wiley, Harvey W.	1080
Wilkes, Lt. Charles	2387
Wilkins, Roy	3501
Willard, Frances E.	872
William T. Sherman	2975q
Williams	
Hank	2723, 2771, 2775
Roger	777
Tennessee	3002
Willie and Joe	2765h
Willkie, Wendell	2192
Wills, Bob	2774, 2778
Willson, Meredith	3349
Wilson, Woodrow	623, 697, 832, 1040, 2218i, 3183k
Win the War	905
Windmills	1738-1742
Winfield Hancock	2975n
Winged	
Airmail Envelope	C79, C83
Globe	C12, C16-C17, C19, C24
Winter	
Aconite	3026
Garden Flowers	2067
Olympic Games '84	2067
Olympic Games '94	2807-2811
Pastime, by Nathaniel Currier	1702
Special Olympics	2142
Wisconsin	1662, 2001, 3206
Statehood	957
Tercentenary	739, 755
(Workman's Compensation Law)	1186
Witherspoon, John	1687c
Wizard of Oz, The	2445
Wolf	
Howlin'	2861
Man, The	3172
Trap Farm National Park	1452, 2018
Wolfe, Thomas	3444
Wolverine	2327
Woman	
American	1152
Clubs, General Federation of	1316
Women	
In Military Service	3174
Join War Effort	2697h
Progress of	959
Suffrage	1406, 2980
Support war effort	3186e
Voting Rights	2980
Women, Armed Services	1013
Women's Rights Movement	3189j
Wonders of the Sea	2863-2866
Wood Carved Figurines	2240-2243
Woodchuck	2307
Wood Duck	2484-2485
Wooden Propeller, Airplane Radiator and	C4

Woodland Caribou	3105l
Woodland Habitats	1924
Woodpecker, Red-headed	3032
Woodson, Carter G.	2073
Woodstock	3188b
Wool Industry, American	1423
Wooly Mammoth	3078
Workmen's Compensation	1186
World	
Columbian Stamp Expo '92	2616, 2624-2629
Cup Soccer Championships	1994, 2834-2837
Exposition, Louisiana	2086
Forestry Congress, Fifth	1156
Health Organization	1194
Peace Through Law	1576
Peace Through World Trade	1129
Of Dinosaurs	3136
Refugee Year	1149
Series rivals	3187j
STAMP EXPO '89	2410, 2433
STAMP EXPO '92, Columbian	2616, 2624-2629
University Games	2748
War I	537, 2154, 2981d-2981j
War II	899-901, 905, 907-908, 909-915, 917-921, 925-926, 929, 934-936, 939-940, 956, 969, 1026, 1289, 1424, 1869, 2186, 2192, 2559, 2697, 2765, 2838, 2981, 3186a
Wide Web	3191n
World's Fair '64	1244
Expo '74	1527
Expo Seattle '62	1196
Knoxville '82	2006-2009
New York	853
Wreath and Toys	1843
Wright	
Airplane	649, C45, C47, C91
Brothers	3182g, C45, C47, C91-C92
Frank Lloyd	1280, 2019
Wrigley Field, Chicago	3519
Wulfenite	2703
Wyeth, N.C.	3502r
Wyoming	1676, 2002
Statehood	2444
Toad	3105g
(Yellowstone National Park)	744, 760, 1453
Yankee Stadium, New York City	3513
Yat-Sen Sun	906, 1188
Year	
International Women's	1571
of the Child, International	1772
of the Disabled, International	1925
2000	3369
Yellow Garden spider	3351d
Yellow Kid, The	3000a
Yellow Lady's -Slipper	2077, 2673
Yellow Popular	3195
Yellowstone National Park	744, 760, 1453
Yellow Skunk Cabbage	2693
Yellow Trumpet	3529
YMCA Youth Camping	2160
York, Alvin C.	3395
Yorktown	
Battle of	703, 1937
Surrender of Cornwallis at	703, 1686
-Virginia Capes, Battle of	703, 1937-1938
Yosemite	
Flag over	2280
National Park	740, 751, 756, 769
Young, CY	3408m
Young, Whitney Moore	1875
Youth	
Camping, YMCA	2160
Salute to	963
Support our	1342
Year, International	2160-2163
Yugoslavia, Oct. 26	917
Yukon-Pacific Expostion, Alaska-	370-371
Zaharias, Babe	1932
Zeppelin	
Between Continents	C14
Century of Progress	C18
over Atlantic	C13
Passing Globe	C15
Zia Pot	1706
Zinnia	2830
Zion National Park	747, 763
ZIP Code	1511

U.S. Postage #1-17
GENERAL ISSUES

1847 – THE FIRST ISSUE
Imperforate

"For every single letter in manuscript or paper of any kind by or upon which information shall be asked or communicated in writing or by marks or signs conveyed in the mail, for any distance under three hundred miles, five cents; and for any distance over three hundred miles, ten cents . . . and every letter or parcel not exceeding half an ounce in weight shall be deemed a single letter, and every additional weight of half ounce, shall be charged with an additional single postage."

With these words, the Act of March 3, 1845, authorized, but not required, the prepayment of postage effective July 1, 1847, and created a need for the first United States postage stamps. Benjamin Franklin, as the first Postmaster General of the United States and the man generally regarded as the "father" of the postal system, was selected for the 5 cent stamp. As the first President of the United States, George Washington was designated for the 10 cent issue.

The 1847 stamps were released July 1, 1847, but were available only in the New York City post office on that date. The earliest known usages are July 7 for the 5 cent and July 2 for the 10 cent.

The best estimates are that 4,400,000 of the 5 cent and 1,050,000 of the 10 cent stamps reached the public. The remaining stocks were destroyed when the stamps were demonetized and could no longer be used for postage as of July 1, 1851.

Like most 19th century United States stamps, the first Issue is much more difficult to find unused than used. Stamps canceled by "handstamp" marking devices—usually carved from cork—are scarcer than those with manuscript, or "pen", cancels.

Issued without gum, the Reproductions of the 1847 issue were printed from entirely new dies for display at the 1876 Centennial Exposition and were not valid for postal use. The issue also was reproduced on a souvenir sheet issued in 1947 to celebrate the centenary of the First Issue. Differences between the 1847 issue, 1875 Reproductions and 1948 stamps are described in the Stamp Identifier at the front of this catalog.

By 1857, improved production techniques and the increasing usage of stamps led to the introduction of perforated stamps that could be more easily separated. The result was the 1857-61 series whose designs are virtually identical to the 1851 set. The 1857-61 perforated stamps were set in the printing plates with very little space between each stamp. As a result, insufficient space was allowed to accommodate the perforations, which often cut into the design on these stamps. In fact, stamps with complete designs and wide margins on all four sides are the exception and command very substantial premiums.

The most fascinating—and most challenging—feature of the 1851-61 stamps is the identification of many major and minor types. An extremely slight design variation can mean a difference of thousands of dollars and collectors even today can apply their knowledge to discover rare, mis-identified types.

The various "Types", identified below by Roman numerals in parentheses, resulted from minor changes in the printing plates caused by wear or plate retouching. The 1851-57 one-cent blue stamp may be the most studied of all the United States issues and is found in seven major catalog-listed Types (14, if we count imperforate and perforated stamps separately), plus countless minor listed and unlisted varieties. A thorough explanation of the differences in the major types for all denominations of the 1857-61 series is contained in the Harris Stamp Identifier in this catalog.

Shortly after the outbreak of the Civil War, the 1851-61 stamps were demonetized to prevent Southern post offices from selling the stamps in the North to raise cash for the Confederate States. After the war, large supplies of unused 1857-61 stamps were located in Southern post offices and purchased by stamp dealers and collectors. This explains the relatively large supply of unused 1857-61 issues that still exist today. The short life and limited use of 90 cent high value, which was issued in 1860, and the 5 cent orange brown, released May 8, 1861, explains why those stamps sell for more used than unused.

1, 3, 948a
Franklin

2, 4, 948b
Washington

5-9, 18-24, 40
Franklin

10, 11, 25, 26, 41
Washington

12, 27-30A, 42
Jefferson

13-16, 31-35, 43
Washington

17, 36, 44
Washington

SCOTT NO.	DESCRIPTION	UNUSED VF	F	AVG	USED VF	F	AVG
		1847 Imperforate					
1	5¢ red brown	6100.00	4400.00	2700.00	825.00	595.00	395.00
1	— Pen cancel	....	....	....	525.00	350.00	275.00
2	10¢ black	27500.00	19500.00	11000.00	1900.00	1350.00	875.00
2	— Pen cancel	....	....	....	950.00	725.00	575.00
		1875 Reprints of 1847 Issues, without gum					
3	5¢ red brown	1395.00	1025.00	850.00	....	....	....
4	10¢ black	1800.00	1200.00	1050.00	....	....	....

1851-61 – THE CLASSIC ISSUES

An act of Congress approved March 3, 1851, enacted new, reduced postage rates, introduced additional rates and made the prepayment of additional postage compulsory. Although the use of postage stamps was not required, the 1851 Act stimulated their use and paved the way for their required usage from July 1, 1855 on.

Under the Act of 1851, the basic prepaid single letter rate (defined as one-half ounce or less) was set at 3 cents. As this would be the most commonly used value, it was decided that a likeness of George Washington should grace the 3 cent stamp. Benjamin Franklin was assigned to the 1 cent stamp, which, among other usages, met the newspaper and circular rates.

Washington also appears on the 10, 12, 24 and 90 cent stamps and Franklin on the 30 cent value. Thomas Jefferson was selected for the new 5 cent stamp that was issued in 1856.

SCOTT NO.	DESCRIPTION	UNUSED VF	F	AVG	USED VF	F	AVG
		1851-57 Imperforate (OG + 75%)					
5	1¢ blue (I)	....	....	....	36500.00	....	....
5A	1¢ blue (Ib)	8000.00	6750.00	5500.00	5800.00	4250.00	3400.00
6	1¢ dark blue (Ia)	23500.00	17750.00	13000.00	9900.00	6800.00	4400.00
7	1¢ blue (II)	750.00	525.00	400.00	225.00	195.00	150.00
8	1¢ blue (III)	7400.00	4800.00	3200.00	2800.00	2150.00	1600.00
8A	1¢ blue (IIIa)	3100.00	2100.00	1300.00	1075.00	850.00	650.00
9	1¢ blue (IV)	580.00	450.00	325.00	175.00	140.00	120.00
10	3¢ orange brown (I)	1700.00	1350.00	1075.00	135.00	105.00	90.00
11	3¢ deep claret (I)	200.00	140.00	100.00	14.50	10.50	9.00
12	5¢ red brown (I)	13000.00	9750.00	6500.00	1550.00	1150.00	875.00
13	10¢ green (I)	10500.00	8000.00	5750.00	925.00	725.00	575.00
14	10¢ green (II)	2300.00	1750.00	1350.00	300.00	210.00	170.00
15	10¢ green (III)	2500.00	1775.00	1300.00	300.00	220.00	170.00
16	10¢ green (IV)	18000.00	12000.00	9500.00	1800.00	1350.00	1050.00
17	12¢ black	3250.00	2500.00	1750.00	500.00	395.00	295.00

> *NOTE: For further details on the various types of similar appearing stamps please refer to our U.S. Stamp Identifier.*

37, 45 *Washington*	38, 46 *Franklin*	39, 47 *Washington*
73, 84, 85B, 87, 93, 103 *Jackson*		77, 85F, 91, 98, 108 *Lincoln*

SCOTT NO.	DESCRIPTION	UNUSED VF	F	AVG	USED VF	F	AVG
\multicolumn{8}{l}{**1857-61 Same design as preceding Issue, Perf. 15-1/2 (†) (OG + 75%)**}
18	1¢ blue (I)	1100.00	800.00	575.00	650.00	450.00	325.00
19	1¢ blue (Ia)	13500.00	9500.00	7000.00	6000.00	4500.00	3000.00
20	1¢ blue (II)	750.00	525.00	400.00	300.00	225.00	165.00
21	1¢ blue (III)	7750.00	5250.00	4000.00	2350.00	1750.00	1150.00
22	1¢ blue (IIIa)	1350.00	950.00	650.00	550.00	400.00	325.00
23	1¢ blue (IV)	4900.00	3400.00	2350.00	725.00	500.00	395.00
24	1¢ blue (V)	175.00	120.00	90.00	72.50	45.00	35.00
25	3¢ rose (I)	1500.00	1100.00	850.00	135.00	75.00	45.00
26	3¢ dull red (II)	85.00	60.00	47.50	12.50	6.00	4.00
26a	3¢ dull red (IIa)	160.00	120.00	85.00	60.00	42.50	30.00
27	5¢ brick red (I)	12500.00	8800.00	6500.00	1450.00	1100.00	800.00
28	5¢ red brown (I)	2300.00	1675.00	1350.00	750.00	550.00	375.00
28A	5¢ Indian red (I)	19500.00	14000.00	10075.00	3500.00	2700.00	1975.00
29	5¢ brown (I)	1400.00	975.00	725.00	450.00	340.00	225.00
30	5¢ orange brown (II)	925.00	650.00	500.00	1250.00	875.00	675.00
30A	5¢ brown (II)	1250.00	975.00	650.00	325.00	240.00	180.00
31	10¢ green (I)	10000.00	7250.00	5250.00	950.00	725.00	550.00
32	10¢ green (II)	3200.00	2150.00	1650.00	320.00	240.00	180.00
33	10¢ green (III)	3200.00	2150.00	1650.00	320.00	240.00	180.00
34	10¢ green (IV)	20500.00	14250.00	11500.00	2600.00	2100.00	1650.00
35	10¢ green (V)	250.00	175.00	135.00	125.00	70.00	45.00
36	12¢ black, Plate I	925.00	675.00	500.00	240.00	165.00	125.00
36b	12¢ black, Plate III	550.00	380.00	250.00	200.00	145.00	110.00
37	24¢ gray lilac	950.00	700.00	475.00	380.00	295.00	220.00
38	30¢ orange	1250.00	850.00	600.00	500.00	375.00	265.00
39	90¢ blue	2150.00	1550.00	1200.00	6500.00	4950.00	3800.00
\multicolumn{8}{l}{**1875 Reprints of 1857-61 Issue. Perf. 12 Without Gum**}
40	1¢ bright blue	900.00	625.00	425.00			
41	3¢ scarlet	3900.00	2600.00	1750.00			
42	5¢ orange brown	1650.00	1100.00	700.00			
43	10¢ blue green	3750.00	2500.00	1600.00			
44	12¢ greenish black	4500.00	3000.00	2000.00			
45	24¢ blackish violet	4875.00	3250.00	2150.00			
46	30¢ yellow orange	4725.00	3150.00	2100.00			
47	90¢ deep blue	7100.00	4750.00	3200.00			

THE 1861-67 ISSUE

The 1861-66 Issue and its 1867 Grilled varieties are among the most interesting and controversial of all stamps. Born out of the need to demonetize previously-issued stamps in the possession of Southern post offices, they were rushed into service shortly after the outbreak of the Civil War.

The controversy begins with the "August Issues", catalog #s 55-62B. It is now generally accepted that all but the 10 and 24 cent values never were issued for use as postage. The set is more aptly described as "First Designs", because they were printed by the National Bank Note Company and submitted to the Post Office Department as fully gummed and perforated sample designs.

| 63, 85A, 86, 92, 107 *Franklin* | 64-66, 74, 79, 82, 83, 85, 85C, 88, 94, 104 *Washington* | 67, 75, 76, 80, 95, 105 *Jefferson* | 62B, 68, 85D, 89, 96, 106 *Washington* |

| 69, 85E, 90, 97, 107 *Washington* | 70, 78, 99, 109 *Washington* | 71, 81, 100, 110 *Franklin* | 72, 101, 111 *Washington* |

(†) means Issue is actually very poorly centered. Perforations may touch the design on "Fine" quality.

SCOTT NO.	DESCRIPTION	UNUSED VF	F	AVG	USED VF	F	AVG
\multicolumn{8}{l}{**1861 First Design (†) Perf. 12 (OG + 75%)**}
62B	10¢ dark green	5000.00	3250.00	2100.00	1050.00	750.00	500.00
\multicolumn{8}{l}{**1861-62 Second Design (†) Perf. 12 (OG + 50%)**}
63	1¢ blue	225.00	150.00	110.00	55.00	35.00	24.00
64	3¢ pink	5200.00	3750.00	2950.00	800.00	600.00	425.00
64b	3¢ rose pink	325.00	250.00	190.00	165.00	115.00	90.00
65	3¢ rose	110.00	65.00	45.00	5.00	3.00	2.25
66	3¢ lake	2850.00	2075.00	1500.00			
67	5¢ buff	10000.00	7000.00	5250.00	850.00	625.00	475.00
68	10¢ yellow green	495.00	350.00	225.00	87.50	50.00	35.00
69	12¢ black	800.00	500.00	325.00	150.00	90.00	60.00
70	24¢ red lilac	1200.00	825.00	600.00	225.00	140.00	105.00
71	30¢ orange	1050.00	725.00	495.00	200.00	150.00	110.00
72	90¢ blue	2100.00	1500.00	1100.00	525.00	395.00	250.00
\multicolumn{8}{l}{**1861-66 (†) (OG + 75%)**}
73	2¢ black	240.00	175.00	110.00	115.00	75.00	45.00
74	3¢ scarlet	7800.00	5250.00	3500.00			
75	5¢ red brown	2800.00	2150.00	1450.00	525.00	395.00	275.00
76	5¢ brown	700.00	495.00	375.00	180.00	125.00	95.00
77	15¢ black	900.00	675.00	485.00	210.00	160.00	100.00
78	24¢ lilac	700.00	550.00	395.00	150.00	110.00	85.00

From 1867 to 1870, grills were embossed into the stamp paper to break the fiber and prevent the eradication of cancellations. The first "A" grilled issues were grilled all over. When postal clerks found that the stamps were as likely to separate along the grill as on the perforations, the Post Office abandoned the "A" grill and tried other configurations, none of which proved to be effective. The Grilled Issues include some of our greatest rarities. The most notable is the 1 cent "Z", only two of which are known to exist. One realized $935,000 in a 1998 auction, making it the most valuable United States stamp. The grills are fully explained and identified in the Harris Stamp Identifier.

SCOTT NO.	DESCRIPTION	UNUSED VF	F	AVG	USED VF	F	AVG
\multicolumn{8}{l}{**1867 Grill with Points Up** / **A. Grill Covering Entire Stamp (†) (OG + 75%)**}
79	3¢ rose		3600.00	3000.00		1375.00	950.00
80	5¢ brown					110000.00	
81	30¢ orange						67500.00
\multicolumn{8}{l}{**B. Grill about 18 x 15 mm. (OG + 75%)**}
82	3¢ rose					170000.00	
\multicolumn{8}{l}{**C. Grill About 13 x 16 mm. (†) (OG + 75%)**}
83	3¢ rose	3700.00	2700.00	1950.00	1000.00	775.00	575.00
\multicolumn{8}{l}{**1867 Grill with Points Down** / **D. Grill About 12 x 14 mm. (†) (OG + 75%)**}
84	2¢ black	11000.00	8500.00	6200.00	2800.00	2000.00	1600.00
85	3¢ rose	3800.00	2600.00	1950.00	1050.00	750.00	575.00
\multicolumn{8}{l}{**Z. Grill About 11 x 14 mm. (†) (OG + 75%)**}
85A	1¢ blue						
85B	2¢ black	5500.00	4000.00	2400.00	1200.00	950.00	700.00
85C	3¢ rose	7000.00	5100.00	3500.00	3200.00	2250.00	1750.00
85D	10¢ green				110000.00	80000.00	
85E	12¢ black	9500.00	6750.00	5500.00	1600.00	1200.00	950.00
85F	15¢ black				250000.00		
\multicolumn{8}{l}{**E. Grill About 11 x 13 mm. (†) (OG + 75%)**}
86	1¢ blue	1700.00	1200.00	950.00	525.00	375.00	285.00
87	2¢ black	750.00	575.00	425.00	160.00	110.00	80.00
88	3¢ rose	495.00	375.00	250.00	32.50	22.50	14.50
89	10¢ green	2900.00	2150.00	1450.00	350.00	275.00	195.00
90	12¢ black	3000.00	2100.00	1200.00	360.00	275.00	195.00
91	15¢ black	5600.00	4000.00	2950.00	775.00	575.00	425.00

U.S. Postage #92-133a

112, 123, 133,133a
Franklin

113, 124
Pony Express Rider

114, 125
Locomotive

115, 126
Washington

SCOTT NO.	DESCRIPTION	VF	UNUSED F	AVG	VF	USED F	AVG
			F. Grill About 9 x 13 mm. (†) (OG + 75%)				
92	1¢ blue	700.00	525.00	375.00	225.00	165.00	115.00
93	2¢ black	275.00	195.00	140.00	95.00	60.00	45.00
94	3¢ red	225.00	165.00	115.00	12.50	7.00	4.75
95	5¢ brown	1800.00	1375.00	950.00	750.00	550.00	395.00
96	10¢ yellow green	1550.00	1150.00	875.00	250.00	180.00	125.00
97	12¢ black	1800.00	1375.00	975.00	275.00	195.00	125.00
98	15¢ black	2100.00	1475.00	1100.00	375.00	285.00	200.00
99	24¢ gray lilac	3400.00	2400.00	1975.00	850.00	625.00	475.00
100	30¢ orange	3750.00	2700.00	1950.00	850.00	625.00	500.00
101	90¢ blue	6000.00	4750.00	3500.00	1600.00	1200.00	975.00

The Re-Issues of the 1861-66 Issue were issued with gum and, while scarce, are found used. They can be distinguished by their bright colors, sharp printing impressions, hard paper and white, crackly original gum.

SCOTT NO.	DESCRIPTION	VF	UNUSED F	AVG	VF	USED F	AVG
			1875. Re-Issue of 1861-66 Issue. Hard White Paper (OG + 75%)				
102	1¢ blue	650.00	550.00	450.00	1200.00	950.00	750.00
103	2¢ black	2100.00	1700.00	1400.00	5250.00	4250.00	3350.00
104	3¢ brown red	2600.00	2000.00	1650.00	5500.00	4850.00	3250.00
105	5¢ brown	1900.00	1600.00	1250.00	3250.00	2700.00	2200.00
106	10¢ green	2000.00	1700.00	1400.00	5250.00	4000.00	3200.00
107	12¢ black	2700.00	2100.00	1700.00	5750.00	4600.00	3500.00
108	15¢ black	2700.00	2150.00	1850.00	6000.00	4800.00	3750.00
109	24¢ deep violet	3200.00	2700.00	2250.00	8250.00	6600.00	5400.00
110	30¢ brownish orange	3400.00	2750.00	2350.00	9500.00	7600.00	6500.00
111	90¢ blue	4500.00	3600.00	2950.00	47500.00	37500.00	30000.00

THE 1869 PICTORIALS

As the first United States series to include pictorial designs, the 1869 issue is one of the most popular today. They were so unpopular that they were removed from sale less than a year after issue. Most protests were directed toward their odd size and the tradition-breaking pictorial designs.

The 1869 issue broke important new ground in the use of two color designs. Not only does this add to their attractiveness; it also is the source for the first United States "Inverted Centers". These inverted errors appear on the bi-colored 15, 24 and 30 cent values. The printing technology of the time required a separate printing pass for each color. On the first pass, the central designs, or vignettes, were printed. The second pass applied the frames.

In a very few instances, the sheets with their central designs already printed were passed upside down through the printing press. As a result, the frames were printed upside down. So the description "inverted center" for the 15 and 24 cent errors is technically incorrect, but the form in which these errors are photographed and displayed is with the center, rather than the frame, inverted.

Used copies of the 1869 Pictorials are not as scarce as might be expected. Any of the stamps above the 3 cent denomination were used on mail to Europe and were saved by collectors overseas. When stamp collecting became popular in the United States and Americans were able to purchase stamps abroad at relatively low prices, many of these used 1869 Pictorials found their way back to this country. On the other hand, because of the short life of the issue in post offices and their sudden withdrawal, unused stamps—particularly the high values—are quite rare.

All values of the 1869 Pictorials are found with the "G" grill. Ungrilled varieties are known on all values except the 6, 10, 12 and type II 15 cent stamps. (The Harris Stamp Identifier describes the difference in the three 15 cent types.)

The 1869 Pictorials were re-issued in 1875 in anticipation of the 1876 Centennial Exposition. Most collectors who had missed the original 1869 issue were delighted to have a second chance to purchase the stamps, which explains why the high value re-issues carry lower prices today than do the original 1869 pictorials. At the time, most collectors did not realize they were buying entirely different stamps. The same designs were used, but the re-issues were issued on a distinctive hard, white paper without grills.

The 1 cent stamp was re-issued a second time, in 1880. This re-issue can be distinguished by the lack of a grill and by the soft, porous paper used by the American Bank Note Company.

116, 127
Shield & Eagle

117, 128
S.S. Adriatic

118, 119, 129
Landing of Columbus

120, 130
Signing of Declaration

121, 131
Shield, Eagle & Flags

122, 132
Lincoln

SCOTT NO.	DESCRIPTION	VF	UNUSED F	AVG	VF	USED F	AVG
			1869 G. Grill measuring 9-1/2 x 9-1/2 mm. (†) (OG + 60%)				
112	1¢ buff	425.00	300.00	240.00	200.00	150.00	120.00
113	2¢ brown	425.00	300.00	240.00	95.00	65.00	42.50
114	3¢ ultramarine	195.00	155.00	120.00	27.00	20.00	15.00
115	6¢ ultramarine	1500.00	1100.00	850.00	275.00	195.00	150.00
116	10¢ yellow	1150.00	900.00	675.00	180.00	135.00	100.00
117	12¢ green	1200.00	900.00	700.00	195.00	145.00	110.00
118	15¢ brown & blue (I)	4500.00	3500.00	2750.00	800.00	550.00	425.00
119	15¢ brown & blue (II)	2100.00	1350.00	1000.00	300.00	240.00	190.00
120	24¢ green & violet	4400.00	2950.00	2100.00	850.00	650.00	475.00
121	30¢ blue & carmine	4400.00	2950.00	2100.00	650.00	450.00	325.00
122	90¢ carmine & black	6000.00	4500.00	3500.00	2800.00	1950.00	1500.00
			1875 Re-Issue of 1869 Issue. Hard White Paper. Without Grill (OG + 60%)				
123	1¢ buff	500.00	350.00	250.00	375.00	275.00	195.00
124	2¢ brown	600.00	450.00	300.00	600.00	425.00	295.00
125	3¢ blue	4500.00	3000.00	2150.00	....	15000.00	....
126	6¢ blue	1200.00	800.00	550.00	1700.00	1050.00	650.00
127	10¢ yellow	1900.00	1300.00	950.00	1800.00	1250.00	875.00
128	12¢ green	2000.00	1500.00	1000.00	2850.00	1825.00	1075.00
129	15¢ brown & blue (III)	1800.00	1250.00	800.00	1100.00	700.00	450.00
130	24¢ green & violet	1800.00	1200.00	750.00	1425.00	875.00	550.00
131	30¢ blue & carmine	2500.00	1600.00	1100.00	2400.00	1600.00	975.00
132	90¢ carmine & black	4500.00	3500.00	2750.00	5800.00	4250.00	3200.00
			1880 Re-Issue. Soft Porous Paper, Issued Without Grill (†) (#133 OG +50%)				
133	1¢ buff	295.00	225.00	180.00	250.00	185.00	145.00
133a	1¢ brown orange (issued w/o gum)	325.00	195.00	150.00	210.00	150.00	100.00

When Quality Counts...

H.E. Harris & Co.®

Serving the Collector Since 1916

THE 1870-88 BANK NOTE ISSUES

The "Bank Notes" are stamps that were issued between 1870 and 1888 by the National, Continental and American Bank Note Companies.

The myriad of varieties, secret marks, papers, grills, re-engravings and special printings produced by the three companies resulted in no less than 87 major catalog listings for what basically amounts to 16 different designs. For collectors, what seems to be the very difficult task of properly identifying all these varieties can be eased by following these guidelines:

1. The chronological order in which the three Bank Note companies produced stamps is their reverse alphabetical order: National, Continental, American.

2. "3, 6, 9" identifies the number of years each of the companies printed stamps within the 18-year Bank Note period. Starting in 1870, National continued its work for 3 more years, until 1873, when the Continental Company began printing stamps. That company served for the next 6 years, until 1879, when American took over the Continental company. Although American printed some later issues, the "Bank Note" period ended 9 years later, in 1888.

3. The first Bank Note issue, the Nationals of 1870-71, continued the practice of grilling stamps. Although some specialists contend there are grilled Continental stamps, for all intents and purposes, if a Bank Note stamp bears a genuine grill, it must be from the 1870-71 National issue.

4. The secret marks on values through the 12 cent, and possibly the 15 cent value, were added when the Continental Company took over. They enabled the government to distinguish between National's work and that of its successor. If a Bank Note stamp did not show a secret mark, the Post Office could identify it as the work of the National Bank Note Company. You can do the same.

5. The paper used by the National and Continental companies is similar, but that of the American Bank Note company is noticeably different from the first two. When held to the light, the thick, soft American paper shows its coarse, uneven texture, while that of its two predecessors is more even and translucent. The American Bank Note paper also reveals a yellowish hue when held to the light, whereas the National and Continental papers are whiter.

6. Experienced collectors also apply a "snap test" to identify American Bank Note paper by gently flexing a Bank Note stamp at one of its corners. The American Bank Note paper will not "snap" back into place. The National and Continental stamps, on the other hand, often give off a noticeable sound when the flex is released.

7. By purchasing one Bank Note design put into use after 1882 (which can only be an American) and one early Bank Note stamp without the secret mark, (which can only be a National), the collector has a reference point against which to compare any other Bank Note stamp. If it is a soft paper, it is an American Bank Note issue; if a harder paper, it is either a National or a Continental—and these two can be classified by the absence (National) or presence (Continental) of the secret marks or other distinguishing features or colors. The Harris Stamp Identifier in this catalog provides illustrations of the secret marks and further information on the distinguishing features of the various Bank Notes. With two reference stamps, some practice and the use of the information in this catalog, collectors can turn the "job" of understanding the Bank Notes into a pleasant adventure.

137, 148, 159, 170,
186, 195, 208
Lincoln

138, 149, 160, 171,
196
Stanton

139, 150, 161, 172,
187, 188, 197, 209
Jefferson

140, 151, 162, 173,
198
Clay

141, 152, 163, 174,
189, 199
Webster

142, 153, 164, 175,
200
Scott

143, 154, 165, 176,
190, 201, 217
Hamilton

144, 155, 166, 177,
191, 202, 218
Perry

SCOTT NO.	DESCRIPTION	UNUSED VF	F	AVG	USED VF	F	AVG
1870 National Bank Note Co., without Secret Marks.							
With H Grill about (10 x 12 mm. or 8-1/2 x 10 mm.) Perf 12. (†)							
(OG + 60%)							
134	1¢ ultramarine	1100.00	725.00	450.00	140.00	100.00	65.00
135	2¢ red brown	700.00	475.00	300.00	85.00	60.00	37.50
136	3¢ green	525.00	325.00	240.00	26.00	16.00	11.00
137	6¢ carmine	2800.00	1650.00	1000.00	625.00	375.00	250.00
138	7¢ vermillion	2100.00	1450.00	875.00	550.00	340.00	225.00
139	10¢ brown	3300.00	2200.00	1450.00	900.00	550.00	350.00
140	12¢ dull violet	16000.00	11000.00	7750.00	3750.00	2250.00	1400.00
141	15¢ orange	3950.00	2300.00	1500.00	1450.00	925.00	575.00
142	24¢ purple	....	....	....	7100.00	5700.00	4100.00
143	30¢ black	8000.00	5500.00	3850.00	2550.00	1575.00	950.00
144	90¢ carmine	9800.00	6000.00	3600.00	1850.00	1025.00	700.00
1870-71. National Bank Note Co., without Secret Marks.							
Without Grill. Perf 12. (†)							
(OG + 60%)							
145	1¢ ultramarine	375.00	230.00	125.00	19.50	12.00	8.50
146	2¢ red brown	235.00	145.00	95.00	12.00	8.00	5.00
147	3¢ green	235.00	145.00	95.00	2.00	1.25	.75
148	6¢ carmine	450.00	280.00	165.00	32.50	18.00	12.00
149	7¢ vermillion	525.00	340.00	200.00	125.00	70.00	42.50
150	10¢ brown	495.00	295.00	175.00	30.00	19.00	12.50
151	12¢ dull violet	1100.00	725.00	450.00	185.00	110.00	75.00
152	15¢ bright orange	1150.00	675.00	395.00	185.00	110.00	75.00
153	24¢ purple	1150.00	675.00	395.00	185.00	110.00	75.00
154	30¢ black	2700.00	1700.00	975.00	210.00	125.00	85.00
155	90¢ carmine	2700.00	1700.00	975.00	375.00	250.00	155.00
1873. Continental Bank Note Co.							
Same designs as 1870-71, with Secret Marks, on thin hard grayish white paper. Perf 12 (†)							
(OG + 60%)							
156	1¢ ultramarine	190.00	110.00	75.00	4.50	3.00	2.00
157	2¢ brown	340.00	195.00	110.00	22.50	13.50	8.00
158	3¢ green	110.00	60.00	35.00	1.00	.50	.30
159	6¢ dull pink	375.00	225.00	125.00	28.00	16.00	11.00
160	7¢ orange vermillion	700.00	475.00	300.00	95.00	65.00	40.00
161	10¢ brown	510.00	295.00	195.00	24.50	14.00	9.75
162	12¢ black violet	1100.00	675.00	380.00	125.00	80.00	52.50
163	15¢ yellow orange	1250.00	700.00	365.00	120.00	75.00	47.50
165	30¢ gray black	1300.00	725.00	450.00	130.00	85.00	50.00
166	90¢ rose carmine	2200.00	1350.00	850.00	310.00	185.00	110.00
1875 Special Printing–On Hard White Wove Paper–Without Gum							
Perf. 12							
167	1¢ ultramarine	11500.00	7250.00	4900.00	....	....	....
168	2¢ dark brown	5500.00	3450.00	2300.00	....	....	....
169	3¢ blue green	16750.00	10500.00	6500.00	....	....	....
170	6¢ dull rose	12750.00	6200.00	4250.00	....	....	....
171	7¢ reddish vermillion	3100.00	2400.00	1750.00	....	....	....
172	10¢ pale brown	11750.00	8250.00	5800.00	....	....	....
173	12¢ dark violet	5200.00	3250.00	2000.00	....	....	....
174	15¢ bright orange	9500.00	5800.00	3900.00	....	....	....
175	24¢ dull purple	2500.00	1600.00	975.00	....	....	....
176	30¢ greenish black	10000.00	7250.00	5100.00	....	....	....
177	90¢ violet carmine	8000.00	6250.00	4000.00	....	....	....

134, 145, 156, 167,
182, 192, 206
Franklin

135, 146, 157, 168,
178, 180, 183, 193,
203
Jackson

136, 147, 158, 169,
184, 194, 207, 214
Washington

NOTE: For further details on the various types of similar appearing stamps please refer to our U.S. Stamp Identifier.

U.S. Postage #178-229

179, 181, 185, 204
Taylor

205, 205C, 216
Garfield

SCOTT NO.	DESCRIPTION	UNUSED VF	F	AVG	USED VF	F	AVG
	1875 Continental Bank Note Co.						
	Hard yellowish paper, Perf 12. (†)						
	(OG + 30%)						
178	2¢ vermillion	260.00	170.00	100.00	12.00	8.50	5.25
179	5¢ blue	340.00	260.00	155.00	21.50	14.00	8.75
	1875 Continental Bank Note Co., Special Printings.						
	Same as 1875, on hard white paper, without gum. Perf 12.						
180	2¢ carmine vermillion	27500.00	20000.00	12000.00	......	......	......
181	5¢ bright blue	44000.00	33000.00	21000.00	......	......	......
	1879 American Bank Note Co.						
	Same designs as 1870-71 Issue (with Secret Marks) and 1875 Issue on soft, porous, coarse, yellowish paper. Perf 12. (†)						
	(OG + 50%)						
182	1¢ dark ultramarine	200.00	135.00	75.00	3.00	1.75	1.25
183	2¢ vermilion	100.00	65.00	37.50	3.00	1.75	1.25
184	3¢ green	85.00	55.00	35.00	.75	.45	.30
185	5¢ blue	395.00	230.00	125.00	17.00	11.00	7.75
186	6¢ pink	650.00	425.00	280.00	24.00	17.00	10.75
187	10¢ brown (no secret mark)	1400.00	825.00	450.00	28.00	19.50	12.75
188	10¢ brown (secret mark)	975.00	575.00	325.00	28.00	19.50	12.75
189	15¢ red orange	300.00	165.00	100.00	28.00	18.50	12.00
190	30¢ full black	800.00	465.00	275.00	77.50	42.50	28.00
191	90¢ carmine	1800.00	1150.00	725.00	325.00	195.00	120.00
	1880 American Bank Note Co., Special Printings.						
	Same as 1879 Issue, on soft, porous paper, without gum. Perf 12.						
192	1¢ dark ultramarine	16000.00	10000.00	6000.00	......	......	......
193	2¢ black brown	7000.00	4700.00	2800.00	......	......	......
194	3¢ blue green	23500.00	15000.00	9500.00	......	......	......
195	6¢ dull rose	17500.00	11000.00	6750.00	......	......	......
196	7¢ scarlet vermillion	4000.00	2500.00	1500.00	......	......	......
197	10¢ deep brown	15500.00	10000.00	6000.00	......	......	......
198	12¢ black purple	7250.00	4500.00	2750.00	......	......	......
199	15¢ orange	14350.00	9000.00	5450.00	......	......	......
200	24¢ dark violet	4750.00	3000.00	1850.00	......	......	......
201	30¢ greenish black	12750.00	8000.00	4850.00	......	......	......
202	90¢ dull carmine	12750.00	8000.00	4850.00	......	......	......
203	2¢ scarlet vermillion	28750.00	17500.00	11250.00	......	......	......
204	5¢ deep blue	51250.00	31500.00	19250.00	......	......	......
	1882 American Bank Note Company Perf 12.						
	(OG + 60%)						
205	5¢ yellow brown	155.00	120.00	85.00	9.75	6.25	4.00
	1882 American Bank Note Co., Special Printing.						
	Same as in 1882 Issue, on soft, porous Paper. Perf 12.						
205C	5¢ gray brown	......	29500.00	......	......	......	......

210, 211B, 213
Washington

211, 211D, 215
Jackson

212
Franklin

SCOTT NO.	DESCRIPTION	UNUSED VF	F	AVG	USED VF	F	AVG
	1881-82 American Bank Note Co.						
	Same designs as 1873, Re-Engraved. On soft, porous paper. Perf 12. (†)						
	(OG + 60%)						
206	1¢ gray blue	52.50	32.50	19.50	1.25	.85	.55
207	3¢ blue green	52.50	32.50	19.50	.70	.45	.30
208	6¢ rose	375.00	240.00	135.00	85.00	60.00	37.50
208a	6¢ brown red	300.00	195.00	110.00	130.00	85.00	50.00
209	10¢ brown	105.00	75.00	47.50	5.50	4.00	2.75
209b	10¢ black brown	340.00	210.00	140.00	55.00	35.00	19.75
210	2¢ red brown	35.00	22.50	15.00	.55	.35	.25
211	4¢ blue green	170.00	110.00	75.00	16.00	11.50	7.50

SCOTT NO.	DESCRIPTION	UNUSED VF	F	AVG	USED VF	F	AVG
	1883 American Bank Note Co. Special Printing.						
	Same design as 1883 Issue, on soft porous paper. Perf 12.						
211B	2¢ pale red brown	500.00	395.00	275.00	......	......	......
211D	4¢ deep blue green	25000.00	......	......	......	......	......
	1887 American Bank Note Co.						
	New designs or colors. Perf 12.						
	(OG + 60%)						
212	1¢ ultramarine	100.00	65.00	40.00	1.75	1.00	.70
213	2¢ green	30.00	18.00	12.00	.60	.35	.25
214	3¢ vermillion	70.00	42.00	25.00	70.00	45.00	28.00

SCOTT NO.	DESCRIPTION	UNUSED O.G. VF	F	AVG	USED VF	F	AVG
	1888 American Bank Note Company.						
	New Colors Perf 12.						
	(NH + 50%)						
215	4¢ carmine	260.00	175.00	100.00	22.00	14.50	9.75
216	5¢ indigo	260.00	175.00	100.00	13.50	9.50	6.25
217	30¢ orange brown	575.00	375.00	210.00	125.00	80.00	52.50
218	90¢ purple	1450.00	950.00	525.00	260.00	175.00	100.00

THE 1890-93 SMALL BANK NOTE ISSUES

Unlike the complex Large Bank Notes, the 1890-93 series is the simplest of the 19th century definitive issues. They were printed by the American Bank Note Company and what few printing varieties there are can easily be determined by using the Harris Stamp Identifier.

The two major printing varieties are the 2 cent carmine with a "cap" on the left 2 (#219a) or both 2s (#219c).

The "cap" appears to be just that—a small flat hat just to the right of center on top of the denomination numeral 2. It was caused by a breakdown in the metal of the transfer roll that went undetected while it was being used to enter the designs into a few printing plates.

219 Franklin — 219D, 220 Washington — 221 Jackson — 222 Lincoln
223 Grant — 224 Garfield — 225 Sherman — 226 Webster

227 Clay — 228 Jefferson — 229 Perry

SCOTT NO.	DESCRIPTION	UNUSED O.G. VF	F	AVG	USED VF	F	AVG
	(NH + 60%)						
219	1¢ dull blue	32.50	21.00	16.50	.50	.30	.20
219D	2¢ lake	250.00	140.00	100.00	1.25	.70	.45
220	2¢ carmine	27.00	19.00	13.75	.50	.30	.25
220a	Cap on left "2"	80.00	55.00	35.50	3.50	2.25	1.50
220c	Cap on both "2"s	300.00	190.00	135.00	22.50	15.00	9.25
221	3¢ purple	80.00	50.00	35.00	9.50	5.25	3.75
222	4¢ dark brown	80.00	50.00	35.00	3.25	2.00	1.25
223	5¢ chocolate	80.00	50.00	35.00	3.25	2.00	1.25
224	6¢ brown red	85.00	52.00	37.50	27.50	18.00	12.50
225	8¢ lilac	62.50	42.50	32.00	16.00	9.75	7.00
226	10¢ green	175.00	110.00	70.00	5.00	3.25	2.00
227	15¢ indigo	220.00	140.00	100.00	27.50	19.50	12.50
228	30¢ black	360.00	240.00	150.00	35.00	22.50	14.00
229	90¢ orange	550.00	375.00	240.00	145.00	85.00	47.50

THE COLUMBIANS

Perhaps the most glamorous of all United States issues is the 1893 Columbians set. Consisting of 16 denominations, the set was issued to celebrate the 1893 World's Columbian Exposition.

Even then, the Post Office Department was aware that stamps could be useful for more than just the prepayment of postage. We quote from an internal Post Office Department report of November 20, 1892:

"During the past summer the determination was reached by the Department to issue, during the progress of the Columbian Exposition at Chicago, a special series of adhesive postage stamps of such a character as would help to signalize the four hundredth anniversary of the discovery of America by Columbus. This course was in accordance with the practice of other great postal administrations on occasions of national rejoicing.

The collecting of stamps is deserving of encouragement, for it tends to the cultivation of artistic tastes and the study of history and geography, especially on the part of the young. The new stamps will be purchased in large quantities simply for the use of collections, without ever being presented in payment of postage; and the stamps sold in this way will, of course, prove a clear gain to the department."

As it turned out, the Columbians issue did sell well, being purchased in large quantities not only by collectors, but by speculators hoping to capitalize on the expected demand for the stamps and the fact that they were supposed to be on sale for only one year, from January 2 to December 31, 1893. (The 8 cent stamp was issued March 3, 1893 to meet the new, reduced Registration fee.)

Although sales of the stamps were brisk at the Exposition site in Chicago, speculation proved less than rewarding. The hordes that showed up on the first day of sale in Chicago (January 3rd) and purchased large quantities of the issue ended up taking losses on most of the stamps.

The set was the most expensive postal issue produced to date by the Post Office. The lower denominations matched those of the previous, "Small" Bank Note issue and the 50 cent Columbian replaced the 90 cent Bank Note denomination. But the $1 through $5 denominations were unheard of at that time. The reason for their release was explained in the November 20, 1892 report: "...such high denominations having heretofore been called for by some of the principal post offices".

The Columbians were an instant success. Businesses did not like the wide size, but they usually could obtain the smaller Bank Note issue. Collectors enjoyed the new stamps, although at least one complained that some of the high values purchased by him had straight edges—and was quickly authorized to exchange "the imperfect stamps" for perfect ones.

The one major variety in this set is the 4 cent blue error of color. It is similar to, but richer in color than, the 1 cent Columbian and commands a larger premium over the normal 4 cent ultramarine color.

The imperforates that are known to exist for all values are proofs which were distributed as gifts and are not listed as postage stamps. The only exception, the 2 cent imperforate, is believed to be printers' waste that was saved from destruction.

SCOTT NO.	DESCRIPTION	UNUSED O.G.			USED		
		VF	F	AVG	VF	F	AVG
1893 COLUMBIAN ISSUE (NH + 75%)							
230	1¢ deep blue ...	33.00	21.00	14.00	.60	.40	.30
231	2¢ brown violet .	30.00	19.00	13.00	.25	.20	.15
231C	2¢ "broken hat" .	95.00	60.00	37.50	1.50	1.00	.60
232	3¢ green	72.00	50.00	35.00	18.00	13.00	9.00
233	4¢ ultramarine ..	110.00	70.00	45.00	11.00	7.25	4.50
234	5¢ chocolate ...	125.00	75.00	50.00	11.00	7.25	4.50
235	6¢ purple	110.00	70.00	45.00	30.00	20.00	14.00
236	8¢ magenta	100.00	65.00	37.50	16.00	10.50	6.25
237	10¢ black brown	175.00	115.00	85.00	12.50	8.25	5.50
238	15¢ dark green .	375.00	240.00	150.00	110.00	65.00	42.50
239	30¢ orange brown	425.00	300.00	195.00	110.00	75.00	52.50
240	50¢ slate blue ..	825.00	575.00	400.00	210.00	135.00	95.00
241	$1 salmon	1900.00	1225.00	975.00	825.00	550.00	340.00
242	$2 brown red ...	2000.00	1300.00	1000.00	825.00	550.00	340.00
243	$3 yellow green .	3350.00	2250.00	1550.00	1450.00	975.00	650.00
244	$4 crimson lake .	4650.00	3250.00	2300.00	1975.00	1325.00	850.00
245	$5 black	5400.00	3100.00	2200.00	2350.00	1400.00	925.00

U.S. Postage #246-284

246, 247, 264, 279
Franklin

248-252, 265-267, 279B
Washington

253, 268
Jackson

254, 269, 280
Lincoln

255, 270, 281
Grant

256, 271, 282
Garfield

257, 272
Sherman

258, 273, 282C, 283
Webster

259, 274, 284
Clay

260, 275
Jefferson

261, 261A, 276, 276A
Perry

262, 277
Madison

263, 278
Marshall

1894-98 THE FIRST BUREAU ISSUES

In 1894, the United States Bureau of Engraving and Printing replaced the American Bank Note Company as the contractor for all United States postage stamps. The "First" Bureau issues, as they are commonly known, actually consist of three series, as follows:

The 1894 Series. In order to expedite the transfer of production to the Bureau, the plates then being used by the American Bank Note Company for the 1890-93 Small Bank Notes were modified, small triangles being added in the upper corners. The 1 cent through 15 cent stamps are otherwise essentially the same as the 1890-93 issue although minor variations have been noted on some values. The 30 cent and 90 cent 1890-93 denominations were changed to 50 cents and $1, respectively, and new $2 and $5 denominations were added.

The 1895 Series. To protect against counterfeiting of United Sates stamps, the Bureau adopted the use of watermarked paper. (A scheme for counterfeiting 2 cent stamps had been uncovered around the same time the watermarked paper was being adopted. Some of these counterfeits are known postally used.) This series is almost exactly the same as the 1984 series except for the presence of watermarks. The watermarks can be difficult t detect on this series, particularly on the light-colored stamps, such as the 50 cent, and on used stamps. Since the 1894 unwatermarked stamps (with the exception of the 2 cent carmine type I) are worth more than the 1895 watermarked stamps, collectors will want to examine their 1894 stamps carefully. (Some collectors feel they can recognize the 1894 stamps by their ragged perforations, caused by difficulties the Bureau encountered when it first took over the produciton of postage stamps. This is not a reliable method.)

The 1898 "Color Changes." With the adoption of a Universal Postal Union code that recommended standard colors for international mail, the United States changed the colors for the lower values in the 1895 Series. The stamps were printed on the same watermarked paper as that used for the 1895 Series. Except for the 2 cent,which was changed from carmine to red, the colors of the 1898 Series are easily differentiated from the 1895 set. The 2 cent value is the most complicated of the First Bureau Issues. In addition to the color changes that took place, three different triangle types are known. The differences are attributed to the possibility that the work of engraving the triangles into the American Bank Note plates was performed by several Bureau engravers.

The 10 cent and $1 types I and II can be distinguished by the circles surrounding the numeral denominations. The Type IIs are identical to the circles of the 1890-93 Small Bank Notes.

All stamps in these series are perf. 12. The Harris Stamp Identifier at the front of this catalog provides additional information on the major types and watermarks of all three series.

SCOTT NO.	DESCRIPTION	UNUSED O.G.			USED		
		VF	F	AVG	VF	F	AVG
1894 Unwatermarked (†)							
(NH + 75%)							
246	1¢ ultramarine ..	34.00	22.00	15.50	7.50	4.75	3.00
247	1¢ blue	75.00	45.00	30.00	4.00	2.50	1.75
248	2¢ pink (I)......	29.00	17.50	12.00	6.00	4.00	2.75
249	2¢ carmine lake (I)	150.00	105.00	70.00	4.00	2.50	1.75
250	2¢ carmine (I) ...	34.00	21.00	14.50	1.00	.65	.40
251	2¢ carmine (II) ..	280.00	185.00	125.00	6.00	4.50	2.25
252	2¢ carmine (III) ..	135.00	80.00	52.50	6.75	3.75	2.75
253	3¢ purple	135.00	80.00	52.50	14.00	8.00	5.50
254	4¢ dark brown ..	155.00	90.00	65.00	7.25	4.00	2.25
255	5¢ chocolate ...	110.00	70.00	50.00	7.75	4.75	3.00
256	6¢ dull brown ...	175.00	115.00	80.00	24.00	18.00	12.00
257	8¢ violet brown .	160.00	110.00	72.50	25.00	15.00	12.00
258	10¢ dark green .	260.00	175.00	110.00	19.50	10.00	7.00
259	15¢ dark blue ...	320.00	225.00	160.00	75.00	45.00	30.00
260	50¢ orange	480.00	325.00	250.00	145.00	90.00	55.00
261	$1 black (I)	1025.00	675.00	475.00	375.00	200.00	140.00
261A	$1 black (II)	2500.00	1750.00	1200.00	825.00	550.00	375.00
262	$2 bright blue ...	3450.00	2300.00	1850.00	1100.00	650.00	475.00
263	$5 dark green ..	5050.00	3350.00	2400.00	2475.00	1550.00	1000.00
1895 Double Line Watermark							
"USPS" (†) (NH + 75%)							
264	1¢ blue	7.75	5.00	3.50	.40	.25	.20
265	2¢ carmine (I) ..	32.00	21.00	14.50	1.20	.75	.50
266	2¢ carmine (II) ..	34.00	23.50	16.50	4.25	2.75	1.50
267	2¢ carmine (III) .	6.50	3.50	2.25	.35	.25	.20
268	3¢ purple	45.00	28.00	20.00	1.85	1.25	.70
269	4¢ dark brown ..	45.00	31.00	19.00	2.25	1.40	.85
270	5¢ chocolate ...	45.00	31.00	19.00	2.95	1.95	1.10
271	6¢ dull brown ...	100.00	65.00	40.00	7.00	4.75	2.75
272	8¢ violet brown .	75.00	40.00	27.50	2.00	1.25	.75
273	10¢ dark green .	90.00	60.00	40.00	2.25	1.40	.80
274	15¢ dark blue ...	250.00	140.00	90.00	12.50	8.25	4.50
275	50¢ orange	325.00	200.00	135.00	28.00	17.00	9.75
276	$1 black (I)	750.00	425.00	300.00	90.00	60.00	38.00
276A	$1 black (II)	1550.00	1000.00	680.00	190.00	125.00	95.00
277	$2 bright blue ...	1350.00	800.00	525.00	400.00	295.00	195.00
278	$5 dark green ..	3000.00	1800.00	1050.00	625.00	400.00	275.00
1898 New Colors							
(NH + 75%)							
279	1¢ deep green ..	13.00	8.00	5.50	.45	.25	.20
279B	2¢ red (IV)	13.00	7.50	5.00	.40	.25	.20
279Bc	2¢ rose carmine (IV)	325.00	195.00	120.00	125.00	80.00	60.00
279Bd	2¢ orange red (IV)	17.50	10.00	7.00	.45	.30	.20
280	4¢ rose brown ..	40.00	27.00	18.00	1.50	.80	.50
281	5¢ dark blue	48.00	29.00	18.00	1.50	.80	.50
282	6¢ lake	60.00	40.00	30.00	4.00	2.25	1.50
282C	10¢ brown (I) ...	230.00	155.00	110.00	4.00	2.25	1.50
283	10¢ orange brown (II)	130.00	80.00	50.00	3.25	1.80	1.20
284	15¢ olive green .	180.00	110.00	68.00	11.00	6.50	4.25

1898 THE TRANS-MISSISSIPPI ISSUE

Issued for the Trans-Mississippi Exposition in Omaha, Nebraska, the "Omahas", as they also are known, did not receive the same welcome from collectors as that accorded the first commemorative set, the 1893 Columbians. Although the uproar was ascribed to the fact that collectors felt put upon by another set with $1 and $2 values, had the $1 to $5 values in the Columbian series appreciated in value, no doubt the protests would have been muted.

On the other hand, the public at large enjoyed the new issue. The Trans-Mississippi issues depict various works of art and are among the most beautiful stamps ever issued by the United States. The 8 and 10 cent values reproduce works by Frederic Remington and the $1 "Western Cattle in Storm", based on a work by J.A. MacWhirter, is regarded as one of our finest examples of the engraver's art.

As appealing as these stamps are in single colors, the set might have been even more beautiful. The original intent was to print each stamp with the vignette, or central design, in black and the frame in a distinctive second color that would be different for each denomination. That plan had to be dropped when the Bureau was called upon to produce large quantities of revenue stamps at the outbreak of the Spanish-American War.

285
Marquette on the Mississippi

286
Farming in the West

287
Indian Hunting Buffalo

288
Fremont on the Rocky Mountains

289
Troops Guarding Train

290
Hardships of Emigration

291
Western Mining Prospector

292
Western Cattle in Storm

293
Eads Bridge over Mississippi River

1901 THE PAN-AMERICAN ISSUE

Issued to commemorate the Pan-American Exposition in Buffalo, N.Y., this set depicts important engineering and manufacturing achievements. The beautiful engraving is showcased by the bicolored printing.

294, 294a
Fast Lake Navigation

295, 295a
Fast Express

296, 296a
Automobile

297
Bridge at Niagara Falls

298
Canal at Sault Ste. Marie

299
Fast Ocean Navigation

SCOTT NO.	DESCRIPTION	UNUSED O.G. VF	F	AVG	USED VF	F	AVG
	1901 Pan-American Issue (NH + 75%)						
294-99	1¢-10¢ (6 varieties, complete)	670.00	385.00	255.00	165.00	95.00	70.00
294	1¢ green & black	26.00	14.00	8.25	5.50	3.75	2.25
294a	same, center inverted	...	12500.00	...	...	6500.00	...
295	2¢ carmine & black	25.00	13.50	7.75	2.00	1.35	.75
295a	same, center inverted	...	37500.00	...	...	16000.00	...
296	4¢ deep red brown & black	115.00	70.00	47.50	24.00	13.50	9.25
296a	same, center inverted	...	10000.00	...	...	...	...
296aS	same, center inverted (Specimen)	...	5500.00	...	...	...	...
297	5¢ ultramarine & black	135.00	80.00	47.50	23.00	13.00	9.25
298	8¢ brown violet & black	165.00	105.00	70.00	85.00	50.00	36.00
299	10¢ yellow brown & black	240.00	125.00	90.00	37.50	22.00	15.25

	UNUSED PLATE BLOCKS OF 6				UNUSED ARROW BLOCKS			
	NH		OG		NH		OG	
	F	AVG	F	AVG	F	AVG	F	AVG
294	365.00	285.00	240.00	180.00	160.00	100.00	65.00	50.00
295	365.00	265.00	235.00	180.00	160.00	100.00	65.00	50.00
296	3750.00	2400.00	2100.00	1650.00	800.00	450.00	350.00	290.00
297	4000.00	2500.00	2600.00	2000.00	825.00	500.00	400.00	325.00
298	7500.00	4650.00	4000.00	3200.00	1050.00	650.00	500.00	375.00
299	10500.00	6500.00	6000.00	4800.00	1500.00	900.00	695.00	500.00

SCOTT NO.	DESCRIPTION	UNUSED O.G. VF	F	AVG	USED VF	F	AVG
	1898 Trans-Mississippi Exposition Issue (†) (NH + 75%)						
285	1¢ dark yellow green	45.00	30.00	19.50	9.75	6.50	4.00
286	2¢ copper red	35.00	22.50	17.50	2.50	1.50	1.00
287	4¢ orange	190.00	120.00	85.00	37.00	22.00	14.00
288	5¢ dull blue	180.00	115.00	80.00	28.00	17.50	10.00
289	8¢ violet brown	250.00	160.00	100.00	52.50	34.00	20.00
290	10¢ gray violet	250.00	160.00	100.00	34.00	19.00	13.00
291	50¢ sage green	900.00	550.00	450.00	255.00	150.00	90.00
292	$1 black	1900.00	1000.00	725.00	750.00	450.00	310.00
293	$2 orange brown	3000.00	1850.00	1300.00	1150.00	775.00	475.00

Insist on Genuine H.E. Harris Products Backed by 89 years of experience

ACCEPT NO SUBSTITUTES!

U.S. Postage #300-322

THE 1902-03 SERIES

The Series of 1902-03 was the first regular issue designed and produced by the United States Bureau of Engraving and Printing, most of the work on the 1894-98 series having been performed by the American Bank Note Company. (When the Bureau was awarded the contract to produce the 1894 series, they added triangles in the upper corners of the American Bank Note designs.)

The new series filled a number of gaps and was the first United States issue to feature a woman—in this case Martha Washington, on the 8 cent value.

Modern collectors consider the 1902-03 issue one of the finest regular series ever produced by the Bureau.

The intricate frame designs take us back to a period when such work still was affordable. In its time, however, the 1902-03 set was looked upon with disdain. The 2 cent Washington, with its ornate frame design and unflattering likeness of George Washington, came in for particular scorn. Yielding to the clamor, in 1903, less than one year after its release, the Post Office recalled the much criticized 2 cent stamp and replaced it with an attractive, less ornate design that cleaned up Washington's appearance, particularly in the area of the nose, and used a shield design that was less ornate.

The issue marked the first time United States stamps were issued in booklet form, the 1 and 2 cent values being printed in panes of six stamps each. Also for the first time since perforating was adopted in 1857, United States stamps were once again deliberately issued in imperforate form for postal use. The intent was to have such stamps available in sheet and coil form for use in vending machines. The manufacturers of such machines could purchase the imperforate stamps and perforate them to fit their equipment. One of these imperforate issues, the 4 cent brown of 1908 (#314A), ranks as one of the great rarities of 20th century philately. It is found only with the private perforations of the Schermack Mailing Machine Company.

Coil stamps intended for use in stamp affixing and vending machines also made their inaugural appearance with this issue. Their availability was not widely publicized and few collectors obtained copies of these coils. All genuine coils from this series are very rare and extremely valuable. We emphasize the word "genuine" because most coils that are seen actually have been faked by trimming the perforated stamps or fraudulently perforating the imperfs.

The only major design types are found on the 1903 2 cent, catalog #s 319 and 320. Identified as Die I and Die II, the differences are described in the Harris Stamp Identifier.

309 Clay
310 Jefferson
311 Farragut
312, 479 Madison
313, 480 Marshall
319-22 Washington

300, 314, 316, 318 Franklin
301 Washington
302 Jackson
303, 314A Grant
304, 315, 317 Lincoln
305 Garfield
306 Martha Washington
307 Webster
308 Harrison

SCOTT NO.	DESCRIPTION	UNUSED O.G. VF	F	AVG	USED VF	F	AVG
		1902-03 Perf. 12 (†) (NH + 75%)					
300	1¢ blue green...	16.00	9.00	5.00	.35	.25	.20
300b	1¢ booklet pane of 6	....	550.00	375.00	....	....	....
301	2¢ carmine.....	18.00	11.50	7.25	.35	.25	.20
301c	2¢ booklet pane of 6	....	475.00	335.00	....	....	....
302	3¢ brown violet .	75.00	42.50	30.00	4.50	3.00	1.75
303	4¢ brown	75.00	42.50	30.00	2.50	1.40	.80
304	5¢ blue	75.00	42.50	30.00	3.00	1.50	.75
305	6¢ claret	90.00	50.00	35.00	5.00	2.75	1.50
306	8¢ violet black ..	60.00	32.00	25.00	3.75	2.00	1.25
307	10¢ pale red brown	85.00	50.00	36.00	3.00	1.60	.95
308	13¢ purple black	60.00	32.00	25.00	13.00	8.25	5.00
309	15¢ olive green .	195.00	120.00	85.00	10.00	6.25	4.00
310	50¢ orange	625.00	375.00	260.00	35.00	22.00	15.75
311	$1 black	925.00	500.00	350.00	80.00	45.00	30.00
312	$2 dark blue....	1550.00	925.00	625.00	300.00	175.00	125.00
313	$5 dark green ..	3200.00	2050.00	1500.00	950.00	575.00	400.00
		1906 Imperforate (NH + 60%)					
	This and all subsequent imperforate issues can usually be priced as unused pairs at double the single price.						
314	1¢ blue green...	30.00	21.00	15.50	22.50	17.00	11.00
314A	4¢ brown	....	35000.00	....	....	26500.00	....
315	5¢ blue	425.00	310.00	195.00	525.00	380.00	275.00
		1908 Coil Stamps. Perf 12 Horizontally					
316	1¢ blue green, pair	....	97500.00	....	....	....	....
317	5¢ blue, pair....	....	15500.00	....	....	....	....
		1908 Coil Stamps. Perf 12 Vertically					
318	1¢ blue green, pair	....	11500.00	....	....	....	....
		1903. Perf. 12 (†) (NH + 60%)					
319	2¢ carmine, Die I	10.00	6.00	4.80	.45	.30	.20
319f	2¢ lake, Die II...	16.00	9.50	6.50	.90	.60	.40
319g	2¢ carmine, Die I, booklet pane of 6	....	160.00	95.00			
		1906 Imperforate (NH + 60%)					
320	2¢ carmine, Die I	30.00	21.50	15.00	28.00	16.00	9.00
320a	2¢ lake, Die I ...	80.00	65.00	45.00	58.00	40.00	27.50
		1908 Coil Stamps. Perf 12 Horizontally					
321	2¢ carmine, pair .	....	....	....	....	....	....
		1908 Coil Stamps. Perf 12 Vertically					
322	2¢ carmine, pair .	....	11500.00	....	....	....	....

SCOTT NO.	UNUSED NH F	AVG	UNUSED OG F	AVG	SCOTT NO.	UNUSED NH F	AVG	UNUSED OG F	AVG
	PLATE BLOCKS OF 6					**CENTER LINE BLOCKS**			
300	280.00	160.00	175.00	110.00	314	300.00	200.00	180.00	135.00
301	325.00	170.00	180.00	120.00	320	305.00	210.00	185.00	145.00
314	365.00	235.00	195.00	195.00		**ARROW BLOCKS**			
319	155.00	90.00	85.00	63.50	314	190.00	140.00	160.00	110.00
320	415.00	290.00	260.00	185.00	320	190.00	140.00	160.00	110.00

1904 THE LOUISIANA PURCHASE ISSUE

Issued to commemorate the Louisiana Purchase Exposition held in St. Louis in 1904, these stamps were not well received. Collectors at the time did not purchase large quantities of the stamps, and the series was on sale for only seven months. As a result, well centered unused stamps are extremely difficult to locate.

323
Robert R. Livingston

324
Jefferson

325
Monroe

326
McKinley

327
Map of Louisiana Purchase

SCOTT NO.	DESCRIPTION	UNUSED O.G. VF	F	AVG	USED VF	F	AVG
	1904 Louisiana Purchase Issue (NH + 60%)						
323-27	1¢-10¢ (5 varieties, complete)	540.00	325.00	225.00	145.00	83.50	53.50
323	1¢ green	48.00	25.00	16.00	8.50	5.00	3.00
324	2¢ carmine	35.00	19.00	12.50	2.50	2.00	1.00
325	3¢ violet	120.00	75.00	50.00	47.50	30.00	18.00
326	5¢ dark blue	140.00	75.00	50.00	36.00	19.00	14.00
327	10¢ red brown	225.00	150.00	110.00	56.00	32.00	20.00

1907 THE JAMESTOWN EXPOSITION ISSUE

This set may be the most difficult United States 20th century issue to find well centered. Issued in April, 1907 for the Jamestown Exposition at Hampton Roads, Virginia, the set was removed from sale when the Exposition closed on November 30th of that year. Very fine copies carry hefty premiums.

328
Capt. John Smith

329
Founding of Jamestown

330
Pocahontas

SCOTT NO.	DESCRIPTION	UNUSED O.G. VF	F	AVG	USED VF	F	AVG
	1907 Jamestown Exposition Issue (NH + 60%)						
328-30	1¢-5¢ (3 varieties, complete)	285.00	135.00	80.00	76.00	33.00	17.50
328	1¢ green	40.00	18.00	10.00	7.50	3.75	2.50
329	2¢ carmine	50.00	25.00	15.00	7.50	4.25	2.00
330	5¢ blue	210.00	100.00	60.00	65.00	27.50	14.00

	UNUSED PLATE BLOCKS OF 6				UNUSED ARROW BLOCKS			
SCOTT NO.	NH F	AVG	OG F	AVG	NH F	AVG	OG F	AVG
323	455.00	260.00	260.00	180.00	200.00	115.00	125.00	80.00
324	455.00	260.00	260.00	180.00	160.00	100.00	95.00	65.00
325	1250.00	750.00	900.00	600.00	550.00	355.00	400.00	265.00
326	1450.00	950.00	990.00	700.00	675.00	380.00	375.00	250.00
327	3000.00	1950.00	1950.00	1450.00	1100.00	715.00	650.00	530.00
328	420.00	230.00	240.00	180.00	125.00	70.00	75.00	50.00
329	590.00	320.00	350.00	240.00	170.00	95.00	90.00	65.00
330	3600.00	1900.00	2000.00	1450.00	765.00	425.00	350.00	250.00

THE WASHINGTON-FRANKLIN HEADS

The Washington-Franklin Heads—so called because all stamps in the regular series featured the busts of George Washington and Benjamin Franklin—dominated the postal scene for almost two decades. Using a variety of papers, denominations, perforation sizes and formats, watermarks, design modifications and printing processes, almost 200 different major catalog listings were created from two basic designs.

The series started modestly, with the issuance of 12 stamps (#331-342) between November 1908 and January 1909. The modest designs on the new set replaced the ornate 1902-03 series. Their relative simplicity might have relegated the set to a secondary position in 20th century United States philately had it not been for the complexity of the varieties and the years of study the Washington-Franklin Heads now present to collectors.

The first varieties came almost immediately, in the form of imperforate stamps (#343-347) and coils, the latter being offered with horizontal (#348-351) or vertical (#352-356) perforations. The imperfs were intended for the fading vending machine technology that required private perforations while the coils were useful in standardized dispensers that were just coming into their own.

Then, in 1909, the Post Office began its experimentation. In this instance, it was the paper. As noted in our introduction to the 1909 Bluish Papers which follows, the Post Office Department and the Bureau of Engraving and Printing hoped that the new paper would reduce losses due to uneven shrinkage of the white wove paper used at the time. The experimental Washington-Franklin Bluish Papers (#357-66) are now among the most valuable in the series and the 8 cent Bluish Paper (#363) is the highest priced of the major listed items.

Attention was next directed to the double line watermark as the cause of the uneven shrinkage, as well as for weakness and thinning in the paper. As a result, a narrower, single line watermark was adopted for sheet stamps (#374-82), imperforates (#383-84), and coils with horizontal perfs (#385-86) and vertical perfs (#387-89).

Even as these experiments were being conducted, the perforation size was being examined to determine if a change was in order. Up until now, the perf 12 gauge had been used on all Washington-Franklin Heads.

The first perforation change was necessitated by the development of new coil manufacturing equipment. Under the increased pressure of the new equipment, the coil strips with the closely-spaced perf 12 gauge were splitting while being rolled into coils. To add paper between the holes, a perf 8-1/2 gauge was adopted for coil stamps and two new major varieties were created: with horizontal perfs (#390-91) and vertical perfs (#392-396).

Necessity was the driving force behind still more changes in 1912, when stamps with numeral denominations were issued to replace the "ONE CENT" and "TWO CENTS" stamps. This responded to the need for numeral denominations on foreign mail and created new sheets (#410-11) and vertically perforated (#412-13) coils. At the same time, a 7 cent value (#407) was issued to meet changing rate requirements.

In conjunction with the introduction of numerals on the 1 and 2 cent stamps, the design of the 1 cent was changed, with the bust of Washington replacing that of Franklin. Meanwhile, the bust of Franklin, which had been used only on the 1 cent stamp, was placed on all values from 8 cents to the $1 (#414-21) and a ribbon was added across their top to make the high value stamp even more noticeable to postal clerks.

As if to add just a little more variety while all the other changes were being made—but in actuality to use up a supply of old double-line watermark paper—50 cent and $1 issues with double-line watermarks (#422-23) were introduced.

The work with perforation changes on coil stamps carried over to sheet stamps in 1914 with the release of a perf 10 series (#424-40). The perf 10 size was then adapted to coils perforated horizontally (#441-42) and vertically (#443-47).

The transition to Rotary Press printing created new coils perforated 10 horizontally (#448-50) and vertically (#452-58). An imperforate Rotary coil (#459) for vending machine manufacturers also was produced.

A perf 10 double-line watermark $1 (#460) and a perf 11 two-cent sheet stamp (#461) added only slightly to the variety, but were followed by completely new runs on unwatermarked paper: perf 10 sheet stamps (#462-478) and imperforates (#481-84) were produced on the flat plate presses, while the Rotary press was used for coils perforated horizontally (#486-489) and vertically (#490-97).

U.S. Postage #331-366

While all this was taking place, the amazing 5 cent carmine error of color (#485) appeared on certain imperf 2 cent sheets. That same error (in rose, #505) was found when perf 11 sheet stamps (#498-518) were issued. The stamps turned out to be too hard to separate. Another strange issue, a 2 cent stamp on double-line watermark paper but perforated 11 (#519), came about when a small supply of old imperfs (#344) were discovered and put into the postal stream.

New $2 and $5 Franklins (#523-24), the former using an erroneous color, were released. To compensate for plate damage being caused by poor quality offset printings, perf 11 (#525-530) and imperforate (#531-535) were tried—and quickly resulted in a whole new series of "types" that had collectors spending more time with their magnifying glasses than with their families.

Odd perf sizes and printings (#538/546) came about as the Bureau cleaned out old paper stock. Then, in one final change, the Bureau corrected the color of the $2 from orange red and black to carmine and black. Almost 200 different stamps, all from two basic designs!

1909 THE BLUISH PAPERS

The Bluish Paper varieties are found on the 1 through 15 cent Washington-Franklin series of 1908-09 and on the 1909 Commemoratives. According to Post Office notices of the period, the experimental paper was a 30% rag stock that was intended to reduce paper waste. After being wet, a preliminary operation in the printing process, the standard white wove paper often would shrink so much that the perforators would cut into the designs. The rag paper did not solve the problem, the experiment was quickly abandoned and the 1909 Bluish Papers became major rarities.

The Harris Stamp Identifier provides further information on identifying the Washington-Franklin Heads.

331, 343, 348, 352, 357, 374, 383, 385, 387, 390, 392
Franklin

332, 344, 349, 353, 358, 375, 384, 386, 388, 391, 393
Washington

333, 345, 359, 376, 389, 394
Washington

334, 346, 350, 354, 360, 377, 395
Washington

335, 347, 351, 355, 361, 378, 396
Washington

336, 362, 379
Washington

337, 363, 380
Washington

338, 356, 364, 381
Washington

339, 365
Washington

340, 366, 382
Washington

341
Washington

342
Washington

NOTE: For further details on the various types of similar appearing stamps please refer to our U.S. Stamp Identifier.

SCOTT NO.	DESCRIPTION	UNUSED O.G. VF	F	AVG	USED VF	F	AVG
	1908-09 Double Line Watermark "USPS" Perf. 12 (NH + 60%)						
331-42	1¢-$1 (12 varieties, complete)	1580.00	920.00	595.00	200.00	125.00	72.00
331	1¢ green	11.00	6.25	4.00	.35	.20	.15
331a	1¢ booklet pane of 6	200.00	145.00	95.00	......	......	......
332	2¢ carmine	10.00	6.00	3.75	.35	.20	.15
332a	2¢ booklet pane of 6	185.00	120.00	85.00	......	......	......
333	3¢ deep violet (I)	50.00	28.00	17.00	4.80	3.25	2.00
334	4¢ orange brown	55.00	34.00	22.00	1.80	1.20	.75
335	5¢ blue	72.00	40.00	24.00	3.25	2.25	1.45
336	6¢ red orange	78.00	45.00	28.00	8.50	5.00	3.15
337	8¢ olive green	60.00	34.00	21.00	5.00	3.00	2.00
338	10¢ yellow	80.00	45.00	36.00	3.00	1.50	.90
339	13¢ blue green	52.50	30.00	20.00	32.00	20.00	11.50
340	15¢ pale ultramarine	82.00	45.00	32.00	10.00	6.50	4.00
341	50¢ violet	440.00	260.00	160.00	30.00	17.50	11.00
342	$1 violet brown	675.00	400.00	260.00	110.00	65.00	40.00
	1908-09 Imperforate (NH + 60%)						
343-47	1¢-5¢ (5 varieties, complete)	138.00	103.50	70.00	110.00	76.00	53.00
343	1¢ green	10.00	7.00	5.00	5.75	4.00	2.75
344	2¢ carmine	12.00	9.50	6.00	5.75	4.00	2.75
345	3¢ deep violet (I)	26.00	20.00	15.00	27.00	19.00	12.50
346	4¢ orange brown	36.00	27.50	18.00	30.00	23.00	17.00
347	5¢ blue	62.00	45.00	30.00	47.00	30.00	21.00
	1908-10 Coil Stamps Perf. 12 Horizontally (NH + 60%)						
348	1¢ green	38.00	23.00	15.50	24.00	15.00	10.00
349	2¢ carmine	75.00	45.00	30.00	15.00	8.00	5.00
350	4¢ orange brown	170.00	105.00	65.00	130.00	85.00	55.00
351	5¢ blue	190.00	120.00	77.50	180.00	115.00	80.00
	NOTE: Counterfeits are common on #348-56 and #385-89						
	1909 Coil Stamps Perf. 12 Vertically (NH + 60%)						
352	1¢ green	78.00	48.00	32.00	50.00	32.50	22.00
353	2¢ carmine	100.00	60.00	40.00	14.00	8.00	5.50
354	4¢ orange brown	200.00	135.00	90.00	100.00	60.00	42.50
355	5¢ blue	210.00	150.00	100.00	140.00	70.00	50.00
356	10¢ yellow	2500.00	1650.00	1000.00	1425.00	975.00	550.00

SCOTT NO.	UNUSED NH F	AVG	UNUSED OG F	AVG	SCOTT NO.	UNUSED NH F	AVG	UNUSED OG F	AVG
	PLATE BLOCKS OF 6					**CENTER LINE BLOCKS**			
331	90.00	60.00	65.00	48.00	343	72.00	50.00	50.00	33.00
332	90.00	70.00	65.00	47.50	344	85.00	60.00	62.00	90.00
333	450.00	325.00	290.00	210.00	345	150.00	105.00	110.00	75.00
334	500.00	340.00	360.00	255.00	346	290.00	200.00	205.00	150.00
335	850.00	635.00	575.00	465.00	347	450.00	315.00	325.00	230.00
337	700.00	495.00	375.00	275.00		**ARROW BLOCKS**			
338	950.00	750.00	700.00	450.00					
339	700.00	575.00	400.00	300.00					
343	110.00	90.00	75.00	50.00	343	45.00	31.50	33.00	22.00
344	160.00	130.00	140.00	100.00	344	60.00	42.00	40.00	40.00
345	300.00	225.00	240.00	190.00	345	110.00	75.00	77.50	55.00
346	400.00	300.00	310.00	260.00	346	185.00	130.00	125.00	82.50
347	525.00	425.00	450.00	325.00	347	290.00	205.00	210.00	150.00

(NH + 60%)

	COIL LINE PAIRS UNUSED OG			COIL PAIRS UNUSED OG		
	VF	F	AVG	VF	F	AVG
348	300.00	200.00	140.00	100.00	70.00	45.00
349	495.00	325.00	210.00	180.00	120.00	80.00
350	1200.00	900.00	650.00	395.00	275.00	175.00
351	1200.00	900.00	650.00	475.00	300.00	185.00
352	575.00	375.00	225.00	200.00	135.00	85.00
353	575.00	375.00	225.00	225.00	145.00	95.00
354	1650.00	1100.00	775.00	500.00	350.00	225.00
355	1650.00	1100.00	775.00	525.00	375.00	240.00
356	11000.00	8500.00	6250.00	5750.00	3750.00	2250.00

SCOTT NO.	DESCRIPTION	UNUSED O.G. VF	F	AVG	USED VF	F	AVG
	1909 Bluish Gray paper Perf. 12 (NH + 60%)						
357	1¢ green	145.00	90.00	65.00	150.00	95.00	60.00
358	2¢ carmine	145.00	90.00	65.00	150.00	95.00	60.00
359	3¢ deep violet (I)	2400.00	1650.00	1200.00	2500.00	1750.00	1100.00
360	4¢ orange brown	......	16000.00	11000.00	......	......	......
361	5¢ blue	5000.00	3250.00	2250.00	9500.00	7000.00	5000.00
362	6¢ red orange	2000.00	1200.00	800.00	2300.00	1550.00	975.00
363	8¢ olive green	......	19500.00	14000.00	......	......	......
364	10¢ yellow	2200.00	1300.00	950.00	2150.00	1400.00	1000.00
365	13¢ blue green	3500.00	2200.00	1500.00	2800.00	1900.00	1275.00
366	15¢ pale ultramarine	2000.00	1100.00	850.00	2000.00	1350.00	875.00

U.S. Postage #367-404

THE 1909 COMMEMORATIVES

After the 16-value Columbian commemorative set, the Post Office Department began gradually reducing the number of stamps in subsequent series. The 1909 commemoratives were the first to use the single-stamp commemorative approach that is now the common practice.

The Lincoln Memorial issue was released on the 100th anniversary of the birth of America's 16th President. The Alaska-Yukon was issued for the Alaska-Yukon Exposition held in Seattle to publicize the development of the Alaska territory. The Hudson-Fulton stamp commemorated Henry Hudson's 1609 discovery of the river that bears his name, the 1809 voyage of Robert Fulton's "Clermont" steamboat and the 1909 celebration of those two events.

As noted earlier, the 1909 Commemoratives were issued on experimental "bluish" paper in addition to the white wove standard. The stamps on white wove paper also were issued in imperforate form for private perforation by vending and stamp-affixing machine manufacturers.

367-369
Lincoln

370, 371
William H. Seward

372, 373
S.S. Clermont

SCOTT NO.	DESCRIPTION	UNUSED O.G. VF	F	AVG	USED VF	F	AVG
	1909 LINCOLN MEMORIAL ISSUE (NH + 50%)						
367	2¢ carmine, perf.	8.00	6.00	4.00	3.50	2.00	1.40
368	2¢ carmine, imperf.	32.00	25.00	18.00	30.00	16.00	12.00
369	2¢ carmine (bluish paper)	300.00	180.00	130.00	300.00	190.00	120.00
	1909 ALASKA-YUKON ISSUE						
370	2¢ carmine, perf.	14.00	8.25	5.50	3.00	1.75	1.00
371	2¢ carmine, imperf.	47.50	35.00	27.50	32.00	20.00	14.00
	1909 HUDSON-FULTON ISSUE						
372	2¢ carmine, perf.	18.00	12.00	9.50	5.00	3.00	2.00
373	2¢ carmine, imperf	42.00	30.00	25.00	32.00	22.00	17.00
	1910-11 Single Line Watermark "USPS" Perf. 12 (NH + 50%)						
374-82	1¢-15¢ (9 varieties, complete)	760.00	475.00	290.00	52.00	33.00	19.75
374	1¢ green	9.00	5.50	3.75	.30	.25	.20
374a	1¢ booklet pane of 6	190.00	130.00	80.00			
375	2¢ carmine	9.00	5.50	3.75	.30	.25	.20
375a	2¢ booklet pane of 6	150.00	105.00	65.50			
376	3¢ deep violet (I)	30.00	17.00	11.00	3.00	1.75	1.10
377	4¢ brown	40.00	24.00	17.50	1.00	.75	.50
378	5¢ blue	40.00	24.00	17.50	1.00	.75	.50
379	6¢ red orange	50.00	30.00	19.00	1.55	.90	.60
380	8¢ olive green	135.00	80.00	47.50	17.00	10.50	6.25
381	10¢ yellow	150.00	95.00	55.00	6.00	4.00	2.65
382	15¢ pale ultramarine	340.00	220.00	130.00	25.00	15.50	8.75
	1911 Imperforate						
383	1¢ green	4.50	3.50	2.00	3.50	2.00	1.25
384	2¢ carmine	7.50	6.50	3.50	3.00	2.00	1.00

SCOTT NO.	UNUSED NH F	AVG	UNUSED OG F	AVG	SCOTT NO.	UNUSED NH F	AVG	UNUSED OG F	AVG
	PLATE BLOCKS OF 6					**CENTER LINE BLOCKS**			
367	175.00	120.00	115.00	85.00	368	200.00	140.00	150.00	95.00
368	300.00	210.00	200.00	150.00	371	285.00	195.00	200.00	135.00
370	320.00	220.00	220.00	150.00	373	305.00	215.00	220.00	150.00
371	390.00	275.00	280.00	190.00	383	42.00	30.00	30.00	20.00
372	380.00	240.00	280.00	190.00	384	75.00	52.50	50.00	30.00
373	415.00	300.00	290.00	200.00		**ARROW BLOCKS**			
374	100.00	65.00	70.00	50.00					
375	105.00	65.00	75.00	50.00	368	170.00	120.00	110.00	75.00
376	200.00	140.00	135.00	100.00	371	220.00	160.00	155.00	110.00
377	240.00	170.00	170.00	120.00	373	250.00	175.00	175.00	120.00
378	300.00	225.00	215.00	140.00	383	21.00	15.00	15.00	10.00
383	80.00	55.00	50.00	36.00	384	31.50	23.00	23.00	15.00
384	210.00	150.00	135.00	95.00					

Very Fine Plate Blocks from this period command premiums.

SCOTT NO.	DESCRIPTION	UNUSED O.G. VF	F	AVG	USED VF	F	AVG
	COIL STAMPS						
	1910 Perf. 12 Horizontally (NH + 75%)						
385	1¢ green	45.00	27.50	17.50	20.00	14.00	10.00
386	2¢ carmine	75.00	47.50	32.50	26.00	17.00	10.00
	1910-11 Perf. 12 Vertically (†)						
387	1¢ green	195.00	125.00	75.00	65.00	45.00	30.00
388	2¢ carmine	1025.00	650.00	525.00	425.00	275.00	160.00
389	3¢ deep violet (I)	......	58000.00	......	......	12400.00	......
	1910 Perf. 8-1/2 Horizontally						
390	1¢ green	6.00	3.50	2.00	7.50	4.75	3.25
391	2¢ carmine	42.00	24.00	16.00	17.00	11.00	7.00
	1910-13 Perf. 8-1/2 Vertically						
392	1¢ green	29.00	19.50	12.00	26.00	15.00	13.50
393	2¢ carmine	50.00	30.00	20.00	14.00	8.00	5.50
394	3¢ deep violet (I)	70.00	40.00	28.00	65.00	40.00	30.00
395	4¢ brown	70.00	40.00	28.00	65.00	40.00	30.00
396	5¢ blue	70.00	40.00	28.00	65.00	40.00	30.00

SCOTT NO.	COIL LINE PAIRS UNUSED OG VF	F	AVG	COIL PAIRS UNUSED OG VF	F	AVG
	(NH + 75%)					
385	450.00	300.00	195.00	100.00	65.00	50.00
386	800.00	550.00	350.00	250.00	165.00	100.00
387	675.00	425.00	275.00	375.00	250.00	175.00
390	50.00	35.00	22.50	20.00	10.00	6.00
391	330.00	235.00	140.00	135.00	60.00	38.00
392	175.00	115.00	75.00	75.00	45.00	35.00
393	325.00	210.00	150.00	160.00	90.00	55.00
394	450.00	295.00	200.00	175.00	110.00	75.00
395	450.00	295.00	200.00	175.00	110.00	75.00
396	450.00	295.00	200.00	175.00	110.00	75.00

THE PANAMA-PACIFIC ISSUE

The Panama-Pacific stamps were issued to commemorate the discovery of the Pacific Ocean in 1513 and the opening of the 1915 Panama-Pacific Exposition that celebrated the completion of the Panama Canal. Released in perf 12 form in 1913, the set of four denominations was changed to perf 10 in 1914. Before the perf change, the 10 cent orange yellow shade was determined to be too light. It was changed to the deeper orange color that is found both perf 12 and perf 10.

Because many collectors ignored the perf 10 stamps when they were issued, these stamps are scarcer than their perf 12 predecessors. In fact, #404 is the rarest 20th century commemorative issue.

397, 401
Balboa

398, 402
Panama Canal

399, 403
Golden Gate

400, 400A, 404
Discovery of San Francisco Bay

SCOTT NO.	DESCRIPTION	UNUSED O.G. VF	F	AVG	USED VF	F	AVG
	1913 Perf. 12 (NH + 75%)						
397-400A	1¢-10¢ (5 varieties, complete)	660.00	350.00	230.00	76.00	42.00	26.00
397	1¢ green	22.50	14.00	10.00	3.00	1.80	1.25
398	2¢ carmine	28.00	15.00	10.00	1.10	.65	.50
399	5¢ blue	100.00	60.00	40.00	14.00	7.50	4.50
400	10¢ orange yellow	180.00	100.00	65.00	32.00	18.00	12.00
400A	10¢ orange	325.00	185.00	120.00	30.00	16.00	10.00
	1914-15 Perf. 10 (NH + 75%)						
401-04	1¢-10¢ (4 varieties, complete)	1563.00	1155.00	760.00	142.00	82.00	54.00
401	1¢ green	35.00	20.00	14.00	9.00	6.50	4.00
402	2¢ carmine	105.00	60.00	45.00	3.25	1.95	1.25
403	5¢ blue	255.00	135.00	95.00	28.00	18.00	12.00
404	10¢ orange	1250.00	1000.00	650.00	110.00	60.00	40.00

Postage #405-447

405/545 Washington | 406/546 Washington | 426/541 Washington | 427, 446, 457, 465, 495, 503 Washington

428, 447, 458, 466, 467, 496, 504, 505 Washington | 429, 468, 506 Washington | 407, 430, 469, 507 Washington | 414, 431, 470, 508 Franklin

415, 432, 471, 509 Franklin | 416, 433, 472, 497, 510 Franklin | 434, 473, 511 Franklin | 417, 435, 474, 512 Franklin

513 Franklin | 418, 437, 475, 514 Franklin | 419, 438, 476, 515 Franklin | 420, 439, 476A, 516 Franklin

421, 422, 440, 477, 517 Franklin | 423, 478, 518 Franklin

SCOTT NO.	DESCRIPTION	UNUSED O.G. VF	F	AVG	USED VF	F	AVG
	1912-14 Single Line Watermark Perf. 12 (NH + 60%)						
405	1¢ green	8.00	4.50	2.75	.30	.20	.15
405b	1¢ booklet pane of 6	95.00	65.00	45.00	......	......	......
406	2¢ carmine (I)	9.00	5.25	3.50	.30	.20	.15
406a	2¢ booklet pane of 6	95.00	65.00	45.00	......	......	......
407	7¢ black	110.00	65.00	45.00	15.00	10.00	6.50
	1912 Imperforate						
408	1¢ green	1.75	1.35	.90	.80	.50	.35
409	2¢ carmine (I)	1.75	1.35	.90	.90	.60	.45

SCOTT NO.	UNUSED NH F	AVG	UNUSED OG F	AVG	SCOTT NO.	UNUSED NH F	AVG	UNUSED OG F	AVG
	PLATE BLOCKS OF 6					**CENTER LINE BLOCKS**			
397	190.00	130.00	140.00	90.00	408	15.50	11.00	11.00	8.50
398	325.00	260.00	215.00	150.00	409	17.00	11.95	14.50	9.50
401	425.00	250.00	275.00	195.00		**ARROW BLOCKS**			
405	140.00	70.00	90.00	60.00					
406	160.00	120.00	100.00	70.00					
408	32.00	24.00	19.00	14.00	408	7.50	8.00	6.00	4.50
409	56.00	40.00	36.00	25.00	409	9.00	9.00	7.25	5.00

SCOTT NO.	DESCRIPTION	UNUSED O.G. VF	F	AVG	USED VF	F	AVG
	COIL STAMPS **1912 Perf. 8-1/2 Horizontally** (NH + 60%)						
410	1¢ green	8.50	5.00	3.50	6.00	3.50	2.10
411	2¢ carmine (I)	14.00	8.50	5.50	5.00	3.25	2.00
	1912 Perf. 8-1/2 Vertically						
412	1¢ green	32.00	22.00	15.00	8.00	5.00	3.50
413	2¢ carmine (I)	55.00	34.00	21.00	2.50	1.75	1.10

	(NH + 60%)					
SCOTT NO.	COIL LINE PAIRS UNUSED OG VF	F	AVG	COIL PAIRS UNUSED OG VF	F	AVG
410	48.00	29.00	18.00	19.00	12.50	8.00
411	70.00	45.00	30.00	30.00	20.00	12.50
412	150.00	100.00	65.00	85.00	65.00	40.00
413	295.00	200.00	135.00	135.00	95.00	65.00

1912-14 Perf. 12 Single Line Watermark (NH + 60%)

414	8¢ pale olive green	60.00	39.00	25.00	2.35	1.30	1.00
415	9¢ salmon red	70.00	45.00	26.50	17.50	11.00	7.25
416	10¢ orange yellow	60.00	38.00	24.00	.65	.45	.25
417	12¢ claret brown	65.00	43.00	28.00	6.50	4.25	2.85
418	15¢ gray	105.00	65.00	42.00	5.60	3.50	2.40
419	20¢ ultramarine	240.00	160.00	100.00	24.00	14.00	10.00
420	30¢ orange red	160.00	105.00	65.00	24.00	14.00	10.00
421	50¢ violet	575.00	340.00	225.00	25.00	16.00	11.00

1912 Double Line Watermark "USPS" Perf 12

422	50¢ violet	350.00	225.00	150.00	26.00	16.50	10.00
423	$1 violet black	675.00	425.00	250.00	85.00	50.00	32.00

1914-15 Single Line Watermark, "USPS" Perf. 10 (NH + 60%)

424-40	1¢-50¢ (16 varieties, complete) ...	2050.00	1250.00	870.00	120.00	79.00	51.00
424	1¢ green	3.75	2.25	1.50	.25	.20	.15
424d	1¢ booklet pane of 6	8.00	4.00	3.00	......	......	......
425	2¢ rose red ..	3.75	1.90	1.25	.25	.20	.15
425e	2¢ booklet pane of 6	30.00	22.50	16.00	......	......	......
426	3¢ deep violet (I)	20.00	12.00	7.50	2.65	1.50	1.00
427	4¢ brown	45.00	28.00	19.75	.90	.55	.40
428	5¢ blue.......	40.00	28.00	17.50	.90	.55	.40
429	6¢ red orange	70.00	45.00	30.00	2.75	1.75	1.00
430	7¢ black	120.00	70.00	52.00	8.00	5.00	3.00
431	8¢ pale olive green	47.50	31.00	19.00	2.95	1.95	1.25
432	9¢ salmon red	70.00	37.50	24.00	14.50	10.00	6.00
433	10¢ orange yellow	67.50	40.00	27.00	1.00	.75	.45
434	11¢ dark green	33.50	22.00	15.50	11.50	7.00	5.00
435	12¢ claret brown	34.50	22.00	15.50	10.00	7.00	4.00
437	15¢ gray	160.00	100.00	75.00	11.50	7.00	4.80
438	20¢ ultramarine	280.00	170.00	120.00	6.95	4.75	3.00
439	30¢ orange red	385.00	210.00	165.00	26.50	17.00	11.50
440	50¢ violet	800.00	500.00	325.00	28.00	18.00	12.00

UNUSED PLATE BLOCKS OF 6

SCOTT NO.	NH F	AVG	OG F	AVG	SCOTT NO.	NH F	AVG	OG F	AVG
414	525.00	350.00	400.00	250.00	429	500.00	300.00	325.00	190.00
415	750.00	525.00	525.00	375.00	430	1200.00	850.00	800.00	550.00
416	650.00	425.00	400.00	280.00	431	500.00	395.00	400.00	280.00
417	700.00	475.00	450.00	300.00	432	800.00	575.00	600.00	425.00
418	900.00	650.00	600.00	450.00	433	800.00	575.00	600.00	425.00
424 (6)	55.00	40.00	30.00	20.00	434	275.00	180.00	200.00	115.00
424 (10)	190.00	120.00	130.00	80.00	435	355.00	200.00	240.00	150.00
425 (6)	30.00	20.00	20.00	15.00	437	1200.00	850.00	850.00	625.00
425 (10)	180.00	120.00	130.00	90.00	438	3850.00	2950.00	2500.00	1950.00
426	200.00	140.00	150.00	100.00	439	5250.00	3750.00	3250.00	2500.00
427	575.00	400.00	425.00	300.00	440	17000.00	11500.00	12500.00	9000.00
428	475.00	300.00	350.00	200.00					

COIL STAMPS
1914 Perf. 10 Horizontally
(NH + 60%)

441	1¢ green	1.75	1.00	.65	1.40	1.00	.65
442	2¢ carmine (I)	14.00	9.00	5.50	11.00	7.20	4.00

1914 Perf.10 Vertically
(NH + 60%)

443	1¢ green	30.00	19.50	13.00	8.50	5.00	3.00
444	2¢ carmine (I)	47.50	28.00	17.25	2.50	1.45	.95
445	3¢ violet (I)...	350.00	225.00	160.00	185.00	120.00	75.00
446	4¢ brown	180.00	120.00	90.00	70.00	42.00	30.00
447	5¢ blue.......	70.00	45.00	32.00	60.00	40.00	25.00

U.S. Postage #448-519

SCOTT NO.	DESCRIPTION	UNUSED O.G. VF	F	AVG	USED VF	F	AVG
	ROTARY PRESS COIL STAMPS 1915-16 Perf. 10 Horizontally (NH + 60%)						
448	1¢ green	9.50	7.00	4.00	5.00	3.50	2.25
449	2¢ red (I)	3500.00	2100.00	1450.00	525.00	395.00	260.00
450	2¢ carmine (III)	13.00	9.25	6.50	6.00	4.00	2.00
	1914-16 Perf. 10 Vertically (NH + 60%)						
452	1¢ green	17.00	12.00	8.75	3.50	2.50	1.75
453	2¢ carmine rose (I)	160.00	90.00	60.00	6.00	3.75	3.00
454	2¢ red (II)	145.00	100.00	65.00	16.00	9.00	6.00
455	2¢ carmine (III)	14.00	9.75	6.50	1.95	1.50	.75
456	3¢ violet (I)	375.00	250.00	160.00	155.00	90.00	60.00
457	4¢ brown	44.00	22.50	16.00	32.00	20.00	12.00
458	5¢ blue......	45.00	30.00	19.50	32.00	20.00	12.00
	1914 Imperforate Coil (NH + 60%)						
459	2¢ carmine (I)	450.00	375.00	300.00	1100.00	800.00	....
	1915 Flat Plate Printing Double Line Watermark Perf. 10 (NH + 60%)						
460	$1 violet black	1250.00	750.00	525.00	135.00	80.00	55.00
	1915 Single Line Watermark "USPS" Perf. 11 (NH + 60%)						
461	2¢ pale carmine red (I)	200.00	115.00	65.00	400.00	210.00	125.00
	1916-17 Unwatermarked Perf. 10 (NH + 60%)						
462	1¢ green	11.50	8.00	5.00	.75	.40	.25
462a	1¢ booklet pane of 6	16.00	10.00	6.00	....	....	....
463	2¢ carmine (I)	6.75	4.50	3.00	.40	.30	.20
463a	2¢ booklet pane of 6	110.00	80.00	55.00	....	....	....
464	3¢ violet (I) ...	120.00	65.00	48.00	21.50	14.00	9.00
465	4¢ orange brown	66.50	42.00	25.00	3.25	2.25	1.35
466	5¢ blue.....	120.00	65.00	40.00	3.25	2.25	1.35
467	5¢ carmine (error)	950.00	575.00	350.00	1000.00	650.00	450.00
468	6¢ red orange	140.00	75.00	45.00	12.50	7.00	4.00
469	7¢ black	180.00	100.00	68.00	20.00	12.00	7.00
470	8¢ olive green	80.00	45.00	30.00	10.50	6.00	4.00
471	9¢ salmon red	90.00	50.00	32.00	22.50	12.50	9.00
472	10¢ orange yellow	160.00	88.00	65.00	2.00	1.50	.90
473	11¢ dark green	55.00	35.00	20.00	30.00	17.00	11.50
474	12¢ claret brown	70.00	45.00	32.50	10.00	6.00	4.00
475	15¢ gray	250.00	175.00	100.00	20.00	11.00	8.00
476	20¢ light ultramarine	400.00	220.00	160.00	20.50	12.00	8.00
476A	30¢ orange red	....	4800.00	....	....	....	....
477	50¢ light violet	1600.00	950.00	625.00	110.00	70.00	45.00
478	$1 violet black.	1175.00	675.00	490.00	31.50	21.50	12.50
	Design of 1902-03						
479	$2 dark blue ..	450.00	310.00	225.00	74.50	42.00	33.50
480	$5 light green .	395.00	250.00	150.00	80.00	45.00	32.00
	1916-17 Imperforate (NH + 60%)						
481	1¢ green	1.50	1.00	.50	1.50	1.00	.50
482	2¢ carmine (I)	2.25	1.75	1.00	2.50	1.50	1.00
483	3¢ violet (I)...	18.50	13.00	9.00	10.00	8.00	6.00
484	3¢ violet (II) ..	14.00	12.00	8.00	6.75	5.25	4.00

		(NH + 60%)					
SCOTT NO.		COIL LINE PAIRS UNUSED OG VF	F	AVG	COIL PAIRS UNUSED OG VF	F	AVG
441		10.00	7.00	4.00	4.50	2.50	2.00
442		90.00	48.00	30.00	32.00	20.00	12.50
443		180.00	120.00	75.00	80.00	55.00	35.00
444		275.00	195.00	110.00	140.00	100.00	60.00
445		1600.00	900.00	600.00	850.00	600.00	400.00
446		900.00	500.00	350.00	450.00	260.00	160.00
447		325.00	185.00	127.00	175.00	110.00	75.00
448		62.00	39.00	25.00	32.00	18.00	12.00
450		90.00	49.00	35.00	40.00	25.50	17.50
452		115.00	65.00	40.00	45.00	25.00	18.00
453		850.00	450.00	350.00	400.00	225.00	160.00
454		900.00	425.00	325.00	350.00	200.00	140.00
455		90.00	50.00	35.00	32.00	18.00	12.00
456		1350.00	900.00	550.00	850.00	500.00	350.00
457		240.00	130.00	90.00	100.00	65.00	45.00
458		250.00	145.00	95.00	115.00	85.00	50.00
459		1800.00	1250.00	900.00	700.00	500.00	375.00

NOTE: For further details on the various types of similar appearing stamps please refer to our U.S. Stamp Identifier.

	UNUSED PLATE BLOCKS OF 6							
SCOTT NO.	NH F	AVG	OG F	AVG	SCOTT NO.	NH F	AVG	OG F	AVG
462	195.00	125.00	125.00	80.00	472	1600.00	1200.00	1200.00	800.00
463	155.00	100.00	100.00	60.00	473	450.00	325.00	300.00	200.00
464	1500.00	1100.00	1150.00	825.00	474	775.00	500.00	500.00	325.00
465	800.00	500.00	600.00	425.00	481	17.00	12.00	12.00	8.00
466	1100.00	850.00	950.00	565.00	482	35.00	22.00	22.50	17.00
470	675.00	500.00	545.00	320.00	483	190.00	150.00	140.00	90.00
471	850.00	675.00	595.00	400.00	484	140.00	90.00	115.00	80.00

CENTER LINE BLOCKS					ARROW BLOCKS				
481	12.00	8.00	7.00	4.00	481	8.00	5.00	4.00	3.00
482	13.00	8.00	8.00	6.00	482	11.00	7.00	7.75	4.75
483	120.00	70.00	75.00	45.00	483	100.00	60.00	65.00	40.00
484	90.00	60.00	65.00	40.00	484	72.00	42.00	50.00	35.00

SCOTT NO.	DESCRIPTION	UNUSED O.G. VF	F	AVG	USED VF	F	AVG
	ROTARY PRESS COIL STAMPS 1916-19 Perf. 10 Horizontally (NH + 60%)						
486	1¢ green	1.50	.80	.50	.40	.30	.20
487	2¢ carmine (II)	24.00	14.00	9.00	7.00	5.00	3.00
488	2¢ carmine (III)	4.75	3.00	1.95	2.40	1.75	1.00
489	3¢ violet (I)...	7.00	4.50	3.00	2.75	1.95	1.00
	1916-22 Perf. 10 Vertically (NH + 60%)						
490	1¢ green	1.00	.60	.40	.35	.25	.15
491	2¢ carmine (II)	2500.00	1600.00	1000.00	800.00	550.00	375.00
492	2¢ carmine (III)	16.00	9.00	6.00	.40	.25	.20
493	3¢ violet (I)...	28.00	16.00	12.00	5.00	3.00	2.00
494	3¢ violet (II)..	16.00	9.00	6.00	1.40	.95	.75
495	4¢ orange brown	18.00	10.00	7.00	6.50	3.75	2.50
496	5¢ blue.....	7.00	4.00	3.00	1.60	1.00	.75
497	10¢ orange yellow	35.00	20.00	15.00	15.00	10.00	5.25

		(NH + 60%)					
SCOTT NO.		COIL LINE PAIRS UNUSED OG VF	F	AVG	COIL PAIRS UNUSED OG VF	F	AVG
486		6.50	4.50	3.50	3.00	2.00	1.25
487		160.00	105.00	75.00	45.00	32.00	20.00
488		28.00	18.00	12.00	12.00	8.00	5.00
489		40.00	30.00	24.00	18.00	11.00	7.00
490		6.00	3.75	1.90	2.80	2.00	1.20
491		....	8000.00	4950.00	5450.00	4000.00	3000.00
492		70.00	50.00	35.00	36.00	24.00	16.00
493		160.00	100.00	70.00	60.00	38.00	28.00
494		90.00	60.00	48.00	36.00	24.00	18.00
495		100.00	75.00	55.00	42.00	26.00	19.00
496		40.00	28.00	19.50	15.00	10.00	6.00
497		160.00	115.00	75.00	80.00	52.00	38.00

	1917-19 Flat Plate Printing Perf. 11 (NH + 60%)						
498/518	(498-99, 501-04, 506-18) 19 varieties	640.00	395.00	265.00	35.00	22.25	16.95
498	1¢ green	.80	.50	.40	.35	.25	.20
498e	1¢ booklet pane of 6	4.50	2.75	2.00	....	....	....
498f	1¢ booklet pane of 30	1200.00	725.00	550.00	....	....	....
499	2¢ rose (I) ...	.80	.40	.30	.35	.25	.20
499e	2¢ booklet pane of 6	7.00	4.50	3.50	....	....	....
500	2¢ deep rose (Ia)	400.00	225.00	165.00	250.00	175.00	100.00
501	3¢ light violet (I)	20.00	12.00	8.00	.35	.25	.20
501b	3¢ booklet pane of 6	95.00	65.00	45.00	....	....	....
502	3¢ dark violet (II)	26.00	15.00	10.00	.80	.55	.35
502b	3¢ booklet pane of 6	80.00	45.00	30.00	....	....	....
503	4¢ brown	18.00	10.00	6.00	.50	.35	.20
504	5¢ blue	14.00	8.00	5.00	.55	.40	.25
505	5¢ rose (error)	680.00	400.00	275.00	700.00	475.00	300.00
506	6¢ red orange	22.00	13.00	8.00	.65	.50	.35
507	7¢ black	42.00	25.00	17.00	2.00	1.45	.80
508	8¢ olive bistre	17.00	10.00	6.00	1.45	1.20	.80
509	9¢ salmon red	24.00	14.00	9.00	3.65	2.30	1.65
510	10¢ orange yellow	28.00	16.00	10.00	.30	.20	.15
511	11¢ light green	14.00	8.00	3.00	5.60	3.50	2.40
512	12¢ claret brown	14.00	8.00	5.00	1.15	.65	.50
513	13¢ apple green	19.00	11.00	7.00	12.00	7.00	6.40
514	15¢ gray	64.00	38.00	26.00	1.60	1.00	.75
515	20¢ light ultramarine	85.00	46.00	34.00	.55	.35	.25
516	30¢ orange red	70.00	40.00	30.00	1.60	1.00	.85
517	50¢ red violet	100.00	75.00	50.00	1.50	.80	.75
518	$1 violet black	95.00	65.00	45.00	3.00	2.00	1.25
	1917 Design of 1908-09 Double Line Watermark Perf. 11						
519	2¢ carmine ...	550.00	325.00	195.00	875.00	575.00	325.00

U.S. Postage #523-550

UNUSED PLATE BLOCKS OF 6

SCOTT NO.	NH F	AVG	OG F	AVG	SCOTT NO.	NH F	AVG	OG F	AVG
498	19.50	14.75	14.00	12.00	511	200.00	110.00	150.00	90.00
499	19.50	14.75	14.00	12.00	512	185.00	100.00	130.00	77.50
501	170.00	128.00	140.00	100.00	513	185.00	105.50	145.00	85.00
502	190.00	175.00	165.00	128.00	514	835.00	465.00	595.00	385.00
503	190.00	150.00	135.00	115.00	515	975.00	565.00	675.00	425.00
504	165.00	100.00	135.00	80.00	516	750.00	440.00	600.00	350.00
506	230.00	155.00	210.00	125.00	517	2000.00	1350.00	1300.00	900.00
507	350.00	265.00	250.00	210.00	518	1500.00	925.00	1050.00	685.00
508	220.00	150.00	175.00	120.00	519	3000.00	1950.00	2285.00	1350.00
509	220.00	150.00	175.00	120.00		**ARROW BLOCK**			
510	260.00	215.00	165.00	125.00	518	450.00	280.00	300.00	225.00

523, 547
Franklin

524
Franklin

SCOTT NO.	DESCRIPTION	UNUSED O.G. VF	F	AVG	USED VF	F	AVG
		1918 Unwatermarked					
523	$2 orange red & black	875.00	600.00	425.00	350.00	240.00	150.00
524	$5 deep green & black	300.00	215.00	150.00	50.00	35.00	20.00
		1918-20 Offset Printing Perf. 11 (NH + 60%)					
525	1¢ gray green	3.00	1.75	1.10	1.25	.85	.50
526	2¢ carmine (IV)	35.00	25.00	13.00	6.00	4.25	2.75
527	2¢ carmine (V)	30.00	19.50	12.00	1.95	1.30	.75
528	2¢ carmine (Va)	14.00	9.00	6.50	.30	.25	.15
528A	2¢ carmine (VI)	70.00	52.50	35.00	2.00	1.00	.80
528B	2¢ carmine (VII)	32.00	21.00	14.50	.45	.30	.20
529	3¢ violet (III)	4.00	3.00	2.40	.45	.30	.20
530	3¢ purple (IV)	2.25	1.50	1.10	.45	.30	.20
		1918-20 Offset Printing Imperforate					
531	1¢ gray green	13.00	8.00	6.00	13.00	8.00	6.00
532	2¢ carmine rose (IV)	55.00	39.00	30.00	40.00	28.00	19.00
533	2¢ carmine (V)	220.00	165.00	120.00	110.00	75.00	55.00
534	2¢ carmine (Va)	16.00	14.00	8.00	10.00	6.25	4.00
534A	2¢ carmine (VI)	55.00	40.00	29.00	44.00	29.00	21.50
534B	2¢ carmine (VII)	2500.00	1800.00	1350.00	1050.00	925.00	600.00
535	3¢ violet (IV)	12.50	8.00	5.50	10.00	6.50	4.00
		1919 Offset Printing Perf. 12-1/2					
536	1¢ gray green	25.00	17.50	10.00	30.00	18.50	12.00

537
"Victory" and Flags

	1919 VICTORY ISSUE (NH + 50%)						
537	3¢ violet	14.00	8.00	4.75	6.50	4.00	2.50
		1919-21 Rotary Press Printings—Perf. 11 x 10 (†) (NH + 50%)					
538	1¢ green	16.00	9.00	6.00	15.00	10.00	7.50
538a	Same, imperf. horizontally	80.00	50.00	35.50	......	......	......
539	2¢ carmine rose (II)	3300.00	2700.00	1800.00	......	3300.00	2300.00
540	2¢ carmine rose (III)	17.50	10.00	6.00	16.00	9.50	6.50
540a	Same, imperf. horizontally	75.00	45.00	35.50	......	......	......
541	3¢ violet (II)	50.00	30.00	23.50	52.00	30.00	22.50
		Perf. 10 x 11					
542	1¢ green	17.00	11.25	7.00	1.60	1.00	.75
		Perf. 10					
543	1¢ green	1.50	.50	.55	.65	.40	.20

SCOTT NO.	DESCRIPTION	UNUSED O.G. VF	F	AVG	USED VF	F	AVG
		Perf. 11					
544	1¢ green (19 x 22-1/2mm)	......	18000.00	14200.00	......	3300.00	2500.00
545	1¢ green (19-1/2 x 22mm)	210.00	140.00	90.00	225.00	140.00	95.00
546	2¢ carmine rose (III)	145.00	95.00	60.00	245.00	150.00	100.00
		1920 Flat Plate Printing Perf. 11					
547	$2 carmine & black	275.00	195.00	130.00	67.50	42.50	32.50

SCOTT NO.	NH F	AVG	OG F	AVG	SCOTT NO.	NH F	AVG	OG F	AVG
	UNUSED PLATE BLOCKS OF 6					**UNUSED PLATE BLOCKS OF (—)**			
525 (6)	29.00	22.50	20.00	14.00	535 (6)	95.00	75.00	65.00	55.00
526 (6)	260.00	200.00	185.00	140.00	536 (6)	200.00	140.00	140.00	90.00
527 (6)	225.00	150.00	140.00	100.00	537 (6)	150.00	105.00	100.00	75.00
528 (6)	125.00	85.00	80.00	50.00	538 (4)	110.00	80.00	75.00	50.00
528A (6)	500.00	350.00	350.00	225.00	540 (4)	130.00	80.00	80.00	50.00
528B (6)	210.00	140.00	145.00	100.00	541 (4)	465.00	325.00	310.00	210.00
529 (6)	75.00	50.00	50.00	35.00	542 (6)	195.00	135.00	135.00	90.00
530 (6)	30.00	20.00	20.00	13.00	543 (4)	23.00	16.00	15.00	10.00
531 (6)	110.00	80.00	85.00	60.00	543 (6)	45.00	32.00	30.00	20.00
532 (6)	400.00	295.00	275.00	190.00	545 (4)	1200.00	800.00	950.00	675.00
533 (6)					546 (4)	1000.00	700.00	700.00	475.00
534 (6)	125.00	90.00	100.00	60.00	547 (8)	5250.00	4000.00	3800.00	2750.00
534A (6)	425.00	295.00	280.00	220.00	548 (6)	55.00	39.50	40.00	30.00
					549 (6)	84.00	58.75	60.00	45.00
					550 (6)	725.00	525.00	475.00	330.00
	CENTER LINE					**ARROW BLOCKS**			
531	80.00	50.00	55.00	35.00	531	50.00	35.00	40.00	28.00
532	275.00	200.00	195.00	145.00	532	230.00	170.00	155.00	120.00
533	900.00	625.00	775.00	540.00	533	775.00	540.00	625.00	440.00
534	90.00	50.00	70.00	45.00	534	90.00	55.00	60.00	45.00
534A	275.00	200.00	185.00	110.00	534A	210.00	150.00	150.00	110.00
535	75.00	45.00	50.00	35.00	535	50.00	35.00	35.00	25.00
547	1400.00	975.00	1175.00	825.00	547	1175.00	830.00	975.00	695.00

548
The "Mayflower"

549
Landing of the Pilgrims

550
Signing of the Compact

SCOTT NO.	DESCRIPTION	UNUSED O.G. VF	F	AVG	USED VF	F	AVG
		1920 PILGRIM TERCENTENARY ISSUE (NH + 50%)					
548-50	1¢-5¢ (3 varieties, complete)	75.00	48.00	37.00	34.75	19.00	16.00
548	1¢ green	6.00	4.00	3.00	5.50	3.00	2.00
549	2¢ carmine rose	11.00	7.00	4.00	3.50	2.00	1.60
550	5¢ deep blue	65.00	40.00	32.00	27.50	15.00	13.50

FOR YOUR CONVENIENCE IN ORDERING, COMPLETE SETS ARE LISTED BEFORE SINGLE STAMP LISTINGS.

U.S. Postage #551-596

551, 653
Nathan Hale

552, 575, 578, 581, 594, 596, 597, 604, 632
Franklin

553, 576, 582, 598, 605, 631, 633
Harding

554, 577, 579, 583, 595, 599-99A, 606, 634-34A
Washington

555, 584, 600, 635
Lincoln

556, 585, 601, 636
Martha Washington

557, 586, 602, 637
Roosevelt

558, 587, 638, 723
Garfield

559, 588, 639
McKinley

560, 589, 640
Grant

561, 590, 641
Jefferson

562, 591, 603, 642
Monroe

563, 692
Hayes

564, 693
Cleveland

565, 695
American Indian

566, 696
Statue of Liberty

567, 698
Golden Gate

568, 699
Niagara Falls

569, 700
Bison

570, 701
Arlington Amphitheatre

571
Lincoln Memorial

572
U.S. Capitol

573
"America"

SCOTT NO.	DESCRIPTION	UNUSED O.G. VF	F	AVG	USED VF	F	AVG
	THE 1922-25 ISSUE Flat Plate Printings Perf. 11 (NH + 60%)						
551-73	1/2¢-$5 (23 varieties, complete) ...	900.00	595.00	443.00	53.75	33.50	22.00
551	1/2¢ olive brown (1925)	.30	.25	.15	.25	.20	.15
552	1¢ deep green (1923)	2.25	1.60	1.20	.25	.20	.15
552a	1¢ booklet pane of 6	8.00	5.25	3.75	....	....	....
553	1-1/2¢ yellow brown (1925)	3.75	2.40	1.80	.50	.35	.25
554	2¢ carmine (1923)	2.70	1.80	1.20	.25	.20	.15
554c	2¢ booklet pane of 6	10.00	7.00	4.50	....	....	....
555	3¢ violet (1923)	24.00	17.00	11.00	1.75	1.00	.75
556	4¢ yellow brown (1923)	24.00	17.00	11.00	.50	.35	.25
557	5¢ dark blue ..	24.00	17.00	11.00	.30	.20	.15
558	6¢ red orange	47.00	30.00	22.00	1.30	.80	.60
559	7¢ black (1923)	12.00	8.00	6.00	1.20	.70	.50
560	8¢ olive green (1923)	62.00	42.00	30.00	1.20	.80	.60
561	9¢ rose (1923)	20.00	12.00	8.00	2.45	1.40	1.00
562	10¢ orange (1923)	28.00	18.00	12.00	.30	.20	.15
563	11¢ light blue .	2.80	2.00	1.25	.75	.50	.30
564	12¢ brown violet (1923)	13.50	7.00	4.50	.30	.20	.15
565	14¢ blue (1923)	9.00	5.00	3.00	1.20	1.00	.60
566	15¢ gray	40.00	23.00	17.50	.25	.20	.15
567	20¢ carmine rose (1923)	32.00	20.00	16.00	.25	.20	.15
568	25¢ yellow green	30.00	19.00	13.00	.90	.55	.40
569	30¢ olive brown (1923)	50.00	35.00	25.00	.80	.50	.35
570	50¢ lilac	85.00	50.00	40.00	.35	.20	.15
571	$1 violet black (1923)	60.00	40.00	30.00	.75	.50	.30
572	$2 deep blue (1923)	140.00	90.00	75.00	16.00	10.00	6.00
573	$5 carmine & blue (1923)	235.00	170.00	125.00	25.00	15.00	10.00
	1923-25 Imperforate						
575	1¢ green	11.00	8.00	6.00	7.75	4.50	3.00
576	1-1/2¢ yellow brown (1925)	2.50	1.60	1.00	3.00	1.60	1.25
577	2¢ carmine ...	3.00	2.00	1.20	3.00	1.75	1.25
	Rotary Press Printings 1923 Perf. 11 x 10 (†) (NH + 60%)						
578	1¢ green	135.00	80.00	55.00	225.00	135.00	100.00
579	2¢ carmine ..	120.00	70.00	50.00	185.00	110.00	75.00
	1923-26 Perf. 10 (†)						
581-91	1¢-10¢ (11 varieties, complete) ...	268.00	152.50	108.50	25.00	15.35	9.75
581	1¢ green	12.00	7.00	4.00	1.20	.85	.60
582	1-1/2¢ brown (1925)	6.00	4.00	3.00	1.20	.85	.60
583	2¢ carmine (1924)	4.00	2.00	1.20	.25	.20	.15
583a	2¢ booklet pane of 6 (1924)	110.00	60.00	40.00	....	....	....
584	3¢ violet (1925)	40.00	24.00	16.50	2.80	2.00	1.20
585	4¢ yellow brown (1925)	24.00	13.00	9.00	.80	.60	.40
586	5¢ blue (1925)	24.00	13.00	9.00	.45	.35	.20
587	6¢ red orange (1925)	16.00	8.50	5.50	1.00	.60	.40
588	7¢ black (1926)	17.00	9.00	6.00	9.00	5.00	3.00
589	8¢ olive green (1926)	40.00	21.00	15.00	5.00	3.25	2.00
590	9¢ rose (1926)	8.00	4.00	3.00	4.50	2.25	1.50
591	10¢ orange (1925)	90.00	55.00	41.50	.45	.35	.25
	Perf. 11 (†)						
594	1¢ green	....	19500.00	14400.00	....	5900.00	4750.00
595	2¢ carmine...	375.00	210.00	165.00	475.00	275.00	185.00
	Perf. 11						
596	1¢ green	....	....	....	....	70000.00	40000.00

When Quality Counts...

H.E. Harris & Co.®

Serving the Collector Since 1916

U.S. Postage #597-619

SCOTT NO.	PLATE BLOCKS (6) UNUSED NH			UNUSED OG		
	VF	F	AVG.	VF	F	AVG.
551	1/2¢ olive brown (1923)	12.00	6.50	5.00	8.50	6.00	4.50
552	1¢ deep green (1923)	52.00	30.00	25.00	32.50	20.00	14.00
553	1-1/2¢ yellow brown (1923)	55.00	40.00	30.00	40.00	30.00	22.00
554	2¢ carmine (1923)	45.00	28.00	20.00	30.00	20.00	14.00
555	3¢ violet (1923)	350.00	225.00	180.00	195.00	150.00	110.00
556	4¢ yellow brown (1923)	350.00	225.00	180.00	195.00	150.00	110.00
557	5¢ dark blue	375.00	240.00	200.00	210.00	160.00	125.00
558	6¢ red orange	750.00	450.00	400.00	500.00	350.00	250.00
559	7¢ black (1923)	150.00	100.00	70.00	100.00	65.00	45.00
560	8¢ olive green (1923)	1100.00	740.00	650.00	750.00	500.00	375.00
561	9¢ rose (1923)	340.00	225.00	160.00	195.00	160.00	130.00
562	10¢ orange (1923)	400.00	290.00	200.00	300.00	200.00	160.00
563	11¢ light blue	55.00	38.00	32.00	45.00	28.00	18.50
564	12¢ brown violet (1923)	170.00	100.00	70.00	145.00	80.00	70.00
565	14¢ blue (1923)	120.00	80.00	57.50	85.00	52.50	42.50
566	15¢ grey	500.00	350.00	240.00	350.00	225.00	175.00
567	20¢ carmine rose (1923) ..	475.00	320.00	240.00	400.00	220.00	190.00
568	25¢ yellow green	420.00	260.00	200.00	325.00	190.00	125.00
569	30¢ olive brown (1923)	550.00	375.00	295.00	325.00	225.00	160.00
570	50¢ lilac	1350.00	1000.00	750.00	850.00	600.00	450.00
571	$1 violet black (1923)	800.00	520.00	400.00	550.00	400.00	300.00
572	$2 deep blue (1923)	2250.00	1500.00	1200.00	1500.00	975.00	800.00
573	$5 carmine + blue (1923) ..	6500.00	4500.00	3250.00	4500.00	2950.00	2200.00

SCOTT NO.		CENTER LINE BLOCKS F/NH F/OG AVG/OG			ARROW BLOCKS F/NH F/OG AVG/OG		
571	$1 violet black	......	......	......	300.00	200.00	130.00
572	$2 deep blue	......	......	......	650.00	450.00	300.00
573	$5 carmine & blue	1050.00	900.00	625.00	1000.00	850.00	595.00
575	1¢ imperforate	58.00	45.00	35.00	45.00	37.50	28.00
576	1-1/2¢ imperforate	19.50	15.00	10.50	11.00	8.00	5.00
577	2¢ imperforate	22.50	17.50	12.00	12.00	9.00	7.00

SCOTT NO.		PLATE BLOCKS UNUSED NH			UNUSED OG		
		VF	F	AVG.	VF	F	AVG.
575 (6)	1¢ green	160.00	110.00	75.00	110.00	70.00	50.00
576 (6)	1-1/2¢ yellow brown (1925)	50.00	33.00	25.00	35.00	22.00	16.00
577 (6)	2¢ carmine	50.00	34.00	25.00	42.00	25.00	18.00
578	1¢ green	1350.00	875.00	675.00	1000.00	625.00	495.00
579	2¢ carmine	1100.00	700.00	525.00	695.00	450.00	350.00
581	1¢ green	225.00	140.00	80.00	120.00	90.00	68.50
582	1-1/2¢ brown (1925)	72.00	45.00	32.00	50.00	34.00	24.00
583	2¢ carmine (1923)	60.00	35.00	28.50	40.00	24.00	18.00
584	3¢ violet (1925)	400.00	260.00	190.00	260.00	190.00	150.00
585	4¢ yellow green (1925)	275.00	190.00	150.00	210.00	160.00	115.00
586	5¢ blue (1925)	300.00	200.00	140.00	225.00	150.00	110.00
587	6¢ red orange (1925)	150.00	100.00	70.00	100.00	70.00	50.00
588	7¢ black (1926)	190.00	110.00	75.00	110.00	79.00	60.00
589	8¢ olive green (1926)	400.00	260.00	190.00	275.00	190.00	125.00
590	9¢ rose (1926)	70.00	48.00	32.00	65.00	40.00	28.00
591	10¢ orange (1925)	1050.00	700.00	500.00	650.00	475.00	380.00

SCOTT NO.	DESCRIPTION	UNUSED VF	F	AVG	USED VF	F	AVG
	1923-29 Rotary Press Coil Stamps (NH + 50%)						
597/606	597-99, 600-06 (10 varieties)	24.50	16.50	11.00	3.50	2.45	1.65
	Perf. 10 Vertically						
597	1¢ green	.50	.30	.20	.25	.20	.15
598	1-1/2¢ deep brown (1925)	1.00	.70	.50	.30	.20	.15
599	2¢ carmine (I) (1923) ...	.60	.40	.30	.25	.20	.15
599A	2¢ carmine (II) (1929)	200.00	110.00	70.00	22.00	13.50	8.50
600	3¢ violet (1924)	10.00	6.50	4.00	.35	.25	.15
601	4¢ yellow brown	5.00	3.50	2.50	1.00	.50	.30
602	5¢ dark blue (1924)	2.40	1.50	1.00	.40	.25	.15
603	10¢ orange (1924)	5.00	3.50	2.40	.35	.20	.15
	Perf. 10 Horizontally						
604	1¢ yellow green (1924)	.45	.30	.20	.25	.20	.15
605	1-1/2¢ yellow brown (1925)	.45	.30	.20	.45	.30	.20
606	2¢ carmine ...	.50	.30	.20	.30	.20	.15

NOTE: For further details on the various types of similar appearing stamps please refer to our U.S. Stamp Identifier.

SCOTT NO.		UNUSED OG (NH + 40%) COIL LINE PAIRS			COIL PAIRS		
		VF	F	AVG.	VF	F	AVG.
597	1¢ green	2.55	1.95	1.40	.95	.55	.35
598	1-1/2¢ brown (1925)	6.75	5.25	4.00	1.85	1.35	.95
599	2¢ carmine (I)	2.15	1.65	1.20	1.10	.75	.55
599A	2¢ carmine (II) (1929)	750.00	575.00	385.00	375.00	215.00	135.00
600	3¢ deep violet (1924)	34.50	26.50	20.50	19.50	12.75	7.85
601	4¢ yellow brown	35.75	27.50	22.00	9.50	6.85	4.85
602	5¢ dark blue (1924)	11.75	9.00	6.00	4.50	2.90	1.95
603	10¢ orange (1924)	28.50	22.00	16.00	9.50	6.85	4.50
604	1¢ green (1924)	3.40	2.60	1.65	.85	.55	.35
605	1-1/2¢ yellow brown (1925)	4.25	3.00	2.00	.85	.55	.35
606	2¢ carmine	2.75	2.00	1.35	.95	.55	.35

610-613
Harding

SCOTT NO.	DESCRIPTION	UNUSED VF	F	AVG	USED VF	F	AVG
	1923 HARDING MEMORIAL ISSUE (NH + 50%)						
610	2¢ black, perf 11 flat	.90	.55	.40	.25	.20	.15
611	2¢ black, imperf	8.75	5.25	4.00	7.50	5.00	3.75
612	2¢ black, perf 10 rotary .	27.00	14.00	12.00	4.00	2.40	1.75
613	2¢ black perf 11 rotary	......	......	......	......	24000.00	19500.00

614
Ship "New Netherlands"

615
Landing at Fort Orange

616
Monument at Mayport, Fla.

1924 HUGUENOT-WALLOON ISSUE (NH + 40%)

614-16	1¢-5¢ (3 varieties, complete) ...	51.75	38.00	28.50	31.75	22.75	17.50
614	1¢ dark green	4.50	3.25	2.50	5.50	3.25	2.50
615	2¢ carmine rose	10.00	6.00	4.00	4.00	2.75	2.00
616	5¢ dark blue . .	40.00	31.00	24.00	24.00	18.00	14.00

617
Washington at Cambridge

618
Birth of Liberty

619
The Minute Man

1925 LEXINGTON-CONCORD SESQUICENTENNIAL (NH + 40%)

617-19	1¢-5¢ (3 varieties, complete) ...	49.50	36.50	27.25	28.50	20.75	14.50
617	1¢ deep green	5.00	3.25	2.75	4.00	2.50	1.75
618	2¢ carmine rose	9.00	6.00	4.00	6.00	4.50	3.50
619	5¢ dark blue . .	38.00	29.00	22.00	20.00	15.00	10.00

U.S. Postage #620-653

SCOTT NO.	DESCRIPTION	UNUSED O.G. VF	F	AVG	USED VF	F	AVG

620 *Sloop "Restaurationen"*

621 *Viking Ship*

1925 NORSE-AMERICAN ISSUE (NH + 40%)

Scott	Description	VF	F	AVG	VF	F	AVG
620-21	2¢-5¢ (2 varieties, complete) . . .	24.25	15.25	10.50	21.25	14.25	10.00
620	2¢ carmine & black	5.75	4.00	2.95	5.50	4.00	2.95
621	5¢ dark blue & black	20.00	12.00	8.25	17.00	11.00	7.75

622, 694 *Harrison*

623, 697 *Wilson*

1925-26 Flat Plate Printings, Perf. 11

622	13¢ green (1926)	24.00	15.00	11.00	1.35	.75	.60
623	17¢ black	28.00	17.00	13.00	.60	.40	.30

PLATE BLOCKS

SCOTT NO.	Description	UNUSED NH VF	F	AVG	UNUSED OG VF	F	AVG
610 (6)	2¢ black perf 11 flat	45.00	30.00	22.00	33.00	23.00	18.00
611 (6)	2¢ black imperf.	210.00	140.00	90.00	160.00	105.00	80.00
611 (4)	2¢ black center line block	110.00	85.00	60.00	77.50	60.00	45.00
611 (4)	2¢ black arrow block	58.00	45.00	32.50	45.00	35.00	25.00
612 (4)	2¢ black perf 10 rotary	500.00	370.00	300.00	390.00	275.00	210.00
614 (6)	1¢ dark green	80.00	54.00	40.00	60.00	39.00	25.00
615 (6)	2¢ carmine rose	150.00	90.00	65.00	110.00	75.00	55.00
616 (6)	5¢ dark blue	620.00	450.00	350.00	510.00	325.00	250.00
617 (6)	1¢ deep green	90.00	50.00	40.00	65.00	40.00	30.00
618 (6)	2¢ carmine rose	160.00	95.00	75.00	115.00	72.50	55.00
619 (6)	5¢ dark blue	510.00	395.00	300.00	410.00	315.00	220.00
620 (8)	2¢ carmine black	325.00	250.00	175.00	235.00	180.00	125.00
621 (8)	5¢ dark blue+black	1050.00	800.00	550.00	815.00	625.00	435.00
622 (6)	13¢ green (1926)	280.00	215.00	150.00	190.00	145.00	105.00
623 (6)	17¢ black	325.00	250.00	175.00	255.00	195.00	136.50

627 *Liberty Bell*

628 *John Ericsson Statue*

629 *Hamilton's Battery*

1926-27 COMMEMORATIVES (NH + 40%)

627/644	627-29, 643-44 (5 varieties, complete)	20.75	15.75	11.25	13.45	10.15	6.85

1926 COMMEMORATIVES

627	2¢ Sesquicentennial	4.00	3.00	2.25	.85	.65	.45
628	5¢ Ericsson Memorial	8.35	6.50	4.50	5.25	3.85	2.75
629	2¢ White Plains	2.95	2.25	1.55	2.55	1.95	1.25
630	White Plains Sheet of 25	600.00	450.00	360.00	550.00	475.00	400.00
630V	2¢ Dot over "S" variety . . .	615.00	475.00	360.00	575.00	500.00	425.00

Rotary Press Printings Designs of 1922-25 1926 Imperforate

631	1-1/2¢ yellow brown	2.65	2.00	1.50	2.40	1.75	1.20
631	1-1/2¢ center line block	26.00	20.00	13.50	......	......	......
631	1-1/2¢ arrow block	12.25	9.50	6.50	......	......	......

1926-28 Perf. 11 x 10 1/2

632/42	1¢-10¢ (632-34, 635-42) 11 varieties	26.75	20.50	15.25	2.60	2.10	1.55
632	1¢ green (1927)	.35	.25	.20	.25	.20	.15
632a	1¢ booklet pane of 6	5.75	4.50	3.35	......	......	......
633	1-1/2¢ yellow brown (1927)	2.95	2.25	1.55	.25	.20	.15
634	2¢ carmine (I)	.35	.25	.20	.25	.20	.15
634	Electric Eye Plate	5.50	4.25	2.75	......	......	......
634d	2¢ booklet pane of 6	2.15	1.65	1.15	......	......	......
634A	2¢ carmine (II) (1928)	450.00	325.00	210.00	24.50	16.50	11.00
635	3¢ violet (1927)	.55	.45	.30	.25	.20	.15
636	4¢ yellow brown (1927)	3.50	2.75	2.20	.25	.20	.15
637	5¢ dark blue (1927)	2.95	2.25	1.65	25	.20	.15
638	6¢ red orange (1927)	2.95	2.25	1.65	25	.20	.15
639	7¢ black (1927)	2.95	2.25	1.65	25	.20	.15
640	8¢ olive green (1927)	2.95	2.25	1.65	25	.20	.15
641	9¢ orange red (1931)	2.95	2.25	1.65	25	.20	.15
642	10¢ orange (1927)	5.75	4.50	3.35	.25	.20	.15

643

644

1927 COMMEMORATIVES

643	2¢ Vermont . .	1.75	1.35	.95	1.55	1.20	.85
644	2¢ Burgoyne .	4.75	3.60	2.60	3.95	3.00	1.95

645

646

647

648

649   650

1928 COMMEMORATIVES (NH + 40%)

645-50	6 varieties, complete	36.00	25.75	18.00	32.50	23.50	16.00
645	2¢ Valley Forge	1.30	1.00	.75	.70	.55	.40
646	2¢ Molly Pitcher	1.35	1.10	.85	1.40	1.10	.75
647	2¢ Hawaii	7.00	4.50	3.00	5.35	4.15	2.50
648	5¢ Hawaii . . .	19.00	13.75	9.50	18.25	14.00	9.50
649	2¢ Aeronautics	2.00	1.35	1.00	1.75	1.00	.70
650	5¢ Aeronautics	8.00	5.50	4.00	7.25	4.00	3.00

651

654-656

657

1929 COMMEMORATIVES (NH + 40%)

651/81	(651, 654-55, 657, 680-81) 6 varieties . . .	5.35	4.15	3.25	5.00	3.70	2.75
651	2¢ George R. Clark	1.00	.60	.50	1.00	.60	.50
	Same, arrow block of 4	4.50	3.35	2.35	......	......	......

1929 Design of 1922-25 Rotary Press Printing Perf. 11x10-1/2

653	1/2¢ olive brown	.30	.25	.20	.25	.20	.15

U.S. Postage #654-690

SCOTT NO.	DESCRIPTION	UNUSED O.G. VF	F	AVG	USED VF	F	AVG
	1929 COMMEMORATIVES						
654	2¢ Edison, Flat, Perf 11	1.10	.85	.65	1.15	.90	.65
655	2¢ Edison, Rotary, 11x10-1/2		.85	.65	.50	.40	.30	.20
656	2¢ Edison, Rotary Press Coil, Perf. 10 Vertically	17.50	13.50	9.00	2.95	2.25	1.35
657	2¢ Sullivan Expedition	1.10	.85	.65	.85	.65	.50
	1929. 632-42 Overprinted Kansas (NH + 50%)						
658-68	1¢-10¢ 11 varieties, complete	370.00	225.00	165.00	245.00	160.00	120.00
658	1¢ green	4.50	2.75	2.00	4.00	2.50	1.75
659	1-1/2¢ brown	6.50	4.50	2.75	5.00	3.00	2.75
660	2¢ carmine	6.50	4.25	2.75	2.00	1.25	.80
661	3¢ violet	32.50	22.00	14.50	22.00	14.00	10.50
662	4¢ yellow brown	29.00	18.50	13.75	15.00	9.75	5.50
663	5¢ deep blue	19.00	11.00	9.00	15.00	9.00	7.00
664	6¢ red orange	45.00	25.00	20.00	27.50	18.00	13.50
665	7¢ black	40.00	25.00	19.00	34.50	23.00	18.00
666	8¢ olive green	147.50	85.00	65.00	100.00	65.00	50.00
667	9¢ light rose	21.00	14.50	10.00	17.50	11.50	8.25
668	10¢ orange yellow	35.00	23.50	17.75	17.00	12.00	9.00
	1929. 632-42 Overprinted Nebraska (NH + 50%)						
669-79	1¢-10¢, 11 varieties, complete	460.00	310.00	215.00	220.00	140.00	97.50
669	1¢ green	6.00	4.00	2.50	3.00	1.90	1.35
670	1-1/2¢ brown	6.00	3.75	2.25	3.50	1.95	1.35
671	2¢ carmine	6.00	3.75	2.25	2.50	1.40	.90
672	3¢ violet	22.00	16.00	10.75	15.00	10.25	7.50
673	4¢ yellow brown	30.00	19.00	14.25	19.00	13.50	9.75
674	5¢ deep blue	25.00	17.50	11.75	22.00	14.00	9.50
675	6¢ red orange	60.00	42.00	31.00	36.00	22.00	15.50
676	7¢ black	35.00	22.50	16.00	26.00	16.00	11.75
677	8¢ olive green	55.00	34.50	21.75	35.00	22.00	15.00
678	9¢ light rose	60.00	37.00	25.50	38.50	23.00	15.75
679	10¢ orange yellow	185.00	125.00	85.00	34.50	21.00	15.00

SCOTT NO.		PLATE BLOCKS UNUSED NH VF	F	AVG.	UNUSED OG VF	F	AVG.
658	1¢ green	60.00	37.50	25.00	40.00	27.50	19.50
659	1-1/2¢ brown	75.00	49.50	30.00	55.00	35.00	22.50
660	2¢ carmine	70.00	45.00	30.00	49.50	33.00	22.50
661	3¢ violet	325.00	200.00	145.00	230.00	150.00	115.00
662	4¢ yellow brown	325.00	200.00	145.00	230.00	150.00	115.00
663	5¢ deep blue	260.00	165.00	120.00	185.00	120.00	90.00
664	6¢ red orange	725.00	450.00	325.00	510.00	330.00	220.00
665	7¢ black	725.00	475.00	325.00	525.00	350.00	250.00
666	8¢ olive green	1350.00	850.00	700.00	1000.00	650.00	475.00
667	9¢ light rose	300.00	195.00	120.00	225.00	150.00	100.00
668	10¢ orange yellow	525.00	325.00	235.00	390.00	260.00	175.00
669	1¢ green	70.00	45.00	35.00	47.50	30.00	20.00
670	1-1/2¢ brown	75.00	47.50	35.00	55.00	35.00	25.00
671	2¢ carmine	65.00	37.50	25.00	47.50	30.00	21.00
672	3¢ violet	280.00	175.00	120.00	230.00	165.00	110.00
673	4¢ yellow brown	350.00	230.00	180.00	245.00	160.00	115.00
674	5¢ deep blue	425.00	265.00	195.00	300.00	190.00	130.00
675	6¢ red orange	825.00	550.00	450.00	585.00	425.00	300.00
676	7¢ black	500.00	375.00	250.00	325.00	215.00	145.00
677	8¢ olive green	650.00	410.00	300.00	475.00	315.00	225.00
678	9¢ light rose	800.00	500.00	375.00	550.00	375.00	265.00
679	10¢ orange yellow	1600.00	1000.00	750.00	1150.00	800.00	600.00

SCOTT NO.	DESCRIPTION	UNUSED O.G. VF	F	AVG	USED VF	F	AVG

680   681

1929 COMMEMORATIVES (NH + 30%)

680	2¢ Fallen Timbers	1.20	.90	.65	1.05	.80	.55
681	2¢ Ohio River Canal	.80	.65	.50	.85	.65	.50

682   683   684, 686   685, 687

1930-31 COMMEMORATIVES

682/703	(682-83, 688-90, 702-03) 7 varieties, complete	5.50	4.10	3.10	5.35	4.15	2.85

1930 COMMEMORATIVES

682	2¢ Massachusetts Bay	.90	.70	.55	.70	.60	.40
683	2¢ Carolina-Charleston	1.65	1.30	1.00	1.75	1.35	1.00

1930 Rotary Press Printing Perf. 11 x 10-1/2 (NH + 30%)

684	1-1/2¢ Harding	.40	.30	.25	.25	.20	.15
685	4¢ Taft	1.05	.80	.50	.25	.20	.15

1930 Rotary Press Coil Stamps Perf. 10 Vertically

686	1-1/2¢ Harding	2.10	1.60	1.05	.25	.20	.15
687	4¢ Taft	4.25	3.35	2.25	.70	.55	.35

688   689   690

1930 COMMEMORATIVES

688	2¢ Braddock's Field	1.30	1.00	.65	1.45	1.00	.70
689	2¢ Von Steuben	.75	.60	.50	.70	.55	.40

1931 COMMEMORATIVES

690	2¢ Pulaski	.40	.30	.25	.25	.20	.15

SCOTT NO.		PLATE BLOCKS UNUSED NH VF	F	AVG.	UNUSED OG VF	F	AVG.
627 (6)	Sesquicentennial	65.00	50.00	35.00	49.50	38.00	26.00
628 (6)	5¢ Ericsson Memorial	145.00	110.00	77.50	110.00	85.00	60.00
629 (6)	2¢ White Plains	67.50	52.00	35.00	52.00	40.00	30.00
631	1-1/2¢ yellow brown	93.00	71.50	50.00	70.00	55.00	40.00
632	1¢ green	3.25	2.25	1.75	2.60	2.00	1.40
633	1-1/2¢ yellow brown (1927)	120.00	92.50	65.00	90.00	70.00	48.00
634	2¢ carmine (1)	2.60	1.95	1.40	2.10	1.70	1.25
635	3¢ violet	15.00	12.50	9.00	10.50	7.50	4.50
636	4¢ yellow brown (1927)	130.00	95.00	70.00	105.00	80.00	55.00
637	5¢ dark blue (1927)	29.50	22.50	15.75	22.75	17.50	12.75
638	6¢ red orange (1927)	29.50	22.50	15.75	22.75	17.50	12.75
639	7¢ black (1927)	29.50	22.50	15.75	22.75	17.50	12.75
640	8¢ olive green (1927)	29.50	22.50	15.75	22.75	17.50	12.75
641	9¢ orange red (1931)	30.00	23.00	16.00	23.00	18.00	13.00
642	10¢ orange (1927)	43.50	33.50	23.00	34.00	26.00	18.25
643 (6)	2¢ Vermont	65.00	50.00	35.00	58.00	42.00	28.00
644 (6)	2¢ Burgoyne	80.00	57.00	42.00	60.00	45.00	30.00
645 (6)	2¢ Valley Forge	58.00	40.00	28.00	41.00	30.00	19.50
646	2¢ Molly Pitcher	60.00	42.50	32.00	42.00	33.00	25.00
647	2¢ Hawaii	205.00	140.00	110.00	145.00	110.00	77.00
648	5¢ Hawaii	425.00	315.00	225.00	335.00	260.00	185.00
649 (6)	2¢ Aeronautics	24.00	18.00	12.00	19.50	14.00	10.00
650 (6)	5¢ Aeronautics	115.00	90.00	65.00	85.00	65.00	47.50
651 (6)	2¢ George R. Clark	19.50	15.00	10.00	14.50	11.00	7.50
653	1/2¢ olive brown	2.75	2.00	1.25	1.95	1.50	.95
654 (6)	2¢ Edison	51.00	39.50	28.00	40.00	31.50	22.50
655	2¢ Edison	70.00	55.00	40.00	58.00	45.00	30.50
657 (6)	2¢ Sullivan Expedition	45.00	35.00	26.50	39.50	30.00	22.50
	LINE PAIR						
656	2¢ Edison, coil	125.00	95.00	65.00	80.00	62.50	45.00

Need Blank Pages For Your Liberty Album?

See page 190 for a full listing of Harris Blank Pages for U.S. and Worldwide Albums.

U.S. Postage #692-725

SCOTT NO.		PLATE BLOCKS UNUSED NH			UNUSED OG		
		VF	F	AVG.	VF	F	AVG.
680 (6)	2¢ Fallen Timbers	48.00	35.00	22.50	36.00	27.50	21.00
681 (6)	2¢ Ohio River Canal	33.75	25.00	15.75	26.00	20.00	12.00
682 (6)	2¢ Massachusetts Bay	58.50	40.00	27.00	39.00	30.00	18.00
683 (6)	2¢ Carolina-Charleston	85.00	60.00	40.00	64.50	49.50	36.00
684	1-1/2¢ Harding	3.65	2.50	1.70	2.90	2.25	1.65
685	4¢ Taft	17.00	12.00	9.00	13.00	10.00	6.00
688 (6)	3¢ Braddock's Field	71.50	47.50	33.00	52.00	40.00	24.00
689 (6)	2¢ Von Steuben	40.00	31.50	18.00	32.50	25.00	15.00
690 (6)	2¢ Pulaski	23.50	17.00	10.75	18.25	14.00	8.50
		LINE PAIR					
686	1-1/2¢ Harding	15.00	10.75	7.50	10.00	8.00	6.00
687	4¢ Taft	24.75	19.00	11.50	20.00	14.00	9.00

SCOTT NO.	DESCRIPTION	UNUSED VF	F	AVG	USED VF	F	AVG
	1931 Designs of 1922-26. Rotary Press Printing. (NH + 35%)						
692-701	11¢ to 50¢ (10 varieties, complete)	136.00	104.00	77.50	3.25	2.50	1.80
	Perf. 11 x 10-1/2						
692	11¢ light blue	4.00	3.00	2.50	.25	.20	.15
693	12¢ brown violet	8.00	6.00	4.00	.25	.20	.15
694	13¢ yellow green	2.55	1.95	1.40	.35	.25	.15
695	14¢ dark blue	5.50	4.25	3.00	.90	.70	.50
696	15¢ gray	11.50	8.75	6.50	.25	.20	.15
	Perf. 10-1/2 x 11						
697	17¢ black	7.50	5.75	4.00	.45	.35	.25
698	20¢ carmine rose	12.50	9.50	7.00	.25	.20	.15
699	25¢ blue green	14.00	11.00	7.50	.25	.20	.15
700	30¢ brown	24.00	18.50	13.50	.25	.20	.15
701	50¢ lilac	53.50	41.50	33.50	.25	.20	.15

702

703

1931 COMMEMORATIVES
(NH + 30%)

702	2¢ Red Cross	.35	.25	.20	.25	.20	.15
702	2¢ arrow block	1.50	1.00	.65	......	......	......
703	2¢ Yorktown	.60	.40	.40	.60	.40	.30
703	2¢ center line block	3.00	2.15	1.75	......	......	......
703	2¢ arrow block	2.75	1.95	1.45	......	......	......

1932 WASHINGTON BICENTENNIAL ISSUE

Planning for this set, which celebrated the 200th anniversary of the birth of George Washington, began more than eight years before its release. Despite many suggestions that a pictorial series be created, the final set depicted 12 portraits of Washington at various stages of his life. For reasons of economy, the stamps were produced in single colors and in the same size as regular issues. Nevertheless, the set was an instant success and it was reported that more than a million covers were mailed from Washington, D.C. on January 1, 1932, the first day of issue.

704 705 706 707

708 709 710 711

712 713 714 715

SCOTT NO.	DESCRIPTION	UNUSED VF	F	AVG	USED VF	F	AVG
	(NH + 40%)						
704-15	1/2¢ to 10¢ (12 varieties, complete)	33.50	24.50	18.00	4.00	3.05	2.40
704	1/2¢ olive brown	.35	.25	.20	.25	.20	.15
705	1¢ green	.35	.25	.20	.25	.20	.15
706	1-1/2¢ brown	.60	.45	.20	.25	.20	.15
707	2¢ carmine rose	.35	.25	.20	.25	.20	.15
708	3¢ deep violet	.85	.65	.45	.25	.20	.15
709	4¢ light brown	.40	.30	.20	.25	.20	.15
710	5¢ blue	2.15	1.65	1.20	.30	.20	.15
711	6¢ red orange	5.00	3.75	2.95	.25	.20	.15
712	7¢ black	.40	.30	.20	.35	.25	.20
713	8¢ olive bistre	5.00	3.10	2.50	1.20	.85	.75
714	9¢ pale red	4.00	2.75	1.95	.40	.30	.25
715	10¢ orange yellow	16.00	12.00	8.50	.25	.20	.15

716 717 718 719

1932 COMMEMORATIVES
(NH + 30%)

716/25	(716-19, 724-25) 6 varieties	7.00	5.30	4.25	2.10	1.55	1.25
716	2¢ Winter Olympics	.65	.50	.35	.40	.30	.25
717	2¢ Arbor Day	.35	.25	.20	.25	.20	.15
718	3¢ Summer Olympics	2.10	1.60	1.35	.25	.20	.15
719	5¢ Summer Olympics	3.25	2.50	1.95	.40	.30	.25

720-722 723

724 725 726

1932 Rotary Press

720	3¢ deep violet	.35	.25	.20	.25	.20	.15
720b	3¢ booklet pane of 6	42.50	30.00	20.00	......	......	......
721	3¢ deep violet coil perf 10 vertically	3.60	2.75	1.90	.25	.20	.15
722	3¢ deep violet coil perf 10 horizontally	1.80	1.40	.90	1.00	.80	.65
723	6¢ Garfield, coil perf 10 vertically	13.00	10.00	6.75	.30	.25	.20

1932 COMMEMORATIVES

724	3¢ Penn	.50	.30	.25	.35	.25	.20
725	3¢ Webster	.75	.45	.35	.55	.40	.30

SCOTT NO.		UNUSED OG (NH + 30%) COIL LINE PAIRS			COIL PAIRS		
		VF	F	AVG.	VF	F	AVG.
686	1-1/2¢ Harding	10.00	8.00	5.50	4.50	3.00	2.00
687	4¢ Taft	20.00	15.00	10.00	8.50	6.50	4.50
721	3¢ deep violet perf 10 vertically	10.75	8.25	5.50	7.00	5.25	4.00
722	3¢ deep violet perf 10 horizontally	7.75	6.00	4.15	4.00	2.75	1.85
723	6¢ Garfield perf 10 vertically	71.50	55.00	33.00	25.00	19.25	13.25

U.S. Postage #726-751a

727, 752   728, 730, 766   729, 731, 767

SCOTT NO.	DESCRIPTION	UNUSED VF	F	AVG	USED VF	F	AVG
	1933 COMMEMORATIVES (NH + 30%)						
726/34	(726-29, 732-34) 7 varieties...	3.40	2.65	2.00	2.40	1.90	1.40
726	3¢ Oglethorpe	.70	.45	.35	.30	.25	.15
727	3¢ Washington's Headquarters	.30	.25	.20	.25	.20	.15
728	1¢ Fort Dearborn	.30	.25	.15	.25	.20	.15
729	3¢ Federal Building	.30	.25	.15	.25	.20	.15
	Special Printing for A.P.S. Convention Imperforate: Without Gum						
730	1¢ yellow green, sheet of 25...	....	36.00	....	....	33.00	....
730a	1¢ yellow green single	.85	.75	.45	.65	.50	.40
731	3¢ violet, sheet of 25	....	31.50	....	....	30.00	....
731a	3¢ violet, single	.65	.60	.45	.55	.45	.35

732   733, 735, 753, 768   734   736

732	3¢ N.R.A	.30	.25	.20	.25	.20	.15
733	3¢ Byrd	.80	.65	.55	.80	.60	.45
734	5¢ Kosciuszko	.90	.70	.55	.45	.35	.25
	1934 NATIONAL PHILATELIC EXHIBITION Imperforate Without Gum						
735	3¢ dark blue, sheet of 6	....	18.50	....	....	15.00	....
735a	3¢ dark blue, single	3.50	3.25	....	2.75	2.10	....

737, 738, 754   739, 755

	1934 COMMEMORATIVES (NH + 30%)						
736-39	4 varieties...	1.30	.90	.75	1.15	.90	.75
736	3¢ Maryland	.35	.25	.20	.30	.25	.20
737	3¢ Mother's Day, rotary, perf 11 x 10-1/2	.35	.25	.20	.30	.25	.20
738	3¢ Mother's Day, flat, perf 11	.35	.25	.20	.30	.25	.20
739	3¢ Wisconsin	.35	.25	.20	.30	.25	.20

FOR YOUR CONVENIENCE IN ORDERING, COMPLETE SETS ARE LISTED BEFORE SINGLE STAMP LISTINGS.

740, 751, 756, 769

742, 750, 758, 770

744, 750

746, 762

748, 764

741, 757

743, 759

745, 761

747, 763

749, 765

SCOTT NO.	DESCRIPTION	UNUSED VF	F	AVG	USED VF	F	AVG
	1934 NATIONAL PARKS ISSUE (NH + 30%)						
740-49	1¢-10¢ (10 varieties, complete)...	15.50	11.40	8.75	9.25	7.10	4.80
740	1¢ Yosemite	.30	.25	.20	.25	.20	.15
741	2¢ Grand Canyon	.30	.25	.20	.25	.20	.15
742	3¢ Mt. Rainier	.35	.25	.20	.25	.20	.15
743	4¢ Mesa Verde	.60	.45	.35	.60	.45	.30
744	5¢ Yellowstone	1.25	.90	.70	.85	.65	.45
745	6¢ Crater Lake	1.75	1.20	.85	1.45	1.10	.70
746	7¢ Acadia	1.10	.75	.55	1.15	.90	.60
747	8¢ Zion	2.95	2.25	1.60	2.75	2.10	1.45
748	9¢ Glacier	2.75	2.00	1.55	.85	.65	.45
749	10¢ Great Smoky Mountains	5.00	3.75	3.05	1.30	1.00	.65
	Special Printing for the A.P.S. Convention & Exhibition of Atlantic City Imperforate Souvenir Sheet (NH + 30%)						
750	3¢ deep violet, sheet of 6	....	45.00	....	....	40.00	....
750a	3¢ deep violet, single	6.50	5.50	....	6.00	5.00	....
	Special Printing for Trans-Mississippi Philatelic Exposition and Convention at Omaha Imperforate Souvenir Sheet (NH + 30%)						
751	1¢ green, sheet of 6	....	16.50	....	....	16.00	....
751a	1¢ green, single	2.75	2.25	....	2.75	2.25	....

U.S. Plate Blocks #692-749

SCOTT NO.		PLATE BLOCKS UNUSED NH			UNUSED OG		
		VF	F	AVG.	VF	F	AVG.
692	11¢ light blue	22.50	16.50	10.00	16.50	12.75	9.50
693	12¢ brown violet	47.50	32.50	20.00	33.00	25.00	19.75
694	13¢ yellow green	21.50	16.50	10.00	16.50	12.75	9.50
695	14¢ dark blue	32.00	24.00	15.00	23.00	17.50	12.50
696	15¢ grey	61.00	45.00	28.25	46.75	36.00	27.00
697	17¢ black	47.50	35.00	22.50	34.50	26.50	18.00
698	20¢ carmine rose	75.00	55.00	40.00	55.00	43.00	30.00
699	25¢ blue green	75.00	55.00	40.00	55.00	42.50	30.00
700	30¢ brown	115.00	80.00	55.00	84.50	65.00	39.00
701	50¢ lilac	335.00	250.00	155.00	250.00	195.00	115.00
702	2¢ Red Cross	4.00	3.00	2.00	3.00	2.50	1.75
703	2¢ Yorktown (4)	5.75	4.00	2.70	4.25	3.35	2.65
704-15	Washington Bicentennial	590.00	435.00	290.00	445.00	335.00	248.50
704	1/2¢ olive brown	7.50	5.00	3.50	5.50	4.00	3.00
705	1¢ green	7.50	5.00	3.50	5.75	4.50	3.25
706	1-1/2¢ brown	34.50	23.50	17.00	25.00	18.00	13.25
707	2¢ carmine rose	3.00	2.00	1.25	2.25	1.60	1.10
708	3¢ deep violet	25.00	18.50	12.50	21.00	15.00	10.50
709	4¢ light brown	11.50	8.00	6.00	8.50	6.00	4.50
710	5¢ blue	30.00	22.00	16.00	23.50	18.00	14.00
711	6¢ red orange	105.00	80.00	49.50	78.00	60.00	46.50
712	7¢ black	12.00	8.50	6.00	9.00	7.00	5.50
713	8¢ olive bistre	105.00	80.00	49.50	78.00	60.00	40.00
714	9¢ pale red	80.00	55.00	40.00	57.50	42.50	30.00
715	10¢ orange yellow	200.00	150.00	100.00	155.00	115.00	90.00
716 (6)	2¢ Winter Olympics	22.00	16.00	11.00	16.95	13.00	9.50
717	2¢ Arbor Day	14.00	10.50	6.50	10.75	8.25	6.00
718	3¢ Summer Olympics	30.00	22.50	15.00	21.00	15.00	11.00
719	5¢ Summer Olympics	45.00	35.00	25.00	35.00	28.00	20.00
720	3¢ deep violet	2.95	2.00	1.40	2.15	1.65	1.10
724 (6)	3¢ Penn	20.00	14.00	9.50	14.00	11.00	9.00
725 (6)	3¢ Daniel Webster	35.75	26.00	14.00	28.00	22.00	16.00
726 (6)	3¢ Oglethorpe	23.50	16.50	11.00	18.00	14.00	10.00
727	3¢ Washington Hdqrs	10.00	7.00	4.50	7.95	6.00	4.50
728	1¢ Fort Dearborn	3.55	2.75	1.65	2.95	2.25	1.65
729	2¢ Federal Building	6.00	4.00	2.75	4.25	3.35	2.25
732	3¢ N.R.A.	2.95	2.00	1.40	2.55	1.95	1.40
733 (6)	3¢ Byrd	27.50	20.00	13.00	21.00	16.00	13.00
734 (6)	3¢ Kosciuszko	60.00	45.00	28.00	42.95	33.00	25.00
736 (6)	3¢ Maryland	17.50	12.50	8.25	13.00	10.00	8.25
737	3¢ Mother's Day, rotary perf. 11 x 10-1/2	2.95	2.00	1.30	2.40	1.75	1.40
738 (6)	3¢ Mother's Day, flat, perf. 11	8.50	6.50	3.95	6.50	5.00	3.85
739 (6)	3¢ Wisconsin	7.00	5.00	3.25	5.75	4.50	3.25
740-49	10 varieties complete	210.00	160.00	96.50	160.00	125.00	94.00
740 (6)	1¢ Yosemite	2.55	1.80	1.15	2.00	1.55	1.10
741 (6)	2¢ Grand Canyon	2.65	1.95	1.25	2.15	1.65	1.20
742 (6)	3¢ Mt. Rainier	3.50	2.75	1.65	3.00	2.30	1.55
743 (6)	4¢ Mesa Verde	15.50	12.00	7.25	13.00	10.00	7.00
744 (6)	5¢ Yellowstone	19.50	15.00	9.00	14.00	11.00	8.25
745 (6)	6¢ Crater Lake	33.50	26.00	15.50	26.50	20.50	15.50
746 (6)	7¢ Acadia	21.50	16.50	10.00	17.25	13.25	10.00
747 (6)	8¢ Zion	33.50	26.00	15.50	26.50	20.50	15.50
748 (6)	9¢ Glacier	33.50	26.00	15.50	26.50	20.50	15.50
749 (6)	10¢ Great Smoky Mountains	53.50	41.25	24.75	39.00	30.00	23.50

SELECTED U.S. COMMEMORATIVE MINT SHEETS

SCOTT NO.	F/NH SHEET	SCOTT NO.	F/NH SHEET
610 (100)	130.00	709 (100)	40.00
614 (50)	255.00	710 (100)	235.00
615 (50)	450.00	711 (100)	490.00
617 (50)	280.00	712 (100)	40.00
618 (50)	420.00	713 (100)	500.00
620 (100)	825.00	714 (100)	400.00
627 (50)	230.00	715 (100)	1750.00
628 (50)	595.00	716 (100)	67.50
629 (100)	365.00	717 (100)	26.00
643 (100)	285.00	718 (100)	195.00
644 (50)	290.00	719 (100)	305.00
645 (100)	175.00	724 (100)	50.00
646 (100)	180.00	725 (100)	82.50
647 (100)	665.00	726 (100)	55.00
648 (100)	1850.00	727 (100)	22.00
649 (50)	85.00	728 (100)	15.00
650 (50)	420.00	729 (100)	22.00
651 (50)	46.50	732 (100)	14.00
654 (100)	130.00	733 (50)	50.00
655 (100)	140.00	734 (100)	110.00
657 (100)	135.00	736 (100)	33.00
680 (100)	140.00	737 (50)	9.00
681 (100)	120.00	738 (50)	15.00
682 (100)	110.00	739 (50)	15.00
683 (100)	205.00	740-49 set	665.00
688 (100)	155.00	740 (50)	6.50
689 (100)	82.50	741 (50)	9.00
690 (100)	45.00	742 (50)	13.00
702 (100)	20.00	743 (50)	33.50
703 (50)	28.00	744 (50)	55.00
704-15 set	3485.00	745 (50)	85.00
704 (100)	16.50	746 (50)	46.50
705 (100)	21.50	747 (50)	120.00
706 (100)	71.50	748 (50)	115.00
707 (100)	14.00	749 (50)	215.00
708 (100)	90.00		

THE FARLEY PERIOD

The 1933-35 period was one of great excitement for the hobby. With a stamp collector in the White House, in the person of President Franklin Delano Roosevelt, it was a period during which special Souvenir Sheets were issued for the A.P.S. Convention in 1933 (catalog #730) and the National Philatelic Exhibition in 1934 (#735). Collectors gloried in the limelight.

But there was a darker side, in the form of rare imperforate sheets that were being released to then Postmaster General James A. Farley, President Roosevelt himself, and a few other prominent personages. The protests against the practice grew to unmanageable proportions when word got around that one of the imperforate sheets of the 1934 Mother's Day issue had been offered to a stamp dealer for $20,000. Adding insult to injury, it was learned shortly thereafter that not only were there individual sheets floating around, but full, uncut sheets also had been presented as gifts to a fortunate few.

The outcry that followed could not be stifled. Congress had become involved in the affair and the demands were mounting that the gift sheets be recalled and destroyed. This being deemed impractical or undesirable, another solution was found—one that comes down to us today in the form of "The Farleys".

The solution was to let everyone "share the wealth", so to speak. Instead of recalling the few sheets in existence, additional quantities of the imperforates were issued in the same full sheet form as the gift sheets. Naturally, this step substantially reduced the value of the original, very limited edition, but it satisfied most collectors and left as its legacy "The Farley Issues".

The Farleys were issued March 15, 1935, and consisted of reprints of 20 issues. They remained on sale for three months, a relatively short time by most standards, but more than enough time for collectors who really cared. Although purists felt then—and some still do now—that President Roosevelt would have saved collectors a considerable sum by having the first few sheets destroyed, the issue has provided us with a wondrous selection of Gutters and Lines, arrow blocks, single sheets and full panes.

The collector on a limited budget can fill the spaces in an album with single imperforates. But the Farleys are such an interesting study that owning and displaying at least one of each variety of any one issue is a must. We illustrate here one of the full sheets of the 1 cent Century of Progress Farley Issue. The full sheets consisted of nine panes of 25 stamps each. The individual panes were separated by wide horizontal (**A**) or vertical (**B**) gutters and the gutters of four adjacent sheets formed a cross gutter (**C**).

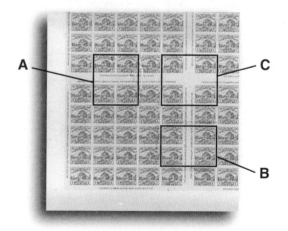

NOTE: For #s 753-765 and 771, lines separated the individual panes. The lines ended in arrows at the top, bottom and side margins.

U.S. Postage #752-784

1935 "FARLEY SPECIAL PRINTINGS"
Designs of 1933-34 Imperforate (#752, 753 Perf.) Without Gum

SCOTT NO.		PLATE BLOCK	CENTER LINE BLOCK	ARROW BLOCK T OR B	ARROW BLOCK L OR R	PAIR WITH V. LINE	PAIR WITH H. LINE	FINE UNUSED	USED
752-71	20 varieties, complete	......	470.00	......	......	135.00	91.50	35.00	29.75
752	3¢ Newburgh	16.00	50.00	16.50	9.50	7.50	4.50	.25	.20
753	3¢ Byrd	(6)19.00	95.00	90.00	4.00	42.50	1.65	.75	.75
754	3¢ Mother's Day	(6)19.00	9.50	4.00	4.25	1.65	1.75	.75	.65
755	3¢ Wisconsin	(6)19.00	9.50	4.00	4.25	1.65	1.75	.75	.65
756-65	1¢-10¢ Parks (10 varieties, complete)	295.00	150.00	140.00	140.00	42.25	43.50	19.50	17.00
756	1¢ Yosemite	(6) 5.00	4.00	1.40	1.10	.60	.50	.30	.25
757	2¢ Grand Canyon	(6) 6.50	5.50	1.55	1.45	.65	.85	.40	.30
758	3¢ Mt. Rainier	(6)16.50	6.50	3.60	4.00	1.55	1.75	.75	.65
759	4¢ Mesa Verde	(6)22.00	11.00	6.00	7.00	2.50	3.10	1.50	1.35
760	5¢ Yellowstone	(6)27.50	16.50	12.00	10.50	5.25	4.75	2.50	2.00
761	6¢ Crater Lake	(6)45.00	22.00	15.00	16.50	6.50	7.50	3.00	2.75
762	7¢ Acadia	(6)36.00	18.00	10.50	12.25	4.50	5.50	2.25	2.00
763	8¢ Zion	(6)45.00	20.00	14.50	12.00	6.25	5.35	2.75	2.25
764	9¢ Glacier	(6)50.00	22.00	13.00	5.75	5.75	6.50	3.00	2.50
765	10¢ Great Smoky Mountains	(6)57.50	33.00	25.00	22.00	11.00	10.00	5.00	4.25
766a-70a	5 varieties, complete	......	80.00	......	......	40.00	35.50	9.45	7.75
766a	1¢ Fort Dearborn	......	16.50	......	......	9.00	6.50	.75	.45
767a	3¢ Federal Building	......	16.50	......	......	9.00	6.50	.75	.45
768a	3¢ Byrd	......	19.00	......	......	7.75	6.50	3.00	2.75
769a	1¢ Yosemite	......	11.00	......	......	5.25	5.00	1.85	1.50
770a	3¢ Mt. Rainier	......	28.00	......	......	11.50	13.00	3.60	3.05
771	16¢ Air Post Special Delivery	(6)80.00	82.50	15.00	16.50	6.75	7.50	3.00	2.75

U.S. FARLEY ISSUE COMPLETE MINT SHEETS

SCOTT NO.	F/NH SHEET	SCOTT NO.	F/NH SHEET
752-71 set	7300.00	762 (200)	420.00
752 (400)	335.00	763 (200)	525.00
753 (200)	635.00	764 (200)	575.00
754 (200)	190.00	765 (200)	900.00
755 (200)	190.00	766 (225)	400.00
756-65 set	3395.00	767 (225)	400.00
756 (200)	67.50	768 (150)	550.00
757 (200)	70.00	769 (120)	240.00
758 (200)	160.00	770 (120)	600.00
759 (200)	280.00	771 (200)	725.00
761 (200)	575.00		

SCOTT NO.	DESCRIPTION	FIRST DAY COVERS SING	FIRST DAY COVERS PL. BLK.	MINT SHEET	PLATE BLOCK F/NH	UNUSED F/NH	USED F

772, 778a

773, 778b

774

775, 778c

1935-36 COMMEMORATIVES

SCOTT NO.	DESCRIPTION	FDC SING	FDC PL.BLK	MINT SHEET	PLATE BLOCK F/NH	UNUSED F/NH	USED F
772/84	(772-77, 782-84) 9 varieties	......	......	......	......	3.60	1.70
772	3¢ Connecticut	12.00	19.50	16.50 (50)	2.25	.40	.20
773	3¢ San Diego	12.00	19.50	16.50 (50)	1.85	.40	.20
774	3¢ Boulder Dam	12.00	19.50	16.50 (50)	(6)2.75	.40	.20
775	3¢ Michigan	12.00	19.50	16.50 (50)	1.85	.40	.20

SCOTT NO.	DESCRIPTION	FIRST DAY COVERS SING	FIRST DAY COVERS PL. BLK.	MINT SHEET	PLATE BLOCK F/NH	UNUSED F/NH	USED F

776, 778d

777

1936 COMMEMORATIVE

776	3¢ Texas	15.00	25.00	16.50 (50)	1.85	.40	.20
777	3¢ Rhode Island	12.00	19.50	25.00 (50)	3.00	.60	.20

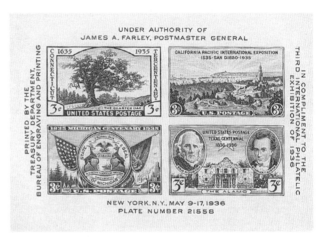

778

782

783

784

1936 THIRD INTERNATIONAL PHILATELIC EXHIBITION
"TIPEX" Imperforate Souvenir Sheet
Designs of 772, 773, 775, 776

778	red violet, sheet of 4	16.50	......	......	......	4.00	4.00
778a	3¢ Connecticut	......	......	......	......	1.00	.95
778b	3¢ San Diego	......	......	......	......	1.00	.95
778c	3¢ Michigan	......	......	......	......	1.00	.95
778d	3¢ Texas	......	......	......	......	1.00	.95
782	3¢ Arkansas Statehood	12.00	19.50	20.00 (50)	1.95	.40	.20
783	3¢ Oregon Territory	12.00	19.50	14.50 (50)	1.75	.40	.20
784	3¢ Suffrage for Women	12.00	19.50	30.00 (100)	1.75	.40	.20

FIRST DAY COVERS:

First Day Covers are envelopes cancelled on the "First Day of Issue" of the stamp used on an envelope. Usually they also contain a picture (cachet) on the left side designed to go with the theme of the stamp. From 1935 to 1949, prices listed are for cacheted, addressed covers. From 1950 to date, prices are for cacheted, unaddressed covers.

U.S. Postage #785-802

785

786

787

788

789

1936-37 ARMY AND NAVY ISSUE

SCOTT NO.	DESCRIPTION	FIRST DAY COVERS SING	PL. BLK.	MINT SHEET	PLATE BLOCK F/NH	UNUSED F/NH	USED F
785-94	10 varieties, complete .	57.50	......	......	59.00	5.50	2.30

ARMY COMMEMORATIVES

785	1¢ green	6.00	12.00	15.00 (50)	1.60	.40	.20
786	2¢ carmine	6.00	12.00	15.00 (50)	1.60	.40	.20
787	3¢ purple	6.00	12.00	25.00 (50)	2.75	.60	.20
788	4¢ gray	6.00	14.50	40.00 (50)	12.00	.60	.30
789	5¢ ultramarine	7.00	14.50	50.00 (50)	13.50	1.00	.30

790

791

792

793

794

NAVY COMMEMORATIVES

790	1¢ green	6.00	12.00	9.00 (50)	1.40	.25	.20
791	2¢ carmine	6.00	12.00	14.00 (50)	1.60	.35	.20
792	3¢ purple	6.00	12.00	18.50 (50)	2.50	.50	.20
793	4¢ gray	6.00	14.50	45.00 (50)	12.00	.75	.30
794	5¢ ultramarine	7.00	14.50	50.00 (50)	13.50	1.00	.35

795

796

1937 COMMEMORATIVES

SCOTT NO.	DESCRIPTION	FIRST DAY COVERS SING	PL. BLK.	MINT SHEET	PLATE BLOCK F/NH	UNUSED F/NH	USED F
795/802	(795-96, 798-802) 7 varieties	......	......	......	......	3.00	1.40
795	3¢ Northwest Ordinance	8.50	16.00	16.50 (50)	1.80	.45	.20
796	5¢ Virginia Dare	8.50	16.00	25.00 (48)	10.00(6)	.45	.30

797

1937 S.P.A. CONVENTION ISSUE
Design of 749 Imperforate Souvenir Sheet

797	10¢ blue green	8.50	......	......	......	1.10	.80

798

799

800

801

802

798	3¢ Constitution	10.00	16.00	37.50 (50)	4.00	.95	.20
799	3¢ Hawaii	10.00	16.00	12.50 (50)	1.85	.35	.20
800	3¢ Alaska	10.00	16.00	12.50 (50)	1.85	.35	.20
801	3¢ Puerto Rico	10.00	16.00	12.50 (50)	1.85	.35	.20
802	3¢ Virgin Islands	10.00	16.00	12.50 (50)	1.85	.35	.20

U.S. Postage #803-834

1938 Presidential Series

In 1938 a new set of definitive stamps was issued honoring the first 29 presidents, Ben Franklin, Martha Washington, and the White House. These were regular issues that effectively replaced the previous definitive issues of the 1922-25 series.

The "Presidential Series" contained 32 denominations ranging from 1/2¢-$5.00. It is an interesting series because various printing methods were employed. The 1/2¢-50¢ values were printed in single colors on rotary presses using both normal and "electric eye" plates. The $1.00 to $5.00 values were printed in two colors on flat plate presses.

The $1.00 value was reprinted twice, once in 1951 on revenue paper watermarked "USIR" (#832b) and again in 1954. The 1954 issue was "dry printed" on thick white paper, with an experimental colorless gum (832c).

This series in regular and coil form was used for 16 years until it was replaced by the new definitive issues of 1954.

SCOTT NO.	DESCRIPTION	FIRST DAY COVERS SING	FIRST DAY COVERS PL. BLK.	MINT SHEET	PLATE BLOCK F/NH	UNUSED F/NH	USED F
	1938 PRESIDENTIAL SERIES						
803-34	1/2¢-$5, 32 varieties, complete	520.00	....	....	900.00	200.00	17.50
803-31	1/2¢-50¢, 29 varieties	110.00	....	....	225.00	50.00	5.90
803	1/2¢ Franklin	2.50	5.50	15.00(100)	1.00	.20	.15
804	1¢ G. Washington	2.50	5.50	20.00(100)	1.00	.25	.15
804b	1¢ booklet pane of 6	14.00	....	....	....	2.25	....
805	1-1/2¢ M. Washington	2.50	5.50	20.00(100)	1.00	.25	.15
806	2¢ J. Adams	2.50	5.50	20.00(100)	1.00	.25	.15
806	E.E. Plate Block of 10	....	....	....	5.00	....	....
806b	2¢ booklet pane of 6	14.00	....	....	....	4.50	....
807	3¢ Jefferson	2.50	5.50	20.00(100)	1.00	.25	.15
807	E.E. Plate Block of 10	....	....	....	28.00	....	....
807a	3¢ booklet pane of 6	14.00	....	....	....	8.25	....
808	4¢ Madison	2.50	5.50	110.00(100)	5.25	1.10	.15
809	4-1/2¢ White House	2.50	5.50	25.00(100)	1.60	.30	.20
810	5¢ J. Monroe	2.50	5.50	30.00(100)	1.75	.35	.15
811	6¢ J.Q. Adams	2.50	5.50	47.50(100)	2.25	.55	.15
812	7¢ A. Jackson	2.50	5.50	47.50(100)	2.25	.55	.15
813	8¢ Van Buren	2.50	5.50	47.50(100)	2.35	.55	.15
814	9¢ Harrison	2.50	5.50	50.00(100)	2.50	.55	.15
815	10¢ Tyler	2.50	5.50	37.50(100)	2.00	.45	.15
816	11¢ Polk	3.75	6.75	85.00(100)	5.00	1.00	.15
817	12¢ Taylor	3.75	6.75	165.00(100)	8.25	2.00	.15
818	13¢ Fillmore	3.75	6.75	185.00(100)	8.50	2.00	.15
819	14¢ Pierce	3.75	6.75	165.00(100)	8.25	2.00	.15
820	15¢ Buchanan	3.75	6.75	65.00(100)	3.50	.75	.15
821	16¢ Lincoln	4.50	8.25	165.00(100)	8.25	2.00	.55
822	17¢ Johnson	4.50	8.25	165.00(100)	8.25	2.00	.20
823	18¢ Grant	4.50	8.25	240.00(100)	11.00	2.50	.25
824	19¢ Hayes	4.50	8.25	210.00(100)	11.00	2.50	.75
825	20¢ Garfield	4.75	11.25	110.00(100)	5.50	1.25	.15
826	21¢ Arthur	5.25	11.25	250.00(100)	12.00	2.75	.25
827	22¢ Cleveland	5.25	11.25	165.00(100)	13.50	2.00	.75
828	24¢ B. Harrison	6.25	11.25	550.00(100)	27.50	6.00	.25
829	25¢ McKinley	6.25	13.75	105.00(100)	5.50	1.20	.15
830	30¢ T. Roosevelt	8.50	13.75	650.00(100)	32.50	7.50	.15
831	50¢ Taft	15.00	30.00	950.00(100)	45.00	10.00	.15
	Flat Plate Printing Perf. 11						
832	$1 Wilson	70.00	150.00	1150.00(100)	55.00	12.00	.15
832	$1 center line block	....	....	....	55.00	....	....
832	$1 arrow block	....	....	....	50.00	....	....
832b	$1 Watermarked "USIR"	....	....	....	....	325.00	70.00
832c	$1 dry print thick paper (1954)	35.00	75.00	725.00(100)	32.50	7.25	.15
833	$2 Harding	135.00	275.00	....	140.00	26.00	6.50
833	$2 center line block	....	....	....	115.00	....	....
833	$2 arrow block	....	....	....	110.00	....	....
834	$5 Coolidge	225.00	400.00	....	525.00	120.00	6.00
834	$5 center line block	....	....	....	525.00	....	....
834	$5 arrow block	....	....	....	500.00	....	....

U.S. Postage #835-868

835

836

837

838

1938-39 COMMEMORATIVES

Scott No.	Description	FDC Sing	FDC Pl. Blk.	Mint Sheet	Plate Block F/NH	Unused F/NH	Used F
835-58	(835-38, 852-58) 11 varieties, complete	....	....	....	....	7.75	2.15
835	3¢ Ratification	10.00	14.00	35.00(50)	7.50	.80	.20
836	3¢ Swedes-Finns	10.00	14.00	14.00(48)	(6)4.00	.35	.20
837	3¢ Northwest Territory	10.00	14.00	35.00(100)	11.50	.35	.20
838	3¢ Iowa Territory	10.00	14.00	24.00(50)	8.50	.35	.20

1939 PRESIDENTIALS ROTARY PRESS COIL

Scott No.	Description	FDC Sing	FDC Pl. Blk.	Line Pair	Line Pair	Unused F/NH	Used F
839-51	13 varieties, complete	67.50	120.00	....	148.50	36.75	5.30

Perforated 10 Vertically

839	1¢ G. Washington	5.00	8.50	....	1.40	.40	.15
840	1-1/2¢ M. Washington	5.00	8.50	....	1.65	.40	.15
841	2¢ J. Adams	5.00	8.50	....	1.75	.40	.15
842	3¢ T. Jefferson	5.00	8.50	....	2.00	.70	.15
843	4¢ J. Madison	5.75	10.50	....	32.50	8.00	.55
844	4-1/2¢ White House	5.75	10.50	....	6.25	.70	.50
845	5¢ J. Monroe	5.75	11.00	....	30.00	5.50	.50
846	6¢ J.Q. Adams	5.75	11.00	....	8.00	1.75	.20
847	10¢ J. Tyler	8.50	16.00	....	50.00	12.00	.90

Perforated 10 Horizontally

848	1¢ G. Washington	5.00	8.50	....	3.75	1.10	.20
849	1-1/2¢ M. Washington	5.00	8.50	....	5.00	1.75	.65
850	2¢ J. Adams	5.00	8.50	....	7.50	3.25	.75
851	3¢ T. Jefferson	5.00	8.50	....	7.00	2.75	.75

852

853

854

855   856

1939 COMMEMORATIVES

852	3¢ Golden Gate	12.00	19.50	15.00(50)	2.00	.40	.20
853	3¢ World's Fair	12.00	19.50	18.00(50)	2.75	.50	.20
854	3¢ Inauguration	12.00	19.50	55.00(50)	(6)8.00	1.10	.20
855	3¢ Baseball	37.50	60.00	150.00(50)	14.00	3.00	.30
856	3¢ Panama Canal	17.50	25.00	25.00(50)	(6)5.00	.60	.20

857

858

1939 COMMEMORATIVES

857	3¢ Printing	12.00	19.50	14.00(50)	1.75	.35	.20
858	3¢ Four States	10.00	14.50	14.00(50)	2.00	.35	.20

859

860

861

862

863

1940 FAMOUS AMERICANS ISSUES

859-93	35 varieties, complete	130.00	....	....	500.00	50.00	23.50

American Authors

859	1¢ Washington Irving	3.00	4.00	20.00(70)	1.75	.35	.20
860	2¢ James F. Cooper	3.00	4.00	20.00(70)	1.75	.35	.20
861	3¢ Ralph W. Emerson	3.00	4.00	22.50(70)	1.85	.35	.20
862	5¢ Louisa May Alcott	4.00	6.00	40.00(70)	13.00	.50	.35
863	10¢ Samuel L. Clemens	7.50	13.50	180.00(70)	52.50	2.50	2.00

864

865

866

867

868

American Poets

864	1¢ Henry W. Longfellow	3.00	4.00	20.00(70)	2.75	.35	.20
865	2¢ John Whittier	3.00	4.00	20.00(70)	2.75	.35	.20
866	3¢ James Lowell	3.00	4.00	22.50(70)	3.25	.35	.20
867	5¢ Walt Whitman	4.00	6.00	50.00(70)	15.00	.80	.35
868	10¢ James Riley	7.50	11.50	225.00(70)	60.00	3.50	2.50

U.S. Postage #869-895

SCOTT NO.	DESCRIPTION	FIRST DAY COVERS SING	FIRST DAY COVERS PL. BLK.	MINT SHEET	PLATE BLOCK F/NH	UNUSED F/NH	USED F

869   870   871

872   873

American Educators

869	1¢ Horace Mann ...	3.00	4.00	20.00(70)	3.50	.35	.20
870	2¢ Mark Hopkins ...	3.00	4.00	20.00(70)	1.75	.35	.20
871	3¢ Charles W. Eliot .	3.00	4.00	22.50(70)	4.00	.40	.20
872	5¢ Frances Willard .	4.00	6.00	55.00(70)	17.50	.75	.35
873	10¢ Booker T. Washington	9.50	13.50	200.00(70)	42.50	3.50	2.00

874   875   876

877   878

American Scientists

874	1¢ John J. Audubon .	3.00	4.00	20.00(70)	1.75	.35	.20
875	2¢ Dr. Crawford Long	3.00	4.00	20.00(70)	1.75	.35	.20
876	3¢ Luther Burbank .	3.00	4.00	22.50(70)	1.85	.40	.20
877	5¢ Dr. Walter Reed .	4.00	6.00	35.00(70)	9.00	.45	.35
878	10¢ Jane Addams ..	6.00	11.50	145.00(70)	30.00	2.25	1.30

879   880   881

882   883

American Composers

879	1¢ Stephen Foster .	3.00	4.00	20.00(70)	1.75	.35	.20
880	2¢ John Philip Sousa	3.00	4.00	20.00(70)	1.75	.35	.20
881	3¢ Victor Herbert ...	3.00	4.00	20.00(70)	1.75	.35	.20
882	5¢ Edward A. MacDowell	4.00	6.00	47.50(70)	14.00	.75	.35
883	10¢ Ethelbert Nevin .	6.00	11.50	370.00(70)	50.00	6.00	2.10

884   885   886

887   888

American Artists

884	1¢ Gilbert Stuart ...	3.00	4.00	20.00(70)	1.75	.40	.20
885	2¢ James Whistler .	3.00	4.00	20.00(70)	1.75	.35	.20
886	3¢ A. Saint-Gaudens	3.00	4.00	22.50(70)	1.75	.40	.20
887	5¢ Daniel C. French .	4.00	6.00	55.00(70)	12.50	1.00	.35
888	10¢ Frederic Remington	6.00	11.50	195.00(70)	40.00	3.00	2.00

889   890   891

892   893

American Inventors

889	1¢ Eli Whitney	3.00	4.00	20.00(70)	3.00	.40	.20
890	2¢ Samuel Morse ..	3.00	4.00	20.00(70)	1.75	.40	.20
891	3¢ Cyrus McCormick	3.00	4.00	32.50(70)	2.50	.55	.15
892	5¢ Elias Howe	4.00	6.00	120.00(70)	20.00	1.75	.20
893	10¢ Alexander G. Bell	8.00	20.00	1150.00(70)	105.00	18.00	3.50

894   895

1940 COMMEMORATIVES

894-902	9 varieties, complete	......	......	......	......	3.55	1.45
894	3¢ Pony Express ...	7.00	11.00	24.00(50)	4.50	.60	.25
895	3¢ Pan Am Union ..	5.00	11.00	24.00(50)	4.50	.60	.20

MINT SHEETS: From 1935 to date, we list prices for standard size Mint Sheets in Fine, Never Hinged condition. The number of stamps in each sheet is noted in ( ).

FAMOUS AMERICANS: Later additions to the Famous American series include #945 Edison, #953 Carver, #960 White, #965 Stone, #975 Rogers, #980 Harris, #986 Poe, and #988 Gompers.

U.S. Postage #896-921

1940 COMMEMORATIVES

Scott No.	Description	FDC Sing	FDC Pl. Blk.	Mint Sheet	Plate Block F/NH	Unused F/NH	Used F
896	3¢ Idaho Statehood	5.00	11.00	17.50(50)	3.00	.35	.20
897	3¢ Wyoming Statehood	5.00	11.00	20.00(50)	2.25	.40	.20
898	3¢ Coronado Expedition	5.00	11.00	20.00(52)	2.25	.40	.20

NATIONAL DEFENSE ISSUE

Scott No.	Description	FDC Sing	FDC Pl. Blk.	Mint Sheet	Plate Block F/NH	Unused F/NH	Used F
899	1¢ Liberty	4.00	7.00	20.00(100)	.65	.30	.15
900	2¢ Gun	4.00	7.00	20.00(100)	.65	.30	.15
901	3¢ Torch	4.00	7.00	22.50(100)	.85	.30	.15
902	3¢ Emancipation	9.00	11.00	27.50(50)	4.75	.50	.35

1941-43 COMMEMORATIVES

Scott No.	Description	FDC Sing	FDC Pl. Blk.	Mint Sheet	Plate Block F/NH	Unused F/NH	Used F
903-08	3¢-5¢ six varieties	....	....	....	....	3.10	.90

1941 COMMEMORATIVES

903	3¢ Vermont	7.00	10.75	22.50(50)	2.25	.40	.20

1942 COMMEMORATIVES

904	3¢ Kentucky	5.00	10.75	18.00(50)	1.85	.35	.20
905	3¢ Win The War	4.50	7.50	24.00(100)	1.00	.30	.15
906	5¢ China Resistance	12.00	20.00	95.00(50)	20.00	1.75	.35

1943 COMMEMORATIVES

907	2¢ Allied Nations	4.50	7.50	15.00(100)	1.00	.30	.15
908	1¢ Four Freedoms	5.00	10.50	15.00(100)	1.00	.30	.15

1943-44 OVERRUN COUNTRIES SERIES

Scott No.	Description	FDC Sing	FDC Pl. Blk.	Mint Sheet	Plate Block F/NH	Unused F/NH	Used F
909-21	13 varieties, complete	50.00	....	....	72.50	6.00	2.85
909	5¢ Poland	5.00	11.75	21.50(50)	8.00	.40	.20
910	5¢ Czechoslovakia	4.00	9.00	17.50(50)	4.00	.40	.20
911	5¢ Norway	4.00	9.00	15.00(50)	2.75	.40	.20
912	5¢ Luxembourg	4.00	9.00	15.00(50)	1.85	.40	.20
913	5¢ Netherlands	4.00	9.00	15.00(50)	1.85	.40	.20
914	5¢ Belgium	4.00	9.00	15.00(50)	1.85	.40	.20
915	5¢ France	4.00	9.00	15.00(50)	1.85	.40	.20
916	5¢ Greece	4.00	9.00	45.00(50)	17.50	1.10	.40
917	5¢ Yugoslavia	4.00	9.00	27.50(50)	8.00	.60	.25
918	5¢ Albania	4.00	9.00	25.00(50)	8.00	.60	.25
919	5¢ Austria	4.00	9.00	20.00(50)	6.00	.40	.25
920	5¢ Denmark	4.00	9.00	27.50(50)	8.00	.60	.25
921	5¢ Korea (1944)	4.00	9.00	17.50(50)	7.00	.40	.25

U.S. Postage #922-947

SCOTT NO.	DESCRIPTION	FIRST DAY COVERS SING	FIRST DAY COVERS PL. BLK.	MINT SHEET	PLATE BLOCK F/NH	UNUSED F/NH	USED F

1944 COMMEMORATIVES

SCOTT NO.	DESCRIPTION	SING	PL. BLK.	MINT SHEET	PLATE BLOCK	UNUSED	USED
922-26	5 varieties					1.90	.95
922	3¢ Railroad	5.00	7.50	20.00(50)	2.25	.40	.20
923	3¢ Steamship	4.00	6.00	20.00(50)	2.25	.40	.20
924	3¢ Telegraph	4.00	6.00	15.00(50)	1.40	.40	.20
925	3¢ Corregidor	4.00	6.00	17.50(50)	1.50	.40	.20
926	3¢ Motion Picture	4.00	6.00	20.00(50)	1.50	.40	.20

1945-46 COMMEMORATIVES

927-38	1¢-5¢ (12 varieties, complete)					3.50	2.25
927	3¢ Florida	4.00	6.00	15.00(50)	1.00	.30	.20
928	5¢ Peace Conference	5.00	7.00	15.00(50)	1.00	.30	.20
929	3¢ Iwo Jima	12.50	15.00	30.00(50)	3.50	.40	.20

930	1¢ FDR & Hyde Park	4.00	6.00	6.00(50)	1.00	.30	.20
931	2¢ FDR & "Little White House"	4.00	6.00	8.50(50)	1.00	.30	.20
932	3¢ FDR & White House	4.00	6.00	10.00(50)	1.00	.30	.20
933	5¢ FDR & Globe (1946)	4.00	6.00	15.00(50)	1.25	.35	.20

934	3¢ Army	6.00	8.00	12.50(50)	1.00	.30	.20
935	3¢ Navy	6.00	8.00	15.00(50)	1.00	.30	.20
936	3¢ Coast Guard	6.00	8.00	12.00(50)	1.00	.30	.20
937	3¢ Al Smith	4.00	6.00	22.00(100)	1.00	.30	.20
938	3¢ Texas Statehood	6.00	8.00	15.00(50)	1.00	.30	.20

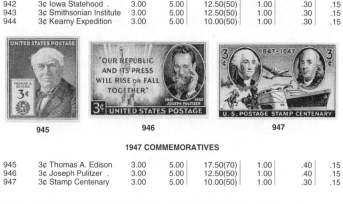

1946-47 COMMEMORATIVES

939/52	(939-47, 949-52) 13 varieties					3.95	1.75
939	3¢ Merchant Marine	6.00	8.00	10.00(50)	1.00	.30	.15
940	3¢ Honorable Discharge	6.00	8.00	22.00(100)	1.00	.30	.15
941	3¢ Tennessee Statehood	3.00	5.00	15.00(50)	1.00	.40	.15
942	3¢ Iowa Statehood	3.00	5.00	12.50(50)	1.00	.30	.15
943	3¢ Smithsonian Institute	3.00	5.00	12.50(50)	1.00	.30	.15
944	3¢ Kearny Expedition	3.00	5.00	10.00(50)	1.00	.30	.15

1947 COMMEMORATIVES

945	3¢ Thomas A. Edison	3.00	5.00	17.50(70)	1.00	.40	.15
946	3¢ Joseph Pulitzer	3.00	5.00	12.50(50)	1.00	.40	.15
947	3¢ Stamp Centenary	3.00	5.00	10.00(50)	1.00	.30	.15

NEVER HINGED: From 1888 to 1935, Unused OG or Unused prices are for stamps with original gum that have been hinged. If you desire Never Hinged stamps, refer to the NH listings.

U.S. Postage #948-970

SCOTT NO.	DESCRIPTION	FIRST DAY COVERS SING	FIRST DAY COVERS PL. BLK.	MINT SHEET	PLATE BLOCK F/NH	UNUSED F/NH	USED F

"CIPEX" SOUVENIR SHEET

948	5¢ & 10¢ Sheet of 2	4.00	......	......	......	1.50	1.00
948a	5¢ blue, single stamp	......	......	......	......	.65	.50
948b	10¢ brown orange, single stamp	......	......	......	......	.65	.50

949	3¢ Doctors	5.00	7.00	10.00(50)	1.00	.30	.15
950	3¢ Utah Centennial	3.00	5.00	10.00(50)	1.00	.30	.15
951	3¢ "Constitution"	6.00	8.00	10.00(50)	1.00	.30	.15
952	3¢ Everglades National Park	3.00	5.00	12.50(50)	1.00	.30	.15

1948 COMMEMORATIVES

953-80	3¢-5¢ (28 varieties, complete)	......	......	......	......	9.25	3.60
953	3¢ George Washington Carver	4.00	6.00	15.00(70)	1.25	.35	.15
954	3¢ Gold Rush	2.40	5.00	12.50(50)	1.25	.35	.15
955	3¢ Mississippi Territory	2.40	5.00	12.50(50)	1.25	.35	.15
956	3¢ Chaplains	3.00	5.00	12.50(50)	1.25	.35	.15
957	3¢ Wisconsin Statehood	2.40	5.00	12.50(50)	1.25	.35	.15

958	5¢ Swedish Pioneer	2.40	5.00	12.50(50)	1.25	.35	.15
959	3¢ Women's Progress	2.40	5.00	12.50(50)	1.25	.35	.15
960	3¢ William White	2.40	5.00	12.50(70)	1.25	.35	.15
961	3¢ U.S.-Canada Friendship	2.40	5.00	12.50(50)	1.25	.35	.15
962	3¢ Francis S. Key	2.40	5.00	12.50(50)	1.25	.35	.15
963	3¢ Salute to Youth	2.40	5.00	12.50(50)	1.25	.35	.15

964	3¢ Oregon Territory	2.40	5.00	12.50(50)	1.25	.35	.15
965	3¢ Harlan Stone	2.40	5.00	12.50(70)	1.25	.35	.15
966	3¢ Mt. Palomar	3.00	5.00	12.50(70)	1.50	.35	.15
967	3¢ Clara Barton	3.00	5.00	12.50(50)	1.25	.35	.15
968	3¢ Poultry	2.40	5.00	12.50(50)	1.25	.35	.15
969	3¢ Gold Star Mothers	2.40	5.00	12.50(50)	1.25	.35	.15
970	3¢ Fort Kearny	2.40	5.00	12.50(50)	1.25	.35	.15

PLATE BLOCKS: are portions of a sheet of stamps adjacent to the number(s) indicating the printing plate number used to produce that sheet. Flat plate issues are usually collected in plate blocks of six (number opposite middle stamp) while rotary issues are normally corner blocks of four.

U.S. Postage #971-997

SCOTT NO.	DESCRIPTION	FIRST DAY COVERS SING	PL. BLK.	MINT SHEET	PLATE BLOCK F/NH	UNUSED F/NH	USED F

971

972

973

974

971	3¢ Volunteer Firemen	4.00	6.00	20.00(50)	3.00	.45	.15
972	3¢ Indian Centennial	2.40	5.00	12.50(50)	1.25	.35	.15
973	3¢ Rough Riders...	2.40	5.00	12.50(50)	1.25	.35	.15
974	3¢ Juliette Low...	5.00	7.00	12.50(50)	1.25	.35	.15

975

976

977

978

979

980

975	3¢ Will Rogers.....	2.40	5.00	12.50(50)	1.25	.35	.15
976	3¢ Fort Bliss......	2.40	5.00	12.50(50)	1.60	.35	.15
977	3¢ Moina Michael..	2.40	5.00	12.50(50)	1.25	.35	.15
978	3¢ Gettysburg Address	3.00	5.00	12.50(50)	1.25	.35	.15
979	3¢ American Turners	2.40	5.00	12.50(50)	1.25	.35	.15
980	3¢ Joel C. Harris...	2.40	5.00	12.50(70)	1.25	.35	.15

981

982

983

984

1949-50 COMMEMORATIVES

981-97	17 varieties, complete	......	......	......	......	5.70	2.20
981	3¢ Minnesota Territory	2.40	4.25	12.50(50)	1.25	.35	.15
982	3¢ Washington & Lee University.........	2.40	4.25	12.50(50)	1.25	.35	.15
983	3¢ Puerto Rico....	3.00	4.25	12.50(50)	1.25	.35	.15
984	3¢ Annapolis......	3.00	4.25	12.50(50)	1.25	.35	.15

985

986

| 985 | 3¢ G.A.R........ | 3.00 | 4.25 | 12.50(50) | 1.25 | .35 | .15 |
| 986 | 3¢ Edgar A. Poe... | 3.00 | 4.25 | 25.00(70) | 2.00 | .45 | .15 |

987

988

989

1950 COMMEMORATIVES

987	3¢ Bankers Association	2.40	4.25	17.50(50)	1.75	.40	.15
988	3¢ Samuel Gompers	2.40	4.25	15.00(70)	1.25	.35	.15
989	3¢ Statue of Freedom	2.40	4.25	12.50(50)	1.25	.35	.15

990

991

992

993

994

995

996

997

990	3¢ Executive Mansion	2.40	4.25	12.50(50)	1.25	.35	.15
991	3¢ Supreme Court.	2.40	4.25	12.50(50)	1.25	.35	.15
992	3¢ United States Capitol	2.40	4.25	12.50(50)	1.25	.35	.15
993	3¢ Railroad.......	4.00	5.25	12.50(50)	1.25	.35	.15
994	3¢ Kansas City....	2.40	4.25	12.50(50)	1.25	.35	.15
995	3¢ Boy Scouts.....	6.00	8.00	12.50(50)	1.25	.35	.15
996	3¢ Indiana Territory.	2.40	4.25	12.50(50)	1.25	.35	.15
997	3¢ California Statehood	2.40	4.25	12.50(50)	1.25	.35	.15

Buy Complete Sets and Save

U.S. Postage #998-1022

SCOTT NO.	DESCRIPTION	FIRST DAY COVERS SING	FIRST DAY COVERS PL. BLK.	MINT SHEET	PLATE BLOCK F/NH	UNUSED F/NH	USED F

1951-52 COMMEMORATIVE

SCOTT NO.	DESCRIPTION	SING	PL. BLK.	MINT SHEET	PLATE BLOCK	UNUSED	USED
998-1016	19 varieties, complete	....	....	....	....	6.40	2.45
998	3¢ Confederate Veterans	3.00	4.25	17.50(50)	1.75	.40	.15
999	3¢ Nevada Settlement	2.00	4.25	12.50(50)	1.25	.35	.15
1000	3¢ Landing of Cadillac	2.00	4.25	12.50(50)	1.25	.35	.15
1001	3¢ Colorado Statehood	2.00	4.25	12.50(50)	1.25	.35	.15
1002	3¢ Chemical Society	2.00	4.25	12.50(50)	1.25	.35	.15
1003	3¢ Battle of Brooklyn	2.00	4.25	12.50(50)	1.25	.35	.15

1952 COMMEMORATIVES

1004	3¢ Betsy Ross	2.50	5.50	17.50(50)	1.75	.40	.15
1005	3¢ 4-H Club	6.00	10.00	17.50(50)	1.75	.40	.15
1006	3¢ B. & O. Railroad	4.00	6.50	17.50(50)	1.75	.40	.15
1007	3¢ AAA	2.00	4.25	17.50(50)	1.75	.40	.15
1008	3¢ NATO	2.00	4.25	17.50(100)	1.25	.35	.15
1009	3¢ Grand Coulee Dam	2.00	4.25	12.50(50)	1.25	.35	.15
1010	3¢ Lafayette	2.00	4.25	17.50(50)	1.75	.40	.15

NOTE: To determine the VF price on stamps issued from 1941 to date, add 20% to the F/NH or F (used) price. All VF unused stamps from 1941 to date will be NH.

1011	3¢ Mt. Rushmore	2.00	4.25	12.50(50)	1.25	.35	.15
1012	3¢ Civil Engineers	2.00	4.25	12.50(50)	1.25	.35	.15
1013	3¢ Service Women	2.25	4.25	12.50(50)	1.25	.35	.15
1014	3¢ Gutenburg Press	2.00	4.25	12.50(50)	1.25	.35	.15
1015	3¢ Newspaper Boys	2.00	4.25	12.50(50)	1.25	.35	.15
1016	3¢ Red Cross	3.00	6.25	12.50(50)	1.25	.35	.15

1953-54 COMMEMORATIVES

1017/63	(1017-29, 1060-63) 17 varieties, complete	....	....	....	....	5.55	2.20
1017	3¢ National Guard	2.00	4.25	12.50(50)	1.25	.35	.15
1018	3¢ Ohio Statehood	2.00	4.25	17.50(70)	1.25	.35	.15
1019	3¢ Washington Territory	2.00	4.25	12.50(50)	1.25	.35	.15
1020	3¢ Louisiana Purchase	2.00	4.25	12.50(50)	1.25	.35	.15
1021	5¢ Opening of Japan	3.00	4.25	17.50(50)	1.75	.40	.15
1022	3¢ American Bar Association	5.00	6.25	12.50(50)	1.25	.35	.15

U.S. Postage #1023-1059A

SCOTT NO.	DESCRIPTION	FIRST DAY COVERS SING	FIRST DAY COVERS PL. BLK.	MINT SHEET	PLATE BLOCK F/NH	UNUSED F/NH	USED F
1023	3¢ Sagamore Hill	2.00	4.25	12.50(50)	1.25	.35	.15
1024	3¢ Future Farmers	2.00	4.25	12.50(50)	1.25	.35	.15
1025	3¢ Trucking Industry	2.50	4.50	12.50(50)	1.25	.35	.15
1026	3¢ Gen. George S. Patton	3.00	4.75	12.50(50)	1.25	.35	.15
1027	3¢ New York City	2.00	4.25	12.50(50)	1.25	.35	.15
1028	3¢ Gadsden Purchase	2.00	4.25	12.50(50)	1.25	.35	.15

1954 COMMEMORATIVE

1029	3¢ Columbia University	2.00	4.25	12.50(50)	1.25	.35	.15

1954-68 LIBERTY SERIES

SCOTT NO.	DESCRIPTION	FIRST DAY COVERS SING	FIRST DAY COVERS PL. BLK.	MINT SHEET	PLATE BLOCK F/NH	UNUSED F/NH	USED F
1030-53	1/2¢-$5, 27 varieties, complete	110.00	235.00	....	525.00	120.00	14.50
1030-51	1/2¢-50¢, 25 varieties	55.00	115.00	....	70.00	17.25	3.50
1030	1/2¢ Benjamin Franklin (1955)	2.00	4.25	9.25(100)	.80	.25	.15
1031	1¢ George Washington	2.00	4.25	6.00(100)	1.00	.25	.15
1031A	1-1/4¢ Palace of Governors (1960)	2.00	4.25	8.00(100)	.80	.25	.15
1032	1-1/2¢ Mount Vernon	2.00	4.25	13.50(100)	2.00	.25	.15
1033	2¢ Thomas Jefferson	2.00	4.25	10.00(100)	.80	.25	.15
1034	2-1/2¢ Bunker Hill (1959)	2.00	4.25	13.50(100)	.80	.25	.15
1035	3¢ Statue of Liberty	2.00	4.25	13.50(100)	.80	.25	.15
1035a	3¢ booklet pane of 6	3.50	....	....	....	5.00	....
1036	4¢ Abraham Lincoln	2.00	4.25	17.00(100)	.80	.25	.15
1036a	4¢ booklet pane of 6	3.00	....	....	....	3.50	....
1037	4-1/2¢ Hermitage (1959)	2.00	4.25	16.50(100)	.80	.25	.15
1038	5¢ James Monroe	2.00	4.25	20.00(100)	.80	.25	.15
1039	6¢ T. Roosevelt (1955)	2.00	4.25	45.00(100)	2.10	.60	.15
1040	7¢ Woodrow Wilson (1956)	2.00	4.25	40.00(100)	1.60	.40	.15
1041	8¢ Statue of Liberty (flat plate)	2.00	4.25	35.00(100)	2.50	.40	.15
1041B	8¢ Statue of Liberty	2.00	4.25	40.00(100)	2.00	.40	.15
1042	8¢ Liberty re-engraved (1958)	2.00	4.25	35.00(100)	1.60	.40	.15
1042A	8¢ John J. Pershing (1961)	2.25	5.00	35.00(100)	1.60	.40	.15
1043	9¢ Alamo (1956)	2.25	5.00	45.00(100)	2.25	.50	.15
1044	10¢ Independence Hall (1956)	2.25	5.00	45.00(100)	2.25	.50	.15
1044A	11¢ Statue of Liberty (1961)	2.25	5.00	45.00(100)	2.25	.50	.15
1045	12¢ Benjamin Harrison (1959)	2.25	5.00	60.00(100)	2.25	.50	.15
1046	15¢ John Jay (1958)	2.50	5.25	120.00(100)	4.95	1.10	.15
1047	20¢ Monticello (1956)	2.50	5.25	90.00(100)	4.00	.95	.15
1048	25¢ Paul Revere (1958)	2.50	5.25	175.00(100)	9.00	2.10	.15
1049	30¢ Robert E. Lee (1955)	3.75	6.00	240.00(100)	10.00	2.35	.15
1050	40¢ John Marshall (1955)	3.75	7.00	295.00(100)	12.50	3.00	.15
1051	50¢ Susan B. Anthony (1955)	5.50	8.50	225.00(100)	10.50	3.00	.15
1052	$1 Patrick Henry (1955)	9.25	17.50	....	32.50	7.50	.25
1053	$5 Alexander Hamilton (1956)	50.00	110.00	....	450.00	105.00	12.50

1954-73 COIL STAMPS
Perf. 10 Vertically or Horizontally

SCOTT NO.	DESCRIPTION	FIRST DAY COVERS SING	FIRST DAY COVERS LINE PAIR	MINT SHEET	PLATE BLOCK LINE PAIR	UNUSED F/NH	USED F
1054-59A	1¢-25¢ (8 varieties, complete)	16.00	29.75	....	29.75	4.65	2.40
1054	1¢ George Washington	2.00	3.75	....	1.25	.30	.15
1054A	1-1/4¢ Palace of Governors(1960)	2.00	3.75	....	3.00	.30	.15
1055	2¢ Thomas Jefferson	2.00	3.75	....	.75	.30	.15
1056	2-1/2¢ Bunker Hill Mon. (1959)	2.00	3.75	....	5.50	.45	.30
1057	3¢ Statue of Liberty	2.00	3.75	....	.85	.25	.15
1058	4¢ Abraham Lincoln (1958)	2.00	3.75	....	.85	.25	.15
1059	4-1/2¢ Hermitage (1959)	2.00	3.75	....	18.00	2.25	1.25
1059A	25¢ Paul Revere (1965)	2.50	5.00	....	3.00	.95	.20

NOTE: Pairs of the above can be priced at two times the single price.

U.S. Postage #1060-1079

SCOTT NO.	DESCRIPTION	FIRST DAY COVERS SING	FIRST DAY COVERS PL. BLK.	MINT SHEET	PLATE BLOCK F/NH	UNUSED F/NH	USED F

1060

1061

1062

1063

1954 COMMEMORATIVES

Scott	Description	FDC Sing	FDC Pl.Blk	Mint Sheet	Plate Block	Unused	Used
1060	3¢ Nebraska Territory	2.00	4.25	12.50(50)	1.25	.35	.15
1061	3¢ Kansas Territory	2.00	4.25	12.50(50)	1.25	.35	.15
1062	3¢ George Eastman	2.00	4.25	15.00(70)	1.25	.35	.15
1063	3¢ Lewis & Clark	2.00	4.25	15.00(50)	1.75	.40	.15

1064

1065

1067

1066

1069

1068

1955 COMMEMORATIVES

Scott	Description	FDC Sing	FDC Pl.Blk	Mint Sheet	Plate Block	Unused	Used
1064-72	3¢-8¢ (9 varieties, complete)	......	......	......	......	2.95	1.20
1064	3¢ Pennsylvania Academy	2.00	4.25	15.00(50)	1.75	.40	.15
1065	3¢ Land Grant Colleges	2.50	4.50	12.50(50)	1.25	.35	.15
1066	8¢ Rotary International	5.00	7.00	20.00(50)	2.00	.50	.15
1067	3¢ Armed Forces Reserve	2.00	4.25	12.50(50)	1.25	.35	.15
1068	3¢ Great Stone Face	2.00	4.25	15.00(50)	1.75	.40	.15
1069	3¢ Soo Locks	2.00	4.25	12.50(50)	1.25	.35	.15

1070

1071

1072

Scott	Description	FDC Sing	FDC Pl.Blk	Mint Sheet	Plate Block	Unused	Used
1070	3¢ Atoms for Peace	2.00	4.25	12.50(50)	1.25	.35	.15
1071	3¢ Fort Ticonderoga	2.00	4.25	12.50(50)	1.25	.35	.15
1072	3¢ Andrew Mellon	2.00	4.25	22.50(70)	1.75	.40	.15

1073

1074

1075

1956 COMMEMORATIVES

Scott	Description	FDC Sing	FDC Pl.Blk	Mint Sheet	Plate Block	Unused	Used
1073/85	(1073-74, 1076-85) 12 varieties	......	......	......	......	3.80	1.50
1073	3¢ Benjamin Franklin	2.00	4.25	14.00(50)	1.25	.35	.15
1074	3¢ Booker T. Washington	3.50	5.50	12.50(50)	1.25	.35	.15
1075	3¢ & 8¢ FIPEX Sheet of 2	6.00	......	......	......	3.25	2.50
1075a	3¢ deep violet, single	......	......	......	......	1.25	1.05
1075b	8¢ violet blue & carmine, single	......	......	......	......	1.75	1.25

1076

1077

1078

1079

Scott	Description	FDC Sing	FDC Pl.Blk	Mint Sheet	Plate Block	Unused	Used
1076	3¢ FIPEX	2.00	4.25	12.50(50)	1.25	.35	.15
1077	3¢ Wild Turkey	2.75	4.50	12.50(50)	1.25	.35	.15
1078	3¢ Antelope	2.75	4.50	12.50(50)	1.25	.35	.15
1079	3¢ Salmon	2.75	4.50	12.50(50)	1.25	.35	.15

PLATE BLOCKS: are portions of a sheet of stamps adjacent to the number(s) indicating the printing plate number used to produce that sheet. Flat plate issues are usually collected in plate blocks of six (number opposite middle stamp) while rotary issues are normally corner blocks of four.

U.S. Postage #1080-1107

SCOTT NO.	DESCRIPTION	FIRST DAY COVERS SING	FIRST DAY COVERS PL. BLK.	MINT SHEET	PLATE BLOCK F/NH	UNUSED F/NH	USED F

1080

1081

1082

1080	3¢ Pure Food & Drug Act	2.00	4.25	12.50(50)	1.25	.35	.15
1081	3¢ "Wheatland"	2.00	4.25	12.50(50)	1.25	.35	.15
1082	3¢ Labor Day	2.00	4.25	12.50(50)	1.25	.35	.15

1083

1084

1085

1083	3¢ Nassau Hall	2.00	4.25	12.50(50)	1.25	.35	.15
1084	3¢ Devil's Tower ...	2.00	4.25	12.50(50)	1.25	.35	.15
1085	3¢ Children of the World	2.00	4.25	12.50(50)	1.25	.35	.15

1086

1087

1088

1089

1090

1091

1957 COMMEMORATIVES

| 1086-99 | 14 varieties, complete | ...... | ...... | ...... | ...... | 4.35 | 1.80 |

1086	3¢ Alexander Hamilton	2.00	4.25	12.50(50)	1.25	.35	.15
1087	3¢ Polio	2.25	4.50	12.50(50)	1.25	.35	.15
1088	3¢ Coast & Geodetic Survey	2.00	4.25	12.50(50)	1.25	.35	.15
1089	3¢ Architects	2.00	4.25	12.50(50)	1.25	.35	.15
1090	3¢ Steel Industry ...	2.00	4.25	12.50(50)	1.25	.35	.15
1091	3¢ International Naval Review	2.00	4.25	12.50(50)	1.25	.30	.15

1092

1093

1094   1095

1096   1097

1092	3¢ Oklahoma Statehood	2.00	4.25	12.50(50)	1.25	.35	.15
1093	3¢ School Teachers	2.25	4.50	12.50(50)	1.25	.35	.15
1094	4¢ 48-Star Flag	2.00	4.25	12.50(50)	1.25	.35	.15
1095	3¢ Shipbuilding Anniversary	2.00	4.25	20.00(70)	1.25	.35	.15
1096	8¢ Ramon Magsaysay	2.50	4.25	12.50(48)	1.40	.35	.15
1097	3¢ Birth of Lafayette	2.00	4.25	12.50(50)	1.25	.35	.15

1098

1099

1100

| 1098 | 3¢ Whooping Cranes | 2.25 | 4.50 | 12.50(50) | 1.25 | .35 | .15 |
| 1099 | 3¢ Religious Freedom | 2.00 | 4.25 | 12.50(50) | 1.25 | .35 | .15 |

1104

1105

1106   1107

1958 COMMEMORATIVES

| 1100-23 | 21 varieties, complete | ...... | ...... | ...... | ...... | 6.70 | 2.70 |

1100	3¢ Gardening & Horticulture	2.00	4.25	12.50(50)	1.25	.35	.15
1104	3¢ Brussels Exhibition	2.00	4.25	12.50(50)	1.25	.35	.15
1105	3¢ James Monroe ..	2.00	4.25	14.00(70)	1.25	.35	.15
1106	3¢ Minnesota Statehood	2.00	4.25	12.50(50)	1.25	.35	.15
1107	3¢ Int'l. Geophysical Year	2.00	4.25	12.50(50)	1.25	.35	.15

U.S. Postage #1108-1129

SCOTT NO.	DESCRIPTION	FIRST DAY COVERS SING PL. BLK.		MINT SHEET	PLATE BLOCK F/NH	UNUSED F/NH	USED F

1108

1109

1110, 1111

1112

1108	3¢ Gunston Hall ...	2.00	4.25	12.50(50)	1.25	.35	.15
1109	3¢ Mackinac Bridge	2.00	4.25	12.50(50)	1.25	.35	.15
1110	4¢ Simon Bolivar ...	2.00	4.25	14.00(70)	1.25	.35	.15
1111	8¢ Simon Bolivar ...	2.00	4.50	19.50(72)	1.85	.35	.15
1112	4¢ Atlantic Cable Centenary	2.00	4.25	12.50(50)	1.25	.35	.15

1113

1114

1115

1116

1113	1¢ Abraham Lincoln (1959)	2.00	4.25	3.75(50)	.75	.30	.15
1114	3¢ Bust of Lincoln (1959)	2.00	4.25	15.00(50)	1.75	.40	.15
1115	4¢ Lincoln-Douglas Debates...........	2.00	4.25	17.50(50)	1.75	.40	.15
1116	4¢ Statue of Lincoln (1959)	2.00	4.25	15.00(50)	1.75	.40	.15

1117, 1118   1119   1120

1117	4¢ Lajos Kossuth ..	2.00	4.25	14.00(70)	1.25	.35	.15
1118	8¢ Lajos Kossuth ..	2.00	4.50	19.50(72)	1.60	.35	.15
1119	4¢ Freedom of Press	2.00	4.25	12.50(50)	1.25	.35	.15
1120	4¢ Overland Mail ..	2.00	4.25	12.50(50)	1.25	.35	.15

Plate blocks will be blocks of 4 stamps unless otherwise noted.

1121   1122   1123

1121	4¢ Noah Webster ..	2.00	4.25	14.00(70)	1.25	.35	.15
1122	4¢ Forest Conservation	2.00	4.25	12.50(50)	1.25	.35	.15
1123	4¢ Fort Duquesne ..	2.00	4.25	12.50(50)	1.25	.35	.15

1124

1125, 1126

1127

1128   1129

1959 COMMEMORATIVES

1124-38	4¢-8¢, 15 varieties .	......	......	......	......	4.95	1.95
1124	4¢ Oregon Statehood	2.00	4.25	12.50(50)	1.25	.35	.15
1125	4¢ José de San Martin	2.00	4.25	14.00(70)	1.25	.35	.15
1126	8¢ José de San Martin	2.00	4.25	19.50(72)	1.40	.35	.15
1127	4¢ NATO	2.00	4.25	12.50(70)	1.25	.35	.15
1128	4¢ Arctic Exploration	2.00	4.25	12.50(50)	1.25	.35	.15
1129	8¢ World Peace & Trade	2.00	4.25	14.00(50)	1.30	.40	.15

1130

1131

1132

1133

1134

1135

U.S. Postage #1130-1163

SCOTT NO.	DESCRIPTION	FIRST DAY COVERS SING	FIRST DAY COVERS PL. BLK.	MINT SHEET	PLATE BLOCK F/NH	UNUSED F/NH	USED F

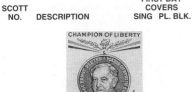
1136, 1137

1138

1130	4¢ Silver Centennial	2.00	4.25	12.50(50)	1.25	.35	.15
1131	4¢ St. Lawrence Seaway	2.00	4.25	12.50(50)	1.25	.35	.15
1132	4¢ 49-Star Flag	2.00	4.25	12.50(50)	1.25	.35	.15
1133	4¢ Soil Conservation	2.00	4.25	12.50(50)	1.25	.35	.15
1134	4¢ Petroleum	2.00	4.25	12.50(50)	1.25	.35	.15
1135	4¢ Dental Health	2.00	4.25	15.00(50)	1.40	.40	.15
1136	4¢ Ernst Reuter	2.00	4.25	14.00(70)	1.25	.35	.15
1137	8¢ Ernst Reuter	2.00	4.25	19.50(72)	1.40	.35	.15
1138	4¢ Dr. Ephraim McDowell	2.00	4.25	12.50(70)	1.25	.35	.15

1139

1140

1141

1142

1143

1144

1960-61 CREDO OF AMERICA SERIES

1139-44	6 varieties, complete	......	......	......	......	1.85	.85
1139	4¢ Credo—Washington	2.00	4.25	12.50(50)	1.25	.35	.15
1140	4¢ Credo—Franklin	2.00	4.25	12.50(50)	1.25	.35	.15
1141	4¢ Credo—Jefferson	2.00	4.25	12.50(50)	1.25	.35	.15
1142	4¢ Credo—Key	2.00	4.25	12.50(50)	1.25	.35	.15
1143	4¢ Credo—Lincoln	2.00	4.25	12.50(50)	1.25	.35	.15
1144	4¢ Credo—Henry (1961)	2.00	4.25	12.50(50)	1.25	.35	.15

1145

1146

1147, 1148

1149

1151

1152

1153

1960 COMMEMORATIVES

1145-73	4¢-8¢, 29 varieties	......	......	......	......	8.50	3.70
1145	4¢ Boy Scouts	8.50	10.50	17.50(50)	1.75	.40	.15
1146	4¢ Winter Olympics	2.00	4.25	10.00(50)	1.00	.30	.15
1147	4¢ Thomas Masaryk	2.00	4.25	14.00(70)	1.00	.30	.15
1148	8¢ Thomas Masaryk	2.00	4.25	19.50(72)	1.40	.35	.15
1149	4¢ World Refugee Year	2.00	4.25	10.00(50)	1.00	.30	.15
1150	4¢ Water Conservation	2.00	4.25	10.00(50)	1.00	.30	.15
1151	4¢ SEATO	2.00	4.25	12.00(70)	1.00	.30	.15
1152	4¢ American Women	2.00	4.25	10.00(50)	1.00	.30	.15
1153	4¢ 50-Star Flag	2.00	4.25	10.00(50)	1.00	.30	.15

1154

1155

1156

1157

1158

1159, 1160

1161

1162

1163

1154	4¢ Pony Express	2.00	4.25	17.50(50)	1.75	.45	.15
1155	4¢ Employ the Handicapped	2.00	4.25	10.00(50)	1.00	.30	.15
1156	4¢ World Forestry Congress	2.00	4.25	10.00(50)	1.00	.30	.15
1157	4¢ Mexican Independence	2.00	4.25	10.00(50)	1.00	.30	.15
1158	4¢ U.S.-Japan Treaty	2.00	4.25	10.00(50)	1.00	.30	.15
1159	4¢ Ignacy Paderewski	2.00	4.25	14.00(70)	1.00	.30	.15
1160	8¢ Ignacy Paderewski	2.00	4.25	19.50(72)	1.40	.35	.15
1161	4¢ Robert A. Taft	2.00	4.25	13.00(70)	1.00	.30	.15
1162	4¢ Wheels of Freedom	2.00	4.25	10.00(50)	1.00	.30	.15
1163	4¢ Boys' Club of America	2.25	4.25	12.00(50)	1.00	.30	.15

Buy Complete Sets and Save

U.S. Postage #1164-1190

1164

1165, 1166

1167

1168, 1169

1170

1171

1172

1173

SCOTT NO.	DESCRIPTION	FIRST DAY COVERS SING	PL. BLK.	MINT SHEET	PLATE BLOCK F/NH	UNUSED F/NH	USED F
1164	4¢ Automated Post Office	2.00	4.25	20.00(50)	1.75	.45	.15
1165	4¢ Gustaf Mannerheim	2.00	4.25	14.00(70)	1.00	.30	.15
1166	8¢ Gustaf Mannerheim	2.00	4.25	19.50(72)	1.40	.35	.15
1167	4¢ Camp Fire Girls	5.00	7.25	17.50(50)	1.75	.45	.15
1168	4¢ Giuseppe Garibaldi	2.00	4.25	14.00(70)	1.00	.30	.15
1169	8¢ Giuseppe Garibaldi	2.00	4.25	19.50(72)	1.40	.35	.15
1170	4¢ Walter George	2.00	4.25	20.00(70)	1.75	.45	.15
1171	4¢ Andrew Carnegie	2.00	4.25	17.50(70)	1.25	.35	.15
1172	4¢ John Foster Dulles	2.00	4.25	17.50(70)	1.25	.35	.15
1173	4¢ "ECHO I" Satellite	3.00	6.50	15.00(50)	1.40	.40	.15

1174, 1175

1176

1177

1961 COMMEMORATIVES

1174/90	(1174-77, 1183-90) 12 varieties					3.80	1.40
1174	4¢ Mahatma Gandhi	2.00	4.25	14.00(70)	1.00	.30	.15
1175	8¢ Mahatma Gandhi	2.00	4.25	19.50(72)	1.40	.35	.15
1176	4¢ Range Conservation	2.00	4.25	10.00(50)	1.00	.30	.15
1177	4¢ Horace Greeley	2.00	4.25	17.50(70)	1.25	.35	.15

1178

1179

1180

1181

1182

1183

1961-65 CIVIL WAR CENTENNIAL SERIES

1178-82	4¢-5¢, 5 varieties, complete					2.75	.60
1178	4¢ Fort Sumter	7.50	10.00	27.50(50)	2.50	.60	.15
1179	4¢ Shiloh (1962)	7.50	10.00	17.50(50)	1.75	.40	.15
1180	5¢ Gettysburg (1963)	7.50	10.00	27.50(50)	2.50	.60	.15
1181	5¢ Wilderness (1964)	7.50	10.00	26.00(50)	2.50	.55	.15
1181	Zip Code Block				1.40		
1182	5¢ Appomattox (1965)	7.50	10.00	40.00(50)	4.00	.75	.15
1182	Zip Code Block				3.50		

1184

1185

1186

1187

1188

1189

1190

1961 COMMEMORATIVES

1183	4¢ Kansas Statehood	2.00	4.25	10.00(50)	1.00	.30	.15
1184	4¢ George W. Norris	2.00	4.25	12.00(50)	1.00	.30	.15
1185	4¢ Naval Aviation	2.00	4.25	10.00(50)	1.00	.30	.15
1186	4¢ Workmen's Compensation	2.00	4.25	10.00(50)	1.00	.30	.15
1187	4¢ Frederic Remington	2.00	4.25	12.00(50)	1.00	.30	.15
1188	4¢ Sun Yat-sen	6.00	10.00	20.00(50)	2.00	.50	.15
1189	4¢ Basketball	9.00	12.00	20.00(50)	2.00	.50	.15
1190	4¢ Nursing	13.50	20.00	20.00(50)	2.10	.50	.15

NOTE: To determine the VF price on stamps issued from 1941 to date, add 20% to the F/NH or F (used) price (minimum .03 per item). All VF unused stamps from 1941 date priced as NH.

U.S. Postage #1191-1233

SCOTT NO.	DESCRIPTION	FIRST DAY COVERS SING	FIRST DAY COVERS PL. BLK.	MINT SHEET	PLATE BLOCK F/NH	UNUSED F/NH	USED F

1191

1192

1193

1194

1962 COMMEMORATIVES

Scott	Description	FDC Sing	FDC Pl.Blk	Mint Sheet	Plate Block	Unused	Used
1191-1207	17 varieties	....	....	....	....	4.65	2.10
1191	4¢ New Mexico Statehood	1.75	4.00	10.00(50)	1.00	.30	.15
1192	4¢ Arizona Statehood	1.75	4.00	10.00(50)	1.00	.30	.15
1193	4¢ Project Mercury	5.00	7.50	12.00(50)	1.10	.30	.15
1194	4¢ Malaria Eradication	1.75	4.00	17.50(50)	1.75	.40	.15

1195

1196

1197

Scott	Description	FDC Sing	FDC Pl.Blk	Mint Sheet	Plate Block	Unused	Used
1195	4¢ Charles Evans Hughes	1.75	4.00	10.00(50)	1.00	.30	.15
1196	4¢ Seattle World's Fair	1.75	4.00	10.00(50)	1.00	.30	.15
1197	4¢ Louisiana Statehood	1.75	4.00	12.00(50)	1.00	.30	.15

1198

1199

1200

1201

1202

1203

1205

1206

1207

Scott	Description	FDC Sing	FDC Pl.Blk	Mint Sheet	Plate Block	Unused	Used
1198	4¢ Homestead Act	1.75	4.00	10.00(50)	1.00	.30	.15
1199	4¢ Girl Scouts	7.00	10.00	10.00(50)	1.00	.30	.15
1200	4¢ Brien McMahon	1.75	4.00	12.50(50)	1.75	.40	.15
1201	4¢ Apprenticeship	1.75	4.00	10.00(50)	1.00	.30	.15
1202	4¢ Sam Rayburn	1.75	4.00	12.50(50)	1.25	.35	.15
1203	4¢ Dag Hammarskjold	1.75	4.00	10.00(50)	1.00	.30	.15
1204	same, yellow inverted	5.00	10.25	10.00(50)	1.00	.30	.15
1205	4¢ Christmas 1962	1.75	4.00	15.00(50)	1.00	.30	.15
1206	4¢ Higher Education	1.75	4.00	10.00(50)	1.00	.30	.15
1207	4¢ Winslow Homer	1.75	4.00	12.50(50)	1.25	.35	.15

1208

1209, 1225

1213, 1229

1962-66 REGULAR ISSUE

Scott	Description	FDC Sing	FDC Pl.Blk	Mint Sheet	Plate Block	Unused	Used
1208	5¢ Flag & White House (1963)	2.00	4.25	27.50(100)	1.35	.30	.15
1209	1¢ Andrew Jackson (1963)	1.75	4.00	10.00(100)	.75	.20	.15
1213	5¢ Washington	1.75	4.00	27.50(100)	1.35	.30	.15
1213a	5¢ b. pane of 5—Slog. I	2.50	....	....	....	6.50	....
1213a	5¢ b. pane of 5—Slog. II (1963)	....	....	....	....	20.00	....
1213a	5¢ b. pane of 5—Slog. III (1964)	....	....	....	....	3.50	....
1213c	5¢ Tagged pane of 5 Slogan II (1963)	....	....	....	....	90.00	....
1213c	5¢ b. p. of 5—Slog. III (1963)	....	....	....	....	2.50	....

Slogan I—Your Mailman Deserves Your Help • Keep Harmful Objects Out of...
Slogan II—Add Zip to Your Mail • Use Zone Numbers for Zip Code.
Slogan III—Add Zip to Your Mail • Always Use Zip Code.

1962-66 COIL STAMPS Perf. 10 Vertically

Scott	Description	FDC Sing	FDC Pl.Blk	Mint Sheet	LINE PAIRS	LINE PAIRS	Unused	Used
1225	1¢ Andrew Jackson (1963)	1.75	3.00	....	3.00		.20	.15
1229	5¢ George Washington	1.75	3.00	....	3.25		1.25	.15

1230

1231

1232

1233

1963 COMMEMORATIVES

Scott	Description	FDC Sing	FDC Pl.Blk	Mint Sheet	Plate Block	Unused	Used
1230-41	12 varieties	....	....	....	....	3.65	1.50
1230	5¢ Carolina Charter	1.75	4.00	17.50(50)	1.75	.40	.15
1231	5¢ Food for Peace	1.75	4.00	10.00(50)	1.00	.30	.15
1232	5¢ West Virginia Statehood	1.75	4.00	10.00(50)	1.00	.30	.15
1233	5¢ Emancipation Proclamation	3.00	4.00	12.50(50)	1.25	.35	.15

U.S. Postage #1234-1257

SCOTT NO.	DESCRIPTION	FIRST DAY COVERS SING	PL. BLK.	MINT SHEET	PLATE BLOCK F/NH	UNUSED F/NH	USED F

1234

1235

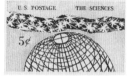
1236

1237

1238

1239 1240

1241

1242

1243

1963 COMMEMORATIVES

1234	5¢ Alliance for Progress	1.75	4.00	10.00(50)	1.00	.30	.15
1235	5¢ Cordell Hull	1.75	4.00	17.50(50)	1.75	.40	.15
1236	5¢ Eleanor Roosevelt	1.75	4.00	12.50(50)	1.25	.35	.15
1237	5¢ The Sciences	1.75	4.00	10.00(50)	1.00	.30	.15
1238	5¢ City Mail Delivery	1.75	4.00	10.00(50)	1.00	.30	.15
1239	5¢ International Red Cross	2.25	4.00	10.00(50)	1.00	.30	.15
1240	5¢ Christmas 1963	1.75	4.00	25.00(100)	1.50	.35	.15
1241	5¢ John J. Audubon	1.75	4.00	10.00(50)	1.00	.30	.15

SCOTT NO.	DESCRIPTION	FIRST DAY COVERS SING	PL. BLK.	MINT SHEET	PLATE BLOCK	UNUSED F/NH	USED

1244

1245

1964 COMMEMORATIVES

1242-60	19 varieties	......	......	......	......	6.95	2.25
1242	5¢ Sam Houston	1.75	4.00	12.50(50)	1.25	.45	.15
1243	5¢ Charles M. Russell	1.75	4.00	12.50(50)	1.25	.35	.15
1244	5¢ New York World's Fair	1.75	4.00	12.50(50)	1.25	.35	.15
1245	5¢ John Muir	1.75	4.00	12.50(50)	1.25	.35	.15

1246

1247

| 1246 | 5¢ John F. Kennedy | 2.50 | 5.00 | 25.00(50) | 2.50 | .75 | .15 |
| 1247 | 5¢ New Jersey Tercentenary | 1.75 | 4.00 | 15.00(50) | 1.25 | .35 | .15 |

1248

1249

1250

1251

1252

1248	5¢ Nevada Statehood	1.75	4.00	12.50(50)	1.25	.35	.15
1249	5¢ Register and Vote	1.75	4.00	8.00(50)	.80	.30	.15
1250	5¢ Shakespeare	1.75	4.00	8.00(50)	.80	.30	.15
1251	5¢ Mayo Brothers	2.50	5.00	16.00(50)	1.50	.40	.15
1252	5¢ American Music	1.75	4.00	8.00(50)	.80	.30	.15

1253

1254

1255

1256

1257

1253	5¢ Homemakers	1.75	4.00	8.00(50)	.80	.30	.15
1254-57	5¢ Christmas, 4 varieties, attached	5.25	7.50	34.00(100)	2.50	2.00	1.25
1254	5¢ Holly	2.75	......	......	......	.60	.15
1255	5¢ Mistletoe	2.75	......	......	......	.60	.15
1256	5¢ Poinsettia	2.75	......	......	......	.60	.15
1257	5¢ Pine Cone	2.75	......	......	......	.60	.15

COMMEMORATIVES: Commemorative stamps are special issues released to honor or recognize persons, organizations, historical events or landmarks. They are usually issued in the current first class denomination to supplement regular issues.

U.S. Postage #1258-1276

1258

1259

1260

1271

1272

1273

SCOTT NO.	DESCRIPTION	FIRST DAY COVERS SING	FIRST DAY COVERS PL. BLK.	MINT SHEET	PLATE BLOCK	UNUSED F/NH	USED
1258	5¢ Verrazano-Narrows Bridge	1.75	4.00	12.50(50)	1.25	.35	.15
1259	5¢ Modern Art	1.75	4.00	8.00(50)	.80	.30	.15
1260	5¢ Radio Amateurs	4.00	6.00	17.50(50)	1.50	.50	.15

SCOTT NO.	DESCRIPTION	FIRST DAY COVERS SING	FIRST DAY COVERS PL. BLK.	MINT SHEET	PLATE BLOCK	UNUSED F/NH	USED
1266	5¢ International Cooperation Year	1.75	4.00	8.00(50)	.80	.30	.15
1267	5¢ Salvation Army	1.75	4.00	8.00(50)	.80	.30	.15
1268	5¢ Dante Alighieri	1.75	4.00	8.00(50)	.80	.30	.15
1269	5¢ Herbert Hoover	1.75	4.00	12.50(50)	1.25	.35	.15
1270	5¢ Robert Fulton	1.75	4.00	8.00(50)	.80	.30	.15
1271	5¢ Florida Settlement	1.75	4.00	8.00(50)	.80	.30	.15
1272	5¢ Traffic Safety	1.75	4.00	8.00(50)	.80	.30	.15
1273	5¢ John S. Copley	1.75	4.00	8.00(50)	.80	.30	.15

1261

1262

1263

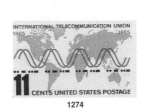
1274

1275

1276

1274	11¢ Telecommunication	1.75	4.00	26.50(50)	7.00	.60	.25
1275	5¢ Adlai Stevenson	1.75	4.00	8.00(50)	.80	.30	.15
1276	5¢ Christmas 1965	1.75	4.00	17.50(100)	.80	.30	.15

1264

1265

1965 COMMEMORATIVES

1261-76	5¢-11¢, 16 varieties					5.15	1.90
1261	5¢ Battle of New Orleans	1.75	4.00	22.50(50)	2.25	.50	.15
1262	5¢ Physical Fitness	1.75	4.00	8.00(50)	.80	.30	.15
1263	5¢ Crusade Against Cancer	4.00	6.00	8.00(50)	.80	.30	.15
1264	5¢ Winston Churchill	1.75	4.00	17.50(50)	1.75	.40	.15
1265	5¢ Magna Carta	1.75	4.00	8.00(50)	.80	.30	.15

1266

1267

1268

1269

1270

Stamp History

Thatcher Ferry Bridge

In 1962, during the regular course of business H.E. Harris purchases, at their 4 cent face value, a pane of 50 stamps honoring the Canal Zone's Thatcher Ferry Bridge. Due to a printing error, the silver bridge has been omitted. Harris discovers that his is the only pane from the sheet of 200 printed that has reached the public. Because a recent error in a Dag Hammerskjold stamp prompted the U.S. Postal Service to reprint thousands in order to make the error worthless, Harris questions how the Canal Zone will handle the bridge error. Flooding the market, he insists, would blunt the fun and excitement of stamp collecting. When the Canal Zone says it will reprint the error, Harris sues.

March 25, 1965, The Federal District Court in Washington rules in Harris' favor, stopping the Canal Zone authorities from reprinting the stamp error. Viewed as a precendent-setting event in philately, the effort won Harris the respect and awards of his fellow collectors.

U.S. Postage #1278-1314

1278, 1299   1279   1280   1281, 1297

1282, 1303   1283, 1304   1283B, 1304C   1284, 1298

1285   1286   1286A   1287

1288, 1288B, 1288d, 1305E, 1305Ei   1289   1290   1291

1292   1293   1294, 1305C

1295   1305

1965-78 PROMINENT AMERICAN SERIES

SCOTT NO.	DESCRIPTION	FIRST DAY COVERS SING	FIRST DAY COVERS PL. BLK.	MINT SHEET	PLATE BLOCK	UNUSED F/NH	USED
1278-95	1¢-$5, 20 varieties, complete (No #1288B or 1288d)	91.50	....	....	118.50	28.50	5.75
1278	1¢ T. Jefferson (1968)	1.75	4.00	5.50(100)	.60	.20	.15
1278a	1¢ bklt.pane of 8	2.50	....	....	....	1.00	....
1278ae	1¢ test gum	90.00	....	....	....	2.00	....
1278b	1¢ bklt pane of 4 (1971)	18.00	....	....	....	.70	....
1279	1¼¢ A. Gallatin (1967)	1.75	4.00	20.00(100)	12.00	.20	.15
1280	2¢ F.L. Wright (1966)	1.75	4.00	6.00(100)	.60	.20	.15
1280a	2¢ bklt pane of 5 (1968)	2.50	....	....	....	1.00	....
1280c	2¢ bklt pane of 6 (1971)	18.00	....	....	....	1.00	....
1280ce	2¢ test gum	125.00	....	....	....	1.00	....
1281	3¢ F. Parkman (1967)	1.75	4.00	12.00(100)	.85	.25	.15
1282	4¢ A. Lincoln	1.75	4.00	18.00(100)	.85	.25	.15
1283	5¢ G. Washington (1966)	1.75	4.00	22.00(100)	.85	.25	.15
1283B	5¢ Washington, redrawn (1967)	1.75	4.00	18.00(100)	1.00	.30	.15
1284	6¢ F. D. Roosevelt(1966)	1.75	4.00	35.00(100)	1.10	.35	.15
1284b	6¢ bklt pane of 8 (1967)	3.00	....	....	....	1.75	....
1284c	6¢ bklt pane of 5 (1968)	150.00	....	....	....	1.60	....
1285	8¢ A. Einstein (1966)	2.00	4.25	45.00(100)	2.25	.50	.15
1286	10¢ A. Jackson (1967)	2.00	4.25	45.00(100)	2.25	.50	.15
1286A	12¢ H. Ford (1968)	2.00	4.25	45.00(100)	2.25	.50	.15
1287	13¢ J.F. Kennedy (1967)	2.50	4.50	67.50(100)	2.75	.70	.15
1288	15¢ O.W. Holmes, die I (1968)	2.25	4.50	55.00(100)	2.25	.60	.15
1288d	15¢ Holmes, die II (1979)	....	....	90.00(100)	14.00	1.10	.15
1288B	same, from bklt pane (1978)	2.25	....	....	....	.60	.15
1288Bc	15¢ bklt pane of 8	3.75	....	....	....	4.75	....
1289	20¢ G.C. Marshall (1967)	2.25	4.50	80.00(100)	3.50	.70	.15
1290	25¢ F. Douglass (1967)	2.50	5.00	95.00(100)	3.50	.85	.15
1291	30¢ J. Dewey (1968)	2.50	5.00	125.00(100)	5.50	1.25	.15
1292	40¢ T. Paine (1968)	2.50	5.00	125.00(100)	6.00	1.50	.15
1293	50¢ L. Stone (1968)	3.75	7.25	200.00(100)	8.00	2.00	.15
1294	$1 E. O'Neil (1967)	6.00	12.50	325.00(100)	14.00	3.50	.15
1295	$5 J. B. Moore (1966)	50.00	115.00	....	60.00	16.00	3.50

BOOKLET PANE SLOGANS

Slogan IV : Mail Early in the Day.   #1278b–Slogans IV and V
Slogan V: Use Zip Code.   #1280a, 1284c–Slogans IV or V

1966-81 COIL STAMPS

SCOTT NO.	DESCRIPTION	FIRST DAY COVERS SING	FIRST DAY COVERS PL. BLK.	MINT SHEET	LINE PAIR PLATE BLOCK	LINE PAIR UNUSED F/NH	USED
1297-1305C	1¢-$1, 9 varieties, (No #1305Ei)	....	....	....	14.00	6.00	2.75
Perf. 10 Horizontally							
1297	3¢ F. Parkman (1975)	1.75	2.75	....	.70	.20	.15
1298	6¢ F.D. Roosevelt (1967)	1.75	2.75	....	1.55	.40	.15
Perf. 10 Vertically							
1299	1¢ T. Jefferson (1968)	1.75	2.75	....	.45	.20	.15
1303	4¢ A. Lincoln	1.75	2.75	....	.70	.25	.15
1304	5¢ G. Washington	1.75	2.75	....	.55	.25	.15
1304C	5¢ Washington, redrawn (1981)	1.75	2.75	....	1.15	.25	.15
1305	6¢ F.D. Roosevelt (1968)	1.75	2.75	....	.85	.40	.15
1305E	15¢ O.W. Holmes, die I (1978)	2.00	3.25	....	1.40	.50	.15
1305Ei	15¢ O.W. Holmes, die II (1979)	....	....	....	3.00	.55	.30
1305C	$1 E. O'Neil (1973)	5.00	9.50	....	7.00	3.95	1.50

1306   1307

1308   1309   1310

1312   1313   1314

1966 COMMEMORATIVES

SCOTT NO.	DESCRIPTION	FIRST DAY COVERS SING	FIRST DAY COVERS PL. BLK.	MINT SHEET	PLATE BLOCK	UNUSED F/NH	USED
1306/22	(1306-10, 1312-22) 16 varieties	....	....	....	....	5.70	1.90
1306	5¢ Migratory Bird Treaty	2.00	4.25	8.00(50)	.80	.30	.15
1307	5¢ A.S.P.C.A.	1.75	4.00	8.00(50)	.80	.30	.15
1308	5¢ Indiana Statehood	1.75	4.00	19.50(50)	2.25	.50	.15
1309	5¢ American Circus	3.00	4.25	14.00(50)	1.50	.45	.15
1310	5¢ SIPEX (single)	1.75	4.00	8.00(50)	.80	.30	.15
1311	5¢ SIPEX, Imperf Souvenir Sheet	2.00	....	....	....	.30	.15
1312	5¢ Bill of Rights	2.25	4.00	8.00(50)	1.00	.30	.15
1313	5¢ Polish Millennium	1.75	4.00	8.00(50)	.80	.30	.15
1314	5¢ National Park Service	1.75	4.00	8.00(50)	.80	.40	.15

U.S. Postage #1315-1337

SCOTT NO.	DESCRIPTION	FIRST DAY COVERS SING	PL. BLK.	MINT SHEET	PLATE BLOCK	UNUSED F/NH	USED

1315

1316

1317

1318

1319

1320

1315	5¢ Marine Corps Reserve	1.75	4.00	8.00(50)	.80	.30	.15
1316	5¢ Women's Clubs	1.75	4.00	8.00(50)	.80	.30	.15
1317	5¢ Johnny Appleseed	1.75	4.00	17.50(50)	1.50	.40	.15
1318	5¢ Beautification	1.75	4.00	8.00(50)	.80	.30	.15
1319	5¢ Great River Road	1.75	4.00	17.50(50)	1.50	.40	.15
1320	5¢ Servicemen– Bonds	1.75	4.00	8.00(50)	.80	.30	.15

1321

1322

| 1321 | 5¢ Christmas 1966 | 1.75 | 4.00 | 18.50(100) | 1.00 | .30 | .15 |
| 1322 | 5¢ Mary Cassatt | 1.75 | 4.00 | 8.00(50) | .85 | .30 | .15 |

1324

1325

1326

1327

1967 COMMEMORATIVES

1323-37	15 varieties, complete	....	....	....	....	7.50	1.90
1323	5¢ National Grange	1.75	4.00	11.50(50)	1.10	.35	.15
1324	5¢ Canada Centennial	1.75	4.00	8.00(50)	.80	.30	.15
1325	5¢ Erie Canal	1.75	4.00	8.00(50)	.80	.30	.15
1326	5¢ Search for Peace	1.75	4.00	8.00(50)	.80	.30	.15
1327	5¢ Henry D. Thoreau	1.75	4.00	17.50(50)	1.50	.40	.15

1328

1329

1330

1328	5¢ Nebraska Statehood	1.75	4.00	8.00(50)	.80	.30	.15
1329	5¢ Voice of America	2.50	4.00	8.00(50)	.80	.30	.15
1330	5¢ Davy Crockett	2.50	4.25	17.50(50)	1.50	.50	.15

1331

1332

1331-32	5¢ Space, attached, 2 varieties	12.50	25.00	60.00(50)	5.75	3.75	1.80
1331	5¢ Astronaut	4.00	....	....	....	1.50	.30
1332	5¢ Gemini 4 Capsule	4.00	....	....	....	1.50	.30

1333

1334

| 1333 | 5¢ Urban Planning | 1.75 | 4.00 | 8.00(50) | .80 | .30 | .15 |
| 1334 | 5¢ Finland Independence | 1.75 | 4.00 | 8.00(50) | .80 | .30 | .15 |

1335

1336

1337

1335	5¢ Thomas Eakins	1.75	4.00	8.00(50)	.80	.30	.15
1336	5¢ Christams 1967	1.75	4.00	8.00(50)	.80	.30	.15
1337	5¢ Mississippi Statehood	1.75	4.00	22.50(50)	2.25	.50	.15

FOR YOUR CONVENIENCE IN ORDERING, COMPLETE SETS ARE LISTED BEFORE SINGLE STAMP LISTINGS.

U.S. Postage #1338-1354

SCOTT NO.	DESCRIPTION	FIRST DAY COVERS SING	FIRST DAY COVERS PL. BLK.	MINT SHEET	PLATE BLOCK	UNUSED F/NH	USED

1338, 1338A, 1338D   1338F, 1338G

GIORI PRESS
1868 Design size: 18½ x 22 mm Perf.11

| 1338 | 6¢ Flag & White House | 1.75 | 4.00 | 17.00(100) | | .90 | .30 | .15 |

HUCK PRESS Design size: 18 x 21 mm
1969 Coil Stamp Perf. 10 Vertically

| 1338A | 6¢ Flag & White House | 1.75 | .... | .... | .... | .30 | .15 |

1970 Perf. 11 x 10½

| 1338D | 6¢ Flag & White House | 2.00 | 4.25 | 17.00(100) | 4.00(20) | .30 | .15 |

1971 Perf. 11 x 10½

| 1338F | 8¢ Flag & White House | 2.00 | 4.25 | 21.50(100) | 4.75(20) | .30 | .15 |

Coil Stamp Perf. 10 Vertically

| 1338G | 8¢ Flag & White House | 2.00 | .... | .... | .... | .30 | .15 |

1339   1340

1968 COMMEMORATIVES

1339/64	(1339-40, 1342-64) 25 varieties	....	....	....	....	12.45	5.30
1339	6¢ Illinois Statehood	1.75	4.00	22.50(50)	2.25	.50	.15
1340	6¢ Hemisfair '68	1.75	4.00	8.25(50)	.80	.30	.15

1341

| 1341 | $1 Airlift to Servicemen | 8.50 | 17.50 | 175.00(50) | 15.00 | 3.95 | 2.75 |

1342   1343   1344

1342	6¢ Support our Youth	1.75	4.00	8.25(50)	.80	.30	.15
1343	6¢ Law and Order	1.75	4.00	19.50(50)	2.25	.50	.15
1344	6¢ Register and Vote	1.75	4.00	8.25(50)	.80	.30	.15

1345   1346

1347   1348

 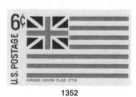

1349   1350

1351   1352

1353   1354

1968 HISTORIC AMERICAN FLAGS

1345-54	10 varieties, complete, attached	11.50	....	25.00(50)	12.00	6.00	....
1345-54	Same, set of singles	57.50	....	....	....	5.25	4.25
1345	6¢ Fort Moultrie Flag	6.00	....	....	....	.55	.45
1346	6¢ Fort McHenry Flag	6.00	....	....	....	.55	.45
1347	6¢ Washington's Cruisers	6.00	....	....	....	.55	.45
1348	6¢ Bennington Flag	6.00	....	....	....	.55	.45
1349	6¢ Rhode Island Flag	6.00	....	....	....	.55	.45
1350	6¢ First Stars & Stripes	6.00	....	....	....	.55	.45
1351	6¢ Bunker Hill Flag	6.00	....	....	....	.55	.45
1352	6¢ Grand Union Flag	6.00	....	....	....	.55	.45
1353	6¢ Philadelphia Light Horse	6.00	....	....	....	.55	.45
1354	6¢ First Navy Jack	6.00	....	....	....	.55	.45

NOTE: All ten varieties of 1345-54 were printed on the same sheet; therefore, plate and regular blocks are not available for each variety separately. Plate blocks of four will contain two each of #1346, with number adjacent to #1345 only; Zip blocks will contain two each of #1353 and #1354, with inscription adjacent to #1354 only; Mail Early blocks will contain two each of #1347-49 with inscription adjacent to #1348 only. A plate strip of 20 stamps, with two of each variety will be required to have all stamps in plate block form and will contain all marginal inscription.

1355   1356

U.S. Postage #1355-1379

1357

1358

1359

1360

1361

1968 COMMEMORATIVES

SCOTT NO.	DESCRIPTION	FIRST DAY COVERS SING	PL. BLK.	MINT SHEET	PLATE BLOCK	UNUSED F/NH	USED
1355	6¢ Walt Disney	30.00	40.00	55.00(50)	5.00	1.50	.30
1356	6¢ Father Marquette	1.75	4.00	19.50(50)	2.25	.50	.15
1357	6¢ Daniel Boone	1.75	4.00	17.50(50)	1.50	.50	.15
1358	6¢ Arkansas River	1.75	4.00	19.50(50)	2.25	.50	.15
1359	6¢ Leif Erikson	1.75	4.00	12.50(50)	1.25	.35	.15
1360	6¢ Cherokee Strip	1.75	4.00	12.50(50)	1.25	.40	.15
1361	6¢ Trumbull Art	1.75	4.00	17.50(50)	1.50	.50	.15

1362

1363

1364

1362	6¢ Waterfowl Conservation	1.75	4.00	17.50(50)	1.75	.40	.15
1363	6¢ Christmas 1968	1.75	....	9.25(50)	2.10(10)	.30	.15
1364	6¢ Chief Joseph	1.75	4.00	20.00(50)	2.50	.50	.15

1365

1366

1367 1368

1969 COMMEMORATIVES

1365-86	22 varieties, complete	....	....	....	....	12.60	3.00
1365-68	Beautification, 4 varieties, attached	6.00	8.50	30.00(50)	4.00	3.25	2.50
1365	6¢ Azaleas & Tulips	3.00	....	....	....	1.00	.20
1366	6¢ Daffodils	3.00	....	....	....	1.00	.20
1367	6¢ Poppies	3.00	....	....	....	1.00	.20
1368	6¢ Crabapple Trees	3.00	....	....	....	1.00	.20

1369

1370 1371

1369	6¢ American Legion	1.75	4.00	8.25(50)	.80	.30	.15
1370	6¢ Grandma Moses	1.75	4.00	8.25(50)	.80	.30	.15
1371	6¢ Apollo 8 Moon Orbit	2.50	5.00	18.00(50)	1.75	.50	.15

1372

1373

1374 1375

1372	6¢ W.C. Handy–Musician	3.50	5.00	22.50(50)	2.25	.50	.15
1373	6¢ California Settlement	1.75	4.00	8.25(50)	.80	.30	.15
1374	6¢ Major J.W. Powell	1.75	4.00	17.50(50)	1.75	.40	.15
1375	6¢ Alabama Statehood	1.75	4.00	17.50(50)	1.75	.40	.15

1376 1377

1378 1379

1376-79	Bontanical Congress, 4 varieties, attached	7.00	9.50	35.00(50)	4.50	3.75	3.00
1376	6¢ Douglas Fir	3.00	....	....	....	1.00	.20
1377	6¢ Lady's-slipper	3.00	....	....	....	1.00	.20
1378	6¢ Ocotillo	3.00	....	....	....	1.00	.20
1379	6¢ Franklinia	3.00	....	....	....	1.00	.20

AVERAGE QUALITY: From 1935 to date, deduct 20% from the Fine price to determine the price for an Average quality stamp.

MINT SHEETS: From 1935 to date, we list prices for standard size Mint Sheets in Fine, Never Hinged condition. The number of stamps in each sheet is noted in ( ).

U.S. Postage #1380-1402

SCOTT NO.	DESCRIPTION	FIRST DAY COVERS SING	FIRST DAY COVERS PL. BLK.	MINT SHEET	PLATE BLOCK	UNUSED F/NH	USED

1380

1381

1382

1383

1380	6¢ Dartmouth College	1.75	4.00	17.50(50)	1.75	.40	.15
1381	6¢ Professional Baseball	16.00	25.00	65.00(50)	6.50	1.50	.20
1382	6¢ College Football	7.00	13.50	27.50(50)	2.25	.75	.20
1383	6¢ Eisenhower	1.75	4.00	5.75(32)	.80	.30	.15

1384

1385

1386

1384	6¢ Christmas 1969	1.75	....	9.00(50)	2.00(10)	.30	.15
1384a	6¢ precancelled set of 4 cities	....	....	225.00(50)	125.00(10)	3.00	....
1385	6¢ Rehabilitation	1.75	4.00	8.00(50)	.80	.30	.15
1386	6¢ William M. Harnett	1.75	4.00	5.75(32)	.80	.30	.15

AMERICAN BALD EAGLE
1387

AFRICAN ELEPHANT HERD
1388

HAIDA CEREMONIAL CANOE
1389

THE AGE OF REPTILES
1390

SCOTT NO.	DESCRIPTION	FIRST DAY COVERS SING	FIRST DAY COVERS PL. BLK.	MINT SHEET	PLATE BLOCK	UNUSED F/NH	USED

1391

1392

1970 COMMEMORATIVES

1387/1422	(1387-92, 1405-22) 24 varieties, (No precancels)	....	....	....	....	11.00	3.20
1387-90	Natural History, 4 varieties, attached	5.00	7.00	10.00(32)	1.75	1.50	.95
1387	6¢ Bald Eagle	2.50	....	....	....	.50	.15
1388	6¢ Elephant Herd	2.50	....	....	....	.50	.15
1389	6¢ Haida Canoe	2.50	....	....	....	.50	.15
1390	6¢ Reptiles	2.50	....	....	....	.50	.15
1391	6¢ Maine Statehood	1.75	4.00	17.50(50)	1.75	.40	.15
1392	6¢ Wildlife–Buffalo	1.75	4.00	17.50(50)	1.75	.40	.15

1393, 1401

1393D

1394

1395, 1402

1396

1397 1398 1399 1400

1970-74 REGULAR ISSUE

1393/1400	6¢-21¢, 8 varieties, complete (No #1395)	....	....	....	....	3.50	1.00
1393	6¢ D. Eisenhower	1.75	4.00	15.50(100)	.80	.30	.15
1393a	6¢ bklt pane of 8	2.75	....	....	....	1.95	....
1393ae	6¢ test gum	90.00	....	....	....	1.90	....
1393b	6¢ bklt pane of 5– Slogan IV or V	3.75	....	....	....	1.40	....
1393D	7¢ B. Franklin (1972)	1.75	4.00	19.75(100)	.95	.30	.15
1394	8¢ Ike–black, blue, red (1971)	1.75	4.00	22.75(100)	1.10	.30	.15
1395	same, deep claret bklt single (1971)	2.50	....	....	....	.45	.15
1395a	8¢ bklt pane of 8	2.50	....	....	....	2.40	....
1395b	8¢ bklt pane of 6	2.25	....	....	....	1.90	....
1395c	8¢ bklt pane of 4, VI & VII (1972)	2.00	....	....	....	1.70	....
1395d	8¢ bklt pane of 7 II or V (1972)	2.50	....	....	....	2.50	....
1396	8¢ Postal Service Emblem (1971)	1.75	4.00	22.50(100)	3.25(12)	.35	.15
1397	14¢ F. LaGuardia (1972)	1.75	4.00	40.00(100)	2.25	.50	.15
1398	16¢ E. Pyle (1971)	2.50	4.50	55.00(100)	2.50	.60	.15
1399	18¢ E. Blackwell (1974)	2.00	4.25	55.00(100)	2.75	.65	.15
1400	21¢ A.P. Giannini (1973)	2.50	4.50	60.00(100)	2.75	.75	.30

1970-71 COIL STAMPS–Perf. 10 Vertically

			LINE PAIR		LINE PAIR		
1401	6¢ D. Eisenhower	1.75	2.75	....	.65	.30	.15
1402	8¢ Eisenhower, claret (1971)	1.75	2.75	....	.70	.35	.15

U.S. Postage #1405-1422

SCOTT NO.	DESCRIPTION	FIRST DAY COVERS SING	FIRST DAY COVERS PL. BLK.	MINT SHEET	PLATE BLOCK	UNUSED F/NH	USED

 1405  1406  1407

 1408  1409

1970 COMMEMORATIVES

SCOTT NO.	DESCRIPTION	SING	PL. BLK.	MINT SHEET	PLATE BLOCK	UNUSED F/NH	USED
1405	6¢ E.L. Master–Poet .	1.75	4.00	17.50(50)	1.75	.40	.15
1406	6¢ Woman Suffrage .	1.75	4.00	9.00(50)	.80	.30	.15
1407	6¢ South Carolina Tercentenary	1.75	4.00	20.00(50)	2.25	.50	.15
1408	6¢ Stone Mountain Memorial	1.75	4.00	22.50(50)	2.25	.50	.15
1409	6¢ Fort Snelling	1.75	4.00	12.50(50)	1.50	.35	.15

 1410  1411

 1412 1413

1410-13	Anti-Pollution, 4 varieties, attached .	5.00	7.00	15.25(50)	3.75(10)	2.50	1.75
1410	6¢ Globe & Wheat . .	2.50	....	....	....	.75	.20
1411	6¢ Globe & City	2.50	....	....	....	.75	.20
1412	6¢ Globe & Bluegill . .	2.50	....	....	....	.75	.20
1413	6¢ Globe & Seagull . .	2.50	....	....	....	.75	.20

 1414

1414	6¢ Nativity	1.75	....	9.00(50)	1.75(8)	.30	.15

 1415  1416

 1417  1418

1415-18	Christmas Toys, 4 varieties, attached .	5.50	....	30.00(50)	6.25(8)	3.00	2.25
1415	6¢ Locomotive	3.00	....	....	....	1.00	.15
1416	6¢ Horse	3.00	....	....	....	1.00	.15
1417	6¢ Tricycle	3.00	....	....	....	1.00	.15
1418	6¢ Doll Carriage	3.00	....	....	....	1.00	.15

Precancelled

1414a	6¢ Nativity (precancelled)	12.00	....	10.25(50)	2.75(8)	.30	.15
1415a-18a	Christmas Toys, precancelled, 4 varieties attached	27.50	....	45.00(50)	9.50(8)	4.25	3.75
1415a	6¢ Locomotive	16.50	....	....	....	1.50	.20
1416a	6¢ Horse	16.50	....	....	....	1.50	.20
1417a	6¢ Tricycle	16.50	....	....	....	1.50	.20
1418a	6¢ Doll Carriage	16.50	....	....	....	1.50	.20

NOTE: *Unused precancels are with original gum, while used are without gum.*

 1419  1420

1419	6¢ U.N. 25th Anniversary	1.75	4.00	9.00(50)	.80	.30	.15
1420	6¢ Pilgrim Landing . .	1.75	4.00	9.00(50)	.80	.30	.15

 1421  1422

1421-22	D.A.V. Servicemen, 2 varieties, attached .	2.00	3.75	9.75(50)	1.75	.50	.35
1421	6¢ Disabled Veterans	1.75	....	....	....	.30	.15
1422	6¢ Prisoners of War .	1.75	....	....	....	.30	.15

FIRST DAY COVERS: First Day Covers are envelopes cancelled on the "First Day of Issue" of the stamp used on the envelope. Usually they also contain a picture (cachet) on the left side designed to go with the theme of the stamp. From 1935 to 1949, prices listed are for cacheted, addressed covers. From 1950 to date, prices are for cacheted, unaddressed covers.

SE-TENANTS: Beginning with the 1964 Christmas issue (#1254-57), the United States has issued numerous Se-Tenant stamps covering a wide variety of subjects. Se-Tenants are issues where two or more different stamp designs are produced on the same sheet in pair, strip or block form. Mint stamps are usually collected in attached blocks, etc.; used are generally saved as single stamps.

U.S. Postage #1423-1443

1971 COMMEMORATIVES

SCOTT NO.	DESCRIPTION	FIRST DAY COVERS SING	FIRST DAY COVERS PL. BLK.	MINT SHEET	PLATE BLOCK	UNUSED F/NH	USED
1423-45	6¢-8¢, 23 varieties complete	....	....	....	....	8.75	3.25
1423	6¢ Sheep	1.75	4.00	9.00(50)	.80	.30	.15
1424	6¢ General D. MacArthur	1.75	4.00	17.50(50)	2.25	.50	.15
1425	6¢ Blood Donors	1.75	4.00	9.00(50)	.80	.30	.15
1426	8¢ Missouri Statehood	1.75	4.00	20.00(50)	5.75(12)	.50	.15

SCOTT NO.	DESCRIPTION	FIRST DAY COVERS SING	FIRST DAY COVERS PL. BLK.	MINT SHEET	PLATE BLOCK	UNUSED F/NH	USED
1427-30	Wildlife Conservation, 4 varieties, attached	3.75	5.50	12.50(32)	2.50	2.00	1.10
1427	8¢ Trout	2.50	....	....	....	.60	.20
1428	8¢ Alligator	2.50	....	....	....	.60	.20
1429	8¢ Polar Bear	2.50	....	....	....	.60	.20
1430	8¢ Condor	2.50	....	....	....	.60	.20

SCOTT NO.	DESCRIPTION	FIRST DAY COVERS SING	FIRST DAY COVERS PL. BLK.	MINT SHEET	PLATE BLOCK	UNUSED F/NH	USED
1431	8¢ Antarctic Treaty	1.75	4.00	11.50(50)	1.25	.35	.15
1432	8¢ American Revolution	1.75	4.00	11.50(50)	1.40	.40	.15
1433	8¢ John Sloan–Artist	1.75	4.00	11.50(50)	1.25	.35	.15

SCOTT NO.	DESCRIPTION	FIRST DAY COVERS SING	FIRST DAY COVERS PL. BLK.	MINT SHEET	PLATE BLOCK	UNUSED F/NH	USED
1434-35	Space Achievements, 2 varieties, attached	2.00	4.50	13.50(50)	1.75	.75	.55
1434	8¢ Moon, Earth, Sun & Landing Craft	1.75	....	....	....	.45	.15
1435	8¢ Lunar Rover	1.75	....	....	....	.45	.15

SCOTT NO.	DESCRIPTION	FIRST DAY COVERS SING	FIRST DAY COVERS PL. BLK.	MINT SHEET	PLATE BLOCK	UNUSED F/NH	USED
1436	8¢ Emily Dickinson	1.75	4.00	17.50(50)	1.75	.40	.15
1437	8¢ San Juan	1.75	4.00	11.25(50)	1.25	.35	.15
1438	8¢ Drug Addiction	1.75	4.00	11.25(50)	1.75(6)	.35	.15
1439	8¢ CARE	1.75	4.00	11.25(50)	2.20(8)	.35	.15

SCOTT NO.	DESCRIPTION	FIRST DAY COVERS SING	FIRST DAY COVERS PL. BLK.	MINT SHEET	PLATE BLOCK	UNUSED F/NH	USED
1440-43	Historic Preservation 4 varieties, attached	3.75	5.50	12.50(32)	2.00	1.75	1.00
1440	8¢ Decatur House	2.50	....	....	....	.60	.15
1441	8¢ Whaling Ship	2.50	....	....	....	.60	.15
1442	8¢ Cable Car	2.50	....	....	....	.60	.15
1443	8¢ Mission	2.50	....	....	....	.60	.15

–Supplies–
Don't forget that Harris offers a complete line of albums, supplies and accessories for all your stamp collecting needs!

U.S. Postage #1444-1463a

1444

1455

SCOTT NO.	DESCRIPTION	FIRST DAY COVERS SING	PL. BLK.	MINT SHEET	PLATE BLOCK	UNUSED F/NH	USED
1444	8¢ Christmas Nativity	1.75	4.00	11.25(50)	3.00(12)	.35	.15
1445	8¢ Christmas Patridge	1.75	4.00	11.25(50)	3.00(12)	.35	.15

1972 COMMEMORATIVES

SCOTT NO.	DESCRIPTION	FIRST DAY COVERS SING	PL. BLK.	MINT SHEET	PLATE BLOCK	UNUSED F/NH	USED
1455	8¢ Family Planning	1.75	4.00	11.25(50)	1.25	.35	.15

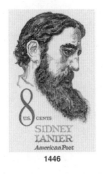

1446

1447

1456

1457

1972 COMMEMORATIVES

Scott	Description						
1446-74	29 varieties, complete	....	....	....	....	10.15	4.10
1446	8¢ Sidney Lanier–Poet	1.75	4.00	17.50(50)	2.25	.50	.15
1447	8¢ Peace Corps	1.75	4.00	12.50(50)	1.80(6)	.35	.15

1458   1459

1448

1449

1452

1456-59	Colonial Craftsmen, 4 varieties, attached	3.75	4.75	15.00(50)	1.75	1.50	.90
1456	8¢ Glassmaker	2.25	....	....	....	.45	.15
1457	8¢ Silversmith	2.25	....	....	....	.45	.15
1458	8¢ Wigmaker	2.25	....	....	....	.45	.15
1459	8¢ Hatter	2.25	....	....	....	.45	.15

1450

1451

1460

1454

1453

1461

1462

1460	6¢ Olympics–Cycling	2.10	4.25	9.25(50)	2.00(10)	.30	.15
1461	8¢ Olympics–Bob Sled Racing	2.10	4.25	12.25(50)	2.80(10)	.35	.15
1462	15¢ Olympics–Foot Racing	2.10	4.25	22.00(50)	4.75(10)	.50	.35

1972 NATIONAL PARKS CENTENNIAL

Scott	Description						
1448-54	2¢-15¢, 7 varieties, complete	....	....	....	....	2.00	.90
1448-51	Cape Hatteras, 4 varieties, attached	1.75	2.50	11.00(100)	.85	.75	.65
1448	2¢ Ship's Hull	....	....	....	....	.25	.10
1449	2¢ Lighthouse	....	....	....	....	.25	.10
1450	2¢ Three Seagulls	....	....	....	....	.25	.10
1451	2¢ Two Seagulls	....	....	....	....	.25	.10
1452	6¢ Wolf Trap Farm Park	1.75	4.00	15.00(50)	1.75	.40	.15
1453	8¢ Yellowstone Park	1.75	4.00	8.50(32)	1.25	.40	.15
1454	15¢ Mount McKinley	1.75	4.00	25.00(50)	2.25	.60	.25

1463

1463	8¢ Parent Teacher Association	1.75	4.00	17.50(50)	1.50	.40	.15
1463a	Same, Reversed Plate Number	1.75	4.00	11.75(50)	1.40	....	....

U.S. Postage #1464-1483

SCOTT NO.	DESCRIPTION	FIRST DAY COVERS SING	PL. BLK.	MINT SHEET	PLATE BLOCK	UNUSED F/NH	USED

1464

1465

1466

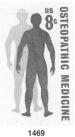
1467

1464-67	Wildlife Conservation, 4 varieties, attached	2.75	3.50	9.00(32)	1.75	1.50	1.10
1464	8¢ Fur Seal	1.75	....	....	....	.45	.15
1465	8¢ Cardinal	1.75	....	....	....	.45	.15
1466	8¢ Brown Pelican	1.75	....	....	....	.45	.15
1467	8¢ Bighorn Sheep	1.75	....	....	....	.45	.15

1468

1469

1470

1468	8¢ Mail Order Business	1.75	4.00	17.50(50)	4.50(12)	.40	.15
1469	8¢ Osteopathic Medicine	2.00	4.25	20.00(50)	2.75(6)	.50	.15
1470	Tom Sawyer–Folklore	1.75	4.00	20.00(50)	2.25	.50	.15

1471

1472

1473

1471	8¢ Christmas–Virgin Mother	1.75	4.00	14.00(50)	3.50(12)	.35	.15
1472	8¢ Christmas–Santa Claus	1.75	4.00	17.50(50)	4.00(12)	.40	.15
1473	8¢ Pharmacy	2.25	4.50	19.50(50)	2.25(4)	.50	.15

1474

1475

| 1474 | 8¢ Stamp Collecting | 2.00 | 4.25 | 9.50(40) | 1.25(4) | .35 | .15 |

1476

1477

1478

1479

1973 COMMEMORATIVES

| 1475-1508 | 34 varieties, complete | .... | .... | .... | .... | 12.00 | 5.30 |
| 1475 | 8¢ "Love" | 2.25 | 5.00 | 17.50(50) | 2.25(6) | .40 | .15 |

COLONIAL COMMUNICATIONS

1476	8¢ Pamphlet Printing	1.75	4.00	15.00(50)	1.75	.40	.15
1477	8¢ Posting Broadside	1.75	4.00	15.00(50)	1.75	.40	.15
1478	8¢ Colonial Post Rider	1.75	4.00	15.00(50)	1.75	.40	.15
1479	8¢ Drummer & Soldiers	1.75	4.00	15.00(50)	1.75	.40	.15

1480

1481

1482

1483

1480-83	Boston Tea Party, 4 varieties, attached	4.50	6.50	13.00(50)	1.75	1.50	1.10
1480	8¢ Throwing Tea	2.25	....	....	....	.45	.15
1481	8¢ Ship	2.25	....	....	....	.45	.15
1482	8¢ Rowboats	2.25	....	....	....	.45	.15
1483	8¢ Rowboats & Docks	2.25	....	....	....	.45	.15

1484

1488

1485

1486

1487

U.S. Postage #1484-1508

SCOTT NO.	DESCRIPTION	FIRST DAY COVERS SING	FIRST DAY COVERS PL. BLK.	MINT SHEET	PLATE BLOCK	UNUSED F/NH	USED
	AMERICAN ARTS						
1484	8¢ George Gershwin–Composer	1.75	4.00	10.25(40)	3.75(12)	.35	.15
1485	8¢ Robinson Jeffers–Poet	1.75	4.00	10.25(40)	3.75(12)	.35	.15
1486	8¢ Henry O. Tanner–Artist	1.75	4.00	10.25(40)	3.75(12)	.35	.15
1487	8¢ Willa Cather–Novelist	1.75	4.00	10.25(40)	3.75(12)	.35	.15
1488	8¢ Nicolaus Copernicus	1.75	4.00	12.25(40)	1.50	.35	.15

1489

1490

1491

1492

1493

1494

1495

1496

1497

1498

1973 POSTAL SERVICE EMPLOYEES

1489-98	10 varieties, complete, attached	6.50	....	18.00(50)	9.00(20)	4.00	2.75
1489-98	Set of singles, complete	22.00	....	....	....	4.25	1.90
1489	8¢ Window Clerk	2.25	....	....	....	.45	.20
1490	8¢ Mail Pickup	2.25	....	....	....	.45	.20
1491	8¢ Conveyor Belt	2.25	....	....	....	.45	.20
1492	8¢ Sacking Parcels	2.25	....	....	....	.45	.20
1493	8¢ Mail Cancelling	2.25	....	....	....	.45	.20
1494	8¢ Manual Sorting	2.25	....	....	....	.45	.20
1495	8¢ Machine Sorting	2.25	....	....	....	.45	.20
1496	8¢ Loading Truck	2.25	....	....	....	.45	.20
1497	8¢ Letter Carrier	2.25	....	....	....	.45	.20
1498	8¢ Rural Delivery	2.25	....	....	....	.45	.20

1499

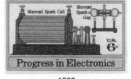
1500

1501

1502

1503

1973 COMMEMORATIVES

1499	8¢ Harry S. Truman	1.75	4.00	14.00(32)	2.25	.50	.15
1500	6¢ Electronics	1.75	4.00	9.50(50)	1.00	.35	.15
1501	8¢ Electronics	1.75	4.00	11.50(50)	1.25	.35	.15
1502	15¢ Electronics	1.75	4.00	25.00(50)	2.50	.60	.40
1503	8¢ Lyndon B. Johnson	1.75	4.00	8.00(32)	3.50(12)	.35	.15

1504

1505

1506

1973-74 RURAL AMERICA

1504	8¢ Angus Cattle	1.75	4.00	11.50(50)	1.25	.35	.15
1505	10¢ Chautauqua (1974)	1.75	4.00	14.00(50)	1.50	.35	.15
1506	10¢ Winter Wheat (1974)	1.75	4.00	14.00(50)	1.50	.35	.15

1507

1508

1973 CHRISTMAS

1507	8¢ Madonna	1.75	3.25	14.50(50)	3.50(12)	.35	.15
1508	8¢ Christmas Tree	1.75	3.25	14.50(50)	3.50(12)	.35	.15

Insist on Genuine H.E. Harris Products Backed by 89 years of experience!

U.S. Postage #1509-1541

SCOTT NO.	DESCRIPTION	FIRST DAY COVERS SING	PL. BLK.	MINT SHEET	PLATE BLOCK	UNUSED F/NH	USED

1509, 1519   1510, 1520   1511   1518

1973-74 REGULAR ISSUES

Scott	Description	FDC Sing	PL BLK	Mint Sheet	Plate Block	Unused	Used
1509	10¢ Crossed Flags	1.75	4.00	33.25(100)	7.25(20)	.35	.15
1510	10¢ Jefferson Memorial	1.75	4.00	30.00(100)	1.50	.35	.15
1510b	10¢ bklt pane of 5— Slogan VIII	1.95	......	......	......	1.85	......
1510c	10¢ bklt pane of 8	1.95	......	......	......	2.50	......
1510d	10¢ bklt pane of 6 (1974)	1.95	......	......	......	8.75	......
1511	10¢ Zip Code Theme (1974)	1.75	4.00	29.50(100)	2.75(8)	.35	.15

BOOKLET PANE SLOGANS
VI–Stamps in This Book....   VII– This Book Contains 25....   VIII–Paying Bills....

COIL STAMPS Perf.10 Vertically

Scott	Description	FDC Sing	LINE PAIR		LINE PAIR	Unused	Used
1518	6.3¢ Liberty Bell	1.75	2.75	......	.70	.30	.15
1519	10¢ Crossed Flags	1.75	......	......	......	.40	.15
1520	10¢ Jefferson Memorial	1.75	2.75	......	.80	.35	.15

1525

1527

1526

1528

1529

1974 COMMEMORATIVES

Scott	Description	FDC Sing	PL BLK	Mint Sheet	Plate Block	Unused	Used
1525-52	28 varieties, complete	......	......	......	......	10.80	4.50
1525	10¢ Veterans of Foreign Wars	1.75	4.00	14.00(50)	1.40	.35	.15
1526	10¢ Robert Frost	1.75	4.00	14.00(50)	1.40	.35	.15
1527	10¢ Environment– EXPO '74	1.75	4.00	14.00(40)	4.00(12)	.35	.15
1528	10¢ Horse Racing	1.75	4.00	14.25(50)	4.00(12)	.35	.15
1529	10¢ Skylab Project	1.75	4.00	14.25(50)	1.40	.35	.15

1530

1531

1532

1533

1534

1535

1536

1537

1974 UNIVERSAL POSTAL UNION

Scott	Description	FDC Sing	PL BLK	Mint Sheet	Plate Block	Unused	Used
1530-37	8 varieties, attached	4.25	......	15.00(32)	7.50(16)	3.50(8)	2.95
1530-37	Set of singles, complete	13.50	......	......	......	3.25	2.25
1530	10¢ Raphael	1.75	......	......	......	.50	.30
1531	10¢ Hokusai	1.75	......	......	......	.50	.30
1532	10¢ J.F. Peto	1.75	......	......	......	.50	.30
1533	10¢ J.E. Liotard	1.75	......	......	......	.50	.30
1534	10¢ G. Terborch	1.75	......	......	......	.50	.30
1535	10¢ J.B.S. Chardin	1.75	......	......	......	.50	.30
1536	10¢ T. Gainsborough	1.75	......	......	......	.50	.30
1537	10¢ F. de Goya	1.75	......	......	......	.50	.30

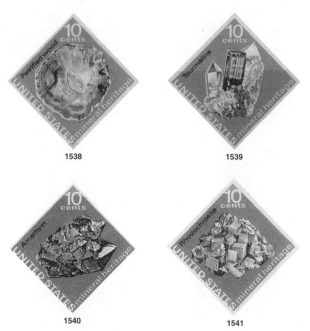

1538   1539   1540   1541

1974 COMMEMORATIVES

Scott	Description	FDC Sing	PL BLK	Mint Sheet	Plate Block	Unused	Used
1538-41	Mineral Heritage, 4 varieties, attached	3.50	5.00	17.50(48)	2.00	1.75	1.25
1538	10¢ Petrified Wood	2.25	......	......	......	.50	.15
1539	10¢ Tourmaline	2.25	......	......	......	.50	.15
1540	10¢ Amethyst	2.25	......	......	......	.50	.15
1541	10¢ Rhodochrosite	2.25	......	......	......	.50	.15

U.S. Postage #1542-1564

SCOTT NO.	DESCRIPTION	FIRST DAY COVERS SING	FIRST DAY COVERS PL. BLK.	MINT SHEET	PLATE BLOCK	UNUSED F/NH	USED

1542

1543

1544

1545

1546

1542	10¢ Fort Harrod Bicentennial	1.75	4.00	20.00(50)	2.00	.45	.15
1543-46	Continental Congress, 4 varieties, attached	2.75	3.75	16.25(50)	2.00	1.75	1.25
1543	10¢ Carpenter's Hall	1.75	....	....	....	.50	.15
1544	10¢ Quote—First Congress	1.75	....	....	....	.50	.15
1545	10¢ Quote—Declaration of Independence	1.75	....	....	....	.50	.15
1546	10¢ Independence Hall	1.75	....	....	....	.50	.15

1547

1548

1549

1547	10¢ Energy Conservation	1.75	4.00	14.00(50)	1.50	.35	.15
1548	10¢ Sleepy Hollow	1.75	4.00	14.00(50)	1.50	.35	.15
1549	10¢ Retarded Children	1.75	4.00	14.00(50)	1.50	.35	.15

1550

1551

1552

1550	10¢ Christmas—Angel	1.75	4.00	14.00(50)	4.00(10)	.35	.15
1551	10¢ Christmas—Currier & Ives	1.75	4.00	14.00(50)	4.50(12)	.35	.15
1552	10¢ Christams— Dove of Peace	1.75	4.00	14.00(50)	7.50(20)	.40	.15
1552	same	....	....	....	4.75(12)	....	....

1553

1554

1555

1975 COMMEMORATIVES

1553-80	8¢-10¢, 28 varieties, complete	....	....	....	....	12.00	4.45
1553	10¢ Benjamin West— Arts	1.75	4.00	20.00(50)	5.00(10)	.45	.15
1554	10¢ Paul Dunbar—Arts	1.75	4.00	20.00(50)	5.00(10)	.45	.15
1555	10¢ D.W. Griffith—Arts	1.75	4.00	20.00(50)	2.00	.45	.15

1556

1557

1558

1556	10¢ Pioneer 10	1.75	4.00	17.00(50)	2.00	.45	.15
1557	10¢ Mariner 10	1.75	4.00	17.00(50)	2.00	.45	.15
1558	10¢ Collective Bargaining	1.75	4.00	14.50(50)	3.00(8)	.40	.15

1559

1560

1561

1562

1559	8¢ Sybil Ludington	1.75	4.00	14.00(50)	4.00(10)	.35	.20
1560	10¢ Salem Poor	1.75	4.00	20.00(50)	5.00(10)	.45	.15
1561	10¢ Haym Salomon	1.75	4.00	20.00(50)	5.00(10)	.45	.15
1562	18¢ Peter Francisco	1.75	4.00	27.50(50)	7.50(10)	.70	.40

1563

1564

| 1563 | 10¢ Lexington-Concord | 1.75 | 4.00 | 15.00(40) | 5.50(12) | .45 | .15 |
| 1564 | 10¢ Battle of Bunker Hill | 1.75 | 4.00 | 15.00(40) | 5.50(12) | .45 | .15 |

U.S. Postage #1565-1580b

SCOTT NO.	DESCRIPTION	FIRST DAY COVERS SING	FIRST DAY COVERS PL. BLK.	MINT SHEET	PLATE BLOCK	UNUSED F/NH	USED
	 1565  1566  1567 1568						
1565-68	Military Uniforms, 4 varieties, attached	2.75	3.75	15.00(50)	5.00(12)	1.75	1.30
1565	10¢ Continental Army	1.75				.50	.20
1566	10¢ Continental Navy	1.75				.50	.20
1567	10¢ Continental Marines	1.75				.50	.20
1568	10¢ American Militia	1.75				.50	.20
	 1569						
	 1570						
1569-70	Apollo-Soyuz Mission, 2 varieties, attached	3.00	4.50	8.00(24)	5.00(12)	.95	.55
1569	10¢ Docked	2.25				.50	.15
1570	10¢ Docking	2.25				.50	.15
	 1571						
1571	10¢ International Women's Year	1.75	4.00	14.00(50)	2.10(6)	.35	.15
	 1572 1573						
	 1574 1575						
1572-75	Postal Service Bicentennial, 4 varieties, attached	2.75	3.75	15.00(50)	5.00(12)	1.85	1.00
1572	10¢ Stagecoach & Trailer	1.75				.50	.15
1573	10¢ Locomotives	1.75				.50	.15
1574	10¢ Airplanes	1.75				.50	.15
1575	10¢ Satellite	1.75				.50	.15

SCOTT NO.	DESCRIPTION	FIRST DAY COVERS SING	FIRST DAY COVERS PL. BLK.	MINT SHEET	PLATE BLOCK	UNUSED F/NH	USED
	 1576						
	 1577  1578						
1576	10¢ World Peace through Law	1.75	4.00	18.00(50)	2.00	.45	.15
1577-78	Banking & Commerce, 2 varieties, attached	2.50	3.75	18.00(40)	2.00	1.00	.70
1577	10¢ Banking	1.75				.60	.15
1578	10¢ Commerce	1.75				.60	.15
	 1579 1580						
1579	(10¢) Madonna	1.75	4.00	18.00(50)	5.00(12)	.45	.15
1580	(10¢) Christams Card	1.75	4.00	18.00(50)	5.00(12)	.45	.15
1580b	(10¢) Christmas Card, perf. 10½ x 11			48.50(50)	15.00(12)	1.00	.30

1581, 1811   1582   1584   1585

1590, 1591, 1616   1592, 1617   1593   1594, 1816

1595, 1618   1596   1597, 1598, 1618C   1599, 1619

1603   1604   1605   1606

U.S. Postage #1581-1632

1608 1610 1611 1612

1622, 1625   1623, 1623b

1975-81 AMERICANA ISSUE

SCOTT NO.	DESCRIPTION	FIRST DAY COVERS SING	PL. BLK.	MINT SHEET	PLATE BLOCK	UNUSED F/NH	USED
1581/1612	1¢-$5, (No #1590, 1590a, 1595, or 1598) 19 varieties, complete	51.50	....	....	155.00	33.50	5.50
1581	1¢ Inkwell & Quill (1977)	1.75	4.00	7.00(100)	.70	.20	.15
1582	2¢ Speaker's Stand (1977)	1.75	4.00	8.25(100)	.70	.20	.15
1584	3¢ Ballot Box (1977)	1.75	4.00	11.50(100)	.70	.20	.15
1585	4¢ Books & Eyeglasses (1977)	1.75	4.00	13.00(100)	.70	.20	.15
1590	9¢ Capitol, from bklt pane (1977)	15.00	....	....	....	1.10	1.10
1590a	same, perf 10 (1977)	....	....	....	....	31.50	....
1590,1623	Attached pair, from bklt pane	....	....	....	....	1.50	....
1590a, 1623b	Attached pair, perf. 10	....	....	....	....	32.50	....
1591	9¢ Capitol, grey paper	1.75	4.00	30.00(100)	1.50	.40	.15
1592	10¢ Justice (1977)	1.75	4.00	32.00(100)	1.50	.40	.15
1593	11¢ Printing Press	1.75	4.00	40.00(100)	1.75	.50	.15
1594	12¢ Torch (1981)	1.75	4.00	42.50(100)	2.25	.50	.15
1595	13¢ Liberty Bell from bklt pane	1.75	....	....	....	.50	.15
1595a	13¢ bklt pane of 6	2.25	....	....	....	3.25	....
1595b	13¢ bklt pane of 7– Slogan VIII	2.50	....	....	....	3.50	....
1595c	13¢ bklt pane of 8	2.50	....	....	....	3.50	....
1595d	13¢ bklt pane of 5– Slogan IX (1976)	1.75	....	....	....	3.50	....

VIII–Paying Bills... IX–Collect Stamps...

1596	13¢ Eagle & Shield	1.75	4.00	45.00(100)	6.00(12)	.50	.15
1597	15¢ Fort McHenry Flag (1978)	1.75	4.00	43.00(100)	9.50(20)	.50	.15
1598	same, from bklt pane (1978)	1.75	....	....	....	.90	.15
1598a	15¢ bklt pane of 8	3.00	....	....	....	8.50	....
1599	16¢ Statue of Liberty (1978)	1.75	4.00	60.00(100)	3.25	.75	.15
1603	24¢ Old North Church	1.75	4.00	80.00(100)	4.00	.95	.15
1604	28¢ Fort Nisqually (1978)	1.75	4.00	85.00(100)	5.00	1.00	.15
1605	29¢ Lighthouse (1978)	1.75	4.00	100.00(100)	5.00	1.20	.20
1606	30¢ School House (1979)	1.75	4.00	100.00(100)	5.00	1.20	.15
1608	50¢ "Betty" Lamp (1979)	2.50	5.25	180.00(100)	8.25	2.00	.15
1610	$1 Rush Lamp (1979)	3.50	17.50	350.00(100)	14.50	3.50	.15
1610c	Same, candle flame inverted	....	....	....	....	14500.00	....
1611	$2 Kerosene Lamp (1978)	7.00	14.50	600.00(100)	27.00	6.25	.70
1612	$5 Conductor's Lantern (1979)	15.00	31.50	1400.00(100)	70.00	15.00	3.00

1613 1614 1615 1615C

1975-79 COIL STAMPS Perforated Vertically

					LINE PR.		
1613-19	3.1¢-16¢, 9 varieties, complete	....	....	....	9.25	3.35	1.25
1613	3.1¢ Guitar (1979)	1.75	2.75	....	.90	.25	.15
1614	7.7¢ Saxhorns (1976)	1.75	2.75	....	1.30	.35	.15
1615	7.9¢ Drum (1976)	1.75	2.75	....	.90	.35	.15
1615C	8.4¢ Piano (1978)	1.75	2.75	....	2.75	.40	.15
1616	9¢ Capitol (1976)	1.75	2.75	....	.90	.40	.15
1617	10¢ Justice (1977)	1.75	2.75	....	.90	.35	.15
1618	13¢ Liberty Bell	1.75	2.75	....	1.00	.45	.15
1618C	15¢ Fort McHenry Flag (1978)	1.75	....	....	....	.50	.15
1619	16¢ Statue of Liberty (1978)	1.75	2.75	....	1.40	.50	.30

COIL LINE PAIRS: are two connected coil stamps with a line the same color as the stamps printed between the two stamps. This line usually appears every 20 to 30 stamps on a roll depending on the issue.

1975-77 REGULAR ISSUES

1622	13¢ Flag & Independence Hall, 11 x 10½	1.75	4.00	35.00(100)	8.50(20)	.45	.15
1622c	same, perf. 11 (1981)	....	....	180.00(100)	90.00(20)	1.20	....
1623	13¢ Flag & Capitol from pane, perf 11 x 10½ (1977)	3.00	....	....	....	.45	.15
1623a	bklt pane of 8 (one–1590, seven–1623)	45.00	....	....	....	2.80	....
1623b	13¢ Flag & Capitol from bklt pane, perf. 10	1.75	....	....	....	.60	.55
1623c	bklt pane of 8 (one–1590a, seven–1623b)	22.50	....	....	....	35.00	....

1975 COIL STAMP

1625	13¢ Flag & Independence Hall	1.75	....	....	....	.55	.15

1629 1630 1631

1632

1976 COMMEMORATIVES

1629/1703	(1629-32, 1683-85, 1690-1703) 21 varieties	....	....	....	....	12.80	3.50
1629-31	Spirit of '76, 3 varieties, attached	3.00	6.00	19.00(50)	6.00(12)	1.75	1.25
1629	13¢ Boy Drummer	2.00	....	....	....	.50	.20
1630	13¢ Older Drummer	2.00	....	....	....	.50	.20
1631	13¢ Fifer	2.00	....	....	....	.50	.20
1632	13¢ Interphil	1.75	4.00	18.75(50)	1.75	.45	.20

1633 1682

1976 BICENTENNIAL STATE FLAGS
Complete Set Printed in One Sheet of 50 Stamps

1633	Delaware	1650	Louisiana	1667	West Virginia
1634	Pennsylvania	1651	Indiana	1668	Nevada
1635	New Jersey	1652	Mississippi	1669	Nebraska
1636	Georgia	1653	Illinois	1670	Colorado
1637	Connecticut	1654	Alabama	1671	North Dakota
1638	Massachusetts	1655	Maine	1672	South Dakota
1639	Maryland	1656	Missouri	1673	Montana
1640	South Carolina	1657	Arkansas	1674	Washington
1641	New Hampshire	1658	Michigan	1675	Idaho
1642	Virginia	1659	Florida	1676	Wyoming
1643	New York	1660	Texas	1677	Utah
1644	North Carolina	1661	Iowa	1678	Oklahoma
1645	Rhode Island	1662	Wisconsin	1679	New Mexico
1646	Vermont	1663	California	1680	Arizona
1647	Kentucky	1664	Minnesota	1681	Alaska
1648	Tennessee	1665	Oregon	1682	Hawaii
1649	Ohio	1666	Kansas		

56 U.S. Postage #1633-1703

1976 BICENTENNIAL STATE FLAGS
Complete Set Printed in One Sheet of 50 Stamps
Continued

SCOTT NO.	DESCRIPTION	FIRST DAY COVERS SING	FIRST DAY COVERS PL. BLK.	MINT SHEET	PLATE BLOCK	UNUSED F/NH	USED
1633-82	13¢ State Flags, 50 varieties, attached	....	....	27.50(50)	....	27.50	....
	Set of 50 singles	95.00	....	....	....	....	18.75
	Singles of above	2.00	....	....	....	.75	.50

1683

1684

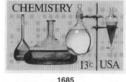
1685

1683	13¢ Telephone	1.75	4.00	20.00(50)	2.10	.50	.15
1684	13¢ Aviation	1.75	4.00	20.00(50)	5.50(10)	.50	.15
1685	13¢ Chemistry	1.75	4.00	25.00(50)	7.50(12)	.60	.15

1686

1687

1976 BICENNTENNIAL SOUVENIR SHEETS

1686-89	4 varieties, complete	32.50	....	....	....	30.00	27.00
1686	13¢ Cornwallis Surrender	6.00	....	....	....	5.00	4.75
1686a-e	13¢ singles, each	3.50	....	....	....	1.20	1.10
1687	18¢ Independence	7.50	....	....	....	7.00	6.50
1687a-e	18¢ singles, each	3.75	....	....	....	1.60	1.50
1688	24¢ Washington Crossing Delaware	9.50	....	....	....	8.75	8.25
1688a-e	24¢ singles, each	4.25	....	....	....	1.90	1.80
1689	31¢ Washington at Valley Forge	11.50	....	....	....	11.00	10.50
1689a-e	31¢ singles, each	5.25	....	....	....	2.40	2.30

1690

1691　1692　1693　1694

SCOTT NO.	DESCRIPTION	FIRST DAY COVERS SING	FIRST DAY COVERS PL. BLK.	MINT SHEET	PLATE BLOCK	UNUSED F/NH	USED
1690	13¢ Benjamin Franklin	1.75	4.00	20.00(50)	1.85	.50	.15
1691-94	Declaration of Independence, 4 varieties, attached	5.00	10.00	30.00(50)	14.50(16)	4.00	2.25
1691	13¢ Delegation members	1.75	....	....	....	1.10	.20
1692	13¢ Adams, etc.	1.75	....	....	....	1.10	.20
1693	13¢ Jefferson, Franklin, etc.	1.75	....	....	....	1.10	.20
1694	13¢ Hancock, Thomson, etc.	1.75	....	....	....	1.10	.20

1695　1696　1697　1698

1695-98	Olympic Games, 4 varieties, attached	2.50	3.50	23.50(50)	6.75(12)	2.40	1.75
1695	13¢ Diving	1.75	....	....	....	.75	.20
1696	13¢ Skiing	1.75	....	....	....	.75	.20
1697	13¢ Running	1.75	....	....	....	.75	.20
1698	13¢ Skating	1.75	....	....	....	.75	.20

1699

1700

1699	13¢ Clara Maass	1.75	4.00	20.00(40)	7.00(12)	.60	.15
1700	13¢ Adolph S. Ochs	1.75	4.00	16.00(32)	2.25	.60	.15

1701

1702, 1703

1701	13¢ Nativity	1.75	....	20.00(50)	6.00(12)	.55	.15
1702	13¢ "Winter Pastime" (Andreati)	1.75	....	20.00(50)	5.25(10)	.55	.15
1703	13¢ "Winter Pastime" (Gravure Int.)	2.25	....	20.00(50)	10.00(20)	.55	.15

U.S. Postage #1704-1724

SCOTT NO.	DESCRIPTION	FIRST DAY COVERS SING	FIRST DAY COVERS PL. BLK.	MINT SHEET	PLATE BLOCK	UNUSED F/NH	USED

1704

1705

1977 COMMEMORATIVES

1704-30	27 varieties, complete	....	....	....	....	13.00	4.00
1704	13¢ Princeton	1.75	4.00	20.00(40)	5.50(10)	.60	.15
1705	13¢ Sound Recording	1.75	4.00	25.00(50)	2.25	.60	.15

1706

1707

1708

1709

1706-09	Pueblo Art, 4 varieties, attached	2.50	....	16.00(40)	5.00(10)	2.00	1.50
1706	13¢ Zia	1.75	....	....	....	.60	.20
1707	13¢ San Ildefonso	1.75	....	....	....	.60	.20
1708	13¢ Hopi	1.75	....	....	....	.60	.20
1709	13¢ Acoma	1.75	....	....	....	.60	.20

1710

1711

| 1710 | 13¢ Transatlantic Flight | 2.00 | 4.25 | 20.00(50) | 5.50(12) | .50 | .15 |
| 1711 | 13¢ Colorado Statehood | 1.75 | 4.00 | 20.00(50) | 5.50(12) | .50 | .15 |

1712   1713

1714

1715

1716

1712-15	Butterflies, 4 varieties, attached	3.50	....	18.75(50)	5.75(12)	2.00	1.75
1712	13¢ Swallowtail	1.75	....	....	....	.60	.20
1713	13¢ Checkerspot	1.75	....	....	....	.60	.20
1714	13¢ Dogface	1.75	....	....	....	.60	.20
1715	13¢ Orange-Tip	1.75	....	....	....	.60	.20
1716	13¢ Lafayette	1.75	4.00	17.00(40)	1.90	.50	.15

1717

1718

1719

1720

1717-20	Skilled Hands, 4 varieties, attached	2.50	....	18.75(50)	5.75(12)	2.00	1.75
1717	13¢ Seamstress	1.75	....	....	....	.60	.20
1718	13¢ Blacksmith	1.75	....	....	....	.60	.20
1719	13¢ Wheelwright	1.75	....	....	....	.60	.20
1720	13¢ Leatherworker	1.75	....	....	....	.60	.20

1721

1722

1723   1724

1721	13¢ Peace Bridge	1.75	4.00	20.00(50)	1.90	.50	.15
1722	13¢ Herkimer at Oriskany	1.75	4.00	17.50(40)	4.75(10)	.50	.15
1723-24	Energy, 2 varieties, attached	2.50	....	15.50(40)	5.25(12)	1.10	.70
1723	13¢ Conservation	1.75	....	....	....	.60	.15
1724	13¢ Development	1.75	....	....	....	.60	.15

MINT SHEETS: From 1935 to date, we list prices for standard size Mint Sheets in Fine, Never Hinged condition. The number of stamps in each sheet is noted in ( ).

U.S. Postage #1725-1752

SCOTT NO.	DESCRIPTION	FIRST DAY COVERS SING	FIRST DAY COVERS PL. BLK.	MINT SHEET	PLATE BLOCK	UNUSED F/NH	USED
1725	13¢ Alta California	1.75	4.00	20.00(50)	1.90	.50	.15
1726	13¢ Articles of Confederation	1.75	4.00	20.00(50)	1.90	.50	.15
1727	13¢ Talking Pictures	1.75	4.00	20.00(50)	1.90	.50	.15
1728	13¢ Surrender at Saratoga	1.75	....	17.50(40)	4.75(10)	.50	.15
1729	13¢ Washington, Christmas	2.50	....	42.50(100)	9.00(20)	.50	.15
1730	13¢ Rural Mailbox, Christmas	2.50	....	42.50(100)	4.75(10)	.50	.15

1978 COMMEMORATIVES

1731/69	(1731-33, 1744-56, 1758-69) 28 varieties	....	....	....	....	14.25	4.25
1731	13¢ Carl Sandburg	1.75	4.00	20.00(50)	1.90	.50	.15
1732-33	Captain Cook, 2 varieties, attached	2.00	....	18.75(50)	8.75(20)	1.25	.80
1732	13¢ Captain Cook (Alaska)	1.75	4.00	....	1.90	.55	.15
1733	13¢ "Resolution" (Hawaii)	1.75	4.00	....	1.90	.55	.15

NOTE: The Plate Block set includes #1732 & 1733 Plate Blocks of four.

1978-80 DEFINITIVES

1734	13¢ Indian Head Penny	1.75	4.00	62.50(150)	2.25	.50	.15
1735	(15¢) "A" Definitive (Gravure)	1.75	4.00	47.50(100)	2.25	.50	.15
1736	same (Intaglio), from bklt pane	1.75	....	....	....	.50	.15
1736a	15¢ "A" bklt pane of 8	3.50	....	....	....	3.85	....
1737	15¢ Roses	1.75	....	....	....	.50	.15
1737a	same, bklt pane of 8	4.00	....	....	....	3.85	....

SCOTT NO.	DESCRIPTION	FIRST DAY COVERS SING	FIRST DAY COVERS PL. BLK.	MINT SHEET	PLATE BLOCK	UNUSED F/NH	USED
1738-42	Windmills, strip of 5, attached (1980)	3.75	....	....	....	3.00	....
1738	15¢ Virginia Windmill	1.75	....	....	....	.70	.15
1739	15¢ Rhode Island Windmill	1.75	....	....	....	.70	.15
1740	15¢ Massachusetts Windmill	1.75	....	....	....	.70	.15
1741	15¢ Illinois Windmill	1.75	....	....	....	.70	.15
1742	15¢ Texas Windmill	1.75	....	....	....	.70	.15
1742a	Same, bklt pane of 10	4.50	....	....	....	5.75	....

1978 COIL STAMP

			LINE PR.		LINE PR.		
1743	(15¢) "A" Definitive	1.75	2.75	....	1.20	.50	.15

1744	13¢ Harriet Tubman	1.75	4.00	28.00(50)	7.50(12)	.65	.15
1745-48	Quilts, 4 varieties, attached	3.50	....	19.50(48)	5.50(12)	1.95	1.50
1745	13¢ Flowers	2.25	....	....	....	.65	.20
1746	13¢ Stars	2.25	....	....	....	.65	.20
1747	13¢ Stripes	2.25	....	....	....	.65	.20
1748	13¢ Plaid	2.25	....	....	....	.65	.20
1749-52	American Dance, 4 varieties, attached	3.50	....	19.50(48)	5.50(12)	1.95	1.50
1749	13¢ Ballet	1.75	....	....	....	.65	.20
1750	13¢ Theater	1.75	....	....	....	.65	.20
1751	13¢ Folk	1.75	....	....	....	.65	.20
1752	13¢ Modern	1.75	....	....	....	.65	.20

U.S. Postage #1775-1798a

SCOTT NO.	DESCRIPTION	FIRST DAY COVERS SING	PL. BLK.	MINT SHEET	PLATE BLOCK	UNUSED F/NH	USED

1775 Pennsylvania Toleware Folk Art USA 15c

1776 Pennsylvania Toleware Folk Art USA 15c

1777 Pennsylvania Toleware Folk Art USA 15c

1778 Pennsylvania Toleware Folk Art USA 15c

Scott	Description	FDC Sing	PL.BLK	Mint Sheet	Plate Block	Unused	Used
1775-78	Pennsylvania Toleware, 4 varieties, attached	3.50	....	19.00(40)	5.50(10)	2.25	1.75
1775	15¢ Coffee Pot	1.75	....	....	....	.75	.20
1776	15¢ Tea Caddy	1.75	....	....	....	.75	.20
1777	15¢ Sugar Bowl	1.75	....	....	....	.75	.20
1778	15¢ Coffee Pot	1.75	....	....	....	.75	.20

1779 Jefferson 1743-1826 Virginia Rotunda Architecture USA 15c

1780 Latrobe 1764-1820 Baltimore Cathedral Architecture USA 15c

1781 Bulfinch 1763-1844 Boston State House Architecture USA 15c

1782 Strickland 1788-1854 Philadelphia Exchange Architecture USA 15c

Scott	Description	FDC Sing	PL.BLK	Mint Sheet	Plate Block	Unused	Used
1779-82	Architecture, 4 varieties, attached	3.50	4.75	27.50(48)	3.50	3.00	1.80
1779	15¢ Virginia Rotunda	1.75	....	....	....	1.00	.20
1780	15¢ Baltimore Cathedral	1.75	....	....	....	1.00	.20
1781	15¢ Boston State House	1.75	....	....	....	1.00	.20
1782	15¢ Philadelphia Exchange	1.75	....	....	....	1.00	.20

1783 Persistent Trillium / 1784 Hawaiian Wild Broadbean / 1785 Contra Costa Wallflower / 1786 Antioch Dunes Evening Primrose

Scott	Description	FDC Sing	PL.BLK	Mint Sheet	Plate Block	Unused	Used
1783-86	Endangered Flora, 4 varieties, attached	3.50	....	23.50(50)	6.75(12)	2.50	1.70
1783	15¢ Trillium	1.75	....	....	....	.75	.20
1784	15¢ Broadbean	1.75	....	....	....	.75	.20
1785	15¢ Wallflower	1.75	....	....	....	.75	.20
1786	15¢ Primrose	1.75	....	....	....	.75	.20

1787 Seeing For Me / 1788 Special Olympics Skill·Sharing·Joy / 1789, 1789a John Paul Jones US Bicentennial / 1790 Olympics 1980 Decathlon

Scott	Description	FDC Sing	PL.BLK	Mint Sheet	Plate Block	Unused	Used
1787	15¢ Guide Dog	1.75	....	28.00(50)	11.50(20)	.70	.15
1788	15¢ Special Olympics	1.75	....	28.00(50)	6.00(10)	.65	.15
1789	15¢ John Paul Jones, perf. 11 x 12	1.75	....	28.00(50)	6.00(10)	.65	.15
1789a	same, perf. 11	1.75	....	40.00(50)	9.00(10)	1.00	.15

NOTE: #1789a may be included in year date sets and special offers and not 1789.

Scott	Description	FDC Sing	PL.BLK	Mint Sheet	Plate Block	Unused	Used
1790	10¢ Summer Olympics, Javelin Thrower	1.75	4.00	14.50(50)	5.00(12)	.40	.15

 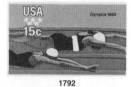

1791 / 1792

1793 / 1794

Scott	Description	FDC Sing	PL.BLK	Mint Sheet	Plate Block	Unused	Used
1791-94	Summer Olympics, 4 varieties, attached	3.50	....	22.50(50)	7.00(12)	2.50	1.75
1791	15¢ Runners	1.75	....	....	....	.80	.20
1792	15¢ Swimmers	1.75	....	....	....	.80	.20
1793	15¢ Rowers	1.75	....	....	....	.80	.20
1794	15¢ Equestrian	1.75	....	....	....	.80	.20

1795 / 1796

1797 / 1798

1980

Scott	Description	FDC Sing	PL.BLK	Mint Sheet	Plate Block	Unused	Used
1795-98	Winter Olympics, 4 varieties, attached	3.50	....	22.50(50)	7.00(12)	2.50	1.75
1795	15¢ Skater	1.75	....	....	....	.85	.20
1796	15¢ Downhill Skier	1.75	....	....	....	.85	.20
1797	15¢ Ski Jumper	1.75	....	....	....	.85	.20
1798	15¢ Hockey	1.75	....	....	....	.85	.20
1795a-98a	same, perf. 11, attached	....	....	49.50(50)	15.00(12)	4.50	....
1795a	15¢ Skater	....	....	....	....	1.20	....
1796a	15¢ Downhill Skier	....	....	....	....	1.20	....
1797a	15¢ Ski Jumper	....	....	....	....	1.20	....
1798a	15¢ Hockey	....	....	....	....	1.20	....

U.S. Postage #1799-1833

SCOTT NO.	DESCRIPTION	FIRST DAY COVERS SING	FIRST DAY COVERS PL. BLK.	MINT SHEET	PLATE BLOCK	UNUSED F/NH	USED

1799

1800

1979 COMMEMORATIVES

| 1799 | 15¢ Christmas–Madonna | 1.75 | .... | 48.00(100) | 6.25(12) | .55 | .15 |
| 1800 | 15¢ Christmas–Santa Claus | 1.75 | .... | 48.00(100) | 6.25(12) | .55 | .15 |

1801

1802

| 1801 | 15¢ Will Rogers | 1.75 | .... | 25.00(50) | 7.00(12) | .55 | .15 |
| 1802 | 15¢ Vietnam Veterans | 2.50 | 5.25 | 30.00(50) | 7.00(10) | .55 | .15 |

1803

1804

1980 COMMEMORATIVES

| 1795/1843 (1795-98, 1803-10, 1821-43) 35 varieties, complete | .... | .... | .... | .... | 21.50 | 5.10 |

| 1803 | 15¢ W.C. Fields | 1.75 | 4.00 | 25.00(50) | 6.50(12) | .55 | .15 |
| 1804 | 15¢ Benjamin Banneker | 1.75 | 4.00 | 35.00(50) | 9.50(12) | .85 | .15 |

1805

1806, 1808, 1810

1807

1809

1805-10	6 varieties, attached	4.50	....	36.00(60)	24.00(36)	4.25	2.75
1805-06	2 varieties, attached	2.50	....	....	....	....	....
1807-08	2 varieties, attached	2.50	....	....	....	....	....
1809-10	2 varieties, attached	2.50	....	....	....	....	....
1805	15¢ "Letters Preserve Memories"	1.75	....	....	....	.75	.15
1806	15¢ claret & multicolor	1.75	....	....	....	.75	.15
1807	15¢ "Letters Lift Spirits"	1.75	....	....	....	.75	.15
1808	15¢ green & multicolor	1.75	....	....	....	.75	.15
1809	15¢ "Letters Shape Opinions"	1.75	....	....	....	.75	.15
1810	15¢ red, white & blue	1.75	....	....	....	.75	.15

1813

1818, 1819, 1820

1980-81 Coil Stamps, Perf. 10 Vertically

SCOTT NO.	DESCRIPTION	FIRST DAY COVERS SING	FIRST DAY COVERS PL. BLK.	MINT SHEET	PLATE BLOCK	UNUSED F/NH	USED
			LINE PR.		LINE PR.		
1811	1¢ Inkwell & Quill	1.75	2.75	....	.50	.20	.15
1813	3.5¢ Two Violins	1.75	2.75	....	1.40	.30	.25
1816	12¢ Torch (1981)	1.75	2.75	....	1.90	.50	.40
1818	(18¢) "B" definitive	2.50	3.50	47.50(100)	2.25	.70	.15
1819	(18¢) "B" definitive, from bklt pane	1.75	....	....	....	1.00	.15
1819a	(18¢) "B" bklt pane of 8	4.00	....	....	....	7.00	....

1981 Coil Stamp Perf. Vertically

| 1820 | (18¢) "B" definitive | 1.75 | 2.75 | .... | 2.00 | .75 | .15 |

1821

1822

1823

1824

1825

1826

1821	15¢ Frances Perkins	1.75	4.00	25.00(50)	2.50	.60	.15
1822	15¢ Dolley Madison	1.75	4.00	70.00(150)	2.50	.60	.15
1823	15¢ Emily Bissell	1.75	4.00	25.00(50)	2.50	.60	.15
1824	15¢ Helen Keller & Anne Sullivan	1.75	4.00	25.00(50)	2.50	.60	.15
1825	15¢ Veterans Administration	1.75	4.00	25.00(50)	2.50	.60	.15
1826	15¢ General Bernardo deGalvez	1.75	4.00	25.00(50)	2.50	.60	.15

1827

1828

1829

1830

1827-30	Coral Reefs, 4 varieties, attached	3.50	....	21.00(50)	6.25(12)	2.25	1.75
1827	15¢ Brain Coral, Virgin Is.	1.75	....	....	....	.80	.20
1828	15¢ Elkhorn Coral, Florida	1.75	....	....	....	.80	.20
1829	15¢ Chalice Coral, American Samoa	1.75	....	....	....	.80	.20
1830	15¢ Finger Coral, Hawaii	1.75	....	....	....	.80	.20

1831

1832

1833

1831	15¢ Organized Labor	1.75	4.00	25.00(50)	6.50(12)	.65	.15
1832	15¢ Edith Wharton	1.75	4.00	27.50(50)	2.75	.65	.15
1833	15¢ Education	1.75	4.00	30.00(50)	3.75(6)	.65	.15

U.S. Postage #1834-1861

SCOTT NO.	DESCRIPTION	FIRST DAY COVERS SING	PL. BLK.	MINT SHEET	PLATE BLOCK	UNUSED F/NH	USED
1834-37	American Folk Art, 4 varieties, attached .	3.50	....	27.00(40)	9.00(10)	3.25	1.85
1834	15¢ Bella Bella Tribe .	1.75	....	....	....	1.00	.20
1835	15¢ Chilkat Tlingit Tribe	1.75	....	....	....	1.00	.20
1836	15¢ Tlingit Tribe	1.75	....	....	....	1.00	.20
1837	15¢ Bella Coola Tribe	1.75	....	....	....	1.00	.20
1838-41	American Architecture, 4 varieties, attached .	2.50	3.75	25.00(40)	3.50	3.00	2.00
1838	15¢ Smithsonian Inst.	1.75	....	....	....	.90	.20
1839	15¢ Trinity Church...	1.75	....	....	....	.90	.20
1840	15¢ Penn Academy..	1.75	....	....	....	.90	.20
1841	15¢ Lyndhurst	1.75	....	....	....	.90	.20
1842	15¢ Madonna	1.75	4.00	22.50(50)	6.50(12)	.55	.15
1843	15¢ Christmas Wreath & Toy	1.75	4.00	23.50(50)	11.75(20)	.55	.15

SE-TENANTS: Beginning with the 1964 Christmas issue (#1254-57), the United States has issued numerous Se-Tenant stamps covering a wide variety of subjects. Se-Tenants are issues where two or more different stamp designs are produced on the same sheet in pair, strip or block form. Mint stamps are usually collected in attached blocks, etc.; used are generally saved as single stamps.

1980-85 GREAT AMERICANS

SCOTT NO.	DESCRIPTION	FIRST DAY COVERS SING	PL. BLK.	MINT SHEET	PLATE BLOCK	UNUSED F/NH	USED
1844-69	1¢-50¢, 26 varieties, complete	....	....	....	....	16.50	5.40
1844	1¢ Dorothea Dix (1983)	1.75	4.00	8.25(100)	3.25(20)	.25	.20
1844a	same, Bullseye perf. .	....	....	....	2.25(20)	.25	....
1845	2¢ Igor Stravinsky (1982)	1.75	4.00	10.00(100)	.80	.25	.20
1846	3¢ Henry Caly (1983)	1.75	4.00	11.25(100)	.80	.25	.20
1847	4¢ Carl Schurz (1983)	1.75	4.00	15.00(100)	.80	.25	.20
1848	5¢ Pearl Buck (1983)	1.75	4.00	17.00(100)	.80	.25	.20
1849	6¢ Walter Lippmann (1985)	1.75	4.00	17.50(100)	3.75(20)	.25	.25
1850	7¢ Abraham Baldwin (1985)	1.75	4.00	30.00(100)	5.50(20)	.35	.20
1851	8¢ Henry Knox (1985)	1.75	4.00	23.50(100)	1.25	.30	.20
1852	9¢ Sylvanus Thayer (1985)	1.75	4.00	35.00(100)	7.00(20)	.40	.20
1853	10¢ Richard Russell (1984)	1.75	4.00	40.00(100)	8.50(20)	.45	.20
1854	11¢ Partridge (1985) .	1.75	4.00	40.00(100)	1.80	.45	.20
1855	13¢ Crazy Horse (1982)	1.75	4.00	45.00(100)	2.25	.50	.40
1856	14¢ Sinclair Lewis (1985)	1.75	4.00	45.00(100)	9.50(20)	.50	.20
1857	17¢ Rachel Carson (1981)	1.75	4.00	50.00(100)	2.50	.60	.20
1858	18¢ George Mason (1981)	1.75	4.00	48.50(100)	3.75	.60	.20
1859	19¢ Sequoyah	1.75	4.00	65.00(100)	3.50	.75	.40
1860	20¢ Ralph Bunche (1982)	1.75	4.00	70.00(100)	4.00	.80	.20
1861	20¢ T. Gallaudet (1983)	1.75	4.00	70.00(100)	4.25	.80	.20

U.S. Postage #1862-1896b

SCOTT NO.	DESCRIPTION	FIRST DAY COVERS SING	FIRST DAY COVERS PL. BLK.	MINT SHEET	PLATE BLOCK	UNUSED F/NH	USED
1862	20¢ Harry Truman (1984)	1.75	4.00	65.00(100)	15.00(20)	.80	.20
1862a	same, Bullseye perf	....	....	....	4.50	.80	....
1863	22¢ J. Audubon (1985)	1.75	4.00	75.00(100)	16.00(20)	.80	.20
1863a	same, Bullseye perf	....	....	....	5.50	.80	....
1864	30¢ F.C. Laubach (1984)	1.75	4.00	90.00(100)	20.00(20)	1.00	.20
1864a	same, Bullseye perf	....	....	....	5.00	1.00	....
1865	35¢ Charles Drew (1981)	2.25	4.50	100.00(100)	5.00	1.20	.20
1866	37¢ Robert Millikan (1982)	2.25	4.50	100.00(100)	4.50	1.20	.20
1867	39¢ Grenville Clark (1985)	2.25	4.50	100.00(100)	24.00(20)	1.20	.20
1867a	same, Bullseye perf	....	....	....	6.25	1.20	....
1868	40¢ Lillian Gilbreth (1981)	2.25	4.50	110.00(100)	25.00(20)	1.35	.20
1868a	same, Bullseye perf	....	....	....	6.25	1.35	....
1869	50¢ Chester Nimitz (1985)	2.25	4.50	145.00(100)	10.00	1.60	.20
1869a	same, Bullseye perf	....	....	....	10.00	1.60	....

1874

1875

1981 COMMEMORATIVES

SCOTT NO.	DESCRIPTION	FDC SING	FDC PL. BLK.	MINT SHEET	PLATE BLOCK	UNUSED F/NH	USED
1874/1945	(1874-79, 1910-45) 42 varieties, complete	....	....	....	....	30.50	6.50
1874	15¢ Everett Dirksen	1.75	4.00	22.00(50)	2.10	.55	.15
1875	15¢ Whitney Moore Young	1.75	4.00	22.00(50)	2.10	.55	.15

1876

1877

1878

1879

SCOTT NO.	DESCRIPTION	FDC SING	FDC PL. BLK.	MINT SHEET	PLATE BLOCK	UNUSED F/NH	USED
1876-79	Flowers, 4 varieties, attached	2.50	3.75	30.00(48)	3.25	3.00	2.60
1876	18¢ Rose	1.75	....	....	....	.80	.20
1877	18¢ Camellia	1.75	....	....	....	.80	.20
1878	18¢ Dahlia	1.75	....	....	....	.80	.20
1879	18¢ Lily	1.75	....	....	....	.80	.20

1880　1881　1882　1883　1884

1885　1886　1887　1888　1889

1981 WILDLIFE DEFINITIVES

SCOTT NO.	DESCRIPTION	FDC SING	FDC PL. BLK.	MINT SHEET	PLATE BLOCK	UNUSED F/NH	USED
1880-89	Wildlife, set of singles	17.00	....	....	....	10.50	1.90
1880	18¢ Bighorned Sheep	1.75	....	....	....	1.10	.20
1881	18¢ Puma	1.75	....	....	....	1.10	.20
1883	18¢ Bison	1.75	....	....	....	1.10	.20
1884	18¢ Brown Bear	1.75	....	....	....	1.10	.20
1885	18¢ Polar Bear	1.75	....	....	....	1.10	.20
1886	18¢ Elk	1.75	....	....	....	1.10	.20
1887	18¢ Moose	1.75	....	....	....	1.10	.20
1888	18¢ White-tailed Deer	1.75	....	....	....	1.10	.20
1889	18¢ Pronghorned Antelope	1.75	....	....	....	1.10	.20
1889a	Wildlife, bklt pane of 10	6.50	....	....	....	11.25	....

1890

1891

1892

1893　1894-1896

1981 FLAG AND ANTHEM ISSUE

SCOTT NO.	DESCRIPTION	FDC SING	FDC PL. BLK.	MINT SHEET	PLATE BLOCK	UNUSED F/NH	USED
1890	18¢ "Waves of Grain"	1.75	4.00	55.00(100)	14.50(20)	.60	.15

1981 Coil Stamp Perf. 10 Vertically

SCOTT NO.	DESCRIPTION	FDC SING	FDC PL. BLK.	MINT SHEET	PLATE# STRIP 3	UNUSED F/NH	USED
1891	18¢ "Shining Sea"	1.75	....	....	6.00	.60	.15

1981

SCOTT NO.	DESCRIPTION	FDC SING	FDC PL. BLK.	MINT SHEET	PLATE BLOCK	UNUSED F/NH	USED
1892	6¢ Stars, from bklt pane	1.75	....	....	....	1.75	.50
1893	18¢ "Purple Mountains" from bklt pane	1.75	....	....	....	.75	.15
1892-93	6¢ & 18¢ as above, attached pair	....	....	....	....	2.75	....
1893a	2-1892, 6-1893 bklt pane of 8	5.25	....	....	....	7.50	....
1894	20¢ Flag & Supreme Court	1.75	4.00	110.00(100)	22.50(20)	1.10	.15
1895	20¢ Flag & Supreme Court	1.75	50.00	....	4.50 (PLATE# STRIP 3)	.65	.15
1896	20¢ Flag & Supreme Court, from bklt pane	1.75	....	....	....	.80	.15
1896a	20¢ bklt pane of 6	3.50	....	....	....	4.25	....
1896b	20¢ bklt pane of 10	5.50	....	....	....	7.00	....

Note: For plate number strips of 5, see page 139

1897

1897A

1898

1898A

1899

1900

1901

1902

1903

1904

1905

1906

U.S. Postage #1897-1924

SCOTT NO.	DESCRIPTION	FIRST DAY COVERS SING	FIRST DAY COVERS PL. BLK.	MINT SHEET	PLATE BLOCK	UNUSED F/NH	USED

1907 — Surrey 1890s USA 18c
1908 — Fire Pumper 1860s USA 20c

NOTE: #1898A—"Stagecoach 1890s" is 19-1/2 mm long.

1981-84 Perf. 10 Vertically
TRANSPORTATION COILS

Scott	Description	FDC Sing	PLATE# STRIP 3		PLATE# STRIP 3	Unused	Used
1897-1908	1¢-20¢, 14 varieties, complete	29.50				4.25	2.60
1897	1¢ Omnibus (1983)	2.25	17.50	....	.70	.20	.20
1897A	2¢ Locomotive (1982)	2.25	25.00	....	.75	.20	.20
1898	3¢ Handcar (1983)	2.25	25.00	....	1.05	.20	.20
1898A	4¢ Stagecoach (1982)	2.25	22.50	....	1.80	.20	.20
1899	5¢ Motorcycle (1983)	2.25	25.00	....	1.25	.20	.20
1900	5.2¢ Sleigh (1983)	2.25	37.50	....	8.00	.30	.20
1901	5.9¢ Bicycle (1982)	2.25	37.50	....	10.00	.30	.20
1902	7.4¢ Baby Buggy (1984)	2.25	25.00	....	9.50	.30	.20
1903	9.3¢ Mail Wagon	2.25	42.50	....	9.00	.30	.20
1904	10.9¢ Hansom Cab (1982)	2.25	40.00	....	21.00	.55	.20
1905	11¢ Caboose (1984)	2.25	40.00	....	4.00	.30	.20
1906	17¢ Electric Car	2.25	37.50	....	3.75	.40	.20
1907	18¢ Surrey	2.25	55.00	....	4.00	.55	.20
1908	20¢ Fire Pumper	2.25	55.00	....	3.75	.55	.20

NOTE: Plate # Strips of 3 and 5 have plate number under center stamp. Some issues have lines between two of the stamps.

PRECANCELLED COILS

The following are for precancelled, unused, never hinged stamps. Stamps without gum sell for less.

SCOTT NO.	Description	PL# STRIP 3	UNUSED
1895b	20¢ Supreme Court	90.00	1.00
1898Ab	4¢ Stagecoach	8.50	.35
1900a	5.2¢ Sleigh	14.00	.30
1901a	5.9¢ Bicycle	50.00	.45
1902a	7.4¢ Baby Buggy	6.25	.40
1903a	9.3¢ Mail Wagon	4.50	.40
1904a	10.9¢ Hansom Cab	40.00	.50
1905a	11¢ Caboose	4.50	.45
1906a	17¢ Electric Car	6.00	.55

1909

1983 EXPRESS MAIL BOOKLET SINGLE

1909	$9.35 Eagle & Moon	95.00	....	....	....	35.00	27.00
1909a	$9.35 bklt pane of 3	300.00	....	....	....	95.00	....

1910

1911

1981 COMMEMORATIVES (Continued)

1910	18¢ American Red Cross	1.75	4.00	27.75(50)	3.25	.60	.15
1911	18¢ Savings & Loans Assoc.	1.75	4.00	25.75(50)	2.75	.60	.15

1912 — Exploring the Moon USA 18c

1913 — Benefiting Mankind USA 18c

1914 — Benefiting Mankind USA 18c

1915 — Understanding the Sun USA 18c

1916 — Probing the Planets USA 18c

1917 — USA 18c Benefiting Mankind

1918 — USA 18c Benefiting Mankind

1919 — Comprehending the Universe USA 18c

Scott	Description	FDC Sing	FDC PL BLK	Mint Sheet	Plate Block	Unused	Used
1912-19	Space Achievement, 8 varieties, attached	6.00	9.00	34.50(48)	7.00(8)	6.50	5.50
1912-19	same, set of singles	15.50	....	....	....	....	1.80
1912	18¢ Exploring the Moon	2.00				.80	.25
1913	18¢ Releasing Boosters	2.00				.80	.25
1914	18¢ Cooling Electric Systems	2.00				.80	.25
1915	18¢ Understanding the Sun	2.00				.80	.25
1916	18¢ Probing the Planets	2.00				.80	.25
1917	18¢ Shuttle and Rockets	2.00				.80	.25
1918	18¢ Landing	2.00				.80	.25
1919	18¢ Comprehending the Universe	2.00				.80	.25

1920 — Professional Management USA 18c

1920	18¢ Professional Management	1.75	4.00	26.50(50)	2.75	.60	.15

1921 — Save Wetland Habitats USA 18c

1922 — Save Grassland Habitats USA 18c

1923 — Save Mountain Habitats USA 18c

1924 — Save Woodland Habitats USA 18c

1921-24	Wildlife Habitats, 4 varieties, attached	2.75	3.75	27.50(50)	3.00	2.75	2.50
1921	18¢ Blue Heron	1.75				.90	.20
1922	18¢ Badger	1.75				.90	.20
1923	18¢ Grizzly Bear	1.75				.90	.20
1924	18¢ Ruffled Grouse	1.75				.90	.20

U.S. Postage #1925-1949d

1925

1926

1927

SCOTT NO.	DESCRIPTION	FIRST DAY COVERS SING	FIRST DAY COVERS PL. BLK.	MINT SHEET	PLATE BLOCK	UNUSED F/NH	USED
1925	18¢ Disabled Persons	1.75	4.00	26.00(50)	2.75	.60	.15
1926	18¢ Edna St. Vincent Millay	1.75	4.00	26.00(50)	2.75	.60	.15
1927	18¢ Alcoholism	1.75	4.00	60.00(50)	47.50(20)	.70	.15

1928

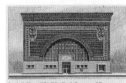
1929

1930

1931

SCOTT NO.	DESCRIPTION	FIRST DAY COVERS SING	FIRST DAY COVERS PL. BLK.	MINT SHEET	PLATE BLOCK	UNUSED F/NH	USED
1928-31	American Architecture, 4 varieties, attached	2.75	3.75	28.50(40)	3.75	3.25	2.75
1928	18¢ New York Univ. Library	1.75	....	....	....	1.00	.20
1929	18¢ Biltmore House	1.75	....	....	....	1.00	.20
1930	18¢ Palace of the Arts	1.75	....	....	....	1.00	.20
1931	18¢ National Farmers Bank	1.75	....	....	....	1.00	.20

1932

1933

1932	18¢ Babe Zaharias	9.00	12.00	38.00(50)	4.50	.90	.30
1933	18¢ Bobby Jones	12.50	15.00	80.00(50)	8.25	1.75	.30

1934

1935

1936

1937   1938

SCOTT NO.	DESCRIPTION	FIRST DAY COVERS SING	FIRST DAY COVERS PL. BLK.	MINT SHEET	PLATE BLOCK	UNUSED F/NH	USED
1934	18¢ Coming Through the Rye	2.25	4.50	26.00(50)	2.75	.60	.15
1935	18¢ James Hoban	1.75	4.00	26.00(50)	2.75	.60	.15
1936	18¢ James Hoban	1.75	4.00	26.00(50)	3.00	.60	.15
1937-38	Yorktown/Virginia Capes, 2 varieties, attached	2.00	4.00	29.00(50)	3.35	1.75	1.25
1937	18¢ Yorktown	1.75	....	....	....	1.00	.30
1938	18¢ Virginia Capes	1.75	....	....	....	1.00	.30

1939

1940

1941

1939	(20¢) Madonna & Child	1.75	4.00	52.00(100)	2.75	.60	.15
1940	(20¢) Christmas Toy	1.75	4.00	27.00(50)	2.75	.60	.15
1941	20¢ John Hanson	1.75	4.00	29.50(50)	3.00	.70	.15

1942

1943

1944

1945

1942-45	Desert Plants, 4 varieties, attached	2.75	3.75	29.50(40)	3.75	3.50	2.50
1942	20¢ Barrel Cactus	1.75	....	....	....	1.00	.20
1943	20¢ Agave	1.75	....	....	....	1.00	.20
1944	20¢ Beavertail Cactus	1.75	....	....	....	1.00	.20
1945	20¢ Saguaro	1.75	....	....	....	1.00	.20

1946-1948

1949

1981-1982 Regular Issues

1946	(20¢) "C" Eagle, 11x10½	1.75	4.00	54.00(100)	2.75	.60	.15
			LINE PAIR		LINE PAIR		
1947	(20¢) "C" Eagle, coil	1.75	2.75	....	2.25	.80	.15
1948	(20¢) "C" Eagle, from pane	1.75	....	....	....	.80	.15
1948a	same, bklt pane of 10	6.00	....	....	....	7.50	....
1949	20¢ Bighorned Sheep, blue, from bklt pane (1982)	1.75	....	....	....	.75	.15
1949a	same, bklt pane of 10	6.00	....	....	....	7.50	....
1949c	Type II, from bklt pane	....	....	....	....	1.75	.20
1949d	same, bklt pane of 10	....	....	....	....	16.00	....

U.S. Postage #1950-2018

SCOTT NO.	DESCRIPTION	FIRST DAY COVERS SING	FIRST DAY COVERS PL. BLK.	MINT SHEET	PLATE BLOCK	UNUSED F/NH	USED

1950   1951   1952   2006   2007

1982 COMMEMORATIVES

Scott	Description	FDC Sing	FDC PB	Mint Sheet	PB	Unused	Used
1950/2030	(1950-52, 2003-04, 2006-30) 30 varieties	....	....	....	....	23.50	4.75
1950	20¢ Franklin D. Roosevelt	1.75	4.00	30.50(48)	5.50	.60	.15
1951	20¢ LOVE, perf. 11	1.85	4.25	30.50(50)	2.90	.65	.15
1951a	same, perf. 11x 10½	....	....	51.75(50)	5.50	1.10	.30

NOTE: Perforations will be mixed on Used #1951.

| 1952 | 20¢ George Washington | 1.75 | 4.00 | 30.50(50) | 2.95 | .65 | .15 |

2008   2009

2006-09	World's Fair, 4 varieties, attached	2.75	3.25	33.50(50)	3.50	3.25	2.00
2006	20¢ Solar Energy	1.75	....	....	....	1.00	.20
2007	20¢ Synthetic Fuels	1.75	....	....	....	1.00	.20
2008	20¢ Breeder Reactor	1.75	....	....	....	1.00	.20
2009	20¢ Fossil Fuels	1.75	....	....	....	1.00	.20

1982 STATE BIRDS AND FLOWERS

1953	Alabama	1978	Montana
1954	Alaska	1979	Nebraska
1955	Arizona	1980	Nevada
1956	Arkansas	1981	New Hampshire
1957	California	1982	New Jersey
1958	Colorado	1983	New Mexico
1959	Connecticut	1984	New York
1960	Delaware	1985	North Carolina
1961	Florida	1986	North Dakota
1962	Georgia	1987	Ohio
1963	Hawaii	1988	Oklahoma
1964	Idaho	1989	Oregon
1965	Illinois	1990	Pennsylvania
1966	Indiana	1991	Rhode Island
1967	Iowa	1992	South Carolina
1968	Kansas	1993	South Dakota
1969	Kentucky	1994	Tennessee
1970	Louisiana	1995	Texas
1971	Maine	1996	Utah
1972	Maryland	1997	Vermont
1973	Massachusetts	1998	Virginia
1974	Michigan	1999	Washington
1975	Minnesota	2000	West Virginia
1976	Mississippi	2001	Wisconsin
1977	Missouri	2002	Wyoming

1966   2002

Perf. 10½ x 11

1953-2002	20¢, 50 varieties, attached	....	....	45.00(50)	....	45.00	....
	set of singles	86.00	....	....	....	....	25.00
	singles of above	2.00	....	....	....	1.10	.65
1953a-2002a	same, perf. 11	....	....	47.50(50)	....	47.50	....
	singles of above	....	....	....	....	1.25	....

NOTE: Used singles will not be sorted by perf. sizes.

2010   2011   2012

2010	20¢ Horatio Alger	1.75	4.00	27.00(50)	2.75	.60	.15
2011	20¢ Aging Together	1.75	4.00	27.00(50)	2.75	.60	.15
2012	20¢ Barrymores	1.75	4.00	30.00(50)	2.75	.60	.15

2013   2014   2015

2013	20¢ Dr. Mary Walker	1.75	4.00	29.50(50)	3.00	.60	.15
2014	20¢ Peace Garden	1.75	4.00	27.00(50)	2.75	.60	.15
2015	20¢ America's Libraries	1.75	4.00	27.00(50)	2.75	.60	.15

2003   2004   2005

| 2003 | 20¢ USA/Netherlands | 1.75 | 4.00 | 34.50(50) | 17.00(20) | .70 | .15 |
| 2004 | 20¢ Library of Congress | 1.75 | 4.00 | 28.00(50) | 2.75 | .60 | .15 |

| | | | | PLATE# STRIP 3 | | PLATE# STRIP 3 | |
| 2005 | 20¢ Consumer Education, Coil | 1.75 | 60.00 | .... | 28.50 | 1.20 | .15 |

2016   2017   2018

2016	20¢ Jackie Robinson	7.00	13.50	110.00(50)	11.00	2.50	.20
2017	20¢ Touro Synagogue	1.75	4.00	40.00(50)	18.00(20)	.85	.15
2018	20¢ Wolf Trap Farm	1.75	4.00	27.00(50)	2.50	.60	.15

PLATE BLOCKS: are portions of a sheet of stamps adjacent to the number(s) indicating the printing plate number used to produce that sheet. Flat plate issues are usually collected in plate blocks of six (number opposite middle stamp) while rotary issues are normally corner blocks of four.

U.S. Postage #2019-2041

2019

2020

2021

2022

SCOTT NO.	DESCRIPTION	FIRST DAY COVERS SING	FIRST DAY COVERS PL. BLK.	MINT SHEET	PLATE BLOCK	UNUSED F/NH	USED
2019-22	American Architecture, 4 varieties, attached	2.30	3.25	35.00(40)	4.50	4.00	2.00
2019	20¢ Fallingwater Mill Run	1.75	....	....	....	1.25	.20
2020	20¢ Illinois Inst. Tech	1.75	....	....	....	1.25	.20
2021	20¢ Gropius House	1.75	....	....	....	1.25	.20
2022	20¢ Dulles Airport	1.75	....	....	....	1.25	.20

2023

2024

2025

2026

2023	20¢ St. Francis of Assisi	1.75	4.00	30.00(50)	3.00	.65	.15
2024	20¢ Ponce de Leon	1.75	4.00	36.00(50)	18.00(20)	.80	.15
2025	13¢ Kitten & Puppy, Christmas	1.75	4.00	19.50(50)	2.25	.50	.15
2026	20¢ Madonna & Child, Christmas	1.75	4.00	30.00(50)	16.50(20)	.65	.15

2027

2028

2029

2030

2027-30	Winter Scenes, Christmas, 4 varieties, attached	2.75	3.25	43.00(50)	5.00	4.25	2.50
2027	20¢ Sledding	1.75	....	....	....	1.25	.20
2028	20¢ Snowman	1.75	....	....	....	1.25	.20
2029	20¢ Skating	1.75	....	....	....	1.25	.20
2030	20¢ Decorating	1.75	....	....	....	1.25	.20

2031

1983 COMMEMORATIVES

SCOTT NO.	DESCRIPTION	FIRST DAY COVERS SING	FIRST DAY COVERS PL. BLK.	MINT SHEET	PLATE BLOCK	UNUSED F/NH	USED
2031-65	13¢-20¢, 35 varieties, complete	....	....	....	....	28.40	6.00
2031	20¢ Science & Industry	1.75	4.00	27.00(50)	2.75	.60	.15

2032

2033 / 2034

2035

2032-35	20¢ Ballooning, 4 varieties, attached	2.75	3.25	27.00(40)	3.75	3.25	2.50
2032	20¢ Intrepid	1.75	....	....	....	1.10	.20
2033	20¢ Red, white, & blue balloon	1.75	....	....	....	1.10	.20
2034	20¢ Yellow, gold & green balloon	1.75	....	....	....	1.10	.20
2035	20¢ Explorer II	1.75	....	....	....	1.10	.20

2036

2037

2038

2036	20¢ USA/Sweden	1.75	4.00	27.00(50)	2.75	.65	.15
2037	20¢ Civilian Conservation Corps	1.75	4.00	27.00(50)	2.75	.65	.15
2038	20¢ Joseph Priestley	1.75	4.00	27.00(50)	2.75	.65	.15

2039

2040

2041

2039	20¢ Volunteerism	1.75	4.00	34.50(50)	18.00(20)	.65	.15
2040	20¢ German Immigrants	1.75	4.00	27.00(50)	2.75	.65	.15
2041	20¢ Brooklyn Bridge	1.75	4.00	30.00(50)	2.75	.65	.15

U.S. Postage #2042-2065

2042

2043

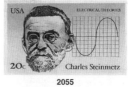
2055

2056

2057

2058

Scott No.	Description	FDC Sing	FDC Pl. Blk.	Mint Sheet	Plate Block	Unused F/NH	Used
2042	20¢ Tennessee Valley Authority	1.75	4.00	34.50(50)	18.00(20)	.65	.15
2043	20¢ Physical Fitness	1.75	4.00	34.50(50)	18.00(20)	.65	.15
2044	20¢ Scott Joplin	1.75	4.00	35.00(50)	3.00	.75	.15
2055-58	Inventors, 4 varieties, attached	2.75	3.25	47.50(50)	5.75	5.00	3.50
2055	20¢ Charles Steinmetz	1.75	......	......	......	1.35	.20
2056	20¢ Edwin Armstrong	1.75	......	......	......	1.35	.20
2057	20¢ Nikola Tesla	1.75	......	......	......	1.35	.20
2058	20¢ Philo T. Farnsworth	1.75	......	......	......	1.35	.20

2045

2046

2047

2059

2060

2045	20¢ Medal of Honor	1.75	4.00	30.00(40)	3.75	.85	.15
2046	20¢ Babe Ruth	8.00	16.00	110.00(50)	10.00	2.50	.20
2047	20¢ Nathaniel Hawthorne	1.75	4.00	32.50(50)	3.25	.75	.20

2061

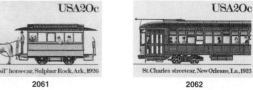
2062

2048

2049

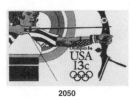
2050

2051

2059-62	Streetcars, 4 varieties, attached	2.75	3.25	37.50(50)	4.75	4.00	3.00
2059	20¢ First Streetcar	1.75	......	......	......	1.25	.20
2060	20¢ Electric Trolley	1.75	......	......	......	1.25	.20
2061	20¢ "Bobtail"	1.75	......	......	......	1.25	.20
2062	20¢ St. Charles Streetcar	1.75	......	......	......	1.25	.20

2048-51	Olympics, 4 varieties, attached	2.75	3.25	30.00(50)	4.00	3.50	2.75
2048	13¢ Discus	1.75	......	......	......	1.00	.30
2049	13¢ High Jump	1.75	......	......	......	1.00	.30
2050	13¢ Archery	1.75	......	......	......	1.00	.30
2051	13¢ Boxing	1.75	......	......	......	1.00	.30

2063

2064

2063	20¢ Madonna	1.75	4.00	27.00(50)	2.75	.60	.15
2064	20¢ Santa Claus	1.75	4.00	34.50(50)	18.00(20)	.60	.15

2052

2053

2054

2065

2052	20¢ Treaty of Paris	1.75	4.00	24.00(40)	3.00	.65	.15
2053	20¢ Civil Service	1.75	4.00	34.50(50)	18.00(20)	.65	.15
2054	20¢ Metropolitan Opera	1.75	4.00	30.00(50)	3.00	.65	.15

MINT SHEETS: From 1935 to date, we list prices for standard size Mint Sheets in Fine, Never Hinged condition. The number of stamps in each sheet is noted in ( ).

2065	20¢ Martin Luther	1.75	4.00	27.00(50)	2.75	.60	.15

U.S. Postage #2066-2091

2066

1984 COMMEMORATIVES

SCOTT NO.	DESCRIPTION	FIRST DAY COVERS SING	FIRST DAY COVERS PL. BLK.	MINT SHEET	PLATE BLOCK	UNUSED F/NH	USED
2066-2109	44 varieties, complete	....	....	....	....	37.20	6.75
2066	20¢ Alaska Statehood	1.75	4.00	27.00(50)	3.00	.60	.15

2067 2068 2069 2070

2067-70	Winter Olympics, 4 varieties, attached .	2.75	3.25	39.00(50)	4.50	4.00	2.00
2067	20¢ Ice Dancing	1.75	....	....	....	1.10	.20
2068	20¢ Downhill Skiing ..	1.75	....	....	....	1.10	.20
2069	20¢ Cross Country Skiing	1.75	....	....	....	1.10	.20
2070	20¢ Hockey	1.75	....	....	....	1.10	.20

2071 2072 2073 2074

2071	20¢ Federal Deposit Insurance Corporation	1.75	4.00	27.00(50)	2.75	.60	.15
2072	20¢ Love	1.95	4.00	34.50(50)	18.00(20)	.65	.15
2073	20¢ Carter G. Woodson	1.75	4.00	30.00(50)	2.00	.60	.15
2074	20¢ Conservatiion ...	1.75	4.00	27.00(50)	2.00	.60	.15

2076

2075

2077

2078 2079

2075	20¢ Credit Union	1.75	4.00	27.00(50)	2.75	.60	.15
2076-79	Orchids, 4 varieties, attd.	2.75	3.25	34.00(48)	3.75	3.25	2.75
2076	20¢ Wildpink	1.75	....	....	....	.95	.20
2077	20¢ Lady's-slipper ...	1.75	....	....	....	.95	.20
2078	20¢ Spreading Pogonia	1.75	....	....	....	.95	.20
2079	20¢ Pacific Calypso .	1.75	....	....	....	.95	.20

2080 2081

2080	20¢ Hawaii Statehood	1.75	4.00	30.00(50)	3.00	.70	.15
2081	20¢ National Archives	1.75	4.00	30.00(50)	3.00	.70	.15

2082 2083 2084 2085

2082-85	Olympics, 4 varieties, attached	2.75	3.25	51.75(50)	6.00	5.50	4.75
2082	20¢ Men's Diving ...	1.75	....	....	....	1.50	.25
2083	20¢ Long Jump	1.75	....	....	....	1.50	.25
2084	20¢ Wrestling	1.75	....	....	....	1.50	.25
2085	20¢ Women's Kayak .	1.75	....	....	....	1.50	.25

2086 2087 2088

2086	20¢ Louisiana Exposition	1.75	4.00	37.50(40)	4.25	.95	.15
2087	20¢ Health Research	1.75	4.00	32.00(50)	3.50	.70	.15
2088	20¢ Douglas Fairbanks	1.75	4.00	36.50(50)	20.00(20)	.70	.15

2089 2090 2091

2089	20¢ Jim Thorpe	4.50	8.00	40.00(50)	4.75	1.00	.30
2090	20¢ John McCormack	1.75	4.00	30.00(50)	3.00	.65	.15
2091	20¢ St. Lawrence Seaway	1.75	4.00	30.00(50)	3.00	.65	.15

SE-TENANTS: Beginning with the 1964 Christmas issue (#1254-57), the United States has issued numerous Se-Tenant stamps covering a wide variety of subjects. Se-Tenants are issues where two or more different stamp designs are produced on the same sheet in pair, strip or block form. Mint stamps are usually collected in attached blocks, etc.—Used are generally saved as single stamps. Our Se-Tenant prices follow in this collecting pattern.

U.S. Postage #2092-2116a

SCOTT NO.	DESCRIPTION	FIRST DAY COVERS SING	PL. BLK.	MINT SHEET	PLATE BLOCK	UNUSED F/NH	USED

2092 2093

| 2092 | Preserving Wetlands | 1.75 | 4.00 | 45.00(50) | 5.00 | .95 | .15 |
| 2093 | Roanoke Voyages | 1.75 | 4.00 | 40.00(50) | 4.00 | .85 | .15 |

2094 2095 2096 2097

2094	20¢ Herman Melville	1.75	4.00	27.00(50)	2.75	.60	.15
2095	20¢ Horace Moses	1.75	4.00	40.00(50)	19.00(20)	.90	.15
2096	20¢ Smokey Bear	1.75	4.00	34.00(50)	3.50	.75	.15
2097	20¢ Roberto Clemente	12.00	20.00	140.00(50)	13.50	2.75	.35

2098 2099

2100 2101

2098-2101	American Dogs, 4 varieties, attached	3.25	3.75	35.00(40)	4.75	4.00	3.25
2098	20¢ Beagle, Boston Terrier	1.75	....	....	....	1.10	.20
2099	20¢ Chesapeake Bay Retriever, Cocker Spaniel	1.75	....	....	....	1.10	.20
2100	20¢ Alaskan Malamute, Collie	1.75	....	....	....	1.10	.20
2101	20¢ Black & Tan Coonhound, American Foxhound	1.75	....	....	....	1.10	.20

2102 2103 2104

2102	20¢ Crime Prevention	1.75	4.00	27.00(50)	2.75	.60	.15
2103	20¢ Hispanic Americans	1.75	4.00	22.00(40)	2.75	.60	.15
2104	20¢ Family Unity	1.75	4.00	45.00(50)	22.00(20)	1.00	.15

SCOTT NO.	DESCRIPTION	FIRST DAY COVERS SING	PL. BLK.	MINT SHEET	PLATE BLOCK	UNUSED F/NH	USED

2105 2106 2107

2105	20¢ Eleanor Roosevelt	1.75	4.00	26.00(40)	3.00	.70	.15
2106	20¢ Nation of Readers	1.75	4.00	37.50(50)	4.00	.85	.15
2107	20¢ Madonna & Child	1.75	4.00	27.00(50)	2.75	.60	.15

2108 2109

| 2108 | 20¢ Santa Claus | 1.35 | 4.00 | 27.00(50) | 2.75 | .60 | .15 |
| 2109 | 20¢ Vietnam Veterans | 1.75 | 4.00 | 45.00(40) | 5.50 | 1.25 | .20 |

2110

1985 COMMEMORATIVES

| 2110/2166 | (2110, 2137-47, 2152-66) 27 varieties | .... | .... | .... | .... | 41.45 | 6.25 |
| 2110 | 22¢ Jerome Kern | 1.75 | 4.00 | 32.00(50) | 3.25 | .70 | .15 |

2111-2113 2114, 2115 2116

1985 REGULAR ISSUES

2111	(22¢) "D" Eagle	1.75	4.00	100.00(100)	35.00(20)	.90	.15
			PLATE# STRIP 3		PLATE# STRIP 3		
2112	(22¢) "D" Eagle, coil	1.75	21.00	....	6.75	.75	.15
2113	(22¢) "D" Eagle from bklt pane	1.75	....	....	....	1.25	.15
2113a	same, bklt pane of 10	5.75	....	....	....	12.00	....
			PLATE BLOCK		PLATE BLOCK		
2114	22¢ Flag over Capitol	1.75	4.00	62.50(100)	3.25	.70	.15
			PLATE# STRIP 3		PLATE# STRIP 3		
2115	22¢ Flag over Capitol, coil	1.75	27.50	....	3.75	.70	.15
2115b	22¢ Flag "T" coil (1985-87)	2.90	....	....	5.50	.80	.15
2116	22¢ Flag over Capitol from bklt pane	1.75	....	....	....	1.00	.15
2116a	same, bklt pane of 5	2.90	....	....	....	4.75	....

U.S. Postage #2117-2141

2117

2118

2119

2120

2121

1985 SEASHELLS FROM BOOKLET PANE

SCOTT NO.	DESCRIPTION	FIRST DAY COVERS SING	FIRST DAY COVERS PL. BLK.	MINT SHEET	PLATE BLOCK	UNUSED F/NH	USED
2117-21	Shells, strip of 5, attached	3.00	....	....	....	4.25	
2117	22¢ Frilled Dogwinkle	1.75	....	....	....	.90	.20
2118	22¢ Reticulated Helmet	1.75	....	....	....	.90	.20
2119	22¢ New England Neptune	1.75	....	....	....	.90	.20
2120	22¢ Calico Scallop	1.75	....	....	....	.90	.20
2121	22¢ Lightning Whelk	1.75	....	....	....	.90	.20
2121a	22¢ Seashells, bklt pane of 10	5.95	....	....	....	8.00	6.50

2122

1985 EXPRESS MAIL STAMP FROM BOOKLET PANE

SCOTT NO.	DESCRIPTION	FIRST DAY COVERS SING	FIRST DAY COVERS PL. BLK.	MINT SHEET	PLATE BLOCK	UNUSED F/NH	USED
2122	$10.75 Eagle & Moon	65.00	....	....	....	32.50	13.50
2122a	same, bklt pane of 3	160.00	....	....	....	95.00	....
2122b	Type II, from bklt pane	....	....	....	....	39.00	14.50
2122c	same, bklt pane of 3	....	....	....	....	115.00	....

2123

2124

2125

2126

2127

2128

2129

2130

2131

2132

2133

2134

2135

2136

TRANSPORTATION COILS 1985-87 PERF. 10

SCOTT NO.	DESCRIPTION	FIRST DAY COVERS SING	FIRST DAY COVERS PL. BLK. PLATE# STRIP 3	MINT SHEET	PLATE BLOCK PLATE# STRIP 3	UNUSED F/NH	USED
2123	3.4¢ School Bus	2.00	11.50	....	1.35	.25	.15
2124	4.9¢ Buckboard	2.00	14.00	....	1.25	.25	.15
2125	5.5¢ Star Route Truck (1986)	2.00	15.00	....	2.50	.25	.15
2126	6¢ Tricycle	2.00	14.00	....	2.00	.25	.15
2127	7.1¢ Tractor (1987)	2.00	15.00	....	3.15	.35	.15
2128	8.3¢ Ambulance	2.00	14.00	....	1.95	.35	.15
2129	8.5¢ Tow Truck (1987)	2.00	12.50	....	3.45	.35	.15
2130	10.1¢ Oil Wagon	2.00	12.50	....	2.75	.40	.20
2131	11¢ Stutz Bearcat	2.00	18.00	....	1.75	.40	.20
2132	12¢ Stanley Steamer	2.00	15.00	....	2.35	.60	.20
2133	12.5¢ Pushcart	2.00	15.00	....	3.00	.40	.20
2134	14¢ Iceboat	2.00	15.00	....	2.30	.40	.20
2135	17¢ Dog Sled (1986)	2.00	12.50	....	3.25	.70	.20
2136	25¢ Bread Wagon (1986)	2.00	15.00	....	4.00	.80	.20

Note: For plate number strips of 5, see page 139

PRECANCELLED COILS

The following are for precancelled, unused, never hinged stamps. Stamps without gum sell for less.

SCOTT NO.		PL# STRIP 3	UNUSED
2123a	3.4¢ School Bus	7.50	.35
2124a	4.9¢ Buckboard	2.35	.35
2125a	5.5¢ Star Route Truck	2.35	.35
2126a	6¢ Tricycle	2.30	.35
2127a	7.1¢ Tractor	4.00	.35
2127b	7.1¢ Tractor, precancel (1989)	2.75	.35
2128a	8.3¢ Ambulance	1.75	.35
2129a	8.5¢ Tow Truck	4.00	.35
2130a	10.1¢ Oil Wagon	3.25	.35
2130b	10.1¢ Oil Wagon, red precancel (1988)	3.00	.35
2132a	12¢ Stanley Steamer	3.00	.60
2132b	12¢ Stanley Steamer "B" Press	28.00	1.85
2133a	12.5¢ Pushcart	4.00	.40

2137

1985 COMMEMORATIVES (continued)

2137	22¢ Mary Bethune	1.75	4.00	42.50(50)	4.25	.95	.15

2138

2139

2140

2141

2138-41	Duck Decoys, 4 varieties, attached	2.75	3.25	100.00(50)	14.00	10.50	8.00
2138	22¢ Broadbill	1.75	....	....	....	2.75	.25
2139	22¢ Mallard	1.75	....	....	....	2.75	.25
2140	22¢ Canvasback	1.75	....	....	....	2.75	.25
2141	22¢ Redhead	1.75	....	....	....	2.75	.25

U.S. Postage #2142-2167

2143

2142

2145

2155 Quarter horse

2156 Morgan

2157 Saddlebred

2158 Appaloosa

SCOTT NO.	DESCRIPTION	FIRST DAY COVERS SING	FIRST DAY COVERS PL. BLK.	MINT SHEET	PLATE BLOCK	UNUSED F/NH	USED
2142	22¢ Winter Special Olympics	1.75	4.00	26.00(40)	3.00	.70	.15
2143	22¢ "LOVE"	1.95	4.00	34.00(50)	3.25	.75	.15
2144	22¢ Rural Electricity .	1.75	. . . .	56.00(50)	35.00(20)	.85	.15
2145	22¢ Ameripex '86 . . .	1.75	4.00	29.00(48)	2.80	.65	.15

2146

2147

2160 YMCA Youth Camping

2161 Boy Scouts

2162 Big Brothers / Big Sisters

2159 Public Education

2163 Camp Fire

2146	22¢ Abigail Adams . .	1.75	4.00	30.00(50)	3.75	.85	.15
2147	22¢ Frederic Bartholdi	1.75	4.00	29.00(50)	3.00	.65	.15

2155-58	American Horses, 4 varieties, attached .	3.00	3.50	125.00(40)	16.00	15.00	8.00
2155	22¢ Quarter Horse . .	1.75	. . . .	. . . .	. . . .	3.50	.50
2156	22¢ Morgan	1.75	. . . .	. . . .	. . . .	3.50	.50
2157	22¢ Saddlebred	1.75	. . . .	. . . .	. . . .	3.50	.50
2158	22¢ Appaloosa	1.75	. . . .	. . . .	. . . .	3.50	.50

2149

2150

1985 REGULAR ISSUE COILS

SCOTT NO.	DESCRIPTION	FIRST DAY COVERS SING	PLATE# STRIP 3		PLATE# STRIP 3	UNUSED F/NH	USED
2149	18¢ George Washington	1.75	50.00	. . . .	4.50	.85	.75
2149a	18¢ George Washington, precancel	. . . .	. . . .	. . . .	4.25	.60	. . . .
2150	21.1¢ Envelope	1.75	32.50	. . . .	4.50	.85	1.00
2150a	21.1¢ Envelope, precancel	. . . .	. . . .	. . . .	4.85	.75	. . . .

2152

2164 Help End Hunger

2165 Christmas Madonna & Child

2153

2154

2166 Season's Greetings

2167 Arkansas Statehood

2152	22¢ Korean War Veterans	1.75	4.00	41.50(50)	5.00	1.00	.15
2153	22¢ Social Security . .	1.75	4.00	29.00(50)	3.50	.70	.15
2154	22¢ World War I Veterans	1.75	4.00	41.50(50)	5.00	1.00	.15

2159	22¢ Public Education	1.75	4.00	70.00(50)	7.00	1.50	.15
2160-63	Youth Year, 4 varieties, attached .	3.00	3.50	61.00(50)	8.00	6.00	3.50
2160	22¢ YMCA	1.75	. . . .	. . . .	. . . .	1.75	.40
2161	22¢ Boy Scouts	1.75	. . . .	. . . .	. . . .	1.75	.40
2162	22¢ Big Brothers & Big Sisters	1.75	. . . .	. . . .	. . . .	1.75	.40
2163	22¢ Camp Fire	1.75	. . . .	. . . .	. . . .	1.75	.40
2164	22¢ Help End Hunger	1.75	4.00	32.75(50)	3.00	.70	.15
2165	22¢ Madonna & Child	1.75	4.00	29.00(50)	3.00	.60	.15
2166	22¢ Poinsettia	1.75	4.00	29.00(50)	3.00	.60	.15
2167	22¢ Arkansas Statehood	1.75	4.00	48.50(50)	4.50	1.00	.15

U.S. Postage #2168-2204

SCOTT NO.	DESCRIPTION	FIRST DAY COVERS SING	FIRST DAY COVERS PL. BLK.	MINT SHEET	PLATE BLOCK	UNUSED F/NH	USED
2189	52¢ Hubert Humphrey (1991)	2.00	4.50	160.00(100)	9.00	1.75	.15
2190	56¢ John Harvard	2.00	4.50	160.00(100)	9.00	1.75	.15
2191	65¢ H.H. Arnold (1988)	2.20	4.25	170.00(100)	9.50	2.00	.15
2192	75¢ Wendell Willkie (1992)	2.75	5.50	190.00(100)	10.00	2.00	.15
2193	$1 Dr. Bernard Revel	5.00	10.00	375.00(100)	19.00	4.00	.15
2194	$1 John Hopkins (1989)	5.00	10.00	60.00(20)	13.50	3.75	.15
2195	$2 William Jennings Bryan	6.00	10.00	525.00(100)	22.50	5.50	.60
2196	$5 Bret Harte (1987)	14.50	28.50	250.00(20)	52.50	13.50	2.00
2197	25¢ Jack London, bklt single (1988)	1.75	....	....	....	.90	.15
2197a	as above bklt pane (6), perf.10	5.00	....	....	....	5.25	....

2198

2199

2200

2201

1986 COMMEMORATIVES

SCOTT NO.	DESCRIPTION	FIRST DAY COVERS SING	FIRST DAY COVERS PL. BLK.	MINT SHEET	PLATE BLOCK	UNUSED F/NH	USED
2167/2245	(2167, 2202-04, 2210-11, 2220-24, 2235-45) 22 varieties	....	....	....	....	23.30	4.75
2198	22¢ Cover & Handstamp	1.75	....	....	....	.90	.40
2199	22¢ Collector with Album	1.75	....	....	....	.90	.40
2200	22¢ No. 836 under magnifier	1.75	....	....	....	.90	.40
2201	22¢ President sheet	1.75	....	....	....	.90	.40
2201a	Stamp Collecting bklt pane, 4 varieties, attached	4.50	....	....	....	3.50	2.60

2202

2203

2204

2202	22¢ LOVE	1.95	4.25	33.00(50)	3.00	.75	.15
2203	22¢ Sojourner Truth	1.75	4.00	40.00(50)	4.25	.90	.15
2204	22¢ Texas Republic	1.75	4.00	33.00(50)	3.00	.75	.15

1986-93 GREAT AMERICANS

SCOTT NO.	DESCRIPTION	FIRST DAY COVERS SING	FIRST DAY COVERS PL. BLK.	MINT SHEET	PLATE BLOCK	UNUSED F/NH	USED
2168	1¢ Margaret Mitchell	1.75	4.00	10.00(100)	.40	.20	.15
2169	2¢ Mary Lyon (1987)	1.75	4.00	10.00(100)	.50	.20	.15
2170	3¢ Dr. Paul D. White	1.75	4.00	12.50(100)	.50	.20	.15
2171	4¢ Father Flanagan	1.75	4.00	14.00(100)	.60	.20	.15
2172	5¢ Hugo L. Black	1.75	4.00	27.50(100)	1.50	.40	.15
2173	5¢ Luis Muñoz Marin (1990)	1.75	4.00	18.00(100)	.90	.20	.15
2175	10¢ Red Cloud (1987)	1.75	4.00	30.00(100)	1.75	.40	.15
2176	14¢ Julia Ward Howe (1987)	1.75	4.00	50.00(100)	2.75	.60	.15
2177	15¢ Buffalo Bill Cody (1988)	1.75	4.00	70.00(100)	4.50	.80	.15
2178	17¢ Belva Ann Lockwood	1.75	4.00	50.00(100)	3.00	.65	.15
2179	20¢ Virginia Apgar (1994)	1.75	4.00	50.00(100)	3.10	.65	.15
2180	21¢ Chester Carlson (1988)	1.75	4.00	60.00(100)	3.50	.65	.50
2181	23¢ Mary Cassatt (1988)	1.75	4.00	65.00(100)	4.00	.75	.15
2182	25¢ Jack London (1988)	1.75	4.00	70.00(100)	4.00	.75	.15
2182a	as above bklt pane of 10	8.00	....	....	....	7.00	....
2183	28¢ Sitting Bull (1989)	1.75	....	90.00(100)	5.25	1.00	.50
2184	29¢ Earl Warren (1992)	1.75	4.00	90.00(100)	5.00	1.00	.15
2185	29¢ Thomas Jefferson (1993)	1.75	4.75	90.00(100)	4.00(4)	1.00	.15
2185b	same, Plate Block of 8	....	....	....	8.00(8)	....	....
2186	35¢ Dennis Chavez (1991)	1.75	4.00	100.00(100)	6.00	1.20	.50
2187	40¢ Claire Lee Chenault (1990)	1.85	4.25	120.00(100)	6.75	1.35	.15
2188	45¢ Dr. Harvey Cushing (1988)	1.85	4.25	130.00(100)	6.75	1.50	.15

BOOKLET PANE SINGLES: Traditionally, booklet panes have been collected only as intact panes since, other than the straight edged sides, they were identical to sheet stamps. However, starting with the 1971 8¢ Eisenhower stamp, many issues differ from the comparative sheet stamp or may even be totally different issues (e.g. #1738-42 Windmills). These newer issues are now collected as booklet singles or panes—both methods being acceptable.

U.S. Postage #2205-2231

SCOTT NO.	DESCRIPTION	FIRST DAY COVERS SING PL. BLK.	MINT SHEET	PLATE BLOCK	UNUSED F/NH	USED

2205

2206

2207

2208

2209

2205	22¢ Muskellunge	1.75	....	....	....	2.50	.25
2206	22¢ Altantic Cod	1.75	....	....	....	2.50	.25
2207	22¢ Largemouth Bass	1.75	....	....	....	2.50	.25
2208	22¢ Bluefin Tuna	1.75	....	....	....	2.50	.25
2209	22¢ Catfish	1.75	....	....	....	2.50	.25
2209a	Fish, bklt pane, 5 varieties, attached	6.50	....	....	....	12.50	6.00

2210

2211

2216

| 2210 | 22¢ Public Hospitals | 1.75 | 4.00 | 34.00(50) | 3.50 | .75 | .15 |
| 2211 | 22¢ Duke Ellington | 1.75 | 4.00 | 35.00(50) | 4.00 | .85 | .15 |

1986 PRESIDENTS MINIATURE SETS
Complete set printed on 4 miniature sheets of 9 stamps each.

- 2216a Washington
- 2216b Adams
- 2216c Jefferson
- 2216d Madison
- 2216e Monroe
- 2216f J.Q. Adams
- 2216g Jackson
- 2216h Van Buren
- 2216i W.H. Harrison
- 2217a Tyler
- 2217b Polk
- 2217c Taylor
- 2217d Fillmore
- 2217e Pierce
- 2217f Buchanan
- 2217g Lincoln
- 2217h A. Johnson
- 2217i Grant
- 2218a Hayes
- 2218b Garfield
- 2218c Arthur
- 2218d Cleveland
- 2218e B. Harrison
- 2218f McKinley
- 2218g T. Roosevelt
- 2218h Taft
- 2218i Wilson
- 2219a Harding
- 2219b Coolidge
- 2219c Hoover
- 2219d F.D. Roosevelt
- 2219e White House
- 2219f Truman
- 2219g Eisenhower
- 2219h Kennedy
- 2219i L.B. Johnson

SCOTT NO.	DESCRIPTION	FIRST DAY COVERS SING PL. BLK.	MINT SHEET	PLATE BLOCK	UNUSED F/NH	USED

1986 AMERIPEX '86 MINIATURE SHEETS

| 2216-19 | 22¢ 36 varieties complete in 4 miniature sheets | 29.95 | .... | .... | .... | 27.50 | 26.00 |
| 2216a-19i | set of 36 singles | 70.00 | .... | .... | .... | .... | 17.50 |

2220

2221

2222

2223

1986 COMMEMORATIVES

2220-23	Explorers, 4 varieties, attached	2.75	3.25	62.00(50)	7.50	6.75	3.00
2220	22¢ Elisha Kent Kane	1.75	....	....	....	1.75	.50
2221	22¢ Adolphus W. Greely	1.75	....	....	....	1.75	.50
2222	22¢ Vilhjalmur Stefansson	1.75	....	....	....	1.75	.50
2223	22¢ R.E. Peary, M. Henson	1.75	....	....	....	1.75	.50

2224

| 2224 | 22¢ Statue of Liberty | 1.75 | 4.00 | 32.50(50) | 3.50 | .80 | .15 |

2225

2226

2228

1986-91 TRANSPORTATION COILS—"B" Press
Perf. 10 Vertically

SCOTT NO.	DESCRIPTION	FDC SING	PLATE# STRIP 3	MINT SHEET	PLATE# STRIP 3	UNUSED	USED
2225	1¢ Omnibus	1.75	6.50	....	.85	.20	.15
2225a	1¢ Omnibus, untagged (1991)	....	....	....	1.25	.20	.15
2226	2¢ Locomotive (1987)	1.75	6.50	....	1.00	.20	.15
2226a	2¢ Locomotive, untagged (1994)	....	....	....	1.10	.20	.15
2228	4¢ Stagecoach	....	....	....	1.75	.20	.15
2228a	same, overall tagging (1990)	....	....	....	15.00	.75	.30
2231	8.3¢ Ambulance precancelled (1986)	....	....	....	8.50	1.35	.30

Note: For plate number strips of 5, see page 139

#2225—"¢" sign eliminated. #1897 has "1¢".
#2226—inscribed "2 USA". #1897A inscribed "USA 2¢".
#2228—"Stagecoach 1890s" is 17 mm long.

U.S. Postage #2235-2266

1986 COMMEMORATIVES (continued)

SCOTT NO.	DESCRIPTION	FIRST DAY COVERS SING	FIRST DAY COVERS PL. BLK.	MINT SHEET	PLATE BLOCK	UNUSED F/NH	USED
2235-38	Navajo Art, 4 varieties, attached	2.75	3.25	60.00(50)	6.50	6.00	3.00
2235	22¢ Navajo Art	1.75	....	....	....	1.75	.20
2236	22¢ Navajo Art	1.75	....	....	....	1.75	.20
2237	22¢ Navajo Art	1.75	....	....	....	1.75	.20
2238	22¢ Navajo Art	1.75	....	....	....	1.75	.20
2239	22¢ T.S. Eliot	1.75	4.00	40.00(50)	4.25	.85	.15
2240-43	Woodcarved Figurines, 4 varieties, attached	2.75	3.25	45.00(50)	5.00	4.25	3.00
2240	22¢ Highlander Figure	1.75	....	....	....	1.10	.20
2241	22¢ Ship Figurehead	1.75	....	....	....	1.10	.20
2242	22¢ Nautical Figure	1.75	....	....	....	1.10	.20
2243	22¢ Cigar Store Figure	1.75	....	....	....	1.10	.20
2244	22¢ Madonna	1.75	4.00	58.00(100)	3.00	.65	.15
2245	22¢ Village Scene	1.75	4.00	58.00(100)	3.00	.65	.15

1987 COMMEMORATIVES

SCOTT NO.	DESCRIPTION	FIRST DAY COVERS SING	FIRST DAY COVERS PL. BLK.	MINT SHEET	PLATE BLOCK	UNUSED F/NH	USED
2246/2368	(2246-51, 2275, 2336-38, 2349-54, 2360-61, 2367-68) 20 varieties	....	....	....	....	19.40	3.25
2246	22¢ Michigan Statehood	1.75	4.00	30.00(50)	3.00	.65	.15
2247	22¢ Pan American Games	1.75	4.00	30.00(50)	3.00	.65	.15
2248	22¢ LOVE	1.95	4.25	57.00(100)	3.00	.65	.15
2249	22¢ Jean Baptiste Pointe du Sable	1.75	4.00	33.00(50)	3.50	.75	.15
2250	22¢ Enrico Caruso	1.75	4.00	33.00(50)	3.50	.75	.15
2251	22¢ Girls Scouts	1.75	4.00	35.00(50)	3.50	.80	.15

1987-93 TRANSPORTATION COILS

SCOTT NO.	DESCRIPTION	FIRST DAY COVERS SING	PLATE# STRIP		PLATE# STRIP	UNUSED F/NH	USED
2252	3¢ Conestoga Wagon (1988)	1.75	9.00	....	1.25	.20	.20
2252a	same, untagged (1992)		9.00		1.75	.20	.20
2253	5¢ Milk Wagon	1.75	9.00		1.50	.20	.20
2254	5.3¢ Elevator, precancel ('88)	1.75	9.00		1.90	.40	.20
2255	7.6¢ Carreta, precancel ('88)	1.75	9.00		3.25	.40	.20
2256	8.4¢ Wheel Chair, precancel (1988)	1.75	9.00		3.25	.40	.20
2257	10¢ Canal Boat	1.75	9.00		2.00	.40	.20
2257a	same, overall tagging (1993)		9.00		3.75	.40	.20
2258	13¢ Police Wagon, precancel (1988)	1.75	9.00		6.50	.80	.25
2259	13.2¢ Railroad Coal Car, precancel (1988)	1.75	9.00		3.50	.40	.20
2260	15¢ Tugboat (1988)	1.75	9.00		3.50	.50	.20
2260a	same, overall tagging (1990)		9.00		5.25	.75	.20
2261	16.7¢ Popcorn Wagon, precancel (1988)	1.75	9.00		4.25	.50	.20
2262	17.5¢ Racing Car	1.75	9.00		4.75	.70	.35
2262a	17.5¢ Racing Car, precancel (1988)		9.00		5.25	.70	.20
2263	20¢ Cable Car (1988)	1.75	9.00		4.50	.70	.20
2263b	same, overall tagging (1990)		9.00		10.00	1.25	.20
2264	20.5¢ Fire Engine, precancel (1988)	1.75	9.00		8.00	1.25	.45
2265	21¢ Railroad Mail Car, precancel (1988)	1.75	9.00		5.50	.70	.45
2266	24.1¢ Tandem Bicycle, precancel (1988)	1.75	9.00		5.50	.85	.45

U.S. Postage #2267-2335

2267   2268   2269

2270   2271   2272

2273   2274

1987 SPECIAL OCCASIONS BOOKLET PANE

Scott	Description	FDC Sing	FDC Pl.Blk.	Mint Sheet	Plate Block	Unused F/NH	Used
2267	22¢ Congratulations!	1.75	....	....	....	2.25	.40
2268	22¢ Get Well!	1.75	....	....	....	2.25	.40
2269	22¢ Thank You!	1.75	....	....	....	2.25	.40
2270	22¢ Love You, Dad!	1.75	....	....	....	2.25	.40
2271	22¢ Best Wishes!	1.75	....	....	....	2.25	.40
2272	22¢ Happy Birthday!	1.75	....	....	....	2.25	.40
2273	22¢ Love You, Mother!	1.75	....	....	....	2.25	.40
2274	22¢ Keep in Touch!	1.75	....	....	....	2.25	.40
2274a	Special Occasions bklt pane of 10, attached	7.00	....	....	....	18.50	....

NOTE: #2274a contains 1 each of #2268-71, 2273-74 and 2 each of #2267 and 2272.

2275

1987 COMMEMORATIVES (continued)

Scott	Description	FDC Sing	FDC Pl.Blk.	Mint Sheet	Plate Block	Unused F/NH	Used
2275	22¢ United Way	1.75	4.00	29.00(50)	3.00	.65	.15

2276, 2276A   2277, 2279, 2282, 2282a   2278, 2285A, 2285Ac

1987-88 REGULAR ISSUE

Scott	Description	FDC Sing	FDC Pl.Blk.	Mint Sheet	Plate Block	Unused F/NH	Used
2276	22¢ Flag & Fireworks	1.75	4.00	58.00(100)	3.25	.65	.15
2276a	bklt pane of 20	12.50	....	....	....	13.50	....
2277	(25¢) "E" Earth (1988)	1.75	4.00	85.00(100)	4.25	.95	.15
2278	25¢ Flag with Clouds (1988)	1.75	4.00	70.00(100)	3.50	.75	.15

2280   2281   2283, 2283a

2284   2285, 2285b

Scott	Description	FDC Sing	FDC Pl.Blk.	Mint Sheet	Plate # Strip 3	Unused F/NH	Used
2279	(25¢) "E" Earth coil (1988)	1.75			7.50	4.50	.75	.15
2280	25¢ Flag over Yosemite, coil (1988)	1.75			7.50	4.50	.85	.15
2280a	25¢ Flag over Yosemite, phosphor (1989)	1.75			....	5.00	.95	.15
2281	25¢ Honey Bee, coil (1988)	1.75			7.50	4.00	.85	.15
2282	(25¢) "E" Earth, bklt single (1988)	1.75			....	....	.85	.15
2282a	(25¢) "E" Earth, bklt pane of 10	7.25			....	....	8.00	....
2283	25¢ Pheasant bklt single (1988)	1.75			....	....	.85	.15
2283a	25¢ Pheasant, bklt pane of 10	7.25			....	....	8.00	....
2283b	25¢ Pheasant, (red omitted) bklt single	....			....	....	10.00	....
2283c	25¢ Pheasant, (red omitted) bklt pane of 10	....			....	....	95.00	....
2284	25¢ Grosbeak, bklt single (1988)	1.75			....	....	.75	.15
2285	25¢ Owl bklt single	1.75			....	....	.75	.15
2285b	25¢ Owl/Grosbeck, bklt pane of 10	7.25			....	....	7.00	....
2285A	25¢ Flag with Clouds, bklt single	1.75			....	....	.90	.15
2285Ac	as above, bklt pane of 6 (1988)	4.00			....	....	5.75	....

2286   2310   2335

1987 AMERICAN WILDLIFE

2286	Barn Swallow	2303	Red-winged Blackbird	2320	Bison
2287	Monarch Butterfly	2304	American Lobster	2321	Snowy Egret
2288	Bighorn Sheep	2305	Black-tailed Jack Rabbit	2322	Gray Wolf
2289	Broad-tailed Hummingbird	2306	Scarlet Tanager	2323	Mountain Goat
2290	Cottontail	2307	Woodchuck	2324	Deer Mouse
2291	Osprey	2308	Roseate Spoonbill	2325	Black-tailed Prairie Dog
2292	Mountain Lion	2309	Bald Eagle	2326	Box Turtle
2293	Luna Moth	2310	Alaskan Brown Bear	2327	Wolverine
2294	Mule Deer	2311	Iiwi	2328	American Elk
2295	Gray Squirrel	2312	Badger	2329	California Sea Lion
2296	Armadillo	2313	Pronghorn	2330	Mockingbird
2297	Eastern Chipmunk	2314	River Otter	2331	Raccoon
2298	Moose	2315	Ladybug	2332	Bobcat
2299	Black Bear	2316	Beaver	2333	Black-footed Ferret
2300	Tiger Swallowtail	2317	White-tailed Deer	2334	Canada Goose
2301	Bobwhite	2318	Blue Jay	2335	Red Fox
2302	Ringtail	2319	Pika		

Scott	Description	FDC Sing	FDC Pl.Blk.	Mint Sheet	Plate Block	Unused F/NH	Used
2286-2335	22¢, 50 varieties, attached	70.00	....	70.00(50)	....	70.00	....
	set of singles	86.00	....	....	....	....	25.00
	singles of above, each	2.00	....	....	....	....	1.00

2336   2337   2338   2339

U.S. Postage #2336-2361

SCOTT NO.	DESCRIPTION	FIRST DAY COVERS SING	PL. BLK.	MINT SHEET	PLATE BLOCK	UNUSED F/NH	USED

1987-90 COMMEMORATIVES

SCOTT NO.	DESCRIPTION	SING	PL. BLK.	MINT SHEET	PLATE BLOCK	UNUSED F/NH	USED
2336	22¢ Delaware Statehood	1.75	4.00	60.00(50)	6.50	1.50	.20
2337	22¢ Pennsylvania Statehood	1.75	4.00	60.00(50)	6.50	1.50	.20
2338	22¢ New Jersey Statehood	1.75	4.00	60.00(50)	6.50	1.50	.20
2339	22¢ Georgia Statehood (1988)	1.75	4.00	60.00(50)	6.50	1.50	.20
2340	22¢ Connecticut Statehood (1988)	1.75	4.00	60.00(50)	6.50	1.50	.20
2341	22¢ Massachusetts Statehood (1988)	1.75	4.00	60.00(50)	6.50	1.50	.20
2342	22¢ Maryland Statehood (1988)	1.75	4.00	60.00(50)	6.50	1.50	.20
2343	25¢ South Carolina Statehood (1988)	1.75	4.00	60.00(50)	6.50	1.50	.20
2344	25¢ New Hampshire Statehood (1988)	1.75	4.00	60.00(50)	6.50	1.50	.20
2345	25¢ Virginia Statehood (1988)	1.75	4.00	60.00(50)	6.50	1.50	.20
2346	25¢ New York Statehood (1988)	1.75	4.00	60.0050	6.50	1.50	.20
2347	25¢ North Carolina Statehood (1989)	1.75	4.00	60.00(50)	6.50	1.50	.20
2348	25¢ Rhode Island Statehood (1990)	1.75	9.00	60.00(50)	6.50	1.50	.20
2349	22¢ Morocco	1.75	4.00	35.00(50)	3.50	.75	.15
2350	22¢ William Faulkner	1.75	4.00	47.50(50)	4.50	1.00	.15

–Supplies–
Don't forget that Harris offers a complete line of albums, supplies and accessories for all your stamp collecting needs!

2351-54	Lacemaking, 4 varieties, attached	2.75	3.25	40.00(40)	5.50	4.25	3.00
2351	22¢ Lace, Ruth Maxwell	1.75				1.25	.25
2352	22¢ Lace, Mary McPeek	1.75				1.25	.25
2353	22¢ Lace, Leslie K. Saari	1.75				1.25	.25
2354	22¢ Lace, Trenna Ruffner	1.75				1.25	.25
2355	22¢ "The Bicentennial"	1.75				1.40	.20
2356	22¢ "We the people"	1.75				1.40	.20
2357	22¢ "Establish justice"	1.75				1.40	.20
2358	22¢ "And secure"	1.75				1.40	.20
2359	22¢ "Do ordain"	1.75				1.40	.20
2359a	Drafting of Constitution bklt pane, 5 varieties, attached	4.60				7.00	3.50
2360	22¢ Signing of U.S. Constitution	1.75	4.00	55.00(50)	5.50	1.25	.15
2361	22¢ Certified Public Accountants	2.50	5.00	170.00(50)	15.00	3.50	.15

U.S. Postage #2362-2385a

LOCOMOTIVES ISSUE

SCOTT NO.	DESCRIPTION	FIRST DAY COVERS SING	FIRST DAY COVERS PL. BLK.	MINT SHEET	PLATE BLOCK	UNUSED F/NH	USED
2362	22¢ "Strourbridge Lion, 1829"	1.75	....	....	....	1.25	.20
2363	22¢ "Best Friend of Charleston, 1830"	1.75	....	....	....	1.25	.20
2364	22¢ "John Bull, 1831"	1.75	....	....	....	1.25	.20
2365	22¢ "Brother Jonathan, 1832"	1.75	....	....	....	1.25	.20
2366	22¢ "Gowan + Marx, 1839"	1.75	....	....	....	1.25	.20
2366a	Locomotives, bklt pane, 5 varieties, attached	4.60	....	....	....	6.00	4.00

SCOTT NO.	DESCRIPTION	FIRST DAY COVERS SING	FIRST DAY COVERS PL. BLK.	MINT SHEET	PLATE BLOCK	UNUSED F/NH	USED
2367	22¢ Madonna	1.75	4.00	58.00(100)	3.00	.65	.15
2368	22¢ Ornament	1.75	4.00	58.00(100)	3.00	.65	.15

1988 COMMEMORATIVES

SCOTT NO.	DESCRIPTION	FIRST DAY COVERS SING	FIRST DAY COVERS PL. BLK.	MINT SHEET	PLATE BLOCK	UNUSED F/NH	USED
2339/2400	(2339-46, 2369-80, 2386-93, 2399-2400) 30 varieties	....	....	....	....	34.25	6.25
2369	22¢ Winter Olympics	1.75	4.00	40.00(50)	3.75	.85	.15
2370	22¢ Australia Bicentennial	1.75	4.00	25.00(50)	3.00	.65	.15
2371	22¢ James Weldon Johnson	1.75	4.00	32.00(50)	3.25	.75	.15
2372-75	Cats, 4 varieties, attached	2.75	3.25	40.00(40)	6.50	5.00	3.00
2372	22¢ Siamese, Exotic Shorthair	1.75	....	....	....	1.35	.30
2373	22¢ Abyssinian, Himalayan	1.75	....	....	....	1.35	.30
2374	22¢ Maine Coon, Burmese	1.75	....	....	....	1.35	.30
2375	22¢ American Shorthair, Persian	1.75	....	....	....	1.35	.30
2376	22¢ Knute Rockne	3.00	6.00	45.00(50)	4.75	1.00	.15
2377	25¢ Francis Ouimet	3.00	6.00	60.00(50)	7.00	1.25	.15
2378	25¢ LOVE	1.75	4.00	68.00(100)	3.50	.75	.15

SCOTT NO.	DESCRIPTION	FIRST DAY COVERS SING	FIRST DAY COVERS PL. BLK.	MINT SHEET	PLATE BLOCK	UNUSED F/NH	USED
2379	45¢ LOVE	1.75	4.00	67.50(50)	7.00	1.50	.20
2380	25¢ Summer Olympics	1.75	4.00	40.00(50)	3.75	.85	.15

SCOTT NO.	DESCRIPTION	FIRST DAY COVERS SING	FIRST DAY COVERS PL. BLK.	MINT SHEET	PLATE BLOCK	UNUSED F/NH	USED
2381	25¢ Locomobile	1.75	....	....	....	2.25	.25
2382	25¢ Pierce-Arrow	1.75	....	....	....	2.25	.25
2383	25¢ Cord	1.75	....	....	....	2.25	.25
2384	25¢ Packard	1.75	....	....	....	2.25	.25
2385	25¢ Duesenberg	1.75	....	....	....	2.25	.25
2385a	Classic Automobiles bklt pane, 5 varieties, attached	4.60	....	....	....	12.00	6.00

BOOKLET PANE SINGLES: Traditionally, booklet panes have been collected only as intact panes since, other than the straight edged sides, they were identical to sheet stamps. However, starting with the 1971 8¢ Eisenhower stamp, many issues differ from the comparative sheet stamp or may even be totally different issues (e.g. #1738-42 Windmills). These newer issues are now collected as booklet singles or panes—both methods being acceptable.

U.S. Postage #2386-2409av

2386

2387

2388

2389

SCOTT NO.	DESCRIPTION	FIRST DAY COVERS SING	PL. BLK.	MINT SHEET	PLATE BLOCK	UNUSED F/NH	USED
2386-89	Antarctic Explorers, 4 varieties, attached	2.75	3.25	57.50(50)	8.00	5.75	3.00
2386	25¢ Nathaniel Palmer	1.75	....	....	....	1.50	.30
2387	25¢ Lt. Charles Wilkes	1.75	....	....	....	1.50	.30
2388	25¢ Richard E. Byrd	1.75	....	....	....	1.50	.30
2389	25¢ Lincoln Ellsworth	1.75	....	....	....	1.50	.30

2390

2391

2392

2393

SCOTT NO.	DESCRIPTION	FIRST DAY COVERS SING	PL. BLK.	MINT SHEET	PLATE BLOCK	UNUSED F/NH	USED
2390-93	Carousel Animals, 4 varieties, attached	2.75	3.25	57.50(50)	6.75	6.00	3.00
2390	25¢ Deer	1.75	....	....	....	1.60	.25
2391	25¢ Horse	1.75	....	....	....	1.60	.25
2392	25¢ Camel	1.75	....	....	....	1.60	.25
2393	25¢ Goat	1.75	....	....	....	1.60	.25

2394

| 2394 | $8.75 Express Mail | 32.00 | 70.00 | 495.00(20) | 120.00 | 27.00 | 10.00 |

2395

2396

2397

2398

SCOTT NO.	DESCRIPTION	FIRST DAY COVERS SING	PL. BLK.	MINT SHEET	PLATE BLOCK	UNUSED F/NH	USED
2395-2398	Special Occasions, bklt singles	7.00	....	....	....	4.50	1.20
2396a	Bklt pane (6) with gutter 3–#2395 + 3–#2396	4.60	....	....	....	6.00	5.00
2398a	Bklt pane (6) with gutter 3–#2397 + 3–#2398	4.60	....	....	....	6.00	5.00

2399

2400

| 2399 | 25¢ Madonna and Child | 1.75 | 4.00 | 32.00(50) | 3.25 | .70 | .15 |
| 2400 | 25¢ One Horse Sleigh | 1.75 | 4.00 | 32.00(50) | 3.25 | .70 | .15 |

2401

2402

1989 COMMEMORATIVES

SCOTT NO.	DESCRIPTION	FIRST DAY COVERS SING	PL. BLK.	MINT SHEET	PLATE BLOCK	UNUSED F/NH	USED
2347/2437	(2347, 2401-04, 2410-14, 2416-18, 2420-28, 2434-37) 26 varieties	....	....	....	....	27.70	3.70
2401	25¢ Montana Statehood	1.75	4.00	45.00(50)	4.50	1.00	.15
2402	25¢ A.P. Randolph	1.75	4.00	41.00(50)	4.00	.90	.15

2403

2404

| 2403 | 25¢ North Dakota Statehood | 1.75 | 4.00 | 42.50(50) | 4.50 | 1.00 | .15 |
| 2404 | 25¢ Washington Statehood | 1.75 | 4.00 | 42.50(50) | 4.50 | 1.00 | .15 |

2405

2406

2407

2408

2409

SCOTT NO.	DESCRIPTION	FIRST DAY COVERS SING	PL. BLK.	MINT SHEET	PLATE BLOCK	UNUSED F/NH	USED
2405	25¢ "Experiment, 1788-90"	1.75	....	....	....	1.40	.25
2406	25¢ "Phoenix, 1809"	1.75	....	....	....	1.40	.25
2407	25¢ "New Orleans, 1812"	1.75	....	....	....	1.40	.25
2408	25¢ "Washington, 1816"	1.75	....	....	....	1.40	.25
2409	25¢ "Walk in the Water, 1818"	1.75	....	....	....	1.40	.25
2409a	Steamboat, bklt pane, 5 varieties, attached	6.00	....	....	....	6.50	4.00
2409av	same, bklt pane, unfolded	....	....	....	....	10.00	....

U.S. Postage #2410-2431

SCOTT NO.	DESCRIPTION	FIRST DAY COVERS SING	FIRST DAY COVERS PL. BLK.	MINT SHEET	PLATE BLOCK	UNUSED F/NH	USED
2410	25¢ World Stamp Expo '89	1.75	4.00	35.00(50)	3.75	.85	.15
2411	25¢ Arturo Toscanini	1.75	4.00	35.00(50)	3.75	.85	.15
2412	25¢ U.S. House of Representatives	1.75	4.00	45.00(50)	4.50	1.00	.15
2413	25¢ U.S. Senate	1.75	4.00	45.00(50)	4.50	1.00	.15
2414	25¢ Executive Branch	1.75	4.00	45.00(50)	5.00	1.00	.15
2415	25¢ U.S. Supreme Court (1990)	1.75	4.00	45.00(50)	4.75	1.00	.15
2416	25¢ South Dakota Statehood	1.75	4.00	42.50(50)	4.00	1.00	.15
2417	25¢ Lou Gehrig	5.00	8.00	55.00(50)	6.00	1.20	.30
2418	25¢ Ernest Hemingway	1.75	4.00	42.50(50)	4.50	1.00	.15
2419	$2.40 Moon Landing	7.50	15.75	160.00(20)	40.00	9.00	5.00
2420	25¢ Letter Carriers	1.75	4.00	26.00(50)	3.25	.70	.15
2421	25¢ Bill of Rights	1.75	4.00	55.00(50)	5.75	1.25	.15
2422-25	Prehistoric Animals, 4 attached	2.75	3.25	52.50(40)	6.25	6.25	3.00
2422	25¢ Tyrannosaurus Rex	1.75	....	....	....	1.50	.20
2423	25¢ Pteranodon	1.75	....	....	....	1.50	.20
2424	25¢ Stegosaurus	1.75	....	....	....	1.50	.20
2425	25¢ Brontosaurus	1.75	....	....	....	1.50	.20
2426	25¢ Kachina Doll	1.75	4.00	32.00(50)	3.25	.70	.15
2427	25¢ Madonna & Child	1.75	4.00	32.00(50)	3.25	.75	.15
2427a	same, bklt pane of 10	7.25	....	....	....	7.50	....
2427av	same, bklt pane, unfolded	....	....	....	....	15.00	....
2428	25¢ Sleigh full of Presents	1.75	4.00	32.00(50)	3.25	.75	.15
2429	25¢ Sleigh full of Presents, bklt single	1.75	....	....	....	.90	.20
2429a	same, bklt pane of 10	7.25	....	....	....	8.00	....
2429av	same, bklt pane, unfolded	....	....	....	....	21.00	....
2431	25¢ Eagle & Shield, self-adhesive	1.95	....	....	....	1.25	.35
2431a	same, bklt pane of 18	13.50	....	....	....	19.50	....
2431	same, coil	....	....	....	3.00(3)	.85	....

U.S. Postage #2433-2468

SCOTT NO.	DESCRIPTION	FIRST DAY COVERS SING	FIRST DAY COVERS PL. BLK.	MINT SHEET	PLATE BLOCK	UNUSED F/NH	USED

2433

| 2433 | $3.60 World Stamp Expo, Imperf. Souvenir Sheet | 15.00 | .... | .... | .... | 25.00 | 17.50 |

 2434  2435

 2436  2437

2434-37	Classic Mail Delivery, 4 attached	2.75	3.25	45.00(40)	6.25	5.50	3.00
2434	25¢ Stagecoach	1.75	....	....	....	1.50	.20
2435	25¢ Paddlewheel Steamer	1.75	....	....	....	1.50	.20
2436	25¢ Biplane	1.75	....	....	....	1.50	.20
2437	25¢ Automobile	1.75	....	....	....	1.50	.20
2438	$1.00 Classic Mail Delivery Imperf. Souvenir Sheet	4.50	....	....	....	8.00	5.00

 2439    2440, 2441   2442

1990 COMMEMORATIVES

2348/2515	(2348, 2415, 2439-40, 2442, 2444-49, 2496-2500, 2506-15, 26 varieties)	....	....	....	....	32.55	5.10
2439	25¢ Idaho Statehood	1.75	4.00	32.00(50)	3.25	.70	.15
2440	25¢ LOVE	1.75	4.00	32.00(50)	3.25	.70	.15
2441	25¢ LOVE, bklt single	1.75	....	....	....	1.25	.15
2441a	25¢ LOVE bklt pane of 10	8.65	....	....	....	12.00	....
2441av	same, bklt pane, unfolded	....	....	....	....	50.00	....
2442	25¢ Ida B. Wells	1.75	4.00	52.50(50)	5.50	1.25	.15

  2443    2444

 2445    2449    2446

 2447   2448

2443	15¢ Umbrella, bklt single	1.75	....	....	....	.50	.15
2443a	15¢ Umbrella, bklt pane of 10	5.75	....	....	....	5.00	3.40
2443av	same, bklt pane, unfolded	....	....	....	....	9.00	....
2444	25¢ Wyoming Statehood	8.00	10.00	37.00(50)	3.75	.80	.15
2445-48	Classic Films, 4 varieties, attached	4.00	6.00	87.00(40)	12.00	10.00	4.50
2445	25¢ Wizard of OZ	4.00	....	....	....	2.75	.25
2446	25¢ Gone with the Wind	4.00	....	....	....	2.75	.25
2447	25¢ Beau Geste	4.00	....	....	....	2.75	.25
2448	25¢ Stagecoach	4.00	....	....	....	2.75	.25
2449	25¢ Marianne Craig Moore	1.75	4.00	32.00(50)	3.25	.70	.15

 2451   2452, 2452B, 2452D   2453, 2454   2457, 2458

 2463   2464   2466   2468

1990-95 TRANSPORTATION COILS

SCOTT NO.	DESCRIPTION	FIRST DAY COVERS SING	PLATE# STRIP 3		PLATE# STRIP 3	UNUSED F/NH	USED
2451	4¢ Steam Carriage (1991)	1.75	6.50	....	1.50	.20	.15
2451b	4¢ Steam Carriage, untagged	....	....	....	1.50	.20	.15
2452	5¢ Circus Wagon	1.75	6.50	....	1.75	.20	.15
2452a	5¢ Circus Wagon, untagged	....	....	....	1.85	.20	.20
2452B	5¢ Circus Wagon, Gravure (1992)	1.75	6.50	....	1.85	.20	.20
2452D	5¢ Circus Wagon, coil (Reissue, 1995 added)	1.95	10.00	....	1.85	.20	.20
2453	5¢ Canoe, precancel, brown (1991)	1.75	6.50	....	1.85	.20	.15
2454	5¢ Canoe, precancel, red (1991)	1.75	6.50	....	1.85	.20	.20
2457	10¢ Tractor Trailer (1991)	1.75	6.50	....	2.75	.30	.15
2458	10¢ Tractor Trailer, Gravure (1994)	1.75	6.50	....	3.25	.35	.20
2463	20¢ Cog Railway Car, coil	1.95	10.00	....	5.00	.50	.15
2464	23¢ Lunch Wagon (1991)	1.75	6.50	....	4.50	.75	.15
2466	32¢ Ferryboat, coil	1.95	10.00	....	7.00	1.00	.15
2468	$1 Seaplane, coil	3.00	10.00	....	9.75	3.00	.85

NOTE: For plate number strips of 5, see page 139

Buy Complete Sets and Save

U.S. Postage #2470-2500

SCOTT NO.	DESCRIPTION	FIRST DAY COVERS SING	FIRST DAY COVERS PL. BLK.	MINT SHEET	PLATE BLOCK	UNUSED F/NH	USED
2470	25¢ Admiralty Head Lighthouse	2.25	....	....	....	1.75	.20
2471	25¢ Cape Hatteras Lighthouse	2.25	....	....	....	1.75	.20
2472	25¢ West Quoddy Head Lighthouse	2.25	....	....	....	1.75	.20
2473	25¢ American Shoals Lighthouse	2.25	....	....	....	1.75	.20
2474	25¢ Sandy Hook Lighthouse	2.25	....	....	....	1.75	.20
2474a	Lighthouse, bklt pane, 5 varieties	4.60	....	....	....	9.00	4.50
2474av	Same, bklt pane, unfolded	....	....	....	....	13.50	....
2475	25¢ ATM Plastic Stamp, single	1.75	....	....	....	1.10	.75
2475a	Same, pane of 12	20.00	....	....	....	13.00	....

1990-95 REGULAR ISSUE

SCOTT NO.	DESCRIPTION	FIRST DAY COVERS SING	FIRST DAY COVERS PL. BLK.	MINT SHEET	PLATE BLOCK	UNUSED F/NH	USED
2476	1¢ Kestrel (1991)	1.75	4.00	6.00(100)	.75	.20	.15
2477	1¢ Kestrel (redesign 1¢, 1995)	1.75	4.00	6.00(100)	.75	.20	.15
2478	3¢ Bluebird (1993)	1.75	4.00	8.00(100)	.75	.20	.15
2479	19¢ Fawn (1993)	1.75	4.00	45.00(100)	4.00	.45	.15
2480	30¢ Cardinal (1993)	1.75	4.00	70.00(100)	4.00	.85	.30
2481	45¢ Pumpkinseed Sunfish (1992)	2.00	4.50	110.00(100)	6.00	1.25	.30
2482	$2 Bobcat	6.00	14.00	100.00(20)	22.50	5.50	.75
2483	20¢ Blue Jay, bklt single (1991)	1.95	....	....	....	.85	.30
2483a	same, bklt pane of 10	6.00	....	....	....	8.25	....
2483av	same, bklt pane, unfolded	....	....	....	....	9.00	....

SCOTT NO.	DESCRIPTION	FIRST DAY COVERS SING	FIRST DAY COVERS PL. BLK.	MINT SHEET	PLATE BLOCK	UNUSED F/NH	USED
2484	29¢ Wood Duck, bklt single (BEP) (1991)	1.75	....	....	....	.95	.20
2484a	same, bklt pane of 10 (BEP)	6.50	....	....	....	8.00	....
2484av	same, bklt pane, unfolded	....	....	....	....	11.00	....
2485	29¢ Wood Duck, bklt single (KCS) (1991)	1.75	....	....	....	1.00	.20
2485a	same, bklt pane of 10 (KCS)	6.50	....	....	....	9.75	....
2485av	same, bklt pane, unfolded	....	....	....	....	12.50	....
2486	29¢ African Violet, bklt single	1.75	....	....	....	.90	.20
2486a	same, bklt pane of 10	6.50	....	....	....	8.75	....
2486av	same, bklt pane, unfolded	....	....	....	....	9.75	....
2487	32¢ Peach, bklt single	1.95	....	....	....	1.00	.25
2488	32¢ Pear, bklt single	1.95	....	....	....	1.00	.25
2488a	32¢ Peach & Pear, bklt pane of 10	7.25	....	....	....	9.50	....
2488av	same, bklt pane, unfolded	....	....	....	....	10.75	....
2489	29¢ Red Squirrel, self-adhesive (1993)	1.75	....	....	....	.95	.45
2489a	same, bklt pane of 18	13.50	....	....	....	15.00	....
2489v	same, coil	....	....	....	3.00(3)	.95	....
2490	29¢ Rose, self-adhesive (1993)	1.75	....	....	....	.95	.40
2490a	same, bklt pane of 18	13.50	....	....	....	15.00	....
2491	29¢ Pine Cone, self-adhesive	1.75	....	....	....	.95	.40
2491a	same, bklt pane of 18	13.50	....	....	....	15.00	....
2492	32¢ Pink Rose, self-adhesive	1.95	....	....	....	.95	.30
2492a	same, bklt pane of 20	14.50	....	....	....	16.00	....
2492b	same, bklt pane of 15	11.50	....	....	....	13.00	....
2493	32¢ Peach, self-adhesive	1.95	....	....	....	.95	.30
2494	32¢ Pear, self-adhesive	1.95	....	....	....	.95	.30
2494a	32¢ Peach & Pear, self-adhesive, bklt pane of 20	14.50	....	....	....	16.00	....
2495	32¢ Peach, self-adhesive coil (1993)	1.95	....	....	7.00(3)	1.20	....
2495A	32¢ Pear, self-adhesive coil	1.95	....	....	....	1.20	....

SCOTT NO.	DESCRIPTION	FIRST DAY COVERS SING	FIRST DAY COVERS PL. BLK.	MINT SHEET	PLATE BLOCK	UNUSED F/NH	USED
2496-2500	Olympians, strip of 5, attached	4.00	12.50	38.00(35)	13.00(10)	7.00	3.00
2496	25¢ Jesse Owens	2.40	....	....	....	1.75	.30
2497	25¢ Ray Ewry	2.40	....	....	....	1.75	.30
2498	25¢ Hazel Wightman	2.40	....	....	....	1.75	.30
2499	25¢ Eddie Eagan	2.40	....	....	....	1.75	.30
2500	25¢ Helene Madison	2.40	....	....	....	1.75	.30

U.S. Postage #2501-2523A

2501

2502

2503

2504

2505

2512

2513

2514

2515, 2516

SCOTT NO.	DESCRIPTION	FIRST DAY COVERS SING	PL. BLK.	MINT SHEET	PLATE BLOCK	UNUSED F/NH	USED
2501	25¢ Assiniboin	2.40	....	....	....	1.25	.20
2502	25¢ Cheyenne	2.40	....	....	....	1.25	.20
2503	25¢ Comanche	2.40	....	....	....	1.25	.20
2504	25¢ Flathead	2.40	....	....	....	1.25	.20
2505	25¢ Shoshone	2.40	....	....	....	1.25	.20
2505a	25¢ bklt pane of 10	7.85	....	....	....	13.00	....
2505av	same, bklt pane, unfolded	....	....	....	....	20.00	....
2512	25¢ Americas Issue (Grand Canyon)	1.75	4.00	40.00(50)	4.25	1.00	.15
2513	25¢ Dwight D. Eisenhower	1.75	4.00	43.00(40)	6.00	1.25	.15
2514	25¢ Madonna & Child– Antonello	1.75	4.00	32.50(50)	3.25	.85	.15
2514a	same, bklt pane of 10	6.50	....	....	....	8.00	....
2514av	same, bklt pane, unfolded	....	....	....	....	15.00	....
2515	25¢ Christmas Tree	1.75	4.00	32.50(50)	3.25	.75	.15
2516	25¢ Christmas Tree bklt single	1.75	....	....	....	1.25	.15
2516a	same, bklt pane of 10	6.00	....	....	....	12.00	....
2516av	same, bklt pane, unfolded	....	....	....	....	19.50	....

2506

2507

2506-07	Micronesia + Marshall Islands 2 varieties, attached	2.50	4.00	39.00(50)	4.00	1.75	1.00
2506	25¢ Micronesia	1.75	....	....	....	1.00	.20
2507	25¢ Marshall Islands	1.75	....	....	....	1.00	.20

2517- 2519, 2520

1991 REGULAR ISSUES

SCOTT NO.	DESCRIPTION	FIRST DAY COVERS SING	PL. BLK.	MINT SHEET	PLATE BLOCK	UNUSED F/NH	USED
2517	(29¢) "F" Flower	1.75	4.25	85.00(100)	4.25	.95	.15
			PLATE # STRIP 3		PLATE# STRIP 3		
2518	(29¢) "F" Flower, coil	1.75	10.00	....	4.25	.85	.15
2519	(29¢) "F" Flower, bklt single (BEP)	1.75	....	....	....	1.00	.15
2519a	same, bklt pane of 10 (BEP)	6.50	....	....	....	10.00	....
2520	(29¢) "F" Flower, bklt single (KCS)	1.75	....	....	....	3.00	.40
2520a	same, bklt pane of 10 (KCS)	6.50	....	....	....	27.50	....

2508

2509

2521

2522

2521	(4¢) "F" Make-up Rate	1.75	4.25	13.00(100)	.75	.20	.15
2522	(29¢) "F" ATM Plastic Stamp, single	1.75	....	....	....	1.25	.65
2522a	same, pane of 12	9.00	....	....	....	12.50	....

2510

2511

1990 REGULAR ISSUES

2508-11	Sea Creatures, 4 varieties, attached	3.00	3.50	40.00(40)	6.00	5.50	4.00
2508	25¢ Killer Whales	2.00	....	....	....	1.25	.20
2509	25¢ Northern Sea Lions	2.00	....	....	....	1.25	.20
2510	25¢ Sea Otter	2.00	....	....	....	1.25	.20
2511	25¢ Common Dolphin	2.00	....	....	....	1.25	.20

2523, 2523A

			PLATE# STRIP 3		PLATE# STRIP 3		
2523	29¢ Flag over Mt. Rushmore, coil	1.75	10.00	....	4.75	.85	.15
2523A	29¢ Falg over Mt. Rushmore, photogravure coil	1.75	10.00	....	4.75	.85	.60

NOTE: For plate number strips of 5, see page 139

U.S. Postage #2524-2544A

SCOTT NO.	DESCRIPTION	FIRST DAY COVERS SING	FIRST DAY COVERS PL. BLK.	MINT SHEET	PLATE BLOCK	UNUSED F/NH	USED

2524-27

| 2524 | 29¢ Flower | 1.75 | 4.25 | 77.50(100) | 4.50 | .85 | .15 |
| 2524A | 29¢ Flower, perf. 13 | .... | .... | 100.00(100) | 6.00 | 1.00 | .30 |

			PLATE# STRIP 3		PLATE# STRIP 3		
2525	29¢ Flower, coil rouletted	1.75	10.00	....	5.50	1.00	.20
2526	29¢ Flower, coil, perf (1992)	1.75	10.00	....	5.50	1.00	.25
2527	29¢ Flower, bklt single	1.75	....	....	....	1.00	.20
2527a	same, bklt pane of 10	6.50	....	....	....	9.50	....
2527av	same, bklt pane, unfolded	....	....	....	....	9.75	....

2528

2529, 2529C

2530

2531

2531A

			PLATE# STRIP 3		PLATE# STRIP3		
2528	29¢ Flag with Olympic Rings, bklt single	1.75	....	....	....	1.00	.15
2528a	same, bklt pane of 10	6.50	....	....	....	10.00	....
2528av	same, bklt pane, unfolded	....	....	....	....	9.00	....
2529	19¢ Fishing Boat Type I	1.75	10.00	....	4.50	.60	.15
2529a	same, Type II (1993)	....	....	....	4.50	.60	.40
2529C	19¢ Fishing Boat (reengraved)	1.75	10.00	....	7.00	.70	.40
2530	19¢ Hot-Air Balloon bklt single	1.75	....	....	....	.60	.25
2530a	same, bklt pane of 10	5.50	....	....	....	5.50	.15
2530av	same, bklt pane, unfolded	....	....	....	....	7.00	....
2531	29¢ Flags on Parade	1.75	4.25	95.00(100)	5.00	1.00	.15
2531A	29¢ Liberty Torch ATM Stamp	1.75	....	....	....	1.10	.30
2531Ab	same, pane of 18	12.50	....	....	....	20.00	....

2532

1991 COMMEMORATIVES

2532/2579	(2532-35, 2537-38, 2550-51, 2553-61, 2567, 2578-79) 29 varieties	....	....	....	....	46.00	11.75
2532	50¢ Switzerland	2.25	5.00	65.00(40)	7.50	1.75	.40

2533

2534

2535, 2536

2537

2538

2539

2533	29¢ Vermont Statehood	1.75	4.25	70.00(50)	7.50	1.50	.20
2534	29¢ Savings Bonds	1.75	4.25	45.00(50)	4.50	1.00	.20
2535	29¢ Love	1.75	4.25	38.00(50)	4.00	.80	.20
2536	29¢ Love, bklt single	1.75	....	....	....	.90	.20
2536a	same, bklt pane of 10	6.50	....	....	....	8.50	....
2536av	same, bklt pane, unfolded	....	....	....	....	9.50	....
2537	45¢ Love	2.25	5.00	65.00(50)	7.00	1.50	.35
2538	29¢ William Saroyan	1.75	4.25	37.00(50)	3.75	.80	.20
2539	$1 USPS/Olympic Rings	3.00	6.50	55.00(20)	12.75	2.75	.80

2540

2540	$2.90 Eagle and Olympic Rings	7.50	16.50	160.00(20)	40.00	9.00	3.50

2541

2542

2541	$9.95 Express Mail	27.00	50.00	500.00(20)	120.00	27.00	11.00
2542	$14.00 Express Mail	35.00	67.50	650.00(20)	140.00	35.00	22.00

2543

2544

2544A

2543	$2.90 Space Vechicle, priority mail	8.00	17.50	275.00(40)	32.50	7.50	2.75
2544	$3 Challenger Shuttle, priority mail (1995)	8.00	17.50	140.00(20)	32.50	7.50	3.00
2544A	$10.75 Endeavour Shuttle, express mail (1995)	27.50	57.50	450.00(20)	100.00	26.50	9.25

U.S. Postage #2545-2561

SCOTT NO.	DESCRIPTION	FIRST DAY COVERS SING	PL. BLK.	MINT SHEET	PLATE BLOCK	UNUSED F/NH	USED
2545	29¢ "Royal Wulff"	1.75	....	....	....	2.00	.20
2546	29¢ "Jock Scott"	1.75	....	....	....	2.00	.20
2547	29¢ "Apte Tarpon"	1.75	....	....	....	2.00	.20
2548	29¢ "Lefty's Deceiver"	1.75	....	....	....	2.00	.20
2549	29¢ "Muddler Minnow"	1.75	....	....	....	2.00	.20
2549a	Fishing Flies, bklt pane, 5 varieties, attached	4.50	....	....	....	9.50	4.50
2549av	same, bklt pane, unfolded	....	....	....	....	13.00	....

2550	29¢ Cole Porter	1.75	4.25	50.00(50)	4.50	1.10	.20
2551	29¢ Desert Storm	1.75	4.25	50.00(50)	4.50	1.10	.20
2552	29¢ Desert Storm, bklt single	1.75	....	....	....	1.10	.20
2552a	same, bklt pane of 5	4.75	....	....	....	5.50	....
2552av	same, bklt pane, unfolded	....	....	....	....	7.50	....

2553-57	Summer Olympics, 5 varieties, attached	4.50	....	35.00(40)	10.50(10)	5.00	4.00
2553	29¢ Pole Vault	1.75	....	....	....	1.10	.20
2554	29¢ Discus	1.75	....	....	....	1.10	.20
2555	29¢ Sprinters	1.75	....	....	....	1.10	.20
2556	29¢ Javelin	1.75	....	....	....	1.10	.20
2557	29¢ Hurdles	1.75	....	....	....	1.10	.20
2558	29¢ Numismatics	1.75	4.25	45.00(50)	4.50	1.00	.20

2559	$2.90 World War II, 1941, souvenir sheet of 10	7.50	....	22.00(20)	....	11.00	8.00
2559a	29¢ Burma Road	1.75	....	....	....	1.10	.50
2559b	29¢ Peacetime Draft	1.75	....	....	....	1.10	.50
2559c	29¢ Lend-Lease Act	1.75	....	....	....	1.10	.50
2559d	29¢ Atlantic Charter	1.75	....	....	....	1.10	.50
2559e	29¢ "Arsenal of Democracy"	1.75	....	....	....	1.10	.50
2559f	29¢ Destroyer "Reuben James"	1.75	....	....	....	1.10	.50
2559g	29¢ Civil Defense	1.75	....	....	....	1.10	.50
2559h	29¢ Liberty Ship	1.75	....	....	....	1.10	.50
2559i	29¢ Pearl Harbor	1.75	....	....	....	1.10	.50
2559j	29¢ Declaration of War on Japan	1.75	....	....	....	1.10	.50

2560	29¢ Basketball	2.00	4.50	48.00(50)	4.75	1.00	.25

2561	29¢ District of Columbia	1.75	4.25	36.00(50)	3.75	.75	.20

U.S. Postage #2562-2592

SCOTT NO.	DESCRIPTION	FIRST DAY COVERS SING	PL. BLK.	MINT SHEET	PLATE BLOCK	UNUSED F/NH	USED
2562	29¢ Laurel and Hardy	1.75	....	....	....	1.00	.20
2563	29¢ Bergen and McCarthy	1.75	....	....	....	1.00	.20
2564	29¢ Jack Benny	1.75	....	....	....	1.00	.20
2565	29¢ Fanny Brice	1.75	....	....	....	1.00	.20
2566	29¢ Abbott and Costello	1.75	....	....	....	1.00	.20
2566a	Comedians, bklt pane of 10	6.00	....	....	....	10.00	6.00
2566av	same, bklt pane, unfolded	....	....	....	....	12.50	....
2567	29¢ Jan Matzeliger	1.75	4.25	40.00(50)	4.75	.90	.20
2568	29¢ Mercury and Mariner 10	1.75	....	....	....	1.50	.30
2569	29¢ Venus and Mariner 2	1.75	....	....	....	1.50	.30
2570	29¢ Earth and Landsat	1.75	....	....	....	1.50	.30
2571	29¢ Moon and Lunar Orbiter	1.75	....	....	....	1.50	.30
2572	29¢ Mars and Viking Orbiter	1.75	....	....	....	1.50	.30
2573	29¢ Jupiter and Pioneer 11	1.75	....	....	....	1.50	.30
2574	29¢ Saturn and Voyager 2	1.75	....	....	....	1.50	.30
2575	29¢ Uranus and Voyager 2	1.75	....	....	....	1.50	.30
2576	29¢ Neptune and Voyager 2	1.75	....	....	....	1.50	.30
2577	29¢ Pluto, "Not Yet Explored"	1.75	....	....	....	1.50	.30
2577a	Space Explorations, bklt pane of 10	7.00	....	....	....	15.00	10.00
2577av	same, bklt pane, unfolded	....	....	....	....	19.00	....
2578	(29¢) Christmas—Traditional	1.75	4.25	35.00(50)	3.50	.80	.20
2578a	same, bklt pane of 10	7.00	....	....	....	8.00	....
2578av	same, bklt pane, unfolded	....	....	....	....	10.50	....
2579	(29¢) Christmas—Contemporary	1.75	4.25	35.00(50)	3.50	.80	.20
2580-85	(29¢) Santa & Chimney set of 6 singles	10.00	....	....	....	12.50	2.00
2581b-85a	same, bklt pane of 4	....	....	....	....	25.00	....
2581-85av	same, bklt pane of 4, unfolded	15.00	....	....	....	32.50	....

NOTE: The far left brick from the top row of the chimney is missing from Type II, No. 2581

1992-95 Regular Issues

SCOTT NO.	DESCRIPTION	FIRST DAY COVERS SING	PL. BLK.	MINT SHEET	PLATE BLOCK	UNUSED F/NH	USED
2587	32¢ James K. Polk (1995)	1.95	4.75	80.00(100)	4.50	1.00	.20
2590	$1 "Surrender at Saratoga" (1994)	3.00	6.50	50.00(20)	12.50	3.00	1.50
2592	$5 Washington & Jackson (1994)	14.50	28.50	240.00(20)	55.00	12.50	4.00

U.S. Postage #2593-2619

2593, 2594

SCOTT NO.	DESCRIPTION	FIRST DAY COVERS SING	FIRST DAY COVERS PL. BLK.	MINT SHEET	PLATE BLOCK	UNUSED F/NH	USED
2593	29¢ Pledge of Allegiance (black) bklt single	1.75	....	....	....	1.00	.15
2593a	same, bklt pane of 10	7.00	....	....	....	9.50	....
2593av	same, bklt pane, unfolded	....	....	....	....	10.50	....
2594	29¢ Pledge of Allegiance (red) bklt single (1993)	1.75	....	....	....	1.00	.15
2594a	same, bklt pane of 10	7.00	....	....	....	9.50	....
2594av	same, bklt pane, unfolded	....	....	....	....	10.50	....

2595-97 **2598** **2599**

1992-94 Self-Adhesive Stamps

SCOTT NO.	DESCRIPTION	FDC SING	FDC PL. BLK.	MINT SHEET	PLATE BLOCK	UNUSED F/NH	USED
2595	29¢ Eagle & Shield (brown) bklt single	1.75	....	....	....	1.00	.30
2595a	same, bklt pane of 17	7.00	....	....	....	16.50	....
2595v	same, coil	2.50	....	....	....	1.00	.30
2596	29¢ Eagle & Shield (green) bklt single	1.75	....	....	....	1.00	.30
2596a	same, bklt pane of 17	7.00	....	....	....	16.50	....
2596v	same, coil	2.50	....	....	....	1.00	.30
2597	29¢ Eagle & Shield (red) bklt single	1.75	....	....	....	1.00	.30
2597a	same, bklt pane of 17	7.00	....	....	....	16.50	....
2597v	same, coil	2.50	....	....	....	1.00	.30
2598	29¢ Eagle (1994)	1.75	....	....	....	1.00	.30
2598a	same, bklt pane of 18	13.50	....	....	....	16.50	....
2598v	29¢ Eagle, coil	2.50	....	....	5.00(3)	1.00	....
2599	29¢ Statue of Liberty (1994)	1.75	....	....	....	1.00	.30
2599a	same, bklt pane of 18	13.50	....	....	....	16.50	....
2599v	29¢ Statue of Liberty, coil	2.50	....	....	5.00(3)	1.00	....

2602 **2603, 2604** **2605**

2606-08 **2609**

1991-93 Regular Issue

SCOTT NO.	DESCRIPTION	FDC SING	PLATE# STRIP 3		PLATE# STRIP 3	UNUSED F/NH	USED
2602	(10¢) Eagle, Bulk-Rate coil	1.75	10.00	....	3.75	.30	.20
2603	(10¢) Eagle, Bulk-Rate coil (orange-yellow) (BEP)	1.75	10.00	....	4.25	.30	.20
2604	(10¢) Eagle, Bulk-Rate coil (Stamp Ventures) (gold) (1993)	1.75	10.00	....	3.00	.40	.20
2605	23¢ Flag, Presort First-Class	1.75	10.00	....	5.00	.70	.30
2606	23¢ USA, Presort First-Class (ABN) (1992)	1.75	10.00	....	5.75	.70	.30
2607	23¢ USA, Presort First-Class (BEP) (1992)	1.75	10.00	....	5.75	.75	.30
2608	23¢ USA, Presort First-Class (Stamp Ventures) (1993)	1.75	10.00	....	5.75	1.00	.30
2609	29¢ Flag over White House, coil (1992)	1.75	10.00	....	6.00	1.00	.30

NOTE: For plate number strips of 5, see page 139

2611 **2612** **2613** **2614** **2615**

1992 COMMEMORATIVES

SCOTT NO.	DESCRIPTION	FDC SING	FDC PL. BLK.	MINT SHEET	PLATE BLOCK	UNUSED F/NH	USED
2611/2720	(2611-23, 2630-41, 2697-2704, 2710-14, 2720) 48 varieties	....	....	....	....	42.50	10.00
2611-15	Winter Olympics, 5 varieties, attached	4.50	....	36.00(35)	10.50(10)	5.00	4.00
2611	29¢ Hockey	1.75	....	....	....	1.00	.20
2612	29¢ Figure Skating	1.75	....	....	....	1.00	.20
2613	29¢ Speed Skating	1.75	....	....	....	1.00	.20
2614	29¢ Skiing	1.75	....	....	....	1.00	.20
2615	29¢ Bobsledding	1.75	....	....	....	1.00	.20

2616 **2617**

SCOTT NO.	DESCRIPTION	FDC SING	FDC PL. BLK.	MINT SHEET	PLATE BLOCK	UNUSED F/NH	USED
2616	29¢ World Columbian Expo	1.75	4.25	37.50(50)	3.75	.85	.20
2617	29¢ W.E.B. Du Bois	1.75	4.25	42.50(50)	4.25	1.00	.20

2618 **2619**

SCOTT NO.	DESCRIPTION	FDC SING	FDC PL. BLK.	MINT SHEET	PLATE BLOCK	UNUSED F/NH	USED
2618	29¢ Love	1.75	4.25	37.50(50)	3.75	.85	.20
2619	29¢ Olympic Baseball	2.50	5.50	57.50(50)	5.50	1.25	.20

ORDER BY MAIL, PHONE (800) 546-2995 OR FAX (256) 246-1116

U.S. Postage #2620-2636

SCOTT NO.	DESCRIPTION	FIRST DAY COVERS SING	FIRST DAY COVERS PL. BLK.	MINT SHEET	PLATE BLOCK	UNUSED F/NH	USED
2620-23	First Voyage of Columbus	3.00	4.25	37.50(40)	5.25	4.25	3.00
2620	29¢ Seeking Isabella's Support	1.75	....	....	....	1.10	.20
2621	29¢ Crossing the Atlantic	1.75	....	....	....	1.10	.20
2622	29¢ Approaching Land	1.75	....	....	....	1.10	.20
2623	29¢ Coming Ashore	1.75	....	....	....	1.10	.20

2624

2625

2626

2627

2628

2629

| 2624-29 | 1¢-$5 Columbian Souvenir Sheets (6) | 55.00 | .... | .... | .... | 40.00 | 37.50 |
| 2624a-29a | same, set of 16 singles | 105.00 | .... | .... | .... | 39.50 | 35.00 |

2630

| 2630 | 29¢ NY Stock Exchange | 1.75 | 4.25 | 28.50(40) | 3.75 | .75 | .20 |

2631   2632   2633   2634

2631-34	Space, US/Russian Joint Issue	3.00	4.75	45.00(50)	5.50	5.00	3.50
2631	29¢ Cosmonaut & Space Shuttle	1.75	....	....	....	1.30	.20
2632	29¢ Astronaut & Mir Space Station	1.75	....	....	....	1.30	.20
2633	29¢ Apollo Lunar Module & Sputnik	1.75	....	....	....	1.30	.20
2634	29¢ Soyuz, Mercury & Gemini Space Craft	1.75	....	....	....	1.30	.20

2635   2636

| 2635 | 29¢ Alaska Highway | 1.75 | 4.75 | 37.50(50) | 3.75 | .85 | .20 |
| 2636 | 29¢ Kentucky Statehood | 1.75 | 4.75 | 37.50(50) | 3.75 | .85 | .20 |

2637

2638   2639

2640   2641

U.S. Postage #2637-2704

2642

2643

2644

2645

2646

Scott No.	Description	First Day Covers Sing	First Day Covers Pl. Blk.	Mint Sheet	Plate Block	Unused F/NH	Used
2637-41	Summer Olympics, 5 varieties, attached	4.50	....	32.50(35)	10.50(10)	5.00	2.75
2637	29¢ Soccer	1.75	....			1.10	.20
2638	29¢ Women's Gymnastics	1.75	....			1.10	.20
2639	29¢ Volleyball	1.75	....			1.10	.20
2640	29¢ Boxing	1.75	....			1.10	.20
2641	29¢ Swimming	1.75	....			1.10	.20
2642	29¢ Ruby-throated Hummingbird	1.75	....			1.10	.20
2643	29¢ Broad-billed Hummingbird	1.75	....			1.10	.20
2644	29¢ Costa's Hummingbird	1.75	....			1.10	.20
2645	29¢ Rufous Hummingbird	1.75	....			1.10	.20
2646	29¢ Calliope Hummingbird	1.75	....			1.10	.20
2646a	29¢ Hummingbirds, bklt pane, 5 vareities, attached	4.50	....			5.00	....
2646av	same, bklt pane, unfolded	....	....			6.00	....

2647

2648

2649

1992 WILDFLOWERS

2647	Indian Paintbrush	2664	Harlequin Lupine	2681	Turk's Cap Lily
2648	Fragrant Water Lily	2665	Twinflower	2682	Dutchman's Breeches
2649	Meadow Beauty	2666	Common Sunflower	2683	Trumpet Honeysuckle
2650	Jack-in-the-Pulpit	2667	Sego Lily	2684	Jacob's Ladder
2651	California Poppy	2668	Virginia Bluebells	2685	Plains Prickly Pear
2652	Large-Flowered Trillium	2669	Ohi'a Lehua	2686	Moss Campion
2653	Tickseed	2670	Rosebud Orchid	2687	Bearberry
2654	Shooting Star	2671	Showy Evening Primrose	2688	Mexican Hat
2655	Stream Violet	2672	Fringed Gentian	2689	Harebell
2656	Bluets	2673	Yellow Lady's Slipper	2690	Desert Five Spot
2657	Herb Robert	2674	Passionflower	2691	Smooth Solomon's Seal
2658	Marsh Marigold	2675	Bunchberry	2692	Red Maids
2659	Sweet White Violet	2676	Pasqueflower	2693	Yellow Skunk Cabbage
2660	Claret Cup Cactus	2677	Round-lobed Hepatica	2694	Rue Anemone
2661	White Mountain Avens	2678	Wild Columbine	2695	Standing Cypress
2662	Sessile Bellwort	2679	Fireweed	2696	Wild Flax
2663	Blue Flag	2680	Indian Pond Lily		

Scott No.	Description	First Day Covers Sing	First Day Covers Pl. Blk.	Mint Sheet	Plate Block	Unused F/NH	Used
2647-96	29¢ Wildflowers, 50 varieties, attached	70.00	....	50.00(50)	....	50.00	....
	set of singles	86.00	....	....	....	....	27.50
	singles of above, each	1.75	....	....	....	1.20	.75

Need Supplements?
See page 125 for a complete list of U.S.Liberty I Album Supplements. Update your album today!

2697

Scott No.	Description	First Day Covers Sing	First Day Covers Pl. Blk.	Mint Sheet	Plate Block	Unused F/NH	Used
2697	$2.90 World War II (1942) Souvenir Sheet of 10	7.50	....	22.00(20)	....	11.00	8.00
2697a	29¢ Tokyo Raid	1.75	....			1.10	.50
2967b	29¢ Commodity Rationing	1.75	....			1.10	.50
2967c	29¢ Battle of Coral Sea	1.75	....			1.10	.50
2967d	29¢ Fall of Corregidor	1.75	....			1.10	.50
2697e	29¢ Japan Invades Aleutians	1.75	....			1.10	.50
2697f	29¢ Allies Break Codes	1.75	....			1.10	.50
2697g	29¢ USS Yorktown Lost	1.75	....			1.10	.50
2697h	29¢ Women Join War Effort	1.75	....			1.10	.50
2697i	29¢ Marines on Guadalcanal	1.75	....			1.10	.50
2697j	29¢ Allies Land in North Africa	1.75	....			1.10	.50

2698

2699

| 2698 | 29¢ Dorothy Parker | 1.75 | 4.75 | 35.00(50) | 3.75 | .80 | .20 |
| 2699 | 29¢ Dr. T. von Karman | 1.75 | 4.75 | 35.00(50) | 3.75 | .80 | .20 |

2700 Azurite

2704

2701 Copper

2702 Variscite

2703 Wulfenite

Scott No.	Description	First Day Covers Sing	First Day Covers Pl. Blk.	Mint Sheet	Plate Block	Unused F/NH	Used
2700-03	Minerals, 4 varieties, attached	3.00	4.75	38.00(40)	4.75	4.25	3.00
2700	29¢ Azurite	1.75	....	....	....	1.10	.20
2701	29¢ Copper	1.75	....	....	....	1.10	.20
2702	29¢ Variscite	1.75	....	....	....	1.10	.20
2703	29¢ Wulfenite	1.75	....	....	....	1.10	.20
2704	29¢ Juan Rodriguez Cabrillo	1.75	4.75	36.00(50)	3.75	.75	.20

U.S. Postage #2705-2723a

2705 Giraffe

2706 Giant Panda

2707 Flamingo

2708 King Penguins

2709 White Bengal Tiger

SCOTT NO.	DESCRIPTION	FIRST DAY COVERS SING	FIRST DAY COVERS PL. BLK.	MINT SHEET	PLATE BLOCK	UNUSED F/NH	USED
2705	29¢ Giraffe	1.75	....	....	....	1.10	.20
2706	29¢ Giant Panda	1.75	....	....	....	1.10	.20
2707	29¢ Flamingo	1.75	....	....	....	1.10	.20
2708	29¢ King Penguins	1.75	....	....	....	1.10	.20
2709	29¢ White Bengal Tiger	1.75	....	....	....	1.10	.20
2709a	29¢ Wild Animals, bklt pane of 5	4.50	....	....	....	5.00	4.50
2709av	same, bklt pane, unfolded	....	....	....	....	6.75	....

2710

2710	29¢ Christmas–Traditional	1.75	4.75	36.00(50)	3.75	.75	.20
2710a	same, bklt pane of 10	7.00	....	....	....	7.75	....
2710av	same, bklt pane, unfolded	....	....	....	....	9.50	....

2711, 2715

2712, 2716, 2719

2713, 2717

2714, 2718

2711-14	Christmas Toys, 4 varieties, attached	3.00	4.75	45.00(50)	4.75	4.25	3.00
2711	29¢ Hobby Horse	1.75	....	....	....	1.10	.20
2712	29¢ Locomotive	1.75	....	....	....	1.10	.20
2713	29¢ Fire Engine	1.75	....	....	....	1.10	.20
2714	29¢ Steamboat	1.75	....	....	....	1.10	.20
2715	29¢ Hobby Horse (gravure) bklt single	1.75	....	....	....	1.50	.20
2716	29¢ Locomotive (gravure) bklt single	1.75	....	....	....	1.50	.20
2717	29¢ Fire Engine (gravure) bklt single	1.75	....	....	....	1.50	.20
2718	29¢ Steamboat (gravure) bklt single	1.75	....	....	....	1.50	.20
2718a	29¢ Christmas Toys (gravure) bklt pane of 4	3.00	....	....	....	6.50	3.25
2718av	same, bklt pane, unfolded	....	....	....	....	7.00	....
2719	29¢ Locomotive ATM, self-adhesive	1.75	....	....	....	1.20	.50
2719a	same, bklt pane of 18	13.50	....	....	....	21.00	....

2720

2720	29¢ Happy New Year	1.75	4.75	22.50(20)	5.50	1.20	.20

2721

2722

2723

1993 COMMEMORATIVES

2721/2806	(2721-30, 2746-59, 2765-66, 2771-74, 2779-89, 2791-94, 2804-06) 48 varieties	....	....	....	....	63.75	16.70
2721	29¢ Elvis Presley	2.00	5.00	35.00(40)	4.50	1.00	.20
2722	29¢ "Oklahoma!"	1.75	4.75	28.50(40)	3.75	.85	.20
2723	29¢ Hank Williams	1.75	4.75	28.50(40)	3.75	.85	.20
2723a	29¢ Hank Williams, perf. 11.2 x 11.4	....	....	950.00(40)	150.00	25.00	4.00

2724, 2731

2725, 2732

2726, 2733

2727, 2734

2728, 2735

2729, 2736

2730, 2737

U.S. Postage #2724-2759

SCOTT NO.	DESCRIPTION	FIRST DAY COVERS SING	FIRST DAY COVERS PL. BLK.	MINT SHEET	PLATE BLOCK	UNUSED F/NH	USED
2724-30	Rock & Roll/Rhythm & Blues, 7 varieties, attached	8.00	....	45.00(35)	12.00(8)	10.00	5.00
2724-30	same, Top Plate Block of 10	....	....	....	16.00(10)	....	....
2724	29¢ Elvis Presley	2.00	....	....	....	1.50	.30
2725	29¢ Bill Haley	2.00	....	....	....	1.50	.30
2726	29¢ Clyde McPhatter	2.00	....	....	....	1.50	.30
2727	29¢ Ritchie Valens	2.00	....	....	....	1.50	.30
2728	29¢ Otis Redding	2.00	....	....	....	1.50	.30
2729	29¢ Buddy Holly	2.00	....	....	....	1.50	.30
2730	29¢ Dinah Washington	2.00	....	....	....	1.50	.30
2731	29¢ Elvis Presley, bklt single	2.00	....	....	....	1.25	.30
2732	29¢ Bill Haley, bklt single	2.00	....	....	....	1.25	.30
2733	29¢ Clyde McPhatter, bklt single	2.00	....	....	....	1.25	.30
2734	29¢ Ritchie Valens, bklt single	2.00	....	....	....	1.25	.30
2735	29¢ Otis Redding, bklt single	2.00	....	....	....	1.25	.30
2736	29¢ Buddy Holly, bklt single	2.00	....	....	....	1.25	.30
2737	29¢ Dinah Washington, bklt single	2.00	....	....	....	1.25	.30
2737a	same, bklt pane of 8	8.00	....	....	....	7.00	....
2737av	same, bklt pane, unfolded	....	....	....	....	9.00	....
2737b	same, bklt pane of 4	5.00	....	....	....	4.00	....
2737bv	same, bklt pane, unfolded	....	....	....	....	5.50	....
2741	29¢ Saturn & 3 Rockets	1.75	....	....	....	1.00	.20
2742	29¢ 2 Flying Saucers	1.75	....	....	....	1.00	.20
2743	29¢ 3 Rocketeers	1.75	....	....	....	1.00	.20
2744	29¢ Winged Spaceship	1.75	....	....	....	1.00	.20
2745	29¢ 3 Space Ships	1.75	....	....	....	1.00	.20
2745a	29¢ Space Fantasy, bklt pane of 5	4.50	....	....	....	4.75	....
2745av	same, bklt pane, unfolded	....	....	....	....	6.00	....
2746	29¢ Percy Lavon Julian	1.75	4.75	42.50(50)	4.50	1.00	.20
2747	29¢ Oregon Trail	1.75	4.75	38.00(50)	3.75	.85	.20
2748	29¢ World University Games	1.75	4.75	38.00(50)	3.75	.85	.20
2749	29¢ Grace Kelly	1.75	4.75	38.00(50)	3.75	.85	.20
2750-53	Circus, 4 varieties, attached	3.00	4.75	42.50(40)	8.00(6)	5.00	4.00
2750	29¢ Clown	1.75	....	....	....	1.35	.25
2751	29¢ Ringmaster	1.75	....	....	....	1.35	.25
2752	29¢ Trapeze Artist	1.75	....	....	....	1.35	.25
2753	29¢ Elephant	1.75	....	....	....	1.35	.25
2754	29¢ Cherokee Strip	1.75	4.75	15.50(20)	3.75	.85	.20
2755	29¢ Dean Acheson	1.75	4.75	38.00(50)	3.75	.85	.20
2756-59	Sporting Horses, 4 varieties, attached	3.00	4.75	38.00(40)	5.00	4.50	3.50
2756	29¢ Steeplechase	1.75	....	....	....	1.25	.25
2757	29¢ Thoroughbred	1.75	....	....	....	1.25	.25
2758	29¢ Harness	1.75	....	....	....	1.25	.25
2759	29¢ Polo	1.75	....	....	....	1.25	.25

U.S. Postage #2760-2778av

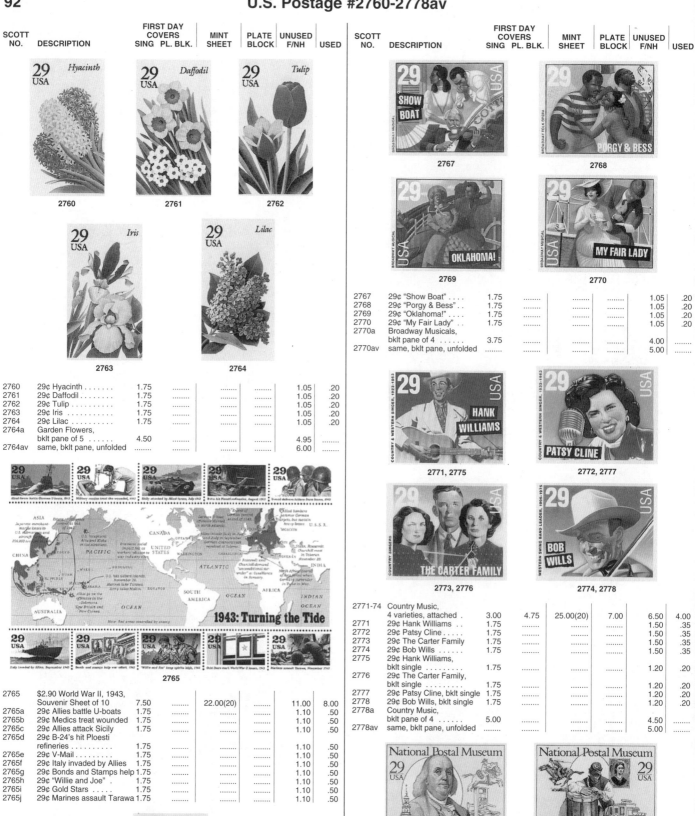

SCOTT NO.	DESCRIPTION	FIRST DAY COVERS SING	PL. BLK.	MINT SHEET	PLATE BLOCK	UNUSED F/NH	USED
2760	29¢ Hyacinth	1.75	....	....	....	1.05	.20
2761	29¢ Daffodil	1.75	....	....	....	1.05	.20
2762	29¢ Tulip	1.75	....	....	....	1.05	.20
2763	29¢ Iris	1.75	....	....	....	1.05	.20
2764	29¢ Lilac	1.75	....	....	....	1.05	.20
2764a	Garden Flowers, bklt pane of 5	4.50	....	....	....	4.95	....
2764av	same, bklt pane, unfolded	....	....	....	....	6.00	....
2765	$2.90 World War II, 1943, Souvenir Sheet of 10	7.50	....	22.00(20)	....	11.00	8.00
2765a	29¢ Allies battle U-boats	1.75	....	....	....	1.10	.50
2765b	29¢ Medics treat wounded	1.75	....	....	....	1.10	.50
2765c	29¢ Allies attack Sicily	1.75	....	....	....	1.10	.50
2765d	29¢ B-24's hit Ploesti refineries	1.75	....	....	....	1.10	.50
2765e	29¢ V-Mail	1.75	....	....	....	1.10	.50
2765f	29¢ Italy invaded by Allies	1.75	....	....	....	1.10	.50
2765g	29¢ Bonds and Stamps help	1.75	....	....	....	1.10	.50
2765h	29¢ "Willie and Joe"	1.75	....	....	....	1.10	.50
2765i	29¢ Gold Stars	1.75	....	....	....	1.10	.50
2765j	29¢ Marines assault Tarawa	1.75	....	....	....	1.10	.50

2766

SCOTT NO.	DESCRIPTION	FIRST DAY COVERS SING	PL. BLK.	MINT SHEET	PLATE BLOCK	UNUSED F/NH	USED
2766	29¢ Joe Louis	1.75	4.75	50.00(50)	5.50	1.10	.20
2767	29¢ "Show Boat"	1.75	....	....	....	1.05	.20
2768	29¢ "Porgy & Bess"	1.75	....	....	....	1.05	.20
2769	29¢ "Oklahoma!"	1.75	....	....	....	1.05	.20
2770	29¢ "My Fair Lady"	1.75	....	....	....	1.05	.20
2770a	Broadway Musicals, bklt pane of 4	3.75	....	....	....	4.00	....
2770av	same, bklt pane, unfolded	....	....	....	....	5.00	....
2771-74	Country Music, 4 varieties, attached	3.00	4.75	25.00(20)	7.00	6.50	4.00
2771	29¢ Hank Williams	1.75	....	....	....	1.50	.35
2772	29¢ Patsy Cline	1.75	....	....	....	1.50	.35
2773	29¢ The Carter Family	1.75	....	....	....	1.50	.35
2774	29¢ Bob Wills	1.75	....	....	....	1.50	.35
2775	29¢ Hank Williams, bklt single	1.75	....	....	....	1.20	.20
2776	29¢ The Carter Family, bklt single	1.75	....	....	....	1.20	.20
2777	29¢ Patsy Cline, bklt single	1.75	....	....	....	1.20	.20
2778	29¢ Bob Wills, bklt single	1.75	....	....	....	1.20	.20
2778a	Country Music, bklt pane of 4	5.00	....	....	....	4.50	....
2778av	same, bklt pane, unfolded	....	....	....	....	5.00	....

U.S. Postage #2779-2811

SCOTT NO.	DESCRIPTION	FIRST DAY COVERS SING	FIRST DAY COVERS PL. BLK.	MINT SHEET	PLATE BLOCK	UNUSED F/NH	USED
2779-82	National Postal Museum, 4 varieties, attached	3.00	4.75	25.00(20)	7.00	6.00	4.00
2779	29¢ Ben Franklin	1.75	....	....	....	1.50	.50
2780	29¢ Soldier & Drum	1.75	....	....	....	1.50	.50
2781	29¢ Lindbergh	1.75	....	....	....	1.50	.50
2782	29¢ Stamps & Bar Code	1.75	....	....	....	1.50	.50
2783-84	American Sign Language/Deaf Communication, 2 varieties, attached	2.50	4.75	17.00(20)	4.25	2.00	1.25
2783	29¢ Mother/Child	1.75	....	....	....	1.10	.20
2784	29¢ Hand Sign	1.75	....	....	....	1.10	.20
2785-88	Youth Classics, 4 varieties, attached	3.00	4.75	50.00(40)	7.00	6.00	4.50
2785	29¢ Rebecca of Sunnybrook Farm	1.75	....	....	....	1.60	.30
2786	29¢ Little House on the Prairie	1.75	....	....	....	1.60	.30
2787	29¢ Adventures of Huckleberry Finn	1.75	....	....	....	1.60	.30
2788	29¢ Little Women	1.75	....	....	....	1.60	.30
2789	29¢ Christmas–Traditional	1.75	4.75	36.00(50)	3.75	.80	.20
2790	29¢ Christmas–Traditional, bklt single	1.75	....	....	....	.85	.20
2790a	same, bklt pane of 4	3.00	....	....	....	3.50	....
2790av	same, bklt pane, unfolded	....	....	....	....	5.25	....
2791-94	Christmas–Contemporary, 4 varieties, attached	3.00	4.75	47.50(50)	5.00	4.25	3.00
2791	29¢ Jack-in-the-Box	1.75	....	....	....	1.10	.20
2792	29¢ Red-Nosed Reindeer	1.75	....	....	....	1.10	.20
2793	29¢ Snowman	1.75	....	....	....	1.10	.20
2794	29¢ Toy Soldier Blowing Horn	1.75	....	....	....	1.10	.20
2795	29¢ Toy Soldier Blowing Horn, bklt single	1.75	....	....	....	1.25	.20
2796	29¢ Snowman, bklt single	1.75	....	....	....	1.25	.20
2797	29¢ Red-Nosed Reindeer, bklt single	1.75	....	....	....	1.25	.20
2798	29¢ Jack-in-the-Box, bklt single	1.75	....	....	....	1.25	.20
2798a	same, bkle pane of 10	7.00	....	....	....	9.75	....
2798av	same, bklt pane, unfolded	....	....	....	....	12.00	....
2799-2802v	Christmas–Contemporary, coil	....	....	....	11.00(8)	5.50(4)	....
2799	29¢ Snowman, self-adhesive (3 buttons)	1.75	....	....	....	1.20	.50
2800	29¢ Toy Soldier Blowing Horn, self-adhesive	1.75	....	....	....	1.20	.50
2801	29¢ Jack-in-the-Box, self-adhesive	1.75	....	....	....	1.20	.50
2802	29¢ Red-Nosed Reindeer, self-adhesive	1.75	....	....	....	1.20	.50
2802a	same, bklt pane of 12	9.00	....	....	....	13.00	....
2803	29¢ Snowman, self-adhesive (2 buttons)	1.75	....	....	....	1.20	.50
2803a	same, bklt pane of 18	13.50	....	....	....	20.00	....
2804	29¢ Commonwealth of North Mariana Islands	1.75	4.75	16.00(20)	4.00	.85	.20
2805	29¢ Columbus Landing in Puerto Rico	1.75	4.75	37.50(50)	4.00	.80	.20
2806	29¢ AIDS Awareness	1.75	4.75	41.00(50)	4.50	.90	.20
2806a	29¢ AIDS Awareness, bklt single	1.75	....	....	....	.95	.20
2806b	same, bklt pane of 5	4.00	....	....	....	4.75	....
2806bv	same, bklt pane, unfolded	....	....	....	....	6.00	....

1994 COMMEMORATIVES

SCOTT NO.	DESCRIPTION	FDC SING	FDC PL. BLK.	MINT SHEET	PLATE BLOCK	UNUSED F/NH	USED
2807/76	(2807-12, 2814C-28, 2834-36, 2838-39, 2841a, 2848-68, 2871-72, 2876) 60 varieties	....	....	....	....	64.50	20.50
2807-11	Winter Olympics, 5 varieties, attached	3.75	....	18.00(20)	10.00(10)	4.75	3.50
2807	29¢ Alpine Skiing	1.75	....	....	....	1.00	.35
2808	29¢ Luge	1.75	....	....	....	1.00	.35
2809	29¢ Ice Dancing	1.75	....	....	....	1.00	.35
2810	29¢ Cross Country Skiing	1.75	....	....	....	1.00	.35
2811	29¢ Ice Hockey	1.75	....	....	....	1.00	.35

U.S. Postage #2812-2833av

2812

2813

2814

2815

1994 COMMEMORATIVES (continued)

SCOTT NO.	DESCRIPTION	FIRST DAY COVERS SING	FIRST DAY COVERS PL. BLK.	MINT SHEET	PLATE BLOCK	UNUSED F/NH	USED
2812	29¢ Edward R. Murrow	1.75	4.75	38.00(50)	3.75	.85	.20
2813	29¢ Love (sunrise), self-adhesive	1.75	....	....	....	1.10	.30
2813a	same, bklt pane of 18	13.50	....	....	....	17.50	....
2813v	29¢ Love (sunrise), self-adhesive coil	2.50	....	....	7.00(3)	1.10	....
2814	29¢ Love (dove), bklt single	1.75	....	....	....	1.10	.30
2814a	same, bklt pane of 10	7.00	....	....	....	10.00	....
2814av	same, bklt pane, unfolded	....	....	....	....	11.00	....
2814C	29¢ Love (dove)	1.75	4.75	45.00(50)	4.75	1.10	.20
2815	52¢ Love (dove)	2.00	4.50	70.00(50)	7.00(4)	1.50	.40
....	same, plate block of 10	....	....	....	16.00(10)	....	....

2816

2817

2818

2816	29¢ Allison Davis	1.75	4.75	16.50(20)	4.25	.90	.20
2817	29¢ Chinese New Year of the Dog	1.75	4.75	32.50(20)	7.50	1.75	.20
2818	29¢ Buffalo Soldiers	1.75	4.75	16.00(20)	4.25	.85	.20

2819

2820

2821

2822

2823

2824

2825

2826

2827

2828

2819	29¢ Rudolph Valentino	1.75	....	....	....	1.10	.35
2920	29¢ Clara Bow	1.75	....	....	....	1.10	.35
2821	29¢ Charlie Chaplin	1.75	....	....	....	1.10	.35
2822	29¢ Lon Chaney	1.75	....	....	....	1.10	.35
2823	29¢ John Gilbert	1.75	....	....	....	1.10	.35
2824	29¢ Zasu Pitts	1.75	....	....	....	1.10	.35
2825	29¢ Harold Lloyd	1.75	....	....	....	1.10	.35
2826	29¢ Keystone Cops	1.75	....	....	....	1.10	.35
2827	29¢ Theda Bara	1.75	....	....	....	1.10	.35
2828	29¢ Buster Keaton	1.75	....	....	....	1.10	.35
2819-28	Silent Screen Stars, 10 varieties, attached	7.00	....	37.50(40)	13.00(10)	11.00	....

2829

2830

2831

2832

2833

2829	29¢ Lily	1.75	....	....	....	1.00	.30
2830	29¢ Zinnia	1.75	....	....	....	1.00	.30
2831	29¢ Gladiola	1.75	....	....	....	1.00	.30
2832	29¢ Marigold	1.75	....	....	....	1.00	.30
2833	29¢ Rose	1.75	....	....	....	1.00	.30
2833a	Summer Garden Flowers, bklt pane of 5	4.50	....	....	....	4.50	3.50
2833av	same, bklt pane, unfolded	....	....	....	....	5.50	....

2834

2835

2836

U.S. Postage #2834-2848

SCOTT NO.	DESCRIPTION	FIRST DAY COVERS SING	FIRST DAY COVERS PL. BLK.	MINT SHEET	PLATE BLOCK	UNUSED F/NH	USED
2834	29¢ World Cup Soccer	1.75	4.75	20.00(20)	4.25	1.00	.20
2835	40¢ World Cup Soccer	1.75	4.75	25.00(20)	5.50	1.25	.30
2836	50¢ World Cup Soccer	1.75	5.50	34.50(20)	6.50	1.75	.40
2837	29¢-50¢ World Cup Soccer Souvenir Sheet	3.50	....	....	....	6.00	4.00
2838	$2.90 World War II, 1944, Souvenir Sheet of 10	7.50	....	22.00(20)	....	11.00	8.00
2838a	29¢ Allied forces retake New Guinea	1.75	....	....	....	1.10	.50
2838b	29¢ P-51s escort B-17s on bombing raids	1.75	....	....	....	1.10	.50
2838c	29¢ Allies in Normandy, D-Day, June 6	1.75	....	....	....	1.10	.50
2838d	29¢ Airborne units spearhead attacks	1.75	....	....	....	1.10	.50
2838e	29¢ Submarines shorten war in Pacific	1.75	....	....	....	1.10	.50
2838f	29¢ Allies free Rome, June 4; Paris, August 25	1.75	....	....	....	1.10	.50
2838g	29¢ U.S. troops clear Saipan bunkers	1.75	....	....	....	1.10	.50
2838h	29¢ Red Ball Express speeds vital supplies	1.75	....	....	....	1.10	.50
2838i	29¢ Battle for Leyte Gulf, October, 23-26	1.75	....	....	....	1.10	.50
2838j	29¢ Bastogne and Battle of the Bulge, December	1.75	....	....	....	1.10	.50
2839	29¢ Norman Rockwell	1.75	4.75	45.00(50)	4.50	1.00	.20
2840	50¢ "Four Freedoms" Souvenir Sheets	5.00	....	....	....	6.50	4.50
2841	29¢ Moon Landing 25th Anniversary, Sheet of 12	....	....	....	....	13.50	....
2841a	29¢ Moon Landing 25th Anniversary, single stamp	1.75	....	....	....	1.25	.30
2842	$9.95 Moon Landing Express Mail Stamp	20.00	50.00	500.00(20)	115.00	28.00	12.50
2843	29¢ Hudson's General	1.75	....	....	....	1.10	.30
2844	29¢ McQueen's Jupiter	1.75	....	....	....	1.10	.30
2845	29¢ Eddy's No. 242	1.75	....	....	....	1.10	.30
2846	29¢ Ely's No. 10	1.75	....	....	....	1.10	.30
2847	29¢ Buchanan's No. 999	1.75	....	....	....	1.10	.30
2847a	Locomotives, bklt pane of 5	4.50	....	....	....	5.50	3.50
2847av	same, bklt pane, unfolded	....	....	....	....	6.50	....
2848	29¢ George Meany	1.75	4.75	37.00(50)	3.75	.80	.20

U.S. Postage #2849-2868

2849

2850

2851   2852

2853

SCOTT NO.	DESCRIPTION	FIRST DAY COVERS SING	FIRST DAY COVERS PL. BLK.	MINT SHEET	PLATE BLOCK	UNUSED F/NH	USED
2849-53	Popular Singers, 5 varieties, attached	4.50	....	24.50(20)	9.50(6)	6.50	4.00
2849	29¢ Al Jolson	1.75	....	....	....	1.35	.50
2850	29¢ Bing Crosby	1.75	....	....	....	1.35	.50
2851	29¢ Ethel Waters	1.75	....	....	....	1.35	.50
2852	29¢ Nat "King" Cole	1.75	....	....	....	1.35	.50
2853	29¢ Ethel Merman	1.75	....	....	....	1.35	.50
....	same, Plate Block of 12	....	....	....	18.00(12)	....	....

2854

2855   2856

2857

2858   2859

SCOTT NO.	DESCRIPTION	FIRST DAY COVERS SING	FIRST DAY COVERS PL. BLK.	MINT SHEET	PLATE BLOCK	UNUSED F/NH	USED

2860

2861

2854-61	Blues & Jazz Singers, 8 varieties, attached	6.00	....	45.00(35)	14.50(10)	13.50	7.50
....	same, Horizontal Plate Block of 10 w/Top Label	....	....	....	15.50(10)	....	....
2854	29¢ Bessie Smith	1.75	....	....	....	1.75	.50
2855	29¢ Muddy Waters	1.75	....	....	....	1.75	.50
2856	29¢ Billie Holiday	1.75	....	....	....	1.75	.50
2857	29¢ Robert Johnson	1.75	....	....	....	1.75	.50
2858	29¢ Jimmy Rushing	1.75	....	....	....	1.75	.50
2859	29¢ "Ma" Rainey	1.75	....	....	....	1.75	.50
2860	29¢ Mildred Bailey	1.75	....	....	....	1.75	.50
2861	29¢ Howlin' Wolf	1.75	....	....	....	1.75	.50

2862

2862	29¢ James Thurber	1.75	4.75	38.00(50)	3.75	.85	.20

2863

2864

2865

2866

2863-66	Wonders of the Sea, 4 varieties, attached	3.00	4.75	27.50(24)	5.25	4.75	3.50
2863	29¢ Diver & Motorboat	1.75	....	....	....	1.20	.25
2864	29¢ Diver & Ship	1.75	....	....	....	1.20	.25
2865	29¢ Diver & Ship's Wheel	1.75	....	....	....	1.20	.25
2866	29¢ Diver & Coral	1.75	....	....	....	1.20	.25

2867

2868

2867-68	Cranes	2.50	4.75	19.50(20)	5.00	2.25	1.50
2867	29¢ Black-Necked Crane	1.75	....	....	....	1.15	.25
2868	29¢ Whooping Crane	1.75	....	....	....	1.15	.25

U.S. Postage #2869-2878

2869 — Legends of the West

2869a	Home on the Range	2869k	Nellie Cashman
2869b	Buffalo Bill Cody	2869l	Charles Goodnight
2869c	Jim Bridger	2869m	Geronimo
2869d	Annie Oakley	2869n	Kit Carson
2869e	Native American Culture	2869o	Wild Bill Hickok
2869f	Chief Joseph	2869p	Western Wildlife
2869g	Bill Pickett	2869q	Jim Beckwourth
2869h	Bat Masterson	2869r	Bill Tilghman
2869i	John Fremont	2869s	Sacagawea
2869j	Wyatt Earp	2869t	Overland Mail

2869g   2870g

Scott No.	Description	FDC Sing	FDC Pl.Blk	Mint Sheet	Plate Block	Unused F/NH	Used
2869	Legends of the West, 20 varieties, attached	....	....	20.00(20)	....	20.00	17.00
	set of singles	31.50	....	....	....	....	12.50
	singles of above, each	....	....	....	....	....	.85
2869v	same as above, uncut sheet of 120 (6 panes)	....	....	100.00(120)	....	100.00	....
	block of 40 with vertical or horizontal, gutter between (2 panes)	....	....	27.50(40)	....	27.50	....
	block of 24 with vertical gutter	....	....	20.75(24)	....	20.75	....
	block of 25 with horizontal gutter	....	....	21.50(25)	....	21.50	....
	cross gutter block of 20	....	....	....	....	31.00	....
	cross gutter block of 4	....	....	....	....	17.00	....
	vertical pair with horizontal gutter	....	....	....	....	2.75	....
	horizontal pair with vertical gutter	....	....	....	....	2.75	....
2870	Legends of the West, (Recalled), 20 varieties, attached	....	....	395.00(20)	....	395.00	....

2871

2872

2873

Greetings 2874

Scott No.	Description	FDC Sing	FDC Pl.Blk	Mint Sheet	Plate Block	Unused F/NH	Used
2871	29¢ Christmas–Traditional	1.75	4.75	37.00(50)	3.75	.80	.20
2871a	29¢ Christmas–Traditional bklt single	1.75	....	....	....	1.10	.20
2871b	same, bklt pane of 10	7.00	....	....	....	10.50	....
2871bv	same, bklt pane, unfolded	....	....	....	....	11.50	....
2872	29¢ Christmas Stocking	1.75	4.75	37.00(50)	3.75	.80	.20
2872v	29¢ Christmas Stocking, bklt single	1.75	....	....	....	.90	.20
2872a	same, bklt pane of 20	....	....	....	....	17.00	....
2872av	same, bklt pane, unfolded	....	....	....	....	20.00	....
2873	29¢ Santa Claus, self-adhesive	1.75	....	....	....	1.20	.20
2873a	same, bklt pane of 12	9.00	....	....	....	13.50	....
2874	29¢ Cardinal in Snow, self-adhesive	1.75	....	....	....	1.20	.30
2874a	same, bklt pane of 18	13.50	....	....	....	20.00	....

2875

Scott No.	Description	FDC Sing	FDC Pl.Blk	Mint Sheet	Plate Block	Unused F/NH	Used
2875	$2 B.E.P. Souvenir Sheet of 4 (Madison)	16.50	....	....	....	24.50	15.00
2875a	single from above ($2 Madison)	6.00	....	....	....	6.25	4.00

2876

Scott No.	Description	FDC Sing	FDC Pl.Blk	Mint Sheet	Plate Block	Unused F/NH	Used
2876	29¢ Year of the Boar	1.75	4.75	22.50(20)	5.75	1.25	.20

2877, 2878

Scott No.	Description	FDC Sing	FDC Pl.Blk	Mint Sheet	Plate Block	Unused F/NH	Used
2877	(3¢) "G" Make-up Rate (ABN, bright blue)	1.75	4.75	8.50(100)	.85	.20	.15
2878	(3¢) "G" Make-up Rate (SVS, dark blue)	1.75	4.75	8.50(100)	.85	.20	.15

H.E. Harris & Co. — Serving the Collector Since 1916

U.S. Postage #2879-2921b

2879, 2880 — Old Glory Postcard Rate
2881-85, 2889-92 — USA G For U.S. addresses only
2886, 2887 — USA G For U.S. addresses only
2888 — USA G First-Class Presort

SCOTT NO.	DESCRIPTION	FIRST DAY COVERS SING	PL. BLK.	MINT SHEET	PLATE BLOCK	UNUSED F/NH	USED
2879	(20¢) "G" Old Glory Postcard Rate (BEP, black "G")	1.75	4.75	65.00(100)	6.00	.75	.20
2880	(20¢) "G" Old Glory Postcard Rate (SVS, red "G")	1.75	4.75	65.00(100)	9.50	.75	.20
2881	(32¢) "G" Old Glory (BEP, black "G")	1.75	4.75	195.00(100)	80.00	1.75	.25
2882	(32¢) "G" Old Glory (SVS, red "G")	1.75	4.75	84.00(100)	5.25	1.00	.20
2883	(32¢) "G" Old Glory, bklt single (BEP, black "G")	1.75	....	....	....	1.10	.20
2883a	same, bklt pane of 10	7.25				11.00	....
2884	(32¢) "G" Old Glory, bklt single (ABN, blue "G")	1.75				1.25	.20
2884a	same, bklt pane of 10	7.25				12.50	....
2885	(32¢) "G" Old Glory, bklt single (KCS, red "G")	1.75				1.50	.20
2885a	same, bklt pane of 10	7.25				15.00	....
2886	(32¢) "G", self-adhesive	1.75				1.10	.30
2886a	same, bklt pane of 18	13.50				18.50	....
2887	(32¢) "G" Old Glory, self-adhesive (blue shading)	1.75				1.10	.40
2887a	same, bklt pane of 18	13.50				18.50	....

SCOTT NO.	DESCRIPTION	FIRST DAY COVERS SING	PL. BLK. PLATE# STRIP 3	MINT SHEET	PLATE BLOCK PLATE# STRIP 3	UNUSED F/NH	USED
2888	(25¢) Old Glory First-Class Presort, coil	1.75	10.00	....	6.25	1.10	.35
2889	(32¢) "G" Old Glory, coil (BEP, black "G")	1.75	10.00		12.50	2.00	.35
2890	(32¢) "G" Old Glory, coil (ABN, blue "G")	1.75	10.00		6.25	1.10	.20
2891	(32¢) "G" Old Glory, coil (SVS, red "G")	1.75	10.00		20.00	2.00	.40
2892	(32¢) "G" Old Glory, coil (SVS, red "G") rouletted	1.75	10.00		7.00	1.10	.20

2893 — Old Glory USA G Nonprofit Presort
2897, 2913-16, 2920, 2921
2902, 2902B
2903, 2904, 2904A, 2904B
2905, 2906 — BULK RATE
2907 — USA Bulk Rate
2908-10 — First-Class Card
2911, 2912, 2912A, 2912B — Presorted First-Class

1995-97 Regular Issues

SCOTT NO.	DESCRIPTION	FIRST DAY COVERS SING	PL. BLK.	MINT SHEET	PLATE BLOCK	UNUSED F/NH	USED
2893	(5¢) "G" Old Glory, Nonprofit, coil	1.95	10.00	....	2.50	.40	.30
2897	32¢ Flag over Porch	1.95	4.75	80.00(100)	4.75	1.00	.20

1995-97 Regular Issue Coils

SCOTT NO.	DESCRIPTION	FIRST DAY COVERS SING	PL. BLK. PLATE# STRIP 3	MINT SHEET	PLATE BLOCK PLATE# STRIP 3	UNUSED F/NH	USED
2902	(5¢) Butte, Nonprofit, coil	1.95	10.00	....	2.00	.30	.20
2902B	(5¢) Butte, self-adhesive coil	1.95	....		2.75	.30	.20
2903	(5¢) Mountain, (BEP, violet 1996)	1.95	10.00		2.00	.30	.20
2904	(5¢) Mountain (SVS, blue 1996)	1.95	10.00		2.00	.30	.20
2904A	(5¢) Mountain, self-adhesive coil	1.95	....		2.75	.30	.20
2904B	(5¢) Mountain, self-adhesive coil (1997)	1.95	....		2.75	.30	.20
2905	(10¢) Automobile, Bulk Rate, coil	1.95	10.00		2.75	.30	.35
2906	(10¢) Automobile, self-adhesive coil	1.95	....		2.75	.30	.20
2907	(10¢) Eagle, bulk-rate, coil (1996)	1.95	....		3.25	.30	.35
2908	(15¢) Auto Tail Fin, Presorted First-Class Card, coil (BEP)	1.95	10.00	....	3.50	.50	.25
2909	(15¢) Auto Tail Fin, Presorted First-Class Card, coil (SVS)	1.95	10.00		3.50	.50	.25
2910	(15¢) Auto Tail Fin, self-adhesive coil	1.95	....		3.75	.55	.30
2911	(25¢) Juke Box, Presorted First-Class, coil (BEP)	1.95	10.00		5.75	.80	.40
2912	(25¢) Juke Box, Presorted First-Class, coil (SVS)	1.95	10.00		5.75	.80	.40
2912A	(25¢) Juke Box, self-adhesive coil	1.95	....		5.75	.80	.30
2912B	(25¢) Juke Box, self-adhesive coil (1997)	1.95	....		5.75	.80	.30
2913	32¢ Flag over Porch, coil (BEP, red date)	1.95	10.00		6.00	1.00	.25
2914	32¢ Flag over Porch, coil (SVS, blue date)	1.95	10.00		6.00	1.00	.25
2915	32¢ Flag over Porch, self-adhesive coil (Die Cut 8.7)	1.95			14.00	1.20	.30
2915A	32¢ Flag over Porch, self-adhesive coil (1996, Die Cut 9.8)	1.95			8.00	1.20	.30
2915B	32¢ Flag over Porch, self-adhesive coil (1996, Die Cut 11.5)	1.95			14.00	1.20	.25
2915C	32¢ Flag over Porch, self-adhesive coil (1996, Die Cut 10.9)	1.95			25.00	2.50	1.00
2915D	32¢ Flag over Porch, self adhesive coil (1997)	1.95			13.00	1.40	.50

Note: For plate number strips of 5, see page 139

2919

1995-97 Booklet Panes

SCOTT NO.	DESCRIPTION	FIRST DAY COVERS SING	PL. BLK.	MINT SHEET	PLATE BLOCK	UNUSED F/NH	USED
2916	32¢ Flag over Porch, bklt single	1.95	....	....	....	1.10	.20
2916a	same, bklt pane of 10	7.25				10.75	....
2916av	same, bklt pane, unfolded	....				1.00	....
2919	32¢ Flag over Field self-adhesive	1.95				1.10	.30
2919a	same, bklt pane of 18	13.50				17.00	....
2920	32¢ Flag over Porch, self-adhesive (large "1995")	1.95				1.10	.30
2920a	same, bklt pane of 20	14.50				21.00	....
2920b	32¢ Flag over Porch, self-adhesive (small "1995")	1.95				7.50	.80
2920c	same, bklt pane of 20	14.50				145.00	....
2920D	32¢ Flag over Porch ("1996" date) self-adhesive	1.95				1.10	.35
2920e	same, Bklt pane of 10	6.95				10.75	....
2921	32¢ Flag over Porch, self-adhesive (Red 1996, Die Cut 9.8)	1.95				1.10	.30
2921a	same, bklt pane of 10	7.00				10.75	....
2921av	same, bklt pane, unfolded	....				11.50	....
2921b	32¢ Flag over Porch, (Red 1997)	1.95				1.10	.30
2921c	same, bklt pane of 10	6.95				10.75	....
2921d	same, bklt pane of 5	5.50				5.50	....

2933 — Milton S. Hershey, Philanthropist
2934 — Cal Farley, Humanitarian
2935 — Henry R. Luce, Editor

2936 — Lila and DeWitt Wallace, Philanthropists
2938 — Ruth Benedict, Anthropologist
2940 — Alice Hamilton, MD, Social Reformer

U.S. Postage #2933-2968

2941

2942

2943

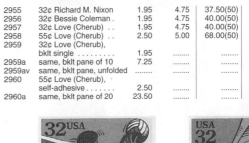
2957, 2959   2958   2960

1995-99 GREAT AMERICANS

SCOTT NO.	DESCRIPTION	FIRST DAY COVERS SING	FIRST DAY COVERS PL. BLK.	MINT SHEET	PLATE BLOCK	UNUSED F/NH	USED
2933	32¢ Milton S. Hershey	1.95	4.75	80.00(100)	4.75	.85	.25
2934	32¢ Carl Farley (1996)	1.95	4.75	80.00(100)	4.75	.85	.25
2935	32¢ Henry R. Luce (1998)	1.95	4.75	16.00(20)	4.75	.85	.25
2936	32¢ Lila & DeWitt Wallace (1998)	1.95	4.75	16.00(20)	4.75	.85	.25
2938	46¢ Ruth Benedict	2.25	5.00	110.00(100)	6.50	1.25	.25
2940	55¢ Alice Hamilton	2.25	5.00	120.00(100)	7.00	1.35	.35
2941	55¢ Justin Morrill (1999)	2.50	5.00	25.00(20)	7.00	1.35	.35
2942	77¢ Mary Breckenridge (1998)	2.95	5.50	35.00(20)	8.50	1.85	.50
2943	78¢ Alice Paul	2.95	5.50	185.00(100)	8.50	2.00	.50

SCOTT NO.	DESCRIPTION	FIRST DAY COVERS SING	FIRST DAY COVERS PL. BLK.	MINT SHEET	PLATE BLOCK	UNUSED F/NH	USED
2955	32¢ Richard M. Nixon	1.95	4.75	37.50(50)	3.95	.90	.20
2956	32¢ Bessie Coleman	1.95	4.75	40.00(50)	3.95	.90	.20
2957	32¢ Love (Cherub)	1.95	4.75	40.00(50)	3.95	.90	.20
2958	55¢ Love (Cherub)	2.50	5.00	68.00(50)	6.75	1.40	.50
2959	32¢ Love (Cherub), bklt single	1.95	....	....	....	1.00	.20
2959a	same, bklt pane of 10	7.25	....	....	....	9.75	....
2959av	same, bklt pane, unfolded	....	....	....	....	10.50	....
2960	55¢ Love (Cherub), self-adhesive	2.50	....	....	....	1.50	.60
2960a	same, bklt pane of 20	23.50	....	....	....	28.50	....

2948

2949

2950

1995 COMMEMORATIVES

2948/3023	(2948, 2950-58, 2961-68, 2974, 2976-92, 2998-99, 3001-07, 3019-23) 50 varieties	....	....	....	....	62.00	22.00
2948	(32¢) Love (Cherub)	1.95	4.75	38.00(50)	3.75	.85	.20
2949	(32¢) Love (Cherub), self-adhesive	1.95	....	....	....	1.10	.25
2949a	same, bklt pane of 20	14.50	....	....	....	20.00	....
2950	32¢ Florida Statehood	1.95	4.75	20.00(20)	5.50	1.10	.20

2961

2962

2963

2964

2965

2951

2952

2953

2954

2961-65	Recreational Sports, 5 varieties, attached	5.50	....	21.00(20)	12.00(10)	5.50	3.00
2961	32¢ Volleyball	1.95	....	....	....	1.20	.35
2962	32¢ Softball	1.95	....	....	....	1.20	.35
2963	32¢ Bowling	1.95	....	....	....	1.20	.35
2964	32¢ Tennis	1.95	....	....	....	1.20	.35
2965	32¢ Golf	1.95	....	....	....	1.20	.35

2951-54	Kids Care About Environment, 4 varieties, attached	4.00	4.75	16.50(16)	5.00	4.50	3.50
2951	32¢ Earth in a Bathtub	1.95	....	....	....	1.20	.35
2952	32¢ Solar Energy	1.95	....	....	....	1.20	.35
2953	32¢ Tree Planting	1.95	....	....	....	1.20	.35
2954	32¢ Beach Clean-Up	1.95	....	....	....	1.20	.35

2966

2967

2968

2966	32¢ POW & MIA	1.95	4.75	16.00(20)	3.95	.90	.20
2967	32¢ Marilyn Monroe	1.95	4.75	26.50(20)	6.50	1.35	.20
2967v	same as above, uncut sheet of 120 (6 panes)	....	....	180.00(120)	....	....	....
....	block of 8 with vertical gutter	....	....	....	....	50.00	....
....	cross gutter block of 8	....	....	....	....	65.00	....
....	vertical pair with horizontal gutter	....	....	....	....	5.50	....
....	horizontal pair with vertical gutter	....	....	....	....	9.50	....
2968	32¢ Texas Statehood	1.95	4.75	20.00(20)	5.50	1.10	.20

2955

2956

U.S. Postage #2969-2981j

SCOTT NO.	DESCRIPTION	FIRST DAY COVERS SING	FIRST DAY COVERS PL. BLK.	MINT SHEET	PLATE BLOCK	UNUSED F/NH	USED
	2969 32¢ Split Rock Lighthouse						
	2970 32¢ St. Joseph Lighthouse						
	2971 32¢ Spectacle Reef Lighthouse						
	2972 32¢ Marblehead Lighthouse						
	2973 32¢ Thirty Mile Point Lighthouse						
	2974 32¢ United Nations						
2969	32¢ Split Rock Lighthouse	1.95	....	....	....	1.10	.25
2970	32¢ St. Joseph Lighthouse	1.95	....	....	....	1.10	.25
2971	32¢ Spectacle Reef Lighthouse	1.95	....	....	....	1.10	.25
2972	32¢ Marblehead Lighthouse	1.95	....	....	....	1.10	.25
2973	32¢ Thirty Mile Point Lighthouse	1.95	....	....	....	1.10	.25
2973a	Great Lakes Lighthouses, bklt pane of 5	5.50	....	....	....	5.25	4.00
2973av	same, bklt pane, unfolded	....	....	....	....	6.00	....
2974	32¢ United Nations	1.75	4.75	16.00(20)	3.95	.90	.20

CIVIL WAR (2975)

2975a	Monitor-Virginia		2975k	Harriet Tubman
2975b	Robert E. Lee		2975l	Stand Watie
2975c	Clara Barton		2975m	Joseph E. Johnston
2975d	Ulysses S. Grant		2975n	Winfield Hancock
2975e	Shiloh		2975o	Mary Chestnut
2975f	Jefferson Davis		2975p	Chancellorsville
2975g	David Farragut		2975q	William T. Sherman
2975h	Frederick Douglass		2975r	Phoebe Pember
2975i	Raphael Semmes		2975s	"Stonewall" Jackson
2975j	Abraham Lincoln		2975t	Gettysburg

SCOTT NO.	DESCRIPTION	FIRST DAY COVERS SING	FIRST DAY COVERS PL. BLK.	MINT SHEET	PLATE BLOCK	UNUSED F/NH	USED
2975	32¢ Civil War, 20 varieties, attached	....	....	28.50(20)	....	28.50	20.00
	set of singles	35.00	....	....	....	15.00	....
	singles of above, each	....	....	....	....	....	1.00
2975v	32¢ Civil War, uncut sheet of 120 (6 panes)	....	....	150.00(120)	....	150.00	....
	cross gutter block of 20	....	....	....	....	40.00	....
	cross gutter block of 4	....	....	....	....	20.00	....
	vertical pair with horizontal gutter	....	....	....	....	4.50	....
	horizontal pair with vertical gutter	....	....	....	....	4.50	....
2976-79	Carousel Horses, 4 varieties, attached	4.00	4.75	21.50(20)	5.25	4.75	2.75
2976	32¢ Palamino	1.95	....	....	....	1.20	.25
2977	32¢ Pinto Pony	1.95	....	....	....	1.20	.25
2978	32¢ Armored Jumper	1.95	....	....	....	1.20	.25
2979	32¢ Brown Jumper	1.95	....	....	....	1.20	.25
2980	32¢ Women's Suffrage	1.95	4.75	30.00(40)	3.95	.85	.20
2981	$3.20 World War II (1945) Souvenir Sheet of 10	8.25	....	25.00(20)	....	12.50	8.50
2981a	32¢ Marines raise flag on Iwo Jima	1.95	....	....	....	1.25	.50
2981b	32¢ Fierce fighting frees Manila	1.95	....	....	....	1.25	.50
2981c	32¢ Okinawa, the last big battle	1.95	....	....	....	1.25	.50
2981d	32¢ U.S. & Soviets link up at Elbe River	1.95	....	....	....	1.25	.50
2981e	32¢ Allies liberate Holocaust survivors	1.95	....	....	....	1.25	.50
2981f	32¢ Germany surrenders at Reims	1.95	....	....	....	1.25	.50
2981g	32¢ By 1945, World War II has uprooted millions	1.95	....	....	....	1.25	.50
2981h	32¢ Truman announces Japan's surrender	1.95	....	....	....	1.25	.50
2981i	32¢ News of victory hits home	1.95	....	....	....	1.25	.50
2981j	32¢ Hometowns honor their returning veterans	1.95	....	....	....	1.25	.50

U.S. Postage #2982-3000

SCOTT NO.	DESCRIPTION	FIRST DAY COVERS SING	FIRST DAY COVERS PL. BLK.	MINT SHEET	PLATE BLOCK	UNUSED F/NH	USED
2982	32¢ Louis Armstrong	1.95	4.75	21.50(20)	5.25	1.25	.20

2983-92	Jazz Musicians	8.25	....	28.00(20)	15.50(10)	14.50	9.00
2983	32¢ Coleman Hawkins	1.95	....	....	....	1.50	.75
2984	32¢ Louis Armstrong	1.95	....	....	....	1.50	.75
2985	32¢ James P. Johnson	1.95	....	....	....	1.50	.75
2986	32¢ "Jelly Roll" Morton	1.95	....	....	....	1.50	.75
2987	32¢ Charlie Parker	1.95	....	....	....	1.50	.75
2988	32¢ Eubie Blake	1.95	....	....	....	1.50	.75
2989	32¢ Charles Mingus	1.95	....	....	....	1.50	.75
2990	32¢ Thelonius Monk	1.95	....	....	....	1.50	.75
2991	32¢ John Coltrane	1.95	....	....	....	1.50	.75
2992	32¢ Erroll Garner	1.95	....	....	....	1.50	.75

ORDER BY MAIL, PHONE (800) 546-2995 OR FAX (256) 246-1116

2993

2994

2995

2996

2997

2998

2999

2993	32¢ Aster	1.95	....	....	....	1.10	.20
2994	32¢ Chrysanthemum	1.95	....	....	....	1.10	.20
2995	32¢ Dahlia	1.95	....	....	....	1.10	.20
2996	32¢ Hydrangea	1.95	....	....	....	1.10	.20
2997	32¢ Rudbeckia	1.95	....	....	....	1.10	.20
2997a	Fall Garden Flowers, bklt pane of 5	5.50	....	....	....	5.25	3.50
2997av	same, bklt pane, unfolded	....	....	....	....	6.00	
2998	60¢ Eddie Rickenbacker	2.25	5.00	80.00(50)	7.00	1.85	.40
2998a	same, large date (1999)	2.25	5.00	70.00(50)	7.25	1.50	.40
2999	32¢ Republic of Palau	1.95	4.75	38.00(50)	3.75	.85	.20

3000
COMIC STRIPS

3000a	The Yellow Kid	3000k	Popeye
3000b	Katzenjammer Kids	3000l	Blondie
3000c	Little Nemo	3000m	Dick Tracy
3000d	Bringing Up Father	3000n	Alley Oop
3000e	Krazy Kat	3000o	Nancy
3000f	Rube Goldberg	3000p	Flash Gordon
3000g	Toonerville Folks	3000q	Li'l Abner
3000h	Gasoline Alley	3000r	Terry and the Pirates
3000i	Barney Google	3000s	Prince Valiant
3000j	Little Orphan Annie	3000t	Brenda Starr

3000	32¢ Comic Strips, 20 varieties, attached	....	....	21.00(20)	....	21.00	15.00
....	set of singles	35.00	....	....	....	....	12.50
....	single of above, each	....	....	....	....	....	.75

U.S. Postage #3000v-3023

COMIC STRIPS (continued)

SCOTT NO.	DESCRIPTION	FIRST DAY COVERS SING	PL. BLK.	MINT SHEET	PLATE BLOCK	UNUSED F/NH	USED
3000v	32¢ Comic Strips, uncut sheet of 120 (6 panes)	....	....	120.00(120)	....	120.00	....
....	cross gutter block of 20	....	....	....	....	40.00	....
....	cross gutter block of 4	....	....	....	....	18.50	....
....	vertical pair with horizontal gutter..........	....	....	....	....	4.50	....
....	horizontal pair with vertical gutter..........	....	....	....	....	4.50	....
3001	32¢ Naval Academy .	1.95	4.75	15.50(20)	3.75	.80	.20
3002	32¢ Tennessee Williams	1.95	4.75	21.00(20)	5.00	1.10	.20
3003	32¢ Madonna & Child	1.95	4.75	38.00(50)	3.75	.80	.20
3003a	32¢ Madonna & Child, bklt single........	1.95	....	....	....	1.10	.20
3003b	same, bklt pane of 10	7.25	....	....	....	10.50	....
3003bv	same, bklt pane, unfolded	....	....	....	....	11.50	....
3004-07	Santa & Children with Toys, 4 varieties, attached .	4.00	4.75	40.00(50)	4.25	3.75	2.75
3004	32¢ Santa at Chimney	1.95	....	....	....	1.10	.25
....	same, bklt single	1.95	....	....	....	1.10	.25
3005	32¢ Girl holding Jumping Jack.............	1.95	....	....	....	1.10	.25
....	same, bklt single	1.95	....	....	....	1.10	.25
3006	32¢ Boy holding Toy Horse	1.95	....	....	....	1.10	.25
....	same, bklt single	1.95	....	....	....	1.10	.25
3007	32¢ Santa working on Sled	1.95	....	....	....	1.10	.25
....	same, bklt single	1.95	....	....	....	1.10	.25
3007b	32¢ Santa & Children with Toys, bklt pane of 10 (3 each of 3004-05)..	7.25	....	....	....	11.50	....
....	same, bklt pane unfolded	....	....	....	....	12.50	....
3007c	32¢ Santa & Children with Toys, bklt pane of 10 (3 each of 3006-07)..	7.25	....	....	....	11.50	....
....	same, bklt pane unfolded	....	....	....	....	12.50	....
3008	32¢ Santa working on Sled, self-adhesive.......	1.95	....	....	....	1.25	.40
3009	32¢ Girl holding Jumping Jack, self-adhesive ..	1.95	....	....	....	1.25	.40
3010	32¢ Santa at Chimney, self-adhesive.......	1.95	....	....	....	1.25	.40
3011	32¢ Boy holding Toy Horse, self-adhesive.......	1.95	....	....	....	1.25	.40
3011a	32¢ Santa & Children with Toys, self-adhesive, pane of 20	14.50	....	....	....	22.50	....
3012	32¢ Midnight Angel, self-adhesive.......	1.95	....	....	....	1.25	.45
3012a	same, bklt pane of 20	14.50	....	....	....	22.50	....
3013	32¢ Children Sledding, self-adhesive.......	1.95	....	....	....	1.25	.30
3013a	same, bklt pane of 18	13.00	....	....	....	20.00	....
3014-17	Santa & Children with Toys, self-adhesive, coil strip of 4	....	....	....	....	5.50	....
3014	32¢ Santa working on Sled, self-adhesive coil	1.95	....	....	....	1.40	.45
3015	32¢ Girl holding Jumping Jack, self-adhesive coil	1.95	....	....	....	1.40	.45
3016	32¢ Santa at Chimney, self-adhesive coil ...	1.95	....	....	....	1.40	.45
3017	32¢ Boy holding Toy Horse, self-adhesive coil ...	1.95	....	....	....	1.40	.45
3018	32¢ Midnight Angel, self-adhesive coil ...	1.95	....	....	....	1.40	.45
3019-23	Antique Automobiles, 5 varieties, attached .	5.50	....	25.00(25)	12.00(10)	5.50	3.50
3019	32¢ 1893 Duryea ...	1.95	....	....	....	1.20	.40
3020	32¢ 1894 Haynes ...	1.95	....	....	....	1.20	.40
3021	32¢ 1898 Columbia .	1.95	....	....	....	1.20	.40
3022	32¢ 1899 Winton	1.95	....	....	....	1.20	.40
3023	32¢ 1901 White	1.95	....	....	....	1.20	.40

3001

3002

3003

3004, 3010, 3016

3005, 3009, 3015

3006, 3011, 3017

3007, 3008, 3014

3012, 3018

3013

3019 / 3020

3021 / 3022

3023

3024

3025 / 3026 / 3027

U.S. Postage #3024-3067

1996 COMMEMORATIVES

SCOTT NO.	DESCRIPTION	FIRST DAY COVERS SING	PL. BLK.	MINT SHEET	PLATE BLOCK	UNUSED F/NH	USED
3024/3118	(3024, 3030, 3058-67, 3069-70, 3072-88, 3090-3104, 3106-11, 3118) 53 varieties	....	....	....	....	56.00	13.80
3024	32¢ Utah Statehood	1.95	4.75	38.00(50)	4.00	.80	.20
3025	32¢ Crocus	1.95	....	....	....	1.20	.20
3026	32¢ Winter Aconite	1.95	....	....	....	1.20	.20
3027	32¢ Pansy	1.95	....	....	....	1.20	.20
3028	32¢ Snowdrop	1.95	....	....	....	1.20	.20
3029	32¢ Anemone	1.95	....	....	....	1.20	.20
3029a	Winter Garden Flowers, bklt pane of 5	5.50	....	....	....	5.50	3.00
3029av	same, bklt pane, unfolded	....	....	....	....	6.50	....
3030	32¢ Love (Cherub), self-adhesive	1.95	....	....	....	1.10	.20
3030a	same, bklt pane of 20	14.50	....	....	....	20.00	....
3030b	same, bklt pane of 15	11.50	....	....	....	15.00	....
3031	1¢ Kestrel, self-adhesive	1.95	....	5.00(50)	.75	.20	.20
3031A	1¢ Kestrel, self-adhesive (2000)	1.95	....	5.00(50)	.75	.20	.20
3032	2¢ Red-headed Woodpecker	1.95	4.75	8.00(100)	.75	.20	.20
3033	3¢ Eastern Bluebird (redesign 3¢)	1.95	4.75	9.50(100)	.75	.20	.20
3036	$1 Red Fox, self-adhesive	3.50	7.50	43.00(20)	10.00	2.25	.65
3036a	$1 Red Fox, 11.75 X 11(2002)	....	....	43.00(20)	10.00	2.25	.65
3044	1¢ Kestrel, coil	1.95	10.00	....	1.00	.20	.20
3044a	1¢ Kestrel, large date, coil(1999)	1.95	10.00	....	1.75	.20	.20
3045	2¢ Red-headed Woodpecker, coil	1.95	....	....	1.00	.20	.20
3048	20¢ Blue Jay, self-adhesive	1.95	....	....	....	.75	.20
3048a	same, bklt pane of 10	5.50	....	....	....	7.25	....
3049	32¢ Yellow Rose, self-adhesive	1.95	....	....	....	1.10	.20
3049a	same, bklt pane of 20	14.50	....	....	....	19.50	....
3050	20¢ Ring-necked Pheasant, self-adhesive	1.95	....	....	....	.70	.20
3050a	same, bklt pane of 10	5.50	....	....	....	6.75	....
3050b	20¢ Pheasant, die cut 11	1.95	....	....	....	.70	.20
3050c	same, bklt pane of 10	5.50	....	....	....	6.75	....
3051	20¢ Ring-necked Pheasant, die cut 10 1/2 x 11, self-adhesive	1.95	....	....	....	1.00	.20
3051a	same, sideways, die cut 10 1/2	1.95	....	....	....	4.50	.35
3051b	same, bklt pane of 5, (4 #3051, 1 #3051a)	3.50	....	....	....	8.50	....
3052	33¢ Coral Pink Rose, self-adhesive	1.95	....	....	....	1.35	.20
3052a	same, bklt pane of 4	3.00	....	....	....	5.25	....
3052b	same, bklt pane of 5	3.75	....	....	....	6.50	....
3052c	same, bklt pane of 6	4.50	....	....	....	7.50	....
3052d	same, bklt pane of 20	14.50	....	....	....	22.50	....
3052E	33¢ Coral Pink Rose, die-cut 10.75 x 10.5, self-adhesive (2000)	1.95	....	....	....	1.00	.20
3052Ef	same, bklt pane of 20	14.50	....	....	....	18.00	....
3053	20¢ Blue Jay, self-adhesive, coil (1996)	1.95	....	....	6.00	1.00	.20
3054	32¢ Yellow Rose, self-adhesive coil (1997)	1.95	....	....	7.50	1.00	.20
3055	20¢ Ring-necked Pheasant, self-adhesive coil (1998)	1.95	....	....	5.00	.75	.20
3058	32¢ Ernest Just	1.95	4.75	19.50(20)	5.00	1.10	.25
3059	32¢ Smithsonian Institution	1.95	4.75	19.50(20)	5.00	1.10	.25
3060	32¢ Year of the Rat	1.95	4.75	22.00(20)	5.50	1.20	.25
3061-64	Pioneers of Communication, 4 varieties, attached	4.00	4.75	18.00(20)	4.75	4.25	2.50
3061	32¢ Eadweard Muybridge	1.95	....	....	....	1.10	.25
3062	32¢ Ottmar Mergenthaler	1.95	....	....	....	1.10	25
3063	32¢ Frederic E. Ives	1.95	....	....	....	1.10	.25
3064	32¢ William Dickson	1.95	....	....	....	1.10	.25
3065	32¢ Fulbright Scholarships	1.95	4.75	50.00(50)	5.00	1.10	.25
3066	50¢ Jacqueline Cochran	2.25	5.00	60.00(50)	5.75	1.25	.50
3067	32¢ Marathon	1.95	4.75	14.50(20)	3.75	.80	.25

U.S. Postage #3068-3082v

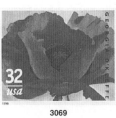

3068

1996 SUMMER OLYMPIC GAMES

3068a	Decathlon	3068k	Beach volleyball	
3068b	Men's canoeing	3068l	Men's rowing	
3068c	Women's running	3068m	Men's sprints	
3068d	Women's diving	3068n	Women's swimming	
3068e	Men's cycling	3068o	Women's softball	
3068f	Freestyle wrestling	3068p	Men's hurdles	
3068g	Women's gymnastics	3068q	Men's swimming	
3068h	Women's sailboarding	3068r	Men's gymnastics	
3068i	Men's shot put	3068s	Equestrian	
3068j	Women's soccer	3068t	Men's basketball	

SCOTT NO.	DESCRIPTION	FIRST DAY COVERS SING PL. BLK.		MINT SHEET	PLATE BLOCK	UNUSED F/NH	USED
3068	32¢ Centennial Olympic Games, 20 varieties, attached	....	....	20.00(20)	....	20.00	16.00
....	set of singles	35.00	....	....	....	....	14.00
....	single of above, each	....	....	....	....	....	.90
3068v	same as above, uncut sheet of 120 (6 panes)	....	....	120.00(120)	....	120.00	....
....	cross gutter block of 20	....	....	....	....	35.00	....
....	cross gutter block of 4	....	....	....	....	19.50	....
....	vertical pair with horizontal gutter	....	....	....	....	4.50	....
....	horizontal pair with vertical gutter	....	....	....	....	4.50	....

3069

3070, 3071

SCOTT NO.	DESCRIPTION	SING	PL. BLK.	MINT SHEET	PLATE BLOCK	UNUSED F/NH	USED
3069	32¢ Georgia O'Keeffe	1.95	....	17.50(15)	5.50	1.25	.25
3070	32¢ Tennessee Statehood	1.95	4.75	38.00(50)	4.00	.80	.25
3071	32¢ Tennessee Statehood, self-adhesive	1.95	....	....	....	1.10	.30
3071a	same, bklt pane of 20	14.50	....	....	....	20.00	....

Is Your U.S. Liberty Album Out of Date?
See page 125 for a complete list of U.S. Liberty I Album Supplements. Update your album today!

3072 **3073** **3074**

3075 **3076**

SCOTT NO.	DESCRIPTION	SING	PL. BLK.	MINT SHEET	PLATE BLOCK	UNUSED F/NH	USED
3072-76	American Indian Dances, 5 varieties, attached	5.50	....	22.50(20)	12.50(10)	6.00	3.50
3072	32¢ Fancy Dance	1.95	....	....	....	1.25	.35
3073	32¢ Butterfly Dance	1.95	....	....	....	1.25	.35
3074	32¢ Traditional Dance	1.95	....	....	....	1.25	.35
3075	32¢ Raven Dance	1.95	....	....	....	1.25	.35
3076	32¢ Hoop Dance	1.95	....	....	....	1.25	.35

3077 **3078**

3079 **3080**

SCOTT NO.	DESCRIPTION	SING	PL. BLK.	MINT SHEET	PLATE BLOCK	UNUSED F/NH	USED
3077-80	Prehistoric Animals, 4 varieties, attached	4.00	4.75	20.00(20)	5.50	5.00	3.50
3077	32¢ Eohippus	1.95	....	....	....	1.25	.25
3078	32¢ Woolly Mammoth	1.95	....	....	....	1.25	.25
3079	32¢ Mastodon	1.95	....	....	....	1.25	.25
3080	32¢ Saber-tooth Cat	1.95	....	....	....	1.25	.25

3081

3082

SCOTT NO.	DESCRIPTION	SING	PL. BLK.	MINT SHEET	PLATE BLOCK	UNUSED F/NH	USED
3081	32¢ Breast Cancer Awareness	1.95	4.75	20.00(20)	5.00	1.10	.25
3082	32¢ James Dean	1.95	4.75	24.00(20)	6.00	1.25	.25
3082v	same as above, uncut sheet of 120 (6 panes)	....	....	120.00(120)	....	120.00(120)	....
....	block of 8 with vertical gutter	....	....	....	....	20.00	....
....	cross gutter block of 8	....	....	....	....	27.50	....
....	vertical pair with horizontal gutter	....	....	....	....	3.50	....
....	horizontal pair with vertical gutter	....	....	....	....	5.50	....

U.S. Postage #3083-3104

SCOTT NO.	DESCRIPTION	FIRST DAY COVERS SING	FIRST DAY COVERS PL. BLK.	MINT SHEET	PLATE BLOCK	UNUSED F/NH	USED
3083-86	Folk Heroes, 4 varieties, attached	4.00	4.75	20.00(20)	5.25	4.75	2.50
3083	32¢ Mighty Casey	1.95				1.20	.25
3084	32¢ Paul Bunyan	1.95				1.20	.25
3085	32¢ John Henry	1.95				1.20	.25
3086	32¢ Pecos Bill	1.95				1.20	.25
3087	32¢ Olympic Discus Thrower	1.95	4.75	27.50(20)	7.00	1.50	.25
3088	32¢ Iowa Statehood	1.95	4.75	38.00(50)	4.00	.80	.25
3089	32¢ Iowa Statehood, self-adhesive	1.95				1.10	.30
3089a	same, bklt pane of 20	14.50				21.00	
3090	32¢ Rural Free Delivery	1.95	4.75	14.75(20)	3.75	.80	.25
3091-95	Riverboats, 5 varieties, attached	5.50		21.50(20)	12.00(10)	5.75	3.00
3091	32¢ Robt. E. Lee	1.95				1.20	.25
3092	32¢ Sylvan Dell	1.95				1.20	.25
3093	32¢ Far West	1.95				1.20	.25
3094	32¢ Rebecca Everingham	1.95				1.20	.25
3095	32¢ Bailey Gatzert	1.95				1.20	.25
3091-95b	32¢ Riverboats, special die cutting, 5 attached				170.00(10)	82.50	
3095b	same, as above, pane of 20			325.00(20)		325.00	

SCOTT NO.	DESCRIPTION	FIRST DAY COVERS SING	FIRST DAY COVERS PL. BLK.	MINT SHEET	PLATE BLOCK	UNUSED F/NH	USED
3096-99	Big Band Leaders, 4 varieties, attached	4.00	4.75	22.00(20)	5.25	4.75	2.50
3096	32¢ Count Basie	1.95				1.25	.35
3097	32¢ Tommy & Jimmy Dorsey	1.95				1.25	.35
3098	32¢ Glenn Miller	1.95				1.25	.35
3099	32¢ Benny Goodman	1.95				1.25	.35
3100-03	Songwriters, 4 varieties, attached	4.00	4.75	22.00(20)	5.25	4.75	2.50
3100	32¢ Harold Arlen	1.95				1.25	.35
3101	32¢ Johnny Mercer	1.95				1.25	.35
3102	32¢ Dorothy Fields	1.95				1.25	.35
3103	32¢ Hoagy Carmichael	1.95				1.25	.35
3104	23¢ F. Scott Fitzgerald	1.95	4.75	31.50(50)	3.25	.70	.25

U.S. Postage #3105-3124a

3105 ENDANGERED SPECIES

3105a	Black-footed ferret	3105i	California condor
3105b	Thick-billed parrot	3105j	Gila trout
3105c	Hawaiian monk seal	3105k	San Francisco garter snake
3105d	American crocodile	3105l	Woodland caribou
3105e	Ocelot	3105m	Florida panther
3105f	Schaus swallowtail butterfly	3105n	Piping plover
3105g	Wyoming toad	3105o	Florida manatee
3105h	Brown pelican		

Scott No.	Description	FDC Sing	FDC Pl.Blk	Mint Sheet	Plate Block	Unused F/NH	Used
3105	32¢ Endangered Species, 15 varieties, attached	....	....	16.00(15)	....	16.00	12.50
	set of singles	27.50	....	....	....	....	9.50
	singles of above, each	....	....	....	....	....	.85

3106

3107, 3112

| 3106 | 32¢ Computer Technology | 1.95 | 4.75 | 30.00(40) | 4.00 | .80 | .25 |
| 3107 | 32¢ Madonna & Child | 1.95 | 4.75 | 38.00(50) | 4.25 | .80 | .20 |

3108, 3113

3109, 3114

3110, 3115

3111, 3116

3108-11	Christmas Family Scenes, 4 varieties, attached	4.00	4.75	50.00(50)	5.50	5.00	2.50
3108	32¢ Family at Fireplace	1.95				1.25	.20
3109	32¢ Decorating Tree	1.95				1.25	.20
3110	32¢ Dreaming of Santa Claus	1.95				1.25	.20
3111	32¢ Holiday Shopping	1.95				1.25	.20
3112	32¢ Madonna & Child, self-adhesive	....	....	....	....	1.00	.30
3112a	same, bklt pane of 20	14.50				18.00	....
3113	32¢ Family at Fireplace, self-adhesive	....	....	....	....	1.20	.30
3114	32¢ Decorating Tree, self-adhesive	....	....	....	....	1.20	.30
3115	32¢ Dreaming of Santa Claus, self-adhesive	....	....	....	....	1.20	.30
3116	32¢ Holiday Shopping, self-adhesive	1.95				1.20	.30
3116a	Christmas Family Scenes, self-adhesive, bklt pane of 20	14.50	....	....	....	18.00	....

3117

3118

3117	32¢ Skaters, self-adhesive	1.95	....	....	....	1.10	.40
3117a	same, bklt pane of 18	13.00				18.50	
3118	32¢ Hanukkah, self-adhesive	1.95	....	14.75(20)	3.75	.80	.25

3119

| 3119 | 50¢ Cycling, sheet of 2 | 3.00 | .... | .... | .... | 3.25 | 2.50 |
| 3119a-b | same, set of 2 singles | 4.25 | | | | 3.00 | 1.80 |

3120

3121

1997 COMMEMORATIVES

3120/75	(3120-21, 3125, 3130-31, 3134-35, 3141, 3143-50, 3152-75) 40 varieties	....	....	....	....	41.50	10.75
3120	32¢ Year of the Ox	1.95	....	22.00(20)	5.00	1.20	.25
3121	32¢ Benjamin O. Davis, Sr.	1.95	4.75	19.50(20)	4.50	1.10	.25

3122

3122	32¢ Statue of Liberty, self-adhesive (1997)	1.95	....	....	....	2.00	.25
3122a	same, bklt pane of 20	14.50				20.00	....
3122b	same, bklt pane of 4	4.75				5.00	....
3122c	same, bklt pane of 5	5.00				6.00	....
3122d	same, bklt pane of 6	5.75				6.50	....
3122E	32¢ Statue of Liberty, die cut 11.5 x 11.8	....	....	....	....	1.40	.25
3122Ef	same, bklt pane of 20	....				40.00	....
3122Eg	same, bklt pane of 6	....				11.00	....

3123

3124

3123	32¢ Swans, self-adhesive	1.95	....	....	....	1.10	.25
3123a	same, bklt pane of 20	14.50				19.50	....
3124	55¢ Swans, self-adhesive	2.50	....	....	....	1.75	.50
3124a	same, bklt pane of 20	19.75				33.50	....

U.S. Postage #3125-3137v

SCOTT NO.	DESCRIPTION	FIRST DAY COVERS SING	FIRST DAY COVERS PL. BLK.	MINT SHEET	PLATE BLOCK	UNUSED F/NH	USED
3125	32¢ Helping Children Learn	1.95	4.75	19.50(20)	5.00	1.10	.25
3126	32¢ Citron, Moth, Larvae, Pupa, Beetle, self-adhesive (Die Cut 10.9 x 10.2)	1.95				1.10	.25
3127	32¢ Flowering Pineapple, Cockroaches, self-adhesive (Die Cut 10.9 x 10.2)	1.95				1.10	.25
3127a	same, bklt pane of 20 (10–#3126, 10–#3127)	14.50				19.50	
3128	32¢ Citron, Moth, Larvae, Pupa, Beetle, self-adhesive (Die Cut 11.2 x 10.8)	1.95				1.10	.25
3128a	same, stamp sideways	1.95				2.00	.50
3128b	same, bklt pane of 5 (2–#3128 & #3129, 1–#3128a)	5.50				6.50	
3129	32¢ Flowering Pineapple, Cockroaches, self-adhesive (Die Cut 11.2 x 10.8)	1.95				1.10	.25
3129a	same, stamp sideways	1.95				3.75	.60
3129b	same, bklt pane of 5 (2–#3128 & #3129, 1–#3129a)	5.50				8.00	
3130-31	32¢ Stagecoach & Ship, (Pacific '97) 2 varieties, attached	3.00	4.75	16.50(16)	5.00	2.25	1.00
3130	32¢ Ship	1.95				1.20	.25
3131	32¢ Stagecoach	1.95				1.20	.25
3130-31v	same, as above, uncut sheet of 96 (6 panes)			90.00(96)			
	block of 32 with vertical or horizontal gutter between (2 panes)			30.00(32)		30.00	
	cross gutter block of 16					30.00	
	vertical pairs with horizontal gutter					8.00	
	horizontal pairs with vertical gutter					8.00	
3132	(25¢) Juke Box, self-adhesive linerless coil	1.95			8.00	.95	.30
3133	32¢ Flag Over Porch, self-adhesive, linerless coil	1.95			8.00	1.10	.45
3134	32¢ Thornton Wilder	1.95	4.75	14.75(20)	3.50	.80	.25
3135	32¢ Raoul Wallenberg	1.95	4.75	14.75(20)	3.50	.80	.25

DINOSAURS

3136a	Ceratosaurus	3136f	Stegosaurus	3136k	Daspletosaurus
3136b	Camptosaurus	3136g	Allosaurus	3136l	Palaeosaniwa
3136c	Camarasaurus	3136h	Opisthias	3136m	Corythosaurus
3136d	Brachiosaurus	3136i	Edmontonia	3136n	Ornithominus
3136e	Goniopholis	3136j	Einiosaurus	3136o	Parasaurolophus

3136	32¢ Dinosaurs, 15 varieties, attached	11.50			16.00	11.50
	set of singles	26.50				10.00
	singles of above, each					.75

3137	32¢ Bugs Bunny, self-adhesive, pane of 10	9.50				8.50	
3137a	same, single from pane	1.95				1.10	.25
3137b	same, pane of 9 (#3137a)					7.00	
3137c	same, pane of 1 (#3137a)					2.50	
3137v	same, top press sheet (6 panes)			525.00		525.00	
3137v	same, bottom press w/ plate# (6 panes)			800.00		800.00	
	pane of 10 from press sheet			95.00		95.00	
	pane of 10 from press sheet w/ plate#			500.00		500.00	

–Supplies–
Don't forget that Harris offers a complete line of albums, supplies and accessories for all your stamp collecting needs!

U.S. Postage #3138-3150

SCOTT NO.	DESCRIPTION	FIRST DAY COVERS SING	FIRST DAY COVERS PL. BLK.	MINT SHEET	PLATE BLOCK	UNUSED F/NH	USED
	1997 COMMEMORATIVES (continued)						
3138	32¢ Bug Bunny, self-adhesive, Die Cut, pane of 10	10.00	....	....	....	200.00	....
3138a	same, single from pane	1.95	....	....	....	....	....
3138b	same, pane of 9 (#3138a)	....	....	....	....	....	....
3138c	same, pane of 1 (#3138a)	....	....	....	....	190.00	....

3139

3140

3139	50¢ Benjamin Franklin, Souvenir Sheet of 12 (Pacific '97)	14.00	....	....	....	18.50	....
3139a	same, single from sheet	2.25	....	....	....	1.60	.80
3140	60¢ George Washington, Souvenir Sheet of 12 (Pacific '97)	16.00	....	....	....	22.00	....
3140a	same, single from sheet	2.25	....	....	....	1.85	1.00

3141

3141	32¢ Marshall Plan	1.95	4.75	14.25(20)	3.50	.75	.25

WE ARE BUYING!
WANTED

Collections, Accumulations, Individual Stamps
Mint or Used

**UNITED STATES, CANADA, WORLDWIDE
TOP PRICES PAID!**

Please phone or fax with details
of what you have to sell.

H.E. Harris & Co.®
Serving the Collector Since 1916

Phone 800-546-2995   Fax 256-246-1116

3142

CLASSIC AMERICAN AIRCRAFT

3142a	Mustang	3142k	Flying Fortress
3142b	Model B	3142l	Stearman
3142c	Cub	3142m	Constellation
3142d	Vega	3142n	Lightning
3142e	Alpha	3142o	Peashooter
3142f	B-10	3142p	Tri-Motor
3142g	Corsair	3142q	DC-3
3142h	Stratojet	3142r	314 Clipper
3142i	GeeBee	3142s	Jenny
3142j	Staggerwing	3142t	Wildcat

3142	32¢ Classic American Aircraft, 20 varieties, attached	....	....	18.50(20)	....	18.50	15.00
....	set of singles	35.00	....	....	....	....	12.00
....	singles of above, each	....	....	....	....	....	.75
3142v	same as above, uncut sheet of 120 (6 panes)	....	....	100.00(120)	....	100.00	....
....	cross gutter block of 20	....	....	....	....	28.00	....
....	cross gutter block of 4	....	....	....	....	18.50	....
....	vertical pair with horizontal gutter	....	....	....	....	3.50	....
....	horizontal pair with vertical gutter	....	....	....	....	3.50	....

3143, 3148

3144, 3149

3145, 3147

3146, 3150

3143-46	Legendary Football Coaches, 4 varieties, attached	4.00	4.75	19.50(20)	5.00	4.50	2.50
3143	32¢ Paul "Bear" Bryant	1.95	....	....	....	1.20	.35
3144	32¢ Glenn "Pop" Warner	1.95	....	....	....	1.20	.35
3145	32¢ Vince Lombardi	1.95	....	....	....	1.20	.35
3146	32¢ George Halas	1.95	....	....	....	1.20	.35
3147	32¢ Vince Lombardi	1.95	4.75	19.50(20)	5.00	1.20	.50
3148	32¢ Paul "Bear" Bryant	1.95	4.75	19.50(20)	5.00	1.20	.50
3149	32¢ Glenn "Pop" Warner	1.95	4.75	19.50(20)	5.00	1.20	.50
3150	32¢ George Halas	1.95	4.75	19.50(20)	5.00	1.20	.50

U.S. Postage #3151-3167

3151 CLASSIC AMERICAN DOLLS

- 3151a "Alabama Baby," and doll by Martha Chase
- 3151b "Columbian Doll"
- 3151c Johnny Gruelle's "Raggedy Ann"
- 3151d Doll by Martha Chase
- 3151e "American Child"
- 3151f "Baby Coos"
- 3151g Plains Indian
- 3151h Doll by Izannah Walker
- 3151i "Babyland Rag"
- 3151j "Scootles"
- 3151k Doll by Ludwig Greiner
- 3151l "Betsy McCall"
- 3151m Percy Crosby's "Skippy"
- 3151n "Maggie Mix-up"
- 3151o Dolls by Albert Schoenhut

SCOTT NO.	DESCRIPTION	FIRST DAY COVERS SING	FIRST DAY COVERS PL. BLK.	MINT SHEET	PLATE BLOCK	UNUSED F/NH	USED
3151	32¢ Classic American Dolls, 15 varieties, attached	....	....	20.00(15)	....	20.00	15.00
	set of singles	26.50	....	....	....	....	10.50
	singles of above, each	....	....	....	....	....	.80
3152	32¢ Humphrey Bogart	1.95	....	19.50(20)	5.00	1.10	.25
3152v	same, as above, uncut sheet of 120 (6 panes)	....	....	110.00(120)	....	110.00	....
	block of 8 with vertical gutter	....	....	....	....	16.50	....
	cross gutter block of 8	....	....	....	....	19.50	....
	vertical pair with horizontal gutter	....	....	....	....	3.50	....
	horizontal pair with vertical gutter	....	....	....	....	5.00	....
3153	32¢ "The Stars & Stripes Forever"	1.95	4.75	40.00(50)	4.25	85	.25
3154-57	Opera Singers, 4 varieties, attached	4.00	4.75	21.50(20)	5.25	4.75	2.50
3154	32¢ Lily Pons	1.95	....	....	....	1.25	.30
3155	32¢ Richard Tucker	1.95	....	....	....	1.25	.30
3156	32¢ Lawrence Tibbett	1.95	....	....	....	1.25	.30
3157	32¢ Rosa Ponselle	1.95	....	....	....	1.25	.30
3158-65	Composers and Conductors, 8 varieties, attached	7.00	....	23.50(20)	12.00(8)	10.00	6.00
3158	32¢ Leopold Stokowski	1.95	....	....	....	1.50	.30
3159	32¢ Arthur Fiedler	1.95	....	....	....	1.50	.30
3160	32¢ George Szell	1.95	....	....	....	1.50	.30
3161	32¢ Eugene Ormandy	1.95	....	....	....	1.50	.30
3162	32¢ Samuel Barber	1.95	....	....	....	1.50	.30
3163	32¢ Ferde Grofé	1.95	....	....	....	1.50	.30
3164	32¢ Charles Ives	1.95	....	....	....	1.50	.30
3165	32¢ Louis Moreau Gottschalk	1.95	....	....	....	1.50	.30
3166	32¢ Padre Félix Varela	1.95	4.75	14.75(20)	3.50	.75	.25
3167	32¢ U.S. Air Force 50th Anniversary	1.95	4.75	14.75(20)	3.50	.75	.25

U.S. Postage #3168-3181

SCOTT NO.	DESCRIPTION	FIRST DAY COVERS SING	FIRST DAY COVERS PL. BLK.	MINT SHEET	PLATE BLOCK	UNUSED F/NH	USED
3168-72	Movie Monster, 5 varieties, attached	5.75	....	21.00(20)	12.00(10)	5.75	3.50
3168	32¢ Lon Chaney as The Phantom of the Opera	1.95	....	....	....	1.20	.30
3169	32¢ Bela Lugosi as Dracula	1.95	....	....	....	1.20	.30
3170	32¢ Boris Karloff as Frankenstein's Monster	1.95	....	....	....	1.20	.30
3171	32¢ Boris Karloff as The Mummy	1.95	....	....	....	1.20	.30
3172	32¢ Lon Chaney Jr. as The Wolfman	1.95	....	....	....	1.20	.30
3168-72v	same, as above, uncut sheet of 180 (9 panes)	....	....	145.00(180)	....	....	....
....	block of 8 with vertical gutter	....	....	....	....	11.00	....
....	block of 10 with horizontal gutter	....	....	....	....	13.00	....
....	cross gutter block of 8	....	....	....	....	18.00	....
....	vertical pair with horizontal gutter	....	....	....	....	3.00	....
....	horizontal pair with vertical gutter	....	....	....	....	3.00	....
3173	32¢ First Supersonic Flight, 50th Anniversary	1.95	4.75	14.75(20)	3.50	.75	.25
3174	32¢ Women in Military Service	1.95	4.75	14.75(20)	3.50	.75	.25
3175	32¢ Kwanzaa	1.95	4.75	37.00(50)	3.75	.80	.25
....	same, as above, uncut sheet of 250 (5 panes)	....	....	725.00(250)	....	....	....
3176	32¢ Madonna & Child, self-adhesive	1.95	....	....	....	1.00	.20
3176a	same, bklt pane of 20	14.50	....	....	....	17.50	....
3177	32¢ American Holly, self-adhesive	1.95	....	....	....	1.00	.20
3177a	same, bklt pane of 20	14.50	....	....	....	17.50	....
3177b	same, bklt pane of 4	3.00	....	....	....	4.50	....
3177c	same, bklt pane of 5	3.75	....	....	....	5.50	....
3177d	same, bklt pane of 6	4.50	....	....	....	6.50	....
3178	$3 Mars Rover Sojourner, Souvenir Sheet	9.50	....	....	....	7.00	6.50
....	same, as above, uncut sheet of 18 souvenir sheets	....	....	195.00(18)	....	195.00	....
3178v	single souvenir sheet from uncut sheet of 18	....	....	....	....	15.00	....

1998 COMMEMORATIVES

SCOTT NO.	DESCRIPTION	FIRST DAY COVERS SING	FIRST DAY COVERS PL. BLK.	MINT SHEET	PLATE BLOCK	UNUSED F/NH	USED
3179/3252	(3179-81, 3192-3203, 3206, 3211-27, 3230-35, 3237-44, 3249-52) 51 varieties	....	....	....	....	50.50	11.75
3179	32¢ Year of the Tiger	1.95	4.75	22.50(20)	5.50	1.20	.25
3180	32¢ Alpine Skiing	1.95	4.75	18.50(20)	4.50	1.00	.25
3181	32¢ Madam C.J. Walker	1.95	4.75	18.50(20)	5.00	1.10	.25

U.S. Postage #3182-3185v

3182

CELEBRATE THE CENTURY 1900's

3182a	Model T Ford	3182i	Immigrants arrive.
3182b	Theodore Roosevelt	3182j	John Muir, preservationist
3182c	"The Great Train Robbery" 1903	3182k	"Teddy" bear created
3182d	Crayola Crayons, introduced, 1903	3182l	W.E.B. DuBois, social activist
3182e	St. Louis World's Fair, 1904	3182m	Gibson Girl
3182f	Pure Food & Drug Act, 1906	3182n	First baseball World Series, 1903
3182g	Wright Brothers first flight, 1903	3182o	Robie House, Chicago
3182h	Boxing match in painting		

Scott No.	Description	FDC Sing	FDC Pl.Blk	Mint Sheet	Plate Block	Unused F/NH	Used
3182	32¢ Celebrate the Century 1900's, 15 varieties, attached	17.50	....	12.00(15)	....	12.00	10.00
	set of singles	26.50	....	....	....	....	8.50
	singles of above, each	....	....	....	....	....	.60
3182v	same as above, uncut sheet of 60 (4 panes)	....	....	65.00(4)	....	65.00	....

3184

CELEBRATE THE CENTURY 1920's

3184a	Babe Ruth	3184i	Radio entertains America
3184b	The Gatsby style	3184j	Art Deco style (Chrysler Building)
3184c	Prohibition enforced	3184k	Jazz flourishes
3184d	Electric toy trains	3184l	Four Horsemen of Notre Dame
3184e	19th Ammendment	3184m	Lindbergh flies the Atlantic
3184f	Emily Post's Etiquette	3184n	American realism
3184g	Margaret Mead, anthropologist	3184o	Stock Market crash, 1929
3184h	Flappers do the Charleston		

Scott No.	Description	FDC Sing	FDC Pl.Blk	Mint Sheet	Plate Block	Unused F/NH	Used
3184	32¢ Celebrate the Century 1920's, 15 varieties, attached	17.50	....	12.00(15)	....	12.00	10.00
	set of singles	26.50	....	....	....	....	8.50
	singles of above, each	....	....	....	....	....	.60
3184v	same, as above, uncut sheet of 60 (4 panes)	....	....	65.00(4)	....	65.00	....

3183

CELEBRATE THE CENTURY 1910's

3183a	Charlie Chaplin as the Little Tramp	3183i	United States enters WWI
3183b	Federal Reserve system created, 1913	3183j	Boy Scouts, 1910
3183c	George Washington Carver	3183k	Woodrow Wilson
3183d	Avant-garde art, 1913	3183l	First crossword puzzle, pub., 1913
3183e	First-Transcontinental telephone line, 1914	3183m	Jack Dempsey wins title, 1919
3183f	Panama Canal opens, 1914	3183n	Construction toys
3183g	Jim Thorpe wins decathlon, 1912	3183o	Child labor reform
3183h	Grand Canyon National Park, 1913		

Scott No.	Description	FDC Sing	FDC Pl.Blk	Mint Sheet	Plate Block	Unused F/NH	Used
3183	32¢ Celebrate the Century 1910's, 15 varieties, attached	17.50	....	12.00(15)	....	12.00	10.00
	set of singles	26.50	....	....	....	....	8.50
	singles of above, each	....	....	....	....	....	.60
3183v	same as above, uncut sheet of 60 (4 panes)	....	....	65.00(4)	....	65.00	....

3185

CELEBRATE THE CENTURY 1930's

3185a	Franklin D. Roosevelt	3185i	"Gone with the Wind"
3185b	Empire State Building	3185j	Jesse Owens
3185c	1st Issue of Life Magazine	3185k	Streamline design
3185d	Eleanor Roosevelt	3185l	Golden Gate Bridge
3185e	FDR's New Deal	3185m	America survives the Depression
3185f	Superman arrives	3185n	Bobby Jones wins Grand Slam
3185g	Household conveniences	3185o	The Monopoly Game
3185h	"Snow White and the Seven Dwarfs"		

Scott No.	Description	FDC Sing	FDC Pl.Blk	Mint Sheet	Plate Block	Unused F/NH	Used
3185	32¢ Celebrate the Century 1930's, 15 varieties, attached	17.50	....	12.00(15)	....	12.00	10.00
	set of singles	26.50	....	....	....	....	8.50
	singles of above, each	....	....	....	....	....	.60
3185v	same as above, uncut sheet of 60 (4 panes)	....	....	65.00(4)	....	65.00	....

U.S. Postage #3186-3189

3186
CELEBRATE THE CENTURY 1940's

3186a	World War II	
3186b	Antibiotics save lives	
3186c	Jackie Robinson	
3186d	Harry S. Truman	
3186e	Women support war effort	
3186f	TV entertains America	
3186g	Jitterbug sweeps nation	
3186h	Jackson Pollock, Abstract Expressionism	
3186i	GI Bill, 1944	
3186j	Big Band Sounds	
3186k	Intl. Style of Architecture	
3186l	Postwar Baby Boom	
3186m	Slinky, 1945	
3186n	"A Streetcar Named Desire" 1947	
3186o	Orson Welles' "Citizen Kane"	

Scott No.	Description	FDC Sing	Mint Sheet	Plate Block	Unused F/NH	Used
3186	33¢ Celebrate the Century 1940's, 15 varieties, attached	17.50	12.00(15)		12.00	10.00
	set of singles	26.50				8.50
	singles of above, each					.60
3186v	same as above, uncut sheet of 60 (4 panes)		65.00(4)		65.00	

3187
CELEBRATE THE CENTURY 1950's

3187a	Polio vaccine developed	
3187b	teen fashions	
3187c	The "Shot Heard Round the World"	
3187d	US launches satellites	
3187e	Korean War	
3187f	Desegregation public schools	
3187g	Tail fins, chrome	
3187h	Dr. Seuss "The Cat in the Hat"	
3187i	Drive-in movies	
3187j	World series rivals	
3187k	Rocky Marciano, undefeated	
3187l	"I Love Lucy"	
3187m	Rock 'n Roll	
3187n	Stock car racing	
3187o	Movies go 3-D	

Scott No.	Description	FDC Sing	Mint Sheet	Plate Block	Unused F/NH	Used
3187	33¢ Celebrate the Century 1950's, 15 varieties, attached	17.50	12.00(15)		12.00	10.00
	set of singles	26.50				8.50
	singles of above, each					.60
3187v	same as above, uncut sheet of 60 (4 panes)		65.00(4)		65.00	

3188
CELEBRATE THE CENTURY 1960's

3188a	"I Have a Dream" Martin Luther King	
3188b	Woodstock	
3188c	Man Walks on the Moon	
3188d	Green Bay Packers	
3188e	Star Trek	
3188f	The Peace Corps	
3188g	The Vietnam War	
3188h	Ford Mustang	
3188i	Barbie Doll	
3188j	The Integrated Circuit	
3188k	Lasers	
3188l	Super Bowl I	
3188m	Peace Symbol	
3188n	Roger Maris, 61 in '61	
3188o	The Beatles "Yellow Submarine"	

Scott No.	Description	FDC Sing	Mint Sheet	Plate Block	Unused F/NH	Used
3188	33¢ Celebrate the Century 1960's, 15 varieties, attached	17.50	12.00(15)		12.00	10.00
	set of singles	26.50				8.50
	singles of above, each					.60
3188v	same as above, uncut sheet of 60 (4 panes)		65.00(4)		65.00	

3189
CELEBRATE THE CENTURY 1970's

3189a	Earth Day Celebrated	
3189b	"All in the Family", TV Series	
3189c	Sesame Street	
3189d	Disco Music	
3189e	Steelers Win Four Super Bowls	
3189f	U.S. Celebrates 200th Birthday	
3189g	Secretariat Wins Triple Crown	
3189h	VCR's Transform Entertainment	
3189i	Pioneer 10	
3189j	Women's Rights Movement	
3189k	1970's Fashion	
3189l	Monday Night Football	
3189m	America Smiles	
3189n	Jumbo Jets	
3189o	Medical Imaging	

Scott No.	Description	FDC Sing	Mint Sheet	Plate Block	Unused F/NH	Used
3189	33¢ Celebrate the Century 1970's, 15 varieties, attached	17.50	12.00(15)		12.00	10.00
	set of singles	26.50				8.50
	singles of above, each					.60
3189v	same as above, uncut sheet of 60 (4 panes)		65.00(4)		65.00	

U.S. Postage #3190-3202   113

SCOTT NO.	DESCRIPTION	FIRST DAY COVERS SING	FIRST DAY COVERS PL. BLK.	MINT SHEET	PLATE BLOCK	UNUSED F/NH	USED

3190
CELEBRATE THE CENTURY 1980's

3190a	Space Shuttle program		3190i	Cabbage Patch Kids
3190b	Cats, Musucal Smash		3190j	"The Cosby Show", Hit Comedy
3190c	San Francisco 49ers		3190k	Fall of the Berlin Wall
3190d	Hostages Come Home		3190l	Video Games
3190e	Figure Skating		3190m	"E.T. The Extra-Terrestrial"
3190f	Cable TV		3190n	Personal Computers
3190g	Vietnam Veterans Memorial		3190o	Hip-hop Culture
3190h	Compact Discs			

3190	33¢ Celebrate the Century 1980's, 15 varieties, attached	17.50	....	12.00(15)	....	12.00	10.00
....	set of singles	26.50	....	....	....	....	8.50
....	singles of above, each	....	....	....	....	....	.60
3190v	same as above, uncut sheet of 60 (4 panes)	....	....	65.00(4)	....	65.00	....

3191
CELEBRATE THE CENTURY 1990's

3191a	New Baseball Records		3191i	Special Olympics
3191b	Gulf War		3191j	Virtual Reality
3191c	"Seinfeld" Sitcom Sensation		3191k	"Jurassic Park"
3191d	Extreme Sports		3191l	"Titanic" Blockbuster Film
3191e	Improving Education		3191m	Sport Utility Vehicles
3191f	Computer Art and Graphics		3191n	World Wide Web
3191g	Recovering Species		3191o	Cellular Phones
3191h	Return to Space			

3191	33¢ Celebrate the Century 1990's, 15 varieties, attached	17.50	....	12.00(15)	....	12.00	10.00
....	set of singles	26.50	....	....	....	....	8.50
....	singles of above, each	....	....	....	....	....	.60
3191v	same as above, uncut sheet of 60 (4 panes)	....	....	65.00(4)	....	65.00	....

3192

| 3192 | 32¢ "Remember the Maine" | 1.95 | 4.75 | 19.50(20) | 5.00 | 1.10 | .25 |

3193   **3194**   **3195**

3196   **3197**

3193-97	Flowering Trees, self-adhesive, 5 varieties, attached	5.75	....	19.50(20)	12.00(10)	5.00	3.75
3193	32¢ Southern Magnolia	1.95	....	....	....	1.10	.25
3194	32¢ Blue Paloverde	1.95	....	....	....	1.10	.25
3195	32¢ Yellow Poplar	1.95	....	....	....	1.10	.25
3196	32¢ Prairie Crab Apple	1.95	....	....	....	1.10	.25
3197	32¢ Pacific Dogwood	1.95	....	....	....	1.10	.25

3198   **3199**

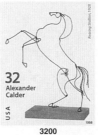  

3200   **3201**   **3202**

3198-3202	Alexander Calder, 5 varieties, attached	5.75	....	19.50(20)	10.50(10)	5.00	2.75
3198	32¢ Black Cascade, 13 Verticals, 1959	1.95	....	....	....	1.10	.25
3199	32¢ Untitled, 1965	1.95	....	....	....	1.10	.25
3200	32¢ Rearing Stallion, 1928	1.95	....	....	....	1.10	.25
3201	32¢ Potrait of a Young Man, c. 1945	1.95	....	....	....	1.10	.25
3202	32¢ Un Effet du Japonais, 1945	1.95	....	....	....	1.10	.25
3198-3202v	same, as above, uncut sheet of 120 (6 panes)	....	....	140.00(120)	....	....	....

U.S. Postage #3203-3211

SCOTT NO.	DESCRIPTION	FIRST DAY COVERS SING	FIRST DAY COVERS PL. BLK.	MINT SHEET	PLATE BLOCK	UNUSED F/NH	USED
3203	32¢ Cinco De Mayo, self-adhesive	1.95	4.75	19.50(20)	5.00	1.10	.25
3203v	same as above, uncut sheet of 180 (9 panes)	....	....	140.00(180)	....	....	....
	cross gutter block of 4	....	....	....	....	16.00	....
	vertical pair with horizontal gutter	....	....	....	....	3.00	....
	horizontal pair with vertical gutter	....	....	....	....	3.00	....
3204	32¢ Sylvester & Tweety, self-adhesive, pane of 10	12.00	....	....	....	9.00	....
3204a	same, single from pane	2.25	....	....	....	1.00	.25
3204b	same, pane of 9 (#3204a)	....	....	....	....	6.50	....
3204c	same, pane of 1 (#3204a)	7.00	....	....	....	2.75	....
	same, top press sheet of 60 (6 panes)	....	....	100.00(60)	....	100.00	....
	same, bottom press sheet of 60 (6 panes)	....	....	175.00(60)	....	175.00	....
	same, pane of 10 from press sheet	....	....	....	....	17.50	....
	same, pane of 10 from press sheet w/ plate #	....	....	....	....	80.00	....
	vert. pair with horiz. gutter	....	....	....	....	10.00	....
	horiz pair with vert. gutter	....	....	....	....	20.00	....
3205	32¢ Sylvester & Tweety, self-adhesive, Die-Cut, pane of 10	17.50	....	....	....	9.50	....
3205a	same, single from pane	....	....	....	....	1.10	....
3205b	same, pane of 9 (#3205a)	....	....	....	....	7.00	....
3205c	same, pane of 1, imperf.	12.00	....	....	....	2.75	....
3206	32¢ Wisconsin, self-adhesive	1.95	4.75	14.75(20)	3.50	.75	.25
3207	(5¢) Wetlands, Nonprofit, coil	1.95	10.00 (PLATE# STRIP 3)	....	2.00 (PLATE# STRIP 3)	.20	.20
3207A	same, self-adhesive coil	1.95	....	....	2.00	.20	.20
	same, plate strip of 5	....	....	....	....	2.50	....
3208	(25¢) Diner, Presorted First-Class, coil	1.95	10.00	....	5.00	.70	.35
3208a	same, self-adhesive coil, die cut 9.7	1.95	....	....	5.00	.70	.35
	same, plate strip of 5	....	....	....	....	5.75	....
3209	1¢-$2 Trans-Mississippi, Souvenir Sheet of 9	8.00	....	....	....	10.00	7.50
	same, set of 9 singles	18.00	....	....	....	9.25	7.25
3209v	block of 9 with horiz. gutter	....	....	....	....	30.00	....
3209v	vert. pair with horiz. gutter	....	....	....	....	12.50	....
3210	$1 Cattle in Storm, Souvenir Sheet of 9	17.50	....	....	....	22.50	17.50
	same, single stamp	....	....	....	....	3.00	2.25
3209-10	same, press sheet of 54 (6 panes, 3-#3209 & 3-#3210)	....	....	175.00(54)	....	175.00	....
3210v	cross gutter block of 12	....	....	....	....	85.00	....
3210v	vert. pair with horiz. gutter	....	....	....	....	12.50	....
3210v	horiz. pair with vert. gutter	....	....	....	....	12.50	....
3211	32¢ Berlin Airlift, 50th Anniversary	1.95	4.75	14.75(20)	3.50	.75	.25

U.S. Postage #3212-3229

3212 · 3213 · 3214 · 3215

SCOTT NO.	DESCRIPTION	FIRST DAY COVERS SING	PL. BLK.	MINT SHEET	PLATE BLOCK	UNUSED F/NH	USED
3212-15	Folk Musicains, 4 varieties, attached	4.00	4.75	19.50(20)	5.00	4.75	2.50
3212	32¢ Huddie "Leadbelly" Ledbetter	1.95	....	....	....	1.25	.35
3213	32¢ Woody Guthrie	1.95	....	....	....	1.25	.35
3214	32¢ Sonny Terry	1.95	....	....	....	1.25	.35
3215	32¢ Josh White	1.95	....	....	....	1.25	.35

3216

3217 · 3218

3219

SCOTT NO.	DESCRIPTION	FIRST DAY COVERS SING	PL. BLK.	MINT SHEET	PLATE BLOCK	UNUSED F/NH	USED
3216-19	Gospel Singers, 4 varieties, attached	4.00	4.75	19.50(20)	5.00	4.75	2.50
3216	32¢ Mahalia Jackson	1.95	....	....	....	1.25	.35
3217	32¢ Roberta Martin	1.95	....	....	....	1.25	.35
3218	32¢ Clara Ward	1.95	....	....	....	1.25	.35
3219	32¢ Sister Rosetta Tharpe	1.95	....	....	....	1.25	.35

3220

3221

SCOTT NO.	DESCRIPTION	FIRST DAY COVERS SING	PL. BLK.	MINT SHEET	PLATE BLOCK	UNUSED F/NH	USED
3220	32¢ Spanish Settlement of the Southwest	1.95	4.75	18.50(20)	4.50	1.00	.25
3221	32¢ Stephen Vincent Benet	1.95	4.75	18.50(20)	4.50	1.00	.25

3222 · 3223

3224 · 3225

SCOTT NO.	DESCRIPTION	FIRST DAY COVERS SING	PL. BLK.	MINT SHEET	PLATE BLOCK	UNUSED F/NH	USED
3222-25	Tropical Birds, 4 varieties, attached	4.00	4.75	22.00(20)	5.00	4.75	2.50
3222	32¢ Antillean Euphonia	1.95	....	....	....	1.25	.25
3223	32¢ Green-throated Carib	1.95	....	....	....	1.25	.25
3224	32¢ Crested Honeycreeper	1.95	....	....	....	1.25	.25
3225	32¢ Cardinal Honeyeater	1.95	....	....	....	1.25	.25

3226

SCOTT NO.	DESCRIPTION	FIRST DAY COVERS SING	PL. BLK.	MINT SHEET	PLATE BLOCK	UNUSED F/NH	USED
3226	32¢ Alfred Hitchcock	1.95	....	16.50(20)	4.00	.90	.25
3226v	same as above, uncut sheet of 120 (6 panes)	....	....	95.00(120)	....	95.00	....
....	block of 8 with vertical gutter	....	....	....	....	15.00	....
....	cross gutter block of 8	....	....	....	....	19.50	....
....	vertical pair with horizontal gutter	....	....	....	....	3.50	....
....	horizontal pair with vertical gutter	....	....	....	....	5.00	....

3227 · 3228, 3229

SCOTT NO.	DESCRIPTION	FIRST DAY COVERS SING	PL. BLK.	MINT SHEET	PLATE BLOCK	UNUSED F/NH	USED
3227	32¢ Organ & Tissue Donation, self-adhesive	1.95	....	19.50(20)	4.00	.90	.25
3228	(10¢) Modern Bicycle, self-adhesive coil, die cut 9.8	1.95	....	....	3.75	.40	.20
....	same, plate strip of 5	....	....	....	....	4.50	....
3229	(10¢) Modern Bicycle, coil	1.95	10.00	....	3.75	.40	.20
....	same, plate strip of 5	....	....	....	....	4.50	....

3230 · 3231

3232 · 3233

116   U.S. Postage #3230-3244a

SCOTT NO.	DESCRIPTION	FIRST DAY COVERS SING	FIRST DAY COVERS PL. BLK.	MINT SHEET	PLATE BLOCK	UNUSED F/NH	USED
	1998 COMMEMORATIVES (continued)						
3230-34	Bright Eyes, self-adhesive, 5 varieties, attached	5.75	....	18.50(20)	10.50(10)	5.00	2.75
3230	32¢ Bright Eyes Dog	1.95	....	....	....	1.25	.30
3231	32¢ Bright Eyes Fish	1.95	....	....	....	1.25	.30
3232	32¢ Bright Eyes Cat	1.95	....	....	....	1.25	.30
3233	32¢ Bright Eyes Parakeet	1.95	....	....	....	1.25	.30
3234	32¢ Bright Eyes Hamster	1.95	....	....	....	1.25	.30
3235	32¢ Klondike Gold Rush	1.95	....	18.50(20)	4.50	1.00	.25

AMERICAN ART

- **3236a** "Portrait of Richard Mather," by John Foster
- **3236b** "Mrs. Elizabeth Freake and Baby Mary," by The Freake Limner
- **3236c** "Girl in Red Dress with Cat and Dog," by Ammi Phillips
- **3236d** "Rubens Peale with Geranium," by Rembrandt Peale
- **3236e** "Long-billed Curlew, Numenius Longrostris," by John James Audubon
- **3236f** "Boatmen on the Missouri," by George Caleb Bingham
- **3236g** "Kindred Spirits," by Asher B. Durand
- **3236h** "The Westwood Children," by Joshua Johnson
- **3236i** "Music and Literature," by William Harnett
- **3236j** "The Fog Warning," by Winslow Homer
- **3236k** "The White Cloud, Head Chief of the Iowas," by George Catlin
- **3236l** "Cliffs of Green River," by Thomas Moran
- **3236m** "The Last of the Buffalo," by Alfred Bierstadt
- **3236n** "Niagara," by Frederic Edwin Church
- **3236o** "Breakfast in Bed," by Mary Cassatt
- **3236p** "Nighthawks," by Edward Hopper
- **3236q** "American Gothic," by Grany Wood
- **3236r** "Two Against the White," by Charles Sheeler
- **3236s** "Mahoning," by Franz Kline
- **3236t** "No. 12," by Mark Rothko

SCOTT NO.	DESCRIPTION	FIRST DAY COVERS SING	FIRST DAY COVERS PL. BLK.	MINT SHEET	PLATE BLOCK	UNUSED F/NH	USED
3236	32¢ American Art, 20 varieties, attached	....	....	24.00(20)	....	24.00	15.00
....	set of singles	35.00	....	....	....	....	12.00
....	same as above, uncut sheet of 120 (6 panes)	....	....	....	....	130.00	....
....	block of 24 with vert. gutter	....	....	....	....	25.00	....
....	block of 25 with horiz. gutter	....	....	....	....	26.00	....
....	cross gutter block of 20	....	....	....	....	35.00	....
....	vert. pair with horiz. gutter	....	....	....	....	7.00	....
	AMERICAN ART (continued)						
....	horiz. pair with vert. gutter	....	....	....	....	9.00	....
....	horiz. blk of 8 with vert. gutter	....	....	....	....	22.50	....
....	vert. blk of 10 with horiz. gutter	....	....	....	....	26.00	....
3237	32¢ Ballet	1.95	....	18.50(20)	4.00	.95	.25
....	same, uncut sheet of 120 (6 panes)	....	....	....	....	100.00	....
....	cross gutter blk of 4	....	....	....	....	13.00	....
....	vert. pair with horiz. gutter	....	....	....	....	3.00	....
....	horiz. pair with vert. gutter	....	....	....	....	3.00	....
3238-42	Space Discovery, 5 varieties, attached	5.75	11.00	19.50(20)	10.50(10)	5.00	2.75
3238	32¢ Space City	1.95	....	....	....	1.25	.35
3239	32¢ Space ship landing	1.95	....	....	....	1.25	.35
3240	32¢ Person in space suit	1.95	....	....	....	1.25	.35
3241	32¢ Space Ship taking off	1.95	....	....	....	1.25	.35
3242	32¢ Large domed structure	1.95	....	....	....	1.25	.35
3238-42v	same, uncut sheet of 180 (9 panes)	....	....	125.00(180)	....	125.00	....
....	cross gutter blk of 10	....	....	....	....	22.50	....
....	vert. blk of 10 with horiz. gutter	....	....	....	....	20.00	....
....	horiz. pair with vert. gutter	....	....	....	....	3.00	....
....	pane of 2 from uncut sheet of 180	....	....	....	....	14.50	....
3243	32¢ Giving and Sharing, self-adhesive	1.95	4.75	16.50(20)	4.00	.95	.25
3244	32¢ Madonna & Child, self-adhesive	1.95	....	....	....	.90	.20
3244a	same, booklet pane of 20	14.50	....	....	....	17.50	....

U.S. Postage #3245-3281b

SCOTT NO.	DESCRIPTION	FIRST DAY COVERS SING	FIRST DAY COVERS PL. BLK.	MINT SHEET	PLATE BLOCK	UNUSED F/NH	USED
	3245, 3249						
	3246, 3250						
	3247, 3251						
	3248, 3252						
3245	32¢ Evergreen Wreath, self-adhesive	1.95	....	....	....	7.00	.35
3246	32¢ Victorian Wreath, self-adhesive	1.95	....	....	....	7.00	.35
3247	32¢ Chili Pepper Wreath, self-adhesive	1.95	....	....	....	7.00	.35
3248	32¢ Tropical Wreath, self-adhesive	1.95	....	....	....	7.00	.35
3248a	32¢ Christmas Wreaths, self-adhesive, bklt pane of 4	4.00	....	....	....	27.50	....
3248b	same, bklt pane of 5	5.00	....	....	....	35.00	....
3248c	same, bklt pane of 6	5.50	....	....	....	42.50	....
3249-52	32¢ Christmas Wreaths, self-adhesive, 4 varieties, attached	4.00	4.75	21.50(20)	6.50	5.50	3.50
3249	32¢ Evergreen Wreath, self-adhesive	1.95	....	....	....	1.30	.35
3250	32¢ Victorian Wreath, self-adhesive	1.95	....	....	....	1.30	.35
3251	32¢ Chili Pepper Wreath, self-adhesive	1.95	....	....	....	1.30	.35
3252	32¢ Tropical Wreath, sel-adhesive	1.95	....	....	....	1.30	.35
3252b	same, bklt pane of 20	14.50	....	....	....	21.50	....
	3257, 3258						
	3259, 3263						
	3260, 3264, 3265, 3266, 3267, 3268, 3269,						
	3261						
	3262						
3257	(1¢) Weather Vane (white USA)	1.95	3.50	3.75(50)	.45	.20	.20
3258	(1¢) Weather Vane (pale blue USA)	1.95	3.50	3.75(50)	.45	.20	.20
3259	22¢ Uncle Sam, self-adhesive	1.95	4.75	9.50(20)	2.50	.55	.20
3260	(33¢) Uncle Sam's Hat	1.95	4.75	45.00(50)	4.50	1.00	.20
3261	$3.20 Space Shuttle Landing, self-adhesive	7.50	26.50	145.00(20)	35.00	7.50	5.00
3262	$11.75 Piggyback Space Shuttle, self-adhesive	28.50	95.00	500.00(20)	110.00	27.50	10.00
3263	22¢ Uncle Sam, self adhesive coil	1.95	....	....	5.50	.75	.25
	same, plate strip of 5	....	....	....	....	6.50	....
3264	(33¢) Uncle Sam's Hat, coil	1.95	10.00	....	8.00	1.00	.30
	same, plate strip of 5	....	....	....	....	9.50	....
3265	(33¢) Uncle Sam's Hat, self-adhesive coil, die cut 9.9	1.95	....	....	10.00	1.00	.30
	same, plate strip of 5	....	....	....	....	11.00	....
3266	(33¢) Uncle Sam's Hat, self-adhesive coil, die cut 9.7	1.95	....	....	8.00	1.10	.30
	same, plate strip of 5	....	....	....	....	10.00	....
3267	(33¢) Uncle Sam's Hat, self-adhesive, die cut 9.9	1.95	....	....	....	1.10	.30
3267a	same, bklt pane of 10	7.25	....	....	....	11.00	....
3268	(33¢) Uncle Sam's Hat, self-adhesive, die cut 11.2 x 11.1	1.95	....	....	....	1.10	.30
3268a	same, bklt pane of 10	7.25	....	....	....	11.00	....
3268b	same, bklt pane of 20	14.50	....	....	....	21.50	....
3269	(33¢) Uncle Sam's Hat, self-adhesive, die cut 8	1.95	....	....	....	1.10	.30
3269a	same, bklt pane of 18	13.50	....	....	....	19.50	....
	3270, 3271						
3270	(10¢) Eagle, Presorted Std. coil	1.95	....	....	4.00	.35	.20
	same, plate strip of 5	....	....	....	....	4.50	....
3271	(10¢) Eagle, Presorted Std., self-adhesive coil	1.95	....	....	4.00	.40	.20
	same, plate strip of 5	....	....	....	....	4.50	....
	3272						
	3273						
	1999 COMMEMORATIVES						
3272/3369	(3272-73, 3276, 3286-92, 3308-09, 3314-3350, 3352, 3354, 3356-59, 2368-69) 56 varieties	....	....	....	....	55.25	15.50
3272	33¢ Year of the Rabbit	1.95	4.75	21.50(20)	5.00	1.10	.25
3273	33¢ Malcolm X, Civil Rights, self-adhesive	1.95	4.75	19.50(20)	5.00	1.10	.25
	3274						
	3275						
3274	33¢ Love, self-adhesive	1.95	....	....	....	1.10	.25
3274a	same, bklt pane of 20	14.50	....	....	....	20.00	....
3275	55¢ Love, self-adhesive	2.50	....	28.50(20)	6.50	1.50	.40
	3276						
	3277, 3278, 3279, 3280, 3281, 3282						
	3283						
3276	33¢ Hospice Care, self-adhesive	1.95	4.75	16.50(20)	4.00	.90	.20
3277	33¢ Flag and City	1.95	4.75	80.00(100)	4.50	.90	.20
3278	33¢ Flag and City, self-adhesive, die cut 11.1	1.95	4.75	16.50(20)	4.00	.90	.20
3278a	same, bklt pane of 4	4.00	....	....	....	4.50	....
3278b	same, bklt pane of 5	5.00	....	....	....	5.25	....
3278c	same, bklt pane of 6	5.50	....	....	....	6.75	....
3278d	same, bklt pane of 10	7.25	....	....	....	9.00	....
3278e	same, bklt pane of 20	14.50	....	....	....	17.50	....
3278F	33¢ Flag and City, self-adhesive, die cut 11.5x11.75	1.95	....	....	....	1.10	.20
3278Fg	same, bklt pane of 20	14.50	....	....	....	20.00	....
3278i	Flag and City, die cut 11.25	1.95	....	....	....	.90	.20
3278j	same, bklt pane of 10	7.25	....	....	....	8.50	....
3279	33¢ Flag and City, self-adhesive, die cut 9.8	1.95	....	....	....	1.10	.20
3279a	same, bklt pane of 10	7.25	....	....	....	10.50	....
3280	33¢ Flag and City, coil	1.95	....	....	4.50	1.00	.20
	same, plate strip of 5	....	....	....	....	6.50	....
3281	33¢ Flag and City, self-adhesive coil (square corners) large date	1.95	....	....	7.50	1.00	.20
	same, plate strip of 5	....	....	....	....	9.00	....
3281c	same, small date	1.95	....	....	9.00	2.00	.20
	same, plate strip of 5	....	....	....	....	12.50	....

U.S. Postage #3282-3308

SCOTT NO.	DESCRIPTION	FIRST DAY COVERS SING	FIRST DAY COVERS PL. BLK.	MINT SHEET	PLATE BLOCK	UNUSED F/NH	USED
3282	33¢ Flag and City, self-adhesive coil (round corners)	1.95	....	....	8.00	1.10	.20
....	same, plate strip of 5	....	....	....	....	10.00	....
3283	33¢ Flag and Chalkboard, self-adhesive	1.95	....	....	....	.95	.20
3283a	same, bklt pane of 18	13.50	....	....	....	17.00	....
3286	33¢ Irish Immigration	1.95	4.75	16.50(20)	4.00	.90	.25
3287	33¢ Alfred Lunt & Lynn Fontanne, Actors	1.95	4.75	16.50(20)	4.00	.90	.25
3288-92	Arctic Animals, 5 varieties, attached	5.75	....	16.50(15)	12.50(10)	6.00	5.00
3288	33¢ Arctic Hare	1.95	....	....	....	1.30	.40
3289	33¢ Arctic Fox	1.95	....	....	....	1.30	.40
3290	33¢ Snowy Owl	1.95	....	....	....	1.30	.40
3291	33¢ Polar Bear	1.95	....	....	....	1.30	.40
3292	33¢ Gray Wolf	1.95	....	....	....	1.30	.40

3293 SONORAN DESERT

3293a	Cactus wren, brittlebush, teddy bear cholla
3293b	Desert tortoise
3293c	White-winged dove, prickly pear
3293d	Gambel quail
3293e	Saquaro cactus
3293f	Desert mule deer
3293g	Desert cottontail, hedgehog cactus
3293h	Gila monster
3293i	Western diamondback rattlesnake, cactus mouse
3293j	Gila woodpecker

SCOTT NO.	DESCRIPTION	FIRST DAY COVERS SING	FIRST DAY COVERS PL. BLK.	MINT SHEET	PLATE BLOCK	UNUSED F/NH	USED
3293	33¢ Sonoran Desert, 10 varieties, attached, self-adhesive	....	....	9.00(10)	....	9.00	7.50
....	set of singles	18.50	....	....	....	....	5.00
3293v	same, uncut sheet of 60 (6 panes)	....	....	45.00(60)	....	45.00	....
3294	33¢ Blueberries, self-adhesive, die cut 11.2 x 11.7	1.95	....	....	....	1.10	.20
3294a	same, dated "2000"	1.95	....	....	....	1.10	.20
3295	33¢ Raspberries, self-adhesive, die cut 11.2 x 11.7	1.95	....	....	....	1.10	.20
3295a	same, dated "2000"	1.95	....	....	....	1.10	.20
3296	33¢ Strawberries, self-adhesive, die cut 11.2x 11.7	1.95	....	....	....	1.10	.20
3296a	same, dated "2000"	1.95	....	....	....	1.10	.20
3297	33¢ Blackberries, self-adhesive, die cut 11.2 x 11.7	1.95	....	....	....	1.10	.20
3297a	same, bklt pane of 20 (3294-97 x 5 of each)	14.50	....	....	....	20.00	....
3297c	same, dated "2000"	1.95	....	....	....	1.10	.20
3297d	same, bklt pane of 20	14.50	....	....	....	20.00	....
3297e	same, block of 4, (#3294a-96a, 3297c)	4.00	....	....	....	4.25	....
3298	33¢ Blueberries, self-adhesive, die cut 9.5 x 10	1.95	....	....	....	1.20	.35
3299	33¢ Strawberries, self-adhesive, die cut 9.5 x 10	1.95	....	....	....	1.20	.35
3300	33¢ Raspberries, self-adhesive, die cut 9.5 x 10	1.95	....	....	....	1.20	.35
3301	33¢ Blackberries, self-adhesive, die cut 9.5 x 10	1.95	....	....	....	1.20	.35
3301a	same, bklt pane of 4 (3298-3301 x 1)	4.00	....	....	....	4.75	....
3301b	same, bklt pane of 5, (3298, 3299, 3301, 3300 x 2)	5.00	....	....	....	5.75	....
3301c	same, bklt pane of 6, (3300, 3301, 3298 x 2, 3299)	6.00	....	....	....	6.75	....
3302-05	33¢ Berries, self-adhesive coil, strip of 4, attached	4.00	....	....	....	4.50	....
3302	33¢ Blueberries, self-adhesive coil	1.95	....	....	....	1.20	.25
3303	33¢ Raspberries, self-adhesive coil	1.95	....	....	....	1.20	.25
3304	33¢ Blackberries, self-adhesive coil	1.95	....	....	....	1.20	.25
3305	33¢ Strawberries, self-adhesive coil	1.95	....	....	....	1.20	.25
3302-05	33¢ Berries, self-adhesive coil, pl# strip of 5 (3302 x 2, 3303-05 x 1)	10.00	....	....	....	6.50	....
3306	33¢ Daffy Duck, self-adhesive, pane of 10	12.00	....	....	....	9.00	....
3306a	same, single from pane	2.25	....	....	....	1.10	.20
3306b	same, pane of 9 (3306a)	....	....	....	....	7.50	....
3306c	same, pane of 1 (3306a)	7.00	....	....	....	2.25	....
3306v	same, top press sheet of 60 (6 panes)	....	....	80.00(60)	....	80.00	....
....	same, bottom press sheet of 60 w/ plate # (6 panes)	....	....	110.00(60)	....	110.00	....
....	same, pane of 10 from press sheet	....	....	....	....	15.00	....
....	same, pane of 10 from press sheet with plate #	....	....	....	....	85.00	....
....	vert. pair with horiz. gutter	....	....	....	....	5.00	....
....	horiz. pair with vert. gutter	....	....	....	....	10.00	....
3307	33¢ Daffy Duck, self-adhesive, die cut, pane of 10	15.00	....	....	....	11.00	....
3307a	same, single from pane	....	....	....	....	1.10	....
3307b	same, pane of 9 (3307a)	....	....	....	....	8.00	....
3307c	same, pane of 1, imperf.	12.00	....	....	....	3.50	....
3308	33¢ Ayn Rand	1.95	4.75	16.40(20)	4.00	.90	.25

U.S. Postage #3309-3332

SCOTT NO.	DESCRIPTION	FIRST DAY COVERS SING	FIRST DAY COVERS PL. BLK.	MINT SHEET	PLATE BLOCK	UNUSED F/NH	USED
3309	33¢ Cinco De Mayo, self-adhesive	1.95	4.75	16.50(20)	4.00	.90	.20
3310-13	33¢ Tropical Flowers, self-adhesive, 4 varieties, attached	4.00	....	....	....	4.00	3.50
3310	33¢ Bird of Paradise, self-adhesive	1.95	....	....	....	1.25	.25
3311	33¢ Royal Poinciana, self-adhesive	1.95	....	....	....	1.25	.25
3312	33¢ Gloriosa Lily, self-adhesive	1.95	....	....	....	1.25	.25
3313	33¢ Chinese Hibiscus, self-adhesive	1.95	....	....	....	1.25	.25
3313a	same, bklt pane of 20 (3310-13 x 5)	14.50	....	....	....	17.50	
3314	33¢ John & William Bartram, Botanists	1.95	4.75	16.50(20)	4.00	.90	.20
3315	33¢ Prostate Cancer Awareness	1.95	4.75	16.50(20)	4.00	.90	.20
3316	33¢ California Gold Rush	1.95	4.75	16.50(20)	4.00	.90	.20
3317-20	Aquarium Fish, self-adhesive, 4 varieties, attached	4.00	....	20.00(20)	11.00(8)	5.00	4.00
3317	33¢ Yellow fish, red fish, cleaner shrimp	1.95	....	....	....	1.35	.30
3318	33¢ Fish, thermometer	1.95	....	....	....	1.35	.30
3319	33¢ Red fish, blue fish	1.95	....	....	....	1.35	.30
3320	33¢ Fish, heater	1.95	....	....	....	1.35	.30
3321-24	Xtreme Sports, self-adhesive, 4 varieties, attached	4.00	....	20.00(20)	5.00	4.50	3.50
3321	33¢ Skateboarding	1.95	....	....	....	1.25	.35
3322	33¢ BMX biking	1.95	....	....	....	1.25	.35
3323	33¢ Snowboarding	1.95	....	....	....	1.25	.35
3324	33¢ Inline skating	1.95	....	....	....	1.25	.35
3325-28	American Glass, 4 varieties, attached	4.00	....	14.00(15)	5.00	4.50	
3325	33¢ Freeblown glass	1.95	....	....	....	1.30	.35
3326	33¢ Mold-blown glass	1.95	....	....	....	1.30	.35
3327	33¢ Pressed glass	1.95	....	....	....	1.30	.35
3328	33¢ Art glass	1.95	....	....	....	1.30	.35
3329	33¢ James Cagney	1.95	4.75	16.50(20)	4.00	.90	.25
3330	55¢ General William "Billy" Mitchell, self-adhesive	2.50	....	27.50(20)	7.00	1.50	.50
3331	33¢ Honoring Those Who Served, self-adhesive	1.95	....	16.50(20)	4.00	.90	.25
3332	45¢ Universal Postal Union	2.25	5.00	23.50(20)	6.00	1.25	.75

U.S. Postage #3333-3350

SCOTT NO.	DESCRIPTION	FIRST DAY COVERS SING	FIRST DAY COVERS PL. BLK.	MINT SHEET	PLATE BLOCK	UNUSED F/NH	USED
3333-37	33¢ Famous Trains, 5 varieties, attached	5.75	11.00	17.50(20)	9.00(8)	5.00	4.00
3333	33¢ Daylight	1.95	....	....	....	1.20	.25
3334	33¢ Congressional	1.95	....	....	....	1.20	.25
3335	33¢ 20th Century Limited	1.95	....	....	....	1.20	.25
3336	33¢ Hiawatha	1.95	....	....	....	1.20	.25
3337	33¢ Super Chief	1.95	....	....	....	1.20	.25
3333-37v	same, uncut sheet of 120 (6 panes)	....	....	95.00(120)	....	95.00	....
....	block of 8 with vertical gutter	....	....	....	....	17.50	....
....	block of 10 with horiz. gutter	....	....	....	....	20.00	....
....	cross gutter block of 8	....	....	....	....	22.50	....
....	horiz. pair with vert. gutter	....	....	....	....	4.00	....
....	vert. pair with horiz. gutter	....	....	....	....	3.00	....
3338	33¢ Frederick Law Olmstead, Landscape Architect	1.95	4.75	16.50(20)	4.00	.90	.25
3339-44	33¢ Hollywood Composers, 6 varieties, attached	6.25	12.00	17.50(20)	7.00(6)	6.00	4.00
....	same, plate block of 8	....	....	....	8.00	....	....
3339	33¢ Max Steiner	1.95	....	....	....	1.10	.45
3340	33¢ Dimitri Tiomkin	1.95	....	....	....	1.10	.45
3341	33¢ Bernard Herrmann	1.95	....	....	....	1.10	.45
3342	33¢ Franz Waxman	1.95	....	....	....	1.10	.45
3343	33¢ Alfred Newman	1.95	....	....	....	1.10	.45
3344	33¢ Erich Wolfgang Korngold	1.95	....	....	....	1.10	.45
3345-50	33¢ Broadway Songwriters, 6 varieties, attached	6.25	12.00	17.50(20)	7.00(6)	6.00	4.00
....	same, plate block of 8	....	....	....	8.00	....	....
3345	33¢ Lra & George Gershwin	1.95	....	....	....	1.10	.45
3346	33¢ Lerner & Loewe	1.95	....	....	....	1.10	.45
3347	33¢ Lorenz Hart	1.95	....	....	....	1.10	.45
3348	33¢ Rodgers & Hammerstein	1.95	....	....	....	1.10	.45
3349	33¢ Meredith Willson	1.95	....	....	....	1.10	.45
3350	33¢ Frank Loesser	1.95	....	....	....	1.10	.45

3351
INSECTS & SPIDERS

3351a	Black Widow	3351k	Monarch butterfly
3351b	Elderberry longhorn	3351l	Eastern hercules beetle
3351c	Lady beetle	3351m	Bombardier beetle
3351d	Yellow garden spider	3351n	Dung beetle
3351e	Dogbane beetle	3351o	Spotted water beetle
3351f	Flower fly	3351p	True Katydid
3351g	Assassin bug	3351q	Spinybacked spider
3351h	Ebony jewelwing	3351r	Periodical cicada
3351i	Velvet ant	3351s	Scorpionfly
3351j	Monarch caterpillar	3351t	Jumping spider

U.S. Postage #3351-3377a

INSECTS & SPIDERS (continued)

SCOTT NO.	DESCRIPTION	FIRST DAY COVERS SING	FIRST DAY COVERS PL. BLK.	MINT SHEET	PLATE BLOCK	UNUSED F/NH	USED
3351	33¢ Insects & Spiders, 20 varieties, attached	....	....	18.50(20)	....	18.50	14.00
	set of singles	37.50	....	....	....	....	10.00
	same, uncut sheet of 80 (4 panes)	....	....	57.50(80)	....	57.50	....
	same, block of 10 with vert. gutter	....	....	....	....	20.00	....
	same, block of 8 with horiz. gutter	....	....	....	....	20.00	....
	same, cross gutter block of 20	....	....	....	....	35.00	....
	same, vert. pair with horiz. gutter	....	....	....	....	3.00	....
	same, horiz. pair with vert. gutter	....	....	....	....	3.00	....
3352	33¢ Hanukkah, self-adhesive	1.95	4.75	16.50(20)	4.00	.90	.25
3353	22¢ Uncle Sam, coil	1.95	....	....	5.00	.70	.30
	same, plate strip of 5	....	....	....	....	6.00	....
3354	33¢ NATO, 50th Anniv.	1.95	4.75	16.50(20)	4.00	.90	.25
3355	33¢ Madonna & Child, self-adhesive	1.95	....	....	....	1.00	.20
3355a	same, bklt pane of 20	14.50	....	....	....	17.50	....

3356, 3360, 3364   3357, 3361, 3365   3358, 3362, 3366   3359, 3363, 3367

SCOTT NO.	DESCRIPTION	FIRST DAY COVERS SING	FIRST DAY COVERS PL. BLK.	MINT SHEET	PLATE BLOCK	UNUSED F/NH	USED
3356-59	33¢ Christmas Deer, self-adhesive	4.00	....	17.50(20)	5.00	4.00	....
3356	33¢ Christmas Deer, gold & red, self-adhesive	1.95	....	....	....	1.10	.20
3357	33¢ Christmas Deer, gold & blue, self-adhesive	1.95	....	....	....	1.10	.20
3358	33¢ Christmas Deer, gold & purple, self-adhesive	1.95	....	....	....	1.10	.20
3359	33¢ Christmas Deer, gold & green, self-adhesive	1.95	....	....	....	1.10	.20
3360	33¢ Christmas Deer, gold & red, bklt single, self-adhesive	1.95	....	....	....	1.20	.20
3361	33¢ Christmas Deer, gold & blue, bklt single, self-adhesive	1.95	....	....	....	1.20	.20
3362	33¢ Christmas Deer, gold & purple, bklt single, self-adhesive	1.95	....	....	....	1.20	.20
3363	33¢ Christmas Deer, gold & green, bklt single, self-adhesive	1.95	....	....	....	1.20	.20
3363a	same, bklt pane of 20	14.50	....	....	....	20.00	....
3364	33¢ Christmas Deer, gold & red, bklt single, (21x19mm), self-adhesive	1.95	....	....	....	1.75	.40
3365	33¢ Christmas Deer, gold & blue, bklt single, (21x19mm), self-adhesive	1.95	....	....	....	1.75	.40
3366	33¢ Christmas Deer, gold & purple, bklt single, (21x19mm), self-adhesive	1.95	....	....	....	1.75	.40
3367	33¢ Christmas Deer, gold & green, bklt single, (21x19mm), self-adhesive	1.95	....	....	....	1.75	.40
3367a	same, bklt pane of 4 (3364-67 x 1)	4.00	....	....	....	7.50	....
3367b	same, bklt pane of 5 (3364, 3366, 3367, 3365 x 2)	5.00	....	....	....	9.00	....
3367c	same, bklt pane of 6 (3365, 3367, 3364 x 2, 3366)	6.00	....	....	....	11.50	....
3368	33¢ Kwanzaa, self-adhesive	1.95	....	16.50(20)	4.00	.90	.25
3369	33¢ Baby New Year, self-adhesive	1.95	....	16.50(20)	4.00	.90	.25

2000 COMMEMORATIVES

SCOTT NO.	DESCRIPTION	FIRST DAY COVERS SING	FIRST DAY COVERS PL. BLK.	MINT SHEET	PLATE BLOCK	UNUSED F/NH	USED
3370/3446	(3370-72, 3379-90, 3393-3402 3414-17, 3438-46) 38 varieties	....	....	....	....	37.50	11.00
3370	33¢ Year of the Dragon	1.95	4.75	17.50(20)	4.50	1.00	.25
3371	33¢ Patricia Roberts Harris, self-adhesive	1.95	....	17.50(20)	4.50	1.00	.25
3372	33¢ Los Angeles Class Submarine (microprint USPS)	1.95	4.75	17.50(20)	4.50	1.00	.25
3373	22¢ S Class Submarine	1.75	....	....	....	....	.75
3374	33¢ Los Angeles Class Submarine (no microprint)	1.95	....	....	....	....	.75
3375	55¢ Ohio Class Submarine	2.50	....	....	....	....	1.25
3376	60¢ USS Holland Submarine	2.50	....	....	....	....	1.25
3377	$3.20 Gato Class Submarine	7.50	....	....	....	....	6.50
3377a	same, bklt pane of 5, (#3373-77)	12.00	....	....	....	25.00	....
	same, complete booklet of 2 panes	....	....	....	....	45.00	....

U.S. Postage #3378-3392c

PACIFIC COAST RAIN FOREST

3378 – Image labeled 3378

PACIFIC COAST RAIN FOREST

3378a	Harlequin duck	
3378b	Dwarf oregongrape, snail-eating ground beetle	
3378c	American dipper	
3378d	Cutthroat trout	
3378e	Roosevelt elk	
3378f	Winter wren	
3378g	Pacific giant salamander, Rough-skinned newt	
3378h	Western tiger swallowtail	
3378i	Douglas squirrel, foliose lichen	
3378j	Foliose lichen, banana slug	

Scott No.	Description	FDC Sing	FDC Pl.Blk	Mint Sheet	Plate Block	Unused F/NH	Used
3378	33¢ Pacific Coast Rain Forest, 10 varieties, attached, self-adhesive	....	....	9.50(10)	....	9.50	8.50
	set of singles	18.50	....	....	....	....	6.00
3378v	same, uncut sheet of 60 (6 panes)	....	....	60.00(60)	....	60.00	....

3379, 3380, 3381, 3382, 3383

Scott No.	Description	FDC Sing	FDC Pl.Blk	Mint Sheet	Plate Block	Unused F/NH	Used
3379-83	33¢ Louise Nevelson, (1899-1988), Sculptor, 5 varieties, attached	5.75	11.00	22.50(20)	11.00(10)	5.00	4.00
3379	33¢ Silent Music I	1.95	....	....	....	1.20	.40
3380	33¢ Royal Tide I	1.95	....	....	....	1.20	.40
3381	33¢ Black Chord	1.95	....	....	....	1.20	.40
3382	33¢ Nightsphere-Light	1.95	....	....	....	1.20	.40
3383	33¢ Dawn's Wedding Chapel I	1.95	....	....	....	1.20	.40

3384 – Eagle Nebula
3385 – Ring Nebula
3386 – Lagoon Nebula
3387 – Egg Nebula
3388 – Galaxy NGC 1316

Scott No.	Description	FDC Sing	FDC Pl.Blk	Mint Sheet	Plate Block	Unused F/NH	Used
3384-88	33¢ Hubble Space Telescope Images, 5 varieties, attached	5.75	11.00	22.50(20)	11.00(10)	5.00	4.00
3384	33¢ Eagle Nebula	1.95	....	....	....	1.20	.40
3385	33¢ Ring Nebula	1.95	....	....	....	1.20	.40
3386	33¢ Lagoon Nebula	1.95	....	....	....	1.20	.40
3387	33¢ Egg Nebula	1.95	....	....	....	1.20	.40
3388	33¢ Galaxy NGC1316	1.95	....	....	....	1.20	.40

3389 – American Samoa
3390 – Library of Congress

Scott No.	Description	FDC Sing	FDC Pl.Blk	Mint Sheet	Plate Block	Unused F/NH	Used
3389	33¢ American Samoa	1.95	4.75	17.50(20)	4.50	1.00	.25
3390	33¢ Library of Congress	1.95	4.75	17.50(20)	4.50	1.00	.25

3391, 3392

Scott No.	Description	FDC Sing	FDC Pl.Blk	Mint Sheet	Plate Block	Unused F/NH	Used
3391	33¢ Road Runner & Wile E. Coyote, self-adhesive, pane of 10	12.00	....	....	....	9.50	....
3391a	same, single from pane	2.25	....	....	....	1.10	.25
3391b	same, pane of 9 (3391a)	....	....	....	....	6.50	....
3391c	same, pane of 1 (3391a)	7.00	....	....	....	2.75	....
	same, top press sheet of 60 (6 panes) w/ plate #	....	....	80.00(60)	....	80.00	....
	same, bottom press sheet of 60 (6 panes) w/ plate #	....	....	80.00(60)	....	80.00	....
	same, pane of 10 from press sheet	....	....	....	....	15.00	....
	same, 2 panes of 10 with plate # on front	....	....	....	....	35.00	....
	same, cross gutter block of 9	....	....	....	....	30.00	....
	vert. pair with horiz. gutter	....	....	....	....	4.00	....
	horiz. pair with vert. gutter	....	....	....	....	8.00	....
3392	33¢ Road Runner & Wile E. Coyote, self-adhesive, die cut, pane of 10	15.00	....	....	....	11.00	....
3392a	same, single from pane	....	....	....	....	1.10	....
3392b	same, pane of 9 (3392a)	....	....	....	....	9.00	....
3392c	same, pane of 1, imperf.	12.00	....	....	....	3.00	....

ORDER BY MAIL, PHONE (800) 546-2995
OR FAX (256) 246-1116

U.S. Postage #3393-3407

SCOTT NO.	DESCRIPTION	FIRST DAY COVERS SING	FIRST DAY COVERS PL. BLK.	MINT SHEET	PLATE BLOCK	UNUSED F/NH	USED
3393-96	33¢ Distinguished Soldiers, 4 varieties, attached	4.00	5.00	20.00(20)	5.00	4.50	3.50
3393	33¢ Major General John L. Hines (1868-1968)	1.95	....	....	....	1.25	.30
3394	33¢ General Omar N. Bradley (1893-1981)	1.95	....	....	....	1.25	.30
3395	33¢ Sergeant Alvin C. York (1887-1964)	1.95	....	....	....	1.25	.30
3396	33¢ Second Lieutenant Audie L. Murphy (1924-71)	1.95	....	....	....	1.25	.30
3397	33¢ Summer Sports	1.95	4.75	17.50(20)	4.50	1.00	.25
3398	33¢ Adoption, self-adhesive	1.95	....	17.50(20)	4.50	1.00	.25
3399-3402	33¢ Youth Team Sports, 4 varieites, attached	4.00	5.00	17.50(20)	5.00	4.50	3.50
3399	33¢ Basketball	1.95	....	....	....	1.25	.30
3400	33¢ Football	1.95	....	....	....	1.25	.30
3401	33¢ Soccer	1.95	....	....	....	1.25	.30
3402	33¢ Baseball	1.95	....	....	....	1.25	.30

3403

THE STARS AND STRIPES

3403a	Sons of Liberty Flag, 1775	3403k	Star-Spangled Banner, 1814
3403b	New England, 1775	3403l	Bennington Flag, c.1820
3403c	Forster Flag, 1775	3403m	Great Star Flag, 1837
3403d	Continental Colors, 1776	3403n	29-Star Flag, 1847
3403e	Francis Hopkinson Flag, 1777	3403o	Fort Sumter Flag, 1861
3403f	Brandywine Flag, 1777	3403p	Centennial Flag, 1876
3403g	John Paul Jones Flag, 1779	3403q	38-Star Flag
3403h	Pierre L'Enfant Flag, 1783	3403r	Peace Flag, 1891
3403i	Indian Peace Flag, 1803	3403s	48-Star Flag, 1912
3403j	Easton Flag, 1814	3403t	50-Star Flag, 1960

SCOTT NO.	DESCRIPTION	FIRST DAY COVERS SING	FIRST DAY COVERS PL. BLK.	MINT SHEET	PLATE BLOCK	UNUSED F/NH	USED
3403	33¢ The Stars & Stripes, 20 varieties, attached, self-adhesive	....	....	19.50(20)	....	19.50	13.00
	set of singles	37.50	....	....	....	....	10.00
3403v	same, uncut sheet of 120 (6 panes)	....	....	120.00(120)	....	120.00	....
....	same, horiz. block of 8 with vert. gutter	....	....	....	....	18.00	....
....	same, vert. block of 10 with horiz. gutter	....	....	....	....	20.00	....
....	same, cross gutter block of 20	....	....	....	....	40.00	....
....	vert. pair with horiz. gutter	....	....	....	....	4.50	....
....	horiz. pair with vert. gutter	....	....	....	....	4.50	....

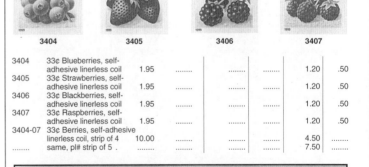

3404	33¢ Blueberries, self-adhesive linerless coil	1.95	....	....	....	1.20	.50
3405	33¢ Strawberries, self-adhesive linerless coil	1.95	....	....	....	1.20	.50
3406	33¢ Blackberries, self-adhesive linerless coil	1.95	....	....	....	1.20	.50
3407	33¢ Raspberries, self-adhesive linerless coil	1.95	....	....	....	1.20	.50
3404-07	33¢ Berries, self-adhesive linerless coil, strip of 4	10.00	....	....	....	4.50	....
....	same, pl# strip of 5	....	....	....	....	7.50	....

Insist on Genuine
H.E. Harris Products
Backed by
89 years of experience

ACCEPT NO SUBSTITUTES!

U.S. Postage #3408-3413

SCOTT NO.	DESCRIPTION	FIRST DAY COVERS SING	FIRST DAY COVERS PL. BLK.	MINT SHEET	PLATE BLOCK	UNUSED F/NH	USED

3408

LEGENDS OF BASEBALL

3408a	Jackie Robinson		3408k	Lefty Grove
3408b	Eddie Collins		3408l	Tris Speaker
3408c	Christy Mathewson		3408m	Cy Young
3408d	Ty Cobb		3408n	Jimmie Foxx
3408e	George Sisler		3408o	Pie Traynor
3408f	Rogers Hornsby		3408p	Satchel Paige
3408g	Mickey Cochrane		3408q	Honus Wagner
3408h	Babe Ruth		3408r	Josh Gibson
3408i	Walter Johnson		3408s	Dizzy Dean
3408j	Roberto Clemente		3408t	Lou Gehrig

SCOTT NO.	DESCRIPTION	SING	PL. BLK.	MINT SHEET	PLATE BLOCK	UNUSED F/NH	USED
3408	33¢ Legends of Baseball, 20 varieties, attached, self-adhesive			19.50(20)		19.50	15.00
	set of singles	37.50					12.00
3408v	same, uncut sheet of 120 (6 panes)			120.00(120)		120.00	
	cross gutter block of 20					40.00	
	block of 8 with vert. gutter					22.50	
	block of 10 with horiz. gutter					22.50	
	vert. pair with horiz. gutter					3.50	
	horiz. pair with vert. gutter					4.50	

3409

3409	60¢ Probing the Vastness of Space, souvenir sheet of 6	10.00				10.00	9.25
3409a	60¢ Hubble Space Telescope	2.50				1.75	1.00
3409b	60¢ National Radio Astronomy Observatory	2.50				1.75	1.00
3409c	60¢ Keck Observatory	2.50				1.75	1.00
3409d	60¢ Cerro Tololo Inter-American Observatory	2.50				1.75	1.00
3409e	60¢ Mt. Wilson Observatory	2.50				1.75	1.00
3409f	60¢ Arecibo Observatory	2.50				1.75	1.00

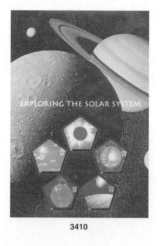

3410

3411

3410	$1 Exploring the Solar System, souvenir sheet of 5	13.50				15.00	12.00
3410a	$1 Solar eclipse	3.50				3.25	2.50
3410b	$1 Cross-section of sun	3.50				3.25	2.50
3410c	$1 Sun and Earth	3.50				3.25	2.50
3410d	$1 Sun & solar flare	3.50				3.25	2.50
3410e	$1 Sun with clouds	3.50				3.25	2.50
3411	$3.20 Escaping the Gravity of Earth hologram, souvenir sheet of 2	16.50				17.50	13.50
3411a	$3.20 International Space Station hologram, from souvenir sheet	7.50				8.75	5.00
3411b	$3.20 Astronauts Working hologram, from souvenir sheet	7.50				8.75	5.00

3412

3412	$11.75 Space Achievement and Exploration hologram, souvenir sheet of 1	27.50				30.00	22.50

3413

3413	$11.75 Landing on the Moon hologram, souvenir sheet of 1	27.50				30.00	22.50

U.S. Postage #3414-3446

SCOTT NO.	DESCRIPTION	FIRST DAY COVERS SING	FIRST DAY COVERS PL. BLK.	MINT SHEET	PLATE BLOCK	UNUSED F/NH	USED
3414-17	33¢ Stampin' the Future, 4 varieties, attached	4.00	5.00	20.00(20)	9.50(8)	4.50	3.50
3414	33¢ Designed by Zachary Canter	1.95	....	....	....	1.25	.30
3415	33¢ Designed by Sarah Lipsey	1.95	....	....	....	1.25	.30
3416	33¢ Designed by Morgan Hill	1.95	....	....	....	1.25	.30
3417	33¢ Designed by Ashley Young	1.95	....	....	....	1.25	.30

2000-2003 DISTINGUISHED AMERICANS

SCOTT NO.	DESCRIPTION	FDC SING	FDC PL. BLK.	MINT SHEET	PLATE BLOCK	UNUSED F/NH	USED
3420	10¢ Joseph W. Stilwell	1.95	4.00	5.00(20)	1.50	.25	.20
3426	33¢ Claude Pepper	1.95	4.75	17.50(20)	4.50	1.00	.25
3431	76¢ Hattie W. Caraway, die cut 11	2.95	5.50	33.50(20)	8.00	1.75	.50
3432	76¢ Hattie W. Caraway, die cut 11.5 x 11	....	....	75.00(20)	18.50	4.00	4.00
3433	83¢ Edna Ferber, die cut 11 x 11.5	2.95	5.50	38.00(20)	9.00	1.95	.75
3434	83¢ Edna Ferber, die cut 11.25 (2003)	2.95	5.50	38.00(20)	9.00	1.95	.75
3438	33¢ California Statehood, self-adhesive	1.95	....	17.50(20)	4.50	1.00	.25

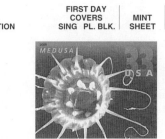

3443

SCOTT NO.	DESCRIPTION	FDC SING	FDC PL. BLK.	MINT SHEET	PLATE BLOCK	UNUSED F/NH	USED
3439-43	33¢ Deep Sea Creatures, 5 varieties attached	5.75	11.00	17.50(20)	....	5.00	4.00
3439	33¢ Fanfin Anglerfish	1.95	....	....	....	1.20	.35
3440	33¢ Sea Cucumber	1.95	....	....	....	1.20	.35
3441	33¢ Fangtooth	1.95	....	....	....	1.20	.35
3442	33¢ Amphipod	1.95	....	....	....	1.20	.35
3443	33¢ Medusa	1.95	....	....	....	1.20	.35

3444   3445   3446

SCOTT NO.	DESCRIPTION	FDC SING	FDC PL. BLK.	MINT SHEET	PLATE BLOCK	UNUSED F/NH	USED
3444	33¢ Thomas Wolfe	1.95	4.75	17.50(20)	4.50	1.00	.25
3445	33¢ White House	1.95	4.75	17.50(20)	4.50	1.00	.25
3446	33¢ Edward G. Robinson	1.95	4.75	17.50(20)	4.50	1.00	.25
....	same, uncut sheet of 120 (6 panes)	....	....	110.00(120)	....	110.00	....
....	cross gutter block of 8	....	....	....	....	25.00	....
....	block of 8 with vert. gutter	....	....	....	....	22.50	....
....	horiz. pair with vert. gutter	....	....	....	....	4.50	....
....	vert. pair with horiz. gutter	....	....	....	....	3.50	....

H.E. Harris & Co.®

LIBERTY® I Supplements

Issued Annually

2001

UNITED STATES LIBERTY® I SUPPLEMENT

Liberty I Supplements include commemorative and regular issues from the United States. Update your album today!

Item #	Year	Retail Price
90922141	2004 Liberty I Supplement	$8.95
90922056	2003 Liberty I Supplement	$7.95
90921806	2002 Liberty I Supplement	$7.95
90921312	2001 Liberty I Supplement	$7.95
90921629	2000 Liberty I Supplement	$7.95
5HRS98	1999 Liberty I Supplement	$7.95
5HRS91	1998 Liberty I Supplement	$7.95
5HRS81	1997 Liberty I Supplement	$7.95
5HRS74	1996 Liberty I Supplement	$7.95

Order from your local dealer or direct from Whitman Publishing, LLC.

U.S. Postage #3447-3481

SCOTT NO.	DESCRIPTION	FIRST DAY COVERS SING	FIRST DAY COVERS PL. BLK.	MINT SHEET	PLATE BLOCK	UNUSED F/NH	USED
	3447						
	3448, 3449, 3450,						
	3451, 3452, 3453						
3447	10¢ New York Public Library Lion, coil	1.95			4.00	.50	.20
....	same, pl# strip of 5 .	....	....	....	....	5.00	....
3448	(34¢) Flag over Farm	1.95	4.75	17.50(20)	4.50	1.00	.45
3449	(34¢) Flag over Farm, self-adhesive	1.95	4.75	20.00(20)	5.50	1.00	.25
3450	(34¢) Flag over Farm, self-adhesive	1.95	....	....	....	1.00	.20
3450a	same, bklt pane of 18	14.00				17.50	
3451	(34¢) Statue of Liberty, self-adhesive	1.95	....	....	....	1.00	.20
3451a	same, bklt pane of 20	14.50				18.50	
3451b	same, bklt pane of 4	4.00				4.50	
3451c	same, bklt pane of 6	5.50				6.50	
3452	(34¢) Statue of Liberty, coil	1.95	....	....	7.00	1.00	.20
....	same, pl# strip of 5 .	....				9.00	
3453	(34¢) Statue of Liberty, self-adhesive coil	1.95	....	....	10.00	1.00	.20
....	same, pl# strip of 5 .	....				12.00	
	3454, 3458, 3465						
	3455, 3459, 3464						
	3456, 3460, 3463						
	3457, 3461, 3462						
3454-57	(34¢) Flowers, self-adhesive, 4 varieties attached	4.25				4.50	3.50
3454	(34¢) Fressia, self-adhesive, die cut 10.25 x 10.75	1.95				1.20	.25
3455	(34¢) Symbidium Orchid, self-adhesive, die cut 10.25 x 10.75	1.95				1.20	.25
3456	(34¢) Longiflorum Lily, self-adhesive, die cut 10.25 x 10.75	1.95				1.20	.25
3457	(34¢) Asian Hydrid, self-adhesive, die cut 10.25 x 10.75	1.95				1.20	.25
3457b	same, bklt pane of 4 (3454-57)	4.00				5.00	
3457c	same, bklt pane of 6 (3456, 3457, 3454 x 2 3455 x 2)	5.50				7.00	
3457d	same, bklt pane of 6 (3454, 3455, 3456 x 2 3457 x 2)	5.50				7.00	
3457e	(34¢) Flowers, bklt pane of 20, self-adhesive (5 each 3457 + label)	14.50				20.00	
3458-61	(34¢) Flowers, self-adhesive, 4 varieties attached	4.25				12.50	
3458	(34¢) Fressia, bklt single, self-adhesive, die cut 11.5 x 11.75	1.95				3.25	.50
3459	(34¢) Symbidium Orchid, bklt single, self-adhesive, die cut 11.5 x 11.75	1.95				3.25	.50
3460	(34¢) Longiflorum Lily, bklt single, self-adhesive, die cut 11.5 x 11.75	1.95				3.25	.50
3461	(34¢) Asian Hybrid Lily, bklt single, self-adhesive, die cut 11.5 x 11.75	1.95				3.25	.50
3461b	same, bklt pane of 20, self-adhesive (2 each 3461a, 3 each 3457a)	14.50				38.00	
3461c	same, bklt pane of 20, self-adhesive (2 each 3457a, 3 each 3461a)	14.50				50.00	
3462	(34¢) Longiflorum Lily, self-adhesive coil	1.95				1.60	.40
3463	(34¢) Asian Hybrid Lily, self-adhesive coil	1.95				1.60	.40
3464	(34¢) Symbidium Orchid, self-adhesive coil	1.95				1.60	.40
3465	(34¢) Fressia, self-adhesive coil	1.95				1.60	.40
3462-65	(34¢) Flowers, self-adhesive coil, strip of 4	4.25				6.50	
....	same, pl# strip of 5 .	....				12.00	

SCOTT NO.	DESCRIPTION	FIRST DAY COVERS SING	FIRST DAY COVERS PL. BLK.	MINT SHEET	PLATE BLOCK	UNUSED F/NH	USED
	3466, 3476, 3477, 3485						
	3467, 3468, 3475, 3484, 3484A						
	3468A, 3475A						
	3469, 3470						
	3471						
	3471A						

2001 REGULAR ISSUES

SCOTT NO.	DESCRIPTION	FIRST DAY COVERS SING	FIRST DAY COVERS PL. BLK.	MINT SHEET	PLATE BLOCK	UNUSED F/NH	USED
3466	34¢ Statue of Liberty, self-adhesive coil, die cut 9.75 (round corners)	1.95	....	....	7.00	1.10	.20
....	same, pl# strip of 5 .	....	....	....	....	9.00	....
3467	21¢ Buffalo	1.95	4.75	60.00(100)	5.00	.65	.20
3468	21¢ Buffalo. self-adhesive	1.95	4.75	12.00(20)	3.00	.65	.20
3468A	23¢ George Washington, self-adhesive	1.95	4.75	12.00(20)	2.75	.65	.20
3469	34¢ Flag over Farm	1.95	4.75	85.00(100)	6.50	1.00	.20
3470	34¢ Flag over Farm, self-adhesive	1.95	4.75	17.50(20)	4.50	.80	.20
3471	55¢ Eagle, self-adhesive	2.50	5.00	27.50(20)	7.00	1.50	.50
3471A	57¢ Eagle, self-adhesive	2.50	5.00	27.50(20)	7.00	1.50	.50
	3472						
	3473						
3472	$3.50 Capitol Dome, self-adhesive	8.00	30.00	175.00(20)	45.00	10.00	5.00
3473	$12.25 Washington Monument, self-adhesive	30.00	98.50	550.00(20)	125.00	30.00	11.00
3475	21¢ Buffalo, self-adhesive coil	1.95	....	....	5.00	.65	.30
....	same, pl# strip of 5 .	....				6.00	
3475A	23¢ George Washington, self-adhesive coil	1.95	....	....	....	.70	.30
....	same, pl# strip of 5 .	....				6.00	
3476	34¢ Statue of Liberty, coil	1.95	....	....	6.00	1.00	.40
....	same, pl# strip of 5 .	....				7.00	
3477	34¢ Statue of Liberty, self-adhesive coil die cut 9.75 (square corners)	1.95	....	....	3.25	1.00	.20
....	same, pl# strip of 5 .	....				6.75	
	3478, 3489						
	3479, 3490						
	3480, 3488						
	3481, 3487						
3478	34¢ Longiflorum, self-adhesive coil	1.95	....	....	....	1.00	.25
3479	34¢ Asain Hybrid Lily, self-adhesive coil	1.95	....	....	....	1.00	.25
3480	34¢ Symbidium Orchid, self-adhesive coil	1.95	....	....	....	1.00	.25
3481	34¢ Fressia, self-adhesive coil	1.95	....	....	....	1.00	.25
3478-81	34¢ Flowers, self-adhesive, coil, strip of 4	4.25	....	....	....	4.50	
....	same, pl# strip of 5 .	....				7.00	

U.S. Postage #3482-3501

SCOTT NO.	DESCRIPTION	FIRST DAY COVERS SING	FIRST DAY COVERS PL. BLK.	MINT SHEET	PLATE BLOCK	UNUSED F/NH	USED

3482, 3483 — 3491, 3493 — 3492, 3494 — 3495

3482	20¢ George Washington, self-adhesive, die cut 11.25	1.95				.65	.30
3482a	same, bklt pane of 10	5.50				6.25	
3482b	same, bklt pane of 4, die cut 11.25 x 11	3.00				3.00	
3482c	same, bklt pane of 6, die cut 11.25 x 11	4.00				4.00	
3483	20¢ George Washington, self-adhesive, die cut 10.5 x 11.25	1.95				2.75	.20
3483a	same, bklt pane of 4 (2 each 3482-3483)	3.00				11.00	
3483b	same, bklt pane of 6 (3 each 3482-3483)	4.00				10.00	
3483c	same, bklt pane of 10, die cut 10.5 x 11 (3482 x 5 at L, 3483 x 5 at R)	5.50				16.50	
3483d	same, bklt pane of 4 (2 each 3482-3483), die cut 11.25 x 11					7.50	
3483e	same, bklt pane of 6 (2 each 3482-3483), die cut 11.25 x 11					10.00	
3483f	same, bklt pane of 10 (5 each 3482-3483), die cut 11.25 x 11					16.50	
3483g	pair, 3482 at left, 3483 at right					3.50	
3483h	pair 3483 at left, 3482 at right					3.50	
3484	21¢ Buffalo, self-adhesive, die cut 11.25	1.95				.65	.35
3484b	same, bklt pane of 4	3.00				2.75	
3484c	same, bklt pane of 6	4.00				4.00	
3484d	same, bklt pane of 10	5.50				6.50	
3484A	21¢ Buffalo, self-adhesive, die cut 10.5 X 11.25	1.95				2.50	.50
3484Ae	same, bklt pane of 4 (3484 x 2 at L, 3484A x 2 at R)					8.50	
3484Af	same, bklt pane of 6 (3484 x 3 at L, 3484A x 3 at R)					12.00	
3484Ag	same, bklt pane of 10 (3484 x 5 at L, 3484A x 5 at R)					13.50	
3484Ah	same, bklt pane of 4 (3484A x 2 at L, 3484 x 2 at R)					8.50	
3484Ai	same, bklt pane of 6 (3484A x 3 at L, 3484 x 3 at R)					12.00	
3484Aj	same, bklt pane of 10 (3484A x 5 at L, 3484 x 5 at R)					13.50	
3484Ak	same, pair (3484 at L, 3484A at R)					3.50	
3484Al	same, pair (3484A at L, 3484 at R)					3.50	
3485	34¢ Statue of Liberty, self-adhesive	1.95				1.00	.20
3485a	same, bklt pane of 10	7.25				9.50	
3485b	same, bklt pane of 20	14.50				18.50	
3485c	same, bklt pane of 4	4.00				4.50	
3485d	same, bklt pane of 6	5.50				6.50	
3487-90	34¢ Flowers, self-adhesive 4 varieties attached	4.25				4.50	2.50
3487	34¢ Fressia, self-adhesive, die cut 10.25 x 10.75	1.95				1.20	.25
3488	34¢ Symbidium Orchid, self-adhesive, die cut 10.25 x 10.75	1.95				1.20	.25
3498	34¢ Longiflorum Lily, self-adhesive, die cut 10.25 x 10.75	1.95				1.20	.25
3490	34¢ Asian Hybrid Lily, self-adhesive, die cut 10.25 x 10.75	1.95				1.20	.25
3490b	same, bklt pane of 4 (3487-90 x 1)	4.00				5.00	
3490c	same, bklt pane of 6 (3489-3490, 3487 x 2, 3488 x 2)	5.50				7.50	
3490d	same, bklt pane of 6 (3487-3488, 3498 x 2 3490 x 2)	5.50				7.50	
3490e	same, bklt pane of 20 (3487-90 x 5 + label)	14.50				22.50	
3491	34¢ Apple, self-adhesive	1.95				1.00	.25
3492	34¢ Orange, self-adhesive	1.95				1.00	.25
3491-92	34¢ Apple & Orange, Pair	2.50				2.00	
3492b	34¢ Apple & Orange, bklt pane of 20, self-adhesive	14.50				19.50	
3493	34¢ Apple, self-adhesive, die cut 11.5 x 10.75	1.95				1.25	.35
3494	34¢ Orange, self-adhesive, die cut 11.5 x 10.75	1.95				1.25	.35
3493-94	34¢ Apple & Orange, Pair	2.50				2.50	
3494b	same, bklt pane of 4 (3493 x 2, 3494 x 2)	4.00				6.50	
3494c	same, bklt pane of 6 (3493 x 3, 3494 x 3) (3493 at UL)	5.50				7.50	
3494d	same, bklt pane of 6 (3493 x 3, 3494 x 3) (3494 at UL)	5.50				7.50	
3495	32¢ Flag over Fram, self-adhesive	1.95				1.00	.30
3495a	same, ATM bklt pane of 18	14.00				17.50	

3496 — 3497, 3498 — 3499

3496	(34¢) LOVE, self-adhesive, die cut 11.75	1.95				1.10	.25
3496a	same, bklt pane of 20	14.50				21.50	
3497	34¢ LOVE, self-adhesive, die cut 11.25	1.95				1.00	.25
3497a	same, bklt pane of 20	14.50				19.50	
3498	34¢ LOVE, self-adhesive, die cut 11.5 x 10.75	1.95				1.10	.20
3498a	same, bklt pane of 4	4.00				4.50	
3498b	same, bklt pane of 6	5.50				6.50	
3499	55¢ LOVE, self-adhesive	2.50	5.00	27.50(20)	6.50	1.50	.50

3500

3501

2001 COMMEMORATIVES

3500/3548	(3500-01, 3503-04, 3507-19, 3521, 3523-33, 3536-40, 3545-48) 38 varieties					38.40	11.95
3500	34¢ Year of the Snake	1.95	4.75	22.50(20)	5.00	1.20	.25
3501	34¢ Roy Wilkins, self-adhesive	1.95	4.75	17.50(20)	4.50	1.00	.25

3502

AMERICAN ILLUSTRATORS

3502a	Marine Corps poster	3502k	"Galahad's Departure"
3502b	"Interlude (The Lute Players)"	3502l	"The First Lesson"
3502c	Advertisement for Arrow Collars and Shirts	3502m	Illustration for cover of McCall's
3502d	Advertisement for Carrier Corp. Refrigeration	3502n	"Back Home for Keeps"
3502e	Advertisement for Luxite Hosiery	3502o	"Something for Supper"
3502f	Illustration for correspondence school lesson	3502p	"A Dash for the Timber"
3502g	"Br'er Rabbit"	3502q	Illustration for "Moby Dick"
3502h	"An Attack on a Galleon"	3502r	"Captain Bill Bones"
3502i	Kewpie and Kewpie Doodle Dog	3502s	Illustration for The Saturday Evening Post
3502j	Illustration for cover of True Magazine	3502t	"The Girl He Left Behind"

U.S. Postage #3502-3519

SCOTT NO.	DESCRIPTION	FIRST DAY COVERS SING	FIRST DAY COVERS PL. BLK.	MINT SHEET	PLATE BLOCK	UNUSED F/NH	USED
	AMERICAN ILLUSTRATORS (Continued)						
3502	34¢ American Illustrators, 20 varieties, attached, self-adhesive	....	....	20.00(20)	....	20.00	15.00
	set of singles	37.50	....	....	....	....	9.50
3502v	same, uncut sheet of 80 (4 panes)	....	....	85.00(80)	....	85.00	....
	cross gutter block of 20	....	....	....	....	40.00	....
	block of 8 with horiz. gutter	....	....	....	....	22.50	....
	block of 10 with vert. gutter	....	....	....	....	22.50	....
	vert. pair with horiz. gutter	....	....	....	....	4.00	....
	horiz. pair with vert. gutter	....	....	....	....	4.00	....
3503	34¢ Diabetes Awareness	1.95	4.75	17.50(20)	4.50	1.00	.25
3504	34¢ Nobel Prize Centenary	1.95	4.75	17.50(20)	4.50	1.00	.25
3505	1¢-80¢ Pan-American Expo. Invert Souvenir Sheet of 7	7.00	....	....	....	10.00	8.50
	same, uncut sheet of 28 (4 panes)	....	....	....	....	45.00	....

GREAT PLAINS PRAIRIE

3506a	Pronghorns, Canada geese	3506f	Western Meadowlark, camel cricket, prairie coneflowers, prairie wild flowers
3506b	Burrowing owls, American buffalos		
3506c	American buffalo, Black-tailed prairie dogs, wild alfalfa	3506g	Badger, Harvester ants
		3506h	Eastern short-horned lizard, plains gopher
3506d	Black-tailed prairie dogs, American Buffalo	3506i	Plains spadefoot, dung beetle, prairie roses
3506e	Painted lady butterfly, American buffalo, prairie coneflowers, prairie wild roses	3506j	Two-striped grasshopper, Ord's kangaroo rat

SCOTT NO.	DESCRIPTION	FIRST DAY COVERS SING	FIRST DAY COVERS PL. BLK.	MINT SHEET	PLATE BLOCK	UNUSED F/NH	USED
3506	34¢ Great Plains Prairie, 10 varieties, attached, self-adhesive	....	....	7.50(10)	....	9.50	7.50
	set of singles	19.50	....	....	....	....	5.00
3506v	same, uncut sheet of 60 (6 panes)	....	....	60.00(60)	....	60.00	....
3507	34¢ Peanuts, self-adhesive	1.95	4.75	28.50(20)	7.00	1.50	.25
3508	34¢ US Veterans, self-adhesive	1.95	4.75	17.50(20)	4.50	1.00	.25
3509	34¢ Frida Kahlo	1.95	4.75	17.50(20)	4.50	1.00	.25

BASEBALL'S LEGENDARY PLAYING FIELDS

3510	Ebbets Field	3515	Forbes Field
3511	Tiger Stadium	3516	Fenway Field
3512	Crosley Field	3517	Comiskey Park
3513	Yankee Stadium	3518	Shibe Park
3514	Polo Grounds	3519	Wrigley Field

SCOTT NO.	DESCRIPTION	FIRST DAY COVERS SING	FIRST DAY COVERS PL. BLK.	MINT SHEET	PLATE BLOCK	UNUSED F/NH	USED
3510-19	34¢ Baseball's Legendary Playing Fields, 10 varieties, self-adhesive	7.25	....	19.50(20)	11.00(10)	10.00	8.50
	set of singles	19.50	....	....	....	....	5.00
3510-19v	same, uncut sheet of 160 (8 panes)	....	....	160.00(160)	....	160.00	....
	cross gutter block of 12	....	....	....	....	25.00	....
	block of 10 with vert. gutter	....	....	....	....	13.00	....
	block of 4 with horiz. gutter	....	....	....	....	6.00	....
	vert. pair with horiz. gutter	....	....	....	....	2.50	....
	horiz. pair with vert. gutter	....	....	....	....	2.50	....

U.S. Postage #3520-3540

SCOTT NO.	DESCRIPTION	FIRST DAY COVERS SING	PL. BLK.	MINT SHEET	PLATE BLOCK	UNUSED F/NH	USED
3520	(10¢) Atlas Statue, coil self-adhesive, die cut 8.5	1.95	....	....	4.00	.30	.25
	same, pl# strip of 5 .	....	....	....	....	4.50	....
3521	34¢ Leonard Bernstein	1.95	4.75	17.50(20)	4.50	1.00	.25
3522	(15¢) Woody Wagon, self-adhesive coil . .	1.95	....	....	4.00	.50	.20
	same, pl# strip of 5 .	....	....	....	....	5.00	....
3523	34¢ Lucille Ball, self-adhesive	1.95	4.75	23.50(20)	6.00	1.25	.25
3523v	same, uncut sheet of 180 (9 panes)	....	....	200.00(180)	....	200.00	....
	cross gutter block of 8	....	....	....	....	30.00	....
	block of 8 with vert. gutter	....	....	....	....	22.50	....
	block of 10 with horiz. gutter	....	....	....	....	22.50	....
	vert. pair with horiz. gutter	....	....	....	....	4.00	....
	horiz. pair with vert. gutter	....	....	....	....	4.00	....
3524-27	34¢ Amish Quilts, 4 varieties attached .	4.25	5.25	20.00(20)	5.00	4.50	3.50
3524	34¢ Diamond in the Square	1.95	....	....	....	1.20	.30
3525	34¢ Lone Star	1.95	....	....	....	1.20	.30
3526	34¢ Sunshine and Shadow	1.95	....	....	....	1.20	.30
3527	34¢ Double Ninepatch Variation	1.95	....	....	....	1.20	.30
3528-31	34¢ Carnivorous Plants, 4 varieties attached ,	4.25	5.25	20.00(20)	5.00	4.50	3.50
3528	34¢ Venus Flytrap . .	1.95	....	....	....	1.20	.30
3529	34¢ Yellow Trumpet	1.95	....	....	....	1.20	.30
3530	34¢ Cobra	1.95	....	....	....	1.20	.30
3531	34¢ English Sundew	1.95	....	....	....	1.20	.30
3532	34¢ "Eid Mubarak", self-adhesive	1.95	4.75	17.50(20)	4.50	1.00	.25
3533	34¢ Enrico Fermi, self-adhesive	1.95	4.75	17.50(20)	4.50	1.00	.25
3534	34¢ That's All Folks, self-adhesive, pane of 10	12.50	....	....	....	9.50	....
3534a	same, single from pane	2.50	....	....	....	1.10	.25
3534b	same, pane of 9 (3534a)	....	....	....	....	6.75	....
3534c	same, pane of 1 (3534a)	7.25	....	....	....	2.75	....
	same, top press sheet of 60 (6 panes) w/ pl# .	....	....	60.00(60)	....	60.00	....
	same, bottom press sheet of 60 (6 panes) w/ pl#	....	....	70.00(60)	....	70.00	....
	same, pane of 10 from press sheet	....	....	....	....	12.00	....
	same, 2 panes of 10 w/ pl# on front	....	....	....	....	25.00	....
	same, cross gutter block of 9	....	....	....	....	20.00	....
	vert. pair with horiz. gutter	....	....	....	....	3.00	....
	horiz. pair with vert. gutter	....	....	....	....	6.00	....
3535	34¢ That's All Folks, die cut, self-adhesive, pane of 10	15.00	....	....	....	11.00	....
3535a	same, single form pane	....	....	....	....	1.10	....
3535b	same, pane of 9 (3435a)	....	....	....	....	9.00	....
3535c	same, pane of 1, imperf.	12.50	....	....	....	3.00	....
3536	34¢ Madonna and Child, self-adhesive	1.95	....	....	....	1.00	.20
3536a	same, bklt pane of 20	14.50	....	....	....	18.50	....
3537-40	34¢ Santas, self-adhesive, 4 varieties attach, large date	4.25	5.25	20.00(20)	5.00	4.50	3.50
3537	34¢ Santa w/ horse, large date	1.95	....	....	....	1.20	.30
3538	34¢ Santa w/ horn, large date	1.95	....	....	....	1.20	.30
3539	34¢ Santa w/ drum, large date	1.95	....	....	....	1.20	.30
3540	34¢ Santa w/ dog, large date	1.95	....	....	....	1.20	.30

U.S. Postage #3537a-3560

SCOTT NO.	DESCRIPTION	FIRST DAY COVERS SING	FIRST DAY COVERS PL. BLK.	MINT SHEET	PLATE BLOCK	UNUSED F/NH	USED
3537a-40a	34¢ Santas, self-adhesive, 4 varieties attach, small date	4.25	5.25	....	....	4.50	3.50
3537a	34¢ Santa w/ horse, small date	1.95				1.20	.30
3538a	34¢ Santa w/ horn, small date	1.95				1.20	.30
3539a	34¢ Santa w/ drum, small date	1.95				1.20	.30
3540a	34¢ Santa w/ dog, small date	1.95				1.20	.30
3540c	same, bklt pane of 20, 3537a-40a x 5 + label	14.50				20.00	....
3541-44	34¢ Santas, self-adhesive, 4 varieties attach, green denom.	4.25				4.50	
3541	34¢ Santa w/ horse, green denom	1.95				1.20	.25
3542	34¢ Santa w/ horn, green denom	1.95				1.20	.25
3543	34¢ Santa w/ drum, green denom	1.95				1.20	.25
3544	34¢ Santa w/ dog, green denom	1.95				1.20	.25
3544b	same, bklt pane of 4 (3541-3544)	4.00				4.50	
3544c	same, bklt pane of 6 (3543-44, 3541-42 x 2)	5.50				6.00	
3544d	same, bklt pane of 6 (3541-42, 3543-44 x 2)	5.50				6.00	

3545

3545	34¢ James Madison	1.95	4.75	17.50(20)	4.50	1.00	.25
3545v	same, uncut sheet of 120 (6 panes)	....	....	110.00(120)	....	110.00	....
....	cross gutter block of 4	....	....	....	....	11.00	....
....	horiz. pair with vert. gutter	....	....	....	....	4.50	....
....	vert. pair with horiz. gutter	....	....	....	....	3.50	....

3547

3548

3546

3546	34¢ We Give Thanks, self-adhesive	1.95	4.75	17.50(20)	4.50	1.00	.25
3547	34¢ Hanukkah, self-adhesive	1.95	4.75	17.50(20)	4.50	1.00	.25
3548	34¢ Kwanzaa, self-adhesive	1.95	4.75	17.50(20)	4.50	1.00	.25

3549, 3549B, 3550, 3550A

3551

3549	34¢ United We Stand, self-adhesive	1.95	....	....	....	1.00	.20
3549a	same, bklt pane of 20	14.50	....	....	....	18.50	....
3549B	34¢ United We Stand, die cut 10.5 x 10.75 on 2 or 3 sides	1.95	....	....	....	1.00	.20
3549Bc	same, bklt pane of 4	4.00	....	....	....	4.50	....
3549Bd	same, bklt pane of 6	5.50	....	....	....	6.50	....
3549Be	same, bklt pane of 20 (double-sided)	....	....	....	....	18.50	....
3550	34¢ United We Stand, self-adhesive coil (square corners)	1.95	....	....	....	1.00	.20
....	same, pl# strip of 5	....	....	....	....	8.00	....
3550A	34¢ United We Stand, self-adhesive coil, (round corners)	1.95	....	....	....	1.00	.20
....	same, pl# strip of 5	....	....	....	....	9.00	....
3551	57¢ Love, self-adhesive	2.50	5.00	27.50(20)	7.00	1.50	.50

3552

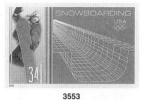

3553

3554

3555

2002 COMMEMORATIVES

3552/3695	(3552-60, 3650-79, 3692, 3695) 41 varieties	....	....	....	....	42.50	10.70
3552-55	34¢ Winter Olympics, self-adhesive, 4 varieties attached	4.25	5.25	20.00(20)	5.00	4.50	3.50
3552	34¢ Ski Jumping	1.95				1.20	.30
3553	34¢ Snowboarding	1.95				1.20	.30
3554	34¢ Ice Hockey	1.95				1.20	.30
3555	34¢ Figure Skating	1.95				1.20	.30
3552-55v	same, uncut sheet of 180 (9 panes)	....	....	185.00(180)	....	185.00	....
....	cross gutter block of 8	....	....	....	....	25.00	....
....	block of 8 with vert. gutter	....	....	....	....	12.50	....
....	block of 8 with horiz. gutter	....	....	....	....	12.50	....
....	vert. pair with horiz. gutter	....	....	....	....	2.50	....
....	horiz. pair with vert. gutter	....	....	....	....	2.50	....

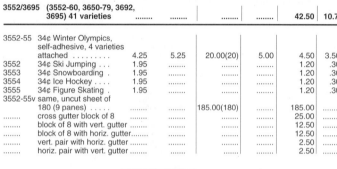

3556   3557   3558

3556	34¢ Mentoring a Child, self-adhesive	1.95	4.75	17.50(20)	4.50	1.00	.25
3557	34¢ Langston Hughes, self-adhesive	1.95	4.75	17.50(20)	4.50	1.00	.25
3558	34¢ Happy Birthday, self-adhesive	1.95	4.75	17.50(20)	4.50	1.00	.25

3559

3560

3559	34¢ Year of the Horse, self-adhesive	1.95	4.75	22.50(20)	5.00	1.20	.25
3560	34¢ Military Academy Bicentennial, self-adhesive	1.95	4.75	17.50(20)	5.00	1.00	.25

Need Blank Pages For Your Liberty Album?

See page 190 for a full listing of Harris Blank Pages for U.S. and Worldwide Albums.

U.S. Postage #3561-3633

3561 — Greetings from Alabama
3610 — Greetings from Wyoming

GREETINGS FROM AMERICA

Scott	State	Scott	State	Scott	State
3561	Alabama	3578	Louisiana	3595	Ohio
3562	Alaska	3579	Maine	3596	Oklahoma
3563	Arizona	3580	Maryland	3597	Oregon
3564	Arkansas	3581	Massachusetts	3598	Pennsylvania
3565	California	3582	Michigan	3599	Rhode Island
3566	Colorado	3583	Minnesota	3600	South Carolina
3567	Connecticut	3584	Mississippi	3601	South Dakota
3568	Delaware	3585	Missouri	3602	Tennessee
3569	Florida	3586	Montana	3603	Texas
3570	Georgia	3587	Nebraska	3604	Utah
3571	Hawaii	3588	Nevada	3605	Vermont
3572	Idaho	3589	New Hampshire	3606	Virginia
3573	Illinois	3590	New Jersey	3607	Washington
3574	Indiana	3591	New Mexico	3608	West Virginia
3575	Iowa	3592	New York	3609	Wisconsin
3576	Kansas	3593	North Carolina	3610	Wyoming
3577	Kentucky	3594	North Dakota		

Scott No.	Description	FDC Sing	FDC Pl. Blk.	Mint Sheet	Plate Block	Unused F/NH	Used
3561-3610	34¢ Greetings from America, self-adhesive, 50 varieties attached	....	....	40.00(50)	....	40.00	....
	set of singles	97.50					30.00

3611 — LONGLEAF PINE FOREST

LONGLEAF PINE FOREST

- 3611a Bachman's sparrow
- 3611b Northern bobwhite, yellow pitcher plants
- 3611c Fox squirrel, red-bellied woodpecker
- 3611d Brown-headed nuthatch
- 3611e Broadhead skink, yellow pitcher plants, pipeworts
- 3611f Eastern towhee, yellow pitcher plants, meadow beauties, toothache grass
- 3611g Gray Fox, gopher tortoise
- 3611h Blind click beetle, sweetbay, pine woods freefrog
- 3611i Rosebuds orchid, pipeworts, southern toad, yellow pitcher plants
- 3611j Grass-pink orchid, yellow-sided skimmer, pipeworts

Scott No.	Description	FDC Sing	FDC Pl. Blk.	Mint Sheet	Plate Block	Unused F/NH	Used
3611	34¢ Longleaf Pine Forest, 10 varieties, attached, self-adhesive	....	....	9.50(10)	....	9.50	7.50
	set of singles	19.50					5.00
3611v	same, uncut sheet of 60 (6 panes)	....	....	75.00(90)	....	75.00	....

3612 — 5¢ Toleware
3613, 3614, 3615 — 3¢ Star
3616, 3617, 3618, 3619 — 23¢ George Washington
3620, 3621, 3622, 3623, 3624, 3625 — 37¢ Flag

Scott No.	Description	FDC Sing	FDC Pl. Blk.	Mint Sheet	Plate Block	Unused F/NH	Used
3612	5¢ Toleware coffee pot, coil	1.95				.25	.20
	same, pl# strip of 5					2.25	
3613	3¢ Lithographed Star (year at LL)	1.95	4.75	4.50(50)	.75	.20	.20
3614	3¢ Photogravure Star (year at LR)	1.95	4.75	4.50(50)	.75	.20	.20
3615	3¢ Star, coil	1.95				.20	.20
	same, pl# strip of 5					2.00	
3616	23¢ George Washington	1.95	4.75	60.00(100)	5.00	.75	.20
3617	23¢ George Washington, self-adhesive coil	1.95	....	....	....	.75	.20
	same pl# strip of 5	....	....	....	....	5.00	
3618	23¢ George Washington, self-adhesive die cut 11.25	1.95	....	....	....	.75	.20
3618a	same, bklt pane of 4	3.00				3.00	
3618b	same, bklt pane of 6	4.00				4.50	
3618c	same, bklt pane of 10	6.75				7.25	
3619	23¢ George Washington, self-adhesive, die cut 10.5 x 11.25	1.95				3.00	.50
3619a	same, bklt pane of 4 (3619 x 2 at L, 3618 x 2 at R)					8.50	
3619b	same, bklt pane of 6 (3619 x 3 at L, 3618 x 3 at R)					13.00	
3619c	same, bklt pane of 4 (3618 x 2 at L, 3619 x 2 at R)					8.50	
3619d	same, bklt pane of 6 (3618 x 3 at L, 3619 x 3 at R)					13.00	
3619g	same, pair (3619 at L, 3618 at R)					4.00	
3619h	same, pair (3618 at L, 3619 at R)					3.00	
3620	(37¢) Flag	1.95	4.75	85.00(100)	4.50	1.00	.20
3621	(37¢) Flag, self-adhesive	1.95	4.75	17.50(20)	4.50	1.00	.20
3622	(37¢) Flag, self-adhesive coil	1.95				1.00	.20
	same, pl# strip of 5					6.75	
3623	(37¢) Flag, self-adhesive, die cut 11.25	1.95				1.00	.20
3623a	same, bklt pane of 20					19.50	
3624	(37¢) Flag, self-adhesive, die cut 10.5 x 10.75	1.95				1.00	.20
3624a	same, bklt pane of 4	4.00				4.25	
3624b	same, bklt pane of 6	5.50				6.00	
3624c	same, bklt pane of 20	15.00				19.50	
3625	(37¢) Flag, self-adhesive, die cut 8	1.95				1.00	.20
3625a	same, ATM bklt pane of 18	15.00				17.50	

3626 — (37¢) Toy mail wagon
3627 — (37¢) Toy locomotive
3628 — (37¢) Toy taxicab
3629 — (37¢) Toy fire pumper

Scott No.	Description	FDC Sing	FDC Pl. Blk.	Mint Sheet	Plate Block	Unused F/NH	Used
3626	(37¢) Toy mail wagon, self-adhesive	1.95				1.00	.30
3627	(37¢) Toy locomotive, self-adhesive	1.95				1.00	.30
3628	(37¢) Toy taxicab, self-adhesive	1.95				1.00	.30
3629	(37¢) Toy fire pumper, self-adhesive	1.95				1.00	.30
3626-29	(37¢) Antique Toys, self-adhesive, 4 varieties attached	4.25				4.50	3.50
3629b	same, bklt pane of 4 (3626-29 x 1)	4.25				4.50	
3629c	same, bklt pane of 6 (3627, 3629, 3626 x 2, 3628 x 2)	5.50				6.50	
3629d	same, bklt pane of 6 (3626, 3628, 3627 x 2, 3629 x 2)	5.50				6.25	
3629e	same, bklt pane of 20	15.00				19.50	
3629F	37¢ Flag	1.95	4.75	85.00(100)	4.50	1.00	.30

3638, 3643 — Toy locomotive
3639, 3642 — Toy mail wagon
3629F, 3630, 3631, 3632, 3632A, 3632C, 3633, 3633A, 3635, 3636, 3637 — Flag
3640, 3645 — Toy fire pumper
3641, 3644 — Toy taxicab

Scott No.	Description	FDC Sing	FDC Pl. Blk.	Mint Sheet	Plate Block	Unused F/NH	Used
3630	37¢ Flag, self-adhesive	1.95	4.75	18.50(20)	4.50	1.00	.30
3631	37¢ Flag, coil	1.95				1.00	.30
	same, pl# strip of 5					8.00	
3632	37¢ Flag, self-adhesive coil, die cut 10 vert.	1.95				1.00	.30
	same, pl# strip of 5					8.00	
3632A	37¢ Flag coil, die cut 10, flag lacking star point	1.95				1.00	.30
	same, pl# strip of 5					8.00	
3632C	37¢ Flag, self-adhesive coil, die cut 11.75 (2004)	1.95				1.00	.30
	same, pl# strip of 5					8.00	
3633	37¢ Flag, self-adhesive coil, die cut 8.5 vert.	1.95				1.00	.30
	same, pl# strip of 5					8.00	

U.S. Postage #3633A-3659

SCOTT NO.	DESCRIPTION	FIRST DAY COVERS SING	FIRST DAY COVERS PL. BLK.	MINT SHEET	PLATE BLOCK	UNUSED F/NH	USED
3633A	37¢ Flag coil, die cut 8.5, right angel corners	1.95	....	....	....	1.00	.30
....	same, pl# strip of 5	....	....	....	....	8.00	....
3634	37¢ Flag, self-adhesive, die cut 11	1.95	....	....	....	1.00	.20
3634a	same, bklt pane of 10	....	....	....	....	9.50	....
3634b	same, self-adhesive, bklt single, dated 2003	1.95	....	....	....	.85	.20
3634c	same, bklt pane of 4 (3634b)	4.25	....	....	....	4.25	....
3634d	same, bklt pane of 6 (3634d)	5.50	....	....	....	5.75	....
3635	37¢ Flag, self-adhesive, die cut 11.25	1.95	....	....	....	1.00	.20
3635a	same, bklt pane of 20	....	....	....	....	19.50	....
3636	37¢ Flag, self-adhesive, die cut 10.5 x 10.75	1.95	....	....	....	1.00	.20
3636c	same, bklt pane of 20	....	....	....	....	19.50	....
3637	37¢ Flag, self-adhesive, die cut 8	1.95	....	....	....	1.00	.20
3637a	same, ATM bklt pane of 18	15.00	....	....	....	17.50	....
3638	37¢ Toy locomotive, self-adhesive coil, die cut 8.5 horiz.	1.95	....	....	....	1.00	.20
3639	37¢ Toy mail wagon, self-adhesive coil, die cut 8.5 horiz.	1.95	....	....	....	1.00	.20
3640	37¢ Toy fire pumper, self-adhesive coil, die cut 8.5 horiz.	1.95	....	....	....	1.00	.20
3641	37¢ Toy taxicab, self-adhesive coil, die cut 8.5 horiz.	1.95	....	....	....	1.00	.20
3638-41	37¢ Antique Toys, self-adhesive coil, strip of 4	4.25	....	....	....	4.50	3.50
....	same, pl# strip of 5	....	....	....	....	7.50	....
3642	37¢ Toy mail wagon, self-adhesive, die cut 11	1.95	....	....	....	1.00	.30
3642a	same, die cut 11x11.25, 2003	1.95	....	....	....	1.00	.30
3643	37¢ Toy locomotive, self-adhesive, die cut 11	1.95	....	....	....	1.00	.30
3643a	same, die cut 11x11.25, 2003	1.95	....	....	....	1.00	.30
3644	37¢ Toy taxicab, self-adhesive, die cut 11	1.95	....	....	....	1.00	.30
3644a	same, die cut 11x11.25, 2003	1.95	....	....	....	1.00	.30
3645	37¢ Toy fire pumper, self-adhesive, die cut 11	1.95	....	....	....	1.00	.30
3645f	same, die cut 11x11.25, 2003	1.95	....	....	....	1.00	.30
3642-45	37¢ Antique Toys, self-adhesive, 4 varieties attach.	4.25	....	....	....	4.50	3.50
3645b	same, bklt pane of 4 (3642-45 x 1)	4.25	....	....	....	4.50	....
3645c	same, bklt pane of 6 (3643, 3645, 3642 x 2, 3644 x 2)	5.50	....	....	....	5.75	....
3645d	same, bklt pane of 6 (3642, 3644, 3642 x 2, 3645 x 2)	5.50	....	....	....	5.75	....
3645e	same, bklt pane of 20	15.00	....	....	....	19.50	....
3645g	37¢ Antique Toys, self-adhesive, blk of 4 (3642a, 3643a, 3644a, 3645f)	4.25	....	....	....	4.25	....
3645h	same, bklt pane of 20	15.00	....	....	....	16.00	....

3646

3648

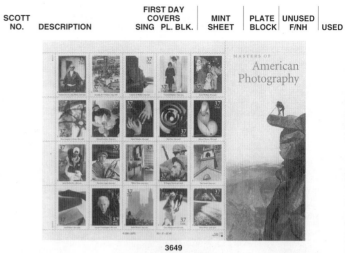
3649

SCOTT NO.	DESCRIPTION	FIRST DAY COVERS SING	FIRST DAY COVERS PL. BLK.	MINT SHEET	PLATE BLOCK	UNUSED F/NH	USED
3646	60¢ Coverlet Eagle, self-adhesive	2.75	5.50	24.50(20)	6.25	1.35	.50
3647	$3.85 Jefferson Memorial, self-adhesive	8.75	35.00	165.00(20)	39.50	8.75	4.50
3647A	same, die cut 11x10.75, dated 2003	8.75	35.00	165.00(20)	39.50	8.75	4.50
3648	$13.65 Capitol Dome, self-adhesive	35.00	105.00	550.00(20)	125.00	29.00	12.00

MASTERS OF AMERICAN PHOTOGRAPHY

3649a	Albert Sands Southworth & Josiah Johnson Hawes		3649k	James VanDerZee
3649b	Timothy H. O'Sullivan		3649l	Dorothea Lange
3649c	Carleton E. Watkins		3649m	Walker Evans
3649d	Getrude Kasebier		3649n	Eugene Smith
3649e	Lewis W. Hine		3649o	Paul Strand
3649f	Alvin Langdon Coburn		3649p	Ansel Adams
3649g	Edward Steichen		3649q	Imogen Cunningham
3649h	Alfred Steiglitz		3649r	Andre Kertesz
3649i	Man Ray		3649s	Garry Winogrand
3649j	Edward Weston		3649t	Minor White

| 3649 | 37¢ Master of American Photography, self-adhesive, 20 varieties attached | .... | .... | 16.00(20) | .... | 19.50 | 15.00 |
| .... | same, set of singles | 39.00 | .... | .... | .... | .... | 12.00 |

3650

3652

3651

SCOTT NO.	DESCRIPTION	FIRST DAY COVERS SING	FIRST DAY COVERS PL. BLK.	MINT SHEET	PLATE BLOCK	UNUSED F/NH	USED
3650	37¢ John James Audubon, self-adhesive	1.95	4.75	17.50(20)	4.50	1.00	.25
3651	37¢ Harry Houdini, self-adhesive	1.95	4.75	17.50(20)	4.50	1.00	.25
3652	37¢ Andy Warhol, self-adhesive	1.95	4.75	17.50(20)	4.50	1.00	.25

3653

3654

3655

3656

3653-56	37¢ Teddy Bears, self-adhesive, 4 varieties attached	4.25	4.75	20.00(20)	5.00	4.50	3.50
3653	37¢ Bruin Teddy Bear	1.95	....	....	....	1.25	.30
3654	37¢ Stick Teddy Bear	1.95	....	....	....	1.25	.30
3655	37¢ Gund Teddy Bear	1.95	....	....	....	1.25	.30
3656	37¢ Ideal Teddy Bear	1.95	....	....	....	1.25	.30

3657

3658

3659

3657	37¢ Love, self-adhesive	1.95	....	....	....	1.00	.20
....	same, bklt pane of 20	15.00	....	....	....	19.50	....
3658	60¢ Love, self-adhesive	2.75	5.50	27.50(20)	7.00	1.50	.50
3659	37¢ Ogden Nash, self-adhesive	1.95	4.75	17.50(20)	4.50	1.00	.25

U.S. Postage #3660-3691

SCOTT NO.	DESCRIPTION	FIRST DAY COVERS SING	FIRST DAY COVERS PL. BLK.	MINT SHEET	PLATE BLOCK	UNUSED F/NH	USED
3660	37¢ Duke Kahanamoku, self-adhesive	1.95	4.75	17.50(20)	4.50	1.00	.25
3661-64	37¢ American Bats, self-adhesive, 4 varieties attached	4.25	4.75	20.00(20)	6.00	4.50	3.50
3661	37¢ Red Bat	1.95	....	....	....	1.20	.30
3662	37¢ Leaf-nosed Bat	1.95	....	....	....	1.20	.30
3663	37¢ Pallid Bat	1.95	....	....	....	1.20	.30
3664	37¢ Spotted Bat	1.95	....	....	....	1.20	.30

3665   3666

3667   3668

SCOTT NO.	DESCRIPTION	SING	PL. BLK.	MINT SHEET	PLATE BLOCK	UNUSED F/NH	USED
3665-68	37¢ Women In Journalism, self-adhesive, 4 varieties attached	4.25	4.75	20.00(20)	5.00	4.50	3.50
3665	37¢ Nellie Bly	1.95	....	....	....	1.20	.30
3666	37¢ Ida M. Tarbel	1.95	....	....	....	1.20	.30
3667	37¢ Ethel L. Payne	1.95	....	....	....	1.20	.30
3668	37¢ Marguerite Higgins	1.95	....	....	....	1.20	.30

3669

| 3669 | 37¢ Irving Berlin, self-adhesive | 1.95 | 4.75 | 17.50(20) | 4.50 | 1.00 | .25 |

3670   3671

3670-71	37¢ Neuter and Spay, self-adhesive, 2 varieites attached	2.95	4.75	22.50(20)	5.50	2.50	1.35
3670	37¢ Kitten	1.95	....	....	....	1.20	.30
3671	37¢ Puppy	1.95	....	....	....	1.20	.30

3672   3673   3674

3672	37¢ Hanukkah, self-adhesive	1.95	4.75	17.50(20)	4.50	1.00	.25
3673	37¢ Kwanzaa, self-adhesive	1.95	4.75	17.50(20)	4.50	1.00	.25
3674	37¢ EID, self-adhesive	1.95	4.75	17.50(20)	4.50	1.00	.25

3675

| 3675 | 37¢ Madonna & Child, self-adhesive | 1.95 | 4.75 | 17.50(20) | 4.50 | 1.00 | .20 |
| .... | same, bklt pane of 20 | 15.00 | .... | .... | .... | 16.00 | .... |

3676, 3683, 3684, 3688   3677, 3680, 3685, 3689   3678, 3681, 3686, 3690   3679, 3682, 3687, 3691

3676-79	37¢ Snowmen, self-adhesive, 4 varieties attached	4.25	4.75	20.00(20)	5.00	4.50	3.50
3676	37¢ Snowman with red and green scarf	1.95	....	....	....	1.20	.30
3677	37¢ Snowman with blue scarf	1.95	....	....	....	1.20	.30
3578	37¢ Snowman with pipe	1.95	....	....	....	1.20	.30
3679	37¢ Snowman with top hat	1.95	....	....	....	1.20	.30
3680	37¢ Snowman with blue scarf, self-adhesive coil	1.95	....	....	....	1.20	.30
3681	37¢ Snowman with pipe, self-adhesive coil	1.95	....	....	....	1.20	.30
3682	37¢ Snowman with top hat, self-adhesive coil	1.95	....	....	....	1.20	.30
3683	37¢ Snowman with red and green scarf, self-adhesive coil	1.95	....	....	....	1.20	.30
3680-83	37¢ Snowmen, self-adhesive coil, strip of 4	4.25	....	....	....	4.50	3.50
....	same, pl# strip of 5	....	....	....	....	6.75	....
3684	37¢ Snowman with red and green scarf, large design	1.95	....	....	....	1.20	.30
3685	37¢ Snowman with blue scarf, large design	1.95	....	....	....	1.20	.30
3686	37¢ Snowman with pipe, large design	1.95	....	....	....	1.20	.30
3687	37¢ Snowman with top hat, large design	1.95	....	....	....	1.20	.30
3684-87	37¢ Snowman, self-adhesive, 4 varieties attached	4.25	....	....	....	4.50	3.50
3687b	same, bklt pane of 20 (3684-87 x 5 + label)	15.00	....	....	....	21.50	....
3688	37¢ Snowman with red and green scarf, small design	1.95	....	....	....	1.20	.30
3689	37¢ Snowman with blue scarf, small design	1.95	....	....	....	1.20	.30
3690	37¢ Snowman with pipe, small design	1.95	....	....	....	1.20	.30
3691	37¢ Snowman with top hat, small design	1.95	....	....	....	1.20	.30
3688-91	37¢ Snowmen, self-adhesive, 4 varieties attached	4.25	....	....	....	4.50	3.50
3691b	same, bklt pane of 4, (3688-91)	4.25	....	....	....	4.50	....
3691c	same, bklt pane of 6 (3690-91, 3688-89 x 2)	5.50	....	....	....	6.00	....
3691d	same, bklt pane of 6 (3688-89, 3690-91 x 2)	5.50	....	....	....	6.00	....

Don't forget Harris offers a complete line of albums, supplies and accessories for all your stamp collecting needs!

U.S. Postage #3692-3772

3693, 3775, 3785   3692   3695   3747   3746   3748

SCOTT NO.	DESCRIPTION	FDC SING	FDC PL. BLK.	MINT SHEET	PLATE BLOCK	UNUSED F/NH	USED
3692	37¢ Cary Grant, self-adhesive	1.95	4.75	17.50(20)	4.50	1.00	.25
3693	(5¢) Sea Coast coil, self-adhesive	1.95				.25	.20
	same, pl# strip of 5					2.50	

2003 COMMEMORATIVES AND REGULAR ISSUES

SCOTT NO.	DESCRIPTION	FDC SING	FDC PL. BLK.	MINT SHEET	PLATE BLOCK	UNUSED F/NH	USED
3746	37¢ Thurgood Marshall, self-adhesive	1.95	4.75	16.00(20)	4.00	.85	.25
3747	37¢ Year of the Ram, self-adhesive	1.95	4.75	17.50(20)	4.50	1.00	.25
3748	37¢ Zora Neale Hurston, self-adhesive	1.95	4.75	16.00(20)	4.00	.85	.25

3694

3750   3751   3757   3766

3769   3771   3770

SCOTT NO.	DESCRIPTION	FDC SING	FDC PL. BLK.	MINT SHEET	PLATE BLOCK	UNUSED F/NH	USED
3694	37¢ Hawaiian Missionary, self-adhesive, souvenir sheet of 4	5.00				5.25	4.00
3694a	37¢ Hawaii 2¢ of 1851	1.95				1.20	.75
3694b	37¢ Hawaii 5¢ of 1851	1.95				1.20	.75
3694c	37¢ Hawaii 13¢ of 1851	1.95				1.20	.75
3694d	37¢ Hawaii 13¢ of 1852	1.95				1.20	.75
3695	37¢ Happy Birthday, self-adhesive	1.95	4.75	17.50(20)	4.50	1.00	.25
3750	4¢ Chippendale Chair, self-adhesive (2004)	1.95	4.75	4.50(20)	.75	.20	.20
3751	10¢ American Clock, self-adhesive	1.95	4.75	4.75(20)	1.35	.30	.20
3757	1¢ Tiffany Lamp, coil	1.95				.25	.20
	same, pl# strip of 5					2.25	
3766	$1 Wisdom, self-adhesive	3.50	7.50	43.00(20)	10.00	2.25	1.25
3769	(10¢) New York Library Lion, perf. 10 vert.	1.95			2.00	.30	.20
	same, pl# strip of 5					2.75	
3770	(10¢) Atlas Statue, self-adhesive coil, die cut 11 dated 2003	1.95				.30	.25
	same, pl# strip of 5					3.00	
3771	80¢ Special Olympics, self-adhesive	3.00	7.00	37.50(20)	8.50	1.95	1.00

3696   3745

GREETINGS FROM AMERICA

3696	Alabama	3713	Louisiana	3730	Ohio
3697	Alaska	3714	Maine	3731	Oklahoma
3698	Arizona	3715	Maryland	3732	Oregon
3699	Arkansas	3716	Massachusetts	3733	Pennsylvania
3700	California	3717	Michigan	3734	Rhode Island
3701	Colorado	3718	Minnesota	3735	South Carolina
3702	Connecticut	3719	Mississippi	3736	South Dakota
3703	Delaware	3720	Missouri	3737	Tennessee
3704	Florida	3721	Montana	3738	Texas
3705	Georgia	3722	Nebraska	3739	Utah
3706	Hawaii	3723	Nevada	3740	Vermont
3707	Idaho	3724	New Hampshire	3741	Virginia
3708	Illinois	3725	New Jersey	3742	Washington
3709	Indiana	3726	New Mexico	3743	West Virginia
3710	Iowa	3727	New York	3744	Wisconsin
3711	Kansas	3728	North Carolina	3745	Wyoming
3712	Kentucky	3729	North Dakota		

SCOTT NO.	DESCRIPTION	FDC SING	FDC PL. BLK.	MINT SHEET	PLATE BLOCK	UNUSED F/NH	USED
3696-3745	37¢ Greetings from America, self-adhesive, 50 varieties attached			40.00(50)		40.00	
	set of singles	97.50					25.00

3772

AMERICAN FILM MAKING

3772a	Screenwriting	3772d	Music	3772g	Cinematography
3772b	Directing	3772e	Make-up	3772h	Film editing
3772c	Costume design	3772f	Art Direction	3772i	Special effects
				3772j	Sound

SCOTT NO.	DESCRIPTION	FDC SING	FDC PL. BLK.	MINT SHEET	PLATE BLOCK	UNUSED F/NH	USED
3772	37¢ American Film Making, self-adhesive, 10 varieties attached			8.00(10)		8.00	6.75
	set of singles	19.50					5.00

U.S. Postage #3773-3801

SCOTT NO.	DESCRIPTION	FIRST DAY COVERS SING	FIRST DAY COVERS PL. BLK.	MINT SHEET	PLATE BLOCK	UNUSED F/NH	USED
3773	37¢ Ohio Statehood, self-adhesive	1.95	4.75	16.00(20)	4.00	.85	.25
3774	37¢ Pelican Island National Wildlife Refuge, self-adhesive	1.95	4.75	16.00(20)	4.00	.85	.25
3775	(5¢) Sea Coast coil, perf. 9.75 vert.	1.95				.25	.20
	same, pl# strip of 5					2.25	
3776	37¢ Uncle Sam on Bicycle	1.95				1.00	.50
3777	37¢ 1888 Pres. Campaign badge	1.95				1.00	.50
3778	37¢ 1893 Silk bookmark	1.95				1.00	.50
3779	37¢ Modern hand fan	1.95				1.00	.50
3780	37¢ Carving of woman with flag & sword	1.95				1.00	.50
3776-80	37¢ Old Glory, self-adhesive, 5 varieties attached	5.00				5.50	
3780b	same, complete booklet of 2 panes					21.50	
3781	37¢ Cesar E. Chavez, self-adhesive	1.95	4.75	16.00(20)	4.00	.85	.25
3782	37¢ Louisiana Purchase, self-adhesive	1.95	4.75	16.00(20)	4.00	.85	.25
3783	37¢ First Flight of the Wright Brothers, self-adhesive	1.95		8.00(10)		.85	.25
3783a	same, bklt pane of 9					7.25	
3783b	same, bklt pane of 1	7.00				2.00	
3784	37¢ Purple Heart, self-adhesive	1.95	4.75	16.00(20)	4.00	.85	.25
3784A	37¢ Purple Heart, self-adhesive, die cut 10.75 x 10.25	1.95	4.75	16.00(20)	4.00	.85	.25
3785	(5¢) Sea Coast coil, four-side die cuts	1.95				.25	.20
	same, pl# strip of 5					2.25	
3786	37¢ Audrey Hepburn, self-adhesive	1.95	4.75	16.00(20)	4.00	.85	.25
3787-91	37¢ Southern Lighthouses, self-adhesive, 5 varieties attached	5.00		22.50(20)		5.50	4.50
3787	37¢ Old Cape Henry, North Carolina	1.95				1.00	.30
3788	37¢ Cape Outlook, North Carolina	1.95				1.00	.30
3788a	same, dropped denomination						
3789	37¢ Morris Island, South Carolina					1.00	.30
3790	37¢ Tybee Island, Georgia	1.95				1.00	.30
3791	37¢ Hillsboro Inlet, Florida	1.95				1.00	.30
3791b	same, strip of 5 (3787, 3788a, 3789-91)						
3792	(25¢) Eagle, gray with gold eagle, coil	1.95				.60	.20
3793	(25¢) Eagle, gold with red eagle, coil	1.95				.60	.20
3794	(25¢) Eagle, dull blue with gold eagle, coil	1.95				.60	.20
3795	(25¢) Eagle, gold with Prussian blue eagle, coil	1.95				.60	.20
3796	(25¢) Eagle, green with gold eagle, coil	1.95				.60	.20
3797	(25¢) Eagle, gold with gray eagle, coil	1.95				.60	.20
3798	(25¢) Eagle, Prussian blue with gold eagle, coil	1.95				.60	.20
3799	(25¢) Eagle, gold with dull blue eagle, coil	1.95				.60	.20
3800	(25¢) Eagle, red with gold eagle, coil	1.95				.60	.20
3801	(25¢) Eagle, gold with green eagle, coil	1.95				.60	.20
3792-3801	(25¢) Eagle, self-adhesive coil, strip of 10	6.00				6.00	
	same, pl# strip of 11					8.50	

— SE-TENANT STAMPS —

Beginning with the 1964 Christmas issue (#1254-57), the United States has issued numerous Se-tenant stamps covering a wide variety of subjects. Se-tenants are issues where two or more different stamp designs are produced on the same sheet in pair, strip or block form. Mint stamps are usually collected in attached blocks, etc. Used are generally saved as single stamps.

U.S. Postage #3802-3820

3802 ARCTIC TUNDRA

3802a	Gyrfalcon	3802f	Caribou & willow ptarmigans
3802b	Gray wolf	3802g	Arctic ground squirrel
3802c	Common raven	3802h	Willow ptarmigan & bearberry
3802d	Musk oxen & caribou	3802i	Arctic grayling
3802e	Grizzly bears & caribou	3802j	Singing vole, thin-legged spider, lingonberry, Labrador tea

Scott No.	Description	FDC Sing	FDC Pl.Blk	Mint Sheet	Plate Block	Unused F/NH	Used
3802	37¢ Arctic Tundra, 10 varieties, attached, self-adhesive				8.00(10)	8.00	6.75
	set of singles		19.50				5.00
3803	37¢ Korean War Veterans, Memorial, self-adhesive	1.95	4.75	16.00(20)	4.00	.85	.20
3804	37¢ Young Mother	1.95				.85	.20
3805	37¢ Children Playing	1.95				.85	.20
3806	37¢ On a Balcony	1.95				.85	.20
3807	37¢ Child in Straw Hat	1.95				.85	.20
3804-07	37¢ Mary Cassatt Paintings, self-adhesive, 4 varieties attached	4.25				3.75	2.75
3807b	same, bklt pane of 20 (3804-07 x 5)		15.00			16.00	

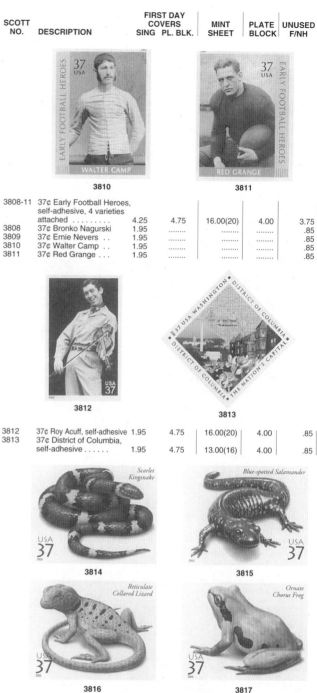

Scott No.	Description	FDC Sing	FDC Pl.Blk	Mint Sheet	Plate Block	Unused F/NH	Used
3808-11	37¢ Early Football Heroes, self-adhesive, 4 varieties attached	4.25	4.75	16.00(20)	4.00	3.75	2.75
3808	37¢ Bronko Nagurski	1.95				.85	.25
3809	37¢ Ernie Nevers	1.95				.85	.25
3810	37¢ Walter Camp	1.95				.85	.25
3811	37¢ Red Grange	1.95				.85	.25
3812	37¢ Roy Acuff, self-adhesive	1.95	4.75	16.00(20)	4.00	.85	.25
3813	37¢ District of Columbia, self-adhesive	1.95	4.75	13.00(16)	4.00	.85	.25

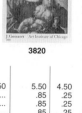

Scott No.	Description	FDC Sing	FDC Pl.Blk	Mint Sheet	Plate Block	Unused F/NH	Used
3814-18	37¢ Reptiles & Amphibians, self-adhesive, 5 varieties attached	5.00	10.50	16.00(20)	11.50	5.50	4.50
3814	37¢ Scarlet Kingsnake	1.95				.85	.25
3815	37¢ Blue-Spotted Salamander	1.95				.85	.25
3816	37¢ Reticulate Lizard	1.95				.85	.25
3817	37¢ Ornate Chorus Frog	1.95				.85	.25
3818	37¢ Ornate Box Turtle	1.95				.85	.25
3819	23¢ George Washington, self-adhesive, die cut 11	1.95	4.75	10.00(20)	2.75	.60	.20
3820	37¢ Madonna & Child, self-adhesive (2003)	1.95				.85	.20
3820a	same, bklt pane of 20					16.00	

U.S. Postage #3821-3843

SCOTT NO.	DESCRIPTION	FIRST DAY COVERS SING	FIRST DAY COVERS PL. BLK.	MINT SHEET	PLATE BLOCK	UNUSED F/NH	USED
	3821, 3825	**3822, 3826**		**3823, 3827**		**3824, 3828**	
3821-24	37¢ Christmas Music Makers, self-adhesive, 4 varieties attached	4.25	4.75	16.00(20)	4.00	3.75	2.75
3821	37¢ Reindeer with Pipes	1.95	....	....	....	.85	.20
3822	37¢ Santa Claus with Drum	1.95	....	....	....	.85	.20
3823	37¢ Santa Claus with Trumpet	1.95	....	....	....	.85	.20
3824	37¢ Reindeer with Horn	1.95	....	....	....	.85	.20
3842b	same, bklt pane of 20, (3821-24 x 5 + label)	15.00	....	....	....	16.00	....
3825	37¢ Reindeer with Pipes, die cut 10.5 x 10.75	1.95	....	....	....	.85	.20
3826	37¢ Santa Claus with Drum, die cut 10.5 x 10.75	1.95	....	....	....	.85	.20
3827	37¢ Santa Claus with Trumpet die cut 10.5 x 10.75	1.95	....	....	....	.85	.20
3828	37¢ Reindeer with Horn, die cut 10.5 x 10.75	1.95	....	....	....	.85	.20
3825-28	37¢ Christmas Music Makers, self-adhesive, 4 varieties attached, die cut 10.5 x 10.75	4.25	....	....	....	3.75	2.75
3828b	same, bklt pane of 4 (3825-28)	4.25	....	....	....	4.25	....
3828c	same, bklt pane of 6 (3827-28, 3825-26 x 2)	5.50	....	....	....	5.75	....
3828d	same, bklt pane of 6 (3825-26, 3827-28 x 2)	5.50	....	....	....	5.75	....
	3829, 3829A, 3830						
3829	37¢ Snowy Egret, self-adhesive coil, die cut 8.5	1.95	....	....	....	.85	.20
....	same, pl# strip of 5	....	....	....	....	6.75	....
3829A	37¢ Snowy Egret, self-adhesive coil, die cut 9.5	1.95	....	....	....	.85	.20
....	same, pl# strip of 5	....	....	....	....	6.75	....

3802 PACIFIC CORAL REEF

- 3831a Emperor angelfish, blue & mound coral
- 3831b Humphead wrasse, Moorish idol
- 3831c Bumphead parrotfish
- 3831d Black-spotted puffer, threadfin butterflyfish
- 3831e Hawksbill turtle, palette surgeonfish
- 3831f Pink anemonefish, sea anemone
- 3831g Snowflake moray eel, Spanish dancer
- 3831h Lionfish
- 3831i Triton's trumpet
- 3831j Oriental sweetlips, bluestreak cleaner wrasse, mushroom coral

2004 COMMEMORATIVES AND REGULAR ISSUES

3830	37¢ Snowy Egret, self adhesive	1.95	....	....	....	.85	.20
....	same, bklt pane of 20	....	....	....	....	16.00	....
3831	37¢ Pacific Coral Reef, 10 varieties, attached, self-adhesive	....	....	8.00(10)	....	8.00	6.75
....	set of singles	19.50	....	....	....	....	5.00

SCOTT NO.	DESCRIPTION	FIRST DAY COVERS SING	FIRST DAY COVERS PL. BLK.	MINT SHEET	PLATE BLOCK	UNUSED F/NH	USED
	3832	**3834**		**3835**			
3832	37¢ Year of the Monkey, self-adhesive	1.95	4.75	16.00(20)	4.00	.85	.25
3833	37¢ Candy Hearts, self-adhesive	1.95	....	....	....	.85	.20
3833a	same, bklt pane of 20	....	....	....	....	16.00	....
3834	37¢ Paul Robeson, self-adhesive	1.95	4.75	16.00(20)	4.00	.85	.20
3835	37¢ Theodore Seuss Geisel (Dr. Seuss) self-adhesive	1.95	4.75	16.00(20)	4.00	.85	.25
	3836	**3833**		**3837**			
3836	37¢ White Lilacs and Pink Roses, self-adhesive	1.95	....	....	....	.85	.20
3836a	same, bklt pane of 20	....	....	....	....	16.00	....
3837	60¢ Five varieties of Pink Roses, self-adhesive	2.75	5.50	24.50(20)	6.25	1.35	.50
	3838	**3839**					
3838	37¢ United States Air Force Academy, self-adhesive	1.95	4.75	16.00(20)	4.00	.85	.20
3839	37¢ Henry Mancini, self-adhesive	1.95	4.75	16.00(20)	4.00	.85	.20
	3840	**3841**					
	3842	**3843**					
3840-43	37¢ American Choreographers, self-adhesive, 4 varieties attached	4.25	4.75	16.00(20)	4.00	3.75	2.75
3840	37¢ Martha Graham	1.95	....	....	....	.85	.20
3841	37¢ Alvin Ailey	1.95	....	....	....	.85	.20
3842	37¢ Agnes de Mille	1.95	....	....	....	.85	.20
3843	37¢ George Balanchine	1.95	....	....	....	.85	.20

U.S. Postage #3844-New Issues

3844, 3845, 3846, 3847, 3848, 3849, 3850, 3851, 3852, 3853

SCOTT NO.	DESCRIPTION	FIRST DAY COVERS SING	FIRST DAY COVERS PL. BLK.	MINT SHEET	PLATE BLOCK	UNUSED F/NH	USED
3844	(25¢) Eagle, gray with gold eagle, coil, perf. 9.75	1.95	....	....	....	.60	.20
3845	(25¢) Eagle, gold with green eagle, coil, perf. 9.75	1.95	....	....	....	.60	.20
3846	(25¢) Eagle, red with gold eagle, coil, perf. 9.75	1.95	....	....	....	.60	.20
3847	(25¢) Eagle, gold with dull blue eagle, coil, perf. 9.75	1.95	....	....	....	.60	.20
3848	(25¢) Eagle, Prussian blue with gold eagle, coil, perf. 9.75	1.95	....	....	....	.60	.20
3849	(25¢) Eagle, gold with gray eagle, coil, perf. 9.75	1.95	....	....	....	.60	.20
3850	(25¢) Eagle, Prussian green with gold eagle, coil, perf. 9.75	1.95	....	....	....	.60	.20
3851	(25¢) Eagle, gold with Prussian blue eagle, coil, perf. 9.75	1.95	....	....	....	.60	.20
3852	(25¢) Eagle, dull blue with gold eagle, coil, perf. 9.75	1.95	....	....	....	.60	.20
3853	(25¢) Eagle, gold with red eagle, coil, perf. 9.75	1.95	....	....	....	.60	.20
3844-3853	(25¢) Eagle, water activated coil, strip of 10, perf. 9.75	6.00	....	....	....	6.00	....
....	same, pl# strip of 11	....	....	....	....	8.50	....

3855

3854

3856

3857

3858

3859

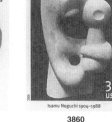

3860

3861

SCOTT NO.	DESCRIPTION	FIRST DAY COVERS SING	FIRST DAY COVERS PL. BLK.	MINT SHEET	PLATE BLOCK	UNUSED F/NH	USED
3857-61	37¢ Isamu Noguchi, self-adhesive, 5 varieties attached	5.00	9.50	16.00(20)	10.00(10)	4.50	3.00
3857	37¢ Akari 25N	1.95	....	....	....	.85	.25
3858	37¢ Margaret La Farge Osborn	1.95	....	....	....	.85	.25
3859	37¢ Black Sun	1.95	....	....	....	.85	.25
3860	37¢ Mother and Child	1.95	....	....	....	.85	.25
3861	37¢ Figure (detail)	1.95	....	....	....	.85	.25

3862

3863

SCOTT NO.	DESCRIPTION	FIRST DAY COVERS SING	FIRST DAY COVERS PL. BLK.	MINT SHEET	PLATE BLOCK	UNUSED F/NH	USED
3854	37¢ Lewis & Clark Bicentennial, self-adhesive	1.95	4.75	16.00(20)	4.00	.85	.25
3855	37¢ Lewis & Clark Bicentennial, Lewis booklet single	2.25	....	....	....	1.25	.30
3856	37¢ Lewis & Clark Bicentennial, Clark booklet single	2.25	....	....	....	1.25	.30
3855-56	37¢ Lewis & Clark, pair	3.75	....	....	....	2.75	....
3856b	37¢ Lewis & Clark: The Corps of Discovery, 1804-06, self-adhesive, bklt pane of 10	....	....	....	....	25.00	....
3862	37¢ National WWII Memorial, self-adhesive	1.95	4.75	16.00(20)	4.00	.85	.20
3863	37¢ 2004 Olympic Games, Athens, Greece, self-adhesive	1.95	4.75	16.00(20)	4.00	.85	.20
....	37¢ Art of Disney: Friendship, self-adhesive, 4 varieties attached	1.95	4.75	16.00(20)	4.00	3.75	2.75
....	37¢ Constellation, self-adhesive	1.95	4.75	16.00(20)	4.00	.85	.20
....	23¢ Wilma Rudolph, self-adhesive	1.95	4.75	16.00(20)	4.75	.60	.20

Liberty® U.S. Plate Block Albums

The Liberty® U.S. Plate Block Albums by H.E. Harris & Co. are published in three volumes. Each volume is formatted and illustrated for U.S. Definitives, Commemoratives, Airpost, Special Delivery, Special Handling, and Certified Mail. Each Volume comes housed in the 3" Traditional blue Lady Liberty Binder.

1HRS3   Plate Block Album – Volume A (1901-63) **$45.99**
1HRS4   Plate Block Album – Volume B (1964-89) **$45.99**
1HRS57   Plate Block Album – Volume C (1990-Current) **$45.99**

1HRS61   Plate Block Three Volume Set – Volume A-C **$124.99**

Continuing the H.E. Harris Tradition for quality...
– *Annual supplements are issued for Plate Block Volume C* –

U.S. Plate Strips of 5, Semi Postal #B1-B3

PLATE NUMBER STRIPS OF 5

SCOTT NO.	UNUSED F/NH	SCOTT NO.	UNUSED F/NH
1891	7.50	2451	1.60
1895	6.00	2451b	1.60
1897	.95	2452	1.80
1897A	.85	2452a	2.00
1898	1.20	2452B	2.00
1898A	2.00	2452D	2.00
1899	1.60	2453	2.00
1900	15.00	2454	2.00
1901	19.00	2457	3.25
1902	13.25	2458	3.75
1903	20.00	2463	5.75
1904	60.00	2464	4.75
1905	5.50	2466	8.00
1906	4.50	2468	14.00
1907	5.25	2495Ab	5.75
1908	5.00	2518	5.50
1898Ab	9.00	2523	6.25
1900A	16.50	2523A	6.50
1901A	52.00	2525	6.00
1902A	7.00	2526	6.00
1903A	5.25	2529	5.00
1904A	42.00	2529a	5.00
1905A	5.25	2529c	8.00
1906A	7.00	2598b	8.50
2005	135.00	2599b	8.50
2112	8.75	2602	4.25
2115	5.50	2603	4.50
2115b	6.75	2604	3.50
2123	1.50	2605	5.25
2124	1.40	2606	6.25
2125	2.75	2607	6.25
2126	2.40	2608	6.25
2127	3.50	2609	6.75
2128	2.75	2802b	8.50
2129	3.75	2813b	8.50
2130	3.50	2886b	6.50
2131	2.00	2888	7.25
2132	2.75	2889	16.50
2133	3.50	2890	7.00
2134	2.50	2891	22.00
2135	4.50	2892	8.00
2136	5.00	2893	2.50
2123A	8.50	2902	2.00
2124A	2.50	2902B	2.75
2125A	2.50	2903	2.50
2126A	2.50	2904	2.50
2127A	4.50	2904A	2.75
2127Av	3.25	2904B	2.75
2128A	2.00	2905	3.50
2129A	4.50	2906	3.00
2130A	3.50	2907	3.50
2130Av	3.25	2908	4.00
2132A	3.50	2909	4.00
2132B	24.00	2910	4.00
2133A	4.50	2911	6.00
2149	5.50	2912	6.00
2149A	5.00	2912A	6.00
2150	5.50	2912B	6.00
2150A	5.25	2913	6.75
2225	.90	2914	6.75
2225a	1.40	2915	16.00
2226	1.10	2915A	10.00
2226a	1.20	2915B	16.50
2228	2.00	2915C	35.00
2228a	16.00	2915D	16.00
2231	9.50	3017a	8.00
2252	1.40	3018	6.50
2252a	1.90	3044	1.50
2253	1.75	3045	1.25
2254	2.50	3053	7.50
2255	3.50	3054	10.00
2256	3.50	3055	6.00
2257	2.25	3132	10.00
2257a	4.00	3133	10.00
2258	7.50	3207	2.25
2259	4.00	3207A	2.25
2260	4.00	3208	5.75
2260a	6.25	3208A	5.75
2261	4.75	3228	3.00
2262	5.00	3229	3.00
2262a	5.50	3263	5.00
2263	5.00	3264	6.00
2263b	12.00	3265	6.00
2264	10.00	3266	6.00
2265	7.50	3270	3.50
2266	6.00	3271	3.50
2279	5.00	3280	6.50
2280	5.00	3281	5.75
2280a	6.00	3282	5.75
2281	4.75	3305A	6.00

SEMI-POSTAL

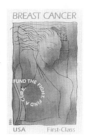
B1

B2

B3

SCOTT NO.	DESCRIPTION	FIRST DAY COVERS SING	FIRST DAY COVERS PL. BLK.	MINT SHEET	PLATE BLOCK	UNUSED F/NH	USED
	1998						
B1	(32¢ + 8¢) Breast Cancer	2.25	5.50	18.00(20)	5.50	1.25	.70
	2001						
B2	(34¢ + 11¢) Heroes of 2001	2.50	5.50	22.50(20)	5.50	1.25	.50
	2003						
B3	(37¢ + 8¢) Stop Family Violence	2.50	5.50	22.50(20)	5.50	1.25	.50

Quality Magnifiers

1029 Gold 10x Triplet Magnifier
Three of the highest quality optical lenses, expertly bonded and ground to form one triplex lens. An excellent loupe when crystal clarity is necessary for critical inspection. Gold-plated and comes packed in its own leather case.
Item# 9ANC3352 .... $31.95

1029RC 10x Triplet Magnifier
Three of the highest quality optical lenses, expertly bonded and ground to form one triplex lens. An excellent loupe when crystal clarity is necessary for critical inspection. Comes packed in its own leather case.
Item# 9ANC3353 .... $31.95

1029 Doublet Magnifier
Manufactured from the highest quality lens and mounted inside a chrome-plated brass rim to protect the lens from scratching. Comes packed in its own leather case.
Item# 9ANC1651 .... $29.95

Reader Magnifiers
Our popular "Sherlock Holmes" readers feature quality lenses mounted in chrome-plated brass rims and solid Ebonite handles.
Item# 9ANC1655 2½" lens $5.89
Item# 9ANC1656 3" lens $7.39
Item# 9ANC1657 3½" lens $9.99
Item# 9ANC1658 4" lens $11.89

Serving the Collector Since 1916

Order from your local dealer or direct from Whitman Publishing, LLC.

U.S. Air Post #C1-C24

SCOTT NO.	DESCRIPTION	UNUSED O.G. VF	F	AVG	USED VF	F	AVG

AIR POST

C1-C3
Curtiss Jenny Biplane

C4
Airplane Propeller

C5
Badge of Air Service

C6
Airplane

1918 (C1-6 NH + 40%)

Scott	Description	VF	F	AVG	VF	F	AVG
C1-3	6¢-24¢, 3 varieties, complete	360.00	270.00	187.50	151.00	105.00	74.75
C1	6¢ orange	100.00	75.00	52.50	42.00	30.00	21.00
C2	16¢ green	140.00	105.00	72.50	52.00	38.50	25.75
C3	24¢ carmine rose & blue	140.00	105.00	72.50	65.00	42.00	32.00
C3a	same, center inverted	....	140000.00	....	....	....	....

SCOTT NO.	DESCRIPTION	CENTER LINE BLOCKS F/NH	F/OG	A/OG	ARROW BLOCKS F/NH	F/OG	A/OG
C1	6¢ orange	350.00	280.00	225.00	300.00	240.00	190.00
C2	16¢ green	500.00	400.00	325.00	450.00	360.00	285.00
C3	24¢ carmine rose & blue	500.00	400.00	325.00	435.00	350.00	275.00

1923

Scott	Description	VF	F	AVG	VF	F	AVG
C4-6	8¢-24¢, 3 varieties, complete	320.00	237.00	160.00	98.50	69.50	47.50
C4	8¢ dark green	40.00	29.50	20.50	20.50	15.00	10.00
C5	16¢ dark blue	142.00	105.00	71.50	42.00	28.00	19.50
C6	24¢ carmine	155.00	115.00	77.50	41.25	30.50	20.50

C7-C9
Map of U.S. and Airplanes

1926-30 (C7-12 NH + 50%)

Scott	Description	VF	F	AVG	VF	F	AVG
C7-9	10¢-20¢, 3 varieties, complete	19.95	15.25	7.60	5.35	4.15	2.80
C7	10¢ dark blue	4.00	3.05	2.20	.55	.40	.25
C8	15¢ olive brown	4.75	3.60	2.75	2.85	2.20	1.50
C9	20¢ yellow green (1927)	14.00	9.75	6.50	2.25	1.75	1.20

C10
Lindbergh's Airplane "Spirit of St. Louis"

1927 LINDBERGH TRIBUTE ISSUE

Scott	Description	VF	F	AVG	VF	F	AVG
C10	10¢ dark blue	10.75	8.25	5.50	2.85	2.20	1.40
C10a	same, bklt pane of 3	125.00	95.00	67.50	....	....	....

C11
Beacon and Rocky Mountains

C12, C16, C17, C19
Winged Globe

1928 BEACON

Scott	Description	VF	F	AVG	VF	F	AVG
C11	5¢ carmine & blue	7.00	4.75	3.00	1.00	.65	.35

1930 Flat Plate Printing, Perf.11

Scott	Description	VF	F	AVG	VF	F	AVG
C12	5¢ violet	15.00	12.00	8.50	.70	.55	.40

C13
Graf Zeppelin

C14

C15

1930 GRAF ZEPPELIN ISSUE (NH + 40%)

Scott	Description	VF	F	AVG	VF	F	AVG
C13-15	65¢-$2.60, 3 varieties, complete	2350.00	1835.00	1480.00	1595.00	1300.00	1110.00
C13	65¢ green	400.00	300.00	260.00	260.00	210.00	175.00
C14	$1.30 brown	800.00	625.00	500.00	495.00	410.00	340.00
C15	$2.60 blue	1275.00	1000.00	800.00	875.00	725.00	625.00

1931-32 Rotary Press Printing. Perf. 10½ x 11, Designs as #C12 (C16-C24 NH + 40%)

Scott	Description	VF	F	AVG	VF	F	AVG
C16	5¢ violet	10.00	7.50	5.50	.80	.55	.35
C17	8¢ olive bistre	3.95	3.25	2.15	.55	.40	.30

C18
Graf Zeppelin

1933 CENTURY OF PROGRESS ISSUE

Scott	Description	VF	F	AVG	VF	F	AVG
C18	50¢ green	125.00	100.00	75.00	95.00	75.00	60.00

1934 DESIGN OF 1930

Scott	Description	VF	F	AVG	VF	F	AVG
C19	6¢ dull orange	4.50	3.25	2.00	.40	.30	.20

C20-22
China Clipper

1935 TRANS-PACIFIC ISSUE

Scott	Description	VF	F	AVG	VF	F	AVG
C20	25¢ blue	1.80	1.40	1.05	1.40	1.00	.70

1937. Type of 1935 Issue, Date Omitted

Scott	Description	VF	F	AVG	VF	F	AVG
C21	20¢ green	13.00	9.75	7.50	2.00	1.65	1.25
C22	50¢ carmine	12.00	10.25	7.75	5.40	4.50	3.50

C23
Eagle

1938

Scott	Description	VF	F	AVG	VF	F	AVG
C23	6¢ dark blue & carmine	.65	.55	.45	.25	.20	.15

C24
Winged Globe

1939 TRANS-ATLANTIC ISSUE

Scott	Description	VF	F	AVG	VF	F	AVG
C24	30¢ dull blue	14.00	12.00	10.50	1.70	1.40	1.10

U.S. Air Post #C25-C47

AIR POST PLATE BLOCKS #C1-C24

SCOTT NO.		UNUSED NH			UNUSED O.G.		
		VF	F	AVG	VF	F	AVG
C1(6)	6¢ orange	1550.00	1150.00	925.00	1115.00	825.00	550.00
C2(6)	16¢ green	2665.00	1975.00	1575.00	2000.00	1485.00	1100.00
C3(12)	24¢ carmine rose & blue	3100.00	2300.00	1825.00	2450.00	1815.00	1250.00
C4(6)	8¢ dark green ...	610.00	450.00	360.00	445.00	330.00	260.00
C5(6)	16¢ dark blue	3845.00	2850.00	2250.00	2975.00	2200.00	1650.00
C6(6)	24¢ carmine	4790.00	3550.00	2825.00	3700.00	2750.00	2100.00
C7(6)	10¢ dark blue	71.50	55.00	44.00	54.00	41.50	27.50
C8(6)	15¢ olive brown ...	85.00	66.00	52.75	65.00	50.00	33.00
C9(6)	20¢ yellow green .	200.00	155.00	125.00	145.00	110.00	85.00
C10(6)	10¢ dark blue	265.00	205.00	165.00	195.00	150.00	110.00
C11(6)	5¢ carmine & blue	82.00	63.25	50.00	60.00	46.50	31.50
C12(6)	5¢ violet	285.00	220.00	175.00	215.00	165.00	120.00
C13(6)	65¢ green	4200.00	3250.00	2500.00	2975.00	2475.00	1950.00
C14(6)	$1.30 brown ...	10000.00	8000.00	5700.00	7250.00	6050.00	4675.00
C15(6)	$2.60 blue	15000.00	12000.00	9500.00	11000.00	9075.00	7250.00
C16(4)	5¢ violet	175.00	135.00	105.00	125.00	95.00	65.00
C17(4)	8¢ olive bistre ...	58.50	45.00	36.00	40.00	30.00	24.00
C18(4)	5¢ green	1075.00	900.00	720.00	955.00	795.00	635.00
C19(4)	6¢ dull orange ...	39.50	33.00	26.00	30.00	25.00	20.00
C20(6)	25¢ blue	33.00	27.50	22.00	26.50	22.00	17.50
C21(6)	20¢ green	185.00	155.00	122.50	150.00	125.00	100.00
C22(6)	50¢ carmine	180.00	150.00	115.00	145.00	120.00	90.00
C23(4)	6¢ dark blue & carmine	11.50	9.50	7.50	8.50	7.15	5.50
C24(6)	30¢ dull blue	250.00	210.00	160.00	200.00	165.00	130.00

SCOTT NO.	DESCRIPTION	FIRST DAY COVERS		MINT SHEET	PLATE BLOCK	UNUSED F/NH	USED
		SING	PL. BLK.				

C25-C31

1941-44 TRANSPORT ISSUE

C25-31	6¢-50¢, 7 varieties, complete	....	....	....	137.00	23.95	5.60
C25	6¢ Transport Plane ..	4.50	8.75	8.35(50)	1.05	.20	.15
C25a	same, bklt pane of 3 .	20.00	....	....	....	4.25	....
C26	8¢ Transport Plane ..	4.50	11.25	11.50(50)	2.20	.25	.15
C27	10¢ Transport Plane .	6.00	12.50	82.50(50)	10.50	1.65	.20
C28	15¢ Transport Plane .	6.00	13.75	150.00(50)	13.95	3.50	.40
C29	20¢ Transport Plane .	8.00	16.00	125.00(50)	12.65	2.60	.35
C30	30¢ Transport Plane .	13.00	27.00	140.00(50)	14.00	3.00	.40
C31	50¢ Transport Plane .	28.50	68.75	625.00(50)	90.00	14.00	4.25

C32

1946

| C32 | 5¢ DC-4 Skymaster .. | 1.75 | 4.25 | 8.00(50) | .75 | .20 | .15 |

C33, C37, C39, C41

C36

C34

C35

SCOTT NO.	DESCRIPTION	FIRST DAY COVERS		MINT SHEET	PLATE BLOCK	UNUSED F/NH	USED
		SING	PL. BLK.				

1947

C33-36	5¢-25¢, 4 varieties, complete	....	....	....	....	2.10	.55
C33	5¢ DC-4 Skymaster ..	1.75	4.25	17.00(100)	.75	.20	.15
C34	10¢ Pan American Bldg.	1.75	4.25	14.00(50)	1.50	.30	.15
C35	15¢ New York Skyline	1.75	4.25	22.50(50)	1.85	.50	.15
C36	25¢ Plane over Bridge	2.00	4.25	50.00(50)	4.75	1.25	.15

1948
Rotary Press Coil–Perf. 10 Horiz.

| | | | LINE PR. | | LINE PR. | | |
| C37 | 5¢ DC-4 Skymaster... | 1.75 | 4.25 | .... | 9.50 | 1.40 | 1.00 |

C38   C40

| C38 | 5¢ New York Jubliee . | 1.75 | 4.25 | 20.00(100) | 5.75 | .25 | .15 |

1949

C39	6¢ DC-4 Skymaster (as #C33)	1.75	4.25	20.00(100)	.75	.25	.15
C39a	same, bklt pane of 6 .	6.50	....	....	....	11.50	....
C40	6¢ Alexandria, Virginia	1.75	4.25	11.00(50)	.95	.25	.15

Rotary Press Coil–Perf. 10 Horiz.

| | | | LINE PR. | | LINE PR. | | |
| C41 | DC-4 Skymaster (as#C37) | 1.75 | 4.25 | .... | 14.00 | 3.50 | .15 |

NOTE: Unused Air Mail coil pairs can be supplied at two times the single price.

C42   C43

C44

1949 U.P.U. ISSUES

C42-44	10¢-25¢, 3 varieties, complete	....	....	....	....	1.90	1.05
C42	10¢ Post Office	1.75	4.25	17.50(50)	1.70	.40	.30
C43	15¢ Globe & Doves ..	2.00	5.00	25.00(50)	1.50	.60	.35
C44	25¢ Plane & Globe ..	2.50	6.25	42.00(50)	7.25	1.00	.50

C45

C46   C47

1949-58

C45-51	7 varieties, complete	....	....	....	....	9.00	2.30
C45	6¢ Wright Brothers (1949)	1.75	4.25	15.00(50)	.80	.40	.15
C46	80¢ Hawaii (1952) ...	15.00	35.00	350.00(50)	35.00	8.00	1.50
C47	6¢ Powered Flight (1953)	1.75	4.25	9.25(50)	.75	.25	.15

142 U.S. Air Post #C48-C69

SCOTT NO.	DESCRIPTION	FIRST DAY COVERS SING	FIRST DAY COVERS PL. BLK.	MINT SHEET	PLATE BLOCK	UNUSED F/NH	USED

C48, C50

1949-58 (continued)

| C48 | 4¢ Eagle (1954) ... | 1.75 | 4.25 | 16.50(100) | 1.95 | .25 | .15 |

C49

C51, C52, C60, C61

C49	6¢ Air Force (1957) .	1.75	4.25	10.00(50)	.75	.25	.15
C50	5¢ Eagle (1958) ...	1.75	4.25	19.50(100)	1.85	.25	.15
C51	7¢ Silhouette of Jet, blue (1958)	1.75	4.25	19.50(100)	1.00	.25	.15
C51a	same, bklt pane of 6	16.00	....	....	12.00	....	....

Rotary Press Coil–Perf. 10 Horiz.

| | | | LINE PR. | | LINE PR. | | |
| C52 | 7¢ Silhouette of Jet, blue | 1.75 | 3.25 | .... | 17.50 | 2.50 | .15 |

C53

C54

1959

C53-56	4 varieties, complete	....	....	....	....	1.30	.70
C53	7¢ Alaska Statehood .	1.75	4.25	14.00(50)	1.25	.30	.15
C54	7¢ Balloon Jupiter ...	1.75	4.25	17.50(50)	1.60	.40	.15

C55

C56

| C55 | 7¢ Hawaii Statehood | 1.75 | 4.25 | 14.00(50) | 1.25 | .30 | .15 |
| C56 | 10¢ Pan-Am Games | 1.75 | 4.25 | 17.50(50) | 1.70 | .40 | .30 |

C57

C58, C63

C59

C62

1959-66 REGULAR ISSUES

| C57/63 | (C57-60, C62-63) 6 varieties........ | .... | .... | .... | .... | 3.90 | 1.65 |

1959-66

C57	10¢ Liberty Bell (1960)	1.75	4.25	85.00(50)	8.00	1.75	1.00
C58	15¢ Statue of Liberty .	1.75	4.25	22.50(50)	1.95	.45	.25
C59	25¢ Abraham Lincoln (1960)	1.75	4.25	40.00(50)	4.00	.90	.15

1960. Design of 1958

| C60 | 7¢ Jet Plane, carmine | 1.75 | 4.25 | 22.50(100) | 1.25 | .30 | .15 |
| C60a | same, bklt pane of 6 . | 9.00 | .... | .... | .... | 15.00 | .... |

Rotary Press Coil–Perf. 10 Horiz.

| | | | LINE PR. | | LINE PR. | | |
| C61 | 7¢ Jet Plane, carmine | 1.75 | 3.25 | .... | 45.00 | 5.00 | .35 |

1961-67

| C62 | 13¢ Liberty Bell ..... | 1.75 | 4.25 | 21.50(50) | 2.10 | .45 | .15 |
| C63 | 15¢ Statue re-drawn . | 1.75 | 4.25 | 27.50(50) | 2.50 | .60 | .15 |

C64, C65

1962-64

| C64/69 | (C64, C66-69) 5 varieties | .... | .... | .... | .... | 2.00 | 1.25 |

1962

C64	8¢ Plane & Capitol ..	1.75	4.25	21.00(100)	1.00	.25	.15
C64b	same, bklt pane of 5, Slogan I	1.95	....	....	....	6.25	....
C64b	bklt pane of 5, Slogan II, (1963)	....	....	....	....	75.00	....
C64b	bklt pane of 5, Slogan III (1964)	....	....	....	....	13.00	....
C64c	bklt pane of 5 tagged, Slogan III (1964)	....	....	....	....	1.85	....

SLOGAN I–Your Mailman Deserves Your Help...   **SLOGAN II–Use Zone Numbers..**

SLOGAN III–Always Use Zip Code....

Rotary Press Coil–Perf. 10 Horiz.

| | | | LINE PR. | | LINE PR. | | |
| C65 | 8¢ Plane & Capitol .. | 1.75 | 3.25 | .... | 5.75 | .45 | .15 |

C66

C68

C67

1963

C66	15¢ Montgomery Blair	1.75	4.25	33.50(50)	4.00	.75	.60
C67	6¢ Bald Eagle	1.75	4.25	16.50(100)	2.25	.20	.15
C68	8¢ Amelia Earhart ...	1.75	4.25	18.50(50)	1.60	.40	.20

C69

1964

| C69 | 8¢ Dr. Robert H. Goddard | 2.00 | 5.00 | 23.75(50) | 2.25 | .50 | .20 |

U.S. Air Post #C70-C90

SCOTT NO.	DESCRIPTION	FIRST DAY COVERS SING	FIRST DAY COVERS PL. BLK.	MINT SHEET	PLATE BLOCK	UNUSED F/NH	USED
C70/76	(C70-72, C74-76) 6 varieties	....	....	....	....	2.85	1.00

1967-68

SCOTT NO.	DESCRIPTION	FDC SING	FDC PL. BLK.	MINT SHEET	PLATE BLOCK	UNUSED F/NH	USED
C70	8¢ Alaska Purchase	1.75	4.25	13.50(50)	1.95	.30	.20
C71	20¢ "Columbia Jays"	1.75	4.25	48.00(50)	4.50	1.00	.15
C72	10¢ 50-Stars (1968)	1.75	4.25	32.50(100)	1.50	.40	.15
C72b	same, bklt pane of 8	3.00	....	....	....	2.50	....
C72c	same, bklt pane of 5, Slogan IV or V	140.00	....	....	....	4.00	....

SLOGAN IV–Mail Early in the Day...   SLOGAN V–Use Zip Code...

1968 Rotary Press Coil–Perf. 10 Vert.

SCOTT NO.	DESCRIPTION	FDC SING	LINE PR.		LINE PR.	UNUSED F/NH	USED
C73	10¢ 50-Star	1.75	3.25		2.25	.35	.15

C74	10¢ Air Mail Anniversary	1.75	4.25	15.00(50)	3.10	.30	.15
C75	20¢ "USA" & Plane	1.75	4.25	28.00(50)	2.50	.55	.20

| C76 | 10¢ Man on the Moon | 6.00 | 14.50 | 15.00(32) | 2.00 | .50 | .20 |

1971-73

C77-81	9¢-21¢, 5 varieties, complete	....	....	....	....	1.95	.80
C77	9¢ Delta Winged Plane	1.75	4.25	25.00(100)	1.25	.30	.25
C78	11¢ Silhouette of Plane	1.75	4.25	35.00(100)	1.60	.40	.15
C78b	same, precanceled	....	....	....	....	....	.50
C78a	11¢ bklt pane of 4	2.25	....	....	....	1.20	....
C79	13¢ Letter (1973)	1.75	4.25	35.00(100)	1.60	.40	.15
C79b	same, precanceled	....	....	....	....	....	.60
C79a	13¢ bklt pane of 5	2.25	....	....	....	1.50	....

C80	17¢ Liberty Head	1.75	4.25	22.50(50)	2.25	.50	.15
C81	21¢ "USA" & Plane	1.75	4.25	24.00(50)	1.95	.50	.15

Rotary Press Coils–Perf. 10 Vert.

			LINE PR.		LINE PR.		
C82	11¢ Silhouette of Jet	1.75	3.25	....	.90	.30	.15
C83	13¢ Letter	1.75	3.25	....	1.15	.35	.15

1972-76

C84-90	11¢-31¢, 7 varieties, complete	....	....	....	....	4.15	1.20

1972

C84	11¢ City of Refuge	1.75	4.25	18.50(50)	1.50	.40	.15
C85	11¢ Olympics	1.75	4.25	18.50(50)	3.10(10)	.40	.15

1973

C86	11¢ Electronics	1.75	4.25	18.50(50)	1.50	.40	.15

1974

C87	18¢ Statue of Liberty	1.75	4.25	27.50(50)	2.50	.60	.40
C88	26¢ Mt. Rushmore	1.75	4.25	35.00(50)	3.25	.80	.15

1976

C89	25¢ Plane & Globes	1.75	4.25	35.0050)	3.25	.80	.15
C90	31¢ Plane, Flag & Globes	1.75	4.25	45.00(50)	4.25	1.00	.15

ORDER BY MAIL, PHONE (800) 546-2995 OR FAX (256) 246-1116

U.S. Air Post #C91-C112

SCOTT NO.	DESCRIPTION	FIRST DAY COVERS SING	FIRST DAY COVERS PL. BLK.	MINT SHEET	PLATE BLOCK	UNUSED F/NH	USED

C91 — 31¢ Wright Brothers & Plane
C92 — 31¢ Wright Brothers & Shed

1978-80

C91-100	21¢-40¢, 10 varieties, complete	....	....	....	....	11.50	4.85
C91-92	Wright Brothers, 2 varieties, attached	2.40	5.00	95.00(100)	5.00	2.10	1.75
C91	31¢ Wright Brothers & Plane	1.75	....	....	....	1.00	.50
C92	31¢ Wright Brothers & Shed	1.75	....	....	....	1.00	.50

C93 — 21¢ Chanute & Plane
C94 — 21¢ Chanute & 2 Planes

1979

C93-94	Octave Chanute, 2 varieties, attached	2.40	5.00	95.00(100)	5.00	2.10	1.75
C93	21¢ Chanute & Plane	1.75	....	....	....	1.00	.50
C94	21¢ Chanute & 2 Planes	1.75	....	....	....	1.00	.50

C95 — 25¢ Post & Plane
C96 — 25¢ Plane & Post

C95-96	Wiley Post, 2 varieties, attached	2.40	5.00	165.00(100)	13.50	3.50	2.25
C95	25¢ Post & Plane	1.75	....	....	....	1.80	1.00
C96	25¢ Plane & Post	1.75	....	....	....	1.80	1.00

C97 — 31¢ High Jumper

| C97 | 31¢ High Jumper | 1.75 | 4.25 | 44.00(50) | 12.00(12) | .95 | .40 |

C98 — 40¢ Philip Mazzei
C99 — 28¢ Blanche S. Scott

1980

| C98 | 40¢ Philip Mazzei | 1.75 | 4.25 | 65.00(50) | 15.00(12) | 1.40 | .25 |
| C99 | 28¢ Blanche S. Scott | 1.75 | 4.25 | 37.00(50) | 9.75(12) | .80 | .25 |

C100 — 35¢ Glenn Curtiss

| C100 | 35¢ Glenn Curtiss | 1.75 | 4.25 | 45.00(50) | 13.00(12) | 1.10 | .25 |

C101 — 28¢ Women's Gymnastics
C102 — 28¢ Hurdles
C103 — 28¢ Women's Basketball
C104 — 28¢ Soccer

1983-85

| C101-16 | 28¢-44¢, 16 varieties, complete | .... | .... | .... | .... | 21.50 | 7.50 |

1983

C101-04	Summer Olympics, 4 varieties, attached	3.50	4.50	64.00(50)	6.50	5.75	3.50
C101	28¢ Women's Gymnastics	1.75	....	....	....	1.50	.50
C102	28¢ Hurdles	1.75	....	....	....	1.50	.50
C103	28¢ Women's Basketball	1.75	....	....	....	1.50	.50
C104	28¢ Soccer	1.75	....	....	....	1.50	.50

C105 — 40¢ Shot Put
C106 — 40¢ Men's Gymnastics
C107 — 40¢ Women's Swimming
C108 — 40¢ Weight Lifting

C105-08	Summer Olympics, 4 varieties, attached	4.50	5.75	60.00(50)	6.75	6.00	2.50
C105	40¢ Shot Put	1.85	....	....	....	1.55	.50
C106	40¢ Men's Gymnastics	1.85	....	....	....	1.55	.50
C107	40¢ Women's Swimming	1.85	....	....	....	1.55	.50
C108	40¢ Weight Lifting	1.85	....	....	....	1.55	.50

C109 — 35¢ Fencing
C110 — 35¢ Cycling
C111 — 35¢ Volleyball
C112 — 35¢ Pole Vault

C109-12	Summer Olympics, 4 varieties, attached	4.00	5.00	68.00(50)	9.50	6.00	4.00
C109	35¢ Fencing	1.75	....	....	....	1.55	.60
C110	35¢ Cycling	1.75	....	....	....	1.55	.60
C111	35¢ Volleyball	1.75	....	....	....	1.55	.60
C112	35¢ Pole Vault	1.75	....	....	....	1.55	.60

U.S. Air Post #C113-C138a

1985

SCOTT NO.	DESCRIPTION	FIRST DAY COVERS SING	FIRST DAY COVERS PL. BLK.	MINT SHEET	PLATE BLOCK	UNUSED F/NH	USED
C113	33¢ Alfred Verville	1.75	4.25	42.00(50)	4.75	1.00	.25
C114	39¢ Lawrence and Elmer Sperry	1.75	4.25	57.50(50)	5.25	1.20	.35
C115	44¢ Transpacific	1.75	4.25	60.00(50)	6.00	1.25	.35
C116	44¢ Junipero Serra	1.75	4.25	70.00(50)	9.50	1.50	.40

1988

SCOTT NO.	DESCRIPTION	FDC SING	FDC PL. BLK.	MINT SHEET	PLATE BLOCK	UNUSED F/NH	USED
C117	44¢ New Sweden	1.75	4.25	75.00(50)	10.00	1.60	.90
C118	45¢ Samuel Langley	1.75	4.25	67.50(50)	6.50	1.50	.30
C119	36¢ Igor Sikorsky	1.75	4.25	55.00(50)	5.25	1.25	.40

1989

SCOTT NO.	DESCRIPTION	FDC SING	FDC PL. BLK.	MINT SHEET	PLATE BLOCK	UNUSED F/NH	USED
C120-25	6 varieties, complete	....	....	....	....	8.60	3.00
C120	45¢ French Revolution	1.75	4.25	37.50(30)	5.50	1.20	.75
C121	45¢ Americas Issue (Key Marco Cat)	1.75	4.25	65.00(50)	6.00	1.35	.45
C122-25	Futuristic Mail Delivery, 4 varieties, attached	5.00	6.00	65.00(40)	7.00	6.50	4.00
C122	45¢ Spacecraft	1.75	....	....	....	1.70	.50
C123	45¢ Air Suspended Hover	1.75	....	....	....	1.70	.50
C124	45¢ Moon Rover	1.75	....	....	....	1.70	.50
C125	45¢ Space Shuttle	1.75	....	....	....	1.70	.50
C126	$1.80 Futuristic Mail Imperf. Souvenir Sheet	6.50	....	....	....	6.50	....

1990

SCOTT NO.	DESCRIPTION	FDC SING	FDC PL. BLK.	MINT SHEET	PLATE BLOCK	UNUSED F/NH	USED
C127	45¢ Americas Issue (Island Beach)	1.75	4.25	85.00(50)	9.00	1.75	.40

1991-93

SCOTT NO.	DESCRIPTION	FDC SING	FDC PL. BLK.	MINT SHEET	PLATE BLOCK	UNUSED F/NH	USED
C128	50¢ Harriet Quimby	1.75	4.25	72.50(50)	7.50	1.60	.50
C128b	50¢ Harriet Quimby, reissue, bullseye perf. (1993)	....	....	85.00(50)	8.50	1.75	.50
C129	40¢ William Piper	1.75	4.25	65.00(50)	6.25	1.35	.50
C130	50¢ Antarctic Treaty	1.75	4.25	70.00(50)	7.00	1.50	.70
C131	50¢ America (Bering Strait) (1991)	1.75	4.25	70.00(50)	7.00	1.50	.65
C132	40¢ William Piper, reissue, bullseye perf. (1993)	....	....	140.00(50)	40.00	2.25	.65

1999

SCOTT NO.	DESCRIPTION	FDC SING	FDC PL. BLK.	MINT SHEET	PLATE BLOCK	UNUSED F/NH	USED
C133	48¢ Niagara Falls	2.25	5.50	25.00(20)	7.50	1.20	.40
C134	40¢ Rio Grande	2.10	5.00	20.00(20)	5.00	1.10	.35

2000-03

SCOTT NO.	DESCRIPTION	FDC SING	FDC PL. BLK.	MINT SHEET	PLATE BLOCK	UNUSED F/NH	USED
C135	60¢ Grand Canyon	2.25	5.00	30.00(20)	8.00	1.65	.40
C136	70¢ Nine-Mile Prairie, Nebraska	2.50	6.00	37.50(20)	8.50	1.95	.60
C137	80¢ Mt. McKinley	2.75	6.50	37.50(20)	9.00	1.95	.70
C138	60¢ Acadia National Park	2.50	5.00	28.00(20)	7.00	1.50	.50
C138a	60¢ Acadia National Park die cut 11.5 x 11.75	2.75	5.50	28.00(20)	7.00	1.50	.50

U.S. Special Delivery #CE1-E23, Registration & Certified

AIR MAIL SPECIAL DELIVERY STAMPS

771, CE1, CE2

SCOTT NO.	DESCRIPTION	PLATE BLOCK F/NH	F	AVG	UNUSED F/NH	F	AVG	USED F	AVG
CE1	16¢ dark blue (1934)	20.50	18.00	14.50	.80	.70	.55	.70	.55
CE2	16¢ red & blue (1936)	8.00	6.00	4.50	.45	.40	.30	.25	.20
CE2	same, center line block	2.75	2.15	1.75	....	....	....	....	....
CE2	same, arrow block of 4	2.50	1.95	1.50	....	....	....	....	....

SPECIAL DELIVERY STAMPS

E1

E2, E3

E4, E5

(E1-E14 for VF Centering–Fine Price + 35%)

SCOTT NO.	DESCRIPTION	UNUSED NH F	AVG	UNUSED OG F	AVG	USED F	AVG

1885 Inscribed "Secures Immediate Delivery at Special Delivery Office" Perf. 12

E1	10¢ blue	400.00	295.00	260.00	165.00	40.00	25.00

1888 Inscribed "Secures Immediate Delivery at any Post Office"

E2	10¢ blue	375.00	270.00	225.00	125.00	12.50	8.00

1893

E3	10¢ orange	250.00	175.00	125.00	80.00	19.00	12.50

1894 Same type as preceding issue, but with line under "Ten Cents" Unwatermarked

E4	10¢ blue	875.00	675.00	550.00	400.00	22.50	14.00

1895 Double Line Watermark

E5	10¢ blue	190.00	140.00	125.00	80.00	3.25	2.00

E6, E8-11

E7

1902

E6	10¢ ultramarine	135.00	90.00	82.50	55.00	3.00	1.95

1908

E7	10¢ green	78.50	62.50	52.50	35.00	29.50	19.50

1911 Single Line Watermark

E8	10¢ ultramarine	120.00	85.00	78.50	50.00	4.75	3.25

1914 Perf. 10

E9	10¢ ultramarine	220.00	160.00	135.00	95.00	5.50	4.00

1916 Unwatermarked Perf. 10

E10	10¢ pale ultra	360.00	280.00	250.00	160.00	24.00	15.00

1917 Perf. 11

E11	10¢ ultramarine	27.50	19.00	14.00	8.50	.45	.30
E11	same, plate block of 6	225.00	175.00	165.00	120.00	....	....

E12, E15   E14, E19

SCOTT NO.	DESCRIPTION	PLATE BLOCK F/NH	F	AVG	UNUSED F/NH	F	AVG	USED F	AVG

1922-25 Flat Plate Printing Perf. 11

E12	10¢ gray violet	(6) 375.00	350.00	220.00	40.00	25.00	13.50	.40	.30
E13	15¢ deep orange (1925)	(6) 375.00	250.00	160.00	32.50	22.50	14.00	.90	.70
E14	20¢ black (1925)	(6) 45.00	31.50	23.00	3.35	2.75	1.70	.90	.70

SCOTT NO.	DESCRIPTION	FIRST DAY COVERS SING	PL. BLK.	MINT SHEET	PLATE BLOCK	UNUSED F/NH	USED

1927-51 Rotary Press Printing Perf. 11 x 10½

E15-19	10¢-20¢, 5 varieties	....	....	....	50.00	8.50	2.60
E15	10¢ gray violet	....	....	42.50(50)	6.75	.85	.15
E16	15¢ orange (1931)	....	....	45.00(50)	4.75	.90	.15
E17	13¢ blue (1944)	9.00	20.00	35.00(50)	4.00	.70	.15
E18	17¢ orange yellow (1944)	12.00	28.00	165.00(50)	28.00	4.00	2.25
E19	20¢ black (1951)	5.00	12.50	97.50(50)	8.00	1.95	.15

E20   E22

1954-57

E20	20¢ deep blue	2.50	6.25	26.00(50)	2.80	.55	.15
E21	30¢ lake (1957)	2.50	6.25	31.50(50)	3.10	.70	.15

1969-71

E22	45¢ carmine & violet blue	2.50	6.25	63.50(50)	7.25	1.40	.35
E23	60¢ violet blue & carmine (1971)	2.75	6.75	55.00(50)	5.25	1.20	.15

REGISTRATION STAMP

SCOTT NO.	DESCRIPTION	UNUSED NH F	AVG	UNUSED OG F	AVG	USED F	AVG

F1

1911 Registration

F1	10¢ ultramarine	95.00	70.00	62.50	40.00	6.50	3.75

U.S. CERTIFIED STAMP

SCOTT NO.	DESCRIPTION	FIRST DAY COVERS SING	PL. BLK.	MINT SHEET	PLATE BLOCK	UNUSED F/NH	USED

FA1

1955 Certified Mail

FA1	15¢ red	2.50	6.25	19.50(50)	5.00	.40	.30

J1-J28

J29-J68

SCOTT NO.	DESCRIPTION	UNUSED NH F	UNUSED NH AVG	UNUSED OG F	UNUSED OG AVG	USED F	USED AVG
	1879 Unwatermarked Perf. 12						
J1	1¢ brown	95.00	67.50	42.50	30.00	7.00	4.75
J2	2¢ brown	495.00	295.00	250.00	140.00	6.75	4.50
J3	3¢ brown	75.00	48.00	40.00	27.50	4.00	2.50
J4	5¢ brown	775.00	550.00	400.00	260.00	38.00	22.00
J5	10¢ brown	750.00	500.00	425.00	230.00	19.00	12.50
J6	30¢ brown	425.00	230.00	210.00	135.00	41.00	26.00
J7	50¢ brown	625.00	375.00	325.00	185.00	52.00	34.00
	1884-89						
J15	1¢ red brown	80.00	47.50	35.00	22.00	3.75	2.25
J16	2¢ red brown	110.00	60.00	47.50	28.00	3.75	2.25
J17	3¢ red brown	1300.00	795.00	675.00	400.00	135.00	80.00
J18	5¢ red brown	725.00	400.00	290.00	175.00	20.00	12.50
J19	10¢ red brown	725.00	400.00	290.00	175.00	14.50	10.00
J20	30¢ red brown	325.00	210.00	130.00	85.00	37.50	23.00
J21	50¢ red brown	2600.00	1750.00	1150.00	725.00	145.00	90.00
	1891						
J22	1¢ bright claret	40.00	25.00	18.00	10.50	.80	.55
J23	2¢ bright claret	55.00	37.50	23.00	14.00	.80	.55
J24	3¢ bright claret	110.00	55.00	45.00	24.50	6.75	3.50
J25	5¢ bright claret	120.00	75.00	50.00	29.00	6.75	3.50
J26	10¢ bright claret . . .	200.00	110.00	85.00	50.00	14.50	9.00
J27	30¢ bright claret . . .	650.00	395.00	290.00	155.00	125.00	70.00
J28	50¢ bright claret . . .	700.00	495.00	310.00	185.00	125.00	70.00
	1894 Unwatermarked Perf. 12 (†)						
J29	1¢ pale vermillion .	1800.00	1150.00	1100.00	650.00	295.00	175.00
J30	2¢ dark vermillion .	700.00	425.00	480.00	300.00	90.00	62.50
J31	1¢ deep claret	55.00	37.50	34.00	21.00	5.25	3.75
J32	2¢ deep claret	50.00	32.00	30.00	16.50	3.25	2.00
J33	3¢ deep claret	190.00	115.00	120.00	75.00	27.50	15.75
J34	5¢ deep claret	275.00	165.00	180.00	100.00	28.00	17.75
J35	10¢ deep claret . . .	275.00	165.00	180.00	100.00	21.00	14.50
J36	30¢ deep claret . . .	475.00	310.00	280.00	170.00	72.50	48.00
J36b	30¢ pale rose	400.00	280.00	240.00	165.00	70.00	45.00
J37	50¢ deep claret . . .	1400.00	875.00	850.00	575.00	180.00	125.00
	1895 Double Line Watermark Perf. 12 (†)						
J38	1¢ deep claret	10.50	7.00	6.75	5.00	.60	.45
J39	2¢ deep claret	10.50	7.00	6.75	5.00	.60	.45
J40	3¢ deep claret	65.00	42.50	40.00	28.00	1.50	1.00
J41	5¢ deep claret	72.50	51.00	42.50	29.00	1.50	1.00
J42	10¢ deep claret . . .	74.00	55.00	45.00	32.00	3.00	2.00
J43	30¢ deep claret . . .	675.00	500.00	400.00	295.00	42.50	31.00
J44	50¢ deep claret . . .	350.00	270.00	225.00	160.00	30.00	21.00
	1910-12 Single Line Watermark Perf. 12						
J45	1¢ deep claret	40.00	28.00	22.00	16.00	2.50	1.80
J46	2¢ deep claret	40.00	28.00	22.00	16.00	.75	.60
J47	3¢ deep claret	800.00	525.00	425.00	300.00	24.00	17.00
J48	5¢ deep claret	120.00	85.00	70.00	52.50	5.50	3.75
J49	10¢ deep claret . . .	155.00	105.00	90.00	70.00	10.00	7.00
J50	50¢ deep claret (1912)	1100.00	775.00	700.00	525.00	100.00	67.50
	1914 Single Line Watermark Perf. 10						
J52	1¢ carmine lake . . .	75.00	60.00	47.50	35.00	9.50	6.25
J53	2¢ carmine lake . . .	58.00	42.00	37.00	24.00	.35	.25
J54	3¢ carmine lake . . .	1100.00	775.00	700.00	525.00	32.00	23.00
J55	5¢ carmine lake . . .	50.00	38.00	29.00	21.00	2.25	1.75
J56	10¢ carmine lake . .	75.00	60.00	47.50	35.00	1.70	1.25
J57	30¢ carmine lake . .	325.00	250.00	195.00	140.00	16.00	11.50
J58	50¢ carmine lake . .	....	....	8800.00	7100.00	700.00	575.00
	1916 Unwatermarked Perf. 10						
J59	1¢ rose	3400.00	2850.00	2000.00	1625.00	280.00	225.00
J60	2¢ rose	210.00	145.00	125.00	90.00	18.00	13.50

SCOTT NO.	DESCRIPTION	PLATE BLOCK (OG) F/NH	PLATE BLOCK (OG) F	PLATE BLOCK (OG) AVG	UNUSED (OG) F/NH	UNUSED (OG) F	UNUSED (OG) AVG	USED F	USED AVG
	1917 Unwatermarked Perf. 11								
J61	1¢ carmine rose . (6)	50.00	40.00	27.50	2.50	1.55	1.10	.20	.15
J62	2¢ carmine rose . (6)	40.00	32.00	25.00	2.35	1.40	.95	.20	.15
J63	3¢ carmine rose . (6)	120.00	95.00	70.00	11.00	7.50	4.75	.20	.15
J64	5¢ carmine . . . . . (6)	120.00	95.00	70.00	11.00	7.50	4.75	.20	.15
J65	10¢ carmine rose (6)	160.00	125.00	100.00	16.50	11.00	5.50	.20	.15
J66	30¢ carmine rose	....	....	....	85.00	50.00	35.00	.55	.35
J67	50¢ carmine rose	....	....	....	100.00	65.00	45.00	.20	.15
	1925								
J68	1/2¢ dull red . . . . (6)	12.50	10.00	7.50	.80	.60	.40	.20	.15

J69-J76, J79-J86

J77, J78, J87

J88-J104

SCOTT NO.	DESCRIPTION	PLATE BLOCK (OG) F/NH	PLATE BLOCK (OG) F	PLATE BLOCK (OG) AVG	UNUSED (OG) F/NH	UNUSED (OG) F	UNUSED (OG) AVG	USED F	USED AVG
	1930 Perf. 11								
J69	1/2¢ carmine . . . (6)	50.00	38.00	30.00	5.00	3.75	2.25	1.25	.85
J70	1¢ carmine . . . . . (6)	37.50	29.00	24.00	3.50	2.60	1.75	.20	.15
J71	2¢ carmine . . . . . (6)	50.00	38.00	30.00	5.00	3.75	2.50	.20	.15
J72	3¢ carmine . . . . . (6)	300.00	240.00	190.00	31.50	22.00	15.00	1.25	.75
J73	5¢ carmine . . . . . (6)	230.00	180.00	145.00	26.00	19.00	13.50	2.10	1.50
J74	10¢ carmine . . . . (6)	475.00	380.00	300.00	58.00	38.00	25.00	.85	.60
J75	30¢ carmine	....	....	....	140.00	95.00	70.00	1.75	1.30
J76	50¢ carmine	....	....	....	230.00	180.00	125.00	.60	.45
J77	$1 scarlet . . . . . . (6)	325.00	260.00	210.00	35.00	22.00	17.00	.20	.15
J78	$5 scarlet . . . . . . (6)	350.00	295.00	220.00	50.00	35.00	24.00	.20	.15
	1931 Rotary Press Printing Perf. 11 x 10 1/2								
J79-86	**1/2¢-50¢, 8 varieties, complete . . . . . .**	....	....	....	**23.00**	**19.00**	**13.50**	**1.50**	**1.15**
J79	1/2¢ dull carmine	25.00	20.00	14.00	1.15	.95	.65	.20	.15
J80	1¢ dull carmine .	2.25	1.80	1.25	.25	.20	.15	.20	.15
J81	2¢ dull carmine .	2.25	1.80	1.25	.25	.20	.15	.20	.15
J82	3¢ dull carmine .	3.10	2.50	1.75	.30	.25	.20	.20	.15
J83	5¢ dull carmine .	4.25	3.40	2.40	.40	.35	.25	.20	.15
J84	10¢ dull carmine	8.50	6.75	4.75	1.25	1.00	.70	.20	.15
J85	30¢ dull carmine	47.50	38.00	26.50	8.50	6.75	4.75	.20	.15
J86	50¢ dull carmine	60.00	48.00	33.50	13.00	9.50	7.00	.20	.15
	1956 Rotary Press Printing Perf. 10 1/2 x 11								
J87	$1 scarlet	260.00	210.00	....	45.00	34.00	....	.20	....

SCOTT NO.	DESCRIPTION	MINT SHEET	PLATE BLOCK F/NH	PLATE BLOCK F	UNUSED F/NH	UNUSED F	USED F
	1959						
J88-101	**1/2¢-$5, 14 varieties, complete**	....	....	....	**16.50**	**14.50**	**3.25**
J88	1/2¢ carmine rose & black	400.00(100)	210.00	175.00	1.70	1.50	1.40
J89	1¢ carmine rose & black	3.25(100)	.40	.35	.20	.15	.15
J90	2¢ carmine rose & black	4.25(100)	.45	.40	.20	.15	.15
J91	3¢ carmine rose & black	6.25(100)	.50	.45	.20	.15	.15
J92	4¢ carmine rose & black	8.00(100)	.85	.75	.20	.15	.15
J93	5¢ carmine rose & black	9.50(100)	.80	.70	.20	.15	.15
J94	6¢ carmine rose & black	11.50(100)	1.10	1.00	.20	.15	.15
J95	7¢ carmine rose & black	13.50(100)	1.20	1.10	.20	.15	.15
J96	8¢ carmine rose & black	16.00(100)	1.60	1.45	.20	.15	.15
J97	10¢ carmine rose & black	18.50(100)	1.70	1.55	.20	.15	.15
J98	30¢ carmine rose & black	57.50(100)	4.75	4.25	.60	.55	.15
J99	50¢ carmine rose & black	90.00(100)	5.75	5.25	1.00	.90	.15
J100	$1 carmine rose & black	175.00(100)	10.00	9.00	2.15	1.95	.15
J101	$5 carmine rose & black	800.00(100)	47.50	42.50	10.00	9.00	.20
	1978-1985						
J102	11¢ carmine rose & black	22.00(100)	4.00	....	.35	....	.20
J103	13¢ carmine rose & black	25.00(100)	2.60	....	.35	....	.25
J104	17¢ carmine rose & black	75.00(100)	33.50	....	.45	....	.35

OFFICES IN CHINA

SHANGHAI
2¢
CHINA

1919
K1-16: U.S. Postage
498-518 surcharged

SHANGHAI
2 Cts.
CHINA

1922
K17-18: U.S. Postage 498-528B
with local surcharge

SCOTT NO.	DESCRIPTION	UNUSED NH F	UNUSED NH AVG	UNUSED OG F	UNUSED OG AVG	USED F	USED AVG
	1919						
K1	2¢ on 1¢ green . . .	35.00	23.00	22.50	14.50	25.00	16.00
K2	4¢ on 2¢ rose	35.00	23.00	22.50	14.50	25.00	16.00
K3	6¢ on 3¢ violet	72.50	48.00	42.00	28.00	55.00	35.00
K4	8¢ on 4¢ brown . . .	75.00	50.00	45.00	28.00	55.00	35.00
K5	10¢ on 5¢ blue	80.00	55.00	52.00	34.00	55.00	35.00
K6	12¢ on 6¢ red orange	110.00	67.50	65.00	42.00	82.50	55.00
K7	14¢ on 7¢ black . . .	115.00	70.00	70.00	45.00	95.00	62.50
K8	16¢ on 8¢ olive bister	82.50	50.00	48.00	30.00	57.50	35.00
K8a	16¢ on 8¢ olive green	72.50	40.00	43.00	27.00	47.50	32.00
K9	18¢ on 9¢ salmon red	82.50	50.00	48.00	31.00	62.50	37.00
K10	20¢ on 10¢ orange yellow	75.00	46.00	45.00	28.00	50.00	31.00
K11	24¢ on 12¢ brown carmine	90.00	57.50	52.50	33.00	58.00	32.00
K11a	24¢ on 12¢ claret brown	120.00	77.50	70.00	42.50	92.50	55.00
K12	30¢ on 15¢ gray . .	110.00	72.50	70.00	45.00	105.00	67.50
K13	40¢ on 20¢ deep ultra.	170.00	130.00	100.00	65.00	160.00	115.00
K14	60¢ on 30¢ orange red	155.00	100.00	95.00	62.50	140.00	95.00
K15	$1 on 50¢ light violet	600.00	475.00	390.00	310.00	460.00	340.00
K16	$2 on $1 violet brown	500.00	360.00	325.00	235.00	400.00	280.00
	1922 LOCAL ISSUES						
K17	2¢ on 1¢ green . . .	165.00	120.00	100.00	62.50	95.00	60.00
K18	4¢ on 2¢ carmine . .	145.00	100.00	87.50	60.00	80.00	62.50

U.S. Official #O1-O113

OFFICIAL STAMPS

O1-O9, O94, O95 / O10-O14 / O15-O24, O96-O103 / O25-O34, O106, O107

Except for the Post Office Department, portraits for the various denominations are the same as on the regular issues of 1870-73

1873 Printed by the Continental Bank Note Co.
Thin hard paper
(OG + 30%)
(O1-O120 for VF Centering–Fine Price + 25%)

DEPARTMENT OF AGRICULTURE

Scott No.	Description	Unused F	Unused AVG	Used F	Used AVG
O1	1¢ yellow	108.00	76.00	103.00	63.25
O2	2¢ yellow	81.50	50.00	41.00	27.00
O3	3¢ yellow	72.50	45.00	7.75	5.00
O4	6¢ yellow	80.50	52.25	33.00	21.50
O5	10¢ yellow	167.50	108.00	132.25	85.50
O6	12¢ yellow	225.00	146.50	165.50	107.50
O7	15¢ yellow	186.00	121.25	143.75	94.75
O8	24¢ yellow	186.75	121.00	132.25	86.25
O9	30¢ yellow	241.50	156.50	186.25	120.75

EXECUTIVE DEPARTMENT

Scott No.	Description	Unused F	Unused AVG	Used F	Used AVG
O10	1¢ carmine	450.00	337.50	287.50	196.00
O11	2¢ carmine	300.00	210.00	128.00	89.50
O12	3¢ carmine	360.00	250.00	125.00	89.50
O13	6¢ carmine	540.00	375.00	340.00	235.00
O14	10¢ carmine	500.00	350.00	400.00	280.00

DEPARTMENT OF THE INTERIOR

Scott No.	Description	Unused F	Unused AVG	Used F	Used AVG
O15	1¢ vermillion	28.00	19.50	6.50	4.50
O16	2¢ vermillion	24.00	16.50	7.25	5.00
O17	3¢ vermillion	38.00	26.50	4.00	2.75
O18	6¢ vermillion	28.00	19.50	4.00	2.75
O19	10¢ vermillion	28.00	19.50	12.00	8.50
O20	12¢ vermillion	40.00	28.00	6.25	4.50
O21	15¢ vermillion	68.00	47.50	13.50	9.50
O22	24¢ vermillion	50.00	35.00	11.25	7.75
O23	30¢ vermillion	68.00	47.50	11.25	7.75
O24	90¢ vermillion	155.00	105.00	30.00	21.00

DEPARTMENT OF JUSTICE

Scott No.	Description	Unused F	Unused AVG	Used F	Used AVG
O25	1¢ purple	84.00	58.75	62.00	43.50
O26	2¢ purple	140.00	98.00	66.00	46.50
O27	3¢ purple	140.00	98.00	13.75	9.50
O28	6¢ purple	128.00	89.50	20.00	14.00
O29	10¢ purple	144.00	100.00	44.00	31.00
O30	12¢ purple	112.00	78.50	30.00	21.00
O31	15¢ purple	220.00	154.00	100.00	70.00
O32	24¢ purple	560.00	395.00	220.00	155.00
O33	30¢ purple	480.00	336.00	128.00	89.50
O34	90¢ purple	720.00	505.00	340.00	238.00

O35-O45 / O47-O56, O108 / O57-O67 / O68-O71

NAVY DEPARTMENT
(OG + 30%)

Scott No.	Description	Unused F	Unused AVG	Used F	Used AVG
O35	1¢ ultramarine	60.00	42.00	30.00	21.00
O36	2¢ ultramarine	48.00	33.50	13.75	9.50
O37	3¢ ultramarine	48.00	33.50	6.50	4.75
O38	6¢ ultramarine	48.00	33.50	11.25	7.75
O39	7¢ ultramarine	300.00	210.00	112.00	78.50
O40	10¢ ultramarine	64.00	44.75	22.00	15.50
O41	12¢ ultramarine	76.00	53.25	20.00	14.00
O42	15¢ ultramarine	140.00	98.00	40.00	28.00
O43	24¢ ultramarine	140.00	98.00	40.00	28.00
O44	30¢ ultramarine	112.00	78.50	22.00	15.50
O45	90¢ ultramarine	560.00	395.00	140.00	98.00

OFFICIAL STAMPS: From 1873 to 1879, Congress authorized the use of Official Stamps to prepay postage on government mail. Separate issues were produced for each department so that mailing costs could be assigned to that department's budget. Penalty envelopes replaced Official Stamps on May 1, 1879.

O72-O82, O109-O113 / O83-O93, O1140-O120

POST OFFICE DEPARTMENT

Scott No.	Description	Unused F	Unused AVG	Used F	Used AVG
O47	1¢ black	10.00	7.00	6.00	4.25
O48	2¢ black	12.75	9.00	5.50	3.75
O49	3¢ black	4.25	3.00	.80	.55
O50	6¢ black	12.75	9.00	4.75	3.25
O51	10¢ black	56.00	39.25	32.00	22.50
O52	12¢ black	28.00	19.50	6.75	4.50
O53	15¢ black	38.00	26.75	11.25	7.75
O54	24¢ black	48.00	33.50	13.50	9.50
O55	30¢ black	48.00	33.50	13.50	9.50
O56	90¢ black	72.00	50.50	11.25	7.75

DEPARTMENT OF STATE

Scott No.	Description	Unused F	Unused AVG	Used F	Used AVG
O57	1¢ dark green	88.00	61.50	32.00	22.50
O58	2¢ dark green	168.00	117.50	48.00	33.50
O59	3¢ bright green	68.00	47.50	13.50	9.50
O60	6¢ bright green	64.00	44.75	15.25	10.50
O61	7¢ dark green	128.00	89.50	32.00	22.50
O62	10¢ dark green	100.00	70.00	22.00	15.50
O63	12¢ dark green	160.00	112.00	66.00	46.25
O64	15¢ dark green	168.00	117.50	44.00	30.75
O65	24¢ dark green	340.00	238.00	112.00	78.50
O66	30¢ dark green	320.00	224.00	88.00	61.50
O67	90¢ dark green	600.00	420.00	200.00	140.00
O68	$2 green & black	680.00	475.00	520.00	365.00
O69	$5 green & black	4800.00	3350.00	2600.00	1825.00
O70	$10 green & black	3200.00	2240.00	1800.00	1260.00
O71	$20 green & black	2600.00	1825.00	1360.00	950.00

TREASURY DEPARTMENT
(OG + 30%)

Scott No.	Description	Unused F	Unused AVG	Used F	Used AVG
O72	1¢ brown	30.00	21.00	3.75	2.50
O73	2¢ brown	38.00	26.50	3.75	2.50
O74	3¢ brown	26.00	18.25	1.00	.75
O75	6¢ brown	34.00	24.00	1.75	1.25
O76	7¢ brown	72.00	50.50	18.00	12.50
O77	10¢ brown	72.00	50.50	6.25	4.50
O78	12¢ brown	72.00	50.50	4.75	3.25
O79	15¢ brown	68.00	47.50	6.25	4.50
O80	24¢ brown	340.00	238.00	52.00	36.50
O81	30¢ brown	116.00	81.25	7.25	5.00
O82	90¢ brown	120.00	84.00	8.00	5.50

WAR DEPARTMENT

Scott No.	Description	Unused F	Unused AVG	Used F	Used AVG
O83	1¢ rose	112.00	78.50	5.75	4.00
O84	2¢ rose	100.00	70.00	7.50	5.25
O85	3¢ rose	105.00	72.50	2.25	1.50
O86	6¢ rose	340.00	238.00	4.75	3.25
O87	7¢ rose	100.00	70.00	58.00	40.50
O88	10¢ rose	34.00	23.75	12.00	8.50
O89	12¢ rose	116.00	81.25	7.25	5.00
O90	15¢ rose	30.00	21.00	8.75	6.25
O91	24¢ rose	30.00	21.00	5.50	3.75
O92	30¢ rose	32.00	22.50	5.50	3.75
O93	90¢ rose	72.00	50.50	32.00	22.50

1879 Printed by American Bank Note Co.
Soft Porous Paper

DEPARTMENT OF AGRICULTURE

Scott No.	Description	Unused F	Unused AVG	Used F	Used AVG
O94	1¢ yellow	2600.00	2000.00	......	......
O95	3¢ yellow	235.00	162.50	44.00	30.75

DEPARTMENT OF INTERIOR

Scott No.	Description	Unused F	Unused AVG	Used F	Used AVG
O96	1¢ vermillion	168.00	117.50	152.00	106.50
O97	2¢ vermillion	3.25	2.25	1.00	.75
O98	3¢ vermillion	2.75	2.00	.75	.60
O99	6¢ vermillion	4.25	3.00	4.50	3.00
O100	10¢ vermillion	52.00	36.50	48.00	33.50
O101	12¢ vermillion	100.00	70.00	72.00	50.50
O102	15¢ vermillion	240.00	168.00	180.00	125.00
O103	24¢ vermillion	2700.00	2200.00	......	......

DEPARTMENT OF JUSTICE

Scott No.	Description	Unused F	Unused AVG	Used F	Used AVG
O106	3¢ bluish purple	68.00	47.50	44.00	30.75
O107	6¢ bluish purple	152.00	106.50	128.00	89.50

POST OFFICE DEPARTMENT

Scott No.	Description	Unused F	Unused AVG	Used F	Used AVG
O108	3¢ black	12.00	8.50	4.00	2.75

TREASURY DEPARTMENT

Scott No.	Description	Unused F	Unused AVG	Used F	Used AVG
O109	3¢ brown	36.00	25.25	5.50	3.75
O110	6¢ brown	68.00	47.50	28.00	19.50
O111	10¢ brown	100.00	70.00	32.00	22.50
O112	30¢ brown	1400.00	1150.00	220.00	192.50
O113	90¢ brown	2200.00	1750.00	220.00	192.50

U.S. Official #O114-O159, Parcel Post, Parcel Post Due, Special Handling

SCOTT NO.	DESCRIPTION	UNUSED F	UNUSED AVG	USED F	USED AVG
	WAR DEPARTMENT				
O114	1¢ rose red	2.75	1.95	2.25	1.50
O115	2¢ rose red	4.00	2.75	2.50	1.75
O116	3¢ rose red	4.00	2.75	1.00	.75
O117	6¢ rose red	3.75	2.50	1.00	.75
O118	10¢ rose red	30.00	21.00	30.00	21.00
O119	12¢ rose red	24.00	16.75	8.00	5.50
O120	30¢ rose red	64.00	45.00	54.00	37.50

SCOTT NO.	DESCRIPTION	UNUSED NH F	UNUSED NH AVG	UNUSED OG F	UNUSED OG AVG	USED F	USED AVG
	O121-O126						
	1910-11						
	Double Line Watermark						
O121	2¢ black	18.00	12.75	11.25	7.75	1.50	1.25
O122	50¢ dark green	180.00	126.00	112.00	78.50	32.00	22.50
O123	$1 ultramarine	168.00	117.50	84.00	60.00	8.75	6.00
	Single Line Watermark						
O124	1¢ dark violet	9.75	6.75	6.00	4.50	1.30	1.00
O125	2¢ black	58.00	40.50	36.00	25.25	4.50	3.00
O126	10¢ carmine	22.00	15.50	14.00	10.50	1.40	1.10

SCOTT NO.	DESCRIPTION	FIRST DAY COVERS SING	FIRST DAY COVERS PL. BLK.	MINT SHEET	PLATE BLOCK	UNUSED	USED
	O127-O136						
	1983-89						
O127	1¢ Great Seal	1.75	4.25	8.25(100)		.45	.20	.20
O128	4¢ Great Seal	1.75	4.25	8.25(100)		.55	.20	.25
O129	13¢ Great Seal	1.75	4.25	35.00(100)	2.25	.50	1.00
O129A	14¢ Great Seal (1985)	1.75	....	38.00(100)	....	.50	.55
O130	17¢ Great Seal	1.75	4.25	60.00(100)	3.50	.60	.50
O132	$1 Great Seal	5.75	14.25	210.00(100)	10.50	2.50	1.25
O133	$5 Great Seal	16.50	41.25	950.00(100)	45.00	11.00	6.00
			PLATE# STRIP 3		PLATE# STRIP 3		
O135	20¢ Great Seal, coil	1.75	80.00	....	19.50	2.00	2.25
O136	22¢ Seal, coil (1985)	1.75	....			.95	2.25
	1985 Non-Denominated Issues						
O138	(14¢) Great Seal, postcard D	1.75	30.00	525.00(100)	45.00	5.50	5.50
O138A	15¢ Great Seal, coil (1988)	1.75	....	....	....	.50	.55
O138B	20¢ Great Seal, coil (1988)	1.75	....	....	....	.50	.40
			PLATE# STRIP 3		PLATE# STRIP 3		
O139	(22¢) Great Seal "D" coil (1985)	1.75	80.00	....	60.00	5.50	3.25
O140	(25¢) Great Seal "E" coil (1988)	1.75	....	....	....	1.20	2.25
O141	25¢ Great Seal, coil (1988)	1.75	....	....	....	.80	.60
O143	1¢ Great Seal (1989)	1.75	....	8.25(100)	....	.20	.25
	1991-94						
O144	(29¢) Great Seal "F" coil	1.75	....	....	....	1.75	.60
O145	29¢ Great Seal, coil	1.75	....	....	....	.95	.50
O146	4¢ Great Seal	1.75	....	9.00(100)	....	.20	.35
O146A	10¢ Great Seal	1.75	....	27.50(100)	....	.30	.50
O147	19¢ Great Seal	1.75	....	45.00(100)	....	.50	.50
O148	23¢ Great Seal	1.75	....	55.00(100)	....	.65	.50

SCOTT NO.	DESCRIPTION	FIRST DAY COVERS SING	FIRST DAY COVERS PL. BLK.	MINT SHEET	PLATE BLOCK	UNUSED	USED
	1993-95						
O151	$1 Great Seal	1.75	....	195.00(100)	....	2.75	2.00
O152	(32¢) Great Seal "G" coil	2.75	....	....	....	.85	
O153	32¢ Official Mail	1.95	....	....	....	.85	
O154	1¢ Official Mail	1.95	....	8.25(100)	....	.20	
O155	20¢ Official Mail	1.95	....	42.00(100)	....	.45	
O156	23¢ Official Mail	1.95	....	49.50(100)	....	.55	
	1999-2002						
O157	33¢ Official Mail, coil	1.95	....	....	....	.75	
O158	34¢ Official Mail, coil	1.95	....	....	....	.80	
O159	37¢ Official Mail, coil	1.95	....	....	....	.90	

PARCEL POST STAMPS — Q1-Q12 Various Designs

PARCEL POST DUE STAMPS — JQ1-JQ5

SPECIAL HANDLING STAMPS — QE1-QE4

SCOTT NO.	DESCRIPTION	UNUSED NH F	UNUSED NH AVG	UNUSED OG F	UNUSED OG AVG	USED F	USED AVG
	(Q1-QE4a for VF Centering–Fine Price + 50%)						
	1912-13 Parcel Post–All Printed in Carmine Rose						
Q1	1¢ Post Office Clerk	9.00	6.00	5.50	4.00	1.50	1.00
Q2	2¢ City Carrier	11.00	7.50	6.50	4.50	1.25	.90
Q3	3¢ Railway Clerk	22.00	14.00	14.00	9.50	6.00	4.25
Q4	4¢ Rural Carrier	60.00	40.00	35.00	25.00	3.00	1.95
Q5	5¢ Mail Train	55.00	38.50	32.00	22.00	2.50	1.95
Q6	10¢ Steamship	80.00	55.00	48.00	32.50	3.25	2.00
Q7	15¢ Auto Service	105.00	75.00	62.50	45.00	12.50	8.00
Q8	20¢ Airplane	215.00	150.00	130.00	95.00	27.50	18.00
Q9	25¢ Manufacturing	105.00	75.00	62.50	45.00	7.00	4.75
Q10	50¢ Dairying	425.00	300.00	250.00	180.00	42.50	27.50
Q11	75¢ Harvesting	150.00	100.00	90.00	65.00	37.50	22.50
Q12	$1 Fruit Growing	550.00	400.00	325.00	225.00	37.50	22.50
	1912 Parcel Post Due						
JQ1	1¢ dark green	14.50	10.00	8.75	6.00	3.75	2.50
JQ2	2¢ dark green	112.00	78.50	68.00	47.50	14.00	9.75
JQ3	5¢ dark green	20.00	14.00	12.00	8.50	4.50	3.00
JQ4	10¢ dark green	235.00	162.50	140.00	98.00	36.00	25.25
JQ5	25¢ dark green	140.00	98.00	84.00	58.50	4.00	2.75
	1925-29 Special Handling						
QE1	10¢ yellow green	1.75	1.25	1.25	.85	1.00	.70
QE2	15¢ yellow green	2.00	1.35	1.40	.95	1.00	.70
QE3	20¢ yellow green	3.00	2.10	1.75	1.20	1.95	1.35
QE4	25¢ yellow green	22.50	15.50	16.50	11.50	8.00	5.00
QE4a	25¢ deep green	31.50	22.00	21.50	14.75	5.00	3.40

POSTAL NOTE STAMPS
PN1-P18
All values printed in black

SCOTT NO.	DESCRIPTION	UNUSED F/NH	UNUSED F/OG	USED F
PN1-18	1¢-90¢, 18 varieties, complete	35.00	24.50	2.50

U.S. Postal Stationery #U1-U73

ENVELOPES

U1-U10
Washington

U19-U24
Franklin

U26, U27
Washington

1853-55

SCOTT NO.	DESCRIPTION	UNUSED ENTIRE	UNUSED CUT SQ.	USED CUT SQ.
U1	3¢ red on white, die 1	1450.00	225.00	19.50
U2	3¢ red on buff, die 1	775.00	78.00	11.50
U3	3¢ red on white, die 2	3600.00	900.00	36.00
U4	3¢ red on buff, die 2	1550.00	240.00	19.50
U5	3¢ red on white, die 3			400.00
U6	3¢ red on buff, die 3	1200.00	240.00	45.00
U7	3¢ red on white, die 4	6350.00	720.00	95.00
U8	3¢ red on buff, die 4	4800.00	1400.00	95.00
U9	3¢ red on white, die 5	100.00	24.00	3.25
U10	3¢ red on buff, die 5	60.00	16.50	3.00
U11	6¢ red on white	270.00	180.00	60.00
U12	6¢ red on buff	220.00	120.00	60.00
U13	6¢ green on white	390.00	225.00	95.00
U14	6¢ green on buff	320.00	190.00	75.00
U15	10¢ green on white, die 1	360.00	210.00	78.00
U16	10¢ green on buff, die 1	228.00	78.00	48.00
U17	10¢ green on white, die 2	440.00	240.00	105.00
U18	10¢ green on buff, die 2	260.00	120.00	60.00

1860-61

U19	1¢ blue on buff, die 1	70.00	33.00	16.50
W20	1¢ blue on buff, die 1	100.00	62.50	52.00
W21	1¢ blue on manila, die 1	100.00	47.00	47.00
W22	1¢ blue on orange, die 1	4650.00	2650.00	
U23	1¢ blue on orange, die 2	600.00	440.00	340.00
U24	1¢ blue on buff, die 3	420.00	220.00	85.00
U26	3¢ red on white	50.00	27.00	16.00
U27	3¢ red on buff	45.00	21.50	13.20
U28	3¢ & 1¢ red & blue on white	725.00	340.00	230.00
U29	3¢ & 1¢ red & blue on buff	675.00	280.00	220.00
U30	6¢ red on white	3600.00	2500.00	1350.00
U31	6¢ red on buff	4200.00	2100.00	875.00
U32	10¢ green on white		1200.00	360.00
U33	10¢ green on buff	3350.00	1075.00	270.00

U34-U37
Washington

U40-U41

1861

U34	3¢ pink on white	50.00	21.00	6.00
U35	3¢ pink on buff	48.00	18.00	6.00
U36	3¢ pink on blue (letter sheet)	200.00	82.50	55.00
U37	3¢ pink on orange	4800.00	3300.00	
U38	6¢ pink on white	180.00	120.00	85.00
U39	6¢ pink on buff	95.00	65.00	62.50
U40	10¢ yellow green on white	72.00	36.00	33.00
U41	10¢ yellow green on buff	65.00	26.00	27.00
U42	12¢ brown & red on buff	460.00	190.00	155.00
U43	20¢ blue & red on buff	470.00	185.00	170.00
U44	24¢ green & red on buff	600.00	190.00	170.00
U45	40¢ red & black on buff	780.00	325.00	310.00

U46-U49

U50-W57
Jackson

1863-64

U46	2¢ black on buff, die 1	65.00	36.00	18.00
W47	2¢ black on dark manila, die 1	78.00	48.50	42.00
U48	2¢ black on buff, die 2	4200.00	2100.00	
U49	2¢ black on orange, die 2	2700.00	1300.00	
U50	2¢ black on buff, die 3	30.00	10.50	9.60
W51	2¢ black on buff, die 3	270.00	155.00	160.00
U52	2¢ black on orange, die 3	27.00	12.00	9.00
W53	2¢ black on dark manila, die 3	132.00	36.00	24.00
U54	2¢ black on buff, die 4	23.00	13.25	10.80
W55	2¢ black on buff, die 4	125.00	70.00	60.00
U56	2¢ black on orange, die 4	19.25	12.00	8.40
W57	2¢ black on light manila, die 4	29.50	13.80	12.00

U58-U61

U66-U67
Washington

1864-65

U58	3¢ pink on white	10.80	7.20	1.80
U59	3¢ pink on buff	11.50	5.40	1.20
U60	3¢ brown on white	78.00	40.00	27.00
U61	3¢ brown on buff	78.00	40.00	27.00
U62	6¢ pink on white	120.00	60.00	28.00
U63	6¢ pink on buff	90.00	33.00	27.00
U64	6¢ purple on white	60.00	48.00	27.00
U65	6¢ purple on buff	69.00	42.50	24.00
U66	9¢ lemon on buff	550.00	420.00	260.00
U67	9¢ orange on buff	170.00	108.00	85.00
U68	12¢ brown on buff	500.00	350.00	230.00
U69	12¢ red brown on buff	165.00	80.00	57.50
U70	18¢ red on buff	210.00	95.00	95.00
U71	24¢ blue on buff	210.00	90.00	84.00
U72	30¢ green on buff	160.00	72.00	65.00
U73	40¢ rose on buff	330.00	84.00	240.00

U74-W77, U108-U121
Franklin

U78-W81, U122-W158
Jackson

U82-U84, U159-U169
Washington

U172-U180
Taylor

U85-U87, U181-U184
Lincoln

U88, U185, U186
Stanton

U89-U92, U187-U194
Jefferson

U93-U95, U195-U197
Clay

U96-U98, U198-U200
Webster

U99-U101, U201-U203
Scott

U102-U104, U204-U210, U336-U341
Hamilton

U105-U107, U211-U217, U342-U347
Perry

NOTE: For details on die or similar appearing varieties of envelopes, please refer to the Scott Specialized Catalogue.

U.S. Postal Stationery #U74-U230

SCOTT NO.	DESCRIPTION	UNUSED ENTIRE	UNUSED CUT SQ.	USED CUT SQ.
	1870-71 REAY ISSUE			
U74	1¢ blue on white	60.00	36.00	30.00
U74a	1¢ ultramarine on white	90.00	50.00	33.00
U75	1¢ blue on amber	60.00	36.00	30.00
U75a	1¢ ultramarine on amber	65.00	54.00	31.00
U76	1¢ blue on orange	30.00	15.50	12.00
W77	1¢ blue on manila	72.00	42.00	36.00
U78	2¢ brown on white	50.00	38.00	15.00
U79	2¢ brown on amber	36.00	18.00	9.00
U80	2¢ brown on orange	15.00	9.60	6.00
W81	2¢ brown on manila	54.00	27.00	21.00
U82	3¢ green on white	13.20	7.20	.90
U83	3¢ green on amber	13.20	5.50	2.00
U84	3¢ green on cream	18.00	9.00	3.60
U85	6¢ dark red on white	33.00	18.50	15.00
U86	6¢ dark red on amber	48.00	25.00	17.00
U87	6¢ dark red on cream	45.00	25.00	16.00
U88	7¢ vermillon on amber	66.00	48.00	200.00
U89	10¢ olive black on white	620.00	490.00	420.00
U90	10¢ olive black on amber	540.00	420.00	420.00
U91	10¢ brown on white	75.00	62.00	72.00
U92	10¢ brown on amber	90.00	72.00	54.00
U93	12¢ plum on white	240.00	105.00	84.00
U94	12¢ plum on amber	210.00	105.00	120.00
U95	12¢ plum on cream	340.00	220.00	220.00
U96	15¢ red orange on white	150.00	72.00	75.00
U97	15¢ red orange on amber	360.00	135.00	175.00
U98	15¢ red orange on cream	330.00	250.00	210.00
U99	24¢ purple on white	155.00	110.00	110.00
U100	24¢ purple on amber	340.00	180.00	290.00
U101	24¢ purple on cream	340.00	180.00	290.00
U102	30¢ black on white	290.00	85.00	95.00
U103	30¢ black on amber	525.00	210.00	260.00
U104	30¢ black on cream	380.00	220.00	390.00
U105	90¢ carmine on white	200.00	150.00	220.00
U106	90¢ carmine on amber	800.00	320.00	425.00
U107	90¢ carmine on cream	925.00	430.00	640.00
	1874-86 PLIMPTON ISSUE			
U108	1¢ dark blue on white, die 1	110.00	90.00	72.00
U109	1¢ dark blue on amber, die 1	170.00	120.00	78.00
U110	1¢ dark blue on cream, die 1	......	900.00	......
U111	1¢ dark blue on orange, die 1	33.00	20.00	18.00
U111a	1¢ light blue on orange, die 1	25.00	24.00	12.00
W112	1¢ dark blue on manila, die 1	78.00	48.00	36.00
U113	1¢ light blue on white, die 2	2.40	1.50	.90
U113a	1¢ dark blue on white, die 2	19.50	8.40	6.00
U114	1¢ light blue on amber, die 2	6.00	4.50	4.80
U115	1¢ blue on cream, die 2	7.20	3.25	3.75
U116	1¢ light blue on orange, die 2	.75	.60	.50
U116a	1¢ dark blue on orange, die 2	8.40	2.00	1.25
U117	1¢ light blue on blue, die 2	8.40	6.00	4.80
U118	1¢ light blue on fawn, die 2	7.20	6.00	4.80
U119	1¢ light blue on manila, die 2	7.20	6.00	3.60
W120	1¢ light blue on manila, die 2	2.40	1.50	1.20
W120a	1¢ dark blue on manila, die 2	12.00	6.50	7.50
U121	1¢ blue on amber manila, die 2	16.00	12.00	10.80
U122	2¢ brown on white, die 1	120.00	100.00	40.00
U123	2¢ brown on amber, die 1	90.00	60.00	48.00
U124	2¢ brown on cream, die 1	......	825.00	......
W126	2¢ brown on manila, die 1	120.00	108.00	60.00
W127	2¢ vermillon on manila, die 1	1600.00	1200.00	260.00
U128	2¢ brown on white, die 2	75.00	44.00	30.00
U129	2¢ brown on amber, die 2	96.00	78.00	42.00
W131	2¢ brown on manila, die 2	24.00	16.50	16.50
U132	2¢ brown on white, die 3	96.00	72.00	30.00
U133	2¢ brown on amber, die 3	260.00	200.00	58.00
U134	2¢ brown on white, die 4	750.00	560.00	140.00
U135	2¢ brown on amber, die 4	520.00	410.00	115.00
U136	2¢ brown on orange, die 4	70.00	44.00	28.00
W137	2¢ brown on manila, die 4	78.00	66.00	36.00
U139	2¢ brown on white, die 5	52.00	40.00	33.00
U140	2¢ brown on amber, die 5	95.00	74.00	64.00
W141	2¢ brown on manila, die 5	42.00	37.00	24.00
U142	2¢ vermillon on white, die 5	7.20	6.00	2.50
U143	2¢ vermillon on amber, die 5	7.20	6.00	2.50
U144	2¢ vermillon on cream, die 5	15.60	12.00	6.00
U146	2¢ vermillon on blue, die 5	195.00	130.00	31.00
U147	2¢ vermillon on fawn, die 5	13.00	7.20	4.80
W148	2¢ vermillon on manila, die 5	7.00	3.75	3.60
U149	2¢ vermillon on white, die 6	62.00	44.00	30.00
U150	2¢ vermillon on amber, die 6	36.00	24.00	16.50
U151	2¢ vermillon on blue, die 6	18.00	13.00	9.50
U152	2¢ vermillon on fawn, die 6	13.80	10.50	4.20
U153	2¢ vermillon on white, die 7	84.00	54.00	24.00
U154	2¢ vermillon on amber, die 7	360.00	280.00	82.00
W155	2¢ vermillon on manila, die 7	42.00	20.00	9.90
U156	2¢ vermillon on white, die 8	800.00	620.00	135.00
W158	2¢ vermillon on manila, die 8	120.00	82.00	60.00
U159	3¢ green on white, die 1	38.50	24.00	6.00
U160	3¢ green on amber, die 1	48.00	28.80	10.80
U161	3¢ green on cream, die 1	54.00	42.00	12.00
U163	3¢ green on white, die 2	2.40	1.20	.40
U164	3¢ green on amber, die 2	2.75	1.50	.60
U165	3¢ green on cream, die 2	10.80	6.60	6.00
U166	3¢ green on blue, die 2	12.00	7.25	4.80
U167	3¢ green on fawn, die 2	8.40	4.80	3.00
U168	3¢ green on white, die 3	1800.00	525.00	52.00
U169	3¢ green on amber, die 3	360.00	240.00	120.00
U172	5¢ blue on white, die 1	11.75	9.00	8.25
U173	5¢ blue on amber, die 1	12.60	8.60	9.00
U174	5¢ blue on cream, die 1	125.00	95.00	40.00
U175	5¢ blue on blue, die 1	37.50	24.00	16.50
U176	5¢ blue on fawn, die 1	225.00	132.00	72.00
U177	5¢ blue on white, die 2	11.40	6.50	6.50
U178	5¢ blue on amber, die 2	13.00	7.20	7.00
U179	5¢ blue on blue, die 2	18.00	13.00	8.40
U180	5¢ blue on fawn, die 2	135.00	96.00	60.00
U181	6¢ red on white	10.80	6.00	6.00
U182	6¢ red on amber	18.00	6.00	6.00
U183	6¢ red on cream	24.00	19.80	12.00
U184	6¢ red on fawn	30.00	21.00	12.00
U185	7¢ vermilion on white	......	1600.00	......
U186	7¢ vermilion on amber	130.00	105.00	62.00
U187	10¢ brown on white, die 1	60.00	36.00	21.00
U188	10¢ brown on amber, die 1	88.00	58.00	33.00
U189	10¢ chocolate on white, die 2	9.60	6.00	3.50
U190	10¢ chocolate on amber, die 2	9.60	7.20	6.50
U191	10¢ brown on buff, die 2	11.10	9.30	7.20
U192	10¢ brown on blue, die 2	14.00	12.00	9.00
U193	10¢ brown on manila, die 2	18.00	15.00	9.00
U194	10¢ brown/amber manila, die 2	19.00	14.00	9.50
U195	12¢ plum on white	228.00	190.00	108.00
U196	12¢ plum on amber	270.00	178.00	160.00
U197	12¢ plum on cream	725.00	240.00	185.00
U198	15¢ orange on white	90.00	42.00	36.00
U199	15¢ orange on amber	180.00	150.00	120.00
U200	15¢ orange on cream	850.00	370.00	370.00
U201	24¢ purple on white	225.00	170.00	130.00
U202	24¢ purple on amber	225.00	170.00	130.00
U203	24¢ purple on cream	690.00	160.00	130.00
U204	30¢ black on white	70.00	62.00	28.00
U205	30¢ black on amber	140.00	75.00	65.00
U206	30¢ black on cream	750.00	380.00	370.00
U207	30¢ black on oriental buff	150.00	100.00	85.00
U208	30¢ black on blue	130.00	105.00	85.00
U209	30¢ black on manila	150.00	95.00	85.00
U210	30¢ black on amber manila	155.00	130.00	85.00
U211	90¢ carmine on white	160.00	130.00	85.00
U212	90¢ carmine on amber	275.00	175.00	240.00
U213	90¢ carmine on cream	2700.00	1700.00	......
U214	90¢ carmine on oriental buff	250.00	210.00	280.00
U215	90¢ carmine on blue	240.00	195.00	260.00
U216	90¢ carmine on manila	240.00	140.00	260.00
U217	90¢ carmine on amber manila	220.00	125.00	220.00

U218-U221, U582
Pony Express Rider and Train

U222-U226
Garfield

Die 1. Single thick line under "POSTAGE"   Die 2. Two thin lines under "POSTAGE"

1876 CENTENNIAL ISSUE

SCOTT NO.	DESCRIPTION	UNUSED ENTIRE	UNUSED CUT SQ.	USED CUT SQ.
U218	3¢ red on white, die 1	70.00	55.00	30.00
U219	3¢ green on white, die 1	60.00	50.00	19.00
U221	3¢ green on white, die 2	80.00	55.00	24.00
	1882-86			
U222	5¢ brown on white	7.20	3.90	2.40
U223	5¢ brown on amber	8.40	4.50	2.75
U224	5¢ brown on oriental buff	150.00	120.00	75.00
U225	5¢ brown on blue	90.00	60.00	40.00
U226	5¢ brown on fawn	320.00	250.00	......

U227-U230
Washington

1883 OCTOBER

U227	2¢ red on white	7.20	3.90	1.80
U228	2¢ red on amber	8.40	4.80	2.10
U229	2¢ red on blue	9.30	6.90	4.80
U230	2¢ red on fawn	15.00	8.00	5.50

U.S. Postal Stationery #U231-U347

SCOTT NO.	DESCRIPTION	UNUSED ENTIRE	UNUSED CUT SQ.	USED CUT SQ.

U231-U249, U260-W292 — *Washington*
U250-U259 — *Jackson*

1883 NOVEMBER
Four Wavy Lines in Oval

Scott	Description	Unused Entire	Unused Cut Sq.	Used Cut Sq.
U231	2¢ red on white	7.20	3.00	1.50
U232	2¢ red on amber	9.00	5.00	4.00
U233	2¢ red on blue	12.00	7.25	7.25
U234	2¢ red on fawn	7.20	6.00	4.50
W235	2¢ red on manila	21.00	16.00	6.50

1884 JUNE

Scott	Description	Unused Entire	Unused Cut Sq.	Used Cut Sq.
U236	2¢ red on white	9.60	6.00	3.60
U237	2¢ red on amber	18.00	11.50	10.00
U238	2¢ red on blue	23.00	18.00	10.00
U239	2¢ red on fawn	16.50	12.50	10.00
U240	2¢ red on white (3-1/2links)	120.00	70.00	42.00
U241	2¢ red on amber (3-1/2links)	1100.00	750.00	340.00
U243	2¢ red on white (2 links)	120.00	90.00	60.00
U244	2¢ red on amber (2links)	220.00	165.00	78.00
U245	2¢ red on blue (2links)	475.00	330.00	145.00
U246	2¢ red on fawn (2links)	420.00	330.00	135.00
U247	2¢ red on white (round O)	2200.00	1600.00	360.00
U249	2¢ red on fawn (round O)	900.00	600.00	360.00

1883-86

Scott	Description	Unused Entire	Unused Cut Sq.	Used Cut Sq.
U250	4¢ green on white, die 1	5.60	3.00	3.00
U251	4¢ green on amber, die 1	6.00	4.20	3.00
U252	4¢ green on buff, die 1	10.80	7.20	9.50
U253	4¢ green on blue, die 1	10.80	7.20	6.00
U254	4¢ green on manila, die 1	12.00	8.50	6.00
U255	4¢ green/amber manila, die 1	30.00	21.00	10.80
U256	4¢ green on white, die 2	12.00	4.80	3.60
U257	4¢ green on amber, die 2	15.75	9.50	6.00
U258	4¢ green on manila, die 2	13.75	9.00	6.00
U259	4¢ green/amber manila, die 2	13.25	9.00	6.00

1884 MAY

Scott	Description	Unused Entire	Unused Cut Sq.	Used Cut Sq.
U260	2¢ brown on white	16.80	13.25	4.95
U261	2¢ brown on amber	14.50	12.00	6.00
U262	2¢ brown on blue	16.80	12.75	9.75
U263	2¢ brown on fawn	14.50	10.80	9.00
W264	2¢ brown on manila	20.50	12.75	9.75

1884 JUNE

Scott	Description	Unused Entire	Unused Cut Sq.	Used Cut Sq.
U265	2¢ brown on white	19.75	13.25	4.95
U266	2¢ brown on amber	77.00	60.00	45.00
U267	2¢ brown on blue	14.50	10.75	6.00
U268	2¢ brown on fawn	18.00	14.50	11.00
W269	2¢ brown on manila	26.00	21.00	14.50
U270	2¢ brown on white (2links)	120.00	90.00	38.00
U271	2¢ brown on amber (2links)	300.00	210.00	95.00
U273	2¢ brown on white (round O)	210.00	165.00	78.00
U274	2¢ brown on amber (round O)	260.00	210.00	78.00
U276	2¢ brown on fawn (round O)	1175.00	810.00	675.00

1884-86
Two Wavy Lines in Oval

Scott	Description	Unused Entire	Unused Cut Sq.	Used Cut Sq.
U277	2¢ brown on white, die 1	.85	.50	.25
U277a	2¢ brown lake on white, die 1	24.00	21.00	14.50
U278	2¢ brown on amber, die 1	1.50	.75	.50
U279	2¢ brown on buff, die 1	4.50	3.00	1.80
U280	2¢ brown on blue, die 1	3.25	2.50	1.50
U281	2¢ brown on fawn, die 1	3.90	3.00	1.80
U282	2¢ brown on manila, die 1	13.80	10.25	3.60
W283	2¢ brown on manila, die 1	7.95	5.50	5.40
U284	2¢ brown/amber manila, die 1	10.25	6.00	6.00
U285	2¢ red on white, die 1	1250.00	600.00	......
U286	2¢ red on blue, die 1	300.00	260.00	......
W287	2¢ red on manila, die 1	170.00	120.00	......
U288	2¢ brown on white, die 2	375.00	160.00	37.50
U289	2¢ brown on amber, die 2	18.00	13.25	12.00
U290	2¢ brown on blue, die 2	1250.00	975.00	150.00
U291	2¢ brown on fawn, die 2	28.00	21.00	19.25
W292	2¢ brown on manila, die 2	27.50	22.00	18.00

NOTE: For details on die or similar appearing varieties of envelopes, please refer to the Scott Specialized Catalogue.

U293 — *Grant* — 1886

Scott	Description	Unused Entire	Unused Cut Sq.	Used Cut Sq.
U293	2¢ green on white Entire letter sheet	28.00	......	17.50

U294-U304, U352-W357 — *Franklin*
U305-U323, U358-U370 — *Washington*

U324-U329 — *Jackson*
U330-U335, U377-U378 — *Grant*

1887-94

Scott	Description	Unused Entire	Unused Cut Sq.	Used Cut Sq.
U294	1¢ blue on white	.90	.60	.25
U295	1¢ dark blue on white	11.40	7.80	3.00
U296	1¢ blue on amber	4.80	3.00	1.50
U297	1¢ dark blue on amber	60.00	48.00	27.00
U300	1¢ blue on manila	1.15	.75	.30
W301	1¢ blue on manila	.90	.50	.30
U302	1¢ dark blue on manila	33.00	24.00	10.75
W303	1¢ dark blue on manila	22.00	14.50	12.00
U304	1¢ blue on amber manila	8.40	4.80	3.25
U305	2¢ green on white, die 1	21.00	12.00	8.50
U306	2¢ green on amber, die 1	30.00	24.00	14.50
U307	2¢ green on buff, die 1	108.00	78.00	36.00
U308	2¢ green on blue, die 1	......	3200.00	1075.00
U309	2¢ green on manila, die 1	7200.00	2400.00	600.00
U311	2¢ green on white, die 2	.60	.30	.15
U312	2¢ green on amber, die 2	.65	.45	.15
U313	2¢ green on buff, die 2	1.00	.60	.25
U314	2¢ green on blue, die 2	1.05	.60	.25
U315	2¢ green on manila, die 2	2.25	1.75	.60
W316	2¢ green on manila, die 2	8.00	3.50	2.50
U317	2¢ green/amber manila, die 2	4.80	2.00	1.80
U318	2¢ green on white, die 3	168.00	120.00	15.00
U319	2¢ green on amber, die 3	192.00	168.00	24.00
U320	2¢ green on buff, die 3	180.00	165.00	50.00
U321	2¢ green on blue, die 3	240.00	198.00	71.50
U322	2¢ green on manila, die 3	190.00	150.00	70.00
U323	2¢ green/amber manila, die 3	390.00	340.00	80.00
U324	4¢ carmine on white	3.60	1.75	1.30
U325	4¢ carmine on amber	4.80	2.40	2.10
U326	4¢ carmine on oriental buff	9.60	6.00	3.00
U327	4¢ carmine on blue	6.75	4.75	4.25
U328	4¢ carmine on manila	9.00	6.85	6.00
U329	4¢ carmine on amber/manila	8.40	4.80	3.00
U330	5¢ blue on white, die 1	6.00	3.60	3.00
U331	5¢ blue on amber, die 1	7.25	3.60	2.25
U332	5¢ blue on oriental buff, die 1	9.90	3.90	3.60
U333	5¢ blue on blue, die 1	14.00	9.00	6.00
U334	5¢ blue on white, die 2	15.00	10.75	5.40
U335	5¢ blue on amber, die 2	16.75	10.75	6.00
U336	30¢ red brown on white	54.00	42.00	48.00
U337	30¢ red brown on amber	60.00	54.00	72.00
U338	30¢ red brown/oriental buff	54.00	42.00	54.00
U339	30¢ red brown on blue	48.00	42.00	48.00
U340	30¢ red brown on manila	54.00	48.00	48.00
U341	30¢ red brown/amber manila	60.00	54.00	36.00
U342	90¢ purple on white	84.00	66.00	84.00
U343	90¢ purple on amber	108.00	84.00	84.00
U344	90¢ purple on oriental buff	108.00	84.00	90.00
U345	90¢ purple on blue	120.00	84.00	96.00
U346	90¢ purple on manila	120.00	84.00	96.00
U347	90¢ purple on amber manila	135.00	90.00	96.00

U.S. Postal Stationery #U348-U445

SCOTT NO.	DESCRIPTION	UNUSED ENTIRE	UNUSED CUT SQ.	USED CUT SQ.

1893 COLUMBIAN ISSUE
U348-U351 — Columbus and Liberty, with Shield and Eagle

U348	1¢ deep blue on white	3.00	2.50	1.25
U349	2¢ violet on white	3.50	2.00	.75
U350	5¢ chocolate on white	15.00	9.60	9.00
U351	10¢ slate brown on white	60.00	35.00	27.50

U371-U373, U374-W376 — Lincoln

1899

U352	1¢ green on white	1.25	.60	.25
U353	1¢ green on amber	7.75	4.80	1.80
U354	1¢ green on oriental buff	14.00	10.80	3.00
U355	1¢ green on blue	15.00	12.00	8.00
U356	1¢ green on manila	6.00	2.10	1.10
W357	1¢ green on manila	8.40	2.10	1.10
U358	2¢ carmine on white, die 1	8.00	2.60	1.10
U359	2¢ carmine on amber, die 1	24.00	18.00	14.50
U360	2¢ carmine on buff, die 1	25.00	16.00	9.60
U361	2¢ carmine on blue, die 1	72.00	60.00	30.00
U362	2¢ carmine on white, die 2	.60	.30	.25
U363	2¢ carmine on amber, die 2	2.75	1.10	.20
U364	2¢ carmine on buff, die 2	2.75	1.10	.20
U365	2¢ carmine on blue, die 2	3.60	1.30	.60
W366	2¢ carmine on manila, die 2	11.40	5.40	3.00
U367	2¢ carmine on white, die 3	9.00	4.80	2.10
U368	2¢ carmine on amber, die 3	14.40	9.00	6.25
U369	2¢ carmine on buff, die 3	31.50	24.00	15.00
U370	2¢ carmine on blue, die 3	24.00	12.00	8.40
U371	4¢ brown on white, die 1	27.00	14.50	13.25
U372	4¢ brown on amber, die 1	33.00	18.00	13.25
U373	4¢ brown on white, die 2	8400.00	6000.00	390.00
U374	4¢ brown on white, die 3	24.00	11.00	8.50
U375	4¢ brown on amber, die 3	51.00	43.00	18.00
W376	4¢ brown on manila, die 3	21.75	16.80	9.00
U377	5¢ blue on white, die 3	15.00	10.25	10.25
U378	5¢ blue on amber, die 3	20.50	15.00	11.50

U379-W384 — Franklin
U385-W389, U395-W399 — Washington
U390-W392 — Grant

U393, U394 — Lincoln
U400-W405, U416, U417 — Franklin
U406-W415, U418, U419 — Washington

1903

U379	1¢ green on white	.90	.60	.25
U380	1¢ green on amber	18.00	12.00	2.25
U381	1¢ green on oriental buff	16.80	12.00	2.30
U382	1¢ green on blue	27.50	18.00	2.75
U383	1¢ green on manila	4.75	3.70	1.00
W384	1¢ green on manila	2.75	1.20	.50
U385	2¢ carmine on white	.75	.45	.20
U386	2¢ carmine on amber	3.60	1.80	.30
U387	2¢ carmine on oriental buff	2.40	1.80	.35
U388	2¢ carmine on blue	2.75	1.50	.60
W389	2¢ carmine on manila	19.25	16.75	8.50
U390	4¢ chocolate on white	24.00	21.00	12.00
U391	4¢ chocolate on amber	24.00	19.25	12.00
W392	4¢ chocolate on manila	24.00	19.25	13.00
U393	5¢ blue on white	24.00	19.25	13.00
U394	5¢ blue on amber	24.00	19.25	12.00

1904 RECUT DIE

U395	2¢ carmine on white	1.15	.50	.25
U396	2¢ carmine on amber	10.80	7.80	1.20
U397	2¢ carmine on oriental buff	7.80	6.00	1.50
U398	2¢ carmine on blue	4.80	3.60	1.10
W399	2¢ carmine on manila	21.00	12.60	10.00

1907-16

U400	1¢ green on white	.45	.30	.15
U401	1¢ green on amber	1.20	.80	.50
U402	1¢ green on oriental buff	6.00	4.50	1.20
U403	1¢ green on blue	6.00	4.80	1.80
U404	1¢ green on manila	4.50	3.30	2.10
W405	1¢ green on manila	.60	.50	.30
U406	2¢ brown red on white	1.70	.85	.20
U407	2¢ brown red on amber	7.50	6.00	3.00
U408	2¢ brown red on oriental buff	10.80	7.50	1.80
U409	2¢ brown red on blue	6.00	4.20	2.10
W410	2¢ brown red on manila	60.00	48.00	36.00
U411	2¢ carmine on white	.60	.25	.20
U412	2¢ carmine on amber	.95	.25	.15
U413	2¢ carmine on oriental buff	.60	.50	.25
U414	2¢ carmine on blue	1.25	.50	.15
W415	2¢ carmine on manila	7.80	4.80	2.40
U416	4¢ black on white	9.00	3.60	1.20
U417	4¢ black on amber	10.80	6.00	3.00
U418	5¢ blue on white	12.00	7.20	2.85
U419	5¢ blue on amber	18.00	14.50	13.25

U420-U428, U440-U442 — Franklin
U429-U439, U443-U445, U481-U485, U529-U531 — Washington

1916-32

U420	1¢ green on white	.25	.20	.20
U421	1¢ green on amber	.55	.45	.35
U422	1¢ green on oriental buff	2.30	1.80	1.20
U423	1¢ green on blue	.70	.50	.20
U424	1¢ green on manila	9.00	7.20	4.80
W425	1¢ green on manila	.40	.30	.20
U426	1¢ green on brown (glazed)	42.00	30.00	19.25
W427	1¢ green on brown (glazed)	75.00	62.50	
U428	1¢ green on brown (unglazed)	12.00	9.00	9.00
U429	2¢ carmine on white	.35	.25	.20
U430	2¢ carmine on amber	.40	.30	.20
U431	2¢ carmine on oriental buff	5.00	2.10	.70
U432	2¢ carmine on blue	.50	.30	.20
W433	2¢ carmine on manila	.55	.30	.20
W434	2¢ carmine on brown (glazed)	120.00	85.00	55.00
W435	2¢ carmine/brown (unglazed)	120.00	85.00	55.00
U436	3¢ dark violet on white	.75	.60	.20
U436f	3¢ purple on white (1932)	.55	.40	.20
U436h	3¢ carmine on white (error)	50.00	35.00	33.00
U437	3¢ dark violet on amber	6.00	2.70	1.20
U437a	3¢ purple on amber (1932)	.70	.35	.20
U437g	3¢ carmine on amber (error)	525.00	470.00	290.00
U437h	3¢ black on amber (error)	220.00	175.00	
U438	3¢ dark violet on buff	30.00	24.00	1.80
U439	3¢ dark violet on blue	10.80	7.20	1.70
U439a	3¢ purple on blue (1932)	.80	.35	.20
U439g	3¢ carmine on blue (error)	440.00	325.00	320.00
U440	4¢ black on white	2.40	1.20	.60
U441	4¢ black on amber	4.80	3.00	.90
U442	4¢ black on blue	5.40	3.00	1.00
U443	5¢ blue on white	6.00	3.20	3.00
U444	5¢ blue on amber	5.50	3.60	1.70
U445	5¢ blue on blue	8.40	4.20	3.50

U.S. Postal Stationery #U446-U531

SCOTT NO.	DESCRIPTION	UNUSED ENTIRE	UNUSED CUT SQ.	USED CUT SQ.
	1920-21 SURCHARGED			
	Type 1 — 2 CENTS / *Type 2*			
U446	2¢ on 3¢ dark violet on white .... (U436)	19.00	12.50	11.75
	Surcharge on Envelopes of 1916-21 Type 2			
U447	2¢ on 3¢ dark violet on white, rose .... (U436)	9.00	8.40	6.60
U448	2¢ on 3¢ dark violet on white .... (U436)	3.00	2.40	2.10
U449	2¢ on 3¢ dark violet on amber .... (U437)	9.00	6.00	6.00
U450	2¢ on 3¢ dark violet on oriental buff ..... (U438)	21.40	14.80	14.80
U451	2¢ on 3¢ dark violet on blue .... (U439)	19.00	12.00	11.00
	Type 3			
	Surcharge on Envelopes of 1874-1921 Type 3 bars 2mm apart			
U454	2¢ on 2¢ carmine on white .... (U429)	105.00	85.00	......
U455	2¢ on 2¢ carmine on amber .... (U430)	1700.00	1200.00	......
U456	2¢ on 2¢ carmine on oriental buff .... (U431)	220.00	185.00	......
U457	2¢ on 2¢ carmine on blue .... (U432)	250.00	220.00	......
U458	2¢ on 3¢ dark violet on white .... (U436)	.75	.55	.40
U459	2¢ on 3¢ dark violet on amber .... (U437)	4.50	3.00	1.20
U460	2¢ on 3¢ dark violet on oriental buff ..... (U438)	3.95	3.15	1.20
U461	2¢ on 3¢ dark violet on blue .... (U439)	6.60	4.80	1.20
U462	2¢ on 4¢ chocolate on white .... (U390)	440.00	370.00	175.00
U463	2¢ on 4¢ chocolate on amber .... (U391)	450.00	390.00	120.00
U464	2¢ on 5¢ blue on white .... (U443)	1200.00	1050.00	......
	Type 4 like Type 3, but bars 1-1/2 mm apart			
U465	2¢ on 1¢ green on white .... (U420)	1200.00	1050.00	......
U466A	2¢ on 2¢ carmine on white .... (U429)	330.00	270.00	......
U467	2¢ on 3¢ green on white .... (U163)	275.00	240.00	......
U468	2¢ on 3¢ dark violet on white .... (U436)	.95	.75	.45
U469	2¢ on 3¢ dark violet on amber .... (U437)	4.80	3.60	2.50
U470	2¢ on 3¢ dark violet on oriental buff ..... (U438)	7.20	5.10	3.00
U471	2¢ on 3¢ dark violet on blue .... (U439)	9.60	4.80	1.50
U472	2¢ on 4¢ chocolate on white .... (U390)	27.00	11.25	9.60
U473	2¢ on 4¢ chocolate on amber .... (U391)	21.00	15.60	10.80
U474	2¢ on 1¢ on 3¢ dark violet on white ...... (U436)	290.00	240.00	......
U475	2¢ on 1¢ on 3¢ dark violet on amber ...... (U437)	290.00	240.00	......
	Type 5 / Type 6 / Type 7			
	Surcharge on Envelope of 1916-21 Type 5			
U476	2¢ on 3¢ dark violet on amber .... (U437)	150.00	120.00	......
	Surcharge on Envelope of 1916-21 Type 6			
U477	2¢ on 3¢ dark violet on white .... (U436)	150.00	120.00	......
U478	2¢ on 3¢ dark violet on amber .... (U437)	240.00	210.00	......
	Surcharge on Envelope of 1916-21 Type 7			
U479	2¢ on 3¢ dark violet on white (black) ..... (U436)	390.00	325.00	......
	1925			
U481	1-1/2¢ brown on white	.60	.20	.20
U481b	1-1/2¢ purple on white (error)	120.00	105.00	......
U482	1-1/2¢ brown on amber	1.75	1.10	.45
U483	1-1/2¢ brown on blue	2.10	1.80	.90
U484	1-1/2¢ brown on manila	13.25	7.25	3.75
W485	1-1/2¢ brown on manila	1.25	.90	.25
	Type 8 — 1½			
	Surcharge on Envelopes of 1887 Type 8			
U486	1-1/2¢ on 2¢ green on white .... (U311)	850.00	700.00	......
U487	1-1/2¢ on 2¢ green on amber .... (U312)	1050.00	775.00	......
	Surcharge on Envelopes of 1899 Type 8			
U488	1-1/2¢ on 1¢ green on white .... (U352)	880.00	575.00	......
U489	1-1/2¢ on 1¢ green on amber .... (U353)	132.00	96.00	70.00
	Surcharge on Envelopes of 1907-10 Type 8			
U490	1-1/2¢ on 1¢ green on white .... (U400)	6.00	4.20	4.20
U491	1-1/2¢ on 1¢ green on amber .... (U401)	13.25	9.00	3.00
U492	1-1/2¢ on 1¢ green on oriental buff ...... (U402a)	240.00	210.00	85.00
U493	1-1/2¢ on 1¢ green on blue .... (U403c)	110.00	85.00	57.50
U494	1-1/2¢ on 1¢ green on manila .... (U404)	270.00	225.00	80.00
	Surcharge on Envelopes of 1916-21 Type 8			
U495	1-1/2¢ on 1¢ green on white .... (U420)	.90	.55	.30
U496	1-1/2¢ on 1¢ green on amber .... (U421)	22.80	16.75	14.00
U497	1-1/2¢ on 1¢ green on oriental buff ...... (U422)	5.40	3.25	2.50
U498	1-1/2¢ on 1¢ green on blue .... (U423)	2.25	1.25	.90
U499	1-1/2¢ on 1¢ green on manila .... (U424)	19.20	12.00	8.40
U500	1-1/2¢ on 1¢ green on brown (unglazed) ... (U428)	72.00	66.00	42.00
U501	1-1/2¢ on 1¢ green on brown (glazed) ..... (U426)	72.00	66.00	36.00
U502	1-1/2¢ on 2¢ carmine on white .... (U429)	360.00	240.00	......
U503	1-1/2¢ on 2¢ carmine on oriental buff .... (U431)	360.00	275.00	......
U504	1-1/2¢ on 2¢ carmine on blue .... (U432)	340.00	275.00	......
	Surcharge on Envelopes of 1925 Type 8			
U505	1-1/2¢ on 1-1/2¢ brown on white .... (U481)	525.00	420.00	......
U506	1-1/2¢ on 1-1/2¢ brown on blue .... (U483)	400.00	350.00	......
	Type 9 — 1½			
	Surcharge on Envelopes of 1899 Type 9			
U508	1-1/2¢ on 1¢ green on amber .... (U353)	72.00	60.00	......
	Surcharge on Envelopes of 1903 Type 9			
U508A	1-1/2¢ on 1¢ green on white .... (U379)	2600.00	2100.00	......
U509	1-1/2¢ on 1¢ green on amber .... (U380)	27.00	12.00	12.00
U509B	1-1/2¢ on 1¢ green on oriental buff ...... (U381)	65.00	55.00	50.00
	Surcharge on Envelopes of 1907-10 Type 9			
U510	1-1/2¢ on 1¢ green on white .... (U400)	3.90	2.50	1.50
U511	1-1/2¢ on 1¢ green on amber .... (U401)	190.00	160.00	80.00
U512	1-1/2¢ on 1¢ green on oriental buff ...... (U402)	10.75	6.60	4.75
U513	1-1/2¢ on 1¢ green on blue .... (U403)	8.25	5.50	3.00
U514	1-1/2¢ on 1¢ green on manila .... (U404)	36.00	21.00	12.00
U515	1-1/2¢ on 1¢ green on white .... (U420)	.65	.35	.25
U516	1-1/2¢ on 1¢ green on amber .... (U421)	60.00	48.00	36.00
U517	1-1/2¢ on 1¢ green on oriental buff ...... (U422)	6.00	4.80	1.50
U518	1-1/2¢ on 1¢ green on blue .... (U423)	6.00	4.80	1.50
U519	1-1/2¢ on 1¢ green on manila .... (U424)	29.00	24.00	12.00
U520	1-1/2¢ on 2¢ carmine on white .... (U429)	370.00	275.00	......
U521	1-1/2¢ on 1¢ green on white, magenta surcharged .... (U420)	5.40	4.80	4.20

U522: Die 1, "E" of "POSTAGE" has center bar shorter than top bar.

U522a: Die 2, "E" of "POSTAGE" has center and top bars same length.

U525: Die 1 "S" of "POSTAGE" even with "T".

U525a: Die 2 "S" of "POSTAGE" higher than "T".

SCOTT NO.	DESCRIPTION	UNUSED ENTIRE	UNUSED CUT SQ.	USED CUT SQ.
	1926 SESQUICENTENNIAL EXPOSITION			
U522	2¢ carmine on white, die 1	2.00	1.50	.60
U522a	2¢ carmine on white, die 2	12.50	8.00	4.50
	1932 WASHINGTON BICENTENNIAL			
U523	1¢ olive green on white	2.00	1.25	1.00
U524	1-1/2¢ chocolate on white	3.25	2.00	2.00
U525	2¢ carmine on white, die 1	.75	.50	.20
U525a	2¢ carmine on white, die 2	100.00	85.00	18.00
U526	3¢ violet on white	3.00	2.50	.50
U527	4¢ black on white	27.50	22.00	18.00
U528	5¢ dark blue on white	7.00	6.00	3.90
	1932 Designs of 1916-32			
U529	6¢ orange on white	10.00	5.75	5.00
U530	6¢ orange on amber	17.50	13.20	9.60
U531	6¢ orange on blue	16.80	13.25	11.00

U.S. Postal Stationery #U532-U564

SCOTT NO.	DESCRIPTION	FIRST DAY COVER	UNUSED ENTIRE	USED CUT SQ.

U532 Franklin
U533 Washington
U535

1950

U532	1¢ green	2.00	8.50	2.00
U533	2¢ carmine	2.00	1.25	.30
U534	3¢ dark violet	2.00	.50	.25

1952

| U535 | 1-1/2¢ brown | ...... | 5.75 | 4.00 |

U537, U538, U552, U556
U539, U540, U545, U553

Surcharge on Envelopes of 1916-32, 1950, 1965, 1971

1958

U536	4¢ red violet	1.75	1.00	.30
U537	2¢ & 2¢ (4¢) carmine .... (U429)	......	4.00	2.00
U538	2¢ & 2¢ (4¢) carmine .... (U533)	......	1.00	.20
U539	3¢ & 1¢ (4¢) purple, die1 .... (U436a)	......	18.50	12.00
U539a	3¢ & 1¢ (4¢) purple, die 7 .... (U436e)	......	15.00	10.00
U539b	3¢ & 1¢ (4¢) purple, die 9 .... (U436f)	......	36.00	16.00
U540	3¢ & 1¢ (4¢) dark violet .... (U534)	......	.70	.15

U541 Franklin
U542 Washington

1960

| U541 | 1-1/4¢ turquoise | 1.75 | .85 | .60 |
| U542 | 2-1/2¢ dull blue | 1.75 | 1.00 | .60 |

U543

| U543 | 4¢ Pony Express | 2.00 | .80 | .40 |

U544 Lincoln
U546

1962

| U544 | 5¢ dark blue | 1.75 | .95 | .25 |

Surcharge on Envelope of 1958

| U545 | 4¢+1¢ red violet .... (U536) | ...... | 1.80 | .60 |

1964

| U546 | 5¢ New York World's Fair | 1.75 | .75 | .45 |

U547, U548, U548A, U566
U549
U550
U551

1965-69

U547	1-1/4¢ brown	1.75	.95	.15
U548	1-4/10¢ brown (1968)	1.75	1.00	.15
U548A	1-6/10¢ orange (1969)	1.75	.90	.15
U549	4¢ bright blue	1.75	.95	.15
U550	5¢ bright purple	1.75	.90	.15
U551	6¢ light green (1968)	1.75	.85	.15

U554

1968
1958 Type Surcharges on Envelopes of 1965

| U552 | 4¢ & 2¢ (6¢) blue .... (U549) | 9.00 | 4.75 | 2.25 |
| U553 | 5¢ & 1¢ (6¢) purple .... (U550) | 9.00 | 4.00 | 2.50 |

1970

| U554 | 6¢ Moby Dick | 1.75 | .60 | .20 |

U555
U557

1971

U555	6¢ Conference on Youth	1.75	.90	.20
U556	1-7/10¢ deep lilac	1.75	.40	.15
U557	8¢ ultramarine	1.75	.50	.15

U561 & U562 Surcharge

| U561 | 6¢ & (2¢) (8¢) green .... (on U551) | 4.00 | 1.25 | .40 |
| U562 | 6¢ & (2¢) (8¢) blue .... (on U555) | 4.00 | 3.00 | 1.75 |

U563
U564

| U563 | 8¢ Bowling | 1.75 | .70 | .15 |
| U564 | 8¢ Conference on Aging | 1.75 | .70 | .15 |

U.S. Postal Stationery #U565-U585

SCOTT NO.	DESCRIPTION	FIRST DAY COVER	UNUSED ENTIRE	USED CUT SQ.

U565

1972

| U565 | 8¢ Transpo '72 | 1.75 | .80 | .15 |

U567

1973

| U566 | 8¢ & 2¢ ultramarine .... (on U557) | 3.00 | .55 | .15 |
| U567 | 10¢ emerald | 1.75 | .45 | .15 |

U568

U569

1974

| U568 | 1-8/10¢ blue green | 1.75 | .35 | .15 |
| U569 | 10¢ Tennis Centenary | 2.50 | .60 | .30 |

U571

U572

U573

U574

U575

1975-76 BICENTENNIAL ERA

U571	10¢ Seafaring	1.75	.55	.20
U572	13¢ Homemaker (1976)	1.75	.55	.20
U573	13¢ Farmer (1976)	1.75	.55	.20
U574	13¢ Doctor (1976)	1.75	.55	.20
U575	13¢ Craftsman (1976)	1.75	.55	.20

CUT SQUARES: From 1947 to date, Unused Envelope Cut Squares can be supplied at the Unused Entire Price.

U576

1975

| U576 | 13¢ orange brown | 1.75 | .50 | .15 |

U577

U578

U579

U580

U581

1976-78

U577	2¢ red	1.75	.35	.15
U578	2.1¢ green (1977)	1.75	.35	.15
U579	2.7¢ green (1978)	1.75	.40	.15
U580	(15¢) "A" orange (1978)	1.75	.60	.20
U581	15¢ red & white (1978)	1.75	.60	.20

1976

| U582 | 13¢ Bicentennial (design of U218) | 1.75 | .55 | .20 |

U583

1977

| U583 | 13¢ Golf | 8.00 | .80 | .20 |

U584

U585

| U584 | 13¢ Energy Conservation | 1.75 | .50 | .20 |
| U585 | 13¢ Energy Development | 1.75 | .50 | .20 |

U.S. Postal Stationery #U586-U606

SCOTT NO.	DESCRIPTION	FIRST DAY COVER	UNUSED ENTIRE	USED CUT SQ.

1978

| U586 | 15¢ on 16¢ blue & white | 1.75 | .55 | .20 |

| U587 | 15¢ Auto Racing | 2.00 | .75 | .20 |
| U588 | 15¢ on 13¢ white, orange brown (U576) | 1.75 | .55 | .20 |

1979

| U589 | 3.1¢ ultramarine & white | 1.75 | .30 | .15 |

1980

| U590 | 3.5¢ purple | 1.75 | .30 | .15 |

1981-82

U591	5.9¢ brown (1982)	1.85	.30	.15
U592	(18¢) "B" violet & white	1.75	.60	.25
U593	18¢ white & dark blue	1.75	.60	.25
U594	(20¢) "C" brown & white	1.75	.60	.15

1979

| U595 | 15¢ Veterinarians | 1.75 | .60 | .20 |
| U596 | 15¢ Moscow Olympics | 1.75 | .90 | .20 |

1980

U597	15¢ Bicycle	1.75	.55	.20
U598	15¢ America's Cup	1.75	.55	.20
U599	15¢ Honeybee	1.75	.55	.20

1981

| U600 | 18¢ Blinded Veterans | 1.75 | .60 | .20 |
| U601 | 20¢ deep magenta & white | 1.75 | .60 | .15 |

1982

| U602 | 20¢ black, blue & magenta | 1.75 | .60 | .15 |
| U603 | 20¢ Purple Heart | 1.75 | .60 | .15 |

1983

| U604 | 5.2¢ orange & white | 1.75 | .50 | .15 |
| U605 | 20¢ Paralyzed Veterans | 1.75 | .60 | .15 |

1984

| U606 | 20¢ Small Business | 2.00 | .60 | .15 |

U.S. Postal Stationery #U607-U624

SCOTT NO.	DESCRIPTION	FIRST DAY COVER	UNUSED ENTIRE	USED CUT SQ.

U607   U608   U609

1985

U607	(22¢) "D"	1.75	.60	.15
U608	22¢ Bison	1.75	.60	.15
U609	6¢ Old Ironsides	1.75	.30	.15

U610

1986

| U610 | 8.5¢ Mayflower | 1.75 | .30 | .15 |

U611   U612

U613

1988

U611	25¢ Stars	1.75	.80	.15
U612	8.4¢ Constellation	1.75	.30	.15
U613	25¢ Snowflake	1.75	1.00	.30

U614   U615

U616   U617, U639

1989

U614	25¢ Stamped Return Envelope	1.75	.55	.30
U615	25¢ "USA" and Stars	1.75	.60	.30
U616	25¢ LOVE	1.75	.60	.30
U617	25¢ Shuttle Docking Hologram	1.75	.80	.30

U618

1990

| U618 | 25¢ Football Hologram | 2.75 | .65 | .30 |

U619

1991

| U619 | 29¢ Star | 1.75 | .70 | .30 |

U620

| U620 | 11.1¢ Birds on Wire | 1.75 | .40 | .20 |

U621

| U621 | 29¢ Love | 1.75 | .70 | .30 |

U622   U623

| U622 | 29¢ Magazine Industry | 1.75 | .70 | .30 |
| U623 | 29¢ Star | 1.75 | .70 | .30 |

U624

| U624 | 26¢ Country Geese | 1.75 | .70 | .70 |

U.S. Postal Stationery #U625-U652

SCOTT NO.	DESCRIPTION	FIRST DAY COVER	UNUSED ENTIRE	USED CUT SQ.

U625

U626

1992

| U625 | 29¢ Space Station | 1.75 | .70 | .30 |
| U626 | 29¢ Saddle & Blanket | 1.75 | .70 | .30 |

U627

U628

| U627 | 29¢ Protect the Environment | 1.75 | .70 | .30 |
| U628 | 19.8¢ Star | 1.75 | .60 | .30 |

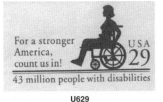
U629

U630

| U629 | 29¢ Americans With Disabilities | 1.75 | .70 | .30 |

1993

| U630 | 29¢ Kitten | 1.75 | .70 | .30 |

U631

U632, U638

1994

| U631 | 29¢ Football | 1.75 | .70 | .30 |

U633, U634

U635

1995

U632	32¢ Liberty Bell	1.95	.75	.35
U633	(32¢) "G" Old Glory (Design size 49x38mm)	1.95	.75	.35
U634	(32¢) "G" Old Glory (Design size 53x44mm)	1.95	.75	.35
U635	(5¢) Sheep, Nonprofit	1.95	.30	.35

U636

U637

U636	(10¢) Graphic Eagle, Bulk Rate	1.95	.40	.35
U637	32¢ Spiral Heart	1.95	.75	.35
U638	32¢ Liberty Bell, security	1.95	.75	.35
U639	32¢ Space Station	1.95	.75	.35

U640

U641

1996

| U640 | 32¢ Save our Environment | 1.95 | .75 | .35 |
| U641 | 32¢ Paralympic Games | 1.95 | .75 | .35 |

U642, U643

U645

U644

1999-2000

U642	33¢ Flag, yellow, blue & red	1.95	.80	.35
U642a	same, tagging bars to right of design	1.95	.80	.35
U643	33¢ Flag, blue & red	1.95	.80	.35
U644	33¢ Love	1.95	.80	.35
U645	33¢ Lincoln, blue & black	1.95	.80	.35

U646

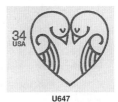
U647

U648

U649

U650

U651

U652

2001-03

U646	34¢ Eagle, blue gray & gray	1.95	.85	.35
U647	34¢ Lovebirds, rose & dull violet	1.95	.85	.35
U648	34¢ Community Colleges, dark blue & orange brown	1.95	.85	.35
U649	37¢ Ribbon Star, red & blue	1.95	.90	.40
U650	(10¢) Graphic Eagle, Presorted Standard	1.95	.40	.35
U651	37¢ Nurturing Love	1.95	.90	.40
U652	$3.85 Jefferson Memorial, pre-paid flat rate	8.75	8.75	5.00

U.S. Postal Stationery Air Mail #UC1-UC36

UC1 — UC2-UC7

Airplane in Circle

Die 1. Vertical rudder not semi-circular, but slopes to the left. Tail projects into "G".
Die 2. Vertical rudder is semi-circular. Tail only touches "G" Die 2a. "6" is 6-1/2mm. wide.
Die 2b. "6" is 6mm. wide.
Die 2c. "6" is 5-1/2mm. wide.
Die 3. Vertical rudder leans forward. "S" closer to "O" than to "T" of "POSTAGE" and "E" has short center bar.

1929-44

SCOTT NO.	DESCRIPTION	UNUSED ENTIRE	UNUSED CUT SQ.	USED CUT SQ.
UC1	5¢ blue, die 1	4.50	3.25	2.00
UC2	5¢ blue, die 2	15.00	12.00	6.00
UC3	6¢ orange, die 2a	1.80	1.50	.50
UC3n	6¢, die 2a, no border	3.00	1.30	.30
UC4	6¢, die 2b, with border	55.00	3.00	2.50
UC4n	6¢, die 2b, no border	4.80	3.00	1.50
UC5	6¢, die 2c, no border	1.25	1.00	.40
UC6	6¢ orange on white, die 3	2.00	1.25	.45
UC6n	6¢, die 3, no border	3.00	1.50	.50
UC7	8¢ olive green	18.00	14.50	4.00

Envelopes of 1916-32 surcharged

1945

UC8	6¢ on 2¢ carmine on white	(U429)	1.75	1.40	.75
UC9	6¢ on 2¢ carmine on white	(U525)	120.00	90.00	45.00

1946

UC10	5¢ on 6¢, die 2a	(UC3n)	4.00	3.00	1.75
UC11	5¢ on 6¢, die 2b	(UC4n)	11.00	10.75	5.50
UC12	5¢ on 6¢, die 2c	(UC5)	1.50	.90	.60
UC13	5¢ on 6¢, die 3	(UC6n)	1.15	.95	.75

UC14, UC15, UC18, UC26
DC-4 Skymaster

UC14: Die 1. Small projection below rudder is rounded.
UC15: Die 2. Small projection below rudder is sharp pointed.

SCOTT NO.	DESCRIPTION	FIRST DAY COVER	UNUSED ENTIRE	USED CUT SQ.
UC14	5¢ carmine, die 1	2.50	1.10	.25
UC15	5¢ carmine, die 2	......	1.10	.30

UC16
DC-4 Skymaster

UC17
Washington and Franklin, Mail-carrying Vehicles

1947

UC16	10¢ red on blue, Entire "Air Letter" on face, 2-line inscription on back	6.00	8.00	6.50
UC16a	Entire, "Air Letter" on face, 4-line inscription on back	......	17.50	......
UC16c	Entire "Air Letter" and "Aerogramme" on face, 4-line inscription on back	......	55.00	......
UC16d	Entire "Air Letter" and "Aerogramme" on face, 3-line inscription on back	......	8.25	......

SCOTT NO.	DESCRIPTION	FIRST DAY COVER	UNUSED ENTIRE	USED CUT SQ.

1947 CIPEX COMMEMORATIVE

UC17	5¢ carmine	3.00	.60	.35

1950 Design of 1946

UC18	6¢ carmine	1.75	.60	.15

ENVELOPE of 1946 Surcharged — ENVELOPE of 1946-47 Surcharged

1951 (Shaded Numeral)

UC19	6¢ on 5¢, die 1	(UC14)	......	1.35	.60
UC20	6¢ on 5¢, die 2	(UC15)	......	1.25	.60

1952 (Solid Numeral)

UC21	6¢ on 5¢, die 1	(UC14)	......	37.50	19.00
UC22	6¢ on 5¢, die 2	(UC15)	......	5.75	2.75
UC23	6¢ on 5¢	(UC17)	......	1900.00	......

UC25

1956 FIPEX COMMEMORATIVE

UC25	6¢ red	1.75	1.10	.60

1958 Design of 1946

UC26	7¢ blue	1.75	1.10	.60

Surcharge on Envelopes of 1934 to 1956

UC27-UC31

1958

UC27	6¢ & 1¢ (7¢) orange, die 2a	(UC3n)	......	320.00	......
UC28	6¢ & 1¢ (7¢), die 2b	(UC4n)	......	90.00	82.50
UC29	6¢ & 1¢ (7¢) orange, die 2c	(UC5)	......	48.50	52.50
UC30	6¢ & 1¢ (7¢) carmine	(UC18)	......	1.35	.60
UC31	6¢ & 1¢ (7¢) red	(UC25)	......	1.40	.60

UC32 — UC33, UC34 — UC35

1958-59

UC32	10¢ blue & red Entire letter sheet, 2-line inscription on back (1959)	......	7.00	5.25
UC32a	Entire letter sheet, 3 line inscription on back	2.25	12.00	5.25

1958

UC33	7¢ blue	1.75	.80	.15

1960

UC34	7¢ carmine	1.75	.75	.15

1961

UC35	11¢ red & blue	3.25	3.00	2.50

UC36

1962

UC36	8¢ red	1.75	.85	.15

U.S. Postal Stationery Air Mail #UC37-UC59

SCOTT NO.	DESCRIPTION	FIRST DAY COVER	UNUSED ENTIRE	USED CUT SQ.

UC37

UC38, UC39

1965

| UC37 | 8¢ red | 1.75 | .60 | .15 |
| UC38 | 11¢ J.F. Kennedy | 1.75 | 4.00 | 3.00 |

UC40

UC41 (surcharge on UC37)

UC51

1976

| UC50 | 22¢ red, white & blue | 1.75 | 1.00 | .50 |

1978

| UC51 | 22¢ blue | 1.75 | .85 | .30 |

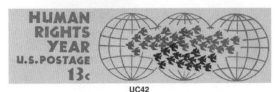

UC42

1967

UC52

UC53, UC54

UC55

| UC39 | 13¢ J.F. Kennedy | 1.75 | 3.50 | 3.00 |

1979

| UC52 | 22¢ Moscow Olympics | 1.75 | 1.70 | .30 |

1968

UC40	10¢ red	1.75	.65	.15
UC41	8¢ & 2¢ (10¢) red	12.00	.95	.20
UC42	13¢ Human Rights Year	1.75	8.00	4.50

1980-81

| UC53 | 30¢ red, blue & brown | 1.75 | .85 | .35 |
| UC54 | 30¢ yellow, magenta, blue & black (1981) | 1.75 | .85 | .35 |

1982

| UC55 | 30¢ Made in U.S.A. | 1.75 | .85 | .35 |

UC43

UC44

1971

UC43	11¢ red & blue	1.75	.70	.15
UC44	15¢ gray, red, white and blue Birds in Flight	1.75	1.60	1.00
UC44a	Aerogramme added	1.75	1.60	1.00

UC56

UC57

1983

| UC56 | 30¢ Communications | 1.75 | .85 | .35 |
| UC57 | 30¢ Olympics | 1.75 | .85 | .35 |

UC45 (surcharge on UC40)

UC47

1971 Revalued

| UC45 | 10 & (1¢) (11¢) red | 6.00 | 2.00 | .25 |

1973

| UC46 | 15¢ Ballooning | 1.75 | .85 | .50 |
| UC47 | 13¢ rose red | 1.75 | 1.50 | .15 |

UC58

1985

| UC58 | 36¢ Landsat Satellite | 1.75 | .85 | .45 |

UC48

UC49

1974

| UC48 | 18¢ red & blue | 1.75 | .85 | .35 |
| UC49 | 18¢ NATO 25th Anniversary | 1.75 | .85 | .30 |

UC59

| UC59 | 36¢ Travel | 1.75 | .85 | .45 |

U.S. Postal Stationery Air Mail #UC60-UC65

SCOTT NO.	DESCRIPTION	FIRST DAY COVER	UNUSED ENTIRE	USED CUT SQ.
UC60	36¢ Mark Twain, Halley's Comet	1.75	.85	.45
	1986			
UC61	39¢ Letters	1.75	.90	.45
	1989			
UC62	39¢ Blair & Lincoln	1.75	.90	.45
UC63	45¢ Eagle	1.75	1.00	.45
	1991			
UC64	50¢ Thaddeus Lowe	1.95	1.10	.50
	1995			
UC65	60¢ Voyagers National Park, Minnesota	1.95	1.35	.65
	1999			

How To Collect Stamps

H.E. Harris Shares The Experience And Knowledge Accumulated Since 1916 In This New, Up-dated Edition.

- Extensive instructions and advice for beginners, including brief history of stamps and stamp collecting
- Philatelic history of all stamp issuing countries
- Detailed guides for identifying U.S. and foreign stamps with many illustrations and maps
- Collector's dictionary defines varieties, formats, grading, condition and other terminology
- Over 200 pages, softbound

Item# 1HRS45
ONLY $5.95

H.E. Harris & Co.®
Serving the Collector Since 1916

Order from your local dealer or direct from Whitman Publishing, LLC.

U.S. Official Postal Stationery #UO1-UO91

UO1-UO13

UO14-UO17

UO18-UO69
Washington

OFFICIAL ENVELOPES
NOTE: For details on similar appearing varieties please refer to the Scott Specialized Catalogue

POST OFFICE DEPARTMENT
1873 SMALL NUMERALS

Scott No.	Description	Unused Entire	Unused Cut Sq.	Used Cut Sq.
UO1	2¢ black on lemon	24.00	16.00	8.50
UO2	3¢ black on lemon	16.00	10.00	6.50
UO4	6¢ black on lemon	24.00	19.00	15.00

1874-79 LARGE NUMERALS

UO5	2¢ black on lemon	10.00	7.00	5.00
UO6	2¢ black on white	100.00	80.00	35.00
UO7	3¢ black on lemon	4.75	3.25	.80
UO8	3¢ black on white	1525.00	1175.00	875.00
UO9	3¢ black on amber	72.00	50.00	37.50
UO12	6¢ black on lemon	15.00	9.50	7.00
UO13	6¢ black on white	1650.00	1200.00	......

1877 POSTAL SERVICE

UO14	black on white	11.00	8.00	4.00
UO15	black on amber	135.00	60.00	30.00
UO16	blue on amber	130.00	55.00	32.50
UO17	blue on blue	12.50	9.00	7.00

Portraits for the various denominations are the same as on the regular issue of 1870-73

WAR DEPARTMENT
1873 REAY ISSUE

UO18	1¢ dark red on white	840.00	650.00	300.00
UO19	2¢ dark red on white	1150.00	875.00	440.00
UO20	3¢ dark red on white	78.00	60.00	48.00
UO22	3¢ dark red on cream	600.00	480.00	210.00
UO23	6¢ dark red on white	260.00	210.00	78.00
UO24	6¢ dark red on cream	4100.00	2200.00	440.00
UO25	10¢ dark red on white	5400.00	3000.00	330.00
UO26	12¢ dark red on white	155.00	120.00	48.00
UO27	15¢ dark red on white	155.00	120.00	54.00
UO28	24¢ dark red on white	165.00	120.00	55.00
UO29	30¢ dark red on white	620.00	475.00	165.00
UO30	1¢ vermillion on white	225.00	150.00	......
WO31	1¢ vermillion on manila	19.00	14.00	13.50
UO32	2¢ vermillion on white	4750.00	290.00	......
WO33	2¢ vermillion on manila	300.00	210.00	......
UO34	3¢ vermillion on white	140.00	80.00	45.00
UO35	3¢ vermillion on amber	240.00	87.50	......
UO36	3¢ vermillion on cream	36.00	15.00	14.00
UO37	6¢ vermillion on white	100.00	75.00	......
UO38	6¢ vermillion on cream	7800.00	420.00	......
UO39	10¢ vermillion on white	325.00	220.00	......
UO40	12¢ vermillion on white	190.00	145.00	......
UO41	15¢ vermillion on white	2700.00	240.00	......
UO42	24¢ vermillion on white	450.00	390.00	......
UO43	30¢ vermillion on white	550.00	480.00	......

1875 PLIMPTON ISSUE

UO44	1¢ red on white	150.00	130.00	85.00
UO45	1¢ red on amber	......	840.00	......
WO46	1¢ red on manila	7.00	4.00	3.00
UO47	2¢ red on white	120.00	102.00	......
UO48	2¢ red on amber	36.00	30.00	15.00
UO49	2¢ red on orange	48.00	42.00	15.00
WO50	2¢ red on manila	110.00	80.00	50.00
UO51	3¢ red on white	16.50	14.00	10.00
UO52	3¢ red on amber	17.50	15.00	9.50
UO53	3¢ red on cream	9.50	7.00	4.00
UO54	3¢ red on blue	5.00	4.00	3.00
UO55	3¢ red on fawn	8.00	4.80	3.00
UO56	6¢ red on white	85.00	42.00	34.00
UO57	6¢ red on amber	90.00	80.00	45.00
UO58	6¢ red on cream	220.00	190.00	92.50
UO59	10¢ red on white	190.00	165.00	90.00
UO60	10¢ red on amber	1500.00	1320.00	......
UO61	12¢ red on white	110.00	42.00	42.00
UO62	12¢ red on amber	750.00	660.00	......
UO63	12¢ red on cream	750.00	640.00	......
UO64	15¢ red on white	210.00	180.00	145.00
UO65	15¢ red on amber	800.00	725.00	......
UO66	15¢ red on cream	775.00	725.00	......
UO67	30¢ red on white	200.00	185.00	132.50
UO68	30¢ red on amber	1275.00	1150.00	......
UO69	30¢ red on cream	1200.00	1100.00	......

UO70-UO72

1911 POSTAL SAVINGS

UO70	1¢ green on white	77.50	65.00	22.00
UO71	1¢ green on oriental buff	240.00	198.00	60.00
UO72	2¢ carmine on white	22.00	13.50	4.50

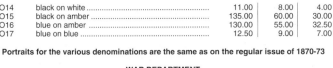

UO73   UO74   UO75

1983

Scott No.	Description	First Day Cover	Unused Cut Sq.	Used Cut Sq.
UO73	20¢ blue and white	2.50	1.40	......

1985

UO74	22¢ blue and white	2.00	.90	......

1987 Design Similar to UO74

UO75	22¢ Savings Bond	3.25	.90	......

UO76   UO77   UO78

UO81   UO83   UO84

1988

UO76	(25¢) "E" black and blue Savings Bonds	2.00	1.25	......
UO77	25¢ black and blue	2.00	.80	......
UO78	25¢ black and blue Savings Bonds	2.00	1.00	......

1990

UO79	45¢ black & blue seal	2.25	1.40	......
UO80	65¢ black & blue seal	3.00	1.95	......
UO81	45¢ Self-sealing Envelope	2.25	1.40	......
UO82	65¢ Self-sealing Envelope	3.00	1.95	......

UO85   UO86, UO87   UO88, UO89, UO90, UO91

1991-92

UO83	(29¢) "F" black and blue Savings Bond	2.00	1.25	......
UO84	29¢ black and blue	2.00	.80	......
UO85	29¢ black and blue Savings Bond	2.00	.80	......
UO86	52¢ Consular Service	2.50	3.00	......
UO87	75¢ Consular Service	3.00	5.00	......

1995

UO88	32¢ red and blue	2.00	.90	......

1999

UO89	33¢ red and blue	2.00	.90	......

2001-02

UO90	34¢ red and blue	2.00	.90	......
UO91	37¢ red & blue	2.00	.95	......

U.S. Postal Stationery #UX1-UX37

POSTAL CARDS

Prices Are For Entire Cards

MINT: As Issued, no printing or writing added.
UNUSED: Uncancelled, with printing or writing added.

UX1, UX3, U65

UX4, UX5, UX7
Liberty

UX6, UX13, UX16

1873

Scott No.	Description	Mint	Unused	Used
UX1	1¢ brown, large watermark	350.00	55.00	19.00
UX3	1¢ brown, small watermark	70.00	22.00	2.25

1875 Inscribed "Write the Address", etc.

| UX4 | 1¢ black, watermarked | 2100.00 | 575.00 | 325.00 |
| UX5 | 1¢ black, unwatermarked | 70.00 | 7.50 | .50 |

1879

| UX6 | 2¢ blue on buff | 28.00 | 12.00 | 18.50 |

1881 Inscribed "Nothing but the Address", etc.

| UX7 | 1¢ black on buff | 67.50 | 6.00 | .50 |

UX8
Jefferson

UX9

UX10, UX11
Grant

1885

| UX8 | 1¢ brown on buff | 50.00 | 10.00 | 1.50 |

1886

| UX9 | 1¢ black on buff | 21.00 | 1.75 | .65 |

1891

| UX10 | 1¢ black on buff | 35.00 | 6.50 | 1.75 |
| UX11 | 1¢ blue on grayish white | 13.50 | 2.50 | 3.00 |

UX12
Jefferson

UX14

UX15
John Adams

1894

| UX12 | 1¢ black on buff Small Wreath | 37.50 | 2.50 | .50 |

1897

| UX13 | 2¢ blue on cream | 135.00 | 70.00 | 82.50 |
| UX14 | 1¢ black on buff Large Wreath | 27.50 | 3.00 | .50 |

1898

| UX15 | 1¢ black on buff | 45.00 | 12.50 | 16.00 |
| UX16 | 2¢ black on buff | 11.00 | 6.25 | 11.00 |

UX18

UX19, UX20
McKinley

UX21

1902 Profile Background

| UX18 | 1¢ black on buff | 13.50 | 1.75 | .40 |

1907

| UX19 | 1¢ black on buff | 40.00 | 2.50 | .60 |

1908 Correspondence Space at Left

| UX20 | 1¢ black on buff | 55.00 | 9.00 | 4.50 |

1910 Background Shaded

| UX21 | 1¢ blue on bluish | 100.00 | 18.00 | 7.00 |

UX22, UX24
McKinley

UX23, UX26
Lincoln

UX25
Grant

White Portrait Background

| UX22 | 1¢ blue on bluish | 13.50 | 1.65 | .30 |

1911

UX23	1¢ red on cream	8.50	3.25	6.00
UX24	1¢ red on cream	10.00	1.50	.35
UX25	2¢ red on cream	1.50	.75	9.00

1913

| UX26 | 1¢ green on cream | 11.00 | 3.00 | 6.50 |

UX27
Jefferson

UX28, UX43
Lincoln

UX29, UX30
Jefferson

UX32, UX33
surcharge

1914

| UX27 | 1¢ green on buff | .35 | .20 | .30 |

1917-18

UX28	1¢ green on cream	1.00	.40	.40
UX29	2¢ red on buff, die 1	42.00	7.00	2.50
UX30	2¢ red on cream, die 2 (1918)	35.00	4.00	1.80

NOTE: On UX29 end of queue slopes sharply down to right while on UX30 it extends nearly horizontally.

1920 UX29 & UX30 Revalued

| UX32 | 1¢ on 2¢ red, die 1 | 55.00 | 16.50 | 13.00 |
| UX33 | 1¢ on 2¢ red, die 2 | 12.50 | 2.75 | 2.25 |

UX37
McKinley

UX38
Franklin

UX39-42
surcharge

1926

| UX37 | 3¢ red on buff | 4.75 | 2.00 | 10.00 |

U.S. Postal Stationery #UX38-UX64

SCOTT NO.	DESCRIPTION	FIRST DAY COVER	MINT	USED
	1951			
UX38	2¢ carmine rose	1.75	.40	.35
	1952 UX27 & UX28 Surcharged by cancelling machine, light green			
UX39	2¢ on 1¢ green	......	.60	.35
UX40	2¢ on 1¢ green	......	.70	.50
	UX27 & UX28 Surcharge Typographed, dark green			
UX41	2¢ on 1¢ green	......	5.00	2.00
UX42	2¢ on 1¢ green	......	5.25	2.75
	1952 Design of 1917			
UX43	2¢ carmine	1.75	.30	1.00
	1956 FIPEX COMMEMORATIVE			
UX44	2¢ deep carmine & dark violet	1.75	.35	1.00
	1956 INTERNATIONAL CARD			
UX45	4¢ deep red & ultramarine	1.75	1.75	45.00
	1958			
UX46	3¢ purple	1.75	.50	.25
	As above, but with printed precancel lines			
UX46c	3¢ purple	......	4.00	2.50
	1958 UX38 Surcharged			
UX47	2¢ & 1¢ carmine rose	......	195.00	280.00
Mint *UX47 has advertising				
	1962-66			
UX48	4¢ red violet	1.75	.30	.25
UX48a	4¢ luminescent (1966)	3.00	.60	.25
	1963			
UX49	7¢ Tourism	1.75	4.00	37.50
	1964			
UX50	4¢ Customs Service	1.75	.50	1.00
UX51	4¢ Social Security	1.75	.50	1.00
	1965			
UX52	4¢ Coast Guard	1.75	.45	1.00
UX53	4¢ Census Bureau	1.75	.45	1.00
	1967 Design of UX49			
UX54	8¢ Tourism	1.75	4.25	37.50
	1968			
UX55	5¢ emerald	1.75	.30	.40
UX56	5¢ Women Marines	1.75	.40	1.00
	1970			
UX57	5¢ Weather Bureau	1.75	.35	1.00
	1971			
UX58	6¢ Paul Revere	1.75	.30	1.00
	Design of UX49			
UX59	10¢ Tourism	1.75	4.50	37.50
	1971			
UX60	6¢ New York Hospital	1.75	.35	1.00
	1972			
UX61	6¢ U.S.F. Constellation	1.75	1.00	3.50
UX62	6¢ Monument Valley	1.75	.45	3.50
UX63	6¢ Gloucester, Massachusetts	1.75	.45	3.50
UX64	6¢ John Hanson	1.75	.35	1.00

U.S. Postal Stationery #UX65-UX89

SCOTT NO.	DESCRIPTION	FIRST DAY COVER	MINT	USED

UX66, UY24

UX67

1973

| UX65 | 6¢ Liberty, magenta, Design of 1873 | 1.75 | .35 | 1.00 |
| UX66 | 8¢ Samuel Adams | 1.75 | .35 | 1.00 |

1974

| UX67 | 12¢ Visit USA | 1.75 | .45 | 35.00 |

UX68, UY25 UX69, UY26

UX70, UY27

1975-76

UX68	7¢ Charles Thomson	1.75	.35	5.00
UX69	9¢ J. Witherspoon	1.75	.35	1.00
UX70	9¢ Caesar Rodney	1.75	.35	1.00

UX71

UX72, UY28

1977

| UX71 | 9¢ Federal Court House | 1.75 | .50 | 1.00 |
| UX72 | 9¢ Nathan Hale | 1.75 | .55 | 1.00 |

UX73

UX74, UX75, UY29, UY30

UX76

UX77

1978

UX73	10¢ Music Hall	1.75	.35	1.00
UX74	(10¢) John Hancock	1.75	.35	1.00
UX75	10¢ John Hancock	1.75	.35	1.00
UX76	14¢ "Eagle"	1.75	.40	17.50
UX77	10¢ multicolored	1.75	.50	.15

SCOTT NO.	DESCRIPTION	FIRST DAY COVER	MINT	USED

UX78

UX79

UX80

1979

UX78	10¢ Fort Sackville	1.75	.35	1.00
UX79	10¢ Casimir Pulaski	1.75	.35	1.00
UX80	10¢ Moscow Olympics	1.75	.60	1.00
UX81	10¢ Iolani Palace	1.75	.35	1.00

UX81

UX82

UX83

UX84 UX85

UX86

1980

UX82	14¢ Winter Olympics	1.75	.60	12.00
UX83	10¢ Salt Lake Temple	1.75	.35	1.00
UX84	10¢ Count Rochambeau	1.75	.35	1.00
UX85	10¢ Kings Mountain	1.75	.35	1.00
UX86	19¢ Sir Francis Drake	1.75	.50	12.00

UX87

UX88, UY31

UX89, UY32

1981

UX87	10¢ Cowpens	1.75	.35	2.75
UX88	"B" (12¢) violet & white	1.75	.35	.50
UX89	12¢ Isaiah Thomas	1.75	.35	.50

U.S. Postal Stationery #UX90-UX117

Nathanael Greene, Eutaw Springs, 1781
UX90

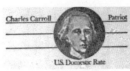
Lewis and Clark Expedition, 1806
UX91

UX92, UY33

UX93, UY34

SCOTT NO.	DESCRIPTION	FIRST DAY COVER	MINT	USED
UX90	12¢ Eutaw Springs	1.75	.35	1.00
UX91	12¢ Lewis & Clark	1.75	.35	3.50
UX92	(13¢) Robert Morris	1.75	.35	.50
UX93	13¢ Robert Morris	1.75	.35	.50

UX105, UX106, UY35, UY36

Clipper *Flying Cloud* 1852
UX107

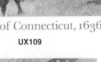
UX108

1985

SCOTT NO.	DESCRIPTION	FIRST DAY COVER	MINT	USED
UX105	(14¢) Charles Carroll	1.75	.35	.60
UX106	14¢ Charles Carroll	1.75	.35	.25
UX107	25¢ Flying Cloud	1.75	.65	6.00
UX108	14¢ George Wythe	1.75	.35	.50

"Swamp Fox" Francis Marion, 1782
UX94

La Salle claims Louisiana, 1682
UX95

Settling of Connecticut, 1636
UX109

Stamps The Universal Hobby USA
UX110

Francis Vigo, Vincennes, 1779
UX111

Settling of Rhode Island, 1636
UX112

1986

UX109	14¢ Connecticut	1.75	.35	.90
UX110	14¢ Stamp Collecting	1.75	.35	.90
UX111	14¢ Francis Vigo	1.75	.35	.90
UX112	14¢ Rhode Island	1.75	.35	.90

UX96 Philadelphia Academy of Music

UX97 Old Post Office St. Louis, Missouri — Historic Preservation

1982

UX94	13¢ Francis Marion	1.75	.35	.65
UX95	13¢ La Salle	1.75	.35	.75
UX96	13¢ Academy of Music	1.75	.35	.75
UX97	13¢ St. Louis Post Office	1.75	.35	.75

Landing of Oglethorpe, Georgia, 1733
UX98

Old Post Office, Washington, D.C.
UX99

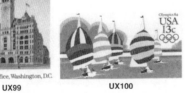
UX100

Wisconsin Territory, 1836
UX113

National Guard Heritage, 1636-1986
UX114

UX113	14¢ Wisconsin	1.75	.35	.90
UX114	14¢ National Guard	1.75	.35	.90

1983

UX98	13¢ General Oglethorpe	1.75	.35	.75
UX99	13¢ Washington Post Office	1.75	.35	.75
UX100	13¢ Olympics	1.75	.35	.75

Ark and Dove, Maryland, 1634
UX101

UX102

Self-scouring steel plow, 1837
UX115

Constitutional Convention, 1787
UX116

Frederic Baraga, Michigan, 1835
UX103

Dominguez Adobe Rancho San Pedro — The California Ranchos 1784-1984
Historic Preservation USA
UX104

UX117

1987

1984

UX101	13¢ "Ark" & "Dove"	1.75	.35	.75
UX102	13¢ Olympics	1.75	.35	.75
UX103	13¢ Frederic Baraga	1.75	.35	.75
UX104	13¢ Historic Preservation	1.75	.35	.75

UX115	14¢ Steel Plow	1.75	.35	.50
UX116	14¢ Constitution	1.75	.35	.50
UX117	14¢ Flag	1.75	.35	.50

U.S. Postal Stationery #UX118-UX144

SCOTT NO.	DESCRIPTION	FIRST DAY COVER	MINT	USED

UX118 — Take Pride in America 14¢
UX119 — Historic Preservation (Timberline Lodge Mt. Hood, Oregon) 14¢

1987 (continued)

| UX118 | 14¢ Take Pride in America | 1.75 | .35 | .50 |
| UX119 | 14¢ Timberline Lodge | 1.75 | .35 | .50 |

UX120 — America the Beautiful 15¢
UX121 — Blair House 15¢

1988

| UX120 | 15¢ America the Beautiful | 1.75 | .35 | .50 |
| UX121 | 15¢ Blair House | 1.75 | .35 | .50 |

UX122 — 28¢ Yorkshire
UX123 — Iowa Territory, 1838 15¢

| UX122 | 28¢ Yorkshire | 1.75 | .65 | 3.50 |
| UX123 | 15¢ Iowa Territory | 1.75 | .35 | .50 |

UX124 — Settling of Ohio, Northwest Territory, 1788 15¢
UX125 — Hearst Castle San Simeon California 15¢

| UX124 | 15¢ Northwest Territory | 1.75 | .35 | .50 |
| UX125 | 15¢ Hearst Castle | 1.75 | .35 | .50 |

UX126 — The Federalist Papers, 1787-88 15¢

| UX126 | 15¢ Federalist Papers | 1.75 | .35 | .50 |

UX127 — America the Beautiful 15¢
UX128 — 15¢

1989

| UX127 | 15¢ The Desert | 1.75 | .35 | .50 |
| UX128 | 15¢ Healy Hall | 1.75 | .35 | .50 |

UX129 — America the Beautiful 15¢
UX130 — Settling of Oklahoma 15¢

| UX129 | 15¢ The Wet Lands | 1.75 | .35 | .50 |
| UX130 | 15¢ Oklahoma Territory | 1.75 | .35 | .50 |

UX131 — America the Beautiful 21¢
UX132 — America the Beautiful 15¢

| UX131 | 21¢ The Mountains | 1.75 | .65 | 3.50 |
| UX132 | 15¢ The Seashore | 1.75 | .35 | .50 |

UX133 — America the Beautiful 15¢
UX134 — 15¢

| UX133 | 15¢ The Woodlands | 1.75 | .35 | .50 |
| UX134 | 15¢ Hull House | 1.75 | .35 | .50 |

UX135 — America the Beautiful 15¢
UX136 — America the Beautiful 15¢

| UX135 | 15¢ Philadelphia Cityscape | 1.75 | .35 | .50 |
| UX136 | 15¢ Baltimore Cityscape | 1.75 | .35 | .50 |

UX137 — America the Beautiful 15¢
UX138 — America the Beautiful 15¢

UX137	15¢ New York Cityscape	1.75	.35	.50
UX138	15¢ Washington Cityscape	1.75	.35	.50
UX139-42	15¢ Cityscape sheet of 4 postcards	8.00	20.00	......

UX143 — 15¢
UX144 — 15¢

| UX143 | 15¢ White House | 1.75 | 1.50 | 1.50 |
| UX144 | 15¢ Jefferson Memorial | 1.75 | 1.50 | 1.50 |

UX145 — 15¢
UX146 — 15¢ The world is an open book.

U.S. Postal Stationery #UX145-UX171

SCOTT NO.	DESCRIPTION	FIRST DAY COVER	MINT	USED

 UX147
 UX148
 UX150
 UX151
 UX152

1990

SCOTT NO.	DESCRIPTION	FIRST DAY COVER	MINT	USED
UX145	15¢ Papermaking	1.75	.35	.40
UX146	15¢ Literacy	1.75	.35	.50
UX147	15¢ Bingham	1.75	1.40	1.50
UX148	15¢ Isaac Royall House	1.75	.50	.50
UX150	15¢ Stanford University	1.75	.50	.50
UX151	15¢ DAR Memorial Hall	1.75	1.40	1.50
UX152	15¢ Chicago Orchestra Hall	1.75	.50	.50

 UX153

 UX154 — Carnegie Hall Centennial 1991
 UX155

1991

UX153	19¢ Flag	1.75	.50	.50
UX154	19¢ Carnegie Hall	1.75	.50	.50
UX155	19¢ Old Red Administration Building	1.75	.50	.50

 UX156 — Ratification of the Bill of Rights
 UX157

UX156	19¢ Bill of Rights	1.75	.50	.50
UX157	19¢ University of Notre Dame, Administration Building	1.75	.50	.50

 UX158 — America the Beautiful
 UX159

SCOTT NO.	DESCRIPTION	FIRST DAY COVER	MINT	USED
UX158	30¢ Niagara Falls	1.75	.90	1.50
UX159	19¢ Old Mill University of Vermont	1.75	.45	.50

 UX160
 UX161
 UX162
 UX163 — America's Cup
 UX164 — Columbia River Gorge
 UX165

1992

UX160	19¢ Wadsworth Atheneum	1.75	.50	.50
UX161	19¢ Cobb Hall University of Chicago	1.75	.50	.50
UX162	19¢ Waller Hall	1.75	.50	.50
UX163	19¢ America's Cup	1.75	1.50	2.00
UX164	19¢ Columbia River Gorge	1.75	.50	.50
UX165	19¢ Great Hall, Ellis Island	1.75	.50	.50

 UX166 — Washington National Cathedral
UX167 — Wren Building, College of William & Mary

1993

UX166	19¢ National Cathedral	1.75	.50	.50
UX167	19¢ Wren Building	1.75	.50	.50

 UX168
 UX169 — Fort Recovery, Ohio

UX168	19¢ Holocaust Memorial	2.00	1.50	2.00
UX169	19¢ Fort Recovery	1.75	.50	.50

 UX170 — Playmakers Theatre, University of North Carolina Bicentennial
 UX171 — O'Kane Hall, College of the Holy Cross Sesquicentennial

UX170	19¢ Playmakers Theatre	1.75	.50	.50
UX171	19¢ O'Kane Hall	1.75	.50	.50

U.S. Postal Stationery #UX172-UX278

SCOTT NO.	DESCRIPTION	FIRST DAY COVER	MINT	USED

UX173

1993 (continued)

| UX172 | 19¢ Beecher Hall | 1.75 | .50 | .50 |
| UX173 | 19¢ Massachusetts Hall | 1.75 | .50 | .50 |

UX174

UX175

UX176

UX177

1994

UX174	19¢ Abraham Lincoln Home	1.75	.50	.50
UX175	19¢ Myers Hall	1.75	.50	.50
UX176	19¢ Canyon de Chelly	1.75	.50	.50
UX177	19¢ St. Louis Union Station	1.75	.50	.50

Legends of the West

UX178	Home on the Range	UX188	Nellie Cashman
UX179	Buffalo Bill	UX189	Charles Goodnight
UX180	Jim Bridger	UX190	Geronimo
UX181	Annie Oakley	UX191	Kit Carson
UX182	Native American Culture	UX192	Wild Bill Hickok
UX183	Chief Joseph	UX193	Western Wildlife
UX184	Bill Pickett	UX194	Jim Beckwourth
UX185	Bat Masterson	UX195	Bill Tilghman
UX186	John Fremont	UX196	Sacagawea
UX187	Wyatt Earp	UX197	Overland Mail

UX178

| UX178-97 | 19¢ Legends of the West, set of 20 | 35.00 | 35.00 | 50.00 |

UX198

UX199

1995

| UX198 | 20¢ Red Barn | 1.75 | .50 | .35 |
| UX199 | (20¢) "G" Old Glory | 1.75 | 1.25 | .35 |

Civil War

UX200	Monitor-Virginia	UX210	Tubman
UX201	Lee	UX211	Watie
UX202	Barton	UX212	Johnston
UX203	Grant	UX213	Hancock
UX204	Shiloh	UX214	Chestnut
UX205	Davis	UX215	Chancellorsville
UX206	Farragut	UX216	Sherman
UX207	Douglass	UX217	Pember
UX208	Semmes	UX218	Jackson
UX209	Lincoln	UX219	Gettysburg

UX200

| UX200-19 | 20¢ Civil War, set of 20 | 35.00 | 42.50 | 50.00 |

UX220

| UX220 | 20¢ American Clipper Ships | 1.75 | .50 | .35 |

American Comic Strips

UX221	Yellow Kid	UX231	Popeye
UX222	Katzenjammer Kids	UX232	Blondie
UX223	Little Nemo	UX233	Dick Tracy
UX224	Bring Up Father	UX234	Alley Oop
UX225	Krazy Kat	UX235	Nancy
UX226	Rube Goldberg	UX236	Flash Gordon
UX227	Toonerville Folks	UX237	Li'l Abner
UX228	Gasoline Alley	UX238	Terry/Pirates
UX229	Barney Google	UX239	Prince Valiant
UX230	Little Orphan Annie	UX240	Brenda Starr

UX221

| UX221-40 | 20¢ American Comic Strips, set of 20 | 35.00 | 60.00 | 50.00 |

UX241

1996

| UX241 | 20¢ Winter Farm Scene | 1.75 | .50 | .35 |

Centennial Olympic Games

UX242	Men's cycling	UX252	Women's softball
UX243	Women's diving	UX253	Women's swimming
UX244	Women's running	UX254	Men's sprints
UX245	Men's canoeing	UX255	Men's rowing
UX246	Decathlon	UX256	Beach volleyball
UX247	Women's soccer	UX257	Men's basketball
UX248	Men's shot put	UX258	Equestrian
UX249	Women's sailboarding	UX259	Men's gymnastics
UX250	Women's gymnastics	UX260	Men's swimming
UX251	Freestyle wrestling	UX261	Men's hurdles

UX242

| UX242-61 | 20¢ Centennial Olympic Games, set of 20 | 35.00 | 50.00 | 50.00 |

UX262

UX263

| UX262 | 20¢ McDowell Hall | 1.75 | .50 | .35 |
| UX263 | 20¢ Alexander Hall | 1.75 | .50 | .35 |

Engandered Species

UX264	Florida panther
UX265	Black-footed ferret
UX266	American crocodile
UX267	Piping plover
UX268	Gila trout
UX269	Florida manatee
UX270	Schaus swallowtail butterfly
UX271	Woodland caribou
UX272	Thick-billed parrot
UX273	San Francisco garter snake
UX274	Ocelot
UX275	Wyoming toad
UX276	California condor
UX277	Hawaiian monk seal
UX278	Brown pelican

UX264

| UX264-78 | 20¢ Endangered Species, set of 15 | 26.50 | 60.00 | 50.00 |

U.S. Postal Stationery #UX279-UX311

SCOTT NO.	DESCRIPTION	FIRST DAY COVER	MINT	USED

UX279

UX280

1997

| UX279 | 20¢ Swans, set of 12 | 20.00(8) | 45.00 | 50.00 |
| UX280 | 20¢ Shepard Hall | 1.75 | .50 | .35 |

UX281

UX282

| UX281 | 20¢ Bugs Bunny | 1.75 | 1.65 | .35 |
| UX282 | 20¢ Golden Gate Bridge | 1.75 | .45 | .50 |

UX283

UX284

| UX283 | 50¢ Golden Gate Bridge at Sunset | 1.95 | 1.40 | 1.25 |
| UX284 | 20¢ Fort McHenry | 1.75 | .50 | .35 |

Classic Movie Monsters
UX285 Lon Chaney as The Phantom of the Opera
UX286 Bela Lugosi as Dracula
UX287 Boris Karloff as Frankenstein's Monster
UX288 Boris Karloff as The Mummy
UX289 Lon Chaney Jr. as The Wolfman

UX285

| UX285 | 20¢ Classic Movie Monsters, set of 5 | 8.75 | 9.00 | 5.00 |
| UX289a | same, bklt of 20 (4 of each) | .... | 35.00 | .... |

UX290

UX291

UX292

1998

UX290	20¢ University of Mississippi	1.75	.50	.35
UX291	20¢ Sylvester & Tweety	1.75	1.75	1.50
UX291a	same, bklt of 10	....	17.00	....
UX292	20¢ Girard College, Philadelphia, PA	1.75	.50	.35

UX293

UX297

UX298

UX293-96	20¢ Tropical Birds, set of 4	7.00	5.00	4.00
UX296a	same, bklt of 20 (5 of each)	....	24.00	....
UX297	20¢ Ballet	1.75	1.75	1.50
UX297a	same, bklt of 10	....	17.00	....
UX298	20¢ Kerr Hall, Northeastern University	1.75	.50	.35

UX299

UX300

UX301

| UX299 | 20¢ Usen Castle, Brandeis University | 1.75 | .50 | .35 |

1999

| UX300 | 20¢ Love, Victorian | 1.75 | 1.00 | .75 |
| UX301 | 20¢ University of Wisc.-Madison-Bascom Hill | 1.75 | .50 | .35 |

UX302

UX303

| UX302 | 20¢ Washington and Lee University | 1.75 | .50 | .35 |
| UX303 | 20¢ Redwood Library & Anthenaum, Newport, RI | 1.75 | .50 | .35 |

UX304

UX305

UX304	20¢ Daffy Duck	1.75	1.75	1.00
UX304a	same, bklt of 10	....	17.00	....
UX305	20¢ Mount Vernon	1.75	.50	.35

UX306

UX307

Famous Trains
UX307 Super Chief
UX308 Hiawatha
UX309 Daylight
UX310 Congressional
UX311 20th Century Limited

1999

UX306	20¢ Block Island Lighthouse	1.75	.50	.35
UX307-11	20¢ Famous Trains, set of 5	8.75	7.00	2.50
UX311a	same, bklt of 20 (4 of each)	....	27.50	....

172 U.S. Postal Stationery #UX312-UX405

SCOTT NO.	DESCRIPTION	FIRST DAY COVER	MINT	USED

UX312

UX313

UX315

UX316

2000

Scott	Description	FDC	Mint	Used
UX312	20¢ University of Utah	1.75	.50	.35
UX313	20¢ Ryman Auditorium, Nashville, Tennessee	1.75	.50	.35
UX314	20¢ Road Runner & Wile E. Coyote	1.75	1.75	1.25
UX314a	same, bklt of 10	....	17.00	....
UX315	20¢ Adoption	1.75	1.75	1.25
UX315a	same, bklt of 10	....	17.00	....
UX316	20¢ Old Stone Row, Middlebury College, Vermont	1.75	.50	.35

UX336

The Stars and Stripes

UX317	Sons of Liberty Flag, 1775	UX327	Star-Spangled Banner, 1814
UX318	New England Flag, 1775	UX328	Bennington Flag, c. 1820
UX319	Forster Flag, 1775	UX329	Great Star Flag, 1837
UX320	Continential Colors, 1776	UX330	29-Star Flag, 1847
UX321	Francis Hopkinson Flag, 1777	UX331	Fort Sumter Flag, 1861
UX322	Brandywine Flag, 1777	UX332	Centennial Flag, 1876
UX323	John Paul Jones Flag, 1779	UX333	38-Star Flag
UX324	Pierre L'Enfant Flag, 1783	UX334	Peace Flag, 1891
UX325	Indian Peace Flag, 1803	UX335	48-Star Flag, 1912
UX326	Easton Flag, 1814	UX336	50-Star Flag, 1960

| UX317-36 | The Stars and Stripes, set of 20 | 35.00 | 32.50 | 25.00 |

UX337

Legends of Baseball

UX337	Jackie Robinson	UX347	Lefty Grove
UX338	Eddie Collins	UX348	Tris Speaker
UX339	Christy Mathewson	UX349	Cy Young
UX340	Ty Cobb	UX350	Jimmie Foxx
UX341	George Sisler	UX351	Pie Traynor
UX342	Rogers Hornsby	UX352	Satchel Paige
UX343	Mickey Cochrane	UX353	Honus Wagner
UX344	Babe Ruth	UX354	Josh Gibson
UX345	Walter Johnson	UX355	Dizzy Dean
UX346	Roberto Clemente	UX356	Lou Gehrig

| UX337-56 | 20¢ Legends of Baseball, set of 20 | 35.00 | 30.00 | 25.00 |

UX357-60

UX361

| UX357-60 | 20¢ Christmas Deer, set of 4 | 7.00 | 6.00 | 2.00 |

2001

| UX361 | 20¢ Connecticut Hall, Yale University | 1.75 | .50 | .35 |

UX362

UX363

UX364

UX362	20¢ University of South Carolina	1.75	.50	.35
UX363	20¢ Northwestern University Sesquicentennial 1851-2001	1.75	.50	.35
UX364	20¢ Waldschmidt Hall, The University of Portland	1.75	.50	.35

UX365

Legendary Playing Fields

UX365	Ebbets Field	UX370	Forbes Field
UX366	Tiger Stadium	UX371	Fenway Park
UX367	Crosley Field	UX372	Comiskey Park
UX368	Yankee Stadium	UX373	Shibe Park
UX369	Polo Grounds	UX374	Wrigley Field

2001

| UX365-74 | 21¢ Legendary Playing Fields, set of 10 | 35.00 | 22.50 | 20.00 |
| UX374a | same, bklt of 10 cards | .... | 22.50 | .... |

UX375

UX376

UX377

UX375	21¢ White Barn	1.75	.50	.35
UX376	21¢ That's All Folks	2.00	1.75	1.75
UX376a	same, bklt of 10	....	17.00	....
UX377-80	21¢ Santas, set of 4	7.50	6.00	....

UX381

UX382

UX386

2002

UX381	23¢ Carlsbad Caverns	1.75	.55	.50
UX382-85	23¢ Teddy Bears, set of 4	7.50	6.00	....
UX386-89	23¢ Christmas Snowmen, set of 4	7.50	6.00	....

UX390

UX395

UX400

2003

UX390-94	23¢ Old Glory, set of 5	8.75	7.00	....
UX394a	same, complete booklet of 20 cards	....	27.50	....
UX395-99	23¢ Southern Lighthouses, set of 5	8.75	7.00	....
UX399a	same, complete booklet of 20	....	27.50	....
UX400	23¢ Ohio University, 200th Anniversary	1.75	.55	.50
UX401-04	23¢ Christmas Music Makers, set of 4	7.50	5.00	....

UX401

UX405

2004

| UX405 | 23¢ Columbia University, 250th Anniversary | 1.75 | .55 | .50 |
| .... | 23¢ Harriton House, 300th Anniversary | 1.75 | .55 | .50 |

U.S. Postal Stationery #UXC1-UXC22

AIR POST POSTAL CARDS

1949

Scott No.	Description	First Day Cover	Mint	Used
UXC1	4¢ orange	2.50	.60	.90

1958 No border on card

| UXC2 | 5¢ red | 2.50 | 2.00 | .90 |

1960 Type of 1958 re-engraved: with border on card

| UXC3 | 5¢ red | 2.50 | 6.25 | 2.50 |

1963

| UXC4 | 6¢ red | 2.50 | .75 | .90 |

1966

| UXC5 | 11¢ SIPEX | 1.75 | .60 | 14.00 |

1967

UXC6	6¢ Virgin Islands	1.75	.40	7.00
UXC7	6¢ Boy Scout Jamboree	2.50	.40	7.00
UXC8	13¢ AAM Convention	1.75	1.40	9.00

1968-71 Precancels

UXC9	8¢ blue & red	1.75	.60	2.50
UXC9at	8¢ luminescent (1969)	20.00	2.25	2.75
UXC10	9¢ red & blue (1971)	1.75	.55	1.00

1971 Inscribed U.S. Air Mail

| UXC11 | 15¢ Travel Service | 1.75 | 2.00 | 14.00 |

1972 Issued with various designs on reverse

| UXC12 | 9¢ Grand Canyon | 1.75 | .50 | 9.00 |
| UXC13 | 15¢ Niagara Falls | 1.75 | .60 | 16.00 |

1974

| UXC14 | 11¢ red & ultramarine | 1.75 | .70 | 2.50 |
| UXC15 | 18¢ Visit USA | 1.75 | .85 | 8.00 |

1975

| UXC16 | 21¢ Visit USA | 1.75 | .80 | 8.50 |

1978

| UXC17 | 21¢ Curtiss Jenny | 1.75 | .80 | 7.00 |

1979

| UXC18 | 21¢ Moscow Olympics | 1.75 | 1.10 | 11.00 |

1981

| UXC19 | 28¢ Pacific Flight | 1.75 | .90 | 5.00 |

1982

| UXC20 | 28¢ Gliders | 1.75 | 1.00 | 3.50 |

1983

| UXC21 | 28¢ Olympics | 1.75 | 1.00 | 2.50 |

1985

| UXC22 | 33¢ China Clipper | 1.75 | 1.10 | 2.50 |

U.S. Postal Stationery #UXC23-UXC28; #UY1-UY8

SCOTT NO.	DESCRIPTION	FIRST DAY COVER	MINT	USED

1986
| UXC23 | 33¢ Ameripex '86 | 1.75 | .85 | 2.00 |

1988
| UXC24 | 36¢ DC-3 | 1.75 | .85 | 1.00 |

1991
| UXC25 | 40¢ Yankee Clipper | 1.75 | .90 | 1.00 |

1995
| UXC26 | 50¢ Soaring Eagle | 1.75 | 1.10 | 2.00 |

1999
| UXC27 | 55¢ Mount Rainier, Washington | 1.75 | 1.35 | 1.00 |

2001
| UXC28 | 70¢ Badlands National Park, South Dakota | 2.25 | 1.60 | 1.00 |

Insist on Genuine
H.E. Harris Products
Backed by
89 years of experience

ACCEPT NO SUBSTITUTES!

PAID REPLY POSTAL CARDS

UY1m, UY3m   UY2m, UY11m   UY4m

UY1r, UY3r   UY2r, UY11r   UY4r

PAID REPLY CARDS: Consist of two halves—one for your message and one for the other party to use to reply.

1892 Card Framed
SCOTT NO.	DESCRIPTION	MINT	UNUSED	USED
UY1	1¢ & 1¢ unsevered	40.00	15.00	9.00
UY1m	1¢ black (Message)	6.50	3.25	1.50
UY1r	1¢ black (Reply)	6.50	3.25	1.50

1893
UY2	2¢ & 2¢ unsevered	20.00	12.00	22.00
UY2m	2¢ blue (Message)	6.00	2.00	6.50
UY2r	2¢ blue (Reply)	6.00	2.00	6.50

1898 Designs of 1892 Card Unframed
UY3	1¢ & 1¢ unsevered	75.00	12.50	15.00
UY3m	1¢ black (Message)	15.50	5.00	3.00
UY3r	1¢ black (Reply)	15.50	5.00	3.00

1904
UY4	1¢ & 1¢ unsevered	50.00	10.00	7.00
UY4m	1¢ black (Message)	10.00	4.00	1.20
UY4r	1¢ black (Reply)	10.00	4.00	1.20

UY5m, UY6m, UY7m, UY13m   UY8m   UY12m

UY5r, UY6r, UY7r, UY13r   UY8r   UY12r

1910
UY5	1¢ & 1¢ unsevered	160.00	45.00	24.00
UY5m	1¢ blue (Message)	12.00	6.00	3.60
UY5r	1¢ blue (Reply)	12.00	6.00	3.60

1911 Double Line Around Instructions
UY6	1¢ & 1¢ unsevered	160.00	70.00	25.00
UY6m	1¢ green (Message)	25.00	12.00	6.00
UY6r	1¢ green (Reply)	25.00	12.00	6.00

1915 Single Frame Line Around Instruction
UY7	1¢ & 1¢ unsevered	1.50	.50	.60
UY7m	1¢ green (Message)	.35	.20	.25
UY7r	1¢ green (Reply)	.35	.20	.25

1918
UY8	2¢ & 2¢ unsevered	85.00	30.00	45.00
UY8m	2¢ red (Message)	24.00	9.00	9.00
UY8r	2¢ red (Reply)	24.00	9.00	9.00

U.S. Postal Stationery #UY9-UY44; UZ1-UZ6

SCOTT NO.	DESCRIPTION	MINT	UNUSED	USED
	1920 UY8 Surcharged			
UY9	1¢/2¢ & 1¢/2¢ unsevered 22.50	9.00	10.00	
UY9m	1¢ on 2¢ red .... (Message)	6.00	2.50	3.00
UY9r	1¢ on 2¢ red .... (Reply)	6.00	2.50	3.00
	1924 Designs of 1893			
UY11	2¢ & 2¢ unsevered	3.00	1.50	32.50
UY11m	2¢ red .... (Message)	.75	.50	12.00
UY11r	2¢ red .... (Reply)	.75	.50	12.00
	1926			
UY12	3¢ & 3¢ unsevered	16.50	5.00	30.00
UY12m	3¢ red .... (Message)	3.25	1.35	7.00
UY12r	3¢ red .... (Reply)	3.25	1.35	7.00

SCOTT NO.	DESCRIPTION	FIRST DAY COVER	MINT	USED
	1951 Design of 1910 Single Line Frame			
UY13	2¢ & 2¢ unsevered	2.10	1.40	2.25
UY13m	2¢ carmine .... (Message)	....	.45	1.00
UY13r	2¢ carmine .... (Reply)	....	.45	1.00
	1952 **UY7 Surcharged by cancelling machine, light green**			
UY14	2¢/1¢ & 2¢/1¢ unsevered	2.00	1.25	
UY14m	2¢ on 1¢ green .... (Message)	....	.50	1.00
UY14r	2¢ on 1¢ green .... (Reply)	....	.50	1.00
	1952 UY7 Surcharge Typographed, dark green			
UY15	2¢/1¢ & 2¢/1¢ unsevered	140.00	120.00	
UY15m	2¢ on 1¢ green .... (Message)	....	20.00	12.00
UY15r	2¢ on 1¢ green .... (Reply)	....	20.00	12.00
	1956 Design of UX45			
UY16	4¢ & 4¢ unsevered	1.75	1.25	55.00
UY16m	4¢ carmine .... (Message)	....	.50	37.50
UY16r	4¢ carmine .... (Reply)	....	.50	32.50
	1958 Design of UX46			
UY17	3¢ & 3¢ purple, unsevered	1.75	4.00	2.50
	1962 Design of UX48			
UY18	4¢ & 4¢ red violet, unsevered	1.75	4.00	2.25
	1963 Design of UX49			
UY19	7¢ & 7¢ unsevered	1.75	3.00	50.00
UY19m	7¢ blue & red .... (Message)	....	1.00	25.00
UY19r	7¢ blue & red .... (Reply)	....	1.00	25.00
	1967 Design of UX54			
UY20	8¢ & 8¢ unsevered	1.75	3.00	50.00
UY20m	8¢ blue & red .... (Message)	....	1.00	25.00
UY20r	8¢ blue & red .... (Reply)	....	1.00	25.00
	1968 Design of UX55			
UY21	5¢ & 5¢ emerald	1.75	1.75	2.00
	1971 Design of UX58			
UY22	6¢ & 6¢ brown	1.75	1.75	2.00
	1972 Design of UX64			
UY23	6¢ & 6¢ blue	1.75	1.25	2.00
	1973 Design of UX66			
UY24	8¢ & 8¢ orange	1.75	1.25	2.00
	1975			
UY25	7¢ & 7¢ design of UX68	1.75	1.25	4.00
UY26	9¢ & 9¢ design of UX69	1.75	1.25	2.00
	1976			
UY27	9¢ & 9¢ design of UX70	1.75	1.25	2.00
	1977			
UY28	9¢ & 9¢ design of UX72	1.75	1.25	2.00
	1978			
UY29	(10¢ & 10¢) design of UX74	3.00	11.00	10.00
UY30	10¢ & 10¢ design of UX75	1.75	1.25	.40
	1981			
UY31	(12¢ & 12¢) "B" Eagle, design of UX88	1.75	1.25	2.00
UY32	12¢ & 12¢ light blue, design of UX89	1.75	1.25	2.00
UY33	(13¢ & 13¢) buff, design of UX92	1.75	1.85	2.00
UY34	13¢ & 13¢ buff, design of UX93	1.75	1.25	.25
	1985			
UY35	(14¢ & 14¢) Carroll, design of UX105	1.75	2.00	2.00
UY36	14¢ & 14¢ Carroll, design of UX106	1.75	1.25	2.00
UY37	14¢ & 14¢ Wythe, design of UX108	1.75	1.25	2.00
	1987			
UY38	14¢ & 14¢ Flag, design of UX117	1.75	1.25	2.00
	1988			
UY39	15¢ & 15¢ America the Beautiful, design of UX120	1.75	1.25	1.00
	1991			
UY40	19¢ & 19¢ Flag	1.75	1.35	1.00
	1995			
UY41	20¢ & 20¢ Red Barn	1.75	1.35	1.00
	1999			
UY42	20¢ & 20¢ Block Island Lighthouse	1.75	1.35	1.00
	2001-02			
UY43	21¢ & 21¢ White Barn	1.75	1.35	1.50
UY44	23¢ & 23¢ Carlsbad Caverns	1.75	1.35	1.50

OFFICIAL POSTAL CARDS

UZ1

SCOTT NO.	DESCRIPTION	FIRST DAY COVER	MINT	USED
	1913			
UZ1	1¢ black (Printed Address)	....	325.00	185.00

UZ2   UZ3

	1983			
UZ2	13¢ Great Seal	1.75	.75	40.00
	1985			
UZ3	14¢ Great Seal	1.75	.75	40.00

UZ4   UZ5   UZ6

	1988			
UZ4	15¢ Great Seal	1.75	.75	40.00
	1991			
UZ5	19¢ Great Seal	1.75	.70	35.00
	1995			
UZ6	20¢ Great Seal	1.75	.50	25.00

U.S. Revenues #R1-R102

1862-71 First Issue

When ordering from this issue be sure to indicate whether the "a", "b" or "c" variety is wanted. Example: R27c. Prices are for used singles.

R1-R4

R5-R15

R16-R42

SCOTT NO.	DESCRIPTION	IMPERFORATE (a) F	AVG	PART PERF. (b) F	AVG	PERFORATED (c) F	AVG
R1	1¢ Express	52.25	27.50	35.75	19.25	1.00	.55
R2	1¢ Playing Cards	742.50	412.50	385.00	230.00	93.50	49.50
R3	1¢ Proprietary	495.00	275.00	99.00	55.00	.40	.25
R4	1¢ Telegraph	275.00	155.00	....	....	7.45	4.15
R5	2¢ Bank Check, blue	.85	.50	1.00	.60	.20	.15
R6	2¢ Bank Check, orange	....	....	71.50	41.25	.20	.15
R7	2¢ Certificate, blue	10.45	5.50	....	....	27.50	12.10
R8	2¢ Certificate, orange	....	....	....	....	24.75	12.10
R9	2¢ Express, blue	10.45	5.50	14.85	8.00	.30	.15
R10	2¢ Express, orange	....	....	....	....	6.00	3.30
R11	2¢ Playing Cards, blue	....	....	110.00	60.50	2.50	1.40
R12	2¢ Playing Cards, orange	....	....	....	....	24.75	13.75
R13	2¢ Proprietary, blue	....	....	93.50	52.25	.35	.20
R14	2¢ Proprietary, orange	....	....	....	....	33.00	17.60
R15	2¢ U.S. Internal Revenue	....	....	....	....	.20	.15
R16	3¢ Foreign Exchange	....	....	143.00	82.50	2.30	1.10
R17	3¢ Playing Cards	....	....	....	....	99.00	52.25
R18	3¢ Proprietary	....	....	181.50	110.00	1.65	.80
R19	3¢ Telegraph	41.25	22.00	13.75	7.70	2.60	1.40
R20	4¢ Inland Exchange	....	....	....	....	1.65	.95
R21	4¢ Playing Cards	....	....	....	....	357.50	181.50
R22	4¢ Proprietary	....	....	181.50	104.50	2.75	1.40
R23	5¢ Agreement	....	....	....	....	.30	.15
R24	5¢ Certificate	2.50	1.40	8.80	4.95	.20	.15
R25	5¢ Express	3.70	2.20	4.70	2.90	.35	.20
R26	5¢ Foreign Exchange	....	....	....	....	.35	.20
R27	5¢ Inland Exchange	3.60	2.15	3.60	2.15	.25	.15
R28	5¢ Playing Cards	....	....	....	....	12.10	6.60
R29	5¢ Proprietary	....	....	....	....	18.70	8.80
R30	6¢ Inland Exchange	....	....	....	....	1.05	.55
R32	10¢ Bill of Lading	46.75	24.75	143.00	77.00	.85	.40
R33	10¢ Certificate	82.50	44.00	110.00	60.50	.35	.20
R34	10¢ Contract, blue	....	....	99.00	55.00	.35	.20
R35	10¢ Foreign Exchange	....	....	....	....	4.70	2.75
R36	10¢ Inland Exchange	120.00	66.00	3.05	1.85	.25	.15
R37	10¢ Power of Attorney	302.50	165.00	18.15	11.00	.40	.25
R38	10¢ Proprietary	....	....	....	....	13.20	6.60
R39	15¢ Foreign Exchange	....	....	....	....	12.10	6.60
R40	15¢ Inland Exchange	24.75	13.75	11.00	6.05	1.00	.55
R41	20¢ Foreign Exchange	42.50	23.65	....	....	29.25	15.40
R42	20¢ Inland Exchange	12.65	7.15	16.50	9.35	.40	.25

R43-R53

R54-R65

R66-R76

SCOTT NO.	DESCRIPTION	IMPERFORATE (a) F	AVG	PART PERF. (b) F	AVG	PERFORATED (c) F	AVG
R43	25¢ Bond	96.25	52.25	5.80	3.50	1.65	.95
R44	25¢ Certificate	6.35	3.30	5.50	3.05	.20	.15
R45	25¢ Entry of Goods	16.50	9.35	33.00	18.15	.55	.30
R46	25¢ Insurance	8.80	4.95	9.90	5.50	.30	.15
R47	25¢ Life Insurance	31.50	17.60	99.00	55.00	4.70	2.50
R48	25¢ Power of Attorney	5.50	3.30	16.50	9.35	.30	.15
R49	25¢ Protest	22.00	12.10	137.50	74.25	5.50	3.05
R50	25¢ Warehouse Receipt	35.75	19.80	137.50	77.00	21.45	11.55
R51	30¢ Foreign Exchange	52.25	23.60	440.00	247.50	33.00	18.25
R52	30¢ Inland Exchange	38.50	22.00	41.25	22.00	2.15	1.20
R53	40¢ Inland Exchange	425.00	247.50	4.15	2.50	2.50	1.40
R54	50¢ Conveyance, blue	9.90	5.50	1.20	.75	.20	.15
R55	50¢ Entry of Goods	....	....	11.00	6.00	.30	.15
R56	50¢ Foreign Exchange	36.85	20.35	31.35	17.50	4.15	2.20
R57	50¢ Lease	21.45	12.10	55.00	30.25	5.25	2.75
R58	50¢ Life Insurance	27.50	15.40	52.25	28.50	.85	.50
R59	50¢ Mortgage	9.35	4.95	1.65	1.00	.40	.25
R60	50¢ Original Process	2.50	1.40	....	....	.35	.20
R61	50¢ Passage Ticket	66.00	35.75	104.50	55.00	.55	.30
R62	50¢ Probate of Will	31.35	17.60	44.00	24.25	16.50	9.35
R63	50¢ Surety Bond, blue	110.00	60.50	2.60	1.45	.30	.15
R64	60¢ Inland Exchange	77.00	42.35	44.00	24.50	4.95	2.75
R65	70¢ Foreign Exchange	291.50	165.00	247.50	137.50	2.50	1.20
R66	$1 Conveyance	10.45	5.80	247.50	137.50	2.50	1.20
R67	$1 Entry of Goods	24.75	13.75	....	....	1.55	.90
R68	$1 Foreign Exchange	49.50	26.95	....	....	.75	.45
R69	$1 Inland Exchange	10.45	5.80	220.00	120.00	.55	.30
R70	$1 Lease	32.45	17.60	....	....	1.40	.85
R71	$1 Life Insurance	137.50	79.75	....	....	4.70	2.50
R72	$1 Manifest	49.50	27.50	....	....	20.90	12.10
R73	$1 Mortgage	15.95	9.35	....	....	126.50	66.00
R74	$1 Passage Ticket	154.00	88.00	....	....	137.50	68.75
R75	$1 Power of Attorney	57.75	31.25	....	....	1.75	1.00
R76	$1 Probate of Will	55.00	30.25	....	....	33.00	18.25

R77-R80

R81-R87

SCOTT NO.	DESCRIPTION	IMPERFORATE (a) F	AVG	PART PERF. (b) F	AVG	PERFORATED (c) F	AVG
R77	$1.30 Foreign Exchange	....	....	....	....	44.00	24.75
R78	$1.50 Inland Exchange	21.00	11.55	....	....	2.90	1.60
R79	$1.60 Foreign Exchange	550.00	302.50	....	....	88.00	46.75
R80	$1.90 Foreign Exchange	1650.00	990.00	....	....	60.50	30.25
R81	$2 Conveyance	88.00	49.50	850.00	550.00	1.90	1.05
R82	$2 Mortgage	77.00	43.35	....	....	2.50	1.40
R83	$2 Probate of Will	....	....	....	....	41.25	22.00
R84	$2.50 Inland Exchange	962.00	535.00	....	....	3.05	1.65
R85	$3 Charter Party	90.75	52.25	....	....	3.60	2.00
R86	$2 Manifest	88.00	49.50	....	....	20.90	11.55
R87	$3.50 Inland Exchange	1000.00	650.00	....	....	44.00	24.75

R88-R96

R97-R101

SCOTT NO.	DESCRIPTION	IMPERFORATE (a) F	AVG	PART PERF. (b) F	AVG	PERFORATED (c) F	AVG
R88	$5 Charter Party	214.50	120.00	....	....	4.70	2.75
R89	$5 Conveyance	30.25	16.50	....	....	4.70	2.75
R90	$5 Manifest	82.50	45.50	....	....	82.50	45.65
R91	$5 Mortgage	79.75	44.00	....	....	16.50	9.10
R92	$5 Probate of Will	375.00	209.00	....	....	16.50	9.10
R93	$10 Charter Party	412.50	220.00	....	....	20.90	11.55
R94	$10 Conveyance	77.00	43.50	....	....	55.00	30.25
R95	$10 Mortgage	302.50	165.00	....	....	20.90	11.55
R96	$10 Probate of Will	935.00	522.50	....	....	20.90	11.55
R97	$15 Mortgage, blue	852.50	478.50	....	....	90.75	49.50
R98	$20 Conveyance	55.00	30.25	....	....	31.35	18.25
R99	$20 Probate of Will	852.50	478.50	....	....	795.00	440.00
R100	$25 Mortgage	700.00	396.00	....	....	82.50	46.75
R101	$50 U.S. Internal Revenue	154.00	88.00	....	....	77.00	44.00

R102

| R102 | $200 U.S. Internal Revenue | 990.00 | 550.00 | .... | .... | 522.50 | 302.50 |

U.S. Revenues #R103-R178

R103, R104,
R134, R135,
R151

R105-R111,
R136-R139

R112-R114

R115-R117,
R142-R143

1871 SECOND ISSUE

NOTE: The individual denominations vary in design from the illustrations shown which are more typical of their relative size.

SCOTT NO.	DESCRIPTION	USED F	AVG
R103	1¢ blue and black	24.75	13.75
R104	2¢ blue and black	1.05	.60
R105	3¢ blue and black	12.10	6.60
R106	4¢ blue and black	41.25	22.00
R107	5¢ blue and black	1.05	.60
R108	6¢ blue and black	66.00	35.75
R109	10¢ blue and black	.90	.50
R110	15¢ blue and black	19.80	11.00
R111	20¢ blue and black	4.40	2.50
R112	25¢ blue and black	.65	.35
R113	30¢ blue and black	49.50	27.50
R114	40¢ blue and black	27.50	15.25
R115	50¢ blue and black	.65	.40
R116	60¢ blue and black	57.75	31.50
R117	70¢ blue and black	23.50	12.95

R118-R122, R144

R123-R126,
R145-R147

SCOTT NO.	DESCRIPTION	USED F	AVG
R118	$1 blue and black	3.05	1.65
R119	$1.30 blue and black	220.00	121.00
R120	$1.50 blue and black	11.00	6.05
R121	$1.60 blue and black	275.00	154.00
R122	$1.90 blue and black	120.00	66.00
R123	$2.00 blue and black	10.45	5.80
R124	$2.50 blue and black	19.25	10.75
R125	$3.00 blue and black	30.25	17.05
R126	$3.50 blue and black	110.00	55.00

R127, R128, R148,
R149

R129-R131, R150

SCOTT NO.	DESCRIPTION	USED F	AVG
R127	$5 blue and black	16.50	9.35
R128	$10 blue and black	82.50	49.50
R129	$20 blue and black	265.00	143.00
R130	$25 blue and black	265.00	143.00
R131	$50 blue and black	302.50	165.00

1871-72 THIRD ISSUE

SCOTT NO.	DESCRIPTION	USED F	AVG
R134	1¢ claret and black	22.00	12.10
R135	2¢ orange and black	.15	.15
R135b	2¢ orange and black (center inverted)	325.00	225.00
R136	4¢ brown and black	27.50	14.85
R137	5¢ orange and black	.30	.15
R138	6¢ orange and black	27.50	15.50
R139	15¢ brown and black	9.90	5.50
R140	30¢ orange and black	10.45	6.00
R141	40¢ brown and black	22.00	12.65
R142	60¢ orange and black	46.75	26.25
R143	70¢ green and black	30.25	16.50
R144	$1 green and black	1.35	.75
R145	$2 vermillion and black	19.80	10.45
R146	$2.50 claret and black	29.15	15.95
R147	$3 green and black	31.35	17.60
R148	$5 vermillion and black	17.60	9.65
R149	$10 green and black	66.00	38.50
R150	$20 orange and black	368.50	203.50

1874 on greenish paper

SCOTT NO.	DESCRIPTION	USED F	AVG
R151	2¢ orange and black	.20	.15
R151a	2¢ orange and black (center inverted)	395.00	295.00

R152
Liberty

I. R.
R153
surcharge

I. R.
R154, R155
surcharge

1875-78

SCOTT NO.	DESCRIPTION	UNUSED F	AVG	USED F	AVG
R152a	2¢ blue on blue silk paper			.20	.15
R152b	2¢ watermarked ("USIR") paper			.20	.15
R152c	2¢ watermarked, rouletted			27.50	13.75

1898 Postage Stamps 279 & 267 Surcharged

R153	1¢ green, small I.R.	1.05	.55	.60	.35
R154	1¢ green, large I.R.	.25	.20	.20	.15
R155	2¢ carmine, large I.R.	.25	.20	.60	.35

DOCUMENTARY STAMPS
Newspaper Stamp PR121 Surcharged

INT. REV.
$5.
DOCUMENTARY.

R159	$5 dark blue, red surcharge reading down	176.00	99.00	126.50	68.75
R160	$5 dark blue, red surcharge reading up	82.50	44.00	55.00	30.25

R161-R172

R173-R178, R182,
R183

1898 Battleships Inscribed "Documentary"

SCOTT NO.	DESCRIPTION	UNUSED F	AVG	USED F	AVG
R161	1/2¢ orange	2.00	3.85	6.05	3.85
R162	1/2¢ dark gray	.25	.20	.20	.15
R163	1¢ pale blue	.25	.20	.20	.15
R164	2¢ carmine	.25	.20	.20	.15
R165	3¢ dark blue	.90	.50	.20	.15
R166	4¢ pale rose	.40	.25	.20	.15
R167	5¢ lilac	.25	.20	.20	.15
R168	10¢ dark brown	.40	.25	.20	.15
R169	25¢ purple brown	.40	.25	.20	.15
R170	40¢ blue lilac (cut cancel .25)	52.25	30.25	1.20	.75
R171	50¢ slate violet	4.15	2.20	.20	.15
R172	80¢ bistre (cut cancel .15)	22.00	13.75	.40	.25
R173	$1 dark green	3.85	2.20	.20	.15
R174	$3 dark brown (cut cancel .20)	9.35	4.95	.45	.30
R175	$5 orange red (cut cancel .25)	11.00	7.15	1.10	.65
R176	$10 black (cut cancel .70)	33.00	20.35	2.75	1.65
R177	$30 red (cut cancel 25.00)	115.50	66.00	74.25	44.00
R178	$50 gray brown (cut cancel 1.50)	55.00	31.35	3.60	1.95

U.S. Revenues #R179-R734

SCOTT NO.	DESCRIPTION	UNUSED F	AVG	USED F	AVG

R179, R225, R246, R248 Washington
R180, R226, R249 Hamilton
R181, R224, R227, R247, R250 Madison

1899 Various Portraits Inscribed "Series of 1898"

Scott	Description	Unused F	AVG	Used F	AVG
R179	$100 yellow brown & black .... (cut cancel 11.50)	57.75	35.75	27.50	15.40
R180	$500 carmine lake & black .. (cut cancel 180.00)	544.50	357.50	440.00	275.00
R181	$1000 green & black .... (cut cancel 95.00)	440.00	265.00	330.00	265.00

1900

| R182 | $1 carmine .... (cut cancel .15) | 6.33 | 3.60 | .55 | .35 |
| R183 | $3 lake .... (cut cancel 7.00) | 66.00 | 38.50 | 41.25 | 24.75 |

R184-R189
R190-R194
Designs of R173-78 surcharged

R184	$1 gray .... (cut cancel .15)	3.60	1.95	.20	.15
R185	$2 gray .... (cut cancel .15)	3.05	1.65	.20	.15
R186	$3 gray .... (cut cancel 1.00)	31.35	16.50	10.45	6.00
R187	$5 gray .... (cut cancel .35)	18.15	10.45	4.40	2.75
R188	$10 gray .... (cut cancel 3.00)	38.50	23.10	9.65	6.00
R189	$50 gray .... (cut cancel 70.00)	550.00	302.50	330.00	181.50

1902

R190	$1 green .... (cut cancel .30)	7.15	3.85	2.20	1.40
R191	$2 green .... (cut cancel .25)	6.60	3.85	1.00	.60
R191a	$2 surcharged as R185	85.00	60.00	85.00	60.00
R192	$5 green .... (cut cancel 1.50)	44.00	24.75	14.85	8.25
R192a	$5 surcharge omitted	70.00	47.50	......	......
R193	$10 green .... (cut cancel 22.50)	214.50	120.00	143.00	77.00
R194	$50 green .... (cut cancel 200.00)	962.50	545.00	687.50	385.00

R195-R216
R217-R223

1914 Inscribed "Series of 1914"
Single Line Watermark "USPS"

R195	1/2¢ rose	4.70	2.75	2.30	1.40
R196	1¢ rose	1.10	.60	.20	.15
R197	2¢ rose	1.10	.60	.15	.15
R198	3¢ rose	27.50	14.85	18.70	10.45
R199	4¢ rose	6.05	3.30	.95	.55
R200	5¢ rose	2.30	1.30	.20	.15
R201	10¢ rose	2.15	1.20	.15	.15
R202	25¢ rose	13.75	7.45	.50	.30
R203	40¢ rose	7.15	4.15	.55	.35
R204	50¢ rose	3.60	1.95	.15	.15
R205	80¢ rose	38.50	20.35	6.00	3.70

1914 Double Line Watermark "USIR"

R206	1/2¢ rose	1.10	.55	.55	.35
R207	1¢ rose	.25	.20	.20	.15
R208	2¢ rose	.25	.20	.20	.15
R209	3¢ rose	1.10	.55	.25	.20
R210	4¢ rose	1.95	1.05	.35	.20
R211	5¢ rose	1.10	.55	.20	.15
R212	10¢ rose	.40	.25	.20	.15
R213	25¢ rose	3.05	1.75	.80	.50
R214	40¢ rose .... (cut cancel .60)	35.75	19.25	7.15	3.85
R215	50¢ rose	7.15	3.85	.20	.15
R216	80¢ rose .... (cut cancel 1.00)	41.25	21.50	8.00	4.80
R217	$1 green .... (cut cancel .15)	13.20	8.25	.20	.15
R218	$2 carmine .... (cut cancel .15)	24.75	13.75	.20	.15
R219	$3 purple .... (cut cancel .25)	35.75	19.25	1.10	.55
R220	$5 blue .... (cut cancel .65)	31.35	16.50	1.95	1.10
R221	$10 orange .... (cut cancel 1.00)	71.50	38.50	4.40	2.65
R222	$30 vermillion .... (cut cancel 2.25)	121.00	71.50	9.65	5.80
R223	$50 violet .... (cut cancel 200.00)	865.00	480.00	632.50	345.00

1914-15 Various Portraits Inscribed "Series of 1914" or "Series of 1915"

R224	$60 brown .... (cut cancel 45.00)	......	......	110.00	66.00
R225	$100 green .... (cut cancel 15.00)	......	......	41.25	22.00
R226	$500 blue .... (cut cancel 200.00)	......	......	495.00	275.00
R227	$1000 orange .... (cut cancel 200.00)	......	......	495.00	275.00

R228-239, R251-256, R260-263

1917 Perf. 11

R228	1¢ carmine rose	.25	.20	.20	.15
R229	2¢ carmine rose	.25	.20	.20	.15
R230	3¢ carmine rose	.30	.20	.25	.15
R231	4¢ carmine rose	.25	.20	.20	.15
R232	5¢ carmine rose	.25	.20	.20	.15
R233	8¢ carmine rose	1.35	.85	.20	.15
R234	10¢ carmine rose	.25	.20	.20	.15
R235	20¢ carmine rose	.35	.20	.20	.15
R236	25¢ carmine rose	.60	.40	.20	.15
R237	40¢ carmine rose	.85	.50	.20	.15
R238	50¢ carmine rose	1.05	.60	.20	.15
R239	80¢ carmine rose	2.75	1.65	.20	.15

R240-245, R257-259

Same design as issue of 1914-15 Without dates.

R240	$1 yellow green	3.85	2.04	.20	.15
R241	$2 rose	8.00	4.70	.20	.15
R242	$3 violet .... (cut cancel .15)	22.00	13.75	.50	.30
R243	$4 yellow brown .... (cut cancel .20)	13.20	7.70	1.10	.65
R244	$5 dark blue .... (cut cancel .10) (perf. in 15)	8.80	4.95	.25	.15
R245	$10 orange	17.60	9.65	.65	.40

Types of 1899 Various Portraits Perf. 12

R246	$30 deep orange, Grant .... (cut cancel .70)	27.50	16.50	2.20	1.35
R247	$60 brown, Lincoln .... (cut cancel .95)	35.75	21.45	7.15	4.40
R248	$100 green, Washington .... (cut cancel .45)	22.00	12.65	.85	.50
R249	$500 blue, Hamilton .... (cut cancel 10.00)	......	......	33.00	19.25
R249a	$500 Numerals in orange	......	......	60.00	42.50
R250	$1000 orange, Madison (Perf. In. 3.00) .... (cut cancel 3.50)	90.75	52.25	11.00	6.60

1928-29 Perf. 10

R251	1¢ carmine rose	1.85	1.10	1.00	.60
R252	2¢ carmine rose	.55	.35	.20	.15
R253	4¢ carmine rose	5.25	2.75	3.30	2.05
R254	5¢ carmine rose	1.10	.50	.35	.20
R255	10¢ carmine rose	1.65	1.00	.95	.60
R256	20¢ carmine rose	5.25	3.05	4.15	2.50
R257	$1 green .... (cut cancel 2.00)	57.75	33.00	27.50	16.50
R258	$2 rose	14.85	8.25	1.65	1.00
R259	$10 orange .... (cut cancel 7.00)	79.75	46.75	24.75	16.50

1929-30 Perf. 11 x 10

R260	2¢ carmine rose	2.50	1.40	1.95	1.20
R261	5¢ carmine rose	1.95	1.20	1.10	.75
R262	10¢ carmine rose	7.15	3.85	6.05	3.85
R263	20¢ carmine rose	13.75	8.25	8.25	4.95

SCOTT NO.	DESCRIPTION	PLATE BLOCK F/NH	UNUSED F/NH	USED F

R733, R734

1962 CENTENNIAL INTERNAL REVENUE. Inscribed "Established 1862"

| R733 | 10¢ violet blue & green .... | 13.50 | 1.25 | .50 |

1964 Without Inscription Date

| R734 | 10¢ violet blue & green .... | 25.00 | 3.50 | .50 |

U.S. Revenues #RB1-RB73, RC1-RC26, RD1-RD24

PROPRIETARY STAMPS

1871-74 Perforated 12

SCOTT NO.	DESCRIPTION	VIOLET PAPER (a) F	AVG	GREEN PAPER (b) F	AVG
RB1	1¢ green & black	3.60	2.15	5.50	3.30
RB2	2¢ green & black	4.15	2.50	12.10	7.15
RB3	3¢ green & black	11.00	6.60	35.75	19.25
RB4	4¢ green & black	6.90	3.85	11.00	6.60
RB5	5¢ green & black	104.50	57.75	110.00	60.50
RB6	6¢ green & black	26.95	15.25	82.50	45.75
RB7	10¢ green & black	143.00	82.50	33.00	18.15
RB8	50¢ green & black (large)	632.50	357.50	900.00	495.00

SCOTT NO.	DESCRIPTION	SILK PAPER (a) F	AVG	WMKD PERF. (b) F	AVG	ROULETTE (c) F	AVG
RB11	1¢ green	1.40	.85	.35	.20	38.50	20.35
RB12	2¢ brown	1.95	1.10	1.20	.65	49.50	27.50
RB13	3¢ orange	8.25	4.40	2.15	1.40	55.00	30.25
RB14	4¢ red brown	4.40	2.50	3.85	2.15	......	......
RB15	4¢ red	......	......	3.85	2.15	55.00	30.25
RB16	5¢ black	96.25	55.00	71.50	35.75	......	101.75
RB17	6¢ violet blue	18.70	11.00	12.65	7.15	148.50	82.50
RB18	6¢ violet	......	......	19.25	11.00	181.50	101.75
RB19	10¢ blue	......	......	187.00	104.50	......	......

1898 Battleship Inscribed "Proprietary"

SCOTT NO.	DESCRIPTION	UNUSED F	AVG	USED F	AVG
RB20	1/8¢ yellow green	.25	.20	.20	.15
RB21	1/4¢ brown	.25	.20	.20	.15
RB22	3/8¢ deep orange	.25	.20	.20	.15
RB23	5/8¢ deep ultramarine	.25	.20	.20	.15
RB24	1¢ dark green	.40	.25	.25	.15
RB25	1-1/4¢ violet	.25	.20	.20	.15
RB26	1-7/8¢ dull blue	2.05	1.10	.85	.50
RB27	2¢ violet brown	.40	.25	.25	.15
RB28	2-1/2¢ lake	.85	.45	.20	.15
RB29	3-3/4¢ olive gray	8.25	4.95	2.95	1.75
RB30	4¢ purple	2.75	1.65	.95	.55
RB31	5¢ brown orange	2.75	1.65	.85	.50

1914 Watermarked "USPS"

RB32	1/8¢ black	.25	.20	.20	.15
RB33	1/4¢ black	1.10	.65	.95	.55
RB34	3/8¢ black	.25	.20	.20	.15
RB35	5/8¢ black	2.30	1.35	1.65	1.00
RB36	1-1/4¢ black	1.50	.95	.75	.45
RB37	1-7/8¢ black	23.65	13.75	14.85	8.80
RB38	2-1/2¢ black	3.30	1.95	2.15	1.65
RB39	3-1/8¢ black	66.00	38.50	46.75	27.50
RB40	3-3/4¢ black	23.65	13.75	17.10	10.45
RB41	4¢ black	41.25	24.75	25.85	15.10
RB43	5¢ black	85.25	49.50	57.75	33.00

1914 Watermarked "USIR"

RB44	1/8¢ black	.25	.20	.20	.15
RB45	1/4¢ black	.25	.20	.20	.15
RB46	3/8¢ black	.60	.35	.35	.20
RB47	1/2¢ black	2.50	1.50	1.95	1.20
RB48	5/8¢ black	.25	.20	.20	.15
RB49	1¢ black	3.30	1.85	2.50	1.40
RB50	1-1/4¢ black	.35	.20	.25	.15
RB51	1-1/2¢ black	3.05	1.75	2.20	1.20
RB52	1-7/8¢ black	.85	.50	.55	.35
RB53	2¢ black	4.70	3.05	3.60	2.15

SCOTT NO.	DESCRIPTION	UNUSED F	AVG	USED F	AVG
RB54	2-1/2¢ black	1.20	.75	1.00	.60
RB55	3¢ black	3.30	1.85	2.50	1.50
RB56	3-1/8¢ black	3.85	2.30	2.75	1.65
RB57	3-3/4¢ black	8.55	4.95	6.90	4.15
RB58	4¢ black	.30	.20	.25	.15
RB59	4-3/8¢ black	9.90	5.80	6.90	4.15
RB60	5¢ black	2.50	1.35	2.15	1.20
RB61	6¢ black	44.00	26.40	35.75	21.45
RB62	8¢ black	12.10	7.15	9.90	6.05
RB63	10¢ black	8.55	4.95	6.60	3.85
RB64	20¢ black	16.50	9.90	13.75	8.25

1919 Offset Printing

RB65	1¢ dark blue	.25	.20	.15	.15
RB66	2¢ dark blue	.25	.20	.15	.15
RB67	3¢ dark blue	.95	.55	.55	.35
RB68	4¢ dark blue	.95	.55	.50	.30
RB69	5¢ dark blue	1.10	.65	.55	.35
RB70	8¢ dark blue	9.90	6.05	8.00	4.70
RB71	10¢ dark blue	2.75	1.85	1.95	1.20
RB72	20¢ dark blue	4.40	3.05	2.75	1.65
RB73	40¢ dark blue	21.75	12.95	9.35	5.50

FUTURE DELIVERY STAMPS

Documentary Stamps of 1917 Overprinted

1918-34 Perforated 11, Type I Overprint Lines 8mm. Apart

RC1	2¢ carmine rose	1.40	.85	.20	.15
RC2	3¢ carmine rose (cut cancel 12.50)	27.50	16.50	19.80	12.10
RC3	4¢ carmine rose	1.75	1.00	.20	.15
RC3A	5¢ carmine rose	35.75	23.65	2.75	1.65
RC4	10¢ carmine rose	4.40	2.75	.20	.15
RC5	20¢ carmine rose	4.40	2.75	.20	.15
RC6	25¢ carmine rose (cut cancel .10)	10.45	6.25	.50	.35
RC7	40¢ carmine rose	10.45	4.50	.50	.35
RC8	50¢ carmine rose	3.60	1.60	.20	.15
RC9	80¢ carmine rose (cut cancel .85)	16.50	10.75	6.00	3.85
RC10	$1 green (cut cancel .10)	......	......	.20	.15
RC11	$2 rose	......	......	.20	.15
RC12	$3 violet (cut cancel .15)	......	......	1.25	.80
RC13	$5 dark blue (cut cancel .10)	......	......	.30	.20
RC14	$10 orange (cut cancel .20)	......	......	.60	.40
RC15	$20 olive bistre (cut cancel .55)	......	......	3.65	2.35

Perforated 12

RC16	$30 vermillon (cut cancel 1.25)	......	......	3.35	2.15
RC17	$50 olive green (cut cancel 1.50)	......	......	1.10	.70
RC18	$60 brown (cut cancel .90)	......	......	1.75	1.10
RC19	$100 yellow green (cut cancel 6.00)	......	......	24.50	16.00
RC20	$500 blue (cut cancel 4.25)	60.00	38.75	9.50	6.25
RC21	$1000 orange (cut cancel 1.75)	......	......	4.25	2.75
RC22	1¢ carmine rose (lines 2mm apart)	.45	.30	.20	.15
RC23	80¢ carmine rose (lines 2mm apart) (cut cancel .25)	......	......	1.50	.95

1925-34 Perforated 11 Type II Overprint

RC25	$1 green (cut cancel .10)	6.00	3.85	.60	.40
RC26	$10 orange (cut cancel 5.75)	......	......	12.00	7.75

STOCK TRANSFER STAMPS

Documentary Stamps Overprinted

1918-22 Perforated 11 Type I Overprint

RD1	1¢ carmine rose	.30	.20	.20	.15
RD2	2¢ carmine rose	.20	.15	.20	.15
RD3	4¢ carmine rose	.20	.15	.20	.15
RD4	5¢ carmine rose	.20	.15	.20	.15
RD5	10¢ carmine rose	.20	.15	.20	.15
RD6	20¢ carmine rose	.25	.20	.20	.15
RD7	25¢ carmine rose (cut cancel .10)	.70	.45	.20	.15
RD8	40¢ carmine rose	.60	.40	.20	.15
RD9	50¢ carmine rose	.30	.20	.20	.15
RD10	80¢ carmine rose (cut cancel .10)	.75	.50	.25	.20
RD11	$1 green (red overprint) (cut cancel .55)	30.00	19.50	7.50	4.75
RD12	$1 green (black overprint)	1.50	.95	.20	.15
RD13	$2 rose	1.50	.95	.20	.15
RD14	$3 violet (cut cancel .25)	5.25	3.50	.90	.60
RD15	$4 yellow brown (cut cancel .10)	3.75	2.50	.20	.15
RD16	$5 dark blue (cut cancel .10)	2.50	1.60	.20	.15
RD17	$10 orange (cut cancel .10)	3.75	2.50	.20	.15
RD18	$20 olive bistre (cut cancel 3.50)	35.00	22.50	17.50	11.50

Perforated 12

RD19	$30 vermillon (cut cancel 1.20)	13.50	8.75	4.25	2.75
RD20	$50 olive green (cut cancel 12.00)	70.00	45.00	35.00	35.00
RD21	$60 brown (cut cancel 6.00)	55.00	35.00	16.50	10.75
RD22	$100 green	14.75	9.50	4.75	3.00
RD23	$500 blue (cut cancel 47.50)	......	......	110.00	70.00
RD24	$1000 orange (cut cancel 27.50)	......	......	77.50	50.00

U.S. Revenues #RD25-RD41, RG1-RG27, RJ1-RJ11

SCOTT NO.	DESCRIPTION	UNUSED F	UNUSED AVG	USED F	USED AVG
	1928 Perforated 10 Type I Overprint				
RD25	2¢ carmine rose	.30	.20	.20	.15
RD26	4¢ carmine rose	.30	.20	.20	.15
RD27	10¢ carmine rose	.35	.25	.20	.15
RD28	20¢ carmine rose	.55	.35	.20	.15
RD29	50¢ carmine rose	1.00	.65	.20	.15
RD30	$1 green	1.65	1.10	.20	.15
RD31	$2 carmine rose	1.65	1.10	.20	.15
RD32	$10 orange .... (cut cancel .10)	7.50	4.75	.20	.15
RD33		2.65	1.75	.50	.35
RD34	10¢ carmine rose	.40	.25	.20	.15
RD35	20¢ carmine rose	.45	.30	.20	.15
RD36	50¢ carmine rose	1.00	.65	.20	.15
RD37	$1 green .... (cut cancel .30)	12.00	7.85	5.50	3.50
RD38	$2 rose .... (cut cancel .30)	8.75	5.75	5.50	3.50
	1920-28 Perforated 10 Type II overprint				
RD39	2¢ carmine rose	2.75	1.75	.30	.20
RD40	10¢ carmine rose	.75	.50	.20	.15
RD41	20¢ carmine rose	1.00	.65	.20	.15
	SILVER TAX STAMPS				
	Documentary Stamps of 1917 Overprinted				
	1934-36				
RG1	1¢ carmine rose	.75	.50	.35	.25
RG2	2¢ carmine rose	1.10	.70	.40	.30
RG3	3¢ carmine rose	1.20	.80	.50	.35
RG4	4¢ carmine rose	1.20	.80	.60	.40
RG5	5¢ carmine rose	1.50	1.00	.90	.60
RG6	8¢ carmine rose	2.00	1.30	1.25	.80
RG7	10¢ carmine rose	2.00	1.30	1.25	.80
RG8	20¢ carmine rose	4.50	2.95	3.00	1.95
RG9	25¢ carmine rose	4.50	2.95	3.50	2.25
RG10	40¢ carmine rose	6.00	3.85	5.25	3.35
RG11	50¢ carmine rose	7.00	4.50	5.75	3.75
RG12	80¢ carmine rose	11.00	7.00	7.00	4.50
RG13	$1 green	11.00	7.00	8.25	5.50
RG14	$2 rose	14.50	9.50	12.00	8.00
RG15	$3 violet	30.00	19.50	25.00	16.00
RG16	$4 yellow brown	20.00	13.00	15.00	10.00
RG17	$5 dark blue	26.50	17.50	14.50	9.50
RG18	$10 orange	45.00	28.75	14.50	9.50
RG19	$30 vermillion .... (cut cancel 20.00)	......	......	35.00	22.50
RG20	$60 brown .... (cut cancel 30.00)	......	......	60.00	38.75
RG21	$100 green	105.00	70.00	35.00	22.50
RG22	$500 blue .... (cut cancel 110.00)	300.00	200.00	235.00	160.00
RG23	$1000 orange .... (cut cancel 70.00)	......	......	120.00	77.50
RG26	$100 green, 11mm spacing	130.00	85.00	60.00	38.75
RG27	$1000 orange, 11mm spacing	......	......	575.00	375.00
	TOBACCO SALE TAX STAMPS				
	Documentary Stamps of 1917 Overprinted				
	1934				
RJ1	1¢ carmine rose	.40	.25	.20	.15
RJ2	2¢ carmine rose	.45	.30	.25	.20
RJ3	5¢ carmine rose	1.40	.90	.45	.30
RJ4	10¢ carmine rose	1.75	1.15	.45	.30
RJ5	25¢ carmine rose	4.75	3.00	1.85	1.20
RJ6	50¢ carmine rose	4.75	3.00	1.85	1.20
RJ7	$1 green	8.00	3.00	1.85	1.20
RJ8	$2 rose	15.00	9.50	2.15	1.40
RJ9	$5 dark blue	17.50	11.00	4.75	3.00
RJ10	$10 orange	30.00	19.00	12.00	7.75
RJ11	$20 olive bistre	70.00	45.00	15.00	9.75

Economically priced
UNITED STATES ALBUMS

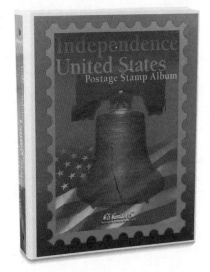

INDEPENDENCE U.S. ALBUM

Contains the same information as the popular U.S. Liberty Album. Pages are printed on both sides to make an excellent, economical album. Colorful illustrated binder. Expandable; loose-leaf. Over 200 pages.

1HRS28—Independence Album **$24.99**
2HRS2—Independence expansion binder, 1-3/4" size **$14.99**

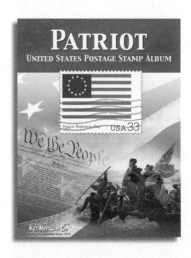

PATRIOT U.S. ALBUM

Ideal for the beginning collector—a quality simplified album for beginning collectors of United States stamps. 64 pages. Colorful, softbound cover.

1HRS27—Patriot Album **$6.99**

Order from your local dealer or direct from Whitman Publishing, LLC.

U.S. Revenues #RW1-RW20
HUNTING PERMIT

SCOTT NO.	DESCRIPTION	UNUSED VF	F	AVG	USED VF	F	AVG

RW1

RW2

RW3

RW4

RW5

1934-1938 Inscribed: DEPARTMENT OF AGRICULTURE (NH + 75%)

RW1	1934 $1 Mallards	575.00	425.00	300.00	180.00	125.00	95.00
RW2	1935 $1 Canvasbacks	500.00	375.00	275.00	225.00	160.00	110.00
RW3	1936 $1 Canada Geese	295.00	185.00	135.00	110.00	72.50	50.00
RW4	1937 $1 Scaup Ducks	200.00	150.00	110.00	65.00	45.00	29.50
RW5	1938 $1 Pintail Drake	250.00	175.00	125.00	75.00	50.00	32.50

RW6

RW7

RW8

RW9

RW10

Note: NH premiums RW6-9 (75%) RW10-16 (50%) RW17-25 (40%)
1939-1958 Inscribed: DEPARTMENT OF INTERIOR

RW6	1939 $1 Green-Winged Teal	150.00	100.00	67.50	60.00	40.00	25.00
RW7	1940 $1 Black Mallards	150.00	100.00	67.50	60.00	40.00	25.00
RW8	1941 $1 Ruddy Ducks	150.00	100.00	67.50	60.00	40.00	25.00
RW9	1942 $1 Baldpates	150.00	100.00	67.50	60.00	40.00	25.00
RW10	1943 $1 Wood Ducks	70.00	50.00	35.00	60.00	40.00	25.00

SCOTT NO.	DESCRIPTION	UNUSED VF	F	AVG	USED VF	F	AVG

RW11

RW12

RW13

RW14

RW15

RW11	1944 $1 White Fronted Geese	60.00	40.00	28.00	33.50	22.00	15.50
RW12	1945 $1 Shoveller Ducks	40.00	27.50	19.50	27.00	18.00	14.00
RW13	1946 $1 Redhead Ducks	40.00	27.50	19.50	21.00	15.00	10.50
RW14	1947 $1 Snow Geese	40.00	27.50	19.50	21.00	15.00	10.50
RW15	1948 $1 Buffleheads	43.00	31.00	20.50	21.00	15.00	10.50

RW16

RW17

RW18

RW19

RW20

RW16	1949 $2 Goldeneye Ducks	46.50	33.50	24.00	15.50	11.00	7.50
RW17	1950 $2 Trumpeter Swans	55.00	38.50	26.00	15.50	11.00	7.50
RW18	1951 $2 Gadwall Ducks	55.00	38.50	26.00	11.50	8.25	5.75
RW19	1952 $2 Harlequin Ducks	55.00	38.50	26.00	11.50	8.25	5.75
RW20	1953 $2 Blue-Winged Teal	55.00	38.50	26.00	11.50	8.25	5.75

Notes on Hunting Permit Stamps
1. Unused stamps without gum (uncancelled) are priced at one-half gummed price.
2. The date printed on the stamp is one year later than the date of issue listed above.
3. #RW1-RW25 and RW31 are plate blocks of 6.

U.S. Revenues #RW21-RW38

SCOTT NO.	DESCRIPTION	UNUSED VF	F	AVG	USED VF	F	AVG

RW21

RW22

RW23

RW24

RW25

SCOTT NO.	DESCRIPTION	VF	F	AVG	VF	F	AVG
RW21	1954 $2 Ringed-Necked Ducks	55.00	38.50	26.00	11.50	8.25	5.75
RW22	1955 $2 Blue Geese	55.00	38.50	26.00	11.50	8.25	5.75
RW23	1956 $2 American Merganser	55.00	38.50	26.00	11.50	8.25	5.75
RW24	1957 $2 Americacn Eider	55.00	38.50	26.00	11.50	8.25	5.75
RW25	1958 $2 Canada Geese	55.00	38.50	26.00	11.50	8.25	5.75

PLATE BLOCKS RW1-RW25

SCOTT NO.	UNUSED NH F	AVG	UNUSED OG F	AVG	SCOTT NO.	UNUSED NH F	AVG	UNUSED OG F	AVG
	PLATE BLOCKS OF 6					PLATE BLOCKS OF 6			
RW1	7000.00	5650.00	5750.00	4200.00	RW14	275.00	220.00	195.00	155.00
RW2	8250.00	6600.00	6750.00	5250.00	RW15	305.00	245.00	205.00	165.00
RW3	3000.00	2400.00	2750.00	2200.00	RW16	325.00	260.00	215.00	170.00
RW4	2100.00	1650.00	1800.00	1400.00	RW17	385.00	305.00	260.00	205.00
RW5	2150.00	1750.00	1850.00	1450.00	RW18	385.00	305.00	260.00	205.00
RW6	1500.00	1200.00	1200.00	950.00	RW19	385.00	305.00	260.00	205.00
RW7	1325.00	1050.00	1100.00	875.00	RW20	385.00	305.00	260.00	205.00
RW8	1200.00	950.00	1000.00	800.00	RW21	385.00	305.00	260.00	205.00
RW9	1200.00	950.00	1000.00	800.00	RW22	385.00	305.00	260.00	205.00
RW10	435.00	350.00	325.00	250.00	RW23	385.00	305.00	260.00	205.00
RW11	415.00	325.00	305.00	240.00	RW24	385.00	305.00	260.00	205.00
RW12	275.00	220.00	195.00	155.00	RW25	385.00	305.00	260.00	205.00
RW13	275.00	220.00	195.00	155.00					

RW26

RW27

RW28

RW29

RW30

1959-1971 (NH + 40%)

		UNUSED VF	F	USED VF	F
RW26	1959 $3 Dog & Mallard	65.00	47.50	11.50	8.25
RW27	1960 $3 Redhead Ducks	65.00	47.50	11.50	8.25
RW28	1961 $3 Mallard Hen & Ducklings	70.00	50.00	11.50	8.25
RW29	1962 $3 Pintail Drakes	80.00	57.50	14.25	10.00
RW30	1963 $3 Brant Ducks Landing	80.00	57.50	14.25	10.00

RW31

RW32

RW33

RW34

RW31	1964 $3 Hawaiian Nene Goose	80.00	57.50	14.25	10.00
RW32	1965 $3 Canvasback Drakes	80.00	57.50	14.25	10.00
RW33	1966 $3 Whistling Swans	80.00	57.50	14.25	10.00
RW34	1967 $3 Old Squaw Ducks	80.00	57.50	14.25	10.00

RW35

RW36

RW37 / RW38

RW35	1968 $3 Hooded Mergansers	50.00	36.00	14.25	10.00
RW36	1969 $3 White-Winged Scoters	50.00	36.00	9.50	6.75
RW37	1970 $3 Ross's Geese	47.00	33.50	9.50	6.75
RW38	1971 $3 Three Cinnamon Teal	33.00	23.75	9.50	6.75

Notes on Hunting Permit Stamps
1. Unused stamps without gum (uncancelled) are priced at one-half gummed price.
2. The date printed on the stamp is one year later than the date of issue listed above.
3. #RW1-RW25 and RW31 are plate blocks of 6.

U.S. Revenues #RW39-RW58

SCOTT NO.	DESCRIPTION	UNUSED NH VF	F	USED VF	F

RW39

RW40

RW41

RW42   RW43

1972-1978

RW39	1972 $5 Emperor Geese	32.00	25.00	9.00	7.50
RW40	1973 $5 Steller's Eider	29.00	22.00	9.00	7.50
RW41	1974 $5 Wood Ducks	22.00	17.00	9.00	7.50
RW42	1975 $5 Canvasbacks	18.75	14.50	9.00	7.50
RW43	1976 $5 Canada Geese	18.75	14.50	9.00	7.50

RW44

RW45

| RW44 | 1977 $5 Pair of Ross's Geese | 18.75 | 14.50 | 9.00 | 7.50 |
| RW45 | 1978 $5 Hooded Merganser Drake | 18.75 | 14.50 | 9.00 | 7.50 |

RW46

RW47

RW48   RW49

1979-1986

RW46	1979 $7.50 Green-Winged Teal	22.00	17.00	9.00	7.50
RW47	1980 $7.50 Mallards	22.00	17.00	9.00	7.50
RW48	1981 $7.50 Ruddy Ducks	22.00	17.00	9.00	7.50
RW49	1982 $7.50 Canvasbacks	22.00	17.00	9.00	7.50

RW50

RW51

RW52

RW53

RW50	1983 $7.50 Pintails	22.00	17.00	9.00	7.50
RW51	1984 $7.50 Widgeon	22.00	17.00	9.00	7.50
RW52	1985 $7.50 Cinnamon Teal	22.00	17.00	9.00	7.50
RW53	1986 $7.50 Fulvous Whistling	22.00	17.00	9.00	7.50

RW54

RW55

RW56

RW57

1987-1991

RW54	1987 $10.00 Redhead Ducks	26.00	21.00	13.00	10.00
RW55	1988 $10.00 Snow Goose	26.00	21.00	13.00	10.00
RW56	1989 $12.50 Lesser Scaup	30.00	24.00	13.00	10.00
RW57	1990 $12.50 Black Bellied Whistling Duck	30.00	24.00	13.00	10.00

RW58

| RW58 | 1991 $15.00 King Eiders | 35.00 | 30.00 | 17.75 | 13.75 |

–Supplies–
Don't forget that Harris offers a complete line of albums, supplies and accessories for all your stamp collecting needs!

U.S. Revenues #RW59-RW70a

RW59

RW60

RW61

RW62

RW63

RW64

RW68

2001

SCOTT NO.	DESCRIPTION	UNUSED NH VF	F	USED VF	F
RW68	2001 $15.00 Northern Pintail	35.00	30.00	17.75	....
RW68a	2001 $15.00 Northern Pintail, self-adhesive, pane of 1	35.00	....	20.00	....

RW69

RW70

2002-2003

SCOTT NO.	DESCRIPTION	UNUSED NH VF	F	USED VF	F
RW69	2002 $15.00 Black Scoters	35.00	30.00	17.75	....
RW69a	2002 $15.00 Black Scoters, self-adhesive, pane of 1	35.00	....	20.00	....
RW70	2003 $15.00 Snow Geese	35.00	30.00	17.75	....
RW70a	2003 $15.00 Snow Geese, self-adhesive, pane of 1	35.00	....	20.00	....

RW65

1992-1998

SCOTT NO.	DESCRIPTION	UNUSED NH VF	F	USED VF	F
RW59	1992 $15.00 Spectacled Eider	35.00	30.00	17.75	13.75
RW60	1993 $15.00 Canvasbacks	35.00	30.00	17.75	13.75
RW61	1994 $15.00 Red-breasted Merganser	35.00	30.00	17.75	13.75
RW62	1995 $15.00 Mallards	35.00	30.00	17.75	13.75
RW63	1996 $15.00 Surf Scoters	35.00	30.00	17.75	13.75
RW64	1997 $15.00 Canada Goose	35.00	30.00	17.75	13.75
RW65	1998 $15.00 Barrow's Goldeneye	35.00	30.00	17.75	13.75
RW65a	1998 $15.00 Barrow's Goldeneye, self-adhesive, pane of 1	35.00	....	20.00	....

RW66

RW67

1999-2000

SCOTT NO.	DESCRIPTION	UNUSED NH VF	F	USED VF	F
RW66	1999 $15.00 Greater Scaup	35.00	30.00	17.75	....
RW66a	1999 $15.00 Greater Scaup, self-adhesive, pane of 1	35.00	....	20.00	....
RW67	2000 $15.00 Mottled Duck	35.00	30.00	17.75	....
RW67a	2000 $15.00 Mottled Duck, self-adhesive, pane of 1	35.00	....	20.00	....

PLATE BLOCKS RW26-RW70

SCOTT NO.			UNUSED NH F	UNUSED OG F
RW26	1959	$3.00 Dog & Mallard	330.00	250.00
RW27	1960	$3.00 Redhead Ducks	330.00	250.00
RW28	1961	$3.00 Mallard Hen & Ducklings	360.00	250.00
RW29	1962	$3.00 Pintail Drakes	415.00	275.00
RW30	1963	$3.00 Brant Ducks Landing	415.00	285.00
RW31(6)	1964	$3.00 Hawaiian Nene Goose	1975.00	1550.00
RW32	1965	$3.00 Canvasback Drakes	385.00	275.00
RW33	1966	$3.00 Whistling Swans	385.00	275.00
RW34	1967	$3.00 Old Squaw Ducks	385.00	275.00
RW35	1968	$3.00 Hooded Mergansers	230.00	175.00
RW36	1969	$3.00 White-Winged Scoters	230.00	175.00
RW37	1970	$3.00 Ross's Geese	230.00	175.00
RW38	1971	$3.00 Three Cinnamon Teal	155.00	110.00
RW39	1972	$5.00 Emperor Geese	110.00	....
RW40	1973	$5.00 Steller's Eider	105.00	....
RW41	1974	$5.00 Wood Ducks	82.50	....
RW42	1975	$5.00 Canvasbacks	60.00	....
RW43	1976	$5.00 Canada Geese	60.00	....
RW44	1977	$5.00 Pair of Ross's Geese	60.00	....
RW45	1978	$5.00 Hooded Merganser Drake	60.00	....
RW46	1979	$7.50 Green-Winged Teal	72.50	....
RW47	1980	$7.50 Mallards	72.50	....
RW48	1981	$7.50 Ruddy Ducks	72.50	....
RW49	1982	$7.50 Canvasbacks	72.50	....
RW50	1983	$7.50 Pintails	72.50	....
RW51	1984	$7.50 Widgeon	72.50	....
RW52	1985	$7.50 Cinnamon Teal	72.50	....
RW53	1986	$7.50 Fulvous Whistling	72.50	....
RW54	1987	$10.00 Redhead Ducks	82.50	....
RW55	1988	$10.00 Snow Goose	82.50	....
RW56	1989	$12.50 Lesser Scaup	100.00	....
RW57	1990	$12.50 Black Bellied Whistling Duck	100.00	....
RW58	1991	$15.00 King Eiders	150.00	....
RW59	1992	$15.00 Spectacled Eider	150.00	....
RW60	1993	$15.00 Canvasbacks	150.00	....
RW61	1994	$15.00 Red-breasted Merganser	150.00	....
RW62	1995	$15.00 Mallards	150.00	....
RW63	1996	$15.00 Surf Scoters	150.00	....
RW64	1997	$15.00 Canada Goose	150.00	....
RW65	1998	$15.00 Barrow's Goldeneye	150.00	....
RW66	1999	$15.00 Greater Scaup	150.00	....
RW67	2000	$15.00 Mottled Duck	150.00	....
RW68	2001	$15.00 Northern Pintail	150.00	....
RW69	2002	$15.00 Black Scoters	150.00	....
RW70	2003	$15.00 Snow Geese	150.00	....

Note: #RW1-RW25 and RW31 are plate blocks of six. All others are plate blocks of four.

State Duck Stamps #AL1-FL25
STATE HUNTING PERMIT

NO.	DESCRIPTION	F-VF NH

ALABAMA
NO.	DESCRIPTION	F-VF NH
AL1	'79 $5 Wood Ducks	10.25
AL2	'80 $5 Mallards	10.25
AL3	'81 $5 Canada Geese	10.25
AL4	'82 $5 Green-Winged Teal	10.25
AL5	'83 $5 Widgeons	11.00
AL6	'84 $5 Buffleheads	11.00
AL7	'85 $5 Wood Ducks	14.00
AL8	'86 $5 Canada Geese	14.00
AL9	'87 $5 Pintails	15.00
AL10	'88 $5 Canvasbacks	11.00
AL11	'89 $5 Hooded Mergansers	10.25
AL12	'90 $5 Wood Ducks	10.25
AL13	'91 $5 Redheads	10.25
AL14	'92 $5 Cinnamon Teal	10.25
AL15	'93 $5 Green-Winged Teal	10.25
AL16	'94 $5 Canvasbacks	10.25
AL17	'95 $5 Canada Geese	10.25
AL18	'96 $5 Wood Ducks	10.25
AL19	'97 $5 Snow Geese	10.25
AL20	'98 $5 Barrows Goldeneye	10.25
AL21	'99 $5 Redheads	10.25
AL22	'00 $5 Buffleheads	10.25
AL23	'01 $5 Ruddy Duck	10.25
AL24	'02 $5 Pintail	10.25
Al25	'03 $5 Wood Duck	10.25

ALASKA
NO.	DESCRIPTION	F-VF NH
AK1	'85 $5 Emperor Geese	14.00
AK2	'86 $5 Steller's Eiders	11.00
AK3	'87 $5 Spectacled Eiders	10.00
AK4	'88 $5 Trumpeter Swans	10.00
AK5	'89 $5 Barrow's Goldeneyes	9.25
AK6	'90 $5 Old Squaws	9.25
AK7	'91 $5 Snow Geese	9.25
AK8	'92 $5 Canvasbacks	9.25
AK9	'93 $5 Tule White Front Geese	9.25
AK10	'94 $5 Harlequin Ducks	9.25
AK11	'95 $5 Pacific Brant	9.25
AK12	'96 $5 Aleutian Canada Geese	9.25
AK13	'97 $5 King Eiders	9.25
AK14	'98 $5 Barrows Goldeneye	9.25
AK15	'99 $5 Pintail	9.25
AK16	'00 $5 Common Eiders	9.25
AK17	'01 $5 Buffleheads	9.25
AK18	'02 $5 Black Scoter	9.25
AK19	'03 $5 Canada Geese	9.25

ARIZONA
NO.	DESCRIPTION	F-VF NH
AZ1	'87 $5.50 Pintails	12.00
AZ2	'88 $5.50 Green-Winged Teal	11.25
AZ3	'89 $5.50 Cinnamon Teal	11.25
AZ4	'90 $5.50 Canada Geese	11.25
AZ5	'91 $5.50 Blue-Winged Teal	11.25
AZ6	'92 $5.50 Buffleheads	11.25
AZ7	'93 $5.50 Mexican Ducks	11.25
AZ8	'94 $5.50 Mallards	11.25
AZ9	'95 $5.50 Widgeon	11.25
AZ10	'96 $5.50 Canvasback	11.25
AZ11	'97 $5.50 Gadwall	11.25
AZ12	'98 $5.50 Wood Duck	11.25
AZ13	'99 $5.50 Snow Geese	11.25
AZ14	'00 $7.50 Ruddy Ducks	13.50
AZ15	'01 $7.50 Redheads	13.50
AZ16	'02 $7.50 Ring-necked ducks	13.50
AZ17	'03 $7.50 Northern Shoveler	13.50

ARKANSAS
NO.	DESCRIPTION	F-VF NH
AR1	'81 $5.50 Mallards	47.50
AR2	'82 $5.50 Wood Ducks	42.50
AR3	'83 $5.50 Green-Winged Teal	60.00
AR4	'84 $5.50 Pintails	26.00
AR5	'85 $5.50 Mallards	14.50
AR6	'86 $5.50 Black Swamp Mallards	12.50
AR7	'87 $7 Wood Ducks	12.50
AR8	'88 $7 Pintails	11.50
AR9	'89 $7 Mallards	11.50
AR10	'90 $7 Black Ducks & Mallards	11.50
AR11	'91 $7 Sulphur River Widgeons	11.50
AR12	'92 $7 Shirey Bay Shovelers	11.50
AR13	'93 $7 Grand Prairie Mallards	11.00
AR14	'94 $7 Canada Goose	11.00
AR15	'95 $7 White River Mallards	11.00
AR16	'96 $7 Black Lab	11.00
AR17	'97 $7 Chocolate Lab	11.00
AR18	'98 $7 Labrador retriever, mallards	11.00
AR19	'99 $7.00 Wood Duck	11.00
AR20	'00 $7 Mallards and golden retriever	11.00
AR21	'01 $7 Canvasback	11.00
AR22	'02 $7 Mallards	11.00
AR23	'03 $7 Mallards & Chesapeake Bay Retriever	11.00

CALIFORNIA
NO.	DESCRIPTION	F-VF NH
CA1	'71 $1 Pintails	850.00
CA2	'72 $1 Canvasbacks	3,250.00
CA3	'73 $1 Mallards	15.00
CA4	'74 $1 White-Fronted Geese	4.50
CA5	'75 $1 Green-Winged Teal	42.50
CA6	'76 $1 Widgeons	19.00
CA7	'77 $1 Cinnamon Teal	50.00
CA8	'78 $5 Cinnamon Teal	9.00
CA9	'78 $5 Hooded Mergansers	150.00
CA10	'79 $5 Wood Ducks	9.50
CA11	'80 $5 Pintails	9.50
CA12	'81 $5 Canvasbacks	9.75
CA13	'82 $5 Widgeons	9.75
CA14	'83 $5 Green-Winged Teal	9.75
CA15	'84 $7.50 Mallard Decoy	12.50
CA16	'85 $7.50 Ring-Necked Ducks	12.50
CA17	'86 $7.50 Canada Goose	12.50
CA18	'87 $7.50 Redheads	12.50
CA19	'88 $7.50 Mallards	12.50
CA20	'89 $7.50 Cinnamon Teal	12.50
CA21	'90 $7.50 Canada Goose	12.50
CA22	'91 $7.50 Gadwalls	12.50
CA23	'92 $7.90 White-Fronted Goose	12.50
CA24	'93 $10.50 Pintails	15.00
CA25	'94 $10.50 Wood Duck	15.00
CA26	'95 $10.50 Snow Geese	15.00
CA27	'96 $10.50 Mallard	15.00
CA28	'97 $10.50 Pintails	15.00
CA29	'98 $10.50 Green-Winged Teal (pair)	35.00
CA30	'99 $10.50 Wood Duck (pair)	35.00
CA31	'00 $10.50 Canada geese, mallard, widgeon	16.00
CA32	'01 $10.50 Redheads	16.00
CA33	'02 $10.50 Pintails	16.00
CA34	'03 $10.50 Mallards	16.00

COLORADO
NO.	DESCRIPTION	F-VF NH
CO1	'90 $5 Canada Geese	12.50
CO2	'91 $5 Mallards	12.50
CO3	'92 $5 Pintails	9.25
CO4	'93 $5 Green-Winged Teal	9.25
CO5	'94 $5 Wood Ducks	9.25
CO6	'95 $5 Buffleheads	9.25
CO7	'96 $5 Cinnamon Teal	9.25
CO8	'97 $5 Widgeon	9.25
CO9	'98 $5 Redhead	9.25
CO10	'99 $5 Blue-winged Teal	9.25
CO11	'00 $5 Gadwalls	9.25
CO12	'01 $5 Ruddy Duck	9.25
CO13	'02 $5 Common Goldeneyes	9.25
CO14	'03 $5 Canvasbacks	9.25

CONNECTICUT
NO.	DESCRIPTION	F-VF NH
CT1	'93 $5 Black Ducks	9.00
CT2	'94 $5 Canvasbacks	9.00
CT3	'95 $5 Mallards	9.00
CT4	'96 $5 Old Squaw	9.00
CT5	'97 $5 Green Winged Teal	9.00
CT6	'98 $5 Mallards	9.00
CT7	'99 $5 Canada Geese	9.00
CT8	'00 $5 Wood Duck	9.00
CT9	'01 Bufflehead	9.00
CT10	'02 Greater Scaups	9.00
CT11	'03 $5.00 Black Duck	9.00

DELAWARE
NO.	DESCRIPTION	F-VF NH
DE1	'80 $5 Black Ducks	95.00
DE2	'81 $5 Snow Geese	85.00
DE3	'82 $5 Canada Geese	80.00
DE4	'83 $5 Canvasbacks	55.00
DE5	'84 $5 Mallards	25.00
DE6	'85 $5 Pintail	14.00
DE7	'86 $5 Widgeons	12.00
DE8	'87 $5 Redheads	12.00
DE9	'88 $5 Wood Ducks	10.50
DE10	'89 $5 Buffleheads	9.75
DE11	'90 $5 Green-Winged Teal	9.75
DE12	'91 $5 Hooded Merganser	9.75
DE13	'92 $5 Blue-Winged Teal	9.75
DE14	'93 $5 Goldeneye	9.75
DE15	'94 $5 Blue Goose	9.75
DE16	'95 $5 Scaup	9.75
DE17	'96 $6 Gadwall	9.75
DE18	'97 $6 White Winged Scoter	9.75
DE19	'98 $6 Blue Winged Teal	9.75
DE20	'99 $6 Tundra Swan	9.75
DE21	'00 $6 American brant	9.75
DE22	'01 $6 Old Squaw	9.75
DE23	'02 $6 Ruddy Duck	9.75
DE24	'03 $9 Ring Necked Duck	14.00

FLORIDA
NO.	DESCRIPTION	F-VF NH
FL1	'79 $3.25 Green-Winged Teal	175.00
FL2	'80 $3.25 Pintails	25.00
FL3	'81 $3.25 Widgeon	25.00
FL4	'82 $3.25 Ring-Necked Ducks	35.00
FL5	'83 $3.25 Buffleheads	60.00
FL6	'84 $3.25 Hooded Merganser	20.00
FL7	'85 $3.25 Wood Ducks	18.00
FL8	'86 $3 Canvasbacks	11.25
FL9	'87 $3.50 Mallards	9.75
FL10	'88 $3.50 Redheads	9.75
FL11	'89 $3.50 Blue-Winged Teal	7.25
FL12	'90 $3.50 Wood Ducks	7.25
FL13	'91 $3.50 Northern Pintails	7.25
FL14	'92 $3.50 Ruddy Duck	7.25
FL15	'93 $3.50 American Widgeon	7.00
FL16	'94 $3.50 Mottled Duck	7.00
FL17	'95 $3.50 Fulvous Whistling Duck	7.00
FL18	'96 $3.50 Goldeneyes	7.00
FL19	'97 $3.50 Hooded Mergansers	7.00
FL20	'98 $3.50 Shoveler	7.00
FL21	'99 $3 Pintail	7.00
FL22	'00 $3.50 Rin-necked duck	7.00
FL23	'01 $3.50 Canvasbacks	7.00
FL24	'02 $3.50 Mottled Duck	7.00
FL25	'03 $3.50 Canvasback	7.00

State Duck Stamps #GA1-LA30

NO.	DESCRIPTION	F-VF NH

GEORGIA
GA1	'85 $5.50 Wood Ducks	13.00
GA2	'86 $5.50 Mallards	10.00
GA3	'87 $5.50 Canada Geese	9.00
GA4	'88 $5.50 Ring-Necked Ducks	9.00
GA5	'89 $5.50 Duckling & Golden Retriever Puppy	12.00
GA6	'90 $5.50 Wood Ducks	9.00
GA7	'91 $5.50 Green-Winged Teal	9.00
GA8	'92 $5.50 Buffleheads	9.00
GA9	'93 $5.50 Mallards	9.00
GA10	'94 $5.50 Ring-Necked Ducks	9.00
GA11	'95 $5.50 Widgeons, Labrador Retriever	9.00
GA12	'96 $5.50 Black Ducks	9.00
GA13	'97 $5.50 Lesser Scaup	9.00
GA14	'98 $5.50 Black Lab with Ringnecks	9.00
GA15	'99 $5.50 Pintails	9.00

HAWAII
HI1	'96 $5 Nene Geese	9.25
HI2	'97 $5 Hawaiian Duck	9.25
HI3	'98 $5 Wild Turkey	9.25
HI4	'99 $5 Ring-necked Pheasant	9.25
HI5	'00 $5 Erckesls Francolin	9.25
HI6	'01 $5 Japanese Green Pheasant	7.00
HI7	'02 $10 Chukar Partridge	18.00
HI8	'03 $10 Nene Geese	18.00

IDAHO
ID1	'87 $5.50 Cinnamon Teal	20.00
ID2	'88 $5.50 Green-Winged Teal	13.50
ID3	'89 $6 Blue-Winged Teal	11.50
ID4	'90 $6 Trumpeter Swans	11.50
ID5	'91 $6 Widgeons	10.00
ID6	'92 $6 Canada Geese	10.00
ID7	'93 $6 Common Goldeneye	10.00
ID8	'94 $6 Harlequin Ducks	10.00
ID9	'95 $6 Wood Ducks	10.00
ID10	'96 $6 Mallard	10.00
ID11	'97 $6.50 Shovelers	10.00
ID12	'98 $6.50 Canada Geese	10.00
ID13		

ILLINOIS
IL1	'75 $5 Mallard	700.00
IL2	'76 $5 Wood Ducks	300.00
IL3	'77 $5 Canada Goose	200.00
IL4	'78 $5 Canvasbacks	110.00
IL5	'79 $5 Pintail	110.00
IL6	'80 $5 Green-Winged Teal	110.00
IL7	'81 $5 Widgeons	110.00
IL8	'82 $5 Black Ducks	80.00
IL9	'83 $5 Lesser Scaup	70.00
IL10	'84 $5 Blue-Winged Teal	70.00
IL11	'85 $5 Redheads	21.00
IL12	'86 $5 Gadwalls	15.50
IL13	'87 $5 Buffleheads	12.50
IL14	'88 $5 Common Goldeneyes	12.50
IL15	'89 $5 Ring-Necked Ducks	10.50
IL16	'90 $10 Lesser Snow Geese	16.00
IL17	'91 $10 Labrador Retriever & Canada Goose	15.50
IL18	'92 $10 Retriever & Mallards	15.00
IL19	'93 $10 Pintail Decoys & Puppy	15.00
IL20	'94 $10 Canvasbacks & Retrievers	15.00
IL21	'95 $10 Retriever, Green-Winged Teal, Decoys	15.00
IL22	'96 $10 Wood Ducks	15.00
IL23	'97 $10 Canvasbacks	15.00
IL24	'98 $10 Canada Geese	15.00
IL25	'99 $10 Canada Geese, black labrador retriever	15.00
IL26	'00 $10 Mallards, golden retriever	15.00
IL27	'01 $10 Canvasback, yellow labrador	15.00
IL28	'02 $10 Canvasbacks, Chesapeake Retriever	15.00
IL29	'03 $10 Chocolate Lab, Green-winged Teal	15.00

INDIANA
IN1	'76 $5 Green-Winged Teal	9.50
IN2	'77 $5 Pintail	9.50
IN3	'78 $5 Canada Geese	9.50
IN4	'79 $5 Canvasbacks	9.50
IN5	'80 $5 Mallard Ducklings	9.50
IN6	'81 $5 Hooded Mergansers	9.50
IN7	'82 $5 Blue-Winged Teal	9.50
IN8	'83 $5 Snow Geese	9.50
IN9	'84 $5 Redheads	9.50
IN10	'85 $5 Pintail	9.50
IN11	'86 $5 Wood Duck	9.50
IN12	'87 $5 Canvasbacks	9.50
IN13	'88 $6.75 Redheads	11.25
IN14	'89 $6.75 Canada Goose	11.25
IN15	'90 $6.75 Blue-Winged Teal	11.25
IN16	'91 $6.75 Mallards	11.25
IN17	'92 $6.75 Green-Winged Teal	11.25
IN18	'93 $6.75 Wood Ducks	11.25
IN19	'94 $6.75 Pintail	11.25
IN20	'95 $6.75 Goldeneyes	11.25
IN21	'96 $6.75 Black Ducks	11.25
IN22	'97 $6.75 Canada Geese	11.25
IN23	'98 $6.75 Widgeon	11.25
IN24	'99 $6.75 Bluebills	11.25
IN25	'00 $6.75 Ring-necked Duck	11.25
IN26	'01 $6.75 Green-winged Teal	11.25
IN27	'02 $6.75 Green-winged Teal	11.25
IN28	'03 $6.75 Shoveler	11.25

IOWA
IA1	'72 $1 Mallards	200.00
IA2	'73 $1 Pintails	47.50
IA3	'74 $1 Gadwalls	100.00
IA4	'75 $1 Canada Geese	130.00
IA5	'76 $1 Canvasbacks	26.00
IA6	'77 $1 Lesser Scaup	26.00
IA7	'78 $1 Wood Ducks	55.00
IA8	'79 $5 Buffleheads	400.00
IA9	'80 $5 Redheads	40.00
IA10	'81 $5 Green-Winged Teal	35.00
IA11	'82 $5 Snow Geese	19.00
IA12	'83 $5 Widgeons	20.00
IA13	'84 $5 Wood Ducks	42.00
IA14	'85 $5 Mallard & Mallard Decoy	25.00
IA15	'86 $5 Blue-Winged Teal	16.50
IA16	'87 $5 Canada Goose	14.50
IA17	'88 $5 Pintails	12.50
IA18	'89 $5 Blue-Winged Teal	12.50
IA19	'90 $5 Canvasbacks	8.50
IA20	'91 $5 Mallards	8.50
IA21	'92 $5 Labrador Retriever & Ducks	10.00
IA22	'93 $5 Mallards	9.25
IA23	'94 $5 Green-Winged Teal	9.25
IA24	'95 $5 Canada Geese	9.25
IA25	'96 $5 Canvasbacks	9.25
IA 26	'97 $5 Canada Geese	9.25
IA27	'98 $5 Pintails	9.25
IA28	'99 $5 Trumpeter Swan	9.25
IA29	'00 $5.50 Hooded Merganser	9.25
IA30	'01 $6 Snow Geese	10.25
IA31	'02 $8.50 Northern Shoveler	13.00
IA32	'03 $8.50 Ruddy Duck	13.00

KANSAS
KS1	'87 $3 Green-Winged Teal	9.00
KS2	'88 $3 Canada Geese	7.00
KS3	'89 $3 Mallards	6.50
KS4	'90 $3 Wood Ducks	6.50
KS5	'91 $3 Pintail	6.50
KS6	'92 $3 Canvasbacks	6.50
KS7	'93 $3 Mallards	6.50
KS8	'94 $3 Blue-Winged Teal	6.50
KS9	'95 $3 Barrow's Goldeneye	6.50
KS10	'96 $3 Widgeon	6.50
KS11	'97 $3 Mallard	6.50
KS12	'98 $3 Mallard	6.50
KS13	'99 $3 Mallard (red)	6.50
KS14	'00 $3 Mallard (purple)	6.50
KS15	'01 $3 Mallard (orange)	6.50
KS16	'02 $5 Pintail (blue)	9.00

KENTUCKY
KY1	'85 $5.25 Mallards	15.00
KY2	'86 $5.25 Wood Ducks	10.00
KY3	'87 $5.25 Black Ducks	10.00
KY4	'88 $5.25 Canada Geese	10.00
KY5	'89 $5.25 Retriever & Canvasbacks	10.00
KY6	'90 $5.25 Widgeons	10.00
KY7	'91 $5.25 Pintails	10.00
KY8	'92 $5.25 Green-Winged Teal	12.50
KY9	'93 $5.25 Canvasbacks & Decoy	15.00
KY10	'94 $5.25 Canada Goose	9.75
KY11	'95 $7.50 Retriever, Decoy, Ringnecks	12.00
KY12	'96 $7.50 Blue-Winged Teal	12.00
KY13	'97 $7.50 Shovelers	12.00
KY14	'98 $7.50 Gadwalls	12.00
KY15	'99 $7.50 Common Goldeneyes	12.00
KY16	'00 $7.50 Hooded Merganser	12.00
KY17	'01 $7.50 Mallard	12.00
KY18	'02 $7.50 Pintails	12.00
KY19	'03 $7.50 Snow Goose	12.00

LOUISIANA
LA1	'89 $5 Blue-Winged Teal	12.50
LA2	'89 $7.50 Blue-Winged Teal	17.00
LA3	'90 $5 Green-Winged Teal	9.25
LA4	'90 $7.50 Green-Winged Teal	13.50
LA5	'91 $5 Wood Ducks	9.75
LA6	'91 $7.50 Wood Ducks	13.50
LA7	'92 $5 Pintails	8.75
LA8	'92 $7.50 Pintails	12.00
LA9	'93 $5 American Widgeon	8.75
LA10	'93 $7.50 American Widgeon	12.00
LA11	'94 $5 Mottled Duck	8.75
LA12	'94 $7.50 Mottled Duck	12.00
LA13	'95 $5 Speckle Bellied Goose	8.75
LA14	'95 $7.50 Speckle Bellied Goose	12.00
LA15	'96 $5 Gadwall	8.75
LA16	'96 $7.50 Gadwell	12.00
LA17	'97 $5.00 Ring Necked Duck	8.75
LA18	'97 $13.50 Ring Necked Duck	18.00
LA19	'98 $5.50 Mallards	8.75
LA20	'98 $13.50 Mallards	18.00
LA21	'99 $5.50 Snow Geese	8.75
LA22	'99 $13.50 Snow Geese	18.00
LA23	'00 $5.50 Lesser Scaup	8.75
LA24	'00 $13.50 Lesser Scaup	18.00
LA25	'01 $5.50 Northern Shoveler	8.75
LA26	'01 $13.50 Northern Shoveler	18.00
LA27	'02 $5.50 Canvasbacks	8.75
LA28	'02 $25 Canvasbacks	32.50
LA29	'03 $5.50 Redhead	8.75
LA30	'03 $25.00 Redhead	32.50

State Duck Stamps #ME1-MT51

MAINE

NO.	DESCRIPTION	F-VF NH
ME1	'84 $2.50 Black Ducks	25.00
ME2	'85 $2.50 Common Eiders	55.00
ME3	'86 $2.50 Wood Ducks	10.00
ME4	'87 $2.50 Buffleheads	8.75
ME5	'88 $2.50 Green-Winged Teal	8.75
ME6	'89 $2.50 Common Goldeneyes	6.50
ME7	'90 $2.50 Canada Geese	6.50
ME8	'91 $2.50 Ring-Necked Duck	6.50
ME9	'92 $2.50 Old Squaw	6.50
ME10	'93 $2.50 Hooded Merganser	6.50
ME11	'94 $2.50 Mallards	6.50
ME12	'95 $2.50 White-Winged Scoters	6.50
ME13	'96 $2.50 Blue-Winged Teal	6.50
ME14	'97 $2.50 Greater Scaup	6.50
ME15	'98 $2.50 Surf Scoters	6.50
ME16	'99 $2.50 Black Duck	6.50
ME17	'00 $2.50 Common Eider	6.50
ME18	'01 $2.50 Wood Duck	6.50
ME19	'02 $2.50 Bufflehead	6.50
ME20	'03 $5.50 Green-winged Teal	11.00

MARYLAND

NO.	DESCRIPTION	F-VF NH
MD1	'74 $1.10 Mallards	14.00
MD2	'75 $1.10 Canada Geese	12.50
MD3	'76 $1.10 Canvasbacks	12.50
MD4	'77 $1.10 Greater Scaup	12.50
MD5	'78 $1.10 Redheads	12.50
MD6	'79 $1.10 Wood Ducks	12.50
MD7	'80 $1.10 Pintail Decoy	12.50
MD8	'81 $3 Widgeon	7.50
MD9	'82 $3 Canvasback	10.50
MD10	'83 $3 Wood Duck	14.50
MD11	'84 $6 Black Ducks	12.50
MD12	'85 $6 Canada Geese	11.25
MD13	'86 $6 Hooded Mergansers	11.25
MD14	'87 $6 Redheads	11.25
MD15	'88 $6 Ruddy Ducks	11.25
MD16	'89 $6 Blue-Winged Teal	10.25
MD17	'90 $6 Lesser Scaup	10.25
MD18	'91 $6 Shovelers	10.25
MD19	'92 $6 Bufflehead	10.25
MD20	'93 $6 Canvasbacks	10.25
MD21	'94 $6 Redheads	10.25
MD22	'95 $6 Mallards	10.25
MD23	'96 $6 Canada Geese	10.25
MD24	'97 $6 Canvasbacks	10.25
MD25	'98 $6 Pintails	10.25
MD26	'99 $5 Wood Ducks	10.25
MD27	'00 $6 Oldsquaws	10.25
MD28	'01 $6 American Widgeon	10.25
MD29	'02 $9 Black Scoters	13.00
MD30	'03 $9 Lesser Scaup	13.00

MASSACHUSETTS

NO.	DESCRIPTION	F-VF NH
MA1	'74 $1.25 Wood Duck Decoy	16.50
MA2	'75 $1.25 Pintail Decoy	12.75
MA3	'76 $1.25 Canada Goose Decoy	12.75
MA4	'77 $1.25 Goldeneye Decoy	12.75
MA5	'78 $1.25 Black Duck Decoy	12.75
MA6	'79 $1.25 Ruddy Turnstone Duck Decoy	12.75
MA7	'80 $1.25 Old Squaw Decoy	12.75
MA8	'81 $1.25 Red-Breasted Merganser Decoy	9.00
MA9	'82 $1.25 Greater Yellowlegs Decoy	9.00
MA10	'83 $1.25 Redhead Decoy	9.00
MA11	'84 $1.25 White-Winged Scoter Decoy	9.00
MA12	'85 $1.25 Ruddy Duck Decoy	9.00
MA13	'86 $1.25 Preening Bluebill Decoy	9.00
MA14	'87 $1.25 American Widgeon Decoy	9.00
MA15	'88 $1.25 Mallard Decoy	9.00
MA16	'89 $1.25 Brant Decoy	9.00
MA17	'90 $1.25 Whistler Hen Decoy	9.00
MA18	'91 $5 Canvasback Decoy	9.00
MA19	'92 $5 Black-Bellied Plover Decoy	9.00
MA20	'93 $5 Red-Breasted Merganser Decoy	9.00
MA21	'94 $5 White-Winged Scoter Decoy	9.00
MA22	'95 $5 Female Hooded Merganser Decoy	9.00
MA23	'96 $5 Eider Decoy	9.00
MA24	'97 $5 Curlew Shorebird	10.25
MA25	'98 $5 Canada Goose	10.25
MA26	'99 $5 Oldsquaw Decoy	10.25
MA27	'00 $5 Merganser Hen decoy	10.25
MA28	'01 $5 Black Duck decoy	10.25
MA29	'02 $5 Bufflehead decoy	10.25
MA30	'03 $5 Green-winged Teal decoy	10.25

MICHIGAN

NO.	DESCRIPTION	F-VF NH
MI1	'76 $2.10 Wood Duck	5.00
MI2	'77 $2.10 Canvasbacks	325.00
MI3	'78 $2.10 Mallards	30.00
MI4	'79 $2.10 Canada Geese	52.00
MI5	'80 $3.75 Lesser Scaup	24.50
MI6	'81 $3.75 Buffleheads	29.00
MI7	'82 $3.75 Redheads	29.00
MI8	'83 $3.75 Wood Ducks	29.00
MI9	'84 $3.75 Pintails	29.00
MI10	'85 $3.75 Ring-Necked Ducks	29.00
MI11	'86 $3.75 Common Goldeneyes	21.50
MI12	'87 $3.85 Green-Winged Teal	11.50
MI13	'88 $3.85 Canada Geese	11.50
MI14	'89 $3.85 Widgeons	8.25
MI15	'90 $3.85 Wood Ducks	8.25
MI16	'91 $3.85 Blue-Winged Teal	7.50
MI17	'92 $3.85 Red-Breasted Merganser	7.50
MI18	'93 $3.85 Hooded Merganser	7.50
MI19	'94 $3.85 Black Duck	7.50
MI20	'95 $4.35 Blue Winged Teal	8.25
MI21	'96 $4.35 Canada Geese	8.25
MI22	'97 $5 Canvasbacks	8.25
MI23	'98 $5 Pintail	8.25
MI24	'99 $5 Shoveler	8.25
MI25	'00 $5 Mallards	8.25
MI26	'01 $5 Ruddy Duck	8.25
MI27	'02 $5 Wigeons	8.25
MI28	'03 $5 Redhead	8.25

MINNESOTA

NO.	DESCRIPTION	F-VF NH
MN1	'77 $3 Mallards	17.50
MN2	'78 $3 Lesser Scaup	11.00
MN3	'79 $3 Pintails	11.00
MN4	'80 $3 Canvasbacks	11.00
MN5	'81 $3 Canada Geese	11.00
MN6	'82 $3 Redheads	11.00
MN7	'83 $3 Blue Geese & Snow Goose	11.00
MN8	'84 $3 Wood Ducks	11.00
MN9	'85 $3 White-Fronted Geese	11.00
MN10	'86 $3 Lesser Scaup	11.00
MN11	'87 $5 Common Goldeneyes	11.50
MN12	'88 $5 Buffleheads	11.50
MN13	'89 $5 Widgeons	11.50
MN14	'90 $5 Hooded Mergansers	17.50
MN15	'91 $5 Ross's Geese	9.25
MN16	'92 $5 Barrow's Goldeneyes	9.25
MN17	'93 $5 Blue-Winged Teal	9.25
MN18	'94 $5 Ringneck Duck	9.25
MN19	'95 $5 Gadwall	9.25
MN20	'96 $5 Greater Scaup	9.25
MN21	'97 $5 Shoveler with Decoy	9.25
MN22	'98 $5 Harlequin Ducks	9.25
MN23	'99 $5 Green-winged Teal	9.25
MN24	'00 $5 Red-beasted Merganser	9.25
MN25	'01 $5 Black Duck	9.25
MN26	'02 $5 Ruddy Duck	9.25
MN27	'03 $5 Long Tailed Duck	9.25

MISSISSIPPI

NO.	DESCRIPTION	F-VF NH
MS1	'76 $2 Wood Duck	24.50
MS2	'77 $2 Mallards	9.25
MS3	'78 $2 Green-Winged Teal	9.25
MS4	'79 $2 Canvasbacks	9.25
MS5	'80 $2 Pintails	9.25
MS6	'81 $2 Redheads	9.25
MS7	'82 $2 Canada Geese	9.25
MS8	'83 $2 Lesser Scaup	9.25
MS9	'84 $2 Black Ducks	9.25
MS10	'85 $2 Mallards	9.25
MS11	'86 $2 Widgeons	9.25
MS12	'87 $2 Ring-Necked Ducks	9.25
MS13	'88 $2 Snow Geese	9.25
MS14	'89 $2 Wood Ducks	7.00
MS15	'90 $2 Snow Geese	14.50
MS16	'91 $2 Labrador Retriever & Canvasbacks	6.00
MS17	'92 $2 Green-Winged Teal	5.25
MS18	'93 $2 Mallards	8.25
MS19	'94 $2 Canvasbacks	8.25
MS20	'95 $5 Blue-Winged Teal	8.25
MS21	'96 $5 Hooded Merganser	8.25
MS22	'97 $5 Wood Duck	9.25
MS23	'98 $5 Pintails	9.25
MS24	'99 $5 Ring-necked Duck	9.25
MS25	'00 $5 Mallards	9.25
MS26	'01 $10 Gadwall	14.50
MS27	'02 $10 Wood Duck	14.50
MS28	'03 $10 Pintail	14.50

MISSOURI

NO.	DESCRIPTION	F-VF NH
MO1	'79 $3.40 Canada Geese	710.00
MO2	'80 $3.40 Wood Ducks	140.00
MO3	'81 $3 Lesser Scaup	72.50
MO4	'82 $3 Buffleheads	62.50
MO5	'83 $3 Blue-Winged Teal	52.50
MO6	'84 $3 Mallards	42.50
MO7	'85 $3 American Widgeons	25.00
MO8	'86 $3 Hooded Mergansers	16.00
MO9	'87 $3 Pintails	12.50
MO10	'88 $3 Canvasback	11.25
MO11	'89 $3 Ring-Necked Ducks	9.25
MO12	'90 $5 Redheads	8.25
MO13	'91 $5 Snow Geese	8.25
MO14	'92 $5 Gadwalls	8.25
MO15	'93 $5 Green-Winged Teal	8.25
MO16	'94 $5 White-Fronted Goose	8.25
MO17	'95 $5 Goldeneyes	8.25
MO18	'96 $5 Black Duck	8.25

MONTANA

NO.	DESCRIPTION	F-VF NH
MT34	'86 $5 Canada Geese	17.50
MT35	'87 $5 Redheads	18.00
MT36	'88 $5 Mallards	14.50
MT37	'89 $5 Black Labrador Retriever & Pintail	10.00
MT38	'90 $5 Blue-Winged & CinnamonTeal	9.00
MT39	'91 $5 Snow Geese	8.50
MT40	'92 $5 Wood Ducks	8.50
MT41	'93 $5 Harlequin Ducks	9.00
MT42	'94 $5 Widgeons	9.00
MT43	'95 $5 Tundra Swans	9.00
MT44	'96 $5 Canvasbacks	9.00
MT45	'97 $5 Golden Retriever	11.00
MT46	'98 $5 Gadwalls	9.00
MT47	'99 $5 Barrow's Goldeneye	9.00
MT48	'00 $5 Mallard decoy, Chesapeake retriever	9.00
MT49	'01 $5 Canada Geese, Steamboat	9.00
MT50	'02 ($5) Sandhill crane	9.00
MT51	'03 $5 Mallards	9.00

State Duck Stamps #NE1-OH22

NO.	DESCRIPTION	F-VF NH

NEBRASKA
NO.	DESCRIPTION	F-VF NH
NE1	'91 $6 Canada Geese	11.50
NE2	'92 $6 Pintails	9.25
NE3	'93 $6 Canvasbacks	9.25
NE4	'94 $6 Mallards	9.25
NE5	'95 $6 Wood Ducks	9.25

NEVADA
NO.	DESCRIPTION	F-VF NH
NV1	'79 $2 Canvasbacks & Decoy	55.00
NV2	'80 $2 Cinnamon Teal	10.00
NV3	'81 $2 Whistling Swans	10.00
NV4	'82 $2 Shovelers	10.00
NV5	'83 $2 Gadwalls	12.50
NV6	'84 $2 Pintails	12.50
NV7	'85 $2 Canada Geese	17.50
NV8	'86 $2 Redheads	16.00
NV9	'87 $2 Buffleheads	12.50
NV10	'88 $2 Canvasbacks	12.50
NV11	'89 $2 Ross's Geese	8.25
NV12	'90 $5 Green-Winged Teal	9.25
NV13	'91 $5 White-Faced Ibis	20.00
NV14	'92 $5 American Widgeon	9.00
NV15	'93 $5 Common Goldeneye	9.00
NV16	'94 $5 Mallards	9.00
NV17	'95 $5 Wood Duck	9.00
NV18	'96 $5 Ring Necked Duck	9.00
NV19	'97 $5 Ruddy Duck	9.00
NV20	'98 $5 Hooded Merganser	9.00
NV21	'99 $5 Canvasback Decoy	9.00
NV22	'00 $5 Canvasbacks	9.00
NV23	'01 $5 Lesser Scaup	9.00
NV24	'02 $5 Cinnamon teal	9.00
NV25	'03 $5 Green-winged Teal	9.00

NEW HAMPSHIRE
NO.	DESCRIPTION	F-VF NH
NH1	'83 $4 Wood Ducks	150.00
NH2	'84 $4 Mallards	110.00
NH3	'85 $4 Blue-Winged Teal	110.00
NH4	'86 $4 Hooded Mergansers	25.00
NH5	'87 $4 Canada Geese	17.50
NH6	'88 $4 Buffleheads	10.00
NH7	'89 $4 Black Ducks	8.50
NH8	'90 $4 Green-Winged Teal	8.25
NH9	'91 $4 Golden Retriever & Mallards	10.50
NH10	'92 $4 Ring-Necked Ducks	8.25
NH11	'93 $4 Hooded Mergansers	8.25
NH12	'94 $4 Common Goldeneyes	8.25
NH13	'95 $4 Northern Pintails	8.25
NH14	'96 $4 Surf Scoters	8.25
NH15	'97 $4 Old Squaws	8.25
NH16	'98 $4 Canada Goose	8.25
NH17	'99 $4 Mallards	8.25
NH18	'00 $4 Black Ducks	8.25
NH19	'01 $4 Blue-winged Teal	8.25
NH20	'02 $4 Pintails	8.25
NH21	'03 $4 Wood Ducks	8.25

NEW JERSEY
NO.	DESCRIPTION	F-VF NH
NJ1	'84 $2.50 Canvasbacks	50.00
NJ2	'84 $5 Canvasbacks	60.00
NJ3	'85 $2.50 Mallards	18.00
NJ4	'85 $5 Mallards	20.00
NJ5	'86 $2.50 Pintails	12.50
NJ6	'86 $5 Pintails	16.00
NJ7	'87 $2.50 Canada Geese	12.50
NJ8	'87 $5 Canada Geese	12.50
NJ9	'88 $2.50 Green-Winged Teal	9.00
NJ10	'88 $5 Green-Winged Teal	10.00
NJ11	'89 $2.50 Snow Geese	6.50
NJ12	'89 $5 Snow Geese	10.50
NJ13	'90 $2.50 Wood Ducks	6.50
NJ14	'90 $5 Wood Ducks	10.00
NJ17	'91 $2.50 Atlantic Brant	6.50
NJ18	'91 $5 Atlantic Brant	10.00
NJ19	'92 $2.50 Bluebills	6.50
NJ20	'92 $5 Bluebills	9.00
NJ21	'93 $2.50 Buffleheads	6.50
NJ22	'93 $5 Buffleheads	9.00
NJ23	'94 $2.50 Black Ducks	6.50
NJ24	'94 $5 Black Ducks	9.00
NJ25	'95 $2.50 Widgeon, Lighthouse	6.50
NJ26	'95 $5 Widgeon, Lighthouse	9.00
NJ27	'96 $2.50 Goldeneyes	8.50
NJ28	'96 $5 Goldeneyes	16.00
NJ29	'97 $5 Oldsquaws	9.00
NJ30	'97 $10 Oldsquaws	16.00
NJ31	'98 $5 Mallards	9.00
NJ32	'98 $10.00 Mallards	16.00
NJ33	'99 $5 Redheads	9.00
NJ34	'99 $10 Redheads	16.00
NJ35	'00 $5 Canvasbacks	9.00
NJ36	'00 $10 Canvasbacks	16.00
NJ37	'01 $5 Tundra Swans	9.00
NJ38	'01 $10 Tundra Swans	16.00
NJ39	'02 $5 Wood Ducks	9.00
NJ40	'02 $10 Wood Ducks	16.00
NJ41	'03 $5 Pintails & Black Lab	9.00
NJ42	'03 $10 Pintails & Black Lab	16.00

NEW MEXICO
NO.	DESCRIPTION	F-VF NH
NM1	'91 $7.50 Pintails	11.50
NM2	'92 $7.50 American Widgeon	11.50
NM3	'93 $7.50 Mallard	11.50
NM4	'94 $7.50 Green-Winged Teal	11.50

NEW YORK
NO.	DESCRIPTION	F-VF NH
NY1	'85 $5.50 Canada Geese	16.00
NY2	'86 $5.50 Mallards	12.00
NY3	'87 $5.50 Wood Ducks	10.00
NY4	'88 $5.50 Pintails	9.50
NY5	'89 $5.50 Greater Scaup	9.50
NY6	'90 $5.50 Canvasbacks	9.00
NY7	'91 $5.50 Redheads	9.00
NY8	'92 $5.50 Wood Ducks	9.00
NY9	'93 $5.50 Blue-Winged Teal	9.00
NY10	'94 $5.50 Canada Geese	9.00
NY11	'95 $5.50 Common Goldeneye	9.00
NY12	'96 $5.50 Common Loon	9.00
NY13	'97 $5.50 Hooded Merganser	9.00
NY14	'98 $5.50 Osprey	9.00
NY15	'99 $5.50 Buffleheads	9.00
NY16	'00 $5.50 Wood Ducks	9.00
NY17	'01 $5.50 Pintails	9.00
NY18	'02 $5.50 Canvasbacks	9.00

NORTH CAROLINA
NO.	DESCRIPTION	F-VF NH
NC1	'83 $5.50 Mallards	85.00
NC2	'84 $5.50 Wood Ducks	55.00
NC3	'85 $5.50 Canvasbacks	35.00
NC4	'86 $5.50 Canada Geese	18.50
NC5	'87 $5.50 Pintails	16.00
NC6	'88 $5.50 Green-Winged Teal	10.50
NC7	'89 $5 Snow Geese	10.50
NC8	'90 $5 Redheads	10.50
NC9	'91 $5 Blue-Winged Teal	9.00
NC10	'92 $5 American Widgeon	9.00
NC11	'93 $5 Tundra Swans	9.00
NC12	'94 $5 Buffleheads	9.00
NC13	'95 $5 Brant, Lighthouse	9.00
NC14	'96 $5 Pintails	9.00
NC15	'97 $5 Wood Ducks	9.00
NC16	'97 $5 Wood Ducks, self-adhesive	9.00
NC17	'98 $5 Canada Geese	9.00
NC18	'98 $5 Canada Geese, self-adhesive	9.00
NC19	'99 $5 Green-winged Teal	9.00
NC20	'99 $5 Green-winged Teal, self-adhesive	9.00
NC21	'00 $10 Green-winged Teal	16.00
NC22	'00 $10 Green-winged Teal, self-adhesive	16.00
NC23	'01 $10 Black Duck, lighthouse	16.00
NC24	'01 $10 Black Duck, lighthouse, self-adhesive	16.00
NC25	'02 $10 Pintails, Hunters, Dog	16.00
NC26	'02 $10 Pintails, Hunters, Dog, self-adhesive	16.00
NC27	'03 $10 Ringneck & Brittney Spaniel	16.00
NC28	'03 $10 Ringneck & Brittney Spaniel, self-adhesive	16.00

NORTH DAKOTA
NO.	DESCRIPTION	F-VF NH
ND32	'82 $9 Canada Geese	150.00
ND35	'83 $9 Mallards	80.00
ND38	'84 $9 Canvasbacks	37.50
ND41	'85 $9 Bluebills	25.00
ND44	'86 $9 Pintails	20.00
ND47	'87 $9 Snow Geese	22.00
ND50	'88 $9 White-Winged Scoters	15.00
ND53	'89 $6 Redheads	12.50
ND56	'90 $6 Labrador Retriever & Mallard	12.50
ND59	'91 $6 Green-Winged Teal	12.00
ND62	'92 $6 Blue-Winged Teal	9.50
ND65	'93 $6 Wood Ducks	9.50
ND67	'94 $6 Canada Geese	9.50
ND69	'95 $6 Widgeon	9.50
ND71	'96 $6 Mallards	9.50
ND73	'97 $6 White Fronted Geese	9.50
ND75	'98 $6 Blue Winged Teal	9.50
ND77	'99 $6 Gadwalls	9.50
ND79	'00 $6 Pintails	9.50
ND81	'01 $6 Canada Geese	9.50
ND82	'02 $6	9.50
ND83	'03 $6 Text, black on green	9.50
ND84	'03 $6 Text, black on green	9.50

OHIO
NO.	DESCRIPTION	F-VF NH
OH1	'82 $5.75 Wood Ducks	85.00
OH2	'83 $5.75 Mallards	85.00
OH3	'84 $5.75 Green-Winged Teal	75.00
OH4	'85 $5.75 Redheads	50.00
OH5	'86 $5.75 Canvasback	32.50
OH6	'87 $6 Blue-Winged Teal	15.00
OH7	'88 $6 Common Goldeneyes	12.50
OH8	'89 $6 Canada Geese	12.50
OH9	'90 $9 Black Ducks	15.00
OH10	'91 $9 Lesser Scaup	15.00
OH11	'92 $9 Wood Duck	14.00
OH12	'93 $9 Buffleheads	14.00
OH13	'94 $11 Mallards	16.50
OH14	'95 $11 Pintails	16.50
OH15	'96 $11 Hooded Mergansers	16.50
OH16	'97 $11 Widgeons	16.50
OH17	'98 $11 Gadwall	16.50
OH18	'99 $11 Mallard	16.50
OH19	'00 $11 Buffleheads	16.50
OH20	'01 $11 Canvasback	16.50
OH21	'02 $11 Ring Neck	16.50
OH22	'03 $11 Hooded Merganser	16.50

State Duck Stamps #OK1-UT12

NO.	DESCRIPTION	F-VF NH

OKLAHOMA
OK1	'80 $4 Pintails	70.00
OK2	'81 $4 Canada Goose	27.50
OK3	'82 $4 Green-Winged Teal	12.00
OK4	'83 $4 Wood Ducks	12.00
OK5	'84 $4 Ring-Necked Ducks	9.50
OK6	'85 $4 Mallards	8.00
OK7	'86 $4 Snow Geese	8.00
OK8	'87 $4 Canvasbacks	8.00
OK9	'88 $4 Widgeons	8.00
OK10	'89 $4 Redheads	8.00
OK11	'90 $4 Hooded Merganser	8.00
OK12	'91 $4 Gadwalls	7.50
OK13	'92 $4 Lesser Scaup	7.50
OK14	'93 $4 White-Fronted Geese	7.50
OK15	'94 $4 Blue-Winged Teal	7.50
OK16	'95 $4 Ruddy Ducks	7.50
OK17	'96 $4 Buffleheads	7.50
OK18	'97 $4 Goldeneyes	7.50
OK19	'98 $4 Shoveler	7.50
OK20	'99 $4 Canvasbacks	7.50
OK21	'00 $4 Pintails	7.50
OK22	'01 $4 Canada Goose	7.50
OK23	'02 $4 Green-winged Teal	7.50
OK24	'03 $10 Wood Duck	14.00

OREGON
OR1	'84 $5 Canada Geese	35.00
OR2	'85 $5 Lesser Snow Goose	45.00
OR3	'86 $5 Pacific Brant	17.50
OR4	'87 $5 White-Fronted Geese	12.00
OR5	'88 $5 Great Basin Canada Geese	10.00
OR7	'89 $5 Black Labrador Retriever & Pintails	10.00
OR8	'90 $5 Mallards & Golden Retriever	12.50
OR9	'91 $5 Buffleheads & Chesapeake Bay Retriever	11.00
OR10	'92 $5 Green-Winged Teal	11.00
OR11	'93 $5 Mallards	11.00
OR12	'94 $5 Pintails	11.00
OR14	'95 $5 Wood Ducks	11.00
OR16	'96 $5 Mallard/Widgeon/Pintail	11.00
OR18	'97 $5 Canvasbacks	11.00
OR20	'98 $5 Pintail	11.00
OR22	'99 $5 Canada Geese	11.00
OR24	'00 $7.50 Canada Geese, Mallard, Widgeon	13.50
OR25	'01 $7.50 Canvasbacks	13.50
OR26	'02 $7.50 American Wigeon	13.50
OR27	'03 $7.50 Wood Duck	13.50

PENNSYLVANIA
PA1	'83 $5.50 Wood Ducks	25.00
PA2	'84 $5.50 Canada Geese	22.50
PA3	'85 $5.50 Mallards	12.00
PA4	'86 $5.50 Blue-Winged Teal	10.00
PA5	'87 $5.50 Pintails	10.00
PA6	'88 $5.50 Wood Ducks	10.00
PA7	'89 $5.50 Hooded Mergansers	9.50
PA8	'90 $5.50 Canvasbacks	9.50
PA9	'91 $5.50 Widgeons	9.50
PA10	'92 $5.50 Canada Geese	9.50
PA11	'93 $5.50 Northern Shovelers	9.00
PA12	'94 $5.50 Pintails	9.00
PA13	'95 $5.50 Buffleheads	9.00
PA14	'96 $5.50 Black Ducks	9.00
PA15	'97 $5.50 Hooded Merganser	9.00
PA16	'98 $5.50 Wood Duck	9.00
PA17	'99 $5.50 Ring-necked Ducks	9.00
PA18	'00 $5.50 Green-Winged Teal	9.00
PA19	'01 $5.50 Pintails	9.00
PA20	'02 $5.50 Snow Geese	9.00
PA21	'03 $5.50 Canvasbacks	9.00

RHODE ISLAND
RI1	'89 $7.50 Canvasbacks	12.50
RI2	'90 $7.50 Canada Geese	12.00
RI3	'91 $7.50 Wood Ducks & Labrador Retriever	14.00
RI4	'92 $7.50 Blue-Winged Teal	12.50
RI5	'93 $7.50 Pintails	11.50
RI6	'94 $7.50 Wood Ducks	11.50
RI7	'95 $7.50 Hooded Mergansers	11.50
RI8	'96 $7.50 Harlequin	11.50
RI9	'97 $7.50 Black Ducks	11.50
RI10	'98 $7.50 Black Ducks	11.50
RI11	'99 $7.50 Common Eiders	11.50
RI12	'00 $7.50 Canvasbacks	11.50
RI13	'01 $7.50 Canvasbacks, Mallard, Lighthouse	11.50
RI14	'02 $7.50 White-winged Scoter	11.50
RI15	'03 $7.50 Oldsquaw	11.50

SOUTH CAROLINA
SC1	'81 $5.50 Wood Ducks	75.00
SC2	'82 $5.50 Mallards	110.00
SC3	'83 $5.50 Pintails	110.00
SC4	'84 $5.50 Canada Geese	70.00
SC5	'85 $5.50 Green-Winged Teal	65.00
SC6	'86 $5.50 Canvasbacks	30.00
SC7	'87 $5.50 Black Ducks	20.00
SC8	'88 $5.50 Widgeon & Spaniel	25.00
SC9	'89 $5.50 Blue-Winged Teal	15.00
SC10	'90 $5.50 Wood Ducks	10.00
SC11	'91 $5.50 Labrador Retriever, Pintails & Decoy	9.00
SC12	'92 $5.50 Buffleheads	9.50
SC13	'93 $5.50 Lesser Scaup	9.00
SC14	'94 $5.50 Canvasbacks	9.00
SC15	'95 $5.50 Shovelers, Lighthouse	9.00
SC16	'96 $5.50 Redheads, Lighthouse	9.00
SC17	'97 $5.50 Old Squaws	9.00
SC18	'98 $5.50 Ruddy Ducks	9.00
SC19	'99 $5.50 Barrow's goldeneye	9.00
SC20	'00 $5.50 Wood Ducks, boykin spaniel	9.00
SC21	'01 $5.50 Mallard, yellow labrador,decoy	9.00
SC22	'02 $5.50 Widgeon, Chocolate Labrador	9.00
SC23	'03 $5.50 Green-winged Teal	9.00

SOUTH DAKOTA
SD3	'76 $1 Mallards	35.00
SD4	'77 $1 Pintails	24.50
SD5	'78 $1 Canvasbacks	15.00
SD6	'86 $2 Canada Geese	12.00
SD7	'87 $2 Blue Geese	8.00
SD8	'88 $2 White-Fronted Geese	6.00
SD9	'89 $2 Mallards	6.00
SD10	'90 $2 Blue-Winged Teal	5.50
SD11	'91 $2 Pintails	5.50
SD12	'92 $2 Canvasbacks	5.50
SD13	'93 $2 Lesser Scaup	5.50
SD14	'94 $2 Redheads	5.50
SD15	'95 $2 Wood Ducks	5.50
SD16	'96 $2 Canada Goose	5.50
SD17	'97 $2 Widgeons	5.50
SD18	'98 $2 Green Winged Teal	5.50
SD19	'99 $2 Tundra Swam	5.50
SD20	'00 $3 Buffleheads	8.00
SD21	'01 $3 Mallards	8.00
SD22	'02 $3 Canvasbacks	8.00
SD23	'03 $3 Pintail	8.00

TENNESSEE
TN1	'79 $2.30 Mallards	175.00
TN2	'79 $5 Mallards, Non-Resident	1,200.00
TN3	'80 $2.30 Canvasbacks	65.00
TN4	'80 $5 Canvasbacks, Non-Resident	525.00
TN5	'81 $2.30 Wood Ducks	50.00
TN6	'82 $6.50 Canada Geese	65.00
TN7	'83 $6.50 Pintails	60.00
TN8	'84 $6.50 Black Ducks	70.00
TN9	'85 $6.50 Blue-Winged Teal	25.00
TN10	'86 $6.50 Mallard	15.00
TN11	'87 $6.50 Canada Geese	15.00
TN12	'88 $6.50 Canvasbacks	15.00
TN13	'89 $6.50 Green-Winged Teal	12.50
TN14	'90 $13 Redheads	19.00
TN15	'91 $13 Mergansers	19.00
TN16	'92 $14 Wood Ducks	19.00
TN17	'93 $14 Pintails & Decoy	19.00
TN18	'94 $16 Mallard	22.50
TN19	'95 $16 Ring-Necked Duck	22.50
TN20	'96 $18 Black Ducks	25.00
TN21	'99 $10 Mallard	18.00
TN22	'00 $10 Bufflehead	18.00
TN23	'01 $10 Wood Ducks	18.00
TN24	'02 $10 Green-winged Teal	18.00
TN25	'03 $10 Canada Geese	18.00

TEXAS
TX1	'81 $5 Mallards	55.00
TX2	'82 $5 Pintails	40.00
TX3	'83 $5 Widgeons	190.00
TX4	'84 $5 Wood Ducks	35.00
TX5	'85 $5 Snow Geese	15.00
TX6	'86 $5 Green-Winged Teal	12.00
TX7	'87 $5 White-Fronted Geese	9.00
TX8	'88 $5 Pintails	9.00
TX9	'89 $5 Mallards	9.00
TX10	'90 $5 American Widgeons	9.00
TX11	'91 $7 Wood Duck	10.00
TX12	'92 $7 Canada Geese	10.00
TX13	'93 $7 Blue-Winged Teal	9.50
TX14	'94 $7 Shovelers	9.50
TX15	'95 $7 Buffleheads	9.50
TX16	'96 $3 Gadwalls	12.00
TX17	'97 $3 Cinnamon Teal	12.00
TX18	'98 $3 Pintail, Labrador Retriever	12.00
TX19	'99 $3 Canvasbacks	12.00
TX20	'00 $3 Hooded Merganser	12.00
TX21	'01 $3 Snow Goose	14.00
TX22	'02 $3 Redheads	14.00
TX23	'03 $3 Mottled Duck	14.00

UTAH
UT1	'86 $3.30 Whistling Swans	10.00
UT2	'87 $3.30 Pintails	8.50
UT3	'88 $3.30 Mallards	8.50
UT4	'89 $3.30 Canada Geese	7.50
UT5	'90 $3.30 Canvasbacks	7.50
UT6	'91 $3.30 Tundra Swans	7.50
UT7	'92 $3.30 Pintails	7.50
UT8	'93 $3.30 Canvasbacks	7.50
UT9	'94 $3.30 Chesapeake Retriever & Ducks	7.50
UT10	'95 $3.30 Green-Winged Teal	7.50
UT11	'96 $7.50 White-Fronted Goose	14.50
UT12	'97 $7.50 Redheads, pair	23.00

State Duck Stamps #VT1-WY20

NO.	DESCRIPTION	F-VF NH

VT1

VERMONT
NO.	DESCRIPTION	F-VF NH
VT1	'86 $5 Wood Ducks	14.00
VT2	'87 $5 Common Goldeneyes	10.00
VT3	'88 $5 Black Ducks	10.00
VT4	'89 $5 Canada Geese	9.50
VT5	'90 $5 Green-Winged Teal	9.50
VT6	'91 $5 Hooded Mergansers	9.50
VT7	'92 $5 Snow Geese	9.50
VT8	'93 $5 Mallards	9.50
VT9	'94 $5 Ring-Necked Duck	8.50
VT10	'95 $5 Bufflehead	8.50
VT11	'96 $5 Bluebills	8.50
VT12	'97 $5 Pintail	8.50
VT13	'98 $5 Blue-Winged Teal	8.50
VT14	'99 $5 Canvasbacks	8.50
VT15	'00 $5 Widgeons	8.50
VT16	'01 $5 Old Squaw	8.50
VT17	'02 $5 Greater Scaups	8.50
VT18	'03 $5 Mallard	8.50

VA1

VIRGINIA
NO.	DESCRIPTION	F-VF NH
VA1	'88 $5 Mallards	15.00
VA2	'89 $5 Canada Geese	18.00
VA3	'90 $5 Wood Ducks	9.50
VA4	'91 $5 Canvasbacks	9.50
VA5	'92 $5 Buffleheads	9.50
VA6	'93 $5 Black Ducks	9.00
VA7	'94 $5 Lesser Scaup	9.00
VA8	'95 $5 Snow Geese	9.00
VA9	'96 $5 Hooded Mergansers	9.00
VA10	'97 $5 Pintail, Labrador Retriever	9.00
VA11	'98 $5 Mallards	9.00
VA12	'99 $5 Green-winged Teal	9.00
VA13	'00 $5 Mallards	9.00
VA14	'01 $5 Blue-winged Teal	9.00
VA15	'02 $5 Canvasbacks	9.00
VA16	'03 $5 Mallard	9.00

WA1

WASHINGTON
NO.	DESCRIPTION	F-VF NH
WA1	'86 $5 Mallards	12.50
WA2	'87 $5 Canvasbacks	16.00
WA3	'88 $5 Harlequin	9.50
WA4	'89 $5 American Widgeons	9.50
WA5	'90 $5 Pintails & Sour Duck	9.50
WA6	'91 $5 Wood Duck	9.50
WA7	'92 $6 Labrador Puppy & Canada Geese	9.50
WA8	'93 $6 Snow Geese	9.50
WA9	'94 $6 Black Brant	9.50
WA10	'95 $6 Mallards	9.50
WA11	'96 $6 Redheads	9.50
WA12	'97 $6 Canada Geese	9.50
WA13	'98 $6 Goldeneye	9.50
WA14	'99 $6 Bufflehead	9.50
WA15	'00 $6 Canada Geese, Mallard, Widgeon	14.00
WA16	'01 $6 Mallards	14.00
WA17	'02 $10 Green-winged Teal	14.00
WA18	'03 $10 Pintail	14.00

WV1

WEST VIRGINIA
NO.	DESCRIPTION	F-VF NH
WV1	'87 $5 Canada Geese	15.00
WV2	'87 $5 Canada Geese, Non-Resident	15.00
WV3	'88 $5 Wood Ducks	12.00
WV4	'88 $5 Wood Ducks, Non-Resident	12.00
WV5	'89 $5 Decoys	13.00
WV6	'89 $5 Decoys, Non-Resident	13.00
WV7	'90 $5 Labrador Retriever & Decoy	12.50
WV8	'90 $5 Labrador Retriever & Decoy, Non-Resident	12.50
WV9	'91 $5 Mallards	10.00
WV10	'91 $5 Mallards, Non-Resident	10.00
WV11	'92 $5 Canada Geese	10.00
WV12	'92 $5 Canada Geese, Non-Resident	10.00
WV13	'93 $5 Pintails	10.00
WV14	'93 $5 Pintails, Non-Resident	10.00
WV15	'94 $5 Green-Winged Teal	10.00
WV16	'94 $5 Green-Winged Teal, Non-Resident	10.00
WV17	'95 $5 Mallards	10.00
WV18	'95 $5 Mallards, Non-Resident	10.00
WV19	'96 $5 American Widgeons	10.00
WV20	'96 $5 Widgeon, Non-Resident	10.00

WI3

WISCONSIN
NO.	DESCRIPTION	F-VF NH
WI1	'78 $3.25 Wood Ducks	125.00
WI2	'79 $3.25 Buffleheads	45.00
WI3	'80 $3.25 Widgeons	15.00
WI4	'81 $3.25 Lesser Scaup	11.00
WI5	'82 $3.25 Pintails	8.00
WI6	'83 $3.25 Blue-Winged Teal	9.00
WI7	'84 $3.25 Hooded Merganser	9.00
WI8	'85 $3.25 Lesser Scaup	11.00
WI9	'86 $3.25 Canvasbacks	11.00
WI10	'87 $3.25 Canada Geese	7.00
WI11	'88 $3.25 Hooded Merganser	7.00
WI12	'89 $3.25 Common Goldeneye	7.00
WI13	'90 $3.25 Redheads	7.00
WI14	'91 $5.25 Green-Winged Teal	9.00
WI15	'92 $5.25 Tundra Swans	9.00
WI16	'93 $5.25 Wood Ducks	9.00
WI17	'94 $5.25 Pintails	9.00
WI18	'95 $5.25 Mallards	9.00
WI19	'96 $5.25 Green-Winged Teal	9.00
WI20	'97 $7 Canada Geese	9.00
WI21	'98 $7 Snow Geese	9.00
WI22	'99 $7 Greater Scaups	11.00
WI23	'00 $7 Canvasbacks	11.00
WI24	'01 $7 Common Goldeneye	11.00
WI25	'02 $7 Shovelers	11.00
WI26	'03 $7 Canvasbacks	11.00

WY10

WYOMING
NO.	DESCRIPTION	F-VF NH
WY1	'84 $5 Meadowlark	45.00
WY2	'85 $5 Canada Geese	45.00
WY3	'86 $5 Antelope	45.00
WY4	'87 $5 Grouse	45.00
WY5	'88 $5 Fish	45.00
WY6	'89 $5 Deer	45.00
WY7	'90 $5 Bear	45.00
WY8	'91 $5 Rams	45.00
WY9	'92 $5 Bald Eagle	25.00
WY10	'93 $5 Elk	20.00
WY11	'94 $5 Bobcat	16.00
WY12	'95 $5 Moose	10.50
WY13	'96 $5 Turkey	10.50
WY14	'97 $5 Rocky Mountain Goats	10.50
WY15	'98 $5 Thunder Swans	10.50
WY16	'99 $5 Brown Trout	10.50
WY17	'00 $5 Buffalo	10.50
WY18	'01 $10 Whitetailed Deer	15.00
WY19	'02 $10 River Otters	20.00
WY20	'03 $10 Mountain Bluebird	17.00

Customize Your Harris Album with Blank Pages for U.S. and Worldwide

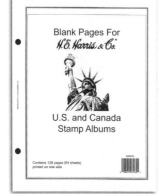

Speed-rille® Album Pages—Faint guide lines help you make neat, attractive arrangements without a lot of measuring. Use them to expand your Harris album or create your own speciality pages. 128 pages (64 sheets) in each package, printed on both sides with borders to match your U.S. or Worldwide Album.

#3HRS17 Speed-rille® Pages for Worldwide **$7.95**
#3HRS15 Speed-rille® Pages for U.S. and Canada **$7.95**

Blank Album Pages—Bordered blank pages to fit your loose-leaf worldwide albums. 128 pages (64 pages) printed on both sides in each package.

#3HRS18 Blank Pages for Worldwide **$7.95**
#3HRS16 Blank Pages for U.S. and Canada **$7.95**

CANAL ZONE

SCOTT NO.	DESCRIPTION	UNUSED NH F	AVG	UNUSED OG F	AVG	USED F	AVG

CANAL ZONE

PANAMA
1904
U.S. Stamp 300, 319, 304, 306-07 overprinted

Scott	Description	NH F	NH AVG	OG F	OG AVG	Used F	Used AVG
4	1¢ blue green	38.00	22.50	25.00	15.00	25.00	15.00
5	2¢ carmine	38.50	23.00	22.00	11.00	20.00	12.00
6	5¢ blue	125.00	75.00	80.00	55.00	65.00	40.00
7	8¢ violet black	205.00	125.00	125.00	70.00	95.00	60.00
8	10¢ pale red brown	225.00	135.00	140.00	80.00	100.00	60.00

CANAL ZONE
1924-25
U.S. Stamps 551-54, 557, 562, 564-66, 569-71 overprinted

Type 1 Flat Tops on Letters "A". Perf. 11

Scott	Description	NH F	NH AVG	OG F	OG AVG	Used F	Used AVG
70	1/2¢ olive brown	1.20	.75	.70	.45	.75	.45
71	1¢ deep green	2.25	1.35	1.50	.95	.50	.30
71e	same, bklt pane of 6	170.00	105.00	130.00	80.00		
72	1-1/2¢ yellow brown	3.00	1.75	2.10	1.10	1.25	.80
73	2¢ carmine	12.00	7.25	8.00	5.50	1.75	1.00
73a	same, bklt pane of 6	210.00	125.00	150.00	90.00		
74	5¢ dark blue	30.00	17.50	21.00	12.50	9.00	5.50
75	10¢ orange	62.00	37.00	40.00	25.00	19.00	11.50
76	12¢ brown violet	55.00	33.00	35.00	22.00	27.00	19.50
77	14¢ dark blue	33.50	19.50	22.00	12.00	17.00	10.00
78	15¢ gray	72.00	43.00	50.00	30.00	33.00	22.00
79	30¢ olive brown	45.00	27.00	33.00	20.00	28.00	16.50
80	50¢ lilac	95.00	57.00	65.00	35.00	42.00	25.00
81	$1 violet brown	335.00	200.00	225.00	135.00	125.00	80.00

CANAL ZONE
1925-28
U.S. Stamps 554-55, 557, 564-66, 623, 567, 569-71, overprinted

Type II Pointed Tops on Letters "A"

Scott	Description	NH F	NH AVG	OG F	OG AVG	Used F	Used AVG
84	2¢ carmine	45.00	27.00	30.00	20.00	10.00	6.00
84d	same, bklt pane of 6	300.00	175.00	220.00	140.00		
85	3¢ violet	6.25	3.75	4.50	2.75	2.75	1.75
86	5¢ dark blue	6.00	3.50	4.00	2.50	2.75	1.75
87	10¢ orange	50.00	30.00	35.00	22.00	10.00	6.00
88	12¢ brown violet	36.50	22.50	25.00	16.50	14.00	9.00
89	14¢ dark blue	32.00	19.25	22.00	14.50	18.00	11.00
90	15¢ gray	10.00	6.00	7.00	4.50	3.35	2.00
91	17¢ black	6.00	3.50	4.25	2.50	3.00	1.95
92	20¢ carmine rose	10.00	6.00	7.00	4.50	4.50	2.65
93	30¢ olive brown	8.50	5.50	6.00	3.75	4.00	2.50
94	50¢ lilac	335.00	200.00	230.00	165.00	140.00	82.50
95	$1 violet brown	150.00	90.00	105.00	72.50	50.00	31.50

1926
Type II overprint on U.S. Stamp 627

Scott	Description	NH F	NH AVG	OG F	OG AVG	Used F	Used AVG
96	2¢ carmine rose	6.75	4.00	4.50	2.60	3.75	2.30

1927
Type II overprint on U.S. Stamp 583-84, 591
Rotary Press Printing, Perf. 10

Scott	Description	NH F	NH AVG	OG F	OG AVG	Used F	Used AVG
97	2¢ carmine	67.50	40.00	45.00	22.00	10.50	6.00
98	3¢ violet	12.50	7.50	9.00	5.25	5.00	3.00
99	10¢ orange	21.50	12.95	15.00	9.25	6.75	4.00

SCOTT NO.	DESCRIPTION	PLATE BLOCK F/NH	F	AVG	UNUSED F/NH	F	AVG	USED F	AVG
100	1¢ green	25.00	20.00	16.00	2.65	1.95	1.15	1.30	.80
101	2¢ carmine	30.00	24.50	19.00	2.75	2.00	1.20	.90	.55
101a	same, bklt pane of 6				275.00	210.00	135.00		
102	3¢ violet (1931)	110.00	85.00	68.00	6.50	4.50	2.25	3.50	2.25
103	5¢ dark blue	185.00	155.00	125.00	30.00	22.00	11.00	11.00	7.25
104	10¢ orange (1930)	225.00	180.00	145.00	25.00	17.00	11.00	12.00	8.00

VERY FINE QUALITY: To determine the Very Fine price, add the difference between the Fine and Average prices to the Fine quality price. For example: if the Fine price is $10.00 and the Average price is $6.00, the Very Fine price would be $14.00. From 1935 to date, add 20% to the Fine price to arrive at the Very Fine price.

1928-40 Builders Issue

Scott	Description	Plate Block F/NH	F	AVG	Unused F/NH	F	AVG	Used F	AVG
105-14	1¢-50¢ complete, 10 varieties				10.40	8.05	4.95	5.70	3.45
105	1¢ Gorgas	1.15(6)	.80	.50	.30	.25	.20	.20	.15
106	2¢ Goethals	3.00(6)	2.25	1.30	.30	.25	.20	.20	.15
106a	same, bklt pane of 6				18.00	13.00	8.50		
107	5¢ Gaillard Cut (1929)	17.00(6)	10.00	6.50	1.70	1.35	.85	.80	.45
108	10¢ Hodges (1932)	8.00(6)	6.00	3.50	.40	.30	.20	.25	.15
109	12¢ Gaillard (1929)	14.50(6)	11.00	6.50	1.35	1.05	.60	.85	.50
110	14¢ Sibert (1937)	11.50(6)	12.50	7.50	1.40	1.10	.70	1.10	.70
111	15¢ Smith (1932)	10.00(6)	6.50	4.00	.65	.50	.30	.50	.30
112	20¢ Rousseau (1932)	11.00(6)	7.50	4.50	.95	.75	.45	.30	.20
113	30¢ Williamson (1940)	13.50(6)	10.00	6.00	1.30	1.00	.60	.95	.55
114	50¢ Blackburn (1929)	22.00(6)	16.00	9.50	2.60	1.95	1.10	.85	.50

1933
Type II overprint on U.S. Stamps 720 & 695
Rotary Press Printing, Perf. 11 x 10-1/2

Scott	Description	Plate Block F/NH	F	AVG	Unused F/NH	F	AVG	Used F	AVG
115	3¢ Washington	37.50	27.00	16.00	4.00	2.75	1.95	.35	.25
116	14¢ Indian	72.50	50.00	36.00	8.00	6.00	4.00	3.35	2.00

1934

Scott	Description	Plate Block F/NH	F	AVG	Unused F/NH	F	AVG	Used F	AVG
117	3¢ Goethals	2.00(6)	1.50	1.00	.30	.25	.20	.20	.15
117a	same, bklt pane of 6				70.00	52.00	35.00		

SCOTT NO.	DESCRIPTION	PLATE BLOCK F/NH	F/OG	UNUSED F/NH	F/OG	USED F

1939 U.S. Stamps 803, 805 overprint

| 118 | 1/2¢ red orange | 2.75 | 2.25 | .30 | .25 | .15 |
| 119 | 1-1/2¢ bistre brown | 2.75 | 2.25 | .30 | .25 | .15 |

FOR CONVENIENCE IN ORDERING, COMPLETE SETS ARE LISTED BEFORE SINGLE STAMP LISTINGS.

Canal Zone #120-157a

SCOTT NO.	DESCRIPTION	PLATE BLOCK F/NH	PLATE BLOCK F/OG	UNUSED F/NH	UNUSED F/OG	USED F

120
Balboa—Before

121
Balboa—After

122	Gaillard Cut—Before			123	After	
124	Bas Obispo—Before			125	After	
126	Gatun Locks—Before			127	After	
128	Canal Channel—Before			129	After	
130	Gamboa—Before			131	After	
132	Pedro Miguel Locks—Before			133	After	
134	Gatun Spillway—Before			135	After	

1939 25th ANNIVERSARY ISSUE

SCOTT	DESCRIPTION	PB F/NH	PB F/OG	Un F/NH	Un F/OG	Used F
120-35	1¢-50¢ complete, 16 varieties	....	....	117.50	82.50	60.00
120	1¢ yellow green	11.00(6)	9.00	.50	.40	.40
121	2¢ rose carmine	12.00(6)	10.00	.60	.50	.50
122	3¢ purple	11.00(6)	9.00	.50	.40	.25
123	5¢ dark blue	20.00(6)	16.00	1.20	.90	.85
124	6¢ red orange	38.50(6)	33.00	2.75	1.95	1.95
125	7¢ black	38.50(6)	33.00	2.75	1.95	1.95
126	8¢ green	50.00(6)	41.00	4.00	2.75	3.00
127	10¢ ultramarine	50.00(6)	41.00	4.00	2.75	2.25
128	11¢ blue hreen	120.00(6)	100.00	9.00	6.75	7.00
129	12¢ brown carmine	100.00(6)	75.00	7.25	5.25	6.00
130	14¢ dark violet	110.00(6)	87.50	8.00	5.50	6.00
131	15¢ olive green	130.00(6)	110.00	12.00	8.00	4.75
132	18¢ rose pink	125.00(6)	105.00	11.00	7.25	8.00
133	20¢ brown	165.00(6)	130.00	14.00	10.50	4.00
134	25¢ orange	275.00(6)	220.00	20.00	15.00	11.50
135	50¢ violet brown	305.00(6)	240.00	26.50	19.50	4.75

136

137

138

139

140

1945-49

SCOTT	DESCRIPTION	PB F/NH	PB F/OG	Un F/NH	Un F/OG	Used F
136-40	1/2¢-25¢ complete, 5 varieties	....	....	2.70	2.15	1.55
136	1/2¢ Major General Davis (1948)	3.00(6)	2.50	.40	.30	.25
137	1-1/2¢ Gov. Magoon (1948)	3.00(6)	2.50	.40	.30	.25
138	2¢ T. Roosevelt (1948)	.70(6)	.50	.25	.20	.15
139	5¢ Stevens	4.00(6)	2.75	.45	.40	.15
140	25¢ J.F. Wallace (1948)	13.50(6)	9.50	1.35	1.10	.85

141

1948 CANAL ZONE BIOLOGICAL AREA

141	10¢ Map & Coat-mundi	14.00(6)	10.00	1.60	1.30	1.10

142

143

144

145

1949 CALIFORNIA GOLD RUSH

SCOTT	DESCRIPTION	PB F/NH	PB F/OG	Un F/NH	Un F/OG	Used F
142-45	3¢-18¢ complete 4 varieties	....	....	6.55	4.85	4.50
142	3¢ "Forty Niners"	7.00(6)	5.00	.80	.65	.45
143	6¢ Journey–Las Cruces	8.25(6)	6.00	.85	.65	.60
144	12¢ Las Cruces–Panama Trail	19.50(6)	13.75	2.20	1.60	1.35
145	18¢ Departure–San Francisco	25.00(6)	21.00	3.05	2.20	2.35

146

147

148

149

150

1951-58

SCOTT	DESCRIPTION	PB F/NH	PB F/OG	Un F/NH	Un F/OG	Used F
146	10¢ West Indian Labor	33.50(6)	25.00	3.60	2.75	2.75
147	3¢ Panama R.R.(1955)	9.00(6)	6.50	.90	.80	.65
148	3¢ Gorgas Hospital (1957)	5.00	3.50	.60	.50	.45
149	4¢ S.S. Ancon (1958)	3.50	2.60	.55	.45	.40
150	4¢ T. Roosevelt (1958)	4.00	3.00	.60	.50	.45

151

152, 154

1960-62

151	4¢ Boy Scout Badge	5.00	3.75	.60	.50	.45
152	4¢ Adminstration Building	1.10	.80	.30	.25	.20

LINE PAIR

153	3¢ G.W. Goethals, coil	1.00	.85	.25	.20	.15
154	4¢ Adminstration Building, coil	1.25	1.05	.25	.20	.20
155	5¢ J.F. Stevens, coil (1962)	1.50	1.20	.35	.30	.20

156

157

PLATE BLOCK

156	4¢ Girl Scout Badge (1962)	3.00	2.20	.45	.40	.35
157	4¢ Thatcher Ferry Bridge (1962)	3.50	2.75	.40	.35	.30
157a	same, silver omitted (bridge)	....	....	85000.00	....	....

158

159

Canal Zone #158-165, #C1-C35

SCOTT NO.	DESCRIPTION	PLATE BLOCK F/NH	F/OG	UNUSED F/NH	F/OG	USED F
		1968-78				
158	6¢ Goethals Memorial	2.50	....	.40	....	.20
159	8¢ Fort San Lorenzo (1971)	3.00	....	.50	....	.25
		LINE PAIR				
160	1¢ W.C. Gorgas, coil (1975)	1.00	....	.20	....	.15
161	10¢ H.F. Hodges, coil (1975)	5.00	....	.80	....	.45
162	25¢ J.F. Wallace, coil (1975)	24.00	....	3.25	....	2.20

163

165

PLATE BLOCK

SCOTT NO.	DESCRIPTION	PLATE BLOCK F/NH	F/OG	UNUSED F/NH	F/OG	USED F
163	13¢ Cascades Dredge (1976)	2.50	....	.50	....	.40
163a	same, bklt pane of 4	....	....	2.75	....	.45
164	5¢ J.F. Stevens (#139) Rotary Press (1977)	5.00	....	1.00	....	.40
165	15¢ Locomotive (1978)	2.20	....	.50	....	.45

SCOTT NO.	DESCRIPTION	PLATE BLOCK F/NH	F	AVG	UNUSED F/NH	F	AVG	USED F	AVG

AIR POST

AIR MAIL

105 & 106 Surcharged

25 CENTS 25

1929-31

C1	15¢ on 1¢ green, Type I	150.00(6)	120.00	85.00	13.50	8.00	5.00	6.25	4.00
C2	15¢ on 1¢ yellow green, Type II (1931)	....	....	....	135.00	100.00	55.00	90.00	55.00
C3	25¢ on 2¢ carmine	140.00	115.00	82.50	6.00	4.00	2.40	2.30	1.35

AIR MAIL

114 & 106 Surcharged

=10c

1929

| C4 | 10¢ on 50¢ lilac | 150.00(6) | 120.00 | 85.00 | 13.50 | 9.50 | 5.50 | 9.00 | 5.25 |
| C5 | 20¢ on 2¢ carmine | 125.00(6) | 100.00 | 70.00 | 9.50 | 6.00 | 3.95 | 2.00 | 1.20 |

C6-C14

1931-49

C6-14	4¢-$1 complete, 9 varieties	....	....	....	28.25	21.25	14.00	7.60	4.80
C6	4¢ Gaillard Cut, red violet (1949)	7.00(6)	5.00	3.35	1.10	.85	.55	.85	.55
C7	5¢ yellow green	5.50(6)	4.50	2.75	.75	.55	.40	.40	.25
C8	6¢ yellow brown (1946)	7.75(6)	5.50	3.35	1.10	.85	.55	.40	.25
C9	10¢ orange	12.50(6)	9.50	6.00	1.30	1.00	.65	.40	.25
C10	15¢ blue	13.50(6)	10.50	7.00	1.60	1.20	.80	.30	.20
C11	20¢ red violet	21.00(6)	16.00	11.00	2.85	2.20	1.40	.30	.20
C12	30¢ rose lake (1941)	40.00(6)	30.00	20.00	4.50	3.25	2.15	1.30	.80
C13	40¢ yellow	40.00(6)	30.00	20.00	4.50	3.50	2.30	1.30	.80
C14	$1 black	105.00(6)	82.50	55.00	12.00	9.00	6.00	2.75	1.75

C15

C16

C17

C18

C19

C20

1939 25th ANNIVERSARY ISSUE

SCOTT NO.	DESCRIPTION	PLATE BLOCK F/NH	F/OG	UNUSED F/NH	F/OG	USED F
C15-20	5¢-$1 complete, 6 varieties	....	....	74.00	54.25	48.00
C15	5¢ Plane over Sosa Hill	35.00(6)	27.00	4.25	3.00	3.00
C16	10¢ Map of Central America	40.00(6)	30.00	4.25	3.00	2.95
C17	15¢ Scene near Fort Amador	44.00(6)	35.00	4.40	3.25	1.30
C18	25¢ Clippper at Cristobal Harbor	170.00(6)	130.00	16.00	12.00	9.00
C19	39¢ Clipper over Gaillard Cut	125.00(6)	95.00	12.50	9.50	8.00
C20	$1 Clipper Alighhting	410.00(6)	300.00	36.50	26.50	26.50

C21-31, C34

1951

C21-26	4¢-80¢ complete, 6 varieties	....	....	29.25	23.25	13.00
C21	4¢ Globe & Wing, red violet	8.00(6)	6.00	1.00	.75	.50
C22	6¢ light brown	6.00(6)	4.50	1.00	.75	.40
C23	10¢ light red orange	10.50(6)	8.50	1.25	1.00	.50
C24	21¢ light blue	90.00(6)	70.00	10.00	8.00	5.00
C25	31¢ cerise	95.00(6)	70.00	10.00	8.00	5.00
C26	80¢ Light gray black	50.00(6)	38.00	7.50	6.00	2.25

1958

C27-31	5¢-35¢ complete, 5 varieties	....	....	28.50	22.90	9.65
C27	5¢ Globe & Wing, yellow green	8.00	5.50	1.40	1.10	.65
C28	7¢ olive	6.00	4.50	1.20	1.00	.65
C29	15¢ brown violet	33.50	26.50	5.50	4.50	2.40
C30	25¢ orange yellow	90.00	72.50	12.00	9.50	3.25
C31	35¢ dark blue	57.50	45.00	10.00	8.00	4.00

C32

C33

C35

1961-63

C32	15¢ Emblem Caribbean School	16.00	13.00	1.95	1.55	1.20
C33	7¢ Anti-Malaria (1962)	4.50	3.35	.80	.60	.55
C34	8¢ Globe & Wing carmine (1968)	6.00	5.00	.85	.65	.40
C35	15¢ Alliance for Progress (1963)	15.00	11.50	1.90	1.50	1.10

Canal Zone #C36-C53, CO1-CO14, J1-J29, O1-O9

SCOTT NO.	DESCRIPTION	PLATE BLOCK F/NH	PLATE BLOCK F/OG	UNUSED F/NH	UNUSED F/OG	USED F

1964 50th ANNIVERSARY ISSUE

(C36 6¢ Cristobal, C37 8¢ Gatun Locks, C38 15¢ Madden Dam, C39 20¢ Gaillard Cut, C40 30¢ Miraflores Locks, C41 80¢ Balboa)

Scott	Description	PB F/NH	PB F/OG	Unused F/NH	Unused F/OG	Used F
C36-41	6¢-80¢ complete 6 varieties	....	....	15.50	11.00	10.00
C36	6¢ Cristobal	3.35	2.75	.60	.45	.55
C37	8¢ Gatun Locks	4.00	3.25	.75	.55	.50
C38	15¢ Madden Dam	9.50	7.75	1.60	1.25	.85
C39	20¢ Gaillard Cut	12.50	10.00	2.50	1.75	1.20
C40	30¢ Miraflores Locks	20.00	16.00	4.00	2.75	3.00
C41	80¢ Balboa	35.00	28.00	7.00	4.95	4.50

C42-C53

1965

Scott	Description	PB F/NH	PB F/OG	Unused F/NH	Unused F/OG	Used F
C42-47	6¢-80¢ complete 6 varieties	....	....	6.95	....	3.60
C42	6¢ Gov. Seal, green & black	2.60	....	.45	....	.40
C43	8¢ rose red & black	3.00	....	.50	....	.20
C44	15¢ blue & black	3.35	....	.50	....	.40
C45	20¢ lilac & black	3.50	....	.90	....	.55
C46	30¢ reddish brown & black	6.00	....	1.20	....	.60
C47	80¢ bistre & balck	19.50	....	3.75	....	1.65

1968-76

Scott	Description	PB F/NH	PB F/OG	Unused F/NH	Unused F/OG	Used F
C48-53	10¢-35¢ complete 6 varieties	....	....	6.40	....	2.70
C48	10¢ Gov. Seal, dull orange & black	2.20	....	.45	....	.25
C48a	same, bklt pane of 4	....	....	4.50	....	....
C49	11¢ Seal, olive & black (1971)	2.75	....	.55	....	.30
C49a	same, bklt pane of 4	....	....	3.50	....	....
C50	13¢ Seal, emerald & black (1974)	6.00	....	1.20	....	.45
C50a	same, bklt pane of 4	....	....	6.00	....	....
C51	22¢ Seal, violet & black (1976)	6.50	....	1.30	....	.55
C52	25¢ Seal, pale yellow green & black	6.50	....	1.30	....	.55
C53	35¢ Seal, salmon & black (1976)	10.50	....	1.60	....	.75

AIR MAIL OFFICIAL STAMPS

C7-14 Overprinted **OFFICIAL PANAMA CANAL**

1941-42 Overprint 19 to 20-1/2 mm. long

Scott	Description	PB F/NH	PB F/OG	Unused F/NH	Unused F/OG	Used F
CO1-7	5¢-$1 complete 7 varieties	....	....	136.50	97.75	49.00
CO1	5¢ Gaillard Cut, yellow green (C7)	....	....	6.50	5.00	2.50
CO2	10¢ orange (C9)	....	....	12.00	9.50	3.15
CO3	15¢ blue (C10)	....	....	15.50	12.00	4.50
CO4	20¢ red violet (C11)	....	....	19.00	15.00	7.00
CO5	30¢ rose lake (1942) (C12)	....	....	23.00	17.50	7.00
CO6	40¢ yellow (C13)	....	....	27.50	20.00	11.00
CO7	$1 black (C14)	....	....	40.00	25.00	16.50

1947 Overprint 19 to 20-1/2mm. long

| CO14 | 6¢ yellow brown (C8) | .... | .... | 15.00 | 11.00 | 6.25 |

SCOTT NO.	DESCRIPTION	UNUSED NH F	UNUSED NH AVG	UNUSED OG F	UNUSED OG AVG	USED F	USED AVG

POSTAGE DUE STAMPS

1914
U.S. Postage Due Stamps J45-46, 49 overprint **CANAL ZONE**

J1	1¢ rose carmine	125.00	105.00	90.00	65.00	17.00	10.00
J2	2¢ rose carmine	410.00	290.00	275.00	200.00	55.00	35.00
J3	10¢ rose carmine	1150.00	925.00	875.00	650.00	55.00	35.00

1924
Type I overprint on U.S. Postage Due Stamps J61-62, 65

J12	1¢ carmine rose	175.00	120.00	120.00	70.00	30.00	20.00
J13	2¢ deep claret	110.00	75.00	65.00	45.00	15.00	9.00
J14	10¢ deep claret	385.00	270.00	260.00	160.00	45.00	30.00

1925
Canal Zone Stamps 71, 73, 75 overprinted **POSTAGE DUE**

J15	1¢ deep green	140.00	95.00	100.00	55.00	19.00	11.50
J16	2¢ carmine	35.00	24.50	25.00	15.00	7.50	4.50
J17	10¢ orange	70.00	49.50	45.00	27.50	11.50	6.50

1925
Type II overprint on U.S. Postage Due Stamps J61-62, 65

J18	1¢ carmine rose	14.00	9.25	9.50	5.50	3.00	1.75
J19	2¢ carmine rose	22.00	15.00	15.00	10.00	5.00	3.00
J20	10¢ carmine rose	175.00	120.00	120.00	75.00	20.00	12.00

1929-39
107 Surcharged **POSTAGE DUE -1-**

J21	1¢ on 5¢ blue	5.50	3.85	4.00	2.75	2.20	1.40
J22	2¢ on 5¢ blue	10.00	7.00	6.50	4.50	3.50	2.00
J23	5¢ on 5¢ blue	10.00	7.00	6.50	4.50	4.00	2.35
J24	10¢ on 5¢ blue	10.00	7.00	6.50	4.50	4.00	2.35

J25

1932-41

J25-29	1¢-15¢ complete, 5 varieties	5.25	3.75	4.15	2.75	3.60	2.50
J25	1¢ claret	.25	.20	.20	.15	.20	.15
J26	2¢ claret	.25	.20	.20	.15	.20	.15
J27	5¢ claret	.60	.45	.50	.35	.35	.25
J28	10¢ claret	2.50	1.75	1.95	1.25	1.75	1.20
J29	15¢ claret (1941)	1.95	1.35	1.50	1.00	1.30	.90

SCOTT NO.	DESCRIPTION	UNUSED F/NH	UNUSED F	USED F

OFFICIAL STAMPS

1941
105, 107, 108, 111, 112, 114, 117, 139 overprinted **OFFICIAL PANAMA CANAL**

"PANAMA" 10mm. Long

O1/9	1¢-50¢ (O1-2, O4-7, O9) 7 varieties	120.00	86.50	23.00
O1	1¢ yellow green (105)	2.25	1.60	.60
O2	3¢ deep violet (117)	4.50	3.35	1.10
O3	5¢ blue (107)	....	....	40.00
O4	10¢ orange (108)	7.50	5.00	2.75
O5	15¢ gray black (111)	17.00	13.00	3.35
O6	20¢ olive brown (112)	20.00	15.00	4.00
O7	50¢ lilac (114)	65.00	45.00	8.00

1947

| O9 | 5¢ deep blue (139) | 11.00 | 8.00 | 4.50 |

ORDER BY MAIL, PHONE (800) 546-2995 OR FAX (256) 246-1116

CANAL ZONE MINT POSTAL STATIONERY ENTIRES

SCOTT NO.	DESCRIPTION	MINT ENTIRES

ENVELOPES

SCOTT NO.	DESCRIPTION	MINT ENTIRES
U16	1934, 3¢ purple	1.30
U17	1958, 4¢ blue	1.50
U18	1969, 4¢ + 1¢ blue	1.50
U19	1969, 4¢ + 2¢ blue	3.00
U20	1971, 8¢ Gaillard Cut	.90
U21	1974, 8¢ + 2¢ Gaillard Cut	1.25
U22	1976, 13¢ Gaillard Cut	.90
U23	1978, 13¢ + 2¢ Gaillard Cut	.90

AIR MAIL ENVELOPES

SCOTT NO.	DESCRIPTION	MINT ENTIRES
UC3	1949, 6¢ DC-4 Skymaster	4.50
UC4	1958, 7¢ DC-4 Skymaster	5.00
UC5	1963, 3¢ + 5¢ purple	7.00
UC6	1964, 8¢ Tail Assembly	2.75
UC7	1965, 4¢ + 4¢ blue	5.00
UC8	1966, 8¢ Tail Assembly	5.50
UC9	1968, 8¢ + 2¢ Tail Assembly	3.25
UC10	1968, 4¢ + 4¢ + 2¢ Tail Assembly	2.50
UC11	1969, 10¢ Tail Assembly	4.50
UC12	1971, 4¢ + 5¢ + 2¢ blue	4.50
UC13	1971, 10¢ + 1¢ Tail Assembly	4.50
UC14	1971, 11¢ Tail Assembly	1.25
UC15	1974, 11¢ + 2¢ Tail Assembly	1.75
UC16	1975, 8¢ + 2¢ + 3¢ emerald	1.50

POSTAL CARDS

SCOTT NO.	DESCRIPTION	MINT ENTIRES
UX10	1935, 1¢ overprint on U.S. #UX27	1.75
UX11	1952, 2¢ overprint on U.S. #UX38	2.50
UX12	1958, 3¢ Ship in Lock	1.75
UX13	1963, 3¢ + 1¢ Ship in Lock	4.50
UX14	1964, 4¢ Ship in Canal	4.00
UX15	1965, 4¢ Ship in Lock	1.25
UX16	1968, 4¢ + 1¢ Ship in Lock	1.25
UX17	1969, 5¢ Ship in Lock	1.25
UX18	1971, 5¢ + 1¢ Ship in Lock	.95
UX19	1974, 8¢ Ship in Lock	.75
UX20	1976, 8¢ + 1¢ Ship in Lock	.60
UX21	1978, 8¢ + 2¢ Ship in Lock	.65

AIR MAIL POSTAL CARDS

SCOTT NO.	DESCRIPTION	MINT ENTIRES
UXC1	1958, 5¢ Plane, Flag & Map	4.00
UXC2	1963, 5¢ + 1¢ Plane, Flag & Map	10.50
UXC3	1965, 4¢ + 2¢ Ship in Lock	4.50
UXC4	1968, 4¢ + 4¢ Ship in Lock	3.25
UXC5	1971, 5¢ + 4¢ Ship in Lock	.90

FIRST DAY COVER ALBUM

Handsome and durable loose-leaf album to protect and display all your covers.

Luxurious leather-look album with gold-stamped title displays first day covers in clear vinyl pages. Two pockets per page; each 20 page album holds 80 covers back to back. Durable two-post loose-leaf binder makes it simple to add extra pages as your collection grows.

1HRS30   Harris First Day Cover Album with slip case *$16.95*

Order from your local dealer or direct from Whitman Publishing, LLC.

CONFEDERATE STATES

1, 4 Jefferson Davis
2, 5 Thomas Jefferson

(Confederate States 1-14 + 40% for VF Centering)

1861

SCOTT NO.	DESCRIPTION	UNUSED OG F	AVG	UNUSED F	AVG	USED F	AVG
1	5¢ green	210.00	150.00	150.00	95.00	120.00	75.00
2	10¢ blue	275.00	155.00	195.00	110.00	150.00	95.00

3 Andrew Jackson
6, 7 Jefferson Davis — 6: Fine Print, 7: Coarse Print

1862

SCOTT NO.	DESCRIPTION	UNUSED OG F	AVG	UNUSED F	AVG	USED F	AVG
3	2¢ green	625.00	475.00	500.00	340.00	525.00	375.00
4	5¢ blue	145.00	85.00	105.00	60.00	80.00	50.00
5	10¢ rose	1100.00	700.00	750.00	475.00	475.00	275.00
6	5¢ light blue, London Print	12.50	9.00	8.00	5.50	26.00	15.00
7	5¢ blue, Local Print	17.50	11.00	13.50	9.00	18.00	12.00

8 Andrew Jackson

1863

SCOTT NO.	DESCRIPTION	UNUSED OG F	AVG	UNUSED F	AVG	USED F	AVG
8	2¢ red brown	65.00	37.50	48.00	31.00	350.00	260.00

9
10, 11 (Die A) Jefferson Davis
12 (Die B)

SCOTT NO.	DESCRIPTION	UNUSED OG F	AVG	UNUSED F	AVG	USED F	AVG
9	10¢ blue (TEN)	975.00	595.00	700.00	425.00	450.00	275.00
10	10¢ blue (with frame line)			2900.00	1875.00	1200.00	700.00
11	10¢ blue (no frame)	12.50	8.50	9.00	6.00	14.00	8.00
12	10¢ blue, filled corner	12.50	8.50	9.00	6.00	14.00	8.00

13 George Washington
14 John C. Calhoun

SCOTT NO.	DESCRIPTION	UNUSED OG F	AVG	UNUSED F	AVG	USED F	AVG
13	20¢ green	49.00	30.50	35.00	22.00	350.00	250.00

1862

SCOTT NO.	DESCRIPTION	UNUSED OG F	AVG	UNUSED F	AVG	USED F	AVG
14	1¢ orange	97.50	63.00	70.00	45.00		

Cuba #221-231, E1-E2, J1-J4, Guam #1-12, E1, Hawaii #23-36

SCOTT NO.	DESCRIPTION	UNUSED NH F	AVG	UNUSED OG F	AVG	USED F	AVG

CUBA
U.S. Administration

1899
U.S. Stamps of 267, 279, 279B, 268, 281, 282C surcharged

221	1¢ on 1¢ yellow green	5.50	3.85	3.65	2.50	.65	.40
222	2¢ on 2¢ carmine	5.50	3.85	3.65	2.50	.55	.35
223	2-1/2¢ on 2¢ carmine	5.00	3.50	2.75	1.95	.65	.40
224	3¢ on 3¢ purple	11.00	7.75	6.50	4.25	1.60	.95
225	5¢ on 5¢ blue	11.00	7.75	6.50	4.25	1.60	.95
226	10¢ on 10¢ brown	26.00	18.25	19.00	12.00	8.00	5.00

227   228   229

230   231

Republic under U.S. Military Rule Watermarked US-C

227	1¢ Columbus	3.65	2.50	2.40	1.60	.25	.15
228	2¢ Coconut Palms	3.65	2.50	2.40	1.60	.25	.15
229	3¢ Allegory "Cuba"	3.65	2.50	2.40	1.60	.35	.20
230	5¢ Ocean Liner	5.50	3.85	3.65	2.75	.40	.25
231	10¢ Cane Field	13.00	9.00	9.00	5.75	.85	.50

SPECIAL DELIVERY
1899
Surcharged of 1899 on U.S. E5

| E1 | 10¢ on 10¢ blue | 135.00 | 95.00 | 95.00 | 60.00 | 85.00 | 50.00 |

E2
Special Delivery Messenger

Republic under U.S. Military Rule
Watermarked US-C Inscribed "Immediate"

| E2 | 10¢ orange | 60.00 | 42.00 | 35.00 | 24.00 | 12.50 | 7.50 |

POSTAGE DUE STAMPS
1899
Surcharge of 1899 on U.S. J38-39, J41-42

J1	1¢ on 1¢ deep claret	35.00	24.50	24.00	16.00	4.00	2.50
J2	2¢ on 2¢ deep claret	35.00	24.50	24.00	16.00	4.00	2.50
J3	5¢ on 5¢ deep claret	35.00	24.50	24.00	16.00	3.50	2.60
J4	10¢ on 10¢ deep claret	35.00	24.50	24.00	16.00	1.75	1.10

GUAM

1899
U.S. Stamps of 279, 267, 268, 272, 280-82C, 284, 275, 276 overprinted

1	1¢ deep green	30.00	21.00	20.00	13.00	30.00	17.00
2	2¢ red	26.50	18.50	19.00	11.00	29.00	17.00
3	3¢ purple	165.00	115.00	110.00	65.00	140.00	90.00
4	4¢ lilac brown	165.00	115.00	110.00	65.00	140.00	90.00
5	5¢ blue	40.00	28.00	25.00	17.00	40.00	22.00
6	6¢ lake	165.00	115.00	110.00	65.00	130.00	85.00
7	8¢ violet brown	165.00	115.00	110.00	65.00	135.00	90.00
8	10¢ brown (Type I)	60.00	36.00	40.00	24.00	60.00	37.50
10	15¢ olive green	175.00	120.00	125.00	70.00	165.00	100.00
11	50¢ orange	305.00	210.00	210.00	125.00	275.00	165.00
12	$1 black (Type I)	500.00	350.00	350.00	210.00	450.00	260.00

SPECIAL DELIVERY
U.S. Stamp E5 overprint

| E1 | 10¢ blue | 205.00 | 140.00 | 130.00 | 80.00 | 170.00 | 110.00 |

SCOTT NO.	DESCRIPTION	UNUSED OG F	AVG	UNUSED F	AVG	USED F	AVG

HAWAII

23, 24   25, 26

1864 Laid Paper

| 23 | 1¢ black | 195.00 | 115.00 | 150.00 | 90.00 | | |
| 24 | 2¢ black | 195.00 | 115.00 | 150.00 | 90.00 | | |

1865 Wove Paper

| 25 | 1¢ dark blue | 200.00 | 125.00 | 150.00 | 95.00 | | |
| 26 | 2¢ dark blue | 175.00 | 110.00 | 135.00 | 85.00 | | |

27-29
King Kamehameha IV

1861-63

| 27 | 2¢ pale rose, horizontal laid paper | 180.00 | 120.00 | 150.00 | 100.00 | 100.00 | 60.00 |
| 28 | 2¢ pale rose, vertical laid paper | 180.00 | 120.00 | 150.00 | 100.00 | 100.00 | 60.00 |

1869 Engraved

| 29 | 2¢ red, thin wove paper | 55.00 | 33.50 | 45.00 | 28.00 | | |

30 *Princess Kamamalu*   31 *King Kamehameha IV*

32, 39, 52C   33   34
King Kamehameha V   *Mataia Kekuanaoa*

1864-71 Wove Paper

30	1¢ purple	8.50	5.50	7.00	4.50	5.50	3.35
31	2¢ rose vermillion	12.00	7.25	10.00	6.00	6.00	3.75
32	5¢ blue	78.00	48.00	65.00	40.00	16.00	11.00
33	6¢ yellow green	19.25	12.00	16.00	10.00	5.50	3.35
34	18¢ dull rose	105.00	55.00	85.00	45.00	13.00	9.00

35, 38, 43   36, 46
King David Kalakaua   *Prince William Pitt Leleichoku*

1875

| 35 | 2¢ brown | 6.60 | 4.00 | 5.50 | 3.35 | 2.20 | 1.40 |
| 36 | 12¢ black | 45.00 | 30.00 | 37.50 | 25.00 | 19.50 | 12.50 |

Hawaii #37-82, O1-O6

SCOTT NO.	DESCRIPTION	UNUSED OG F	UNUSED OG AVG	UNUSED F	UNUSED AVG	USED F	USED AVG
	37, 42 Princess Likelike						
	40, 44, 45 King David Kalakaua						
	41 Queen Kapiolani						
	47 Statue of King Kamehameha I						
	48 King William Lunalilo						
	49 Queen Emma Kaleleonalani						
	1882						
37	1¢ blue	4.50	3.00	3.75	2.50	6.00	4.00
38	2¢ lilac rose	90.00	60.00	75.00	50.00	28.00	18.00
39	5¢ ultramarine	13.75	9.00	11.50	7.50	2.10	1.40
40	10¢ black	26.50	18.00	22.00	15.00	15.00	9.50
41	15¢ red brown	45.00	28.75	37.50	24.00	22.00	13.50
	1883-86						
42	1¢ green	2.50	1.65	2.10	1.40	1.40	.80
43	2¢ rose	4.00	2.50	3.35	2.10	.85	.50
44	10¢ red brown	21.00	12.50	17.50	10.50	6.50	4.25
45	10¢ vermillion	26.50	15.00	22.00	12.50	11.50	7.75
46	12¢ red lilac	66.00	42.00	55.00	35.00	30.00	19.50
47	25¢ dark violet	95.00	60.00	80.00	50.00	41.50	26.50
48	50¢ red	155.00	105.00	130.00	85.00	70.00	45.00
49	$1 rose red	235.00	145.00	195.00	120.00	85.00	50.00
	52 Queen Liliuokalani						
	1890-91						
52	2¢ dull violet	7.25	3.00	6.00	2.50	1.20	.80
52C	5¢ deep indigo	135.00	70.00	100.00	60.00	72.50	45.00
	Provisional GOVT. 1893						
	1893 Provisional Government Red Overprint						
53	1¢ purple	4.75	2.85	4.00	2.40	3.40	2.10
54	1¢ blue	4.75	2.85	4.00	2.40	6.00	3.40
55	1¢ green	1.80	1.05	1.50	.85	2.75	1.65
56	2¢ brown	6.00	3.35	5.00	2.75	10.50	7.00
57	2¢ dull violet	1.80	1.10	1.50	.90	1.30	.85
58	5¢ deep indigo	10.75	6.25	9.00	5.25	16.00	10.50
59	5¢ ultramarine	5.50	3.35	4.50	2.75	3.25	1.95
60	6¢ green	11.50	6.50	9.50	5.50	17.00	11.00
61	10¢ black	7.75	4.50	6.50	3.75	8.00	5.00
62	12¢ black	8.75	5.30	7.25	4.50	12.00	7.50
63	12¢ red lilac	145.00	85.00	120.00	72.50	155.00	95.00
64	25¢ dark violet	24.00	14.50	20.00	12.00	25.00	17.00
	Black Overprint						
65	2¢ rose vermillion	55.00	36.00	45.00	30.00	45.00	30.00
66	2¢ rose	1.45	.95	1.20	.80	2.50	1.50
67	10¢ vermillion	12.00	7.75	10.00	6.50	20.00	12.00
68	10¢ red brown	7.25	4.50	6.00	3.75	10.00	6.00
69	12¢ red lilac	250.00	155.00	210.00	130.00	285.00	175.00
70	15¢ red brown	19.25	12.50	16.00	10.50	28.75	17.50
71	18¢ dull rose	25.00	14.50	21.00	12.00	33.75	20.00
72	50¢ red	62.50	36.00	52.50	30.00	85.00	51.50
73	$1 rose red	120.00	72.50	100.00	60.00	140.00	85.00
	74, 80 Coat of Arms						
	75, 81 View of Honolulu						
	76 Statue of King Kamehameha I						
	1894						
74	1¢ yellow	3.00	2.10	2.00	1.20	1.40	.85
75	2¢ brown	3.10	2.20	2.15	1.25	.80	.45
76	5¢ rose lake	6.00	4.20	4.00	2.40	1.90	1.20
	77 Star and Palm						
	78 S.S. "Arawa"						
	79 Pres. S.B. Dole						
77	10¢ yellow green	7.25	5.00	5.00	3.00	5.00	3.00
78	12¢ blue	16.00	11.00	10.00	6.00	12.00	7.25
79	25¢ deep blue	16.00	11.00	10.00	6.00	12.00	7.25
	82 Statue of King Kamehameha I						
	1899						
80	1¢ dark green	2.50	1.75	1.60	1.00	1.30	.85
81	2¢ rose	2.50	1.75	1.60	1.00	1.30	.85
82	5¢ blue	7.25	5.00	5.00	3.00	3.35	2.00
	O1 Lorrin A. Thurston						
	1896 OFFICIAL STAMPS						
O1	2¢ green	45.00	31.50	30.00	18.00	18.00	11.75
O2	5¢ black brown	45.00	31.50	30.00	18.00	18.00	11.75
O3	6¢ deep ultramarine	60.00	42.00	40.00	22.00	18.00	11.75
O4	10¢ bright rose	45.00	31.50	30.00	18.00	18.00	11.75
O5	12¢ orange	95.00	65.00	60.00	35.00	18.00	11.75
O6	25¢ gray violet	120.00	85.00	82.50	50.00	18.00	11.75

MARSHALL ISLANDS

The Marshall Islands are a part of the U.S. administered Trust Territories of the Pacific formed in 1947. They were granted postal autonomy in 1984 on their way to independence.

SCOTT NO.	DESCRIPTION	UNUSED F/NH

1984 COMMEMORATIVES

| 31-34 | 20¢ Postal Independence, attached | 2.75 |

1984-85 MAPS & NAVIGATION

35-49A	**1¢-$1, 16 varieties**	**11.00**
35	1¢ Mili Atoll	
36	3¢ Likiep Atoll	
37	5¢ Ebon Atoll	
38	10¢ Jaluit Atoll	
39	13¢ Alinginae Atoll	
40	14¢ Wotho Atoll (1985)	
41	20¢ Kwajalein Atoll	
42	22¢ Enewetok (1985)	
43	28¢ Ailinglaplap Atoll	
44	30¢ Majuro Atoll	
45	33¢ Namu Atoll (1985)	
46	37¢ Rongelap Atoll	
47	39¢ Utirik & Taka (1985)	
48	44¢ Ujelang Atoll (1985)	
49	50¢ Maloelap & Aur (1985)	
49A	$1.00 Arno Atoll	

1984-85 BOOKLET PANES

39a	13¢ Ailingingae (10)	10.00
40a	14¢ Wotho Atoll (10)	10.00
41a	20¢ Kwajalein (10)	10.00
41b	13¢ (5) & 20¢ (5)	13.00
42a	22¢ Eniwetok (10)	10.00
42b	14¢ (5) & 22¢ (5)	13.00

1984 COMMEMORATIVES

| 50-53 | 40¢ U.P.U.—Hamburg, attached | 3.50 |
| 54-57 | 20¢ Dolphins, attached | 2.25 |

| 58 | 20¢ Christmas, strip of 4 | 2.50 |
| 59-62 | 20¢ Constitution, attached | 2.25 |

1985 COMMEMORATIVES

63-64	22¢ Audubon Birds, attached	1.40
65-69	22¢ Seashells, attached	2.75
70-73	22¢ Decade for Women, attached	2.25

| 74-77 | 22¢ Reef Fish, attached | 2.25 |
| 78-81 | 22¢ Youth Year, attached | 2.25 |

82-85	14¢-44¢ Christmas, 4 varieties	2.75
86-90	22¢ Halley's Comet, strip of 5	6.00
91-94	22¢ Medicinal Plants, attached	2.25

1986-87 MAPS & NAVIGATION

107	$2 Wotje & Erikub	5.50
108	$5 Bikini Atoll	12.00
109	$10 Stick Chart (1987)	19.50

1986 COMMEMORATIVES

| 110-13 | 14¢ Marine Invertebrates, attached | 2.10 |
| 114 | $1 AMERIPEX '86 Souvenir Sheet | 3.40 |

115-18	22¢ Operation Crossroads, Atomic Tests, attached	2.50
119-23	22¢ Seashells, designs as #65-69, attached	2.50
124-27	22¢ Game Fish, attached	2.25
128-31	22¢ Christmas, Peace, attached	3.00

1987 COMMEMORATIVES

| 132-35 | 22¢ Whaling Ships, attached | 2.50 |
| 136-41 | 33¢, 39¢, 44¢ Historic Aircraft, 3 attached pairs | 5.50 |

Marshall Islands #142-220

SCOTT NO.	DESCRIPTION	UNUSED F/NH
142	$1 CAPEX '87 Souvenir Sheet	3.00
143-51	14¢-44¢ U.S. Constitution, 3 attached strips of 3	5.25
152-56	22¢ Seashells, attached	2.50
157-59	44¢ Copra Industry, attached	2.75
160-63	14¢-44¢ Christmas	2.75

1988

SCOTT NO.	DESCRIPTION	UNUSED F/NH
164-67	44¢ Marine Birds	4.25

1988-89 Definitives

SCOTT NO.	DESCRIPTION	UNUSED F/NH
168-83	1¢-$5 Fish, 16 singles complete set	22.50
184	$10 Blue Jack (1989)	19.25

Booklet Panes 1987-89

SCOTT NO.	DESCRIPTION	UNUSED F/NH
170a	14¢ Hawkfish pane (10)	4.50
171a	15¢ Balloonfish pane (10)	6.25
173a	22¢ Lyretail wrasse pane (10)	5.50
173b	5 (14¢) & 5 (22¢) pane (10)	5.50
174a	25¢ Parrotfish pane (10)	7.50
174b	5 (15¢) & 5 (25¢) pane (10)	7.50

SCOTT NO.	DESCRIPTION	UNUSED F/NH
188-89	15¢-25¢ Olympics 2 attached strip of 5	5.00
190	25¢ Stevenson, sheetlet of 9	7.00
191-94	25¢ Ships & Flags, attached	2.75
195-99	25¢ Christmas, strip of 5	3.00
200-04	25¢ J.F.K. Tribute, strip of 5	3.50
205-08	25¢ Space Shuttle, strip of 4	2.75

1989 COMMEMORATIVES

SCOTT NO.	DESCRIPTION	UNUSED F/NH
209-12	45¢ Links to Japan, attached	4.25
213-15	45¢ Alaska Anniv., strip of 3	3.00
216-20	25¢ Seashells, strip of 5	3.25

Marshall Islands #221-380

1989 COMMEMORATIVES (continued)

Scott No.	Description	Unused F/NH
221	$1 Japanese Art Souvenir Sheet	2.40
222-25	45¢ Migrant Birds, attached	4.00
226-29	45¢ Postal Service, attached	4.00
230	$1.50 PHILEX-FRANCE Souv. Sheet	12.00
231	$1.00 Postal Service Centenary Souvenir Sheet	12.00
232-38	25¢-$1 20th Anniversary First Moon Landing	20.00
238a	booklet pane of 232-38	20.50

1989 WWII Anniversary Issues

Scott No.	Description	Unused F/NH
239	25¢ Invasion of Poland	.75
240	45¢ Sinking of HMS Royal Oak	1.25
241	45¢ Invasion of Finland	1.25
242-45	45¢ Battle of River Plate, 4 attached	5.00

1990 WWII Anniversary Issues

Scott No.	Description	Unused F/NH
246-47	25¢ Invasion of Denmark and Norway	1.40
248	25¢ Katyn Forest Massacre	.60
249-50	25¢ Bombing of Rotterdam/25¢ Invasion of Belgium	1.20
251	45¢ Winston Churchill	1.25
252-53	45¢ Evacuation at Dunkirk, 2 attached	2.50
254	45¢ Occupation of Paris	1.25
255	25¢ Battle of Mers-el-Kebir	.75
256	25¢ Battles for Burma Road	.75
257-60	45¢ U.S. Destroyers, 4 attached	5.00
261-64	45¢ Battle for Britain, 4 attached	5.00
265	45¢ Tripartite Pact 1940	1.25
266	25¢ Roosevelt Reelected	.75
267-70	25¢ Battle of Taranto, 4 attached	2.75

1991 WWII Anniversary Issues

Scott No.	Description	Unused F/NH
271-74	30¢ Roosevelt's Four Freedoms of Speech, 4 attached	3.25
275	30¢ Battle of Beda Fomm	.80
276-77	29¢ Invasion of Greece and Yugoslavia, 2 attached	1.40
278-81	50¢ Sinking of the Bismarck, 4 attached	5.50
282	30¢ Germany Invades Russia	.90
283-84	29¢ Atlantic Charter, 2 attached	1.75
285	29¢ Siege of Moscow	.90
286-87	30¢ Sinking of the USS Reuben James, 2 attached	1.75
288-91	50¢ Japanese Attack Pearl Harbor, 4 attached	7.00
288-91b	same, 2nd printing (1 title corrected)	17.50
292	29¢ Japanese Capture Guam	.90
293	29¢ Fall of Singapore	.90
294-95	50¢ Flying Tigers, 2 attached	2.75
296	29¢ Fall of Wake Island	.90

1992 WWII Anniversary Issues

Scott No.	Description	Unused F/NH
297	29¢ Arcadia Conference	.90
298	50¢ Fall of Manila	1.50
299	29¢ Japanese take Rabaul	.90
300	29¢ Battle of Java Sea	.90
301	50¢ Fall of Rangoon	1.50
302	29¢ Japanese on New Guinea	.90
303	29¢ MacArthur evacuated from Corregidor	.90
304	29¢ Raid on Saint-Nazaire	.90
305	29¢ Bataan/Death March	.90
306	50¢ Doolittle Raid on Tokyo	1.50
307	29¢ Fall of Corregidor	.90
308-11	50¢ Battle of the Coral Sea, 4 attached	7.00
308-11b	same, 2nd printing (4 titles corrected)	17.50
312-15	50¢ Battle of Midway, 4 attached	6.00
316	29¢ Village of Lidice destroyed	.90
317	29¢ Fall of Sevastopol	.90
318-19	29¢ Convoy PQ 17 Destroyed, 2 attached	1.75
320	29¢ Marines on Guadalcanal	.90
321	29¢ Battle of Savo Island	.90
322	29¢ Dieppe Raid	.90
323	50¢ Battle of Stalingrad	1.50
324	29¢ Battle of Eastern Solomons	.90
325	50¢ Battle of Cape Esperance	1.50
326	29¢ Battle of El Alamein	.90
327-28	29¢ Battle of Barents Sea, 2 attached	1.75

1993 WWII Anniversary Issues

Scott No.	Description	Unused F/NH
329	29¢ Casablanca Conference	.90
330	29¢ Liberation of Kharkov	.90
331-34	50¢ Battle of Bismarck Sea, 4 attached	6.00
335	50¢ Interception of Admiral Yamamoto	.90
336-37	29¢ Battle of Kursk, 2 attached	2.25

1989

Scott No.	Description	Unused F/NH
341-44	25¢ Christmas 1989, 4 attached	4.50
345	45¢ Milestones in space (25)	40.00

1990

Scott No.	Description	Unused F/NH
346-65A	1¢/$2 Birds (21)	32.50
361a	Essen '90 Germany, miniature sheet of 4 (347, 350, 353, 361)	4.95
366-69	25¢ Children's Games, 4 attached	3.50
370-76	25¢, $1 Penny Black, singles	17.50
376a	booklet pane of 370-76	18.00
377-80	25¢ Endangered Wildlife, 4 attached	5.00

MARSHALL ISLANDS #381-503

SCOTT NO.	DESCRIPTION	UNUSED F/NH
381	25¢ Joint Issue (US & Micronesia)	1.00
382	45¢ German Reunification	1.40
383-86	25¢ Christmas 1990, 4 attached	3.50
387-90	25¢ Breadfruit, 4 attached	3.50

1991

391-94	50¢ 10th Anniversary of Space Shuttle, 4 attached	5.00
395-98	52¢ Flowers, 4 attached	5.00
398a	52¢ Phila Nippon, sheet of 4	5.00
399	29¢ Operation Desert Storm	1.25
400-06	29¢, $1 Birds, set of 7 singles	25.00
406a	same, booklet pane of 7	26.00
407-10	12¢-50¢ Air Marshall Islands Aircraft, set of 4	4.25
411	29¢ Admission to the United Nations	.85
412	30¢ Christmas 1991, Dove	.85
413	29¢ Peace Corps	.85

1992

414-17	29¢ Ships, strip of 4	5.25
418-24	50¢, $1 Columbus, set of 7 singles	16.00
424a	same, booklet pane of 7	17.00
425-28	29¢ Handicrafts, 4 attached	3.50
429	29¢ Christmas, 1992	.85
430-33	9-45¢ Birds, set of 4	3.75

1993

434-40	50¢, $1 Reef Life, set of 7 singles	17.50
440a	same, booklet pane of 7	18.00

1993-95

441-66B	10¢-$10 Ships & Sailing Vessels, 28 varieties.	85.00
466C	"Hong Kong '94" miniature sheet of 4 (#464d-64g)	4.00

1993 WWII Anniversary Issues (continued)

467-70	52¢ Invasion of Sicily, 4 attached	5.75
471	50¢ Bombing of Schweinfurt	1.50
472	29¢ Liberation of Smolensk	.90
473	29¢ Landings at Bougainville	.90
474	50¢ Invasion of Tarawa	1.50
475	52¢ Teheran Conference, 1943	1.50
476-77	29¢ Battle of North Cape, 2 attached	2.50

1994 WWII Anniversary Issues

478	29¢ Gen. Dwight D. Eisenhower	.90
479	50¢ Invasion of Anzio	1.50
480	52¢ Siege of Leningrad lifted	1.50
481	29¢ US Liberates Marshall Islands	.90
482	29¢ Japanese Defeated at Truk	.90
483	52¢ US Bombs Germany	1.50
484	50¢ Lt. Gen. Mark Clark, Rome Falls to the Allies	1.50
485-88	75¢ D Day – Allied Landings at Normandy, 4 attached	12.00
485-88b	same, 2nd printing (3 titles corrected)	20.00
489	50¢ V-1 Bombardment of England Begins	1.50
490	29¢ US Marines Land on Saipan	.90
491	50¢ 1st Battle of Philippine Sea	1.50
492	29¢ US Liberates Guam	.90
493	50¢ Warsaw Uprising	1.50
494	50¢ Liberation of Paris	1.50
495	29¢ US Marines land on Peliliu	1.50
496	52¢ MacArthur returns to the Philippines	1.50
497	52¢ Battle of Leyte Gulf	1.50
498-99	50¢ Battleship Tirpitz Sunk, 2 attached	3.50
500-03	50¢ Battle of the Bulge, 4 attached	9.50

MARSHALL ISLANDS #504-589

Scott No.	Description	Unused F/NH
	1995 WWII Anniversary Issues	
504	32¢ Yalta Conference Begins	1.25
505	55¢ Bombing of Dresden	2.00
506	$1 Iwo Jima Invaded by US Marines	3.50
507	32¢ Remagen Bridge Taken by US Forces	1.25
508	55¢ Okinawa Invaded by US Forces	2.00
509	50¢ Death of F.D.R.	2.00
510	32¢ US/USSR troops meet at Elbe River	1.25
511	60¢ Russian troops capture Berlin	2.00
512	55¢ Allies liberate concentration camps, 1945	2.00
513-16	75¢ VE Day, 4 attached	17.50
517	32¢ UN Charter signed	1.25
518	55¢ Potsdam Conference convenes	2.00
519	60¢ Churchill resigns	2.00
520	$1 Enola Gay drops atomic bomb on Hiroshima, 1945	2.00
521-24	75¢ VJ Day, 4 attached	17.50
	1994 WWII Anniversary Issues (continued)	
562	$1 MacArthur returns to the Philippines, souvenir sheet	3.25
563	$1 Harry S. Truman/UN Charter souvenir sheet	3.25

567

1993 (continued)

567-70	29¢ New Capitol	2.60

571

572   576

571	50¢ Super Tanker "Eagle" souvenir sheet	1.10
572-75	29¢ Life in the 1800s, 4 attached	2.75
576	29¢ Christmas 1993	1.00

577

1994

577	$2.90 15th Anniversary Constitution souvenir sheet	6.25

578

578	29¢ 10th Anniversary Postal Service souvenir sheet	.70

579   583

582a

579-80	50¢ World Cup Soccer, 2 attached	4.75
582	50¢ Solar System, Planets, sheetlet of 12	16.50
583-86	75¢ 25th Anniversary of First Moon Landing, 4 attached	6.25
586b	$3 25th Anniversary of First Moon Landing, souvenir sheet	6.25

587a   588

587	"PHILAKOREA '94" souvenir sheet of 3	4.00
588	29¢ Christmas 1994	.70

589

1995

589	50¢ New Year 1995 (Year of the Boar)	2.50

Marshall Islands #590-609

SCOTT NO.	DESCRIPTION	UNUSED F/NH

590a 591a 592a

1995

590	55¢ Marine Life, 4 attached	6.00
591	55¢ John F. Kennedy, strip of 6	7.50
592	75¢ Marilyn Monroe, 4 attached	7.25

593a 594a

| 593 | 32¢ Cats, 4 attached | 3.00 |
| 594 | 75¢ Space Shuttle, 4 attached | 6.25 |

595a

| 595 | 60¢ Pacific Game Fish, 8 attached | 16.00 |

596a 597a

| 596 | 32¢ Island Legends, 4 attached, plus 4 labels | 3.00 |
| 597 | 32¢ Orchids (Singapore '95), miniature sheet of 4 | 3.00 |

598

| 598 | 50¢ Suzhou Gardens souvenir sheet | 1.10 |

SCOTT NO.	DESCRIPTION	UNUSED F/NH

599 600a 601

599	32¢ Christmas 1995	.75
600	32¢ Jet Fighter Planes, sheetlet of 25	18.75
601	32¢ Yitzhak Rabin	.75

603a 604a

1996

602	50¢ New Year 1996 (Year of the Rat)	1.10
603	32¢ Native Birds, 4 attached	6.00
604	55¢ Wild Cats, 4 attached	4.75

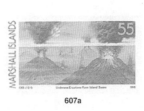 

605a 606a

607a 608

605	32¢ Sailing Ships, sheetlet of 25	18.75
606	60¢ Olympic Games Centenary, 4 attached	5.50
607	55¢ History of the Marshall Islands, sheetlet of 12	15.00
608	32¢ Elvis Presley First #1 Hit 40th Anniversary	1.25

609

| 609 | 50¢ The Palance Museum, Shenyang souvenir sheet | 1.50 |

Marshall Islands #610-650

SCOTT NO.	DESCRIPTION	UNUSED F/NH

610 611a 612a

1996 (continued)

610	32¢ James Dean	1.25
611	60¢ Automobiles, sheet of 8	11.00
612	32¢ Island Legends 1996, 4 attached	3.00

613a

614a 615

613	55¢ Steam Locomotives, sheet of 12	14.50
614	32¢ Marine Life (Taipei '96), miniature sheet of 4	3.00
615	$3 Stick Chart, Canoe & Flag of the Republic	6.75

616 617a 618a

616	32¢ Christmas 1996	.75
617	32¢ World's Legendary Biplanes, sheet of 25	18.50
618	32¢ Native Crafts, 4 attached	3.00

620 622a

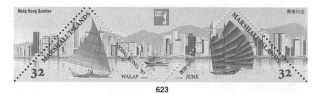

623

1997

619	60¢ New Year 1997 (Year of the Ox)	1.50
620-21	32¢-60¢ Amata Kabua, President of Marshall Islands, set of 2	2.00
622	32¢ Elvis Presley, strip of 3	2.25
623-24	32¢ Hong Kong '97, 2 sheets of 2	3.00

625a 627a 628

625	60¢ The Twelve Apostles, sheet of 12	17.50
626	$3 Rubens "The Last Supper", souvenir sheet	6.75
627	60¢ First Decade of the 20th Century, sheet of 15	21.50
628	60¢ Deng Xiaoping (1904-97), Chinese Leader	1.35

629, 630 638 640a

629	32¢ Native Crafts (1996), 4 attached, self-adhesive, Die-Cut	3.00
630	32¢ Native Crafts (1996), 4 attached, self-adhesive, perf.	3.00
631-37	50¢-$1 Anniv. 1st US & Marshall Islands Stamps, booklet of 7	9.00
638	16¢ Bristle-Thighed Curlew, strip of 4	1.45
639	50¢ Bank of China, Hong Kong, souvenir sheet	1.25
640	32¢ Canoes, strip of 4	2.95

641a 642a 643a

641	32¢ Legendary Aircraft, sheet of 25	20.00
642	32¢ "Old Ironsides" Bicentennial	.80
643	32¢ Island Legends, 4 attached	3.00

644 646a

647-48 649a

644	60¢ Marine Life, 4 attached	5.50
645	60¢ Princess Diana, strip of 3	4.50
646	60¢ Events of the 20th Century, 1910-19, sheetlet of 15	22.50
647-48	32¢ Christmas, Angel, pair	1.50
649	20¢ US State-Named Warships, sheet of 50	25.00
650	50¢ Treasure Ship, Shanghai '97, souvenir sheet	1.50

Marshall Islands #651-721

1998

Scott No.	Description	Unused F/NH
651	60¢ Year of the Tiger, souvenir sheet	1.50
652	32¢ Elvis Presley's 1968 Television Special, strip of 3	2.25
653	32¢ Sea Shells, strip of 4	3.00
654	60¢ Events of the 20th Century, 1920-29, sheetlet of 15	21.50
655	32¢ Canoes of the Pacific, sheetlet of 8	6.25
656	60¢ Berlin Airlift, 4 attached	5.50
657	60¢ Events of the 20th Century, 1930-39, sheetlet of 15	20.00
658-64	60¢-$3 Tsar Nicholas II, bklt of 7 (60¢ x 6, $3 x 1)	19.75
665	32¢ Babe Ruth	.80
666	32¢ Legendary Aircraft of the US Navy, sheetlet of 25	18.75
667	60¢ Chevrolet Automobiles, sheetlet of 8	11.00
668	33¢ Marshalese Language and Alphabet, sheetlet of 24	18.75
669	33¢ New Buildings in Marshall Islands, strip of 3	2.40
670	32¢ Midnight Angel	.80
671-77	60¢-$3 John Glenn's Return to Space, bklt of 7 (60¢ x 6, $3 x 1)	16.00
678	$3.20 Airplane delivering supplies, souvenir sheet	7.25
679	60¢ Events of the 20th Century, 1940-49, sheetlet of 15	20.00
680	33¢ Warships, sheetlet of 25	19.00

1999

Scott No.	Description	Unused F/NH
681	60¢ Year of the Rabbit, souvenir sheet	1.35
682-89	1¢-¢10 Birds (8)	26.50
690	33¢ Canoes of the Pacific, sheetlet of 8	6.25
691-98	same, self-adhesive, block of 10 (691-97 x 1, 698 x 3)	7.50
699	60¢ Great American Indian Chiefs, sheetlet of 12	16.50
700	33¢ Marshall Islands National Flag	.80
701	33¢ Flowers of the Pacific, 6 attached	4.75
702	60¢ Events of the 20th Century, 1950-59, sheetlet of 15	20.00
703	$1.20 HMAS Australia, souvenir sheet	2.75
704	33¢ Elvis Presley	.80
705	60¢ IBRA '99 Exhibition, sheetlet of 4	5.50
706	33¢ Marshall Islands Constitution, 20th Anniversary	.80
707	33¢ Marshall Islands Postal Service, 15th Anniversary, 4 attached	3.25
708	33¢ Legendary Aircraft, sheetlet of 25	19.00
709	$1 PHILEXFRANCE '99, souvenir sheet	2.50
710	60¢ Tanker Alrehab, souvenir sheet	1.45
711	60¢ Events of the 20th Century, 1960-69, sheetlet of 15	20.00
712	33¢ 1st Manned Moonlanding, 30th Anniversary, sheetlet of 3	2.40
713	33¢ Ships, 4 attached	3.25
714-21	5¢-$5 Birds, set of 8	29.00

Marshall Islands #722-791

SCOTT NO.	DESCRIPTION	UNUSED F/NH

722   728a   729a

1999 (continued)

722	33¢ Christmas	.80
723	60¢ Events of the 20th Century, 1970-79, sheetlet of 15	20.00
724-25	33¢ Millenium, 2 attached	1.60

2000

726	60¢ Events of the 20th Century, 1980-89, sheetlet of 15	20.00
727	60¢ New Year 2000 (Year of the Dragon), souvenir sheet	1.45
728	33¢ Legendary Aircraft, sheetlet of 25	19.00
729	33¢ Roses, 6 attached	4.75
730	60¢ Events of the 20th Century, 1990-99, sheetlet of 15	20.00

731a   739a

731	33¢ Pandas, 6 attached	4.75
732-38	1¢-42¢ American Presidents, 7 sheetlets of 6	20.00
739	33¢ First Zepplin Flight, 4 attached	3.25

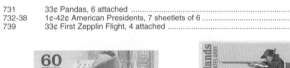

740   747a

740-46	60¢-$1 Sir Winston Churchill, bklt of 7 (60¢ x 6, $1 x 1)	10.25
747	33¢ US Military 225th Anniversary, 3 attached	2.50

748a   749a   750a

748	33¢ National Government, 4 attached	3.25
749	60¢ Ships, 6 attached	8.00
750	60¢ Queen Mother's 100th birthday, 4 attached	5.35

752a   754a

751	33¢ Reef Life, sheetlet of 8	6.50
752	60¢ Butterflies, sheetlet of 12	16.00
753	33¢ Reunification of Germany, 10th Anniversary	.80
754	33¢ Submarines, 4 attached	3.25
755	33¢ Christmas	.80
756	60¢-$1 Sun Yat-sen, bklt of 7 (60¢ x 6, $1 x 1)	10.50

758

2001

757	80¢ Year of the Snake, souvenir sheet	1.95
758	34¢ Carnations, stamp + label	.85
759	34¢ Violets, stamp + label	.85
760	34¢ Jonguil, stamp + label	.85
761	34¢ Sweet Pea, stamp + label	.85
762	34¢ Lily of the Valley, stamp + label	.85
763	34¢ Rose, stamp + label	.85
764	34¢ Larkspur, stamp + label	.85
765	34¢ Poppy, stamp + label	.85
766	34¢ Aster, stamp + label	.85
767	34¢ Marigold, stamp + label	.85
768	34¢ Chrysanthemum, stamp + label	.85
769	34¢ Poinsettia, stamp + label	.85

770   772   777a

770-71	$5-$10 Sailing Canoes	38.50
772-75	34¢-$1 Famous People, set of 4	6.75
776	80¢ Butterflies, sheetlet of 12	9.75
777	34¢ Fairy Tales, 7 varieties attached	5.75

778a   780a

778	34¢ Watercraft Racing, 4 attached	3.25
779	80¢ Manned Spacecraft 40th Anniv, 4 attached	7.25
780	34¢ Stamp Day	.85
781	80¢ American Achievements in Space, 4 attached	7.25
782	34¢ Marine Life, 4 attached	3.25

783a   788a   785a

783	34¢ Sports, 4 attached	3.25
784	57¢ Atlan Anien	1.35
785	34¢ Zodiac Signs, sheetlet of 12	10.00
786	80¢ Phila Nippon 2001, sheetlet of 12	24.00
787	80¢ US Naval Heroes in WWII Pacific Theater, sheetlet of 9	17.50
788	34¢ Classic Cars, 8 attached	6.50
789	34¢-¢1 Remembrance of Victims of Sept. 11, bklt of 7 (34¢ x 6, $1 x 1)	7.50
790	34¢ Christmas, 4 attached	3.25
791	80¢ Airplanes, 10 attached	19.50

Marshall Islands #792-825; B1; C1-C25b; UX1-UX7

SCOTT NO.	DESCRIPTION	UNUSED F/NH
	2002	
792	80¢ Year of the Horse, souvenir sheet	1.95
793	34¢ Shells, 6 attached	4.75
794	80¢ Reign of Queen Elizabeth, 50th Anniv., souvenir sheet	1.95
795	34¢ United We Stand	.85
796	34¢ Classic Cars, 8 attached	6.50
797	34¢ Corals, 4 attached	6.50
798	80¢ Butterflies, sheet of 12	22.50
799	34¢ Horses in Art, sheet of 12	10.00
800	80¢ Horses in Art, souvenir sheet	1.95
801	37¢ Russian Fairy Tale The Frog Princess, sheet of 12	12.50
802	80¢ Carousel Figures, 4 attached	7.25
803	37¢ Birds, sheet of 16	14.75
804	80¢ Benjamin Franklin, 2 attached	3.75
805	37¢ Sea Turtles, 4 attached	3.75
806	80¢ Intl. Federation of Stamp Dealers, 50 Anniv., 6 attached	11.25
807	37¢ U.S. Navy Ships, 6 attached	5.25
808	23¢ Insects and Spiders, sheet of 20	11.00
809	80¢ Classic Cars, 8 attached	14.50
810	80¢ Queen Mother, redrawn, 4 attached	7.25
811	80¢ Regal Princess Cruise Ship, souvenir sheet	1.95
812	80¢ World War I Heroes, 8 attached	14.50
813	37¢ Snowman cookies, 2 attached	1.95
	2003	
814	80¢ Year of the Ram, souvenir sheet	1.95
815	60¢ UN Membership, 12th Anniv.	1.50
816	50¢ Folktales, block of 4	4.75
817-19	37¢-$13.65 Famous People	37.50
820	37¢ Marshallese Culture, block of 8	7.50
821	80¢ Butterflies, sheetlet of 12	9.75
822	37¢ Powered Flight Centenary, blk of 10	9.50
823	37¢ Classic Cars, 8 attached	7.50
824	37¢ Marshallese Culture, part 2, 8 attached	7.50
825	37¢ Christmas Ornaments, 4 attached	4.75

SEMI-POSTAL

SCOTT NO.	DESCRIPTION	UNUSED F/NH
	1996	
B1	32¢+8¢ 50th Anniv. of Nuclear Testing, sheet of 6	5.50

AIR POST

	1985	
C1-2	44¢ Audubon Birds, attached	3.00
	1986	
C3-6	44¢ AMERIPEX '86, attached	4.25
C7	44¢ Operation Crossroads, souvenir sheet	5.00
C8	44¢ Statue of Liberty, Peace	1.25
C9-12	44¢ Girl Scouts, attached	3.75
	1987	
C13-16	44¢ Marine Birds, attached	3.75
C17-20	44¢ CAPEX '87, attached	3.75
	1988-89	
C21	45¢ Space Shuttle	1.10
C22-25	12¢-45¢ Aircraft	2.75

Booklet Panes

C22a	12¢ Dornier DO288, pane (10)	5.00
C23a	36¢ Boeing 737, pane (10)	12.00
C24a	39¢ Hawker 748, pane (10)	13.00
C25a	45¢ Boeing 727, pane (10)	15.00
C25b	5 (36¢) & 5 (45¢), pane (10)	14.00

POSTAL STATIONERY

UX1	20¢ Elvis Presley, postal card (1996)	3.00
UX2-5	20¢ Canoes, set of 4	5.00
UX6	20¢ Heavenly Angels, Christmas (1996)	1.50
UX7	32¢ Turtle (1997)	1.50

Micronesia #1-55; C4-27
FEDERATED STATES OF MICRONESIA

Micronesia, formed from the major portion of the Caroline Islands, became postally autonomous in 1984. It forms part of the U.S. administered Trust Territories of the Pacific.

SCOTT NO.	DESCRIPTION	UNUSED F/NH
	1984 COMMEMORATIVES	
1-4	20¢ Postal Service, attached	2.50
	1984 DEFINITIVES	
5-20	1¢-$5 16 varieties, singles, complete set	22.50
5	1¢ Pedro de Quiros	
6	2¢ Louis Duperrey	
7	3¢ Fyedor Lutke	
8	4¢ Dumont d'Urville	
9	5¢ Men's House, Yap	
10	10¢ Sleeping Lady Hill	
11	13¢ Liduduhriab Waterfall	
12	17¢ Tonachau Peak	
13	19¢ Pedro de Quiros	
14	20¢ Louis Duperrey	
15	30¢ Fyedor Lutke	
16	37¢ Dumont d'Urville	
17	50¢ Devil Mask, Truk	
18	$1 Sokeh's Rock	
19	$2 Canoes	
20	$5 Stone Money	
	1984 COMMEMORATIVES	
21 & C4-6	20¢-40¢ AUSIPEX '84, 4 varieties	3.75
22 & C7-9	20¢-40¢ Christmas '84, 4 varieties	5.00
	1985 COMMEMORATIVES	
23 & C10-12	22¢-44¢ Ships, 4 varieties	4.00
24 & C13-14	22¢-44¢ Christmas '85, 3 varieties	4.00
25-28 & C15	22¢ Audubon, booklet of 4 attached, & 44¢ airmail	4.00
25-28 & C15	22¢ Audubon, booklet of 4 attached, & 44¢ airmail	4.00
	1985-88 DEFINITIVES	
31-39 & C34-36	12 varieties, singles, complete set	27.50
31	3¢ Long-billed	
32	14¢ Truk Monarch	
33	15¢ Waterfall	
34	22¢ Tall Ship Senyavin	
35	22¢ Pohnpei Mountain starling	
36	25¢ Tonachau Peak	
37	36¢ Tall Ship	
38	45¢ Sleeping Lady	
39	$10 National Seal	
C34	33¢ Great truk white-eye	
C35	44¢ Blue-faced parrotfinch	
C36	$1 Yap monarch	
	Booklet Panes 1988	
33a	15¢ booklet pane of (10)	4.25
36a	25¢ booklet pane of (10)	7.00
36b	booklet pane of (10), 5—15¢ & 5—25¢	5.50
	1985 COMMEMORATIVES & AIR MAILS	
45 & C16-18	22¢-44¢ Nan Mandol Ruins, 4 varieties	4.00
	1986 COMMEMORATIVES & AIRMAILS	
46 & C19-20	22¢, 44¢ Peace Year	4.50
48-51	22¢ on 20¢ Postal Service, block of 4 attached	2.50
52 & C21-24	22¢-44¢ AMERIPEX '86, 5 varieties	5.50
53	22¢ Passport	.80
54-55 & C26-27	5¢-44¢ Christmas, 4 varieties	4.00

Micronesia #56-145; C28-C38

SCOTT NO.	DESCRIPTION	UNUSED F/NH

1987 COMMEMORATIVES & AIR MAILS

56 & C28-30	22¢-44¢ Shelter for Homeless, 4 varieties	4.25
57	$1 CAPEX '87 souvenir sheet	3.25
58 & C31-33	22¢-44¢ Christmas, 4 varieties	3.75

1988 COMMEMORATIVES & AIR MAILS

59-62 & C37-38	22¢, 44¢ Colonial Flags, 7 varieties	5.75
63-66	25¢ & 45¢ Summer Olympics, 2 pairs	3.00
67-70	25¢ Christmas, block of 4 attached	2.25
71	25¢ Truk Lagoon, souvenir sheet of 18 varieties	9.50

1989 COMMEMORATIVES

72-75	45¢ Flowers, block of 4 attached	3.75
76	$1 Japanese Art souvenir sheet	2.10
77-80	25¢, 45¢ Sharks, attached, 2 pairs	3.00
81	25¢ Space Achievements souvenir sheet of 9	5.50
82	$2.40 Priority Mail	4.75
83-102	1¢-$5 Seashells (12)	23.50
85a	15¢ Commercial trochus pane (10)	3.25
88a	25¢ Triton's trumpet pane (10)	5.50
88b	5 (15¢) + 5 (25¢) pane 10	4.50
103	25¢ Fruits & Flowers, sheet of 18	9.50
104-05	Christmas	1.50

1990 COMMEMORATIVES

106-09	World Wildlife Fund (4 varieties)	1.75
110-13	45¢ Whaling Ships & Artifacts, 4 attached	3.75
114	$1 Whaling Souvenir Sheet	2.50
115	$1 Penny Black Anniversary Souvenir Sheet	2.50
116-20	25¢ P.A.T.S. strip of 5	2.75
121	$1 Expo '90 Souvenir Sheet	2.50
122-23	25¢ & 45¢ Loading Mail	1.75
124-26	25¢ Joint Issue, 3 attached	2.00
127-30	45¢ Moths, 4 attached	3.75
131	25¢ Christmas, sheetlet of 9	5.00

1991

132	25¢+45¢ Government bldgs., Souvenir Sheet of 2	1.75
133	$1 New Capitol Souvenir Sheet	2.25
134-37	29¢+50¢ Turtles, 2 pairs	6.50
138-41	29¢ Operation Desert Storm, 4 attached	2.50
142	$2.90 Operation Desert Storm Priority Mail	6.00
142a	$2.90 Operation Desert Storm Souvenir Sheet	6.50
143	29¢ Phila Nippon Souvenir Sheet of 3	1.80
144	50¢ Phila Nippon Souvenir Sheet of 3	3.10
145	$1 Phila Nippon Souvenir Sheet	2.25

Micronesia #146-198

SCOTT NO.	DESCRIPTION	UNUSED F/NH

146   149a

1991 (continued)

146-48	29¢ Christmas 1991 set of 3	2.75
149	29¢ Pohnpei Rain Forest, sheetlet of 18	14.75

 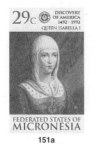

150a   151a

1992

150	29¢ Peace Corps/Kennedy, strip of 5	3.25
151	29¢ Columbus, strip of 3	2.10

152   154

152-53	29¢, 50¢ UN Membership Anniversary	1.75
153a	same, Souvenir Sheet of 2	1.75
154	29¢ Christmas, 1992	.70

155a   156

1993

155	29¢ Pioneers of Flight I, 8 attached	5.00

1993-94

156-67	10¢-$2.90, Fish, 16 varieties	22.50

168a   172   173

177a   179   182

1993

168	29¢ Sailing Ships, sheetlet of 12	7.50
172	29¢ Thomas Jefferson	.70
173-76	29¢ Canoes, 4 attached	2.75
177	29¢ Local Leaders I, strip of 4	2.75
178	50¢ Pioneers of Flight II, 8 attached	8.75
179-80	29¢, 50¢ Tourist Attractions, Pohnpei	1.75
181	$1 Tourist Attractions, Souvenir Sheet	2.25
182-83	29¢, 50¢ Butterflies, 2 pairs	3.75

184   186a

184-85	29¢-50¢ Christmas 1993	1.75
186	29¢ Micronesia Culture, sheetlet of 18	15.00

192a   193a   194

1994

187-89	29¢-50¢ Tourist Attractions, Kosrae	2.75
190	"Hong Kong '94" miniature sheet of 4 (#182a, 182b, 183a, 183b)	4.00
191	29¢ Pioneers of Flight III, 8 attached	5.00
192	29¢ 1994 Micronesian Games, 4 attached	2.75
193	29¢ Native Costumes, 4 attached	2.75
194	29¢ Constitution, 15th Anniversary	.90

195a   198a   196

195	29¢ Flowers, strip of 4	2.75
196-97	50¢ World Cup Soccer, pair	2.25
198	29¢ 10th Anniv. Inauguration Postal Service, 4 attached	2.75

Micronesia #199-249

211

SCOTT NO.	DESCRIPTION	UNUSED F/NH

 199a   201a  202

199	"PHILAKOREA '94" Dinosaur, miniature sheet of 3	4.25
200	50¢ Pioneers of Flight IV, 8 attached	8.75
201	29¢ Migratory Birds, 4 attached	3.95
202-03	29¢, 50¢ Christmas 1994	2.50
204-07	32¢ Local Leaders II, set of 4	3.95

 208

1995

| 208 | 50¢ New Year 1995 (Year of the Boar) | 1.50 |

 209a  211a  228a

209	32¢ Chuuk Lagoon, 4 attached	3.50
210	32¢ Pioneers of Flight V, 8 attached	5.75
211	32¢ Dogs, 4 attached	3.00
213-26	32¢-$5.00 Fish, set of 7	26.00
227	32¢ Fish, sheetlet of 25 (1996)	25.00
228	32¢ Flowers II, strip of 4	3.00
229	$1 UN 50th Anniversary Souvenir Sheet	2.25

 230a  231a

230	32¢ Orchids (Singapore '95), min. sheet of 4	3.00
231	60¢ US Warships, 4 attached	5.50
232	50¢ Temple of Heaven Souvenir Sheet	1.50
233	60¢ Pioneers of Flight VI, 8 attached	11.50

SCOTT NO.	DESCRIPTION	UNUSED F/NH

 234  236

| 234-35 | 32¢-60¢ Christmas Poinsettias | 2.00 |
| 236 | 32¢ Yitzhak Rabin | .75 |

 238a  239a

 240a  241a

1996

237	50¢ New Year 1996 (Year of the Rat)	1.50
238	32¢ Pioneers of Flight VII, 8 attached	5.75
239	32¢ Tourism in Yap, 4 attached	3.00
240	55¢ Sea Stars, 4 attached	6.00
241	60¢ Olympic Games Centenary, 4 attached	5.50
242	50¢ The Tarrying Garden, Suzhou Souvenir Sheet	1.50

 243  245a

| 243-44 | 32¢ Marine Vessels, 2 attached | 1.50 |
| 245 | 55¢ Automobile, sheet of 8 | 12.00 |

 247  249a

247	32¢ Police Drug Enforcement Dog	.75
248	32¢ Citrus Fruit, strip of 4	4.50
249	60¢ Pioneers of Flight VIII, 8 attached	14.50

SCOTT NO.	DESCRIPTION	UNUSED F/NH

250a   251

253

1996 (continued)

250	32¢ Fish (Taipei '96), miniature sheet of 4	3.00
251-52	32¢-60¢ Christmas 1996, set of 2	2.00
253	$3 Canoe & Flag of Micronesia	6.75

257, 258

1997

254	60¢ Deng Xiaoping, sheet of 4	5.50
255	$3 Deng Xiaoping, souvenir sheet	6.50
256	$2 Bridge to the Future, salute to Hong Kong, souvenir sheet	4.50
257	32¢ Year of the Ox	.75
258	$2 Year of the Ox, souvenir sheet	4.50

259

259	60¢ Return of Hong Kong to China, sheet of 6	9.00
260	$3 Return of Hong Kong to China, souvenir sheet	6.50
261	32¢ Sea Goddesses of the Pacific, sheet of 6	4.25

262

| 262-64 | 20¢-60¢ Hiroshige, 3 sheetlets of 3 | 9.00 |
| 265-66 | $2 Hiroshige, souvenir sheets(2) | 9.25 |

SCOTT NO.	DESCRIPTION	UNUSED F/NH

267a   268a   269a

267	32¢ 2nd Federated States of Micronesia Games, 4 attached	3.00
268	50¢ Elvis Presley, sheetlets of 6	7.00
269	32¢ Undersea Exploration, sheetlet of 9	6.50
270-72	$2 Undersea Exploration, souvenir sheets (3)	14.50

273a   274a

| 273 | 60¢ Princess Diana | 1.35 |
| 274 | 50¢ World Wildlife Fund, Butterfly Fish, 4 attached | 4.50 |

275-76

277-78

| 275-76 | 32¢ Christmas Paintings, Fra Angelico, pair | 1.50 |
| 277-78 | 60¢ Christmas Paintings, Simon Marmion, pair | 2.75 |

279

1998

279-80	50¢ Year of the Tiger, souvenir sheets (2)	3.00
281	$1 Micronesia's Admission to the UN, souvenir sheet	2.25
282	32¢ Disney's Winnie the Pooh, sheetlet of 8	6.25
283-84	$1 Disney's Winnie the Pooh, souvenir sheets (2)	9.00

Micronesia #285-394

SCOTT NO.	DESCRIPTION	UNUSED F/NH
285	32¢ 1998 World Cup Soccer Championships, sheetlet of 8	6.00
286-87	$2 1998 World Cup, souvenir sheets (2)	8.50
288	$3 Olympics, souvenir sheet	7.00
289-91	32¢-60¢ Old Testament Bible Stories, 3 sheetlets of 3	8.50
292-94	$2 Old Testament Bible Stories, souvenir sheets (3)	13.00
295	32¢ International Year of the Ocean, sheetlet of 9	6.75
296-98	$2 International Year of the Ocean, souvenir sheets (3)	13.50
299	50¢ Native Birds, 4 attached	4.50
300	$3 Native Birds, souvenir sheet	6.50
301-19A	1¢-$10.75 Fish, 20 varieties	52.50
320	32¢ Fala, FDR's Dog, sheetlet of 6	4.25
321-22	32¢-60¢ Christmas, 20th Century Art, 2 sheetlets of 3	6.25
323	$2 Christmas, 20th Century Art, souvenir sheet	4.50
324-25	60¢ John Glenn's Return to Space 2 sheets of 6	22.00
326-27	$2 John Glenn's Return to Space 2 souvenir sheets	9.50

1999

SCOTT NO.	DESCRIPTION	UNUSED F/NH
328-33	33¢-$11.75 Fish, 6 varieties	35.00
334	33¢ Russian Space Exploration, sheetlet of 20	16.00
335-36	$2 Russsian Space Exploration 2 souvenir sheets	9.50
337-38	33¢-50¢ "Romance of the 3 Kingdoms" by Lo Kuan-chung, 2 sheetlets of 5	9.25
339	$2 "Romance of the 3 Kingdoms", souvenir sheet	4.50
340-41	55¢ IBRA '99 Exhibition, set of 2	2.50
342	$2 IBRA '99 Exhibition, souvenir sheet	4.50
343	33¢ Voyages of the Pacific, sheetlet of 20	16.00
344	33¢ Space Achievements, sheetlet of 20	16.00
345-46	$2 Space Achievemnets, 2 souvenir sheets	9.50
347	33¢ Earth Day-Endangered Species, sheetlet of 20	16.00
348-49	$2 Earth Day-Endangered Species, 2 souvenir sheets	9.50
350-51	33¢ Hokusai Paintings, 2 sheetlets of 6	9.75
352-53	$2 Hokusai Paintings, 2 souvenir sheets	9.50
354	50¢ Flowers, photomosaic of Princess Diana, sheetlet of 8	9.00
355	20¢ Highlights of the 12th Century, sheetlet of 17	8.25
356	33¢ Science & Technology of Ancient China, sheetlet of 17	13.50
357	33¢ Costumes, sheetlet of 20	16.00
358-60	33¢-$2 Christmas-Van Dyck Paintings	7.00
361	$2 Christmas-Van Dyck Paintings, souvenir sheet	4.75
362	33¢ Millenium-Airplanes, sheetlet of 15	12.00
363-64	$2 Millenium-Airplanes, 2 souvenir sheets	9.50

2000

SCOTT NO.	DESCRIPTION	UNUSED F/NH
365-67	33¢ Orchids, 3 sheetlets of 6	14.50
368-69	$1 Orchids, 2 souvenir sheets	4.75
370	33¢ Leaders of the 20th Century, sheetlet of 12	9.50
371	$2 New Year 2000 (Year of the Dragon), souvenir sheet	4.75
372-73	20¢-55¢ Butterflies, 2 sheetlets of 6	9.75
374-76	$2 Butterflies, 3 souvenir sheets	14.25
377	20¢ Highlights of the 1920's, sheetlet of 17	8.25
378	33¢ Millennium 2000	.80
379	33¢ Peacemakers, sheetlet of 24	19.25
380	33¢ Philantropists, sheetlet of 16	12.75
381-82	33¢ Mushrooms, 2 sheetlets of 6	9.75
383-34	$2 Mushrooms, 2 souvenir sheets	9.50
385	33¢ Flowers of the Pacific, sheetlet of 6	4.75
386	33¢ Wildflowers, sheetlet of 6	4.75
387	$2 Flowers of the Pacific, souvenir sheet	4.75
388	$2 Wildflowers, souvenir sheet	4.75
389	33¢ 2000 Summer Olympics, Sydney, souvenir sheet of 4	3.25
390	33¢ Zeppelins & Airships, sheetlet of 6	4.75
391-92	$2 Zeppelins & Airships, 2 souvenir sheets	9.50
393	33¢ Queen Mother Flower Photomosaic, sheet of 8	6.50
394	33¢-$1 2000 Summer Olympics, Sydney, souvenir sheet of 3	4.00

Micronesia #395-506

SCOTT NO.	DESCRIPTION	UNUSED F/NH

395

395-98	33¢ Fish, set of 4	3.25
399-400	33¢ Fish, 2 sheetlets of 9	14.50
401-02	$2 Fish, 2 souvenir sheets	9.50
403	50¢ Pope John Paul II Photomosaic, sheet of 8	10.50

404

408a

404-07	20¢-$3.20 2000 Christmas, set of 4	9.25
408-09	33¢ Dogs & Cats, 2 sheetlets of 6	9.75
410-11	$2 Dogs & Cats, 2 souvenir sheets	9.50

414a

416a

2001

412-13	60¢ Year of the Snake, 2 souvenir sheets	2.75
414	50¢ Pokemon, sheet of 6	7.95
415	$2 Farfetch'd, souvenir sheet	4.75
416-17	50¢-60¢ Whales, 2 sheetlets of 6	15.95
418-19	$2 Whales, 2 souvenir sheets	9.50

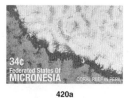
420a

424

420	34¢ Ecology, sheetlet of 6	5.00
421	60¢ Ecology, sheetlet of 4	5.50
422-23	$2 Ecology, 2 souvenir sheets	9.50
424-28	11¢-$3.50 Fish, set of 5	12.75
429	$12.25 Blue-spotted boxfish	30.00
430-35	34¢ Japanese Art, set of 6	5.00
436	34¢ Japanese Art, sheetlet of 6	5.00
437-38	$2 Japanese Art, 2 imperf sheets	9.50
439	60¢ Toulouse-Lautrec Paintings, sheetlets of 3	4.25
440	$2 Toulouse-Lautrec Paintings, souvenir sheet	4.75
441	60¢ Queen Victoria, sheetlet of 6	8.50
442	$2 Queen Victoria, souvenir sheet	4.75
443	60¢ Queen Elizabeth II, 75th Birthday, sheet of 6	8.50
444	$2 Queen Elizabeth II, 75th Birthday, souvenir sheet	4.75

445

449

457a

SCOTT NO.	DESCRIPTION	UNUSED F/NH
445-46	60¢ Marine Life, 2 sheetlets of 6	17.00
447-48	$2 Marine Life, 2 souvenir sheets	9.50
449-52	60¢ Prehistoric Animals, set of 4	5.50
453-54	60¢ Prehistoric Animals, 2 sheetlets of 6	17.00
455-56	$2 Prehistoric Animals, 2 souvenir sheets	9.50
457-58	50¢ Shells, 2 sheetlets of 6	13.75
459-60	$2 Sheets, 2 souvenir sheets	9.50

461

469a

473

461-64	5¢-$2.10 Birds, set of 4	6.00
465-66	60¢ Birds, 2 sheetlets of 6	17.00
467-68	$2 Birds, 2 souvenir sheets	9.50
469-70	60¢ Nobel Prizes Cent., 2 sheetlets of 6	17.00
471-72	$2 Nobel Prizes Cent., 2 souvenir sheets	9.50
473-76	22¢-$1 Christmas, set of 4	5.00
477	$2 Christmas, souvenir sheet	4.75
478-79	60¢ Attack on Pearl Harbor, 60th Anniv., 2 sheetlets of 6	17.00
480-81	$2 Attack on Pearl Harbor, 60th Anniv., 2 souvenir sheets	9.50

485

492a

494a

2002

482	60¢ Year of the Horse, sheetlet of 5	7.00
483	80¢ Reign of Queen Elizabeth II, 50th Anniv., sheetlet of 4	7.25
484	$2 Reign of Queen Elizabeth II, 50th Anniv., souvenir sheet	4.75
485	$1 United We Stand	2.25
486-87	$1 2002 Winter Olympics, set of 2	4.75
488-89	60¢ Japanese Art, 2 sheetlets of 6	17.00
490-91	$2 Japanese Art, 2 souvenir sheets	9.50
492	80¢ Intl. Year of Mountains, sheet of 4	7.25
493	$2 Intl. Year of Mountains, souvenir sheet	4.75
494	60¢ President John F. Kennedy, sheet of 4	5.50
495	$2 President John F. Kennedy, souvenir sheet	4.75
496	60¢ Princess Diana, sheetlet of 6	8.50
497	$2 Princess Diana, souvenir sheet	4.75

498a

502

504

498	80¢ International Year of Eco-Tourism, sheet of 6	10.50
499	$2 International Year of Eco-Tourism, souvenir sheet	4.75
500	$1 20th World Boy Scout Jamboree, Thailand, sheet of 3	6.75
501	$2 20th World Boy Scout Jamboree, Thailand, souvenir sheet	4.75
502-03	$1 2002 Winter Olympics, redrawn smaller rings, set of 2	4.75
503a	$2 2002 Winter Olympics, redrawn smaller rings, souvenir sheet	4.75
504	37¢ Xavier High School, 50th Anniversary	.90

507a

509

525

Micronesia #507-577; C1-C49; U1-U3; UX1-UX4

507	80¢ Teddy Bear Centennial, sheet of 4	7.00
508	37¢ Elvis Presley (1935-77), sheetlet of 6	5.50
509-13	15¢-$1 Christmas, set of 5	6.75
514	$2 Christmas, souvenir sheet	4.75
515-19	37¢-80¢ Flora, Fauna & Mushrooms, set of 5 sheets of 6	39.50
520-24	$2 Flora, Fauna & Mushrooms, set of 5 souvenir sheets	23.75
525-37	3¢-$13.65 Bird Definitives, set of 13	59.50

538a

539a

543a

2003

538	60¢ 1st Non-Stop Solo Transatlantic Flight 75th Anniversary, sheet of 6	8.00
539	37¢ Year of the Ram, sheet of 6	5.50
540	37¢ Astronauts Killed in Shuttle Columbia, In Memoriam, sheet of 7	6.40
541	$1 Coronation of Queen Elizabeth II, 50th Anniversary, sheet of 3	6.75
542	$2 Coronation of Queen Elizabeth II, 50th Anniversary, souvenir sheet	4.75
543	$1 Prince Williams, 21st Birthday, sheet of 3	6.75
544	$2 Prince Williams, 21st Birthday, souvenir sheet	4.75
545-46	37¢ Operation Iraqi Frredom, set of 2 sheets of 6	11.00
547	60¢ Tour de France Bicycle Race, Centenary, sheet of 4	5.50
548	$2 Tour de France Bicycle Race, Centenary, souvenir sheet	4.75
549	$1 International Year of Freshwater, sheet of 3	6.75
550	$2 International Year of Freshwater, souvenir sheet	4.75
551	55¢ Powered Flight Centenary, sheet of 6	7.50
552	$2 Powered Flight Centenary, souvenir sheet	4.75
553-54	80¢ Circus Performers, set of 2 sheets of 4	14.00
555	80¢ Paintings of Boy Scouts by Norman Rockwell, sheet of 4	7.00
556	$2 Paintings of Boy Scouts by Norman Rockwell, souvenir sheet, imperf.	4.75
557	80¢ Paintings by Paul Gauguin, sheet of 4	7.00
558	$2 Paintings by Paul Gauguin, souvenir sheet, imperf.	4.75
559-62	37¢-80¢ Paintings by James McNeill Whistler, set of 4	5.25
563	$1 Paintings by James McNeill Whistler, sheet of 3	6.75
564	$2 Paintings by James McNeill Whistler, souvenir sheet, imperf.	4.75
565-68	37¢-80¢ Christmas, set of 4	5.25
569	$2 Christmas, souvenir sheet	4.75
570-73	80¢ Cats, Dogs, Birds & Amphibians, set of 4 sheets of 4	28.00
574-77	$2 Cats, Dogs, Birds & Amphibians, set of 4 souvenir sheets	19.00

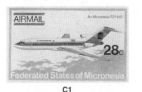
C1

C39

1984-94 AIR MAIL

C1-3	28¢-40¢ Aircraft, set of 3	2.50
C25	$1 Ameripex '86 Souvenir Sheet	4.25
C39-42	45¢ State Flags, block of 4 attached	3.75

C43

C43-46	22¢-45¢ Aircraft Serving Micronesia (4 varieties)	3.10
C47-48	40¢, 50¢ Aircraft and Ships	1.95
C49	$2.90 25th Anniv. First Moon Landing, souvenir sheet	6.50

Postal Stationery

U1	20¢ National Flag	16.50
U2	22¢ Tail Ship Senyavin	10.00
U3	29¢ on 30¢ New Capitol	4.50

Postal Cards

UX1-4	20¢ Scenes, set of 4	6.50

Palau #1-98

REPUBLIC OF PALAU

Palau is a Strategic Trust of the United States; a designation granted by the United Nations after World War II. It is the first Trust Territory to be granted postal independence, which became effective November 1, 1982. The first stamps were issued March 10, 1983.

SCOTT NO.	DESCRIPTION	UNUSED F/NH

1983 COMMEMORATIVES

| 1-4 | 20¢ Art and Preamble, attached | 3.25 |
| 5-8 | 20¢ Birds, attached | 2.25 |

1983-84 DEFINITIVES

9-21	1¢-$5, 13 varieties, singles, complete set	25.00
9	1¢ Sea Fan	
10	3¢ Map Cowrie	
11	5¢ Jellyfish	
12	10¢ Hawksbill Turtle	
13	13¢ Giant Clam	
14	20¢ Parrotfish	
15	28¢ Chambered Nautilus	
16	30¢ Dappled Sea Cucumber	
17	37¢ Sea Urchin	
18	50¢ Starfish	
19	$1 Squid	
20	$2 Dugong (1984)	
21	$5 Pink Sponge (1984)	

1983-84 Booklet Panes

13a	13¢ Giant Clam (10)	12.00
13b	13¢ (5) & 20¢ (5)	14.50
14b	20¢ Parrotfish (10)	14.00

24

28

33

1983 COMMEMORATIVES

24-27	20¢ Whales, attached	2.50
28-32	20¢ Christmas, strip of 5	4.00
33-40	20¢ When Different Worlds Meet, attached	4.75

41

51

1984 COMMEMORATIVES

41-50	20¢ Seashells, attached	4.50
51-54	40¢ Explorer Ships, attached	4.00
55-58	20¢ Fishing, attached	2.25
59-62	20¢ Christmas, Flowers, attached	2.25

1985 COMMEMORATIVES

| 63-66 | 22¢ Audubon—Birds, attached | 2.75 |
| 67-70 | 22¢ Canoes, attached | 2.50 |

1985 DEFINITIVES

75-85	14¢-$10, 7 varieties, singles complete set	30.00
75	14¢ Trumpet Triton	....
76	22¢ Parrotfish	....
77	25¢ Damsel Fish	....
79	33¢ Clownfish	....
80	39¢ Sea Turtle	....
81	44¢ Sailfish	....
85	$10 Spinner Dolphins	....

1985 Booklet Panes

75a	14¢ Trumpet Triton (10)	10.00
76a	22¢ Parrotfish (10)	13.00
76b	14¢ (5) & 22¢ (5)	14.00

94

95

1985 COMMEMORATIVES

86-89	44¢ Youth Year, attached	3.75
90-93	14¢-44¢ Christmas, 4 varieties	3.25
94	$1 Trans-Pacific, souvenir sheet	3.50
95-98	44¢ Halley's Comet, attached	4.00

Palau #99-218; C17

SCOTT NO.	DESCRIPTION	UNUSED F/NH

99, 104

1986 COMMEMORATIVES

99-102	44¢ Songbirds, attached	4.00
103	14¢ World of Sea and Reef, Ameripex '86 sheet of 40	47.50
104-08	22¢ Seashells, strip of 5	3.25

109, 113, 117

109-12, C17	22¢ International Peace Year, 4 attached, 44¢ Airmail	4.00
113-16	22¢ Reptiles, attached	2.50
117-21	22¢ Christmas, attached	2.50

121B, 122, 126

1987 COMMEMORATIVES

| 121B-E | 44¢ Butterflies, attached | 4.50 |
| 122-25 | 44¢ Fruit Bats, attached | 4.50 |

1987-88 FLOWER DEFINITIVES

126-42	1¢-$5, 17 varieties, single complete set	55.00
126	1¢ Kerdeu	......
127	3¢ Ngemoel	......
128	5¢ Uror	......
129	10¢ Woody Vine	......
130	14¢ Rur	......
131	15¢ Jaml (1988)	......
132	22¢ Denges	......
133	25¢ Ksid (1988)	......
134	36¢ Meldii (1988)	......
135	39¢ Emeridesh	......
136	44¢ Eskeam	......
137	45¢ Shrub (1988)	......
138	50¢ Rriu	......
139	$1 Koranges	......
140	$2 Meliin	......
141	$5 Orchid	......
142	$10 Flower Bouquet (1988)	19.00

1987 Booklet Panes

130a	14¢ Bikkia Palauensis (10)	5.00
132a	22¢ Bruguiera Gymnorhiza (10)	8.50
132b	14¢ (5) and 22¢ (5)	8.50

1988 Booklet Panes

131a	15¢ Limnophila (10)	4.50
133a	25¢ Ksid (10)	6.50
133b	15¢ (5) 25¢ (5)	6.50

146, 155

1987 COMMEMORATIVES (continued)

146-49	22¢ Capex '87, attached	2.25
150-54	22¢ Seashells, strip of 5	3.00
155-63	14¢-44¢ U.S. Bicentennial 3 attached, strips of 3	5.50
164-67	12¢-44¢ Japan Links	2.75
168	$1 Japan souvenir sheet	2.50

173, 178

| 173-77 | 22¢ Christmas, attached | 3.10 |
| 178-82 | 22¢ Marine Species, attached | 3.10 |

187, 196a, 198

1988 COMMEMORATIVES

183-86	44¢ Butterflies, attached	4.00
187-90	44¢ Birds, attached	4.00
191-95	25¢ Seashells, strip of 5	3.00
196	25¢ Finlandia sheetlet of 6	3.25
197	45¢ PRAGA '88, sheetlet of 6	6.00
198-202	25¢ Christmas, strip of 5	3.00
203	25¢ Chambered Nautilus, sheetlet of 5	3.50

204, 208

1989 COMMEMORATIVES

204-07	45¢ Endangered Birds, attached	4.00
208-11	45¢ Mushrooms, attached	4.00
212-16	25¢ Seashells, strip of 5	3.50
217	$1 Japanese Art souvenir sheet	2.50
218	25¢ Apollo 11 mission, sheetlet of 25	14.50

Palau #219-299

SCOTT NO.	DESCRIPTION	UNUSED F/NH

219   220a   222

1989 COMMEMORATIVES (continued)

219	$2.40 Priority Mail	5.00
220	25¢ Literacy (block of 10)	6.25
221	25¢ Stilt Mangrove Fauna, sheetlet of 20	14.00
222-26	25¢ Christmas (strip of 5)	3.00

227   231

1990 COMMEMORATIVES

| 227-30 | 25¢ Soft Coral (4 attached) | 2.50 |
| 231-34 | 45¢ Forest Birds (4 attached) | 4.00 |

235a   237

235	Prince Boo Visit (sheet of 9)	5.00
236	$1 Penny Black Ann.	2.50
237-41	45¢ Tropical Orchids (strip of 5)	4.75

242   249   254

242-45	45¢ Butterflies II (4 attached)	3.75
246	25¢ Lagoon Life, sheet of 25	16.50
247-48	45¢ Pacifica, pair	2.75
249-53	25¢ Christmas, strip of 5	2.75
254-57	45¢ U.S. Forces in Palau, attached	4.00
258	$1 U.S. Peleliu, souvenir sheet	2.35

259   263a   267

1991

| 259-62 | 30¢ Hard Corals, attached | 2.75 |
| 263 | 30¢ Angaur—The Phosphate Island sheet of 16 | 12.00 |

1991-92

| 266-83 | 1¢-$10 Birds, 18 varieties | 50.00 |

1991 Booklet Panes

269b	19¢ Palau fantail booklet pane (10)	4.75
272a	Booklet pane of 10, 19¢ (5) + 29¢ (5)	6.00
272b	29¢ Palau fruit dove booklet pane (10)	6.00

288a   289a

290a   294a

1991 (continued)

288	29¢ Christianity in Palau, sheetlet of 6	3.50
289	29¢ Marine Life, sheetlet of 20	16.75
290	20¢ Operation Desert Storm, sheetlet of 9	4.50
291	$2.90 Operation Desert Storm Priority Mail	6.00
292	$2.90 Operation Desert Storm Souvenir Sheet	6.00
293	29¢ 10th Anniversary of Independence sheetlet of 8	5.50
294	50¢ Giant Clams, Souvenir Sheet of 5	5.50

295a   297a

295	29¢ Japanese Heritage in Palau, sheet of 6	4.00
296	$1.00 Phila Nippon, Souvenir Sheet	2.10
297	29¢ Peace Corps, sheetlet of 6	4.00

299a

| 298 | 29¢ Christmas, 1991, strip of 5 | 3.25 |
| 299 | 29¢ Pearl Harbor/WWII, sheetlet of 10 | 6.75 |

Palau #300-348

SCOTT NO.	DESCRIPTION	UNUSED F/NH
	1992	
300	50¢ Butterflies, attached	4.50
301	29¢ Shells, strip of 5	3.25
302	29¢ Columbus & Age of Discovery, sheetlet of 20	14.00
303	29¢ World Environment, sheetlet of 24	16.50
304-09	50¢ Olympians, set of 6 Souvenir Sheets	7.50
310	29¢ Elvis Presley, sheetlet of 9	6.50
311	50¢ WWII Aircraft, sheet of 10	10.00
312	29¢ Christmas, strip of 5	3.25
	1993	
313	50¢ Fauna, 4 attached	4.00
314	29¢ Seafood, 4 attached	2.25
315	50¢ Sharks, 4 attached	4.00
316	29¢ WWII in the Pacific, sheetlet of 10	6.50
317	29¢ Christmas 1993, strip of 5	3.75
318	29¢ Prehistoric Sea Creatures, sheet of 25	16.50
319	29¢ International Year of Indigenous People, sheet of 2	2.75
320	$2.90 Quarrying of Stone Money, souvenir sheet	6.00
321	29¢ Jonah and the Whale, sheet of 25	16.50
	1994	
322	40¢ Rays "Hong Kong '94", 4 attached	3.50
323	20¢ Estuarine Crocodile, 4 attached	2.00
324	50¢ Large Seabirds, 4 attached	4.00
325	29¢ Action in the Pacific, 1944, sheet of 10	6.50
326	50¢ D-Day, sheet of 10	15.00
327	29¢ Pierre de Coubertin	.70
328-33	50¢-$2 Winter Olympic medalists, souvenir sheet of 1 (6)	15.00
334	29¢ PHILAKOREA '94 (Fish), sheetlet of 8	5.25
335	40¢ PHILAKOREA '94 (Mammals), sheetlet of 8	7.00
336	50¢ PHILAKOREA '94 (Birds), sheetlet of 8	8.00
337	29¢ 25th Anniversary First Manned Moon Landing, sheet of 20	14.00
338	29¢ Independence Day, strip of 5	3.25
339	$1 50th Anniv. of Invasion of Peleliu, souvenir sheet	2.50
340	29¢ Disney Characters Visit Palau, sheetlet of 9	5.75
341-42	$1 Mickey, Donald visiting Palau, souvenir sheet of 1 (2)	5.00
343	$2.90 Pluto, Mickey in Boat, souvenir sheet	6.00
344	20¢ Int. Year of the Family, sheetlet of 12	5.50
345	29¢ Christmas, strip of 5	3.25
346-48	29¢-50¢ World Cup '94, 3 sheetlets of 12	30.00

Palau #350-400

SCOTT NO.	DESCRIPTION	UNUSED F/NH

351

1995

| 350 | 32¢ Elvis Presley, sheetlet of 9 | 6.25 |
| 351-65 | 1¢-$10 Palau Fishes, set of 15 | 47.50 |

1995 Booklet Panes

366a	20¢ Magenta dottyback (10)	4.50
367a	32¢ Reef Lizardfish (10)	7.50
367b	same, 20¢ (5) & 32¢ (5)	6.00

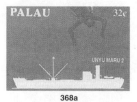
368a

369a

370a

372a

1995 (continued)

368	32¢ WWII Japanese Sunken Ships, sheetlet of 18	12.25
369	32¢ Flying Dinosaurs, sheetlet of 18	12.25
370	50¢ Experimental Aircraft (Jets), sheetlet of 12	12.50
371	$2 Experimental Aircraft (Concorde) souvenir sheet	4.50
372	32¢ Underwater Submersibles, sheetlet of 18	12.25

373a

374a

373	32¢ Marine Life (Singapore '95), 4 attached	3.00
374	60¢ UN, FAO, 50th Anniversary, 4 attached	5.50
375-76	$2 UN Emblem souvenir sheet (2)	9.00
377-78	20¢-32¢ Independence Anniversary, min. sheet of 4 & single	2.50
379-80	32¢-60¢ 50th End of WWII, sheetlets of 12 & 5	16.00

381

382a

384

381	$3 B-29 Nose souvenir sheet	6.50
382	32¢ Christmas 1995, strip of 5	3.75
383	32¢ Life Cycle of the Sea Turtle, sheetlet of 12	9.00
384	32¢ John Lennon	.75

385a

388a

389a

1996

385	10¢ New Year 1996 (Year of the Rat), strip of 4	1.00
386	60¢ New Year 1996 (Year of the Rat), min. sheet of 2	2.95
387	32¢ UNICEF, 50th Anniversary, 4 attached	3.00
388	32¢ Marine Life, strip of 5	3.75
389-90	32¢-60¢ The Circumnavigators, 2 sheetlets of 9	19.25
391-92	$3 The Circumnavigators, 2 souvenir sheets	15.00
392A-F	1¢-6¢ Disney Sweethearts, set of 6	.55

393a

396a

393	60¢ Disney Sweethearts, sheetlet of 9	15.00
394-95	$2 Disney Sweethearts, 2 souvenir sheets	9.00
396	20¢ Jerusalem Bible Studies, sheetlet of 30	15.00

397-98

399-400

| 397-98 | 40¢ 1996 Summer Olympics, pair | 1.80 |
| 399-400 | 60¢ 1996 Summer Olympics, pair | 2.70 |

401a

403a

407-08

Palau #401-478

SCOTT NO.	DESCRIPTION	UNUSED F/NH

409a

1996 (continued)

Scott	Description	Price
401	32¢ 1996 Summer Ollympics, sheet of 20	16.00
402	50¢ Birds over the Palau Lagoon, sheet of 20	27.00
403	40¢ Military Spy Aircraft, sheet of 12	12.00
404	60¢ Weird & Wonderful Aircraft, sheet of 12	17.00
405	$3 Stealth Bomber, souvenir sheet	6.75
406	$3 Martin Marietta X-24B, souvenir sheet	6.75
407-08	20¢ Independence, 2nd Anniversary, pair	.90
409	32¢ Christmas 1996, strip of 5	3.75
410	32¢ Voyage to Mars, sheet of 12	8.50
411-12	$3 Mars rover & Water probe, 2 souvenir sheets	14.00

415

422a

420a

1997

Scott	Description	Price
412A	$2 Year of the Ox, souvenir sheet	4.50
413	$1 50th Anniv. of South Pacific Commission, souvenir sheet	2.25
414-19	1¢-$3 Flowers (Hong Kong '97), set of 6	7.00
420	32¢ Shoreline Plants (Hong Kong '97), 4 attached	3.00
421	50¢ Shoreline Plants (Hong Kong '97), 4 attached	4.50
422-23	32¢-60¢ Bicentennial of the Parachute, sheet of 8	19.50
424-25	$2 Bicentennial of the Parachute, 2 souvenir sheets	9.00
426	20¢ Native Birds & Trees, sheet of 12	5.25

427a

428a

431a

Scott	Description	Price
427-28	32¢-60¢ 50th Anniv. of UNESCO, sheet of 8 & 5	13.50
429-30	$2 50th Anniv. of UNESCO, 2 souvenir sheets	9.00
431	32¢ Prints of Hiroshige, sheet of 5	3.50
432-33	$2 Prints of Hiroshige, 2 souvenir sheets	9.00

–SUPPLIES–
Don't forget that Harris offers a complete line of albums, supplies and accessories for all your stamp collecting needs!

434a   435

Scott	Description	Price
434	32¢ Volcano Goddesses, sheet of 6	4.25
435	32¢ 3rd Anniversary of Independence	.75

436a

440a

450a

Scott	Description	Price
436	32¢ Oceanographic Research, sheetlet of 9	6.50
437-39	$2 Oceanographic Research, souvenir sheets (3)	15.00
440	60¢ Princess Diana	1.35
441-46	1¢-10¢ Disney "Let's Read"	1.20
447	32¢ Disney Characters "Reading", sheetlet of 9	6.00
448	$2 Daisy "The library is for everyone" souvenir sheet	5.00
449	$3 Mickey "Books are magical" souvenir sheet	6.75
450	32¢ Children singing Christmas carol, strip of 5	3.75

453a

457a

458a

1998

Scott	Description	Price
451-52	50¢ Year of the Tiger, souvenir sheets (2)	2.50
453	32¢ Hubble Space Telescope, sheetlet of 6	4.50
454-56	$2 Hubble Space Telescope, souvenir sheets (3)	15.00
457	60¢ Mother Teresa, sheetlet of 4	5.00
458	32¢ Deep Sea Robots, sheetlet of 18	14.00
459-60	$2 Deep Sea Robots, souvenir sheets (2)	9.00

461a

463a

466a

Scott	Description	Price
461	20¢ Israel Stamp Expo ovpt. on Sc. #396, sheetlet of 30	14.50
462	40¢ Legend of Orachel, sheetlet of 12	11.50
463	50¢ 1998 World Cup Soccer, sheetlet of 8	9.00
464	$3 1998 World Cup Soccer, souvenir sheet	6.50
465	32¢ 4th Micronesian Games, sheetlet of 9	6.50
466	32¢ Christmas, Rudolph the Red Nosed Reindeer, strip of 5	3.75
467-70	20¢-60¢ Disney's " A Bug's Life" 4 sheets of 4	16.75
471-74	$2 Disney's "A Bug's Life" 4 souvenir sheets	21.00
475-76	60¢ John Glenn's Return to Space, 2 sheets of 8	22.50
477-78	$2 John Glenn's Return to Space, 2 souvenir sheets	9.50

Palau #479-593

SCOTT NO.	DESCRIPTION	UNUSED F/NH

480a

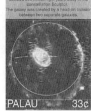
495a

507a

564a

568a

564-65	33¢ Marine Life, 2 sheetlets of 6	10.00
566-67	$2 Marine Life, 2 souvenir sheets	9.50
568	20¢ Millennium, sheetlet of 6	2.75
569	55¢ Millennium, sheetlet of 6	8.25

1999

479	33¢ Environmentalists, sheetlet of 16	12.00
480	33¢ MIR Space Station, sheetlet of 6	4.50
481-84	$2 MIR Space Station, 4 souvenir sheets	19.00
485-94	1¢-$3.20 US & Palau Personalities, set of 10	14.00
495	33¢ Australia '99 World Stamp Expo, sheetlet of 12	9.00
496-97	$2 Australia '99, 2 souvenir sheets	9.50
501	33¢ Exploration of Mars, sheetlet of 6	4.50
502-05	$2 Exploration of Mars, 4 souvenir sheets	19.00
506	33¢ Pacific Insects, Earth Day, sheetlet of 20	15.00
507	33¢ International Space Station, sheetlet of 6	4.50
508-11	$2 International Space Station, 4 souvenir sheets	19.00

570a

574a

570-71	33¢ New and Recovering Species, 2 sheetlets of 6	10.00
572-73	$2 New and Recovering Species, 2 souvenir sheets	9.50
574	20¢ Dinosaurs, sheetlet of 6	2.75
575	33¢ Dinosaurs, sheetlet of 6	5.00
576-77	$2 Dinosaurs, 2 souvenir sheets	9.50
578-79	55¢ Queen Mother's 100th birthday, 2 sheetlets of 4	11.00
580	$2 Queen Mother's 100th birthday, souvenir sheet	4.75

512a

512	33¢ 20th Century Visionaries, sheetlet of 25	18.75
513-14	33¢ Hokusai Paintings, 2 sheetlets of 6	9.75
515-16	$2 Hokusai Paintings, 2 souvenir sheets	9.50

517a

524a

517	33¢ Apollo 11, 30th Anniversary, sheetlet of 6	5.00
518-21	$2 Apollo 11, 30th Anniversary, 4 souvenir sheets	19.00
522	60¢ Queen Mother (b.1900), sheetlet of 4	5.00
523	$2 Queen Mother (b.1900), souvenir sheet	4.75
524	33¢ Hubble Space Telescope Images, sheetlet of 6	5.00
525-28	$2 Hubble Space Telescope Images, 4 souvenir sheets	19.00
530	33¢ Love for Dogs, sheetlet of 10	8.00
531-32	$2 Love for Dogs, 2 souvenir sheets	9.50

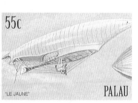
581a

584a

581	55¢ First Zeppelin Flight, sheetlet of 6	8.25
582-83	$2 First Zeppelin Flight, 2 souvenir sheets	9.50
584	33¢ Millennium, sheetlet of 17	16.00
585	50¢ Pope John Paul II, sheetlet of 8	10.00
586-87	60¢ Year of the Snake, 2 souvenir sheets	3.00

553a

557a

2000

533	55¢ Futuristic Space probes, sheetlet of 6	8.25
534-37	$2 Fururistic Space Probes, 4 souvenir sheets	19.00
538-39	20¢ Highlights of 1800-50 and Highlights of 1980-89, 2 Millenium sheetlets of 17	15.50
540	$2 New Year 2000 (Year of the Dragon)	4.75
541-45	$1-$11.75 US Presidents	49.50
546	20¢ 20th Century Discoveries about Prehistoric Life, sheetlet of 20	9.00
547	33¢ 2000 Summer Olympics, Sydney, sheetlet of 4	3.25
548	33¢ Future of Space Exploration, sheetlet of 6	5.00
549-52	$2 Future of Space Exploration, 4 souvenir sheets	19.00
553-54	20¢-33¢ Birds, 2 sheetlets of 6	7.50
555-56	$2 Birds, 2 souvenir sheets	9.50
557	33¢ Visionaries of the 20th Century, sheetlet of 20	16.00
558-61	33¢ 20th Century Science and Medicine Advances, 4 sheetlets of 5	16.00
562-63	$2 20th Century Science and Medicine Advances, 2 souvenir sheets	9.50

589a

592a

588	55¢ Pacific Ocean Marine Life, sheetlet of 6	8.25
589	20¢ Atlantic Ocean Fish, sheetlet of 6	2.75
590-91	$2 Atlantic Ocean Fish, 2 souvenir sheets	9.50
592	33¢ Pacific Arts Festival, sheetlet of 9	7.50
593	33¢ National Museum, 45th anniv., sheetlet of 12	10.00

ORDER BY MAIL, PHONE (800) 546-2995 OR FAX (256) 246-1116

Palau #594-716

SCOTT NO.	DESCRIPTION	UNUSED F/NH

594

602a

594-97	33¢ Butterflies, set of 4 singles	3.35
598-99	33¢ Butterflies, 2 sheetlets of 6	10.00
600-01	$2 Butterflies, 2 souvenir sheets	9.50
602-03	33¢ Flora and Fauna, 2 sheetlets of 6	10.00
604-05	$2 Flora and Fauna, 2 souvenir sheets	9.50

616

607

630a

2001

606	11¢ Lazarus Salil	.30
607-09	70¢-$12.25 Personalities, set of 3	32.50
610-11	60¢ Phila Nippon, Japan, 2 sheetlets of 5	14.00
612	60¢ Phila Nippon, Japan, sheetlet of 6	8.50
613-15	$2 Phila Nippon, Japan, 3 souvenir sheets	14.00
616-19	20¢-$1 Moths, set of 4	5.25
620-21	34¢-70¢ Moths, 2 sheetlets of 6	15.00
622-23	$2 Moths, 2 souvenir sheets	9.50
624-26	34¢-80¢ Nobel Prizes Cent., 3 sheetlets of 6	26.50
627-29	$2 Nobel Prizes Cent., 3 souvenir sheets	14.25
630-31	34¢-80¢ 2002 World Cup Soccer, 2 sheetlets of 6	16.50
632-33	$2 2002 World Cup Soccer, 2 souvenir sheets	9.50

634

638a

641

634-35	20¢-34¢ Christmas, set of 2	1.35
636	60¢ Queen Mother redrawn, sheet of 4 + label	5.50
637	$2 Queen Mother redrawn, souvenir sheet	4.75
638	60¢ Year of the Horse	1.35
639-40	55¢-60¢ Birds, 2 sheetlets of 6	16.25
641-42	$2 Birds of Palau, 2 souvenir sheets	9.50

643

648

670

2002

643-44	20¢-30¢ Palau-Japan Friendship Bridge, 2 sheets of 30	36.50
645	$1 United We Stand	2.25
646	80¢ Reign of Queen Elizabeth II, 50th Anniv., sheet of 4	7.25
647	$2 Reign of Queen Elizabeth II, 50th Anniv., souvenir sheet	4.75
648-669	1¢-$10 Birds, set of 22	70.00
670-73	20¢-80¢ Flowers, set of 4	4.50
674-75	60¢ Flowers, 2 sheetlets of 6	17.00
676-77	$2 Flowers, 2 souvenir sheets	9.50

678

680a

678-79	$1 2002 Winter Olympics, set of 2	4.75
680-81	50¢ Cats & Dogs, 2 sheetlets of 6	13.75
682-83	$2 Cats & Dogs, 2 souvenir sheets	9.50
684	80¢ Intl. Year of Mountains, sheet of 4	7.25
685	$2 Intl. Year of Mountains, souvenir sheet	4.75
686	37¢ Flags of Palau and its States, sheet of 17	15.75

696a 688

705a

687-88	$1 2002 Winter Olympics, redrawn, set of 2	4.75
689	60¢ Intl. Year of Ecotourism, sheet of 6	8.50
690	$2 Intl. Year of Ecotourism, souvenir sheet	4.75
691	60¢ Japanese Art, sheet of 6	8.50
692-93	80¢ Japanese Art, 2 sheets of 4	14.50
694-95	$2 Japanese Art, 2 souvenir sheets	9.50
696	60¢ Popeye, sheet of 6	8.50
697	$2 Popeye, souvenir sheet	4.75
698	37¢ Elvis Presley, sheet of 6	5.75
699-703	23¢-$1 Christmas, set of 5	6.75
704	$2 Christmas, souvenir sheet	4.75
705	60¢ Teddy Bears, Centenary, sheet of 4	5.75
706	80¢ Queen Mother, sheet of 4	7.25
707	$2 Queen Mother, souvenir sheet	4.75

708a

710a

712a

2003

708	60¢ 20th World Scout Jamboree, Thailand, sheet of 6	8.50
709	$2 20th World Scout Jamboree, Thailand, souvenir sheet	4.75
710	60¢ Shells, sheet of 6	8.50
711	$2 Shells, souvenir sheet	4.75
712	37¢ Year of the Ram, vert. strip of 3	2.75

714

713	80¢ President John F. Kennedy, sheet of 4	7.25
714-15	26¢-37¢ Birds, unserifed numerals	1.50
716	37¢ Astronauts, Space Shuttle Columbia, sheet of 7	6.50

Palau #717-749; B1-B4; C1-C23; U1-UC1; UX1

SCOTT NO.	DESCRIPTION	UNUSED F/NH

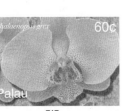
717a

723a

717	60¢ Orchids, sheet of 6	8.50
718	$2 Orchids, souvenir sheet	4.75
719	60¢ Insects, sheet of 6	8.50
720	$2 Insects, souvenir sheet	4.75
721	60¢ 1st Non-Stop Solo Transatlantic Flight, 75th Anniversary, sheet of 6	8.50
722	80¢ President Ronald Reagn, sheet of 4	7.25
723	80¢ Pricess Diana (1961-97), sheet of 4	7.25
724	$1 Coronation of Queen Elizabeth II, 50th Anniversary, sheet of 3	6.75
725	$2 Coronation of Queen Elizabeth II, 50th Anniversary, souvenir sheet	4.75
726	37¢ Operation Iraqi Freedom, sheet of 6	5.50
727	$1 Prince Williams, 21st Birthday, sheet of 3	6.75
728	$2 Prince Williams, 21st Birthday, souvenir sheet	4.75
729	60¢ Tour de France Bicycle Race Centenary, sheet of 4	7.25
730	$2 Tour de France Bicycle Race Centenary, souvenir sheet	4.75
731	55¢ Powered Flight, sheet of 6	7.50
732	$2 Powered Flight, souvenir sheet	4.75
733-36	37¢-$1 Paintings by James McNeil Whistler, set of 4	5.75
737	80¢ Paintings by James McNeil Whistler, sheet of 4	7.25
738	$2 Paintings by James McNeil Whistler, souvenir sheet	4.75
739-40	80¢ Circus Performers, set of 2 sheets of 4	14.50
741-44	37¢-$1 Christmas, set of 4	5.75
745	$2 Christmas, souvenir sheet	4.75

2004

746	60¢ Sea Turtles, sheet of 6	8.50
747	$2 Sea Turtles, souvenir sheet	4.75
748	80¢ Paintings of Norman Rockwell, sheet of 4	7.25
749	$2 Paintings of Norman Rockwell, souvenir sheet	4.75

B1

C1

C6

1988 SEMI POSTAL

| B1-B4 | (25¢ + 5¢) + (45¢ + 5¢) Olympics, 2 pairs | 4.50 |

AIR MAILS
1984 AIR MAILS

| C1-4 | 40¢ Seabirds, attached | 3.75 |

1985 AIR MAILS

C5	44¢ Audubon Birds	1.50
C6-9	44¢ German Links, attached	4.50
C10-13	44¢ Transpacific, attached	4.10

C14

SCOTT NO.	DESCRIPTION	UNUSED F/NH

C17

C18

C23a

| C14-16 | 44¢ Remeliik, strip of 3 | 4.00 |
| C17 | 44¢ Statue of Liberty | 1.25 |

1989 AIR MAILS

| C18-20 | 36¢-45¢ Aircraft, complete set of 3 | 2.75 |

1991 AIR MAILS

| C21 | 50¢ 10th Anniv. Airmail, self-adhesive | 1.75 |

1989 BOOKLET PANES

C18a	36¢ Aircraft pane (10)	8.00
C19a	39¢ Aircraft pane (10)	8.50
C20a	45¢ Aircraft pane (10)	10.00
C20b	5 (36¢) + 5 (45¢) Aircraft pane (10)	8.50

1995

| C22 | 50¢ World War II, Aircraft, sheetlet of 10 | 14.50 |
| C23 | 50¢ Birds (Swallows), 4 attached | 5.00 |

1985 ENVELOPE ENTIRES

U1	22¢ Marine Life	4.00
U2	22¢ Spear Fishing	7.00
U3	25¢ Chambered Nautilus	1.25
UC1	36¢ Bird, air letter sheet	6.00

1985 POSTAL CARDS

| UX1 | 14¢ Marine Life | 3.00 |

MASTER Worldwide Album Supplements

Master Supplements are designed to update the Harris Masterwork Deluxe and Standard, Citation and Senior Statesman Albums. Update your album today!

Item #	Year	Retail Price
90922060	2003 Master Supplement	$17.95
90921809	2002 Master Supplement	$16.95
90921315	2001 Master Supplement	$16.95
90921632	2000 Master Supplement	$16.95
5HRS102	1999 Master Supplement	$16.95
5HRS97	1998 Master Supplement	$16.95

Philippines #212-240; E1; J1-J7; Puerto Rico #210-216; J1-J3

SCOTT NO.	DESCRIPTION	UNUSED NH F	UNUSED NH AVG	UNUSED OG F	UNUSED OG AVG	USED F	USED AVG
	PHILIPPINES						
	U.S. Stamps of various issues overprinted						
	1899						
	On 260. Unwatermarked						
212	50¢ orange	550.00	345.00	385.00	265.00	190.00	130.00
	On 279, 279d, 267-68, 281, 282C, 283, 284, 275						
	Double Line Watermarked						
213	1¢ yellow green	5.00	3.25	3.60	2.15	1.10	.65
214	2¢ orange red	2.25	1.35	1.40	.95	.85	.50
215	3¢ purple	9.00	6.25	5.75	3.75	2.10	1.30
216	5¢ blue	8.25	5.00	5.50	3.40	1.75	1.05
217	10¢ brown (Type I)	27.00	16.00	17.00	11.25	4.75	3.10
217A	10¢ orange brown (Type II)	295.00	205.00	195.00	115.00	45.00	27.50
218	15¢ olive green	48.00	29.50	35.00	21.50	8.75	5.25
219	50¢ orange	170.00	105.00	115.00	70.00	45.00	27.50
	1901						
	On 280, 282, 272, 276-78						
220	4¢ orange brown	32.50	23.00	22.50	14.00	6.00	3.75
221	6¢ lake	40.00	25.00	27.00	16.50	7.50	5.00
222	8¢ violet brown	45.00	27.50	30.00	18.50	8.00	4.75
223	$1 black (Type I)	565.00	375.00	375.00	230.00	240.00	150.00
223A	$1 black (Type II)	3200.00	2150.00	2200.00	1450.00	1100.00	695.00
224	$2 dark blue	810.00	495.00	550.00	360.00	330.00	215.00
225	$5 dark green	1895.00	1250.00	1295.00	850.00	910.00	595.00
	1903-04						
	On 300-313						
226	1¢ blue green	6.50	4.25	4.40	2.90	.50	.35
227	2¢ carmine	10.95	7.25	7.50	5.00	2.10	1.25
228	3¢ bright violet	105.00	70.00	72.00	46.50	17.50	11.50
229	4¢ brown	110.00	75.00	75.00	48.00	27.00	16.50
230	5¢ blue	18.00	11.00	12.00	7.75	1.50	.95
231	6¢ brownish lake	117.50	77.50	80.00	52.50	24.50	15.95
232	8¢ violet black	55.00	36.00	38.50	26.00	15.00	9.75
233	10¢ pale red brown	30.00	18.50	20.00	12.50	3.75	2.25
234	13¢ purple black	55.00	35.75	35.00	22.75	17.00	11.00
235	25¢ olive green	85.00	55.00	60.00	35.00	14.50	9.50
236	50¢ orange	215.00	140.00	140.00	90.00	42.50	27.50
237	$1 black	750.00	455.00	500.00	325.00	275.00	175.00
238	$2 dark blue	2150.00	1395.00	1425.00	950.00	900.00	585.00
239	$5 dark green	2300.00	1550.00	1625.00	1050.00	1100.00	715.00
	On 319						
240	2¢ carmine	8.25	5.35	5.50	3.65	2.75	1.75
	SPECIAL DELIVERY STAMPS						
	1901						
	U.S. E5 Surcharged						
E1	10¢ dark blue	140.00	90.00	95.00	62.50	115.00	75.00
	POSTAGE DUE STAMPS						
	1899						
	U.S. J38-44 overprinted						
J1	1¢ deep claret	7.50	4.75	4.75	3.10	1.95	1.25
J2	2¢ deep claret	7.10	4.50	4.50	2.95	2.00	1.35
J3	5¢ deep claret	17.50	11.50	11.50	7.50	3.50	2.25
J4	10¢ deep claret	22.50	14.50	14.00	9.00	6.75	4.40
J5	50¢ deep claret	215.00	140.00	145.00	95.00	97.50	63.50
	1901						
J6	3¢ deep claret	22.50	14.75	14.25	9.25	9.75	6.50
J7	30¢ deep claret	250.00	165.00	165.00	105.00	95.00	57.50

SCOTT NO.	DESCRIPTION	UNUSED NH F	UNUSED NH AVG	UNUSED OG F	UNUSED OG AVG	USED F	USED AVG
	PUERTO RICO						
	1899						
	U.S. Stamps 279-79B, 281, 272, 282C overprinted						
210	1¢ yellow green	9.50	5.85	6.50	4.10	1.75	1.15
211	2¢ carmine	8.75	5.75	6.00	3.95	1.65	1.05
212	5¢ blue	12.50	8.00	8.50	5.50	2.50	1.65
213	8¢ violet brown	45.00	28.50	27.50	18.00	17.50	11.50
214	10¢ brown (I)	30.00	19.25	19.00	12.25	6.00	3.95
	1900						
	U.S. 279, 279B overprinted						
215	1¢ yellow green	8.50	5.65	6.00	4.25	1.95	1.15
216	2¢ carmine	7.95	5.15	5.50	3.60	1.50	.95
	POSTAGE DUE STAMPS						
	1899						
	U.S. Postage Due Stamps J38-39, J41 overprinted						
J1	1¢ deep claret	32.50	21.00	22.50	13.50	8.25	5.35
J2	2¢ deep claret	22.50	14.50	14.00	9.00	7.00	4.75
J3	10¢ deep claret	215.00	140.00	140.00	90.00	60.00	36.50

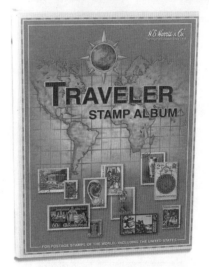

The Traveler® Worldwide Album provides spaces for thousands of stamps that beginning collectors are most likely to own or acquire. Headings feature the philatelic history of each stamp-issuing country. Brightly colored 2-post binder. Over 300 pages (150 sheets) printed on both sides.

1HRS18 Traveler® Album $24.99
2HRS9   Traveler® expansion binder $14.99

Order from your local dealer or direct from Whitman Publishing, LLC

Need Stamp Supplies?

Don't forget H.E. Harris offers a complete line of Albums, Supplies and Accessories for all your Stamp Collecting needs!

Ryukyu Islands #1-26

The Ryukyu Islands were under U.S. administration from April 1, 1945 until May 15, 1972. Prior to the General Issues of 1948, several Provisional Stamps were used.

SCOTT NO.	DESCRIPTION	UNUSED F/NH	F	SCOTT NO.	DESCRIPTION	UNUSED F/NH	F

RYUKYU ISLANDS

1, 1a, 3, 3a   2, 2a, 5, 5a   4, 4a, 6, 6a   7, 7a

1951

14	3y Ryukyu University	65.00	50.00
15	3y Pine Tree	55.00	42.50
16	10y on 50s (no. 8) Type II	14.00	10.25
16a	same, Type I	45.00	30.00
16b	same, Type III	50.00	35.00
17	100y on 2y (no. 10)	2150.00	1700.00
18	3y Govt. of Ryukyu	150.00	10.00

1949 Second Printing
White gum & paper, sharp colors; clean perfs.

1-7	5s to 1y 7 varieties, complete	28.00	22.00
1	5s Cycad	2.00	1.65
2	10s Lily	6.75	5.00
3	20s Cycad	4.50	3.35
4	30s Sailing Ship	2.75	2.00
5	40s Lily	2.25	1.75
6	50s Sailing Ship	5.00	3.75
7	1y Farmer	6.75	5.00

Type I—Bars are narrow spaced; "10" normal
Type II—Bars are wide spaced; "10" normal
Type III—Bars are wide spaced; "10" wide spaced

14   15

1948 First Printing
Thick yellow gum; gray paper; dull colors; rough perfs.

1a-7a	5s to 1y, 7 varieties, complete	525.00	400.00
1a	5s Cycad	3.75	2.70
2a	10s Lily	2.10	1.60
3a	20s Cycad	2.10	1.60
4a	30s Sailing Ship	3.75	2.70
5a	40s Lily	55.00	45.00
6a	50s Sailing Ship	3.75	2.70
7a	1y Farmer	460.00	360.00

16, 16a-b, 17   18

8   9   10

19   20   21

11   12   13

1952-53

19-26	1y to 100y, 8 varieties, complete		50.00
19	1y Mandanbashi Bridge		.35
20	2y Main Hall of Shun Castle		.50
21	3y Shurei Gate		.60
22	6y Stone Gate, Sogenji Temple		2.50
23	10y Benzaiten-do Temple		3.75
24	30y Altar at Shuri Castle		12.00
25	50y Tamaudun Shuri		15.00
26	100y Stone Bridge, Hosho Pond		18.00

1950

8-13	50s to 5y, 6 varieties, complete	80.00	62.50
8	50s Tile Roof	.30	.20
9	1y Ryukyu Girl	3.50	2.50
10	2y Shun Castle	16.00	12.50
11	3y Dragon Head	33.50	27.50
12	4y Women at Beach	20.00	16.00
13	5y Seashells	9.50	7.50

NOTE: The 1950 printing of #8 is on toned paper and has yellowish gum. A 1958 printing exhibits white paper and colorless gum.

27   28

Ryukyu Islands #27-63

Scott No.	Description	Unused F/NH
	1953	
27	3y Reception at Shuri Castle	15.00
28	6y Perry and Fleet	1.40
29	4y Chofu Ota and Pencil	13.00
	1954	
30	4y Shigo Toma & Pen	14.00
	1954-55	
31	4y Pottery	1.10
32	15y Lacquerware (1955)	3.50
33	20y Textile Design (1955)	2.50
	1955	
34	4y Noguni Shrine & Sweet Potato Plant	15.00
	1956	
35	4y Stylized Trees	13.50
36	5y Willow Dance	1.00
37	8y Straw Hat Dance	2.50
38	14y Group Dance	2.95
39	4y Dial Telephone	18.50
40	2y Garland, Bamboo & Plum	2.00
	1957	
41	4y Map & Pencil Rocket	1.00
42	2y Phoenix	.30
	1958	
43	4y Ryukyu Stamps	1.00
44-53	1/2¢ to $1.00, 10 varieties, complete, ungummed	65.00
44	1/2¢ Yen, Symbol & Denom., orange	.95
45	1¢ same, yellow green	1.55
46	2¢ same, dark blue	1.95
47	3¢ same, deep carmine	1.95
48	4¢ same, bright green	2.75
49	same, orange	5.00
50	10¢ same, aquamarine	7.00
51	25¢ same, bright violet blue	8.00
51a	25¢ same, bright violet blue (with gum)	10.00
52	50¢ same, gray	18.00
52a	50¢ same, gray (with gum)	12.00
53	$1 same, rose lilac	14.00
54	3¢ Gate of Courtesy	1.40
55	1-1/2¢ Lion Dance	.30
	1959	
56	3¢ Mountains & Trees	.85
57	3¢ Yonaguni Moth	1.30
58-62	1/2¢ to 17¢, 5 varieties, complete	35.00
58	1/2¢ Hibiscus	.35
59	3¢ Moorish Idol	1.00
60	8¢ Seashell	10.00
61	13¢ Dead Leaf Butterfly	3.25
62	17¢ Jellyfish	20.00
63	1-1/2¢ Toy (Yakaji)	.80

 33

 34

 35

 36

 37

 38

 54

 55

 56

 57

 58, 76

 63

Ryukyu Islands #64-105

SCOTT NO.	DESCRIPTION	UNUSED F/NH
	1960	
64	3¢ University Badge	1.10
	DANCES II	
65-68	1¢-10¢, 4 varieties, complete	5.50
65	1¢ Munsunu	1.40
66	2-1/2¢ Nutwabushi	2.40
67	5¢ Hatomabushi	.90
68	10¢ Hanafubushi	.95

64

65, 81

72

73

74

75

SCOTT NO.	DESCRIPTION	UNUSED F/NH
	3¢ Torch & Nago Bay	7.50
72		
73	8¢ Runners	1.10
74	3¢ Egret & Sun	6.00
75	1-1/2¢ Bull Fight	1.95

1960-61 REDRAWN INSCRIPTION

76-80	1/2¢ to 17¢, 5 varieties, complete	14.50
76	1/2¢ Hibiscus	.50
77	3¢ Moorish Idol	1.45
78	8¢ Seashell	1.45
79	13¢ Dead Leaf Butterfly	2.00
80	17¢ Jellyfish	9.50

88

89

90

91

92

93

95

97

98

WITH "RYUKYUS" ADDED
1961-64

Scott No.	Description	Unused F/NH
81-87	1¢ to $1.00, 8 varieties, Dancers, complete	11.25
81	1¢ Munsuru	.20
82	2-1/2¢ Nutwabushi (1962)	.25
83	5¢ Hatomabushi (1962)	.45
84	10¢ Hanafubushi (1962)	.85
84A	20¢ Shundun (1964)	1.25
85	25¢ Hanagasabushi (1962)	1.50
86	50¢ Nubui Kuduchi	3.00
87	$1 Kutubushi	5.00

1961

88	3¢ Pine Tree	1.75
89	3¢ Naha, Steamer & Sailboat	2.25
90	3¢ White Silver Temple	2.25
91	3¢ Books & Bird	1.60
92	1-1/2¢ Eagles & Rising Sun	2.75

1962

93	1-1/2¢ Steps, Trees & Building	.75
94	3¢ GRI Building	1.25
95	3¢ Malaria Eradication	.70
96	8¢ Eradication Emblem	1.45
97	3¢ Children's Day	1.50

103

104

105

106

107

108

109

110

111

98-102	1/2¢ to 17¢ varieties, Flowers, complete	2.95
98	1/2¢ Sea Hibiscus	.18
99	3¢ Indian Coral Tree	.40
100	8¢ Iju	.50
101	13¢ Touch-Me-Not	.75
102	17¢ Shell Flower	1.25
103	3¢ Earthenware	4.00
104	3¢ Japanese Fencing	5.25
105	1-1/2¢ Bingata Cloth	1.25

VERY FINE QUALITY: From 1935 to date, add 20% to the Fine price. Minimum of 3¢ per stamp.

Ryukyu Islands #106-150

1963

Scott No.	Description	Unused F/NH
106	3¢ Stone Relief	1.20
107	1-1/2¢ Gooseneck Cactus	.20
108	3¢ Trees & Hills	1.20
109	3¢ Map of Okinawa	1.50
110	3¢ Hawks & Islands	1.25
111	3¢ Shioya Bridge	1.25
112	3¢ Lacquerware Bowl	3.00
113	3¢ Map of Far East	1.00
114	15¢ Mamaomoto	1.10
115	3¢ Nakagusuku Castle Site	.95
116	3¢ Human Rights	1.00
117	1-1/2¢ Dragon	.40

1964

Scott No.	Description	Unused F/NH
118	3¢ Mothers' Day	.50
119	3¢ Agricultural Census	.50
120	3¢ Minsah Obi, rose pink	.65
120a	same, deep carmine	.90
121	3¢ Girl Scout & Emblem	.40
122	3¢ Shuri Relay Station	1.00
122a	3¢ same, inverted "1"	27.50
123	8¢ Antenna & map	1.50
124	3¢ Olympic Torch & Emblem	.40

1964-65

Scott No.	Description	Unused F/NH
125	3¢ Karate, "Naihanchi"	.70
126	3¢ Karate, "Makiwara" (1965)	.60
127	3¢ Karate, "Kumite" (1965)	.60

1964

Scott No.	Description	Unused F/NH
128	3¢ Miyara Dunchi	.40
129	1-1/2¢ Snake & Iris	.20

1965

Scott No.	Description	Unused F/NH
130	3¢ Boy Scouts	.60
131	3¢ Onoyama Stadium	.30
132	3¢ Samisen of King Shoko	.60
133	3¢ Kin Power Plant	.30
134	3¢ ICY and United Nations	.25
135	3¢ Naha City Hall	.25

1965-66

Scott No.	Description	Unused F/NH
136	3¢ Chinese Box Turtle	.40
137	3¢ Hawksbill Turtle (1966)	.30
138	3¢ Asian Terrapin (1966)	.30

1965

Scott No.	Description	Unused F/NH
139	1-1/2¢ Horse	.20

1966

Scott No.	Description	Unused F/NH
140	3¢ Woodpecker	.30
141	3¢ Sika Deer	.35
142	3¢ Dugong	.35
143	3¢ Swallow	.25
144	3¢ Memorial Day	.20
145	3¢ University of Ryukyus	.20
146	3¢ Lacquerware	.25
147	3¢ UNESCO	.25
148	3¢ Government Museum	.20
149	3¢ Nakasone T. Genga's Tomb	.20
150	1-1/2¢ Ram in Iris Wreath	.20

Ryukyu Islands #151-200

SCOTT NO.	DESCRIPTION	UNUSED F/NH
	1966-67	
151-55	5 varieties, Fish, complete	1.60
151	3¢ Clown Fish	.30
152	3¢ Young Boxfish (1967)	.30
153	3¢ Forceps Fish (1967)	.35
154	3¢ Spotted Triggerfish (1967)	.35
155	3¢ Saddleback Butterflyfish (1967)	.40
	1966	
156	3¢ Tsuboya Urn	.25
	1967-68	
157-61	5 varieties, Seashells, complete	1.95
157	3¢ Episcopal Miter	.30
158	3¢ Venus Comb Murex	.30
159	3¢ Chiragra Spider	.35
160	3¢ Green Turban	.35
161	3¢ Euprotomus Bulla	.75
162	3¢ Roofs & ITY Emblem	.25
163	3¢ Mobile TB Clinic	.25
164	3¢ Hojo Bridge, Enkaku Temple	.30
165	1-1/2¢ Monkey	.20
166	3¢ TV Tower & Map	.35
	1968	
167	3¢ Dr. Nakachi & Helper	.30
168	3¢ Pill Box	.45
169	3¢ Man, Library, Book & Map	.45
170	3¢ Mailmen's Uniforms & 1948 Stamp	.40
171	3¢ Main Gate, Enkaku Temple	.40
172	3¢ Old Man's Dance	.40
	1968-69	
173-77	5 varieties, Crabs, complete	3.75
173	3¢ Mictyris Longicarpus	.60
174	3¢ Uca Dubia Stimpson (1969)	.70
175	3¢ Baptozius Vinosus (1969)	.70
176	3¢ Cardisoma Carnifex (1969)	.95
177	3¢ Ocypode (1969)	.95
	1968	
178	3¢ Saraswati Pavilion	.40
179	3¢ Tennis Player	.40
180	1-1/2¢ Cock & Iris	.20
	1969	
181	3¢ Boxer	.40
182	3¢ Ink Slab Screen	.60
183	3¢ Antennas & Map	.30
184	3¢ Gate of Courtesy & Emblems	.30

SCOTT NO.	DESCRIPTION	UNUSED F/NH
	1969-70	
185-89	5 varieties, Folklore, complete	3.45
185	3¢ Tug of War Festival	.55
186	3¢ Hari Boat Race	.55
187	3¢ Izaiho Ceremony	.55
188	3¢ Mortardrum Dance (1970)	1.00
189	3¢ Sea God Dance	1.00
	1969	
190	1/2¢ on 3¢ (no. 99) Indian Coral Tree	.30
191	3¢ Nakamura-Ke Farm House	.30
192	3¢ Statue & Maps	.40
193	1-1/2¢ Dog & Flowers	.20
194	3¢ Sake Flask	.50
195-99	5 varieties, Classic Opera, complete	3.50
195	3¢ "The Bell"	.80
196	3¢ Child & Kidnapper	.80
197	3¢ Robe of Feathers	.80
198	3¢ Vengeance of Two Sons	.65
199	3¢ Virgin & the Dragon	.65
195-99a	5 varieties, complete, sheets of 4	23.75
195a	3¢ sheet of 4	5.50
196a	3¢ sheet of 4	5.00
197a	3¢ sheet of 4	4.75
198a	3¢ sheet of 4	4.75
199a	3¢ sheet of 4	4.75
200	3¢ Underwater Observatory	.40

Ryukyu Islands #201-E1

SCOTT NO.	DESCRIPTION	UNUSED F/NH

1970-71 Portraits

201	3¢ Noboru Jahana	.55
202	3¢ Saion Gushichan Bunjaku	1.50
203	3¢ Choho Giwan (1971)	.65

1970

204	3¢ Map & People	.30
205	3¢ Great Cycad of Une	.35
206	3¢ Flag, Diet & Map	1.10
207	1-1/2¢ Boar & Cherry Blossoms	.20

1971

208-12	5 varieties, Workers, complete	2.55
208	3¢ Low Hand Loom	.45
209	3¢ Filature	.45
210	3¢ Farmer with Raincoat & Hat	.45
211	3¢ Rice Huller	.80
212	3¢ Fisherman's Box & Scoop	.55
213	3¢ Water Carrier	.55
214	3¢ Old & New Naha	.30
215	2¢ Caesalpinia Pulcherrima	.20
216	3¢ Madder	.20

1971-72 Government Parks

217	3¢ View from Mabuni Hill	.40
218	3¢ Mt. Arashi from Haneji Sea	.40
219	4¢ Yabuchi Is. from Yakena Port	.45

1971

220	4¢ Dancer	.20
221	4¢ Deva King	.25
222	2¢ Rat & Chrysanthemums	.20
223	4¢ Student Nurse	.35

1972

224	5¢ Birds & Seashore	.55
225	5¢ Coral Reef	.55
226	5¢ Sun Over Islands	.65
227	5¢ Dove & Flags	.95
228	5¢ Antique Sake Pot	.70

AIR MAIL STAMPS

1950

C1	8y Dove & Map, bright blue	160.00
C2	12y same, green	33.50
C3	16y same, rose carmine	24.00

1951-54

C4-8	13y to 50y, 5 varieties, complete	30.00
C4	13y Heavenly Maiden, blue	2.50
C5	18y same, green	3.50
C6	30y same, cerise	6.75
C7	40y same, red violet (1954)	9.00
C8	50y same, yellow orange (1954)	10.00

1957

C9-13	15y to 60y, 5 varieties, complete	85.00
C9	15y Maiden Playing Flute, blue green	10.00
C10	20y same, rose carmine	14.00
C11	35y same, yellow green	18.50
C12	45y same, reddish brown	21.50
C13	60y same, gray	25.00

1959

C14-18	9¢ to 35¢, 5 varieties, complete	51.50
C14	9¢ on 15y (no. C9)	3.00
C15	14¢ on 20y (no. C10)	4.50
C16	19¢ on 35y (no. C11)	8.50
C17	27¢ on 45y (no. C12)	20.00
C18	35¢ on 60y (no. C13)	18.00

1960

C19-23	9¢ to 35¢, 5 varieties, complete	31.00
C19	9¢ on 4y (no. 31)	4.00
C20	14¢ on 5y (no. 36)	5.50
C21	19¢ on 15y (no. 32)	4.00
C22	27¢ on 14y (no. 38)	11.00
C23	35¢ on 20y (no. 33)	8.00

1961

C24-28	9¢ to 35¢, 5 varieties, complete	8.75
C24	9¢ Heavenly Maiden	.55
C25	14¢ Maiden Playing Flute	.70
C26	19¢ Wind God	.95
C27	27¢ Wind God	4.00
C28	35¢ Maiden Over Tree Tops	3.00

1963

| C29 | 5-1/2¢ Jet & Gate of Courtesy | .25 |
| C30 | 7¢ Jet Plane | .30 |

SPECIAL DELIVERY

1950

| E1 | 5y Dragon & Map | 32.50 |

U.N. Postage #1-87
UNITED NATIONS (NEW YORK)

SCOTT NO.	DESCRIPTION	FIRST DAY COVERS SING	INSC. BLK	INSRIP BLK-4	UNUSED F/NH	USED F

1, 6
2, 10, UX1-2
3, 11
4, 7, 9
5
8
12
13-14

1951
| 1-11 | 1¢ to $1 Definitives | 85.00 | 150.00 | 40.00 | 8.00 | 7.00 |

1952-1953
| 12-22 | 1952-53 Issues, complete (11) | ...... | ...... | ...... | 8.75 | ...... |

1952
| 12 | 5¢ United Nations Day | 1.20 | 2.50 | 1.40 | .25 | .20 |
| 13-14 | 3¢ & 5¢ Human Rights Day | 2.00 | 5.00 | 3.00 | .60 | .50 |

1953
15-16	3¢ & 5¢ Refugee Issue	1.80	4.50	7.75	1.00	.80
17-18	3¢ & 5¢ U.P.U. Issue	3.00	7.50	11.50	2.30	1.20
19-20	3¢ & 5¢ Technical Assistance	1.75	4.40	6.95	1.50	.95
21-22	3¢ & 5¢ Human Rights Day	7.75	18.50	12.75	2.50	1.25

1954
23-30	1954 Issues, complete (8)	......	......	22.00		
23-24	3¢ & 8¢ Food & Agriculture	2.05	5.15	9.15	2.00	1.00
25-26	3¢ & 8¢ International Labor	2.75	6.85	18.50	4.00	1.50
27-28	3¢ & 8¢ Geneva	4.00	10.00	25.00	5.00	2.50
29-30	3¢ & 8¢ Human Rights Day	7.75	18.50	55.00	12.25	4.00

1955
31/40	1955 Issues, (9) (No #38)	......	......		12.25	
31-32	3¢ & 8¢ Int. Civil Aviation Org.	3.95	9.85	24.25	4.95	2.25
33-34	3¢ & 8¢ UNESCO	2.00	5.00	7.95	1.70	1.10
35-37	3¢ to 8¢ United Nations	2.85	7.15	24.25	4.95	2.25
38	same, souvenir sheet	85.00			175.00	55.00

15-16
17-18
19-20
21-22
23-24
25-26
27-28
57-58
59-60
61-62
63-64
65-66

SETS ONLY: Prices listed are for complete sets as indicated. We regrettably cannot supply individual stamps from sets.

| 38 var | Second print, retouched | ...... | ...... | | 180.00 | 65.00 |
| 39-40 | 3¢ & 8¢ Human Rights Day | 2.00 | 5.00 | 6.25 | 1.30 | .90 |

1956
41-48	1956 Issues, complete (8)	......	......	......	3.20	......
41-42	3¢ & 8¢ International Telecommunications	2.00	5.00	6.25	1.30	.90
43-44	3¢ & 8¢ World Health Org.	2.00	5.00	6.25	1.30	.90
45-46	3¢ & 8¢ United Nations Day	1.25	3.15	1.35	.35	.25
47-48	3¢ & 8¢ Human Rights Day	1.25	3.15	1.25	.40	.30

1957
49-58	1957 Issues, complete (10)	......	......	......	1.65	......
49-50	3¢ & 8¢ Meteorological Org.	1.25	3.15	1.35	.35	.25
51-52	3¢ & 8¢ Emergency Force	1.25	3.15	1.35	.35	.25
53-54	same, re-engraved	......	......	1.40	.35	.25
55-56	3¢ & 8¢ Security Council	1.25	3.15	1.35	.35	.25
57-58	3¢ & 8¢ Human Rights Day	1.25	3.15	1.35	.35	.25

67-68
69-70
71-72
73-74
75-76
77-78
79-80
81-82
83-85
86-87

1958
59-68	1958 Issues, complete (10)	......	......	......	1.65	......
59-60	3¢ & 8¢ Atomic Energy Agency	1.25	3.15	1.35	.35	.25
61-62	3¢ & 8¢ Central Hall	1.25	3.15	1.35	.35	.25
63-64	4¢ & 8¢ U.N. Seal	1.25	3.15	1.35	.35	.25
65-66	4¢ & 8¢ Economic & Social Council	1.25	3.15	1.35	.35	.25
67-68	4¢ & 8¢ Human Rights Day	1.21	3.15	1.35	.356	.21

1959
69-76	1959 Issues, complete (8)	......	......	......	1.35	......
69-70	4¢ & 8¢ Flushing Meadows	1.25	3.15	1.40	.35	.25
71-72	4¢ & 8¢ Economic Commission Europe	1.25	3.15	1.40	.35	.25
73-74	4¢ & 8¢ Trusteeship Council	1.25	3.15	1.40	.35	.25
75-76	4¢ & 8¢ World Refugee Year	1.25	3.15	1.40	.35	.25

1960
77/87	1960 Issues, (10) (No #85)	......	......	......	1.65	......
77-78	4¢ & 8¢ Palais de Chaillot	1.25	3.15	1.40	.35	.25
79-80	4¢ & 8¢ Economic Commission Asia	1.25	3.15	1.40	.35	.25
81-82	4¢ & 8¢ 5th World Forestry Congress	1.25	3.15	1.40	.35	.25
83-84	4¢ & 8¢ 15th Anniversary	1.25	3.15	1.40	.35	.25
85	same, souvenir sheet	4.25	......	......	2.10	1.80
85 var	Broken "V" Variety	135.00	......	......	72.50	67.50
86-87	4¢ & 8¢ International Bank	1.25	3.15	1.40	.35	.25

FIRST DAY COVERS: Prices for United Nations First Day Covers are for cacheted, unaddressed covers with each variety in a set mounted on a separate cover. Complete sets mounted on one cover do exist and sell for a slightly lower price.

U.N. Postage #88-174
UNITED NATIONS (NEW YORK)

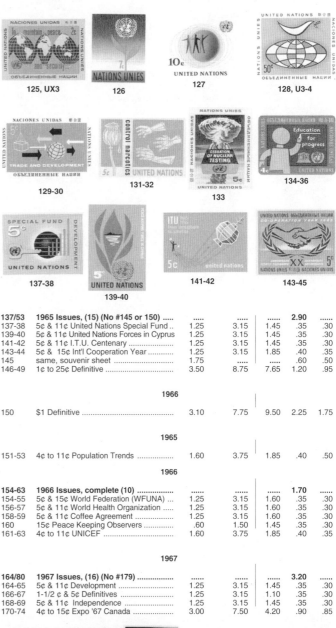

SCOTT NO.	DESCRIPTION	FIRST DAY COVERS SING	FIRST DAY COVERS INSC. BLK	INSRIP BLK-4	UNUSED F/NH	USED F
	1961					
88-99	1961 Issues, complete (12)	......	......	......	2.65	......
88-89	4¢ & 8¢ International Court of Justice	1.25	3.15	1.35	.35	1.25
90-91	4¢ & 7¢ Int. Monetary Fund	1.25	3.15	1.35	.35	1.25
92	30¢ Abstract Flags	1.25	3.15	2.70	.60	.35
93-94	4¢ & 11¢ Economic Commission Latin America	1.25	3.15	2.70	.60	.35
95-96	4¢ & 11¢ Economic Commission Africa	1.25	3.15	1.40	.35	.35
97-99	3¢, 4¢ & 13¢ Children's Fund	1.25	3.50	2.55	.55	.40
	1962					
100-13	1962 Issues, complete (14)	......	......	......	2.95	......
100-01	4¢ & 7¢ Housing & Community Development	1.25	3.15	1.40	.35	.25
102-03	4¢ & 11¢ Malaria Eradication	1.25	3.15	2.35	.50	.35
104-07	1¢ to 11¢ Definitives	2.00	4.00	2.75	.55	.35
108-09	5¢ & 15¢ Memorial Issue	1.25	3.15	3.40	.70	.55
110-11	4¢ & 11¢ Operation in the Congo	1.25	3.15	3.25	.65	.55
112-13	4¢ & 11¢ Peaceful Uses of Outer Space	1.25	3.15	1.70	.35	.30
	1963					
114-22	1963 Issues, complete (9)	......	......	......	2.10	......
114-15	5¢ & 11¢ Science & Technology	1.25	3.15	1.85	.40	.35
116-17	5¢ & 11¢ Freedom From Hunger	1.25	3.15	1.85	.40	.35
118	25¢ UNTEA	1.10	3.00	2.70	.60	.35
119-20	5¢ & 11¢ General Assem. Bldg.	1.25	3.15	1.85	.40	.35
121-22	5¢ & 11¢ Human Rights	1.25	3.15	1.85	.40	.35
	1964					
123-36	1964 Issues, complete (14)	......	......	......	2.95	......
123-24	5¢ & 11¢ Maritime Organization (IMCO)	1.25	3.15	1.85	.40	.35
125-28	2¢ to 50¢ Definitives	3.25	7.75	6.65	1.30	.85
129-30	5¢ & 11¢ Trade & Development	1.25	3.15	1.85	.40	.35
131-32	5¢ & 11¢ Narcotics Control	1.25	3.45	1.85	.40	.35
133	5¢ Cessation of Nuclear Testing	.60	1.30	.65	.20	.15
134-36	4¢ to 11¢ Education for Progress	1.30	3.25	1.85	.40	.35
	1965					
137/53	1965 Issues, (15) (No #145 or 150)	......	......	......	2.90	......
137-38	5¢ & 11¢ United Nations Special Fund	1.25	3.15	1.45	.35	.30
139-40	5¢ & 11¢ United Nations Forces in Cyprus	1.25	3.15	1.45	.35	.30
141-42	5¢ & 11¢ I.T.U. Centenary	1.25	3.15	1.45	.35	.30
143-44	5¢ & 15¢ Int'l Cooperation Year	1.25	3.15	1.85	.40	.30
145	same, souvenir sheet	1.75	......	......	.60	.50
146-49	1¢ to 25¢ Definitive	3.50	8.75	7.65	1.20	.95
	1966					
150	$1 Definitive	3.10	7.75	9.50	2.25	1.75
	1965					
151-53	4¢ to 11¢ Population Trends	1.60	3.75	1.85	.40	.50
	1966					
154-63	1966 Issues, complete (10)	......	......	......	1.70	......
154-55	5¢ & 15¢ World Federation (WFUNA)	1.25	3.15	1.60	.35	.30
156-57	5¢ & 11¢ World Health Organization	1.25	3.15	1.60	.35	.30
158-59	5¢ & 11¢ Coffee Agreement	1.25	3.15	1.60	.35	.30
160	15¢ Peace Keeping Observers	.60	1.50	1.45	.35	.30
161-63	4¢ to 11¢ UNICEF	1.60	3.75	1.85	.40	.35
	1967					
164/80	1967 Issues, (16) (No #179)	......	......	......	3.20	......
164-65	5¢ & 11¢ Development	1.25	3.15	1.45	.35	.30
166-67	1-1/2 ¢ & 5¢ Definitives	1.25	3.15	1.10	.35	.30
168-69	5¢ & 11¢ Independence	1.25	3.15	1.45	.35	.30
170-74	4¢ to 15¢ Expo '67 Canada	3.00	7.50	4.20	.90	.85

160

161-63

164-65

166

U.N. Postage #175-225
UNITED NATIONS (NEW YORK)

SCOTT NO.	DESCRIPTION	FIRST DAY COVERS SING	INSC. BLK	INSRIP BLK-4	UNUSED F/NH	USED F
175-76	5¢ & 15¢ International Tourist Year	1.25	3.15	1.65	.35	.25
177-78	6¢ & 13¢ Towards Disarmament	1.25	3.15	1.90	.40	.35
179	36¢ Chagall Window souvenir sheet	1.25	......	......	.65	.60
180	6¢ Kiss of Peace	.60	......	.65	.25	.15

1968

181-91	1968 Issues, complete (11)	......	......	......	4.00	......
181-82	6¢ & 13¢ Secretariat	1.25	3.15	1.80	.40	.35
183-84	6¢ & 75¢ H. Starcke	6.25	15.00	7.50	1.75	1.50
185-86	6¢ & 13¢ Industrial Development	1.25	3.15	1.65	.35	.30
187	6¢ Definitive	.60	1.50	.65	.25	.15
188-89	6¢ & 20¢ Weather Watch	1.25	3.15	2.30	.50	.40
190-91	6¢ & 13¢ International Year—Human Rights	1.25	3.15	2.30	.50	.40

1969

192-202	1969 Issues (11)	......	......	......	2.35	......
192-93	6¢ & 13¢ Institute Training Research	1.25	3.15	1.85	.40	.35
194-95	6¢ & 15¢ U.N. Building—Chile	1.25	3.15	2.15	.45	.40
196	13¢ Definitive	.60	1.50	1.40	.30	.25
197-98	6¢ & 13¢ Peace Through International Law	1.25	3.15	1.85	.40	.35
199-200	6¢ & 20¢ Labor & Development	1.25	3.15	2.35	.50	.45
201-02	6¢ & 13¢ Tunisian Mosaics	1.25	3.15	1.90	.40	.35

1970

203/14	1970 Issues, (11) (No #212)	......	......	......	3.25	......
203-04	6¢ & 25¢ Japanese Peace Bell	1.25	3.15	2.45	.55	.50
205-06	6¢ & 13¢ L. Mekong Delta Devel.	1.25	3.15	1.65	.35	.30
207-08	6¢ & 13¢ Fight Cancer	1.25	3.15	1.65	.35	.30
209-11	6¢ to 25¢ Peace & Progress	1.70	4.25	4.10	.90	.80
212	same, souvenir sheet	1.40	......	......	.90	.85
213-14	6¢ & 13¢ Peace, Justice & Prog.	1.25	3.15	1.65	.35	.30

1971

215-25	1971 Issues (11)	......	......	......	3.25	......
215	6¢ Peaceful Uses Sea-Bed	.60	1.50	.65	.20	.15
216-17	6¢ & 13¢ Support Refugees	1.25	3.15	1.65	.35	.30
218	13¢ World Food Programme	.60	1.50	1.20	.25	.20
219	20¢ Universal Postal Union Building	.70	1.75	1.65	.35	.35
220-21	8¢ & 13¢ Anti-Discrimination	1.25	3.15	1.85	.40	.35
222-23	8¢ & 60¢ Definitives	2.50	6.25	5.70	1.25	1.10
224-25	8¢ & 21¢ International School	1.25	3.15	2.75	.60	.55

183-84

185-86

187, U5

188-89

190-91

192-93

194-95

196

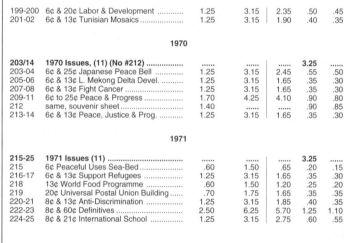

SETS ONLY: Prices listed are for complete sets as indicated. We regrettably cannot supply individual stamps from sets.

INSCRIPTION BLOCKS: Each corner of United Nations complete sheets contains the U.N. Emblem plus the name of the issue in the selvage. These are offered as Inscription Blocks of Four.

U.N. Postage #226-303
UNITED NATIONS (NEW YORK)

SCOTT NO.	DESCRIPTION	FIRST DAY COVERS SING	FIRST DAY COVERS INSC. BLK	INSRIP BLK-4	UNUSED F/NH	USED F
	1972					
226-33	1972 Issues, complete (8)	......	......	......	3.55	......
226	95¢ Definitive	2.75	6.85	8.65	1.90	1.50
227	8¢ Non-Proliferation	.60	1.50	.80	.20	.15
228	15¢ World Health Org.	.60	1.50	1.40	.30	.25
229-30	8¢ & 15¢ Environment	1.25	3.15	2.15	.45	.40
231	21¢ Economic Commission Europe	.75	1.85	2.10	.45	.40
232-33	8¢ & 15¢ Art—Sert Ceiling	1.25	3.15	2.15	.45	.40
	1973					
234-43	1973 Issues, complete (10)	......	......	......	2.60	......
234-35	8¢ & 15¢ Disarmament Decade	1.25	3.15	2.15	.45	.40
236-37	8¢ & 15¢ Drug Abuse	1.25	3.15	2.50	.55	.50
238-39	8¢ & 21¢ Volunteers Programme	1.25	3.15	2.75	.60	.50
240-41	8¢ & 15¢ Namibia	1.25	3.15	2.55	.55	.50
242-43	8¢ & 21¢ Human Rights	1.25	3.15	2.75	.60	.55
	1974					
244-55	1974 Issues, complete (12)	......	......	......	3.20	......
244-45	10¢ & 21¢ ILO Headquarters	1.30	3.25	3.25	.70	.65
246	10¢ Universal Postal Union	.60	1.50	.95	.20	.15
247-48	10¢ & 18¢ Brazil Peace Mural	1.25	3.15	2.55	.55	.50
249-51	2¢ to 18¢ Definitives	1.65	4.15	2.75	.60	.55
252-53	10¢ & 18¢ World Population Year	1.35	3.35	2.55	.55	.50
254-55	10¢ & 26¢ Law of the Sea	1.35	3.35	3.45	1.75	.70
	1975					
256/66	1975 Issues, (10) (No #262)	......	......	......	4.05	......
256-57	10¢ & 26¢ Peaceful Uses of Space	1.35	3.35	3.45	.75	.70
258-59	10¢ & 18¢ Int'l. Women's Year	1.25	3.15	2.55	.55	.50
260-61	10¢ & 26¢ Anniversary	1.30	3.35	3.00	.60	.60
262	same, souvenir sheet	1.55	......	......	1.00	.80
263-64	10¢ & 18¢ Namibia	1.25	3.15	2.55	.55	.50
265-66	13¢ & 26¢ Peacekeeping	1.35	3.35	3.45	.75	.70
	1976					
267-80	1976 Issues, complete (14)	......	......	......	7.90	......
267-71	3¢ to 50¢ Definitives	3.10	7.75	7.45	1.60	1.35
272-73	13¢ & 26¢ World Federation	1.50	3.75	3.25	.70	.65
274-75	13¢ & 31¢ Conf. on Trade & Dev.	1.45	3.65	4.70	.85	.75
276-77	13¢ & 25¢ Conference on Human Settlements	1.25	3.15	4.00	.85	.75
278-79	13¢ & 31¢ Postal Admin.	9.50	23.50	18.75	4.00	2.25
280	13¢ World Food Council	.60	1.50	1.40	.30	.25
	1977					
281-90	Issues, complete (10)	......	......	......	3.60	......
281-82	13¢ & 31¢ WIPO	1.40	3.50	4.20	.90	.80
283-84	13¢ & 25¢ Water Conference	1.35	3.40	3.95	.85	.75
285-86	13¢ & 31¢ Security Council	1.50	3.75	4.05	.65	.60
287-88	13¢ & 25¢ Combat Racism	1.35	3.40	3.50	.75	.70
289-90	13¢ & 18¢ Atomic Energy	1.25	3.15	3.00	.65	.60
	1978					
291-303	1978 Issues, complete (13)	......	......	......	5.65	......
291-93	1¢, 25¢ & $1 Definitives	4.00	10.00	9.90	2.20	1.90
294-95	13¢ & 31¢ Smallpox Eradication	1.40	3.50	4.40	.95	.85
296-97	13¢ & 18¢ Namibia	1.25	3.15	2.70	.60	.55
298-99	13¢ & 25¢ ICAO	1.30	3.25	3.50	.75	.70
300-01	13¢ & 18¢ General Assembly	1.25	3.15	2.70	.60	.55
302-03	13¢ & 31¢ TCDC	1.50	3.75	4.00	.85	.75

U.N. Postage #304-416

UNITED NATIONS (NEW YORK)

SCOTT NO.	DESCRIPTION	FIRST DAY COVERS SING	FIRST DAY COVERS INSC. BLK	INSRIP BLK-4	UNUSED F/NH	USED F
	1979					
304-15	1979 Issues, complete (12)	......	......	......	4.15	......
304-07	5¢, 14¢, 15¢ & 20¢ Definitives	2.00	5.00	4.40	.95	.85
308-09	15¢ & 20¢ UNDRO	1.35	3.40	3.25	.70	.65
310-11	15¢ & 31¢ I.Y.C.	3.75	9.40	4.95	1.10	.95
312-13	15¢ & 31¢ Namibia	1.55	3.85	4.00	.85	.75
314-15	15¢ & 20¢ Court of Justice	1.40	3.50	3.50	.75	.60

1980 World Flags
- 326 Luxembourg
- 327 Fiji
- 328 Viet Nam
- 329 Guinea
- 330 Surinam
- 331 Bangladesh
- 332 Mali
- 333 Yugoslavia
- 334 France
- 335 Venezuela
- 336 El Salvador
- 337 Madagascar
- 338 Cameroon
- 339 Rwanda
- 340 Hungary

SCOTT NO.	DESCRIPTION	FIRST DAY COVERS SING	FIRST DAY COVERS INSC. BLK	INSRIP BLK-4	UNUSED F/NH	USED F
	1980					
316/42	1980 Issues, (26) (No #324)	......	......	......	7.95	......
316-17	15¢ & 31¢ Economics	1.65	4.15	4.00	.85	.75
318-19	15¢ & 20¢ Decade for Women	1.35	3.40	3.50	.75	.60
320-21	15¢ & 31¢ Peacekeeping	1.60	4.00	4.20	.90	.80
322-23	15¢ & 31¢ Anniversary	1.55	3.90	4.00	.85	.75
324	same, souvenir sheet	1.45	......	......	.95	.90
325-40	15¢ 1980 World Flags, 16 varieties	10.00	......	13.50	3.00	2.75
341-42	15¢ & 20¢ Economic & Social Council	1.30	3.25	3.50	.75	.60

1981 World Flags
- 350 Djibouti
- 351 Sri Lanka
- 352 Bolivia
- 353 Equatorial Guinea
- 354 Malta
- 355 Czechoslovakia
- 356 Thailand
- 357 Trinidad
- 358 Ukraine
- 359 Kuwait
- 360 Sudan
- 361 Egypt
- 362 United States
- 363 Singapore
- 364 Panama
- 365 Costa Rica

SCOTT NO.	DESCRIPTION	FIRST DAY COVERS SING	FIRST DAY COVERS INSC. BLK	INSRIP BLK-4	UNUSED F/NH	USED F
	1981					
343-67	1981 Issues, complete (25)	......	......	......	9.25	......
343	15¢ Palestinian People	.75	1.85	1.60	.35	.30
344-45	20¢ & 35¢ Disabled Persons	1.70	4.25	4.75	1.00	.90
346-47	20¢ & 31¢ Fresco	1.60	4.00	4.75	1.00	.90
348-49	20¢ & 40¢ Sources of Energy	1.90	4.75	5.45	1.20	1.00
350-65	20¢ 1981 World Flags, 16 varieties	13.50	......	22.00	5.00	4.50
366-67	18¢ & 28¢ Volunteers Program	1.55	3.85	5.50	1.20	.85
	1982					
368-91	1982 Issues, complete (24)	......	......	......	9.75	......
368-70	17¢, 28¢ & 49¢ Definitives	2.50	6.25	9.25	2.00	1.55
371-72	20¢ & 40¢ Human Environment	1.95	4.85	7.00	1.40	1.15
373	20¢ Space Exploration	.90	2.25	3.25	.70	.40
374-89	20¢ World Flags, 16 varieties	13.00	......	22.00	5.00	4.50
390-91	20¢ & 28¢ Nature Conservation	1.75	4.35	5.75	1.20	1.00

1982 World Flags
- 374 Austria
- 375 Malaysia
- 376 Seychelles
- 377 Ireland
- 378 Mozambique
- 379 Albania
- 380 Dominica
- 381 Solomon Islands
- 382 Philippines
- 383 Swaziland
- 384 Nicaragua
- 385 Burma
- 386 Cape Verde
- 387 Guyana
- 388 Belgium
- 389 Nigeria

1983 World Flags
- 399 United Kingdom
- 400 Barbados
- 401 Nepal
- 402 Israel
- 403 Malawi
- 404 Byelorussian SSR
- 405 Jamaica
- 406 Kenya
- 407 China
- 408 Peru
- 409 Bulgaria
- 410 Canada
- 411 Somalia
- 412 Senegal
- 413 Brazil
- 414 Sweden

SCOTT NO.	DESCRIPTION	FIRST DAY COVERS SING	FIRST DAY COVERS INSC. BLK	INSRIP BLK-4	UNUSED F/NH	USED F
	1983					
392-416	1983 Issues, complete (25)	......	......	......	12.50	......
392-93	20¢ & 40¢ World Communications Year	2.05	5.15	6.75	1.40	1.10
394-95	20¢ & 37¢ Safety at Sea	1.95	4.75	6.75	1.40	1.10
396	20¢ World Food Program	.85	2.10	3.95	.85	.50
397-98	20¢ & 28¢ Trade & Development	1.60	4.00	7.25	1.60	1.00
399-414	20¢ World Flags, 16 varieties	13.00	......	25.00	6.00	7.00
415-16	20¢ & 40¢ Human Rights	2.50	6.25	9.00	2.00	1.50

1984 World Flags
- 425 Burundi
- 426 Pakistan
- 427 Benin
- 428 Italy
- 429 Tanzania
- 430 United Arab Emirates
- 431 Ecuador
- 432 Bahamas
- 433 Poland
- 434 Papua New Guinea
- 435 Uruguay
- 436 Chile
- 437 Paraguay
- 438 Bhutan
- 439 Central African Republic
- 440 Australia

U.N. Postage #417-545
UNITED NATIONS (NEW YORK)

SCOTT NO.	DESCRIPTION	FIRST DAY COVERS SING	INSC. BLK	INSRIP BLK-4	UNUSED F/NH	USED F
	1984					
417-42	1984 Issues, complete (25)	......	......	......	20.40	......
417-18	20¢ & 40¢ Population	2.10	5.25	8.50	1.75	1.25
419-20	20¢ & 40¢ Food Day	2.10	5.25	9.50	2.00	1.25
421-22	20¢ & 50¢ Heritage	2.25	5.50	10.50	2.25	1.50
423-24	20¢ & 50¢ Future for Refugees	2.25	5.50	9.00	2.00	1.35
425-40	20¢ 1984 World Flags, 16 varieties	13.00	......	47.50	11.50	10.00
441-42	20¢ & 35¢ Youth Year	2.10	5.25	9.00	2.00	1.25

1985 World Flags
450	Grenada	458	Liberia
451	Germany-West	459	Mauritius
452	Saudi Arabia	460	Chad
453	Mexico	461	Dominican Republic
454	Uganda	462	Oman
455	Sao Tome & Principe	463	Ghana
456	U.S.S.R.	464	Sierra Leone
457	India	465	Finland

443
444
445

1985

SCOTT NO.	DESCRIPTION	SING	INSC. BLK	BLK-4	F/NH	F
443/67	1985 Issues, (24) (No #449)	......	......	......	25.00	......
443	23¢ ILO—Turin Centre	1.00	2.50	3.70	.85	.50
444	50¢ United Nations University in Japan	1.65	4.15	7.75	1.65	1.10
445-46	22¢ & $3 Definitives	8.00	20.00	23.00	5.50	4.50
447-48	22¢ & 45¢ 40th Anniversary	2.30	5.75	8.75	1.75	1.50
449	same, souvenir sheet	2.50	......	......	2.50	1.50
450-65	22¢ 1985 World Flags, 16 varieties	14.00	......	52.50	12.50	10.00
466-67	22¢ & 33¢ Child Survival	2.25	5.65	7.95	1.75	1.10

1986 World Flags
477	New Zealand	485	Iceland
478	Lao PDR	486	Antigua & Barbuda
479	Burkina Faso	487	Angola
480	Gambia	488	Botswana
481	Maldives	489	Romania
482	Ethiopia	490	Togo
483	Jordan	491	Mauritania
484	Zambia	492	Colombia

446   447   448   466   441   468

469   473   475   476

1986

SCOTT NO.	DESCRIPTION	SING	INSC. BLK	BLK-4	F/NH	F
468-92	1986 Issues (25)	......	......	......	24.50	......
468	22¢ African Crisis	1.05	2.60	3.25	.70	.40
469-72	22¢ Development, 4 varieties, attached	2.50	3.25	10.50	9.00	......
473-74	22¢ & 44¢ Philately	2.30	5.75	8.65	1.75	1.00
475-76	22¢ & 33¢ Peace Year	2.25	5.65	8.65	1.90	1.00
477-92	22¢ 1986 World Flags, 16 varieties	14.00	......	52.50	12.50	10.00

493a   494   495   497

1987 World Flags
499	Comoros	507	Argentina
500	Democratic Yemen	508	Congo
501	Mongolia	509	Niger
502	Vanuatu	510	St. Lucia
503	Japan	511	Bahrain
504	Gabon	512	Haiti
505	Zimbabwe	513	Afghanistan
506	Iraq	514	Greece

515   517

SCOTT NO.	DESCRIPTION	FIRST DAY COVERS SING	INSC. BLK	INSRIP BLK-4	UNUSED F/NH	USED F
	1986					
493	22¢ to 44¢ World Federation of United Nations Associations Souvenir sheet of 4	4.00	......	......	5.50	4.00
	1987					
494-518	1987 Issues (25)	......	......	......	19.00	......
494	22¢ Trygve Lie	1.05	2.60	5.00	1.00	.75
495-96	22¢ & 44¢ Shelter Homeless	2.25	5.65	8.50	1.75	1.75
497-98	22¢ & 33¢ Anti-Drug Campaign	2.25	5.65	8.25	1.65	1.65
499-514	22¢ 1987 World Flags, 16 varieties	14.00	......	52.50	12.50	10.00
515-16	22¢ & 39¢ United Nations Day	2.30	5.75	7.50	1.50	1.30
517-18	22¢ & 44¢ Child Immunization	2.35	5.70	9.00	2.10	2.00

519   521   522

1988 World Flags
528	Spain
529	St. Vincent & Grenadines
530	Ivory Coast
531	Lebanon
532	Yemen
533	Cuba
534	Denmark
535	Libya
536	Qatar
537	Zaire
538	Norway
539	German Democratic Republic
540	Iran
541	Tunisia
542	Samoa
543	Belize

524   544-45   526

546   548   549   550

1988

SCOTT NO.	DESCRIPTION	SING	INSC. BLK	BLK-4	F/NH	F
519/44	1988 Issues (24) (No #522-23)	......	......	......	19.25	......
519-20	22¢ & 33¢ World without Hunger	2.25	5.65	10.50	2.35	1.75
521	3¢ For a Better World	.90	2.25	.90	.20	.20
					Sheetlets	
522-23	25¢ & 44¢ Forest Conservation (set of 6, includes Geneva and Vienna)	15.00	40.00	130.00	27.50	25.00
524-25	25¢ & 50¢ Volunteer Day	2.60	6.50	10.50	2.25	2.00
526-27	25¢ & 38¢ Health in Sports	2.30	5.75	12.00	2.75	2.00
528-43	25¢ 1988 World Flags, 16 varieties	14.50	......	52.50	12.50	10.00
544	25¢ Human Rights	1.75	4.25	4.00	.75	.45
545	$1 Human Rights souvenir sheet	2.75	......	......	2.50	2.00

552   553   570-71   572   573-74

1989 World Flags
554	Indonesia
555	Lesotho
556	Guatamala
557	Netherlands
558	South Africa
559	Portugal
560	Morocco
561	Syrian Arab Republic
562	Honduras
563	Kampuchea
564	Guinea-Bissau
565	Cyprus
566	Algeria
567	Brunei
568	St. Kitts & Nevis
569	United Nations

U.N. Postage #546-654
UNITED NATIONS (NEW YORK)

SCOTT NO.	DESCRIPTION	FIRST DAY COVERS SING	FIRST DAY COVERS INSC. BLK	INSRIP BLK-4	UNUSED F/NH	USED F
	1989					
546-71	1989 Issues (26)	......	......	......	30.00	......
546-47	25¢ & 45¢ World Bank	2.60	6.50	12.00	2.75	2.00
548	25¢ Nobel Peace Prize	1.10	1.65	5.75	1.10	.95
549	45¢ United Nations Definitive	1.40	2.10	5.75	1.10	.95
550-51	25¢ & 36¢ Weather Watch	2.30	5.75	15.00	3.50	2.50
552-53	25¢ & 90¢ U.N. Offices in Vienna	3.75	9.25	23.50	5.50	5.00
554-69	25¢ 1989 World Flags, 16 varieties	14.50	......	57.50	13.50	10.00
				Sheetlets (12)		
570-71	25¢ & 45¢ Human Rights 40th Ann. (strips of 3 with tabs)	2.60	6.50	21.00	5.00	......
	1990					
572/83	1990 Issues (11) (No #579)	......	......	......	25.50	......
572	25¢ International Trade Center	1.75	2.95	10.50	2.10	1.80
573-74	25¢ & 40¢ AIDS	2.60	6.50	12.25	2.75	2.25
575-76	25¢ & 90¢ Medicinal Plants	3.75	9.25	16.00	3.50	2.50
577-78	25¢ & 45¢ United Nations 45th Anniversary	2.60	6.50	18.50	4.00	3.50
579	25¢ & 45¢ United Nations 45th Anniversary Souvenir Sheet	2.10	......	......	5.50	4.50
580-81	25¢ & 36¢ Crime Prevention	2.30	5.75	18.00	4.00	3.00
				Sheetlets (12)		
582-83	25¢ & 45¢ Human Rights (strips of 3 with tabs)	2.60	6.50	23.00	5.00	......
	1991					
584-600	1991 Issues (17)	......	......	......	27.50	......
584-87	30¢ Econ. Comm. for Europe, 4 varieties, attached	4.50	5.50	5.25	4.50	4.00
588-89	30¢ & 50¢ Namibia—A New Nation	3.50	8.75	10.50	2.35	2.00
590-91	30¢ & 50¢ Definitives	4.00	10.00	10.50	2.35	2.35
592	$2 Definitive	5.50	13.50	19.00	4.00	3.00
593-94	30¢ & 70¢ Children's Rights	4.00	10.00	12.50	3.00	2.75
595-96	30¢ & 90¢ Banning of Chemical	4.25	10.50	17.00	3.50	3.00
597-98	30¢ & 40¢ 40th Anniversary of UNPA	3.50	8.75	10.50	2.35	2.25
				Sheetlets (12)		
599-600	30¢ & 50¢ Human Rights (strips of 3 with tabs)	3.00	7.50	31.50	7.00	......
	1992					
601-17	1992 Issues (17)	......	......	......	23.00	......
601-02	29¢-50¢ World Heritage—UNESCO	3.60	9.00	11.25	2.00	1.75
603-04	29¢ Clean Oceans, 2 varieties, attached	2.50	4.95	4.50	1.60	1.50
605-08	29¢ Earth Summit, 4 varieties, attached	3.50	4.25	3.50	2.75	2.50
609-10	29¢ Mission to Planet Earth, 2 varieties, attd	2.50	4.95	14.50	6.00	6.00
611-12	29¢-50¢ Science and Technology	3.60	9.00	8.75	1.95	1.75
613-15	4¢-40¢ Definitives	3.40	8.50	9.75	2.00	1.75
				Sheetlets (12)		
616-17	20¢-50¢ Human Rights (strips of 3 with tabs)	3.00	9.50	22.50	5.50	......
	1993					
618-36	1993 Issues (19)	......	......	......	18.50	......
618-19	29¢-52¢ Aging	3.00	9.50	8.75	1.95	1.75
620-23	29¢ Endangered Species, 4 attached	3.50	4.25	3.50	2.75	2.50
624-25	29¢-50¢ Health Environment	3.60	9.00	8.75	1.95	1.75
626	5¢ Definitive	2.00	4.00	1.00	.20	.20
	Sheetlets (12)					
627-28	29¢-35¢ Human Rights (strips of 3 with tabs)	3.00	9.50	18.50	6.25	......
629-32	29¢ Peace, 4 attached	3.50	4.25	3.50	4.00	3.50
633-36	29¢ Environment—Climate, strip of 4	3.50	7.00	6.25(8)	2.75	2.50
	1994					
637-54	1994 Issues (18)	......	......	......	13.60	......
637-38	29¢-45¢ International Year of the Family	2.25	8.50	8.50	1.95	1.75
639-42	29¢ Endangered Species, 4 attached	3.00	4.25	3.50	2.50	2.25
643	50¢ Refugees	1.75	5.75	5.00	1.20	1.00
644-46	10¢-$1 Definitives (3)	3.50	12.50	12.00	2.75	2.25
647-50	29¢ International Decade for Natural Disaster Reduction, 4 attached	3.00	4.25	3.50	2.50	2.25
651-52	29¢-52¢ Population and Development	2.25	9.00	8.75	1.75	1.50
653-54	29¢-50¢ Development through Partnership	2.25	9.00	8.75	1.75	1.50

U.N. Postage #655-760
UNITED NATIONS (NEW YORK)

SCOTT NO.	DESCRIPTION	FIRST DAY COVERS SING	FIRST DAY COVERS INSC. BLK	INSRIP BLK-4	UNUSED F/NH	USED F

656

661

663

666

668

669a

671

672

673

1995

Scott	Description	Sing	Insc Blk	Blk-4	F/NH	Used F
655/69	1995 Issues (14) (No #665)	......	......	......	30.95	......
655	32¢ 50th Anniversary of the UN	1.75	4.00	3.50	.75	.65
656	50¢ Social Summit	1.75	5.75	5.00	1.10	.85
657-60	29¢ Endangered Species, 4 attached	3.00	4.25	3.50	2.75	2.25
661-62	32¢-55¢ Youth: Our Future	2.50	9.00	8.00	1.80	1.50
663-64	32¢-50¢ 50th Anniversary of the UN	2.50	9.00	8.00	1.95	1.50
665	82¢ 50th Anniversary of the UN, Souvenir Sheet	2.50	......	......	2.10	1.95
666-67	32¢-40¢ 4th World Conference on Women	2.50	9.00	8.00	1.75	1.50
668	20¢ UN Headquarters	1.75	......	1.75	.40	.45
669	32¢ 50th Anniversary, Miniature Sheet of 12	......	......	......	20.00	......
669a-l	32¢ 50th Anniversary of the UN, booklet single	1.75	......	......	.75	.25
670	same, Souvenir booklet of 4 panes of 3	......	......	......	22.00	......

1996

Scott	Description	Sing	Insc Blk	Blk-4	F/NH	Used F
671/89	1996 Issues (18) (No 685)	......	......	......	14.20	......
671	32¢ WFUNA 50th Anniversary	1.75	4.00	3.50	.75	.65
672-73	32¢-60¢ Definitives	2.50	9.00	8.00	2.00	1.60
674-77	32¢ Endangered Species, 4 attached	3.00	4.25	3.50	2.75	2.25
678-82	32¢ City Summit (Habitat II), strip of 5	3.75	5.00	9.00	3.50	3.00
683-84	32¢-50¢ Sport & the Environment	2.50	9.00	8.50	1.95	1.50
685	82¢ Sport & the Environment souvenir sheet	2.50	......	......	2.10	1.95
686-87	32¢-60¢ A Plea for Peace	2.50	9.00	9.00	2.00	1.75
688-89	32¢-60¢ UNICEF 50th Anniversary	2.50	9.00	9.00	2.00	1.75

1997 World Flags

690	Tadjikistan	694	Liechtenstein
691	Georgia	695	South Korea
692	Armenia	696	Kazakhstan
693	Namibia	697	Latvia

687

686

688

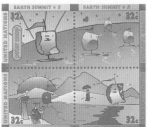
704-07

700-03

698

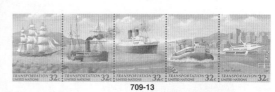
709-13

714

716

1997

Scott	Description	Sing	Insc Blk	Blk-4	F/NH	Used F
690/717	1997 Issues (27) (No. #708, 708A)	......	......	......	20.50	......
690-97	1997 World Flags, 8 varieties	12.50	......	24.50	5.75	5.00
698-99	8¢-55¢ Flowers, UN headquarters	2.25	8.00	8.00	1.85	1.50
700-03	32¢ Endangered Species, 4 attached	3.00	4.25	3.50	2.75	2.25
704-07	32¢ Earth Summit +5, 4 attached	3.00	4.25	3.50	3.00	2.25
708	$1 Earth Summit +5, souvenir sheet	2.50	......	......	2.25	1.75
708a	$1 1997 Pacific '97 overprint on #708	15.00	......	......	19.50	15.00
709-13	32¢ Transporation, strip of 5	3.75	5.00	9.00(10)	4.00	3.50
714-15	32¢-50¢ Tribute to Philately	2.50	9.00	8.00	1.75	1.50
716-17	32¢-60¢ Terracota Warriors	2.50	9.00	8.25	1.85	1.75
718	same, Souvenir bklt of 6 panes of 4	......	......	......	5.50	......

1998 World Flags

719	Micronesia
720	Slovakia
721	Dem. People's Rep. of Korea
722	Azerbaijan
723	Uzbekistan
724	Monaco
725	Czeh Republic
726	Estonia

727

734a

730-33

1998

Scott	Description	Sing	Insc Blk	Blk-4	F/NH	Used F
719-26	1998 World Flags, 8 varieties	12.50	......	24.50	6.00	5.00
727-29	1¢-21¢ Definitives	4.50	10.00	3.00	.70	.60
730-33	32¢ Endangered Species, 4 attached	3.00	4.25	3.50	3.00	2.25
734	32¢ Intl. Year of the Ocean, sheetlet of 12	15.00	......	......	8.50	......
735	32¢ Rain Forest, Jaguar	1.75	4.25	3.50	.70	.40
736	$2 Rain Forest, Jaguar, souvenir sheet	7.00	......	......	5.00	4.00
737-38	32¢-40¢ 50 Year of Peacekeeping	3.75	9.00	7.50	1.60	1.40
739-40	32¢-50¢ 50th of the Dec. of Human Rights	4.00	9.50	8.00	1.75	1.60
741-42	32¢-60¢ Schonbrunn Castle	4.25	10.00	8.50	2.00	1.75
743	same, souvenir bklt of 6 panes	......	......	......	7.00	......

1999 World Flags

744	Lithuania	748	Moldova
745	San Marino	749	Kyrgyzstan
746	Turkmenistan	750	Bosnia & Herzegovia
747	Marshall Islands	751	Eritrea

754

757-60

1999

Scott	Description	Sing	Insc Blk	Blk-4	F/NH	Used F
744-51	1999 World Flags, 8 varieties	12.50	......	25.00	6.00	5.00
752-53	33¢-$5 Definitives	12.00	30.00	45.00	11.50	9.50
754-55	33¢-60¢ World Heritage Sites, Australia	4.25	10.00	9.00	2.25	1.75
756	same, souvenir bklt of 6 panes	......	......	......	6.00	......
757-60	33¢ Endangered Species, 4 attached	3.00	4.25	3.50	3.00	2.25

U.N. Postage #761-New Issues
UNITED NATIONS (NEW YORK)

761-62

764-67

SCOTT NO.	DESCRIPTION	FIRST DAY COVERS SING	INSC. BLK	INSRIP BLK-4	UNUSED F/NH	USED F
761-62	33¢ Unispace III Conference	1.75	4.25	3.75	1.50	1.10
763	$2 Unispace III Conference, souvenir sheet	7.00	....	....	5.00	4.00
764-67	33¢ Universal Postal Union	1.75	4.25	3.75	3.00	2.25

770-71

768	33¢ In Memorium	1.75	4.25	3.75	.75	.40
769	$1 In Memorium, souvenir sheet	3.25	....	....	2.25	1.10
770-71	33¢-60¢ Education-Keystone to the 21st Century	4.25	10.00	9.00	2.25	1.75

772

773-76

2000

772	33¢ International Year of Thanksgiving	1.75	4.25	3.75	.75	.40
773-76	33¢ Endangered Species, 4 attached	3.00	4.25	3.75	3.00	2.25

777

787

782

777-78	33¢-60¢ Our World 2000	4.25	10.00	9.00	2.25	1.75
779-80	33¢-55¢ 55th Anniversary of the UN	4.25	10.00	9.00	2.25	1.75
781	same, 33¢-55¢ souvenir sheet	....	....	....	2.25	1.75
782	33¢ International Flag of Peace	1.75	4.25	3.75	.75	.40
783	33¢ United Nations in the 21st Century	1.75	4.25	3.75	.75	.40
784-85	33¢-60¢ World Heritage Sites, Spain	4.25	10.00	9.00	2.25	1.75
786	same, souvenir bklt of 6 panes of 4	....	....	....	6.00	....
787	23¢ Respect for Refuges	1.75	4.25	3.75	.75	.40
788	$1 Respect for Refuges, souvenir sheet	3.25	....	....	2.25	1.10

793

789-92

2001

789-92	34¢ Endangered Species, 4 attached	3.00	4.25	3.75	3.00	2.25
793-94	34¢-80¢ Intl. Volunteers Year	4.50	10.00	11.00	2.75	2.00
795-802	2001 World Flags, 8 varieties	12.50	....	25.00	6.00	5.00
803-04	7¢-34¢ Definitives	3.50	8.50	5.00	1.00	.60
805-06	34¢-70¢ World Heritage Sites, Japan	4.50	10.00	10.00	2.50	2.00
807	same, souvenir bklt of 6 panes of 4	....	....	....	7.00	....

808

816

809

808	80¢ Dag Hammarskjold	2.50	4.00	8.00	1.95	1.00
809-10	34¢-80¢ 50th Anniv. of the UNPA	4.50	10.00	11.00	2.75	2.00
811	same, $2.40 souvenir sheet	6.50	....	....	6.00	5.00
812-15	34¢ Climate Change, strip of 4	3.00	4.25	3.75	3.00	2.25
816	34¢ Nobel Peace Prize	1.75	4.25	3.75	.75	.40

817

822

832

2002

817	80¢ Children and Stamps	2.50	4.00	8.00	1.95	1.00
818-21	34¢ Endangered Species, 4 attached	3.00	4.25	3.75	3.00	2.25
822-23	34¢-57¢ Independence of East Timor	4.00	9.00	9.00	2.25	1.90
824-27	34¢-80¢ Intl. Year of Mountains, 2 pairs	5.00	11.00	5.50	4.75	4.00
828-31	37¢-60¢ Johannesburg Summit, 2 pairs	4.50	10.00	4.75	4.00	3.00
832-33	34¢-80¢ World Heritage Sites, Italy	4.50	10.00	11.00	2.75	2.00
834	same, souvenir bklt of 6 panes of 4	....	....	....	7.00	....
835	70¢ UNAIDS Awareness, semi postal	2.25	3.75	7.50	1.75	1.00
B1	37¢ + 6¢ UNAIDS Awareness, souv. sheet	2.00	....	....	1.25	1.00

837

842-45

2003

836	37¢ Indigenous Art, sheet of 6	7.00	....	....	5.50	3.50
837-39	23¢-70¢ Definitives	3.50	4.50	12.50	3.00	1.75
840-41	23¢-70¢ Centenary of First Flight, 2 attach.	3.00	4.00	4.50	2.00	1.10
842-45	37¢ Endangered Species, 4 attached	3.50	4.50	4.25	3.50	2.50
846-47	23¢-37¢ Intl. Year of Freshwater, 2 attach.	2.25	3.75	6.00	1.50	1.00
848	37¢ Ralph Bunche	1.75	4.50	4.25	.95	.50
849	60¢ In Memoriam, UN Complex Bombing in Iraq	2.25	4.50	6.00	1.50	.85
850-51	37¢-80¢ World Heritage Sites, United States	4.25	9.50	9.75	2.50	1.75
852	same, souvenir bklt of 6 panes of 4	....	....	....	8.00	....
853-57	37¢ UN Headquarters + labels, vert strip of 5	....	....	....	8.50	....
....	same, sheet of 4 (853-57)	....	....	....	35.00	....

2004

859-61	37¢ Endangered Species, 4 attached	4.00	6.00	4.25	3.50	2.50
862	37¢ Indigenous Art, sheet of 6	7.50	....	....	5.25	4.00
863-64	37¢-70¢ Road Safety	4.50	10.00	10.75	2.75	2.00
....	80¢ Japanese Peace Bell, 50th Anniv.	2.50	5.00	8.00	2.00	1.25

U.N. Air Post #C1-C23

AIR POST ISSUE

SCOTT NO.	DESCRIPTION	FIRST DAY COVERS SING	FIRST DAY COVERS INSC. BLK	INSRIP BLK-4	UNUSED F/NH	USED F

C1-2, UC5   C3-C4, UC1-2

1951-77

| C1-C23 | AIR MAILS, complete (23) | ...... | ...... | 38.50 | 7.85 | ...... |

C5-6, UXC1, UXC3   C7, UC4

1951-59

| C1-4 | 6¢, 10¢, 15¢ & 20¢ | 24.50 | 60.00 | 9.00 | 2.00 | 2.00 |
| C5-7 | 4¢, 5¢ & 7¢ (1957-59) | 1.65 | 4.15 | 2.25 | .55 | .45 |

C8, UXC4   C10

C9, UC6, UC8

C11

1963-77

| C8-12 | 6¢, 8¢, 13¢, 15¢, & 25¢ (1963-64) | 3.25 | 8.00 | 7.50 | 1.65 | 1.25 |

C13   C14

| C13-14 | 10¢ & 20¢ (1968-69) | 2.00 | 4.95 | 3.65 | .75 | .60 |

C16, UC10   C15, UXC8   C17, UXC10

C18

| C15-18 | 9¢, 11¢, 17¢, & 21¢ (1972) | 2.40 | 6.00 | 5.25 | 1.15 | .95 |

C19, UC11   C20, UXC11

C21

| C19-21 | 13¢, 18¢, & 26¢ (1974) | 2.75 | 6.95 | 5.25 | 1.10 | 1.00 |

C22   C23

| C22-23 | 25¢ & 31¢ (1977) | 2.50 | 6.25 | 5.25 | 1.10 | 1.05 |

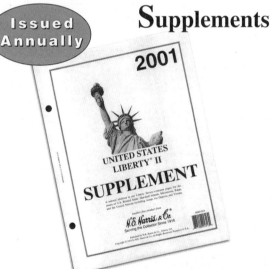

Liberty II Supplements include issues from UN, US Possessions and Trust Territories. Update your album today!

Item #	Year	Retail Price
90922057	2003 Liberty II Supplement	$7.95
90921807	2002 Liberty II Supplement	$7.95
90921313	2001 Liberty II Supplement	$7.95
90921630	2000 Liberty II Supplement	$7.95
5HRS99	1999 Liberty II Supplement	$7.95
5HRS92	1998 Liberty II Supplement	$7.95
5HRS82	1997 Liberty II Supplement	$7.95
5HRS75	1996 Liberty II Supplement	$7.95
5HRS64	1995 Liberty II Supplement	$7.95
5HRS56	1994 Liberty II Supplement	$5.95

Order from your local dealer or direct from Whitman Publishing, LLC.

U.N. Postal Stationery #U1-U19; UC1-UC23

ENVELOPES AND AIR LETTER SHEETS

SCOTT NO.	DESCRIPTION	FIRST DAY COVER	UNUSED ENTIRE
	1953		
U1	3¢ blue	4.50	1.00
	1958		
U2	4¢ ultramarine	.95	.75
	1963		
U3	5¢ multicolored (design #128)	1.00	.30
	1969		
U4	6¢ multicolored (design #128)	.85	.25
	1973		
U5	8¢ multicolored (design #187)	.85	1.00
	1975		
U6	10¢ multicolored (design #250)	.95	.50
	1985		
U7	22¢ Strip Bouquet	2.00	9.50
	1989		
U8	25¢ U.N. Headquarters	2.50	3.00
U9	25¢+4¢ surcharge (U8)	2.00	2.50
U9a	25¢+7¢ surcharge (U8)	7.50	3.25
	1997		
U10	32¢ Cripticandina (79x38mm)	1.35	2.50
U11	32¢ Cripticandina (89x44mm)	1.35	1.75
	1999		
U12	32¢+1¢ surcharge (U10)	1.40	1.75
U13	32¢+1¢ surcharge (U11)	1.40	1.75
	2001		
U14	34¢ NY Headquarters (34x34mm)	1.40	1.75
U15	34¢ NY Headquarters (36x36mm)	1.40	1.75
	2002		
U16	34¢+3¢ surcharge (U14)	1.50	1.95
U17	34¢+3¢ surcharge (U15)	1.50	1.95
	2003		
U18	37¢ U.N. Headquarters (37X47mm)	1.50	1.95
U19	37¢ U.N. Headquarters (40X52mm)	1.50	1.95

AIRMAILS

SCOTT NO.	DESCRIPTION	FIRST DAY COVER	UNUSED ENTIRE
	1952		
UC1	10¢ blue, air letter (design #C3)	8.00	27.50
	1954		
UC2	10¢ royal blue, white borders aerogramme (design of #C3)	......	8.00
	1958		
UC2a	10¢ royal blue, no border (design #C3)	......	7.50
	1959		
UC3	7¢ blue	1.00	2.00
	1960		
UC4	10¢ ultramarine on bluish, letter sheet (design of #C7)	.95	.75
	1961		
UC5	11¢ ultramarine on bluish, letter sheet (design of #C1)	.85	1.00
	1965		
UC5a	11¢ dark blue on green, letter sheet (design of #C1)	......	2.25
	1963		
UC6	8¢ multicolored (design #C9)	1.00	.75
	1958		
UC7	13¢ shades-blue, letter sheet	.95	.45
	1969		
UC8	10¢ multicolored (design #C9)	.95	.40
	1972-73		
UC9	15¢ shades-blue, letter sheet	.95	.90
UC10	11¢ multicolored (design #C16)	.95	.75
	1975		
UC11	13¢ multicolored (design #C19)	1.00	.45
UC12	18¢ multicolored, aerogramme (design of #222)	1.00	.55
	1977		
UC13	22¢ multicolored, aerogramme	1.25	.90
	1982		
UC14	30¢ black, aerogramme	3.00	2.00
	1988-89		
UC15	30¢ & 6¢ Surcharge on #UC14	11.50	45.00
UC16	39¢ U.N. Headquarters aerogramme	2.25	5.00
UC17	39¢+6¢ Surcharge on #UC16	2.25	19.00
	1982		
UC18	45¢ Winged Hand	1.95	2.50
	1995		
UC19	45¢+5¢ Surcharge on #UC18	5.00	7.00
	1997/1999		
UC20	50¢ Cherry Blossoms	1.65	2.00
UC21	50¢+10¢ surcharge on #UC20	1.75	2.00
	2001		
UC22	50¢+20¢ on UC9	1.75	2.00
UC23	70¢ Cherry Blossoms	1.75	2.00

U.N. Postal Stationery #UX1-UX33; UXC1-UXC12
POSTAL CARDS

SCOTT NO.	DESCRIPTION	FIRST DAY COVER	UNUSED ENTIRE
	1952		
UX1	2¢ blue on buff (design of #2)	1.65	.25
	1958		
UX2	3¢ gray olive on buff (design of #2)	.85	.25
	1963		
UX3	4¢ multicolored (design of #125)	.85	.25
	1969		
UX4	5¢ blue & black	.90	.25
	1973		
UX5	6¢ multicolored	.85	.25
	1975		
UX6	8¢ multicolored	1.00	.50
	1977		
UX7	9¢ multicolored	1.00	.75
	1982		
UX8	13¢ multicolored	1.10	.50
	1989		
UX9	15¢ UN Complex	1.10	1.35
UX10	15¢ UN Complex with trees	1.10	1.35
UX11	15¢ Flags	1.10	1.35
UX12	15¢ General Assembly	1.10	1.35
UX13	15¢ UN Complex from East River	1.10	1.35
UX14	36¢ UN Complex and Flags	1.50	1.75
UX15	36¢ Flags	1.50	1.75
UX16	36¢ UN Complex at Dusk	1.50	1.75
UX17	36¢ Security Council	1.50	1.75
UX18	36¢ UN Complex and Sculpture	1.50	1.75
UX19	40¢ UN Headquarters	1.60	3.00
	1998		
UX20	21¢ Secretariat Bldg., Roses	1.75	1.40
UX21	50¢ UN Complex	1.75	1.35
	2001		
UX22	70¢ NY Headquarters	1.75	2.00
	2003		
UX24	23¢ Equestrian Statue	1.75	1.40
UX25	23¢ Lobby	1.75	1.40
UX26	23¢ U.N. Headquarters	1.75	1.40
UX27	23¢ Meeting Room	1.75	1.40
UX28	23¢ Post Office	1.75	1.40
UX29	70¢ Meeting Room	1.75	2.00
UX30	70¢ Peace Bell	1.75	2.00
UX31	70¢ Statue	1.75	2.00
UX32	70¢ U.N. Headquarters	1.75	2.00
UX33	70¢ General Assembly	1.75	2.00

AIR MAILS

SCOTT NO.	DESCRIPTION	FIRST DAY COVER	UNUSED ENTIRE
	1957		
UXC1	4¢ maroon on buff (design of #C5)	.60	.25
	1959		
UXC2	4¢ & 1¢ (on UXC1)		.75
UXC3	5¢ crimson on buff (design of #C6)	.70	1.00
UXC4	6¢ black & blue (design of #C8)	.85	.50
	1965		
UXC5	11¢ multicolored	1.00	.50
	1968		
UXC6	13¢ yellow & green	.95	.50
	1969		
UXC7	8¢ multicolored	.90	.40
	1972		
UXC8	9¢ multicolored (design of #C15)	1.00	.50
UXC9	15¢ multicolored	1.00	.55
	1975		
UXC10	11¢ shades—blue (design of #C17)	1.00	.40
UXC11	18¢ multicolored (design of #C20)	1.20	.55
	1982		
UXC12	28¢ multicolored	1.40	.70

U.N. Geneva #1-112

UNITED NATIONS;
OFFICES IN GENEVA, SWITZERLAND
Denominations in Swiss Currency

NOTE: Unless illustrated, designs can be assumed to be similar to the equivalent New York or Vienna issues

SCOTT NO.	DESCRIPTION	FIRST DAY COVERS SING	INSC. BLK	INSRIP BLK-4	UNUSED F/NH	USED F
	1969-70					
1-14	5¢ to 10fr Definitives	45.00	110.00	50.00	11.00	10.00
	1971					
15-21	1971 Issues, complete (7)	......	......	......	3.80	......
15	30¢ Peaceful Uses Sea Bed	.95	2.40	1.40	.30	.25
16	50¢ Support for Refugees	1.10	2.75	1.95	.45	.40
17	50¢ World Food Programme	1.40	3.50	2.65	.55	.45
18	75¢ U.P.U. Building	2.75	6.85	4.00	.80	.80
19-20	30¢ & 50¢ Anti-Discrimination	2.25	5.65	4.25	.90	.60
21	1.10fr International School	3.65	9.00	4.75	1.00	1.15
	1972					
22-29	1972 Issues, complete (8)	......	......	......	5.95	......
22	40¢ Definitive	1.10	2.75	1.90	.40	.35
23	40¢ Non Proliferation	2.15	5.40	3.50	.75	.75
24	80¢ World Health Day	2.15	5.40	3.75	.85	.85
25-26	40¢ & 80¢ Environment	3.75	9.50	7.95	1.75	1.40
27	1.10fr Economic Committee Europe	3.25	8.15	7.50	1.60	1.35
28-29	40¢ & 80¢ Art—Sert Ceiling	3.50	8.75	8.45	1.85	1.65
	1973					
30-36	1973 Issues, complete (6)	......	......	......	4.60	......
30-31	60¢ & 1.10fr Disarmament Decade	3.50	8.75	7.00	1.50	1.50
32	60¢ Drug Abuse	2.00	5.00	2.65	.60	.65
33	80¢ Volunteer	2.50	6.25	3.50	.75	.75
34	60¢ Namibia	2.05	5.15	2.75	.60	.75
35-36	40¢ & 80¢ Human Rights	2.65	6.65	6.50	1.40	1.00
	1974					
37-45	1974 Issues, complete (9)	......	......	......	6.05	......
37-38	60¢ & 80¢ ILO Headquarters	2.75	6.85	4.95	1.10	1.00
39-40	30¢ & 60¢ U.P.U. Centenary	2.25	5.65	4.95	1.10	.90
41-42	60¢ & 1fr Brazil Peace Mural	3.00	7.50	7.00	1.50	1.45
43-44	60¢ & 80¢ World Population Year	2.50	6.25	6.25	1.35	1.25
45	1.30fr Law of the Sea	2.25	5.65	5.95	1.30	1.15
	1975					
46/56	1975 Issues, (10) (No #52)	......	......	......	8.45	......
46-47	60¢ & 90¢ Peaceful Use of Space	2.40	6.00	6.45	1.40	1.30
48-49	60¢ & 90¢ International Women's Year	2.75	6.85	7.50	1.60	1.40
50-51	60¢ & 90¢ 30th Anniversary	2.25	5.65	6.45	1.40	1.25
52	same, souvenir sheet	2.50	......	......	1.50	1.40
53-54	50¢ & 1.30fr Namibia	2.50	6.25	7.45	1.60	1.40
55-56	60¢ & 70¢ Peacekeeping	2.10	5.25	6.45	1.40	1.20
	1976					
57-63	1976 Issues, (7)	......	......	......	8.95	......
57	90¢ World Federation	1.80	4.50	4.45	1.00	.90
58	1.10fr Conference T.& D.	2.10	5.25	4.75	1.05	1.00
59-60	40¢ & 1.50fr Human Settlement	3.00	7.50	7.75	1.65	1.50
61-62	80¢ & 1.10fr Postal Administration	12.00	29.50	22.50	5.00	4.50
63	70¢ World Food Council	1.40	3.50	3.50	.75	.65
	1977					
64-72	1977 Issues, complete (9)	......	......	......	6.95	......
64	80¢ WIPO	1.40	3.50	3.75	.80	.70
65-66	80¢ & 1.10fr Water Conference	3.00	7.50	7.75	1.65	1.45
67-68	80¢ & 1.10fr Security Council	3.00	7.50	7.75	1.65	1.45
69-70	40¢ & 1.10fr Combat Racism	2.50	6.25	7.25	1.50	1.40
71-72	80¢ & 1.10fr Atomic Energy	3.00	7.50	7.75	1.65	1.45
	1978					
73-81	1978 Issues, complete (9)	......	......	30.95	6.50	......
73	35¢ Definitive	.95	2.40	2.20	.45	.40
74-75	80¢ & 1.10fr Smallpox Eradication	2.95	7.50	7.70	1.65	1.45
76	80¢ Namibia	1.50	3.75	4.75	.90	.80
77-78	70¢ & 80¢ ICAO	2.25	5.65	6.25	1.35	1.20
79-80	70¢ & 1.10fr General Assembly	3.00	7.50	7.70	1.65	1.35
81	80¢ TCDC	1.40	3.50	3.95	.85	.75
	1979					
82-88	1979 Issues, complete (7)	......	......	......	6.55	......
82-83	80¢ & 1.50fr UNDRO	3.10	7.75	9.75	2.15	1.95
84-85	80¢ & 1.10fr I.Y.C.	4.75	11.85	9.50	2.00	1.40
86	1.10fr Namibia	1.90	4.75	4.75	1.05	.95
87-88	80¢ & 1.10fr Court of Justice	3.00	7.50	7.95	1.70	1.55
	1980					
89/97	1980 Issues, (8) (No #95)	......	......	......	5.15	......
89	80¢ Economics	1.50	3.75	3.95	.85	.75
90-91	40¢ & 70¢ Decade for Women	1.95	4.95	5.25	1.15	1.00
92	1.10fr Peacekeeping	1.85	4.65	5.25	1.15	1.00
93-94	40¢ & 70¢ 35th Anniversary	2.00	5.00	5.15	1.15	1.00
95	Same, Souvenir Sheet	2.75			1.40	1.25
96-97	40¢ & 70¢ Economic & Social Council	1.85	4.65	5.15	1.15	1.00
	1981					
98-104	1981 Issues, complete (7)	......	......	......	5.50	......
98	80¢ Palestinian People	1.70	4.25	4.00	.85	.70
99-100	40¢ & 1.50fr Disabled People	2.75	6.85	7.65	1.70	1.45
101	80¢ Fresco	1.50	3.75	4.50	.95	.75
102	1.10fr Sources of Energy	1.50	3.75	5.25	1.15	1.00
103-04	40¢ & 70¢ Conservation	1.75	4.50	5.25	1.15	1.00
	1982					
105-12	1982 Issues, complete (8)	......	......	......	6.45	......
105-06	30¢ & 1fr Definitives	2.10	5.25	6.50	1.40	1.40
107-08	40¢ & 1.20fr Human Environment	2.40	6.00	7.65	1.70	1.45
109-10	80¢ & 1fr Space Exploration	2.65	6.65	8.50	1.75	1.50
111-12	40¢ & 1.50fr Conservation	2.75	6.95	8.95	1.95	1.50

U.N. Geneva #113-243

SCOTT NO.	DESCRIPTION	FIRST DAY COVERS SING	FIRST DAY COVERS INSC. BLK	INSRIP BLK-4	UNUSED F/NH	USED F
	1983					
113-20	1983 Issues, complete (8)	......	......	......	8.35	......
113	1.20fr World Communications	1.75	4.40	7.25	1.55	1.15
114-15	40¢ & 80¢ Safety at Sea	1.75	4.40	7.25	1.55	1.15
116	1.50fr World Food Program	2.25	5.65	8.00	1.70	1.45
117-18	80¢ & 1.10fr Trade & Development	2.75	6.95	8.95	1.95	1.70
119-20	40¢ & 1.20fr Human Rights	3.50	8.75	10.50	2.05	1.80
	1984					
121-28	1984 Issues, complete (8)	......	......	......	9.20	......
121	1.20fr Population	1.75	4.50	10.15	1.50	1.25
122-23	50¢ & 80¢ Food Day	1.75	4.50	8.50	1.75	1.25
124-25	50¢ & 70¢ Heritage	1.75	4.50	10.25	2.25	1.25
126-27	35¢ & 1.50fr Future for Refugees	2.75	6.95	10.50	2.25	1.75
128	1.20fr Youth Year	1.75	4.50	8.95	1.95	1.25
	1985					
129/39	1985 Issues, (10) (No #137)	......	......	......	11.50	......
129-30	80¢-1.20fr Turin Centre	2.75	6.95	12.95	2.75	1.75
131-32	50¢-80¢ U.N. University	2.00	5.00	8.95	1.95	1.25
133-34	20¢-1.20fr Definitives	2.25	5.65	9.75	2.10	1.25
135-36	50¢-70¢ 40th Anniversary	2.00	5.80	8.95	1.95	1.25
137	same, souvenir sheet	2.75	......	......	2.25	1.35
138-39	50¢-1.20fr Child Survival	5.75	14.50	15.25	3.40	2.50
	1986					
140-49	1986 Issues (10)	......	......	......	17.25	......
140	1.40fr Africa in Crisis	2.00	5.00	11.00	2.50	1.25
141-44	35¢ Development, 4 varieties, attached	2.00	2.75	12.00	10.50	5.00
145	5¢ Definitive	1.10	2.75	.85	.20	.15
146-47	50¢ & 80¢ Philately	1.85	4.65	9.50	2.00	.95
148-49	45¢ & 1.40fr Peace Year	2.75	6.95	13.50	3.00	1.50
150	35¢-70¢ WFUNA, souvenir sheet	2.75	......	......	5.50	2.75
	1987					
151-61	1987 Issues (11)	......	......	......	12.75	......
151	1.40fr Trygve Lie	2.00	5.00	10.15	2.00	1.75
152-53	90¢-1.40fr Definitive	3.50	8.75	13.00	2.00	1.75
154-55	50¢-90¢ Shelter Homeless	2.00	5.00	9.50	1.95	1.75
156-57	80¢-1.20fr Anti-Drug Campaign	2.75	6.95	13.00	2.00	1.75
158-59	35¢-50¢ United Nations Day	3.50	8.75	8.50	1.50	1.25
160-61	90¢-1.70fr Child Immunization	1.85	4.65	19.50	4.00	3.50
	1988					
162/172	1988 Issues, (8) (No #165-66, 172)	......	......	......	9.00	......
162-63	35¢-1.40fr World without Hunger	2.50	6.25	13.00	2.75	2.00
164	50¢ For a Better World	1.25	3.15	4.00	.85	.75
				Sheetlets (12)		
165-66	50¢-1.10fr Forest Conservation (set of 6, includes NY and Vienna)	15.00	40.00	130.00	27.50	25.00
167-68	80¢-90¢ Volunteer Day	2.50	6.25	12.00	2.40	2.00
169-70	50¢-1.40fr Health in Sports	2.75	6.95	13.50	2.25	2.00
171	90¢ Human Rights 40th Anniversary	2.00	5.00	7.00	1.25	1.00
172	2fr Human Rights 40th Anniversary souvenir sheet	2.75	......	......	3.25	3.00
	1989					
173-81	1989 Issues (9)	......	......	......	19.50	......
173-74	80¢ & 1.40fr. World Bank	2.75	6.95	18.50	4.00	3.00
175	90¢ Nobel Peace Prize	1.50	3.75	8.00	1.40	1.10
176-77	90¢ & 1.10fr World Weather Watch	2.75	6.95	18.50	3.75	2.00
178-79	50¢ & 2fr UN Offices in Vienna	4.00	10.00	20.00	4.50	4.25
				Sheetlets (12)		
180-81	35¢ & 80¢ Human Rights 40th Ann. (strips of 3 w/tabs)	1.85	4.65	24.00	7.00	......
	1990					
182/94	1990 Issues, No #190 (12)	......	......	......	33.50	......
182	1.50fr International Trade	2.15	5.40	14.00	3.00	2.50
183	5fr Definitive	7.75	19.50	33.50	6.00	5.00
184-85	50¢ & 80¢ SIDA (AIDS)	2.15	5.50	14.00	3.25	2.75
186-87	90¢ & 1.40fr Medicinal Plants	3.60	9.00	18.00	3.50	3.00
188-89	90¢ & 1.10fr Anniversary of U.N	3.00	7.50	18.50	3.50	3.00
190	same, souvenir sheet	3.00	......	......	5.00	4.50
191-92	50¢ & 2fr Crime Prevention	4.15	10.50	19.50	3.75	3.25
				Sheetlets (12)		
193-94	35¢ & 90¢ Human Rights (strips of 3 w/tabs)	1.95	4.95	28.50	7.50	......
	1991					
195-210	1991 Issues (17)	......	......	......	30.00	......
195-98	90¢ Econ. Comm. for Europe, 4 varieties, attached	5.75	6.75	7.75	5.50	4.50
199-200	70¢ & 90¢ Namibia—A New Nation	3.85	9.60	15.00	3.25	3.00
201-02	80¢ & 1.50fr Definitives	5.00	12.50	18.50	4.00	3.50
203-04	80¢ & 1.10fr Children's Rights	4.50	11.25	17.50	3.50	3.25
205-06	80¢ & 1.40fr Banning of Chemical Weapons	5.00	12.50	19.50	3.75	3.25
207-08	50¢ & 1.60fr 40th Anniv. of the UNPA	4.75	11.95	19.50	3.75	3.25
				Sheetlets (12)		
209-10	50¢ & 90¢ Human Rights (strips of 3 w/tabs)	2.75	7.50	32.50	8.00	......
	1992					
211-25	1992 Issues (15)	......	......	......	30.00	......
211-12	50¢-1.10fr. World Heritage—UNESCO	3.60	9.00	18.75	3.75	3.50
213	3fr Definitive	6.00	15.00	21.25	3.75	3.50
214-15	80¢ Clean Oceans, 2 varieties, attached	2.75	5.35	7.50	2.50	2.00
216-19	75¢ Earth Summit, 4 varieties, attached	4.00	4.95	5.50	4.50	4.00
220-21	1.10fr Mission to Planet Earth, 2 varieties, attached	4.00	6.95	12.50	5.00	4.50
222-23	90¢-1.60fr Science and Technology	4.75	11.75	18.00	4.00	3.50
				Sheetlets (12)		
224-25	50¢-90¢ Human Rights (strips of 3 w/tabs)	2.75	6.50	32.50	8.00	......
	1993					
226-43	1993 Issues (18)	......	......	......	28.00	......
226-27	50¢-1.60fr Aging	3.60	9.00	23.50	4.00	3.50
228-31	80¢ Endangered Species, 4 attached	4.00	5.00	6.50	5.00	4.50
232-33	60¢-1fr Healthy Environment	3.00	8.00	11.00	2.50	2.00
				Sheetlets (12)		
234-35	50¢-90¢ Human Rights (strips of 3 w/tabs)	3.00	7.00	33.00	8.00	......
236-39	60¢ Peace, 4 attached	3.50	4.50	5.00	4.00	3.50
240-43	1.10fr Environment—Climate, strip of 4	3.50	8.00	14.00(8)	6.00	5.00

245

U.N. Geneva #244-350

SCOTT NO.	DESCRIPTION	FIRST DAY COVERS SING	INSC. BLK	INSRIP BLK-4	UNUSED F/NH	USED F
	1994					
244-61	1994 Issues (18)	......	......	......	21.25	......
244-45	80¢-1fr Intl. Year of the Family	3.50	12.50	12.50	3.25	3.00
246-49	80¢ Endangered Species, 4 attached	4.50	5.00	4.75	4.25	4.00
250	1.20fr Refugees	2.50	9.25	9.00	2.00	4.85
251-54	60¢ Intl. Decade for Natural Disaster Reduction, 4 attached	3.50	4.25	3.75	3.25	3.00
255-57	60¢-1.80fr Definitives (3)	5.00	17.50	17.50	4.50	4.00
258-59	80¢-80¢ Population and Development	2.75	10.00		2.35	2.00
260-61	80¢-1fr Development through Partnership	3.50	12.50	12.50	2.75	2.50
	1995					
262/75	1995 Issues (13) (No #272)	......	......	......	47.00	......
262	80¢ 50th Anniversary of the UN	1.75	6.50	6.00	1.25	1.00
263	1fr Social Summit	2.25	7.50	7.00	1.95	1.75
264-67	80¢ Endangered Species, 4 attached	4.50	5.00	7.00	6.50	6.00
268-69	80¢-1fr Youth: Our Future	3.50	12.50	13.50	3.25	3.00
270-71	60¢-1.80fr 50th Anniversary of the UN	4.75	12.50	15.50	4.00	3.50
272	2.40fr 50th Anniversary of the UN, souvenir sheet	4.50	......	......	4.25	4.00
273-74	60¢-1fr 4th Conference on Women	3.00	10.00	13.00	2.95	2.75
275	30¢ 50th Anniversary, min. sheet of 12	......	......	......	26.00	....
276	same, souvenir booklet of 4 panes of 3	......	......	......	29.00	......
	1996					
277/95	1996 Issues (18) (No 291)	......	......	......	26.35	......
277	80¢ WFUNA 50th Anniversary	1.75	6.50	6.00	1.25	1.00
278-79	40¢-70¢ Definitives	2.75	10.00	10.50	2.25	2.00
280-83	80¢ Endangered Species, 4 attached	4.50	5.00	7.00	6.50	6.00
284-88	80¢ City Summit (Habitat II), strip of 5	5.00	15.00	17.00	8.00	7.00
289-90	70¢-1.10fr Sport & the Environment	3.50	12.50		3.25	3.00
291	1.80fr Sport & the Environment souvenir sheet	3.50	......	......	3.75	3.00
292-93	80¢-1fr A Plea for Peace	3.50	12.50	13.50	3.25	3.00
294-95	80¢-1fr UNICEF 50th Anniversary	3.50	12.50	13.50	3.25	3.00

SCOTT NO.	DESCRIPTION	FIRST DAY COVERS SING	INSC. BLK	INSRIP BLK-4	UNUSED F/NH	USED F
	1997					
296/315	1997 Issues (19) (No.# 306)	......	......	......	22.50	......
296-97	10¢-$1 10fr. Definitives	2.75	10.00	11.75	2.75	2.00
298-301	80¢ Endangered Species, 4 attached	4.50	5.00	7.00	6.50	6.00
302-05	45¢ Earth Summit +5, 4 attached	2.50	2.75	4.00	3.25	2.80
306	1.10Fr Earth Summit, souvenir sheet	2.40	......	......	2.00	1.75
307-11	70¢ Transporation, strip of 5	5.50	13.50	11.60(10)	5.50	5.00
312-13	70¢-1.10Fr Tribute to Philately	3.50	12.50	13.50	3.25	3.00
314-15	45¢-70¢ Terracota Warriors	2.75	10.00	10.50	2.50	2.25
316	same, Souvenir bklt of 6 pane of 4	......	......	......	5.25	......
	1998					
317	2fr Definitive	4.00	9.00	14.00	3.00	2.75
318-21	80¢ Endangered Species, 4 attached	4.50	5.00	6.50	5.50	5.00
322	45¢ Intl. Year of the Ocean, sheetlet of 12	15.00	......	......	9.00	4.00
323	70¢ Rain Forests, Orangutans	2.00	4.50	6.00	1.50	1.40
324	3fr Rain Forests, Orangutans, souvenir sheet	7.00	......	......	5.00	4.00
325-26	70¢-90¢ 50 Years of Peacekeeping	4.00	9.00	13.00	3.25	3.00
327-28	90¢-1.80fr 50th of the Dec. of Human Rights	6.75	15.00	21.00	5.50	5.00
329-30	70¢-1.10fr Schonbrunn Castle	4.50	10.00	14.50	3.65	3.25
331	same, souvenir bklt of 6 panes	......	......	......	7.00	......
	1999					
332	1.70fr Denfinitive	4.00	9.00	13.00	3.25	2.75
333-34	90¢-1.10fr World Heritage Sites, Australia	4.50	10.00	15.00	3.85	3.25
335	same, souvenir bklt of 6 panes	......	......	......	6.50	......
336-39	90¢ Endangered Species, 4 attached	4.50	5.00	7.00	6.00	5.00
340-41	45¢ Unispace III Conference	1.95	4.00	4.25	2.00	.80
342	2fr Unispace III Conference, souvenir sheet	6.00	......	......	3.75	3.00
343-46	70¢ Universal Postal Union	2.00	4.50	6.00	1.50	1.40
347	1.10fr In Memoriam	2.40	5.00	8.00	2.00	1.75
348	2fr In Memoriam, souvenir sheet	3.75	......	......	3.50	2.75
349-50	70¢-1.80fr Education-Keystone to the 21st Century	6.50	14.00	19.50	5.00	4.50

U.N. Geneva #351-New Issues; #UC1; UX1-UX15

AIR LETTER SHEETS & POSTAL CARDS

SCOTT NO.	DESCRIPTION	FIRST DAY COVERS SING	FIRST DAY COVERS INSC. BLK	INSRIP BLK-4	UNUSED F/NH	USED F
	2000					
351	90¢ International Year of Thanksgiving	1.95	4.00	6.60	1.65	1.25
352-55	90¢ Endangered Species, 4 attached	4.50	5.00	7.00	6.00	5.00
356-57	90¢-1.10fr Our World 2000		10.00	15.00	3.85	3.25
358-59	90¢-1.40fr 55th Anniversary of the UN	4.75	11.00	16.50	4.00	3.25
360	same, 90¢-1.40fr souvenir sheet				4.00	3.25
361	45¢ United Nations in the 21st Century	1.75	3.75	4.50	1.00	.75
362-63	1fr-1.20fr World Heritage Sites, Spain	5.25	11.50	18.00	4.50	4.00
364	same, souvenir bklt of 6 panes				9.25	
365	80¢ Respect for Regugees	1.75	6.50	6.00	1.25	1.00
366	1.80fr Respect for Refugees, souvenir sheet	3.50			3.25	2.50
	2001					
367-70	90¢ Endangered Species, 4 attached	4.50	5.00	7.00	6.00	5.00
371-72	90¢-1.10fr Intl. Volunteers Year		10.00	15.00	3.85	3.25
373-74	1.20fr-1.80fr World Heritage Sites, Japan	6.00	12.50	22.00	5.50	5.00
375	same, souvenir bklt of 6 panes				10.00	
376	2fr Dag Hammarskjold	3.50	7.50	14.00	3.50	2.75
377-78	90¢-1.30fr 50th Anniv. of UNPA	4.50	10.00	15.00	3.85	3.25
379	same, 3.50fr souvenir sheet	4.50			6.00	5.50
380-83	90¢ Climate Change, strip of 4	4.50	5.00	7.00	6.00	5.00
384	90¢ Nobel Peace Prize	1.95	4.00	6.60	1.65	1.25
	2002					
385	1.30fr Palais des Nations	2.75	6.00	10.00	2.50	2.00
386-89	90¢ Endangered Species, 4 attached	4.50	5.00	7.00	6.00	5.00
390-91	90¢-1.30fr Independence of East Timor	4.50	7.50	14.00	3.50	2.75
392-95	70¢-1.20fr Intl. Year of Mountains, 2 pairs	4.50	5.00	7.00	6.00	5.00
396-99	90¢-1.80fr Johannesburg Summit, 2 pairs	6.00	7.00	10.00	8.50	7.00
400-01	90¢-1.30fr World Heritage Sites, Italy	4.50	7.50	14.00	3.50	2.75
402	same, souvenir bklt of 6 panes of 4				10.00	
403	1.30fr UNAIDS Awareness, semi postal	2.75	6.00	10.00	2.50	2.00
404	3fr Entry of Switzerland into United Nations	7.00	15.00	20.00	5.00	4.00
B1	90¢+30¢ UNAIDS Awareness, souvenir sheet	2.40			2.25	2.00
	2003					
405	90¢ Indigenous Art, sheet of 6	11.00			8.50	4.50
406	90¢ Interparliamentary Union	1.95	4.00	6.60	1.65	1.25
407-10	90¢ Endangered Species, 4 attached	4.50	5.00	7.00	6.00	5.00
411-12	70¢-1.30fr Intl. Year of Freshwater, 2 attached	4.25	9.50	14.00	3.50	2.75
413	1.80fr Ralph Bunche	3.75	9.50	12.00	3.00	2.25
415-16	90¢-1.30fr World Heritage Sites, United States	4.50	7.50	14.00	3.50	2.75
417	same, souvenir bklt of 6 panes of 4				10.00	
	2004					
418-21	1fr Endangered Species, 4 attached	8.00	10.00	8.00	7.50	5.00
422	1fr Indigenous Art, sheet of 6	12.00			11.25	7.50
423-24	85¢-1fr Road Safety	4.25	8.00	13.00	3.25	2.50
	1.30fr Japanese Peace Bell, 50th Anniv.	3.00	7.75	9.00	2.25	1.75

SCOTT NO.	DESCRIPTION	FIRST DAY COVER	UNUSED ENTIRE
	1969		
UC1	65¢ ultramarine & light blue	4.50	1.75
	1969		
UX1	20¢ olive green & black	1.65	.35
UX2	30¢ violet blue, blue, light & dark green	1.65	.35
	1977		
UX3	40¢ multicolored	1.25	.55
UX4	70¢ multicolored	1.65	1.25
	1985		
UX5	50¢ Six languages	1.25	1.00
UX6	70¢ Birds & Rainbow	1.65	4.75
	1986		
UX7	70¢+10¢ Surcharge on UX6	8.00	2.50
	1992-93		
UX8	90¢ U.N. Buildings	1.75	2.00
UX9	50¢ + 10¢ Surcharge on UX5	1.75	3.00
UX10	80¢ Postal Card	1.75	3.00
	1997		
UX11	50¢+20¢ Surcharge on UX5	1.75	1.95
UX12	80¢+30¢ Surcharge on UX10	2.00	1.95
	1998		
UX13	70¢ Assembly Hall	2.00	1.75
UX14	1.10fr Palais des Nations	2.50	2.25
	2001		
UX15	1.30fr Palais des Nations	2.75	2.50

U.N. Vienna #1-109
UNITED NATIONS:
OFFICES IN VIENNA, AUSTRIA
Denominations in Austrian Currency

NOTE: Unless illustrated, designs can be assumed to be similar to the equivalent New York or Geneva issue

SCOTT NO.	DESCRIPTION	FIRST DAY COVERS SING	INSC. BLK	INSRIP BLK-4	UNUSED F/NH	USED F
	1979					
1-6	50g to 10s Definitives	6.75	16.95	10.00	2.25	2.50
	1980					
7/16	1980 Issues, (9) (No #14)	......	......	......	6.35	......
7	4s International Economic Order	3.75	9.50	11.50	1.25	1.20
8	2.50s International Economic Definitive	.85	2.15	(B)1.75	.40	.30
9-10	4s & 6s Decade for Women	3.10	7.75	6.50	1.25	1.40
11	4s Peacekeeping	1.95	4.85	5.25	1.15	1.05
12-13	4s & 6s 35th Anniversary	3.15	7.85	6.50	1.25	1.40
14	same, souvenir sheet	3.85	......	......	1.40	1.40
15-16	4s & 6s Economic and Social Council	2.35 5.85	6.50	1.40	1.20	
	1981					
17-23	1981 Issues, complete (7)	......	......	......	4.90	......
17	4s Palestinian People	1.55	3.85	3.75	.85	.75
18-19	4s & 6s Disabled Persons	2.40	6.00	5.50	1.25	1.15
20	6s Fresco	1.45	3.65	3.45	.80	.75
21	7.50s Sources of Energy	1.95	4.85	3.95	.85	.70
22-23	5s & 7s Volunteers Program	2.75	6.85	6.75	1.40	1.25
	1982					
24-29	1982 Issues, complete (6)	......	......	......	4.85	......
24	3s Definitive	.85	2.15	3.00	.65	.45
25-26	5s & 7s Human Environment	2.50	6.25	9.00	1.95	1.40
27	5s Space Exploration	1.25	3.15	3.95	.85	.70
28-29	5s & 7s Nature Conservation	2.50	6.25	7.75	1.65	1.40\
	1983					
30-38	1983 Issues, complete (9)	......	......	......	7.00	......
30	4s World Communications	.85	2.15	3.95	.85	.55
31-32	4s & 6s Safety at Sea	2.15	5.35	6.15	1.40	1.25
33-34	5s & 7s World Food Program	2.60	6.50	4.45	1.65	1.40
35-36	4s & 8.50s Trade & Develop.	2.75	6.95	8.95	1.95	1.55
37-38	5s & 7s Human Rights	3.15	7.85	8.95	1.95	1.45
	1984					
39-47	1984 Issues, complete (9)	......	......	......	8.55	......
39	7s Population	1.40	3.50	4.50	1.00	.95
40-41	4.50s & 6s Food Day	1.85	4.65	7.25	1.50	1.50
42-43	3.50s & 15s Heritage	3.50	8.75	10.50	2.25	2.25
44-45	4.50s & 8.50s Future for Refugees	2.25	5.65	10.50	2.25	1.75
46-47	3.50s & 6.50s Youth Year	1.80	4.50	9.00	2.00	1.65
	1985					
48/56	1985 Issues, (8) (No #54)	......	......	......	10.90	......
48	7.50s I.L.O. Turin Centre	1.25	3.15	6.45	1.40	1.00
49	8.50s U.N. University	1.35	3.40	6.95	1.50	1.10
50-51	4.50s & 15s Definitives	3.15	7.95	13.75	3.25	2.35
52-53	6.50s & 8.50s 40th Anniversary	2.50	6.25	10.00	2.35	2.35
54	Same, Souvenir Sheet	3.25	......	......	3.00	2.50
55-56	4s-6s Child Survival	2.15	5.40	14.00	3.00	1.70
	1986					
57-65	1986 Issues (9)	......	......	......	17.00	......
57	8s Africa in Crisis	1.35	3.40	7.50	1.50	.90
58-61	4.50s Development, 4 varieties, attached	3.05	7.65	13.00	12.00	2.25
62-63	3.50s & 6.50s Philately	1.95	4.95	9.75	2.00	1.15
64-65	5s & 6s Peace Year	2.25	5.65	12.00	2.50	1.95
66	4s to 7s WFUNA, souvenir sheet	3.05	......	......	5.50	4.00
	1987					
67-77	1987 Issues (11)	......	......	......	13.40	......
67	8s Trygve Lie	1.35	3.40	7.50	1.10	1.00
68-69	4s & 9.50s Shelter Homeless	2.35	5.95	11.00	2.25	2.00
70-71	5s & 8s Anti-Drug Campaign	2.25	5.65	10.25	2.25	2.00
72-73	2s & 17s Definitives	3.45	8.65	16.00	2.75	2.25
74-75	5s & 6s United Nations Day	2.25	5.65	12.00	2.75	2.00
76-77	4s & 9.50s Child Immunization	2.35	5.95	14.00	3.00	2.50
	1988					
78/86	1988 Issues, (7) (No #80-81, 87)	......	......	......	8.30	......
78-79	4s & 6s World Without Hunger	2.25	5.65	9.50	2.00	1.50
					Sheetlets	
80-81	4s & 5s Forest Conservation (set of 6, includes NY and Geneva)	22.50	65.00	130.00	27.50	25.00
82-83	6s & 7.50s Volunteer Day	2.35	5.95	14.00	2.75	2.00
84-85	6s & 8s Health in Sports	2.50	6.25	14.50	3.25	2.00
86	5s Human Rights 40th Anniversary	1.00	2.50	7.50	1.50	.60
87	11s Human Rights 40th Anniversary souvenir sheet	1.75	......	......	3.00	2.25
	1989					
88-96	1989 Issues (9)	......	......	......	18.75	......
88-89	5.50s & 8s World Bank	2.35	5.95	16.50	3.50	3.00
90	6s Nobel Peace Prize	1.25	3.15	6.75	1.35	1.00
91-92	4s & 9.50s World Weather Watch	2.35	5.95	19.50	4.00	3.50
93-94	5s & 7.50s UN Office in Vienna	2.25	5.65	24.00	5.50	5.00
					Sheetlets(12)	
95-96	4s & 6s Human Rights, 40th Ann. (strips of 3 w/tabs)	2.25	5.65	25.00	5.50	......
	1990					
97/109	1990 Issues, (12) (No #105)	......	......	......	26.95	......
97	12s Int'l. Trade Center	2.15	5.40	10.50	2.00	1.50
98	1.50s Definitive	.85	2.15	1.80	.40	.30
99-100	5s & 11s AIDS	2.75	6.95	17.00	3.50	3.00
101-02	4.50s & 9.50s Medicinal Plants	2.50	6.25	18.00	3.50	3.00
103-04	7s & 9s 45th Anniv. of U.N.	2.75	6.95	18.00	4.00	3.50
105	same, souvenir sheet	2.75	......	......	4.50	4.00
106-07	6s & 8s Crime Prevention	2.50	6.25	18.00	4.00	3.25
					Sheetlets(12)	
108-09	4.50s & 7s Human Rights (strips of 3 w/tabs)	2.35	5.95	30.00	6.50	......

U.N. Vienna #110-232

SCOTT NO.	DESCRIPTION	FIRST DAY COVERS SING	FIRST DAY COVERS INSC. BLK	INSRIP BLK-4	UNUSED F/NH	USED F
	1991					
110-24	1991 Issues, (15)	....	....	....	28.95	....
110-13	5s Econ. Comm. for Europe, 4 varieties, attached	5.50	13.75	6.50	5.00	4.50
114-15	6s & 9.50s Namibia—A New Nation	4.50	11.25	19.50	4.00	3.50
116	20s Definitive Issue	4.75	11.85	19.50	3.75	3.00
117-18	7s & 9s Children's Rights	4.50	11.25	14.50	3.25	3.00
119-20	5s & 10s Chemical Weapons	4.75	11.95	15.00	3.50	3.00
121-22	5s & 8s 40th Anniv. of U.N.P.A.	4.15	10.35	15.00	3.50	3.00
				Sheetlets (12)		
123-24	4.50s & 7s Human Rights (strips of 3 w/tabs)	2.50	6.25	34.50	7.50	....
	1992					
125-40	1992 Issues, (17)	....	....	....	31.50	....
125-26	5s-9s World Heritage—UNESCO	4.25	10.75	15.00	3.25	3.00
127-28	7s Clean Oceans, 2 varieties, attached	4.25	5.50	7.50	3.00	2.50
129-32	5.50s Earth Summit, 4 varieties, attached	4.25	5.25	4.95	5.50	5.00
133-34	10s Mission to Planet Earth, 2 varieties, attached	4.25	5.50	13.00	6.00	5.50
135-36	5.50s-7s Science & Technology	4.00	10.25	13.00	2.75	2.25
137-38	5.50s-7s Definitives	4.00	10.25	13.00	2.75	2.50
				Sheetlets (12)		
139-40	6s-10s Human Rights (strips of 3 w/tabs)	2.75	6.95	38.00	10.00	....
	1993					
141-59	1993 Issues, (19)	....	....	....	31.00	....
141-42	5.50s-7s Aging	4.00	10.25	11.00	2.50	2.25
143-46	7s Endangered Species, 4 attached	5.00	6.00	7.50	6.00	5.00
147-48	6s-10s Healthy Environment	4.00	11.50	13.00	3.00	2.50
149	13s Definitive	4.00	10.25	12.50	3.00	2.50
				Sheetlets (12)		
150-51	5s-6s Human Rights	3.00	7.00	35.00	8.00	....
152-55	5.50s Peace, 4 attached (strips of 3 w/tabs)	2.50	6.00	5.50	4.50	4.00
156-59	7s Environment—Climate, strip of 4	4.00	7.00	12.50(8)	6.00	5.50
	1994					
160-77	1994 Issues (18)	....	....	....	24.50	....
160-61	5.50s-8s Intl. Year of the Family	3.00	10.75	10.50	2.75	2.50
162-65	7s Endangered Species, 4 attached	6.25	7.50	7.50	6.00	5.00
166	12s Refugees	3.50	12.00	11.75	2.25	1.75
167-69	50g-30s Definitives (3)	8.50	33.50	32.50	6.00	5.00
170-73	6s Intl. Decade for Natural Disaster Reduction, 4 attached	5.50	6.50	6.00	4.00	3.50
174-75	5.50s-7s Population and Development	3.00	10.25	10.00	2.50	2.25
176-77	6s-7s Development through Partnership	3.50	10.25	10.25	2.40	2.25

SCOTT NO.	DESCRIPTION	FIRST DAY COVERS SING	FIRST DAY COVERS INSC. BLK	INSRIP BLK-4	UNUSED F/NH	USED F
	1995					
178/91	1995 Issues (13) (No #188)	....	....	....	49.95	....
178	7s 50th Anniversary of the UN	2.00	7.25	7.00	1.60	1.25
179	14s Social Summit	3.50	12.50	13.00	3.00	2.25
180-83	7s Endangered Species, 4 attached	6.25	7.50	8.00	7.00	6.00
184-85	6s-7s Youth: Our Future	3.50	10.25	11.50	2.75	2.50
186-87	7s-10s 50th Anniversary of the UN	4.00	11.50	13.50	3.25	3.00
188	17s 50th Anniversary of the UN, souvenir sheet	3.50	....	....	3.50	3.00
189-90	5.50s-6s 4th World Conference on Women	3.25	10.50	10.50	2.50	2.25
191	3s 50thAnniversary, min. sheet of 12	....	....	....	29.00	....
192	same, souvenir booklet of 4 panes of 3	....	....	....	31.00	....
	1996					
193/211	1996 Issues (18) (No 207)	....	....	....	27.15	....
193	7s WFUNA 50th Anniversary	2.00	7.25	7.00	1.60	1.25
194-95	1s-10s Definitives	3.25	10.50	10.50	2.50	2.25
196-99	7s Endangered Species, 4 attached	6.25	7.50	8.00	7.00	6.00
200-04	6s City Summit (Habitat II), strip of 5	6.75	16.50	18.00	8.75	8.00
205-06	6s-7s Sport & the Environment	3.50	10.25	11.50	2.75	2.50
207	13s Sport & theEnvrinronment souvenir sheet	3.25	....	....	2.50	2.25
208-09	7s-10s A Plea for Peace	4.00	11.50	13.50	3.25	3.00
210-11	5.5s-8s UNICEF 50th Anniversary	3.50	10.25	11.50	2.75	2.50
	1997					
212/31	1997 Issues (19) (No. #222)	....	....	....	24.50	....
212-13	5s-6s Definitives	3.25	10.50	10.50	2.50	2.25
214-17	7s Endangered Species, 4 attached	6.25	7.50	8.00	7.00	6.00
218-21	3.5s Earth Summit +5, 4 attached	3.25	3.75	4.00	3.50	3.00
222	11s Earth Summit +5, souvenir sheet	2.50	....	....	2.50	2.00
223-27	7s Transportation, strip of 5	6.75	9.50	16.00(10)	7.75	7.00
228-29	6.50s-7s Tribute to Philately	3.50	10.25	11.50	2.75	2.50
230-31	3s-6s Terracota Warriors	2.75	8.25	9.00	2.35	2.00
232	same, Souvenir bklt of 6 panes of 4	....	....	....	6.00	....

U.N. Vienna #233-New Issues

SCOTT NO.	DESCRIPTION	FIRST DAY COVERS SING	INSC. BLK	INSRIP BLK-4	UNUSED F/NH	USED F

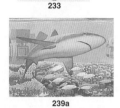
233

235-38

239a

1998

233-34	6.50-9s Definitives	3.75	8.00	13.50	3.00	2.75
235-38	7s Endangered Species, 4 attached	6.25	7.50	7.00	6.00	5.50
239	3.50s Intl. Year of the Ocean, sheetlet of 12	15.00			8.50	
240	6.50s Rain Forest, Ocelot	2.00	4.50	6.75	1.50	1.25
241	22s Rain Forests, Ocelet, souvenir sheet	6.50			4.50	4.00
242-43	4s-7.50s 50 Years of Peacekeeping	3.25	7.00	11.00	2.50	2.25
244-45	4.50s-7s 50th of the Dec. of Human Rights	3.25	7.00	11.00	2.50	2.25
246-47	3.50s-7s Schonbrunn Castle	3.00	6.50	10.00	2.35	2.10
248	same, souvenir bklt of 6 panes				6.75	

253-56

249

266

264

1999

249	8s Definitive	2.50	6.75	7.50	2.00	1.50
250-51	4.50s-6.50s World Heritage Sites, Australia	3.00	6.50	10.00	2.35	2.10
252	same, souvenir bklt of 6 panes				7.25	
253-56	7s Endangered Species, 4 attached	6.25	7.50	7.00	6.00	5.50
257-58	3.50s Unispace III Conference	1.95	4.50	4.00	.95	.75
259	13s Unispace III Conference, souvenir sheet	3.50			3.00	2.75
260-63	6.50s Universal Postal Union	2.00	4.50	6.75	1.50	1.25
264	3.50s In Memorium	1.95	4.50	4.00	.95	.75
265	14s In Memorium	3.50			2.75	2.00
266-67	7s-13s Education-Keystone to the 21st Century	5.00	11.50	20.00	4.75	4.00

268

269-72

2000

268	7s International Year of Thanksgiving	1.95	4.50	5.50	1.25	.95
269-72	7s Endangered Species, 4 attached	6.25	7.50	7.00	6.00	5.50

273

275

273-74	7s-8s Our World 2000	4.50	10.50	17.00	4.00	3.00
275-76	7s-9s 55th Anniversary of the UN	4.50	10.50	17.00	4.00	3.00
277	same, 7s-9s souvenir sheet				4.00	3.00
278	3.50s United Nations in the 21st Century	1.75	4.50	4.50	1.00	.75
279-80	4.50s-6.50s World Heritage Sites, Spain	3.00	6.50	10.00	2.35	2.10
281	same, souvenir bklt of 6 panes				7.25	
282	7s Respect for Refugees	1.95	4.50	5.50	1.25	.95
283	25s Respect for Refugees, souvenir sheet	7.00			5.00	2.45

284-87

293

2001

284-87	7s Endangered Species, 4 attached	6.25	7.50	7.00	6.00	5.50
288-89	10s-12s Intl. Volunteers Year	5.50	12.50	21.00	5.00	4.00
290-91	7s-15s World Hertiage Sites, Japan	4.00	8.00	19.00	4.75	4.00
292	same, souvenir bklt of 6 panes				8.00	
293	7s Dag Hammarskjold	1.95	4.50	5.50	1.25	.95
294-95	7s-8s 50th Anniv. of the UNPA	4.50	10.50	17.00	4.00	3.00
296	same, 28s souvenir sheet	7.50			5.50	4.50
297-300	7s Climate Change, strip of 4	6.25	7.50	7.00	6.00	5.50
301	7s Nobel Peace Prize	1.95	4.50	5.50	1.25	.95

302

312

322

2002

302-07	e0.07-e2.03 Austrian Tourist Attractions	5.50	15.00	21.00	5.00	4.00
308-11	e0.51 Endangered Species, 4 attached	5.00	6.00	5.50	4.75	4.00
312-13	e0.51-1.09 Independence of East Timor	3.50	8.00	16.00	3.75	3.00
314-17	e0.22-0.51 Intl. Year of Mountains, 2 pairs	3.50	4.50	16.00	3.75	3.00
318-21	e0.51-0.58 Johannesburg Summit, 2 pairs	4.50	5.50	6.00	5.00	4.00
322-23	e0.51-0.58 World Heritage Sites, Italy	2.25	7.00	3.00	2.50	2.00
324	same, souvenir bklt of 6 panes of 4				6.50	
325	e1.53 UNAIDS Awareness, semi-postal	3.00	8.00	14.00	3.50	3.00
B1	e0.55-0.25 UNAIDS Awareness, souvenir sheet	2.25			2.00	1.50

2003

326	e0.51 Indigenous Art, sheet of 6	9.50			7.50	4.00
327-28	e0.25-e1.00 Austrian Tourist Attractions	2.50	7.50	3.25	2.75	2.25
329-32	e0.51 Endangered Species, 4 attached	5.00	6.00	5.50	4.75	4.00
333-34	e0.55-e0.75 Intl. Year of Freshwater, 2 attach	2.50	7.50	3.25	2.75	2.25
335	e0.04 Schloss Eggenberg, Graz	1.75	4.50	4.50	1.00	.75
336	e2.10 Ralphe Bunche	3.75	9.50	18.00	4.50	3.50
337	e2.10 In Memoriam, UN Complex Bomding in Iraq	3.75	9.50	18.00	4.50	3.50
338-39	e0.51-e0.75 World Heritage Sites, United States	2.50	8.00	11.00	2.75	2.00
340	same, souvenir bklt of 6 panes of 4				6.50	

2004

341	e0.55 Schloss Schonbrunn, Vienna	2.10	4.00	7.50	1.75	.85
342-45	e0.55 Endangered Species, 4 attached	7.00	9.00	7.00	6.50	4.50
346	e0.55 Indigenous Art	10.50			9.75	6.50
347-48	e0.55-e0.75 Road Safety	2.50	8.00	11.00	2.75	2.25
	e2.10 Japanese Peace Bell, 50th Anniv.	3.75	9.50	18.00	4.50	3.50

U.N. Vienna #U1-U7; UC1-UC5; UX1-UX15
AIR LETTER SHEETS & POSTAL CARDS

SCOTT NO.	DESCRIPTION	FIRST DAY COVER	UNUSED ENTIRE

UX1   UX2   UX3   UX7

U1

1995

| U1 | 6s Vienna International Center | 1.75 | 3.50 |
| U2 | 7s Vienna Landscape | 1.75 | 1.75 |

1998

| U3 | 13s multicolored | 4.00 | 3.00 |

2002

| U4 | e0.51 Vienna International Center | 2.50 | 1.75 |
| U5 | e1.09 Vienna International Center | 3.75 | 3.00 |

2003

| U6 | e0.51+e0.4 surcharged envelope (U4) | 2.50 | 1.75 |
| U7 | e1.09+e0.16 surcharged envelope (U5) | 3.75 | 3.00 |

SCOTT NO.	DESCRIPTION	FIRST DAY COVERS SING / INSC. BLK	INSRIP BLK-4	UNUSED F/NH	USED F

1982

| UX1 | 3s multicolored | | | .55 | 1.50 |
| UX2 | 5s multicolored | | | 1.75 | 1.00 |

1985

| UX3 | 4s U.N. Emblem | | | .85 | 3.00 |

1992

| UX4 | 5s+1s surcharged | | | ...... | 20.00 |
| UX5 | 6s Reg Schek Painting | | | 1.75 | 3.00 |

1993

| UX6 | 5s Postal Card | | | 1.75 | 8.50 |
| UX7 | 6s Postal Card | | | 1.75 | 3.50 |

1994

| UX8 | 5s + 50g surcharge on UX6 | | | 1.75 | 4.00 |

UC1   UC5   UC3

UX11

1962

| UC1 | 9s multicolored | 4.00 | 4.00 |

1967

UC2	9s+2s surcharge on UC1	18.50	37.50
UC3	11s Birds in Flight	3.50	3.50
UC4	11s+1s surcharged	3.50	35.00
UC5	12s Vienna Office	4.00	2.50

1997

| UX9 | 6s+50s surcharge on UX5 | | | 2.50 | 2.50 |
| UX10 | 6s+1s surcharge on UX7 | | | 2.50 | 2.50 |

1998-2003

UX11	6.50s multicolored			2.00	1.50
UX12	7s The Gloriette			2.00	1.50
UX13	7s multicolored, type of 1983			2.00	1.50
UX14	e0.51 Clock tower Graz, Austria			1.75	1.50
UX15	e0.51+e0.04 surcharged postal card (UX14)			1.75	1.50

STATESMAN® DELUXE ALBUM
Round out your Collection with our Newly Designed Statesman® Worldwide Album.

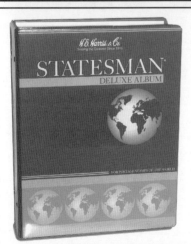

Our most popular loose-leaf album! Covers all stamp-issuing countries, with space for more than 25,000 stamps. Includes interesting historical and geographical information. Vinyl 3" loose-leaf binder. Over 650 pages (325 sheets) printed on both sides.

1HRS15—Statesman® Traditional Album (3")..............$45.99
2HRS6—Statesman® Traditional Expansion Binder (3").............$14.99

H.E. Harris & Co.®
Serving the Collector Since 1916

Order from your local dealer or direct from Whitman Publishing, LLC. • www.whitmanbooks.com

Canada Postage #1-40c
CANADA

SCOTT NO.	DESCRIPTION	UNUSED VF	UNUSED F	UNUSED AVG	USED VF	USED F	USED AVG
	1851 Laid paper, Imperforate (OG + 75%)						
1	3p red 13300.00	9975.00	5900.00	800.00	575.00	350.00	
2	6p grayish purple 12750.00	9500.00	5700.00	1400.00	875.00	525.00	
	1852-55 Wove paper						
4	3p red 1275.00	950.00	700.00	200.00	140.00	95.00	
4d	3p red (thin paper) 1275.00	950.00	700.00	200.00	140.00	95.00	
5	6p slate gray 8800.00	6100.00	3750.00	1100.00	850.00	525.00	
	1855						
7	10p blue 6250.00	4750.00	3200.00	1225.00	875.00	600.00	
	1857						
8	1/2p rose 700.00	475.00	325.00	470.00	325.00	210.00	
9	7-1/2p green 6900.00	4800.00	2850.00	1950.00	1350.00	975.00	
	Very thick soft wove paper						
10	6p reddish purple 14400.00	10200.00	6400.00	3100.00	2300.00	1400.00	
	1858-59 Perf. 12						
11	1/2p rose 2200.00	1650.00	1000.00	925.00	650.00	425.00	
12	3p red 3400.00	2550.00	1500.00	495.00	335.00	225.00	
13	6p brown violet 8200.00	6250.00	4500.00	4350.00	3200.00	2400.00	
	1859 (OG + 35%)						
14	1¢ rose 295.00	210.00	150.00	55.00	35.00	22.00	
15	5¢ vermillion 375.00	220.00	145.00	29.00	22.00	15.00	
16	10¢ black brown 9200.00	6600.00	3950.00	2750.00	1800.00	1250.00	
17	10¢ red lilac 700.00	480.00	325.00	85.00	55.00	33.00	
18	12-1/2¢ yellow green 700.00	480.00	325.00	85.00	55.00	33.00	
19	17¢ blue 825.00	575.00	400.00	135.00	80.00	50.00	
	1864						
20	2¢ rose 440.00	310.00	195.00	210.00	125.00	70.00	

SCOTT NO.	DESCRIPTION	UNUSED VF	UNUSED F	UNUSED AVG	USED VF	USED F	USED AVG
	1868-75 Wove paper, Perf. 12, unwkd. (OG + 35%)						
21	1/2¢ black 70.00	45.00	31.00	41.50	25.00	16.00	
22	1¢ brown red 495.00	350.00	245.00	66.00	40.00	28.00	
23	1¢ yellow orange 745.00	495.00	325.00	135.00	80.00	50.00	
24	2¢ green 495.00	350.00	245.00	55.00	33.00	22.00	
25	3¢ red 795.00	525.00	360.00	30.00	17.00	10.00	
26	5¢ olive gr. (pf. 11-1/2x12) ... 925.00	600.00	410.00	185.00	115.00	75.00	
27	6¢ dark brown 1300.00	875.00	550.00	80.00	50.00	32.00	
28	12-1/2¢ blue 650.00	440.00	275.00	95.00	60.00	40.00	
29	15¢ gray violet 67.50	45.00	28.00	35.00	20.00	14.00	
29b	15¢ red lilac 740.00	525.00	320.00	90.00	55.00	32.00	
30	15¢ gray 70.00	48.00	30.00	35.00	20.00	14.00	
	1873-74 Wove paper. Perf. 11-1/2 x 12, unwatermarked						
21a	1/2¢ black 70.00	48.00	30.00	41.50	25.00	16.00	
29a	15¢ gray violet 875.00	595.00	360.00	155.00	95.00	57.50	
30a	15¢ gray 900.00	620.00	375.00	155.00	95.00	57.50	
	1868 Wove paper. Perf. 12 watermarked						
22a	1¢ brown red	1450.00	800.00	......	175.00	115.00	
24a	2¢ green	2000.00	1250.00	......	240.00	175.00	
25a	3¢ red	2200.00	1450.00	......	240.00	175.00	
27b	6¢ dark brown	3600.00	2450.00	......	900.00	650.00	
28a	12-1/2¢ blue	1250.00	675.00	......	145.00	95.00	
29c	15¢ gray violet	3600.00	2500.00	......	550.00	375.00	
	1868 Laid Paper (OG + 20%)						
31	1¢ brown red 11000.00	6600.00	3400.00	2300.00	1425.00		
33	3¢ bright red 10000.00	6000.00	......	675.00	495.00		
	1870-89 Perf. 12						
34	1/2¢ black 9.00	6.25	3.75	7.50	4.50	3.00	
35	1¢ yellow 28.00	19.00	12.00	1.00	.70	.45	
35a	1¢ orange 85.00	57.50	35.00	10.00	6.00	3.50	
36	2¢ green 35.00	23.50	14.75	1.75	1.20	.75	
36d	2¢ blue green 67.50	45.00	28.50	4.25	2.50	1.50	
37	3¢ dull red 74.00	50.00	31.00	2.85	1.75	.90	
37c	3¢ orange red 67.50	45.00	25.00	1.75	1.00	.70	
37d	3¢ copper red, pf. 12-1/2 ... 4725.00	2800.00	1025.00	700.00	425.00		
38	5¢ slate green 395.00	275.00	170.00	20.00	12.00	8.25	
39	6¢ yellow brown 320.00	225.00	135.00	20.00	12.00	8.25	
40	10¢ dull rose lilac 425.00	295.00	175.00	47.50	28.00	19.00	
	1873-79 Perf. 11-1/2 x 12 (OG + 20%)						
35d	1¢ orange 180.00	125.00	75.00	16.00	9.50	6.00	
36e	2¢ green 250.00	170.00	110.00	22.00	13.50	9.00	
37e	3¢ red 220.00	150.00	92.50	9.75	5.75	3.75	
38a	5¢ slate green 480.00	325.00	200.00	37.00	22.00	15.00	
39b	6¢ yellow brown 510.00	345.00	220.00	37.00	22.00	15.00	
40c	10¢ pale milky rose lilac . 900.00	610.00	380.00	325.00	195.00	130.00	

Original Gum: Prior to 1897, the Unused price is for stamps either without gum or with partial gum. If you require full original gum, use the OG premium. Never hinged quality is scarce on those issues. Please write for specific quotations for NH.

Canada Postage #41-108a

SCOTT NO.	DESCRIPTION	VF	UNUSED F	AVG	VF	USED F	AVG
	1888-93 Perf. 12						
41	3¢ bright vermillion	27.50	18.75	11.50	.75	.45	.25
41a	3¢ rose carmine	340.00	230.00	145.00	10.00	6.00	4.00
42	5¢ gray	77.50	52.00	32.50	5.00	3.00	1.60
43	6¢ red brown	67.50	46.00	28.50	12.50	8.50	5.00
43a	6¢ chocolate	190.00	130.00	80.00	30.00	21.00	12.50
44	8¢ gray	80.00	55.00	33.00	4.50	3.25	1.85
45	10¢ brown red	145.00	98.50	60.00	35.00	22.00	13.75
46	20¢ vermillion	300.00	210.00	125.00	90.00	55.00	35.00
47	50¢ deep blue	305.00	205.00	135.00	80.00	50.00	30.00

46, 47

50-65
Queen Victoria in 1837 & 1897

SCOTT NO.	DESCRIPTION	VF	UNUSED OG F	AVG	VF	USED F	AVG
	1897 Jubilee Issue (NH + 150%)						
50	1/2¢ black	90.00	60.00	35.00	80.00	55.00	37.50
51	1¢ orange	16.00	10.00	7.00	9.00	6.00	4.00
52	2¢ green	19.00	13.00	8.00	12.25	8.25	5.00
53	3¢ bright rose	11.00	7.50	4.50	2.25	1.50	.90
54	5¢ deep blue	35.00	23.50	14.75	22.50	15.00	8.25
55	6¢ yellow brown	175.00	120.00	74.00	150.00	110.00	75.00
56	8¢ dark violet	37.50	25.50	15.75	32.50	19.50	12.00
57	10¢ brown violet	75.00	50.00	27.50	75.00	50.00	28.00
58	15¢ steel blue	165.00	110.00	75.00	150.00	110.00	75.00
59	20¢ vermillion	180.00	122.50	75.00	150.00	110.00	75.00
60	50¢ ultramarine	180.00	120.00	75.00	165.00	110.00	65.00
61	$1 lake	625.00	405.00	250.00	500.00	400.00	200.00
62	$2 dark purple	1000.00	650.00	450.00	550.00	360.00	220.00
63	$3 yellow bistre	1200.00	775.00	500.00	900.00	600.00	450.00
64	$4 purple	1200.00	775.00	500.00	900.00	600.00	450.00
65	$5 olive green	1200.00	775.00	500.00	900.00	600.00	450.00

66-73   74-84   85-86
Queen Victoria   Map Showing British Empire

77: 2¢ Die I. Frame of four thin lines
77a: 2¢ Die II. Frame of thick line between two thin lines

	1897-98 Maple Leaves (NH + 150%)						
66	1/2¢ black	6.75	4.50	2.75	5.50	3.75	2.20
67	1¢ blue green	15.25	10.25	6.50	1.10	.70	.45
68	2¢ purple	16.00	10.75	6.75	1.65	1.10	.70
69	3¢ carmine (1898)	19.50	13.25	8.25	.45	.30	.25
70	5¢ dark blue, bluish paper	80.00	57.50	40.00	5.75	3.75	2.20
71	6¢ brown	67.50	45.00	28.00	26.50	17.00	11.00
72	8¢ orange	150.00	95.00	60.00	9.00	6.00	3.75
73	10¢ brown violet (1898)	185.00	120.00	75.00	67.50	45.00	30.00
	1898-1902 Numerals (NH + 150%)						
74	1/2¢ black	2.75	1.80	1.10	1.60	1.10	.65
75	1¢ gray green	16.00	10.50	7.00	.30	.20	.15
76	2¢ purple (I)	16.00	10.50	7.00	.30	.20	.15
77	2¢ carmine (I) (1899)	15.50	10.50	6.00	.30	.20	.15
77a	2¢ carmine (II)	18.00	11.00	6.50	.45	.30	.20
78	3¢ carmine	25.00	16.00	9.50	.50	.40	.30
79	5¢ blue, bluish paper	110.00	70.00	45.00	1.40	1.00	.55
80	6¢ brown	92.50	62.50	35.00	40.00	22.00	11.50
81	7¢ olive yellow (1902)	75.00	50.00	35.00	17.00	10.00	6.50
82	8¢ orange	125.00	80.00	50.00	19.00	11.50	7.50
83	10¢ brown violet	180.00	122.50	76.00	17.00	10.00	6.50
84	20¢ olive green (1900)	365.00	250.00	155.00	80.00	47.00	32.50
	1898 IMPERIAL PENNY POSTAGE COMMEMORATIVE						
85	2¢ black, lavender & carmine	25.00	17.00	12.00	7.25	5.00	3.25
86	2¢ black, blue & carmine	25.00	17.00	12.00	7.25	5.00	3.25
	1899						
	69 & 78 surcharged						
87	2¢ on 3¢ carmine	9.25	6.25	4.00	5.50	3.50	2.50
88	2¢ on 3¢ carmine	14.50	10.00	6.00	4.00	2.50	1.75s

89-95
King Edward VII

SCOTT NO.	DESCRIPTION	UNUSED NH F	AVG	UNUSED OG F	AVG	USED F	AVG
	1903-08						
89	1¢ green	25.00	17.00	15.00	10.00	.20	.15
90	2¢ carmine	25.00	17.00	15.00	10.00	.20	.15
90a	2¢ carmine, imperf. pair	35.00	25.00	25.00	17.00	......	......
91	5¢ blue, blue paper	125.00	85.00	50.00	30.00	2.00	1.35
92	7¢ olive bistre	100.00	65.00	40.00	25.00	2.00	1.35
93	10¢ brown lilac	175.00	125.00	85.00	60.00	4.50	3.00
94	20¢ olive green	495.00	350.00	325.00	250.00	16.00	11.50
95	50¢ purple (1908)	675.00	500.00	300.00	200.00	55.00	35.00

96   97   98
Princess and Prince of Wales in 1908   Jacques Cartier and Samuel Champlain   Queen Alexandra and King Edward

99   100   101
Champlain's Home in Quebec   Generals Montcalm and Wolfe   View of Quebec in 1700

102   103   104-34, 136-38, 184
Champlain's Departure for the West   Arrival of Cartier at Quebec   King George V

Never Hinged: From 1897 to 1949, Unused OG is for stamps with original gum that have been hinged. If you desire Never Hinged stamps, order from the NH listings.

1908 QUEBEC TERCENTENARY ISSUE

96-103	1/2¢-20¢ complete, 8 varieties	715.00	515.00	310.00	208.25	275.00	185.00
96	1/2¢ black brown	5.00	3.15	2.50	1.40	3.00	1.95
97	1¢ blue green	13.00	8.00	6.00	4.50	3.00	1.95
98	2¢ carmine	23.50	18.00	9.00	6.50	.95	.55
99	5¢ dark blue	55.00	35.00	24.00	17.00	22.50	13.50
100	7¢ olive green	135.00	95.00	55.00	40.00	40.00	30.00
101	10¢ dark violet	135.00	95.00	55.00	40.00	45.00	30.00
102	15¢ red orange	160.00	110.00	75.00	45.00	72.50	45.00
103	20¢ yellow brown	225.00	175.00	100.00	65.00	105.00	62.50

1912-25

104-22	1¢-$1 complete, 18 varieties	947.00	702.00	376.50	258.75	31.75	19.25
104	1¢ green	11.50	8.00	5.00	3.00	.20	.15
104a	same, booklet pane of 6	24.00	16.75	18.00	10.50	......	......
105	1¢ yellow (1922)	11.50	8.00	5.00	3.00	.20	.15
105a	same, booklet pane of 4	55.00	38.00	35.00	25.00	......	......
105b	same, booklet pane of 6	45.00	35.00	28.50	20.00	......	......
106	2¢ carmine	11.00	7.50	4.50	3.00	.20	.15
106a	same, booklet pane of 6	33.50	23.00	20.00	14.00	......	......
107	2¢ yellow green (1922)	8.00	5.50	3.50	2.25	.20	.15
107b	same, booklet pane of 4	60.00	45.00	35.00	23.50	......	......
107c	same, booklet pane of 6	275.00	200.00	190.00	145.00	......	......
108	3¢ brown (1918)	14.00	10.00	5.75	3.50	.20	.15
108a	same, booklet pane of 4	85.00	59.50	50.00	33.50	......	......

Canada Postage #109-161

SCOTT NO.	DESCRIPTION	UNUSED NH F	AVG	UNUSED OG F	AVG	USED F	AVG
109	3¢ carmine (1923)	8.00	6.00	3.25	2.20	.20	.15
109a	same, booklet pane of 4	50.00	37.50	35.00	23.00	.....	.....
110	4¢ olive bistre (1922)	35.00	27.50	14.00	10.00	1.95	1.25
111	5¢ dark blue	120.00	95.00	50.00	35.00	.35	.20
112	5¢ violet (1922)	23.00	18.00	9.00	6.50	.35	.20
113	7¢ yellow ochre	45.00	35.00	18.00	13.00	1.40	.85
114	7¢ red brown (1924)	22.50	15.00	9.00	7.00	5.50	4.00
115	8¢ blue (1925)	38.00	28.50	15.00	9.50	5.00	4.00
116	10¢ plum	275.00	200.00	85.00	60.00	1.05	.60
117	10¢ blue (1922)	44.50	30.00	19.50	12.00	1.15	.75
118	10¢ bistre brown (1925)	40.00	30.00	17.50	12.50	1.00	.65
119	20¢ olive green	85.00	60.00	35.00	25.00	.90	.55
120	50¢ black brown (1925)	85.00	60.00	37.50	25.00	1.75	1.15
120a	50¢ black	180.00	120.00	75.00	50.00	2.20	1.30
122	$1 orange (1923)	120.00	95.00	60.00	40.00	6.00	3.75
	1912 Coil Stamps; Perf. 8 Horizontally						
123	1¢ dark green	105.00	60.00	51.00	31.50	25.00	14.00
124	2¢ carmine	105.00	60.00	51.00	31.50	25.00	14.00
	1912-24 Perf. 8 Vertically						
125-30	1¢-3¢ complete, 6 varieties	133.00	93.00	74.50	45.75	14.75	9.50
125	1¢ green	17.00	10.00	8.50	5.25	1.00	.65
126	1¢ yellow (1923)	10.00	8.00	5.50	3.25	5.50	3.75
126a	1¢ block of 4	50.00	35.00	30.00	20.00	.....	.....
127	2¢ carmine	22.00	15.00	12.00	7.25	.90	.60
128	2¢ green (1922)	14.00	8.00	8.00	5.50	.90	.60
128a	2¢ block of 4	50.00	35.00	30.00	20.00	.....	.....
129	3¢ brown (1918)	12.00	7.00	7.00	4.00	.90	.60
130	3¢ carmine (1924)	65.00	50.00	50.00	23.00	6.50	4.00
130a	3¢ block of 4	600.00	400.00	375.00	250.00	.....	.....
	1915-24 Perf. 12 Horizontally						
131	1¢ dark green	6.50	4.50	3.75	2.50	7.00	4.25
132	2¢ carmine	20.00	13.00	11.00	8.00	7.00	5.00
133	2¢ yellow green (1924)	82.50	57.00	50.00	30.00	45.00	28.00
134	3¢ brown (1921)	8.00	6.00	4.50	3.25	4.50	2.60

135
Quebec Conference of 1867

1917 CONFEDERATION ISSUE

135	3¢ brown	42.00	25.00	18.00	12.00	.75	.50

1924 Imperforate

136	1¢ yellow	45.00	30.00	31.00	22.00	35.00	23.00
137	2¢ green	45.00	30.00	31.00	22.00	35.00	23.00
138	3¢ carmine	24.00	17.00	15.00	10.00	16.00	12.00

1926 — 109 Surcharged

| 139 | 2¢ on 3¢ carmine | 55.00 | 37.50 | 35.00 | 25.00 | 37.00 | 26.00 |

109 Surcharged

| 140 | 2¢ on 3¢ carmine | 24.00 | 18.00 | 17.00 | 12.00 | 16.00 | 11.00 |

141 — Sir John Macdonald
142 — The Quebec Conference of 1867
143 — The Parliment Building at Ottawa

144 — Sir Wilfred Laurier
145 — Map of Canada

1927 CONFEDERATION ISSUE

SCOTT NO.	DESCRIPTION	UNUSED NH F	AVG	UNUSED OG F	AVG	USED F	AVG
141-45	1¢-12¢ complete, 5 varieties	36.25	24.75	21.75	15.25	8.25	5.10
141	1¢ orange	3.00	2.25	1.95	1.30	.65	.40
142	2¢ green	2.00	1.25	1.10	.75	.20	.15
143	3¢ brown carmine	8.25	5.50	5.50	3.75	3.50	2.10
144	5¢ violet	5.00	3.25	3.35	2.20	1.80	1.10
145	12¢ dark blue	20.00	14.00	11.00	8.00	3.00	1.85

146 — Thomas McGee
147 — Sir Wilfred Laurier and Sir John Macdonald
148 — Robert Baldwin and L.H. Lafontaine

1927 HISTORICAL ISSUE

146-48	5¢-20¢ complete, 3 varieties	35.50	25.60	20.25	14.00	6.90	4.40
146	5¢ violet	5.00	3.00	2.35	1.75	1.40	.85
147	12¢ green	9.50	7.00	6.00	4.00	3.00	2.00
148	20¢ brown carmine	23.00	17.00	13.00	9.00	3.50	2.20

149-154, 160, 161 — King George V
155 — Mt. Hurd
156 — Quebec Bridge

157 — Harvesting Wheat
158 — Fishing Schooner "Bluenose"
159 — The Parliament Building at Ottawa

1928-29

149-59	1¢-$1 complete, 11 varieties	618.75	444.25	364.00	253.75	94.00	60.50
149-55	1¢-10¢, 7 varieties	80.25	51.95	41.00	26.45	17.15	10.15
149	1¢ orange	3.00	2.00	1.50	1.25	.25	.20
149a	same, booklet pane of 6	19.00	12.00	13.00	8.00	.....	.....
150	2¢ green	1.25	.95	.75	.60	.20	.15
150a	same, booklet pane of 6	22.00	15.00	15.00	10.00	.....	.....
151	3¢ dark carmine	22.00	16.00	12.00	8.00	8.00	4.50
152	4¢ bistre (1929)	14.25	8.75	8.50	5.25	3.50	2.10
153	5¢ deep violet	10.00	7.00	6.00	4.00	2.00	1.30
153a	same, booklet pane of 6	110.00	80.00	70.00	50.00	.....	.....
154	8¢ blue	17.00	10.00	7.00	4.25	4.00	2.30
155	10¢ green	17.00	10.00	7.50	4.50	.80	.50
156	12¢ gray (1929)	24.00	18.00	12.00	7.25	4.50	2.60
157	20¢ dark carmine (1929)	38.00	25.00	18.00	12.00	7.75	5.00
158	50¢ dark blue (1929)	230.00	170.00	140.00	95.00	42.50	30.00
159	$1 olive green (1929)	275.00	200.00	170.00	125.00	50.00	32.50

1929 Coil Stamps. Perf. 8 Vertically

160	1¢ orange	30.00	9.00	15.00	10.00	15.50	9.75
161	2¢ green	24.00	17.00	12.00	7.50	1.95	1.10

162-172, 178-183 — King George V
173 — Parliament Library at Ottawa

2¢ Die I. Above "POSTAGE" faint crescent in ball of ornament. Top letter "P" has tiny dot of color.

2¢ Die II. Stronger and clearer crescent, spot of color in "P" is larger.

Canada Postage #162-210

SCOTT NO.	DESCRIPTION	UNUSED NH F	AVG	UNUSED OG F	AVG	USED F	AVG

174 The Old Citadel at Quebec   **175** Harvesting Wheat on the Prairies

176 The Museum at Grand Pre and Monument to Evangeline   **177** Mt. Edith Cavell

VERY FINE QUALITY: To determine the Very Fine price, add the difference between the Fine and Average prices to the Fine quality price. For example: if the Fine price is $10.00 and the Average price is $6.00, the Very Fine price would be $14.00. From 1935 to date, add 20% to the Fine price to arrive at the Very Fine price.

1930-31

Scott	Description	NH F	NH AVG	OG F	OG AVG	Used F	Used AVG
162-77	1¢-$1 complete, 16 varieties	480.25	304.00	278.25	188.25	46.00	31.00
162-72	1¢-8¢, 11 varieties	49.80	37.35	30.25	20.10	14.00	9.30
162	1¢ orange	1.00	.65	.70	.45	.40	.30
163	1¢ deep green	1.30	.80	.85	.50	.20	.15
163a	same, booklet pane of 4	100.00	70.00	70.00	50.00	.....	.....
163c	same, booklet pane of 6	20.00	13.00	14.00	9.00	.....	.....
164	2¢ dull green	1.10	.65	.55	.40	.20	.15
164a	same, booklet pane of 6	33.00	27.00	20.00	13.00	.....	.....
165	2¢ deep red, die II	1.50	.90	1.00	.60	.20	.15
165a	2¢ deep red, die I	1.40	.85	.95	.55	.20	.15
165b	same, booklet pane of 6	22.00	13.00	15.00	9.50	.....	.....
166	2¢ dark brown, die II (1931)	1.60	1.10	.90	.70	.20	.15
166a	same, booklet pane of 4	95.00	70.00	70.00	50.00	.....	.....
166b	2¢ dark brown, die I (1931)	4.00	2.50	2.75	1.75	2.60	1.75
166c	same, booklet pane of 6	31.00	20.00	21.00	16.00	.....	.....
167	3¢ deep red (1931)	2.25	1.45	1.55	.95	.20	.15
167a	same, booklet pane of 4	35.00	21.00	24.00	17.00	.....	.....
168	4¢ yellow bistre	10.00	6.00	6.50	4.50	3.50	2.20
169	5¢ dull violet	6.00	4.00	3.35	2.20	2.75	1.75
170	5¢ dull blue	3.75	2.00	1.80	1.20	.20	.15
171	8¢ dark blue	18.00	12.00	11.00	7.50	5.00	3.25
172	8¢ red orange	6.00	3.50	3.70	2.50	2.50	1.60
173	10¢ olive green	10.00	7.00	5.50	3.40	.80	.45
174	12¢ gray black	17.00	12.00	9.50	5.50	4.00	2.50
175	20¢ brown red	26.00	18.00	16.00	11.00	.35	.20
176	50¢ dull blue	200.00	125.00	110.00	75.00	10.00	6.00
177	$1 dark olive green	200.00	125.00	120.00	82.00	17.50	10.00

Coil Pairs for Canada can be supplied at double the single price

1930-31 Coil Stamps. Perf. 8-1/2 Vertically

Scott	Description	NH F	NH AVG	OG F	OG AVG	Used F	Used AVG
178-83	1¢-3¢ complete, 6 varieties	70.25	41.75	42.75	27.00	14.20	9.00
178	1¢ orange	13.00	8.00	8.50	5.25	6.50	4.00
179	1¢ deep green	7.00	3.50	4.00	2.50	3.25	2.25
180	2¢ dull green	6.00	3.00	3.50	2.20	2.50	1.40
181	2¢ deep red	20.00	13.00	12.00	7.25	1.80	1.25
182	2¢ dark brown (1931)	10.00	5.50	7.00	4.75	.45	.30
183	3¢ deep red (1931)	18.00	11.00	10.25	6.50	.45	.30

1931 Design of 1912-25. Perf. 12x8

Scott	Description	NH F	NH AVG	OG F	OG AVG	Used F	Used AVG
184	3¢ carmine	5.50	3.75	3.00	2.00	2.00	1.25

1931

| 190 | 10¢ dark green | 11.00 | 8.00 | 5.00 | 3.30 | .20 | .15 |

1932 165 & 165a surcharged

| 191 | 3¢ on 2¢ deep red, die II | 1.00 | .70 | .75 | .40 | .20 | .15 |
| 191a | 3¢ on 2¢ deep red, die I | 2.25 | 1.55 | 1.60 | .95 | 1.10 | .95 |

190 Sir George Etienne Cartier   **192** King George V   **193** Prince of Wales   **194** Allegorical Figure of Britannia Surveying the British Empire

1932 OTTAWA CONFERENCE ISSUE

Scott	Description	NH F	NH AVG	OG F	OG AVG	Used F	Used AVG
192-94	3¢-13¢ complete, 3 varieties	14.00	9.50	10.00	6.00	5.50	3.75
192	3¢ deep red	.80	.55	.55	.35	.20	.15
193	5¢ dull blue	6.00	4.25	4.00	2.70	1.60	1.10
194	13¢ deep green	8.00	5.25	6.00	3.25	4.00	2.70

195-200, 205-207 King George V   **201** The Old Citadel at Quebec

1932

Scott	Description	NH F	NH AVG	OG F	OG AVG	Used F	Used AVG
195-201	1¢-31¢ complete, 7 varieties	105.30	72.00	62.00	40.40	8.65	5.70
195	1¢ dark green	.80	.60	.60	.35	.20	.15
195a	same, booklet pane of 4	95.00	70.00	65.00	40.00	.....	.....
195b	same, booklet pane of 6	25.00	17.50	20.00	12.00	.....	.....
196	2¢ black brown	.95	.55	.65	.40	.20	.15
196a	same, booklet pane of 4	95.00	70.00	65.00	40.00	.....	.....
196b	same, booklet pane of 6	22.00	13.00	16.00	11.00	.....	.....
197	3¢ deep red	1.10	.65	.85	.50	.20	.15
197a	same, booklet pane of 4	30.00	20.00	22.00	16.00	.....	.....
198	4¢ ochre	38.00	25.00	24.00	16.00	3.95	2.50
199	5¢ dark blue	8.00	5.00	4.00	2.80	.20	.15
200	8¢ red orange	22.00	15.00	13.50	9.00	2.75	1.80
201	13¢ dull violet	40.00	26.00	22.00	13.50	1.95	1.20

202 Parliament Buildings at Ottawa   **203**   **204** S.S. Royal William

208   **209**   **210**

1933-34 COMMEMORATIVES

Scott	Description	NH F	NH AVG	OG F	OG AVG	Used F	Used AVG
202/10	(202-04, 208-10), 6 varieties	77.00	47.25	50.65	34.20	21.25	12.95

1933

202	5¢ Postal Union	8.00	4.75	5.50	4.00	2.20	1.45
203	20¢ Grain Exhibition	35.00	21.00	25.00	16.00	10.00	5.50
204	5¢ Trans-Atlantic Crossing	9.00	5.25	5.75	4.00	2.20	1.45

1933 Coil Stamps Perf. 8-1/2 Vertically

205	1¢ dark green	16.00	9.50	11.00	7.00	1.60	1.10
206	2¢ black brown	18.00	10.50	12.50	8.00	.50	.35
207	3¢ deep red	14.00	9.00	8.00	5.50	.25	.15

1934

208	3¢ Jacques Cartier	4.00	2.25	2.20	1.60	1.00	.60
209	10¢ Loyalists Monument	23.00	15.00	13.50	9.50	5.50	3.75
210	2¢ New Brunswick	2.10	1.50	1.40	.90	1.40	.80

Canada #211-248

SCOTT NO.	DESCRIPTION	PLATE BLOCKS F/NH	PLATE BLOCKS AVG	UNUSED OG F/NH	UNUSED OG AVG	USED F

211 212 213

214 215 216

1935 SILVER JUBILEE ISSUE

Scott	Description	PB F/NH	PB AVG	Unused F/NH	Unused AVG	Used F
211-16	1¢-13¢ complete, 6 varieties	.....	.....	21.35	15.00	8.25
211	1¢ Princess Elizabeth	4.00	3.00	.40	.30	.25
212	2¢ Duke of York	8.25	6.95	.70	.60	.20
213	3¢ George & Mary	16.00	12.50	1.90	1.40	.20
214	5¢ Prince of Wales	41.00	30.00	5.00	3.60	2.25
215	10¢ Windsor Castle	50.00	36.00	6.00	4.50	2.00
216	13¢ Royal Yacht	62.50	42.50	8.50	5.50	4.00

217-22, 228-30 223 224
King George V

225 226 227

1935

Scott	Description	PB F/NH	PB AVG	Unused F/NH	Unused AVG	Used F
217-27	1¢-$1 complete, 11 varieties	.....	.....	147.00	96.50	13.95
217	1¢ green	2.75	2.20	.30	.25	.20
217a	same, booklet pane of 4	.....	.....	50.00	33.00	.....
217b	same, booklet pane of 4	.....	.....	25.00	16.50	.....
218	2¢ brown	4.00	3.00	.40	.30	.20
218a	same, booklet pane of 4	.....	.....	50.00	33.00	.....
219	3¢ dark carmine	5.50	4.50	.55	.45	.20
219a	same, booklet pane of 4	.....	.....	16.50	11.00	.....
220	4¢ yellow	23.00	17.50	2.95	2.20	.40
221	5¢ blue	20.00	15.50	2.50	1.95	.20
222	8¢ deep orange	22.00	16.50	2.95	2.20	1.50
223	10¢ Mounted Policeman	53.00	37.00	7.25	5.25	.120
224	13¢ Conference of 1864	55.00	38.50	7.25	5.25	.55
225	20¢ Niagara Falls	195.00	145.00	25.00	16.50	.40
226	50¢ Parliament Building	260.00	175.00	33.00	22.00	4.00
227	$1 Champlain Monument	500.00	325.00	72.50	45.00	7.75

1935 Coil Stamps Perf. 8 Vertically

Scott	Description	PB F/NH	PB AVG	Unused F/NH	Unused AVG	Used F
228-30	1¢-3¢ coils, complete, 3 varieties	.....	.....	34.20	22.50	2.30
228	1¢ green	.....	.....	14.00	9.00	2.00
229	2¢ brown	.....	.....	11.00	7.25	.70
230	3¢ dark carmine	.....	.....	11.50	7.50	.40

231-236, 238-240 237 241
King George VI

242 243

244 245 246

247 248

1937

Scott	Description	PB F/NH	PB AVG	Unused F/NH	Unused AVG	Used F
231-36	1¢-8¢ complete, 6 varieties	.....	.....	8.30	6.40	1.30
231	1¢ green	2.50	2.05	.40	.35	.20
231a	same, booklet pane of 4	.....	.....	11.00	7.50	.....
231b	same, booklet pane of 6	.....	.....	1.65	1.10	.....
232	2¢ brown	3.00	2.50	.55	.40	.20
232a	same, booklet pane of 4	.....	.....	13.00	7.50	.....
232b	same, booklet pane of 6	.....	.....	7.00	5.00	.....
233	3¢ carmine	2.75	2.25	.55	.45	.20
233a	same, booklet pane of 4	.....	.....	2.25	1.65	.....
234	4¢ yellow	12.50	11.00	2.50	1.95	.20
235	5¢ blue	12.00	9.50	2.25	1.65	.20
236	8¢ orange	12.00	9.00	2.50	1.95	.40
237	3¢ Coronation	1.90	1.55	.25	.20	.20

Coil Stamps Perf. 8 Vertically

Scott	Description	PB F/NH	PB AVG	Unused F/NH	Unused AVG	Used F
238-40	1¢-3¢ coils, complete, 3 varieties	.....	.....	6.85	5.25	1.25
238	1¢ green	.....	.....	1.10	.85	.85
239	2¢ brown	.....	.....	1.95	1.40	.30
240	3¢ carmine	.....	.....	4.15	3.30	.20

1938

Scott	Description	PB F/NH	PB AVG	Unused F/NH	Unused AVG	Used F
241-45	10¢-$1 complete, 5 varieties	.....	.....	120.00	77.50	9.10
241	10¢ Memorial Hall	23.50	16.50	5.00	3.60	.20
242	13¢ Halifax Harbor	41.50	27.50	8.25	5.50	.40
243	20¢ Fort Garry Gate	82.50	52.50	16.50	11.00	.30
244	50¢ Vancouver Harbor	125.00	77.00	22.00	14.00	3.50
245	$1 Chateau de Ramezay	350.00	230.00	75.00	47.50	5.50

1939 Royal Visit

Scott	Description	PB F/NH	PB AVG	Unused F/NH	Unused AVG	Used F
246-48	1¢-3¢ complete, 3 varieties	4.00	3.15	.70	.55	.40
246	1¢ Princess Elizabeth & Margaret	1.40	1.10	.25	.20	.15
247	2¢ War Memorial	1.40	1.10	.25	.20	.15
248	3¢ King George VI & Queen Elizabeth	1.40	1.10	.25	.20	.15

249, 255, 250, 254, 264, 253 256
263, 278   267, 279, 281
           King George VI

Canada Postage #249-283

257

258, 259

260

261

262

271

272

273

1946 PEACE ISSUE

SCOTT NO.	DESCRIPTION	PLATE BLOCKS F/NH	AVG	UNUSED OG F/NH	AVG	USED F
268-73	8¢-$1 complete, 6 varieties	......	......	60.50	41.25	5.15
268	8¢ Farm Scene	5.80	4.40	1.10	.95	.55
269	10¢ Great Bear Lake	6.35	5.50	1.25	1.05	.20
270	14¢ Hydro-Electric Power Station	13.75	11.00	2.75	2.20	.20
271	20¢ Reaper & Harvester	17.60	13.75	3.30	2.75	.20
272	50¢ Lumber Industry	84.15	61.60	16.50	12.10	1.65
273	$1 New Train Ferry	181.50	129.25	38.50	27.50	2.75

1942-43 WAR ISSUE

SCOTT NO.	DESCRIPTION	PLATE BLOCKS F/NH	AVG	UNUSED OG F/NH	AVG	USED F
249-62	1¢-$1 complete, 14 varieties	......	......	128.50	85.25	13.75
249	1¢ green	.95	.75	.25	.20	.15
249a	same, booklet pane of 4	......	......	4.50	3.05	.....
249b	same, booklet pane of 6	......	......	1.65	1.40	.....
249c	same, booklet pane of 3	......	......	1.65	1.10	.....
250	2¢ brown	1.95	1.40	.40	.30	.15
250a	same, booklet pane of 4	......	......	4.50	3.05	.....
250b	same, booklet pane of 6	......	......	4.50	3.05	.....
251	3¢ dark carmine	2.35	1.85	.40	.30	.15
251a	same, booklet pane of 4	......	......	1.95	1.40	.....
252	3¢ rose violet (1943)	1.95	1.40	.40	.30	.15
252a	same, booklet pane of 4	......	......	1.65	1.10	.....
252b	same, booklet pane of 3	......	......	2.25	1.80	.....
252c	same, booklet pane of 6	......	......	4.50	3.05	.....
253	4¢ Grain Elevators	11.00	8.00	1.40	.90	.50
254	4¢ dark carmine (1943)	2.05	1.50	.40	.30	.15
254a	same, booklet pane of 6	......	......	1.95	1.40	.....
254b	same, booklet pane of 3	......	......	1.95	1.40	.....
255	5¢ deep blue	5.00	3.30	1.00	.65	.15
256	8¢ Farm Scene	10.50	7.25	1.95	1.40	.40
257	10¢ Parliament Buildings	17.50	13.00	3.85	2.75	.15
258	13¢ "Ram" Tank	25.00	18.25	5.00	3.60	3.00
259	14¢ "Ram" Tank (1943)	36.00	27.00	7.75	5.50	.30
260	20¢ Corvette	27.50	21.00	8.00	5.50	.20
261	50¢ Munitions Factory	125.00	80.00	30.00	18.00	1.65
262	$1 Destroyer	345.00	235.00	75.00	50.00	6.50

Coil Stamps Perf. 8 Vertically

SCOTT NO.	DESCRIPTION	PLATE BLOCKS F/NH	AVG	UNUSED OG F/NH	AVG	USED F
263-67	1¢-4¢ complete, 5 varieties	......	......	9.00	6.00	1.75
263	1¢ green	......	......	.90	.65	.35
264	2¢ brown	......	......	1.30	.95	.75
265	3¢ dark carmine	......	......	1.30	.95	.75
266	3¢ rose violet (1943)	......	......	2.50	1.65	.25
267	4¢ dark carmine (1943)	......	......	3.50	2.20	.20

274

275

276 277

282

283

268

269

270

1947-49 COMMEMORATIVES

SCOTT NO.	DESCRIPTION	PLATE BLOCKS F/NH	AVG	UNUSED OG F/NH	AVG	USED F
274/83	274-77, 282-83, complete, 6 varieties	4.00	3.40	1.25	.85	.95
274	4¢ Alexander G. Bell	.70	.60	.20	.15	.15
275	4¢ Canadian Citizen	.70	.60	.20	.15	.15

1948

| 276 | 4¢ Princess Elizabeth | .70 | .60 | .20 | .15 | .15 |
| 277 | 4¢ Parliament Building | .70 | .60 | .20 | .15 | .15 |

Designs of 1942-43
Coil Stamps Perf. 9-1/2 Vertically

278-81	1¢-4¢ complete, 4 varieties	......	......	25.00	22.50	10.50
278	1¢ green	......	......	2.90	2.50	1.65
279	2¢ brown	......	......	9.90	9.00	7.00
280	3¢ rose violet	......	......	5.25	4.75	1.95
281	4¢ dark carmine	......	......	8.25	7.50	2.15

1949

| 282 | 4¢ Cabot's "Matthew" | .70 | .60 | .20 | .15 | .15 |
| 283 | 4¢ Founding of Halifax | .70 | .60 | .20 | .15 | .15 |

COMMEMORATIVES: Commemorative stamps are special issues released to honor or recognize persons, organizations, historical events or landmarks. They are usually issued in the current first class denomination to supplement regular issues.

VERY FINE QUALITY: From 1935 to date, add 20% to the FIne price. Minimum of 3¢ per stamp.

Canada Postage #284-343

SCOTT NO.	DESCRIPTION	PLATE BLOCK F/NH	UNUSED F/NH	USED F

284, 289, 295, 297 / **285, 290, 298, 305, 309** / **286, 291, 296, 299** / **287, 292, 300, 306, 310** / **288, 293**

King George VI

1949 (with "Postes-Postage")

Scott	Description	Plate Block	Unused	Used
284-88	1¢-5¢ complete, 5 varieties	10.45	2.10	.70
284	1¢ green	.75	.20	.15
284a	same, booklet pane of 3	......	1.25	......
285	2¢ sepia	1.25	.25	.15
286	3¢ rose violet	1.50	.30	.15
286a	same, booklet pane of 3	......	1.50	......
286b	same, booklet pane of 4	......	1.75	......
287	4 dark carmine	2.00	.50	.15
287a	same, booklet pane of 3	......	12.00	......
287b	same, booklet pane of 6	......	13.50	......
288	5¢ deep blue	5.50	1.00	.15

1950 Type of 1949 (without "Postes-Postage")

Scott	Description	Plate Block	Unused	Used
289-93	1¢-5¢ complete, 5 varieties	9.50	1.65	2.05
289	1¢ green	.65	.20	.15
290	2¢ sepia	1.95	.25	.20
291	3¢ rose violet	.85	.20	.15
292	4¢ dark carmine	1.10	.25	.15
293	5¢ deep blue	5.50	1.05	.75
294	50¢ Oil Wells, Alberta	60.50	12.65	1.05

Coil Stamps Perf. 9-1/2 Vertically

Scott	Description	Plate Block	Unused	Used
295-300	1¢-4¢ complete, 6 vars.	......	17.00	3.30

(without "Postes-Postage")

| 295 | 1¢ green | ...... | .50 | .30 |
| 296 | 3¢ rose violet | ...... | .75 | .55 |

(with "Postes-Postage")

297	1¢ green	......	.35	.25
298	2¢ sepia	......	2.25	1.40
299	3¢ rose violet	......	1.50	.20
300	4¢ dark carmine	......	12.65	.75
301	10¢ Fur Resources	4.00	.75	.15
302	$1 Fishing	300.00	65.00	12.00

294 / **301** / **302** / **303**

304 / **311** / **314** / **315**

1951

1951-52 COMMEMORATIVES

Scott	Description	Plate Block	Unused	Used
303/19	(303-04, 311-15, 317-19) complete, 10 vars.	26.10	5.25	2.90
303	3¢ Sir Robert L. Borden	1.10	.20	.15
304	4¢ William L.M. King	1.25	.25	.15

(with "Postes-Postage")

305	2¢ olive green	.80	.20	.15
306	4¢ orange vermillion	1.00	.20	.15
306a	same, booklet pane of 3	......	2.50	......
306b	same, booklet pane of 6	......	2.75	......

Coil Stamps Perf. 9-1/2 Vertically

| 309 | 2¢ olive green | ...... | 1.10 | .60 |
| 310 | 4¢ orange vermillion | ...... | 2.50 | .70 |

1951 "CAPEX" Exhibition

311	4¢ Trains of 1851 & 1951	2.50	.55	.15
312	5¢ Steamships	8.25	1.65	1.35
313	7¢ Stagecoach & Plane	5.00	1.00	.35
314	15¢ "Three Pence Beaver"	5.50	1.00	.30
315	4¢ Royal Visit	.95	.20	.15

---

317 / **318** / **319** / **316**

1952

Scott	Description	Plate Block	Unused	Used
316	20¢ Paper Production	7.00	1.35	.15
317	4¢ Red Cross	.95	.20	.15
318	3¢ J.J.C. Abbott	.95	.20	.15
319	4¢ A. Mackenzie	1.10	.25	.10

1952-53

| 320 | 7¢ Canada Goose | 1.80 | .35 | .15 |
| 321 | $1 Indian House & Totem Pole (1953) | 55.00 | 12.00 | .80 |

1953-54 COMMEMORATIVES

322/50	(322-24, 330, 335-36, 349-50) complete, 8 varieties	8.95	1.90	1.15
322	2¢ Polar Bear	.80	.20	.15
323	3¢ Moose	.90	.20	.15
324	4¢ Bighorn Sheep	1.10	.25	.15

320 / **321** / **322** / **323** / **324**

1953

325-29	1¢-5¢ complete, 5 vars.	4.50	1.10	.70
325	1¢ violet brown	.70	.20	.15
325a	same, booklet pane of 3	.60	......	.15
326	2¢ green	.70	.20	.15
327	3¢ carmine rose	.85	.20	.15
327a	same, booklet pane of 3	1.40	......	......
327b	same, booklet pane of 4	1.40	......	......
328	4¢ violet	1.10	.25	.15
328a	same, bklt. pane of 3	......	1.65	......
328b	same, bklt. pane of 6	......	1.95	......
329	5¢ ultramarine	1.40	.30	.15
330	4¢ Queen Elizabeth II	.95	.20	.15

Coil Stamps Perf. 9-1/2 Vertically

331-33	2¢-4¢ complete, 3 vars.	......	4.90	3.45
331	2¢ green	......	1.20	1.00
332	3¢ carmine rose	......	1.20	1.00
333	4¢ violet	......	2.75	1.65
334	50¢ Textile Industry	21.00	4.70	.20

325-29, 331-33 / **330** / **334** / **335**

336 / **337-342, 345-348** / **343**

1954

335	4¢ Walrus	1.40	.30	.15
336	5¢ Beaver	1.65	.35	.15
336a	same, booklet pane of 5	......	1.95	......
337-43	1¢-15¢ cpl., 7 vars.	10.65	2.35	1.00
337	1¢ violet brown	.70	.20	.15
337a	same, booklet pane of 5	......	.75	......
338	2¢ green	.70	.20	.15
338a	mini pane of 25	......	4.40	......
338a	sealed pack of 2	......	8.80	......
339	3¢ carmine rose	.70	.20	.15
340	4¢ violet[1]	.85	.20	.15
340a	same, booklet pane of 5	......	1.65	......
340b	same, booklet pane of 6	......	5.50	......
341	5¢ bright blue	1.10	.20	.15
341a	same, booklet pane of 5	......	1.65	......
341b	mini sheet of 20	......	8.25	......
342	6¢ orange	1.65	.35	.15
343	15¢ Gannet	5.50	1.10	.15

Canada Postage #345-392

SCOTT NO.	DESCRIPTION	PLATE BLOCK F/NH	UNUSED F/NH	USED F
	Coil Stamps Perf. 9-1/2 Vertically			
345-48	2¢-4¢ complete, 3 vars.	......	3.40	.60
345	2¢ green	......	.35	.20
347	4¢ violet	......	1.25	.25
348	5¢ bright blue	......	2.00	.20
349	4¢ J.S.D. Thompson	1.30	.25	.15
350	5¢ M. Bowell	1.30	.25	.15
	1955			
351	10¢ Eskimo in Kayak	1.65	.35	.15
	1955-56 COMMEMORATIVES			
352/64	(352-61, 364 (complete, 11 varieties)	15.10	3.25	1.60
352	4¢ Musk Ox	1.30	.30	.15
353	5¢ Whooping Cranes	1.30	.30	.15
	1955			
354	5¢ Intl. Civil Aviation Org.	1.50	.30	.15
355	5¢ Alberta-Saskatchewan	1.50	.30	.15
356	5¢ Boy Scout Jamboree	1.50	.30	.15
357	4¢ R.B. Bennett	1.50	.30	.15
358	5¢ C. Tupper	1.50	.30	.15
	1956			
359	5¢ Hockey Players	1.50	.30	.15
360	4¢ Caribou	1.50	.35	.15
361	5¢ Mountain Goat	1.50	.35	.15
362	20¢ Paper Industry	6.60	1.35	.15
363	25¢ Chemical Industry	8.25	1.65	.15
364	5¢ Fire Prevention	1.30	.30	.15
	1957 COMMEMORATIVES			
365-74	complete, 10 varieties	17.50(7)	4.80	3.15
365-68	Recreation, attached	1.90	1.45	1.60
365	5¢ Fishing	......	.40	.20
366	5¢ Swimming	......	.40	.20
367	5¢ Hunting	......	.40	.20
368	5¢ Skiing	......	.40	.20
369	5¢ Loon	1.20	.30	.15
370	5¢ D. Thompson, Explorer	1.20	.30	.15
371	5¢ Parliament Building	1.20	.30	.15
372	15¢ Posthorn & Globe	11.00	2.20	1.75
373	5¢ Coal Miner	1.00	.25	.15
374	5¢ Royal Visit	1.00	.25	.15
	1958 COMMEMORATIVES			
375-82	complete, 8 varieties	10.75(6)	1.95	1.15
375	5¢ Newspaper	......	.30	.15
376	5¢ Int'l. Geophysical Year	......	.25	.15
377	5¢ Miner Panning Gold	2.00	.25	.15
378	5¢ La Verendrye, Explorer	1.50	.25	.15
379	5¢ S. deChamplain	3.50	.25	.15
380	5¢ National Health	1.50	.25	.15
381	5¢ Petroleum Industry	1.50	.25	.15
382	5¢ Speaker's Chair & Mace	1.50	.25	.15
	1959 COMMEMORATIVES			
383-88	complete, 6 varieties	9.65	1.45	.85
383	5¢ Old & Modern Planes	1.50	.25	.15
384	5¢ NATO Anniversary	1.35	.25	.15
385	5¢ Woman Tending Tree	1.10	.25	.15
386	5¢ Royal Tour	1.10	.25	.15
387	5¢ St. Lawrence Seaway	4.00	.25	.15
387a	same, center inverted	...	9250.00	8500.00
388	5¢ Plains of Abraham	1.10	.25	.15
	1960-62 COMMEMORATIVES			
389-400	complete, 12 varieties	12.50	2.85	1.70
389	5¢ Girl Guides Emblem	1.10	.25	.15
390	5¢ Battle of Long Sault	1.10	.25	.15
	1961			
391	5¢ Earth Mover	1.10	.25	.15
392	5¢ E.P. Johnson	1.10	.25	.15

Canada Postage #393-444

SCOTT NO.	DESCRIPTION	PLATE BLOCK F/NH	UNUSED F/NH	USED F
393	5¢ A. Meighen	1.10	.25	.15
394	5¢ Colombo Plan	1.10	.25	.15
395	5¢ Natural Resources	1.10	.25	.15

1962

396	5¢ Education	1.10	.25	.15
397	5¢ Red River Settlement	1.10	.25	.15
398	5¢ Jean Talon	1.10	.25	.15
399	5¢ Victoria, B.C.	1.10	.25	.15
400	5¢ Trans-Canada	1.10	.25	.15

393, 395, 396, 394

397, 398, 399

400, 401-09

1962-63

401-05	1¢-5¢ complete, 5 varieties	6.50	1.00	.70
401	1¢ deep brown (1963)	.45	.20	.15
401a	same, booklet pane of 5	......	3.30	......
402	2¢ green (1963)	3.60	.20	.15
402a	mini pane of 25	......	4.70	......
402a	same, sealed pack of 2	......	10.50	......
403	3¢ purple (1963)	.70	.20	.15
404	4¢ carmine (1963)	1.00	.20	.15
404a	same, booklet pane of 5	......	3.30	......
404b	mini pane of 25	......	8.00	......
405	5¢ violet blue	1.20	.25	.15
405a	same, booklet pane of 5	......	5.00	......
405b	mini pane of 20	......	12.00	......

1963-64 Coil Stamps, Perf. 9-1/2 Horiz.

406-09	2¢-5¢ complete, 4 varieties	......	13.75	4.30
406	2¢ green	......	4.00	1.55
407	3¢ purple (1964)	......	2.50	1.25
408	4¢ carmine	......	4.00	1.25
409	5¢ violet blue	......	4.00	.50

1963-64 COMMEMORATIVES

410/35	(410, 412-13, 416-17, 431-35) 10 varieties	10.20	2.35	1.45
410	5¢ Sir Casimir S. Gzowski	1.10	.25	.15
411	$1 Export Trade	74.25	15.00	2.50
412	5¢ Sir M. Frobisher, Explorer	1.10	.25	.15
413	5¢ First Mail Routes	1.10	.25	.15

1963-64

414	7¢ Jet Takeoff (1964)	1.50	.35	.55
415	15¢ Canada Geese	11.00	2.20	.20

1964

416	5¢ World Peace	1.10	.25	.15
417	5¢ Canadian Unity	1.10	.25	.15

410, 411, 412, 413

414, 430, 436 — 415 — 416 — 417

COATS OF ARMS & FLORAL EMBLEMS

- 419 Quebec & White Garden Lily
- 420 Nova Scotia & Mayflower
- 421 New Brunswick & Purple Violet (1965)
- 422 Manitoba & Prairie Crocus (1965)
- 423 British Columbia & Dogwood (1965)
- 424 Prince Edward Island & Lady's Slipper (1965)
- 425 Saskatchewan & Prairie Lily (1966)
- 426 Alberta & Wild Rose (1966)
- 427 Newfoundland & Pitcher Plant (1966)
- 428 Yukon & Fireweed (1966)
- 429 Northwest Territories & Mountain Avens (1966)

418 — Ontario & White Trillium — 429A — Canada & Maple Leaf

1964-66

SCOTT NO.	DESCRIPTION	PLATE BLOCK F/NH	UNUSED F/NH	USED F
418-29A	complete, 13 varieties	13.60	3.10	2.00
418	5¢ red brown, buff & green	1.10	.25	.15
419	5¢ green, yellow & orange	1.10	.25	.20
420	5¢ blue, pink & green	1.10	.25	.15
421	5¢ carmine, green & violet	1.10	.25	.15
422	5¢ red brown, lilac & green	1.10	.25	.15
423	5¢ lilac, green & bistre	1.10	.25	.15
424	5¢ violet, green & deep rose	1.10	.25	.15
425	5¢ sepia, orange & green	1.10	.25	.20
426	5¢ green, yellow & carmine	1.10	.25	.15
427	5¢ black, green & carmine	1.10	.25	.15
428	5¢ dark blue, rose & green	1.10	.25	.15
429	5¢ olive, yellow & green	1.10	.25	.20
429A	5¢ dark blue & red (1966)	1.10	.25	.15

1964 Surcharged on 414

430	8¢ on 7¢ Jet Takeoff	1.65	.35	.35
431	5¢ Charlottetown Conference	1.10	.25	.15
432	5¢ Quebec Conference	1.10	.20	.15
433	5¢ Queen Elizabeth's Visit	1.10	.25	.15
434	3¢ Christmas	.85	.20	.15
434a	mini sheet of 25	......	7.50	......
434a	same, sealed pack of 2	......	15.50	......
435	5¢ Christmas	1.10	.25	.15

Jet Type of 1964

436	8¢ Jet Takeoff	1.65	.35	.25

1965 COMMEMORATIVES

437-44	8 varieties	7.80	1.85	1.15
437	5¢ I.C.Y.	1.00	.25	.15

431, 432, 433, 434, 435

437, 438, 439, 440

441, 442, 443-44

438	5¢ Sir Wilfred Grenfell	1.00	.25	.15
439	5¢ National Flag	1.00	.25	.15
440	5¢ Winston Churchill	1.00	.25	.15
441	5¢ Inter-Parliamentary	1.00	.25	.15
442	5¢ Ottawa, National Capital	1.00	.25	.15
443	3¢ Christmas	.80	.20	.15
443a	mini pane of 25	......	6.50	......
443a	same, sealed pack of 2	......	13.00	......
444	5¢ Christmas	1.40	.25	.15

Canada Postage #445-486

SCOTT NO.	DESCRIPTION	PLATE BLOCK F/NH	UNUSED F/NH	USED F
	1966 COMMEMORATIVES			
445-52	8 varieties	7.75	1.80	1.15
445	5¢ Alouette II Satellite	1.10	.25	.15
446	5¢ La Salle Arrival	1.10	.25	.15
447	5¢ Highway Safety	1.10	.25	.15
448	5¢ London Conference	1.10	.25	.15
449	5¢ Atomic Reactor	1.10	.25	.15
450	5¢ Parliamentary Library	1.10	.25	.15
451	3¢ Christmas	.70	.20	.15
451a	mini pane of 25	......	4.50	......
451a	same, sealed pack of 2	......	9.00	......
452	5¢ Christmas	.85	.20	.15
	1967 COMMEMORATIVES			
453/77	(453, 469-77) complete, 10 varieties	10.00	2.30	.45
453	5¢ National Centennial	1.10	.25	.15
	Regional Views & Art Designs			
	1967-72 Perf.12 except as noted			
454-65B	1¢-$1 complete, 14 varieties	95.50	18.25	2.50
454-64	1¢-20¢, 11 varieties	21.00	3.35	1.45
454	1¢ brown	.90	.20	.15
454a	same, booklet pane of 5	......	.90	......
454b	booklet pane, 1¢(1), 6¢(4)	......	3.00	......
454c	booklet pane, 1¢(5), 3¢(5)	......	3.85	......

NOTE—#454d, 454e, 456a, 457d, 458d, 460g, and 460h are Booklet Singles

454d	1¢ perf. 10 (1968)	......	.25	.20
454e	1¢ 12-1/2 x 12 (1969)	......	.45	.15
455	2¢ green	1.40	.20	.15
455a	booklet pane 2¢(4), 3¢(4)	......	1.65	......
456	3¢ dull purple	1.20	.20	.15
456a	3¢ 12-1/2 x 12 (1971)	......	1.10	.45
457	4¢ carmine rose	1.65	.20	.15
457a	same, booklet pane 5	......	1.50	......
457b	miniature pane of 25	......	20.00	......
457c	same, booklet pane of 25	......	8.00	......
457d	4¢ perf.10 (1968)	......	.70	.30
458	5¢ blue	.85	.20	.15
458a	same, booklet pane of 5	......	6.50	......
458b	miniature pane of 20	......	30.00	......
458c	booklet pane of 20, perf.10	......	7.75	......
458d	5¢ perf. 10 (1968)	......	.70	.30
459	6¢ orange, perf. 10 (1968)	3.85	.35	.15
459a	same, booklet pane of 25	......	10.00	......
459b	6¢ orange 12-1/2x12 (1969)	3.30	.35	.15
460	6¢ black, 12-1/2x12 (1970)	1.95	.25	.15
460a	booklet pane of 25, perf.10	......	15.40	......
460b	booklet pane of 25, 12-1/2x12	......	18.50	......
460c	6¢ black, 12-1/2x12 (1970)	2.20	.30	.15
460d	booklet pane of 4, 12-1/2x12	......	5.50	......
460e	booklet pane of 4, perf.10	......	10.00	......
460f	6¢ black, perf. 12 (1972)	2.50	.50	.15
460g	6¢ black, perf. 10 (I)	......	1.75	.40
460h	6¢ black, perf. 10 (II)	......	4.00	.85

460, 460a, b,& g: Original Die. Weak shading lines around 6.
460 c, d, e, & h: Reworked plate lines strengthened, darker.
460f: Original Die. Strong shading lines, similar to 468B, but Perf 12x12 .

SCOTT NO.	DESCRIPTION	PLATE BLOCK F/NH	UNUSED F/NH	USED F
461	8¢ "Alaska Highway"	2.00	.35	.20
462	10¢ "The Jack Pine"	1.80	.35	.15
463	15¢ "Bylot Island"	3.30	.55	.15
464	20¢ "The Ferry, Quebec"	3.30	.70	.15
465	25¢ "The Solemn Land"	6.90	1.40	.15
465A	50¢ "Summer Stores"	22.00	4.40	.15
465B	$1 "Imp. Wildcat No. 3"	49.50	9.90	.80
	1967-70 Coil Stamps			
466-68B	3¢-6¢ complete, 5 varieties	......	4.50	3.35
	Perf. 9-1/2 Horizontally			
466	3¢ dull purple	......	1.55	.95
467	4¢ carmine rose	......	.90	1.55
468	5¢ blue	......	1.65	.70
	Perf. 10 Horizontally			
468A	6¢ orange (1969)	......	.35	.15
468B	6¢ black (1970)	......	.35	.15

NOTE : See #543-50 for similar issues

1967

469	5¢ Expo '67	1.10	.25	.15
470	5¢ Women's Franchise	1.10	.25	.15
471	5¢ Royal Visit	1.10	.25	.15
472	5¢ Pan-American Games	1.10	.25	.15
473	5¢ Canadian Press	1.10	.25	.15
474	5¢ George P. Vanier	1.10	.25	.15
475	5¢ View of Toronto	1.10	.25	.15
476	3¢ Christmas	.90	.20	.15
476a	miniature pane of 25	......	4.25	......
476a	same, sealed pack of 2	......	8.50	......
477	5¢ Christmas	.85	.20	.15

1968 COMMEMORATIVES

478-89	complete, 12 varieties	22.00	4.30	2.70
478	5¢ Gray Jays	4.15	.45	.15
479	5¢ Weather Map & Inst	1.10	.25	.15
480	5¢ Narwhal	1.10	.25	.15
481	5¢ Int'l Hydro. Decade	1.10	.25	.15
482	5¢ Voyage of "Nonsuch"	1.40	.25	.15
483	5¢ Lacrosse Players	1.10	.25	.15
484	5¢ G. Brown, Politician	1.10	.25	.15
485	5¢ H. Bourassa, Journalist	1.10	.25	.15
486	15¢ W.W.I Armistice	8.25	1.65	1.20

NOTE: Beginning with #478, some issues show a printer's inscription with no actual plate number.

Canada Postage #487-542

SCOTT NO.	DESCRIPTION	PLATE BLOCK F/NH	UNUSED F/NH	USED F
487	5¢ J. McCrae	1.10	.25	.15
488	5¢ Eskimo Family	.85	.20	.15
488a	same, booklet pane of 10		3.15	
489	6¢ Mother & Child	1.10	.25	.15

1969 COMMEMORATIVES

490-504	complete, 15 varieties	48.25	11.25	7.15
490	6¢ Game of Curling	1.10	.25	.15
491	6¢ V. Massey	1.10	.25	.15
492	50¢ A. deSuzor-Cote, Artist	17.60	3.85	2.20
493	6¢ I.L.O.	1.10	.25	.15
494	15¢ Vickers Vimy Over Atlantic	8.80	2.85	1.65
495	6¢ Sir W. Osler	1.10	.25	.15
496	6¢ White Throated Sparrows	1.65	.35	.15
497	10¢ Ipswich Sparrow	3.85	.75	.50
498	25¢ Hermit Thrush	8.25	1.65	1.55
499	6¢ Map of Prince Edward Island	1.10	.25	.15
500	6¢ Canada Games	1.10	.25	.15
501	6¢ Sir Isaac Brock	1.10	.25	.15
502	5¢ Children of Various Races	.85	.20	.15
502a	booklet pane of 10		2.75	
503	6¢ Children Various Races	.85	.20	.15
504	6¢ Stephen Leacock	1.20	.25	.15

1970 COMMEMORATIVES

505/31	(505-18, 531) 15 varieties	24.50	11.75	11.00
505	6¢ Manitoba Cent.	.85	.20	.15
506	6¢ N.W. Territory Centenary	.85	.20	.15
507	6¢ International Biological	.85	.20	.15
508-11	Expo '70 attached	9.90	8.80	8.80
508	25¢ Emblems		2.15	2.15
509	25¢ Dogwood		2.15	2.15
510	25¢ Lily		2.15	2.15
511	25¢ Trilium		2.15	2.15

512	6¢ H. Kelsey—Explorer	.85	.20	.15
513	10¢ 25th U.N. Anniversary	3.30	.70	.45
514	15¢ 25th U.N. Anniversary	4.95	1.00	1.10
515	6¢ L. Riel—Metis Leader	.85	.20	.15
516	6¢ Sir A. Mackenzie-Explorer	.85	.20	.15
517	6¢ Sir O. Mowat Confederation Father	.85	.20	.15
518	6¢ Isle of Spruce	.85	.20	.15

519-30	5¢-15¢ complete, 12 varieties	16.75	5.50	2.45
519-23	5¢ Christmas, attached	4.95(10)	2.25	2.00
519	5¢ Santa Claus		.40	.15
520	5¢ Sleigh		.40	.15
521	5¢ Nativity		.40	.15
522	5¢ Skiing		.40	.15
523	5¢ Snowman & Tree		.40	.15
524-28	6¢ Christmas, attached	6.00(10)	2.50	2.25
524	6¢ Christ Child		.45	.15
525	6¢ Tree & Children		.45	.15
526	6¢ Toy Store		.45	.15
527	6¢ Santa Claus		.45	.15
528	6¢ Church		.45	.15

NOTE: We cannot supply blocks or pairs of the 5¢ & 6¢ Christmas designs in varying combinations of designs.

529	10¢ Christ Child	2.20	.40	.20
530	15¢ Snowmobile & Trees	4.50	.85	.90
531	6¢ Sir Donald A. Smith	.85	.20	.15

1971 COMMEMORATIVES

532/58	(532-42, 552-58) complete, 18 varieties	29.75	6.10	7.00
532	6¢ E. Carr—Painter & Writer	.85	.20	.15
533	6¢ Discovery of Insulin	.85	.20	.15
534	6¢ Sir E. Rutherford—Physicist	.85	.20	.15
535-38	6¢-7¢ Maple Leaves	4.00	.90	.50
535	6¢ Maple Seeds	1.10	.25	.15
536	6¢ Summer Leaf	1.10	.25	.15
537	Autumn Leaf	1.10	.25	.15
538	7¢ Winter Leaf	1.10	.25	.15
539	6¢ L. Papineau—Polit. Reform	.85	.20	.15
540	6¢ Copper Mine Expedition	.85	.20	.15
541	15¢ Radio Canada Int'l	7.70	1.65	1.40
542	6¢ Census Centennial	.85	.20	.15

Canada Postage #543-610

SCOTT NO.	DESCRIPTION	PLATE BLOCK F/NH	UNUSED F/NH	USED F

1971

543	7¢ Trans. & Communication	3.30	.30	.15
543a	bklt. pane 7¢(3), 3¢(1), 1¢(1)	......	3.05	......
543b	bklt. pane 7¢(12), 3¢(4), 1¢(4)	......	7.70	......
544	8¢ Parliamentary Library	3.30	.30	.15
544a	bklt. pane 8¢(2), 6¢(1), 1¢(3)	......	1.95	......
544b	bklt. pane 8¢(11), 6¢(1), 1¢(6)	5.80		
544c	bklt. pane 8¢(5), 6¢(1), 1¢(4)	......	2.50	......

1971 Coil Stamps Perf.10 Horizontally

549	7¢ Trans. & Communication	......	.40	.15
550	8¢ Parliamentary Library	......	.35	.15
552	7¢ B.C. Centennial	.85	.20	.15
553	7¢ Paul Kane	2.50	.35	.15
554-57	6¢-15¢ Christmas	8.00	1.65	1.50
554	6¢ Snowflake, dark blue	.85	.20	.15
555	7¢ same, bright green	1.10	.25	.15
556	10¢ same, deep carmine & silver	2.20	.45	.40
557	15¢ same, light ultramarine, deep carmine & silver	4.00	.85	.85
558	7¢ P. Laporte	2.65	.25	.15

1972 COMMEMORATIVES

559/610	(559-61, 582-85, 606-10) 12 varieties	47.85(9)	9.75	7.55
559	8¢ Figure Skating	1.10	.25	.15
560	8¢ W.H.O. Heart Disease	1.40	.30	.15
561	8¢ Frontenac & Ft. St. Louis	1.10	.25	.15

VERY FINE QUALITY: From 1935 to date, add 20% to the Fine price. Minimum of 3¢ per stamp.

1972-76 INDIAN PEOPLES OF CANADA

562-81	complete, 20 varieties	14.00	5.90	2.85
562-63	Plains, attached	1.65	.70	.60
562	8¢ Buffalo Chase	......	.30	.15
563	8¢ Indian Artifacts	......	.30	.15
564-65	Plains, attached	1.65	.70	.60
564	8¢ Thunderbird Symbolism	......	.30	.15
565	8¢ Sun Dance Costume	......	.30	.15
566-67	Algonkians, attached (1973)	1.65	.70	.60
566	8¢ Algonkian Artifacts	......	.30	.15
567	8¢ Micmac Indians	......	.30	.15
568-69	Algonkians, attached (1973)	1.65	.70	.60
568	8¢ Thunderbird Symbolism	......	.30	.15
569	8¢ Costume	......	.30	.15
570-71	Pacific, attached (1974)	1.65	.70	.50
570	8¢ Nootka Sound House	......	.30	.15
571	8¢ Artifacts	......	.30	.15
572-73	Pacific, attached (1974)	1.65	.70	.50
572	8¢ Chief in Chilkat Blanket	......	.30	.15
573	8¢ Thunderbird—Kwakiutl	......	.30	.15
574-75	Subarctic, attached (1975)	1.20	.50	.45
574	8¢ Canoe & Artifacts	......	.25	.15
575	8¢ Dance—Kutcha-Kutchin	......	.25	.15
576-77	Subarctic, attached (1975)	1.20	.50	.45
576	8¢ Kutchin Costume	......	.25	.15
577	8¢ Ojibwa Thunderbird	......	.25	.15
578-79	Iroquois, attached (1976)	1.20	.50	.45
578	10¢ Masks	......	.25	.15
579	10¢ Camp	......	.25	.15
580-81	Iroquois, attached (1976)	1.20	.50	.45
580	10¢ Iroquois Thunderbird	......	.25	.15
581	10¢ Man & Woman	......	.25	.15

1972 EARTH SCIENCES

582-85	Sciences, attached	38.50(16)	7.50	7.50
582	15¢ Geology	......	1.80	1.50
583	15¢ Geography	......	1.80	1.50
584	15¢ Photogrammetry	......	1.80	1.50
585	15¢ Cartography	......	1.80	1.50

NOTE: Plate Block Price is for a miniature pane of 16 Stamps.

1973-76 DEFINITIVE ISSUE PERF. 12 x 12-1/2

586-93A	1¢-10¢, 9 varieties	6.85	1.75	1.30
586	1¢ Sir J. Macdonald	.70	.20	.15
586a	bklt. pane 1¢(3), 6¢(1), 8¢(2)	......	1.00	......
586b	bklt. pane 1¢(6), 6¢(1), 8¢(11)	......	3.00	......
586c	bklt. pane 1¢(2), 2¢(4), 8¢(4)	......	1.30	......
587	2¢ Sir W. Laurier	.70	.20	.15
588	3¢ Sir R.L. Borden	.70	.20	.15
589	4¢ W.L. Mackenzie King	.70	.20	.15
590	5¢ R.B. Bennett	.80	.20	.15
591	6¢ L.B. Pearson	.80	.20	.15
592	7¢ L. St. Laurent (1974)	.85	.20	.15
593	8¢ Queen Elizabeth	.85	.20	.15
593b	same (pf. 13x13-1/2) (1976)	4.95	.80	.45
593A	10¢ Queen Elizabeth (perf 13x13-1/2) (1976)	1.10	.25	.15
593c	10¢ same, perf 12x12-1/2 booklet single	......	.35	.20

1972-73 Photogravure & Engraved Perf. 12-1/2x12

594-99	10¢-$1, 6 varieties	23.60	5.00	1.25
594	10¢ Forests	1.10	.25	.15
595	15¢ Mountain Sheep	1.55	.35	.15
596	20¢ Prairie Mosaic	2.30	.50	.15
597	25¢ Polar Bears	2.55	.55	.15
598	50¢ Seashore	5.25	1.10	.15
599	$1 Vancouver Skyline (1973)	12.10	2.50	.55

NOTE: #594-97 exist with 2 types of phosphor tagging. Prices are for Ottawa tagged. Winnipeg tagged are listed on page 320.

1976-77 Perf. 13

594a	10¢ Forests	1.40	.30	.15
595a	15¢ Mountain Sheep	1.85	.40	.25
596a	20¢ Prairie Mosaic	2.65	.55	.15
597a	25¢ Polar Bears	2.50	.75	.15
598a	50¢ Seashore	8.00	1.65	.15
599a	$1 Vancouver Skyline (1977)	12.10	2.50	.45

1972 Lithographed & Engraved Perf. 11

| 600 | $1 Vancouver Skyline | 22.00 | 4.95 | 1.95 |
| 601 | $2 Quebec Buildings | 19.80 | 4.15 | 2.50 |

1974-76 Coil Stamps

| 604 | 8¢ Queen Elizabeth | ...... | .25 | .15 |
| 605 | 10¢ Queen Elizabeth (1976) | ...... | .30 | .15 |

1972

606-09	6¢-15¢ Christmas	7.00	1.45	1.25
606	6¢ Five candles	.85	.20	.15
607	8¢ same	1.10	.25	.15
608	10¢ Six candles	1.95	.40	.25
609	15¢ same	3.30	.70	.80
610	8¢ C. Krieghoff—Painter	1.10	.25	.15

562

564

582

586

593, 593b, 593A, 604-605

594, 594a, 594B

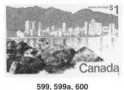
599, 599a, 600

606, 607

608, 609

610

611

Canada Postage #611-680

SCOTT NO.	DESCRIPTION	PLATE BLOCK F/NH	UNUSED F/NH	USED F
	1973 COMMEMORATIVES			
611-28	18 varieties, complete	27.40	6.15	4.95
611	8¢ Monseignor De Laval	1.00	.25	.15
612	8¢ G.A. French & Map	1.35	.30	.15
613	10¢ Spectrograph	1.65	.35	.35
614	15¢ "Musical Ride"	3.30	.70	.60
615	8¢ J. Mance—Nurse	1.00	.25	.15
616	8¢ J. Howe	1.00	.25	.15
617	15¢ "Mist Fantasy" Painting	2.75	.55	.50
618	8¢ P.E.I. Confederation	1.00	.25	.15
619	8¢ Scottish Settlers	1.00	.25	.15
620	8¢ Royal Visit	1.00	.25	.15
621	15¢ same	3.10	.70	.60
622	8¢ Nellie McClung	1.00	.25	.15
623	8¢ 21st Olympic Games	1.00	.25	.15
624	15¢ same	2.75	.55	.60
625-28	6¢ to 15¢ Christmas	5.75	1.20	1.10
625	6¢ Skate	.80	.20	.15
626	8¢ Bird Ornament	1.00	.25	.15
627	10¢ Santa Claus	1.40	.30	.30
628	15¢ Shepherd	2.75	.55	.60
	1974 COMMEMORATIVES			
629-55	complete, 27 varieties	22.40(16)	9.15	6.25
629-32	Summer Olympics, attached	1.65	1.40	1.35
629	8¢ Children Diving	……	.35	.20
630	8¢ Jogging	……	.35	.20
631	8¢ Bicycling	……	.35	.20
632	8¢ Hiking	……	.35	.20
633	8¢ Winnipeg Centenary	1.00	.25	.15
634-39	Postal Carriers, attached	3.60(6)	3.00	2.75
634	8¢ Postal Clerk & Client	……	.40	.35
635	8¢ Mail Pick-up	……	.40	.35
636	8¢ Mail Handler	……	.40	.35
637	8¢ Sorting Mail	……	.40	.35
638	8¢ Letter Carrier	……	.40	.35
639	8¢ Rural Delivery	……	.40	.35
640	8¢ Agriculture Symbol	1.00	.25	.15
641	8¢ Antique to Modern Phones	1.00	.25	.15
642	8¢ World Cycling Championship	1.00	.25	.15
643	8¢ Mennonite Settlers	1.00	.25	.15
644-47	Winter Olympics, attached	1.65	1.40	1.20
644	8¢ Snowshoeing	……	.35	.20
645	8¢ Skiing	……	.35	.20
646	8¢ Skating	……	.35	.20
647	8¢ Curling	……	.35	.20
648	8¢ U.P.U. Cent.	1.00	.25	.15
649	15¢ same	2.75	.55	.50
650-53	6¢ to 15¢ Christmas	5.65	1.25	1.10
650	6¢ Nativity	.80	.20	.15
651	8¢ Skaters in Hull	.80	.20	.15
652	10¢ The Ice Cone	1.60	.35	.35
653	15¢ Laurentian Village	2.75	.55	.50
654	8¢ G. Marconi—Radio Inventor	1.00	.25	.15
655	8¢ W.H. Merritt & Welland Canal	1.00	.25	.15
	1975 COMMEMORATIVES			
656-80	complete, 25 varieties	67.50(18)	16.40	12.00
656	$1 "The Sprinter"	11.00	2.50	1.95
657	$2 "The Plunger"	25.35	5.75	4.40
658-59	Writers, attached	1.05	.45	.40
658	8¢ L.M. Montgomery—Author	……	.20	.15
659	8¢ L. Hemon—Author	……	.20	.15
660	8¢ M. Bourgeoys—Educator	1.00	.25	.15
661	8¢ A. Desjardins—Credit Union	1.00	.25	.15
662-63	Religious, attached	1.05	.45	.45
662	8¢ S Chown & Church	……	.20	.20
663	8¢ J. Cook & Church	……	.20	.20
664	20¢ Pole Vaulter	3.30	.75	.50
665	25¢ Marathon Runner	3.85	.85	.55
666	50¢ Hurdler	6.60	1.50	1.10
667	8¢ Calgary Centenary	1.10	.25	.15
668	8¢ Int'l. Women's Year	1.10	.25	.15
669	8¢ "Justice"	1.10	.25	.15
670-73	Ships, attached	2.75	2.20	1.85
670	8¢ W.D. Lawrence	……	.55	.35
671	8¢ Beaver	……	.55	.35
672	8¢ Neptune	……	.55	.35
673	8¢ Quadra	……	.55	.35
674-79	6¢ to 15¢ Christmas	4.50(4)	1.35	1.25
674-75	Christmas, attached	.85	.40	.35
674	6¢ Santa Claus	……	.20	.15
675	6¢ Skater	……	.20	.15
676-77	Christmas, attached	1.05	.40	.35
676	8¢ Child	……	.20	.15
677	8¢ Family & Tree	……	.20	.15
678	10¢ Gift	1.10	.25	.15
679	15¢ Trees	1.65	.35	.35
680	8¢ Horn & Crest	1.10	.25	.15

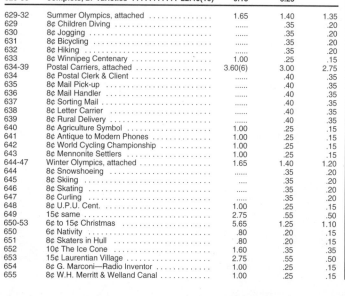

Canada Postage #681-737

SCOTT NO.	DESCRIPTION	PLATE BLOCK F/NH	UNUSED F/NH	USED F

674 676 679 680

681 687

689 690 684 691

1976 COMMEMORATIVES

Scott	Description	Plate Block	Unused	Used
681-703	complete, 23 varieties	75.00(18)	18.15	14.25
681	8¢ Olympic Flame	1.05	.25	.15
682	20¢ Opening Ceremony	2.60	.55	.55
683	25¢ Receiving Medals	3.30	.75	.75
684	20¢ Communication Arts	4.40	1.00	.60
685	25¢ Handicraft Tools	4.95	1.10	.75
686	50¢ Performing Arts	8.25	1.85	1.30
687	$1 Notre Dame & Tower	11.00	2.50	1.95
688	$2 Olympic Stadium	25.85	5.80	4.40
689	20¢ Olympic Winter Games	3.30	.75	.70
690	20¢ "Habitat"	2.20	.50	.45
691	10¢ Benjamin Franklin	1.20	.30	.25
692-93	Military College, attached	1.05	.40	.35
692	8¢ Color Parade	......	.20	.15
693	8¢ Wing Parade	......	.20	.15
694	20¢ Olympiad—Phys. Disabled	3.14	.65	.60
695-96	Authors, attached	1.05	.40	.35
695	8¢ R.W. Service—Author	......	.20	.15
696	8¢ G. Guevremont—Author	......	.20	.15
697	8¢ Nativity Window	.85	.20	.15
698	10¢ same	1.05	.25	.15
699	20¢ same	2.15	.45	.45
700-03	Inland Vessels, attached	1.75	1.40	1.30
700	10¢ Northcote	......	.35	.30
701	10¢ Passport	......	.35	.30
702	10¢ Chicora	......	.35	.30
703	10¢ Athabasca	......	.35	.30

692 693 694 695

696 697 700 704

1977 COMMEMORATIVES

Scott	Description	Plate Block	Unused	Used
704/51	(704, 732-51) complete, 21 varieties	20.85(14)	6.10	4.65
704	25¢ Silver Jubilee	3.05	.65	.55

705, 781, 781a   713, 713a, 716, 716a, 789, 789a, 791, 792   714, 715, 729, 730, 790, 797, 800, 806

1977-79 Definitives
Perf. 12x12-1/2

Scott	Description	Plate Block	Unused	Used
705-27	1¢ to $2 complete, 22 varieties	66.50	14.85	5.75
705	1¢ Bottle Gentian	.65	.20	.15
707	2¢ Western Columbine	.65	.20	.15
708	3¢ Canada Lily	.65	.20	.15
709	4¢ Hepatica	.65	.20	.15
710	5¢ Shooting Star	.65	.20	.15
711	10¢ Lady's Slipper	.80	.20	.15
711a	same, perf.13 (1978)	1.10	.25	.15
712	12¢ Jewelweed, perf 13x13-1/2 (1978)	1.45	.30	.15
713	12¢ Queen Elizabeth II, perf.13x13-1/2	1.30	.30	.15
713a	same, perf.12x12-1/2	......	.35	.20
714	12¢ Parliament, perf.13	1.20	.25	.15
715	14¢ same, perf.13 (1978)	1.35	.30	.15
716	14¢ Queen Elizabeth II perf. 13x13-1/2	1.35	.30	.15
716a	14¢ same, perf 12x12-1/2	......	.30	.20
716b	same, booklet pane of 25	......	6.25	......

NOTE: 713a and 716a are from booklet panes. 713a will have one or more straight edges, 716a may or may not have straight edges.

717   723, 723A   726

Perforated 13-1/2

Scott	Description	Plate Block	Unused	Used
717	15¢ Trembling Aspen	1.80	.40	.15
718	20¢ Douglas Fir	1.55	.35	.15
719	25¢ Sugar Maple	2.00	.45	.15
720	30¢ Oak Leaf	2.50	.55	.25
721	35¢ White Pine (1979)	2.75	.60	.35
723	50¢ Main Street (1978)	4.25	.95	.30
723A	50¢ same, 1978 Lic. Plate	4.70	1.00	.25
724	75¢ Row Houses (1978)	6.35	1.40	.50
725	80¢ Maritime (1978)	7.15	1.50	.55
726	$1 Fundy Park (1979)	8.80	1.95	.45
727	$2 Kluane Park (1979)	17.60	3.85	1.30

1977-78 Coil Stamps Perf. 10 Vert.

Scott	Description	Plate Block	Unused	Used
729	12¢ Parliament	......	.25	.15
730	14¢ same (1978)	......	.30	.15

732   733   735

736   737

1977 COMMEMORATIVES

Scott	Description	Plate Block	Unused	Used
732	12¢ Cougar	1.20	.25	.15
733-34	Thomson, attached	1.20	.50	.45
733	12¢ Algonquin Park	......	.25	.15
734	12¢ Autumn Birches	......	.25	.15
735	12¢ Crown & Lion	1.20	.25	.15
736	12¢ Badge & Ribbon	1.20	.25	.15
737	12¢ Peace Bridge	1.20	.25	.15

265

Canada Postage #738-820

SCOTT NO.	DESCRIPTION	PLATE BLOCK F/NH	UNUSED F/NH	USED F
738-39	Pioneers, attached	1.20	.50	.45
738	12¢ Bernier & CGS Arctic	......	.25	.15
739	12¢ Fleming & RR Bridge	......	.25	.15
740	25¢ Peace Tower	3.30	.75	.75
741	10¢ Braves & Star	1.05	.25	.15
742	12¢ Angelic Choir	1.20	.25	.10
743	25¢ Christ Child	2.45	.50	.50
744-47	Sailing Ships	1.30	1.00	.95
744	12¢ Pinky	......	.25	.20
745	12¢ Tern	......	.25	.20
746	12¢ Five Masted	......	.25	.20
747	12¢ Mackinaw	......	.25	.20
748-49	Inuit, attached	1.20	.50	.45
748	12¢ Hunting Seal	......	.25	.20
749	12¢ Fishing	......	.25	.20
750-51	Inuit, attached	1.20	.50	.45
750	12¢ Disguised Archer	......	.25	.20
751	12¢ Hunters of Old	......	.25	.20

1978 COMMEMORATIVES

SCOTT NO.	DESCRIPTION	PLATE BLOCK F/NH	UNUSED F/NH	USED F
752/79	(No #756a)28 varieties	33.00(19)	9.15	6.30
752	12¢ Peregrine Falcon	1.20	.25	.15
753	12¢ CAPEX Victoria	1.10	.25	.15
754	14¢ CAPEX Cartier	1.35	.25	.15
755	30¢ CAPEX Victoria	2.65	.55	.55
756	$1.25 CAPEX Albert	8.25	2.00	1.40
756a	$1.69 CAPEX sheet of 3	......	3.00	2.15
757	14¢ Games Symbol	1.15	.25	.15
758	30¢ Badminton Players	2.50	.55	.35
759-60	Comm. Games, attached	1.20	.50	.45
759	14¢ Stadium	......	.25	.15
760	14¢ Runners	......	.25	.15
761-62	Comm. Games, attached	2.45	1.05	.95
761	30¢ Edmonton	......	.45	.35
762	30¢ Bowls	......	.45	.35
763-64	Captain Cook, attached	1.15	.50	.45
763	14¢ Captain Cook	......	.25	.15
764	14¢ Nootka Sound	......	.25	.15
765-66	Resources, attached	1.20	.50	.45
765	14¢ Miners	......	.25	.15
766	14¢ Tar Sands	......	.25	.15
767	14¢ CNE 100th Anniversary	1.15	.25	.15
768	14¢ Mere d'Youville	1.15	.25	.15
769-70	Inuit, attached	1.20	.50	.45
769	14¢ Woman Walking	......	.25	.15
770	14¢ Migration	......	.25	.15
771-72	Inuit, attached	1.20	.50	.45
771	14¢ Plane over Village	......	.25	.15
772	14¢ Dog Team & Sled	......	.25	.15
773	12¢ Mary & Child w/pea	1.05	.25	.15
774	14¢ Mary & Child w/apple	1.15	.25	.15
775	30¢ Mary & Child w/goldfinch	2.50	.55	.35
776-79	Ice Vessels, attached	1.20	1.00	.95
776	14¢ Robinson	......	.25	.15
777	14¢ St. Roch	......	.25	.15
778	14¢ Northern Light	......	.25	.15
779	14¢ Labrador	......	.25	.15

1979 COMMEMORATIVES

SCOTT NO.	DESCRIPTION	PLATE BLOCK F/NH	UNUSED F/NH	USED F
780/846	(780, 813-20, 833-46) complete, 23 varieties	27.10(16)	8.20	4.55
780	14¢ Quebec Winter Carnival	1.15	.25	.15

1977-83 Definitives Perf 13x13 1/2

SCOTT NO.	DESCRIPTION	PLATE BLOCK F/NH	UNUSED F/NH	USED F
781-92	1¢-32¢ complete, 11 varieties	13.00	3.15	1.60
781	1¢ Gentian (1979)	.65	.20	.15
781a	1¢ same, perf 12x12-1/2	......	.20	.15
781b	booklet pane, 1¢ (2—781a), 12¢ (4—713a)	......	.85	......
782	2¢ Western Columbine (1979)	.65	.20	.15
782a	booklet pane, 2¢ (4—782b), 12¢ (3—716a)	......	.80	
782b	2¢ same, perf 12x121/2 (1978)	......	.20	.15
783	3¢ Canada Lily (1979)	.65	.20	.15
784	4¢ Hepatica (1979)	.65	.20	.15
785	5¢ Shooting Star (1979)	.65	.20	.15
786	10¢ Lady's-Slipper (1979)	.90	.20	.15
787	15¢ Violet (1979)	1.35	.30	.15
789	17¢ Queen Elizabeth II (1979)	1.50	.35	.15
789a	17¢ same, 12x12-1/2 (1979)	......	.35	.15
789b	booklet pane of 25	......	7.45	......
790	17¢ Parliament Bldg. (1979)	1.50	.30	.15
791	30¢ Queen Elizabeth II (1982)	2.50	.55	.15
792	32¢ Queen Elizabeth II (1983)	2.75	.60	.15

NOTE: 781a, 782b, 797 & 800 are from booklet panes and will have one or more straight edges. 789a may or may not have straight edges.

1979 Perf 12x12-1/2

SCOTT NO.	DESCRIPTION	PLATE BLOCK F/NH	UNUSED F/NH	USED F
797	1¢ Parliament Building	......	.35	.30
797a	booklet pane 1¢ (1—797), 5¢ (3—800), 17¢ (2—789a)	......	.90	......
800	5¢ Parliament Building	......	.20	.15

1979 Coil Stamps Perf 10 Vertical

SCOTT NO.	DESCRIPTION	PLATE BLOCK F/NH	UNUSED F/NH	USED F
806	17¢ Parliament Building, slate green	......	.50	.15

1979

SCOTT NO.	DESCRIPTION	PLATE BLOCK F/NH	UNUSED F/NH	USED F
813	17¢ Turtle	1.50	.30	.15
814	35¢ Whale	3.05	.65	.35
815-16	Postal Code, attached	1.65	.65	.45
815	17¢ Woman's Finger	......	.30	.15
816	17¢ Man's Finger	......	.30	.15
817-18	Writers, attached	1.65	.65	.45
817	17¢ "Fruits of the Earth"	......	.30	.15
818	17¢ "The Golden Vessel"	......	.30	.15
819-20	Colonels, attached	1.65	.65	.45
819	17¢ Charles de Salaberry	......	.30	.15
820	17¢ John By	......	.30	.15

Canada Postage #821-889

SCOTT NO.	DESCRIPTION	PLATE BLOCK F/NH	UNUSED F/NH	USED F
	PROVINCIAL FLAGS			
821	Ontario			
822	Quebec			
823	Nova Scotia			
824	New Brunswick			
825	Manitoba			
826	British Columbia			
827	Prince Edward Island			
828	Saskatchewan			
829	Alberta			
830	Newfoundland			
831	Northern Teritories			
832	Yukon Territory			
832a	17¢ Sheet of 12 varieties, attached	......	4.00	......
821-32	set of singles	......	......	2.00
Any	17¢ single		.30	.20
833	17¢ Canoe—kayak	1.50	.30	.15
834	17¢ Field Hockey	1.50	.30	.15
835-36	Inuit, attached	1.60	.65	.60
835	17¢ Summer Tent	......	.30	.20
836	17¢ Igloo	......	.30	.20
837-38	Inuit, attached	1.60	.65	.60
837	17¢ The Dance	......	.30	.20
838	17¢ Soapstone Figures	......	.30	.20
839	15¢ Wooden Train	1.00	.25	.15
840	17¢ Horse Pull Toy	1.30	.30	.15
841	35¢ Knitted Doll	2.75	.60	.30
842	17¢ I.Y.C.	1.50	.30	.15
843-44	Flying Boats, attached	1.60	.65	.50
843	17¢ Curtiss, HS2L	......	.30	.20
844	17¢ Canadair CL215	......	.30	.20
845-46	Flying Boats, attached	3.55	1.50	1.40
845	35¢ Vichers Vedette	......	.70	.50
846	35¢ Consolidated Canso	......	.70	.50

833

834

839

835-36

842

843

847

848

1980 COMMEMORATIVES

847-77	complete, 31 varieties	42.25(23)	12.35	6.30
847	17¢ Arctic Islands Map	1.50	.30	.15
848	35¢ Olympic Skiing	2.90	.60	.55
849-50	Artists, attached	1.60	.65	.50
849	17¢ School Trustees	......	.30	.15
850	17¢ Inspiration	......	.30	.15
851-52	Artists, attached	3.05	1.30	1.10
851	35¢ Parliament Bldgs	......	.60	.35
852	35¢ Sunrise on the Saguenay	......	.60	.35
853	17¢ Atlantic Whitefish	1.55	.35	.15
854	17¢ Greater Prairie Chicken	1.55	.35	.15

859 | 870 | 860 | 862

863 | 865 | 873

866-67 | 878 | 877

855	17¢ Gardening	1.50	.30	.15
856	17¢ Rehabilitation	1.50	.30	.15
857-58	"O Canada", attached	1.60	.65	.50
857	17¢ Bars of Music	......	.30	.15
858	17¢ Three Musicians	......	.30	.15
859	17¢ John Diefenbaker	1.50	.30	.15
860-61	Musicians, attached	1.60	.65	.50
860	17¢ Emma Albani	......	.30	.15
861	17¢ Healy Willan	......	.30	.15
862	17¢ Ned Hanlan	1.50	.30	.15
863	17¢ Saskatchewan	1.50	.30	.15
864	17¢ Alberta	1.50	.30	.15
865	35¢ Uranium Resources	2.95	.60	.35
866-67	Inuit, attached	1.75	.70	.50
866	17¢ Sedna	......	.35	.15
867	17¢ Sun	......	.35	.15
868-69	Inuit, attached	3.05	1.30	1.10
868	35¢ Bird Spirit	......	.60	.35
869	35¢ Shaman	......	.60	.35
870	15¢ Christmas	1.35	.30	.15
871	17¢ Christmas	1.50	.30	.15
872	35¢ Christmas	2.95	.60	.35
873-74	Aircraft	1.65	.75	.65
873	17¢ Avro Canada CF-100	......	.35	.15
874	17¢ Avro Lancaster	......	.35	.15
875-76	Aircraft, attached	3.25	1.40	1.20
875	35¢ Curtiss JN-4	......	.65	.35
876	35¢ Hawker Hurricane	......	.65	.35
877	17¢ Dr. Lachapelle	1.50	.30	.15

1981 COMMEMORATIVES

878-906	complete, 29 varieties	32.45(19)	10.35	5.45
878	17¢ Antique Instrument	1.50	.30	.15
879-82	Feminists, attached	1.65	1.40	1.10
879	17¢ Emily Stowe	......	.35	.20
880	17¢ Louise McKinney	......	.35	.20
881	17¢ Idola Saint-Jean	......	.35	.20
882	17¢ Henrietta Edwards	......	.35	.20
883	17¢ Marmot	1.50	.30	.15
884	35¢ Bison	3.30	.75	.40
885-86	Women, attached	1.60	.65	.50
885	17¢ Kateri Tekakwitha	......	.30	.15
886	17¢ Marie de L'Incarnation	......	.30	.15
887	17¢ "At Baie Saint-Paul"	1.50	.30	.15
888	17¢ Self-Portrait	1.50	.30	.15
889	35¢ Untitled No. 6	2.95	.60	.40

879 | 883

885 | 887

Canada Postage #890-969

SCOTT NO.	DESCRIPTION	PLATE BLOCK F/NH	UNUSED F/NH	USED F
890-93	Canada Day, attached	1.65(8)	1.40	1.30
890	17¢ Canada in 1867	......	.35	.20
891	17¢ Canada in 1873	......	.35	.20
892	17¢ Canada in 1905	......	.35	.20
893	17¢ Canada in 1949	......	.35	.20
894-95	Botanists, attached	1.60	.65	.35
894	17¢ Frere Marie Victorin	......	.30	.15
895	17¢ John Macoun	......	.30	.15
896	17¢ Montreal Rose	1.65	.30	.15
897	17¢ Niagara-on-the-Lake	1.65	.30	.15
898	17¢ Acadians	1.65	.30	.15
899	17¢ Aaron Mosher	1.65	.30	.15
900	15¢ Christmas Tree in 1781	1.30	.30	.15
901	15¢ Christmas Tree in 1881	1.30	.30	.15
902	15¢ Christmas Tree in 1981	1.30	.30	.15
903-04	Aircraft, attached	1.65	.75	.50
903	17¢ Canadair CL-41 Tutor	......	.35	.15
904	17¢ de Havilland Tiger Moth	......	.35	.15
905-06	Aircraft, attached	3.25	1.40	1.20
905	35¢ Avro Canada C-102	......	.65	.40
906	35¢ de Havilland Canada Dash-7	......	.65	.40
907	(30¢) "A" Maple Leaf	2.60	1.55	.15
908	(30¢) "A" Maple Leaf, Coil	......	1.90	.15

1982 COMMEMORATIVES

Scott	Description	Plate	Unused	Used
909/75	(909-16, 954, 967-75) 18 varieties, complete	51.25(16)	11.95	4.35
909	30¢ 1851 Beaver	2.65	.55	.15
910	30¢ 1908 Champlain	2.65	.55	.15
911	35¢ 1935 Mountie	3.15	.65	.35
912	35¢ 1928 Mt. Hurd	3.15	.65	.35
913	60¢ 1929 Bluenose	6.35	1.30	.55
913a	$1.90 Phil. Exhib. sheet of 5	......	3.60	......
914	30¢ Jules Leger	2.65	.55	.15
915	30¢ Terry Fox	2.65	.55	.15
916	30¢ Constitution	2.65	.55	.15

1982-87 DEFINITIVES

Scott	Description	Plate	Unused	Used
917-37	1¢-$5 complete, 23 varieties	135.00	27.50	9.00
917a-21a	1¢-10¢, 5 varieties	4.10	1.00	.70
917	1¢ Decoy	.80	.20	.15
917a	1¢ perf.13x13-1/2 (1985)	.80	.20	.15
918	2¢ Fishing Spear	.80	.20	.15
918a	2¢ perf.13x13-1/2 (1985)	.80	.20	.15
919	3¢ Stable Lantern	.80	.20	.15
919a	3¢ perf.13x13-1/2 (1985)	.80	.20	.15
920	5¢ Bucket	.80	.20	.15
920a	5¢ perf.13x13-1/2 (1984)	.80	.20	.15
921	10¢ Weathercock	1.10	.25	.15
921a	10¢ perf.13x13-1/2 (1985)	1.10	.25	.15
922	20¢ Ice Skates	2.25	.45	.15
923	30¢ Maple Leaf, blue & red, perf.13x13-1/2	2.55	.55	.15
923a	30¢ booklet pane (20) perf 12x12-1/2	......	10.50	......
923b	as above, single	......	.20	.20
924	32¢ Maple Leaf, red & brown, perf.13x13-1/2 (1983)	2.55	.55	.15
924a	32¢ booklet pane (25) perf. 12x12-1/2	......	14.00	......
924b	as above, single	......	.60	.20
925	34¢ Parliament (multicolored, perf.13x13-1/2 (1985)	2.75	.60	.15
925a	34¢ booklet pane (25) perf.13x13-1/2	......	14.00	......
925b	34¢ single, perf 13-1/2x14	......	.75	......
926	34¢ Elizabeth II (1985), perf.13x13-1/2	2.75	.60	.15
926A	36¢ Elizabeth II (1987) perf. 13x13-1/2	20.00	4.00	.55
926B	36¢ Parliament Library (1987)	3.05	.65	.25
926Bc	as above, booklet pane (10)	......	6.00	......
926Bd	as above, booklet pane (25)	......	15.50	......
926Be	Booklet single (perf. 13-1/2x14)	......	.75	......
927	37¢ Plow (1983)	3.15	.60	.25
928	39¢ Settle bed (1985)	3.30	.75	.25
929	48¢ Cradle (1983)	4.15	.80	.30
930	50¢ Sleigh (1985)	4.40	.85	.30
931	60¢ Ontario Street	4.95	.95	.35
932	64¢ Stove (1983)	5.80	1.00	.40
933	68¢ Spinning Wheel (1985)	1.80	1.10	.40
934	$1 Glacier Park (1984)	8.80	1.75	.25
935	$1.50 Waterton Lakes	12.25	2.50	.80
936	$2 Banff Park (1985)	17.20	3.50	1.10
937	$5 Point Pelee (1983)	41.25	8.50	2.50

1982-87 BOOKLET SINGLES

Scott	Description	Plate	Unused	Used
938-948	1¢-36¢ complete, 11 varieties	......	4.00	3.00
938	1¢ East Block (1987)	......	.20	.15
939	2¢ West Block (1985)	......	.20	.15
940	5¢ Maple Leaf (1982)	......	.20	.15
941	5¢ East Block (1985)	......	.20	.20
942	6¢ West Block (1987)	......	.20	.15
943	8¢ Maple Leaf (1983)	......	.20	.35
944	10¢ Maple Leaf (1982)	......	.25	.35
945	30¢ Maple Leaf, red perf. 12x12-1/2 (1982)	......	.75	.45
945a	booklet pane 2# 940, 1 #944, 1 #945	......	1.20	......
946	32¢ Maple Leaf, brown on white, perf.12x12-1/2 (1983)	......	.65	.35
946b	booklet pane 2 #941, 1 #943, 1 #946	......	1.10	......
947	34¢ Library, slate blue, perf.12x12-1/2 (1985)	......	.60	.45
947a	booklet pane, 3 #939, 2 #941, 1 #947	......	1.40	......
948	36¢ Parliament Library (1987)	......	.75	.45
948a	booklet pane, 2 #938, 2 #942, #948	......	1.35	......

1982-1987 COILS

Scott	Description	Plate	Unused	Used
950-53	30¢-36¢ complete, 4 varieties	......	2.65	.55
950	30¢ Maple Leaf (1982)	......	.95	.15
951	32¢ Maple Leaf (1983)	......	.60	.15
952	34¢ Parliament (1985)	......	.60	.15
953	36¢ Parliament (1987)	......	.65	.15

Paintings

956 Quebec
957 Newfoundland
958 Northwest Territories
959 Prince Edward Island
960 Nova Scotia
961 Saskatchewan
962 Ontario
963 New Brunswick
964 Alberta
965 British Columbia
966 Manitoba

1982 COMMEMORATIVES

Scott	Description	Plate	Unused	Used
954	30¢ Salvation Army	2.65	.55	.15
955-66	set of singles	......	8.00	6.50
......	same, any 30¢ single	......	.95	.50
966a	sheet of 12 varieties, attached	......	8.50	......
967	30¢ Regina	2.65	.55	.15
968	30¢ Henley Regatta	2.21	.55	.15
969-70	30¢ Aircraft, attached	2.65	1.00	.90
969	30¢ Fairchild FC-2W1	......	.45	.15

Canada Postage #970-1031

SCOTT NO.	DESCRIPTION	PLATE BLOCK F/NH	UNUSED F/NH	USED F
970	30¢ De Havilland Canada Beaver	....	.45	.15
971-72	Aircraft, attached	6.20	2.20	2.10
971	60¢ Noorduyn Norseman		1.00	.50
972	60¢ Fokker Super Universal	....	1.00	.50
973	30¢ Joseph, Mary & Infant	2.65	.55	.15
974	35¢ Shepherds	3.05	.65	.25
975	60¢ Wise Men	5.25	1.10	.45

973

976

978

999

1003

1004

1007

977

1009

1010

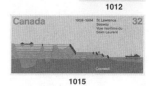
1011

1012

1983 COMMEMORATIVES

976/1008	(976-82, 993-1008) complete, 23 varieties	80.25(20)	22.25	9.30
976	32¢ World Comm. Year	2.85	.60	.25
977	$2 Commonwealth Day	35.00	10.00	4.00
978-79	Poet/Author, attached	2.85	1.20	1.10
978	32¢ Laure Conan	....	.55	.25
979	32¢ E.J. Pratt	....	.55	.25
980	32¢ St.John Ambulance	3.10	.60	.25
981	32¢ University Games	3.10	.60	.25
982	64¢ University Games	3.10	1.20	.45

Forts

984	Ft. William		989	Ft. Chambly
985	Ft. Rodd Hill		990	Ft. No. 1 Pt. Levis
986	Ft. Wellington		991	Ft. at Coteau-du-Lac
987	Fort Prince of Wales		992	Fort Beausejour
988	Halifax Citadel			

992a	32¢ Forts, pane of 10	....	7.00	6.50
983-92	set of singles	....	6.50	6.00
......	Any 32¢ single Fort	....	.75	.30
993	32¢ Boy Scouts	2.75	.60	.25
994	32¢ Council of Churches	2.75	.60	.25
995	32¢ Humphrey Gilbert	2.75	.60	.25
996	32¢ Nickel	2.75	.60	.25
997	32¢ Josiah Henson	2.75	.60	.25
998	32¢ Fr. Antoine Labelle	2.75	.60	.25

999-1000	Steam Trains, attached	2.75	1.10	1.00
999	32¢ Toronto 4-4-0	....	.55	.25
1000	32¢ Dorchester 0-4-0	....	.55	.25
1001	37¢ Samson 0-6-0	3.10	.65	.30
1002	64¢ Adam Brown 4-4-0	5.50	1.10	.52
1003	32¢ Law School	2.75	.60	.25
1004	32¢ City Church	2.75	.60	.25
1005	37¢ Family	3.05	.65	.30
1006	64¢ County Chapel	5.50	1.10	.52
1007-08	Army Regiment, attached	2.75	1.10	1.00
1007	32¢ Canada & Br.Reg.	....	.55	.25
1008	32¢ Winn. & Dragoons	....	.55	.25

1984 COMMEMORATIVES

1009/44	(1009-15, 1028-39, 1040-44) complete, 24 varieties	60.15(20)	14.25	6.25
1009	32¢ Yellowknife	2.75	.60	.25
1010	32¢ Year of the Arts	2.75	.60	.25
1011	32¢ Cartier	2.75	.60	.25
1012	32¢ Tall Ships	2.75	.60	.25
1013	32¢ Canadian Red Cross	2.75	.60	.25
1014	32¢ New Brunswick	2.75	.60	.25
1015	32¢ St. Lawrence Seaway	2.75	.60	.25

PROVINCIAL LANDSCAPES BY JEAN PAUL LEMIEUX

1017 British Columbia
1018 Yukon Territory
1019 Quebec
1020 Manitoba
1021 Alberta
1022 Prince Edward Island
1023 Saskatchewan
1024 Nova Scotia
1025 Northwest Territories
1026 Newfoundland
1027 Ontario

1027a	sheet of 12 varieties attached	....	8.50	8.50
1016-27	set of singles	....	8.25	4.75
.....	Any 32¢ single Provinces	....	.75	.30
1028	32¢ Loyalists	2.75	.60	.25
1029	32¢ Catholicism	2.75	.60	.25
1030	32¢ Papal Visit	2.75	.60	.25
1031	64¢ Papal Visit	5.25	1.10	.52

980

981

983 Ft. Henry

993

994

995

1016 New Brunswick

1028

998

1030

1032

Canada Postage #1032-1107b

SCOTT NO.	DESCRIPTION	PLATE BLOCK F/NH	UNUSED F/NH	USED F
1032-35	Lighthouses, attached	2.75	2.25	1.75
1032	32¢ Louisbourg	......	.60	.25
1033	32¢ Fisgard	......	.60	.25
1034	32¢ Ile Verte	......	.60	.25
1035	32¢ Gilbraltar Point	......	.60	.25
1036-37	Locomotives, attached	2.75	1.20	1.00
1036	32¢ Scotia 0-6-0	......	.60	.15
1037	32¢ Countess of Dufferin 4-4-0	......	.60	.15
1038	37¢ Grand Trunk 2-6-0	3.15	.65	.30
1039	64¢ Canadian Pacific 4-6-0	5.25	1.10	.52
1039a	Locomotive Souvenir Sheet	......	3.25	2.75
1040	32¢ Christmas	2.75	.60	.25
1041	37¢ Christmas	3.15	.60	.30
1042	64¢ Christmas	5.25	1.10	.52
1043	32¢ Royal Air Force	2.75	1.00	.25
1044	32¢ Newspaper	2.75	1.00	.25

1985 COMMEMORATIVES

1045/76	(1045-49, 1060-66, 1067-76) complete, 21 varieties	49.40(16)	13.75	6.00
1045	32¢ Youth Year	2.75	.60	.25
1046	32¢ Canadian Astronaut	2.75	.60	.25
1047-48	Women, attached	2.75	1.20	1.00
1047	32¢ T. Casgrain	......	.60	.25
1048	32¢ E. Murphy	......	.60	.25
1049	32¢ G. Dumont	2.75	.60	.25
1059a	34¢ Forts pane of 10	......	8.00	8.00
1050-59	set of singles	......	8.50	7.50
......	any Fort single	......	.70	.30
1060	34¢ Louis Hebert	2.75	.60	.27
1061	34¢ Inter-Parliamentary	2.75	.60	.27
1062	34¢ Girl Guides	2.75	.60	.27
1063-66	Lighthouses, attached	2.75	2.50	2.00
1063	34¢ Sisters Islets	......	.60	.27
1064	34¢ Pelee Passage	......	.60	.27
1065	34¢ Haut-fond Prince	......	.60	.27
1066	34¢ Rose Blanche	......	.60	.27
1066b	Lighthouse Souvenir Sheet	......	2.95	2.50
1067	34¢ Christmas	2.75	.60	.27
1068	39¢ Christmas	3.60	.75	.40
1069	68¢ Christmas	6.05	1.35	.60
1070	32¢ Christmas, booklet single	......	.80	......
1070a	same, booklet pane of 10	......	8.00	......
1071-72	Locomotives, attached	2.75	1.25	.75
1071	34¢ GT Class K2	......	.60	.27
1072	34¢ CP Class P2a	......	.60	.27
1073	39¢ CMoR Class 010a	3.30	.75	.40
1074	68¢ CGR Class H4D	6.05	1.35	.75
1075	34¢ Royal Navy	2.75	.60	.27
1076	34¢ Montreal Museum	2.75	.60	.27

FORTS

1050	Lower Ft. Garry	1051	Fort Anne	1052	Fort York
1053	Castle Hill	1054	Fort Whoop Up	1055	Fort Erie
1056	Fort Walsh	1057	Fort Lennox	1058	York Redoubt
1059	Fort Frederick				

1986 COMMEMORATIVES

1077/1121	(1077-79, 1090-1107,1108-16, 1117-21) complete, 35 varieties	70.50	22.10	11.60
1077	34¢ Computer Map	2.75	.60	.27
1078	34¢ Expo '86	2.75	.60	.27
1079	39¢ Expo '86	3.30	.75	.32

1987 HERITAGE ARTIFACTS

1080	25¢ Butter Stamp	2.00	.60	.20
1081	42¢ Linen Chest	3.75	1.00	.35
1082	55¢ Iron Kettle	5.25	1.20	.45
1083	72¢ Hand-drawn Cart	7.75	1.50	.60

1986-87 Definitive

1084	$5 La Mauricie	39.50	8.50	3.50

1986 COMMEMORATIVES

1090	34¢ Philippe Aubert de Gaspe	2.75	.60	.27
1091	34¢ Molly Brant	2.75	.60	.27
1092	34¢ Expo '86	2.75	.60	.27
1093	68¢ Expo '86	6.00	1.30	.55
1094	34¢ Canadian Forces Postal Service	2.75	.60	.27
1095-98	Birds, attached	4.75	4.00	3.00
1095	34¢ Great Blue Heron	......	1.10	.45
1096	34¢ Snow Goose	......	1.10	.45
1097	34¢ Great Horned Owl	......	1.10	.45
1098	34¢ Spruce Grouse	......	1.10	.45
1099-1102	Science & Technology, attached	3.00	2.75	2.25
1099	34¢ Rotary Snowplow	......	.75	.30
1100	34¢ Canadarm	......	.75	.30
1101	34¢ Anti-gravity Flight Suit	......	.75	.30
1102	34¢ Variable-pitch Propeller	......	.75	.30
1103	34¢ CBC	2.75	.60	.27
1104-07	Exploration, attached	3.00	2.75	2.25
1104	34¢ Continent	......	.75	.30
1105	34¢ Vikings	......	.75	.30
1106	34¢ John Cabot	......	.75	.30
1107	34¢ Hudson Bay	......	.75	.30
1107b	CAPEX souvenir sheet	......	3.00	2.75

Canada Postage #1108-1180c

SCOTT NO.	DESCRIPTION	PLATE BLOCK F/NH	UNUSED F/NH	USED F
1108-09	Frontier Peacemakers, attached	2.75	1.25	1.00
1108	34¢ Crowfoot	......	.60	.27
1109	34¢ J.F. Macleod	......	.60	.27
1110	34¢ Peace Year	2.75	.60	.27
1111-12	Calgary, attached	2.75	1.25	1.00
1111	34¢ Ice Hockey	......	.60	.27
1112	34¢ Biathlon	......	.60	.27
1113	34¢ Christmas Angels	2.75	.60	.27
1114	39¢ Christmas Angels	3.30	.75	.32
1115	68¢ Christmas Angels	6.00	1.30	.55
1116	29¢ Christmas Angels, booklet singles	......	.60	.25
1116a	same, booklet pane of 10	......	6.10	......
1117	34¢ John Molson	2.75	.60	.27
1118-19	Locomotive, attached	3.75	1.25	1.00
1118	34¢ CN V1a	......	.60	.27
1119	34¢ CP T1a	......	.60	.27
1120	39¢ CN U2a	4.25	.95	.75
1121	68¢ CP H1c	6.75	1.50	1.25

1987 COMMEMORATIVES

1122/54	(1122-25, 1126-54) complete, 33 varieties	68.75	23.25	12.35
1122	34¢ Toronto P.O.	2.75	.60	.27

1987 CAPEX EXHIBITION

1123	36¢ Nelson-Miramichi: Post Office	3.00	.60	.30
1124	42¢ Saint Ours P.O.	4.00	.80	.40
1125	72¢ Battleford P.O.	6.50	1.50	1.25
1125A	CAPEX Souvenir Sheet	......	3.00	2.50
1126-29	Exploration, attached	4.00	3.50	3.25
1126	34¢ Brule	......	.95	.45
1127	34¢ Radisson	......	.95	.45
1128	34¢ Jolliet	......	.95	.45
1129	34¢ Wilderness	......	.95	.45
1130	36¢ Calgary Olympics	2.85	.60	.30
1131	42¢ Calgary Olympics	3.30	.80	.40
1132	36¢ Volunteers	4.00	.60	.30
1133	36¢ Charter of Freedom	2.85	.60	.30
1134	36¢ Engineering	2.85	.60	.30

1987 COMMEMORATIVES

1135-38	Science & Tech., attached	3.00	2.45	2.20
1135	36¢ Reginald A. Fessenden	......	.75	.35
1136	36¢ Charles Fenerty	......	.75	.35
1137	36¢ Desbarats & Leggo	......	.75	.35
1138	36¢ Frederick N. Gisborne	......	.75	.35
1139-40	Steamships, attached	3.00	1.25	1.10
1139	36¢ Segwun	......	.75	.35
1140	36¢ Princess Marguerite	......	.75	.35
1141-44	Historic Shipwrecks, att'd.	3.50	3.00	2.75
1141	36¢ Hamilton & Scourge	......	.85	.35
1142	36¢ San Juan	......	.85	.35
1143	36¢ Breadalbane	......	.85	.35
1144	36¢ Ericsson	......	.85	.35
1145	36¢ Air Canada	2.85	.60	.30
1146	36¢ Quebec Summit	2.85	.60	.30
1147	36¢ Commonwealth Mtg.	2.85	.60	.30
1148	36¢ Christmas	2.85	.60	.30
1149	42¢ Christmas	3.30	.75	.40
1150	72¢ Christmas	6.35	1.40	1.00
1151	31¢ Christmas booklet single	......	.75	.50
1151a	same, booklet pane of 10	......	6.00	......
1152-53	Calgary Olympics, attached	2.85	1.35	1.10
1152	36¢ Cross-Country Skiing	......	.60	.30
1153	36¢ Ski Jumping	......	.60	.30
1154	36¢ Grey Cup	2.85	.60	.30

1987-91 DEFINITIVE ISSUES

1155	1¢ Flying Squirrel	.80	.20	.15
1156	2¢ Porcupine	.80	.20	.15
1157	3¢ Muskrat	.80	.20	.15
1158	5¢ Hare	.80	.20	.15
1159	6¢ Red Fox	.80	.20	.15
1160	10¢ Skunk	1.00	.25	.15
1160a	same, perf. 13x12-1/2	22.00	5.00	.50
1161	25¢ Beaver	2.00	.50	.20
1162	37¢ Elizabeth II	3.05	.75	.30
1163	37¢ Parliament	3.05	.75	.30
1163a	same, bklt. pane of 10 (1988)	......	7.50	7.50
1163b	same, bklt. pane of 25 (1988)	......	18.80	15.00
1163c	37¢, perf. 13-1/2x14 (1988)	......	1.20	......
1164	38¢ Elizabeth II (1988)	3.30	.75	.30
1164a	38¢, perf. 13x13-1/2	......	1.50	.75
1164b	same, booklet pane of 10	......	7.50	6.00
1165	38¢ Clock Tower (1988)	3.30	.65	.15
1165a	same, booklet pane of 10	......	8.00	6.00
1165b	same, booklet pane of 25	......	20.00	18.75
1166	39¢ Flag & Clouds	3.30	.75	.15
1166a	same, booklet pane of 10	......	7.50	6.75
1166b	same, booklet pane of 25	......	22.50	18.75
1166c	same, perf. 12-1/2x13	......	15.00	1.00
1167	39¢ Elizabeth II	3.30	.75	.15
1167a	same, booklet pane of 10	......	10.00	6.00
1167b	39¢, perf. 13 (1990)	70.00	16.00	.50
1168	40¢ Elizabeth II (1990)	3.30	.75	.15
1168a	same, booklet pane of 10	......	8.00	6.75
1169	40¢ Flag and Mountains (1990)	3.30	.70	.15
1169a	same, booklet pane of 25	......	26.25	18.75
1169b	same, booklet pane of 10	......	8.00	6.75
1170	43¢ Lynx	4.50	1.00	.30
1171	44¢ Walrus (1989)	4.50	1.00	.20
1171a	44¢, perf. 12-1/2x13	......	3.00	.30
1171b	same, booklet pane of 5	......	12.00	......
1172	45¢ Pronghorn (1990)	4.50	.95	.30
1172b	same, booklet pane of 5	7.50	1.50	.30
1172d	45¢, perf. 13	80.00	18.00	1.20
1172A	46¢, Wolverine (1990)	3.85	1.00	.30
1172Ac	46¢, perf. 12-1/2x13	......	.85	.30
1172Ae	same, booklet pane of 5	......	1.15	.30
1172Ag	same, perf. 14-1/2x14	25.00	5.00	......
1173	57¢ Killer Whale	4.90	1.15	.35
1174	59¢ Musk-ox (1989)	4.90	1.15	.35
1174a	same, booklet pane of 5	37.50	10.00	.60
1175	61¢ Timber Wolf (1990)	5.65	1.15	.40
1175a	61¢, perf. 13	325.00	70.00	.50
1176	63¢ Harbor Porpoise	6.00	1.35	.40
1176a	63¢, perf. 13	32.50	6.00	.60
1177	74¢ Wapiti (1988)	7.50	1.50	.60
1178	76¢ Grizzly Bear (1989)	6.00	1.35	.40
1178a	76¢, perf. 12-1/2x13	......	2.50	.35
1178b	same, booklet pane of 5	......	16.00	......
1178c	same, perf. 13	225.00	50.00	2.75
1179	78¢ Beluga (1990)	7.50	1.50	.55
1179a	same, booklet pane of 5	......	12.00	......
1179b	78¢, perf. 13	195.00	40.00	2.65
1179c	same, perf. 12-1/2x13	15.00	3.00	.60
1180	80¢ Peary caribou (1990)	8.50	2.00	.60
1180a	80¢, perf. 12-1/2x13	6.60	2.00	.55
1180b	same, booklet pane of 5	......	17.50	......
1180c	80¢, perf. 14-1/2x14	24.00	6.50	.60

Canada Postage #1181-1263

SCOTT NO.	DESCRIPTION	PLATE BLOCK F/NH	UNUSED F/NH	USED F
1181	$1 Runnymede Library	7.50	1.50	.80
1182	$2 McAdam Train Station	15.00	3.00	1.50
1183	$5 Bonsecours Market	40.00	8.50	4.00

BOOKLET STAMPS

1184	1¢ Flag, booklet single (1990)	......	.20	.15
1185	5¢ Flag, booklet single (1990)	......	.20	.15
1186	6¢ Parliament East (1989)	......	.25	.15
1187	37¢ Parliament booklet single	......	.65	.25
1187a	booklet pane (4), 1 #938, 2 #942, 1 #1187	......	1.50	......
1188	38¢ Parliament Library booklet single (1989)	......	.65	.25
1188a	booklet pane (5), 3 #939a, 1 #1186, 1 #1188	......	1.50	......
1189	39¢ Flag booklet single (1990)	......	.75	.30
1189a	booklet pane (4), 1 #1184, 2 #1185, 1 #1189	......	2.00	......
1190	40¢ Flag booklet single (1990)	......	1.50	.50
1190a	booklet pane (4) 2 #1184, 1 #1185, 1 #1190	......	2.50	......

SELF-ADHESIVE BOOKLET STAMPS

1191	38¢ Flag, forest (1989)	......	1.15	.60
1191a	same, booklet pane of 12	......	13.75	......
1192	39¢ Flag field (1990)	......	1.15	.60
1192a	same, booklet pane of 12	......	13.75	......
1193	40¢ Flag, seacoast (1991)	......	1.15	.60
1193a	same, booklet pane of 12	......	13.75	......

COIL STAMPS

1194	37¢ Parliament Library (1988)	......	.85	.25
1194A	38¢ Parliament Library (1989)	......	.85	.25
1194B	39¢ Flag (1990)	......	.85	.25
1194C	40¢ Flag (1990)	......	.85	.25

1988 COMMEMORATIVES

1195/1236	(1195-1225, 1226-36) complete, 39 varieties	74.75	33.25	14.75
1195-96	Calgary Olympics, att'd.	3.05	1.50	1.15
1195	37¢ Alpine Skiing	......	.65	.30
1196	37¢ Curling	......	.65	.30
1197	43¢ Figure Skating	3.30	.75	.60
1198	74¢ Luge	5.80	1.50	.95
1199-1202	Explorers, attached	3.05	3.00	2.25
1199	37¢ Anthony Henday	......	.65	.30
1200	37¢ George Vancouver	......	.65	.30
1201	37¢ Simon Fraser	......	.65	.30
1202	37¢ John Palliser	......	.65	.30
1203	50¢ Canadian Art	5.00	1.10	.95
1204-05	Wildlife Conservation, att'd.	3.30	1.40	.95
1204	37¢ Ducks Unlimited	......	.65	.30
1205	37¢ Moose	......	.65	.30
1206-09	Science & Technology, att'd.	3.75	3.25	2.50
1206	37¢ Kerosene	......	.85	.35
1207	37¢ Marquis Wheat	......	.85	.35
1208	37¢ Electron Microscope	......	.85	.35
1209	37¢ Cancer Therapy	......	.85	.35
1210-13	Butterflies, attached	4.00	3.50	2.50
1210	37¢ Short-tailed Swallowtail	......	.85	.35
1211	37¢ Northern Blue	......	.85	.35
1212	37¢ Macoun's Arctic	......	.85	.35
1213	37¢ Tiger Swallowtail	......	.85	.35
1214	37¢ Harbor Entrance	3.05	.65	.25
1215	37¢ 4-H Club Anniv.	3.05	.65	.25
1216	37¢ Les Forges Du St. Maurice	3.05	.65	.25
1217-20	Dogs, attached	5.00	4.50	3.00
1217	37¢ Tahltan Bear Dog	......	1.20	.45
1218	37¢ Nova Scotia Retriever	......	1.20	.45
1219	37¢ Canadian Eskimo Dog	......	1.20	.45
1220	37¢ Newfoundland Dog	......	1.20	.45
1221	37¢ Baseball	4.15	.65	.25
1222	37¢ Christmas Nativity	3.50	.75	.25
1223	43¢ Virgin & Child	4.00	.90	.75
1224	74¢ Virgin & Child	6.00	1.15	.95
1225	32¢ Christmas Icons booklet single	......	.75	.30
1225a	same, booklet pane of 10	......	7.00	5.25
1226	37¢ Charles Inglis	3.05	.65	.25
1227	37¢ Ann Hopkins	3.05	.65	.25
1228	37¢ Angus Walters	3.05	.65	.25
1229-32	Small Craft Series, attached	3.30	2.70	2.25
1229	37¢ Chipewyan Canoe	......	.65	.25
1230	37¢ Haida Canoe	......	.65	.25
1231	37¢ Inuit Kayak	......	.65	.25
1232	37¢ Micmac Canoe	......	.65	.25
1233-36	Explorers, attached	3.30	3.00	2.25
1233	38¢ Matonabbee	......	.65	.25
1234	38¢ Sir John Franklin	......	.65	.25
1235	38¢ J.B.Tyrrell	......	.65	.25
1236	38¢ V. Stefansson	......	.65	.25

1989 COMMEMORATIVES

1237/63	(1237-56, 1257, 1258, 1259, 1260-63) complete, 26 varieties	......	18.25	7.40
1237-40	Canadian Photography, att'd.	3.30	3.00	2.25
1237	38¢ W. Notman	......	.65	.25
1238	38¢ W.H. Boorne	......	.65	.25
1239	38¢ A. Henderson	......	.65	.25
1240	38¢ J.E. Livernois	......	.65	.25
1241	50¢ Canadian Art	5.00	1.10	.95
1243-44	19th Century Poets, att'd.	3.30	1.40	.95
1243	38¢ L.H.Frechette	......	.65	.25
1244	38¢ A. Lampman	......	.65	.25
1245-48	Mushrooms, attached	3.30	3.00	2.25
1245	38¢ Cinnabar Chanterelle	......	.85	.30
1246	38¢ Common Morel	......	.85	.30
1247	38¢ Spindell Coral	......	.85	.30
1248	38¢ Admirable Boletus	......	.85	.30
1249-50	Canadian Infantry, attached	195.00	1.50	1.15
1249	38¢ Light Infantry	......	.65	.25
1250	38¢ Royal 22nd Regiment	......	.65	.25
1251	38¢ International Trade	3.30	.65	.25
1252-55	Performing Arts, attached	3.30	2.70	2.25
1252	38¢ Dance	......	.65	.25
1253	38¢ Music	......	.65	.25
1254	38¢ Film	......	.65	.25
1255	38¢ Theatre	......	.65	.25
1256	38¢ Christmas 1989	3.30	.65	.25
1256a	same, booklet single	......	3.75	.75
1256a	same, booklet pane of 10	45.00	......	......
1257	44¢ Christmas 1989	4.60	.85	.40
1257a	same, booklet single	......	4.50	.75
1257a	same, booklet pane of 5	22.50	......	......
1258	76¢ Christmas 1989	7.00	1.40	.70
1258a	same, booklet single	......	5.50	.75
1258a	same, booklet pane of 5	30.00	......	......
1259	33¢ Christmas, booklet single	......	.70	.25
1259a	same, booklet pane of 10	......	6.75	5.25
1260-63	WWII 50th Anniversary, att'd.	3.30	3.00	2.25
1260	38¢ Declaration of War	......	.65	.25
1261	38¢ Army Mobilization	......	.65	.25
1262	38¢ Navy Convoy System	......	.65	.25
1263	38¢ Commonwealth Training	......	.65	.25

Canada Postage #1264-1348

SCOTT NO.	DESCRIPTION	PLATE BLOCK F/NH	UNUSED F/NH	USED F

1990 COMMEMORATIVES

SCOTT NO.	DESCRIPTION	PLATE BLOCK F/NH	UNUSED F/NH	USED F
1264/1301	(1264-73, 1274-94, 1295, 1296, 1297, 1298-1301) complete, 38 vars.		62.25	29.10	16.25
1264-65	Norman Bethune, attached	3.50	2.00	1.50
1264	39¢ Bethune in Canada	......	1.10	.50
1265	39¢ Bethune in China	......	1.10	.50
1266-69	Small Craft Series, att'd.	3.50	3.00	2.50
1266	39¢ Dory	......	.85	.35
1267	39¢ Pointer	......	.85	.35
1268	39¢ York Boat	......	.85	.35
1269	39¢ North Canoe	......	.85	.35
1270	39¢ Multiculturalism	3.30	.70	.25
1271	50¢ Canadian Art,"The West Wind"	5.00	1.10	.95
1272-73	Canada Postal System 39¢ booklet pair	......	1.50	1.00
1273a	same, booklet pane of 8	......	7.00	......
1273b	same, booklet pane of 9	......	8.00	......
1274-77	Dolls of Canada, attached	4.00	3.00	2.50
1274	39¢ Native Dolls	......	.85	.35
1275	39¢ Settlers' Dolls	......	.85	.35
1276	39¢ Four Commercial Dolls	......	.85	.35
1277	39¢ Five Commercial Dolls	......	.85	.35
1278	39¢ Canada/Flag Day	3.30	.75	.25
1279-82	Prehistoric Life, attached	4.00	3.00	2.50
1279	39¢ Trilobite	......	.85	.35
1280	39¢ Sea Scorpion	......	.85	.35
1281	39¢ Fossil Algae	......	.85	.35
1282	39¢ Soft Invertebrate	......	.85	.35
1283-86	Canadian Forests, attached	4.00	3.25	2.75
1283	39¢ Acadian	......	.85	.35
1284	39¢ Great Lakes—St.Lawrence	......	.85	.35
1285	39¢ Coast	......	.85	.35
1286	39¢ Boreal	......	.85	.35
1287	39¢ Climate Observations	3.30	.70	.25
1288	39¢ Int'l. Literacy Year	3.30	.70	.25
1289-92	Can. Lore & Legend, attached	4.00	3.25	2.75
1289	39¢ Sasquatch	......	.85	.35
1290	39¢ Kraken	......	.85	.35
1291	39¢ Werewolf	......	.85	.35
1292	39¢ Ogopogo	......	.85	.35
1293	39¢ Agnes Macphail	3.30	.70	.25
1294	39¢ Native Mary & Child	3.20	.75	.25
1294a	same, booklet pane of 10	......	10.00	......
1295	45¢ Inuit, Mother & Child	5.00	1.10	..75
1295a	same, booklet pane of 5	......	9.50	......
1296	78¢ Raven Children	8.00	1.75	1.00
1296a	same, booklet pane of 5	......	15.00	......
1297	34¢ Christmas, booklet sgl.	......	.65	.25
1297a	same, booklet pane of 10	......	7.00	......
1298-1301	World War II—1940, att'd.	5.00	4.25	4.00
1298	39¢ Home Front	......	1.10	.95
1299	39¢ Communal War Efforts	......	1.10	.95
1300	39¢ Food Production	......	1.10	.95
1301	39¢ Science and War	......	1.10	.95

1991 COMMEMORATIVES

SCOTT NO.	DESCRIPTION	PLATE BLOCK F/NH	UNUSED F/NH	USED F
1302-43, 1345-48, 46 varieties		41.75	37.00	17.75
1302-05	Canadian Doctors, att'd.	4.00	3.00	2.25
1302	40¢ Jennie Trout	......	.85	.35
1303	40¢ Wilder Penfield	......	.85	.35
1304	40¢ Sir Frederick Banting	......	.85	.35
1305	40¢ Harold Griffith	......	.85	.35
1306-09	Prehistoric Life, attached	4.00	3.50	2.75
1306	40¢ Microfossils	......	.95	.35
1307	40¢ Early tree	......	.95	.35
1308	40¢ Early fish	......	.95	.35
1309	40¢ Land reptile	......	.95	.35
1310	50¢ Canadian Art, "Forest, British Columbia"	4.50	.95	.75
1311	40¢ The Butchart Gardens, attached booklet single	......	.95	.35
1312	40¢ International Peace Garden, booklet single	......	.95	.35
1313	40¢ Royal Botanical Garden, booklet single	......	.95	.35
1314	40¢ Montreal Botanical Garden, booklet single	......	.95	.35
1315	40¢ Halifax Public Gardens, booklet single	......	.95	.35
1315a	Public Gardens, strip of 5	......	4.00	3.00
1315b	Public Gardens, attached booklet pane of 10	......	8.00	......
1316	40¢ Canada Day	3.50	.75	.25
1317-20	Small Craft Series, attached	3.50	3.00	2.25
1317	40¢ Verchere Rowboat	......	.85	.35
1318	40¢ Touring Kayak	......	.85	.35
1319	40¢ Sailing Dinghy	......	.85	.35
1320	40¢ Cedar Strip Canoe	......	.85	.35
1321	40¢ South Nahanni River	......	.95	.45
1322	40¢ Athabasca River	......	.95	.45
1323	40¢ Voyageur Waterway	......	.95	.45
1324	40¢ Jacques Cartier River	......	.95	.45
1325	40¢ Main River	......	1.95	.45
1325a	Canadian Rivers, strip of 5	......	4.00	3.00
1325b	Canadian Rivers, attached booklet pane of 10	......	8.00	......
1326-29	Arrival of the Ukrainians, attached	4.00	3.00	2.25
1326	40¢ Leaving	......	.85	.35
1327	40¢ Winter in Canada	......	.85	.35
1328	40¢ Clearing Land	......	.85	.35
1329	40¢ Growing Wheat	......	.85	.35
1330-33	Dangerous Public Service Occupations, attached	5.00	4.00	2.50
1330	40¢ Ski Patrol	......	1.10	.35
1331	40¢ Police	......	1.10	.35
1332	40¢ Firefighters	......	1.10	.35
1333	40¢ Search & Rescue	......	1.10	.35
1334-37	Folktales, attached	4.00	3.00	2.25
1334	40¢ Witched Canoe	......	.85	.35
1335	40¢ Orphan Boy	......	.85	.35
1336	40¢ Chinook Wind	......	.85	.35
1337	40¢ Buried Treasure	......	.85	.35
1338	40¢ Queen's University, booklet, single	......	.85	.25
1338a	Same booklet pane of 10	......	8.00	......
1339	40¢ Santa at Fireplace	3.60	.75	.25
1339a	Same, booklet pane of 10	......	8.00	......
1340	46¢ Santa with White horse, tree	4.10	.85	.40
1340a	Same, booklet pane of 5	......	5.00	......
1341	80¢ Sinterklaas, girl	7.00	1.50	1.00
1341a	Same, booklet pane of 5	......	9.00	......
1342	35¢ Santa with Punchbowl, booklet, single	......	.85	.25
1342a	Same, booklet pane of 10	......	8.00	......
1343	40¢ Basketball Centennial	4.00	.85	.25
1344	40¢-80¢ Basketball Souvenir Sheet of 3	......	5.00	......
1345-48	World War II—1941, att'd.	5.00	4.00	3.75
1345	40¢ Women's Armed Forces	......	1.10	.95
1346	40¢ War Industry	......	1.10	.95
1347	40¢ Cadets and Veterans	......	1.10	.95
1348	40¢ Defense of Hong Kong	......	1.10	.95

1302

1311

1316

1321

1326

1330

1334

1338

1343 1349 1339 1342

Canada Postage #1349-1445a

SCOTT NO.	DESCRIPTION	PLATE BLOCK F/NH	UNUSED F/NH	USED F
	1991-96 Regular Issue			
1349	1¢ Blueberry (1992)	.80	.20	.15
1350	2¢ Wild Strawberry (1992)	.80	.20	.15
1351	3¢ Black Crowberry (1992)	.80	.20	.15
1352	5¢ Rose Hip (1992)	.80	.20	.15
1353	6¢ Black Raspberry (1992)	.80	.20	.15
1354	10¢ Kinnikinnick (1992)	1.00	.25	.15
1355	25¢ Saskatoon berry (1992)	2.00	.50	.15
1356	42¢ Flag + Rolling Hills	3.20	.75	.20
1356a	Same, booklet pane of 10	....	7.50	6.00
1356b	Same, booklet pane of 50	....	80.00	33.75
1356c	Same, booklet pane of 25	....	18.75	15.00
1357	42¢ Queen Elizabeth II (Karsh)	3.20	.75	.20
1357a	Same, booklet pane of 10	....	7.50	6.00
1358	43¢ Queen Elizabeth II (Karsh) (1992)	4.15	.95	.20
1358a	Same, booklet pane of 10	....	9.40	7.50
1359	43¢ Flag + Prairie (1992)	4.15	.95	.20
1359a	Same, booklet pane of 10	....	7.50	6.00
1359b	Same, booklet pane of 25	....	22.50	18.75
1360	45¢ Queen Elizabeth II (Karsh) (1995)	3.20	.75	.20
1360a	Same, booklet pane of 10	....	8.00	6.00
1361	45¢ Flag & Building (1995)	3.20	.75	.20
1361a	Same, booklet pane of 10	....	9.40	7.50
1361b	Same, booklet pane of 25	....	28.00	22.50
1362	45¢ Flag & Building, perf. 13½ x 13	3.20	.75	.20
1362a	Same, booklet pane of 10	....	8.00	6.00
1362b	Same, booklet pane of 30	....	20.00	15.00
1363	48¢ McIntosh Apple Tree, perf. 13	4.15	.95	.25
1363a	Same, perf. 14½ x 14	....	1.25	.30
1363b	Same, booklet pane of 5	....	7.00	4.50
1364	49¢ Delicious Apple perf.13 (1992)	4.15	.95	.25
1364a	Same, perf. 14½ x 14	3.95	1.25	.30
1364b	Same, booklet pane of 5	....	7.00	4.50
1365	50¢ Snow Apple (1994)	3.95	.95	.30
1365b	Same, perf. 14½ x 14	3.95	1.75	.25
1365a	Same, booklet pane of 5	....	9.00	....
1366	52¢ Gravenstein apple (1995)	3.95	.95	.25
1366a	Same, booklet pane of 5	....	9.00	4.50
1366b	52¢ Gravenstein apple, perf. 14½ x 14	3.95	2.50	.30
1366c	Same, booklet pane of 5	....	12.00	....
1367	65¢ Black Walnut Tree	4.90	1.15	.35
1368	67¢ Beaked Hazelnut (1992)	4.90	1.15	.35
1369	69¢ Shagbark Hickory (1994)	4.90	1.15	.35
1370	71¢ American Chestnut (1995)	4.90	1.10	.35
1371	84¢ Stanley Plum Tree, perf. 13	5.65	1.35	.40
1371a	Same, perf. 14½ x 14	....	2.00	.50
1371b	Same, booklet pane of 5	....	10.00	....
1372	86¢ Bartlett Pear, perf. 13 (1992)	9.00	2.65	.60
1372a	Same, perf. 14½ x 14	13.15	3.00	.60
1372b	Same, booklet pane of 5	....	15.00	....
1373	88¢ Westcot Apricot (1994)	6.40	1.50	.50
1373b	Same, perf. 14½ x 14	6.75	3.00	.60
1363bc	Same, booklet pane of 5	....	15.00	....
1374	90¢ Elberta Peach (1995)	6.00	1.90	.45
1374a	Same, booklet pane of 5	....	10.00	....
1374b	Same, booklet pane of 5, perf. 14½ x 14	....	12.00	....
1375	$1 Yorkton Court House (1994)	6.75	1.50	.55
1376	$2 Provincial Normal School, Nova Scotia (1994)	13.15	3.00	1.05
1378	$5 Carnegie Public Library, Victoria	33.75	8.00	2.25
1388	42¢ Flag and Mountains, quick-stick (1992)	....	.80	.30
1388a	Same, booklet pane of 12	....	10.00	....
1389	43¢ Flag, estuary shore (1993)	....	.80	.30
1394	42¢ Canadian Flag + Rolling Hills, coil	....	.80	.30
1395	43¢ Canadian Flag, coil (1992)	....	.80	.30
1396	45¢ Canadian Flag, coil (1995)	....	.80	.20

1361

1399

1404

1992 COMMEMORATIVES

1399-1455, 57 varieties	44.15	56.10	22.25	
1399	42¢ Ski Jumping	....	.95	.25
1400	42¢ Figure Skating	....	.95	.25
1401	42¢ Hockey	....	.95	.25
1402	42¢ Bobsledding	....	.95	.25
1403	42¢ Alpine Skiing	....	.95	.25
1403a	Olympic Winter Games, Strips of 5	....	4.50	3.00
1403b	Olympic Winter Games, booklet pane of 10	....	8.00	5.00
1404-05	350th Anniversary of Montreal, attached	3.60	1.50	1.00
1404	42¢ Modern Montreal	....	.80	.25
1405	42¢ Early Montreal	....	.80	.25
1406	48¢ Jaques Cartier	3.95	.90	.40
1407	84¢ Columbus	7.65	1.65	.60
1407a	42¢-84¢ Canada '92, Souvenir Sheet of 4	....	4.00	....
1408	42¢ The Margaree River	....	.85	.25
1409	42¢ Eliot or West River	....	.85	.25
1410	42¢ Ottowa River	....	.85	.25
1411	42¢ Niagara River	....	.85	.25
1412	42¢ South Saskatchewan River	....	.85	.25
1412a	Canadian Rivers II, Strip of 5	....	4.00	3.00
1412b	Canadian Rivers II, booklet pane of 10	....	8.00	5.00

1413

1420

SCOTT NO.	DESCRIPTION	PLATE BLOCK F/NH	UNUSED F/NH	USED F
1413	42¢ 50th Anniversary of the Alaska Highway	3.60	.80	.25
1414	42¢ Gymnastics	....	.95	.25
1415	42¢ Track and Field	....	.95	.25
1416	42¢ Diving	....	.95	.25
1417	42¢ Cycling	....	.95	.25
1418	42¢ Swimming	....	.95	.25
1418a	Olympic Summer Games, Strip of 5, attached	....	4.50	3.00
1418b	Olympic Summer Games, booklet pane of 10	....	8.00	5.00
1419	50¢ Canadian Art "Red Nasturtiums"	4.40	.95	1.00
1420	Nova Scotia	....	2.10	1.00
1421	Ontario	....	2.10	1.00
1422	Prince Edward Island	....	2.10	1.00
1423	New Brunswick	....	2.10	1.00
1424	Quebec	....	2.10	1.00
1425	Saskatchewan	....	2.10	1.00
1426	Manitoba	....	2.10	1.00
1427	Northwest Territories	....	2.10	1.00
1428	Alberta	....	2.10	1.00
1429	British Columbia	....	2.10	1.00
1430	Yukon	....	2.10	1.00
1431	Newfoundland	....	2.10	1.00
1431a	42¢ 125th Anniversary of Canada, 12 various attached	....	24.00	22.00

1432

1436

1432-35	Canadian Folk Heroes, attached	3.60	3.00	2.25
1432	42¢ Jerry Potts	....	.80	.25
1433	42¢ Capt. William Jackman	....	.80	.25
1434	42¢ Laura Secord	....	.80	.25
1435	42¢ Joseph Montferrand	....	.80	.25
1436	42¢ Copper	....	.85	.25
1437	42¢ Sodalite	....	.85	.25
1438	42¢ Gold	....	.85	.25
1439	42¢ Galena	....	.85	.25
1440	42¢ Grossular	....	.85	.25
1440a	Minerals, Strip of 5	....	4.00	3.00
1440b	Minerals, booklet pane of 10	....	8.00	5.00

1441

1443a

1441-42	Canadian Space Exploration, attached	3.60	1.50	1.15
1441	42¢ Anik E2 Satellite	....	.80	.25
1442	42¢ Earth, Space Shuttle	....	.80	.25
1443-45	National Hockey League, booklet singles	....	2.40	.75
1443a	Skates, Stick, booklet pane of 8	....	6.40	....
1444a	Team Emblems, booklet pane of 8	....	6.40	....
1445a	Goalie's Mask, booklet pane of 9	....	7.20	....

Canada Postage #1446-1508

SCOTT NO.	DESCRIPTION	PLATE BLOCK F/NH	UNUSED F/NH	USED F

1446-47

1452

1446-47	Order of Canada + D. Michener, attached	3.60	1.50	1.15
1446	42¢ Order of Canada	....	.80	.25
1447	42¢ Daniel Roland Michener	....	.80	.25
1448-51	World War II—1942, att'd.	3.60	3.00	2.25
1448	42¢ War Reporting	......	.80	.50
1449	42¢ Newfoundland Air Bases	......	.80	.50
1450	42¢ Raid on Dieppe	......	.80	.50
1451	42¢ U-boats offshore	......	.80	.50
1452	42¢ Jouluvana—Christmas	3.90	.80	.25
1452a	Same, perf. 13½	3.90	.80	.25
1452b	Same, booklet pane of 10	......	7.75	......
1453	48¢ La Befana—Christmas	3.95	.90	.30
1453a	Same, booklet pane of 5	......	4.50	......
1454	84¢ Weihnachtsmann	6.75	1.50	.50
1454a	Same, booklet pane of 5	......	8.00	......
1455	37¢ Santa Claus	......	.70	.25
1455a	Same, booklet pane of 10	......	8.00	......

1455

1456

1460

1993 COMMEMORATIVES

1456-89, 1491-1506, 50 varieties			41.00	41.50	19.50
1456-59	Canadian Women, attached	3.60	3.00	2.25
1456	43¢ Adelaide Sophia Hoodless	....	.80	.25
1457	43¢ Marie-Josephine Gerin-Lajoie	....	.80	.25
1458	43¢ Pitseolak Ashoona	....	.80	.25
1459	43¢ Helen Kinnear	....	.80	.25
1460	43¢ Stanley Cup Centennial	3.60	.80	.25

1461

1467

1461	43¢ Coverlet "Bed Rugg", New Brunswick	....	.85	.25
1462	43¢ Pieced Quilt, Ontario	....	.85	.25
1463	43¢ Doukhobor Bedcover, Saskatchewan	....	.85	.25
1464	43¢ Kwakwaka'wakw ceremonial robe, British Columbia	....	.85	.25
1465	43¢ Boutonne coverlet, Quebec	....	.85	.25
1465a	Handcrafted Textiles, Strip of 5	....	4.00	3.00
1465b	Handcrafted Textiles, booklet pane of 10	....	8.00	5.00
1461-65	Same, set of 5 singles	....	3.90	......
1466	86¢ Canadian Art—"Drawing for the Owl"	6.75	1.50	.95
1467	43¢ Empress Hotel, Victoria, B.C.	....	.85	.25
1468	43¢ Banff Springs Hotel, Banff, Alberta	....	.85	.25
1469	43¢ Royal York Hotel, Toronto, Ontario	....	.85	.25
1470	43¢ Chateau Frontenac, Quebec City, Quebec	....	.85	.25
1471	43¢ Algonquin Hotel, St. Andrews, N.B.	....	.85	.25
1471a	Canadian Pacific Hotels, strip of 5	....	4.00	3.00
1471b	Canadian Pacific Hotels, booklet pane of 10	....	8.00	5.00

1472

1490a

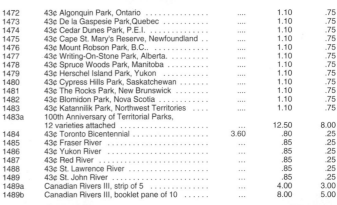
1484

SCOTT NO.	DESCRIPTION	PLATE BLOCK F/NH	UNUSED F/NH	USED F
1472	43¢ Algonquin Park, Ontario	....	1.10	.75
1473	43¢ De la Gaspesie Park, Quebec	....	1.10	.75
1474	43¢ Cedar Dunes Park, P.E.I.	....	1.10	.75
1475	43¢ Cape St. Mary's Reserve, Newfoundland	....	1.10	.75
1476	43¢ Mount Robson Park, B.C.	....	1.10	.75
1477	43¢ Writing-On-Stone Park, Alberta	....	1.10	.75
1478	43¢ Spruce Woods Park, Manitoba	....	1.10	.75
1479	43¢ Herschel Island Park, Yukon	....	1.10	.75
1480	43¢ Cypress Hills Park, Saskatchewan	....	1.10	.75
1481	43¢ The Rocks Park, New Brunswick	....	1.10	.75
1482	43¢ Blomidon Park, Nova Scotia	....	1.10	.75
1483	43¢ Katannilik Park, Northwest Territories	....	1.10	.75
1483a	100th Anniversary of Territorial Parks, 12 varieties attached	....	12.50	8.00
1484	43¢ Toronto Bicentennial	3.60	.80	.25
1485	43¢ Fraser River	....	.85	.25
1486	43¢ Yukon River	....	.85	.25
1487	43¢ Red River	....	.85	.25
1488	43¢ St. Lawrence River	....	.85	.25
1489	43¢ St. John River	....	.85	.25
1489a	Canadian Rivers III, strip of 5	....	4.00	3.00
1489b	Canadian Rivers III, booklet pane of 10	....	8.00	5.00

1491

1495

1499

1490	43¢-86¢ Canadian Motor Vehicles souvenir sheet of 6	....	7.50	6.00
1491-94	Canadian Folklore—Folk Songs, attached	3.60	3.00	2.25
1491	43¢ The Alberta Homesteader	....	.80	.25
1492	43¢ Les Raftmans	....	.80	.25
1493	43¢ I'se the B'y that Builds the Boat	....	.80	.25
1494	43¢ Bear Song	....	.80	.25

1502

1507

1495-98	Dinosaurs, attached	4.00	3.50	2.50
1495	43¢ Massospondylus (Jurassic period)	....	.95	.35
1496	43¢ Styracosaurus (Cretaceous period)	....	.95	.35
1497	43¢ Albertosaurus (Cretaceous period)	....	.95	.35
1498	43¢ Platecarpus (Cretaceous period)	....	.95	.35
1499	43¢ Santa Claus—Poland	3.60	.80	.25
1499a	same, booklet pane of 10	....	8.00	...
1500	49¢ Santa Claus—Russia	3.90	.90	.30
1500a	same, booklet pane of 5	....	4.50	...
1501	86¢ Father Christmas, Australia	7.00	1.50	.50
1501a	same, booklet pane of 5	....	7.50	...
1502	38¢ Santa Claus	....	.70	.25
1502a	same, booklet pane of 10	....	7.00	...
1503-06	World War II—1943	3.60	3.00	2.25
1503	43¢ Aid to Allies	....	.80	.50
1504	43¢ Canada's Bomber Force	....	.80	.50
1505	43¢ Battle of the Atlantic	....	.80	.50
1506	43¢ Invasion of Italy	....	.80	.50

1994

1507-08	43¢ Greeting booklet (10 stamps w/35 stickers)	....	10.00	

Canada Postage #1509-1573

1509

1510

1517

1994 COMMEMORATIVES

SCOTT NO.	DESCRIPTION	PLATE BLOCK F/NH	UNUSED F/NH	USED F
1509-22, 1524-26, 1528-40, 41 varieties		32.50	31.25	13.75
1509	43¢ Jeanne Sauve	3.60	.80	.25
1510	43¢ T. Eaton Prestige	3.60	.80	.25
1510a	43¢ T. Eaton Prestige, booklet of 10	...	8.00	...
1511	43¢ Saguenay River	...	.95	.35
1512	43¢ French River	...	.95	.35
1513	43¢ Mackenzie River	...	.95	.35
1514	43¢ Churchill River	...	.95	.35
1515	43¢ Columbia River	...	.95	.35
1515a	Canadian Rivers IV, strip of 5	...	5.00	4.00
1515b	Canadian Rivers IV, booklet pane of 10	...	10.00	...
1516	88¢ Canadian Art "Vera"	8.00	1.50	1.00

1523a

1524a

1525

1517-18	Commonwealth Games, attached	3.60	1.50	.60
1517	43¢ Lawn Bowls	...	.80	.25
1518	43¢ Lacrosse	...	.80	.25
1519-20	Commonwealth Games, attached	3.60	1.50	.60
1519	43¢ Wheelchair Marathon	...	.80	.25
1520	43¢ High Jump	...	.80	.25
1521	50¢ Commonwealth Games (Diving)	4.00	.90	.35
1522	88¢ Commonwealth Games (Cycling)	6.75	1.50	.75
1523	43¢ Intl. Year of the Family, souvenir sheet of 5	...	5.00	4.00
1524	Canada Day—Maple Trees, 12 varieties, attached	...	9.00	6.00
1525-26	Famous Canadians, attached	3.60	1.50	1.15
1525	43¢ Billy Bishop, Fighter Ace	...	.80	.25
1526	43¢ Mary Travers, Folk Singer	...	.80	.25
1527	43¢-88¢ Historic Motor Vehicles, souvenir sheet of 6	...	8.00	5.75

1528

1533

1536

1528	43¢ 50th Anniversary of ICAO	3.60	.80	.25
1529-32	Dinosaurs, attached	3.60	3.00	2.25
1529	43¢ Coryphodon	...	.80	.25
1530	43¢ Megacerops	...	.80	.25
1531	43¢ Short-Faced Bear	...	.80	.25
1532	43¢ Woolly Mammoth	...	.80	.25
1533	43¢ Family Singing Carols	3.60	.80	.25
1533a	same, booklet pane of 10	...	7.75	...
1534	50¢ Choir	3.95	.90	.30
1534a	same, booklet pane of 5	...	4.50	...
1535	88¢ Caroling	6.75	1.50	.75
1535a	same, booklet pane of 5	...	7.50	...
1536	38¢ Caroling Soloist, booklet single	...	.85	.25
1536a	same, booklet pane of 10	...	8.50	...
1537-40	World War II—1944, attached	3.60	3.00	2.25
1537	43¢ D-Day Beachhead	...	.80	.25
1538	43¢ Artillery—Normandy	...	.80	.25
1539	43¢ Tactical Air Forces	...	.80	.25
1540	43¢ Walcheren and Scheldt	...	.80	.25

1995 COMMEMORATIVES

SCOTT NO.	DESCRIPTION	PLATE BLOCK F/NH	UNUSED F/NH	USED F
1541-51, 1553-58, 1562-67, 1570-90, 47 varieties		51.50	33.85	10.40
1541-44	World War II—1945, attached	3.60	3.00	2.25
1541	43¢ Veterans Return Home	...	.80	.25
1542	43¢ Freeing the POW	...	.80	.25
1543	43¢ Libertation of Civilians	...	.80	.25
1544	43¢ Crossing the Rhine	...	.80	.25
1545	88¢ Canadian Art "Floraison"	6.75	1.50	.75
1546	(43¢) Canada Flag over Lake	3.60	.85	.25
1547	(43¢) Louisbourg Harbor, ships near Dauphin Gate	...	.85	.25
1548	(43¢) Walls, streets & buildings of Louisbourg	...	.85	.25
1549	(43¢) Museum behind King's Bastion	...	.85	.25
1550	(43¢) Drawing of King's Garden, Convent, Hospital & barracks	...	.85	.25
1551	(43¢) Partially eroded fortifications	...	.85	.25
1551a	(43¢) Fortress of Louisbourg, strip of 5	...	4.00	3.00
1551b	(43¢) Fortress of Louisbourg, booklet pane of 10	...	8.00	5.00
1552	43¢-88¢ Historic Land Vehicles/Farm and Frontier souvenir sheet of 6	...	6.00	5.75
1553	43¢ Banff Springs Golf Club	...	.85	.25
1554	43¢ Riverside Country Club	...	.85	.25
1555	43¢ Glen Abbey Golf Club	...	.85	.25
1556	43¢ Victoria Golf Club	...	.85	.25
1557	43¢ Royal Montreal Golf Club	...	.85	.25
1557a	43¢ Royal Canadian Golf Assoc., strip of 5	...	4.00	3.00
1557b	43¢ Royal Canadian Golf Assoc., booklet pane of 10	...	8.00	5.00
1558	43¢ Lunenberg Academy Centennial	3.60	.80	.25
1559-61	43¢ Group of Seven 75th Anniv. 3 souv. sheets (2 w/3 stamps and 1 w/4 stamps)	...	8.00	7.50
1562	43¢ Winnipeg, Manitoba 125th Anniversary	3.60	.80	.25
1563-66	Migratory Wildlife, attached	3.60	3.00	2.25
1563, 65-67	Migratory Wildlife, attached (revised inscription)	3.60	3.00	2.25
1563	45¢ Monarch Butterfly	...	.80	.25
1564	45¢ Belted Kingfisher	...	.80	.25
1565	45¢ Northern Pintail	...	.80	.25
1566	45¢ Hoary Bat	...	.80	.25
1568-69	45¢ Canadian Memorial College, Toronto, Greetings Booklet (10 stamps w/15 stickers)	...	10.00	...
1570-73	45¢ Canadian Bridges, attached	3.60	3.00	2.25
1570	45¢ Quebec Bridge, Quebec	...	.80	.25
1571	45¢ Highway 403-401-410 interchange, Ontario	...	.80	.25
1572	45¢ Hartland Covered Wooden Bridge, New Brunswick	...	.80	.25
1573	45¢ Alex Fraser Bridger, British Columbia	...	.80	.25

1546

1547

1553

1558

1559a

1562

1563

1570

1574

Canada Postage #1574-1615e

SCOTT NO.	DESCRIPTION	PLATE BLOCK F/NH	UNUSED F/NH	USED F
1574	45¢ Polar bear, caribou	....	.80	.25
1575	45¢ Arctic poppy, cargo canoe	....	.80	.25
1576	45¢ Inuk man, igloo, sled dogs	....	.80	.25
1577	45¢ Dog-sled team, ski plane	....	.80	.25
1578	45¢ Children	....	.80	.25
1578a	45¢ Canadian Arctic, strip of 5	....	4.00	3.00
1578b	45¢ Canadian Arctic, booklet pane of 10	....	8.00	5.00
1579	45¢ Superman	....	.80	.25
1580	45¢ Johnny Canuck	....	.80	.25
1581	45¢ Nelvana	....	.80	.25
1582	45¢ Captain Canuck	....	.80	.25
1583	45¢ Fleur de Lys	....	.80	.25
1583a	45¢ Comic Book Characters, strip of 5	....	4.00	3.00
1583b	45¢ Comic Book Characters, booklet pane of 10	....	8.00	5.00
1584	45¢ United Nations, 50th Anniversary	3.60	.80	.25
1585	45¢ The Nativity	3.60	.80	.25
1585a	same, booklet pane of 10	....	8.00	....
1586	52¢ The Annunciation	4.10	.95	.30
1586a	same, booklet pane of 5	....	4.75	....
1587	90¢ Flight to Egypt	6.95	1.55	.50
1587a	same, booklet pane of 5	....	7.75	....
1588	40¢ Holly, booklet single	....	.80	.25
1588a	same, booklet pane of 10	....	7.50	....
1589	45¢ La Francophonie's Agency, 25th Anniversary	3.60	.80	.25
1590	45¢ End of the Holocaust, 50th Anniversary	3.60	.80	.25

SCOTT NO.	DESCRIPTION	PLATE BLOCK F/NH	UNUSED F/NH	USED F
	1996 COMMEMORATIVES			
1591-98, 1602-03, 1606-14, 1617-21, 1622-29, 36 varieties		41.25	32.10	13.25
1591-94	Birds, attached	3.60	3.00	2.00
1591	45¢ American Kestrel	....	.85	.35
1592	45¢ Atlantic Puffin	....	.85	.35
1593	45¢ Pileated Woodpecker	....	.85	.35
1594	45¢ Ruby-throated Hummingbird	....	.85	.35
1595-98	High Technology Industries, attached	3.60	4.00	3.00
1595	45¢ Ocean technology	....	1.10	.45
1596	45¢ Aerospace technology	....	1.10	.45
1597	45¢ Information technology	....	1.10	.45
1598	45¢ Biotechnology	....	1.10	.45
1600-01	Special Occasions, Greetings Booklet (10 stamps w/35 stickers)	....	10.00	....
1602	90¢ Canadian Art—"The Spirit of Haida Gwaii"	6.95	1.55	.50
1603	45¢ AIDS Awareness	3.60	.80	.25
1604	45¢-90¢ Historic Canadian Industrial & Commercial Vehicles souvenir sheet of 6	....	6.50	5.00
1605	5¢-45¢ CAPEX '96 souvenir pane of 25 vehicle stamps	....	8.00	5.00
1606	45¢ Yukon Gold Rush centennial, strip of 5	....	4.00	3.00
1606a	45¢ Jim Mason's discovery on Rabbit Creek, 1896	....	1.10	.45
1606b	45¢ Miners trekking to gold fields, boats on Lake Laberge	....	1.10	.45
1606c	45¢ Supr. Sam Steele, North West Mounted Police	....	1.10	.45
1606d	45¢ Dawson, boom town, city of entertainment	....	1.10	.45
1606e	45¢ Klondike gold fields	....	1.10	.45
1607	45¢ Canada Day (Maple Leaf), self-adhesive	....	.80	.25
1607a	same, pane of 12	....	12.00	....
1608	45¢ Ethel Catherwood, high jump, 1928	....	1.10	.45
1609	45¢ Etienne Desmarteau, 56 lb. weight throw, 1904	....	1.10	.45
1610	45¢ Fanny Rosenfeld, 100m, 400m relay, 1928	....	1.10	.45
1611	45¢ Gerald Ouellette, smallbore, rifle, prone, 1956	....	1.10	.45
1612	45¢ Percy Williams, 100m, 200m, 1928	....	1.10	.45
1612a	45¢ Canadian Gold Medalists, strip of 5	....	4.00	3.00
1612b	45¢ Canadian Gold Medalists, booklet pane of 10	....	10.00	....
1613	45¢ 125th Anniv. of British Columbia's Entry into Confederation	3.60	.80	.25
1614	45¢ Canadian Heraldy	3.60	.80	.25
1615	45¢ Motion Pictures Centennial, self-adhesive, sheet of 5	....	3.75	2.75
1615a	45¢ L'arrivee d'un train en gate, Lumiere cinematography, 1896	....	.80	.50
1615b	45¢ Back to God's Country, Nell & Ernest Shipman, 1919	....	.80	.50
1615c	45¢ Hen Hop, Norman McLaren, 1942	....	.80	.50
1615d	45¢ Pour la suite du monde, Pierre Perrault, Michel Brault, 1963	....	.80	.50
1615e	45¢ Goin' Down the Road, Don Shebib, 1970	....	.80	.50

1579

1585

1584

1588

1589

1590

1591

1595

1600

1602

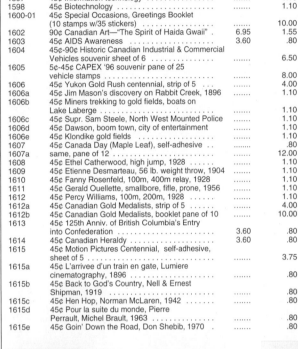

1603

1604a

1607

1606a

1608

1613

1614

1615a

1617

Canada Postage #1616-1707b

1618

1622

1627

1645

1647

1650

SCOTT NO.	DESCRIPTION	PLATE BLOCK F/NH	UNUSED F/NH	USED F
1616	45¢ Motion Pictures Centennial, self-adhesive, sheet of 5	....	3.75	2.00
1616a	45¢ Mon oncle Antoine, Claude Jutra, 1971	....	.80	.25
1616b	45¢ The Apprenticeship of Duddy Kravitz, Ted Kotcheff, 1974	....	.80	.25
1616c	45¢ Les Ordres, Michel Brault, 1974	....	.80	.25
1616d	45¢ Les Bons Debarras, Francis Mankiewicz, 1980	....	.80	.25
1616e	45¢ The Grey Fox, Phillip Borsos, 1982	....	.80	.25
1617	45¢ Edouard Montpetit, Educator	3.60	.80	.25
1618-21	Winnie the Pooh, attached	3.60	2.70	1.50
1618	45¢ Winnie, Lt. Colebourne, 1914	....	.80	.25
1619	45¢ Winnie, Christopher Robin, 1925	....	.80	.25
1620	45¢ Milne and Shepard's Winnie the Pooh, 1926	....	.80	.25
1621	45¢ Winnie the Pooh at Walt Disney World, 1996	....	.80	.25
1621b	same, souvenir sheet of 4 (#1618-21)	....	3.00	2.50
......	same, booklet pane of 8 (2 blocks, #1618-21)	....	5.50	4.50
......	same, 2 booklet panes plus souvenir book	....	10.75	....
1622	45¢ Margaret Laurence (1926-1987)	....	.80	.25
1623	45¢ Donald G. Creighton (1902-1979)	....	.80	.25
1624	45¢ Gabrielle Roy (1909-1983)	....	.80	.25
1625	45¢ Felix-Antoine Savard (1896-1982)	....	.80	.25
1626	45¢ Thomas C. Haliburton (1796-1865)	....	.80	.25
1626a	45¢ Canadian Authors, strip of 5	....	3.75	2.00
1626b	45¢ Canadian Authors, booklet pane of 10	....	7.50	4.00
1627	45¢ Children on snowshoes, sled	3.60	.80	.25
1627a	same, booklet pane of 10	....	7.50	....
1628	52¢ Santa Claus skiing	4.10	.95	.30
1628a	same, booklet pane of 5	....	4.75	....
1629	90¢ Children skating	6.95	1.55	.50
1629a	same, booklet pane of 5	....	7.75	....

1997 COMMEMORATIVES

SCOTT NO.	DESCRIPTION	PLATE BLOCK F/NH	UNUSED F/NH	USED F
1630, 1631-48, 1649-72, 43 varieties		90.00	34.00	11.50
1630	45¢ New Year 1997 (Year of the Ox)	....	1.10	.60
1630a	same, souvenir sheet of 2	....	2.25	2.10
......	same, souvenir sheet of 2, with Hong Kong '97 overprint	....	6.00	....
1631-34	Birds of Canada, attached	3.75	2.70	1.50
1631	45¢ Mountain bluebird	....	.80	.25
1632	45¢ Western grebe	....	.80	.25
1633	45¢ Northern gannet	....	.80	.25
1634	45¢ Scarlet tanager	....	.80	.25
1635	90¢ Canadian Art "York Boat on Lake Winnipeg"	6.95	1.55	.50
1636	45¢ Canadian Tire, 75th Anniv.	3.75	.80	.25
1637	45¢ Father Charles-Emile Gadbois (1906-1981)	3.75	.80	.25
1638	45¢ Blue poppy	....	.80	.25
1638a	same, booklet pane of 12	....	9.50	....
1639	45¢ Victorian Order of Nurses	3.75	.80	.25
1640	45¢ Law Society of Upper Canada	3.75	.80	.25
1641-44	45¢ Ocean Fish, attached	3.75	3.00	1.75
1641	45¢ Great White Shark	....	.80	.25
1642	45¢ Pacific Halibut	....	.80	.25
1643	45¢ Atlantic Sturgeon	....	.80	.25
1644	45¢ Bluefin Tuna	....	.80	.25
1645-46	45¢ Confederation Bridge, attached	3.75	1.55	.90
1645	45¢ Lighthouse and Bridge	....	.80	.25
1646	45¢ Bridge and Bird	....	.80	.25
1647	45¢ Gilles Villeneuve, Formula 1 driver	3.75	.80	.25
1648	90¢ Gilles Villeneuve, Formula 1 d iver	7.25	1.60	.80
1648b	45¢-90¢ Gilles Villeneuve, souvenir sheet of 8	....	8.50	....
1649	45¢ John Cabot	3.75	.80	.25
1650-53	45¢ Canada's scenic highways (Canada Day), attached	3.75	3.00	1.75
1650	45¢ Sea to Sky Highway, British Columbia	....	.80	.25
1651	45¢ The Cabot Trail, Nova Scotia	....	.80	.25
1652	45¢ The Wine Route, starting in Ontario	....	.80	.25
1653	45¢ The Big Muddy, Saskatchewan	....	.80	.25
1654	45¢ Industrial Design	3.75	.80	.25
1654v	same, sheet of 24 w/12 different Labels	....	18.75	....
1655	45¢ Highland Games	3.75	.80	.25
1656	45¢ Knights of Columbus in Canada	3.75	.80	.25
1657	45¢ World Congress of the PTT	3.75	.80	.25
1658	45¢ Canada's Year of Asia Pacific	3.60	.80	.25
1659-60	45¢ Ice Hockey "Series of the Century", bklt singles	....	1.60	.70
1660a	same, bklt pane of 10 (5 of each)	....	8.00	....
1661-64	Famous Politicians, attached	3.75	3.00	1.75
1661	45¢ Martha Black	....	.80	.25
1662	45¢ Lionel Chevrier	....	.80	.25
1663	45¢ Judy LaMarsh	....	.80	.25
1664	45¢ Real Caouette	....	.80	.25
1665-68	Supernatural, 4 attached	3.75	3.00	1.75
1665	45¢ Vampire	....	.80	.25
1666	45¢ Werewolf	....	.80	.25
1667	45¢ Ghost	....	.80	.25
1668	45¢ Goblin	....	.80	.25
1669	45¢ Christmas, Stained Glass Window	3.60	.80	.25
1669a	same, bklt pane of 10	....	7.50	....
1670	52¢ Christmas, Stained Glass Window	4.10	.95	.30
1670a	same, bklt pane of 5	....	4.75	....
1671	90¢ Christmas, Stained Glass Window	6.95	1.55	.50
1671a	same, bklt pane of 5	....	7.75	....
1672	45¢ 75th Royal Agriculture Winter Fair, Toronto	3.60	.80	.25

1997-2000 Regular Issues

SCOTT NO.	DESCRIPTION	PLATE BLOCK F/NH	UNUSED F/NH	USED F
1673	1¢ Bookbinding	.80	.20	.15
1674	2¢ Ironwork	.80	.20	.15
1675	3¢ Glass blowing	.80	.20	.15
1676	4¢ Oyster farmer	.80	.20	.15
1677	5¢ Weaving	.80	.20	.15
1678	9¢ Quilting	1.00	.25	.15
1679	10¢ Artistic woodworking	1.10	.25	.15
1680	25¢ Leatherworking	2.00	.50	.15
1682	46¢ Queen Elizabeth II	3.75	.80	.25
1683	47¢ Queen Elizabeth II(2000)	3.75	.85	.25
1687	46¢ Flag over Mountains	3.75	.80	.25
1687a	same, bklt pane of 10	....	8.00	....
1692	55¢ Maple Leaf	4.75	1.10	.35
1692a	same, bklt pane of 5	....	5.50	....
1694	73¢ Maple Leaf	5.00	1.20	.35
1696	95¢ Maple Leaf	6.25	1.50	.50
1696a	same, bklt pane of 5	....	7.50	....
1697	$1 Loon	7.50	1.50	1.00
1698	$2 Polar Bear	14.50	3.25	2.50
1700	$8 Grizzly Bear	65.00	14.00	6.50
1703	46¢ Flag, coil	....	.80	.25
1705	46¢ Flag over Mountains, self-adhesive	....	.80	.25
1705a	same, bklt pane of 30	....	24.00	....
1706	46¢ Maple Leaf, self-adhesive	....	.80	.25
1706a	same, bklt pane of 18	....	14.50	....
1707	47¢ Flag and Inukshuk, self-adhesive	....	.85	.25
1707a	same, bklt pane of 10	....	8.25	....
1707b	same, bklt pane of 30	....	24.00	....

1630

1631

1635

1636

1637

1638

1639

1640

1641

1659

1661

1665

Canada Postage #1708-1777b

1708

1709a

1710

1750

1756

1761

1764

1714

1715

1721

1722

1723

1735

1736

1739

1767

1770

1998 COMMEMORATIVES

No.	Description			
1708	45¢ Year of the Tiger	3.60	.80	.25
1708a	same, souvenir sheet of 2	....	1.65	1.30
1709	45¢ Provincial Leaders, sheetlet of 10	....	8.50	7.00
1710-13	Birds, attached	3.75	3.00	1.75
1710	45¢ Hairy Woodpecker	....	.80	.25
1711	45¢ Great Crested Flycatcher	....	.80	.25
1712	45¢ Eastern Screech Owl	....	.80	.25
1713	45¢ Gray Crowned Rosy-Finch	....	.80	.25
1714	45¢ Maple Leaf, self-adhesive, bklt single	....	1.50	.95
1714a	same, bklt pane of 18	....	25.00	....
1714B	45¢ Maple Leaf, self-adhesive, die cut perf. 13	....	.80	.25
1715-20	Fly Fishing, strip of 6, from bklt pane	....	4.75	4.00
1715	45¢ Coquihalla orange, steelhead trout	....	.80	.25
1716	45¢ Steelhead bee, steelhead trout	....	.80	.25
1717	45¢ Dark Montreal, brook trout	....	.80	.25
1718	45¢ Lady Amherst, Atlantic salmon	....	.80	.25
1719	45¢ Coho blue, coho salmon	....	.80	.25
1720	45¢ Cosseboom special, Atlantic salmon	....	.80	.25
1720a	same, bklt pane of 12	....	9.25	....
1721	45¢ Canadian Inst. of Mining Centennial	3.60	.80	.25
1722	45¢ Imperial Penny Post Centennial	3.60	.80	.25
1723-24	Sumo Wrestling Tournament, attached	3.60	1.60	1.50
1723	45¢ Rising sun, Mapleleaf and two wrestlers	....	.80	.25
1724	45¢ Rising sun, Mapleleaf and Sumo champion	....	.80	.25
1724b	45¢ Sumo Wrestling Tournament, souvenir sheet of 2	....	1.75	1.60
1725	45¢ St. Peters Canal, Nova Scotia	....	.80	.60
1726	45¢ St. Ours Canal, Quebec	....	.80	.60
1727	45¢ Port Carling Lock, Ontario	....	.80	.60
1728	45¢ Locks, Rideau Canal, Ontario	....	.80	.60
1729	45¢ Peterborough lift lock, Trent-Severn Waterway, Ontario	....	.80	.60
1730	45¢ Chambly Canal, Quebec	....	.80	.60
1731	45¢ Lachine Canal, Quebec	....	.80	.60
1732	45¢ Ice skating on Rideau Canal, Ottawa	....	.80	.60
1733	45¢ Boat on Big Chute Marine Railway, Trent-Severn Waterway	....	.80	.60
1734	45¢ Sault Ste. Marie Canal, Ontario	....	.80	.60
1734a	45¢ Canals of Canada, bklt pane of 10 plus labels	....	8.00	....
1735	45¢ Health Professionals	....	.80	.25
1736-37	Royal Canadian Mounted Police 125th Anniv. attd.	3.60	1.60	1.50
1736	45¢ Male mountie, native horse	....	.80	.25
1737	45¢ Female mountie, helicopter, cityscape	....	.80	.25
1737b	same, souvenir sheet of 2	....	3.00	2.75
1737c	same, souvenir sheet of 2 with signature	....	4.00	3.50
1737d	same, souvvenir sheet of 2 with Portugal '98 emblem	....	4.00	3.50
1737e	same, souvenir sheet of 2 with Italia '98 emblem	....	4.00	3.50
1738	45¢ William Roue, designer of Bluenose	3.60	.80	.25
1739-42	Scenic Highways, 4 attached	3.60	3.00	1.75
1739	45¢ Dempster Highway, Yukon	....	.80	.25
1740	45¢ Dinosaur Trail, Alberta	....	.80	.25
1741	45¢ River Valley, Scenic Drive, New Burnswick	....	.80	.25
1742	45¢ Blue Heron Route, Prince Edward Isalnd	....	.80	.25
1743	45¢ "Peinture", Jean-Paul Riopelle, self-adhesive	....	.80	.25
1744	45¢ "La demiere campagne de Napolean", Fernand Leduc, self-adhesive	....	.80	.25
1745	45¢ "Jet fulignieux sur noir torture", Jean -Paul Monusseau, self-adhesive	....	.80	.25
1746	45¢ "Le fond du garde-robe", Pierre Gauvreau, self-adhesive	....	.80	.25
1747	45¢ "Jean lacustre", Paul-Emile Borduas, self-adhesive	....	.80	.25
1748	45¢ "Syndicat des gens de met", Marcelle Ferron, self-adhesive	....	.80	.25
1749	45¢ "Le tumulte a la machoire crispee", Marcel Barbeau, self-adhesive	....	.80	.25
1749a	45¢ The Automatists, 50th Anniversary, self-adhesive, bklt pane of 7	....	5.75	....
1750-53	Canadian Legendary Heroes, 4 attached	3.60	3.00	1.75
1750	45¢ Napoleon-Alexandre Comeau (1848-1923) outdoorsman	....	.80	.25
1751	45¢ Phyllis Munday (1894-1990), mountaineer	....	.80	.25
1752	45¢ Bill Mason (1929-1988), film maker	....	.80	.25
1753	45¢ Harry "Red" Foster (1905-1985), sports enthusiast	....	.80	.25
1754	90¢ Canadian Art "The Farmer's Family"	6.95	1.55	.50
1755	45¢ Housing in Canada, sheetlet of 9	....	7.50	6.00
1756	45¢ University of Ottawa, 150th Anniversary	3.60	.80	.25
1757	45¢ Elephant, bear performing tricks	....	.80	.25
1758	45¢ Women standing on horse, aerial act	....	.80	.25
1759	45¢ Lion tamer	....	.80	.25
1760	45¢ Contortionists, acrobats	....	.80	.25
1760a	45¢ The Circus, bklt pane of 12	....	9.75	....
1760b	same, souvenir sheet of 4	....	3.00	2.50
1761	45¢ John Peters Humphrey, Human Rights author	3.60	.80	.25
1762-63	Canadian Naval Reserve, 75th Anniversary, attached	3.75	1.55	.90
1762	45¢ HMCS Sackville	....	.80	.25
1763	45¢ HMCS Shawinigan	....	.80	.25
1764	45¢ Christmas, Sculpted wooden angels	3.60	.80	.25
1764a	same, bklt pane of 10	....	7.50	....
1765	52¢ Christmas, Sculpted wooden angels	4.10	.95	.30
1765a	same, bklt pane of 5	....	4.75	....
1766	90¢ Christmas, Sculpted wooden angels	6.95	1.55	.50
1766a	same, bklt pane of 5	....	7.75	....

1999 COMMEMORATIVES

No.	Description			
1767	46¢ New Year 1999, Year of the Rabbit	3.60	.80	.25
1768	same, souvenir sheet of 2	....	1.75	1.25
1769	46¢ Le Theatre du Rideau Vert, 50th Anniversary	3.60	.80	.25
1770-73	Birds, 4 attached	3.60	3.00	1.75
1770	46¢ Northern goshawk	....	.80	.25
1771	46¢ Red-winged blackbird	....	.80	.25
1772	46¢ American goldfinch	....	.80	.25
1773	46¢ Sandhill crane	....	.80	.25
1774	46¢ Northern goshawk, self-adhesive	....	.80	.25
1775	46¢ Red-winged blackbird, self-adhesive	....	.80	.25
1776	46¢ American goldfinch, self-adhesive	....	.80	.25
1777	46¢ Sandhill crane, self-adhesive	....	.80	.25
1777a	same, bklt pane of 6 (1774 x 2, 1775 x 2, 1777 x 1), self-adhesive	....	4.90	....
1777b	same, bklt pane of 6 (1774 x 1, 1775 x 1, 1776 x 2, 1777 x 2), self-adhesive	....	4.90	....

Canada Postage #1778-1817a

1999 COMMEMORATIVES (continued)

SCOTT NO.	DESCRIPTION	PLATE BLOCK F/NH	UNUSED F/NH	USED F
1778	46¢ Univ. of British Columbia Museum of Anthropology, 50th Anniversary	3.60	.80	.25
1779	46¢ Sailing Ship Marco Polo	3.60	.80	.25
1779a	same, souvenir sheet of 2 (1779 x 1, Australia 1631 x 1)	....	2.25	....
1780-83	Canada's Scenic Highways, 4 attached	3.60	3.00	1.75
1780	46¢ Gaspe Peninsula, Highway 132, Quebec	....	.80	.25
1781	46¢ Yellowhead Highway (PTH 16), Manitoba	....	.80	.25
1782	46¢ Dempster Highway 8, Northwest Territories	....	.80	.25
1783	46¢ Discovery Trail, Route 230N, Newfoundland	....	.80	.25
1784	46¢ Creation of the Nunavnt Territory	3.60	.80	.25
1785	46¢ International Year of Older Persons	3.60	.80	.25
1786	46¢ Baisakhi, Religious Holiday of Sikh Canadians, 300 th Anniversary	3.60	.80	.25
1787	46¢ Canadian orchid, Arethusa bulbosa, self-adhesive	....	.80	.25
1788	46¢ Canadian orchid, Amerorchis rotundifolia, self-adhesive	....	.80	.25
1789	46¢ Canadian orchid, Platanthera psycodes, self-adhesive	....	.80	.25
1790	46¢ Canadian orchid, Cypripedium pubescens, self-adhesive	....	.80	.25
1790a	same, bklt pane of 12 (1787-90 x 3)	....	9.50	....
1790b	same, souvenir sheet of 4 w/ China '99 emblem	....	4.00	3.50
1791-94	Horses, 4 attached	3.60	3.00	1.75
1791	46¢ Northern Dancer, thorough-bred race horse	....	.80	.25
1792	46¢ Kingsway Skoal, bucking horse	....	.80	.25
1793	46¢ Big Ben, show horse	....	.80	.25
1794	46¢ Ambro Flight, harness race horse	....	.80	.25
1795	46¢ Northern Dancer, thorough-bred race horse, self-adhesive	....	.80	.25
1796	46¢ Kingsway Skoal, bucking horse, self-adhesive	....	.80	.25
1797	46¢ Big Ben, show horse, self-adhesive	....	.80	.25
1798	46¢ Ambro Flight, harness race horse, self-adhesive	....	.80	.25
1789a	same, bklt of 12 (1795-98 x 3)	....	9.50	....
1799	46¢ Quebec Bar Association, 150th Anniversary	3.60	.80	.25
1800	95¢ Canadian Art "Unicorn Rooster"	7.25	1.65	.50
1801-04	46¢ Pan-American Games XIII, 4 attached	3.60	.80	.25
1801	46¢ Track & Field	....	.80	.25
1802	46¢ Cycling, weight lifting, gymnastics	....	.80	.25
1803	46¢ Swimming, sailboarding, kayaking	....	.80	.25
1804	46¢ Soccer, tennis, medals winners	....	.80	.25
1805	46¢ World Rowing Championships	3.60	.80	.25
1806	46¢ Universal Postal Union	3.60	.80	.25
1807	46¢ Canadian Int. Air Show, 50th Anniv., sheetlet of 4	....	3.25	3.00
1807a	46¢ Fokker DR-1, CT-114 Tutors	....	.80	.25
1807b	46¢ Tutors, H101 Salto sailplane	....	.80	.25
1807c	46¢ De Havilland DH100 Vampire MKIII	....	.80	.25
1807b	46¢ Stearman A-75	....	.80	.25
1808	46¢ Royal Canadian Air Force, 75th Anniv, sheetlet of 6	....	12.75	11.00
1808a	46¢ De Havilland Mosquito FVBI	....	.80	.25
1808b	46¢ Sopwith F1 Camel	....	.80	.25
1808c	46¢ De Havilland Canada DHC-3 Otter	....	.80	.25
1808d	46¢ De Havilland Canada CC-108 Caribou	....	.80	.25
1808e	46¢ Canadair DL-28 Argus MK 2	....	.80	.25
1808f	46¢ North American F86 Sabre 6	....	.80	.25
1808g	46¢ McDonnell Douglas CF-18 Hornet	....	.80	.25
1808h	46¢ Sopwith SF-1 Dolphin	....	.80	.25
1808i	46¢ Armstrong Whitworth Siskin IIIA	....	.80	.25
1808j	46¢ Canadian Vickers (Northrop) Delta II	....	.80	.25
1808k	46¢ Sikorsky CH-124A Sea King Helicopter	....	.80	.25
1808l	46¢ Vickers-Armstrong Wellington MKII	....	.80	.25
1808m	46¢ Avro Anson MKI	....	.80	.25
1808n	46¢ Canadair (Lockheed) CF-104G Starfighter	....	.80	.25
1808o	46¢ Burgess-Dunne seaplane	....	.80	.25
1808p	46¢ Avro 504K	....	.80	.25
1809	46¢ NATO, 50th Anniversary	3.60	.80	.25
1810	46¢ Frontier College, 100th Anniversary	3.60	.80	.25
1811	33¢ Kites, bklt pane of 8	....	6.50	....
1811a	33¢ Master Control, sport kite by Lam Hoac (triangular)	....	.80	.25
1811b	33¢ Indian Garden Flying Carpet, edo kite by Skye Morrison (trapezoidal)	....	.80	.25
1811c	33¢ Gibson Girl, Manufactured box kite (rectangular)	....	.80	.25
1811d	33¢ Dragon centipede kite by Zhang tian Wei (oval)	....	.80	.25
1812	Holographic Dove & 2000	....	.80	.25
....	same, pane of 4	....	3.25	....
1813	55¢ Girl & Dove	....	.95	.30
....	same, pane of 4	....	3.80	....
1814	95¢ Millenium Dove	....	1.55	.50
....	same, pane of 4	....	6.25	....
1815	46¢ Christmas, Angel, drum	3.60	.80	.25
1815a	same, bklt pane of 10	....	7.50	....
1816	55¢ Christmas, Angel, toys	4.10	.95	.30
1816a	same, bklt pane of	....	4.75	....
1817	95¢ Christmas, Angel, candle	6.95	1.55	.50
1817a	same, bklt pane of 5	....	7.75	....

Canada Postage #1818-1831d

SCOTT NO.	DESCRIPTION	PLATE BLOCK F/NH	UNUSED F/NH	USED F

1818a   1819a   1820a

SCOTT NO.	DESCRIPTION	PLATE BLOCK F/NH	UNUSED F/NH	USED F
1818	46¢ Millenium Collection-Media Tech. sheet of 4	....	3.25	....
1818a	46¢ IMAX Movies	....	.80	.25
1818b	46¢ Softimage animation software	....	.80	.25
1818c	46¢ Ted Rogers Sr. (1900-39) and radio tube	....	.80	.25
1818d	46¢ Invention of radio facsimile device by Sir William Stephenson (1896-1989)	....	.80	.25
1819	46¢ Millenium Collection-Canadian Entertainment, sheet of 4	....	3.25	....
1819a	46¢ Calgary Stampede	....	.80	.25
1819b	46¢ Performers from Cirque du Soleil	....	.80	.25
1819c	46¢ Hockey Night in Canada	....	.80	.25
1819d	46¢ La Soiree du Hockey	....	.80	.25
1820	46¢ Millenium Collection-Entertainers, sheet of 4	....	3.25	....
1820a	46¢ Portia White (1911-68), singer	....	.80	.25
1820b	46¢ Glenn Gould (1932-82), pianist	....	.80	.25
1820c	46¢ Guy Lombardo (1902-77), band leader	....	.80	.25
1820d	46¢ Felix Leclerc (1914-88), singer, guitarist	....	.80	.25

1821a   1822a   1823a

SCOTT NO.	DESCRIPTION	PLATE BLOCK F/NH	UNUSED F/NH	USED F
1821	46¢ Millenium Collection-Fostering Canadian Talent, sheet of 4	....	3.25	....
1821a	46¢ Royal Canadian Academy of Arts (men viewing painting)	....	.80	.25
1821b	46¢ Canada Council (sky, musical staff, "A")	....	.80	.25
1821c	46¢ National Film Board of Canada	....	.80	.25
1821d	46¢ Canadian Broadcasting Corp.	....	.80	.25
1822	46¢ Millenium Collection-Medical Innovators, sheet of 4	....	3.25	....
1822a	46¢ Sir Frederic Banting (1891-1941), co-discoverer of insulin, syringe and dog	....	.80	.25
1822b	46¢ Dr. Armand Frappier (1904-91), microbiologist, holding flask	....	.80	.25
1822c	46¢ Dr. Hans Selye (1907-82), endocrinologist and molecular diagram	....	.80	.25
1822d	46¢ Maude Abbott (1869-1940), pathologist, and roses	....	.80	.25
1823	46¢ Millenium Collection-Social Progress, sheet of 4	....	3.25	....
1823a	46¢ Nun, doctor, hospital	....	.80	.25
1823b	46¢ Statue of women holding decree	....	.80	.25
1823c	46¢ Alphonse Desjardins (1854-1920) and wife, credit union founders	....	.80	.25
1823d	46¢ Father Moses Coady (1882-1959), educator of adults	....	.80	.25

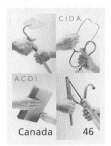   

1824a   1825a

SCOTT NO.	DESCRIPTION	PLATE BLOCK F/NH	UNUSED F/NH	USED F
1824	46¢ Millenium Collection-Charity, sheet of 4	....	3.25	....
1824a	46¢ Canadian Inter. Development Agency (hand and tools)	....	.80	.25
1824b	46¢ Dr. Lucille Teasdale (1929-96), hospital administrator in Uganda	....	.80	.25
1824c	46¢ Marathon of Hope inspired by Terry Fox (1958-81)	....	.80	.25
1824d	46¢ Meals on Wheels program	....	.80	.25
1825	46¢ Millenium Collection-Humanitarians and Peacekeepers, sheet of 4	....	3.25	....
1825a	46¢ Raoul Dandurand (1861-1942)	....	.80	.25
1825b	46¢ Pauline Vanier (1898-1991), Elizabeth Smellie (1884-1968) nurses	....	.80	.25
1825c	46¢ Lester B. Pearson (1897-1972), prime minister and Nobel Peace Prize winner	....	.80	.25
1825d	46¢ Amputee and shadow (Ottawa Convention on Land Mines)	....	.80	.25

1826a   1827a   1828a

2000 COMMEMORATIVES

SCOTT NO.	DESCRIPTION	PLATE BLOCK F/NH	UNUSED F/NH	USED F
1826	46¢ Millenium Collection-Canada's First People, sheet of 4	....	3.25	....
1826a	46¢ Chief Pontiac (c.1720-69)	....	.80	.25
1826b	46¢ Tom Longboat (1887-1949), marathon runner	....	.80	.25
1826c	46¢ Inuit sculpture of shaman	....	.80	.25
1826d	46¢ Medicine man	....	.80	.25
1827	46¢ Millenium Collection-Canada's Cultural Fabric, sheet of 4	....	3.25	....
1827a	46¢ Norse boat, L'Anse aux Meadows	....	.80	.25
1827b	46¢ Immigrants on Halifax Pier 21	....	.80	.25
1827c	46¢ Neptune Theater, Halifax (head of Neptune)	....	.80	.25
1827d	46¢ Stratford Festival (actor and theater)	....	.80	.25
1828	46¢ Millenium Collection-Literary Legends, sheet of 4	....	3.25	....
1828a	46¢ W.O. Mitchell (1914-98), novelist, and prairie scene	....	.80	.25
1828b	46¢ Gratien Gelinas (1909-99), actor and playwright, and stars	....	.80	.25
1828c	46¢ Le Cercle du Livre de France book club	....	.80	.25
1828d	46¢ Harlequin paperback books	....	.80	.25

1829a   1830a   1831a

SCOTT NO.	DESCRIPTION	PLATE BLOCK F/NH	UNUSED F/NH	USED F
1829	46¢ Millenium Collection-Great Thinkers, sheet of 4	....	3.25	....
1829a	46¢ Marshall McLuhan (1911-80), philosopher, and television set	....	.80	.25
1829b	46¢ Northrop Frye (1912-91), literary critic, and word "code"	....	.80	.25
1829c	46¢ Roger Lemelin (1919-92), novelist, and cast of "The Plouffe Family" TV series	....	.80	.25
1829d	46¢ Hilda Marion Neatby (1904-75), historian, and farm scene	....	.80	.25
1830	46¢ Millenium Collection-A Tradition of Generosity, sheet of 4	....	3.25	....
1830a	46¢ Hart Massey (1823-96), Hart House, University of Toronto	....	.80	.25
1830b	46¢ Dorothy (1899-1965) & Izaak Killam (1885-1955), philantropists	....	.80	.25
1830c	46¢ Eric Lafferty Harvive (1892-1975), philantropist, and mountain scene	....	.80	.25
1830d	46¢ Macdonald Stewart Foundation	....	.80	.25
1831	46¢ Millenium Collection-Engineering and Tech. Marvels, sheet of 4	....	3.25	....
1831a	46¢ Map of Roger Pass, locomotive and tunnel diggers	....	.80	.25
1831b	46¢ Manic Dams	....	.80	.25
1831c	46¢ Canadian satellites, Remote Manipulator Arm	....	.80	.25
1831d	46¢ CN Tower	....	.80	.25

Canada Postage #1832-1877

SCOTT NO.	DESCRIPTION	PLATE BLOCK F/NH	UNUSED F/NH	USED F

1832a

1833a

1834a

SCOTT NO.	DESCRIPTION	PLATE BLOCK F/NH	UNUSED F/NH	USED F
1832	46¢ Millenium Collection-Fathers of Invention, sheet of 4	....	3.25	....
1832a	46¢ George Klein (1904-92), gearwheels	....	.80	.25
1832b	46¢ Abraham Gesner (1797-1864), beaker of kerosene and lamp	....	.80	.25
1832c	46¢ Alexander Graham Bell (1847-1922), passenger-carrying kite, hydrofoil	....	.80	.25
1832d	46¢ Joseph-Armand Bombardier (1907-64), snowmobile	....	.80	.25
1833	46¢ Millenium Collection-Food, sheet of 4	....	3.25	....
1833a	46¢ Sir Charles Saunders (1867-1937), Marquis wheat	....	.80	.25
1833b	46¢ Pablum	....	.80	.25
1833c	46¢ Dr. Archibald Gowanlock Huntsman (1883-1973), marketer of frozen fish	....	.80	.25
1833d	46¢ Products of McCain Foods, Ltd., tractor	....	.80	.25
1834	46¢ Millenium Collection-Enterprising Giants, sheet of 4	....	3.25	....
1834a	46¢ Hudson's Bay Company (Colonist, Indian, canoe)	....	.80	.25
1834b	46¢ Bell Canada Enterprises (earth, satellite, string of binary digits)	....	.80	.25
1834c	Vachon Co., snack cakes	....	.80	.25
1834d	46¢ George Weston Limited (Baked Goods, eggs)	....	.80	.25

1837a

1838a

1835	46¢ Millenium-2000	3.60	.80	.25
1836	46¢ New Year 2000, Year of the Dragon	3.60	.80	.25
1837	95¢ New Year 2000, Year of the Dragon, souvenir sheet of 1	....	1.75	1.60
1838	46¢ 50th National Hockey League All-Star, sheet 6	....	4.75	3.75
1838a	46¢ Wayne Gretsky (Oilers jersey No. 99)	....	.80	.25
1838b	46¢ Gordie Howe (Red Wings jersey No. 9)	....	.80	.25
1838c	46¢ Maurice Richard (red, white and blue Canadians jersey No. 9)	....	.80	.25
1838d	46¢ Doug Harvey (Canadiens jersey No. 2)	....	.80	.25
1838e	46¢ Bobby Orr (Bruins jersey No. 4)	....	.80	.25
1838f	46¢ Jacques Plante (Canadiens jersey No. 1)	....	.80	.25

1839

1847

1839-42	46¢ Birds, 4 attached	3.60	3.00	1.75
1839	46¢ Canada warbler	....	.80	.25
1840	46¢ Osprey	....	.80	.25
1841	46¢ Pacific Loon	....	.80	.25
1842	46¢ Blue Jay	....	.80	.25
1843	46¢ Canada warbler, self-adhesive	....	.80	.25
1844	46¢ Osprey, self-adhesive	....	.80	.25
1845	46¢ Pacific Loon, self-adhesive	....	.80	.25
1846	46¢ Blue Jay, self-adhesive	....	.80	.25
1846a	same, bklt pane of 6 (1843x2, 1844x2, 1845x1, 1846x1)	....	4.75	....
1846b	same, bklt pane of 6 (1843x1, 1844x1, 1845x2, 1846x2)	....	4.75	....
1847	46¢ Supreme Court, 125th Anniversary	3.60	.80	.25

1850

1854a

1848	46¢ Ritual of the Calling of an Engineer, 75 Anniv.	3.60	.80	.25
1848a	same, tete-beche pair	....	1.60	.50
1849	46¢ Decorated Rural Mailboxes, Ship, fish, house designs	....	.80	.25
1850	same, Flower, cow and church designs	....	.80	.25
1851	same, Tractor design	....	.80	.25
1852	same, Goose head, house designs	....	.80	.25
1852a	same, bklt pane of 12 (1849-52x3)	....	9.50	....
1853	46¢ Picture Frame, self-adhesive	....	.80	.25
1853a	same, bklt pane of 5 plus 5 labels	....	4.00	....
1853b	same, pane of 25	....	20.00	....
1854	55¢ Fresh Waters, bklt pane of 5, self-adhesive	....	4.75	....
1855	95¢ Fresh Waters, bklt pane of 5, self-adhesive	....	8.00	....

1856

1858

1856	46¢ Queen Mother's 100th Birthday	3.60	.80	.25
1857	46¢ Boys' and Girls' clubs, Centennial	3.60	.80	.25
1858	46¢ Seventh Day Adventists	3.60	.80	.25

1859

1866

1859-62	46¢ Stampin' the Future, 4 attached	3.60	3.00	1.75
1859	46¢ Rainbow, Spacevechile, astronauts, flag	....	.80	.25
1860	46¢ Children in space vechile, children on ground	....	.80	.25
1861	46¢ Children and map of Canada	....	.80	.25
1862	46¢ Two astronauts in space vechile, planets	....	.80	.25
1863	95¢ Canadian Artists, The Artist at Niagara	7.50	1.75	.50
1864-65	46¢ Tall Ships in Halifax Harbor, 2 attached	3.60	1.60	.95
1865a	same, bklt of 10 (1864-65 x 5)	....	8.25	....
1866	46¢ Department of Labor	3.60	.80	.25
1867	46¢ Petro-Canada, 25th anniversary	....	.80	.25
1867a	same, bklt pane of 12	....	9.50	....
1867b	same, die cut inverted (2 points at TL)	....	3.75	3.75

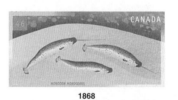
1868

1873

1876-77

1868-71	46¢ Centaceans, 4 attached	3.60	3.00	1.75
1868	46¢ Monodon monoceros	....	.80	.25
1869	46¢ Balaenoptera musculus	....	.80	.25
1870	46¢ Balaena mysticetus	....	.80	.25
1871	46¢ Delphinapterus leucas	....	.80	.25
1872	46¢ Christmas frame	....	.80	.25
1872a	same, bklt pane of 5 + 5 labels	....	4.00	....
1873	46¢ Adoration of the shepherds	3.60	.80	.25
1873a	same, bklt pane of 10	....	7.50	....
1874	55¢ Creche	4.10	.95	.30
1874a	same, bklt pane of 6	....	5.60	....
1875	95¢ Flight into Egypt	6.95	1.55	.50
1875a	same, bklt pane of 6	....	9.25	....
1876-77	46¢ Regiments, 2 attached	3.60	1.60	.95
1876	46¢ Lord Stratchcona's Horse Regiment	....	.80	.25
1877	46¢ Les Voltigeurs de Quebec	....	.80	.25

Canada Postage #1878-1924a

SCOTT NO.	DESCRIPTION	PLATE BLOCK F/NH	UNUSED F/NH	USED F
1878	47¢ Maple leaves, coil	....	.85	.25
1879	60¢ Red fox, coil	....	1.00	.40
1879a	same, bklt pane of 6	....	6.00	....
1880	75¢ Gray wolf, coil	....	1.25	.50
1881	$1.05 White-tailed deer, coil	....	1.50	.50
1881a	same, bklt pane of 6	....	9.00	....
1882	47¢ Picture Frame, self-adhesive	....	.85	.25
1882a	same, bklt pane of 5 + 5 labels	....	4.25	....
1883	47¢ Year of the Snake	3.75	.85	.25
1884	$1.05 Year of the Snake, souvenir sheet	....	1.50	.75

2001 COMMEMORATIVES

SCOTT NO.	DESCRIPTION	PLATE BLOCK F/NH	UNUSED F/NH	USED F
1885	47¢ National Hockey League, sheet of 6 + 3 labels	....	5.00	4.00
1885a	47¢ Jean Beliveau (Canadiens jersey No. 4)	....	.85	....
1885b	47¢ Terry Sawchuk (goalie in Red Wings uniform)	....	.85	....
1885c	47¢ Eddie Shore (Bruins jersey No.2)	....	.85	....
1885d	47¢ Denis Potvin (Islanders jersey No. 5)	....	.85	....
1885e	47¢ Bobby Bull (Black Hawks jersey No.9)	....	.85	....
1885f	47¢ Syl Apps, Sr. (Toronto Maple leafs jersey)	....	.85	....
1886-89	47¢ Birds, 4 attached	3.75	3.25	1.95
1886	47¢ Golden Eagle	....	.85	.25
1887	47¢ Arctic tern	....	.85	.25
1888	47¢ Rock ptarmigan	....	.85	.25
1889	47¢ Lapland longspur	....	.85	.25
1890	47¢ Golden Eagle, self-adhesive	....	.85	.25
1891	47¢ Artic tern, self-adhesive	....	.85	.25
1892	47¢ Rock ptarmigan, self-adhesive	....	.85	.25
1893	47¢ Lapland longspur, self-adhesive	....	.85	.25
1893a	same, bklt pane of 6 (1890 x 2, 1891 x 2, 1892 x 1, 1893 x 1)	....	5.00	....
1893b	same, bklt pane of 6 (1892 x 2, 1893 x 2, 1890 x 1, 1891 x 1)	....	5.00	....
1894-95	47¢ Games of La Francophonie, 2 attached	3.75	1.65	1.00
1894	47¢ High jumper	....	.85	.25
1895	47¢ Dancer	....	.85	.25
1896-99	47¢ World Figure Skating, 4 attached	3.75	3.25	1.95
1896	47¢ Pairs	....	.85	.25
1897	47¢ Ice dancing	....	.85	.25
1898	47¢ Men's singles	....	.85	.25
1899	47¢ Women's singles	....	.85	.25
1900	47¢ First Canadian postage stamp	3.75	.85	.25
1901	47¢ Toronto Blue Jays Baseball Team, 25th anniv.	....	.85	.25
1901a	same, bklt pane of 8	....	6.75	....
1902	47¢ Summit of the Americans, Quebec	3.75	.85	.25
1903	60¢ Tourist Attractions, bklt pane of 5, self-adhesive	....	6.00	....
1904	$1.05 Tourist Attraction, bklt pane of 5, self-adhesive	....	9.00	....
1905	47¢ Armemian Apostolic Church	3.75	.85	.25
1906	47¢ Royal Military College	3.75	.85	.25
1907-08	47¢ Intl. Amateur Athletic Federation World Championship, 2 attached	3.75	1.65	1.00
1907	47¢ Pole Vault	....	.85	.25
1908	47¢ Runner	....	.85	.25
1909	47¢ Pierre Elliot Trudeau	3.75	.85	.25
1909a	same, souvenir sheet of 4	....	3.25	....
1910	47¢ Canadian Roses, souvenir sheet of 4	....	3.25	1.95
1911	47¢ Morden Centennial Rose	....	.85	.25
1912	47¢ Agnes Rose	....	.85	.25
1913	47¢ Champion Rose	....	.85	.25
1914	47¢ Canadian White Star Rose	....	.85	.25
1914a	same, bklt pane of 4 (1911-14)	....	3.25	....
....	same, complete booklet (1914a x 3)	....	9.50	....
1915	47¢ Great Peace of Montreal	3.75	.85	.25
1916	$1.05 Canadian Artists, "The Space Between Columns"	8.50	1.95	.75
1917	47¢ Shriners	3.75	.85	.25
1918	47¢ Picture Frame, bklt pane of 5 + 5 labels	....	4.25	....
1919-20	47¢ Theater Anniversaries, 2 attached	3.75	1.65	1.00
1919	47¢ Theatre du Nouveau Monde	....	.85	.25
1920	47¢ Grand Theater	....	.85	.25
1921	47¢ Hot Air Balloons, self-adhesive, bklt of 8	....	6.75	....
1922	47¢ Horse-drawn sleigh	3.75	.85	.25
1922a	same, bklt pane of 10	....	8.25	....
1923	60¢ Skaters	5.25	1.20	.50
1923a	same, bklt pane of 6	....	7.00	....
1924	$1.05 Children making snowman	8.50	1.95	.75
1924a	same, bklt pane of 6	....	11.50	....

Canada Postage #1927-1955

1927

1931

1928 1929 1930

2002 COMMEMORATIVES

SCOTT NO.	DESCRIPTION	PLATE BLOCK F/NH	UNUSED F/NH	USED F
1927	48¢ Maple Leaves, self-adhesive coil	....	.85	.30
1928	65¢ Jewelry making, coil	....	1.25	.60
1928a	same, bklt pane of 6	....	7.25	....
1929	77¢ Basket weaving, coil	....	1.40	.75
1930	$1.25 Sculpture, coil	....	2.00	.95
1930a	same, bklt pane of 6	....	11.50	....
1931	48¢ Flag & Canada Post Headquarters	....	.85	.30
1931a	same, bklt pane of 10	....	8.25	....
1931b	same, bklt pane of 30	....	24.00	....

1932

1933

1932	48¢ Regin of Queen Elizabeth, 50th Anniv.	3.75	.85	.30
1933	48¢ Year of the Horse	3.75	.85	.30
1934	$1.25 Year of the Horse, souvenir sheet	....	2.00	.95

1935a

1935	48¢ National Hockey League Stars, sheet of 6 + 3 labels	....	5.00	4.00
1935a	48¢ Tim Horton	....	.85	.30
1935b	48¢ Guy Lafleur	....	.85	.30
1935c	48¢ Howie Morenz	....	.85	.30
1935d	48¢ Glenn Hall	....	.85	.30
1935e	48¢ Red Kelly	....	.85	.30
1935f	48¢ Phil Esposito	....	.85	.30

1936

1940

1936-39	48¢ 2002 Winter Olympics, 4 attached	3.75	3.25	1.95
1936	48¢ Short track speed skating	....	.85	.30
1937	48¢ Curling	....	.85	.30
1938	48¢ Freestyle aerial skiing	....	.85	.30
1939	48¢ Women's hockey	....	.85	.30
1940	48¢ Appoint. of First Canadian Governor General	3.75	.85	.30

1941

1942

1941	48¢ University of Manitoba	....	.85	.30
1941a	same, bklt pane of 8	....	6.75	....
1942	48¢ Laval University	....	.85	.30
1942a	same, bklt pane of 8	....	6.75	....
1943	48¢ University of Trinity College	....	.85	.30
1943a	same, bklt pane of 8	....	6.75	....
1944	48¢ Saint Mary's University, Halifax	....	.85	.30
1944a	same, bklt pane of 8	....	6.75	....

1945

1946a

1945	$1.25 Canadian Art, Church and Horse	8.50	2.00	.95
1946	48¢ Canadian Tulips, bklt pane of 4, self-adhesive	....	3.25	1.95
1946a	48¢ City of Vancouver tulip	....	.85	.30
1946b	48¢ Monte Carlo tulip	....	.85	.30
1946c	48¢ Ottawa tulip	....	.85	.30
1946d	48¢ The Bishop tulip	....	.85	.30
1947	48¢ Canadian Tulips, souvenir sheet of 4, perforted	....	3.25	1.95

1948

1948-51	48¢ Corals, 4 attached	3.75	3.25	1.95
1948	48¢ Dendronepthea Giagantea & Dendronepthea Corals	....	.85	.30
1949	48¢ Tubastrea & Echinogorgia Corals	....	.85	.30
1950	48¢ North Atlantic Pink Tree, Pacific Orange Cup & North Pacific Horn Corals	....	.85	.30
1951	48¢ North Atlantic Giant Orange Tree & Black Coral	....	.85	.30
1951a	same, souvenir sheet of 4	....	3.25	1.95

1954-55

1952	65¢ Tourists Attractions, bklt pane of 5, self-adhesive	....	6.00	4.00
1952a	65¢ Yukon Quest, Yukon Territory	....	1.25	.60
1952b	65¢ Icefields Parkway, Alberta	....	1.25	.60
1952c	65¢ Agawa Canyon, Ontario	....	1.25	.60
1952d	65¢ Old Port of Montreal, Quebec	....	1.25	.60
1952e	65¢ Kings Landing, New Burnswick	....	1.25	.60
1953	$1.25 Tourists Attractions, bklt pane of 5, self-adhesive	....	9.75	6.50
1953a	$1.25 Northern Lights, Northwest Territories	....	2.00	.95
1953b	$1.25 Stanley Park, Vancouver, British Columbia	....	2.00	.95
1953c	$1.25 Head-Smashed-In Buffalo Jump, Alberta	....	2.00	.95
1953d	$1.25 Saguenay Fjord, Quebec	....	2.00	.95
1953e	$1.25 Peggy's Cove, Nova Scotia	....	2.00	.95
1954-55	48¢ Sculpture, Lumberjacks & Embacle, 2 attached	3.75	1.65	1.00
1954	48¢ Sculpture "Embacle" by Charles Daudelin	....	.85	.30
1955	48¢ Sculpture "Lumberjacks" by Leo Mol	....	.85	.30

Canada Postage #1956-1988

SCOTT NO.	DESCRIPTION	PLATE BLOCK F/NH	UNUSED F/NH	USED F

1956

1957

1956	48¢ Canadian Postmasters & Assistants Assoc.	3.75	.85	.30
1957	48¢ World Youth Day, self-adhesive		.85	.30
1957a	48¢ World Youth Day, bklt pane of 8, self-adhesive		6.75	

1958

1959

1958	48¢ Public Services International World Congress	3.75	.85	.30
1959	48¢ Public Pensions, 75th Anniv.	3.75	.85	.30
1960	48¢ Mountains, 8 attached	7.25	6.50	4.00
1960a	48¢ Mt. Logan ,Canada		.85	.30
1960b	48¢ Mt. Elbrus, Russia		.85	.30
1960c	48¢ Puncak Java, Indonesia		.85	.30
1960d	48¢ Mt. Everest, Nepal & China		.85	.30
1960e	48¢ Mt. Kilimanjaro, Tanzania		.85	.30
1960f	48¢ Vinson Massif, Antarctica		.85	.30
1960g	48¢ Mt. Aconcagua, Argentina		.85	.30
1960h	48¢ Mt. Mckinley, Alaska		.85	.30

1961

1962

| 1961 | 48¢ World Teacher's Day | 3.75 | .85 | .30 |
| 1962 | 48¢ Toronto Stock Exchange | 3.75 | .85 | .30 |

1963-64

1963-64	48¢ Communication Technology Centenaries, 2 attach	3.75	1.65	1.00
1963	48¢ Sir Sandford Fleming 91827-1915, cable-laying ship		.85	.30
1964	48¢ Guglielmo Marconi 1874-19370, radio and transmission towers		.85	.30

Order By Mail, Phone (800) 546-2995 Or Fax (256) 246-1116

SCOTT NO.	DESCRIPTION	PLATE BLOCK F/NH	UNUSED F/NH	USED F

1965

1968

1965	48¢ "Genesis" by Daphne Odjig	3.75	.85	.25
1965a	same, bklt pane of 10		8.25	
1966	65¢ "Winter Travel" by Cecil Youngfox	5.25	1.20	.50
1966a	same, bklt pane of 6		7.00	
1967	$1.25 "Mary and Child" sculpture by Irene Katak Angutitaq	8.50	1.95	.75
1967a	same, bklt pane of 6		11.50	
1968	48¢ Quebec Symphony Orchestra Centenary	3.75	.85	.30

1969

1971a, 1972a

1973

2003 COMMEMORATIVES

1969	48¢ Year of the Ram	3.75	.85	.30
1970	$1.25 Year of the Ram, souvenir sheet		1.95	.95
1971	48¢ National Hockey League All-Star Game, sheet of 6		5.00	4.00
1971a	48¢ Frank Mahovlich		.85	.30
1971b	48¢ Raymond Bourque		.85	.30
1971c	48¢ Serge Savard		.85	.30
1971d	48¢ Stan Mikita		.85	.30
1971e	48¢ Mike Bossy		.85	.30
1971f	48¢ Bill Durnan		.85	.30
1972	48¢ National Hockey League All-Star Game, sheet of 6, self-adhesive		5.00	4.00
1972a	48¢ Frank Mahovlich, self-adhesive		.85	.30
1972b	48¢ Raymond Bourque, self-adhesive		.85	.30
1972c	48¢ Serge Savard, self-adhesive		.85	.30
1972d	48¢ Stan Mikita, self-adhesive		.85	.30
1972e	48¢ Mike Bossy, self-adhesive		.85	.30
1972f	48¢ Bill Durnan, self-adhesive		.85	.30
1973	48¢ Bishop's University, Quebec, 150th Anniv.		.85	.30
1973a	same, bklt pane of 8		6.75	
1974	48¢ University of Western Ontario, 125th Anniv.		.85	.30
1974a	same, bklt pane of 8		6.75	
1975	48¢ St. Francis Xavier University, Antigonis, 150th Anniv.		.85	.30
1975a	same, bklt pane of 8		6.75	
1976	48¢ Macdonald Institute, Guelph, Ont., Centennial		.85	.30
1976a	same, bklt pane of 8		6.75	
1977	48¢ University of Montreal, 125th Anniversary		.85	.30
1977a	same, bklt pane of 8		6.75	

1979

1984

1979-82	Bird paintings by John James Audubon, 4 attached	3.75	3.25	1.95
1979	48¢ Leach's Storm Petrel		.85	.30
1980	48¢ Brant		.85	.30
1981	48¢ Great Cormorant		.85	.30
1982	48¢ Common Murre		.85	.30
1983	65¢ Gyfalcon, self-adhesive		1.25	.60
1983a	same, bklt pane of 6		7.25	
1984	48¢ Canadian Rangers	3.75	.85	.30
1985	48¢ American Hellenic Educational Progressive Assoc. in Canada, 75th Anniversary	3.75	.85	.30
1986	48¢ Volunteer Firefighters	3.75	.85	.30
1987	48¢ Coronation of Queen Elizabeth II, 50th Anniv.	3.75	.85	.30
1988	48¢ Pedro da Silva, First Courier in New France	3.75	.85	.30

Canada Postage #1989-New Issues

SCOTT NO.	DESCRIPTION	PLATE BLOCK F/NH	UNUSED F/NH	USED F

1992

1991

1993

SCOTT NO.	DESCRIPTION	PLATE BLOCK F/NH	UNUSED F/NH	USED F
1989	65¢ Tourist Attractions, bklt pane of 5, self-adhesive	....	6.00	....
1989a	65¢ Wilbeforce Falls, Nunavult	....	1.25	.60
1989b	65¢ Inside Passage, B.C.	....	1.25	.60
1989c	65¢ Royal Canadian Mounted Police Depot Division	....	1.25	.60
1989d	65¢ Casa Loma, Toronto	....	1.25	.60
1989e	65¢ Gatineau Park, Quebec	....	1.25	.60
1990	$1.25 Tourist Attractions, bklt pane of 5, self-adhesive	....	9.75	6.50
1990a	$1.25 Dragon boat races, Vancouver, B.C.	....	2.00	.95
1990b	$1.25 Polar bear watching, Manitoba	....	2.00	.95
1990c	$1.25 Nigara Falls, Ontario	....	2.00	.95
1990d	$1.25 Magdalen Islands, Quebec	....	2.00	.95
1990e	$1.25 Charlottestown, P.E.I.	....	2.00	.95
1991	48¢ "Vancouver 2010" overprint	....	.85	.30
1991a	same, bklt pane of 10	....	8.25	....
1991b	same, bklt pane of 20	....	16.50	....
1992	48¢ Lutheran World Federation 10th Assem	3.75	.85	.30
1993	48¢ Korean War Armistice, 50th Anniv.	3.75	.85	.30

1998

1994

SCOTT NO.	DESCRIPTION	PLATE BLOCK F/NH	UNUSED F/NH	USED F
1998	48¢ World Road Cycling Championships, Hamilton, Ont.	....	.85	.30
1998a	same, bklt pane of 8	....	6.75	....
1991C-Da	($1.25) Canada-Alaska Cruise Scenes, self-adhesive, 2 attached	....	3.95	2.00
1991C	($1.25) Mountains and Totem Pole	....	1.95	1.00
1991D	($1.25) Mountains and Whale's Tail	....	1.95	1.00
1994-97	48¢ National Library, 50th Anniv. 4 attached	....	3.25	1.95
1994	48¢ Anne Hebert (1916-2000)	....	.85	.30
1995	48¢ Hector de Saint-Denys Garneau (1912-43)	....	.85	.30
1996	48¢ Morley Callaghan (1903-90)	....	.85	.30
1997	48¢ Susanna Moodie (1803-85), Catharine Parr Trail (1802-99)	....	.85	.30
1997b	same, bklt pane of 8 (1994-97 x 2)	....	6.50	....
1999	48¢ Canadian Astronauts, self-adhesive, sheet of 8	....	6.50	....
1999a	48¢ Marc Garneau, self-adhesive	....	.85	.30
1999b	48¢ Roberta Bondar, self-adhesive	....	.85	.30
1999c	48¢ Steve MacLean, self-adhesive	....	.85	.30
1999d	48¢ Chris Hadfield, self-adhesive	....	.85	.30
1999e	48¢ Robert Thrisk, self-adhesive	....	.85	.30
1999f	48¢ Bjarni Tryggvason, self-adhesive	....	.85	.30
1999g	48¢ Dave Williams, self-adhesive	....	.85	.30
1999h	48¢ Julie Payette, self-adhesive	....	.85	.30

2000-01

2002a

SCOTT NO.	DESCRIPTION	PLATE BLOCK F/NH	UNUSED F/NH	USED F
2000-01	48¢ Trees of Canada and Thailand, 2 attached	3.75	1.65	1.00
2000	48¢ Acer Saccharum leaves (Canada)	....	.85	.30
2001	48¢ Cassia fistula (Thailand)	....	.85	.30
2001b	48¢ Trees of Canada and Thailand, souvenir sheet of 2	....	1.65	1.00
2002	48¢ L'Hommage a Rosa Luxemburg by Jean-Paul Riopelle, sheet of 6	....	5.00	4.00
2002a	48¢ Red & Blue dots between birds at LR	....	.85	.30
2002b	48¢ Bird with yellow beak at center	....	.85	.30
2002c	48¢ Three birds in circle at R	....	.85	.30
2002d	48¢ Sun at UR	....	.85	.30
2002e	48¢ Birds with purple outlines ar L	....	.85	.30
2002f	48¢ Birds with red outline in circle at R	....	.85	.30
2003	$1.25 Pink bird in red circle at R, souvenir sheet	....	1.95	.75

2004

SCOTT NO.	DESCRIPTION	PLATE BLOCK F/NH	UNUSED F/NH	USED F
2004	48¢ Gift boxes and Ice skates	3.75	.85	.25
2004a	same, bklt pane of 6	....	5.00	....
2005	65¢ Gift boxes and Teddy bear	5.25	1.20	.50
2005a	same, bklt pane of 6	....	7.00	....
2006	$1.25 Gift boxes and Toy duck	8.50	1.95	.75
2006a	same, bklt pane of 6	....	11.50	....
2007	$5 Moose	37.50	8.50	5.00
2008	49¢ Maple Leaf and Samara, self-adhesive, coil	....	.90	.40
2009	80¢ Maple Leaf on Twig, self-adhesive, coil	....	1.35	.75
2010	$1.40 Maple Leaf on Twig, self-adhesive, coil	....	2.50	1.25
2011	49¢ Flag over Edmonton, Alberta, self-adhesive	....	.90	.40
2011a	same, bklt pane of 10	....	9.00	....
2012	49¢ Queen Elizabeth II, self-adhesive	....	.90	.40
2012a	same, bklt pane of 10	....	9.00	....
2013	80¢ Maple Leaf on Twig, self-adhesive	....	1.35	.75
2013a	same, bklt pane of 6	....	8.00	....
2014	$1.40 Maple Leaf Twig, self-adhesive	....	2.50	1.25
2014a	same, bklt pane of 6	....	15.00	....

2015

2024

2026

2004 Commemoratives

SCOTT NO.	DESCRIPTION	PLATE BLOCK F/NH	UNUSED F/NH	USED F
2015	49¢ Year of the Monkey	4.00	.90	.40
2016	$1.40 Year of the Monkey souvenir sheet	....	2.75	1.50
2017	49¢ National Hockey League Stars, sheet of 6	....	5.50	4.00
2017a	49¢ Larry Robinson	....	.90	.40
2017b	49¢ Marcel Dionne	....	.90	.40
2017c	49¢ Ted Lindsay	....	.90	.40
2017d	49¢ Johnny Bower	....	.90	.40
2017e	49¢ Brad Park	....	.90	.40
2017f	49¢ Milt Schmidt	....	.90	.40
2018	49¢ National Hockey League Stars, sheet of 6, self-adhesive	....	5.50	4.00
2018a	49¢ Larry Robinson, self-adhesive	....	.90	.40
2018b	49¢ Marcel Dionne, self-adhesive	....	.90	.40
2018c	49¢ Ted Lindsay, self-adhesive	....	.90	.40
2018d	49¢ Johnny Bower, self-adhesive	....	.90	.40
2018e	49¢ Brad Park, self-adhesive	....	.90	.40
2018f	49¢ Milt Schmidt, self-adhesive	....	.90	.40
2019	49¢ Quebec Winter Carnival, self-adhesive	....	.90	.40
2019a	same, bklt pane of 6	....	5.50	....
2024	49¢ Governor General Ramon John Hnatyshyn	4.00	.90	.40
2025	49¢ Royal Canadian Army Cadets, 125th Anniv, self-adhesive	....	.90	.40
2025a	same, bklt pane of 4	....	3.60	....
2026	49¢ The Farm, Ship of Otto Sverdrup, Arctic Explorer	4.00	.90	.40
2027	$1.40 The Farm, Ship of Otto Sverdrup, Arctic Explorer, souvenir sheet	....	2.75	1.50
2028-31	49¢ Urban Transit & Light Rail Systems, 4 attached	4.00	3.60	4.00
2028	49¢ Toronto Transit Commission	....	.90	.40
2029	49¢ Translink Skytrain, Vancouver	....	.90	.40
2030	49¢ Societe de Transport de Montreal	....	.90	.40
2031	49¢ Calgary Transit Light Rail	....	.90	.40
....	49¢ St. Joseph Oratory, Montreal, self-adhesive	....	.90	.40
....	same bklt pane of 6	....	5.50	....
....	49¢ Home Hardware, 40th Anniv., self-adhesive	....	.90	.40
....	same, bklt pane of 10	....	9.00	....
....	49¢ University of Sherbrooke, 50th Anniv.	....	.90	.40
....	same, bklt pane of 8	....	7.25	....
....	49¢ Montreal Children's Hospital Centenary, self-adhesive	....	.90	.40
....	same, bklt pane of 8	....	7.25	....
....	49¢ University of Prince Edwards Island, BiCenn	....	.90	.40
....	same, bklt pane of 8	....	7.25	....
....	49¢ Bird Paintings by John James Audubon, 4 attache	4.00	3.60	.40
....	80¢ Lincoln's Sparrow by J.J. Audubon, self-adhesive	....	1.50	.75
....	same, bklt pane of 6	....	9.00	....
....	49¢ Shipping Line Pioneers, 2 attached	4.00	1.80	1.00
....	49¢ Montreal International Jazz Festival, self-adhesive	....	.90	.40
....	same, bklt pane of 6	....	5.50	....

Canada Phospher Tagged Issues; Canada Postage #B1-B13a; C1-C9a

SCOTT NO.	DESCRIPTION			UNUSED F/NH

CANADA PHOSPHOR TAGGED ISSUES
Overprinted with barely visible phosphorescent ink

TYPES OF TAGGING

I = Wide Side Bars
II = Wide Bar in Middle
III = Bar at Right or Left
IV = Narrow Bar in Middle
V = Narrow Side Bars

1962-63 Queen Elizabeth II

SCOTT NO.	DESCRIPTION		Unused	F/NH
337-41p	1¢-5¢ Elizabeth	(5)	52.50	10.60
401-5p	1¢-5¢ Elizabeth	(5)	10.75	1.75
404pIV	4¢ Carmine—IV		6.00	1.25
404pII	4¢ Carmine—II		17.50	4.00
405q	5¢ Elizabeth, mini. pane of 25		......	41.25

1964-67

434-35p	3¢-5¢ 1964 Christmas	(2)	13.00	2.25
434q	3¢ mini. pane of 25		......	12.10
434q	same, sealed pack of 2		......	25.00
443-44p	3¢-5¢ 1965 Christmas	(2)	3.50	.65
443q	3¢ mini. pane of 25		......	7.70
443q	same, sealed pack of 2		......	15.75
451-52p	3¢-5¢ 1966 Christmas	(2)	3.50	.80
451q	3¢ mini. pane of 25		......	5.15
451q	same, sealed pack of 2		......	10.50
453p	5¢ Centennial		2.25	.45

1967-72 Queen Elizabeth II

454-58pI	1¢-5¢—I	(4)	12.50	1.75
454-58pII	1¢-5¢—II	(4)	12.50	1.65
454-57pV	1¢-5¢—V	(4)	7.75	.95
454ep	1¢ booklet single—V			.25
457p	4¢ carmine—III		2.75	.35
458q	5¢ mini. pane of 20		......	65.00
459p	6¢ orange, perf.10—I		4.50	.65
459bp	6¢ orange, perf.12-1/2x12—I		4.50	.65
460p	6¢ black, perf 12-1/2x12—I		5.50	.40
460cp	6¢ black, perf 12-1/2x12—II		4.25	.50
460gp	6¢ black, booklet single, perf.10—V		......	.75
460pII	6¢ black, perf. 12—II		4.00	.55
460pV	6¢ black, perf. 12—V		4.00	.50

1967 Views

| 462-65pI | 10¢-25¢—I | (4) | 45.00 | 9.00 |
| 462-63pV | 10¢-15¢—V | (2) | 12.50 | 2.00 |

1967-69

476-77p	3¢-5¢ 1967 Christmas	(2)	3.50	.65
476q	3¢ mini. pane of 25		......	3.30
476q	same, sealed pack of 2		......	7.00
488-89p	5¢-6¢ 1968 Christmas	(2)	3.75	.70
488q	5¢ booklet pane of 10		......	4.15
502-3p	5¢-6¢ 1969 Christmas	(2)	3.50	.60
502q	5¢ booklet pane of 10		......	3.85

1970-71

505p	6¢ Manitoba		1.75	.35
508-11p	25¢ Expo '70	(4)	12.50	11.00
513-14p	10¢-15¢ U.N.	(2)	20.00	3.15
519-30p	5¢-15¢ Christmas	(12)	23.50	6.05
541p	15¢ Radio Canada		17.25	3.05

1971 Queen Elizabeth II

543-44p	7¢-8¢—I	(2)	9.25	1.05
544q	booklet pane, 8¢(2), 6¢(1), 1¢(3)		......	2.20
544r	booklet pane, 8¢(11), 6¢(1), 1¢(6)		......	6.05
544s	booklet pane, 8¢(5), 6¢(1), 1¢(4)		......	2.75
544pV	8¢ slate—V		4.25	.60
550p	8¢ slate, coil		......	.30

1971-72

554-57p	6¢-15¢ Christmas	(4)	11.00	2.50
560p	8¢ World Health Day		3.25	.65
561p	8¢ Frontenac		5.75	.95
562-63p	8¢ Indians	(2)	3.75	1.20
564-65p	8¢ Indians	(2)	3.75	1.20
582-85p	15¢ Sciences	(4)	16.00	13.20

1972 Pictorials

| 594-97 | 10¢-25¢—V | (4) | 10.50 | 2.25 |
| 594-97p I | 10¢-25¢—I | (4) | 35.00 | 7.50 |

1972

606-09p	6¢-15¢ Christmas—V	(4)	12.75	2.65
606-09pI	6¢-15¢ Christmas—I	(4)	15.00	3.50
610p	8¢ Krieghoff		3.50	.40

SCOTT NO.	DESCRIPTION	PLATE BLOCK F/NH	UNUSED F/NH	USED F

SEMI-POSTAL STAMPS

1974-76

| B1-12 | Olympics, 12 varieties | 28.50 | 5.95 | 5.95 |

1974

B1-3	Emblems, 3 varieties	7.50	1.75	1.75
B1	8¢ + 2¢ Olympic Emblem	1.75	.55	.55
B2	10¢ + 5¢ same	2.65	.55	.55
B3	15¢ + 5¢ same	3.40	.75	.75

1975

B4-6	Water Sports, 3 varieties	7.25	1.50	1.50
B4	8¢ + 2¢ Swimming	1.75	.35	.50
B5	10¢ + 5¢ Rowing	2.65	.55	.55
B6	15¢ + 5¢ Sailing	3.40	.75	.75
B7-9	Combat Sports, 3 varieties	7.25	1.50	1.50
B7	8¢ + 2¢ Fencing	1.75	.35	.35
B8	10¢ + 5¢ Boxing	2.65	.55	.55
B9	15¢ + 5¢ Judo	3.40	.75	.75

1976

B10-12	Team Sports, 3 varieties	8.00	1.50	1.50
B10	8¢ + 2¢ Basketball	1.75	.35	.35
B11	10¢ + 5¢ Gymnastics	2.65	.50	.55
B12	20¢ + 5¢ Soccer	3.85	.85	.85

1997

| B13 | 45¢ + 5¢ Literacy | .... | .90 | .40 |
| B13a | same, booklet pane of 10 | .... | 10.00 | .... |

SCOTT NO.	DESCRIPTION	UNUSED NH VF F AVG	UNUSED OG VF F AVG	USED VF F AVG

AIR POST STAMPS

C1   C2   C5

1928

| C1 | 5¢ brown olive | 16.50 11.25 6.95 | 11.00 7.50 4.75 | 3.75 2.60 1.75 |

1930

| C2 | 5¢ olive brown | 65.00 44.00 27.50 | 42.00 28.50 17.75 | 21.00 15.50 10.00 |

1932

| C3 | 6¢ on 5¢ brown olive | 11.25 7.75 4.75 | 8.00 5.50 3.25 | 3.50 2.60 1.50 |
| C4 | 6¢ on 5¢ olive brown | 28.00 19.00 11.95 | 18.00 12.25 7.75 | 11.50 8.75 5.50 |

SCOTT NO.	DESCRIPTION	PLATE BLOCK F/NH F/OG	UNUSED F/NH F/OG	USED F

C6   C7   C9

1935

| C5 | 6¢ red brown | 14.00 11.50 | 2.40 1.75 | .85 |

1938

| C6 | 6¢ blue | 16.50 13.25 | 3.40 2.50 | .20 |

1942-43

| C7 | 6¢ deep blue | 13.75 11.00 | 2.75 2.05 | .75 |
| C8 | 7¢ deep blue (1943) | 2.75 2.20 | .55 .45 | .15 |

1946

| C9 | 7¢ deep blue | 2.65 2.20 | .55 .45 | .15 |
| C9a | same, booklet pane of 4 | ... 2.20 | 1.80 ... | ... |

SCOTT NO.	DESCRIPTION	PLATE BLOCK F/NH	F/OG	UNUSED F/NH	F/OG	USED F

AIR POST SPECIAL DELIVERY

CE1

CE3

1942-43

| CE1 | 16¢ bright ultramarine | 12.50 | 9.50 | 2.20 | 1.65 | 1.50 |
| CE2 | 17¢ bright ultramarine (1943) | 14.00 | 10.75 | 2.75 | 2.10 | 1.95 |

1946

| CE3 | 17¢ bright ultramarine (circumflex "E") | 23.10 | 17.60 | 5.50 | 3.75 | 3.60 |

1947

| CE4 | 17¢ bright ultramarine (grave "E") | 23.10 | 17.60 | 5.50 | 3.75 | 3.60 |

SCOTT NO.	DESCRIPTION	UNUSED NH VF	F	AVG	UNUSED O.G. VF	F	AVG	USED VF	F	AVG

SPECIAL DELIVERY STAMPS

E1

E2

E3

1898

| E1 | 10¢ blue green | 180.00 | 110.00 | 80.00 | 70.00 | 47.50 | 29.50 | 11.00 | 7.50 | 5.00 |

1922

| E2 | 20¢ carmine | 140.00 | 90.00 | 65.00 | 70.00 | 47.50 | 29.50 | 8.75 | 6.50 | 4.00 |

1927

| E3 | 20¢ orange | 31.00 | 21.00 | 13.00 | 16.50 | 11.25 | 6.95 | 12.50 | 8.75 | 5.00 |

1930

| E4 | 20¢ henna brown | 90.00 | 59.50 | 40.00 | 48.00 | 32.50 | 20.25 | 16.50 | 11.25 | 6.95 |

1933

| E5 | 20¢ henna brown | 90.00 | 61.25 | 38.00 | 48.00 | 32.50 | 20.25 | 19.00 | 13.00 | 8.25 |

E4

E6

E7

E10

SCOTT NO.	DESCRIPTION	PLATE BLOCK F/NH	F/OG	UNUSED F/NH	F/OG	USED F

1935

| E6 | 20¢ dark carmine | 72.50 | 46.50 | 10.00 | 6.10 | 4.50 |

1938-39

E7	10¢ dark green(1939)	24.75	19.25	5.00	3.85	2.75
E8	20¢ dark carmine	247.25	178.25	32.50	22.00	22.50
E9	10¢ on 20¢ dark carmine (#E8) (1939)	36.95	26.50	5.50	3.85	3.85

1942

| E10 | 10¢ green | 11.50 | 9.00 | 2.50 | 1.95 | 1.50 |

1946

| E11 | 10¢ green | 8.00 | 6.75 | 1.65 | 1.40 | .90 |

SCOTT NO.	DESCRIPTION	UNUSED NH F	AVG	UNUSED F	AVG	USED F	AVG

WAR TAX STAMPS

MR1

MR3

2¢ + 1¢ Die I. Below large letter "T" there is a clear horizontal line of color.
Die II. Right side of line is replaced by two short lines and five dots.

1915

| MR1 | 1¢ green | 18.00 | 12.50 | 9.00 | 6.50 | .20 | .15 |
| MR2 | 2¢ carmine | 18.00 | 12.50 | 9.00 | 6.50 | .25 | .20 |

1916 Perf 12

MR3	2¢ + 1¢ carmine (I)	23.00	15.00	11.50	8.00	.20	.15
MR3a	2¢ + 1¢ carmine (II)	165.00	110.00	80.00	60.00	4.00	2.50
MR4	2¢ + 1¢ brown (II)	18.00	12.00	10.00	7.00	8.50	5.00
MR4a	2¢ + 1¢ brown(I)	375.00	275.00	195.00	150.00	8.50	6.50

Perf 12 x 8

| MR5 | 2¢ + 1¢ carmine | 55.00 | 40.00 | 27.00 | 20.00 | 20.00 | 14.00 |

Coil Stamps Perf. 8 Vertically

MR6	2¢ + 1¢ carmine (I)	125.00	85.00	75.00	50.00	7.00	5.00
MR7	2¢ + 1¢ brown (II)	27.00	20.00	13.00	9.00	.90	.60
MR7a	2¢ + 1¢ brown (I)	170.00	120.00	85.00	65.00	7.00	5.00

SCOTT NO.	DESCRIPTION	UNUSED O.G. VF	F	AVG	UNUSED VF	F	AVG	USED VF	F	AVG

REGISTRATION STAMPS

F1

1875-88 Perf. 12 (NH+50%)

F1	2¢ orange	85.00	56.00	34.00	70.00	46.75	28.50	4.00	2.75	1.55
F1a	2¢ vermillion	100.00	66.00	39.50	82.50	55.00	33.00	9.50	6.35	3.40
F1b	2¢ rose carmine	195.00	130.00	79.50	165.00	110.00	66.00	110.00	72.50	40.00
F1d	2¢ orange, perf 12x11-1/2	365.00	245.00	158.00	305.00	203.50	132.50	88.00	58.85	32.50
F2	5¢ dark green	100.00	66.00	41.50	82.50	55.00	34.50	4.50	3.25	1.95
F2d	5¢ dark green, perf 12x11-1/2	1140.00	960.00	500.00	950.00	800.00	450.00	185.00	125.00	67.50
F3	8¢ blue	550.00	365.00	245.00	455.00	305.00	205.00	410.00	275.00	148.50

Canada Postage #J1-O27

POSTAGE DUE STAMPS

J1

J11

J6

J15

J21

SCOTT NO.	DESCRIPTION	UNUSED NH F	AVG	UNUSED F	AVG	USED F	AVG
	1906-28						
J1	1¢ violet	14.75	9.25	8.50	5.25	3.50	1.95
J2	2¢ violet	14.75	9.25	8.50	5.25	.75	.50
J3	4¢ violet (1928)	59.50	37.00	34.00	21.00	16.00	10.00
J4	5¢ violet	14.75	9.25	8.50	5.25	1.35	.95
J5	10¢ violet (1928)	38.75	23.75	22.00	13.50	11.00	7.50
	1930-32						
J6	1¢ dark violet	10.25	6.50	5.75	3.50	3.00	1.75
J7	2¢ dark violet	7.50	4.50	4.25	2.50	.75	.50
J8	4¢ dark violet	14.25	8.75	8.50	5.25	3.00	1.75
J9	5¢ dark violet	14.25	8.75	8.50	5.25	5.00	1.65
J10	10¢ dark violet (1932)	88.50	54.50	51.00	31.50	7.00	4.00
	1933-34						
J11	1¢ dark violet (1934)	12.00	7.50	6.75	4.00	5.00	2.95
J12	2¢ dark violet	4.75	2.95	2.75	1.50	.90	.60
J13	4¢ dark violet	11.00	6.75	6.25	3.75	5.00	3.25
J14	10¢ dark violet	20.50	12.75	12.00	7.50	4.00	2.50

SCOTT NO.	DESCRIPTION	UNUSED NH F	AVG	UNUSED F	AVG	USED F
	1935-65					
J15-20	1¢-10¢ complete, 7 varieties	40.00	36.50	5.50	4.95	3.35
J15	1¢ dark violet	.80	.55	.20	.15	.15
J16	2¢ dark violet	.80	.55	.20	.15	.15
J16B	3¢ dark violet (1965)	13.75	9.60	1.95	1.35	1.00
J17	4¢ dark violet	1.35	.95	.20	.15	.15
J18	5¢ dark violet (1948)	2.20	1.55	.35	.25	.25
J19	6¢ dark violet (1957)	13.75	9.60	1.95	1.35	1.00
J20	10¢ dark violet	1.55	1.10	.25	.20	.15

POSTAGE DUES

SCOTT NO.	DESCRIPTION	PLATE BLOCK F/NH	UNUSED F/NH	USED F
	1967 Perf. 12 Regular Size Design 20mm X 17mm			
J21-27	1¢-10¢ cpl., 7 vars.	18.00	3.50	3.40
J21	1¢ carmine rose	1.40	.25	.25
J22	2¢ carmine rose	1.40	.25	.25
J23	3¢ carmine rose	1.40	.25	.25
J24	4¢ carmine rose	2.20	.45	.25
J25	5¢ carmine rose	8.25	1.65	1.35
J26	6¢ carmine rose	2.15	.40	.25
J27	10¢ carmine rose	2.15	.40	.25
	1969-78 Perf. 12 (White or Yellow Gum) Modular Size Design 20mm x 15-3/4 mm			
J28/37 (J28-31, J33-37) 9 vars.		6.50	1.95	1.60
J28	1¢ carmine rose (1970)	.65	.20	.15
J29	2¢ carmine rose (1972)	.65	.20	.15
J30	3¢ carmine rose (1974)	.65	.20	.15
J31	4¢ carmine rose (1969)	.65	.20	.15
J32a	5¢ carmine rose (1977)	125.00	24.75	24.75
J33	6¢ carmine rose (1972)	.65	.20	.15
J34	8¢ carmine rose	.80	.20	.15
J35	10¢ carmine rose (1969)	1.00	.20	.20
J36	12¢ carmine rose (1969)	1.10	.25	.25
J37	16¢ carmine rose (1974)	1.65	.40	.35
	1977-78 Perf. 12-1/2 X 12			
J28a-40	1¢-50¢ cpl., 9 vars.	24.00	5.05	4.75
J28a	1¢ carmine rose	.65	.20	.15
J31a	4¢ carmine rose	.65	.20	.15
J32	5¢ carmine rose	.65	.20	.15
J34a	8¢ carmine rose (1978)	1.95	.40	.25
J35a	10¢ carmine rose	.90	.20	.15
J36a	12¢ carmine rose	11.00	2.25	1.40
J38	20¢ carmine rose	1.95	.40	.35
J39	24¢ carmine rose	2.55	.50	.45
J40	50¢ carmine rose	4.95	1.00	1.95
	OFFICIAL STAMPS **1949-50** #249, 250, 252, 254, 269-73 overprinted O.H.M.S.			
O1-10	1¢-$1 complete, 9 vars.	......	290.00	165.00
O1-8	1¢-20¢, 7 varieties	......	47.50	18.50
O1	1¢ green	10.45	2.15	1.65
O2	2¢ brown	110.00	15.40	18.00
O3	3¢ rose violet	10.75	2.20	1.10
O4	4¢ dark carmine	14.85	3.30	.70
O6	10¢ olive	18.70	4.05	.55
O7	14¢ black brown	29.45	6.45	1.85
O8	20¢ slate black	79.75	16.50	2.50
O9	50¢ dark blue green	962.50	203.50	100.00
O10	$1 red violet	247.50	52.25	35.75
	1950 #294 overprinted O.H.M.S.			
O11	50¢ dull green	148.50	30.75	16.50
	1950 #284-88 overprinted O.H.M.S.			
O12-15A	1¢-5¢ cpl., 5 vars.	26.75	4.90	2..50
O12	1¢ green	3.50	.30	.30
O13	2¢ sepia	3.80	.80	.75
O14	3¢ rose violet	4.95	1.00	.40
O15	4¢ dark carmine	4.95	1.00	.15
O15A	5¢ deep blue	11.00	2.05	1.10
	1950 #284-88, 269-71, 294, 273 overprinted G			
O16-25	1¢-$1 complete, 10 vars.	......	115.00	60.00
O16-24	1¢-50¢, 9 varieties	......	37.00	8.00
O16	1¢ green	1.75	.25	.15
O17	2¢ sepia	5.50	1.00	.65
O18	3¢ rose violet	4.95	1.00	.15
O19	4¢ dark carmine	5.25	1.10	.15
O20	5¢ deep blue	11.00	1.20	.75
O21	10¢ olive	12.10	2.60	.40
O22	14¢ black brown	31.35	7.15	1.65
O23	20¢ slate black	74.25	14.85	.90
O24	50¢ dull green	49.50	9.90	3.60
O25	$1 red violet	368.50	82.50	55.00
	1950-51 #301, 302 overprinted G			
O26	10¢ black brown	6.05	1.30	.20
O27	$1 bright ultramarine	395.00	74.25	55.00

Canada Postage #O22-EO2; British Columbia & Vancouver Island #1-18

SCOTT NO.	DESCRIPTION	PLATE BLOCK F/NH	UNUSED F/NH	USED F
	1951-53 #305-06, 316, 320-21 overprinted G			
O28	2¢ olive green	1.85	.40	.15
O29	4¢ orange vermillion ('52)	3.60	.65	.15
O30	20¢ gray (1952)	9.35	2.10	.15
O31	7¢ blue (1952)	14.60	3.15	.80
O32	$1 gray (1953)	60.50	12.65	7.45
	1953 #325-29, 334 overprinted G			
O33-37	1¢-5¢ complete, 5vars.	8.40	1.90	.70
O33	1¢ violet brown	1.35	.30	.15
O34	2¢ green	1.55	.35	.15
O35	3¢ carmine	1.55	.35	.15
O36	4¢ violet	2.20	.50	.15
O37	5¢ ultramarine	2.20	.50	.15
O38	50¢ lightgreen	24.20	5.25	1.00
	1955 #351 overprinted G			
O39	10¢ violet brown	3.55	.80	.15
	1955-56 #337, 338, 340, 341, 362 overprinted G			
O40-45	1¢-20¢ cpl., 5vars.	17.00	3.55	.80
O40	1¢ violet brown (1956)	1.30	.30	.25
O41	2¢ green (1956)	1.65	.35	.15
O43	4¢ violet (1956)	5.35	1.00	.15
O44	5¢ bright blue	2.05	.45	.15
O45	20¢ green (1956)	7.70	1.65	.15
	1963 #401, 402, 404, 405 overprinted G			
O46-49	1¢-5¢ cpl., 4 vars.	14.60	2.30	2.30
O46	1¢ deep brown	2.75	.60	.60
O47	2¢ green	2.75	.60	.60
O48	4¢ carmine	7.15	.75	.75
O49	5¢ violet blue	2.75	.45	.45
	1949-50 AIR POST OFFICIAL STAMPS			
CO1	7¢ deep blue, O.H.M.S. (C9)	38.50	8.25	2.65
CO2	7¢ deep blue, G (C9)	88.00	18.15	13.75
	1950 SPECIAL DELIVERY OFFICIAL STAMPS			
EO1	10¢ green, O.H.M.S.(E11)	99.00	20.35	12.25
EO2	10¢ green, G (E11)	130.00	30.00	25.00

SCOTT NO.	DESCRIPTION	UNUSED O.G. VF	UNUSED O.G. F	UNUSED O.G. AVG	UNUSED VF	UNUSED F	UNUSED AVG	USED VF	USED F	USED AVG
	1860 Imperforate									
1	2-1/2p dull rose	...	...	...	...	2750.00	1750.00	...	...	...
	1860 Perforated 14									
2	2-1/2p dull rose	895.00	450.00	260.00	475.00	250.00	140.00	300.00	150.00	95.00
	VANCOUVER ISLAND									
	1865 Imperforate									
3	5¢ rose	....	....	....	....	....	....	....	....	....
4	10¢ blue	4500.00	2450.00	1650.00	2450.00	1350.00	900.00	1350.00	725.00	450.00
	Perforated 14									
5	5¢ rose	850.00	450.00	250.00	450.00	240.00	140.00	300.00	150.00	95.00
6	10¢ blue	850.00	450.00	250.00	450.00	240.00	140.00	300.00	150.00	95.00
	BRITISH COLUMBIA									
	1865									
7	3p blue	265.00	140.00	90.00	140.00	75.00	50.00	140.00	75.00	50.00
	New Values surcharged on 1865 design									
	1867-69 Perforated 14									
8	2¢ brown	325.00	175.00	95.00	180.00	95.00	50.00	180.00	95.00	55.00
9	5¢ bright red	550.00	300.00	175.00	325.00	175.00	95.00	300.00	160.00	95.00
10	10¢ lilac rose	4500.00	2450.00	1300.00	2450.00	1300.00	700.00	...	...	...
11	25¢ orange	600.00	325.00	180.00	325.00	170.00	95.00	300.00	160.00	95.00
12	50¢ violet	2000.00	1075.00	650.00	1075.00	575.00	350.00	1075.00	575.00	325.00
13	$1 green	3500.00	1850.00	1050.00	1900.00	1000.00	550.00	...	...	...
	1869 Perforated 12-1/2									
14	5¢ bright red	4500.00	2400.00	1475.00	2400.00	1250.00	775.00	1700.00	900.00	550.00
15	10¢ lilac rose	2500.00	1400.00	800.00	1400.00	750.00	450.00	1450.00	750.00	450.00
16	25¢ orange	1450.00	800.00	400.00	850.00	450.00	250.00	850.00	450.00	250.00
17	50¢ violet	2000.00	1100.00	600.00	1100.00	600.00	350.00	1125.00	600.00	350.00
18	$1 green	4000.00	2250.00	1275.00	2250.00	1175.00	675.00	2250.00	1175.00	675.00

Queen Victoria (designs 1, 3, 4)
Seal (design 7)

Newfoundland #1-23

SCOTT NO.	DESCRIPTION	UNUSED O.G. VF	UNUSED O.G. F	UNUSED O.G. AVG	UNUSED VF	UNUSED F	UNUSED AVG	USED VF	USED F	USED AVG

 1, 15A, 16    2, 11, 17    3, 11A    4, 12, 18    6, 13, 20

 7, 21    8, 22    9, 15, 23    24, 38 *Codfish*    25, 26, 40 *Seal*

1857 Imperforate, Thick Paper

Scott	Description	VF (OG)	F (OG)	AVG (OG)	VF	F	AVG	VF (Used)	F (Used)	AVG (Used)
1	1p brown violet	107.50	82.50	57.75	72.50	55.00	38.50	140.00	100.00	70.00
2	2p scarlet vermillion	13000.00	9000.00	6750.00	10000.00	7200.00	5400.00	4400.00	3125.00	2200.00
3	3p green	540.00	410.00	260.00	360.00	275.00	175.00	425.00	300.00	225.00
4	4p scarlet vermillion	8200.00	6150.00	4625.00	7700.00	5750.00	4350.00	3200.00	2000.00	1500.00
5	5p brown violet	250.00	187.50	145.00	200.00	150.00	112.50	325.00	245.00	175.00
6	6p scarlet vermillion	12800.00	9175.00	6500.00	12000.00	9000.00	6750.00	3450.00	2475.00	1750.00
7	6-1/2p scarlet vermillion	3100.00	2325.00	1750.00	2800.00	2100.00	1575.00	2475.00	1775.00	1240.00
8	8p scarlet vermillion	275.00	210.00	155.00	225.00	168.75	125.00	395.00	300.00	205.00
9	1sh scarlet vermillion	15100.00	10750.00	7550.00	14800.00	11100.00	8325.00	5400.00	3800.00	2700.00

1860 Thin Paper

Scott	Description	VF	F	AVG	VF	F	AVG	VF	F	AVG
11	2p orange	275.00	210.00	155.00	225.00	168.75	125.00	325.00	245.00	185.50
11A	3p green	80.00	62.00	39.50	53.50	41.25	26.40	100.00	83.00	55.00
12	4p orange	2600.00	1950.00	1475.00	2400.00	1800.00	1350.00	1200.00	900.00	675.00
12A	5p violet brown	127.50	100.00	49.50	85.00	66.00	33.00	180.00	138.00	88.00
13	6p orange	3900.00	3000.00	2250.00	2600.00	2000.00	1500.00	715.00	550.00	385.00

1861-62 Thin Paper

Scott	Description	VF	F	AVG	VF	F	AVG	VF	F	AVG
15	1sh orange	27000.00	19250.00	12500.00	21500.00	15450.00	10900.00	8050.00	5750.00	4600.00
15A	1p violet brown	195.00	150.00	100.00	130.00	100.00	66.00	175.00	138.00	105.00
16	1p reddish brown	4725.00	3375.00	2375.00	3775.00	2700.00	1950.00	...	...	...
17	2p rose	195.00	150.00	100.00	130.00	100.00	66.00	175.00	138.00	83.00
18	4p rose	58.75	45.00	25.50	39.25	30.25	17.00	65.00	50.00	24.00
19	5p reddish brown	64.50	44.50	33.00	43.00	33.00	22.00	71.50	55.00	34.65
20	6p rose	32.25	24.75	13.20	21.50	16.50	8.80	69.00	53.00	35.75
21	6-1/2p rose	96.75	74.25	39.60	64.50	49.50	26.40	320.00	240.00	180.00
22	8p rose	82.50	63.50	33.00	55.00	42.35	22.00	320.00	240.00	180.00
23	1sh rose	48.50	37.00	19.75	32.00	24.75	13.20	320.00	240.00	180.00

 27 *Prince Albert*    28, 29 *Queen Victoria*    30 *Fishing Ship*

 31 *Queen Victoria*    32, 32A, 37 *Prince of Wales*    35, 36 *Queen Victoria*

Newfoundland #24-60

SCOTT NO.	DESCRIPTION	UNUSED O.G. VF	F	AVG	UNUSED VF	F	AVG	USED VF	F	AVG
				1865-94 Perforate 12 Yellow Paper						
24	2¢ green	74.50	57.25	39.25	57.25	44.00	30.25	32.00	24.75	13.75
24a	2¢ green (white paper)	56.00	43.00	26.50	43.00	33.00	20.35	22.75	17.60	9.90
25	5¢ brown	560.00	430.00	300.00	430.00	330.00	230.00	285.00	220.00	148.00
26	5¢ black (1868)	280.00	215.00	143.00	215.00	165.00	110.00	120.00	93.00	60.50
27	10¢ black	280.00	215.00	143.00	215.00	165.00	110.00	71.50	55.00	38.50
27a	10¢ black (white paper)	130.00	100.00	64.50	100.00	77.00	49.50	43.00	33.00	18.15
28	12¢ pale red brown	345.00	265.00	175.00	265.00	204.00	137.50	165.00	126.50	87.50
28a	12¢ pale red brown (white paper)	45.50	35.00	18.50	35.00	26.95	14.30	35.00	26.95	14.30
29	12¢ brown (1894)	45.50	35.00	18.50	35.00	26.95	14.30	32.00	24.75	13.20
30	13¢ orange	110.00	85.00	57.25	85.75	66.00	44.00	57.25	44.00	30.25
31	24¢ blue	37.50	28.50	20.00	28.75	22.00	15.40	26.50	20.35	13.75
				1868-94						
32	1¢ violet	37.00	28.50	18.50	28.50	22.00	14.30	28.50	22.00	11.00
32A	1¢ brown lilac, re-engraved (1871)	56.00	43.00	23.00	43.00	33.00	17.60	43.00	33.00	17.60
33	3¢ vermillion (1870)	345.00	265.00	180.00	265.00	203.50	137.50	165.00	26.50	71.50
34	3¢ blue (1873)	280.00	215.00	143.00	215.00	165.00	110.00	23.00	17.60	9.90
35	6¢ dull rose (1870)	16.00	12.15	7.15	12.15	9.35	5.50	12.25	9.35	5.50
36	6¢ carmine lake (1894)	18.50	14.25	10.00	14.25	11.00	7.70	14.25	11.00	7.70
				1876-79 Rouletted						
37	1¢ brown lilac (1877)	52.00	40.00	40.00	40.00	30.25	30.75	21.50	16.50	11.00
38	2¢ green (1879)	63.00	48.50	48.50	48.50	37.40	37.40	35.75	27.50	17.60
39	3¢ blue (1877)	170.00	130.00	100.00	130.00	99.00	99.00	10.00	770	5.25
40	5¢ blue	110.00	85.75	85.75	85.75	66.00	66.00	10.00	7.70	5.25

41-45
Prince of Wales

46-48
Codfish

53-55
Seal

56-58
Newfoundland Dog

SCOTT NO.	DESCRIPTION	UNUSED O.G. VF	F	AVG	UNUSED VF	F	AVG	USED VF	F	AVG
				1880-96 Perforate 12						
41	1¢ violet brown	15.50	10.50	5.65	13.00	8.80	4.70	9.25	7.15	3.60
42	1¢ gray brown	15.50	10.50	5.65	13.00	8.80	4.70	9.25	7.15	3.60
43	1¢ brown (Reissue) (1896)	35.00	23.75	13.25	29.50	19.80	11.00	23.50	18.15	10.20
44	1¢ deep green (1887)	9.90	6.60	3.95	8.25	5.50	3.30	3.60	2.75	1.65
45	1¢ green (Reissue) (1897)	10.75	7.25	4.50	9.00	6.05	3.85	6.50	4.95	2.75
46	2¢ yellow green	19.75	13.25	7.95	16.50	11.00	6.60	13.50	10.45	5.50
47	2¢ green (Reissue) (1896)	44.50	29.50	15.85	37.00	24.75	13.20	19.25	14.85	8.25
48	2¢ red orange (1887)	16.75	11.25	5.95	14.00	9.35	4.95	7.50	5.80	3.30
49	3¢ blue	24.00	16.50	9.95	20.00	13.75	8.25	4.25	3.30	1.85
51	3¢ umber brown (1887)	19.75	13.25	8.50	16.50	11.00	7.15	4.25	3.30	1.85
52	3¢ violet brown (Reissue) (1896)	52.50	35.00	18.50	43.75	29.15	15.40	38.00	29.15	15.40
53	5¢ pale blue	290.00	198.00	120.00	245.00	165.00	99.00	11.25	8.80	4.95
54	5¢ dark blue (1887)	120.00	79.00	46.25	100.00	66.00	38.50	8.50	6.60	3.60
55	5¢ bright blue (1894)	24.50	16.50	9.95	20.50	13.75	8.25	6.50	4.95	2.50

59
Schooner

60
Queen Victoria

1897
60a surcharged in black

61
Queen Victoria

62
John Cabot

63
Cape Bonavista

SCOTT NO.	DESCRIPTION	UNUSED O.G. VF	F	AVG	UNUSED VF	F	AVG	USED VF	F	AVG
				1887-96						
56	1/2¢ rose red	7.25	5.65	3.30	6.10	4.70	2.75	5.75	4.40	2.50
57	1/2¢ orange red (1896) 38.50	29.75	15.85	32.00	24.75	13.20	34.00	26.40	15.40	
58	1/2¢ black (1894)	6.00	4.60	2.45	5.00	3.85	2.05	5.00	3.85	2.05
59	10¢ black	55.75	43.00	26.50	46.50	35.75	22.00	43.00	33.00	17.60
				1890						
60	3¢ slate	9.40	7.25	3.95	7.85	6.05	3.30	.85	.65	.40

Newfoundland #61-85

SCOTT NO.	DESCRIPTION	UNUSED O.G. VF	F	AVG	UNUSED VF	F	AVG	USED VF	F	AVG

64 Caribou Hunting   **65** Mining   **66** Logging   **67** Fishing   **68** Cabot's Ship

69 Ptarmigan   **70** Seals   **71** Salmon Fishing   **72** Seal of Colony   **73** Coast Scene   **74** King Henry VII

1897 CABOT ISSUE

Scott	Description	VF	F	AVG	VF	F	AVG	VF	F	AVG
61-74	1¢-60¢ complete, 14 varieties	360.00	275.00	170.00	206.00	149.00	97.50	153.50	118.00	64.75
61	1¢ deep green	2.70	2.10	1.40	1.55	1.20	.80	1.55	1.20	.65
62	2¢ carmine lake	3.40	2.60	1.75	1.95	1.50	1.00	1.55	1.20	.65
63	3¢ ultramarine	5.00	3.85	2.50	2.85	2.20	1.45	1.45	1.10	.60
64	4¢ olive green	8.15	6.30	4.00	4.65	3.60	2.30	3.55	2.75	1.65
65	5¢ violet	8.15	6.30	4.00	4.65	3.60	2.30	3.55	2.75	1.65
66	6¢ red brown	7.45	5.75	3.85	4.25	3.30	2.20	4.30	3.30	2.00
67	8¢ red orange	16.20	12.50	7.70	9.25	7.15	4.40	6.45	4.95	2.75
68	10¢ black brown	22.50	17.25	10.50	12.85	9.90	6.05	6.10	4.70	2.60
69	12¢ dark blue	23.50	18.25	11.50	13.50	10.45	6.60	7.50	5.80	3.15
70	15¢ scarlet	23.50	18.25	11.50	13.50	10.45	6.60	8.25	6.35	3.50
71	24¢ gray violet	23.50	18.25	11.50	13.50	10.45	6.60	8.50	6.60	3.60
72	30¢ slate	68.25	53.00	31.75	39.00	30.25	18.15	35.75	27.50	15.40
73	35¢ red	150.00	115.00	70.00	85.75	66.00	40.15	64.75	49.50	26.40
74	60¢ black	16.85	12.50	7.70	9.65	7.15	4.40	8.50	6.60	3.60

1897

Scott	Description	VF	F	AVG	VF	F	AVG	VF	F	AVG
75	1¢ on 3¢ gray lilac, Type a	35.00	26.25	19.75	30.00	22.50	15.00	18.00	13.50	10.00
76	1¢ on 3¢ gray lilac, Type b	140.00	105.00	78.75	120.00	90.00	67.50	140.00	105.00	78.75
77	1¢ on 3¢ gray lilac, Type c	525.00	395.00	295.00	450.00	337.50	255.00	480.00	360.00	270.00

78 Edward, Prince of Wales   **79, 80** Queen Victoria   **81, 82** King Edward VII   **83** Queen Alexandria   **84** Queen Mary   **85** King George V

1897-1901 ROYAL FAMILY ISSUE

Scott	Description	VF	F	AVG	VF	F	AVG	VF	F	AVG
78-85	1/2¢-5¢ complete, 8 varieties	105.00	80.50	52.50	58.00	44.75	29.00	18.40	14.00	8.10
78	1/2¢ olive green	3.85	3.00	2.00	2.15	1.65	1.10	2.65	2.05	1.10
79	1¢ carmine rose	5.40	4.10	2.80	3.00	2.30	1.55	3.55	2.75	1.55
80	1¢ yellow green (1898) 3.25	2.50	1.70	1.80	1.40	.95	.25	.20	.15	
81	2¢ orange	6.40	4.95	3.15	3.55	2.75	1.75	4.30	3.30	2.00
82	2¢ vermillion (1898) 11.60	8.90	5.95	6.45	4.95	3.30	.75	.55	.35	
83	3¢ orange (1898)	20.60	15.85	10.00	11.45	8.80	5.60	.75	.55	.35
84	4¢ violet (1901)	27.00	20.75	13.85	15.00	11.55	7.70	4.30	3.30	1.85
85	5¢ blue (1899)	32.00	24.75	15.85	17.85	13.75	8.60	2.85	2.20	1.20

Newfoundland #86-103

SCOTT NO.	DESCRIPTION	UNUSED O.G. VF	F	AVG	UNUSED VF	F	AVG	USED VF	F	AVG

 86 Map of Newfoundland
 87 King James I
 88 Arms of the London & Bristol Company
 89 John Guy
 90 Guy's Ship the "Endeavour"
 91 View of the Town of Cupids

 92, 92A, 98 Lord Bacon
 93, 99 View of Mosquito Bay
 94, 100 Logging Camp
 95, 101 Paper Mills
 96, 102 King Edward VII

1908

| 86 | 2¢ rose carmine | 25.75 | 19.75 | 13.85 | 14.30 | 11.00 | 7.70 | 1.45 | 1.10 | .70 |

1910 JOHN GUY ISSUE—Lithographed Perf. 12

87/97	(87-92, 92A, 93-97) 12 varieties	475.00	350.00	195.00	285.00	219.00	145.00	320.00	245.00	129.00
87	1¢ deep green, perf. 12x11	2.30	1.75	1.25	1.45	1.10	.80	1.10	.85	.50
87a	1¢ deep green	5.25	4.00	2.65	6.80	2.50	1.65	2.15	1.65	1.00
87b	1¢ deep green, perf. 12x14	4.00	3.10	1.90	2.55	1.95	1.20	1.95	1.50	.95
88	2¢ carmine	8.00	6.15	4.25	5.00	3.85	2.65	.85	.65	.40
88a	2¢ carmine, perf. 12x14	5.75	4.40	2.95	3.55	2.75	1.85	.85	.65	.40
88c	2¢ carmine, perf. 12x11-1/2	210.00	160.00	105.00	129.00	99.00	66.00	85.00	66.00	35.75
89	3¢ brown olive	13.65	10.50	7.00	8.55	6.60	4.40	10.75	8.25	4.40
90	4¢ dull violet	22.75	17.60	11.45	14.25	11.00	7.15	9.30	7.15	3.60
91	5¢ ultramarine, perf. 14x12	9.00	7.00	4.75	5.75	4.40	2.95	3.50	2.75	1.50
91a	5¢ ultramarine	20.50	15.85	11.45	12.85	9.90	7.15	4.30	3.30	1.85
92	6¢ claret (I)	91.00	70.00	46.50	57.25	44.00	29.15	57.25	44.00	23.60
92A	6¢ claret (II)	34.50	26.50	17.60	21.45	16.50	11.00	25.75	19.80	11.00
93	8¢ pale brown	57.25	44.00	29.00	35.75	27.50	18.15	45.00	34.65	17.60
94	9¢ olive green	57.25	44.00	29.00	35.75	27.50	18.15	45.00	34.65	17.60
95	10¢ violet black	57.25	44.00	29.00	35.75	27.50	18.15	40.00	30.25	15.95
96	12¢ lilac brown	57.25	44.00	29.00	35.75	27.50	18.15	45.00	34.65	17.60
97	15¢ gray black	68.50	52.75	35.00	43.00	33.00	22.00	55.75	42.90	22.00

#92 Type I. "Z" of "COLONIZATION" is reversed. #92A Type II. "Z" is normal

 97, 103 King George V
 104 Queen Mary
 105 King George
 106 Prince of Wales
 107 Prince Albert
 108 Princess Mary
 109 Prince Henry

1911 Engraved. Perf. 14

98-103	6¢-15¢ complete, 6 varieties	450.00	345.00	310.00	285.00	216.00	132.00	280.00	216.00	117.50
98	6¢ brown violet	27.95	21.50	14.95	21.50	13.45	9.35	17.15	13.20	8.80
99	8¢ bistre brown	68.50	52.75	34.25	43.00	33.00	21.45	43.00	33.00	21.45
100	9¢ olive green	57.25	44.00	28.00	35.75	27.50	17.60	35.25	27.50	17.60
101	10¢ violet black	115.00	88.00	52.00	71.50	55.00	32.50	71.50	55.00	17.60
102	12¢ red brown	103.00	79.25	46.50	64.50	49.50	29.15	64.50	49.50	29.15
103	15¢ slate brown	103.00	79.25	46.50	64.50	49.50	29.15	64.50	49.50	29.15

Newfoundland #104-126

| | 110
Prince George | 111
Prince John | 112
Queen Alexandria | 113
Duke of Connaught | 114
Seal of Colony |

1911 ROYAL FAMILY ISSUE

SCOTT NO.	DESCRIPTION	UNUSED O.G. VF	UNUSED O.G. F	UNUSED O.G. AVG	UNUSED VF	UNUSED F	UNUSED AVG	USED VF	USED F	USED AVG
104-14	1¢-15¢ complete, 11 varieties	347.00	268.00	175.00	178.00	137.00	91.25	170.00	130.00	85.00
104	1¢ yellow green	2.95	2.25	1.60	1.45	1.10	.80	.25	.20	.15
105	2¢ carmine	3.60	2.75	1.75	1.80	1.40	.90	.25	.20	.15
106	3¢ red brown	33.75	26.00	16.50	17.15	13.20	8.80	17.15	13.20	8.80
107	4¢ violet	25.00	19.50	13.50	12.85	9.90	7.15	11.45	8.80	6.05
108	5¢ ultramarine	14.25	11.00	7.50	7.15	5.50	3.60	1.80	1.40	.75
109	6¢ black	25.00	19.50	13.50	12.85	9.90	7.15	12.85	9.90	7.15
110	8¢ blue (paper colored)	94.25	72.50	44.00	47.95	36.85	23.65	47.95	36.85	23.65
110a	8¢ peacock blue (white paper)	99.50	76.50	48.00	50.00	38.50	24.75	50.00	38.50	24.75
111	9¢ blue violet	35.00	27.00	18.00	17.85	13.75	8.80	17.85	13.75	8.80
112	10¢ dark green	45.00	35.00	24.00	23.50	18.15	12.10	23.50	18.15	12.10
113	12¢ plum	45.00	35.00	24.00	23.50	18.15	12.10	23.50	18.15	12.10
114	50¢ magenta	41.50	32.00	21.50	21.45	16.50	11.00	21.45	16.50	11.00

| | 115 | 116 | 72
surcharged | 70 & 73
surcharged |

| | 131 | 132 | 133 | 134 |

| | 135 | 136 | 137 | 138 | 139 | 140 |

1919 TRAIL OF THE CARIBOU ISSUE

SCOTT NO.	DESCRIPTION	UNUSED O.G. VF	UNUSED O.G. F	UNUSED O.G. AVG	UNUSED VF	UNUSED F	UNUSED AVG	USED VF	USED F	USED AVG
115-26	1¢-36¢ complete, 12 varieties	240.00	186.00	120.00	138.00	106.50	69.50	123.50	94.50	61.35
115	1¢ green	2.30	1.75	1.15	1.30	1.00	.65	.40	.30	.20
116	2¢ scarlet	2.55	1.95	1.45	1.45	1.10	.80	.55	.40	.25
117	3¢ red brown	3.20	2.45	1.65	1.80	1.40	.90	.35	.25	.15
118	4¢ violet	5.00	3.85	2.50	2.85	2.20	1.45	1.45	1.10	.65
119	5¢ ultramarine	5.75	4.40	2.70	3.25	2.50	1.55	1.45	1.10	.65
120	6¢ gray	26.00	20.25	13.50	15.00	11.55	7.70	15.00	11.55	7.70
121	8¢ magenta	20.00	15.50	10.50	11.45	8.80	6.05	10.75	8.25	5.50
122	10¢ dark green	15.00	11.55	6.75	8.50	6.60	3.85	3.50	2.75	1.65
123	12¢ orange	50.00	38.50	25.00	28.50	22.00	14.30	25.00	19.25	12.65
124	15¢ dark blue	41.25	31.75	20.25	23.50	18.15	11.55	23.50	18.15	11.00
125	24¢ bistre	46.00	35.50	23.00	26.50	20.35	13.20	26.50	20.35	13.20
126	36¢ olive green	37.35	28.75	19.25	21.45	16.50	11.00	21.50	16.50	11.00

Newfoundland #127-144

SCOTT NO.		UNUSED OG F	AVG	UNUSED F	AVG	USED F	AVG
		1920					
127	2¢ on 30¢ slate	6.90	4.25	4.95	3.05	4.95	3.05
		Bars 10-1/2mm apart					
128	3¢ on 15¢ scarlet	247.50	150.00	165.00	104.50	181.50	104.50
		Bars 13-1/2mm apart					
129	3¢ on 15¢ scarlet	11.55	6.95	8.25	6.05	8.25	6.05
130	3¢ on 35¢ red	11.55	6.95	8.25	6.05	8.25	6.05

141

142

143

144

145, 163, 172
Map of Newfoundland

146, 164, 173
S.S. Caribou

1923-24 PICTORIAL ISSUE

		F	AVG	F	AVG	F	AVG
131-44	1¢-24¢ complete, 14 varieties	121.00	73.00	85.00	50.95	77.00	47.00
131	1¢ gray green	2.65	1.60	1.95	1.05	.25	.15
132	2¢ carmine	1.75	1.05	1.30	.65	.20	.15
133	3¢ brown	2.65	1.60	1.95	1.05	.20	.15
134	4¢ brown violet	2.20	1.35	1.65	.90	1.55	.95
135	5¢ ultramarine	3.85	2.30	2.75	1.50	1.75	1.10
136	6¢ gray black	4.80	2.85	3.30	1.75	3.30	1.75
137	8¢ dull violet	3.85	2.30	2.75	1.50	2.60	1.40
138	9¢ slate green	24.75	14.85	16.50	10.45	16.50	10.45
139	10¢ dark violet	4.25	2.55	3.05	1.65	1.75	1.10
140	11¢ olive green	7.70	4.60	5.50	3.05	5.50	3.05
141	12¢ lake	8.00	4.80	5.80	3.15	5.80	3.15
142	15¢ deep blue	9.10	5.45	6.60	3.85	6.35	3.60
143	20¢ red brown (1924)	8.80	5.25	6.35	3.30	4.95	2.75
144	24¢ black brown (1924)	44.00	26.50	30.25	19.80	30.25	19.80

147, 165, 174
Queen Mary and King George

148, 166, 175
Prince of Wales

149, 167, 176
Express Train

150, 168, 177
Newfoundland Hotel, St. John's

151, 178
Town of Heart's Content

152
Cabot Tower, St. John's

153, 169, 179
War Memorial, St. John's

154
Post Office, St. John's

156, 170, 180
First Airplane to Cross Atlantic Non-Stop

157, 171, 181
House of Parliament, St. John's

159, 182
Grand Falls, Labrador

Newfoundland #145-211

SCOTT NO.	DESCRIPTION	UNUSED O.G. F	UNUSED O.G. AVG	UNUSED F	UNUSED AVG	USED F	USED AVG
	1928 Tourist Publicity Issue Unwatermarked. Thin paper, dull colors						
145-59	1¢-30¢ complete, 15 varieties	97.85	58.75	67.25	38.25	51.00	30.25
145	1¢ deep green	1.65	1.00	1.05	.55	.55	.35
146	2¢ deep carmine	2.15	1.30	1.50	.85	.55	.35
147	3¢ brown	2.75	1.65	1.85	1.00	.35	.20
148	4¢ lilac rose	3.30	2.00	2.10	1.40	1.65	1.00
149	5¢ slate green	6.35	3.80	4.40	2.50	3.05	1.85
150	6¢ ultramarine	4.70	2.80	3.30	1.95	2.75	1.50
151	8¢ light red brown	6.35	3.80	4.40	2.50	3.60	1.95
152	9¢ myrtle green	7.45	4.50	5.50	2.75	4.40	2.50
153	10¢ dark violet	7.45	4.50	5.50	2.75	3.85	2.20
154	12¢ brown carmine	5.50	3.30	3.85	2.20	3.05	1.65
155	14¢ red brown	7.45	4.50	5.50	2.75	3.05	2.20
156	15¢ dark blue	8.00	4.80	6.05	3.05	4.95	2.65
157	20¢ gray black	7.45	4.50	5.50	3.05	3.30	1.85
158	28¢ gray green	24.75	14.85	14.85	9.90	13.75	8.80
159	30¢ olive brown	7.70	4.50	5.50	3.05	4.95	2.65
	1929						
160	3¢ on 6¢ gray black	3.50	2.10	2.95	1.75	2.95	1.75
	1929-31 Tourist Publicity Issue Types of 1928 re-engraved Unwatermarked. Thicker paper, brighter colors						
163-71	1¢-20¢ complete, 9 varieties	123.00	73.95	78.00	44.00	50.25	27.00
163	1¢ green	1.75	1.05	1.30	.65	.45	.30
164	2¢ deep carmine	1.75	1.05	1.30	.65	.20	.15
165	3¢ deep red brown	2.00	1.20	1.45	.80	.20	.15
166	4¢ magenta	2.95	1.75	2.10	1.10	1.00	.60
167	5¢ slate green	4.40	2.65	3.15	1.75	1.00	.60
168	6¢ ultramarine	11.55	6.95	8.25	4.40	6.60	3.60
169	10¢ dark violet	6.05	3.65	4.40	2.50	1.65	1.00
170	15¢ deep blue (1930)	41.25	24.95	24.75	14.30	23.10	12.10
171	20¢ gray black (1931)	57.75	34.75	35.75	20.35	18.70	9.90
	1931 Tourist Publicity Issue Types of 1928 re-engraved, watermarked, coat of arms Thicker paper, brighter colors						
172-82	1¢-30¢ complete, 11 varieties	195.00	114.00	130.00	71.50	93.50	50.50
172	1¢ green	2.50	1.40	1.65	.95	.90	.55
173	2¢ red	3.85	2.30	2.50	1.40	1.20	.75
174	3¢ red brown	3.85	2.30	2.50	1.40	.90	.55
175	4¢ rose	4.95	3.00	3.35	1.85	1.35	.85
176	5¢ greenish gray	9.90	5.95	7.15	3.85	6.05	3.30
177	6¢ ultramarine	22.00	13.25	15.40	8.80	13.75	7.70
178	8¢ light red brown	22.00	13.25	15.40	8.80	13.75	7.70
179	10¢ dark violet	11.55	6.95	8.25	4.40	6.05	3.30
180	15¢ deep blue	41.25	24.75	27.50	14.85	24.75	13.20
181	20¢ gray black	44.00	26.00	29.15	15.40	8.80	4.40
182	30¢ olive brown	38.50	21.00	24.75	13.20	20.90	11.00

SCOTT NO.	DESCRIPTION	UNUSED O.G. F	UNUSED O.G. AVG	UNUSED F	UNUSED AVG	USED F	USED AVG
	1932-37 RESOURCES ISSUE Perf. 13-1/2						
183-99	1¢-48¢ complete, 17 varieties	93.50	56.00	57.00	36.50	37.95	25.75
183	1¢ green	1.50	.95	1.05	.65	.35	.25
184	1¢ gray black	.35	.20	.25	.20	.20	.15
185	2¢ rose	1.50	.90	1.05	.65	.20	.15
186	2¢ green	1.50	.90	1.00	.65	.20	.15
187	3¢ orange brown	1.20	.75	.85	.55	.20	.15
188	4¢ deep violet	4.95	2.90	3.60	2.30	1.40	.90
189	4¢ rose lake	.55	.35	.40	.30	.20	.15
190	5¢ violet brown (I)	6.60	3.95	4.40	2.75	.90	.55
191	5¢ deep violet (II)	1.00	.60	.65	.50	.20	.15
191a	5¢ deep violet (I)	10.45	6.25	7.00	5.25	.60	.40
192	6¢ dull blue	11.00	6.60	7.15	5.35	7.15	5.35
193	10¢ olive black	1.40	.85	.95	.60	.60	.40
194	14¢ black	2.75	1.65	1.95	1.30	1.65	1.10
195	15¢ magenta	2.75	1.65	1.95	1.30	1.65	1.10
196	20¢ gray green	2.75	1.65	2.95	1.30	.85	.55
197	25¢ gray	3.05	1.85	2.10	1.40	1.75	1.15
198	30¢ ultramarine	30.25	18.15	20.35	12.10	18.15	12.10
199	48¢ red brown (1937)	14.85	8.95	10.45	6.60	4.25	2.75

197, 265 Sealing Fleet

198 Fishing Fleet

208 The Duchess of York

209, 259 Corner Brook Paper Mills

210, 264 Loading Iron Ore, Bell Island

1932 Perf. 13-1/2

SCOTT NO.	DESCRIPTION	UNUSED O.G. F	UNUSED O.G. AVG	UNUSED F	UNUSED AVG	USED F	USED AVG
208-10	7¢-24¢ complete, 3 varieties	6.60	4.00	4.70	3.15	4.50	3.10
208	7¢ red brown	1.55	.95	1.10	.75	1.10	.75
209	8¢ orange red	1.55	.95	1.10	.75	1.00	.65
210	24¢ light blue	3.85	2.30	2.75	1.85	2.65	1.85

1933 LAND & SEA OVERPRINT

211	15¢ brown	10.00	6.00	7.15	4.40	5.75	3.55

THREE CENTS

160 *136 surcharged in red*

183, 253 Codfish

185, 186 King George

187 Queen Mary

188, 189 Prince of Wales

190, 191, 257 Caribou

192 Princess Elizabeth

193, 260 Salmon

194, 261 Newfoundland Dog

195, 262 Northern Seal

196, 263 Trans-Atlantic Beacon

L. & S. Post.

211 No. C9 with Overprint and Bars

212 Sir Humphrey Gilbert

213 Compton Castle, Devon

214 The Gilbert Arms

216 Token to Gilbert from Queen Elizabeth

215 Eton College

217 Gilbert Commissioned by Queen Elizabeth

218 Gilbert's Fleet Leaving Plymouth

219 The Fleet Arriving at St. John's

220 Annexation of Newfoundland

221 Coat of Arms of England

Newfoundland #212-251

SCOTT NO.	DESCRIPTION	UNUSED O.G. F	UNUSED O.G. AVG	UNUSED F	UNUSED AVG	USED F	USED AVG
	1933 SIR HUMPHREY GILBERT ISSUE						
212-25	1¢-32¢ complete, 14 varieties	144.00	86.75	98.75	65.95	94.75	67.50
212	1¢ gray black	.95	.60	.75	.50	.55	.40
213	2¢ green	1.20	.75	.95	.60	.55	.40
214	3¢ yellow brown	1.65	1.00	1.30	.85	.95	.65
215	4¢ carmine	1.65	1.00	1.30	.85	.40	.30
216	5¢ dull violet	2.10	1.30	1.65	1.10	.95	.65
217	7¢ blue	15.95	9.50	10.45	6.60	12.65	8.25
218	8¢ orange red	8.25	5.00	5.80	3.85	5.80	4.15
219	9¢ ultramarine	9.35	5.60	6.35	4.15	6.30	4.40
220	10¢ red brown	8.25	5.00	5.80	3.85	4.95	3.60
221	14¢ black	18.15	10.95	12.65	8.25	11.55	8.25
222	15¢ claret	18.15	10.95	12.40	8.00	11.00	8.25
223	20¢ deep green	11.00	6.60	8.25	5.50	7.70	5.25
224	24¢ violet brown	27.50	16.50	18.15	12.65	18.15	13.20
225	32¢ gray	27.50	16.50	18.15	12.65	18.15	13.20

222
Gilbert on the "Squirrel"

223
1624 Map of Newfoundland

224
Queen Elizabeth I

225
Gilbert Statue at Truro

226
Windsor Castle and King George

SCOTT NO.	DESCRIPTION	UNUSED F/NH	UNUSED F	USED F
	1935 SILVER JUBILEE			
226-29	4¢-24¢ complete, 4 varieties	11.00	8.40	8.00
226	4¢ bright rose	1.10	.85	.60
227	5¢ violet	1.10	.85	.75
228	7¢ dark blue	2.75	2.20	2.20
229	24¢ olive green	6.60	4.95	4.95
	1937 CORONATION ISSUE			
230-32	2¢-5¢ complete, 3 varieties	1.90	1.55	1.40
230	2¢ deep green	.55	.45	.40
231	4¢ carmine rose	.55	.45	.35
232	5¢ dark violet	.90	.75	.75

230
King George VI and Queen Elizabeth

233

234
Die I: Fine Impression
Die II: Coarse Impression

235

236

237

238

239

240

242

243

245, 254
King George VI

SCOTT NO.	DESCRIPTION	UNUSED F/NH	UNUSED F	USED F
	1937 LONG CORONATION ISSUE			
233-43	1¢-48¢ complete, 11 varieties	30.25	20.95	17.85
233	1¢ Codfish	.50	.35	.25
234	3¢ Map, die I	2.05	1.40	.60
234a	3¢ same, die II	1.85	1.20	.45
235	7¢ Caribou	2.20	1.55	1.35
236	8¢ Paper Mills	2.20	1.55	1.50
237	10¢ Salmon	4.15	2.75	2.50
238	14¢ Newfoundland Dog	3.30	2.30	2.05
239	15¢ Northern Seal	3.30	2.30	2.05
240	20¢ Cape Race	2.75	1.95	1.65
241	24¢ Bell Island	3.60	2.55	2.30
242	25¢ Sealing Fleet	3.60	2.55	2.20
243	48¢ Fishing Fleet	4.15	2.75	2.50

249

250
249 surcharged

SCOTT NO.	DESCRIPTION	UNUSED F/NH	UNUSED F	USED F
	1938 ROYAL FAMILY Perf. 13-1/2			
245-48	2¢-7¢ complete, 4 varieties	6.55	4.45	1.65
245	2¢ green	1.65	1.10	.15
246	3¢ dark carmine	1.85	1.10	.15
247	4¢ light blue	1.95	1.40	.15
248	7¢ dark ultramarine	1.65	1.10	1.20
249	5¢ violet blue	.85	.60	.60
	249 SURCHARGED			
250	2¢ on 5¢ violet blue	1.30	.95	.95
251	4¢ on 5¢ violet blue	1.00	.75	.75

Newfoundland #252-270; C2-C12

SCOTT NO.	DESCRIPTION	UNUSED F/NH	F	USED F	SCOTT NO.	DESCRIPTION	UNUSED F/NH	F	USED F

267

267

TWO CENTS
268
267 surcharged

269

1941 GRENFELL ISSUE

| 252 | 5¢ dull blue | .45 | .35 | .35 |

1941-44 RESOURCES ISSUE
Designs of 1931-38. Perf. 12-1/2

253-66	1¢-48¢ complete, 14 varieties	16.25	10.25	10.30
253	1¢ dark gray	.30	.20	.15
254	2¢ deep green	.30	.20	.15
255	3¢ rose carmine	.30	.25	.15
256	4¢ blue	.65	.45	.15
257	5¢ violet	.65	.50	.15
258	7¢ violet blue (1942)	1.00	.65	.85
259	8¢ red	.85	.65	.60
260	10¢ brownish black	.85	.55	.55
261	14¢ black	1.65	1.10	1.20
262	15¢ pale rose violet	1.65	1.10	1.20
263	20¢ green	1.65	1.10	1.20
264	24¢ deep blue	1.95	1.35	1.55
265	25¢ slate	1.95	1.35	1.55
266	48¢ red brown (1944)	3.30	2.20	1.40

270

1943-47

267	30¢ Memorial University	1.45	1.05	.95
268	2¢ on 30¢ University (1946)	.35	.30	.30
269	4¢ Princess Elizabeth (1947)	.35	.30	.15
270	5¢ Cabot (1947)	.35	.30	.15

AIR POST STAMPS

SCOTT NO.	DESCRIPTION	UNUSED O.G. VF	F	AVG	UNUSED VF	F	AVG	USED VF	F	AVG

Trans-Atlantic AIR POST, 1919. ONE DOLLAR.
C2
70 surcharged

AIR MAIL to Halifax, N.S. 1921
C3
73 overprinted

Air Mail DE PINEDO 1927
C4
74 overprinted

Trans-Atlantic AIR MAIL By B. M. "Columbia" September 1930 Fifty Cents
C5
126 surcharged

C6, C9
Airplane and Dog Team

1919
| C2 | $1 on 15¢ scarlet | 200.00 | 150.00 | 112.50 | 175.00 | 131.25 | 98.00 | 180.00 | 135.00 | 105.00 |
| C2a | same without comma after "POST" | 240.00 | 180.00 | 135.00 | 210.00 | 157.50 | 120.00 | 225.00 | 170.00 | 125.00 |

1921
| C3 | 35¢ red | 180.00 | 135.00 | 105.00 | 140.00 | 105.00 | 78.75 | 140.00 | 105.00 | 78.75 |
| C3a | same with period after "1921" | 200.00 | 150.00 | 112.50 | 175.00 | 131.25 | 98.00 | 180.00 | 135.00 | 105.00 |

C7, C10
First Trans-atlantic Airmail

C8, C11
Routes of Historic Trans-atlantic Flights

TRANS-ATLANTIC WEST TO EAST Per Dornier DO-X May, 1932. One Dollar and Fifty Cents
C12
C11 surcharged

C13

1931 Unwatermarked
C6	15¢ brown	12.85	9.90	5.95	8.50	6.60	4.40	8.50	6.60	4.40
C7	50¢ green	32.15	24.75	15.00	21.50	16.50	11.00	23.50	18.15	12.65
C8	$1 blue	85.75	66.00	39.50	57.25	44.00	30.25	60.00	46.75	31.35

Watermarked Coat of Arms
C9	15¢ brown	10.00	7.70	4.56	7.15	5.50	3.30	7.15	5.50	3.30
C10	50¢ green	50.00	38.50	23.00	32.15	24.75	16.50	30.75	23.65	15.95
C11	$1 blue	120.00	93.50	56.00	78.50	60.50	42.35	75.00	57.75	38.50

1932 TRANS-ATLANTIC FLIGHT
| C12 | $1.50 on $1 blue | 470.00 | 360.00 | 225.00 | 360.00 | 275.00 | 181.50 | 360.00 | 275.00 | 181.50 |

299

Newfoundland #C13-C19; J1-J7

SCOTT NO.	DESCRIPTION	UNUSED O.G. VF	F	AVG	UNUSED VF	F	AVG	USED VF	F	AVG

C14

C15

1933 LABRADOR ISSUE

Scott	Description	VF	F	AVG	VF	F	AVG	VF	F	AVG
C13-17	5¢-75¢ complete, 5 varieties	206.00	172.50	103.50	135.00	112.50	75.00	135.00	112.50	75.00
C13	5¢ "Put to Flight"	15.85	13.20	7.95	9.90	8.25	5.75	9.90	8.25	5.80
C14	10¢ "Land of Heart's Delight"	23.75	19.80	11.85	13.75	11.55	8.00	13.75	11.55	8.00
C15	30¢ "Spotting the Herd"	39.50	33.00	19.75	26.50	22.00	14.85	26.50	22.00	14.85
C16	60¢ "News from Home"	69.25	57.75	34.75	46.25	38.50	24.75	46.25	38.50	24.75
C17	75¢ "Labrador, The Land of Gold"	69.25	57.75	34.75	46.25	38.00	25.85	46.25	38.00	25.85

C16

C17

1933 GEN. BALBO FLIGHT. $4.50
C18
C17 Surcharged

C19

1933 BALBOA FLIGHT ISSUE

Scott	Description	VF	F	AVG	VF	F	AVG	VF	F	AVG
C18	$4.50 on 75¢ bistre	650.00	545.00	330.00	460.00	385.00	302.50	460.00	385.00	302.50

1943

C19	7¢ St. John's	.55	.45	.40	.50	.40	.35	.30	.25	.15

POSTAGE DUE STAMPS

SCOTT NO.	DESCRIPTION	UNUSED F/NH	F	USED F	SCOTT NO.	DESCRIPTION	UNUSED F/NH	F	USED F

J1

1939 Unwatermarked, Perf. 10-1/2x10

J1	1¢ yellow green	2.50	1.65	1.65
J2	2¢ vermillion	3.85	2.50	2.50
J3	3¢ ultramarine	4.95	3.30	3.30
J4	4¢ yellow orange	6.05	4.15	4.15
J5	5¢ pale brown	4.15	2.75	2.75
J6	10¢ dark violet	3.85	2.65	2.65

1946-49 Unwatermarked, Perf. 11

J1a	1¢ yellow green	4.95	3.30	3.30

Unwatermarked, Perf. 11x9

J2a	2¢ vermillion	4.95	3.30	3.30
J3a	3¢ ultramarine	5.50	3.85	3.85
J4a	4¢ yellow orange	7.15	4.95	4.95

Watermarked, Perf. 11

J7	10¢ dark violet	9.35	6.35	6.35

New Brunswick #1-11

SCOTT NO.	DESCRIPTION	UNUSED O.G. VF	UNUSED O.G. F	UNUSED O.G. AVG	UNUSED VF	UNUSED F	UNUSED AVG	USED VF	USED F	USED AVG

1
Crown of Great Britain surrounded by Heraldic Flowers of the United Kingdom

6, 7, 8, 9, 10, 11

1851 PENCE ISSUE. Imperforate

Scott	Description	VF	F	AVG	VF	F	AVG	VF	F	AVG
1	3p red	2025.00	1565.00	865.00	1350.00	1045.00	577.50	425.00	320.00	240.00
2	6p olive yellow	4800.00	3700.00	2250.00	3200.00	2475.00	1495.00	775.00	580.00	440.00
3	1sh bright red violet	16750.00	11200.00	8000.00	10000.00	8000.00	5000.00	3800.00	2850.00	2150.00
4	1sh dull violet	14000.00	10500.00	7700.00	10000.00	7700.00	4800.00	4800.00	3600.00	2700.00

1860-63 CENTS ISSUE
(NH + 50%)

Scott	Description	VF	F	AVG	VF	F	AVG	VF	F	AVG
6	1¢ Locomotive	40.00	30.00	22.50	30.00	22.50	17.00	28.00	21.00	15.50
7	2¢ Queen Victoria, orange (1863)	15.00	11.25	8.50	12.50	9.50	7.00	14.00	10.50	7.75
8	5¢ same, yellow green	15.00	11.25	8.50	12.50	9.50	7.00	14.00	10.50	7.75
9	10¢ same, vermillion	45.00	33.75	25.25	42.00	31.50	23.75	45.00	33.75	25.00
10	12-1/2¢ Ships	70.00	52.50	39.50	60.00	45.00	33.75	70.00	52.50	39.50
11	17¢ Prince of Wales	45.00	33.75	25.25	42.00	31.50	23.75	45.00	33.75	25.00

Nova Scotia #1-13

1

2, 3
Royal Crown and Heraldic Flowers of the United Kingdom

1851-53 PENCE ISSUE
Imperf. Blue Paper

Scott	Description	VF	F	AVG	VF	F	AVG	VF	F	AVG
1	1p Queen Victoria	2600.00	1950.00	1450.00	2200.00	1650.00	1250.00	500.00	375.00	280.00
2	3p blue	725.00	550.00	400.00	575.00	430.00	300.00	140.00	105.00	73.50
3	3p dark blue	950.00	715.00	500.00	800.00	600.00	420.00	190.00	142.50	100.00
4	6p yellow green	3485.00	2675.00	2050.00	3000.00	2200.00	1500.00	430.00	330.00	220.00
5	6p dark green	7650.00	5885.00	4535.00	6200.00	4650.00	3250.00	850.00	637.50	450.00
6	1sh reddish violet	18000.00	13500.00	9450.00	14000.00	10500.00	7350.00	3550.00	2675.00	1850.00
7	1sh dull violet	18500.00	13875.00	9725.00	15000.00	11250.00	7875.00	3900.00	2925.00	2050.00

8, 11, 13
Queen Victoria

1860-63 CENTS ISSUE
White or Yellowish Paper, Perf. 12
(NH + 50%)

Scott	Description	VF	F	AVG	VF	F	AVG	VF	F	AVG
8	1¢ black	6.50	4.30	2.65	5.40	3.60	2.20	4.95	3.30	2.20
9	2¢ lilac	8.85	5.95	3.95	7.40	4.95	3.30	7.40	4.95	3.30
10	5¢ blue	340.00	230.00	150.00	285.00	192.50	126.50	11.50	7.70	4.25
11	8-1/2¢ green	5.95	3.95	2.65	4.95	3.30	2.20	19.75	13.20	8.25
12	10¢ vermillion	8.85	5.95	3.95	7.40	4.95	3.30	7.40	4.95	3.30
13	12-1/2¢ black	29.75	19.75	15.00	24.75	16.50	12.65	24.75	16.50	11.55

Prince Edward Island #1-16

SCOTT NO.	DESCRIPTION	UNUSED O.G. VF	UNUSED O.G. F	UNUSED O.G. AVG	UNUSED VF	UNUSED F	UNUSED AVG	USED VF	USED F	USED AVG

Queen Victoria

1861 PENCE ISSUE, Perf. 9

SCOTT NO.	DESCRIPTION	VF	F	AVG	VF	F	AVG	VF	F	AVG
1	2p dull rose	375.00	280.00	197.50	325.00	245.00	170.00	190.00	142.50	100.00
2	3p blue	855.00	660.00	130.00	700.00	525.00	370.00	400.00	300.00	210.00
3	6p yellow green	1375.00	1025.00	725.00	1200.00	900.00	625.00	800.00	600.00	425.00

1862-65 PENCE ISSUE, Perf. 11 to 12
(NH + 50%)

SCOTT NO.	DESCRIPTION	VF	F	AVG	VF	F	AVG	VF	F	AVG
4	1p yellow orange	25.00	19.25	13.50	19.25	14.85	10.45	26.00	19.50	13.75
5	2p rose	7.50	5.75	3.60	5.75	4.40	2.75	5.75	4.40	2.75
6	3p blue	12.00	7.85	4.30	9.30	6.05	3.30	12.00	9.00	6.25
7	6p yellow green	90.00	53.50	35.75	69.50	41.25	27.50	70.00	52.50	36.75
8	9p violet	60.50	35.75	23.50	46.50	27.50	18.15	58.00	43.50	30.00

1868-70 PENCE ISSUE
(NH + 50%)

SCOTT NO.	DESCRIPTION	VF	F	AVG	VF	F	AVG	VF	F	AVG
9	4p black	10.25	7.85	5.40	7.85	6.05	4.15	19.25	14.85	9.35
10	4-1/2p brown (1870)	46.50	35.75	25.00	35.75	27.50	19.25	43.00	33.00	22.00

Queen Victoria

1872 CENTS ISSUE
(NH + 40%)

SCOTT NO.	DESCRIPTION	VF	F	AVG	VF	F	AVG	VF	F	AVG
11	1¢ brown orange	6.00	4.60	3.00	5.00	3.85	2.50	9.30	7.15	4.70
12	2¢ ultramarine	12.90	9.90	6.60	10.75	8.25	5.50	23.50	18.15	12.10
13	3¢ rose	20.75	15.85	10.55	17.25	13.20	8.80	15.00	11.55	7.70
14	4¢ green	6.90	5.25	3.65	5.75	4.40	3.05	26.50	20.35	13.75
15	6¢ black	5.75	4.30	3.30	4.75	3.60	2.75	23.50	18.15	12.10
16	12¢ violet	6.50	5.00	3.30	5.40	4.15	2.75	35.75	27.50	20.35

NOTES

Our Premier U.S. Stamp Album
LIBERTY®
by H.E. Harris & Co.

A leader for years among top quality, fully comprehensive U.S. Albums. Our latest editions are priced within reach of ALL collectors.

The Liberty® I Album by H.E. Harris & Co. contains more than 900 pages, printed on one side only. Provides thousands of spaces for U.S. definitives, commemoratives, airpost, special delivery, postage dues, officials and hunting permit stamps. Also contains an illustrated U.S. Stamp Identifier. Available in the traditional blue Lady Liberty Binder or the elegant Heirloom U.S. binder.

1HRS1A	Liberty® Album – 3" Traditional binder	$45.99
1HRS53	Liberty® Album – 3-1/2" Heirloom binder	$49.99

Continuing the H.E. Harris Tradition for quality...
– Annual supplements are issued for all Liberty Albums –

Order from your local dealer or direct from Whitman Publishing, LLC.

FIRST DAY COVER ALBUM

Handsome and durable loose-leaf album to protect and display all your covers.

Luxurious leather-look album with gold-stamped title displays first day covers in clear vinyl pages. Two pockets per page; each 20 page album holds 80 covers back to back. Durable two-post loose-leaf binder makes it simple to add extra pages as your collection grows.

1HRS30   Harris First Day Cover Album (binder & slip case) *$16.95*

Order from your local dealer or direct from Whitman Publishing, LLC.

Note: Coupon ONLY valid with order of $50.00 or more from the H.E. Harris 2005 US/BNA Catalog. Copies of coupon will not be accepted. Please include this coupon with order and payment. Coupon expires December 31, 2005.

HOW TO WRITE YOUR ORDER

Please use order form

1. Print all requested information (name, address, etc.)
2. Indicate quantity, country (U.S, UN, CAN or province), catalog number, item description (sgle., pt. block, F.D. cover, etc.)
3. Specify condition (F, VF, NH etc.) and check whether mint or used.
4. Enter price as listed in this catalog.
5. Total all purchases, adding shipping/handling charge from table below. Alabama and Georgia residents (only) also add sales tax.
6. Payment may be made by check, money order, or credit card (VISA, Discover or MasterCard accepted). ORDERS FROM OUTSIDE THE U.S. MUST BE PAID BY CREDIT CARD, and all payment must be in U.S. funds.

SHIPPING AND HANDLING CHARGES*
Safe delivery is guaranteed. We assume all losses.
If "TOTAL ALL PAGES" AMOUNT IS:

If ordering STAMPS ONLY	add $3.50
$75.00 or less	add $3.95
$300.00 or less	add $6.95
OVER $300.00	add $9.95

*The following charges may not fully cover the actual postage or freight, insurance and handling cost for foreign orders, and additional charges may be added.

The H.E. HARRIS PERFORMANCE PLEDGE

- All stamps are genuine, exactly as described, and have been inspected by our staff experts.
- H.E. Harris & Co. upholds the standards set forth by the American Philatelic Society and the American Stamp Dealers Association.
- If you have any problem with your order, phone us at 1-800-546-2995. We will handle it to your complete satisfaction.
- 30 day return privilege on all merchandise.

H.E. Harris & Co.®
Serving the Collector Since 1916
4001 Helton Drive, Bldg. A • Florence, AL 35630

You may also order by phone 1-800-546-2995 or Fax 1-256-246-1116

30 day Money-back Guarantee on every item.
Sorry, no CODs.

Make payment in U.S. dollars by personal check, money order, Visa, Master Card, Discover or American Express. Please do not send cash.

Orders for shipment outside the U.S. must be paid by credit card and shipping charges will be added.

We Thank You For Your Order!

RUSH SHIPMENT TO:

Name _____

Address _____

City/State/Zip _____

Phone *(in case of question about your order)* _____

FAST CREDIT CARD ORDERING

☐ VISA ☐ MasterCard ☐ DISCOVER ☐ American Express

Card # _____

Expiration Date _____

Signature _____

Catalog or Stock No.	Qty.	Description	Mint	Used	Unit Price	Total Price

---

Shipping & Handling

If ordering STAMPS ONLY .... add $3.50
If order includes supply items and totals
    $75 or less .... add $3.95
    $300 or less .... add $6.95
    Over $300 .... add $9.95
Foreign orders: S&H will be added separately.

For Office Use Only

TOTAL FRONT	
TOTAL REVERSE	
DISCOUNTS–If applicable	
SUBTOTAL	
SHIPPING CHARGE	
AL & GA RESIDENTS ADD SALES TAX	
TOTAL PURCHASE	

2005USBNA

Catalog or Stock No.	Qty.	Description	Mint	Used	Unit Price	Total Price
Catalog or Stock No.	Qty.					
				TOTAL THIS SIDE		

Serving the Collector Since 1916
4001 Helton Drive, Bldg. A • Florence, AL 35630

You may also order by phone 1-800-546-2995 or Fax 1-256-246-1116

30 day Money-back Guarantee on every item.
Sorry, no CODs.

Make payment in U.S. dollars by personal check, money order, Visa, Master Card, Discover or American Express. Please do not send cash.

Orders for shipment outside the U.S. must be paid by credit card and shipping charges will be added.

We Thank You For Your Order!

RUSH SHIPMENT TO:

Name _____
Address _____
City/State/Zip _____
Phone *(in case of question about your order)* _____

FAST CREDIT CARD ORDERING

☐ VISA ☐ MasterCard ☐ DISCOVER ☐ AMERICAN EXPRESS

Card # _____
Expiration Date _____
Signature _____

Catalog or Stock No.	Qty.	Description	Mint	Used	Unit Price	Total Price

Shipping & Handling

If ordering STAMPS ONLY .... add $3.50
If order includes supply items and totals
        $75 or less .... add $4.95
        $300 or less .... add $6.95
        Over $300 .... add $9.95
Foreign orders: S&H will be added separately.

For Office Use Only

TOTAL FRONT	
TOTAL REVERSE	
DISCOUNTS–If applicable	
SUBTOTAL	
SHIPPING CHARGE	
AL & GA RESIDENTS ADD SALES TAX	
TOTAL PURCHASE	

2005USBNA

Catalog or Stock No.	Qty.	Description	Mint	Used	Unit Price	Total Price

Catalog or Stock No.	Qty.	Description	Mint	Used	Unit Price	Total Price
			TOTAL THIS SIDE			

H.E. Harris & Co.®
Serving the Collector Since 1916
4001 Helton Drive, Bldg. A • Florence, AL 35630

You may also order by phone 1-800-546-2995 or Fax 1-256-246-1116

30 day Money-back Guarantee on every item.
Sorry, no CODs.

Make payment in U.S. dollars by personal check, money order, Visa, Master Card, Discover or American Express. Please do not send cash.

Orders for shipment outside the U.S. must be paid by credit card and shipping charges will be added.

We Thank You For Your Order!

RUSH SHIPMENT TO:

Name _____
Address _____
City/State/Zip _____
Phone *(in case of question about your order)* _____

FAST CREDIT CARD ORDERING

☐ VISA ☐ MasterCard ☐ DISCOVER ☐ AMERICAN EXPRESS

Card # _____
Expiration Date _____
Signature _____

Catalog or Stock No.	Qty.	Description	Mint	Used	Unit Price	Total Price

Shipping & Handling
If ordering STAMPS ONLY .... add $3.50
If order includes supply items and totals
    $75 or less .... add $4.95
    $300 or less .... add $6.95
    Over $300 .... add $9.95
Foreign orders: S&H will be added separately.

For Office Use Only

TOTAL FRONT	
TOTAL REVERSE	
DISCOUNTS–If applicable	
SUBTOTAL	
SHIPPING CHARGE	
AL & GA RESIDENTS ADD SALES TAX	
TOTAL PURCHASE	

2005USBNA

Catalog or Stock No.	Qty.	Description	Mint	Used	Unit Price	Total Price
Catalog or Stock No.	Qty.	Description	Mint	Used	Unit Price	Total Price
			TOTAL THIS SIDE			